UNDERSTANDING ABNORMAL BEHAVIOR

UNDERSTANDING ABNORMAL BEHAVIOR

FOURTH EDITION

DAVID SUE

Western Washington University

DERALD SUE

California State University, Hayward

STANLEY SUE

University of California, Los Angeles

HOUGHTON MIFFLIN COMPANY   BOSTON   TORONTO

Geneva, Illinois   Palo Alto   Princeton, New Jersey

To our parents, Tom and Lucy Sue, who never suspected they would produce three psychologists, and to our wives and families, who provided the emotional support that enabled us to complete this edition.

Senior sponsoring editor: Michael DeRocco
Development editor: Susan Yanchus
Senior project editor: Carol Newman
Production/design coordinator: Sarah Ambrose
Senior manufacturing coordinator: Marie Barnes
Marketing manager: Becky Dudley

Cover design: Darci Mehall

Cover art by Glenn Bradshaw/Courtesy of Neville-Sargent Gallery, Chicago, *Blue Squared, 1991.* Casein on watercolor, 24½ × 38½.

All other credits appear in the Credits section at the end of the text.

Printed in the U.S.A.

Library of Congress Catalog Card Number: 93-78705

ISBN: 0-395-67659-2

3 4 5 6 7 8 9-DW-97 96 95

Brief Contents

Contents

5 The Scientific Method in Abnormal Psychology   **135**

PART 2 ANXIETY AND STRESS

6 Anxiety Disorders   **161**

7 Dissociative Disorders and Somatoform Disorders   **197**

11 Sexual and Gender Identity Disorders   **319**

Gender Identity Disorders 320
Etiology of Gender Identity Disorders 322
Treatment of Gender Identity Disorders 323

Paraphilias 324
Paraphilias Involving Nonhuman Objects 325
Paraphilias Involving Nonconsenting Others 327
Pedophilia 328
Paraphilias Involving Pain or Humiliation (Sadism and Masochism) 330

Etiology and Treatment of Paraphilias 332

Other Deviations Involving Sex 334
Rape 334
Incest 337
Treatment for Incest Offenders and Rapists 338

Sexual Dysfunction 339
The Sexual Response Cycle 341
Sexual Desire Disorders 344
Sexual Arousal Disorders 346
Female Orgasmic Disorder (Inhibited Female Orgasm) 347
Male Orgasmic Disorder (Inhibited Male Orgasm) 348
Premature Ejaculation 349
Sexual Pain Disorders 349
Etiology and Treatment of Sexual Dysfunctions 349

Homosexuality 353

Aging and Sexual Activity 354

Summary 355

Key Terms 356

PART 4 SEVERE DISORDERS OF MOOD AND THOUGHT

12 Mood Disorders   **359**

The Symptoms of Depression and Mania 360
Clinical Symptoms of Depression 360
Clinical Symptoms of Mania 362

Classification of Mood Disorders 363
Depressive Disorders 363
Bipolar Disorders 365
Other Mood Disorders 365
Symptom Features and Course Specifiers 365
Comparison Between Unipolar and Bipolar Disorders 366

The Etiology of Mood Disorders 366
The Causes of Depression 366
Biological Perspectives on Mood Disorders 376
Evaluating the Causation Theories 379

The Treatment of Mood Disorders 379
Biomedical Treatments for Unipolar Disorders 380
Cognitive-Behavioral Treatment for Unipolar Disorders 381
Biomedical Treatment for Bipolar Disorders 385

Summary 387

Key Terms 388

13 Suicide   **391**

Problems in the Study of Suicide 393

Hopelessness, Depression, and Suicide 393

Other Psychological Factors and Suicide 396

The Dynamics of Suicide 397
Sociocultural Explanations 397
Intrapsychic Explanations 398
Biochemical Factors in Suicide 399

The Victims of Suicide 400
Suicide Among Children and Adolescents 400
College Student Suicides 402
Suicide Among the Elderly 404
The Other Victims of Suicide 405

Preventing Suicide 407
Clues to Suicidal Intent 408
Crisis Intervention 408

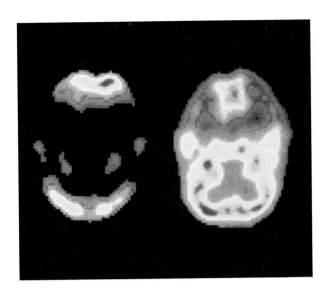

Features

FIRST PERSON NARRATIVES

CRITICAL THINKING DISCUSSIONS

DISORDER CHARTS

Preface

This is an exciting time to be learning about abnormal behavior, its causes, and its treatment. Researchers have made major advances in understanding genetic and other biological influences on mental disorders. At the same time, psychological models of psychopathology have become increasingly sophisticated, and much research has been conducted on effective forms of psychotherapy. In our society, health-care reform is altering the provision of mental health services, and new ethical issues concerning the delivery of mental health interventions have been raised. Looking beyond our society, we are becoming more familiar with other cultures and peoples, and more aware of variability in the way emotional distress is expressed and in the way problems are treated. This dynamic environment is the context in which we study abnormal behavior.

In writing and revising this book we have sought to engage students in the exciting process of understanding abnormal behavior and the ways that mental health professionals study and attempt to treat it. In pursuing this goal, we have been guided by three major objectives.

1. To provide students with scholarship of the highest quality

2. To offer an evenhanded treatment of abnormal psychology as both a scientific and a clinical endeavor, giving students the opportunity to explore topics thoroughly and responsibly

3. To make our book inviting and stimulating to a wide range of students

In each edition we have strived to achieve these objectives, working with comments from many students and instructors and our own work in teaching, research, and therapy. The Fourth Edition, we believe, builds on the achievements of previous editions and surpasses them.

OUR APPROACH

We are pleased to provide instructors and students with the most current information contained in the fourth edition of the *Diagnostic and Statistical Manual of Mental Disorders* (DSM-IV). We've provided readers with comprehensive, integrated coverage of changes in the DSM-IV diagnostic categories as well as analysis of those changes throughout the text. The DSM nosological system has generated much controversy, which we discuss as we examine the system's strengths, weaknesses, and evolution. This thorough integration of DSM distinguishes our text as an up-to-date and useful resource for student learning.

The text covers the major categories of disorders listed in DSM-IV, but is not a reiteration of DSM. We take an eclectic, multicultural approach to the field, drawing on important contributions from various disciplines and theoretical stances. We believe that different combinations of life experiences and constitutional factors influence behavioral disorders, and we project this view throughout the text. One vital aspect of life experience is cultural norms, values, and expectations. Because we are convinced that cross-cultural comparisons of abnormal behavior and treatment methods can greatly enhance our understanding of disorders, we pay special attention to cultural phenomena. For example, our analysis of mood disorders carefully examines gender and culture as factors in diagnosing and treating depression.

As psychologists (and professors) we know that learning is enhanced whenever material is presented in a lively and engaging manner. We achieve these qualities in part by providing case vignettes and clients' descriptions of their experiences to complement and illustrate research-based explanations. Controversial topics are highlighted and explored in depth. Among these are:

◆ Rape and symptoms of posttraumatic stress disorder (Chapter 6)

◆ Processes of addiction (Chapter 10)

◆ Eating disorders (Chapter 17)

◆ Cultural bias in psychotherapy (Chapter 18)

◆ Assisted suicide and the "right to die" (Chapter 20)

Complex material is presented with clarifying examples. The intriguing symptoms of multiple personality disorder emerge as an experienced therapist describes a client in detail (p. 202). The various factors that affect clients with mood disorders are carefully examined (p. 384). We try to encourage students to think critically about the knowledge they acquire in hope that they will develop an appreciation of the study of abnormal behavior rather than merely assimilate a collection of facts and theories.

SPECIAL FEATURES

Contributing to the strength of the Fourth Edition are a number of features popularized in earlier editions. Among these is the extended case study of Steven V., a unique device that translates theory into reality by interpreting the problems of a troubled college student through different theoretical perspectives. The case appears in four chapters, reflecting many of the issues presented in the text, such as the relationships among theoretical stances and the way therapists diagnose and treat mental illness. Steven's background and clinical history are discussed in Chapter 1. He is viewed from the biogenic, psychoanalytic, and humanistic-existential perspectives in Chapter 2, and from the behavioral and family systems perspectives in Chapter 3. The case culminates in Chapter 18, where Steven's therapist discusses his mental state, treatment, and prognosis from a systematic eclectic perspective. Other helpful features appearing in the previous edition include:

◈ Discussions of treatment approaches in each of the chapters on disorders as well as in a separate chapter

◈ Disorder charts that illustrate the relationships among categories of disorder in every chapter, based on DSM-IV criteria

◈ A separate chapter on suicide

◈ Two chapters devoted to schizophenia

◈ Focus boxes highlighting high-interest topics

◈ "First Person" essays that demonstrate therapy issues and the range of careers available in the field of psychopathology

◈ A chapter outline on the first page of every chapter

◈ Chapter summaries reinforcing important concepts and ideas

◈ Key terms with definitions listed at the end of each chapter, plus a glossary at the back of the book that defines all key terms

NEW TO THE FOURTH EDITION

Our foremost objective in preparing this edition was to update thoroughly and present the latest trends in research and clinical thinking. Most significantly, we have included information from the DSM-IV in all topical coverage of disorders. We also introduce and provide a thorough overview of the DSM's evolution in Chapter 4.

Throughout the text we have expanded our coverage of dozens of topics, including:

◈ Biochemical research and treatment perspectives for many of the disorders, including the use of drugs such as Prozac (in all chapters)

◈ An overview of biological research methods and techniques (Chapter 5)

◈ Cognitive therapies and their use in conjunction with drug treatment (Chapter 18)

◈ Cultural, gender, and stress factors involved in mood disorders (Chapter 12)

◈ Research on the process of addiction (Chapter 10)

◈ Eating disorders and cultural factors that may contribute to them (Chapter 17)

◈ Alzheimer's disease: its diagnosis, treatment, and effects (Chapter 16)

◈ Stress and the effects of Acquired Immune Deficiency Syndrome (Chapter 8)

◈ Delusions and hallucinations as symptoms of schizophrenia (Chapter 14)

A new feature, Critical Thinking, encourages students to evaluate and analyze a high-interest topic such as the causes of rape or the "right" to die. Each Critical Thinking box provides factual evidence and thought-provoking questions that raise key issues in research, examine widely held assumptions about abnormal behavior, or challenge the student's own understanding of the text material. The Critical Thinking feature is designed to prompt students to begin thinking about issues as a psychologist would, weighing the evidence and applying theoretical perspectives and personal experiences to arrive at an evaluation. The feature should also be helpful in sparking lively class discussion.

New First Person narratives discuss

- A case of multiple personality disorder
- Family counseling for families of Alzheimer's patients
- Battered women and their symptoms of PTSD
- AIDS and the diagnosis and treatment of a mood disorder
- A therapy program for women with eating disorders
- A psychologist's perspective on the issue of cross-cultural counseling.

New Focus box topics include

- Our ability to predict dangerous behavior in serial killers
- The relatively fast recovery from schizophrenia among people in developing countries
- The psychology of women from a feminist perspective
- The relationship between psychotherapy and cultural bias
- Reasons for early onset Alzheimer's disease

ORGANIZATION OF THE TEXT

In the Fourth Edition, we have reorganized some key material to make it more useful for professors and students alike, although the text continues to be organized into six major sections. Part I (Chapters 1 through 5) provides a context for viewing abnormal behavior and treatment by introducing students to historical contributions and to the diverse theoretical perspectives that currently are used to explain deviant behaviors. Biogenic and psychogenic models are presented in Chapter 2. We have moved an expanded discussion of basic brain structure and function to this introductory chapter, allowing fuller and more understandable explanations of biochemical processes through the entire remainder of the text. Behavioral and family systems models are presented in Chapter 3, including expanded coverage of cognitive perspectives. Chapter 4, which discusses the new edition of DSM, has also been restructured to present

an overview of assessment before moving into issues of classification. This logical progression encourages students to think about the relationship between assessment, classification, and diagnosis and the skills and methods involved in each of these activities. Chapter 5 examines research methods, including biological techniques that psychologists use in studying abnormal behavior.

The bulk of the text, Chapters 6 through 17, presents the major disorders covered in DSM-IV. In each chapter, symptoms are presented first, followed by diagnosis, theoretical perspectives, etiology, and treatment.

Part II contains three chapters that deal with anxiety and stress. Anxiety disorders are discussed in Chapter 6, somatoform and dissociative disorders in Chapter 7, and psychophysiological disorders in Chapter 8.

Part III includes chapters dealing with personality and impulse control disorders (Chapter 9), substance abuse (Chapter 10), and psychosexual disorders and dysfunctions (Chapter 11).

Part IV contains four chapters that deal with mood disorders (Chapter 12), suicide (Chapter 13), and schizophrenia (Chapters 14 and 15).

Part V encompasses cognitive impairment disorders (Chapter 16) and developmental disorders and mental retardation (Chapter 17). We have included the topic of mental retardation in Chapter 17 to bring it in line with the classification system of DSM and focusing on the essential characteristics—both causes and treatments—for this condition.

Part VI comprises three chapters. The first two, Chapters 18 and 19, examine treatment and community intervention. Although the therapies used to treat specific disorders are discussed in the disorders themselves, the different approaches can be more easily contrasted in a separate chapter. The chapter on community psychology (Chapter 19) explores the argument that community and institutional forces have a major impact on emotional well-being and that community interventions can be used to promote mental health. The final chapter (Chapter 20) deals with legal and ethical issues. Because of growing concern over such matters as the insanity defense, patients' rights, confidentiality, and mental health practices in general, we believe it is important to understand the issues and controversies surrounding these topics.

ANCILLARIES

We once again thank Richard L. Leavy of Ohio Wesleyan University for continuing his outstanding work on the ancillary package. He has substantially revised the *Instructor's Resource Manual* and *Study Guide*, and written approximately 1000 new questions for the *Test Bank*. All three of these key ancillaries are unified by the same set of learning objectives.

For each chapter of the text, the *Instructor's Resource Manual* includes an extended chapter outline, a set of learning objectives, discussion topics, classroom exercises, handouts, and a list of supplementary readings and audiovisual resources. New in the fourth edition of this manual are diagnostic problems that present a case study, a sample diagnostic "tree" or flow chart, and questions to prompt the student's clinical ability to make a correct diagnosis of disorder.

The *Instructor's Resource Manual* also includes a conversion chart to facilitate instructors' use of the new edition. This chart highlights new material and revisions to topic organization. It also provides a list of new disorder charts and their location throughout the text.

The enlarged *Test Bank* now includes one hundred multiple-choice questions per chapter, of which 50 percent are new (marked by an *) to this edition. (In items repeated from the previous edition, answer choices have been scrambled.) For each question, the corresponding learning objective, text page number, question type (fact/concept or application), and page number are provided. The new test questions provide a greater emphasis on application and higher-order thinking skills.

The *Study Guide* provides a complete review of each chapter in the text through the use of chapter outlines, learning objectives, a fill-in-the-blank review of key terms, and practice multiple-choice questions. The answers to the test questions include an explanation of each incorrect answer as well as the right answer; we know of no other study guide in abnormal psychology that contains this valuable pedagogical device.

A *Computerized Test Bank* available in both IBM and Macintosh formats allows instructors to create their own exams from the *Test Bank* questions and integrate their own questions with those on disk.

Finally, a selection of videos on topics in abnormal psychology is available to instructors with a minimum order of new books. Your Houghton Mifflin sales representative can provide the details.

ACKNOWLEDGMENTS

We'd like to express our thanks to Sumie Okazaki and Chi-Ah Chun, both of the University of California, Los Angeles, who assisted in the preparation of the new edition.

We continue to appreciate the feedback provided by reviewers and colleagues. The following individuals reviewed the manuscript for the Fourth Edition and shared valuable insights, opinions, and recommendations with us.

Ira W. Bernstein, University of Texas

Thomas Bradbury, University of California-Los Angeles

Mira M. Braunstein, New England College

Frank L. Collins, Oklahoma State University

Lorry J. Cology, Owens Technical College

Marcie Coulter, Holy Cross College

Robert Doan, University of Central Oklahoma

Lennis G. Echterling, James Madison University

A. Fazio, University of Wisconsin

Kenneth France, Shippensburg University

Fay Terris Friedman, D'Youville College

William F. Gayton, University of Southern Maine

R. Walter Heinrichs, York University

William L. Hoover, Suffolk County Community College

Arlene Confalone Lacombe, Chestnut Hill College

Alan R. Lang, Florida State University

Scott O. Lilienfeld, State University of New York-Albany

John Moritsugu, Pacific Lutheran University

Leslie Morey, Vanderbilt University

Michael W. O'Hara, University of Iowa

Denis Nissim-Sabat, Mary Washington College

Susan Schenck, Texas A&M University

Norman R. Simonson, University of Massachusetts, Amherst

Joseph J. Tecce, Boston College

Stephen Tiffany, Purdue University

Elaine F. Walker, Emory University

We would also like to acknowledge the continuing support and high quality of work by Houghton Mifflin personnel; in particular, Senior Sponsoring Editor Mike DeRocco for his vision regarding our book, Development Editor Susan Yanchus for her helpful comments and suggestions; and Senior Project Editor Carol Newman for her dedication and attentive supervision of the production process.

D.S.
D.S.
S.S.

UNDERSTANDING ABNORMAL BEHAVIOR

Abnormal Behavior

The study of abnormal psychology is a journey into known and unknown territories of the mind. To help you understand the scope and dynamics of this field, we would like to start by introducing you to Steven V. Steve is a 21-year-old college student who exemplifies many of the issues we discuss in this text. We begin his story in the office of his therapist.

Steven V. had been suffering from a crippling and severe bout of depression. Eighteen months earlier, Steve's woman friend, Linda, had broken off her relationship with Steve. Steve had fallen into a crippling depression. During the past few weeks, however, with the encouragement of his therapist, Steve had begun to open up and express his innermost feelings. His depression had lifted, but it was replaced by a deep anger and hostility toward Linda. In today's session, Steve had become increasingly loud and agitated as he recounted his complaints against Linda. Minutes ago, with his hands clenched into fists, his knuckles white, he had abruptly lowered his voice and looked his therapist in the eye. "She doesn't deserve to live," Steve had said. "I swear, I'm going to kill her."

The therapist could feel himself becoming tense, apprehensive, and uncertain: How should he interpret the threat? How should he act on it? One wheel of his swivel chair squealed sharply, breaking the silence, as he backed away from his client.

Until this session, the therapist had not believed Steve was dangerous. Now he wondered whether Steve could be the one client in ten thousand to act out such a threat. Should Linda or the police be told of what Steve had said?

Steve V. had a long psychiatric history, beginning well before he first sought help from the therapist at the university's psychological services center. (In fact, his parents wanted their son to continue seeing a private therapist, but Steve stopped therapy during his junior year at the university.) Steve had actually been in and out of psychotherapy since kindergarten; while in high school, he was hospitalized twice for depression.

His case records, nearly two inches thick, contained a number of diagnoses, including labels such as *schizoid personality, paranoid schizophrenia*, and *manic-depressive psychosis* (now referred to as a bipolar mood disorder). Although his present therapist did not find these labels particularly helpful, Steve's clinical history did provide some clues to the causes of his problems.

Steven V. was born in a suburb of San Francisco, California, the only child of an extremely wealthy couple. His father was a prominent businessman who worked long hours and traveled frequently. On those rare occasions when he was at home, Mr. V. was often preoccupied with business matters and held himself quite aloof from his son. The few interactions they had were characterized by his constant ridicule and criticism of Steve. Mr. V. was greatly disappointed that his son seemed so timid, weak, and withdrawn. Steve was extremely bright and did well in school, but Mr. V. felt that he lacked the "toughness" needed to survive and prosper in today's world. Once, when Steve was about ten years old, he came home from school with a bloody nose and bruised face, crying and complaining of being picked on by his schoolmates. His father showed no sympathy but instead berated Steve for losing the fight. In his father's presence, Steve usually felt worthless, humiliated, and fearful of doing or saying the wrong thing.

Mrs. V. was very active in civic and social affairs, and she too spent relatively little time with her son. Although she treated Steve more warmly and lovingly than his father did, she seldom came to Steve's defense when Mr. V. bullied him. She generally allowed her husband to make family decisions.

When Steve was a child, his mother at times had been quite affectionate. She had often allowed Steve to sleep with her in her bed when her husband was away on business trips. She usually dressed minimally on these occasions and was very demonstrative—holding, stroking, and kissing Steve. This behavior had continued until Steve was twelve, when his mother abruptly refused to let

Steve into her bed. The sudden withdrawal of this privilege had confused and angered Steve, who was not certain what he had done wrong. He knew, though, that his mother had been quite upset when she awoke one night to find him masturbating next to her.

Most of the time, however, Steve's parents seemed to live separately from one another and from their son. Steve was raised, in effect, by a full-time maid. He rarely had playmates of his own age. His birthdays were celebrated with a cake and candles, but the only celebrants were Steve and his mother. By age ten, Steve had learned to keep himself occupied by playing "mind games," letting his imagination carry him off on flights of fantasy. He frequently imagined himself as a powerful figure—Superman or Batman. His fantasies were often extremely violent, and his foes were vanquished only after much blood had been spilled.

As Steve grew older, his fantasies and heroes became increasingly menacing and evil. When he was fifteen, he obtained a pornographic videotape that he viewed repeatedly on a video player in his room. Often, Steve would masturbate as he watched scenes of women being sexually violated. The more violent the acts against women, the more aroused he became. He was addicted to the *Nightmare on Elm Street* films, in which the villain, Freddie Kruger, disemboweled or slashed his victims to death with his razor-sharp glove. Steve now recalls that he spent much of his spare time between the ages of fifteen and seventeen watching X-rated videotapes or violent movies, his favorite being *The Texas Chainsaw Massacre*, in which a madman saws and hacks women to pieces. Steve always identified with the character perpetrating the outrage; at times, he imagined his parents as the victims.

At about age sixteen, Steve became convinced that external forces were controlling his mind and behavior and were drawing him into his fantasies. He was often filled with guilt and anxiety after one of his mind games. Although he was strongly attracted to his fantasy world, he also felt that something was wrong with it and with him. After seeing the movie *The Exorcist*, he became convinced that he was possessed by the devil.

Until this time, Steve had been quiet and withdrawn. In kindergarten the school psychologist had described his condition as autisticlike because Steve seldom spoke, seemed unresponsive to the environment, and was socially isolated. His parents had immediately hired a prominent child psychiatrist to work with Steve. The psychiatrist had assured them that Steve was not autistic but would need intensive treatment for several years. And throughout these years of treatment, Steve never acted out any of his fantasies. With the development of his interest in the occult and in demonic possession, however, he became outgoing, flamboyant, and even exhibitionistic. He read extensively about Satanism, joined a "Church of Satan" in San Francisco, and took to wearing a black cape on weekend journeys into that city. Against his will, he was hospitalized twice by his parents with diagnoses of, respectively, bipolar affective disorder and schizophrenia in remission.

Steve was twenty-one years old when he met Linda at an orientation session for first-year university students. Linda struck him as different from the other women students: unpretentious, open, and friendly. He quickly became obsessed with their relationship. But although Linda dated Steve frequently over the next few months, she did not seem to reciprocate his intense feelings. She took part in several extracurricular activities, including the student newspaper and student government, and her willingness to be apart from him confused and frustrated Steve. When her friends were around, Linda seemed almost oblivious to Steve's existence. In private, however, she was warm, affectionate, and intimate. She would not allow sexual intercourse, but she and Steve did engage in heavy petting.

Even while he and Linda were dating, Steve grew increasingly insecure about their relationship. He felt slighted by Linda's friends and began to believe that she disliked him. Several times he accused her of plotting against him and deliberately making him feel inadequate. Linda continually denied these allegations. Finally (on one occasion), feeling frightened and intimidated by Steve, she acquiesced to having sex with him. Unfortunately, Steve could not maintain an erection. When he blamed her for this "failure" and became verbally and physically abusive, Linda put an end to their relationship and refused to see him again.

During the next year and a half, Steve suffered from severe bouts of depression and twice attempted suicide by drug overdose. For the past six months, up to the time of his threat, he had been seeing a therapist regularly at the university's psychological services center.

What do you make of Steven V.? His behavior is certainly beyond almost anyone's definition of normal. But is he a dangerous person from whom society must be protected? Is he a pathetic figure, doomed to fail in relationships with others as he did with Linda? Or is his major problem simply a lack of social skills that, once learned, will enable him to interact comfortably and confidently with other people?

In a sense, the purpose of this book, *Understanding Abnormal Behavior,* is to help you answer such questions. But at this point these questions are premature. Let's first examine some basic aspects of the study of abnormal behavior, including some of its history. Then, at the end of this chapter, we'll again discuss the case of Steven V. and its place in this book.

THE CONCERNS OF ABNORMAL PSYCHOLOGY

Abnormal psychology is the scientific study whose objectives are to describe, explain, predict, and control behaviors that are considered strange or unusual. Its subject matter ranges from the bizarre and spectacular to the more commonplace—from the violent homicides and "perverted" sexual acts that are widely reported by the news media to such unsensational (but more prevalent) behaviors as stuttering, depression, ulcers, and anxiety about examinations.

Describing Abnormal Behavior

The description of a particular case of abnormal behavior must be based on systematic observations by an attentive professional. These observations, usually paired with the results of psychological tests and with the person's psychological history, become the raw material for a **psychodiagnosis,** an attempt to describe, assess, and systematically draw inferences about an individual's psychological disorder.

Diagnosis is obviously an important early step in the treatment process. But a diagnosis that is not de-

During a therapy session, the therapist not only hears about the client's problems, but also carefully observes the client's behavior and emotional reactions. These observations can help to form the basis of a psychodiagnosis.

veloped with great care can end up as nothing more than a label that tends to hinder rather than aid treatment. Such labels present two major problems. First, a term such as *manic-depressive* (a term once used to refer to a particular mood disorder), which was originally used to describe Steven V., can cover a wide range of behaviors, so this label may mean different things to different psychologists. A label may therefore be too general—it may describe something other than a client's specific behaviors. Additionally, it describes only a current condition rather than a past or changing circumstance. Third, a person's (especially a young person's) psychological problems are likely to change over time. A previous diagnosis can quickly become obsolete, a label that no longer describes that person. To guard against these problems, sensitive therapists ensure that labels, either old or new, are not substitutes for careful investigation of a client's condition.

Explaining Abnormal Behavior

To explain abnormal behavior, the psychologist must identify its causes and determine how they led to the described behavior. This information, in turn, bears heavily on how a program of treatment is chosen.

As you will see in later chapters, explanations of abnormal behavior do vary, depending on the psychologist's theoretical orientation. For example, Steve's therapist might stress his client's loneliness, lack of self-esteem, and feelings of worthlessness brought about by his parents' actions—primarily his father's—and his lack of companions his own age. To make up for what was missing from his life (the therapist might contend), Steve created a fantasy world in which he could feel powerful, freely express his anger toward his parents, and experience a sense of self-worth. But when Steve became disturbed by his own anger and hatred toward his parents, he protected himself by adopting the belief that these feelings were implanted by a demon and beyond his (Steve's) control.

Explanations offered by other psychologists might be more biological in nature, emphasizing genetics or a biochemical imbalance. Still other psychologists might focus on Steve's inadequate interpersonal skills: he cannot make friends or develop meaningful relationships because he has never learned how to act around others. And still others might see and treat Steve's behavior as resulting from a combination of these causes.

Predicting Abnormal Behavior

If a therapist can correctly identify the source of a client's difficulty, he or she should be able to predict the kinds of problems the client will face during therapy and the symptoms the client will display. The therapist should try to predict the process to prepare the client for potential problems. But therapists have difficulty predicting the future course of many disorders. Even an experienced professional finds it hard to foretell how a particular client will behave.

For example, consider Steve's threat to kill Linda. Was it an empty threat—just Steve's way of venting his anger—or was it serious? Research shows that mental health professionals do a poor job of answering such questions; they tend to greatly overpredict violence.

Steve's threat raises another important issue—that of the therapist's legal and ethical responsibilities. Psychologists routinely grapple with questions of social responsibility. In particular, should Steve's therapist make the threat known? And if he does, how will it affect the therapeutic process? These issues are discussed more fully in Chapter 20.

In a landmark legal case (*Tarasoff v. Regents of the University of California*, 1974), the California Supreme Court ruled that, if a therapist hears a client threaten someone and does not inform the threatened person, and if the threat is carried out, then the injured person has the right to sue the therapist. Some therapists believe that the ruling weakens the principle of confidentiality that is central to the client-therapist relationship because it stipulates conditions under which a client's confidentiality must be violated. As one therapist remarked, "No one wants a shrink who's a fink." Naturally, no therapist wants a client to hurt or kill anyone either. As we will discuss in Chapter 20, the therapist has both a legal and ethical obligation to balance the trust of the client-therapist relationship with the cost of a human life (protection of society).

Controlling Abnormal Behavior

Abnormal behavior may be controlled through **therapy,** which is a program of systematic intervention whose purpose is to modify a client's behavioral, affective (emotional), or cognitive state. For example, many therapists believe that allowing Steve to vent his anger at Linda reduces the chances of his harming her. Others might also recommend family therapy, social skills training, or medication. As we have noted, the treatment for abnormal behavior generally follows from its explanation. Just as there are many

By most people's standards, this man's outfit would probably be considered unusual at best and bizarre at worst. It certainly can't be considered normal everyday wear. Yet, despite the way he dresses, this person may be very functional in his work and personal life.

ways to explain abnormal behaviors, many ways have been proposed to control them.

DEFINING ABNORMAL BEHAVIOR

Implicit in our discussion so far is the one overriding concern of abnormal psychology: abnormal behavior itself. But what exactly is abnormal behavior, and how do psychologists recognize it?

We will examine four types of criteria that may be used to define or characterize behaviors as abnormal. Two of them—statistical criteria and criteria for ideal mental health—define abnormal behavior as, essentially, deviations from what is considered normal. The third considers multicultural factors in defining abnormality. The fourth type—consisting of the practical criteria—takes account of the effect of the behavior on the person exhibiting it or on others.

Statistical Criteria

Statistical criteria equate normality with those behaviors that occur most frequently in the population. Abnormality is therefore defined in terms of those behaviors that occur least frequently. For example, data on IQ scores may be accumulated and an average calculated. Then IQ scores near that average are considered normal, and relatively large deviations from the norm (in either direction) are considered abnormal. In spite of the word *statistical,* however, these criteria need not be quantitative in nature: People who talk to themselves incessantly, undress in public, or laugh uncontrollably for no apparent reason are considered abnormal according to statistical criteria simply because most people do not behave that way.

Statistical criteria may seem adequate in some specific instances, but they have many problems. One problem is that they fail to take into account differences in place, community standards, and cultural values. For example, some lifestyles that are acceptable in San Francisco and New York may be judged abnormal by community standards in other parts of the nation. Likewise, if deviations from the majority are considered abnormal, then many ethnic and racial minorities that show strong subcultural differences from the majority must be classified as abnormal. When we use a statistical definition, the dominant or most powerful group generally determines what constitutes normality and abnormality.

In addition, the statistical criteria do not provide any basis for distinguishing between desirable and undesirable deviations from the norm. An IQ score of 100 is considered normal or average. But what constitutes an abnormal deviation from this average? More important, is abnormality defined in only one direction or in both? An IQ score of 55 is considered abnormal by most people; but should people with IQ scores of 145 or higher also be considered abnormal? How does one evaluate such personality traits as assertiveness and dependence in terms of statistical criteria?

Two other central problems also arise. First, people who strike out in new directions—artistically, politically, or intellectually—may be seen as candidates for psychotherapy simply because they do not conform to normative behavior. Second, statistical criteria may "define" quite widely distributed but undesirable characteristics, such as anxiety, as normal.

In spite of these weaknesses, statistical criteria remain among the most widely used determinants of normality and abnormality. Not only do they underlie the layperson's evaluation of behaviors, they are the most frequently used criteria in psychology. Many psychological tests and much diagnosis and classification of behavior disorders are based in part on statistical criteria.

Criteria for Ideal Mental Health

The concept of ideal mental health has been proposed as a criterion of normality by humanistic psychologists Carl Rogers and Abraham Maslow. Deviations from the ideal are taken to indicate varying degrees of abnormality.

Such criteria stress the importance of attaining some positive goal. Maslow and his followers have suggested *self-actualization* or *creativity.* Psychoanalytically oriented psychologists have used the concept of *consciousness* (awareness of motivations and behaviors) and *balance of psychic forces* as criteria for normality. Aspects of maturity such as *competence, autonomy,* and *resistance to stress* have also been proposed. But using any of these constructs as the sole criterion for defining normality leads to a number of problems.

First, which particular goal or ideal should be used? The answer depends largely on the particular theoretical frame of reference or values embraced by those proposing the criterion. Second, most of these goals are vague; they lack clarity and precision. If resistance to stress is the goal, are the only healthy persons those who can always adapt? Recent experiences with prisoners of war indicate that, under repeated stress, many eventually break down. Should we label them as unhealthy? Third, ideal criteria exclude too many people: Most persons would be considered mentally unhealthy by these definitions.

Multicultural Criteria

The traditional view of abnormal psychology is based on the assumption that a fixed set of mental disorders

Mother Teresa and the Reverend Martin Luther King, Jr. are perceived by many to be self-actualized people, who have made extensive commitments and contributions to society—Mother Teresa to the poor in India and other Third World countries, providing shelter and medical care; Reverend King to the Civil Rights movement in the United States.

exists, whose obvious manifestations cut across cultures (Draguns, 1985; D. W. Sue & D. Sue, 1990; Triandis, 1983). This psychiatric tradition dates back to Emil Kraepelin (to be discussed shortly), who believed that depression, sociopathic behavior, and especially schizophrenia were universal disorders that appeared in all cultures and societies. Early research supported the belief that these disorders occurred worldwide, had similar processes, and were more similar than dissimilar (Howard, 1991; Wittkower & Rin, 1965). Such **cultural universality** has led to the belief that a disorder such as depression is similar in origin, process, and manifestation in Asian, black, Hispanic, or white clients. As a result, no modifications in diagnosis and treatment need be made; western concepts of normality and abnormality could be considered universal and equally applicable across cultures.

At the other extreme were social scientists who stressed **cultural relativism**. This concept arose from anthropological tradition and stressed the importance of diversity in the manifestation of abnormal symptoms. Deviant behavior was seen to reflect the lifestyle, cultural values, and world views of the afflicted peoples. For example, a body of research supports the conclusion that "acting-out" behaviors associated with mental disorders are much higher in the United States than in Asia, and even Asian Americans in the United States are less likely to express symptoms via "acting out" (Leong, 1986). Researchers have proposed that Asian cultural values (restraint of feelings, emphasis on self-control, and need for subtlety in approaching problems) all contribute to their restraint. Furthermore, cultures seem to vary in what they consider to be normal or abnormal behavior. In some societies and cultural groups, hallucinating is considered normal in specific situations. Yet in the United States, hallucinating is generally perceived to be a manifestation of a disorder.

Which of these views is correct? Are the criteria used to determine normality and abnormality culturally universal or specific? Few mental health professionals today embrace the extreme of either position, although most gravitate toward one or the other. Proponents of cultural universality focus on the disorder and minimize cultural factors, and proponents of cultural relativism focus on the culture and on how the disorder is manifested within it. Both views have validity. It is naive to believe that no disorders cut across different cultures and share universal char-

Why Do Mental Disorders Vary Across Populations?

Do men and women differ in the type of mental disorders they are likely to suffer? Does belonging to a particular racial or ethnic minority group place an individual at higher or lower risk for a disorder? What about such variables as age, place of residence, social class, and religious background? More and more, we are beginning to recognize that the types of mental problems likely to come to the attention of mental health practitioners and professionals are powerfully affected by these and many other factors.

For example, it is quite clear that men are more likely to evidence alcohol abuse or dependence and drug abuse or dependence problems, whereas women are more likely to suffer depressive and anxiety disorders. Drug problems are more prevalent in persons between eighteen and twenty-four years of age; alcohol and depression in persons between twenty-five and forty-four years of age; and cognitive impairments in persons sixty-five years and older (Regier et al., 1988). Some evidence exists that people in lower socioeconomic classes are likely to be identified as severely disturbed when they suffer an emotional disorder (Lopez, 1989).

Similar influences have been found with respect to racial or ethnic minority group membership. Native Americans have been found to have higher rates of alcohol abuse and dependence than the general population (Red Horse, 1982; Rhoades et al., 1980). Statistics also show inordinately high suicide rates in the Native American population (Shore, 1988). Likewise, Hispanic Americans have been identified as suffering more severe cognitive impairment than European Americans and may somaticize (express psychological problems via bodily complaints) more (Lopez, 1989; Lopez & Hernandez, 1987).

What do all of these differences mean? Are the differences real or are they artifacts that can be explained in other possible ways? Although these questions will no doubt continue to be debated, several conclusions can apparently be drawn. First, it appears that all groups are probably equally susceptible to psychological distress. Furthermore, considerable evidence exists suggesting that social conditioning, cultural factors, sociopolitical influences, and diagnostic bias may all affect the identification and manifestation of a behavior disorder.

1. *Social conditioning* How we are raised, what values are instilled in us, and how we are expected to behave in fulfilling our roles seem to have a major effect on the type of disorder we are most likely to exhibit. In the case of gender, for example, the roles we are expected to play and what is considered appropriate or inappropriate sex-role behavior may account for why some differences exist between men and women in mental disorders. In our culture, men are raised to fulfill the masculine role: independent, assertive, courageous, active, unsentimental, and objective. Women, in contrast, are raised to be dependent, helpful, fragile, self-abnegating, conforming, empathetic, and emotional. As a result, some mental health professionals believe that women are more likely to internalize their conflicts (resulting in anxiety and depression), whereas men are more likely to externalize and act out (resulting in drug or alcohol abuse and dependence). Although sex roles have begun to change, their effects continue to be widely felt.

2. *Cultural values and influences* How culture affects the manifestation of behavior disorders is also becoming a much researched area in the field of psychopathology. Mental health professionals now recognize that types of mental disorders differ from country to country, and that var-

acteristics. For example, even though hallucinating may be viewed as normal in one culture, proponents of cultural universality argue that it still represents a breakdown in biological-cognitive processes. Likewise, it is equally naive to believe that the relative frequencies and manner of symptom formation for various disorders do not reflect dominant cultural values and the lifestyles of a society. A third point to consider is that some common disorders, such as depression, are manifested similarly in different cultures. A more fruitful approach to studying multicultural criteria of abnormality is to explore two ques-

ious racial and ethnic minority groups in the United States may possess major differences likely to influence susceptibility to certain emotional disorders. Among Asian Americans, experiencing physical complaints (somaticizing) is a common and culturally accepted means of expressing psychological and emotional stress (S. Sue & Morishima, 1982; D.W. Sue & D. Sue, 1990). It is believed that physical problems cause emotional disturbances, and that the emotional disturbances will disappear as soon as appropriate treatment for the physical illness is instituted. In addition, mental illness among Asians is seen as a source of shame and disgrace, although physical illness is acceptable. Asian values also stress restraint of strong feelings. Thus when stress is encountered, the mental health professional is likely to hear complaints involving headaches, fatigue, restlessness, and disturbances of sleep and appetite.

3. *Sociopolitical influences* In response to the history of prejudice, discrimination, and racism, many minorities have adopted various behaviors (in particular, behaviors toward whites) that have proved important for survival in a racist society (Grier & Cobbs, 1986; D.W. Sue & D. Sue, 1990). These behaviors may be seen by mental health professionals as being abnormal and deviant. Yet, when seen from the minority group perspective, they may be viewed as healthy functional survival mechanisms. For example, "playing it cool" has been identified as one means by which

minorities may conceal their true thoughts and feelings. An African American who is experiencing conflict, anger, or even rage may be skillful at appearing serene and composed. This tactic is a survival mechanism aimed at reducing one's vulnerability to harm and exploitation in a hostile environment. Early personality studies of blacks concluded that, as a group, blacks tend to appear more "suspicious," "mistrustful," and "paranoid" than their white counterparts. But are African Americans inherently pathological, as studies suggest, or are they making healthy responses? Members of minority groups who have been victims of discrimination and oppression in a society not yet free of racism have good reasons to be suspicious and distrustful of white society. The "paranoid orientation" may reflect not only survival skills but also *accurate reality testing*. We are pointing out that certain behaviors and characteristics need to be evaluated not only by an absolute standard, but by the sociopolitical context in which it arises.

4. *Bias in diagnosis and classification* Epidemiological studies reporting the distribution and types of mental disorders that occur in the population may be prone to bias of the clinician and researcher. The mental health professional is not immune from inheriting the prejudicial attitudes, biases, and stereotypes of the larger society. Even the most enlightened and well-intentioned mental health professional may be the victim of race, gender, and social class bias.

Several forms of bias appear to be operative when clinicians are identifying certain disorders. One is the tendency to attribute the disorders of one group as being more severe than they are because cultural values or lifestyles may differ markedly from the clinician's own. This may be the case with respect to lower socioeconomic clients and racial or ethnic minority groups. Overpathologizing the severity of disorders has been found to exist for African Americans, Hispanic Americans, and women (Lopez & Hernandez, 1986). Equally disturbing, a second bias can be identified: underpathologizing a disorder. For example, some studies reveal a minimizing bias in the diagnosis of psychotic symptoms for mentally retarded individuals (it is more "normal" for them) (Reiss, Levitan & Szyszko, 1982). Women who present symptoms perceived to be related to their gender role (emotionality and depression) may be seen as less disturbed (Horwitz & White, 1987). Third, biases may be linked to overdiagnosis and underdiagnosis of specific disorders. Being black or Hispanic may increase a patient's chances of being misdiagnosed as schizophrenic when in fact he or she is suffering from a bipolar disorder (Mukherjee et al., 1983).

In closing, mental health professionals must exercise caution in interpreting epidemiological statistics related to the incidence and prevalence of psychopathology in the population.

tions. First, what is universal in human behavior that is also relevant to understanding psychopathology? Second, what is the relationship between cultural norms, values, and attitudes, and the incidence and manifestation of behavior disorders? These are important questions (see Critical Thinking) that we hope you will constantly ask as we continue our journey into the field of abnormal psychology.

Practical Criteria

Practical, or clinical, criteria are subject to many of the same criticisms as other criteria. Nonetheless, according to Buss (1966), they are often the basis on which people who are labeled abnormal or unhealthy come to the attention of psychologists or other mental health specialists. Moreover, clinicians often must act primarily on the basis of pragmatic manifestations. The practical criteria for abnormality include subjective discomfort, bizarreness, and inefficiency.

Discomfort   Most people who see clinicians are suffering physical or psychological discomfort. Many physical reactions stem from a strong psychological component; among them are disorders such as asthma, hypertension, and ulcers as well as physical symptoms such as fatigue, nausea, pain, and heart palpitations. Discomfort can also be manifested in extreme or prolonged emotional reactions, of which anxiety and depression are the most prevalent and common. Of course, it is normal for a person to feel depressed after suffering a loss or a disappointment. But if the reaction is so intense, exaggerated, and prolonged that it interferes with the person's capacity to function adequately, it is likely to be considered abnormal.

Bizarreness   As a practical criterion for abnormality, bizarreness is closely related to statistical criteria. Bizarre or unusual behavior is an abnormal deviation from an accepted standard of behavior (such as an antisocial act) or a false perception of reality (such as a hallucination). This criterion is extremely subjective; it depends on the individual being diagnosed, the diagnostician, and, as we have just seen, on the particular culture.

Certain sexual behaviors, delinquency, and homicide are examples of acts that our society considers abnormal. But social norms are far from static, and behavioral standards cannot be considered absolute. Changes in our attitudes toward human sexuality provide a prime example. During the Victorian era, women wore six to eight undergarments to make sure that every part of the body from the neck down was covered. Exposing an ankle was roughly equivalent to wearing a topless bathing suit today. Taboos against publicly recognizing sexuality dictated that words be chosen carefully to avoid any sexual connotation. Victorians said "limb" instead of "leg" because the word *leg* was considered too erotic. (Even pianos and tables were said to have limbs.) People who did not adhere to these strict codes of conduct were considered immoral or even perverted.

Nowadays, however, magazines and films openly exhibit the naked human body, and topless and bottomless nightclub entertainment is hardly newsworthy. Various sex acts are explicitly portrayed in X-rated movies. Women are freer to question traditional sex roles and to act more assertively in initiating sex. Such changes in behavioral standards make it difficult to subscribe to absolute standards of normality.

Nevertheless, some behaviors can usually be judged abnormal in most situations. Among these are hallucinations, delusions, and severe disorientation. *Hallucinations* are false impressions that involve the senses. People who have hallucinations (they may be pleasant or unpleasant) may hear, feel, or see things that are not really there, such as voices accusing them of vile deeds, insects crawling on their bodies, or monstrous apparitions. *Delusions* are false beliefs steadfastly held by the individual despite contradictory objective evidence. A delusion of grandeur is a belief that one is an exalted personage, such as Jesus Christ or Joan of Arc; a delusion of persecution is a belief that one is controlled by others or is the victim of a conspiracy. Schroth and Sue (1975) reported the following example of a delusionary system involving both grandiosity and persecution:

A young schizophrenic believed that there was an elaborate plot to kill him because he was, in truth, Jesus Christ. The plotters had discovered his true identity and were themselves agents of Israel. He believed he was sent to earth to save humanity from Communist and Jewish foolishness. He said God had told him personally of his role but requested him to maintain secrecy while saving the world. Somehow the word got out, even to his relatives, who had been corrupted by his enemies, and they were trying to keep him in the hospital. (p. 291)

Disorientation is confusion with regard to identity, place, or time. People who are disoriented may not know who they are, where they are, or what historical era they are living in.

Inefficiency   In everyday life, people are expected to fulfill various roles—as students or teachers, as workers and caretakers, as parents, lovers, and marital partners. Emotional problems sometimes interfere with the performance of these roles, and the resulting role inefficiency may be used as an indicator of abnormality.

One way to assess efficiency (or inefficiency) is to compare an individual's performance with the requirements of the role. Another related means of assessment is to compare the individual's performance

Cult leader David Koresh convinced his followers that he was Jesus Christ, had a special gift for deciphering the Holy Scriptures, could foretell the end of the world, and believed his "exalted" personage allowed him special favors from women. Was he delusional? Koresh, along with most of his followers, died in a blazing fire in their Branch Davidian compound in Waco, Texas in 1993.

with his or her potential. An individual with an IQ score of 150 who is failing in school can be labeled inefficient. (The label *underachiever* is often hung on students who possess high intelligence but obtain poor grades in school.) Similarly, a productive worker who suddenly becomes unproductive may be experiencing emotional stress. The major weakness of this approach is that it is difficult to accurately assess potential. How do we know whether a person is performing at his or her peak? To answer such questions, psychologists, educators, and the business sector have relied heavily on testing. Tests of specific abilities and intelligence are attempts to assess potential and to predict performance in schools or jobs.

The Concept of Multiple Perspectives

Different definitions of abnormality carry different implications, and there is no easy consensus on a best definition. All the criteria we have discussed have shortcomings. Some are more precise than others in specifying what behaviors are or are not considered abnormal, some seem to fit our beliefs about abnor-

mality better than others, and all are sensitive to such variables as psychological orientation and societal and individual value systems.

Perhaps, then, abnormality should not be viewed from a single perspective or measured in accordance with a single criterion. Two researchers (Strupp & Hadley, 1977) working together have proposed a three-part method that can be used to define normality and abnormality. They identify three vantage points from which to judge a person's mental health: (1) that of society, (2) that of the individual, and (3) that of the mental health professional. Each "judge" operates from a different perspective, perhaps using different criteria. At times, three people taking these viewpoints would agree that a person is either mentally disturbed or mentally healthy. At other times, they might disagree. Nonetheless, using multiple criteria alleviates the problems inherent in imposing a single criterion.

We must carefully consider two important points as we assess the value of the multiple-perspectives concept. First, a person who feels subjectively contented—mentally sound—may be perceived as unhealthy from a societal perspective. For example, people who commit antisocial acts such as rape, murder, or robbery may not feel remorseful but may be quite contented with their acts. Likewise, an artist living a very unconventional lifestyle may be judged maladapted from society's perspective; from that individual's perspective and the perspective of many health professionals, however, he or she is intact and sound. Second, a judgment must be recognized as stemming from one of the three vantage points. Otherwise, even greater confusion could result.

Recently, Wakefield (1992) has advocated defining the concept of mental disorder from the perspective of biological facts and social values. He argues that a mental disorder is a "harmful dysfunction," wherein the term *harmful* is based on social norms, and *dysfunction* is a scientific term referring to the "failure of a mental mechanism to perform a natural function for which it was designed by evolution." This definition considers several things as important: (1) understanding dysfunction requires identifying the natural functions of an organ or organ system (the function of the heart is to pump blood); (2) distinguishing between functions and effects (the sound of a beating heart is an effect and not a function—thus a quiet heart is not a dysfunction); (3) we must ultimately look for our definition of disorder in the biological sciences; and (4) dysfunction must involve the harm requirement (social and cultural perspectives). This latter point is important to understand. Wakefield argues that dysfunctions must cause significant harm to the person according to current environmental and cultural standards. For example, a man whose aging mechanism suffers a dysfunction and slows the aging process would not be considered disordered but lucky! Thus albinism, reversal of heart position, and fused toes would not be considered disorders even though they involve a breakdown of natural functions. Likewise, hallucinations may be a manifestation of a mental disorder because they represent a *dysfunction* of a normal biological process. Yet, a cultural group which values "visions" would not consider them harmful, but a positive development.

A truly adequate understanding of mental illness and health can be reached through comprehensive evaluation from all points of view. It may not be enough to rely solely on the judgments of mental health professionals, who are not immune to biases and shortcomings.

A Definition of Abnormal Behavior

Thus we may define **abnormal behavior** as behavior that departs from some norm and that harms the affected individual or others. This definition encompasses—or at least allows room for—the various criteria and perspectives on behavior. It also accurately implies that no precise, universally acknowledged line delineates normal behavior from abnormal behavior.

Somewhat more loosely, we will speak of *mentally disturbed people* as those individuals who display abnormal behavior. And by a *mental disorder* or *mental disturbance* we mean some recognizable pattern of abnormal behavior.

THE INCIDENCE OF ABNORMAL BEHAVIOR

A student once asked one of the authors, "How crazy is this nation?" This question, put in somewhat more scientific terms, has occupied psychologists for some time. Psychiatric epidemiology provides insights into factors that contribute to the occurrence of specific mental disorders. From this information, we can find out how frequently or infrequently various disturbances occur in the population; how the prevalence of disorders varies by ethnicity, gender, and age; and whether current mental health practices are sufficient and effective (Lopez, 1989; Watkins & Peterson, 1986).

Current Research into the Epidemiology of Mental Disorders

An early but highly regarded and frequently cited study, the Midtown Manhattan Study, was performed in 1950 (Srole et al., 1962). Fifteen hundred New Yorkers were interviewed and rated on their psychological health. The results were startling: Approximately 25 percent of those interviewed showed severe impairment, about 55 percent were mildly impaired, and only 20 percent (one in five) were rated unimpaired.

Some social commentators contend that our mental health has deteriorated since the Midtown Manhattan Study was conducted. They point to such "evidence" as the mushrooming of cults, a revival of belief in the supernatural, the increased incidence of mass and serial murders, and attempts at political assassination. To ascertain whether the population's

According to research done in 1984, almost one out of every five Americans suffers from some kind of mental disorder. This incidence rate was about the same in 1950. What is alarming, though, is that fewer than one-third of those suffering from a mental disorder are receiving mental health services.

mental health was deteriorating, a similar study was carried out in the 1970s (Srole & Fisher, 1980). Although the investigators found no support for this contention, neither did they find any evidence that the mental health of Americans had improved in the intervening decades!

A number of other studies have found equally disheartening tendencies (Dohrenwend & Dohrenwend, 1982; Dohrenwend et al., 1980; Mechanic, 1978; and Regier, Goldberg & Taube, 1978). These studies estimate that some 25 to 40 million Americans, or approximately 15 percent of the population, suffer from serious emotional disorders. Counting both severe and milder disturbances, estimates are that 44 million Americans suffer from symptoms of depression, 20 million have drug-related problems, 4 to 9 million have some form of phobic or anxiety disturbance, 6 million are mentally retarded, and 2 million suffer from schizophrenia. In addition, some 25,000 to 60,000 people commit suicide each year, and another 200,000 attempt it. These estimates do not include disorders such as child abuse, sexual dysfunctions, and pathological expressions of violence, which could increase the total substantially. For example, every year 20,000 murders are committed in the United States; an average of 10 out of every

100,000 Americans will be murdered (Thiers, 1988). Crime statistics also show that 456,000 acts of family violence are reported each year in the United States, and that figure probably grossly underestimates the number of acts committed because many such acts go unreported.

Perhaps the most thorough and comprehensive study of the incidence of mental disorders in the U.S. adult population (eighteen years and older) was conducted by the National Institute of Mental Health (NIMH; Eaton et al., 1984; Freedman, 1984; Myers et al., 1984; Regier et al., 1988; Robbins et al., 1984). The NIMH epidemiological study included data collected in three major cities: New Haven, Baltimore, and St. Louis. The study had several features that distinguished it from others. It included a large sample of approximately 20,000 persons, and it used the categories in the *Diagnostic and Statistical Manual* of the American Psychiatric Association in the construction of the research instruments.

Like the previous studies cited, subjects reported a high rate of disorders. Approximately 29 to 38 percent (percentage range accounts for variations in the three cities) of the sample reported that they experienced at least one mental disorder! Alcohol abuse or dependence was the most prevalent disorder (11

F O C U S   1 . 1

The Psychologizing of America

In his book, *The Shrinking of America* (1983), psychologist Bernie Zilbergeld contends that Americans seem to have set out to psychologize almost every aspect of their lives. A main theme of Zilbergeld's is that our national history and cultural values have prepared us for this psychology-minded orientation. He notes that our culture is strongly committed to the following propositions:

◆ We are endowed with an unalienable right to the pursuit of happiness.
◆ We have a duty to better ourselves.
◆ Individual freedom is important.

◆ There are no limits to what we can do in life.
◆ We are highly malleable.

Solutions to an individual's problems do exist, and finding a cure is possible.

Accepting these basic tenets, thousands of people each year try to banish all conceivable forms of failure and misfortune from their lives. They spend millions of dollars and countless hours of effort in attempts to improve their behavior, attitudes, personality, and moods. Zilbergeld argues that the following beliefs underlie what he calls our "therapeutic sensibility":

1. *The world is best understood in psychological terms.* It appears that psychology has become the most important way of understanding our internal and external world. When we think of ourselves or others, we often think of psychological characteristics—anxiety, insecurity, passivity, depression, paranoia, hostility, and unconscious processes. When some important person is assassinated or a bizarre killing is reported, the media call on mental health experts to analyze the slayer's state of mind. On radio and television programs and in newspaper columns, mental health professionals dispense advice to callers or readers. High on the best-seller lists are many self-help psychology books.

to 16 percent), and phobic disorders were a clear second (8 to 23 percent) followed by several other disturbances with averages greater than 5 percent (depressive episodes, drug abuse, and dependence). Schizophrenia, often one of the most severe mental disturbances, affects 1 percent of the population, or approximately 2.5 million Americans. Researchers also found that although men and women were equally likely to suffer from mental disorders, they differ in the kinds of disorders they experience. For example, alcohol abuse or dependence occurs in 24 percent of men and only 4 percent of women; men are more likely to abuse drugs; and depression and anxiety are more likely to occur in women. Age was also an important factor. Alcoholism and depression are most prominent in the 25- to 44-year-old age group; drug dependence in the 18- to 24-year-old age group; and cognitive impairment in people age 65 and older. Phobias, however, were equally represented at all ages.

These epidemiological findings are troubling, to say the least. Clearly, mental disturbances are widespread, and many persons are currently suffering from them. What is even more troubling is that the study reveals that less than one-third of people suffering from a mental disorder are receiving mental health services!

The Psychologically Oriented Society

Afflicted people and their families and friends pay a huge price in human suffering. In addition, the U.S. public spends increasing amounts each year in either direct or indirect expenses for mental health care. In 1974 we spent $40 billion, of which nearly 40 percent went for direct care, including therapy and hospitalization (Levine & Willner, 1976); from 1974 to 1985 the number of psychologists in health care increased by more than 100 percent (Dorken, Stapp & VandenBos, 1986; Enright et al., 1990). A recent report of The National Behavioral Science Research Agenda Committee (Observer, 1992) indicates that when the costs of mental health problems are calculated to include decreased productivity in the workplace, educational problems, our aging society, drug and alcohol abuse, and health and violence in the United States, we are literally speaking about hundreds of billions of dollars. And as Americans have become more oriented toward understanding behav-

2. *There is much more to behavior than meets the eye.* Unconscious processes and hidden meanings have become important in our belief system. Such thinking was popularized through the writings of Sigmund Freud, who claimed that hidden purposes lay behind nearly all human behavior: a desire for bananas, hot dogs, or carrots may represent unfulfilled sexual cravings. A person's charity work may be an expression of repressed hostility. Illness may be a result of the need to be loved and cared for. As a result of this emphasis, insight into one's own motives and behaviors has become highly valued.

3. *People are not OK.* In general, mental health professionals tend to focus on disorders rather than on healthy characteristics. People are often described in terms of their inadequacies or deficiencies. A large portion of the public seems to have accepted a fantasy model of well-being and mental health that none of us can attain.

4. *Individuals need to be liberated.* People are basically good, creative, and aspiring, but their nature has been blocked, inhibited, distorted, or repressed by the traditions and institutions of society. Excessive guilt may be caused by religious teachings, confining family ties, or rigid sex roles. We need to liberate ourselves to be whole, free, and well.

5. *Everyone needs and can benefit from therapy.* The number of people who sought some form of counseling or therapy increased threefold between 1957 and 1976, and the trend seems to be continuing. When other forms of treatment such as en-counter groups, Weight Watchers, EST (Earhardt Seminar Training), and TM (transcendental meditation) are included, it becomes obvious that this belief has been widely taken to heart.

6. *The therapist is an expert and knows best.* Ours is a highly credentialed society, and the title "therapist" evokes the image of a person with much wisdom and knowledge. Even though therapy is supposed to free the client and allow him or her to advance and grow, however, therapists may inadvertently foster reliance on their "expert" judgment. Zilbergeld may be correct in asserting that "psychological man reigns supreme." To the question, "Whatever became of sin?" he answers, "It was psychologized away."

---

iors and motives of the self and others, their demand for various forms of mental health treatment has increased. This demand is evident in the following statistics:

- The proportion of Americans seeking mental health consultation increased from 4 to 14 percent between 1957 and 1976. Among the college-educated, the increase has been even greater—from 9 to 21 percent.

- Mental health professionals seem to believe in what they do, as they are the heaviest consumers of therapy. Seventy-four percent have been in treatment, one-third have been treated more than once, and the average time spent in treatment was 4½ years.

- More than 5 million persons have taken part in encounter or sensitivity groups in the past 15 years; more than one million have learned transcendental meditation; more than one million have participated in marriage enrichment programs; and countless millions have entered nonprofessional therapeutic programs for drug, alcohol, smoking, and weight control (Zilbergeld, 1983).

Focus 1.1 examines some of the beliefs that underlie this enthusiasm for psychological therapy and self-enhancement.

Stereotypes About the Mentally Disturbed

Despite our "psychology-mindedness" and our belief in the efficacy of various therapies, Americans tend to regard people with mental disturbance with suspicion. Are most of them really maniacs who at any moment may be seized by uncontrollable urges to murder, rape, or maim? Such portrayals seem to emerge from the news media and the entertainment industry, but they are rarely accurate. Like other minority groups in the United States, people with mental disturbances are the subject of rampant stereotyping and popular misconceptions. It is worthwhile at this point to dispel the most common of these misconceptions or myths.

Myth: "Mentally disturbed people can always be recognized by their consistently deviant abnormal behavior."

Reality: Mentally disturbed people are not always distinguishable from others on the basis of consistently unusual behavior. Even in an outpatient clinic or a psychiatric ward, distinguishing patients from staff on the basis of behavior alone is often difficult. There are two main reasons for this difficulty. First, as already noted, no sharp dividing line usually exists between "normal" and "abnormal" behaviors. Rather, the spectrum of behaviors is continuous, ranging from abnormal to normal. Depending on the situational context and the perspective of the person judging the behavior, many behaviors could be considered either normal or deviant. Second, even when people are suffering from some form of emotional disturbance, that experience may not always be detectable in their behavior.

Myth: "The mentally disturbed have inherited their disorders. If one member of a family has an emotional breakdown, other members will probably suffer a similar fate."

Reality: The belief that insanity runs in certain families has caused misery and undue anxiety for many people. Although the data are far from conclusive, heredity does not seem to play a major role in most mental disorders, except for some cases of schizophrenia and depression, certain types of mental retardation, and the bipolar disorders. Evidence suggests that, even though heredity may predispose an individual to certain disorders, environmental factors are extremely important. When many family members suffer from mental disorders, a stress-producing environment is usually acting on the family predisposition. If the environment is benign, however, or predisposed individuals modify a stressful environment, psychopathology may never occur.

Myth: "The mentally disturbed person can never be cured and will never be able to function normally or hold jobs in the community."

Reality: This erroneous belief has caused great distress to many people who have at some time been labeled mentally ill. Former mental patients have endured social discrimination and have been denied employment because of the public perception that "once insane, always insane." Unfortunately, this myth may keep former mental patients or those currently experiencing emotional problems from seeking help. Although most people don't hesitate to consult a doctor, dentist, or lawyer for help, many who need mental health services are fearful and anxious about the social stigma attached to being labeled "mentally ill." According to several studies (U.S. Department of Health and Human Services, 1985; World Health Organization, 1973a), however, nearly three-fourths of clients with severe disorders who are hospitalized improve and go on to lead productive lives. Many recovered mental patients make excellent employees, and employers frequently report that they outperform other workers in attendance and punctuality. Some famous examples of persons who have recovered from mental illnesses are President Abraham Lincoln, philosopher William James, Senator Thomas Eagleton, singer Rosemary Clooney, and golfer Bert Yancy (DHHS, 1985).

Myth: "People become mentally disturbed because they are weak-willed. To avoid emotional disorders or cure oneself of them, one need only exercise will power."

Reality: These statements show that the speaker does not understand the nature of mental disorders. Needing help to resolve difficulties does not indicate a lack of will power. In fact, recognizing one's own need for help may be seen as a sign of strength rather than a sign of weakness. Many problems stem from situations that are not under the individual's immediate control, such as the death of a loved one or the loss of a job. Other problems stem from lifelong patterns of faulty learning; it is naive to expect that a simple exercise of will can override years of experience.

Myth: "Mental illness is always a deficit and the person suffering from it can never contribute anything of worth until cured."

Reality: Many persons who suffered from mental illness were never "cured" but made great contributions to humanity. Ernest Hemingway, one of the greatest writers of our time and who won the Nobel Prize for literature in 1954, suffered from lifelong depressions, alcoholism, and frequent hospitalizations. In 1961 he put a shotgun in his mouth and killed himself. The famous Dutch painter, Vincent van Gogh, produced great works of art despite the fact that he was severely disturbed. Not only did he lead an unhappy and tortured life, he frequently heard voices, cut off a piece of his left ear as a gift to a prostitute, and finally committed suicide. Others like Pablo Picasso and Edgar Allen Poe contributed major works to humanity while seriously disturbed. The point of these examples is not to illustrate that madness and genius go hand in hand, but that many who are less severely disturbed can continue to lead productive and worthwhile lives. Because people suffer from psychological problems does not mean that their ideas and contributions are less worthy of consideration.

Myth: "The mentally disturbed person is unstable and potentially dangerous."

Reality: This misconception has been perpetuated by the mass media. Many murderers on television are labeled "psychopathic," and the news media concentrate on the occasional mental patient who kills. But the thousands of mental patients who do not commit crimes, do not harm others, and do not get into trouble with the law are not news. An important study of the issue does not support the notion that mental patients are seriously dangerous (Rabkin, 1979). Unfortunately, the myth persists.

The Mental Health Professions

The traditional therapy fields have grown along with the demand for mental health treatment. In 1968 there were 12,000 clinical psychologists in the United States; today there are more than 40,000. We now have approximately 280,000 professional therapists (primarily in clinical psychology, counseling psychology, psychiatry, psychoanalysis, social work, and marriage and family counseling). As one writer observed, there are more professional therapists than librarians, firefighters, or mail carriers and twice as many therapists as dentists and pharmacists (Zilbergeld, 1983). The qualifications, training, and functions of the people who work within these specialties are briefly described below.

Clinical Psychology Clinical psychology is the professional field concerned with the study, assessment, treatment, and prevention of abnormal behavior in disturbed individuals. ("Abnormal psychology" is the name, not of a professional field, but of a course of study.) Clinical psychologists must hold the Ph.D. degree from a university or the Psy.D. (doctor of psychology) degree, a more practitioner-oriented degree granted by several institutions. Their training includes coursework in psychopathology, personality, diagnosis, psychological testing, psychotherapy, and human physiology. Apart from these and other course requirements, there are two additional requirements for the Ph.D. degree. First, the candidate must complete a doctoral dissertation, which is an original research study on some aspect of the candidate's area of specialization—therapy, diagnosis, or test interpretation, for example. Second, a practicum experience or internship, usually one year at a psychiatric hospital or mental health center, is also required.

Clinical psychologists work in a variety of settings, but most commonly they provide therapy to clients in hospitals and clinics and in private practice. Some choose to work in an academic setting where they can concentrate on teaching and research. Other clinical psychologists are hired by government or private organizations to do research. It is not unusual, however, for clinical psychologists to assume a number of different roles. For example, many professors not only teach and do research but engage in part-time clinical work as well.

Counseling Psychology To a great extent, a description of clinical psychology applies to counseling psychology as well. The academic and internship requirements are similar, but the emphasis differs. Whereas clinical psychologists are trained to work specifically with a disturbed client population, counseling psychologists are usually more immediately concerned with the study of life problems in relatively normal people. Furthermore, counseling psychologists are more likely to be found in educational settings than in hospitals and clinics. These are not rigid distinctions, however, because counseling psychologists can choose to practice in the clinical setting.

Psychiatry Psychiatrists hold the M.D. degree. Their education includes the four years of medical school required for that degree, along with an additional three or four years of training in psychiatry. Of all the specialists involved in mental health care, only psychiatrists can prescribe drugs in the treatment of mental disorders.

Psychoanalysis Psychoanalysis has been associated with medicine and psychiatry because its founder, Sigmund Freud, and his major disciples were physicians. But Freud was quite adamant in stating that one need not be medically trained to be a good psychoanalyst. Nevertheless, most psychoanalysts hold either the M.D. or the Ph.D. degree. In addition, psychoanalysts receive intensive training in the theory and practice of psychoanalysis at an institute devoted to the field. This training includes the individual's own analysis by an experienced analyst.

Psychiatric Social Work   Those entering psychiatric social work are trained in a school of social work, usually in a two-year graduate program leading to a master's degree. Included in this program is a one-year internship in a social-service agency, sometimes a mental health center. Some social workers go on to earn the D.S.W. (doctor of social work) degree, which requires additional training and a dissertation. Traditionally, psychiatric social workers work in family counseling services or community agencies, where they specialize in intake (assessment and screening of clients), take psychiatric histories, and deal with other agencies.

Marriage and Family Counseling   In the past, the counseling of married couples was usually performed by the clergy or social workers in churches, public welfare agencies, and family-service organizations. Counseling and clinical psychologists may also work with couples and families. A specialty in marriage and family counseling has recently emerged, however, with its own professional organizations, journals, and state licensing requirements. Marriage and family counselors have varied professional backgrounds, but their training usually includes a master's degree in counseling and many hours of supervised clinical experience.

HISTORICAL PERSPECTIVE ON ABNORMAL BEHAVIOR

In this section and the next, we briefly review the historical development of western thought concerning abnormal behavior. This task is extremely difficult for several reasons. First, the information and data we have are necessarily incomplete. We lack specific facts about the historical past and must piece them together. Often these gaps in our knowledge lead us to mistaken conclusions until other information is uncovered. For example, disagreements now exist over the psychiatric interpretation of witchcraft. Second, historical interpretation depends on the perspective of the researcher. For example, an anthropological approach to the study of history may be different from a psychological one. Within each discipline, one's biases and point of view may affect how an interpretation is made. Even with these limitations in mind, it appears that many current attitudes to-

ward abnormal behavior, as well as modern ideas about its causes and treatment, have been influenced by early beliefs. In fact, some psychologists contend that modern societies have, in essence, adopted more sophisticated versions of earlier concepts. For example, the use of electroconvulsive therapy to treat depression is in some ways similar to ancient practices of exorcism in which the body was physically assaulted. The Greek physician Hippocrates, 2,500 years ago, believed that many abnormal behaviors were caused by imbalances and disorders in the brain and the body, a belief shared by many contemporary psychologists.

Most ideas about abnormal behavior are firmly rooted in the system of beliefs that is operative in a given society at a given time. Perhaps for that reason, change—especially in the form of new ideas—does not come quickly or easily. People who dare to voice ideas that differ from the prevalent beliefs of their time are often made outcasts; in some periods, some were even executed. Yet in spite of the difficulties, we have evolved a humanistic and scientific explanation of abnormal behavior. It remains to be seen whether such an explanation will still be thought valid in decades to come. (Much of this history section is based on discussions of deviant behavior by Alexander & Selesnick, 1966; Hunter & Macalpine, 1963; Neugebauer, 1979; Spanos, 1978; and Zilboorg & Henry, 1941).

Prehistoric and Ancient Beliefs

Prehistoric societies some half a million years ago did not distinguish sharply between mental and physical disorders. Abnormal behaviors, from simple headaches to convulsive attacks, were attributed to evil spirits that inhabited or controlled the afflicted person's body. According to historians, these ancient peoples attributed many forms of illness to demonic possession, sorcery, or the behest of an offended ancestral spirit. Within this system of belief, called *demonology*, the victim was usually held at least partly responsible for the misfortune.

It has been suggested that Stone Age cave dwellers may have treated behavior disorders with a surgical method called **trephining**, in which part of the skull was chipped away to provide an opening through which the evil spirit could escape. People may have believed that when the evil spirit left, the person

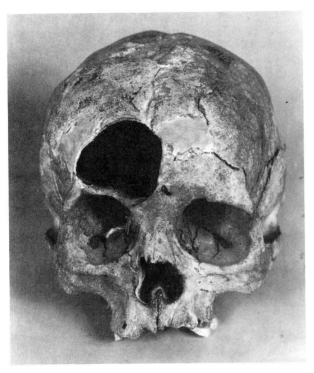

There are two theories about trephining. The most widely accepted postulates that trephining was a form of surgery that enabled an evil spirit to leave the body. The other theory rejects this idea, proposing instead that the holes were actually wounds received when one person clubbed another over the head during a fight.

would return to his or her normal state. Surprisingly, some trephined skulls have been found to have healed over, indicating that some patients survived this extremely crude operation. As pointed out earlier, however, disputes often arise from the interpretation of historical data: a different explanation of trephining is that it was used to remove bone splinters and blood clots resulting from blows to the head in fights between men (Maher & Maher, 1985). This explanation is consistent with findings that most trephined skulls were of men and many had fractures (suggesting a vigorous blow).

Another treatment method used by the early Greeks, Chinese, Hebrews, and Egyptians was exorcism. In an **exorcism**, elaborate prayers, noises, emetics (drugs that induce vomiting), and extreme measures such as flogging and starvation were marshaled to cast the evil spirit out of the afflicted person's body.

Naturalistic Explanations (Greco-Roman Thought)

In the ancient world, then, both physical and mental illness was thought to be supernatural in origin. But with the flowering of Greek civilization and its continuation into the era of Roman rule (500 B.C.–A.D. 500), naturalistic explanations gradually became distinct from supernatural ones. Early thinkers, such as Hippocrates (460–370 B.C.), a physician who is often called the father of medicine, actively questioned prevailing superstitious beliefs and proposed much more rational and scientific explanations for mental disorders.

The beliefs of many thinkers of this era were based on incorrect assumptions. They all relied heavily on observations and explanations, however, which form the foundation of the scientific method. Also, they denied the intervention of demons in the development of abnormality and instead stressed organic causes, so the treatment they prescribed for mental disorders tended to be more humane than previous treatments.

Hippocrates believed that, because the brain was the central organ of intellectual activity, deviant behavior was caused by **brain pathology**—that is, a dysfunction or disease of the brain. He also considered heredity and environment important factors in psychopathology. He classified mental illnesses into three categories—mania, melancholia, and phrenitis (brain fever)—and for each category gave detailed clinical descriptions of such disorders as paranoia, alcoholic delirium, and epilepsy. Many of his descriptions of symptoms are still used today, eloquent testimony to his keen powers of observation.

To treat melancholia, Hippocrates recommended tranquility, moderate exercise, a careful diet, abstinence from sexual activity, and bloodletting if necessary. His belief in environmental influences on behavior sometimes led him to separate disturbed patients from their families. He seems to have gained insight into a theory popular among psychologists today: that the family constellation often fosters deviant behavior in its own members.

Other thinkers who contributed to the organic explanation of behavior were the philosopher Plato and Greek physician Galen, who practiced in Rome. Plato (429–347 B.C.) carried on the thinking of Hippocrates; he insisted that the mentally disturbed were

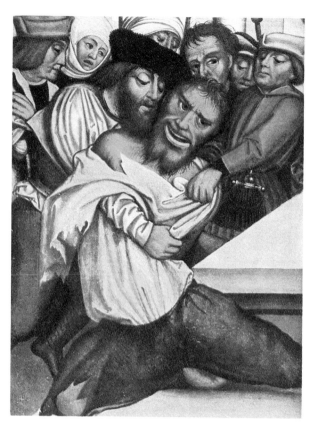

In primitive societies, mental illness was attributed to the demonic possession of a person's soul. During the Greco-Roman period, demonology gave rise to more naturalistic explanations. However, these views were repressed during the Dark and Middle Ages, when mental illness was again believed to be caused by supernatural forces.

the responsibility of the family and should not be punished for their behavior. Galen (A.D. 129–199) made major contributions through his scientific examination of the nervous system and his explanation of the role of the brain and central nervous system in mental functioning. His greatest contribution may have been his codification of all medical knowledge from Hippocrates's to his own time.

Reversion to Superstition (the Middle Ages)

With the collapse of the Roman Empire and the rise of Christianity, rational and scientific thought gave way to a reemphasis on the supernatural. Religious dogma included the beliefs that nature was a reflection of divine will and beyond human reason, and

that earthly life was a prelude to the "true" life (after death). Scientific inquiry—attempts to understand, classify, explain, and control nature—was less important than accepting nature as a manifestation of God's will. Early Christianity did little to promote science and in many ways actively discouraged it. The church demanded uncompromising adherence to its tenets. Christian fervor brought with it the concepts of heresy and punishment; certain truths were deemed sacred, and those who challenged them were denounced as heretics. Scientific thought that was in conflict with church doctrine was not tolerated. Because of this atmosphere, rationalism and scholarly scientific works went underground for many years, preserved mainly by Arab scholars and European monks. Natural and supernatural explanations of illness became fused.

People came to believe that many illnesses were the result of supernatural forces, although they had natural causes. In many cases, the mentally ill were treated gently and with compassion in monasteries and at shrines where they were prayed over and allowed to rest. In other cases, treatment could be quite brutal, especially if illnesses were believed to be due to God's wrath. Relief could come only through atonement or repentance. Because illness was perceived as punishment for sin, the sick person was assumed to be guilty of wrongdoing.

In some cases, treatment of the mentally ill during this period consisted of torturous exorcistic procedures seen as appropriate to combat Satan and eject him from the possessed person's body. Prayers, curses, obscene epithets, and the sprinkling of holy water—as well as such drastic and painful "therapy" as flogging, starving, and immersion in hot water—were used to drive out the devil. The humane treatments that Hippocrates had advocated centuries earlier were challenged severely. A time of trouble for everyone, the Dark Ages (A.D. 400–900) were especially bleak for the mentally ill.

Mass Madness (Thirteenth Century)

Belief in the power of the supernatural became so prevalent and intense that it frequently affected whole populations. Beginning in Italy early in the thirteenth century, large numbers of people were affected by various forms of group hysteria, or **mass madness.** One of the better known manifestations of this disorder was *tarantism*, a dance mania characterized by wild raving, jumping, dancing, and convulsions. The hysteria was most prevalent during the height of the summer and was attributed to the sting of a tarantula. A victim would leap up and run out into the street or marketplace, jumping and raving, to be joined by others who believed that they had also been bitten. The mania soon spread throughout the rest of Europe, where it became known as St. Vitus's Dance.

Another form of mass madness was *lycanthropy*, a mental disorder in which victims imagine themselves to be wolves and imitate wolves' actions. (Motion pictures about werewolves—people who assume the physical characteristics of wolves during the full moon—are modern reflections of this delusion.)

How can these phenomena be explained? Stress and fear are often associated with outbreaks of mass hysteria. During the thirteenth century, for example, there was enormous social unrest. The bubonic plague had decimated half the population of Europe. War, famine, and pestilence were rampant, and the social order of the times was crumbling.

A more recent example was evident in the small town of Berry, Alabama, where elementary school children became ill. A fifth-grader came to school with a rash and began scratching vigorously and uncontrollably. Other classmates began to scratch at an imaginary itch. The incident resulted in more than 150 schoolchildren afflicted with a frenzy of scratching, fainting, vomiting, numbness, crying, and screaming. Medical authorities concluded after months of study that the culprit could not be an infectious disease or food poisoning. Rather, the symptom pattern, onset, and manifestation suggested mass hysteria (Kramer, 1983).

Witchcraft (Fifteenth Through Seventeenth Centuries)

During the fifteenth and sixteenth centuries, the authority of the church was increasingly challenged by social and religious reformers. Reformers such as Martin Luther attacked the corruption and abuses of the clergy, precipitating the Protestant Reformation of the sixteenth century. Church officials saw such protests as insurrection and believed that their power was threatened. According to the church, Satan himself fostered these attacks. By doing battle with Satan and with people supposedly influenced or possessed by Satan, the church actively endorsed an already popular belief in demonic possession and witches.

To counter the threat, Pope Innocent VIII issued a papal bull (decree) in 1484 calling on the clergy to identify and exterminate witches. Means of detecting witches were publicized. For example, red spots on the skin (birthmarks) were supposedly made by the claw of the devil in sealing a blood pact and thus were damning evidence of a contract with Satan. Such birth defects as club foot and cleft palate also aroused suspicion.

The church initially recognized two forms of demonic possession: unwilling and willing. God let the devil seize an unwilling victim as punishment for a sinful life. A willing person, who made a blood pact with the devil in exchange for supernatural powers, was able to assume animal form and cause disasters such as floods, pestilence, storms, crop failures, and sexual impotence. Although an unwilling victim of possession was at first treated with more sympathy than one who willingly conspired with the devil, this distinction soon evaporated.

People whose actions were interpreted as peculiar were often suspected of witchcraft. It was acceptable to use torture to obtain confessions from suspected witches, and many victims confessed because they preferred death to prolonged agony. Thousands of innocent men, women, and even children were beheaded, burned alive, or mutilated.

Witch hunts occurred in both colonial America and Europe. The witchcraft trials of 1692 in Salem, Massachusetts, were infamous. Authorities there acted on statements taken from children who may have been influenced by the sensational stories told by an old West Indian servant. Several hundred people were accused, many were imprisoned and tortured, and twenty were killed. It has been estimated that some 20,000 people were killed as witches in Scotland alone, and that more than 100,000 throughout Europe were executed as witches during the middle of the fifteenth to the end of the seventeenth century.

It would seem reasonable to assume that the mentally ill would be especially prone to being perceived as witches. Indeed, most psychiatric historians argue that mental disorders were at the roots of witchcraft persecutions (Alexander & Selesnick, 1966; Deutsch, 1949; Zilboorg & Henry, 1941). Support for the belief that many accused witches were mentally ill was based on the following evidence: (1) some witches claimed that they could do impossible acts (such as fly and cause floods) and thus must have been deluded (schizophrenic); (2) they participated in sabbats (nocturnal orgies) and must have been psychopaths or nymphomaniacs; (3) they evidenced localized sensitivity to pain in various parts of their bodies and must have been hysterics; and (4) they evidenced symptoms associated with high suggestibility, delusions, or hallucinations. Spanos (1978), however, in a comprehensive critical analysis concluded that very little support could be found to indicate that accused witches were insane.

Indeed, the lines of evidence just mentioned do not have a basis in fact or were misinterpreted. For example, sabbats seem to have existed only in the imaginations of the witch-hunters, claims of supernatural powers from the accused were obtained only after prolonged and painful torture, and trickery was often used to diminish body sensitivity. It appears that while some accused witches may have been mentally ill, most were sane (Schoeneman 1984).

The Rise of Humanism (the Renaissance)

A resurgence of rational and scientific inquiry during the Renaissance (fifteenth and seventeenth centuries) led to great advances in science and **humanism,** a philosophical movement that emphasizes human welfare and the worth and uniqueness of the individual. Until this time, most asylums were at best custodial centers where the mentally disturbed were chained, caged, starved, whipped, and even exhibited to the public for a small fee, much like animals in a zoo. But if people were "mentally ill" and not possessed, then they should be treated as though they were sick. A number of new methods for treating the mentally ill reflected this humanistic spirit.

In 1563 Johann Weyer (1515–1588), a German physician, published a revolutionary book that challenged the foundation of witchcraft. Weyer asserted that many people who were tortured, imprisoned, and burned as witches were mentally disturbed, not possessed by demons. The emotional agonies he was made to endure for committing this heresy are well documented. His book was severely criticized and banned by both church and state, but it proved to be a forerunner of the humanitarian perspective on mental illness. Others eventually followed his lead.

The Reform Movement (Eighteenth and Nineteenth Centuries)

In France, Philippe Pinel (1745–1826), a physician, was put in charge of La Bicêtre, a hospital for insane men in Paris. Pinel instituted what came to be known as the **moral treatment movement.** He ordered that inmates' chains be removed, replaced dungeons with sunny rooms, encouraged exercise outdoors on hospital grounds, and treated patients with kindness and reason. Surprising many disbelievers, the freed patients did not become violent; instead, this humane treatment seemed to foster recovery and improved behavior. Pinel later instituted similar equally successful reforms at La Salpêtrière, a large mental hospital for women in Paris.

In England William Tuke (1732–1822), a prominent Quaker tea merchant, established a retreat at York for the "moral treatment" of mental patients. At this pleasant country estate, the patients worked, prayed, rested, and talked out their problems—all in an atmosphere of kindness quite unlike that of the lunatic asylums of the time.

In the United States, three individuals made important contributions to the moral-treatment movement: Benjamin Rush, Dorothea Dix, and Clifford Beers. Benjamin Rush (1745–1813), widely acclaimed as the father of U.S. psychiatry, attempted to train physicians to treat mental patients and to introduce more humane treatment policies into mental hospitals. He insisted that patients be accorded respect and dignity and that they be gainfully employed while hospitalized, an idea that anticipated the modern concept of work therapy. Yet Rush was not unaffected by the established practices and beliefs of his times: his theories were influenced by astrology, and his remedies included bloodletting and purgatives.

Dorothea Dix (1802–1887), a New England schoolteacher, was the preeminent American social reformer of the nineteenth century. While teaching Sunday school to female prisoners, she became familiar with the deplorable conditions in which jailed mental patients were forced to live. (Prisons and poorhouses were commonly used to incarcerate these patients.) For the next forty years, Dix worked tirelessly for the mentally ill. She campaigned for reform legislation and funds to establish suitable mental hospitals and asylums. She raised millions of dollars, es-

As skeptics look on, Philippe Pinel orders the chains removed from the inmates of La Bi-cêtre. Jean-Baptiste Pussin, an untrained ward superintendent, actually abolished the chaining of inmates. Pinel introduced even more radical changes, such as talking with patients to give them comfort and advice.

tablished more than thirty modern mental hospitals, and greatly improved conditions in countless others. But the struggle for reform was far from over. Although the large hospitals that replaced jails and poorhouses had better physical facilities, the humanistic, personal concern of the moral treatment movement was lacking.

That movement was given further impetus in 1908 with the publication of *A Mind That Found Itself,* a book by Clifford Beers (1876–1943) about his own mental collapse. His book describes the terrible treatment he and other patients experienced in three mental institutions, where they were beaten, choked, spat on, and restrained with straitjackets. His vivid account aroused great public sympathy and attracted the interest and support of the psychiatric establishment, including such eminent figures as psychologist-philosopher William James. Beers founded the National Committee for Mental Hygiene, an organization dedicated to educating the public about mental illness and about the need to treat the mentally ill rather than punish them for their unusual behaviors.

It would be naive to believe that these reforms have totally eliminated inhumane treatment of the mentally disturbed. Books like Mary Jane Ward's *The Snake Pit* (1946) and films like Frederick Wiseman's *Titicut Follies* (1967) continue to document harsh treatment of mental patients. Even the severest critic of the mental health system, however, would have to admit that conditions and treatment for the mentally ill have improved in this century.

CAUSES: EARLY VIEWPOINTS

Paralleling the rise of humanism in the treatment of mental illness was an inquiry into its causes. Two schools of thought emerged. The organic viewpoint holds that mental disorders are the result of physiological damage or disease; the psychological viewpoint stresses an emotional basis for mental illness. It is important to note that most people were not extreme adherents of one or the other. Rather, they tended to combine elements of both, which predated the biopsychosocial model widely used today.

Dorothea Dix was an exceptional contributor to the social reform movements of the nineteenth century—an era when women were discouraged from political participation.

The Organic Viewpoint

Hippocrates' suggestion of an organic explanation for abnormal behavior was ignored during the Middle Ages but revived after the Renaissance. Not until the nineteenth century, however, did the organic or **biogenic view** become important. The ideas of Wilhelm Griesinger (1817–1868), a German psychiatrist who believed that all mental disorders had physiological causes, received considerable attention. Emil Kraepelin (1856–1926), a follower of Griesinger, observed that certain symptoms tend to occur regularly in clusters, called **syndromes**; he believed that each cluster of symptoms represented a mental disorder with its own unique—and clearly specifiable—cause, course, and outcome. He attributed all disorders to one of four organic causes: metabolic disturbance, endocrine difficulty, brain disease, or heredity. In his *Textbook of Psychiatry* (1923 [1883]), Kraepelin outlined a system for classifying mental illnesses on the basis of their organic causes. That system was

the original basis for the diagnostic categories in the *Diagnostic and Statistical Manual of Mental Disorders* (DSM), the classification system of the American Psychiatric Association.

The acceptance of an organic cause for mental disorders was accelerated by medical breakthroughs in the study of the nervous system. The effects of brain disorders, such as cerebral arteriosclerosis, on mental retardation, senile psychoses, and certain other psychoses, led many scientists to suspect or advocate organic factors as the sole cause of all mental illness. And, as we will see in Chapter 2, the drug revolution of the 1950s made medication available for almost every disorder. The issue of their therapeutic effectiveness and how they work, however, is still hotly debated today.

The organic viewpoint gained even greater strength with the discovery of the organic basis of general paresis, a progressively degenerative and irreversible physical and mental disorder. Several breakthroughs had led scientists to suspect that the deterioration of mental and physical abilities exhibited by certain mental patients might actually be caused by an organic disease. The work of Louis Pasteur (1822–1895) established the germ theory of disease (invasion of the body by parasites). Then in 1897 Richard von Krafft-Ebing (1840–1902), a German neurologist, inoculated paretic patients with pus from syphilitic sores; when the patients failed to develop the secondary symptoms of syphilis, Krafft-Ebing concluded that the subjects had been previously infected by that disease. Finally, in 1905 a German zoologist, Fritz Schaudinn (1871–1906), isolated the microorganism that causes syphilis and thus paresis. These discoveries convinced many scientists that every mental disorder might eventually be linked to an organic cause.

The Psychological Viewpoint

Some scientists noted, however, that certain types of emotional disorders were not associated with any organic disease in the patient. Such observations led to another view that stressed psychological factors rather than organic factors as the cause of many disorders. For example, the inability to attain personal goals and resolve interpersonal conflicts could lead to intense feelings of frustration, depression, failure, anger, and consequent disturbed behavior.

Mesmerism and Hypnotism   The unique and exotic techniques of Friedrich Anton Mesmer (1734–1815), an Austrian physician who practiced in Paris, presented an early challenge to the organic point of view. It is important to note, however, that Mesmer was really an anomaly and not part of mainstream scientific thinking. Mesmer developed a highly controversial treatment that came to be called *mesmerism* and was the forerunner of the modern practice of hypnotism.

Mesmer performed his most miraculous cures in the treatment of *hysteria*—the appearance of symptoms such as blindness, deafness, loss of bodily feeling, and paralysis that seem to have no organic basis. According to Mesmer, hysteria was a manifestation of the body's need to redistribute the magnetic fluid that determined a person's mental and physical health. His techniques for curing this illness involved inducing a sleeplike state, during which his patients became highly susceptible to suggestion. During this state, their symptoms often disappeared.

Mesmer's dramatic and theatrical techniques earned him censure as well as fame. A committee of prominent thinkers, including U.S. ambassador Benjamin Franklin, investigated Mesmer and declared him a fraud. He was finally forced to leave Paris.

Although Mesmer's basic assumptions were discredited, the power of suggestion proved to be a strong therapeutic technique in the treatment of hysteria. The cures he effected stimulated scientific interest in and much bitter debate about the **psychogenic view**—that is, that mental disorders are caused by psychological and emotional rather than organic factors.

An English physician, James Braid (1795–1860), renamed mesmerism *neurohypnotism* (later shortened to hypnotism) because he believed that the technique induced sleep by producing paralysis of the eyelid muscles. (The Latin word *hypnos* means "sleep.") Braid's trance-inducing technique of having a subject gaze steadily at an object has now become almost a standard procedure in hypnosis.

The Nancy School   About ten years after Mesmer died, a number of researchers began to experiment actively with hypnosis. Jean-Martin Charcot (1825–1893), a neurosurgeon at La Salpêtrière Hospital in Paris and the leading neurologist of his time, was among them. His initial experiments with hypnosis led him to abandon it in favor of more traditional methods of treating hysteria, which he claimed was caused by organic damage to the nervous system. Other experimenters had more positive results using hypnosis, however, which convinced him to try it again. His subsequent use of the technique in the study of hysteria did much to legitimize the application of hypnosis in medicine.

The experimenters most instrumental in Charcot's conversion were two physicians practicing in the city of Nancy, in eastern France. First working separately, Ambroise-Auguste Liébeault (1823–1904) and Hippolyte-Marie Bernheim (1840–1919) later came together to work as a team. As a result of their experiments, they hypothesized that hysteria was a form of self-hypnosis. The results they obtained in treating patients attracted other scientists, who collectively became known as the "Nancy school." In treating hysterical patients under hypnosis, they were often able to remove symptoms of paralysis, deafness, blindness, and anesthesia. They were also able to produce these symptoms in normal persons through hypnosis. Their work demonstrated impressively that suggestion could cause certain forms of mental illness; that is, symptoms of mental and physical disorders could have a psychological rather than an organic explanation. This conclusion represented a major breakthrough in the conceptualization of mental disorders.

Breuer and Freud   The idea that psychological processes could produce mental and physical disturbances began to gain credence among several physicians who were using hypnosis. Among them was the Viennese doctor Josef Breuer (1842–1925). He discovered accidentally that, after one of his female patients spoke quite freely about her past traumatic experiences while in a trance, many of her symptoms abated or disappeared. He achieved even greater success when the patient recalled previously forgotten memories and relived their emotional aspects. This latter technique became known as the **cathartic method**. It foreshadowed psychoanalysis, one of the major theories of psychopathology, whose founder, Sigmund Freud (1856–1939), was influenced by Charcot and was a colleague of Breuer. Freud's theories have had a great and lasting influence in the field of abnormal psychology.

While psychoanalysis offered an intrapsychic explanation of abnormal behavior, another viewpoint emerged during the latter part of this period that was more firmly rooted in laboratory science: *behaviorism*. The behavioristic perspective stressed the importance of directly observable behavior and the conditions or stimuli that evoked, reinforced, and extinguished them. As we will see in Chapter 3, behaviorism not only offered an alternative explanation of the development of both normal and abnormal behavior, it also demonstrated a high degree of success in treating maladaptive behaviors.

The Contemporary Viewpoint: A Biopsychosocial Approach

Earlier, we made the statement that much of our explanations of abnormal behavior were heavily influenced by the beliefs of the past. Much has also changed, however, in our understanding and treatment of psychopathological disorders. Twentieth-century views of abnormality evolved from the effects of three major events: (1) the drug revolution in psychiatry, (2) increased appreciation for research in abnormal psychology, and (3) increased belief that abnormal behavior may be the result of multiple factors acting in combination with one another.

Many mental health professionals consider the introduction of psychiatric drugs in the 1950s as one of the great medical advances in the twentieth century (Andreasen, 1984; Lickey & Gordon, 1991). Although some might find such a statement excessive, it is difficult to overemphasize the impact that drug therapy has had. It started in 1949 when an Australian psychiatrist, John F. J. Cade, reported on his successful experiments with lithium (a drug currently used for persons with bipolar affective disorders) in radically calming manic patients who had been hospitalized for years. Several years later, French psychiatrists Jean Delay and Pierre Deniker discovered that the drug chlorpromazine (brand name, Thorazine) was extremely effective in treating agitated schizophrenics. Within a matter of years, drugs were developed to treat disorders such as depression, schizophrenia, phobias, obsessive-compulsive disorders, and anxiety. Large classes of drugs were developed for depression (antidepressant drugs), anxiety (antianxiety drugs), and grossly impaired thinking (antipsychotic drugs).

These drugs were considered revolutionary because they rapidly and dramatically decreased or eliminated troublesome symptoms experienced by patients. As a result, other forms of therapy became available to the mentally ill (they were more able to focus their attention on the therapy), their stays in mental hospitals were shortened and were more cost effective than prolonged hospitalizations, and they were allowed to return home for treatment. The new drug therapies were credited with the depopulation of mental hospitals, often referred to as deinstitutionalization (see discussion in Chapter 20).

Statistics on mental health care between 1905 and 1986 reveal drug therapy's impact. The number of patients residing in mental institutions continued to steadily rise to a high of 550,000 until 1956 when drugs were introduced. At that point, the upward trend was reversed, and in 1986, only 111,000 patients were hospitalized. The decline was not attributed to a decrease in new admissions, but rather shorter stays and earlier releases (Lickey & Gordon, 1991). To handle the large increase of patients returning to the community, outpatient treatment became the primary mode of service for the severely disturbed. In addition to changing the landscape by which therapy was dispensed, the introduction of psychiatric drugs revived strong belief in the biological bases of mental disorders.

Along with the introduction of drug therapies emerged another contemporary trend: an increased appreciation for the role of research in the study of abnormal behavior. The success of psychopharmacology spawned renewed interest and research into brain-behavior relationships. Indeed, it appears that more and more researchers are now turning to an exploration of the biological bases (chemical and structural) of abnormal behavior. Within recent years, biological factors have been associated with depression, suicide, certain forms of schizophrenia, learning disabilities, alcoholism, and Alzheimer's disease. On the other hand, many researchers focus on aspects of mental illness that are primarily psychological rather than biological. As we shall see in Chapter 3, the behavioral school of thought and the recent interest and work in cognitive psychology have been instrumental in not only expressing this point of view, but in advocating the use of scientific research in understanding human behavior (Hollon, DeRubeis & Seligman, 1992; Lipman & Kendall,

1992). Currently, insight into the most effective means of understanding and treating specific disorders is being sought in the comparison studies concerning the effectiveness of drug treatment versus cognitive treatment.

We would like to make clear our position concerning the multiple views of abnormal psychology. In reality, few contemporary psychologists or psychiatrists take the extreme of either position. Indeed, most psychologists believe that mental illness probably springs not only from a combination of biological and psychological factors, but from societal and environmental influences as well. The realization that biological, psychological, and social factors all need to be considered in explaining and treating mental disorders has been termed the **biopsychosocial approach.** It would be a serious oversight to neglect the powerful impact on mental health of family upbringing and influence, the stresses of modern society (unemployment, poverty, loss of a loved one, adapting to technological change, and so on), experiences of oppression (prejudice, discrimination, stereotyping), effects of natural disasters (earthquakes, floods, hurricanes), and human-made conflicts such as wars.

WHAT LIES AHEAD IN THIS TEXT

The first part of this text is intended to acquaint you with the study of abnormal psychology. In Chapter 1, we have marked out the boundaries of our subject and surveyed its historical antecedents. In Chapters 2 and 3, we discuss several explanations of abnormal behavior, including those that have their roots in the organic, psychological, and environmental views of mental disorders. Chapter 4 examines the contemporary means by which abnormal behavior is classified and individual problems are assessed. Then, to help you understand and evaluate the psychological research cited and described in this text, Chapter 5 explains the use of scientific methods in abnormal psychology.

The next four parts of this book cover specific disorders. Part 2 contains three chapters on disorders that are characterized predominantly by anxiety and stress. In Part 3, we examine disorders commonly associated with social problems: faulty interpersonal relationships, alcohol and drug abuse, and psychosexual problems. Part 4 covers disorders that often have an exceptional impact on individual functioning and that used to be labeled *psychotic disorders*—schizophrenia and the affective disorders. Suicide is also discussed in Part 4. Part 5 is devoted primarily to organic brain dysfunction, mental retardation, and disorders of childhood and adolescence.

Finally, in Part 6, we discuss and evaluate the major approaches to therapy, as well as community psychology, a field that seeks to identify and implement ways to prevent the occurrence of disorders. Our final chapter is a discussion of some of the major legal and ethical issues raised in our study of abnormal psychology.

In Chapters 2 and 3, we continue to discuss the case of Steven V. Gradually we uncover more and more of his past. You will be able to take part in searching through the details of Steve's life for clues to his current condition. Then, in Chapter 18, we discuss a therapeutic approach to Steve's problems. There you will also see how Steve's therapist solved the dilemma brought about by Steve's threat against Linda.

Steve's behaviors are, by any definition, abnormal. But Steve does not suffer from every mental disorder known to psychology. His problems are different from those faced, for example, by a mentally retarded child, by an 80-pound teenager suffering from anorexia nervosa, or by an older person deteriorating from Alzheimer's disease. Why do we spend so much time with Steven V.?

There are two good reasons to dwell on Steve. The first is to emphasize that abnormal behavior is nonetheless human behavior. We hope that Steve will become for you a real, live human being rather than a specimen exhibiting strange behavior. (Steve is actually a composite character based on various clients whom we, the authors, have treated.)

Second, through Steve's psychological history we can examine a variety of concerns and issues that arise in virtually every case of abnormal behavior. For example, what are the most important features of the behavior? Would all psychologists diagnose a given condition similarly? What kind of treatment, in what setting, would promise the best results? Steve's case provides a format for discussing such questions more explicitly and concretely than we could in the more conventional textbook discourse.

We would like to close this chapter with a word of caution. To be human is to encounter difficulties

"I Have It Too": The Medical Student Syndrome

Medical students probably caught it first. As they read about physical disorders and listened to lecturers describe illnesses, some students began to imagine that they themselves had one disorder or another. "Diarrhea? Fatigue? Trouble sleeping? That's me!" In this way, a cluster of symptoms—no matter how mild or how briefly experienced—can lead some people to suspect that they are very sick.

Students who take a course that examines psychopathology may be equally prone to believe that they have a mental disorder that is described in their text. It is possible, of course, that some of these students do suffer from a disorder and would benefit from counseling or therapy. Most, however, are merely experiencing an exaggerated sense of their susceptibility to disorders. In one study, it was found that one of every five individuals responded yes to the question "Have you ever felt that you were going to have a

nervous breakdown?" Of course, most of those people never suffered an actual breakdown (U.S. Department of Health, Education and Welfare, 1971).

Two influences in particular may make us susceptible to these imagined disorders. One is the universality of the human experience. All of us have experienced misfortunes in life. We can all remember and relate to feelings of anxiety, unhappiness, guilt, lack of self-confidence, and even thoughts of suicide. In most cases, however, these feelings are normal reactions to stressful situations, not symptoms of disease. Depression that follows the loss of a loved one or anxiety before giving a speech to a large audience may be perfectly normal and appropriate. Another influence is our tendency to compare our own functioning with our perceptions of how other people are functioning. The outward behaviors of fellow students may lead us to conclude that they experience

few difficulties in life, are self-assured and confident, and are invulnerable to mental disturbance. If we were privy to their inner thoughts and feelings, however, we might be surprised to find that they share our apprehension and insecurities.

If you see yourself anywhere in the pages of this book, we hope that you will take the time to discuss the matter with a friend or with one of your professors. You may be responding to pressures that you have not encountered before—a heavy course load, for example—and to which you have not yet adjusted. Other people can help point out these pressures to you. If your discussion supports your suspicion that you have a problem, however, then by all means consider getting a professional evaluation.

and problems in life. A course in abnormal psychology dwells on human problems—many familiar. As a result, we may be prone to the "medical student syndrome": reading about a disorder may lead us to suspect that we have the disorder or that a friend or relative has it (see Focus 1.2). This reaction to the study of abnormal behavior is common, but one that it pays to guard against.

SUMMARY

1. The objectives of abnormal psychology are to describe, explain, predict, and control behaviors that

are strange or unusual. Various criteria may be used to define such behaviors. Statistical criteria define abnormality in terms of those behaviors that occur least frequently in the population. Ideal mental health criteria characterize abnormality as an inability to attain some positive goal. The multicultural criteria stress cultural influences in the process and manifestation of a disorder. The various practical criteria define abnormality on the basis of discomfort, either physical or psychological, suffered by the affected individual; the bizarreness of the person's actions; or his or her inefficiency in filling life roles. It may be that a single criterion or viewpoint is not sufficient but that abnormality should be defined from the combined vantage points of society, the individual, and the mental health professional.

2. Mental health problems are widespread in the United States, and more and more Americans are seeking professional help. The result has been a gigantic growth in the number of mental health professionals practicing in the United States. These professionals include clinical psychologists, counseling psychologists, psychiatrists, psychoanalysts, psychiatric social workers, and marriage and family counselors.

3. Many of our current concepts of mental illness have their roots in past beliefs and practices. Ancient people believed in demonology and attributed abnormal behaviors to evil spirits that inhabited the victim's body. Treatment consisted of trephining or exorcism. Rational and scientific explanations of abnormality emerged during the Greco-Roman era. Especially influential was the thinking of Hippocrates, who believed that abnormal behavior was due to a dysfunction or disease of the brain. With the collapse of the Roman Empire and the increased influence of the church and its emphasis on divine will and the hereafter, however, rationalist thought was suppressed and belief in the supernatural began to flourish again. During the Middle Ages, famine, pestilence, and dynastic wars caused enormous social upheaval. Forms of mass hysteria affected groups of people. In the fifteenth century, the church endorsed witch hunts both in response to fear generated by social unrest and as a way to deal with those opposing its authority. Among the numerous men, women, and children who were tortured and killed as witches were some whom we would today call mentally ill. The Renaissance brought a return to rational and scientific inquiry along with a heightened interest in humanitarian methods of treating the mentally ill.

4. In the nineteenth and twentieth centuries, major medical breakthroughs fostered a belief in the organic roots of mental illness. The discovery of the microorganism that caused general paresis was especially important in this regard. Scientists believed that they would eventually find organic causes for all mental disorders. Mesmerism and later hypnosis supported another view, however. The uncovering of a relationship between hypnosis and hysteria corroborated the belief that psychological processes could produce emotional disturbances.

KEY TERMS

abnormal behavior Behavior that departs from some norm and that harms the affected individual or others.

abnormal psychology The scientific study whose objectives are to describe, explain, predict, and control behaviors that are considered strange or unusual

biogenic view The belief or theory that mental disorders have a physical or physiological basis

biopsychosocial model An approach to understanding and explaining human behavior by recognizing the influence of biological, psychological, and social factors

brain pathology Dysfunction or disease of the brain

cathartic method The therapeutic use of verbal expression to release pent-up emotional conflicts

cultural relativism The belief that lifestyles, cultural values, and world views affect the expression and determination of deviant behavior

cultural universality The belief that many behavior disorders cut across lifestyles, cultural norms, and world views

exorcism Ritual in which prayer, noise, emetics, and extreme measures such as flogging and starvation were used to cast evil spirits out of an afflicted person's body

humanism An emphasis on human welfare and on the worth and uniqueness of the individual

mass madness Group hysteria

moral treatment movement A shift to more humane treatment of the mentally disturbed; its initiation is generally attributed to Philippe Pinel

psychodiagnosis An attempt to describe, assess, and systematically draw inferences about an individual's psychological disorder

psychogenic view The belief or theory that mental disorders are caused by psychological and emotional factors

syndrome A cluster of symptoms that tend to occur together and are believed to indicate a particular disorder

therapy A program of systematic intervention whose purpose is to modify a client's behavioral, affective, or cognitive state

trephining An ancient surgical technique in which part of the skull was chipped away to provide an opening through which evil spirits could escape

CHAPTER 2

Biogenic and Psychogenic Models of Abnormal Behavior

In Chapter 1, we described the rise of humanism in society's attitude toward mental disorders. As rational thought replaced superstition in the eighteenth and nineteenth centuries, the mentally disturbed were increasingly regarded as unfortunate human beings who deserved respectful and humane treatment, not as monsters inhabited by the devil.

This humanistic view gave rise, in the late nineteenth and early twentieth centuries, to two different schools of thought about the causes of mental disorders. According to one group of thinkers, mental disorders are primarily biogenic—that is, caused by biological problems. The disturbed individual, this group contended, is displaying symptoms of physical disease or damage. A second group of theorists found organic explanations inadequate. These thinkers believed that abnormal behavior is essentially psychogenic, rooted not in cells and tissues but in the invisible complexities of the human mind.

In this chapter, we continue to trace the evolution of these two schools of thought and bring them up to date. We begin with the biogenic perspective and then examine three psychogenic perspectives: the psychoanalytic theory first articulated by Sigmund Freud and the more recent humanistic and existential perspectives. Later, in Chapter 3, we discuss three additional perspectives on abnormal behavior, the behavioral, cognitive, and family systems theories. It

A Diversity Perspective on Models of Psychopathology

Models of psychopathology are often culture-bound; they may evaluate and view things from a world view not shared by other cultural groups. For example, mental health professionals in the United States may hold values, assumptions, and biases about human behavior that affect the manner in which they judge normality and abnormality among various racial and ethnic minorities. A number of multicultural experts (Parham & White, 1990; Ponterotto & Casas, 1990; D. W. Sue & D. Sue, 1990) have identified three primary models that have emerged in the mental health field that are used to explain differences between various minority groups and their white counterparts: (1) the inferiority model, (2) the deprivations/deficit model, and (3) the multicultural model. Each tends to

view minority differences from a different perspective.

1. *Inferiority model*   The inferiority model generally contends that racial and ethnic minorities are inferior in some respect to the majority population. Low academic achievement and higher unemployment rates among African Americans and Latino Americans are attributed to heredity. For example, de Gobineau's (1915) *Essay on the Inequality of the Human Races* and Darwin's (1859) *On the Origin of Species by Means of Natural Selection* were used to support the genetic intellectual superiority of whites and the genetic inferiority of the "lower races."

The assertions of racial inferiority continued well into the 1900s and were promoted by leading psychologists. For example, Cyril Burt,

an eminent British psychologist, believed that intelligence is inherited and that African Americans have inherited inferior brains. Although his data were later found to have been fabricated (Dorfman, 1978; Gillie, 1977) and questions have been raised regarding his integrity, many other psychologists (Hernstein, 1971; Jensen, 1969; Shockley, 1972; Shuey, 1966) have voiced similar beliefs.

2. *Deprivations/deficit model*   The deprivations/deficit model arose during the 1950s and 1960s when well-meaning social scientists began to actively question whether the differences that existed between blacks and whites were encoded in the genes or whether environmental factors could account for them. One explanation was that years of racism and discrimination had deprived

is important to note, however, that the psychogenic models in Chapter 2 are concerned primarily with the individual human mind. Models in Chapter 3 tend to examine the relationship between the mind and the environment.

The six theories we examine in Chapters 2 and 3 are by no means the only possible explanations of abnormal behavior. One survey identified more than 130 such theories in the United States alone (National Institute of Mental Health, 1975). Many of these are variants of the more basic theories discussed here, however, and others have never gained widespread acceptance.

To help bring the major theories to life, and to show how they can be applied to individual problems, we continue to explore the case of Steven V. in Chapters 2 and 3. Immediately after our discussion of each major approach, we examine Steve's prob-

lems through the eyes and insights of a hypothetical follower of that approach.

Let's begin by clarifying two terms that we use frequently. The first is **psychopathology,** which clinical psychologists use as a synonym for abnormal behavior. The second is *model*, a term that requires a more elaborate explanation.

MODELS IN THE STUDY OF PSYCHOPATHOLOGY

Scientists who need to discuss a phenomenon that is difficult to describe or explain often make use of an analogy in which they liken the phenomenon to something more concrete. A **model** is such an analogy, and it is most often used to describe something

blacks of the opportunity to develop a positive self-esteem. Related to this explanation was that the deficits observed in black people were the result of "cultural deprivation." Reissman's (1962) widely read book *The Culturally Deprived Child* indicated that minority groups performed poorly on tests or exhibited deviant characteristics because they were "culturally impoverished." Although Reissman meant his concept to add balance to understanding minority groups and to ultimately improve their conditions, it was conceptually inaccurate. First, the term *culturally deprived* means to lack a cultural background (which conceptually means Africans arrived in America without a culture!), but everyone inherits a culture. Second, such terms cause conceptual and theoretical confusion because they imply that we should infuse "white values" into minority groups to solve the problems. White middle-class values are perceived as superior. Third, these deviations in values be-

come equated with disorder because a group's cultural values are seen as pathological. In some respects, instead of blaming the genes, the deprivations/deficit model blamed the lifestyles and values of various ethnic groups.

3. *Multicultural model* Within the last ten years, a new and conceptually different model has emerged in the literature. Often referred to as the "multicultural model" (Johnson, 1990; Parham & White, 1990), "culturally different model" (Katz, 1985; Sue, 1981), "culturally pluralistic model or culturally diverse model" (Ponterotto & Casas, 1990), the new model makes several assumptions. First and foremost is the explicit belief that to be culturally different does not equal deviancy, pathology, or inferiority. The model recognizes that each culture has strengths and limitations and that differences are inevitable. Behaviors must be evaluated from the perspective of a group's value system as well as other standards

used in determining normality and abnormality.

The 1990 U.S. Census revealed that the United States is fast undergoing some radical demographic changes. The current population trend can be referred to as the "diversification of America" with projections that by the year 2000, more than one-third of the population will be a member of a racial or ethnic minority and that by the year 2010 (less than twenty years from now), European Americans will constitute a numerical minority. The reality of cultural diversity in the United States has already had tremendous impact on educational, political, economic, and social systems. The mental health professions and the models we use to explain both normal and abnormal behavior are also experiencing a major revolution.

that cannot be observed directly. In an analogy, terms, concepts, or principles are borrowed from one field and applied to another. The person who likens the heart to a pump or the eye to a camera is making use of a model.

When psychologists speak of deviant behavior as "mental illness" or refer to their "patients," they are borrowing the terminology of medicine and essentially applying a *medical model* of abnormal behavior. They may also describe certain external symptoms as being visible signs of deep underlying conflict. Again, the medical analogy is clear: just as fevers, rashes, perspiration, or infections may be symptoms of a bacterial or viral invasion of the body, bizarre behavior may be a symptom of a mind "invaded" by unresolved conflicts. Psychologists have used models extensively to help them conceptualize the causes of abnormal behavior, ask probing ques-

tions, determine what information or data are relevant, and interpret data. Each model is a means of viewing abnormal behavior, and it generally embodies a particular theoretical approach. Hence we tend to use the terms *model, theory, viewpoint,* and *perspective* somewhat interchangeably.

Every model, however apt, is limited in its usefulness. (See Focus 2.1) None provides all the answers. The complexity of human behavior and the relatively shallow understanding of it prevent psychologists from developing *the* definitive model. Most theorists do not believe that the models they construct will correspond in every respect to the phenomena they are studying. Rather, models are used to visualize psychopathology as if it truly worked in the manner described by the models (Millon, 1973).

In reality, most practicing clinicians do not adhere rigidly to any one model. In a survey of clinical psychologists, 64 percent identified themselves as having an **eclectic approach** (Garfield & Kurtz, 1976, 1977). These therapists remain open to all perspectives, borrowing diagnostic techniques and treatment strategies from all approaches and using them selectively with clients. To the eclectic therapist, the important question is always, "What theories will work best with this particular client, in what setting, and with what expected therapeutic outcome?"

To be sure, the eclectic approach has disadvantages (Brammer & Shoestrom, 1984; Norcross & Prochaska, 1988). Because often it is not rooted in a carefully constructed system of concepts and assumptions, the eclectic approach may result in uncritical picking and choosing: one therapeutic technique from Column A, another from Column B, and so on down the menu of theories. Furthermore, any novel mixture of concepts and techniques necessarily lacks a substantial base of research to prove how effective it is; essentially, it is educated guesswork. And finally, therapists who do not associate themselves with a traditional theory of psychopathology may be especially prone to embrace the fad therapy of the moment.

Despite these potential shortcomings, eclecticism is inevitable because we have no single "true" model of abnormal behavior. In fact, most psychologists see considerable value in an eclectic approach (discussed more fully in Chapter 18). They recognize that different models of psychopathology do not completely contradict each other on every point. Rather, the elements of various models can complement each other to produce a broad and detailed explanation of a person's condition (Corey, 1991).

THE BIOGENIC MODEL

The idea that mental disorders are caused by organic problems was proposed by Hippocrates around 400 B.C., but this organic viewpoint was not generally accepted until the late eighteenth and early nineteenth centuries. The contributions of Wilhelm Griesinger, Emil Kraepelin, and other pioneers; Pasteur's formulation of the germ theory of disease; and Fritz Schaudinn's discovery of the microorganism that caused general paresis all reinforced the belief that abnormal behavior is symptomatic of organic disease. And if every mental disorder has a physiological

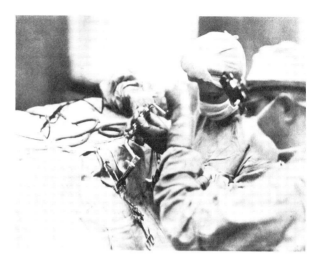

During a prefrontal lobotomy, surgeons used a drill to open the skull. Because of severe side-effects, lobotomies have rarely been used since the 1950s.

source, every mental disorder should also have an organic cure. This reasoning is the essence of the **biogenic model** of psychopathology (Cottone, 1992; Harris, 1980).

Modern biogenic explanations of normal and abnormal behavior continue to share certain assumptions: (1) human thoughts, emotions, and behaviors are associated with nerve cell activities of the brain and spinal cord; (2) a change in any of these domains is associated with a change in activity or structure (or both) of the brain; (3) a mental disorder is highly correlated with some form of brain dysfunction; and (4) mental disorders can be treated by drugs or somatic intervention. As we have seen, the introduction of drugs in the 1950s and advances in the understanding of brain chemistry lend credence to this line of reasoning.

The biogenic models have been heavily influenced by the neurosciences, a group of subfields that focus on brain structure, function, and disorder. Understanding biogenic explanations of human behavior requires knowledge about structure and function of the central nervous system (composed of the brain and spinal cord). Especially important is knowledge about how the brain is organized, how it works, and especially the chemical reactions that enhance or diminish normal brain actions.

The Human Brain

The brain is composed of billions of **neurons,** or nerve cells that transmit messages throughout the body. The brain is responsible for three very important and highly complicated functions. It receives information from the outside world, it uses the information to decide on a course of action, and it implements decisions by commanding muscles to move and glands to secrete. Weighing approximately three pounds, this relatively small organ continues to amaze and mystify biological researchers.

The brain is separated into two hemispheres. A disturbance in either one (such as by a tumor or by electrical stimulation with electrodes) may produce specific sensory or motor effects. Each hemisphere controls the opposite side of the body. For example, paralysis on the left side of the body indicates a dysfunction in the right hemisphere. In addition, the right hemisphere is associated with visual-spatial abilities and emotional behavior. The left hemisphere controls the language functions for nearly all right-handed people and for most left-handed ones (Golden & Vincente, 1983).

Viewed in cross section, the brain has three parts: forebrain, midbrain, and hindbrain. Although each part is vital for functioning and survival, the forebrain is probably the most relevant to a discussion of abnormality. The *forebrain* probably controls all the higher mental functions associated with human consciousness learning, speech, thought, and memory. Within the forebrain are the thalamus, hypothalamus, reticular activating system, limbic system, and cerebrum (see Figure 2.1). The specific functions of these structures are still being debated, but we can discuss their more general functions with some confidence. The *thalamus* appears to serve as a "relay station," transmitting nerve impulses from one part of the brain to another. The *hypothalamus* ("under the thalamus") regulates bodily drives (such as hunger, thirst, and sex) and body conditions such as temperature and hormone balance. The *reticular activating system* is a network of nerve fibers that controls bodily states such as sleep, alertness, and attention. The *limbic system* is involved in experiencing and expressing emotions and motivation—pleasure, fear, aggressiveness, sexual arousal, and pain.

The largest structure in the brain is the *cerebrum,* with its most visible part, the cerebral cortex, covering the midbrain and thalamus. The other two regions of the brain also have distinct functions. The *midbrain* is involved in vision and hearing. It is also partially involved with the hindbrain in the control of sleep, alertness, and pain. Of interest to mental health professionals is its role in the manufacture of certain chemicals: serotonin, norepinephrine, and dopamine, which have been implicated in certain mental disorders. The *hindbrain* also manufactures serotonin and appears to control vegetative functions such as heart rate, sleep, and respiration.

Because the brain controls all aspects of human functioning, it is not difficult to conclude that damage or interruption of normal brain function and activity could lead to observable mental disorders. There are, of course, many biological causes for psychological disorders. Damage to the nervous system is one: as Schaudinn demonstrated, general paresis results from brain damage caused by parasitic microorganisms. Tumors, strokes, excessive intake of alcohol or drugs, and external trauma (such as a blow to the head) have also been linked to cognitive, emotional, and behavioral disorders. Two specific biological sources deserve special attention here, however, for they have given rise to important biogenic theories of psychopathology. These causes are body chemistry and heredity.

Biochemical Theories

Most physiological and mental processes, from sleeping and digestion to reading and thinking, involve chemical actions within the body. Thus it seems likely that body chemistry has considerable effect on behavior. The basic premise of the biochemical theories is that chemical imbalances underlie mental disorders. Support for these theories has been provided by research into anxiety disorders, mood disorders (both depression and bipolar disorder), and schizophrenia (Davis & Greenwald, 1991; Lickey & Gordon, 1991; McGeer & McGeer, 1980; Seiver, Davis & Gorman, 1991; Snyder, 1986). To understand how biochemical imbalances in the brain can result in abnormal behavior, we need to briefly explain how messages in the brain are transmitted from nerve cell to nerve cell.

While nerve cells (neurons) vary in function throughout the brain and may appear different, they

FIGURE 2.1 The Internal Structure of the Brain

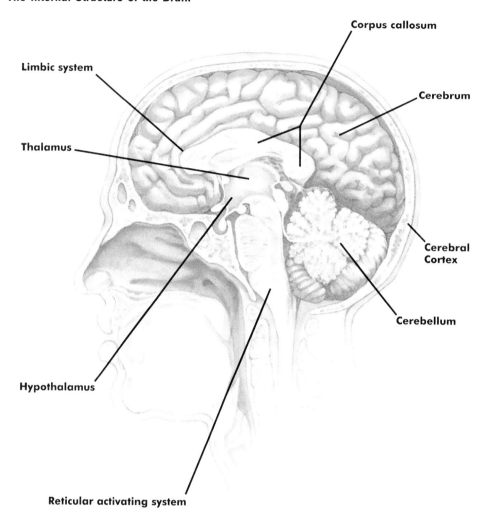

do possess similarities. Neurons possess a cell membrane that separates it from the outside environment and regulates the chemical contents within it. On one side of the cell are numerous short rootlike structures called **dendrites** whose function is to receive signals from other neurons. At the other end is a much longer extension called an **axon,** which sends signals to neurons a considerable distance away. Under an electron microscope dendrites can be distinguished from axons because dendrites usually have many short branches (see Figure 2.2). Messages travel through the brain by electrical impulses via neurons: An incoming message is received by a neuron's dendrites and is sent down the axon to bulblike swellings called *axon terminals*, usually located near dendrites of another neuron. It is important to note that neurons do not touch one another. A minute gap (called the **synapse**) exists between the axon terminal and the dendrites of the receiving neuron. The electrical impulse crosses the synapse by the release of chemicals called **neurotransmitters.** When they reach the dendrites of the receiving neuron they attach themselves to receptors and a binding occurs (see Figures 2.3 and 2.4). The binding of transmitters to receptors in the neuron triggers either a synaptic excitation (encouragement to produce other nerve impulses) or synaptic inhibition (prevents production of nerve impulses).

FIGURE 2.2   Major Parts of a Neuron

The major parts of a neuron include dendrites, the cell body, the axon, and the axon terminals.

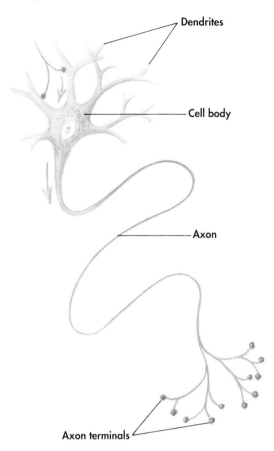

Dendrites

Cell body

Axon

Axon terminals

There are many different kinds of chemical transmitters in the body and they differ in the effects they have on the neurons (see Table 2.1). An imbalance of certain neurotransmitters in the brain is believed to be implicated in mental disorders. As discussed in Chapter 1, the search for chemical causes and cures for mental problems accelerated tremendously in the early 1950s with the discovery of psychoactive drugs. The lines of evidence supporting this belief were very convincing. First, it was found that antipsychotic drugs have beneficial effects on schizophrenics, that lithium is useful in controlling affective disorders, and that tricyclic and monoamine oxidase inhibitors alleviate symptoms of severely depressed patients. Second, biochemical studies (Andreasen, 1984;

Lickey & Gordon, 1991) indicate that these drugs seem to work by blocking or facilitating neurotransmitter activity at receptor sites. Most of the current psychiatric drugs seem to affect one of five different transmitters: norepinephrine, dopamine, serotonin, acetylcholine, and gamma aminobutyric acid (GABA).

Last, evidence began to accumulate that certain chemical imbalances were disorder-specific. For example, we have already discussed the finding that insufficient dopamine is a possible cause of Parkinson's disease. Ironically, an excess of dopamine has been implicated in the development of schizophrenia (Cooper et al., 1986; Davis & Greenwald, 1991; Snyder, 1986). It is hypothesized that schizophrenics may have too many postsynaptic dopamine receptors (structural explanation) or that their receptors may be supersensitive to dopamine. Likewise, it has been found that drugs used to treat depression alter norepinephrine and serotonin sensitivity and receptivity at the receptor sites; drugs used in the treatment of anxiety affect receptor reactivity to GABA.

Research into biochemical mechanisms involved in mental disorders holds great promise for our understanding and treatment of these disorders. It appears likely, however, that biochemistry alone cannot provide completely satisfactory explanations of the biological bases of abnormal behavior. Researchers should instead expect to find hundreds—or perhaps thousands—of pieces in the biogenic puzzle.

Genetic Explanations

Genetics are also clearly important in the development of certain abnormal conditions. For instance, past research has shown that "nervousness" can be inherited in animals by breeding generations of dogs that were either fearful or friendly (Murphree & Dykman, 1965). Evidence supports the contention that autonomic nervous system (ANS) reactivity may be inherited in human beings as well; that is, a person may be born with an ANS that makes an unusually strong response to stimuli (Andreasen, 1984; Baker & Clark, 1990). Recent studies (Cloninger et al., 1986; Gatz, 1990; Neale & Oltmanns, 1980; Paykel, 1982; Plonin, 1989) now implicate heredity as a causal factor in alcoholism, schizophrenia, and depression. To show that a particular disorder is inherited, however, researchers must show that it could

FIGURE 2.3 Synaptic Transmission

Messages travel via electrical impulses from one neuron to another. The impulse crosses the synapse in the form of chemicals called *neurotransmitters.* Note that the axon terminals and the receiving dendrites do not touch.

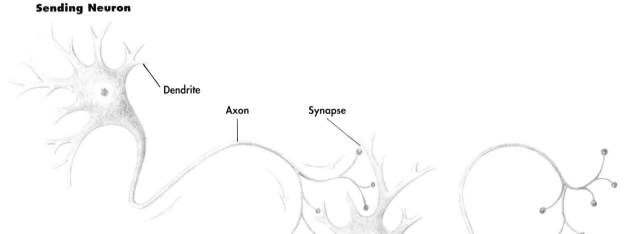

Sending Neuron

Dendrite

Axon

Synapse

Axon terminal

Dendrites

Axon

Receiving Neuron

not be caused by environmental factors alone, that closer genetic relationships produce greater similarity of the disorder in human beings, and that people with these problems have similar biological and behavioral patterns (Siegel, 1990).

Biological inheritance is transmitted by the genes. A person's genetic makeup is called his or her **geno-type;** interaction between the genotype and the environment results in the person's **phenotype,** or physical and behavioral characteristics. At times, however, it is difficult to determine which influence predominates. For example, characteristics such as eye color are determined solely by the coding of the genes (genotype). But other physical characteristics, such as height, are determined partly by the genetic code and partly by environmental factors. Undernourished children may become grownups who are shorter than the height they were genetically capable of reaching. On the other hand, even the most effective nutrition cannot spur people to grow taller than their "programmed" height limit.

Twin Studies As is detailed more fully in Chapter 15, one of the most useful procedures for studying the contributions of heredity is to compare the degree of similarity between identical twins and same-sex nonidentical twins. **Monozygotic (MZ)** or **identical twins** are derived from a single egg; they have the same genetic makeup. We assume that differences between MZ twins are due to their environment. **Dizygotic (DZ)** or **fraternal twins,** derived from two eggs, do not share the same genes.

Many studies of human twins indicate that MZ twins tend to be more alike on autonomic (that part of the nervous system concerned with involuntary bodily functions and changes) measures than DZ twins (Pogue-Geile & Rose, 1985; Siegel, 1990). Several studies of emotionality among pairs of MZ twins and pairs of DZ twins also found strong evidence for an inherited component to distress, fear, anger, activity, and sociability (Buss & Plonin, 1986; Plonin et al., 1988). The MZ twins consistently evidenced greater similarity in these traits.

FIGURE 2.4   Neurotransmitter Binding

Neurotransmitters are released into the synapse and travel to the receiving dendrite. Each transmitter has a specific shape that corresponds to a receptor site. Like a jigsaw puzzle, binding occurs if the transmitter fits into the receptor site.

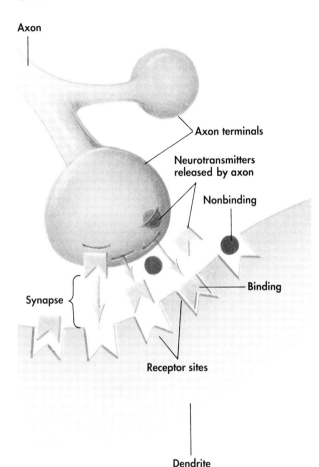

Axon

Axon terminals

Neurotransmitters released by axon

Nonbinding

Binding

Synapse

Receptor sites

Dendrite

Table 2.1

Neurotransmitters and Their Effects

Neurotransmitter	Source and Function
Acetylcholine (ACh)	One of the most widespread neurotransmitters. Occurs in systems that control the muscles and in circuits related to attention and memory.
Dopamine	Concentrated in small areas of the brain, one of which is involved in the control of the muscles. In excess, dopamine can cause hallucinations.
Endorphins	Found in the brain and spinal cord. Suppresses pain.
Gamma amino-butyric acid (GABA)	Widely distributed in the brain. Works against other neurotransmitters, particularly dopamine.
Norepinephrine	Occurs widely in the central nervous system. May increase arousal and alertness and regulates mood.
Serotonin	Occurs in the brain. Works more or less in opposition to norepinephrine, suppressing activity and causing sleep.

Although twin studies seem to strongly implicate heredity, most studies examine only a few pairs of twins. Thus we must be cautious in interpreting their implications. Furthermore, these results do not explain why, in 35 percent of MZ twins, one identical twin became disordered and the other did not. It seems, however, that interactions between heredity and environment can either facilitate or retard the manifestation of disorders. For example, a person with an inherited predisposition to anxiety may be born into a benign environment, peopled with supportive parents and friends, that retards anxiety development.

Overall, it is clear that heredity influences autonomic reactions, that heredity contributes to the development of anxiety reactions, and that individual exposure to the environment can moderate the effects of an inherited predisposition to anxiety.

Correlation Studies   A strong correlation also appears to exist between (1) genetic inheritance and (2) the development of bipolar disorder, some forms of schizophrenia, and certain kinds of mental retardation. Down syndrome, for example, is a result of chromosomal aberrations. Except in specific cases, however, the exact influence of genes is difficult to ascertain. Because law and basic morality prohibit selective breeding of human beings, we rely on *correlation studies* when seeking the relationship between heredity and mental disorders. But such studies are really just comparisons of existing frequencies of mental disorders in various populations; no matter how strong the correlations they reveal, they do not

These pairs of identical twins are all from the same family. The physical similarities are striking and make it easy for us to assume that genetics may play a powerful role in determining other personality characteristics as well. Evidence is strong that certain disorders have a genetic link.

demonstrate cause-and-effect relationships. For that reason, they must be interpreted cautiously.

Criticisms of the Biogenic Model

The biogenic model of abnormal behavior, which drifted out of favor when psychoanalysis was at the peak of its influence in the 1940s, has regained its popularity. Indeed, it is rare that a week goes by without news reports linking genetics to alcohol abuse, learning disabilities, temperament, personality, or susceptibility to stress. Structural differences in the brain have been linked to schizophrenia, and new "miracle" drugs are being discovered for various disorders. But the biogenic model has some major shortcomings if viewed as the sole explanation for mental disorders.

First, one of its basic tenets is that abnormal behavior results from an underlying physical condition, such as damage to the brain or malfunction of neural processes. The model implies that treatment should be aimed at controlling the underlying disease by changing the individual's biochemistry or removing toxic substances. This approach ignores the many empirical findings that emphasize the importance of environmental factors. It doesn't acknowledge the interpersonal and social causes of abnormal behavior.

Nor does it adequately account for abnormal behavior for which no organic etiology, or cause, can be found. For example, although some mental disorders, such as bipolar and unipolar psychotic mood states and schizophrenia, may have primary biological causes, strong evidence exists that phobias and eating disorders have a predominantly social cause. Many disorders are probably a mix of predisposition and environment.

Second, the biogenic model implicitly assumes a correspondence between organic dysfunction and mental dysfunction. Environmental or cultural influences are thought to have minimal impact. But rarely are the equations of human behavior so uncomplicated. More often there are a multitude of causes behind any human behavior, and environmental factors seem to play as important a role as any other. Increasingly, mental health research has focused on the diathesis-stress theory, originally proposed by Meehl (1962) and developed further by Rosenthal (1970). The **diathesis-stress theory** holds that it is not a particular abnormality that is inherited but rather a *predisposition to develop illness* (diathesis). Certain environmental forces, called *stressors*, may activate the predisposition, resulting in a disorder. Alternatively, in a benign and supportive environment, the abnormality may never materialize.

A third shortcoming, related to the preceding one, is revealed by our accumulating knowledge that biochemical changes often occur because of environmental forces. We know, for example, that stress-produced fear and anger cause the secretion of adrenalin and noradrenalin. Similarly, schizophrenia could cause the excess amounts of chemicals such as dopamine in persons with the disorder rather than result from it.

Last, wholesale adoption of the biogenic model could foster helplessness in the patient by eliminating patient responsibility in the treatment process. The patient might be seen—both by the therapist and by himself or herself—as a passive participant, to be treated only with appropriate drugs and medical interventions. For patients who are already suffering from feelings of helplessness or loss of control, such an approach could be devastating.

◆ A BIOGENIC VIEW OF STEVEN V.

How would a psychologist oriented toward biogenic explanations view the case of Steven V.? If Steve's therapist were so oriented, we believe that he would discuss Steve's behavior in the following terms.

Before I interpret the symptoms displayed by Steven V. and speculate on what they mean, I must stress my belief that many "mental disorders" have a strong biological basis. I do accept the importance of environmental influences; but, in my view, the biological bases of abnormality are too often overlooked by psychologists. This seems clearly to be the case with Steven V.

Much of Steve's medical history is missing from his case records, along with important information about his biological and developmental milestones. We do not have the data necessary to chart a family tree, which would show whether other members of his family have suffered from a similar disorder. This lack of information about possible inherited tendencies in Steve's current behavior pattern is a serious shortcoming.

At age fifteen, Steve was given a diagnosis of bipolar affective disorder (formerly called *manic-depressive psychosis*). Pharmacological treatment was moderately effective in controlling his symp-

toms. After Steve's condition became stabilized, lithium carbonate treatment was instituted for a period of time, and Steve was free of symptoms during that period. Unfortunately, Steve apparently disliked taking medication and did so only sporadically.

In any case, evidence documents and supports a diagnosis of bipolar affective disorder. Steve displays the behaviors associated with this disorder, ranging from manic episodes (elevated mood characterized by expansiveness, hyperactivity, flight of ideas, and inflated self-esteem) to depressive episodes (depressed mood characterized by loss of interest, feelings of worthlessness, and thoughts of death or suicide). These symptoms are not of recent origin but probably were evident very early in his life. Steve's first contact with a mental health professional was with the school psychologist in kindergarten, who described him as "autistic-like." I believe the child psychiatrist whom Steve subsequently visited was correct in saying that Steve was not autistic. The chief symptoms described in his early years, which appeared to indicate autism (social isolation and unresponsiveness), are similar to those of depression. I suspect Steve was experiencing a major depressive episode as early as kindergarten, and it may not have been his first. Unfortunately, we do not have access to Steve's pediatrician, who may have observed even earlier signs of bipolar disorder. What we do have, however, are several statements from his parents indicating that "even at birth, Steve did not respond in a normal way."

Thus the following conclusions can be drawn: Steve's disorder was evident early in his life, and he suffered from a chemical imbalance. In spite of a shortage of information, there is some indication that some of Steve's relatives may have suffered from a similar disorder. The most defensible diagnosis is bipolar affective disorder. The most effective way to treat this disorder is through drug therapy.

These conclusions strongly support a biological interpretation of the patient's psychopathology. Heredity seems to have played a part; we have some evidence that relatives may have suffered a similar disorder. The precise biological mechanism that triggered the disorder is probably within one of the two major classes of neurotransmitters (catecholamines and indoleamines). If this diagnosis is accurate, the patient should resume taking medication. Of course, stressful life events may also be contributing to Steve's emotional problems, and I intend to continue psychotherapy with him. But I believe that many of Steve's depressive episodes would have occurred regardless of *psychological* intervention. And they will probably continue to occur unless Steve controls his biological problem with medication. I am not an M.D. and therefore cannot prescribe drugs, so I have arranged for Steve to visit a physician at the college medical center. Only when Steve's organic problem is under control can I or any other therapist begin to make headway with Steve's problems in relating to other people.

THE PSYCHOANALYTIC MODEL

The **psychoanalytic model** of abnormal behavior has two main distinguishing features. First, this approach places strong emphasis on childhood experiences to explain adult behavior. Psychoanalysts view disorders in adults as the result of traumas or anxieties experienced in childhood. Second, the psychoanalytic model holds that many of these childhood-based anxieties operate unconsciously; because they are too threatening for the adult to face, they are repressed through mental defense mechanisms. As a result, people exhibit symptoms they are unable to understand. To eliminate the symptoms, the therapist must make the patient aware of these unconscious anxieties or conflicts.

The early development of psychoanalytic theory is generally credited to Sigmund Freud (1938, 1949), a Viennese neurologist. Before he developed the technique of psychoanalysis, Freud had already made major contributions in neurology. He was acquainted with the methods of the Nancy school (see Chapter 1) and had worked with Josef Breuer, a colleague who was successfully using hypnosis to treat hysterical patients (those who exhibited physical symptoms for which no organic cause could be found). This background led his creative and tenacious mind into the field of psychiatry. During his clinical work, Freud became convinced that powerful mental processes could remain hidden from consciousness and could cause abnormal behaviors. He believed that the

Sigmund Freud (1856–1939) began his career as a neurologist. He became increasingly intrigued with the relationship between illness and mental processes when he worked with Josef Breuer, who successfully used hypnotism to treat hysterical patients.

therapist's role was to help the patient achieve insight into these unconscious processes. Although he originally relied on hypnosis for this purpose, Freud soon dropped it in favor of other techniques. He felt that cures were more likely to be permanent if patients became aware of their problems without the aid of hypnosis. This view eventually led Freud to his formulation of **psychoanalysis.**

Although critics have vehemently attacked the psychoanalytic view on the grounds that it is not a scientific theory, it has undoubtedly had a profound impact on Western thought (Joseph, 1991; Smith, 1982). Not only is it an extremely popular explanation of abnormal behavior among lay people, but many other theories of psychopathology are derivatives of or reactions to its basic tenets. "Slips of the tongue" or pen, the dynamic workings of the unconscious, the importance of childhood experiences, "defense mechanisms," and countless other concepts and terms that permeate our thinking and language have their roots in the work of Sigmund Freud.

Personality Structure

Freud believed that the personality is composed of three major components and that all behavior is a product of their interaction. He called these mental structures the *id,* the *ego,* and the *superego.* The *id* is the original component of the personality present at birth from which the ego and superego eventually develop. It is impulsive, subjective, and pleasure seeking; it is completely selfish and seeks immediate gratification of instinctual needs. Although the id operates from the **pleasure principle,** the *ego* is influenced by the **reality principle;** it represents the realistic and rational part of the mind. The ego comes into existence because the human personality must be able to cope with the external world if it is to survive. Its decisions are dictated by realistic considerations rather than moral judgment. Moral judgments and moralistic considerations are the domain of the *superego;* they often represent society's ideals or values as interpreted by our parents. It is composed of the *conscience,* which instills guilt feelings about engaging in immoral or unethical behavior, and the ego *ideal,* which rewards altruistic or moral behavior with feelings of pride.

Take the case of a young soldier who has been raised to respect the value of human life. He may find the act of killing abhorrent even in a war. Witnessing the death of several of his closest friends in bloody hand-to-hand combat, however, may cause the soldier to feel severe conflict. Filled with anger and a desire to avenge the death of his friends (id impulses), he may also feel guilty about having these thoughts (superego versus id). Now suppose that the young soldier suddenly spots an enemy soldier aiming a rifle at him from behind a tree. Here the soldier experiences a conflict between superego and ego. His superego tells him not to kill because it is "bad" (a moralistic consideration), whereas his ego tells him to defend himself (a realistic consideration).

Instincts

Instincts are the energy system from which the personality operates. Instincts give rise to our thoughts and actions and fuel their expression. Freud postulated the existence of two groups of instincts: the life instincts and the death instincts. The *life instincts,* also referred to by the Greek term *eros,* consist of self-preservation and sexual drives. Freud focused mainly on sexual drives as the most important human motivation. The manifestation of sexual instincts, called the *libido,* plays a central role in his theory of abnormal behavior.

During his later years Freud became convinced that there was a second group of instincts. He termed these the *death instincts* (collectively called *thanatos,* the ancient Greek word for death). The death instincts function in opposition to the life instincts and are manifested as aggression and hostility.

Freud emphasized sex and aggression as the dominant human instincts because he recognized that the society of his times placed strong prohibitions on these drives and that, as a result, people were taught to inhibit them. A profound need to express one's instincts is often frightening and can lead one to deny their existence. Indeed, Freud felt that even though most impulses are hidden from consciousness, they nonetheless determine human actions.

Psychosexual Stages

According to psychoanalytic theory, all human beings develop through a sequence of five stages. Each **psychosexual stage** brings a unique challenge. If unfavorable circumstances prevail, the personality may be drastically affected. Because Freud stressed the importance of early childhood experiences, he saw the human personality as largely determined in the first five years of life—during the oral, anal, and phallic stages. The last two psychosexual stages are the latency (approximately 6 to 12 years of age), and genital (beginning in puberty) stages.

Oral Stage   The first year of life is characterized by a focus of instincts on the *oral* cavity. For infants, the mouth is not only the primary source of pleasurable sensations, as in sucking and feeding, but also the mechanism with which they can respond to and deal with the outside world.

The importance of the oral stage for later development lies in how much fixation occurs during that stage. (*Fixation* is the arresting of emotional development at a particular psychosexual stage.) If the infant is traumatized (harmed) in some way during this period, much fixation can occur; that is, some of the infant's instinctual energy becomes trapped and doesn't move on to more mature stages. Consequently, the personality of such an adult retains strong features of the oral stage. Passivity, helplessness, obesity, chronic smoking, and alcoholism may all be characteristics of an oral personality.

Anal Stage   Toward the end of the first year of life, the *anal* region becomes the zone of pleasurable

During the oral stage, the first stage of psychosexual development, the infant not only receives nourishment but also derives pleasure from sucking and being close to its mother.
Later, during the anal stage, toilet training can be a time of
intense emotional conflict between parent and child, or it
can be a time of cooperation.

sensations, and the second psychosexual stage begins. During the anal stage, parents demand that
the child control what is a normal biological and
innate urge—evacuation of feces. Toilet training is
rarely achieved smoothly, and the child may react
in ways that can manifest themselves in later adulthood as passive-aggressive or obsessive-compulsive
behaviors.

Phallic Stage   During the third and fourth years of
life, the genitals (the boy's penis and the girl's clitoris)
become the focus of pleasurable sensations. In both
sexes, incestuous feelings for the opposite-sex parent
become very strong. Freud concentrated on male development and used the term *Oedipus complex* to
describe male sexuality at the phallic stage. The term
is taken from the ancient Greek myth in which Oedipus killed his father and married his mother (both
unwittingly).

In essence, the Oedipus complex is a *conflict:* a
wish for a form of sexual possession of the mother
(for her warmth, nurturance, and so on) countered
by a *fear* of reprisal from a powerful rival for the
mother's affection, the father. (*Castration anxiety* is
the young boy's fear that the father will punish him

for his forbidden desires by cutting off the guilty organ, his penis.)

For the girl, according to Freud, the phallic stage
is characterized by *penis envy*, the girl's desire to
have a penis. Because she lacks the valued organ, the
girl believes castration has already taken place, as a
punishment by the mother. The child sees her mother
as a hostile rival in competition for the father's penis.
As in the Oedipus complex, the conflict becomes very
intense for the girl. She resolves it in the same way
and for the same reasons as the boy resolves his conflict—by identifying with the same-sex parent.

The phallic stage of development is crucial to sexual identity in later adult life. According to psychoanalytic theory, if incomplete resolution occurs, impotence, frigidity, promiscuity, and homosexuality may
result. Because this stage is characterized by development of the superego, anxiety disorders and personality disorders have their roots in this stage.

Latency Stage   Freud believed that the years from
ages six to twelve (*latency* stage) were generally devoid of sexual motivations. Developmental skills, activities, and interests are the primary concern during
this latency stage. Sexuality is repressed because of

According to psychoanalytic theory, the resolution of the Oedipus complex—the central issue of the phallic stage—occurs when a young boy begins to identify with his father, adopting many of his characteristics, values, and mannerisms.

During the latency stage, sexuality is repressed and activities that develop the child's skills and enhance his or her ability to deal with the world are the primary focus. Sexual urges reemerge during the genital stage, which is characterized by rapid physical and emotional changes in the child.

strong social taboos against its expression. Children of this age may become upset on encountering overt sexual displays.

Genital Stage   The reawakening of sexual urges during puberty and adolescence ushers in the *genital* stage. Physiological and physical changes occur that drastically affect heterosexual relationships. The child's first relationship is generally *narcissistic:* affection is directed toward one's own body. True heterosexual love does not develop until the emotional investment can be transferred to a member of the opposite sex. That is, intense interest in one's own body and concern with its health indicate a "self"

orientation rather than the "other" orientation needed for interpersonal relationships.

Freud believed that a person who could transcend the various fixations would develop into a normal, healthy individual. Heterosexual interests, stability, vocational planning, marriage, and other social activities would become a person's prime concern during the genital stage.

Anxiety and Psychopathology

Anxiety is at the root of Freud's theory of psychopathology. The three-part personality structure that Freud postulated can produce a number of conflict situations. Freud identified three types of anxiety (shown diagrammatically in Figure 2.5). *Realistic anxiety* occurs when there is potential danger from the external environment. For example, when you smell smoke in a building, your ego warns you to take action to protect yourself from physical harm. *Moralistic anxiety* results when someone does not live up to his or her own moral standards or engages in unethical conduct. In this case, the ego warns of possible retaliation from the superego. *Neurotic anx-*

FIGURE 2.5 Three Types of Anxiety
Freud believed that people suffer from three types of anxiety, arising from conflicts involving the id, ego, and superego. Each type of anxiety is, in essence, a signal of impending danger.

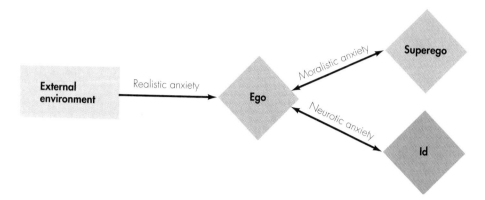

iety often results when id impulses seem to be getting out of hand, bursting through ego controls. In all these cases, anxiety is a signal that something bad is about to happen and that appropriate steps should be taken to reduce the anxiety.

Although Freud studied and treated all three types of anxiety, he concentrated mainly on neurotic anxiety. We shall do the same, although much of our discussion applies to the other two types of anxiety as well. Changes in the later editions of the *Diagnostic and Statistical Manual of Mental Disorders* of the American Psychiatric Association like DSM-IV replaced the traditional subcategories of neurotic behavior with other, more refined concepts, but we use the term *neurotic* because of its importance to Freud's theory.

Defense Mechanisms

Neurotic behavior develops from the threat of overwhelming anxiety, which may lead to full-scale panic. To forestall this panic, the ego often resorts to defense mechanisms to reduce anxiety. **Defense mechanisms** are ways of preventing awareness of anxiety-arousing impulses and thoughts. These mechanisms have three characteristics in common: they protect the individual from anxiety, they operate unconsciously, and they distort reality.

All individuals use strategies such as defense mechanisms to reduce anxiety. The defense mechanisms discussed here are considered maladaptive, however, when they are overused—that is, when they become the predominant means of coping with stress and when they interfere with one's ability to handle life's everyday demands. The difference is one of degree, not of kind.

Repression *Repression* is the blocking of forbidden or dangerous desires and thoughts to keep them from entering one's consciousness. According to Freud, it is the most basic defense mechanism and is generally the first used. However, simply forcing this material into what Freud called the *unconscious* does not eliminate it. Unconscious material continually seeks consciousness, which means the ego must constantly expend energy to keep it hidden. This draining of psychic energy leaves the person less energy to use for more adaptive functions. Moreover, unconscious material often tends to increase in energy and strength.

According to Freud, unconscious material can become conscious in two ways: by overpowering the forces of repression, or by circumventing them. Overpowering repressive forces results in a break with reality (psychotic episode), and circumventing these forces occurs during states of ego weakness when the ego's guard is relaxed. For example, when you are asleep or very tired, your ego defenses are weakened and unconscious impulses often surface. Dreams and slips of the tongue and pen express unconscious material that has escaped during a period of ego weakness.

As well as preventing dangerous and unacceptable desires from reaching consciousness, repression expels painful or traumatic memories from consciousness. Here is a case example.

> Mr. X was a 35-year-old veteran who complained of listlessness, occasional anxiety, and inability to taste the flavor of foods. In addition, he complained of numbness throughout his body and a ringing in his ear that correlated with certain mood states. For example, a high pitch meant he was angry, and a low pitch meant he would become elated. A thorough neurological exam revealed no significant organic problem, so he was referred to the psychology service for further evaluation. Subsequent interviews revealed a strange obsession on the part of Mr. X. For the past two months he had found himself drawn to reading the obituary column of the local newspaper, although he found such activity extremely frightening. He could not make sense of his obsession, nor could he ever recall anything related to this preoccupation. Under hypnosis, Mr. X was finally able to recall that as an adolescent he had broken into several cemeteries and had dug up graves as a prank. One night he broke into a coffin containing the body of a young female and found himself sexually aroused by the body. The thought of being sexually attracted to a corpse was so abhorrent to him that he . . . repressed the entire memory from consciousness. However, his repressive mechanisms were beginning to fail. (Schroth & Sue, 1975, pp. 253–254)

Reaction Formation   In *reaction formation*, dangerous impulses are repressed and then converted to their direct opposite. Feelings of hate may be converted to superficial love, sexual desires to rigid morality, and pessimism to optimism. The extremely overprotective mother who is afraid to let her seven-year-old child play anywhere but in the back yard may be masking unconscious resentment and hostility toward an unwanted child who has tied her down for years. Because mothers are supposed to love their children, she cannot admit these feelings and converts them to their opposite by showering the child with superficial attention.

Projection   The defensive reaction in which people rid themselves of threatening desires or thoughts by attributing them to others is called *projection*. Projection can be manifested in two ways. First, a person

may blame his or her mistakes or shortcomings on some external source. For example, a worker may mask unpleasant feelings of inadequacy by blaming his or her poor performance on the incompetence of fellow workers. Second, in extreme cases a person may form a *delusional system,* in which the person believes that enemies are disrupting his or her life.

Rationalization   *Rationalization* is a common defense in which a person gives well thought-out and socially acceptable reasons for certain behavior—but these reasons do not happen to be the real ones. For example, a student may explain flunking a test as follows: "I'm not interested in the course and don't really need it to graduate. Besides, I find the teacher extremely dull." These may be plausible and rational statements. However, the student has failed to mention that she did not try hard because she was afraid that the course was too difficult for her to pass. In essence, rationalization helps people justify their behavior and softens disappointments connected with unattainable goals.

It can be very difficult for rationalizer and listener alike to tell the difference between objective truths and rationalizations. People who rationalize frequently become upset when their reasons are questioned. They never tire of dredging up justifications. A common example of rationalization is the myriad of reasons that smokers can generate to justify their habit.

Displacement   *Displacement* is the directing of an emotion such as hostility or anxiety toward a substitute target. For example, a meek clerk who is constantly belittled by his boss may build up tremendous resentment. If he were to express this anger openly at work, he might be fired. Instead, he snaps at family members or teases the dog at home. Commonly referred to as *scapegoating*, displacement occurs when the expression of feelings toward their real source is too threatening. Displacement is generally directed toward a less powerful object (human being or pet). Prejudice and discrimination against certain identifiable groups may be partly explained as displacement.

Displacement can also be self-directed; that is, people may unconsciously turn their anger in on themselves. In most cases, such people have inhibited personalities and can be described as passive. They let others take advantage of them and then build up a great deal of resentment. On the subconscious level, these people castigate themselves for not being able to stand up to others. A poor self-image begins to form, accompanied by self-hatred that is manifested in self-recriminations and strong guilt feelings. Some clinicians believe that people who are depressed harbor a great deal of hostility that needs to be expressed. Psychoanalytically oriented therapists believe that a strong relationship exists between depression and aggression.

Undoing In most cases, *undoing* can be viewed as a symbolic attempt to right a wrong or negate some disapproved thought, impulse, or act. It tends to be ritualistic and repetitive. In Shakespeare's play, Lady Macbeth goaded her husband into slaying the king, and then tried to cleanse herself of sin by constantly going through the motions of washing her hands. More commonplace examples of this defense mechanism may be seen in the superstitious behaviors people engage in to ward off bad luck and to maximize good luck—for example, knocking on wood. Some clinicians believe that compulsive behaviors are associated with undoing.

Regression *Regression* is a retreat to an earlier developmental level that demands less mature responses and aspirations. Freud believed that a person using this defense generally moves back to his or her most fixated psychosexual stage. Whether this interpretation is true or not, many people, when faced with severe stress, often resort to immature or infantile behavior. They seem to want to remove themselves from the threatening situation by regressing to a stage in which they were allowed to be dependent, helpless, and irresponsible.

Examples of regression may be found everywhere, from the child who reverts to infantile behavior, such as thumb sucking or bed wetting when a sibling is born, to the dignified college president who whoops it up at a reunion with college classmates. Regression becomes extremely pathological, however, when the person begins to live in the state to which he or she has regressed and cannot function as a mature individual. In severe forms, the individual loses contact with reality. From the psychoanalytic perspective, certain forms of schizophrenia, such as *catatonia*, represent the ultimate in regression. In catatonia, the person withdraws completely into his or her own world and becomes mute and deaf. A person with catatonia frequently assumes rigid postures—often the fetal position—for long periods of time.

Psychoanalytic Therapy

Besides occurring in the natural states of sleep and excessive fatigue, ego weakness can be externally induced. To rid people of maladaptive behaviors, psychoanalytic therapy, better known as **psychoanalysis,** induces ego weakness through such techniques as hypnosis and *projective tests*, in which ambiguous stimuli such as ink blots, word associations, or pictures provoke revealing verbal responses. These techniques give the therapist (called a *psychoanalyst* or just an *analyst*) some access to unconscious material. This material is used to help patients achieve insight into their own inner motivations and desires. The basic premise of psychoanalysis is that a cure can be effected only in this way. (Psychoanalytic methods are discussed in Chapter 18.)

Neo-Freudian Perspectives

Freud's psychoanalytic movement attracted many followers. Some of Freud's disciples, however, came to disagree with his insistence that the sex instinct is the major determinant of behavior. Many of his most gifted adherents broke with him and formulated coherent psychological models of their own. These thinkers have since become known as **neo-Freudians** (or post-Freudians) because, despite their new ideas, they remained strongly influenced by Freud's constructs. For example, nearly all of them continued to believe in the power of the unconscious, in the use of "talking" methods of psychotherapy that rely heavily on the patient's introspection, in the three-part structure of personality, and in the one-to-one analyst-patient approach to therapy.

The major differences between the various neo-Freudian theories and psychoanalytic theory lie in the emphasis that the neo-Freudians placed on five areas:

1. Freedom of choice and the importance of future goals
2. Consciousness and ego autonomy
3. The influence of social forces on psychological functioning
4. Importance of significant others (object relations)
5. The need to treat the seriously disturbed individual

Let us look at each of these areas in greater detail.

Carl Jung (1875–1961) proposed the collective unconscious to represent the cumulative experience that all humans share. Unlike Freud's psychoanalysis, Jung's theory took an optimistic view of human beings.

Choice and Future Goals Two of the first pupils to break with Freud were Alfred Adler (1870–1937) and Carl Jung (1875–1961). Adler developed his own approach, called *individual psychology*. He contended that human beings are much less at the mercy of instinctual unconscious motivations than Freud had indicated. Adler deemphasized biological drives and stressed social drives instead. Psychologically healthy people, Adler believed, have some freedom of choice in their actions; their behavior is directed toward goals they value and is guided in part by their vision of what they want their future to become. Adler thought psychopathology resulted from inappropriate child-rearing practices, and he thought therapists should focus on the social context of their patients' lives.

Like Adler, Carl Jung believed that human beings are goal directed and future oriented and that these characteristics help guide behavior. Although he shared Freud's premise that the unconscious is a powerful force, Jung was more optimistic in outlook. He asserted that the unconscious comprises two parts: the individual unconscious, as in the Freudian theory, and the collective unconscious. The **collective unconscious** contains positive attributes and spiritual elements; it is a kind of storehouse of religious and aesthetic values derived from the cumulative experience of the human species. In addition, Jung viewed the id as a creative force and not a regressive one that needed to be controlled.

More than any other prominent psychologist, Jung was a student of history. His writings on mythology, religion, folklore, ancient symbols and rituals, dreams, and visions have had a great impact on art, literature, and sociology. In addition, his concepts of introversion and extroversion have permeated psychological thinking. Jung's work continues to be popular among college students.

Ego Autonomy Whereas Adler and Jung moved contemporary psychoanalytic theory toward a more optimistic, less deterministic, and less biological orientation, others, such as Heinz Hartmann (1894–1970), Freud's daughter Anna Freud (1895–1982), and Erik Erikson (born 1902), emphasized the role, operation, and importance of the ego. Thus they and their followers are often called *ego psychologists*. Ego psychologists accept Freud's three-part division of the personality, but they believe that the ego is an autonomous component. The ego is not at the mercy of the id; it is able to be creative while remaining independent of the sexual and aggressive drives.

In his book *Ego Psychology and the Problems of Adaptation* (1958), Hartmann argued persuasively that the ego is independent from the id, that it is a creative force, and that the manifestations of memory, perception, and learning are not simple manifestations of id impulses. Like Hartmann, Anna Freud focused on ego functions as the executive of the personality—that part that controls the gateways to action by mediating id, superego, and environmental demands. Her major contributions were made in the study of ego defenses and the pioneering psychoanalytic treatment of children.

Eric Erikson is perhaps the most influential of the ego theorists. His outstanding contribution was formulating the stages of ego development from infancy to late adulthood—one of the first truly developmental examinations of personality structures and

Erik Erikson (b. 1902) studied with Anna Freud (Freud's daughter). He formulated an important theory of psychosocial ego development from infancy to late adulthood.

Karen Horney (1885–1952), one of the first feminist psychologists, developed a theory of personality development and pathology based on the social relationship between parent and child.

processes. His analyses of identity crises in youth are held in especially high regard. Unlike Freud, Erikson considered personality to be flexible and capable of growth and change throughout the adult years. He believed, in other words, that we need not remain imprisoned in our past.

Social Forces A third major influence in contemporary psychoanalytic theory came from thinkers such as Erich Fromm (1900–1980), Karen Horney (1885–1952), and Harry Stack Sullivan (1892–1949). Despite considerable differences among their ideas, all three agreed on the primary role of interpersonal relationships in the development of the personality.

Although Erich Fromm drew heavily on psychoanalytic concepts, his major themes emphasize the social and interpersonal aspects of psychological development. According to Fromm, people have become separated from nature and have lost a sense of community. In his book *Escape from Freedom* (1941), Fromm points out that the price of greater freedom and individuation is loneliness. Thus people

attempt to escape freedom, which has become a negative condition (see Focus 2.2). To find meaning in their lonely lives, they have two choices: unite in a spirit of love and shared work or seek security through submission and conformity. The former leads to the development of a better society; the latter may lead to behavior disorders.

Karen Horney argued that the cause of behavior disorder is *basic anxiety*, a disturbance of the child's security resulting from parental rejection or overprotection. This interpersonal childhood disturbance may lead to the development of a need to move *closer* to people, a need to move *away from* people, or a need to move *against* people. Neurotic behavior then results from this need.

Horney is also considered by many to be the first feminist psychologist. She rejected Freud's concept of penis envy, denying that feminine psychology had anything to do with either male or female anatomy (see Focus 2.3). She also rejected the concept of psychopathology as a sexual-aggressive conflict resulting from an Oedipus or Electra (female child's incestuous attraction to the father) complex.

Cults: Escape from Freedom?

What do the followers of Bhagwan Shree Rajneesh and Reverend Sun Myung Moon, the Hare Krishnas, and the members of an estimated 2,500 other cults in the United States have in common? If Erich Fromm were alive today, he might well view young people's joining cults as an "escape from freedom." Confronted with the many choices of life and the need to establish greater independence and individual identity, some young people have found only unbearable insecurity and loneliness. Cult membership has often been their answer.

An analysis of cult followers that reiterates Fromm's escape-from-freedom theme is Saul V. Levine's *Radical Departures: Desperate Detours to Growing Up* (1984). Levine's study of cults began in the 1960s. He studied more than a thousand individuals belonging to fifteen different groups—drug groups, religious cults, political organizations, and therapy groups. To augment this broad perspective, Levine concentrated on nine young men and women as they journeyed into and out of communal groups.

Levine did not find the typical group member to be a loner, a failure, a substance abuser, or a misfit. Nor did he find that members were controlled, duped, or held captive.

Group members by and large

showed no serious signs of disorder, came from pleasant homes, were raised by concerned parents, were well off financially, and had much to look forward to. These "radical departers," as Levine prefers to call the group members, are generally between eighteen and twenty-six years old, unmarried, affluent, well-educated, white, and from intact families.

Levine's findings seem to make the radical departer's sudden leave-taking from the family strange and puzzling. He believes that joining a cult may represent a desperate attempt to avoid choice and responsibility. To understand the framework of his analysis, we need to recognize the pressures that adolescents experience as they enter adulthood.

In our middle-class culture, we stress the importance of children growing up, separating from their parents, and establishing their own independence and identity. As children become teenagers, their parents begin to relinquish control, allowing them greater freedom and decision-making power. Parents make it clear that adult responsibilities loom ahead. Young adults must think about college, make career choices, and leave home. Not only do adolescents feel a sense of loss and loneliness as this occurs, they also grope with identity issues. In the normal

course of growing up, they seek intimacy with friends and lovers. But radical departers seem to have been unable to form satisfactory relationships with others or to commit themselves to a value system. Separation from parents then involves pain, and cults seem to offer a magical solution: separation without accompanying pain. Submission and conformity to a group bring temporary security. For as long as this commitment lasts, the struggle to form an independent self is given up in favor of a flawless "group self." Radical departers, then, are escaping from freedom—making a temporary retreat from growing up.

Levine does not believe, however, that joining a cult is wholly negative. He observes, for example, that more than 90 percent of radical departers return home within two years and that virtually all eventually abandon their groups. A radical departure thus may represent a rehearsal for separation from the parents. Levine also argues that joining a cult and voluntarily separating can be a therapeutic process. He warns against "deprogramming," which involves kidnapping the member and then systematically assailing the values and beliefs the group has instilled. Deprogramming interferes with the natural and normal departure process.

Harry Stack Sullivan's major contribution was his interpersonal theory of psychological disorders. Sullivan believed that the individual's psychological functions could be understood only in the context of his or her social relationships. We say considerably more about Sullivan and his interpersonal theory in Chapter 3.

Object Relations One contemporary trend in the psychodynamic perspective has been the contributions of the object relations theorists. The technical term **object relations** is roughly equivalent to "past interpersonal relationships." It refers to how people develop patterns of living from their early relations with significant others, particularly their mothers.

The Psychology of Women: A Feminist Viewpoint

Modern feminist psychologists (Chesler, 1972; Chodorow, 1978; Dworkin, 1984; Gilligan, 1982; Holroyd, 1980; Williams, 1977) have not limited their criticisms to psychoanalytic theory alone, but have taken the mental health profession to task for implicitly and explicitly accepting sex role stereotypes. They point out several sociocultural factors (rather than inferior biology) that contribute to the denigration of women. First, images of women throughout history have been unflattering or fearful. Women were portrayed as seductress-enchantresses or as powerful mother goddesses. In most cases, women were perceived as evil, lustful, and depraved, needing to be controlled, subordinated, and devalued. Such images justified men's need to control them (women were burned as witches), to treat them as property, and to exclude them from positions of power (Williams, 1977). Second, socialization was seen as one way to "keep them in their place." From the time of birth, boys are taught to be clever, independent, brave, rational, and assertive whereas girls are taught to be docile, kind, dependent, emotional, and nurturant. Sex roles for adults also parallel those taught to children. Men are supposed to be providers, strong, independent, competitive, and rational

beings. Women are supposed to be emotional, irrational, weak, and passive. No wonder women may regard the man's role highly.

The major problem facing women in our society not only includes unflattering stereotypes and sex-role conditioning, but a tendency on the part of society to view the female role and the differences (both biological and cultural) as less desirable than male biology and behavior. Most theories of identity development use the "white male standard" to judge normality and abnormality. For example, not only did Erik Erickson (1968) link a woman's attractiveness and her search for a mate to identity, but he used the male experience as the model for healthy adult identity (McBride, 1990). Feminist psychologists believe that the role ascribed to women is not only less desirable in our society but also has drastic implications for their mental health. Feminist thinking recognizes that women's sex roles may make them "sick," particularly when the role of wife or mother is at odds with their needs. Furthermore, one early study (Broverman et al., 1972) found that clinicians often viewed behaviors associated with the male role to be an ideal standard of mental health but that the female role (weakness, irrationality, submission to authority,

and dependency) was equated with unhealthiness. Yet, if a woman exhibits traits of autonomy, independence, and assertiveness ("healthy male characteristics"), she is often seen as "castrating," "too aggressive," and "unladylike." It appears that women in our society are placed in a double-bind: if they behave in traditional feminine roles, they are considered less healthy than their male counterparts; if, however, they behave in the traditional male role, they are also considered in a negative light.

In 1975, the American Psychological Association (*Report on Sex Bias and Sex-Role Stereotyping in Psychotherapeutic Practice*) engaged in a comprehensive study of the research literature on this topic, surveyed women psychologists, and obtained case studies of such practices. They concluded that strong therapy bias in the area of fostering traditional sex roles, devaluating of women, sexist use of psychoanalytic concepts, and responding to women as sex objects (including seduction of women in therapy) were present. The subjugation of women in our society, and not inferior biological makeup or intrapsychic dynamics, may account for much of the differences we see between men and women.

In the 1930s, Melanie Klein (1975) and Harry Guntrip (1968) began to formulate object relations theory. These researchers theorized that small children may identify with and incorporate the symbolic representation of important figures. As adults, the object or symbol may influence the way they experience, behave, or interpret events. Because fixed personality characteristics tend to develop quite early, the goal of therapy is to understand how these childhood patterns are repeated in many variations in adult life. For example, a young boy who has been neglected and unloved by his mother (object) may experience severe unmet needs for nurturance. The relationship he forms with his mother (constant seeking to be taken care of and loved) forms the core of his relationship with women. When he grows up, his distorted idealized representation of nurturing women is at odds with the real women he meets. When he marries, he may be disappointed by the discrepancy between his wife and his distorted image of the ideal woman. As a result, he may go through numerous divorces and relationships.

Additional contributions to object relations theory are attributed to Margaret Mahler (Mahler et al., 1975, 1979). She concentrated on the psychological aspects of how a child separates from the mother. Although the newborn seems to differentiate little between its own existence and that of the mother, the process of *separation* and *individuation* in the development of the child is crucial for further growth. Many factors may disrupt the differentiation process, but how the mother and other significant figures in the child's life handle the situation is very important.

Two other individuals important to object relations theory are Otto Kernberg and Heinz Kohut. Kernberg (1980) is especially known for his studies of the borderline personality (discussed more fully in Chapter 9). He observed many clients who seemed to have difficulty in establishing stable relationships. These individuals often appeared to have internalized but nonintegrated pathological objects in their past. Because they have been unable to synthesize contradictory self-images and object images, these people find it difficult to form consistent relationships with others (object constancy).

Heinz Kohut (Kohut & Wolf, 1978), however, emphasized emotional support of the child by the parents. If a child's emotional needs are not met, then the child's psyche may be damaged. The result may be a *narcissistic personality* (also discussed further in Chapter 9), which is a constant and exaggerated need to satisfy the self.

It is important to note that the object relations movement differs from traditional psychodynamic theory in several ways. First, it deemphasizes the id and ego and instead concentrates on the significant early figures of the child; especially important is the mother. Second, biological factors are downplayed in favor of interpersonal or social forces. Third, while it does stress the importance of early childhood experiences, object relations approaches are strongly centered on discovering current and consistent patterns of behavior and thinking in the here and now.

Treatment of the Seriously Disturbed During the 1950s and 1960s, a number of psychoanalysts admitted that classical psychoanalysis had certain inherent weaknesses. For example, Freud disqualified from psychoanalysis a large percentage of the population that he considered "analytically unfit." That is, they did not have sufficient contact with reality or possess characteristics that would make psychoanalysis suitable for them. Very seriously disturbed people, particularly those with schizophrenia, were viewed as unfit because they did not respond to the "verbal interpretive" techniques advocated by Freud. In addition, certain narcissistic neurotic patients were too isolated (not psychologically minded) to respond to verbal therapy.

Under the rubric of modern psychoanalysis, Hyman Spotnitz (1963, 1968, 1976) and his colleagues have introduced new treatment techniques that do not require the patient to be emotionally or intellectually capable of understanding interpretations. These techniques essentially involve reflection or mirroring in which the analyst actively provides feedback to the patient. The patient is then helped to resolve conflicts by experiencing the conflicts rather than understanding them. Although Spotnitz's work is not well known outside the psychoanalytic movement, it has become an important contribution to contemporary psychoanalysis.

Criticisms of the Psychoanalytic Model

Psychoanalytic theory has had a tremendous impact on the field of psychology. Psychoanalysis and its variations are very widely employed. Nonetheless, the usefulness of the psychoanalytic view in explaining and treating behavior disorders has been challenged. Three major criticisms are often leveled at psychoanalysis (Hall & Lindzey, 1970; Joseph, 1991), as follows:

Lack of Scientific Rigor First, the empirical procedures by which Freud validated his hypotheses have grave shortcomings. His observations about human behavior were often made under uncontrolled conditions (Edelson et al., 1985). For example, he relied heavily on case studies and on his own self-analysis as a basis for formulating theory. His patients, from whom he drew conclusions about universal aspects of personality dynamics and behavior, tended to represent a narrow spectrum of people. Although case studies are often a rich source of clinical data, Freud's lack of verbatim notes means that his recollections were subject to distortions and omissions. Furthermore, he seldom checked the accuracy of the material related by his patients through any form of external corroboration (relatives, friends, test data, documents, or medical records). Using such private and uncontrolled methods of inquiry as a basis for theory is fraught with hazards.

Freud failed to make explicit the line of reasoning by which he drew inferences and conclusions. In his numerous writings, he presented the end results of his thinking without giving the original data on which they were based, his method of analysis, or any systematic presentation of his empirical findings. It is difficult, if not impossible, to replicate many of Freud's investigations. Thus the reliability of his observations is impossible to evaluate. Did he really find a relationship between alcoholism and orality, between obsessive-compulsive behavior and anality, and between hysteria and phallic fixation? Did he read into his cases only what he wanted to find? How much was he influenced by his own personal biases and needs? Freud's reluctance to follow the conventions of full scientific reporting leaves many people skeptical about his concepts and explanations.

Much of psychoanalytic theory, then, cannot be empirically validated. A "good" theory should clearly and precisely explain phenomena, specifying the relationship between events and forces. It should also be capable of predicting what will happen, given certain conditions. Psychoanalysis falls short on both scores. Certain relationships are presented vaguely, which makes them virtually useless. What exactly is the relationship between the superego and the Oedipus complex? How intense must an experience be to become traumatic? Exactly how strong must instinctual forces be to overcome the ego? Not only does psychoanalytic theory lack specificity, it cannot adequately predict what will happen. For example, the concept of a death instinct can be used to explain certain events such as suicides and wars after the fact. Yet such a vague concept is of little use in understanding or predicting such events.

Biased Application to Women Is a theory of human behavior adequate if it does not apply to more than one-half the population of the world? Freud's theory of female sexuality and personality has drawn

heavy criticisms from feminists for many years. Phallic-stage dynamics, penis envy, unfavorable comparisons of the clitoris to the penis, the woman's need for a male child as penis substitute, and the belief that penetration is necessary for the woman's sexual satisfaction all rest on assumptions that are biologically questionable and that fail to consider social forces shaping women's behavior. Such theories, at face value, seem to depreciate female sexuality and legitimize male sexuality (McBride, 1990; Schaef, 1981). "Since man is the measure of all things—man, literally, rather than human beings—we have all tended to measure ourselves by men" (Miller, 1976, p. 69).

One of the earliest psychoanalytic critics of the penis envy notion was Karen Horney, who argued persuasively that psychoanalysis was a creation of male bias and that almost all those who had developed Freud's ideas were men (1965). Horney believed that the desire to be a man did not reflect penis envy, but reflected the sociocultural devaluation of women. She called for anthropological studies in other cultures to investigate whether penis envy was universal, and whether social conditioning and sex-limited roles might not account for this phenomenon. For example, the well-known anthropologist, Margaret Mead (1949), provided a vivid description of the traditional emotional characteristics of men and women in three societies of New Guinea. Among the Arapesh, both men and women display emotional characteristics that in our society would be considered distinctly feminine. Both sexes are trained to be unaggressive, cooperative, kind, noncompetitive, and responsive to the needs of other people. The river-dwelling Mundugmur, however, present a sharp contrast. In their society, both men and women are violent, combative, ruthless, and competitive: fighting has become a way of life for them, in which they take great delight.

Perhaps the most interesting pattern is that of the lakeshore community of the Tchambuli, where the sex role stereotypes typical of our culture seem completely reversed. The women hold the positions of power and are responsible for fishing and manufacturing the tribes's chief articles of trade. The men are engaged predominantly in the arts and have become skilled in dancing, carving, and painting. Tchambuli women are described as impersonal, practical, and efficient, and the men are reported to be humanistically oriented, artistic, timid, and submissive. Interestingly, in the Tchambuli society the "masculine" man and the "effeminate" women are considered to be deviants! Thus it becomes clear that the psychoanalytic model may not be completely applicable to women. Interestingly, this very criticism may be equally applicable to the mental health profession in general.

Limitations to Other Populations and Problems

A third criticism of psychoanalysis is that there is a wide range of disturbed people to which it cannot be applied. Individuals who have speech disturbances or are inarticulate (talking is important in therapy); people who have urgent, immediate problems (classical psychoanalysis requires much time); and people who are very young or old may not profit from psychoanalysis (Fenichel, 1945). Research studies have shown that psychoanalytic therapy is best suited to well-educated people of the middle and upper socioeconomic classes who exhibit anxiety disorders rather than psychotic behavior. It is more limited in therapeutic value with people of lower socioeconomic levels and with people who are less verbal, less intelligent, and more severely disturbed (Sloane et al., 1975).

◆ A PSYCHOANALYTIC VIEW OF STEVEN V.

Let us hypothesize again. Suppose that Steven V.'s therapist had a psychoanalytical orientation. Here is what we believe that he or she might have to say about Steve.

In Steve's case records, I see many possible explanations for his continuing problems. I will focus on four areas that I find particularly important: Steve's early childhood experiences; his repression of conflicts, intense feelings, and other impulses; the oedipal dynamics that seem to be at work; and the unconscious symbolism behind his relationship with Linda.

Steve did not receive the love and care, at crucial psychosexual stages, that a child needs to develop into a healthy adult. He was neglected, understimulated, and left on his own. The result was that he felt unloved and rejected. We have evidence that he was prone to "accidents"—being hit on the head by a swing, burning himself severely on an electric range, numerous falls. I believe that these were not really accidents. They represented Steve's unconscious attempts to gain attention and to test his parents' love for him. Furthermore, I believe that his proneness to accidents was the forerunner of his attempts at suicide, a reflection of the death instinct and a desire to punish himself. Although Steve may not have been conscious of his feelings or able to verbalize them, it is obvious that he was deeply affected by his parents' negative attitudes. It must be an awful experience for a young child to believe that he or she is unloved. For many of us, it is easier to deny or repress this belief than to face up to it.

Steve may have been the victim of marital unhappiness between his mother and father. The records indicate that they lived rather separate lives and that Mr. V. kept several mistresses whom he saw on his frequent "business trips." In one therapy session, when Mrs. V. was seen alone, she stated that she knew of her husband's extramarital affairs but never confronted him about them. Apparently she was fearful of his dominating and abusive manner at home, and she avoided potential conflicts by playing a passive role. When Mr. V. belittled Steve, she chose not to intervene; secretly, however, she identified with her son's predicament. Unable to form an intimate relationship with her husband, she became physically seductive toward Steve. As you recall, Mrs. V. frequently caressed and kissed her son and even had him sleep with her. To a youngster still groping his way through oedipal conflicts, nothing could have been more damaging. Steve's sexual feelings toward the mother were no doubt intensified by her actions.

Mr. V.'s verbal abuse of Steve also aggravated Steve's problems. One of his father's common remarks to Steve was "You've got no balls." Abuse such as this deepened and prolonged Steve's oedipal feelings of rivalry with and fear of his father. Steve's oedipal conflict was never adequately resolved. His continued feelings of inadequacy and anger, and his sexual drives as well, have remained repressed and are expressed symbolically.

Steve's repressed anger is certainly present in both his fantasies and behavior. His violent "mind games" and his preference for sadistic pornographic films are an indirect expression of anger at his father, whom he continues to see as a powerful feared rival (he has failed to identify with his father in resolution of the oedipal conflict), and at his mother, who never came to his defense and suddenly withdrew his "bed privileges" when she became aware of Steve's sexual excitement. There also appears to be a strong relationship between Steve's anger and his depression. Steve's periodic bouts of depression are probably the result of anger turned inward. His frequent accidents, his episodic depression, and his attempts at suicide are classic manifestations of the death instinct.

Steve's early childhood experiences continue to affect his behavior with women. Note the similarities between his woman friend, Linda, and his mother. Linda is described as being active in student affairs; the mother was always involved with civic activities. Linda seemed oblivious to Steve's existence in the presence of others, and he felt slighted by her friends; the mother seems never to have introduced Steve to her friends and relatives. Linda was "warm, affectionate, and intimate" in private; the mother, when "alone with Steve," was quite affectionate. Linda would consent to "heavy petting" but drew the line short of intercourse; the mother suddenly withdrew "bed privileges" when Steve showed incestuous sexual interest. It is clear that Steve continues to search for a "mother figure" and unconsciously selected a woman who is most like his mother. His impotence with Linda is additional evidence that Steve unconsciously views her as his mother. (In our society, incest is an unthinkable act.)

If Steve is to become a healthier individual, he must commit himself to intensive, long-term therapy aimed at helping him gain insight into his deep conflicts and repressed experiences. Resolving past traumas, overcoming resistance, and working through a transference relationship with the therapist will be crucial components of his therapy.

HUMANISTIC AND EXISTENTIAL APPROACHES

The humanistic and existential approaches evolved as a reaction to the determinism of other behavioral models. For example, many proponents of these approaches were disturbed that Freudian psychology did not focus on the inner world of the client but rather categorized the client according to a set of preconceived diagnoses (May, 1967). Psychoanalysts, these critics said, described clients in terms of blocked instinctual forces and psychic complexes that made them victims of some mechanistic and deterministic personality structure.

It is important to note that the humanistic and existential perspectives represent many schools of thought. But they do share a set of assumptions that distinguish them from other approaches or viewpoints.

First, both perspectives view an individual's reality as a product of that person's unique perceptions of the world. How the individual experiences the world determines his or her behavior. Hence, to understand why a person behaves as he or she does, the psychologist must reconstruct the world from that individual's vantage point. Moreover, the subjective universe of this person—how he or she construes events—is more important than the events themselves. Second, both humanistic and existential theorists stress that individuals have the ability to make free choices and are responsible for their own decisions. Third, these theorists believe in the "wholeness" or integrity of the person. Attempts to reduce human beings to a set of formulas, to be explained simply by measuring responses to certain stimuli, are viewed as pointless. And last, according to the humanistic and existential perspectives, people have the ability to become what they want, to fulfill their capacities, and to lead the lives best suited to themselves.

The Humanistic Perspective

The psychoanalytic view of personality strongly emphasizes unconscious determinants of behavior. And, if unconscious forces determine behavior, then free choice is not really available. As we have noted, a number of theorists take issue with these concepts, emphasizing instead people's conscious experiences and their ability to choose among alternatives.

Carl Rogers (1902–1987) is perhaps the best known of the humanistic psychologists. Rogers's theory of personality (1959) reflects his concern with human welfare and his deep conviction that humanity is basically "good," forward-moving, and trust-

Carl Rogers (1902–1987) believed people need both positive regard from others and positive self-regard. When positive regard is given unconditionally, a person can develop freely and become self-actualized.

Abraham Maslow (1908–1970) proposed that people are motivated toward self-actualization once more basic needs are met. He based his ideas on his study of self-actualized, healthy people such as Einstein, Spinoza, and Eleanor Roosevelt.

worthy. One of the major contributions of the **humanistic perspective** has been this positive view of the individual.

Besides being concerned with treating the mentally ill, psychologists such as Rogers (1961, 1981, 1987) and Abraham Maslow (1954) have focused on improving the mental health of the person who is considered normal. This focus has led humanistic psychologists and others to explore the characteristics of the healthy personality (see Focus 2.4).

The Actualizing Tendency Instead of concentrating exclusively on behavior disorders, the humanistic approach is concerned with helping people *actualize* their potential and with bettering the state of humanity. The quintessence of humanistic psychological theory is the concept of **self-actualization.** This term, popularized by Maslow, implies that people are motivated not only to fill their biological needs (for food,

warmth, and sex) but also to cultivate, maintain, and enhance the self. The *self* is one's image of oneself, the part one refers to as "I" or "me."

The humanistic psychologist believes that all people are born with an inherent tendency to become actualized or fulfilled. This tendency can be defined as the impetus to achieve one's inherent potential as a fully functioning person. As one psychologist has pointed out, the actualizing tendency can be viewed as fulfilling a grand design or a genetic blueprint (Maddi, 1972). This thrust of life that pushes people forward is manifested in such qualities as curiosity, creativity, and joy of discovery. According to Rogers (1961), this inherent force is common to all living organisms; its psychological manifestation is *self-actualization* (Maslow, 1954; Rogers, 1959). How

The Healthy Personality

One major contribution by humanistic psychologists has been their optimistic perception of people. Rather than focusing on disorder, they stress our assets and strengths. Psychologist Abraham Maslow has identified characteristics of mental health in well-known figures, including Thomas Jefferson, Albert Einstein, and Eleanor Roosevelt. Other studies have provided additional information about healthy individuals. Here are some of the traits that are most prominent in the healthy personality—traits that, according to humanists, distinguish human beings from other species.

1. *An ability to accept oneself, others, and nature* Self-actualizers accept their shortcomings and are not ashamed of being what they are. They have a positive self-image and believe that they are making contributions to the world. They are also receptive to others—even others who are different.

2. *An adequate perception of and comfortable attitude toward reality* Self-actualizers prefer to cope with unpleasant realities rather than avoid or deny them. They waste little time in feeling sorry for themselves. They base decisions on how things really are rather than on how they wish they were.

3. *Spontaneity* Healthy individuals are relatively spontaneous in behavior, thoughts, and inner impulses. They tend to behave naturally.

4. *Focus on external problems* Most healthy people tend to focus on external problems rather than worrying about themselves or their personal problems and concerns. For example, Maslow's subjects were concerned with the major world issues of the day and were also interested in developing a philosophy of life. Not overly self-conscious, they could devote their attention to a task that seemed particularly appropriate for them.

5. *A need for privacy* Self-actualizers seem to enjoy solitude and privacy more than others. Other people may perceive them as being somewhat aloof, reserved, and unruffled by events that disturb most people. But although they do need time to be by themselves, they also appreciate other people and enjoy being around them.

6. *Independence from the environment* Mentally healthy people remain relatively stable and secure in spite of harsh environmental conditions. They can maintain happiness in circumstances that might upset others. In other words, they are able to withstand severe forms of stress such as economic deprivation, the loss of a loved one, or physical hardships.

7. *A continued freshness of appreciation* Self-actualizers have the capacity to appreciate again and again the basic joys of nature. They have an ability to see uniqueness and wonder in many apparently commonplace experiences. In essence, the mentally healthy person is creative, open, and possesses a strong feeling of "belongingness" with all humanity.

In evaluating these traits, however, we must bear two cautions in mind. First, in almost all cases where criteria for mental health are used (as here), the issue of values and subjectivism arises. The fact that the researchers and their subjects do not represent a cross-section of socioeconomic classes or subcultures in our society may result in overgeneralizations. Second, as noted in Chapter 1, mental health can be viewed from several perspectives. For example, one healthy trait is spontaneity—the uninhibited expression of thoughts and feelings. Yet various cultural groups value restraint with regard to feelings and discourage their direct expression.

Sources: Barron, 1963; Coelho et al., 1963; Jahoda, 1958; Korchin & Ruff, 1964; Maslow, 1954; Rogers, 1961; Ruff & Korchin, 1964; Sibler et al., 1961; Wild, 1965.

one views the self, how others relate to the self, and what values are attached to the self constitute one's **self-concept.**

During the course of their development, children increase their awareness of the world and gain experience in it. From various encounters they learn of two needs that affect the self-concept: the need for *positive regard* (how they think others perceive them) and the need for *positive self-regard* (how they perceive themselves). All people are sensitive to and influenced by others' opinions and reactions; group or peer pressure can be extremely powerful. People need positive feedback from others and feel frustration when they are looked on with disapproval. Each person also needs to approve of his or her self and feels distress when that need goes unmet. Both needs define how the actualizing tendency will be expressed.

Development of Abnormal Behavior

Rogers believes that if people were left unencumbered by societal restrictions and allowed to grow and develop freely, the result would be self-actualized, fully functioning people. In such a case, the self-concept and the actualizing tendency would be congruent.

However, society frequently imposes *conditions of worth* on its members. These conditions are standards by which people determine whether they have worth. They are transmitted via *conditional positive regard*. That is, significant others (such as parents, peers, friends, and spouse) in a person's life accept some but not all of that person's actions, feelings, and attitudes. The person's self-concept becomes defined as having worth only when others approve. But this reliance on others forces the individual to develop a distorted self-concept that is inconsistent with his or her self-actualizing potential, inhibiting that person from being self-actualized. A state of disharmony or *incongruence* is said to exist between the person's inherent potential and his or her self-concept (as determined by significant others).

According to Rogers, behavior disorders are a result of this state of incongruence. The developing child who attempts to become what others wish is at odds with what he or she wants or was meant to be. This conflict forms the basis of abnormal behavior.

Rogers believed that fully functioning people have been *allowed to grow* toward their potential. The environmental condition most suitable for this growth is called *unconditional positive regard* (Rogers, 1951). In essence, people who are significant figures in someone's life value and respect that person *as a person*. Giving unconditional positive regard is valuing and loving regardless of behavior. People may disapprove of someone's actions, but they still respect, love, and care for that someone. The assumption that humans need unconditional positive regard has many implications for child rearing and psychotherapy. For parents, it means creating an open and accepting environment for the child. For the therapist, it means fostering conditions that will allow clients to grow and fulfill their potential; this approach has become known as *nondirective* or *person-centered* therapy.

Person-Centered Therapy

Carl Rogers emphasized that therapist attitudes are more important than specific counseling techniques. The therapist needs a strong positive regard for the client's ability to deal constructively with all aspects of life. The more willing the therapist is to rely on the client's strengths and potential, the more likely the client is to discover such strengths and potential. The therapist cannot help the client by explaining the client's behavior or by prescribing actions. Therapy techniques involve expressing and communicating respect, understanding, and acceptance. The therapist tries to understand the client's internal frame of reference by thinking, feeling, and exploring with him or her. Indeed, Rogers shuns the term *patient* because it denotes a helpless and disabled person in need of help to "cure" the disorder. The therapist needs to avoid seeing the person as "sick," which is why Rogers moved to the term *client*. In his later years, he changed the description of his therapy as *client centered* to *person centered*. He believed that the term *person* was broader and more holistic than *client*. Instead of a client-to-helper relationship, Rogers prefers a person-to-person relationship.

The way the person-centered therapist most commonly communicates understanding of the client's subjective world is through *reflecting feelings*. In "saying back" to the client what he or she understood the client to say, the therapist provides a "mirror" for the client. The client can then actively evaluate thoughts and feelings with less distortion. Even in very strained situations, the person-centered therapist relies on reflection of feelings and on acceptance in working with the client. The following dialogue between client (S) and counselor (C), transcribed by Rogers (1951, pp. 211–213), illustrates the technique:

S: (Silent for two minutes. Then begins to talk in hard, flat voice, quite unlike her usual tone. Does not look at counselor. There is much repetition but the following excerpts give the major thoughts.) You feel I want to come, but I don't! I'm not coming anymore. It doesn't do any good. I don't like you. I hate you! I wish you never were born.

C: You hate me very bitterly.

S: I think I'll throw you in the lake. I'll cut you up!

You think people like you, but they don't. . . . I wish you were dead.

C: You detest me and you'd really like to get rid of me.

S: You think my father did bad things to me, but he didn't! You think he wasn't a good man, but he was. You think I want intercourse, but I don't.

C: You feel I absolutely misrepresent all your thoughts.

You might well sense a lack of direction here and wonder where this conversation is leading. The therapist, as you can see, is not steering this exchange but is using a standard technique of humanistic therapy, the understanding reflection of the client's feelings. It is the client who will ultimately move on his or her own in the direction of health; the client, that is, *wants* to be healthy.

The Existential Perspective

The **existential approach** is really not a systematized school of thought but a set of attitudes. It shares with humanistic psychology an emphasis on individual uniqueness, a quest for meaning in life and for freedom and responsibility, a phenomenological approach to understanding the person, and a belief that the individual has positive attributes that will eventually be expressed unless they are distorted by the environment.

The existential and humanistic approaches differ from one another in several dimensions. First, existentialism is less optimistic than humanism; it focuses on the irrationality, difficulties, and suffering encountered in life. Although humanism allows the clear possibility of self-fulfillment and freedom, existentialism deals with human alienation from the social and spiritual structures that no longer provide meaning in an increasingly technological and impersonal world. Second, humanists focus on the individual. Humanistic therapists attempt to reconstruct the subjective world of their clients through empathy. Although phenomenology is also stressed among existentialists, the perspective is slightly different. The individual must be viewed within the context of the human condition, and moral, philosophical, and ethical considerations are part of the relationship. Last, humanism stresses individual responsibility; that is, the individual is ultimately responsible for what he or she becomes. Existentialism also stresses individual responsibility but it stresses responsibility to others as well. Self-fulfillment is not enough.

Existentialists contend that many of the problems encountered by people are due to the loss of our connectedness with the world. Modern society has reduced us to "cogs in the machine," which has led to questioning of old values and a search for meaning in life.

Roots of Existentialism Existential psychology has its roots in the nineteenth and twentieth century and is an outgrowth of the European existential thought of Kierkegaard, Heidegger, and Sartre. Some Europeans who have made important contributions to existential psychology are Viktor Frankl, J. H. van den Berg, and R. D. Laing. Frankl developed his system of logotherapy (from the Greek word *logos*, meaning *word* or *thought*) as a direct result of experiences suffered in a Nazi concentration camp. Not only did he witness horrible atrocities, but he also observed prisoners who were able to transcend pain, torture, and suffering. Those who transcended the camp experience were generally able to find spiritual meaning in life. They exhibited a "will to meaning," a capacity to find reasons for their existence.

Van den Berg contributed much to the existential movement by focusing on the concept of "being-in-the-world." People are in unity with the world and, as such, disorder is often strongly influenced by sociocultural forces. In modern society, loneliness and isolation are fostered by the direction of our social structure: fragmentation, individualism, and separateness. Like van den Berg, Laing also stressed the interconnectedness of our social being with the world. He, however, believed that the primary problem of modern human beings was the split between the false self (fostered by our society) and the true inner unexpressed self.

Psychologist Rollo May was especially influential in developing an existential perspective in the United States (May, 1958, 1961, 1983, 1987; May, Angel & Ellenberger, 1958). He, like his European counterparts, stressed that rapidly accelerating technology, a reliance on science to solve pressing human problems, increasing urbanization, and emphasis on naturalistic rather than religious or spiritual explanations of human nature have led to great personal confusion and strain. Both literature and the media have explored this theme in books such as *Future Shock* (Alvin Toffler) and *The Stranger* (Albert Camus) and in movies such as *Star Wars*, *Making Mr. Right*, *Short Circuit*, *Robocop*, and *The Terminator*. Technology and all the accoutrements of a modern society have reduced people to "cogs in the machine." Such rapid and dehumanizing change has led to a questioning of old values, of the meaning of life, and of basic human nature.

Existential Concepts Many therapists *have* observed an increase in the number of patients complaining about the meaninglessness of life and reporting a sense of emptiness. Such symptoms as loneliness, alienation, isolation, detachment, and depersonalization have increased. Many psychotherapists find American psychology's naturalistic view of people inadequate for helping patients or clients. They believe that essential human characteristics—awareness of self (existence) and self-directed, goal-oriented striving (becoming)—have been ignored. Many find that the concepts underlying existential analysis fill this void.

Three concepts are essential to existential thought: being, nonbeing, and being-in-the-world.

1. *Being* The distinctive character of human existence is that human beings are aware of themselves and their experience of being (existence) at a particular point in time and space. Because people are *conscious* of their existence, existentialists say, they are *responsible* for it and are capable of *choosing* their direction. They are *free*, and such factors as heredity, environment, and culture are merely excuses for not experiencing the process of "becoming"—attaining their potential.

2. *Nonbeing* Most people also know that at some future time they will cease to exist (not be). Awareness of eventual nonbeing or nonexistence is necessary to fully understand and experience being. Death gives life reality because it is an absolute fact that must be confronted. Impending nonbeing is the source of anxiety, aggression, and hostility. Because the threat is always present, the anxiety it produces is considered normal. This anxiety is frequently called *existential anxiety* because it represents a conflict between being and nonbeing. When a person cannot accept this condition without repression, that person's choices become restricted and his or her actualization of potentials is thwarted.

3. *Being-in-the-world* We are all "beings in the world." The "world" can be described as the structure of meaningful relationships in which all people must function. One major problem caused by the complexity of contemporary society is that many people have lost their world. This loss is reflected in alienation—estrangement from other human beings or from the natural world. The French writer Albert Camus brilliantly portrays this modern predicament in his novel *The Stranger* (1946, p. 85):

[The modern human is] a man who is a stranger in his world, a stranger to other people to whom he speaks or pretends to love; he moves about in a state of homelessness, vagueness, and haze as though he has no direct connection with his world but were in a foreign country where he does not know the language and has no hope of learning it, and is always doomed to wander in quiet despair, incommunicado, homeless, a stranger.

Development of Abnormal Behavior   Abnormal behavior, say the existentialists, results from conflicts between people's essential nature and the demands they make on themselves or others make on them. The more alienated a person becomes from his or her total being, the fewer alternatives are available: behavior becomes increasingly stereotyped, inhibited, conforming, and morally rigid. The potential for disturbance is ever present.

Anxiety stems from two main sources: the threat of imminent nonbeing, of losing oneself to nothingness, and the inability to relate to all the ways of our world. When these two conflicts (nonbeing and being-in-the-world) are not confronted and adequately resolved, crippling anxiety results. This anxiety leaves one with a sense of living a meaningless life; ultimately, it causes despair.

Existential Therapy   The goal of the existential approach to therapy is to help the individual become aware of his or her own potential for growth, for choice, and for finding meaning in life. The existential approach is not a fixed system of therapy or a set of techniques; it is a means of understanding and illuminating the patient's being-in-the-world through exploration by therapist and patient together. People who are being helped are not placed in theoretical categories because categories are inconsistent with the existential situation. Therapy techniques are de-emphasized in favor of the therapist's ability to see the patient's "reality" from the patient's perspective. In fact, because techniques must evolve from an understanding of the patient, the approach used may be derived from almost any school of therapy.

May (1961) lists six characteristics of existential therapy.

1. Techniques vary from patient to patient; the goal is to illuminate the person's being-in-the-world.

2. Although therapists use terms such as *transference*, *repression*, and *resistance*, they always re-

late these psychoanalytic concepts to the existential situation of the patient's immediate life.

3. Therapists emphasize that the patient is not a subject but an "existential partner" with the therapist in a genuine encounter.

4. The therapist attempts to avoid behavior that would impede or terminate the genuine quality of the relationship. A full encounter with a person can create anxiety even within the therapist. Overreliance on therapy techniques permits a therapist to avoid the full encounter and is therefore undesirable.

5. Therapy is aimed at having the patient experience and become aware of the fact that his or her existence is redefined at each moment.

6. For the patient, increased awareness of potentialities and the possibility of commitment will enable the patient to make decisions and to implement actions.

These characteristics of existential psychotherapy may seem excessively vague and insubstantial. Nowhere is there any systematic explanation of existential therapy and its procedures and techniques. Indeed, no single existential therapy exists. Instead, the therapy springs from a collaborative and shared venture between therapist and patient. Both are open to experience, are honest with each other, and act as authentically as possible. What matters is what the therapist is, rather than what he or she does. The therapist's task is to understand the private meaning of the patient's existence (being-in-the-world), and the patient's task is to be responsible for accepting his or her existential being. Each client is the author of his or her world and is responsible for his or her life and future.

Criticisms of the Humanistic and Existential Approaches

Many psychologists have criticized the formulations of the humanistic and existential perspectives (Holt, 1962; Millon, 1973; Smith, 1950). Although these phenomenological approaches have been extremely creative in describing the human condition, they have been less successful in constructing theory. Moreover, they are not suited to scientific or experimental investigation. The emphasis on subjective understanding rather than prediction and control, on intuition and empathy rather than objective investigation, and on the individual rather than the more general case, all tend to hinder empirical study.

Carl Rogers has certainly expressed many of his ideas as researchable propositions, but it is difficult to verify scientifically the humanistic concept of people as rational, inherently good, and moving toward self-fulfillment. The existential perspective can be similarly criticized for its lack of scientific grounding because of its reliance on the unique subjective experiences of individuals to describe the inner world. Such data are difficult to quantify and test. Nevertheless, the existential concepts of freedom, choice, responsibility, being, and nonbeing have had a profound influence on contemporary thought beyond the field of psychology.

Another major criticism leveled at the humanistic and existential approaches is that they do not work well with severely disturbed clients. They seem to be most effective with intelligent, well-educated, and relatively "normal" individuals who may be suffering adjustment difficulties. In fact, Carl Rogers's person-centered counseling originated from his work with college students who were bright, articulate, and psychology-minded—what some psychologists described as the "worried well." This limitation, along with the occasional vagueness of humanistic and existential thought, has made applying these ideas broadly to abnormal psychology difficult.

◆ A HUMANISTIC-EXISTENTIAL VIEW OF STEVEN V.

A therapist who strongly endorses the humanistic or existential approach would see Steven V. quite differently from the way a psychoanalyst or a proponent of the biogenic model would see Steve. If Steve's therapist were so oriented, we believe that he or she would consider the case of Steven V. very much as follows.

I must begin by stressing a point that is likely to be underemphasized by many other psychologists. Steven V. is not merely the sum of the voluminous case records I have before me. Steve is a flesh-and-blood person, alive, organic, and moving, with thoughts, feelings, and emotions. How could anyone hope to understand Steve by reading a pile of material that is static and inorganic and occasionally seeks to pigeonhole him into diagnostic categories? To classify Steve as schizophrenic, manic-depressive, or suicidal does not help me understand him. Indeed, such labels might serve as barriers to the development of a therapeutic relationship with him.

I intend to develop such a relationship with Steve, to engage him in a dialogue that will require no pretenses or self-justifications, and to travel with him on a journey whose destination neither of us will know until we get there. What makes me so sure that such a journey will be worthwhile? Almost everything I know of Steve, I learned from Steve himself. Here, for example, is an entry from Steve's diary, written when he was in his junior year in high school.

> Seems like I can't do anything right. Why does he always pick on me? Came home with top scores on my SAT. Mother was impressed. Showed Dad. Wouldn't even look up from his newspaper. All he's interested in is the *Wall Street Journal*. Make money, that's the goal!!
>
> Tried to tell him at dinner again. Got top score, Dad!! Don't you care?? Of course not! Said he expected it from me. Said he wanted me to do better next time. Said I should sit up and not slurp my soup. . . . Said I should learn better table manners. . . . Said I was an asshole!!! I am an asshole, I am, I am, who am I? Who cares?

Steve expresses strong feelings and emotions in this passage. Steve is deeply hurt by his father, he is angry at his father, and he seems to be seeking approval and validation from his father; he is also grappling with identity issues. These themes, but especially that of seeking approval from his father, are sounded throughout Steve's diary. His self-image and self-esteem seem to depend on his father's reaction to him. He clings to this perception of himself because he is afraid that without it he would not know who he is. This is illustrated in his questions: "Who am I? Who cares?" Until Steve knows who he is, he cannot understand what he might become. Now here is another diary entry, this one during his senior year in high school:

> Hello diary! Another do-nothing day! Parents won't let me do anything. Maybe I should jack off. . . . Got another good porno tape. This room's like a prison. Hello walls. . . . hello

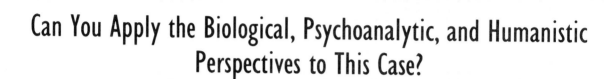

Can You Apply the Biological, Psychoanalytic, and Humanistic Perspectives to This Case?

Bill was born in Indiana to extremely religious parents who raised him in a rather strict moralistic manner. His father, a Baptist minister, often told him and his two sisters to "keep your mind clean, heart pure, and body in control." He forbade Bill's sisters from ever dating while they lived at home. Bill's own social life and contacts were extremely limited, and he recalls how anxious he would become around girls.

Bill's memories of his father always included feelings of fear and intimidation. No one in the family dared disagree with the father openly, lest they be punished and ridiculed. The father appeared to be hardest on Bill's two sisters, es-

pecially when they expressed interest in boys. The arguments and conflicts between father and daughters were often loud and extreme, disrupting the typical quietness of the home. Although it was never spoken of, Bill was aware that one of his sisters suffered from depression like his mother; twice she had attempted suicide.

His recollections of his mother were unclear, except that she was always sick with what the father referred to as "the dark cloud," which seemed to visit her periodically. His relationships with his sisters, who were several years older, were uncomfortable. When younger, they teased him mercilessly, and when he reached adolescence, they seemed to take sadistic

delight in arousing his raging hormones by flaunting their partially exposed bodies. The result was that Bill became obsessed with having sex with one of his sisters, and he tended to compulsively masturbate. Throughout his adolescence and early adulthood he was tortured by feelings of guilt and believed himself to be, as his father put it, "an unclean and damned sinner."

By all external standards, Bill was a quiet, obedient, and well-behaved child. He did well in school, attended Sunday school without fail, never argued or spoke against his parents, and seldom ventured outside of the home. Although he did exceptionally well in high school—obtain-

desk . . . hello fly . . . hello hell! Ha, that's a good one . . .

> Every day's the same.
> When you're in the well!
> Every day's a game.
> When you're in hell.

This passage reveals another aspect of what is happening with Steve. He feels trapped, immobilized, lonely, and unable to change his life. He has never recognized or accepted the responsibility of making choices. He externalizes his problems and views himself as a passive victim. In this way Steve evades responsibility for choosing and protects himself by staying in the safe, known environment of his room.

Steve needs to realize that he is responsible for his own actions, that he cannot find his identity in others. He needs to get in touch with, and express directly, his feelings of anxiety, guilt, shame, and anger. And he needs to be open to new experiences. All this can be accomplished through a free, open, and unstructured client-therapist relationship.

Thus far, three basic models used to explain abnormal behavior have been introduced in this chapter: biogenic, psychoanalytic, and humanistic. As we have mentioned, there are considerable variations even within each school of thought. We would like

ing nearly straight A's—some of his teachers were concerned about his introverted behavior and occasional bouts of depression. When the depression was brought to the attention of his father, however, Mr. M. seemed unconcerned and dismissed it as no reason to worry. Indeed, Mr. M. complimented Bill on his good grades and nonobtrusive behavior, rewarding him occasionally with small privileges (a larger portion of dessert or the choice of a television program). To some degree of awareness, Bill felt that his worth as a person was dependent only on "getting good grades" and "staying out of trouble."

As a young child, Bill had exhibited excellent artistic potential, and his teachers tried to encourage him in that direction. In elementary school he won several awards with his drawings and was frequently asked by teachers to paint murals in their classrooms or to draw and design flyers and posters for school events. His artistic interests continued into high school, where his art instructor entered one of Bill's drawings in a state

contest. His entry won first prize. Unfortunately, the father discouraged Bill from his interests and talents and told him that "God calls you in another direction." Attempting to please his father, Bill became less involved in art during his junior and senior years in favor of concentrating on math and sciences. He did exceptionally well in these subjects, obtaining nearly straight A's at the finish of his high school years.

When Bill entered college, his prime objective was to remain a straight-A student. Although he had originally loved the excitement of learning, achieving, and mastering new knowledge, he now became cautious and obsessed with "safety"; he was fearful of upsetting his father. As his string of perfect grades became longer and longer, safety (not risking a B grade) became more and more important. He began to choose safe and easy topics for essays, to enroll in very easy courses, and to take "incompletes" or withdrawals when courses appeared tough.

Toward the end of his sophomore year, Bill suffered a mental

breakdown characterized by pessimism and hopelessness. He became very depressed and was subsequently hospitalized after he tried to take his own life.

Remember, your task is not only to explain Bill's behavior from three different perspectives, but to compare and contrast each theoretical orientation. Some hints that may be of help are the following: (1) What do each of the theories propose as the basis for the development of a mental disorder? (2) What type of data does each perspective consider most important? (3) Compare and contrast only after each perspective has been developed. Notice how the adoption of a particular framework influences the type of data that you consider important. Is it possible that all three models may hold some semblance of truth? Are their positions necessarily contradictory? Is it possible to integrate them into a unified explanation of Bill? Why don't you try your hand at this task?

to pause, at this point, to allow you an opportunity to apply these models to a case study just as we have done in the example of Steven V. You may wish to reread the analysis of Steve from all three perspectives and then try your hand with the case related in the Critical Thinking section. One suggestion is to ask yourself these questions: "If I were a biologically oriented mental health professional, how would I make sense of Bill?" "If I were psychoanalytically oriented, how might I explain the dynamics of Bill?" "How would a humanistic psychologist explain Bill's disorder?" We have found that dividing into small groups for discussion is a useful learning experience.

SUMMARY

1. Psychologists use theories, or models, to explain behavior. Each model is built around its own set of assumptions. The model one adopts determines not only how the therapist explains abnormal behavior but also what treatment methods he or she is likely to use. Most clinicians, however, take an eclectic approach, blending and using components of various models.

2. Biogenic models cite various organic causes of psychopathology. Damage to the nervous system is one such cause. Another is biochemical imbalances; several types of disturbances have been found to re-

spond to drugs. In addition, a good deal of biochemical research has focused on identifying the role of neuroregulators in abnormal behavior. Still another biogenic theory cites heredity in mental disorders: correlations have been found between genetic inheritance and certain psychopathologies.

3. Psychoanalytic theory emphasizes childhood experiences and the role of the unconscious in determining present behavior. Sigmund Freud, the founder of psychoanalysis, believed that personality has three components: the id, which represents the impulsive, selfish, pleasure-seeking part of the person; the ego, which represents the rational part; and the superego, which represents society's values and ideals. Each component checks and balances the others. The life instincts and the death instincts are the energy system from which the personality operates. These instincts manifest themselves in various ways during the five different periods of life, or psychosexual stages, through which people pass: the oral, anal, phallic, latency, and genital stages. Each stage poses unique challenges that, if not adequately resolved, can result in maladaptive adult behaviors.

4. According to Freud, neurotic behavior results from the threat that unconscious thoughts will attain consciousness. To repress forbidden thoughts and impulses, the ego uses defense mechanisms: repression, reaction formation, projection, rationalization, displacement, undoing, and regression. Psychoanalytic therapy induces an ego weakness that allows access to unconscious material, which the therapist uses to help the patient achieve insight into his or her unconscious.

5. Neo-Freudians have adapted traditional psychoanalytic theory. While accepting basic psychodynamic tenets, they differ along several dimensions. First, they place greater emphasis on freedom of choice and the importance of future goals. Second, they see consciousness and ego autonomy as equally important to id processes. Third, they recognize the influence of social forces as important. Fourth, they highlight important people or object relations in the past. And, last, they give increasing attention to adapting psychoanalytic techniques in working with seriously disturbed people.

6. Psychoanalytic theory has been criticized for several reasons. First, critics point out that it lacks scientific rigor and is difficult to validate empirically. Second, gender bias is clearly evident in how it conceptualizes the feminine psyche. Last, psychoanalytic theory appears less effective with people who are experiencing pressing, immediate problems; those who are less verbal; and those who are psychotic as opposed to less severely disturbed clients.

7. Advocates of the humanistic approaches see people as capable of making free choices and fulfilling their potential. This viewpoint emphasizes conscious rather than unconscious processes. Perhaps the best-known humanistic formulation is Carl Rogers's person-centered approach. Rogers believes that people are motivated not only to meet their biological needs but also to grow and to enhance the self, to become actualized or fulfilled. Behavior disorders result when a person is forced to develop a self-concept that is at odds with his or her actualizing tendency. In person-centered therapy, the therapist projects a strong belief in the client's ability to deal with life, to grow, and to reach his or her potential.

8. Existentialists believe that rapidly accelerating technology and an emphasis on naturalistic rather than spiritual explanations of the world have led to much personal trauma. Loneliness, alienation, isolation, and depersonalization have all been increased in contemporary times, as a direct result of society's treating people like objects. Three concepts essential to existentialism are being (human awareness of existence), nonbeing (human awareness of death), and being-in-the-world (existing in a social context). Existentialists see behavior disorders as a product of the conflict between people's essential natures and the demands made on them by themselves and others. Existential therapy is an unstructured collaborative venture between therapist and patient; its object is to illuminate the patient's being-in-the-world.

9. Humanistic and existential perspectives have been characterized as possessing a vagueness of thought and being too subjective. As such, the perspectives may not be suited for empirical investigation. In addition, these approaches may not work well with severely disturbed clients.

KEY TERMS

axon A long, thin extension attached to a neuron that transmits impulses to other neurons

biogenic model The theory or expectation that every mental disorder has an organic basis and cure

collective unconscious A term devised by Jung that refers to ancient, primordial memories common to all humanity

defense mechanism In psychoanalytic theory, the unconscious and automatic means by which the ego is protected from anxiety-provoking conflicts

dendrites Rootlike structures attached to the body of the neuron that receive impulses from other neurons

diathesis-stress theory The theory that a predisposition to develop mental illness is inherited and that this predisposition may or may not be activated by environmental factors

dizygotic (DZ) or **fraternal twins** Twins from two separate eggs; such twins share about 50 percent of the same genes

eclectic approach An openness to all models of abnormal behavior, along with a willingness to borrow and integrate techniques from all approaches and to use them selectively with clients

existential approach The belief that contemporary society has a dehumanizing effect and that mental disorders result from a conflict between essential human nature and the demands made on people by themselves and others

genotype The genetic component of a trait or characteristic

humanistic perspective The optimistic viewpoint that people are born with the ability to fulfill their potential and that abnormal behavior results from disharmony between the person's potential and self-concept

model An analogy most often used to describe or explain something that cannot be directly observed

monozygotic (MZ) or **identical twins** Genetically identical twins who developed from one fertilized egg

neo-Freudians Psychologists whose ideas are strongly influenced by Freud's psychoanalytic model but who have modified that model in various ways

neurons Nerve cells that transmit messages throughout the body

neurotransmitters Chemical substances involved in the transmission of neural impulses between neurons

object relations Past interpersonal relations that shape and affect the individual's current interactions with people

phenotype The observable results of the interaction of the genotype and the environment

pleasure principle The impulsive, pleasure-seeking aspect of our being usually associated with the id, which seeks immediate gratification regardless of moral or realistic concerns

psychoanalysis Therapy based on the Freudian view that unconscious conflicts must be aired and understood by the patient if abnormal behavior is to be eliminated

psychoanalytic model The view that adult disorders arise from the unconscious operation of repressed anxieties originally experienced during childhood

psychopathology Abnormal behavior

psychosexual stages In psychoanalytic theory, the sequence of stages—oral, anal, phallic, latency, and genital—through which human personality develops

reality principle In Freudian theory, awareness of the demands of the environment and adjustment of behavior to meet these demands; acts to modify the pleasure principle and is part of the ego structure

self-actualization An inherent tendency in people to strive toward the realization of their full potential

self-concept An individual's assessment of his or her own value and worth

synapse A small gap between the axon terminal of the transmitting neuron and the dendrites of the receiving neuron

CHAPTER 3

Behavioral, Cognitive, and Family Systems Models of Psychopathology

This is the second of two chapters concerned with models of abnormal behavior. Recall that such models are idealized constructs or analogies; their purpose is to provide insight into the causes of abnormal behavior and thus to suggest methods of treatment. In Chapter 2, we discussed the biogenic model and three psychogenic models. The biogenic model of abnormal behavior emphasizes an organic basis for mental disorders and, therefore, medical therapies. The psychogenic models look primarily to the mind, or psyche, for both causes and treatment.

The models discussed in this chapter focus more on the environment or cognitive processes (the process and content of thought) than on the intrapsychic inner life of the individual. The behavioral and cognitive models hold that all behavior and cognitions—normal and abnormal—are learned through interaction between the person and the environment. The mentally disturbed person either has learned the "wrong" behaviors and thoughts or has not learned the "right" ones. Therapy should be directed toward helping the client replace inappropriate behaviors or learn appropriate ones.

The family systems model of abnormal behavior concentrates on a particular part of the total environment. According to its proponents, individual identity and the quality of our relationships with others are largely the result of our family experiences. When psychopathology occurs, the therapist must look to the family for causes and possible solutions.

ENVIRONMENTAL DETERMINANTS OF ABNORMAL BEHAVIOR

Although the models of psychopathology discussed in the previous chapter do acknowledge the role of environmental factors in the development of behavior disorders, they tend to downplay their importance. Most of these models strongly emphasize the innate importance of internal factors (biological predispositions, unconscious urges and conflicts, or innate humanistic values), which determine the type of personality and abnormality most likely to emerge. These models tend to place less emphasis on environmental influences; for example, the psychoanalytic theories propose that learning and the effects of environmental constraints are less important after early childhood (that is, after the child has passed through the oedipal stage). Personality is believed to be relatively fixed after a particular point in the development of the individual.

The theories in this chapter, however, focus more on the environmental or sociocultural conditions that affect behavior throughout the lifespan. The behavioral schools of thought focus more on how an organism responds to stimuli in the environment through the principles of learning (reinforcement, punishment, and extinction). For example, a young girl who is always rewarded when she maintains her "slender figure" and is constantly admonished to "look nice and pretty" may develop an eating disorder such as anorexia or bulimia. A young child who is attacked and traumatized by a neighborhood dog may eventually develop a phobia to certain animals. In both cases, the development of these disorders is determined to a large extent by that person's interactions with the immediate environment.

Increasingly, psychologists have recognized that our most important interactions are likely to occur in two primary domains: (1) our interpersonal environment and (2) our sociocultural environment. First, there can be no doubt that we are social beings and that what we become is a function of our relationships with others. Central to this statement is the role of the family as a powerful determinant of human behavior. Although families attempt to instill in children the values, beliefs, and behaviors that will maximize their successes in society, they may also contribute to their children's difficulties. This is especially true if the family is dysfunctional; the structure, rules, role-relationships, and communication patterns force members to behave in maladaptive ways. Thus a number of psychologists are beginning to adopt a family systems approach to the explanation and treatment of psychopathology.

Second, attention to environmental determinants has also made psychologists more aware of larger social, cultural, and political forces that may shape behavior. We have already seen how social and cultural conditioning may affect the manifestation of behavior disorders in men and women and in racial and ethnic minorities. A person's social class, whether upperclass or lowerclass, can have major consequences on his or her adaptation to society. Thus powerful variables such as racism, sexism, poverty, and societal values and institutions may all affect behavior (see Chapter 19, Community Psychology).

It would be a mistake, however, to believe that the theories discussed in this chapter neglect the internal mechanisms that mediate an individual's interactions with the environment. The cognitive models of psychopathology offer a useful bridge between environmental forces and behavior by studying the content and process of human thought. We are not passive organisms who simply respond to incoming stimuli. We are active participants capable of analyzing, thinking, and interpreting the meaning of our experiences. When the content of our thoughts and the manner by which we process information are distorted or maladaptive, abnormal behavior may be the result.

BEHAVIORAL MODELS OF PSYCHOPATHOLOGY

The behaviorist approach to psychology was suggested in 1913 by John B. Watson (1878–1958) in a lecture delivered at Columbia University. Watson said that if psychology were ever to become a science, it must be limited to the study of directly observable and measurable events. Furthermore, he declared that there was no place in psychology for the subjective study of mind, emotions, and thought processes. (In this, Watson's view contrasted with the intrapsychic approach of Freud.) The single goal of the science of psychology, Watson said, should be the prediction and control of human *behavior.*

At the time, several scientists were doing laboratory experiments on *conditioning,* or basic learning processes. Watson saw such experimentation as a proper part of the science of psychology, and he viewed these investigators' results as closely related to the study of behavior. Watson himself began to experiment with conditioning, and learning became the primary focus of behaviorism.

The **behavioral models** of psychopathology are thus concerned with the role of learning in abnormal behavior. The differences among them lie mainly in their explanations of how learning occurs. Although some models disagree, they generally tend to complement each other. That is, each of the three learning models discussed here is, for the most part, applied to a different type of behavior.

The Classical Conditioning Model

Principles of Classical Conditioning   Early in the twentieth century, Ivan Pavlov (1849–1936), a Russian physiologist, discovered an associative learning process that is known as **classical conditioning** or **respondent**. This process involves the involuntary responses (such as reflexes, emotional reactions, and sexual arousal), which are controlled by the autonomic nervous system.

Pavlov's discovery was accidental. He was measuring dogs' salivation as part of a study of their digestive processes when he discovered that the dogs would begin to salivate at the sight of an assistant carrying their food. The dogs' salivation in response to a stimulus other than food placed in their mouths puzzled Pavlov and led to his formulation of classical conditioning. He reasoned that food is an **unconditional stimulus (UCS)** that, in the mouth, automatically elicits salivation; this salivation is an unlearned or **unconditioned response (UCR)** to the food. Pavlov then presented a previously *neutral* stimulus (one that does not initially elicit salivation, such as the sound of a bell) to the dogs just before presenting the food. He found that, after a number of repetitions, the sound of the bell alone elicited salivation. This learning process is based on association: the neutral stim-

Ivan Pavlov (1849–1936), a Russian physiologist, discovered the associative learning process we know as classical conditioning, while he was studying salivation in dogs. Pavlov won the Nobel Prize in physiology and medicine in 1904 for his work on the principal digestive glands.

ulus acquires some of the properties of the unconditioned stimulus when they are repeatedly paired. When the bell alone can provoke this response, it is called a **conditioned stimulus (CS),** and the salivation it elicits is termed a **conditioned response (CR).** Each time the conditioned stimulus is paired with the unconditioned stimulus, the conditioned response is said to be *reinforced,* or strengthened. Pavlov's conditioning process is illustrated in Figure 3.1.

Pavlov also discovered other principles governing classical conditioning. If he presented the bell many times without following it with the food, the animals would gradually salivate less and less in response to the bell. This process, by which a response is eliminated when it is not reinforced, is called *extinction.* Pavlov also observed that the dogs salivated when he presented stimuli that were similar to the original conditioned stimulus. For example, a bell with a somewhat different tone might elicit salivation. This process is called **generalization.** The reverse of gener-

FIGURE 3.1 A Basic Classical Conditioning Process
Dogs normally salivate when food is provided (left drawing). With his laboratory dogs,
Ivan Pavlov paired the ringing of a bell with the presentation of food (middle drawing).
Eventually, the dogs would salivate to the ringing of the bell alone, when no food was
near (right drawing).

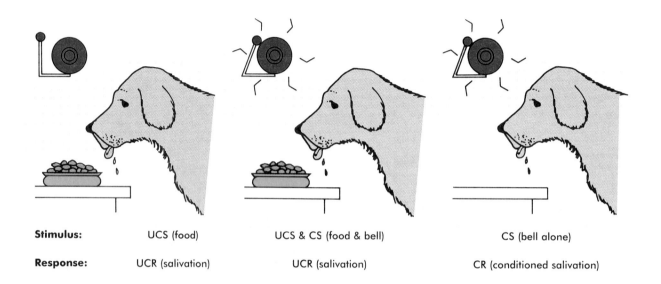

Stimulus:	UCS (food)	UCS & CS (food & bell)	CS (bell alone)
Response:	UCR (salivation)	UCR (salivation)	CR (conditioned salivation)

alization, **stimulus discrimination,** is learning *not* to respond to a stimulus that is different from the conditioned stimulus.

For example, most people have learned to respond favorably to a smile, even on a face that they have never seen before; however, they do not respond so favorably to a frown. When the occurrence or nonoccurrence of a particular behavior is controlled by a preceding stimulus, that behavior is said to be under *stimulus control.*

Classical Conditioning in Psychopathology Pavlov never fully explored the implications of classical conditioning for human behavior; John B. Watson is credited with recognizing the importance of associative learning in the explanation of abnormal behavior. In a classic and oft-cited experiment, Watson (Watson & Rayner, 1920), using classical conditioning principles, attempted to condition a fear response in a young child named Albert. Jones (1924) reported:

Albert, eleven months of age, was an infant with phlegmatic disposition, afraid of nothing "under the

sun" except a loud sound made by striking a steel bar. This made him cry. By striking the bar at the same time that Albert touched a white rat, the fear was transferred to the white rat. After seven combined stimulations, rat and sound, Albert not only became greatly disturbed at the sight of a rat, but this fear had spread to include a white rabbit, cotton, wool, a fur coat, and the experimenter's hair. It did not transfer to his wooden blocks and other objects very dissimilar to the rat. (pp. 308–309)

In other words, Watson was able to demonstrate that the acquisition of a *phobia* (an exaggerated, seemingly illogical fear of a particular object or class of objects) could be explained by classical conditioning. Today, however, conditioning fear in human beings is considered highly unethical.

Originally, Watson had intended to "decondition" Albert to the fear, but because he was an adopted child from out of town, this feat was never accomplished. Mary Cover Jones (1924), a student of Watson's, was able to demonstrate how fear could be unlearned through classical conditioning principles. By using food as a stimulus to counteract the

Most behaviorists believe that fear of animals is not an innate response, but a conditioned one. The young girl on the left is obviously not afraid of snakes (unconditioned response), while the young boy on the right exhibits a conditioned fear of horses.

fear response, Jones described vividly how this could be done:

> During a period of craving for food, the child is placed in a high chair and given something to eat. The feared object is brought in, starting a negative response. It is then moved away gradually until it is at a sufficient distance not to interfere with the child's eating. The relative strength of the fear impulse may be gauged by the distance to which it is necessary to remove the feared object. While the child is eating, the object is slowly brought nearer to the table, then placed upon the table and, finally, as the tolerance increases, it is brought close enough to be touched. Since we could not interfere with the regular schedule of meals, we chose the time of the mid-morning lunch for the experiment. This usually assured some degree of interest in the food and corresponding success in our treatment. (pp. 388–389)

The positive aspects of food eventually overcame the negative (fear-arousing) aspects of the object. The pairing of a negative stimulus to elicit the undesirable response (fear) with a pleasant stimulus (food) to elicit a pleasurable response is called **counterconditioning**; it is a major form of therapy used by many behaviorists.

As we shall see in later chapters, classical conditioning has provided explanations for the acquisition of fears (phobias), certain unusual sexual attractions, and other extreme emotional reactions and has served as a basis for effective treatment techniques. Yet the "passive nature" of associative learning was limited as an explanatory and treatment tool. Most human behavior, both normal and abnormal, tends to be much more active and voluntary. To explain how these behaviors are acquired or eliminated necessitates an understanding of operant conditioning.

The Operant Conditioning Model

An **operant behavior** is a voluntary and controllable behavior, such as walking or thinking, that "operates" on an individual's environment. Suppose that you are in an extremely warm room. It would be very difficult for you to consciously control your sweating—to "will" your body not to perspire. You could, however, decide to change your environment by simply walking out of the uncomfortably warm room.

Most human behavior is operant in nature. The concept of **operant conditioning** was first formulated by Edward Thorndike (1874–1949), although he used the term *instrumental conditioning*. In working with cats, Thorndike observed that they would repeat certain behaviors when those behaviors were asso-

In operant conditioning, positive consequences increase the likelihood and frequency of a desired response. This is particularly important in a classroom setting where a child knows that appropriate behavior will be rewarded and inappropriate behavior will be punished.

ciated with positive consequences. Likewise, if the consequences were unpleasant, the behaviors would be discouraged and reduced. This principle became known as the **law of effect.** Some fifty years later, B. F. Skinner (1904–1990) started a revolution in the field by innovatively applying Thorndike's law of effect, which he renamed *reinforcement.*

This type of learning differs from classical conditioning primarily in two ways. First, classical conditioning is involved in the development of involuntary behaviors such as fear, whereas operant conditioning is related to voluntary behaviors.

Second, as we discussed earlier, behaviors based on *classical* conditioning are controlled by stimuli, or events *preceding* the response: salivation occurs only when it is preceded by a UCS (food in the mouth) or a CS (the thought of a sizzling, juicy steak covered

with mushrooms). In *operant* conditioning, however, behaviors are controlled by events that *follow* them. Positive consequences increase the likelihood and frequency of a response. But when the consequences are negative, the behavior is less likely to be repeated. For example, a student is likely to raise his or her hand in class often if the teacher recognizes the student, smiles, and seems genuinely interested in the student's comments. If the instructor frowns, looks disgusted, or yawns, however, the student's hand-raising behavior will probably become less frequent.

Principles of Operant Conditioning The principles of operant conditioning are statements about the relationships between behavior and consequences (also called *contingencies*). Let us look at some of the most basic of these principles.

Reinforcement Anything that increases the frequency or magnitude of the behavior it follows is called a **reinforcer.** A **positive reinforcer** provides a positive, wanted, or pleasant consequence; it may be tangible (money, food, sexual activity) or social (attention, praise, a smile).

Whether a consequence is a reinforcer depends only on its effect. Certain consequences that are aversive to most people can function as reinforcement to others. One study of classroom behavior recorded the number of times schoolchildren left their seats and the number of teacher reprimands (Madsen et al., 1970). To assess the relationship between these two variables, teachers were asked to triple the frequency of reprimands. Amazingly, the out-of-seat behaviors increased. The greater the number of commands to sit down, the more often children stood up! In this situation, reprimands functioned as a reinforcer; that is, they increased the frequency of the response.

A **negative reinforcer** increases the frequency of a behavior by removing an aversive (unpleasant or punishing) event. Suppose that near dinner time a small child wants a cookie. The mother, afraid that the cookie will spoil the child's appetite, says no. Out of frustration and anger, the child throws a temper tantrum (which is aversive to the mother). Because the mother is fearful that the child will be injured, she gives in and grants the child's demand. Although it is easy for us to see that the mother has positively reinforced the child's tantrum behavior, it is more difficult to see that the mother has been negatively

Table 3.1

Increasing and Decreasing the Frequency of Behavior Through Operant Conditioning

These Increase the Frequency of a Behavior	These Decrease the Frequency of a Behavior
Positive Reinforcement: Presentation of a positive reinforcer	*Punishment:* Presentation of an aversive stimulus or removal of a positive reinforcer
Negative Reinforcement: Removal of an aversive event	*Extinction:* Removal of a positive reinforcer

reinforced. Once the child gets the cookie, the aversive behavior ends (removal of aversive stimulus) and the mother is negatively reinforced (the probability of her giving in increases).

Punishment A **punishment** is either the removal of a positive reinforcer or the presentation of an aversive stimulus. Both reduce the probability of the response. (Note that negative reinforcement increases the probability.) In the first kind of punishment, privileges such as use of the car, television viewing, or access to games may be withdrawn after an inappropriate action is performed. This is often referred to as *response cost*. The second kind of punishment involves the presentation of an aversive consequence such as a reprimand or a spanking.

Extinction You have already seen how extinction works in classical conditioning: after the conditioned stimulus is presented repeatedly without the unconditioned stimulus, the conditioned response disappears. In operant conditioning, **extinction** is the process of eliminating a behavior through nonreinforcement. When the reinforcement for a behavior is discontinued, the behavior usually disappears.

These four basic components of operant conditioning are listed and distinguished in Table 3.1. In addition, you should be aware of two more concepts that are important in the operant conditioning model: discriminative stimulus and shaping.

Discriminative stimulus A cue that is usually present when reinforcement occurs is known as a **discriminative stimulus**. For example, through experience people learn that success is more likely when they address a request to a person who is smiling than when they approach one who looks angry. Most

people are more likely to cross a street when the light is green than when it is red because of the consequences associated with the color of the light. In other words, the smile and the green light indicate that reinforcement is likely to follow.

Shaping **Shaping** is the process of developing a new or complex behavior by reinforcing successive behaviors that increasingly approximate the final goal desired by the experimenter. Many responses are very complex and do not usually occur spontaneously. In these cases, the experimenter can break down a response into a series of small steps and can reinforce each step.

Operant Conditioning in Psychopathology Studies have demonstrated a relationship between environmental reinforcers and certain abnormal behaviors. For example, self-injurious behavior, such as head banging, is a dramatic form of psychopathology that is often reported in psychotic and mentally retarded children. It has been hypothesized that some forms of head banging may be linked to reinforcing features in the environment (Schaefer, 1970; Schaefer & Martin, 1969). To test this hypothesis, a self-injurious behavior (head hitting) was shaped in two monkeys through successive approximations. First the raising of the animal's paw was reinforced, then holding the paw over the head, and finally bringing the paw down on the head. This sequence of behaviors was shaped in about sixteen minutes in both monkeys. The discriminative stimulus for reinforcement comprised the words "Poor boy! Don't do that! You'll hurt yourself." Head hitting occurred whenever these words were spoken by the experimenter because they had been associated with reinforcement (bananas). It seems clear from these findings that self-injurious behaviors can be developed and maintained through reinforcement.

Although positive reinforcement can account for some forms of self-injurious behaviors, in some instances other variables seem more important (Carr, 1977). Negative reinforcement, for example, can also strengthen and maintain unhealthy behaviors. Consider a student who has enrolled in a class in which the instructor requires oral reports. The thought of doing an oral presentation in front of a class produces feelings of anxiety, sweating, an upset stomach, and trembling in the student. Having these feelings is aversive. To stop the unpleasant reaction, the student switches to another section whose instructor does not require oral presentations. The student's behavior is reinforced by escape from aversive feelings, and such avoidance responses to situations involving "stage fright" will increase in frequency.

As in classical conditioning, operant conditioning principles have proven invaluable in the treatment of psychopathology. In many cases, the therapist must be ingenious in devising successful strategies. In later chapters on specific psychological disorders, and in Chapter 18 on treatment approaches, we discuss a variety of ways in which operant conditioning has been applied to the treatment of abnormal behaviors.

The Observational Learning Model

The traditional behavioral theories of learning—classical conditioning and operant conditioning—require that the individual actually perform behaviors to learn them. **Observational learning theory** suggests that an individual can acquire new behaviors by simply watching them performed (Bandura, 1969; Bandura & Walters, 1963). The process of learning by observing models (and later imitating them) is called *vicarious conditioning* or **modeling.** Direct and tangible reinforcement (giving praise, etc.) for imitation of the model is not necessary, although reinforcers are necessary to maintain behaviors learned in this manner. Observational learning can involve both respondent and operant behaviors, and its discovery has had such an impact in psychology that it has been proposed as a third form of learning.

Vicarious Classical Conditioning   You would probably not be surprised to hear that an eight-year-old boy who has never left his hometown of Seattle is afraid of snakes, elephants, and monsters, none of which he has ever met. Some of these fears can be explained by the phenomenon of *generalization:* the boy perhaps generalized fears of animals he had encountered, or had been warned about, to creatures

Observational learning is based on the theory that behavior can be learned by observing it. Research indicates that a direct relationship exists between actual aggression and violence viewed on television. But as this photograph shows, observational learning can also be positive.

he had never seen. However, people may also acquire fears by seeing others exhibit fear or arousal (through vicarious classical conditioning).

In one study, subjects watched a person go through a classical conditioning procedure in which a neutral stimulus was presented and followed by an electric shock (Berger, 1962). The model displayed pain cues (grimaces and jerks) in response to the shock (UCS). The observers, whose emotional reactions were monitored, also developed responses to the conditioned stimulus, although they never received a shock.

Vicarious Operant Conditioning   Operant behavior can also be learned through modeling. Some of the most compelling research in this area has examined the acquisition of aggressive behaviors in children.

The finding that symbolic representations of aggressive action in films and television can increase aggression in children has alarmed parents, educators, and researchers. Heavy viewing of aggressive programs, including cartoon shows, on television appears to be related to overt aggression in preschool children (Singer & Singer, 1983). The National Institute of Mental Health also found a relationship between the viewing of violent fare on television and aggressive behavior in children (Pearl, Bouthilet & Lazar, 1982). In a long-term study, L. D. Eron (1963) surveyed hundreds of third-grade students to assess their television-viewing habits and found that children who preferred violent programs were more likely than children who preferred nonviolent fare to be rated aggressive by peers. A follow-up study of this same sample of children ten years later (when the subjects were approximately nineteen years old) again found a correlation between preference for violent programs and aggressiveness ratings (Eron et al., 1972).

Although these studies were correlational, the link between modeled television violence and aggressive behavior has also been demonstrated experimentally. In one study, children were exposed to either a violent television program or a sports show of track events. When the researchers later observed both groups of children playing, they saw significantly more aggression among the children who had watched the violent programs (Liebert & Baron, 1972).

Observational learning does not, however, have to be negative. Prosocial behaviors such as cooperation, empathy, friendliness, and delay of gratification can be increased through appropriate modeling (Rubinstein, 1983).

Observational Learning in Psychopathology   Observational learning approaches, like those emphasizing classical and operant conditioning, assume that abnormal behaviors are learned in the same manner as normal behaviors; exposure to disturbed models is likely to produce disturbed behaviors. For example, when monkeys watched other monkeys respond with fear to an unfamiliar object, they learned to respond in a similar manner (Cook et al., 1986). Observational learning can have four possible effects on the observers (Spiegler, 1983): (1) new behaviors can be acquired by watching a model; (2) a model may serve to elicit particular behaviors by providing observers with cues to engage in those behaviors; (3) behaviors that are inhibited because of anxiety or other negative reactions may be performed after they are observed; and (4) a behavior may become inhibited in the observer if the model's similar behavior resulted in aversive consequences.

Criticisms of the Behavioral Models

Behavioral approaches to psychopathology are a strong force in psychology today (Franks, 1990; Liberman, Mueser & DeRisi, 1989). The behaviorist perspectives have had tremendous impact in the areas of cause and therapy. Some of these contributions have been (1) to question the adequacy of the organic model of psychological disorders, (2) to stress the importance of external influences on behavior, (3) to require strict adherence to scientific methods, and (4) to encourage continuing evaluation of the techniques employed by psychologists. These features endow behaviorism with a degree of effectiveness and accountability that is lacking in the insight-oriented perspectives.

A behavioral orientation may often, however, neglect or place low importance on the inner determinants of behavior. This exclusion has been criticized, as has the behaviorists' extension to human beings of results obtained from animal studies. A lack of attention to human values in relation to behavior has also led to the charge that the behaviorist perspective is mechanistic, viewing people as "empty organisms"

(Hayes & Zettle, 1979, p. 5). Some critics also complain that behaviorists are not open minded and that they tend to dismiss out of hand the advances and data accumulated by other approaches to therapy (Hayes & Zettle, 1979; Lazarus, 1977). Criticism that behavioral approaches ignore the person's inner life are less applicable to proponents of modeling. As we will shortly discuss, a recent trend among behaviorists is to place increasing importance on cognitive processes and deemphasize the importance of intrapsychic dynamics. This has led to the development of cognitive-behavioral models. Many theorists and practitioners, however, find it hard to believe that clients can help themselves by simply changing their thinking.

There is, in fact, a movement among some therapists to seek the best ideas and techniques from all the psychotherapies. They believe that both psychoanalysts and behavior therapists could offer a more complete form of psychotherapy if they listened more carefully to each other and borrowed useful ideas from one another (Wachtel, 1977). Cognitive learning theorists are now stressing the importance of internal mediating processes (the individual's perception of events), which has always been emphasized by humanistic psychologists.

It is clear from recent writings and research publications that a major evolution, or revolution, is occurring in behaviorism. This movement may lead to an integration of some of the currently contrasting views on treatment and psychopathology, in line with the eclectic approach discussed in Chapter 2. Such integration is a long way off, however, and there are still strong fundamental differences among the major schools of psychotherapy.

◆ A BEHAVIORAL VIEW OF STEVEN V.

In the previous chapter we included three treatment approaches to the case of Steven V., as a therapist might apply them. Now suppose that Steve's therapist is strongly oriented toward the behavioral models. He or she would then discuss Steve's problems in terms very much like the following. (Before going on, you may find it useful to refresh your memory by rereading the discussion of Steve's case at the beginning of Chapter 1.)

Let me start by drawing an analogy between behavior and music. In music, all the songs a performer has learned make up the performer's repertoire. Quite similarly, all an individual's behaviors—all the responses the person has learned to make in each situation—constitute the person's behavioral repertoire.

The roots of Steve's problems can be traced to his behavioral repertoire. Many of the behaviors he has learned are inappropriate (much like songs that nobody wants to hear), and his repertoire lacks useful, productive behaviors.

Many of Steve's troubles stem from his deficiency in, or lack of, social skills. He has had little practice in social relationships, and so has difficulty distinguishing between appropriate and inappropriate behavior. You can see evidence of these problems in his withdrawn behavior when he is in the company of relatives or his parents' or Linda's friends. Steve himself reports that he feels apprehensive and anxious in the company of others (for example, Linda's friends) and finds himself with no idea of what to do or say. While others seem to have no difficulty making "small talk," Steve remains silent. When he does speak, his statements are usually perfunctory, brief, and inappropriate. I think this deficiency stems from Steve's early social isolation, which prevented him from developing interpersonal skills, and from his lack of good role models. His parents seldom interacted with one another or with Steve. Recall that Mr. V.'s manner of relating to his son was generally antagonistic; he did not model effective and appropriate skills.

I am also interested in exploring Steve's bouts of depression, but I need to know several things: first, through what specific behaviors is Steve's depression made manifest? Does he withdraw from social contact? Lose his appetite? Weep? Make negative statements? If we are to help Steve change his behavior, we must know what behavior we are talking about. Too often terms such as *depression, passivity,* and *anxiety* are used without a common referent. For example, when a client calls himself "shy," we must be sure that both therapist and client understand the term in the same way.

Second, what situations tend to elicit his depression? If the events share common characteristics, then we may be able to control or alter them to Steve's advantage. Again, it appears that Steve experiences depression when he believes himself to be worthless: when rejected by his woman friend, when belittled by his father, and on becoming impotent in his first sexual encounter. Steve may be able to master such situations by developing more effective behaviors. He might benefit, for example, from learning to respond to his father's bullying by telling his father how hurt and angry he feels when his father belittles him. A behavioral program designed to enhance Steve's sexual functioning could also prove helpful in combatting his depression. And Steve must learn to challenge his own irrational beliefs—for example, the belief that his father's failure to acknowledge Steve's academic achievements is somehow Steve's fault.

Steve's heterosexual anxiety and impotence must also be addressed. I believe that Steve has a conditioned or learned anxiety toward women and especially toward sexual intercourse. This anxiety not only blocks his ability to relate to members of the opposite sex but also directly affects his autonomic nervous system, so that his sexual arousal is impaired. We must teach Steve through classical conditioning how to subtract anxiety from the sexual encounter. Counterconditioning techniques seem to offer promise in treating Steve's impotence; relaxation could be used as a response that is antagonistic to his anxiety about sexual intercourse.

I have purposefully saved the discussion of Steve's delusions for last. Perhaps you find it difficult to imagine a behavioral analysis of delusions. But I am not concerned with the phenomena of Steve's imagination; my concern is with the behaviors that are alleged to express a delusional system. Many people display inappropriate behaviors that are considered aversive, odd, or unusual but that may be somehow reinforced. Steve's repeated assertion that he is controlled by demonic forces and his continual thinking about Satanism disturb many people. But the people who call him crazy and are occasionally frightened by him may actually be reinforcing these behaviors.

When Steve behaves in this way, he garners much attention from his parents, peers, and onlookers. Fully seven pages of a ten-page psycho-logical report, prepared by a therapist two years ago, are devoted to Steve's delusions. I submit that by finding the topic fascinating and spending a lot of time talking with Steve about his delusions, the therapist thus reinforced the client's verbal behavior! I am not the only behaviorist who contends that psychoanalytically oriented therapists make this mistake. Many behavioral therapists believe, for example, that psychoanalysts elicit so much sexual material from their clients precisely because they unwittingly reinforce this concentration on sex. Is it possible that Steve's verbal and other behavioral evocations of Satanism would diminish if people ignored them? It is more than possible.

In sum, a behavioral program including modeling, role playing, and assertiveness training could be used to enhance Steve's social skills. I would use cognitive strategies and teach him behaviors through which he may more adequately control his environment to combat his depression. His heterosexual anxiety and impotence would be treated via counterconditioning methods and relaxation training. Finally, the use of extinction strategies might reduce his excessive concern with Satanism.

COGNITIVE MODELS OF PSYCHOPATHOLOGY

The cognitive perspective probably originated with the Stoic philosopher Epictetus, who noted, "Men are disturbed not by events, but by the views they take of them." The **cognitive model** is based on the assumption that people actually create their own problems (and symptoms as well) by the way they interpret events and situations. For example, one person who fails to be hired for a job may become severely depressed, blaming himself for the failure. Another might only become mildly irritated, believing that failure to get the job had nothing to do with personal inadequacy. For both people, the situations (not being hired for a job) are identical but the responses are very different. Why is this so? To explain this phenomenon, we have to look at *mediating processes*—thoughts, perceptions, and self-evaluations that determine the reactions and behaviors of people.

Traditionally, behaviorists have dismissed events that cannot be observed and have not considered internal mediating processes important in modifying behavior. By the mid-1970s, however, cognitive-behavioral and cognitive approaches became popular and prevalent. At that time, three theories were solidly formulated: George Kelly's (1955) personal construct approach, Albert Ellis's (1962) rational-emotive therapy (popularly designated RET), and Aaron T. Beck's (1963, 1970) cognitive therapy. That number has increased to at least twenty (Mahoney & Lyddon, 1988), and, although most cognitively oriented theorists are also behaviorists, the development of the cognitive schools has progressed so far that they deserve to be considered as independent models in their own right. All are based on the premise that the way an individual perceives, anticipates, or evaluates an event—rather than the event itself—has the greatest impact on that individual's behavior. Further, cognitive theories argue that modifying thoughts and feelings is essential to changing behavior. How people label a situation and how they interpret events profoundly affect their emotional reactions and behavior. How a person interprets events is a function of his or her **schema**—underlying assumptions held by the person and heavily influenced by experiences, values, and perceived capabilities. The job hunters' reactions may suggest where cognitive psychologists would attribute the causes of psychopathology: (1) it may reside in the actual irrational and maladaptive contents of thoughts or (2) it may be due to distortions of the actual thought process. Although many theorists have contributed greatly to this area, we will concentrate primarily on three individuals who are credited with having a profound influence on the cognitive perspective: Albert Ellis, Aaron Beck, and Donald Meichenbaum.

Irrational and Maladaptive Assumptions and Thoughts

Almost all cognitive theorists stress heavily that disturbed individuals have both irrational and maladaptive thoughts. Ellis (1962, 1984, 1987) labels these "irrational" assumptions; Beck (1976, 1991) calls them dysfunctional "automatic thoughts"; and Meichenbaum (1977, 1986) refers to them as counterproductive "self-statements." As a practicing therapist for many years, Beck became interested in how many of his clients would engage in an almost rigid, inflexible, and automatic interpretation of events they had experienced. These negative thoughts

seemed to "just happen," as if by reflex, even in the face of objective contrary evidence. For example, Beck believes that depression revolves around firmly entrenched "negative views of self, experience and the future" and the paranoid individual persists in assuming that other people are deliberately abusive, interfering, or critical (Beck & Weishaar, 1989).

In working with his clients, Beck concluded that cognitive content is organized in a hierarchy along three levels. First, voluntary thoughts are those cognitions that we have the greatest ability to control and summon at will. They are the most accessible and least stable, and they are constantly subject to change. Clients suffering from an anxiety disorder, for example, are readily able to describe their symptoms and offer superficial causes and solutions. They do not, however, have ready access to the second level of cognitions that involve automatic thoughts. Automatic thoughts occur spontaneously, and the person is not necessarily aware of them. They are triggered by circumstances and intercede between an event or stimulus and the individual's emotional and behavioral reactions. A student who must make an oral presentation in class may think that "everyone will see I'm nervous." Such thoughts are given credibility without being challenged and usually derive from the third level of cognitions: underlying assumptions about ourselves and the world around us. These assumptions are quite stable and almost always outside of the person's awareness.

One of the most prominent psychologists associated with implicating the role of irrational beliefs and assumptions in maladaptive emotions and behaviors is Albert Ellis (Dryden, 1989; Ellis 1979, 1989). According to Ellis, psychological problems are produced by irrational thought patterns that stem from the individual's belief system. Unpleasant emotional responses that lead to anger, unhappiness, depression, fear, and anxiety result from the *thoughts* about an event rather than from the *event itself* (see Focus 3.1). These irrational thoughts have been conditioned through early childhood, but we also add to the difficulty by reinstilling these false beliefs in ourselves by autosuggestion and self-repetition. Ellis hypothesized that irrational thinking operates from dogmatic, absolutist "shoulds," "musts," and "oughts." Some examples are self-statements such as "I must be loved by my mother or father," "I ought to be able to succeed in everything," and "If I don't get what I want,

FOCUS 3.1

Some Common Irrational Assumptions

Rational-emotive therapy (RET) is based on the principle that psychological problems are produced by irrational assumptions such as those listed here. Making such irrational assumptions, RET advocates contend, results in anger, fear, anxiety, or depression.

1. It is necessary to be loved or approved by virtually every significant other.

2. One should be thoroughly competent, adequate, and achieving in all possible respects if one is to consider oneself worthwhile.

3. Certain people are bad, wicked, or villainous, and they should be severely blamed and punished for their villainy.

4. It is awful and catastrophic when things are not the way one would like them to be.

5. Human unhappiness is externally caused, and people have little or no ability to control their sorrows and disturbed behavior.

6. If something is or may be dangerous or fearsome, a person should be terribly concerned about it and should constantly dwell on the possibility of its occurring.

7. It is easier to avoid than to face certain responsibilities and difficulties in your life.

8. Each person should be dependent on others; people need

someone stronger than themselves to rely on.

9. A person's past history is the all-important determinant of his or her present behavior. Because something once strongly affected a person's life, it should have a similar effect indefinitely in the future.

10. People should become emotionally involved in other people's problems and disturbances.

_____

Source: Adapted from A. Ellis, 1962.

Albert Ellis (b. 1913) believes that psychological problems occur because of irrational thought processes. In his rational-emotive therapy, the therapist disputes the client's irrational beliefs and helps the client to replace them with more reasonable ideas.

it will be awful." Cynically, Ellis has referred to the many "musts" that cause human misery as "musturbatory activities." Although being accepted and loved by everyone is desirable, an unrealistic and irrational idea such as this creates dysfunctional feelings and behaviors. A student who becomes depressed after an unsuccessful date develops the depression not because of the failure but because of an irrational belief regarding the failure. An appropriate emotional response in such an unsuccessful dating situation might be frustration and temporary disappointment, but a more severe depression develops only if the student adds irrational thoughts, such as "Because this person turned me down, I am worthless. . . . I will never succeed with anyone of the opposite sex. . . . I am a total failure."

Distortions of Thought Processes

The study of cognitions as a cause of psychopathology has led many therapists to concentrate on the process (as opposed to the content) of thinking that characterizes both normal and abnormal individuals.

FIGURE 3.2 Ellis's A-B-C Theory of Personality

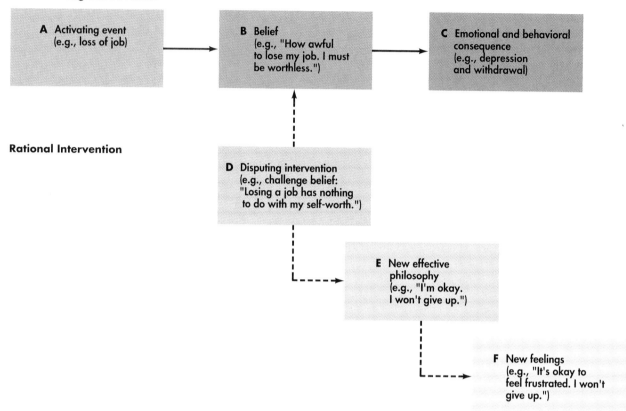

Ellis (1962, 1971, 1975) believed that human beings are born with potential for rational and irrational thinking. The irrational thoughts acquired through interactions with significant others are described in his *A-B-C* theory of personality. *A* is an event, fact, or the individual's behavior or attitude. *C* is the person's emotional or behavioral reaction. The activating event *A* never causes the emotional or behavioral consequence *C*. Instead, *B*, the person's beliefs about *A*, causes *C*. Think back to the two job hunters. Job hunter 1, who has been turned down for the position (activating event *A*), may think to himself (irrational beliefs *B*), "How awful to be rejected! I must be worthless. I'm no good." Thus he may become depressed and withdraw (emotional and behavioral consequence *C*). Job hunter 2, on the other hand,

reacts to the activating event *A* by saying (rational beliefs *B*), "How unfortunate to get rejected. It's frustrating and irritable. I'll have to try harder" (healthy consequence *C*). The assumptions and expectations of each individual are very different. One blamed himself and was overcome with feelings of worthlessness; the other recognized that not every person is right for every job (or vice versa), and left the situation with self-esteem intact. Job hunter 1 interprets the rejection as "awful and catastrophic" and, as a result, reacts with depression and may cease looking for a job. Job hunter 2 does not interpret the rejection personally, reacts with mild irritation and annoyance, and redoubles efforts to seek employment. Figure 3.2 illustrates the *A-B-C* relationship and provides a clue as to a cognitive approach to treatment.

Although the cognitive model proposed by Ellis applies to both rational and irrational thinking, interest has increased in identifying the types of cognitive distortions that lead to abnormal functioning. Beck's work on depression has led him to formulate six types of faulty thinking processes that seem to operate in most psychological disorders (Beck et al., 1979; Beck & Weishaar, 1989).

1. *Arbitrary inference* Arbitrary inference occurs when people draw conclusions about themselves or the world without sufficient and relevant information. In clinical practice, this is often referred to as *catastrophizing,* or picturing the worst-case scenario. The person who was not hired by a potential employer perceives himself as "totally worthless" and believes that he will probably never find employment of any sort.

2. *Selective abstraction* Selective abstraction refers to conclusions drawn from very isolated details and events without considering the larger context or picture. A depressed student who receives a C on an exam becomes depressed and gives up even though he or she may have A's and B's in all other courses. In this case, the student measures his or her worth by failures, errors, and weaknesses rather than by successes or strengths.

3. *Overgeneralization* Overgeneralization is the process of holding extreme beliefs on the basis of a single incident and applying it to a different or dissimilar and inappropriate situation. For example, a depressed person who has relationship problems with her boss may believe that she is a failure in all other types of relationships.

4. *Magnification and exaggeration* Magnification and exaggeration is the process of overestimating the significance of negative events. For example, experiencing shortness of breath will be interpreted as a major health problem, or worse yet, an indication of imminent death.

5. *Personalization* Personalization is a process by which people relate external events to themselves when no objective basis for such a connection is apparent. A student who raises his hand in class and is not called on by the professor may believe that the instructor dislikes or is biased against him.

6. *Polarized thinking* Polarized thinking is an "all-or-nothing" approach to viewing the world. Things are perceived in extremes or in "good and bad," "either-or" terms. For example, at one extreme is a student who perceives herself as "perfect" and immune from making mistakes, and at the other extreme is the student who believes that he is a total flop, an incompetent. In both students, polarized thinking leads to irrational and dysfunctional beliefs and attitudes.

Cognitive Approaches to Therapy

Almost all cognitive approaches to psychotherapy share commonalities. These have been summarized by Beck & Weishaar (1989):

> Cognitive therapy consists of highly specific learning experiences designed to teach patients (1) to monitor their negative, automatic thoughts (cognitions); (2) to recognize the connections between cognition, affect, and behavior; (3) to examine the evidence for and against distorted automatic thoughts; (4) to substitute more reality-oriented interpretations for these biased cognitions; and (5) to learn to identify and alter the beliefs that predispose them to distort their experiences. (p. 308)

Cognitive Restructuring All cognitive theorists emphasize the importance of **cognitive restructuring** in their therapeutic approaches. The assumption is that an individual's cognitive system can be changed directly and that this change will result in an altered and more appropriate set of rational behaviors. Among those most noted for this orientation is Aaron Beck (Beck, 1967, 1976). Beck contended that specific emotions such as depression are a product of situational interpretations made by the person. He tries to help clients identify the ways in which they distort their own thinking. Typical distortions include dichotomous reasoning (things are all good or all bad with no in-between), overgeneralization (if my husband leaves me, I'm totally alone), magnification (perceiving things as worse than they are), and faulty reasoning.

In his approach to cognitive restructuring, Beck first attempts to understand what the client is thinking. Faulty reasoning and irrational ideas are then identified, and the client is assisted in recognizing these debilitating thinking patterns. This may be done by challenging the person's ideas and supplying

Donald H. Meichenbaum (b. 1940) suggests that problematic behavior, especially stress-related behavior, can be changed for the better if the person learns new behavior strategies and uses more productive self-statements.

another frame of reference (restructuring the cognition) from which to view the situation. The last step involves feedback to see whether the changes developed in the client's reasoning more accurately reflect the situation.

Coping Strategies One prominent cognitive theorist, Donald H. Meichenbaum (1976), suggested that therapists should not only deal with clients' specific problems but also teach them cognitive and behavioral skills—*coping strategies*—that can be applied in a variety of stressful situations. He has developed a training program that can be used to "inoculate" clients against future problems and facilitate the development of self-control. His program involves determining his clients' thought patterns and strategies in stressful situations and teaching them more productive self-statements. Table 3.2 gives some examples of coping self-statements designed to be used in a variety of situations. The therapist teaches the client

when to use these statements in combatting stress and anxiety.

Learning to replace irrational self-statements with more productive ones allows the client both to adopt problem-solving strategies when faced with a problem and to self-reinforce the appropriate use of these strategies. The program has been used successfully with schizophrenics, who were trained to monitor their own behavior and thinking and to be sensitive to cues from other people that they were displaying psychotic symptoms. With this internal approach, the schizophrenics were able to improve their performance in reducing "sick talk," in proverb abstraction, and in ink-blot tests. The self-statements included comments such as "Be relevant," "Be coherent," "Make myself understood," and "Give healthy talk" (Meichenbaum, 1977).

Meichenbaum (1985) developed a more sophisticated approach to teaching coping strategies called *stress inoculation training* (SIT), which is based on the premise that self-statements influence attitudes and feelings. The idea is not to judge the statements immediately, but to test their assumptions in terms of rationality and, in doing so, transform them into more positive self-statements. Although similar to many cognitive strategies in basic assumptions and practice, SIT is aimed at teaching clients the cognitive and physical skills to deal with future problems. SIT operates like its medical counterpart, vaccines, which defend the body against future disease. SIT is used to prepare people to deal with anticipated stresses, anxieties, tensions, and a wide variety of potentially traumatic or debilitating situations. Thus it is both proactive and future oriented.

Rational-Emotive Therapy Rational-emotive therapy (RET) is based on the principle that psychological problems are produced by irrational assumptions. These thoughts continually sustain and regenerate negative emotions. If the client were to eradicate the irrational self-statements, the negative emotional reactions would also be eradicated. The RET therapist asks the client to discriminate between the real event and the unrealistic assumptions. "Not succeeding with the opposite sex is frustrating," the therapist might point out, "but the conclusion that you are a worthless failure and will never succeed does not follow. The idea that you will always fail in future encounters is an irrational belief that is producing your depression."

Table 3.2

Examples of Coping Self-Statements

Preparing for a Stressful Situation

What is it you have to do?

You can develop a plan to deal with it.

Just think about what you can do about it. That's better than getting anxious.

No negative self-statements; just think rationally.

Don't worry; worry won't help anything.

Maybe what you think is anxiety is eagerness to confront it.

Confronting and Handling a Stressful Situation

Just "psych" yourself up—you can meet this challenge.

One step at a time; you can handle the situation.

Don't think about fear; just think about what you have to do. Stay relevant.

This anxiety is what the therapist said you would feel. It's a reminder to use your coping exercises.

This tenseness can be an ally, a cue to cope.

Relax; you're in control. Take a slow deep breath.

Ah, good.

Coping with the Feeling of Being Overwhelmed

When fear comes, just pause.

Keep the focus on the present; what is it you have to do?

Label your fear from 0 to 10 and watch it change.

Coping with the Feeling of Being Overwhelmed (continued)

You should expect your fear to rise.

Don't try to eliminate fear totally; just keep it manageable.

You can convince yourself to do it. You can reason your fear away.

It will be over shortly.

It's not the worst thing that can happen.

Just think about something else.

Do something that will prevent you from thinking about fear.

Describe what is around you. That way you won't think about worrying.

Reinforcing Self-Statements

It worked; you did it.

Wait until you tell your therapist about this.

It wasn't as bad as you expected.

You made more out of the fear than it was worth.

Your damn ideas—that's the problem. When you control them, you control your fear.

It's getting better each time you use the procedures.

You can be pleased with the progress you're making.

You did it!

Source: D. H. Meichenbaum, 1976.

Once the client understands and accepts this interpretation, he or she is trained to eliminate such thoughts and to replace them with more reasonable notions. The client is also assigned "homework" tasks, such as asking others out on dates. It is emphasized that failure is possible until the client develops more social skills or meets more compatible dating partners. However, he or she is to consider these unsuccessful ventures as part of the learning experience—perhaps unpleasant, but necessary.

Ellis (1957) claimed a 90 percent success rate using RET, with an average of twenty-seven therapy sessions. Other studies (Beck, 1985; Meichenbaum, Gilmore & Fedoravicius, 1971) have also reported success. Most of the experimental support for RET has involved treatment of mild fears in college students, however; few controlled studies involve clinical populations.

Criticisms of the Cognitive Models

In many respects, the cognitive-behavioral model resembles the psychogenic models examined in Chapter 2. However, this approach shares many characteristics of the traditional behavioral models. They emphasize learned cognitions that occur within people as they interact with internally generated stimuli and external events. Altering behavior is stressed, childhood experiences are deemphasized, and insight into a problem is not considered necessary to alleviate it (Beck, 1970; Rimm & Masters, 1979). In addition, successful treatment is measured by changes in overt behavior, and therapists rely on experimental methods to validate techniques.

Yet it appears that some behaviorists remain quite skeptical of the cognitive schools. Skinner (1990), just before his death, warned that cognitions were not observable phenomena and could not form the foundations of empiricism. In this respect, he echoed the historical beliefs of John B. Watson who stated that the science of psychology was observable behaviors, not "mentalistic concepts." Although Watson's reference was to the intrapsychic dynamics of the mind postulated by Freud, Watson might have viewed cognitions in the same manner.

Cognitive theories have also been attacked by more humanistically oriented psychologists who believe that human behavior is more than thoughts and beliefs (Corey, 1991). They object to the mechanistic manner by which human beings are reduced to the sum of their cognitive parts. Do thoughts and beliefs really cause disturbances, or do the disturbances themselves distort thinking?

Criticisms have also been leveled at the therapeutic approach taken by cognitive therapists. The nature of an approach such as RET makes the therapist a teacher, expert, and authority figure. The therapist is quite direct and confrontive in identifying and attacking irrational beliefs and processes. As such, clients can readily be intimidated into acquiescing to the therapist's power and authority. Thus the therapist may misidentify the disorder suffered by the client and the client may be hesitant to challenge the beliefs of the therapist.

Although more evaluative research must be conducted before the cognitive learning approach can be evaluated, this approach, with its emphasis on the powerful influence of internal mediating processes, seems to offer an exciting new direction for behaviorists. One proponent goes so far as to speculate that psychology is undergoing a "revolution" in that cognitive and behavioral approaches are being integrated into mainstream psychological thought (Mahoney, 1977).

◆ A COGNITIVE VIEW OF STEVEN V.

What if Steve was working with a cognitively oriented therapist? How would the therapist view Steve's problems and how would he or she help him?

In essence, it is important to show Steve that the psychological problems he is experiencing derive from the many irrational beliefs that he uses to judge himself and others. First, it is very easy for us to conclude that the problems he now encounters are a function of unrealistic and illogical standards that he learned from his family and significant others in his life. This would be simplistic, however, because the real problem is not the learned values in his childhood, but rather the many dogmatic, rigid "musts," "shoulds," and "oughts" that he has creatively constructed around these standards and around the unfortunate events that occur in his life. Second, as a practicing cognitive therapist, I would attempt to work with Steve in a highly didactic, cognitive, and behavior-oriented manner, stressing Steve's need to (1) recognize the role thinking and belief systems play in his problems; (2) identify self-statements, belief systems, or assumptions that are irrational and maladaptive and rationally dispute them; and (3) learn to replace irrational self-statements with productive ones. Let us use an example to illustrate this approach.

As you recall, Steve first came to the attention of the university therapist after a breakup with his woman friend, Linda. Initially, he became severely depressed and withdrew from almost all social activities. Most of us, including Steve, could easily conclude that the reason he became depressed was because of the breakup of a valued relationship. However, this simple cause-effect analysis negates the importance of Steve's internal cognitions. Ending a relationship is certainly unpleasant and unfortunate. Most people do not feel good about such an event, and the negative reactions we experience might even be normal and expected. Nevertheless, Steve's reactions to the breakup are too severe, intense, and prolonged to be considered normal.

The breakup with Linda must have other personal significance and meaning to him, contained in irrational beliefs he holds. Using Ellis's *A-B-C* theory of personality we might say that the breakup with Linda is the activating event *A* and Steve's depression and withdrawal is the consequence *C*. Steve's beliefs and interpretations *B* about *A*, however, cause his psychological reactions *C*. It is quite clear that Steve has irrational beliefs about himself and others that are the basis of his problems. He might be saying something like this to himself: "Linda's rejection of me shows me how inadequate and worthless I am. I'll never be able to find another woman again. I'm a miserable failure as a man. No one will ever love me again." These thoughts are very active in Steve and he keeps telling himself that they are true. Some of the irrational assumptions that seem to be operating in Steve's thought processes are as follows:

1. "I should always please my parents. I must live up to their expectations or I will be a failure as a son and person."

2. "If everyone doesn't love me and approve of me, it would be awful. I'm a worthless and miserable person."

3. "I must be perfect in school. I must get straight A's. If I don't get good grades, I am stupid."

4. "A real 'man' would never be rejected by a woman. A real 'man' should always be able to perform sexually."

5. "I'm a prisoner of my past. No matter what I do I cannot change how screwed up I am. I can't help being crazy. My future looks bleak."

These irrational beliefs are at the basis of much of Steve's problems. He must be helped to distinguish between the real event and the unrealistic assumptions he makes about its consequences. Because human beings have the capacity for both rational and irrational thinking, I would utilize Steve's capacity for rational thinking to attack his belief system. Logic could help Steve recognize and dispute faulty assumptions and reasoning, using statements such as "Where is it written that one's self-worth is based on being universally loved?" He could be taught realistic and productive self-statements to replace irrational ones: "I'm catastrophizing again. It's okay to flub up occasionally. I'm a worthwhile person even though my father doesn't approve." Having Steve understand the cognitive source of his problems, helping him attack these irrational beliefs, replacing them with realistic values and standards, and correcting his faulty logic will go a long way to help Steve become a more productive and healthy individual.

THE FAMILY SYSTEMS MODEL OF PSYCHOPATHOLOGY

The biogenic and psychogenic approaches to psychopathology focus on the individual. Even the behavioral and cognitive schools of thought, though they are concerned with external or cognitive determinants of behavior, are mainly involved with assessing and altering individual behavior. Given the American emphasis on individual achievement and responsibility—our "rugged individualism"—it is not surprising that these approaches have been very popular in the United States.

The family systems model of psychopathology represents a new and emerging paradigm that redefines many traditional concepts; it does not isolate the individual as other theories do. As the term *family systems* indicates, this viewpoint holds that all members of a family are enmeshed in a network of interdependent roles, statuses, values, and norms. What one member does directly affects the entire family system. Correspondingly, people typically behave in ways that reflect family influences. Thus the **family systems model** concentrates on the family's influence on individual behavior.

We can identify three distinct characteristics of the family systems approach (Foley, 1989; Robinson, 1975). First, personality development is ruled largely by the attributes of the family, especially the way parents behave toward and around their children. Second, abnormal behavior in the individual is usually a reflection or "symptom" of unhealthy family dynamics and, more specifically, of poor communication among family members. Third, the therapist must focus on the family system, not solely on the individual, and must strive to involve the entire family in therapy (see Critical Thinking). As a result, the locus of disorder is not seen to reside within the individual, but within the family system.

Development of Personality and Identity Within the Family

One of the earliest individuals to emphasize the importance of family influences was American psychiatrist Harry Stack Sullivan (1892–1949). Sullivan started out with a strong psychoanalytic orientation but eventually broadened his focus to include inter-

Can Psychopathology Serve a Family Function?

Family systems practitioners commonly observe that when two siblings are raised under the same pathological influences, one may be normal and the other quite disturbed. Common sense, however, would lead us to expect that all siblings should be affected equally by pathological family dynamics. Why aren't they?

Can you think of any possible explanations for this phenomena? Could it be that the family systems approach is misguided and that influences outside the family are more powerful shapers of behavior than the family itself? Indeed, this is one possible explanation. Our journey into understanding abnormal behavior has shown us that biology may play a powerful role in accounting for these individual differences. Perhaps one sibling was born with a bio-

logical predisposition for the disorder while another inherited a biological apparatus that makes him or her less vulnerable to psychopathology. Or, we could use a learning analysis of the two individuals and speculate that one was the victim of faulty learning whereas the other learned more healthy and adaptive ways of dealing with the world. What other explanations might you propose?

In Chapter 2 we discuss the role of models in understanding human behavior. Paradigms, to some extent, are much broader ways of viewing the human condition. The paradigm we adopt will often determine how we view a problem. Those who see the differences in the siblings as problematic to the family systems approach have adopted a paradigm related to causality; a linear cause-

effect relationship. In psychology, when therapists speak about biochemical imbalance as causing disorders, irrational thoughts as causing negative emotions, fixations as causing regressions, or stimuli as causing responses, they have adopted a linear cause-and-effect perspective. That may be the reason why the paradoxical observation that one sibling develops a disorder while the other does not appears to negate the family systems perspective.

Now take some time and think about this question critically. How does the family systems approach explain causality? Is it linear? If not, how would you characterize it?

Family systems theory subscribes to a circular and reciprocal explanation of cause and effect. In the linear model, A causes B. In the circular

personal relations. He proposed that our concepts of self, identity, and self-esteem are formed through our interactions with "significant others," typically parents, siblings, and peers (Sullivan, 1953). Parents, of course, have the major share of responsibility for socializing the child. If parents behave toward the child as though he or she is worthwhile, the child is likely to develop a positive self-image and sense of self-worth. This sense of self, in turn, provides the emotional resilience that all people need if they are to persevere through defeats, conflicts, and the many other stressors of day-to-day life. Those parents who do not see their child as a worthwhile person and who belittle or antagonize the child may cause the child to develop a negative self-image. This negative self-image can lead to the child's making self-statements such as "I am worthless" and "If I try, I'll only fail."

Another neo-Freudian, Erik Erikson, also stressed child-parent relationships. He pointed out that parental love and attention are important for the child to develop a sense of trust (Erikson, 1968). We all need a few people on whom we can rely and in whom we can confide with confidence. Without this trust, we are likely to see the world as dangerous, hostile, and threatening. As a result, we may shun close personal relationships and avoid even casual social interactions. How trust develops in a child depends very much on the parents, as is illustrated in the following case.

Jonathan R. first came to the attention of juvenile authorities at the age of thirteen, when he was picked up for vandalism and repeated truancy from school. At age fifteen, he was arrested again, this time for shoplifting and assaulting a clerk. At first Jonathan refused to give his name or cooperate with the police in any

model, A is influenced by B, which in turn was influenced by A in the first place. Therapists bound to the linear model will look for direct correlates of behavior, and those subscribing to the circular model will view the family in relational terms and from a wholistic perspective. Does this help you any? Can the family systems theory explain the phenomenon of siblings with and without disorders? If you are still having difficulty, don't feel bad. Shifting focus from linear to circular causality and from the family as a collection of individuals to a wholistic system has proven difficult for many psychologists.

Actually, family systems theorists can account for this perplexing situation. According to family systems theory, each family has a wholeness or unity greater than the sum of its parts. An individual child may develop symptoms of a disorder not from internal conflict, but from the unhealthy values and pressures of family life. Some theorists assert that this pathological behavior may actually serve a family function. Scottish psychiatrist R. D. Laing (1965) has

applied the term *mystification* to this phenomenon. Deviances in a family, Laing contends, have meaning and purpose in the context of family interactions. A family member's "madness" may actually preserve the fragile equilibrium of the family. For example, a husband and wife who are experiencing marital discord may avoid potentially damaging conflicts in their marriage by "forcing" one of their children to play the "sick role." In this way, attention is diverted from the parents' unhappiness and unfulfilled needs. Identifying one member of the family as the problem seems to relieve the entire family system. Parents can avoid their marital conflicts, and siblings can pursue their own development.

Some family systems theorists also assert that if the identified patient is treated individually and gets better, another family member may show stronger signs of disorder. This tendency to regain a kind of family equilibrium has been called *family homeostasis*. Many families exist in a closed system: an accepted state of equilibrium or balance has been attained,

and change is unwelcome. When a child is treated outside the system and improvement occurs, it unbalances the system. The husband and wife in conflict can no longer use their "sick" child as an excuse to avoid marital conflicts. To restore balance to the system, the child may be forced to play the sick role again; the family may go to great lengths to undermine the child's treatment and consequent improvement! If this approach does not work, another sibling may begin to exhibit symptoms that represent family disorder. Or the husband and wife may begin to express their conflicts with each other in other unhealthy ways, creating an atmosphere of strife and discord.

If such analyses are accurate, an individual's abnormal behavior can serve a function in the family. This phenomenon certainly dramatizes the assertion of family therapists that treating one individual in an unhealthy family system is unproductive. The entire family should be the focus of treatment.

way. Finally, when the prospect of incarceration was raised, he relented, giving his name and the names of his parents. He was referred to a child welfare agency.

The social worker assigned to the case found Jonathan guarded, openly hostile, and suspicious of her. He responded noncommittally, disclosed a minimum of information about himself, and would not submit to any diagnostic tests until told their purpose. When a psychiatric evaluation was ordered by the court, he refused to say anything to the examining psychiatrist. During the administration of psychological tests, Jonathan appeared apprehensive and frequently stated that he knew "what you're trying to do."

A workup of Jonathan's family revealed an unemployed father who himself had numerous run-ins with the law, a mother who worked as a clerk, and two younger brothers who also attended school sporadically. The family atmosphere appeared to be extremely defensive in that all members perceived the

outside world as hostile. This was demonstrated during the social worker's first visit to Jonathan's home. When she rang the doorbell, the social worker heard noises behind the door—and the sounds of people scurrying around. After a few moments, she rang the bell again. This time she noticed curtains moving slightly as though someone were peeking at her. When she called out, asking whether anyone was home, a male voice from behind the door asked her what she wanted. She said she was the social worker who had called earlier. The voice asked if she had identification. She pushed her business card through the mail slot, and the man asked for further identification. At this point, the social worker became angry and threatened to leave, informing the man that he and his family would then have to visit the agency. At that point, she was allowed into the home.

As the social worker became familiar with the family, it became increasingly clear to her that many of

Jonathan's problems stemmed from his pathological family identity and upbringing. The father in particular raised his children to trust no one. The parents had no identifiable friends, kept primarily to themselves, and seldom ventured out of their home.

Jonathan manifested many of the behavioral characteristics of the family. His mistrust of people, tendency to be a loner, and inability to form close relationships with others were clearly evident during the time he spent at juvenile hall. When other boys made efforts to include him in their activities, he rebuffed them. In group therapy, Jonathan usually contributed only statements indicating that "You've got to look out for number one!" and "You can't trust no one."

As the case of Jonathan R. illustrates, personality and identity depend heavily on the attitudes of parents toward their children, the values they instill, and the models they provide.

Family Dynamics

By **family dynamics** we mean the day-to-day "operation" of the family system, including communication among its members. Inconsistent communication or distorted patterns of operation can cause children to develop a misconception of reality.

Early theorists proposed that psychopathology (especially schizophrenia) was the result of inconsistency in family communications (Bateson et al., 1956; Weakland, 1960). Most communications occur at two levels—verbal and nonverbal. The verbal content of a message can be enhanced or negated by its nonverbal content. For example, a father who insists, "I'm not angry!"—and raises his voice, clenches his fists, and pounds the table—is physically contradicting his verbal message. Inconsistency may also result when family members continually disqualify one another's messages. For example, a mother who tells her child one thing may have her message negated by the father: "Your mother doesn't know what she's talking about." Such contradictions create a *double bind* within the child, which may result in an inability to communicate, social withdrawal, and eventually schizophrenia (Abels, 1975, 1976; Bateson, 1978; Nichols, 1984; Smith, 1972). The process is discussed in greater detail in Chapter 15. Although the double-bind theory was very popular in the 1950s and 1960s, it has since fallen into disrepute. As a specific explanation of schizophrenia, it has been found seriously lacking. Nevertheless, faulty and dis-

torted communications continue to be strongly emphasized in family system approaches.

Communication Approaches   Among those who have emphasized the importance of clear and direct communications for healthy family system development is Virginia Satir (Bandler & Grinder, 1979; Satir, 1967). Her *conjoint family therapeutic approach* stresses the importance of teaching message-sending and message-receiving skills to family members. Like other family therapists, Satir believes that the identified patient is really a reflection of the family system gone awry. Problematic behaviors or symptoms always involve at least two people: the "feeder" and the one "fed." Satir strongly believes that the family is truly an individualized system of feeders and those fed, directors and the directed, supporters and the supported.

Satir believes that group or family communication takes place at two levels: the literal and the metacommunicative. The *metacommunicative* level can best be described as the message about the message because it reflects the sender's feelings about and intentions toward the receiver. When metacommunication contradicts literal meaning and allows no opportunity or receptivity for clarification, it can be considered dysfunctional. Pathological family systems are often the result of dysfunctional communication patterns.

The goal of family therapy is to teach families and its members healthy communication patterns. According to Satir, the therapist must clearly discern five groups of communication patterns.

1. The literal message is one of agreement; the affective (feeling tone) message is pleasing and placating.

2. The literal message is disagreement; the affective message is blaming and attacking.

3. The literal message is changing the subject; the affective message is being irrelevant or withdrawing.

4. The literal message is being reasonable; the affective message is conniving.

5. The literal message is reporting oneself; the affective message is making a place for others.

Only pattern 5 is considered to be a healthy communication pattern. All other patterns or their com-

Family interaction patterns can exert tremendous influence on a child's personality development, determining the child's sense of self-worth and the acquisition of appropriate social skills. This picture shows an Inupiat (Eskimo) family in Kotzebue, Alaska during a meal. Notice the attentiveness of the parents toward their children (communicating a sense of importance to them) and how every family member is present during the meal (emphasizing family cohesion and belonging).

binations may lead to dysfunction in the family. For example, when Father plays the "pleaser" (pattern 1), Mother plays the "blamer" (pattern 2), and the child plays "irrelevant" and withdraws (pattern 3), we may be looking at a schizophrenic family. Certain communication patterns condition children's behavior. When the communications are pathological, deconditioning is essential. Satir considers communication training to be a central feature in therapy. She believes that the effective communicator firmly states his or her case, clarifies and qualifies meaning, and asks for and considers feedback. Ineffective or dysfunctional communicators are vague and send incomplete and inconsistent messages.

Strategic Approaches The term *strategic* as applied to family therapy grew out of the ideas of Don Jackson and Jay Haley (Haley, 1963, 1977, 1987). Therapy is conceived as a power struggle between client and therapist. The crucial issue is one of control. According to this viewpoint, the identified patient is in control, making other family members around him or her feel helpless. The role of the therapist is to reestablish boundaries and restructure the family system (Haley, 1980). To shift the balance of power, the therapist must devise strategies to effect

(hence the term *strategic*) change. The word *change* best summarizes the work of the strategic therapy group. The group's general approach is to define the family problem (noting that the problem is a family problem and not only that of the symptomatic individual), determine what the family has done about it (what has and hasn't worked), establish family goals (not those of the therapist), and construct strategic interventions that disrupt the patterns that sustain the problem.

Much of the techniques developed in this approach come from the distinguished psychiatrist Milton Erickson. There have been attempts to codify the strategic ideas of Erickson and others (Watzlawick, Weakland & Fish, 1974).

Structural Approaches In the structural family approach advocated by Salvatore Minuchin (1974), disorder is seen simply as a result of a system of relationships that need to be strategically changed or restructured. Most family problems arise because members are either too involved or too little involved with each other. The following case study illustrates how family members may be too enmeshed with one another, thereby supporting a disorder within the family.

Cultural Definitions of the Family

Increasingly, family system advocates have had to work with culturally different families. Most of the concepts, principles, and techniques of family system approaches, however, have been derived from white middle-class norms. For example, we need only look at our concept of the family structure to ascertain that middle-class European Americans define the family as being composed of the biological mother, father, and children (the nuclear family). Yet almost all other minority groups have traditionally operated from an extended family system (Ho, 1987; McGoldrick, Pearce & Giordano, 1982; D. W. Sue & D. Sue, 1990). Hispanic American families consider godparents to be an intimate part of the family (they are responsible for

the moral, ethical, and religious upbringing of the child); African Americans have a family structure that may include aunts, uncles, and male and female friends; Asian Americans operate from an extended family system that may include ancestor worship; and Native Americans may subscribe to a communal family system. As a result, transferring children from one nuclear family to another within the extended system is a common practice that white therapists may not understand and consider a form of child abuse or neglect.

For example, Ho (1987) reported the case of a Native American child who had been originally taken away from the parents on recommendations of a social worker. It was ob-

served that the parents "were negligent in raising their child and did not provide proper food and shelter." The conclusion was reached after observing a very common practice in the tribe in which the child would spend one week with one family and several weeks with another. In Native American culture and custom, this was considered acceptable.

Mental health professionals need to be aware of a number of major cultural differences among minority group family values to accurately assess and understand the minority family system. These cultural values are often very difficult for European Americans to understand and may cause major difficulties in family system analysis and treatment.

Nadine G. was a victim of child abuse and incest from her father when she came to the attention of the Child Protective Services. Her high school teacher had periodically observed bruises on her neck, face, and arms throughout the school year. The fifteen-year-old would always have a seemingly good reason for the injuries, but they occurred too often. After reading a poem written by Nadine as part of a homework assignment, the teacher became convinced that Nadine was being sexually abused. In the poem, Nadine had expressed in metaphorical language the pain, fear, and agony of a young girl raped and repeatedly beaten by a trusted adult. The suspected case of child abuse was reported to the local Child Protective Services, and Nadine was subsequently removed from the family and placed in a foster home.

A former marine sergeant, Nadine's father had started sexually molesting her when she was five years old. During her younger years, Mr. G. would only engage in petting, touching, and rubbing his body against Nadine. This finally progressed to masturbation, oral sex, and at age ten, intercourse. After each of these encounters, the father would warn Nadine not to tell anyone. He threatened her with physical

harm and the break-up of the family. His abuse was not only sexual, but consisted of regular beatings and psychological torment. Mr. G. also had two older sons (ages seventeen and eighteen), whom he also beat regularly. He demanded complete obedience from the family, including his wife. The wife catered to Mr. G.'s every wish and admonished her children to do the same.

When charges of child abuse were brought against Mr. G. by the school, he vehemently denied them. He called a family meeting including his wife and two sons. During that meeting he informed them that the family was being threatened by outsiders who wanted to break them apart. In a highly agitated manner, he threatened to sue the school, and lashed out at his wife for allowing Nadine to make such false accusations. He enlisted the aid of his wife who was allowed to see the daughter. During that meeting, Mrs. G. admonished her daughter to "tell the truth" and deny the charges because "they're all in your sick mind." When Nadine indirectly inferred that she had been sexually molested, the mother became highly agitated: "Shut your mouth and never let anything like that come out again." Mrs. G. staunchly defended her hus-

1. Studies indicate that ethnic minority extended family ties are more cohesive and extensive than kinship relationships among European Americans. Most middle-class European Americans prefer individual autonomy, whereas ethnic minorities prefer collectivity. Primary allegiance is to the family, and individual autonomy and identity are downplayed for the good of the family unit. A traditional Asian American college student who desires to consult with parents before making a vocational choice may not be manifesting dependency or immaturity.

2. Many ethnic minority families are patriarchal. That is, the male partner is the primary decision maker and the female partner is relegated to a lesser role. This is particularly true of traditional Hispanic American, Asian American, and Native American cultures, and is less true for African Americans. European Americans prefer an egalitarian relationship that may not be desired among minority couples.

3. Communication patterns between parent and child in traditional white society tend to be more egalitarian than many minority groups. In Asian and Hispanic groups, however, communication may be more rigidly hierarchical (parent to child). For example, a child speaks when spoken to and is discouraged from initiating conversations. Conjoint family therapy, whose sessions are characterized by free and open expression, may be a violation of cultural norms.

4. Sibling relationships in minority families may also differ radically from their white counterparts. Traditional Asian and Hispanic cultures, for example, have firm hierarchial standards determined by age and sex. The older the sibling, the more status, responsibility, and influence he or she possesses. Also, gender is an important determinant of status. Historically, male children are more valued than female children.

Other cultural differences exist, such as how various ethnic groups view divorce and intermarriage. The mental health professional who is unaware of cultural differences may actually view these differences as pathological and deviant. It may not be that the techniques and methods of family approaches are culturally biased, so much as they are inappropriately applied. For example, Munuchin's (1974) structural approach has been used effectively with black families. This is because he recognizes that different cultures have different patterns of what is "close" and "too close" (enmeshed) and handles the issue of restructuring differently.

band, pointing out how Mr. G. worked hard for a living, that he was only a strict disciplinarian for their own good, that there was nothing wrong with him, and that they would ultimately become better people as a result of his rules and standards. Nadine was made to feel guilty for having caused the crisis.

In the short term, the charges were never proven and Nadine was returned to the family. Nadine left the family at age twenty-two, went through two marriages, and finally entered therapy at age thirty-seven, when recollections of her abuse were reported. To this day, Mr. G. continues to deny the accusations of incest with the support of his wife and two adult sons.

The dynamics of the G. family are typical of an unbalanced relationship. Here the husband exhibits a serious disorder that dominates the family, and the wife supports the husband's interpretation of reality. Suggestions that something may be wrong within the family are flatly denied. As a result, the children are daily subjected to a deviant picture of reality. Among children from such a background, the risk of psychopathology is relatively high. Minuchin might say that this family's therapeutic task is to restructure its power and rules with the ultimate goal of balancing enmeshment and detachment.

Criticisms of the Family Systems Model

The family systems approach has added an important social dimension to our understanding of abnormal behavior, and there is no denying that we are social creatures. In fact, much evidence shows that unhealthy family relationships can contribute to the development of disorders. But the family systems model is subject to a number of criticisms. For one thing, the definition of the family used by these models may be culture-bound (see Focus 3.2). Also, its basic tenets and its specific applications are difficult to study and quantify. As you will see in Chapter 15, the double-bind hypothesis is very controversial, and the controversy intensifies when the hypothesis is applied to the acquisition of severe disorders such as schizophrenia. For example, it is often difficult to obtain agreement among psychologists on whether a double bind actually exists within a given family. Then there is the fact that not all siblings raised in a pathological family environment become disturbed. It seems that factors beyond family life may be equally influential on mental health.

As we have stated frequently, a psychologist who places too much emphasis on any one model may overlook the influence of factors that are not included in that model. But exclusive emphasis on the family systems model may have particularly unpleasant consequences. Too often, psychologists have pointed an accusing finger at the parents of children who suffer from certain disorders, despite an abundance of evidence that parental influence may not be a factor in those disorders. The parents are then burdened with guilt over a situation they could not have controlled. (We discuss this problem in greater detail when we examine childhood and adolescent disorders in Chapter 17.)

Perhaps the most credible attack on the family systems theory, however, comes from the feminist perspective (Cottone, 1992). Bolgrad (1984, 1986) uses the issue of wife-battering and incest as examples of subtle biases against women in the family systems approach. This bias can be found in the language and assumptions of the systems approach. These assumptions are that (1) sexual and physical abuse serves a functional role in the family; (2) all members actively participate in perpetuating the dysfunctional system; and (3) the abused wife or sexually molested daughter is viewed as a symptom of a sick system. In essence, the family systems approach, with its emphasis on the interrelationship of parts to the whole and the belief in balance (homeostasis), may inadvertently minimize acts of violence against women. Bolgrad (1984) stated the following:

> Feminist values are clear regarding the allocation of responsibility for wife battering incidents: (1) no woman deserves to be beaten; (2) men are solely responsible for their actions. . . . From a feminist perspective, a systemic formulation is biased if it can be employed to implicate the battered woman or to excuse the abusive man. (pp. 560–561)

Such reasoning necessitates a return to linear thinking: abusive men are to be blamed for abusive incidents, and women should not be blamed. Bolgrad believes that the systemic circular causality of family systems theory breaks down in this case, especially when applied to a two- or three-year-old who is sexu-

ally abused. To even suggest that young children may have contributed to their own sodomy or rape is to truly blame the victim.

A FAMILY SYSTEMS VIEW OF STEVEN V.

What if Steven V.'s therapist were a proponent of the family systems model? We believe that he or she would view Steve and his family very much as follows.

Officially, only Steve is my client. In reality, however, Steve's father and mother are also suffering, and their pathological symptoms are reflected in Steve. My attempts to help Steve must therefore focus on the entire family. It is obvious that the relationships between Steve and his father, between Steve and his mother, and between his father and mother are unhealthy. Let me comment briefly on each of these relationships.

Relationship Between Steve and His Father   If we accept that a person's identity, self-concept, and feelings of self-worth are based on how significant others treat the person, it is not hard to see why Steve has very low self-esteem. It appears that he could do nothing right in his father's eyes. Mr. V. constantly derogated his son, seldom praised him, and always focused on Steve's inadequacies and mistakes. Steve's case records are filled with examples of this negative interaction.

- Steve had many medical problems as a young child. He was prone to ear infections and colds, had multiple allergies, and seemed to contract an unusual number of childhood illnesses. He also seemed accident prone and one time suffered a near-fatal injury when he walked into a playground swing. Instead of expressing concern and sympathy when his son was ill or hurt, Mr. V. became irritated and angry at Steve. He teased him, called him a "weakling," and blamed him for the illness or injury.

- At school Steve was frequently the butt of his classmates' pranks and was constantly teased and beaten by them. His father's reaction to these incidents was to call his son a "sissy," someone who was unmasculine and "didn't have the guts to defend himself."

Even when Steve had successes (academically he was outstanding), Mr. V. did not praise him but instead emphasized that Steve could do better still. Early in his life his father labeled him a "bookworm," a social isolate who would "never amount to anything."

As a result of this consistently negative interaction, Steve's self-concept is negative. He sees himself as inadequate and ineffectual. For this reason he withdraws from social interactions, neglects to learn new behaviors, and has a fatalistic outlook on life.

Relationship Between Steve and His Mother

This relationship is more complicated than Steve's relationship with his father. On the surface it appears that his mother was affectionate, warm, and loving toward Steve. But much of this behavior seems to have been stimulated by, or to have arisen out of, the mother's unfulfilled needs. We have considerable evidence that the mother continually gave inconsistent messages to Steve. I submit that Mrs. V. actually had a deep-seated hostility toward her son but masked it in socially appropriate ways. For example, Steve's childhood illnesses seemed to upset Mrs. V. quite a bit—not out of concern for her child, but because these illnesses interfered with her own social plans. She sent double messages to Steve: on the one hand, "I'm worried about you. Are you okay?" and, on the other, "Why did you have to get sick? Now I can't go to the theater this evening." One message is "I love and care about you," and the other is "I don't love you." Consider the confusing double bind Steve experiences. If he responds to the first message, he must deceive himself into believing that his mother loves him—a distortion of reality. If he responds to the second and more accurate message, he must acknowledge that he is unloved. He's damned if he does and damned if he doesn't. Another example of a double message is the mother's alternately seductive and withdrawing behavior toward Steve. Mrs. V. was physically seductive in having him sleep with her when she was scantily clothed, but she withdrew and punished him when he became sexually aroused.

Relationship Between Husband and Wife

Mr. and Mrs. V. had a relationship that we can characterize as isolative. Each seemed to live a separate life, even when they were together in the same house. Both had unfulfilled needs, and both denied and avoided interactions and conflicts with one another. Publicly they maintained the façade of the ideal family, but privately they seemed to care little for one another. Neither wanted to confront their unfulfilling relationship: the wife knew of the husband's extramarital affairs but pretended she didn't, and the husband knew of the wife's unhappiness but never mentioned it. To avoid dealing with their marital disappointments, the parents made Steve their scapegoat. As long as Steve was the "identified patient" and was seen as "the problem," Mr. and Mrs. V. could continue in their mutual self-deception that all was well between them.

Even though Steve does not live at home while college is in session, his psychological roots remain there, and his parents are still enormously influential in his life. It would therefore be most desirable to include the entire family in a program of therapy.

A FINAL NOTE ABOUT THE MODELS OF PSYCHOPATHOLOGY

Table 3.3 compares the models of psychopathology that we have discussed in Chapter 2 and this chapter. Each model has devout supporters who, in turn, are influenced by the model they support. But even though theory building and the testing of hypotheses are critical to psychology as a science, it seems evident that we can best understand abnormal behavior only by integrating the various approaches. We are all biological, psychological, and social beings. To neglect any one of these aspects of human life would be to deny an important part of our existence.

SUMMARY

1. The behaviorist approach evolved in the early twentieth century, at a time when the existing theories of psychology emphasized the subjective analysis of the inner—and unobservable—workings of the mind. John B. Watson proposed that psychology's goal should be the prediction and control of human behavior and that, as a science, psychology should be limited to observable and measurable events. Tra-

Table 3.3

A Comparison of the Most Influential Models of Psychopathology

	Biogenic	Psychoanalytic	Humanistic
Motivation for Behavior	State of biological integrity and health	Unconscious influences	Self-actualization
Basis for Assessment	Medical tests, self-reports, and observable behaviors	Indirect data, oral self-reports	Subjective data, oral self-reports
Theoretical Foundation	Animal and human research, case studies, and other research methods	Case studies, correlational methods	Case studies, correlational and experimental methods
Source of Abnormal Behavior	Biological trauma, heredity, biochemical imbalances	Internal: early childhood experiences	Internal: Incongruence between self and experiences
Treatment	Biological interventions (drugs, ECT, surgery, diet)	Dream analysis, free association, transference; locating unconscious conflict from early childhood; resolving the problem and reintegrating the personality	Nondirective reflection, no interpretation; providing unconditional positive regard; increasing congruence between self and experience

ditional behaviorists are concerned primarily with the influence of environmental factors on behavior through the processes of learning.

2. The traditional behavioral models of psychopathology hold that abnormal behaviors are acquired through association (classical conditioning) or reinforcement (operant conditioning). Negative emotional responses such as anxiety can be learned through classical conditioning: a formerly neutral stimulus evokes a negative response after it has been presented along with a stimulus that already evokes that response. Negative voluntary behaviors may be learned through operant conditioning if those behaviors are reinforced (rewarded) when they occur.

3. Some psychologists assert that the acquisition of many complex behaviors cannot be explained solely by classical or operant conditioning. These behaviors may, however, be acquired through observational learning, in which a person learns behaviors by observing them in other people, who act as models, and then imitating them. Pathological behavior results when inappropriate behavior is imitated or when normal behavior is inappropriately applied.

4. Cognitive models developed partly as a reaction to the criticism that traditional behaviorists ignore the influence of thought processes on behavior. According to the cognitive model, perceptions of events are mediated by thoughts and feelings, and the perception may have a greater influence on behavior than the event itself. Despite this emphasis on cognition, cognitive perspective shares many characteristics with the traditional behavioral models. Cognitive therapeutic approaches, such as cognitive restructuring, coping strategies, and rational-emotive therapy, are generally aimed at normalizing the client's perception of events.

5. The family systems model asserts that family interactions guide an individual's development of

Table 3.3 *(continued)*			
A Comparison of the Most Influential Models of Psychopathology			
Existential	**Behavioral**	**Cognitive**	**Family Systems**
Capacity for self-awareness; freedom to decide one's fate; search for meaning in a meaningless world	External influences	Interaction of external and cognitive influences	Interaction with significant others
Subjective data, oral self-reports, experiential encounter	Observable, objective data, overt behaviors	Self-statements, alterations in overt behaviors	Observation of family dynamics
An approach to understanding the human condition rather than a firm theoretical model	Animal research, case studies, experimental methods	Human research, case studies, experimental methods	Case studies, social psychological studies, experimental methods
Failure to actualize human potential; avoidance of choice and responsibility	External: learning maladaptive responses or not acquiring appropriate responses	Internal: learned pattern of irrational or negative self-statements	External: faulty family interactions (family pathology and inconsistent communication patterns)
Provide conditions for maximizing self-awareness and growth, to enable clients to be free and responsible	Direct modification of the problem behavior; analysis of the environmental factors controlling the behavior and alteration of the contingencies	Understanding relationship between self-statements and problem behavior; modification of internal dialogue	Family therapy involving strategies aimed at treating the entire family, not just the identified patient

personal identity as well as his or her sense of reality. Abnormal behavior is viewed as the result of distortion or faulty communication or unbalanced structural relationships within the family. Children who receive faulty messages from parents, or who are subjected to structurally abnormal family constellations may develop behavioral and emotional problems. Therapeutic techniques generally focus on the family as a whole, rather than on one disturbed individual.

KEY TERMS

behavioral models Theories of psychopathology that are concerned with the role of learning in abnormal behavior

classical conditioning or **respondent** A principle of learning, involving involuntary behaviors, in which responses to new stimuli are learned through association

cognitive model A principle of learning holding that conscious thought mediates, or modifies, an individual's behavior in response to a stimulus

cognitive restructuring An attempt to alter problematic cognitions by replacing them with more rational and positive thoughts

conditioned response (CR) In classical conditioning, the response made to a previously neutral stimulus

conditioned stimulus (CS) In classical conditioning, a previously neutral stimulus

counterconditioning A therapeutic means of eliminating anxiety by gradually pairing the fear-producing stimulus with a pleasant stimulus

discriminative stimulus A cue that is usually present when reinforcement occurs

extinction In classical and operant conditioning, the

process by which a response is gradually eliminated by not being reinforced

family dynamics The day-to-day "operation" of the family system

family systems model A model of psychopathology that emphasizes the influence of the family on individual behavior

generalization Responding in a similar manner to different stimuli that share common characteristics

law of effect An increase in behaviors associated with positive consequences and a reduction when associated with unpleasant ones

modeling The process of learning by observing models

negative reinforcer Increases the frequency of a behavior by removing an aversive event

observational learning theory A theory of learning that holds that people can learn new behaviors by watching other people perform those behaviors and then imitating them

operant behavior A voluntary and controllable behavior that "operates" on an individual's environment

operant conditioning A theory of learning, applying primarily to voluntary behaviors, that holds that these behaviors are controlled by the consequences that follow them

positive reinforcer Increases the frequency of the behavior it follows by providing a positive, wanted, or pleasant consequence

punishment Either the removal of a positive reinforcer or the presentation of an aversive stimulus

rational-emotive therapy (RET) The system of therapy developed by Albert Ellis that stresses that psychological problems are produced by irrational thought patterns

reinforcer In operant conditioning, a consequence that increases the frequency or magnitude of the behavior it follows; may be positive or negative

schema The underlying assumptions held by a person that are influenced by experiences, values, and perceived capabilities and by how he or she interprets events

shaping The process of developing a new or complex behavior by reinforcing successive behaviors that increasingly approximate the final goal desired by the experimenter

stimulus discrimination Being able to differentiate differences between similar stimuli

unconditioned response (UCR) In classical conditioning, the response first made to the unconditioned stimulus

unconditioned stimulus (UCS) In classical conditioning, the stimulus that elicits an unconditioned response

CHAPTER 4

Assessment and Classification of Abnormal Behavior

Among the most important tasks in the mental health field are to find the nature and rate of mental disorders, factors that cause or affect mental disorders, and effective means to treat and prevent disorders. To accomplish these tasks, therapists must collect information on the well-being of individuals and organize the information about a person's or patient's condition. Among the assessment tools available to the clinician are observation, conversations and interviews, a variety of psychological tests, and the reports of the patient and his or her relatives and friends. When the data gathered from all sources are combined and analyzed, the therapist can gain a good picture of the patient's behavior and mental state. In most cases, the information-gathering process results in a rather bulky file on the patient. The information needs to be sorted and integrated—reduced to its essentials and categorized by its similarities or how the data relate to one another.

As noted in Chapter 1, the evaluation of the information leads to a *psychodiagnosis,* which involves describing and drawing inferences about an individual's psychological state. Psychodiagnosis is often an early step in the treatment process. It is for many psychotherapists the basis on which a program of therapy is first formulated.

It usually involves obtaining a clear description of the client's behavioral patterns and classifying them based on the symptom picture that emerges. This classification of behaviors and information performs several functions. First, it helps clarify the therapist's "picture" of the client's mental state; once the data are organized, they are easier to analyze. Second, if the classification scheme is an effective one, it can lead the therapist to possible treatment programs. Third, the names of the categories within a classification scheme provide concise descriptions of, or referents to, symptoms and disorders; these descriptions facilitate communication among psychologists who try to use the same categories to convey information about clients. Finally, using a classification scheme standardizes psychological assessment procedures. That is, if particular information is required for classification, therapists tend to use the assessment techniques that provide that information. Thus classification may affect the entire psychodiagnostic process as well as the therapy that follows it. Classification is at the heart of science (Barlow, 1991).

RELIABILITY AND VALIDITY

To be useful, assessment tools and classification systems must demonstrate reliability and validity. **Reliability** refers to the degree to which evaluation tools or classification schemes yield the same results repeatedly, under the same circumstances. There are many types of reliability (Robinson, Shaver & Wrightsman, 1991). In *test-retest reliability*, a measure is given to individuals at two different points in time. For example, if we administer a measure of anxiety to individuals in the morning and then readminister the measure later in the day, the results of a reliable measure will show consistency or stability from one point in time to another. Similarly, if the items are effectively measuring anxiety, we expect the items to be related to one another. If a measure has many items that are thought to measure anxiety but the items are not correlated, the measure may be unreliable or have poor internal consistency because the items may be measuring different things. Finally, in *interrater reliability*, the consistency of different judges or raters is determined. For example, let us imagine that two clinicians are trained to diagnose individuals according to a certain classification scheme. Yet, one clinician diagnoses a patient as schizophrenic and the other diagnoses mental retardation. This classification scheme may not be amenable to making reliable diagnoses. Obviously, in interrater reliability, one clinician may simply be a poor judge; and in test-retest reliability, inconsistent re-

sults may reflect real changes in the mood of individuals. Nevertheless, in such circumstances, the reliability of the classification scheme or measurement instrument is open to question.

Validity is the extent to which a test or procedure actually performs the function that it was intended to perform. If a measure is intended to assess depression, but instead it assesses anxiety, the measure demonstrates poor validity for depression. As in the case of reliability, there are several ways to determine reliability. The most important ways are to examine criterion-related and construct validity. *Criterion-related validity* determines if a measure is related to the phenomenon in question. For example, if we devise a measure that is intended to tell us if recovering alcoholics are likely to return to drinking, and we find that those who score high on the measure start drinking again compared to those who score low, then the measure is valid. Determining *construct validity* is actually a series of tasks, all designed to see if a measure is related to expected phenomena. Let us say that a researcher has developed a questionnaire to measure anxiety. To determine construct validity, the researcher should show that the questionnaire is correlated with other measures (e.g., questionnaires or tests) of anxiety. Furthermore, we would have increased confidence that the questionnaire is measuring anxiety if it is related to other phenomena that appear in anxious people such as muscle tension, sweating, tremors, and startle responses. The questionnaire should also be unrelated to characteristics that are not consistently associated with anxiety, such as paranoia.

Questions of reliability and validity are essential to address in assessment tools and in any diagnostic system. In this chapter, we examine assessment methods and the use of assessment tools by clinicians. We also discuss the most widely employed diagnostic classification system, DSM-IV, as well as the issues of reliability and validity.

THE ASSESSMENT OF ABNORMAL BEHAVIOR

Assessment is the process of gathering information and drawing conclusions about the traits, skills, abilities, emotional functioning, and psychological problems of the individual, generally for use in developing a diagnosis. Assessment tools are necessary to the study and practice of mental health. Without them, data could not be collected, and psychologists could not conduct meaningful research, develop theories, or engage in psychotherapy. Data collection necessarily involves the use of tools to systematically record the observations, behaviors, or self-reports of individuals. Four principal means of assessment are available to clinicians: observations, interviews, psychological tests, and neurological tests. As indicated in Critical Thinking, the various methods of assessment are essential to the work of researchers and clinicians.

Observations

Observations of overt behavior provide the most basic method of assessing abnormal behavior; indeed, observation is the most basic tool in all of science. Research methods are examined in Chapter 5; we concentrate here on clinical observations. These can be either controlled or naturalistic. *Controlled observations* are made in a laboratory, clinic, or other contrived setting. *Naturalistic observations*, which are much more characteristic of the clinician's work, are observations made in a natural setting—a schoolroom, an office, a hospital ward, or a home—rather than in a laboratory. Although we primarily focus in our discussion on observing a client alone, observing interpersonal interactions, such as between client and family, are also important to determine the factors that produce and maintain disturbed behaviors (Guerin & Chabot, 1992).

Observations of behavior are usually made in conjunction with an interview, although verbal interaction is not necessary. A trained clinical psychologist watches for external signs or cues and expressive behaviors that may have diagnostic significance (Kleinmuntz, 1967). The client's general mode of dress (neat, conventional, sloppy, flashy), significant scars or tattoos, and even the type of jewelry worn may be correlated with personality traits or perhaps with disorder. Likewise, people's expressive behaviors, such as body posture, facial expression, body type, language and verbal patterns, handwriting, and self-expression through graphic art, may all reveal certain characteristics of their lives. Here is an example.

> Margaret is a 37-year-old depressive patient who was seen by one of the authors in a hospital psychiatric ward. She had recently been admitted for treatment.

It was obvious from even a casual glance that Margaret had not taken care of herself for weeks. Her face and hands were dirty. Her long hair, which had originally been done up in a bun, had shaken partially loose on one side of her head and now hung down her left shoulder. Her beat-up tennis shoes were only halfway on her stockingless feet. Her unkempt and disheveled appearance and her stooped body posture would lead one to believe she was much older than her actual age.

When first interviewed, she sat as though she did not have the strength to straighten her body. She avoided eye contact with the interviewer and stared at the floor. When asked questions, she usually responded in short phrases: "Yes," "No," "I don't know," "I don't care." There were long pauses between the questions and her answers. Each response seemingly took great effort on her part.

Some psychologists rely on trained raters or on parents, teachers, or other third parties to make the observations and gather information for assessment and evaluation. Others prefer their own observations to those of a third party. Two problems may occur when conducting an observation (Sundberg et al., 1983). First, observers must check the validity of their own interpretations of the patient's behaviors. This is particularly important when the patient is from a culture different from that of the observer. Second, if the patient is aware of being observed, he or she may behave differently, a phenomenon called **reactivity**. Observers must try to minimize the impact of their observation on the patient's behaviors.

Interviews

The clinical interview is a time-honored tradition as a means of psychological assessment. It lets the therapist observe the client as well as collect data about the person's life situation and personality. Verbal and nonverbal behaviors, as well as the content (what the client is saying) and process (how the client is communicating—with anxiety, hesitation, or anger) of communications are important to analyze (Reiser, 1988).

Depending on the particular disciplinary training of the interviewer, the interview's frame of reference and its emphasis may vary considerably. (This variability has been a source of inconsistency and error in the assessment of clients.) Psychiatrists, being trained in medicine, may be much more interested in

CRITICAL THINKING

Why Is Assessment So Important in Clinical Psychology?

To address the question of assessment's importance, we must first examine assessment in general. Obviously, all of us engage in some kind of assessment whenever we encounter someone. When we encounter strangers, we frequently ask ourselves, "What kind of person is this? Is this person friendly or unfriendly, honest or dishonest? Do I like this person?" Often, decisions are based on the appraisals that are made. Choice of a dating partner, buying a car from a salesperson, hiring staff for one's business, and type of negotiating style to use with another individual are all influenced by our assessment of the other person. Clinical psychologists are interested in assessing the feelings, attitudes, and behaviors of human beings to understand the causes of behavior and mental disorders and to prevent and treat these disorders or to promote human welfare. We know that in evaluations, errors are often

made. We misjudge people. Therefore, psychologists attempt to find reliable and valid assessment tools with which to evaluate others.

How do we know what assessment tools should be used to evaluate someone? From the wide array of assessmemt tools (observations, interviews, psychological tests, and neurological tests), clinicians must make decisions as to the tools that should be used. How are these decisions made? Most clinicians have to consider a number of issues. First, they must find out what the referral question is. What is the purpose of the evaluation—is it to assess cognitive functioning, determine the presence of depression, render a formal diagnosis, or identify organic brain damage? Specifying the referral question is important because it helps determine what clinicians look for in their assessment tools as well as which tools to use. For example, if the task is to

determine if a client is depressed, a clinical interviewer might ask about the client's moods, energy level, and sleeping patterns. Psychological tests designed to assess depression would be more appropriate to use than tests for brain damage, unless the clinician suspected that the client had organic brain damage as well. Second, the clinician must decide on the specific tools to use. Most will interview the client and make behavioral observations. With respect to the kinds of tests to use, much depends on factors such as the theoretical orientation, familiarity and expertise with the particular tests being considered, cost and ease of administration, and demonstated reliability and validity of the instrument. Because tests can only provide samples of behavior, several tests may be used. This gives a more complete and comprehensive picture of the client. Sometimes, a test battery is given. A *test battery* is a group

biological or physical variables. Social workers may be more concerned with life history data and the socioeconomic environment of the client. Clinical psychologists may be most interested in establishing rapport with clients as a form of therapy.

Likewise, variations within the discipline of psychology affect the interview. Because of their strong belief in the unconscious origin of behavior, psychoanalysts may be more interested in psychodynamic processes than in the surface content of the client's words. They are also more likely to pay particular attention to life history variables and dreams. Behaviorists are more likely to concentrate on current envi-

ronmental conditions related to the client's behavior. It should be noted, however, that in practice mental health practitioners with different therapeutic orientations can also exhibit a great deal of similarity in psychotherapeutic style.

Standardization Interviews vary in the degree to which they are structured and consistently conducted in the same manner. In some interviews, the patient is given considerable freedom about what to say and when to say it. The clinician does little to interfere with conversation or direct its flow. Psychoanalysts, who use free association, and Rogerians, who carry

of tests and measures that clinicians may routinely give to clients. In general, clinicians must evaluate the value of using additional tests. Third, the selected tests must be capable of eliciting appropriate responses from the testee or client. For example, it would not be appropriate to give a structured interview to a client who was mute, the Wechsler Adult Intelligence Scale to a young child, or the English version of the MMPI-2 to a non-English-speaking client. Based on these criteria, what assessment instruments might be used with a 23-year-old white female who has been referred after complaining of sleeplessness and feelings of panic?

Can we accurately assess the status of members of different cultural groups? Problems in assessment often occur in trying to assess members of ethnic minority groups or individuals from different cultures. Brislin (1993) has identified several major problems, including the equivalence of concepts and scales. First, certain concepts may not be equivalent across cultures. For instance, Americans and the Baganda of East Africa have different concepts of intelligent behavior. In the United States, one indicator of intelligence is quickness in mental reasoning; in East Africa,

slow, deliberate thought is considered a part of intelligence. Obviously, tests of intelligence devised in the two cultures would differ. Individuals taking the tests could be considered intelligent on one culture's measure but not the other. Second, scalar or metric equivalence refers to whether scores on assessment instruments are really equivalent in cross-cultural research. For example, many universities use the Scholastic Aptitude Test (SAT), which has a verbal and quantitative component, as a criterion for admissions. Do the tests scores mean the same thing for different groups in terms of assessing academic potential, achievements, and ability to succeed? SAT scores do tend to moderately predict subsequent university grades. Sue and Abe (1988), however, found that the ability of the SAT score to predict success varies according to ethnicity and the components of the SAT. Whereas the SAT verbal component was a good predictor of university grades for whites, the SAT quantitative portion was a good predictor of grades for Asian American students. Thus, Asian American and white students who have the same SAT scores may receive very different grades. What are the implications of these findings?

How are tests and assessments interpreted? After collecting the results of interviews and tests, the clinician must interpret the data. Some measures, such as the MMPI-2, can provide interpretations of the client through a formal scoring of the client's responses; for others, the clinician may primarily rely on clinical judgments to interpret the responses. The information is integrated by trying to draw generalities suggested by the findings and to explain consistencies and inconsistencies in the data. Many clinicians form hypotheses derived from one measure to see if the hypotheses are confirmed on other measures. This is important because our assessment tools are not perfectly valid. If test results are inconsistent, further tests may be administered. Can you think of some reasons why test results vary?

Finally, on the basis of the assessment, the clinician may decide to conduct further evaluations or come to some conclusion about the client's diagnosis, appropriate treatments, and prognosis. The entire process of assessment is complex, entailing a great deal of skill and judgment. We hope that by raising these questions you'll begin to develop the skills necessary for assessment.

on nondirective therapy, tend to conduct highly unstructured interviews. Behaviorists tend to use more structured interviews.

The most highly structured interview is the formal standardized interview. The questions are usually arranged as a checklist, complete with scales for rating answers. The interviewer uses the checklist to ask the same set of questions of each interviewee, so that errors are minimized. One of the most complex structured interviews is the Structured Clinical Interview for DSM-III-R (SCID). The purpose of the interview is to enable a clinical interviewer to arrive at a diagnosis. Slightly different forms are available for in-

patients, outpatients, and nonpatients. The clinician asks open-ended questions and then makes clinical judgments; the clinician asks follow-up questions depending on the client's previous responses (McReynolds, 1989).

Errors In the field of mental health, straightforward questions do not always yield usable or accurate information. Believing personal information to be private, patients may refuse to reveal it, may distort it, or may lie about themselves. Furthermore, many patients may not be able to articulate their inner thoughts and feelings. The interview should

During the clinical interview the therapist can observe and gather information about the client. Moreover, the client can use the interview to gather important information about the therapist, such as his or her training, theoretical orientation, licensure status, and overall manner and style.

therefore be considered a measurement device that is fallible and subject to error (Wiens, 1983).

Three sources of interviewing errors were summarized by Kleinmuntz (1967). One is the interview process itself and the relationship between the interviewer and interviewee. If either the client or the clinician does not respect the other, or if one or the other is not feeling well, information exchange may be blocked. A second source of error may be intense anxiety or preoccupation on the part of the interviewee; his or her revelations may be inconsistent or inaccurate. Third, the interviewer may be a source of error. A clinician's unique style, degree of experience, and theoretical orientation definitely will affect the interview.

Psychological Tests

Psychological tests have been used to assess personality, maladaptive behavior, development of social skills, intellectual abilities, vocational interests, and

brain damage. Tests have also been developed for the purpose of understanding personality dynamics and conflicts. They vary in form (that is, they may be oral or written and may be administered to groups or to individuals), structure, degree of objectivity, and content. Most do, however, share two characteristics. First, they provide a standard situation in which certain kinds of responses are elicited. The same instructions are given to all who take the same test, the same scoring is applied, and similar environmental conditions are maintained to ensure that the responses are due to each test taker's unique attributes rather than to differences in situations. Second, by comparing responses with norms, the therapist uses these responses to make inferences about the underlying traits of the person. For instance, a person who answers yes to questions such as "Is someone trying to control your mind?" more frequently than most other people answer yes might be assumed to be responding in a manner similar to diagnosed paranoids.

In the remainder of this section, we examine two different types of personality tests (projective and objective) and tests of intelligence and brain damage.

Projective Personality Tests   In a **projective personality test,** the test taker is presented with ambiguous stimuli, such as inkblots, pictures, or incomplete sentences, and asked to respond to them. The stimuli are generally novel, and the test is relatively unstructured. Conventional or stereotyped patterns of response usually do not fit the stimuli. The person must "project" his or her attitudes, motives, and other personality characteristics into the situation. The nature of the appraisal is generally well disguised: subjects are often unaware of the true nature or purpose of the test and usually do not recognize the significance of their responses. Based largely on a psychoanalytic perspective, projective tests presumably tap into the individual's unconscious needs and motivations.

No matter which form of test is used, the goal of projective testing is to get a multifaceted view of the total functioning person, rather than a view of a single facet or dimension of personality. We will concentrate on inkblot descriptions and storytelling because they are both popular and typical of projective tests.

The *Rorschach technique* was devised by Swiss psychiatrist Hermann Rorschach in 1921 for personality appraisal. A Rorschach test consists of ten cards

The Rorschach technique uses a number of cards, with each showing a symmetrical inkblot design. The earlier cards in the set are black and white, while the later cards are more colorful. A client's responses to the inkblots are interpreted according to assessment guidelines and can be compared by the therapist to the responses that other clients have made.

displaying symmetrical inkblot designs. The cards are presented one at a time to subjects, who are asked (1) what they see in the blots and (2) what characteristics of the blots make them see that. Inkblots are considered appropriate stimuli because they are ambiguous, are nonthreatening, and do not elicit learned responses.

What people see in the blots, whether they attend to large areas or details, whether they respond to color, and whether their perceptions suggest movement are assumed to be symbolic of inner promptings, motivations, and conflicts. Subjects react in a personal and "unlearned" fashion because there are no right or wrong answers. These reactions are interpreted by the psychologist. Both the basic premise of the Rorschach test and the psychologist's interpretation of the symbolism within the patient's responses are strongly psychoanalytic. For example, seeing eyes or buttocks may imply paranoid tendencies; fierce animals may imply aggressive tendencies; blood may imply strong uncontrolled emotions; food may imply dependency needs; and masks may imply avoidance of personal exposure (Klopfer & Davidson, 1962).

There are actually a variety of approaches to interpreting and scoring Rorschach responses. The most extensive and recent is that of Exner (1983, 1990), whose scoring system is based on reviews of research findings and studies of the Rorschach technique. Exner thinks of the Rorschach technique as a problem-solving task; test takers are presented with ambiguous stimuli that they interpret according to their preferred mode of perceptual-cognitive processing. Exner's system has also yielded indexes of specific disorders such as depression, although the adequacy of the Rorschach technique in assessing specific disorders is a matter of continuing research (Ball et al., 1991). Because it relies on research findings and normative data, Exner's system is becoming the standard for scoring the Rorschach test (Weiss, 1988).

The *Thematic Apperception Test (TAT)* was first developed by Henry Murray in 1935 (Murray & Morgan, 1938). It consists of thirty picture cards, each typically depicting two human figures. Their poses and actions are vague and ambiguous enough to be open to different interpretations. Some cards

In the Thematic Apperception Test, clients tell a story about each of a series of pictures they are shown. These pictures—often depicting one, two, or three people doing something—are less ambiguous than Rorschach inkblots.

are designated for specific age levels or for a single sex, and some are appropriate for all groups. Like the Rorschach technique, the TAT taps underlying motives, drives, and personality processes through projection. Most clinicians agree, however, that the TAT is best at uncovering aspects of interpersonal relationships.

Generally, twenty TAT cards are shown to the subject, one at a time, with instructions to tell a story about each picture. Typically, the tester says, "I am going to show you some pictures. Tell me a story about what is going on in each one, what led up to it, and what its outcome will be." The entire story is recorded verbatim. There is usually no limit on time or the length of the stories.

The subject's responses are interpreted by a trained clinician, either subjectively or by using a formal scoring system. Both interpretations usually take

into account the style of the story (length, organization, and so on); recurring themes such as retribution, failure, parental domination, aggression, and sexual concerns; the outcome of the story in relationship to the plot; primary and secondary identification (the choice of hero or secondary person of importance); and the handling of authority figures and sex relationships. The purpose is to gain insight into the subject's conflicts and worries as well as clues about his or her core personality structure.

Other types of projective tests include the sentence-completion test and draw-a-person tests. In the *sentence-completion test*, the subject is given a list of partial sentences and is asked to complete each of them. Typical partial sentences are "My ambition," "My mother was always," and "I can remember." Clinicians try to interpret the meaning of the subject's responses. In *draw-a-person tests* such as the Machover D-A-P (Machover, 1949), the subject is actually asked to draw a person. Then he or she may be asked to draw a person of the opposite sex. Finally, the subject may be instructed to make up a story about the characters that were drawn or to describe the first character's background. Many clinicians analyze these drawings for size, position, detail, and so on, assuming that the drawings provide diagnostic clues. For example, persons suffering from organic brain disorders may draw disproportionately large heads. The validity of such assumptions is open to question, and well-controlled studies cast doubt on diagnostic interpretations (Anastasi, 1982).

The analysis and interpretation of responses to projective tests are subject to wide variation. Clinicians given the same data frequently disagree with one another about scoring. Much of this disparity is caused by differences in clinicians' orientation, skills, and personal style. But, as noted earlier, the demonstrably low reliability and validity of these instruments means that they should be used with caution and in conjunction with other assessment measures (Weiss, 1988). And even when projective tests exhibit reliability, they may still have low validity. For example, many clinicians agree that certain specific responses to the Rorschach inkblots indicate repressed anger. The fact that many clinicians agree makes the test reliable, but those specific responses could indicate something other than repressed anger. Illusory correlations may exist, and clinicians may erroneously link a patient's response to the existence of a syndrome (Chapman & Chapman, 1967). In general, projective tests may yield important information when they are interpreted by clinicians who are highly skilled and insightful in their use. Because many projective tests are subjectively interpreted by clinicians in accordance with their intuition, however, overall validity of the tests is low.

Objective Personality Inventories Unlike projective tests, **objective personality tests** supply the test taker with a list of alternatives from which an answer is selected. The "questions" are usually self-descriptive statements with which subjects are asked to either agree or disagree. Because a predetermined score is assigned to each possible answer, human judgmental factors in scoring and interpretation are minimized. In addition, subjects' responses and scores can be compared readily.

Perhaps the most widely used personality inventory is the *Minnesota Multiphasic Personality Inventory*, or *MMPI* (Hathaway & McKinley, 1943). The MMPI was recently revised by Butcher and colleagues into the MMPI-2 (see Butcher, 1990; Graham, 1990; Greene, 1991). The revisions were intended to restandardize the inventory, refine the wording of certain items, eliminate items that were considered outdated, and include appropriate representation of ethnic minority groups. Table 4.1 shows the possible responses to ten sample items and the kinds of responses that contribute to a high rating on each scale. This test consists of 567 statements; subjects are asked to indicate whether each statement is true or false as it applies to them. There is also a "cannot say" alternative, but clients are strongly discouraged from using this category because too many such responses can invalidate the test.

The test taker's MMPI-2 results are rated on ten clinical scales and three validity scales. The clinical scales were originally constructed by analyzing the responses of different types of diagnosed psychiatric patients (and the responses of normal subjects) to the 567 test items to determine what kinds of responses each of the various types of psychiatric patients usually made. The validity scales assess the degree of candor, confusion, and falsification. They help the clinician detect potential faking or special circumstances that may affect the outcome of other scales.

A basic assumption of the original version of the MMPI was that people whose MMPI answers are similar to those of diagnosed patients are likely to behave similarly to those patients. However, single-scale interpretations are fraught with hazards. Although a person with a high rating on Scale 6 may be labeled paranoid, many persons with paranoia are not detected by this scale. Interpretation of the MMPI-2 scales can be quite complicated and require special training. Generally, multiple-scale interpretations (pattern analysis) and characteristics associated with the patterns are examined. The MMPI-2 should be used by clinicians who have mastered its intricacies and who understand relevant statistical concepts (Graham, 1990; Newmark, 1985).

A number of criticisms have been leveled against personality inventories:

1. The fixed number of alternatives offered can limit subjects in presenting a true picture of themselves. Being asked to answer true or false to the statement "I am suspicious of people" does not permit an individual to qualify the item in any way.

2. Although some personality tests are devised to measure "normal" psychological traits, most clinicians tend to be most alert to responses that may signal disorder. Thus the best the subject can do is avoid a "bad" score.

3. Many individuals are able to fake their scores in a direction they see as desirable (for example, to secure a psychiatric discharge from the army or to get a job).

4. A subject's unique response style or response set may distort the results. For example, many people have a pressing need to present themselves in a favorable light, and this can cause them to give answers that are socially acceptable but inaccurate.

5. Interpretations of responses of people from different cultural groups may not be accurate if norms for these groups have not been developed.

Despite these objections, personality inventories are widely used. Some, like the MMPI-2, have been extensively researched and their validity in many cases has been established. Sophisticated means have also been found to control for response sets (the tendency to respond to test items in a certain way irrespective of content) and for faking, and, as noted earlier, attempts have been made to establish the

Table 4.1

The Ten MMPI-2 Clinical Scales and Sample MMPI-2 Test Items

Sample Items

Ten MMPI Clinical Scales with Simplified Descriptions	I like mechanics magazines.	I have a good appetite.	I wake up fresh and rested most mornings.	I think I would like the work of a librarian.	I am easily awakened by noise.	I like to read newspaper articles on crime.	My hands and feet are usually warm enough.	My daily life is full of things that keep me interested.	I am about as able to work as I ever was.	There seems to be a lump in my throat much of the time.
1. Hypochondriasis (Hs)—Individuals showing excessive worry about health with reports of obscure pains.		NO	NO					NO	NO	
2. Depression (D)—People suffering from chronic depression, feelings of uselessness, and inability to face the future.		NO		YES				NO	NO	
3. Hysteria (Hy)—Individuals who react to stress by developing physical symptoms (paralysis, cramps, headaches, etc.)		NO	NO			NO	NO	NO	NO	YES
4. Psychopathic Deviate (Pd)—People who show irresponsibility, disregard social conventions, and lack deep emotional responses.								NO		
5. Masculinity-Femininity (Mf)—People tending to identify with the opposite sex rather than their own.	NO			YES						
6. Paranoia (Pa)—People who are suspicious, sensitive, and feel persecuted.										
7. Psychasthenia (Pt)—People troubled with fears (phobias) and compulsive tendencies.			NO					NO		YES
8. Schizophrenia (Sc)—People with bizarre and unusual thoughts or behavior.								NO		
9. Hypomania (Ma)—People who are physically and mentally overactive and who shift rapidly in ideas and actions.										
10. Social Introversion (Si)—People who tend to withdraw from social contacts and responsibilities.										

Source: Adapted from Dahlstrom & Welsh, 1965.
Note: The answers shown on the grid contribute to high ratings on the related clinical scales. Item 5 illustrates a male's response.

cross-cultural validity of instruments such as the MMPI-2. In general, inventories are easier to administer than projective tests, are inexpensive, and can be scored without much difficulty compared with projective tests. (In fact, some inventories are now scored and interpreted by computer.) These features make the use of objective personality inventories desirable, especially in the busy clinic or hospital environment.

Moreover, although progress has been agonizingly slow, the predictive ability and validity of personality assessment have been improved. **Psychometrics**—the techniques used in making mental measurements—are becoming increasingly sophisticated. Further refinement will be achieved when situational variables that help determine behaviors can be taken into account and when fluctuations in mood and other more stable personality processes can be measured.

Intelligence Tests Intelligence testing has two primary diagnostic functions and one secondary function. First, it is used to obtain an estimate of a person's current level of cognitive functioning, called the *intelligence quotient (IQ)*. An IQ score indicates an individual's level of performance relative to the performance level of others of the same age. As such, it is an important aid in predicting school performance and detecting mental retardation. (Through statistical procedures, IQ test results are converted into numbers such that 100 is the mean, or average, score. An IQ score of about 130 indicates performance exceeding that of 95 percent of all same-aged peers.) Second, intelligence testing is used to assess intellectual deterioration in organic or functional psychotic disorders. Third, an individually administered intelligence test may yield additional useful data for the clinician. The therapist may also find important observations of how the subject approached the task (systematic versus disorganized), handled failure (depression, frustration, or anger), and persisted in (or gave up) the task.

The two most widely used intelligence tests are the *Wechsler Scales* (Wechsler, 1981b) and the *Stanford-Binet Scales* (Terman & Merrill, 1960; Thorndike, Hagen & Sattler, 1986). The Wechsler Adult Intelligence Scale (the WAIS and its revised version WAIS-R) is administered to persons aged sixteen and older, although two other forms are appropriate for

Intelligence tests provide valuable information about intellectual functioning and can help psychologists to assess mental retardation and intellectual deterioration. Although many of these tests have been severely criticized as being culturally biased, they can be beneficial tools, if used appropriately.

children aged six to sixteen (WISC-R) and four to six (WPPSI-R). The WAIS-R consists of six verbal and five performance scales, which yield verbal and performance IQ scores. These scores are combined to present a total IQ score. Table 4.2 shows subtest items similar to those used in the WAIS-R.

The Stanford-Binet Scale is used for people aged two and older. Much more complicated in administration and scoring, and not standardized on an adult population, the Stanford-Binet requires considerable skill in its use. The test procedure is designed to establish a basal age (the subject passes all subtests for that age) and a ceiling age (the subject fails all subtests for that age), from which an IQ score is calculated. In general, the WISC-R is preferred over the

Table 4.2

Simulated Items for the Wechsler Adult Intelligence Scale—Revised (WAIS—R)

Information

1. How many nickels make a dime?
2. What is steam made of?
3. What is pepper?

Comprehension

1. Why do some people save sales receipts?
2. Why is copper often used in electrical wire?

Arithmetic (all calculated "in the head")

1. Sue had 2 pieces of candy and Joe gave her 4 more. How many pieces of candy did Sue have altogether?
2. If 2 pencils cost 15¢, how much will a dozen pencils cost?

Similarities

In what way are the following alike?

1. lion/tiger
2. saw/hammer
3. circle/square

Vocabulary

What is the meaning of the following words?

1. chair
2. mountain
3. guilt
4. building
5. foreboding
6. prevaricate
7. plethora

Source: Wechsler Adult Intelligence Scale—Revised. Copyright © 1981, 1955 by The Psychological Corporation. Reproduced by permission. All rights reserved.

Stanford-Binet for school-age children (LaGreca & Stringer, 1985). It is easier to administer and yields scores on different cognitive skills (such as verbal and performance subtests).

Some interesting research has been conducted on possible physiological measures of intelligence. When individuals are exposed to an auditory stimulus, brain reactions to the stimulus can be monitored by electroencephalogram (EEG) recordings of the brain waves. Matarazzo (1992) has noted that brain wave patterns have been found to be strongly correlated with IQ scores on the WAIS. Moreover, his review of research also showed that measures of intellectual functioning were related to the rate of glucose metabolism in certain brain regions, as revealed by positron emission tomography (a technique described later in this chapter). Even if the findings prove to be valid, interpretations of such results are difficult to make. We cannot assume that physiological measures are somehow "superior" indicators of intelligence compared to performance on the WAIS-R.

IQ testing (and some other standardized testing) has come under attack by many ethnic groups. There are four major issues. First, some investigators believe that IQ tests have been popularized as a means of measuring innate intelligence, when in truth the tests largely reflect cultural and social factors (Garcia, 1981; Williams, 1974). The tests may therefore bestow an unfair advantage on members of the groups whose culture they reflect. Second, and related to the first point, is the issue of the predictive validity of IQ tests. That is, do IQ test scores accurately predict the future behaviors or achievements of different cultural groups? Proponents and critics disagree on this point (Anastasi, 1982). Third, investigators have disagreed over criterion variables (in essence, what is actually being predicted by IQ tests). For example, two investigators may be interested in the ability of IQ tests to predict future success. The first may try to find a correlation between test scores and grades subsequently received in school. The second investigator may argue that grades are a poor indicator of success—that leadership skills and ability to work with people are better indicators of success. Fourth, some researchers have questioned whether our current conceptions of IQ tests and intelligence are adequate. A number of researchers have proposed that intelligence is a multidimensional attribute. Taylor (1990) stated that an important aspect of intelligence, and one that cannot be adequately assessed using IQ tests, is social intelligence or competency. Social skills may be important in areas such as problem solving, adaptation to life, ability to utilize resources, and social knowledge. The controversies over the validity and usefulness of IQ testing may never fully subside. Some continue to claim that IQ tests demonstrate predictive validity for many important attributes including future success (Barrett & Depinet, 1991), although others maintain that such tests are biased and limited (Helms, 1992). It is beyond the scope of this chapter to fully discuss intelligence testing.

Reliance on IQ scores has resulted in discriminatory actions. In California, for example, black or African American children were in the past disproportionately assigned to classes for the educable mentally retarded on the basis of IQ results. Mercer (1979) has argued that all cultural groups have the same average intellectual potential. On a given IQ test, members of a cultural minority may score low, not because of mental retardation, but because they are less familiar with the tasks required on such tests. She has developed the System of Multicultural Pluralistic Assessment, through which performance on the WISC-R is assessed in relation to that of groups with similar social and cultural backgrounds. In other words, a person is compared with others who have similar backgrounds, rather than with others from different backgrounds. This assessment procedure results in fewer children who represent ethnic minorities being assigned to classes for the mentally retarded.

The Kaufman Assessment Battery for Children (K-ABC)   An increasingly popular means of evaluating the intelligence and achievement of children aged 2½ to 12½ years is the *Kaufman Assessment Battery for Children (K-ABC)*. Based on theories of mental processing developed by neuropsychologists and cognitive psychologists, the K-ABC is intended for use with both the general population and special populations. For example, the assessment battery has been employed with children who have hearing or speech impairments and who have learning disabilities. Because of its reliance on visual stimuli, however, the K-ABC is unsuitable for the visually impaired (Kaufman et al., 1985).

The K-ABC can also be used with exceptional children and members of ethnic minority groups. Its applicability to diverse groups has been attributed to

measures that (1) are less culturally dependent than those found on traditional tests and (2) focus on the process used to solve problems rather than on the specific content of test items. Children are administered a wide variety of tasks, such as copying a sequence of hand movements performed by the examiner, recalling numbers, assembling triangles to match a model, and demonstrating reading comprehension, and verbal performance and nonverbal performance are assessed. For certain language-disordered children or those who do not speak English, nonverbal performance can be used to estimate intellectual functioning.

A Spanish-language version of the K-ABC is available, and norms for black and Hispanic children have been developed. Interestingly, differences in performance between white and ethnic minority children are much lower on the K-ABC than on traditional IQ tests. Kaufman and Kaufman (1983) and Kaufman and colleagues (1985) reported that the K-ABC has high reliability and validity, and Reynolds, Kamphaus, and Rosenthal (1989) proposed that the K-ABC will continue to provide a comprehensive, unique, and useful assessment tool for children. This approach offers promise in the effort to devise more culturally unbiased tests of intelligence. Taylor (1990) also believes that the K-ABC is more likely than traditional IQ tests to assess social intelligence because many of the subscales measure performance using social information.

Tests for Brain Damage   Clinical psychologists, and especially those who work in a hospital setting, are concerned with detecting and assessing **organicity** (damage to the central nervous system). Organic brain damage can sometimes be identified by the use of individual intelligence tests such as the WAIS-R. On the WAIS-R, discrepancy between an individual's verbal and performance scores or the pattern of scores on the individual subtests often suggests possible organicity. For example, a difference of twenty points between verbal and performance scores on the WAIS-R may indicate the possibility of brain damage. Subtests that measure verbal concept formation or abstracting ability (comparison and comprehension) can also reveal brain damage. Because impaired abstract thinking may be characteristic of organicity, a lower score on this scale (when accompanied by other signs) must be investigated.

FIGURE 4.1 The Nine Bender Designs

The figures presented to subjects are shown on the left. The distorted figures drawn by subjects are possibly indicative of organicity (brain damage) and are shown on the right.

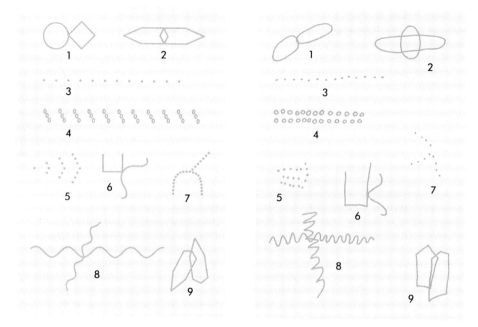

Source: The American Orthopsychiatric Association, 1938.

One of the routine means of assessing organicity is the *Bender-Gestalt Visual-Motor Test,* developed by Bender (1938) and shown in Figure 4.1. Nine geometric designs, each drawn in black on a piece of white cardboard, are presented one at a time to the subject, who is asked to copy them on a piece of paper. Certain errors in the copies are characteristic of neurological impairment. Among these are rotation of figures, perseveration (continuation of a pattern to an exceptional degree), fragmentation, oversimplification, inability to copy angles, and reversals.

The *Halstead-Reitan Neuropsychological Test Battery,* developed by Reitan from the earlier work of Halstead, has been used successfully to differentiate patients with brain damage from those without brain damage and to provide valuable information about the type and location of the damage (Boll, 1983). The full battery consists of eleven tests, although several are often omitted. Clients are presented with a series of tasks that assess sensorimotor, cognitive, and perceptual functioning, including abstract concept formation, memory and attention, and auditory perception. The full battery takes more than six hours to administer, so it is a relatively expensive

and time-consuming assessment tool. Versions of the Halstead-Reitan Battery are available for children aged five and older (Nussbaum & Bigler, 1989), and normative data for children have been collected.

A less costly test for organicity is the *Luria-Nebraska Neuropsychological Battery,* which requires about 2½ hours to administer and is more standardized in content, administration, and scoring than the Halstead-Reitan Battery. Developed by Golden and colleagues (1981), this battery includes twelve scales that assess motor functions, rhythm, tactile functions, visual functions, receptive and expressive speech, memory, writing, intellectual processes, and other functions. Validation data indicate that the battery is highly successful in screening for brain damage and quite accurate in pinpointing damaged areas (Anastasi, 1982). A children's version has been developed (Golden, 1989). Although the battery has been shown to differentiate brain-damaged from normal children, its ability to discriminate between different types of learning disabilities has been questioned (Morgan & Brown, 1988). Golden (1989) suggested that other tests be used in conjunction with the Luria-Nebraska when clinicians must make detailed analysis of specific diagnostic decisions.

Recent neurological tests have dramatically improved our ability to study the brain and to assess brain damage. In magnetic resonance imaging, radio waves are used to produce detailed pictures of a person's brain.

Neurological Tests

In addition to psychological tests, a variety of neurological medical procedures are available for diagnosing brain damage. For example, brain x-ray studies can often detect tumors. A more sophisticated procedure, *computerized axial tomography (CAT) scan*, involves repeatedly scanning different areas of the brain with beams of x-rays. With the assistance of a computer, a three-dimensional image of the structure of the brain emerges, and the results of the CAT scan provide a detailed view of brain deterioration or abnormality. In addition to the study of brain damage, CAT scans have also been used to study brain tissue abnormalities among patients diagnosed with schizophrenia, affective disorders, Alzheimer's disease, and alcoholism (Coffman, 1989). More recently, *positron emission tomography (PET) scan* has been developed to study the physiological and biochemical processes of the brain, rather than the anatomical structures seen in the CAT scan. In PET scans, a radioactive substance is injected into the patient's bloodstream. The scanner detects the substance as it is metabolized in the brain. Information can then be gained about brain functioning. As in the case of CAT scans, PET scans have been used with a variety of mental disorders and brain diseases. Characteristic metabolic patterns have been observed in many of these disorders (Holcomb et al., 1989). A widely used examination involves the *electroencephalograph (EEG)*, in which electrodes are attached to the skull. The electrical activity (brain waves) is recorded from the electrodes, and abnormalities in the activity can provide information as to the presence of tumors or other brain conditions. Finally, *magnetic resonance imaging (MRI)* can produce an amazingly clear "picture" of the brain and its tissues. By creating a magnetic field around the patient and using radio waves, abnormalities in the brain can be detected. The pictures are reminiscent of postmortem brain slices. Because of its superior clear pictures, MRI may eventually supplant CAT scans (Andreasen, 1989).

These neurological techniques, coupled with psychological tests, are increasing our diagnostic accuracy and understanding of brain functioning and disorders. Matarazzo (1992) predicted that in the future such techniques will allow therapists to make more precise diagnoses and to pinpoint precise areas of the brain that are affected by disorders such as Alzheimer's and Huntington's diseases.

The Ethics of Assessment

In recent years, a strong antitesting movement has developed in the United States. Issues such as the confidentiality of a client's records, invasion of privacy, client welfare, cultural bias, and unethical practices have increasingly been raised (Bersoff, 1981). In assessing and treating emotionally disturbed people, the clinical psychologist must often ask embarrassing questions or use tests that may be construed as invasions of privacy. In many cases, the clinician may not know beforehand whether the results of the tests will prove beneficial to the client. Yet to exclude testing because it may offend the client or place him or her in an uncomfortable position could ultimately deprive the client of the test's long-range benefits.

Some people strongly criticize tests on the grounds that they can have undesirable social consequences. They ask, "Who will use the test results, and for what purpose is the test employed?" Test results may be used to the client's detriment in some instances. Tests may also be inaccurate, causing serious misdiagnosis and its consequences. Note the fears and concerns over the possible widespread use of tests to detect antibodies to the HIV virus (AIDS) and drug abuse, as well as the use of the polygraph in job settings.

Psychological testing has ethical, legal, and societal implications that go beyond the field of psychology. Psychologists should be aware of these implications and should guard against the misuse of test results. They should also carefully weigh the consequences of permitting such considerations to interfere with devising, improving, and applying tests that will benefit their patients. The mental health professions and the general public are increasingly aware of the need to guard against possible abuses and to continually refine and improve classification systems and assessment procedures.

As indicated in Focus 4.1, more sophisticated use of computers in the mental health professions may be likely in the near future (Sundberg et al., 1983). At least one clinician has predicted that assessment and psychological testing will be applied more and more broadly as computer use spreads (Cummings, 1984).

Finally, there is also the problem of using psychological tests or assessment procedures to assess the status of individuals from different cultures. Do therapists of different ethnicities evaluate the same client behaviors differently? This question was examined in one study. Li-Repac (1980) had five Chinese American and five European American male therapists rate Chinese- and European American male clients who appeared on a videotaped interview. The results revealed that therapists evaluate clients of other ethnicities more negatively than they evaluate clients of their own ethnicities. European American therapists rated Chinese American clients as anxious, awkward, confused, and nervous, while Chinese American therapists perceived the same clients as alert, ambitious, adaptable, honest, and friendly. The European American clients, who were deemed active, aggressive, rebellious, and outspoken by Chinese American therapists, were seen as affectionate, adventurous, sincere, and easy-going by European American therapists. In addition, European American therapists rated Chinese American clients as more depressed, more inhibited, less socially poised, and having lower capacity for interpersonal relationships than did Chinese American therapists. Similarly, Chinese American therapists rated European American clients as more severely disturbed than did European American therapists. These findings suggest that judgments about psychological functioning depend at least in part on whether therapists are of the same ethnic background as their clients. Because tests or procedures may not be normed, standardized, or widely used on individuals from different cultural groups or because of cultural biases, clinicians should consider some of the recommendations discussed in Critical Thinking.

THE CLASSIFICATION OF ABNORMAL BEHAVIOR

The goal of having a **classification system** for abnormal behaviors is to provide distinct categories, indicators, and nomenclature for different patterns of behavior, thought processes, and emotional disturbances. Thus the pattern of behavior that is classified as *paranoid schizophrenia* should be clearly different from the pattern named *borderline personality*. At the same time, the categories should be constructed in such a way as to accommodate wide variation in these patterns. That is, the clinician should be able to categorize paranoid schizophrenic behavior as such, even when the patient does not show the "perfect" or "textbook" paranoid schizophrenic pattern.

Computer Assessment: A Substitute for Clinicians?

For decades, computers have been used to score the test results of clients and to provide psychological profiles of clients. More recently, computer programs have become available to administer clinical interviews, IQ tests, personality inventories, and projective tests. They may also interpret responses of clients or other persons such as applicants for jobs. The computers are programmed, for example, to simulate a structured clinical interview. Individuals who are being assessed sit before a keyboard and answer questions shown on the computer screen.

Using computer assessment has some advantages. First, with the rising costs of mental health care, this technique can free up the time of clinicians and other personnel who have traditionally administered the interviews or tests. Scoring and interpretation can be easily performed by the computer. Second, the motivation and attention of clients may be increased because clients often enjoy using a computer. Third, because clinicians often differ in interviewing styles and backgrounds, computer assessment may provide superior standardization of procedures. But the important questions are how valid are computer assessments, and can the computer be a substitute for face-to-face assessment between client and clinician?

Some studies of computer assessment have yielded encouraging results. Farrell, Stiles-Camplair, and McCullough (1987) evaluated the ability of a computer interview to assess the target complaints of clients. The clients were given a computer interview in which various questions were presented. They were told to answer the questions by pressing the appropriate keys on the keyboard that corresponded to their feelings. Depending on their answers, further programmed questions were asked to refine their responses. Clients were also given a traditional clinical interview and psychological tests, so that the results of the computer interview could be compared with the results of the traditional forms of assessment. The researchers were encouraged by the results. The computer interview findings generally agreed with those of the traditional clinical interview and test results. Furthermore, clients had little difficulty on the keyboard and many found it easier to answer questions on the computer than to be interviewed by the clinician. However, most of them preferred to see the clinician for an interview. Matarazzo (1992) speculated that computers will increasingly play a role not only in the assessment of individuals but also in providing computerized interpretations of background information and test results for individuals.

Although some studies have provided positive results, critics of computer assessment are concerned about the proliferation of computer assessment techniques and the paucity of research studies that have established their validity, as noted by Matarazzo (1986). Computer assessment should not be extensively used until the concerns over validity, use and abuse of test results, and ethical issues such as privacy are addressed. Assessment is an intimate and important process that often requires extensive training, flexibility, and human judgment that can be provided by trained clinicians. Individual differences between clients may not be fully appreciated by computer software. Also, by popularizing computer assessment, there is the risk that untrained individuals, or even clients themselves, may not be aware of the limits of this form of assessment and may misinterpret the meaning of the findings. It is clear that research into computer assessment should be strongly encouraged and the application of computer techniques should be guided by research and the social or ethical consequences.

Problems with Early Diagnostic Classification Systems

As indicated in Chapter 1, the first effective classification scheme for mental disorders was devised by Emil Kraepelin toward the end of the nineteenth century. Kraepelin held the organic view of psychopathology, and his system had a distinctly biogenic slant. Classification was based on the patient's symptoms, as in medicine. It was hoped that disorders (similar groups of symptoms) would have a common **etiology** (cause or origin), would require similar treatments, would respond to those treatments

In an 1883 publication, the psychiatrist Emil Kraepelin (1856–1926) proposed that mental disorders could be directly linked to organic brain disorders, and further proposed a diagnostic classification system for disorders. Kraepelin is also noted for being a pioneer in experimental abnormal psychology. He established his own laboratory where he conducted research on mental illness.

similarly, and would progress similarly if left untreated.

Many of these same expectations were held for the first edition of the *Diagnostic and Statistical Manual of Mental Disorders* (DSM-I), published by the American Psychiatric Association in 1952 and based on Kraepelin's system. These expectations, however, were not realized in DSM-I. The DSM was revised in 1968 (DSM-II), 1980 (DSM-III), 1987 (DSM-III-R), and 1993 (DSM-IV). Each revision was made to increase the reliability, validity, and usefulness of the classification scheme (Spitzer & Williams, 1987). As mentioned previously, reliability and validity are crucial to any diagnostic scheme and, in fact, to any scientific construct.

Reliability   With respect to reliability, early studies of the DSM that compared the diagnoses of pairs of clinicians found poor agreement (interrater reliability) between the members of each pair (Ash, 1949; Schmidt & Fonda, 1956). The greatest disagreement was found in specific categories, even though, in about 80 percent of the pairs, both clinicians agreed on which general category (organic, psychotic, or personality disturbance) a particular disorder belonged in. As a rule, reliability is higher for broad rather than for fine distinctions (Phares, 1984).

In other reliability studies, the same information was presented to clinicians on two occasions or at different times (test-retest reliability). These studies showed that the clinicians' later diagnoses often did not agree with their earlier ones (Beck, 1962; Wilson & Meyer, 1962). Thus even a single clinician's diagnosis was not very reliable over time.

Much unreliability of early DSM editions can be attributed to the diagnostic categories themselves. Three sources of diagnostic error have been identified: Of the errors, 5 percent were attributable to the patients, who gave different material to different interviewers. Nearly one-third (32.5 percent) of the errors were due to inconsistencies among diagnosticians in interview techniques, in interpreting similar data, and in judging the importance of symptoms. Most significantly, however, 62.5 percent of the errors derived from inadequacies of the diagnostic system (Ward et al., 1962). It was simply not clear which behavior patterns belonged in which categories.

In view of these problems, DSM-III and DSM-III-R were developed to have greater interrater reliability. Results of field trials indicated that good to excellent interrater reliability could be obtained for many, but not all, of the major classes of disorders (Widiger et al., 1991).

Validity   Many critics questioned the validity and usefulness of psychiatric classification (Ferster, 1965; Jones, Kahn & Langsley, 1965; Kanfer & Phillips, 1969; Ullmann & Krasner, 1965). They claimed that DSM did not adequately convey information about underlying causes, processes, treatment, and prognosis. (A **prognosis** is a prediction of the future course of a particular disorder.) The problem arose because early versions of DSM were strongly influenced by the biogenic model of mental illness, in which cause is supposed to be a basis of classification. With the exception of the categories of organic mental disorders (brain damage), which may parallel diseases, most other DSM categories were purely descriptive. In addition, having high reliability is a prerequisite for high validity. Because the early versions of DSM had questionable reliability, validity of the DSM was limited. Indeed, it is difficult to talk about the validity of the entire diagnostic system because different categories within the system show different reliabilities and validities. Carson (1991) noted that empirical tests of the construct validity of DSM have been largely absent.

DSM-III-R tried to take into account new research findings (Spitzer & Williams, 1987). Although Kraepelin's concepts still formed the basis for some of its categories, DSM-III-R contained substantial revisions. For example, to improve reliability the exact criteria to be used in making a diagnosis were specified. Clinical usefulness and suitability for research studies were also considered. DSM-III-R was intended to be atheoretical and descriptive, making it more useful to clinicians of varying orientations. In a survey of use and attitudes among mental health professionals in forty-two countries, DSM-III-R was widely used and considered useful, although certain diagnostic categories such as personality disorders were felt to be very problematic (Maser, Kaelber & Weise, 1991).

The Current System: DSM-IV

DSM-IV is a revision of DSM-III-R that takes into account the accumulating research on psychopathology and diagnosis. The adequacy of DSM-IV has been under investigation. Particularly important is the large-scale research being conducted on thousands of clinicians and clients. In this research, videotapes are made of interviews of clients with different disorders. Clinicians will be asked to evaluate and diagnose the clients. Factors (such as degree of training with DSM-IV among clinicians and type of symptoms shown by the clients) that may affect the ability to make a reliable diagnosis are being studied (Nelson-Gray, 1991). Other field trials or studies are being conducted on certain diagnostic categories, and the results are not yet available (Kline et al., 1993).

DSM-IV recommends that the individual's mental state be examined and evaluated with regard to five factors or dimensions (called *axes* in the manual). The five-axis evaluation is intended to provide com-

prehensive and useful information. Axes I, II, and III deal with the individual's present mental and medical condition. Axes IV and V provide additional information about the person's life situation and functioning.

- *Axis I—Clinical syndromes and other conditions that may be a focus of clinical attention* Any mental disorder (except those included on Axis II) listed in the manual are indicated on Axis I—clinical syndromes. If an individual has more than one mental disorder, they are all listed. The principal disorder is listed first.

- *Axis II—Personality disorders* Patients may also have personality disorders, and these disorders are listed on Axis II. They may be present with or without a mental disorder from Axis I. If more than one personality disorder is present, they are all listed.

- *Axis III—General medical conditions* Listed on Axis III are any medical conditions that are potentially relevant to understanding and treating the person.

- *Axis IV—Psychosocial and environmental problems* These problems may affect the diagnosis, treatment, and prognosis of mental disorders. For example, the client may be experiencing the death of a family member, social isolation, homelessness, extreme poverty, and inadequate health services. These problems are listed by the clinician if they have been present during the year preceding the current evaluation or if they occurred before the previous year and are clearly contributory to the disorder or have become a focus of treatment. The clinician has various categories in which to classify the type of problems.

- *Axis V—Global assessment of functioning* The clinician provides a rating of the psychological, social, and occupational functioning of the person. Normally, the rating is made for the level of functioning at the time of the evaluation. The clinician uses a 100-point scale in which 1 indicates severe impairment in functioning (for example, the individual is in persistent danger of severely hurting self or others or is unable to maintain minimal personal hygiene) and 100 refers to superior functioning with no symptoms.

Table 4.3 lists the disorders (categories) for Axes I and II that are included in DSM-IV. Focus 4.2 pro-

Table 4.3

DSM-IV Classification: Categories for Axes I and II (abbreviated)

DISORDERS USUALLY FIRST DIAGNOSED IN INFANCY, CHILDHOOD, OR ADOLESCENCE

Mental retardation

Mild mental retardation
Moderate retardation
Severe mental retardation
Profound mental retardation
Mental retardation, severity unspecified

Learning disorders (academic skills disorder)

Reading disorder (developmental reading disorder)
Mathematics disorder (developmental arithmetic disorder)
Disorder of written expression (developmental expressive writing disorder)
Learning disorder NOS

Motor skills disorder

Developmental coordination disorder

Pervasive developmental disorders

Autistic disorder
Rett's disorder
Childhood disintegrative disorder
Pervasive developmental disorder NOS (including atypical autism)

Disruptive behavior and attention-deficit disorders

Attention-deficit/hyperactivity disorder
predominantly inattentive type
predominantly hyperactive-impulsive type
combined type

Attention-deficit/hyperactive disorder NOS
Oppositional defiant disorder
Conduct disorder
Disruptive behavior disorder NOS

Feeding and eating disorders of infancy or early childhood

Pica
Rumination disorder
Feeding disorder of infancy or early childhood

Tic disorders

Tourette's disorder
Chronic motor or vocal tic disorder
Transient tic disorder
Tic disorder NOS

Communication disorders

Expressive language disorder (developmental expressive language disorder)
Mixed receptive/expressive language disorder (developmental receptive language disorder)
Phonological disorder (developmental articulation disorder)
Stuttering
Communication disorder NOS

Elimination disorders

Encopresis
Enuresis

Other disorders of infancy, childhood, or adolescence

Separation anxiety disorder
Selective mutism (elective mutism)
Reactive attachment disorder of infancy or early childhood

Stereotypic movement disorder (stereotypy/habit disorder)
Disorder of infancy, childhood, or adolescence NOS

DELIRIUM, DEMENTIA, AMNESTIC AND OTHER COGNITIVE DISORDERS

Deliria

Delirium due to general medical condition
Substance-induced delirium
Delirium due to multiple etiologies
Delirium NOS

Dementias

Dementia of the Alzheimer's type
With early onset (if onset at age 65 or below)
uncomplicated
with delirium
with delusions
with depressed mood
with hallucinations
with perceptual disturbance
with behavioral disturbance
with communication disturbance
With late onset (if onset after age 65)
uncomplicated
with delirium
with delusions
with depressed mood
with hallucinations
with perceptual disturbance
with behavioral disturbance

with communication disturbance
Vascular dementia
uncomplicated
with delirium
with delusions
with depressed mood
with hallucinations
with perceptual disturbance
with behavioral disturbance
with communication disturbance

Dementias due to other general medical conditions

Dementia due to HIV disease
Dementia due to head trauma
Dementia due to Parkinson's disease
Dementia due to Huntington's disease
Dementia due to Pick's disease
Dementia due to Creutzfeldt-Jakob disease
Dementia due to other general medical condition
Substance-induced persisting dementia
Dementia due to multiple etiologies
Dementia NOS

Amnestic disorders

Amnestic disorder due to a general medical condition
Substance-induced persisting amnestic disorder
Amnestic disorder NOS
Cognitive disorder NOS

Table 4.3

DSM-IV Classification: Categories for Axes I and II (abbreviated) *(continued)*

MENTAL DISORDERS DUE TO A GENERAL MEDICAL CONDITION NOT ELSEWHERE CLASSIFIED

Catatonic disorder due to a general medical condition
Personality change due to a general medical condition
Mental disorder NOS due to a general medical condition

SUBSTANCE RELATED DISORDERS

Alcohol use disorders

Alcohol dependence
Alcohol abuse
Alcohol intoxication
Alcohol withdrawal
Alcohol delirium
Alcohol persisting dementia
Alcohol psychotic disorder
  with delusions
  with hallucinations
Alcohol mood disorder
Alcohol anxiety disorder
Alcohol sexual dysfunction
Alcohol sleep disorder
Alcohol use disorder NOS

Amphetamine (or related substance) use disorders

Amphetamine (or related substance) dependence
Amphetamine (or related substance) abuse
Amphetamine (or related substance) intoxication
Amphetamine (or related substance) withdrawal
Amphetamine (or related substance) delirium
Amphetamine (or related substance) psychotic disorder
  with delusions
  with hallucinations

Amphetamine (or related substance) mood disorder
Amphetamine (or related substance) anxiety disorder
Amphetamine (or related substance) sexual dysfunction
Amphetamine (or related substance) sleep disorder
Amphetamine (or related substance) use disorder NOS

Caffeine use disorders

Caffeine intoxication
Caffeine anxiety disorder
Caffeine sleep disorder
Caffeine use disorder NOS

Cannabis use disorders

Cannabis dependence
Cannabis abuse
Cannabis intoxication
Cannabis delirium
Cannabis psychotic disorder
  with delusions
  with hallucinations
Cannabis anxiety disorder
Cannabis use disorder NOS

Cocaine use disorders

Cocaine dependence
Cocaine abuse
Cocaine intoxication
Cocaine withdrawal
Cocaine delirium
Cocaine psychotic disorder
  with delusions
  with hallucinations
Cocaine mood disorder
Cocaine anxiety disorder
Cocaine sexual dysfunction
Cocaine sleep disorder
Cocaine use disorder NOS

Hallucinogen use disorders

Hallucinogen dependence
Hallucinogen abuse
Hallucinogen intoxication
Hallucinogen persisting perception disorder

Hallucinogen delirium
Hallucinogen psychotic disorder
  with delusions
  with hallucinations
Hallucinogen mood disorder
Hallucinogen anxiety disorder
Hallucinogen use disorder NOS

Inhalant use disorders

Inhalant dependence
Inhalant abuse
Inhalant intoxication
Inhalant delirium
Inhalant dementia
Inhalant psychotic disorder
  with delusions
  with hallucinogens
Inhalant mood disorder
Inhalant anxiety disorder
Inhalant use disorder NOS

Nicotine disorders

Nicotine dependence
Nicotine withdrawal
Nicotine use disorder NOS

Opioid use disorders

Opioid dependence
Opioid abuse
Opioid intoxication
Opioid withdrawal
Opioid delirium
Opioid psychotic disorder
  with delusions
  with hallucinations
Opioid mood disorder
Opioid sleep disorder
Opioid sexual dysfunction
Opioid use disorder NOS

Phencyclidine (or related substance) use disorders

Phencyclidine (or related substance) dependence
Phencyclidine (or related substance) abuse
Phencyclidine (or related substance) intoxication

Phencyclidine (or related substance) delirium
Phencyclidine (or related substance) psychotic disorder
  with delusions
  with hallucinations
Phencyclidine (or related substance) mood disorder
Phencyclidine (or related substance) anxiety disorder
Phencyclidine (or related substance) use disorder NOS

Sedative, hypnotic, or anxiolytic substance use disorders

Sedative, hypnotic, or anxiolytic dependence
Sedative, hypnotic, or anxiolytic abuse
Sedative, hypnotic, or anxiolytic intoxication
Sedative, hypnotic, or anxiolytic withdrawal
Sedative, hypnotic, or anxiolytic delirium
Sedative, hypnotic, or anxiolytic persisting dementia
Sedative, hypnotic, or anxiolytic persisting amnestic disorder
Sedative, hypnotic, or anxiolytic psychotic disorder
  with delusions
  with hallucinations
Sedative, hypnotic, or anxiolytic mood disorder
Sedative, hypnotic, or anxiolytic anxiety disorder
Sedative, hypnotic, or anxiolytic sleep disorder
Sedative, hypnotic, or anxiolytic sexual dysfunction
Sedative, hypnotic, or anxiolytic use disorder NOS

Table 4.3

DSM-IV Classification: Categories for Axes I and II (abbreviated) (continued)

SUBSTANCE RELATED DISORDERS (continued)

Polysubstance use disorder

Polysubstance dependence

Other (or unknown) substance dependence use disorders

Other (or unknown) substance dependence
Other (or unknown) substance abuse
Other (or unknown) substance intoxication
Other (or unknown) substance withdrawal
Other (or unknown) substance delirium
Other (or unknown) substance persisting dementia
Other (or unknown) substance persisting amnestic disorder
Other (or unknown) substance psychotic disorder
Other (or unknown) substance mood disorder
Other (or unknown) substance anxiety disorder
Other (or unknown) substance sexual dysfunction
Other (or unknown) substance sleep disorder
Other (or unknown) substance use disorder NOS

SCHIZOPHRENIA AND OTHER PSYCHOTIC DISORDERS

Schizophrenia
  paranoid type
  disorganized type
  catatonic type
  undifferentiated type
  residual type
Schizophreniform disorder

Schizoaffective disorder
Delusional disorder
Brief psychotic disorder
Shared psychotic disorder
  (folie a deux)
Psychotic disorder due to a general medication condition
  with delusions
  with hallucinations
Substance-induced psychotic disorder
Psychotic disorder NOS

MOOD DISORDERS

Depressive disorders

Major depressive disorder
  single episode
  recurrent
Dysthymic disorder
Depressive disorder NOS

Bipolar disorders

Bipolar I disorder
  single manic episode
  most recent episode hypomanic
  most recent episode manic
  most recent episode mixed
  most recent episode depressed
  most recent episode unspecified
Bipolar II disorder (recurrent major depressive episodes with hypomania)
Cyclothymic disorder
Bipolar disorder NOS

Mood disorder due to a general medical condition
Substance-induced mood disorder
Mood disorder NOS

ANXIETY DISORDERS

Panic disorder
  without agoraphobia
  with agoraphobia

Agoraphobia without history of panic disorder
Specific phobia (simple phobia)
Social phobia (social anxiety disorder)
Obsessive-compulsive disorder
Posttraumatic stress disorder
Acute stress disorder
Generalized anxiety disorder (includes overanxious disorder of childhood)
Anxiety disorder due to a general medical condition
Substance-induced anxiety disorder
Anxiety disorder NOS

SOMATOFORM DISORDERS

Somatization disorder
Conversion disorder
Hypochondriasis
Body dysmorphic disorder
Pain disorder
  associated with psychological factors
  associated with both psychological factors and a general medical condition
Undifferentiated somatoform disorder
Somatoform disorder NOS

FACTITIOUS DISORDERS

Factitious disorder
  with predominantly psychological signs and symptoms
  with predominantly physical signs and symptoms
  with combined psychological and physical signs and symptoms
Factitious disorder NOS

DISSOCIATIVE DISORDERS

Dissociative amnesia

Dissociative fugue
Dissociative identity disorder (multiple personality disorder)
Depersonalization disorder
Dissociative disorder NOS

SEXUAL AND GENDER IDENTITY DISORDERS

Sexual dysfunctions

Sexual desire disorders

Hypoactive sexual desire disorder
Sexual aversion disorder

Sexual arousal disorders

Female sexual arousal disorder
Male erectile disorder

Orgasm disorders

Female orgasmic disorder (inhibited female orgasm)
Male orgasmic disorder (inhibited male orgasm)
Premature ejaculation

Sexual pain disorders

Dyspareunia
Vaginismus

Sexual dysfunctions due to a general medical condition

Male erectile disorder due to a general medical condition
Male dyspareunia due to a general medical condition
Female dyspareunia due to a general medical condition
Male hypoactive sexual desire disorder due to a general medical condition
Female hypoactive sexual desire disorder due to a general medical condition

Table 4.3

DSM-IV Classification: Categories for Axes I and II (abbreviated) *(continued)*

SEXUAL AND GENDER IDENTITY DISORDERS *(continued)*

Other male sexual dysfunction due to a general medical condition
Other female sexual dysfunction due to a general medical condition
Substance-induced sexual dysfunction
Sexual dysfunction NOS

Paraphilias

Exhibitionism
Fetishism
Frotteurism
Pedophilia
Sexual masochism
Sexual sadism
Voyeurism
Transvestic fetishism
Paraphilia NOS

Sexual disorder NOS

Gender identity disorders

Gender identity disorder
 in children
 in adolescents and adults
Gender identity disorder
 NOS

EATING DISORDERS

Anorexia nervosa
Bulimia nervosa
Eating disorder NOS

SLEEP DISORDERS

Primary sleep disorders

Dyssomnias

Primary insomnia
Primary hypersomnia
Narcolepsy
Breathing-related sleep disorder

Circadian rhythm sleep disorder (sleep-wake schedule disorder)
Dyssomnia NOS

Parasomnias

Nightmare disorder (dream anxiety disorder)
Sleep terror disorder
Sleepwalking disorder
Parasomnia NOS

Sleep disorders related to another mental disorder

Insomnia related to [Axis I or Axis II disorder]
Hypersomnia related to [Axis I or Axis II disorder]

Other sleep disorders

Sleep disorder due to a general medical condition
 insomnia type
 hypersomnia type
 parasomnia type
 mixed type
Substance-induced sleep disorder

IMPULSE CONTROL DISORDERS NOT ELSEWHERE CLASSIFIED

Intermittent explosive disorder
Kleptomania
Pyromania
Pathological gambling
Trichotillomania
Impulse control NOS

ADJUSTMENT DISORDERS

Adjustment disorder
 with anxiety
 with depressed mood
 with disturbance of conduct
 with mixed disturbance of emotions and conduct

with mixed anxiety and depressed mood
Unspecified

PERSONALITY DISORDERS

Note: Personality disorders are coded in Axis II.
Paranoid personality disorder
Schizoid personality disorder
Schizotypal personality disorder
Antisocial personality disorder
Borderline personality disorder
Histrionic personality disorder
Narcissistic personality disorder
Avoidant personality disorder
Dependent personality disorder
Obsessive-compulsive personality disorder
Personality disorder NOS

OTHER CONDITIONS THAT MAY BE A FOCUS OF CLINICAL ATTENTION

(Psychological factors) affecting medical condition

Medication-induced movement disorders

Neuroleptic-induced Parkinsonism
Neuroleptic malignant syndrome
Neuroleptic-induced acute dystonia
Neuroleptic-induced acute akathisia
Neuroleptic-induced tardive dyskinesia

Medication-induced postural tremor
Medication-induced movement disorder NOS
Adverse effects of medication NOS

Relational problems

Relational problem related to a mental disorder or general medical condition
Parent-child relational problem
Partner relational problem
Sibling relational problem
Relational problem NOS

Problems related to abuse or neglect

Physical abuse of child
Sexual abuse of child
Neglect of child
Physical abuse of adult
Sexual abuse of adult

Additional conditions that may be a focus of clinical attention

Bereavement
Borderline intellectual functioning
Academic problem
Occupational problem
Childhood or adolescent antisocial behavior
Adult antisocial behavior
Malingering
Phase of life problem
Noncompliance with treatment of a mental disorder
Identity problem
Religious or spiritual problem
Acculturation problem
Age-associated memory decline

Source: The DSM-IV categories were based on *DSM-IV Draft Criteria.*
NOS = Not otherwise specified

An Example of Classification Using DSM-IV

The client: Mark is a 56-year-old machine operator who was referred for treatment by his supervisor. The supervisor noted that Mark's performance at work had deteriorated during the past four months. Mark was frequently absent from work, had difficulty getting along with others, and often had a strong odor of liquor on his breath after his lunch break. The supervisor knew Mark was a heavy drinker and suspected that Mark's performance was affected by alcohol consumption. In truth, Mark could not stay away from drinking. He consumed alcohol every day; during weekends, he averaged about 16 ounces of Scotch per day. Although he had been a heavy drinker for thirty years, his consumption had increased after his wife divorced him six months ago. She claimed that she could no longer tolerate his drinking, extreme jealousy, and unwarranted suspicions concerning her marital fidelity.

Co-workers avoided Mark because he was a cold, unemotional person who distrusted others.

During interviews with the therapist, Mark revealed very little about himself. He blamed others for his drinking problems: if his wife had been faithful or if others were not out to get him, he would drink less. Mark appeared to overreact to any perceived criticisms of himself. A medical examination revealed that Mark was developing cirrhosis of the liver as a result of his chronic and heavy drinking.

The evaluation: Mark's heavy use of alcohol, which interfered with his functioning, resulted in an alcohol abuse diagnosis on Axis I. Mark also exhibited a personality disorder, which was diagnosed as paranoid personality on Axis II because of his suspiciousness, hypervigilance, and other behaviors. Cirrhosis of the liver was noted on Axis

III. The clinician noted Mark's divorce and difficulties in his job on Axis IV. Finally, Mark was given a 54 on the Global Assessment of Functioning scale (GAF), used in Axis V to rate his current level of functioning, mainly because he was exhibiting moderate difficulty at work and in his social relationships. Mark's diagnosis, then, was as follows:

Axis I—Clinical syndrome: alcohol abuse

Axis II—Personality disorder: paranoid personality

Axis III—Physical disorder: cirrhosis

Axis IV—Psychosocial and environmental problems: (1) Problems with primary support group (divorce), (2) occupational problems

Axis V—Current GAF, 54

vides an example of the diagnoses that result from the five-axis evaluation.

DSM-IV Mental Disorders

The task of making a diagnosis of mental disorder involves classifying individuals on Axes I and II. Most clients have a disorder that is listed under either Axis I or Axis II. Sometimes, clients may be diagnosed as having disorders in both axes or more than one on each axis. The following are the broad categories of mental disorders, most of which are discussed in this book:

Disorders usually first diagnosed in infancy, childhood, or adolescence Included in the category of disorders that begin before maturity is a variety of problems. The problems involve impairment in

cognitive and intellectual functioning, language or motor deficiencies, disruptive behaviors, poor social skills, anxiety, eating disorders, and so on (see Chapter 17).

Delirium, dementia, amnestic, and other cognitive disorders The essential feature of the cognitive impairment disorders is a psychological or behavioral abnormality that is associated with a transient or permanent, identifiable dysfunction of the brain. Included in this category are cognitive, emotional, and behavioral problems that arise from head injuries, ingestion of toxic or intoxicating substances, brain degeneration or disease, and so on (see Chapter 16).

Mental disorders due to a general medical condition Medical conditions can be an important cause of mental disorders. When there is evidence that gen-

There is a fine line between mental disorders and extreme but normal behavior. Shy children could easily be diagnosed as disordered, when instead their social development may simply be delayed.

eral medical conditions are causally related to and explain a disorder, the client is considered to have a mental disorder due to a general medical condition. For example, hypothyroidism can be a direct cause of major depressive disorder. In that case, the diagnosis would be "major depressive disorder due to a general medical condition (hypothyroidism)." Many of the major diagnostic categories (mood disorders or anxiety disorders) have categories that include disorders caused by medical conditions.

Substance-related disorders Psychoactive substances, such as alcohol, amphetamines, marijuana, cocaine, and nicotine, are those that affect the central nervous system. Whenever use of these substances

continues despite social, occupational, psychological, or physical problems, it is considered a mental disorder. Individuals with substance use disorders are often unable to control intake and have a persistent desire to use the substance (see Chapter 10). Some disorders (anxiety or mood) occur because of the ingestion of substances. In these cases, they are considered substance-induced disorders and are listed by DSM-IV not in the section on substance-related disorders but in the section for those disorders that share the same symptoms (for example, substance-induced major depressive disorder would be classified under mood disorders).

Schizophrenia and other psychotic disorders The disorder known as schizophrenia is marked by severe impairment in thinking and perception. Speech may be incoherent, and the person often has delusions (false belief systems), hallucinations (such as hearing imaginary voices), and inappropriate affect. Schizophrenia as well as other psychotic disorders seriously disrupts social, occupational, and recreational functioning (see Chapters 14 and 15).

Mood disorders A separate class of disorders is composed of disturbances in mood or affect. The mood may be one of serious depression, in which the person shows marked sadness, diminished interest, and loss of energy. Extreme elation or mania is also included in these disorders. People with mania frequently have grandiosity, decreased need for sleep, flight of ideas, and impairment in functioning. Severity of mood disorders can vary, and sometimes, in bipolar conditions, both depression and mania are exhibited (see Chapter 12).

Anxiety disorders Anxiety is the predominant symptom in anxiety disorders, and avoidance behaviors are almost always present. For example, in phobias people fear an object or situation and avoid encountering the feared object. In other anxiety disorders, people may not know the reasons for their extreme feelings of anxiety or may exhibit obsessions (recurrent thoughts) or compulsions (repetitive behaviors), which, when not performed, cause marked distress (see Chapter 6).

Somatoform disorders Symptoms of a physical disorder that cannot be fully explained by a known general medical condition are usually classified as somatoform disorders. Individuals with these disorders usually complain of bodily problems or dysfunctions, are preoccupied with beliefs of having a disease or health problem, or experience pain. Yet the symptoms may be inconsistent with anatomical structures, and the discrepancy suggests a psychological basis for the symptoms (see Chapter 7).

Factitious disorders In factitious disorders, there is intentional feigning of physical or psychological symptoms. The individual with this disorder is motivated not by external incentives (economic gain, avoiding legal responsibility) but by the assumption of a sick role.

Dissociative disorders The essential feature of these disorders is a disturbance or alteration in memory, identity, or consciousness. The disturbance may be reflected in people who cannot remember who they are, who assume new identities, who have two or more distinct personalities, or who experience feelings of depersonalization in which the sense of reality is lost (see Chapter 7).

Sexual and gender identity disorders Two main groups of disturbances are included in sexual disorders: paraphilias and sexual dysfunctions. Paraphilias are characterized by intense sexual arousal and fantasies involving nonhuman objects, suffering or humiliation of oneself or one's partner, or children or nonconsenting people. They are considered disorders only if the person has acted on the fantasies or is markedly distressed by them. Sexual dysfunctions may involve inhibitions in sexual desires, inhibited orgasms, premature ejaculations among males, or recurrent pain during the process of sexual intercourse. In gender identity disorders, there is a strong cross-gender identification and a desire to be the other sex coupled with a persistent discomfort with one's own sex (see Chapter 11).

Eating disorders Included in this category are disorders involving eating, such as refusal to maintain body weight above a minimally normal weight, and binge eating and purging (that is, eating excessively and then intentionally vomiting).

Sleep disorders The primary symptoms in these disorders involve sleeping difficulties: problems in initiating or maintaining sleep, excessive sleepiness, sleep disruptions, repeated awakening from sleep associated with extremely frightening nightmares, sleepwalking, and so on.

Impulse control disorders not elsewhere classified A separate class of disorders involves the failure to resist an impulse or temptation to perform some act that is harmful to the individual or others. Included are disorders involving loss of control of impulses over aggression, stealing, gambling, fire setting, and hair pulling. Disorders of impulse control that are listed under other disorders (such as drug use or paraphilias) are not classified in this group of disorders (see Chapter 9).

Adjustment disorders These disorders are characterized by marked and excessive distress, or significant impairment in social, occupational, or academic functioning because of a recent stressor. The symptoms do not meet the criteria for Axis I or II disorders and do not include bereavement.

Personality disorders Whenever personality traits are inflexible and maladaptive and notably impair functioning or cause subjective distress, a diagnosis of personality disorder is likely. The patterns of these disorders are usually evident by adolescence. They typically involve odd or eccentric behaviors, excessive dramatic and emotional behaviors, or anxious and fearful behaviors (see Chapter 9).

Throughout DSM-IV, there are categories entitled "Not Otherwise Specified." The categories are intended to include disorders that do not fully meet the criteria for a particular disorder. For example, a disorder that is cognitive in nature but does not meet all of the criteria for delirium, demential, amnestic, or other specified cognitive disorders would be considered a cognitive disorder not otherwise specified. Furthermore, after each diagnosed disorder, clinicians can use modifiers that indicate severity and remission status. Severity is rated as mild, moderate, or severe, depending on the symptoms and degree of impairment. *Remission* refers to a disorder in which the full criteria for making the diagnosis were met at one time but the current symptoms or signs of the disorder only partially (partial remission) or no longer (full remission) remain.

Finally, DSM-IV emphasizes cross-cultural assessment issues far more than previous versions of DSM. It warns clinicians to exercise caution in using the DSM-IV classification with individuals from different ethnic or cultural groups. It also tries to indicate cultural variations in the symptoms of disorders and describes culture-bound syndromes (disorders that are unique to a particular cultural group). These improvements make DSM-IV far more culturally sensitive than previous editions.

Evaluation of the DSM Classification System

It is too soon to provide a comprehensive evaluation of DSM-IV because it was so recently developed. Extensive research needs to be conducted on its reliability and validity with different populations; the social and research consequences of its use need to be studied as well. Many sections of DSM-IV are basically unchanged from those of DSM-III-R. Because research findings helped to shape DSM-IV, it is likely that reliability and validity are stronger than in the previous versions.

Most objections have been directed to DSM in general, and many are applicable to DSM-IV. For example, some clinicians and researchers believe that DSM has a strong medical orientation, even though more than one-half of the disorders listed are not attributable to known or presumed organic causes and should not be considered biogenic in nature (Nelson-Gray, 1991; Schacht, 1985; Schacht & Nathan, 1977). Some psychologists believe that the medical emphasis of DSM is in part a response to psychiatrists' need to define abnormality more strongly within their profession. A survey of psychotherapists who are psychologists rather than psychiatrists indicated that there was little enthusiasm for DSM (Smith & Kraft, 1983). Most of the respondents rejected the notion that mental disorders form a subset of medical disorders. They preferred a social and interpersonal, rather than a medical, approach to mental disorder. However, no such alternative to DSM enjoys widespread use at present.

Other psychologists question the usefulness of the DSM classification scheme for research. Some of the categories were created out of compromises between conflicting views or were rooted in practical considerations such as ease of application and acceptability to practitioners. Schacht (1985) believes that political and practical aspects of DSM are inseparable from scientific considerations. For example, certain diagnostic categories in DSM have been characterized as being sexist. In other words, specific behaviors sometimes seen among women may be inappropriately in-

terpreted as signs of mental disorders (D. Franklin, 1987; M. Kaplan, 1983; see Focus 4.3 and Critical Thinking in Chapter 9). Some researchers (Persons, 1986) have argued that the study of the symptoms of a disorder is more valuable than research on diagnosed disorders because many patients may be misdiagnosed. Furthermore, by placing patients in diagnosed categories, important information regarding the severity of symptoms is lost. Carson (1991) questioned whether a diagnostic system that uses categories for disorders is appropriate. He prefers a model that views disorders on dimensions (that is, having more or less of certain characteristics) rather than one that categorizes disorders. For these reasons, the DSM (in any revision) may be difficult to use for scientific purposes.

Millon (1983) has tried to clarify the intent of DSM and respond to critics. He noted that the classification system was not intended to imply that all mental disorders have an organic basis. To Millon, the important question is whether the DSM revised editions are a substantial improvement over past systems. He believes they are. Millon also pointed out that constructing a diagnostic classification system is an ongoing process, requiring continual revision and improvement. The limitations in the usefulness of DSM may therefore partly reflect holes in our knowledge of psychopathology (Goldman & Foreman, 1988). It should also be noted that nosological or classification systems such as DSM-IV are constructed by people. This means that issues concerning the philosophical and scientific orientation and cultural beliefs of the developers of a nosological system are important to examine. One can imagine that a group of individuals who believe that spiritual forces influence human behavior would devise a completely different nosological system than DSM-IV. Even within DSM-IV, critics have believed that the psychopathology found in non-Western societies may not be easily classified. This points to the need to continually attend to issues of cross-cultural usefulness (Frances et al., 1991).

The debates over the usefulness of the DSM system have been valuable in suggesting new research directions, increasing the role of research in developing the system, and stimulating the examination of conceptual, methodological, philosophical, and clinical assumptions in the classification of mental disorders. Future research, particularly that examining

Gender Bias in DSM?

From its very inception, DSM has encountered a great deal of criticism. One criticism has focused on gender issues. Kaplan (1983) argued that some diagnostic categories in the DSM are biased in favor of masculine traits. These biases tend to view certain behaviors of women as being unhealthy or disturbed, biases that were denied by those who helped formulate versions of DSM (Williams & Spitzer, 1983).

Proposals to establish the DSM diagnostic categories of self-defeating personality disorder and premenstrual dysphoric disorder illustrate the controversies over gender bias. The essential feature of self-defeating personality disorder is a pervasive pattern of self-defeating behavior, in which the person avoids or undermines pleasurable encounters and is drawn to situations in which he or she will experience suffering. Critics were concerned that this category of disorders might

unfairly be applied to battered women. The women could be diagnosed as having a mental disorder when they were actually victims of abuse. Furthermore, women are often socialized into the roles of being more nurturant, deferential, and willing to delay gratification. These behaviors could be interpreted as being masochistic—a sign of a mental disorder (Caplan, 1984; D. Franklin, 1987). DSM-III-R listed self-defeating personality disorder as a possible disorder to be further examined. Because of the controversy over its inclusion and because subsequent research did not establish the usefulness of this disorder, it was not included as a disorder in DSM-IV.

Premenstrual dysphoric disorder, many times associated with women experiencing premenstrual syndrome (PMS), has also been a hotly debated category (Tavris, 1991). According to DSM-IV, the diagnosis

classified under depressive disorders (NOS) involves symptoms such as marked changes in mood, persistent anger, depression, or anxiety often accompanied by complaints of breast tenderness and bodily aches. There is often an avoidance of social activities, increased interpersonal conflicts, and marked interference with work or social activities and relationships. These symptoms occur in a cyclical pattern a week before menses and remit a few days afterward. Although critics of this category acknowledge that many women have some of these symptoms, they believe that the disorder should be treated strictly as a physical or gynecological disorder. Labeling it as a psychiatric disorder stigmatizes women as being emotional and controlled by "raging hormones." It also suggests that being a woman is per se a risk factor in developing psychiatric disorders (Holden, 1986).

construct validity of the DSM, is essential to evaluate the usefulness of the system.

An Alternative Approach: Behavioral Classification

Some alternatives to the traditional (DSM) classification and diagnostic procedures have gained support; the most developed ones are behavioral. Behavioral approaches tend to examine the interactions between a person's behaviors and situation (Phares, 1984). In their classification scheme, Goldfried and Davison (1976) categorized deviant behaviors according to the variables that are maintaining these behaviors (see Table 4.4). They use five categories to classify

disorders. The first involves stimulus control: either (1) different stimuli do not produce different (and appropriate) behaviors, or (2) particular stimuli produce inappropriate behaviors. For example, a child may learn to be physically aggressive while playing football and then bring such behavior into the classroom. Stimulus control is defective because the behavior does not conform to the appropriate stimulus (i.e., the child should be nonphysically aggressive in the classroom). The change of stimuli (playing field to classroom) fails to change the child's behavior. Or an innocuous stimulus or situation, such as the classroom, may elicit a strong and aversive emotional response such as fear. In this case, the stimulus (i.e., the classroom) is inappropriately controlling the behavior of fear.

Table 4.4

A Behavioral Approach to Classification

I. Difficulties in stimulus control of behavior

Environmental stimuli may fail to control maladaptive instrumental behavior or some stimuli may elicit maladaptive emotional reactions.

A. Defective stimulus control. The individual possesses an adequate behavioral repertoire but is unable to respond to socially appropriate discriminative stimuli.

B. Inappropriate stimulus control. The individual has intensive aversive emotional reactions that are elicited by objectively innocuous cues.

II. Deficient behavioral repertoires

The individual lacks social skills needed to effectively cope with situational demands.

III. Aversive behavioral repertoires

Maladaptive behavior patterns that are aversive to other people are included here.

IV. Difficulties with incentive systems (reinforcers)

Deviant behaviors that are functionally tied to reinforcing consequences would be placed in this category.

A. Defective incentive system in individual. The person's behavior is not under the control of social stimuli that are reinforcing to most people.

B. Inappropriate incentive system in the individual. This category includes individuals for whom the incentive system itself is maladaptive. Those things reinforcing are harmful and/or culturally disapproved.

C. Absence of incentives in environment. The person's environment is lacking in reinforcement.

D. Conflicting incentives in environment. In this category are maladaptive behavior patterns stemming from conflicting environmental consequences.

V. Aversive self-reinforcing systems

It is assumed that cognitive processes can maintain behavior so that the presence or absence of self-reinforcement influences behaviors and emotions.

Source: Goldfried & Davison, 1976.

The second category comprises deficiencies in the range of skills required for day-to-day living. When one or more of these skills are lacking, an individual is said to exhibit a "deficient behavioral repertoire."

The third category involves aversive behaviors—those that are unpleasant, irritating, or harmful to others.

Difficulties with incentive systems, or reinforcers for appropriate behavior, are included in the fourth category. As Table 4.4 indicates, these difficulties are of four types: the reinforcers may be defective or weak, they may themselves be inappropriate, some reinforcers may be missing, or various reinforcers may conflict with each other.

Finally, the fifth category involves aversive self-reinforcement or the absence of positive reinforcement. People who have unrealistically high standards of behavior, for instance, may be very critical of their own performance. As a result, they may fail to appreciate their accomplishments and become depressed or feel inadequate.

Obviously, an individual may manifest problems that can be classified in several of these categories. Nevertheless, because this system emphasizes the variables that maintain behavioral patterns, it lets the therapist isolate those variables for treatment purposes (Goldfried & Davison, 1976).

Evidence shows that the behavioral classification approach is superior to DSM in reliability and validity (Bellack & Hersen, 1980). Although clinicians often do not use the formal categories proposed by Goldfried and Davison (1976), behavioral approaches to assessment are in widespread use (for example, see Hersen & Van Hasselt, 1992). However, many clinicians and therapists prefer a psychodynamic (rather than a purely behavioral) approach to mental disorder and thus to assessment and classification as well.

Objections to Classification and Labeling

Diagnostic classification has been criticized on the grounds that it fosters belief in an erroneous all-or-nothing quality of psychopathology. As we noted in Chapter 1, behaviors lie on a spectrum from normality to abnormality. To place a diagnostic label on someone categorizes that person as "abnormal" and implies that he or she is qualitatively different from normal. Many psychologists now perceive that, for many disorders, the differences between normal and abnormal are differences of degree, not of kind (Persons, 1986).

In Chapter 1, we also touched on two problems that can arise when a diagnosis becomes a label. Here are three more:

1. *A label can cause people to interpret all activities of the affected individual as pathological.* A young psychology intern, training in the psychiatric ward of a VA hospital, talked very openly about his feelings of inadequacy. Most people have such feelings, but his openness gave him the reputation of being anxious. On the basis of this prejudgment and label, his supervisor became concerned about the young intern's competence and watched him very closely. One of the supervisor's chief complaints about the intern was that his anxiety prevented him from acquiring sufficient information during interviews with patients. Frustrated by his inability to shake this impression from the supervisor's mind, the intern took copious notes on all his patients. When he was next scheduled to present a case to his supervisor, the young intern prepared thoroughly and memorized details of the patient's life. He displayed a remarkable knowledge of the patient's life history to his supervisor that day, but the supervisor's response was not at all what he expected. The supervisor felt that the intern's anxiety had caused him to become so compulsive in obtaining information from patients that he was not listening to their feelings! Thus a label can predispose the observer to distort even contradictory evidence to fit into the frame of reference suggested by the label.

2. *A label may lead others to treat a person differently even when he or she is perfectly normal.* A study by Rosenthal and Jacobson (1968) showed how responses to a label can cause differential treatment. They tested schoolchildren and then randomly assigned them to either of two groups. Teachers were told that tests of one group indicated that they were potential intellectual "bloomers" (gaining in competence and maturity); the other group was not given this label. After a one-year interval, children from both groups were retested. Children identified as bloomers showed dramatic gains in IQ scores. How did this occur? Many have speculated that the label led teachers to have higher intellectual expectations for the bloomers and thus to treat them differently. Even though there was no significant difference in IQ levels between the two groups to begin with, differences were present by the end of the year. The Rosenthal and Jacobson study has been criticized on the basis of its methodology and statistical analysis. Nevertheless, other studies have yielded similar results (Rappaport & Cleary, 1980).

3. *A label may lead those who are labeled to believe that they do indeed possess such characteristics.* In these cases, the label becomes a self-fulfilling prophecy. In the Rosenthal and Jacobson study just cited, the label not only caused teachers to behave differently but also affected the children. It is possible that when people are constantly told by others that they are stupid or smart, they may come to believe such labels. For example, if people ascribe certain stereotypical traits to a racial minority or an ethnic group, then it is reasonable to believe that they will behave differently toward that group and cause cognitive and behavioral changes among members of that group. Rosenhan (1973) showed how people labeled mentally ill can become trapped by this label. Rosenhan's most renowned research study is discussed in Focus 4.4. Another case of labeling is presented in the First Person narrative. The narrative raises the question of what would have happened to a boy's self-image had the initial labels concerning his intellectual and social impairment persisted. The effect of labeling may be pronounced among children who are forming their self-identities and self-concepts. Reschly (1992) noted that labeling a child as mentally retarded is not only demeaning but problematic in that many people believe that the condition is a biological anomaly, permanent disability, and gross intellectual handicap. Such beliefs and the accompanying reactions may have a profound effect on the self-images of children.

Normal or Abnormal: The Consequences of Labeling?

Can "normal" people be diagnosed as disturbed? To find out, psychologist D. L. Rosenhan (1973) sent eight experimenters as pseudopatients to different psychiatric hospitals. Their assignment was first to simulate psychiatric symptoms to gain admission into psychiatric wards and, once there, to behave in a normal manner. Rosenhan wanted the pseudopatients to record their experiences as patients without hospital staff members becoming aware of the experiment.

Several interesting and provocative findings emerged. First, no one on the ward staff in the hospitals ever detected that the pseudopatients were normal—despite the

fact that many *patients* suspected the pseudopatients were not abnormal but were merely "checking up on the hospital." In fact, the pseudopatients' length of hospitalization ranged from seven to fifty-two days. Second, nearly all pseudopatients were initially diagnosed as schizophrenic. And many of their normal behaviors on the ward were subsequently interpreted as manifestations of schizophrenia; one example was "excessive note-taking." Third, the staff failed to interact much with patients, who were treated as powerless, irresponsible individuals.

Rosenhan concluded that it is difficult to distinguish normal and disturbed behaviors in persons in men-

tal hospitals, that the labels applied to patients often outlive their usefulness, and that the hospital environment is harsh and frequently maintains maladaptive behaviors. His study has generated a great deal of controversy (Millon, 1975; Weiner, 1975). One critic argued that, because patients did report abnormal symptoms at the time of hospital admission, it is understandable that they were hospitalized (Spitzer, 1975). And, although the pseudopatients were not detected by the staff, they were all released within sixty days. All were said to be "in remission."

SUMMARY

1. Assessment and classification of disorders are essential in the mental health field. In developing assessment tools and useful classification schemes, researchers and clinicians have been concerned with issues regarding reliability and validity.

2. Clinicians primarily use four methods of assessment: observations, interviews, psychological tests, and neurological tests. Observations of external signs and expressive behaviors are often made during an interview and can have diagnostic significance. Interviews, the oldest form of psychological assessment, involve a face-to-face conversation after which the interviewer differentially weighs and interprets verbal information obtained from the interviewee. Psychological tests provide a more formalized means of obtaining information. Most testing situations have two characteristics in common. They provide a standard situation in which certain responses are elicited, and responses from subjects are measured and used to make inferences about underlying traits. In personality testing, projective techniques or objec-

tive tests (personality inventories) may be used. In the former, the stimuli are ambiguous; in the latter, the stimuli are much more structured. Two of the most widely used projective techniques are the Rorschach inkblot technique and the Thematic Apperception Test (TAT). Unlike projective tests, objective personality inventories, such as the MMPI-2, supply the test taker with a list of alternatives from which to select an answer. Intelligence tests can be used to obtain an estimate of a person's current level of cognitive functioning and to assess intellectual deterioration. Behavioral observations of how a person takes the test are additional sources of information about personality attributes. The WAIS, Stanford-Binet, and Bender-Gestalt tests can be used to assess brain damage. The Halstead-Reitan and Luria-Nebraska test batteries are tests that specifically assess brain dysfunction. Neurological medical procedures, including x-rays, CAT and PET scans, EEG, and MRI have added highly important and sophisticated means to detect brain damage.

3. The first edition of DSM was based to a large extent on the biogenic model of mental illness. It as-

FIRST PERSON

Eddy Regnier

Early in my training, when I was learning about psychological assessment tools, diagnostic criteria, and nomenclature, I became aware of the limitations of methodology. This discovery occurred because of a case I had as a graduate student. During my graduate training, I worked with a ten-year-old boy who as an infant

and a child had been through the most horrendous experiences. He had, perhaps for years, been sexually assaulted by his father in a dark, confined space. Furthermore, he had watched an older sibling being similarly abused.

I met Steven (not his real name) after he had been hospitalized for a year. When I was assigned to be his primary therapist, he had already undergone a variety of psychological tests that included behavioral observations, intelligence tests and projectives, such as the Rorschach, Thematic Apperception, and Harris-Goodenough Draw-A-Person tests. The results of these tests suggested that Steven was intellectually below average and functioning emotionally in the pervasive developmental disorder range, which is characterized by impaired social interactions and communication skills. My supervi-

sors cautioned me against getting too attached to Steven, probably because they thought he was unlikely to ever improve. He had not shown any social response during the year he had been hospitalized, and held himself aloof from everyday affairs. Although he ate and slept, he refused all overtures of friendship by the staff and the other boys on the ward. Their attempts to involve him in games and activities actually seemed to frighten him. He had an odd quality about him, and drove most people away. At our first meeting, I was immediately drawn to his eyes. They had the distant, faraway expression of a person who had been in hell. I believe he thought that at any moment he would be returned to the fiendish world he had come from. My first goal was to re-evaluate his intellectual and emotional functioning. But I didn't

sumed that people classified in a psychodiagnostic category show similar symptoms that stem from a common cause, should be treated in a certain manner, and have similar prognoses. Critics questioned the reliability and validity of earlier versions of DSM. In the current version, DSM-IV, detailed diagnostic criteria are given; research findings and expert judgments were used to help construct this latest version. As a result, its reliability appears to be higher than that of the previous manuals. Furthermore, data are collected on five axes so that much more information about the patient is systematically examined. General objections to classification are primarily based on the problems involved in labeling.

4. In addition to issues involving reliability and validity, a number of ethical questions have been raised about classifying and assessing people through tests. These include questions about confidentiality, privacy, and cultural bias. Concerned with these issues, psychologists have sought to improve classification and assessment procedures and to define the

appropriate conditions for testing and diagnosis. In spite of the problems and criticisms, classification and assessment are necessary to psychological research and practice.

KEY TERMS

assessment With regard to psychopathology, the process of gathering information and drawing conclusions about the traits, skills, abilities, emotional functioning, and psychological problems of an individual

classification system With regard to psychopathology, a system of distinct categories, indicators, and nomenclature for different patterns of behavior, thought processes, and emotional disturbances

etiology The causes or origins of a disorder

objective personality test An inventory of personality attributes in which the test taker either agrees

know how to engage him sufficiently to get a true sample of his abilities. Usually a psychologist has only a limited amount of time to complete such an evaluation. In this instance, because I was a student and also seeing Steven for therapy, that time was extended.

I thought how frightening it must be for a baby to be born into a violent world of bright lights, sensations, and rapid change and wondered whether it was equally difficult for Steven to re-engage our world. I spent as much time with him as I could, and slowly he began to trust me. As he opened up to me, we started to communicate through a game we developed, which can be described as "Draw what you are feeling." This game involved his drawing a picture, usually a family scene; I would then try to guess what was happening in it. To shape

his drawings to more closely approximate the themes (sexual and physical abuse) I thought he was trying to convey, I made wild guesses about what was going on in his pictures to encourage him to reveal much more of what he had experienced. Responding to my incorrect guesses, Steven added more detail to his pictures, thus clarifying his experiences. I was eventually able to complete an evaluation using standard psychological tools, and I discovered that Steven had above-normal intellectual functioning.

By today's standards, Steven would have been diagnosed as having posttraumatic stress disorder because his traumatic experiences were so far outside the range of usual human experience. A person experiencing extremely traumatic events may show such symptoms as depression and anxiety, poor

social interactions, and somatic changes. So it isn't hard to understand how Steven could have been misdiagnosed.

Once Steven was correctly diagnosed and given appropriate therapy, he began to get better. I have watched him grow from a terrified little boy into a wonderful, bright adolescent. He's lost that sad look in his eyes, and I'm grateful that I've had the chance to play a small part in his development.

Eddy Regnier is director of the day treatment program at the Fuller Mental Health Center in Boston, Massachusetts.

or disagrees with specific self-descriptive statements; administration, scoring, and interpretation are largely independent of the test giver's subjectivity

organicity Brain damage or deterioration

prognosis A prediction of the future course of a particular disorder

projective personality test A personality assessment technique in which the test taker is presented with ambiguous stimuli and is asked to respond to them in some way

psychological test Any test instrument used to assess personality, maladaptive behavior, development

of social skills, intellectual abilities, vocational interests, and brain damage

psychometrics Mental measurement, including its study and techniques

reactivity A situation in which people who know they are being observed or assessed change the way they respond

reliability The degree to which a procedure or test yields the same result repeatedly, under the same circumstances

validity The degree to which a procedure or test actually performs the function that it was designed to perform

The Scientific Method in Abnormal Psychology

As individuals interested in abnormal psychology, we are constantly bombarded with simplified, eye-catching headlines. The following were obtained from the *New York Times*:

> "Study identified part of brain as important site of anxiety"

> "Beliefs on depression in women contradicted"

> "Aggression in men: Hormone levels are a key"

> "Scientists trace aberrant sexuality"

> "A key to post-traumatic stress lies in brain chemistry, scientists find"

All of the articles that accompanied these headlines seemed highly convincing. Yet, how can we determine how believable the findings are?

Scientists who work in the field of abnormal psychology seek as their primary goal to understand abnormal behavior and to use that understanding to describe, explain, predict, and control such behavior. Unfortunately, the methods used in studying abnormal behavior are often fraught with problems. Finding answers is difficult—despite the convincing headlines. In this chapter, we will discuss the components of the scientific method and the ways to evaluate research. Common means of studying abnormal behavior include experiments, correlations, analogue studies, single-subject studies, and epidemiological and other forms of research. Understanding different research designs and their shortcomings is necessary to be able to critically evaluate reported findings in abnormal psychology.

Have We Found the Gene That Causes Alcoholism?

An article appeared in the *New York Times* stating the following:

The biological approach took a big step forward in April, when researchers reported the identification of a specific gene that may play a key role in some forms of alcoholism, as well as other addictions. . . . The discovery, announced by researchers at the University of Texas and the University of California at Los Angeles, is a gene linked to the receptors for dopamine, a brain chemical involved in the sensation of pleasure. (Goldman, 1990, p. 5)

This article was based in part on a study by Blum and colleagues (1990) who were looking for specific genetic characteristics in alcoholics. They believed that the genetic link involved the A1 allele of DRD2. In their study, twenty-four (69 percent) of thirty-five alcoholics were found to carry this genetic characteristic as compared with only seven (20 percent) of thirty-five nonalcoholics. Their analysis was based on examination of the brain tissue of deceased individuals. The alcoholics were characterized as being treatment failures and had died of alcoholic-related problems.

Had they found the gene respon-

sible for alcoholism? Any conclusions have to be interpreted cautiously. First, thirty-one percent of the alcoholics did not show this genetic characteristic and 20 percent of nonalcoholics did. Thus causes other than the identified genetic characteristic have to be involved. Second, the sample sizes are small. Because of this, the findings must be considered preliminary until larger samples can be assessed. Third, the characteristics (treatment failures and death from alcohol-related problems) of these alcoholics may not be representative of alcoholics in general. Fourth, although a normal control group was included, we need to

Scientists are often described as skeptics. The conclusions from any one study are rarely accepted. Instead, we demand that the results be *replicated* or repeated by other researchers. Replication lessens the chance that the findings were due to experimenter bias, methodological flaws, or sampling errors. The following are examples of findings that were initially reported as "conclusive" by the mass media and their current status after further investigation:

- Taraxein, a substance found in the blood of schizophrenics, is responsible for this condition. Heath and associates (1970) reported that when this substance was injected into nonschizophrenic volunteers, they displayed schizophrenic behaviors. *Status:* Other researchers were unable to replicate the findings.

- Autism is related to an underdevelopment of the cerebellum region known as the vermis (Courchesne et al., 1988). *Status:* Unclear. Another researcher reported finding no differences between autistic individuals and controls in that brain region.

- Hyperactivity in children is due to reactions to specific food groups or food additives. *Status:* Probably not supported. In general, experimental studies using biological challenge or double-blind (described later in chapter) methods have reported no change in behavior as a result of food or additives.

- An individual's attitude or personality can influence both the development and course of diseases such as cancer. *Status:* Unresolved. Little evidence exists that attitude or personality influences the development of cancer.

- Specific negative family communication patterns may be responsible for the development of schizophrenia. *Status:* Little support exists for this view, although a negative family environment might be associated with relapses and increased stress for a number of disorders.

- Childhood sexual abuse is a major causal factor in the development of eating disorders. *Status:* When methodological problems are controlled for, there is little support for this position (Conners & Morse, 1993; Pope & Hudson, 1992).

determine if the gene is specific (pathognomonic) to alcoholism. If it is also present in other disorders, the relationship between the gene and alcoholism would be weakened. To find the answers, replication of the study was necessary.

Conflicting findings were soon reported. Gelernter and associates (1991) found no difference in the prevalence of the A1 allele in controls and alcoholics in their sample. They suggested that the significant differences presented in the earlier study were due to "falsely low estimates" of its prevalence in control groups. In a review of six studies on the A1 allele, Cloninger (1991) did find a larger percentage of alcoholics (45 percent) with the A1 allele than control groups (26 percent). There is evidence, therefore, that the A1 allele is found in nearly one-half of the alcoholics studied; it is also found in more than one-fourth of the persons in the control groups. Is the genetic characteristic also found in other psychiatric populations? Comings and coworkers (1991) reported the same genetic characteristic in the following groups: controls (24.5 percent); Tourette's syndrome (44.9 percent); attention deficit hyperactive disorder (46.2 percent); autistic disorder (54.5 percent); alcoholism (42.3 percent); and posttraumatic stress disorder (45.7 percent).

It is clear from a review of the research that the A1 allele is neither sufficient nor necessary in the development of alcoholism. Less than 50 percent of alcoholics carry this genetic characteristic. This characteristic is also not specific or pathognomonic to alcoholism because it is associated with a number of different behavior disorders. The A1 allele may act as a modifying influence, perhaps making a number of disorders worse. But this is only speculation that must be determined with further research.

Not finding that the A1 allele is responsible for alcoholism does not mean that a gene will not be found. As Cloninger observed, however, "It was surprising that a single gene could be so strongly associated with a common disorder that is known to be developmentally complex and genetically heterogeneous" (p. 1833). These studies demonstrate the self-corrective feature of the scientific method—the need to replicate original findings.

As you can see, the search for "truth" is a long and tortuous journey. Answers to the causes of abnormal behavior have come and gone. For an example of a scientific investigation, see Focus 5.1.

THE SCIENTIFIC METHOD IN CLINICAL RESEARCH

The **scientific method** is a method of inquiry that provides for the systematic collection of data through controlled observation and for the testing of hypothesis. (A **hypothesis** is a conjectural statement, usually describing a relationship between two variables.) Perhaps the unique and most general characteristic of the scientific method is its potential for self-correction. Under ideal conditions, data and conclusions are freely exchanged and experiments are replicable (reproducible), so that all are subject to discussion, testing, verification, and modification. As a result, the knowledge developed is as free as possible from the scientist's personal beliefs, perceptions, biases, values, attitudes, and emotions. Another characteristic of the scientific method is that it attempts to identify and explain (hypothesize) the relationship between variables. Examples of hypotheses are statements such as "some seasonal forms of depressions may be due to decreases in light," "autism (a severe disorder beginning in childhood) is a result of poor parenting," and "eating disorders are a result of specific family interaction patterns." Different theories may result in different hypotheses for the same phenomenon. (A **theory** is a group of principles and hypotheses that together explain some aspect of a particular area of inquiry.) For example, hypothesized reasons for eating disorders have included biological or neurochemical causes, fear of sexual maturity, societal demands for thinness in women, and pathological family relationships. Each of these hypotheses reflects a different theory.

Elements of Clinical Research

Clinical research can proceed only when the relationship expressed in a hypothesis is clearly and systematically stated and when the variables of concern are measurable and defined. We need to define clearly what we are studying and make sure that the vari-

The scientific method involves the collection of data through controlled observations. In this case, the child's responses are videotaped through a one-way mirror.

ables are measured with reliable and valid instruments. Clinical research relies on these additional characteristics of the scientific method—use of operational definitions, consideration of reliability and validity, and acknowledgment of base rates.

Operational Definitions   Operational definitions are definitions of the variables under study. For example, an operational definition of depression could involve responses to a self-report questionnaire (that is, depression is defined as a certain score on a depression inventory), ratings by an observer on a depression checklist, or the identification of specific neurochemical changes. Operational definitions are important because they force an experimenter to clearly define what he or she means by the variable. This allows others to agree or disagree with the way the variable was defined. When operational definitions of a phenomenon differ, comparing research is problematic and conclusions can be faulty.

Let us consider the recent studies or reports linking child sexual abuse with panic disorder, phobias, depression, alcohol and substance abuse, multiple personality and dissociative disorders, and bulimia and anorexia nervosa (Briere, 1992; Pribor & Dinwiddie, 1992; Terr, 1991). Unfortunately, these studies do not employ the same operational definition.

Consider the following different definitions of child sexual abuse:

"Any sexual activity, overt or covert, between a child and an adult (or older child), where the younger child's participation is obtained through seduction or coercion (Ratican, 1992)

"Any self-reported contact—ranging from fondling to sexual intercourse—experienced by a patient on or before age 18 and initiated by someone 5 or more years senior or by a family member at least 2 years senior (Brown & Anderson, 1991, p. 56)

Other definitions of child sexual abuse include "any unwanted sexual experience before 14," "any attempted or completed rape before 18 years," and "contact between someone under 15 and another person 5 years older" (Briere, 1992). The use of so many different definitions of child sexual abuse makes any general conclusions difficult.

Operational definitions need to be clear and precise. How can "any unwanted sexual experience before 14" be interpreted? What behaviors can this definition include? It is no wonder that the reported prevalence rate of sexual abuse in different studies ranges from 6 to 62 percent for females and from 3 to 31 percent for males (Watkins & Bentovim, 1992).

The operational definition of eating disorders has varied from study to study resulting in conflicting findings (Conners & Morse, 1993; Pope & Hudson, 1992). In evaluating or comparing research, the operational definition of the phenomenon must be considered.

Reliability and Validity of Measures and Observations   The scientific method requires that the measures we use be reliable or consistent. **Reliability** refers to the degree to which a measure or procedure will yield the same results repeatedly. In other words, individuals diagnosed as antisocial personality with a questionnaire that is reliable should receive the same diagnosis if they take the questionnaire again. Consistent results are necessary if we are to have any faith in them. Diagnostic reliability is low for many of the childhood disorders and some of the personality disorders.

Even if consistent results are obtained, questions can arise over the validity of a measure. Does the test really measure what it was developed to measure? If we claim to have developed a test that identifies multiple personality disorder, we have to demonstrate that it can accomplish this task. Many of the clinical tests used in studies have not been evaluated to determine their validity. Examples of this will be discussed later in the chapter.

Base Rates   The **base rate** is the phenomenon's natural occurrence in the population studied. When the base rate is not known or considered, problems in interpretation can occur. For example, unwanted sexual events and eating problems are reported by a high percentage of females (Conners & Morse, 1993; Pope & Hudson, 1992). Because of this, clinicians may find that the majority of individuals treated for eating problems report a history of sexual abuse. An investigator, not recognizing that these are both high-frequency behaviors (high base rates), may mistakenly conclude that one is the cause of the other.

Knowing how frequent a phenomenon is can be important in how it is interpreted. For example, before survey data were obtained, masturbation was viewed as a relatively rare and harmful behavior. The finding that the majority of both sexes engage in this behavior forced a change in how it was viewed. As another example, persons with severe mental disorders are thought to have "unusual" thoughts or reactions. On a psychotic traits questionnaire, however,

the following percentage of a normal control group answered positively to the following questions:

> Are you bothered by the feeling that people are watching you? (29 percent)
>
> Have you ever thought you heard people talking only to discover it was in fact a nondescript noise? (30 percent)
>
> Have you ever felt that you were communicating with someone else telepathically? (37 percent)
>
> Have you ever felt the urge to injure yourself? (24 percent)
>
> Are your thoughts about sex often odd or bizarre? (23 percent)

Although individuals with schizophrenia are twice as likely as normal persons to endorse these statement (Jackson & Claridge, 1991), nonpsychiatric controls also report disturbing thoughts and urges, "paranoid ideation," and "magical thinking." That an individual or client reports having odd or bizarre thoughts of sex or being bothered by the feeling of being watched may therefore not be indicative of a disorder. Many "normal" individuals also report these thoughts.

Another problem when base rates are not considered is illustrated in the following example. Suppose that you developed a new therapy that involves having clients write stories about the causes of their problems and then scenarios of different solutions. They then are asked to dream about the solutions to their problems. After ten weeks, nearly two-thirds of your clients improve. Can you consider the new technique successful? Probably not. We know that even without treatment as many as two-thirds of people with problems "spontaneously improve." We would have to evaluate the new therapy on this standard of improvement.

Statistical Versus Clinical Significance   Research is evaluated by its ability to find *statistical significance,* or how likely it is that the relationship being studied is due to chance. What may be statistically significant may not be of practical significance. For example, various articles based on a study by Phillips, Van Voorhess, and Ruth (1992) recently stated that women were more likely to die the week after their birthdays than any other week of the year. This seemed to show that psychological factors have a powerful effect on biological processes. The study involved 2,745,149 persons, and the findings were statistically significant (not due to chance). The excess in deaths for the week after the birthday, however, was only 3.03 percent more than expected. Thus psychological factors associated with deaths and birthdays, although statistically significant, play a relatively small role in deaths among women. When evaluating research, you must determine if the statistical significance reported is really "clinically" significant. This problem is most likely to occur in studies with large sample sizes.

EXPERIMENTS

The **experiment** is perhaps the best tool for testing cause-and-effect relationships. In its simplest form, the experiment involves the following:

1. An **experimental hypothesis,** which is the prediction concerning how an independent variable affects a dependent variable in an experiment

2. An **independent variable** (the possible cause), which the experimenter manipulates to determine its effect on a dependent variable

3. A **dependent variable** that, according to the hypothesis, is somehow controlled by the independent variable

As we noted, the experimenter is also concerned with controlling extraneous variables. Let us clarify these concepts with an example.

Melinda N. was a nineteen-year-old sophomore who sought help from a university psychology clinic for panic attacks. At least four times a month she had severe bouts of anxiety during which she felt that she was dying. Although she could never predict when the attacks would occur, she always became highly anxious before and during class examinations. Fear of having panic attacks interfered with her ability to perform. The therapist had heard that an antidepressant, alprazolam, and psychological methods (relaxation training and changing thoughts about the attacks) were both successful in treating this disorder. Before deciding which treatment to use, she searched the research literature to determine if comparative effectiveness studies had been done on the two approaches.

A study by Janet Klosko and her colleagues (1990) seemed to provide an answer. The experiment included fifty-seven individuals who were diagnosed as suffering from a panic disorder according to the Anxiety Disorders Interview Schedule-Revised (ADIS-R) and DSM-III. These subjects were randomly assigned to one of the following groups: (1) alprazolam, (2) behavior therapy, (3) placebo treatment, and (4) waiting list control.

The Experimental Group

An experimental group is the group that is subjected to the independent variable. In the study by Klosko and her colleagues, two experimental groups were created: one exposed to behavioral treatment for fifteen weeks and the other exposed to alprazolam for fifteen weeks. The behavioral treatment included cognitive, relaxation, and breathing training.

Because the investigators were interested in how treatment affects level of anxiety and reports of panic attacks, the dependent variables were measured in two ways: (1) self-monitoring (subjects kept a daily record of each episode of anxiety above a certain level and indicated whether they thought it was a panic attack), and (2) rating by clinicians on anxiety and frequency of panic attacks. Pretesting occurred before treatment, and posttesting occurred after fifteen weeks. In this way, it was possible to evaluate how much improvement was made on the measures after treatment.

The Control Group

If subjects in the two experimental groups show a reduction of anxiety and panic attacks on the outcome measures from pretesting to posttesting, can we conclude that the treatments are effective forms of therapy? The answer would be no. Students may have shown less anxiety and fewer panic attacks merely as a result of the passage of time or as a function of completing the assessment measures. The use of a control group enables one to eliminate these possibilities.

A *control group* is a group that is similar in every way to the experimental group except for the manipulation of the independent variable. In the study by Klosko and colleagues the control group also took the pretest measures, were placed on a fifteen-week waiting list for treatment, and took the posttest measures. They did not receive any of the experimental treatments.

The Placebo Group

You should note that the results of the experiment may also be challenged for another reason. For example, what if the subjects in the treated, experimental groups improved not because of the treatment but because they had faith or an expectancy that they would improve? Some researchers have found that if subjects expect to improve from treatment, this expectancy—rather than specific treatment—is responsible for the outcome.

One method to induce an expectancy in students without using the specific treatment is to have a placebo control group. In the study by Klosko and coworkers subjects in the placebo control group were told that they were taking a medication for anxiety. In actuality, they were given an inert drug or placebo that could have no chemical impact on their anxiety. If the therapy groups improved more than the placebo control group, then one can be more confident that therapy, rather than expectancy, was responsible for the results. Results indicated that both experimental groups showed fewer panic attacks than did the waiting-list control and placebo groups. The percentage free from panic attacks after the study were as follows: persons receiving behavior therapy (87 percent), persons receiving alprazolam (50 percent), persons receiving placebo (36 percent), and waiting-list control (33 percent). The behavior therapy package was more effective than alprazolam in reducing anxiety and specific panic symptoms. In working with the client with panic disorder, the therapist could choose between either of the two effective treatments.

Additional Concerns in Clinical Research

Although we hope to control expectations of outcome through the use of the placebo control group, two types of problems can occur. First, the placebo control group may also report significant improvements. In a group of fifty patients with mild depression, all reported that they were "much or very much" improved after taking a placebo (Rabkin et al., 1990). This finding would make it difficult to separate treatment from expectancy effects. Second, subjects may "guess" correctly that they are receiving a placebo, thereby reducing any expectancy effects.

Experimenter expectations can also influence the outcome of a study. In genetic studies, interviews or diagnoses are often made with the patients' relatives to determine if they have the same or related disorders. When clinicians are aware that they are interviewing the patient's relatives, higher rates of psychopathology are reported than when they are not aware (Gottesman & Shields, 1982). Expectancy can therefore influence diagnosis. To control for this, the experimenter may use a *blind design*, in which the clinicians doing the interviewing are not aware of the purpose of the study. Even in this case we may not be totally satisfied that clinician ratings are not influenced in some way. In family history studies, relatives are often contacted by the researcher or the patient (Alexander, Lerer & Baron, 1992). The knowledge that they are participating in a genetic study could cause the relatives of the patients to behave differently than a control subject during the interview. These behavioral differences may be picked up by the clinician and influence diagnostic decisions.

A method to reduce the impact of both experimenter and subject expectations is the *double-blind design*. In this procedure, neither the individual working directly with the subject nor the subject is aware of the experimental conditions. However, the effectiveness of this design is dependent on the "blindness" of the participants, which may not always be ensured. In a randomized, double-blind study (Margraf et al., 1991), patients with panic disorder were given one of two antidepressants (alprazolam or imipramine) or a placebo. All of the substances were dispensed in identical capsules. Were the patients and physicians "blind" to the conditions? Apparently not. The great majority of patients and physicians were able to accurately rate whether an antidepressant was being taken. Further, the physicians were able to distinguish between the two types of active drugs on the reaction of the patients. These findings indicate the need to modify experimental designs trials so the degree of "blindness" is increased. Otherwise, the results may be influenced by both client and experimenter expectations. Interestingly, in an analysis of twenty-two studies of the effectiveness of antidepressants chosen for their emphasis on blindness (included both a placebo and standard antidepressant controls), Greenberg and colleagues found that (1) patients rated the antidepressants as no more effective than the placebo and (2) physicians rated antidepressants significantly but only slightly more than placebos. These studies indicate the need to develop even more procedures that increase the effectiveness of blind design studies. This is necessary if we are to adequately evaluate therapies.

CORRELATIONS

A **correlation** is the extent to which variations in one variable are accompanied by increases or decreases in a second variable. As opposed to experiments, the variables are not manipulated. Instead, a statistical analysis is performed to determine if increases in one variable are accompanied by increases or decreases in the other. It is expressed as a statistically derived *correlation coefficient,* symbolized by the symbol r, which has a numerical value between -1 and $+1$. In a positive correlation, an increase in one variable is accompanied by an increase in the other. When an increase in one variable is accompanied by a decrease in the other variable, it is a negative correlation. The greater the value of r, positive or negative, the stronger the relationship. Thus the correlation expressed by $r = 0.88$ is much stronger than that expressed by $r = 0.15$. See Figure 5.1 for examples of correlations.

Let us consider a study reported in the *American Journal of Psychiatry,* "Dissociation and Childhood Trauma in Psychologically Disturbed Adolescents." The researchers (Sanders & Giolas, 1991) hypothesized that dissociation (disturbance or change in function of identity, memory, or consciousness) during adolescence is positively correlated with childhood stress and abuse. Their subjects were a group of institutionalized adolescents (thirty-five females and twelve males) between the ages of thirteen and seventeen. They completed the Dissociative Experiences Scale and a questionnaire on child abuse and trauma. Statistically significant correlations were obtained between these measures ($r = 0.38$, $p > 0.01$). The researchers concluded that "these findings support the view that dissociation represents a reaction to early negative experience." If we adopt the scientific method, what are some of the questions that we might raise about the study? We must first remember that correlations do not necessarily imply a cause-and-effect relationship. Many alternative reasons for the relationship may exist. A third variable such as environmental stress might make it more likely for parents to use physical abuse and for the child to develop a range of problem behaviors. Poverty or poor living conditions may cause both the dissocia-

Depression is often inversely related to activity level. The more depressed a person is, the less likely he or she is to engage in any activities, particularly physical ones. It is not surprising then that research continues to show that jogging or other aerobic activity helps to reduce depression.

FIGURE 5.1 Possible Correlation Between Two Variables

The more closely the data points approximate a straight line, the greater the magnitude of the correlation coefficient *r*. The slope of the regression line rising from left to right in example (a) indicates a positive perfect correlation between two variables, whereas example (b) reveals a negative correlation. Example (c) shows a lower positive correlation. Example (d) shows no relationship whatsoever.

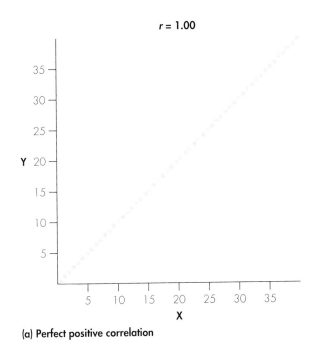

(a) Perfect positive correlation

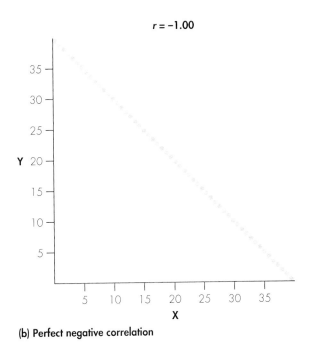

(b) Perfect negative correlation

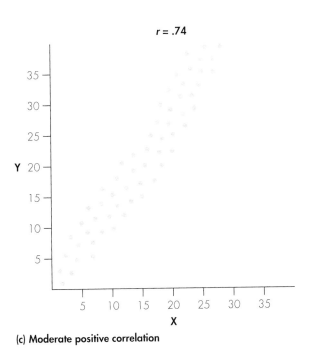

(c) Moderate positive correlation

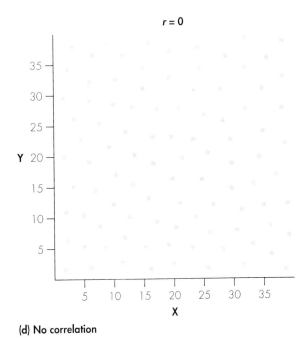

(d) No correlation

tion in the adolescent and abusive behavior on the part of the parents. Such third-variable possibilities in correlations are numerous. Consider the following actual observations. What third-variable explanations can you suggest for them?

> The number of storks nesting on rooftops in certain New England communities is positively correlated with the human birthrate.
>
> The number of violent crimes committed in a community is positively correlated with the number of churches in the community.

In correlations, it is also often difficult to determine the direction of the causation. If the findings of Sanders and Giolas are accepted, we must then determine if the physical abuse caused dissociation or did early dissociative behaviors in a child result in more negative parenting?

This study also raises other issues. Do we agree or disagree with how the variables were defined in the study (the operational definitions)? How were dissociation and trauma measured? Sanders and Giolas used the Dissociative Experiences Scale (DES) to measure dissociation and developed a child abuse and trauma questionnaire. Although the DES is one of the more frequently used research instruments to study dissociative experiences, not all researchers believe that it is a valid instrument. In a review of several studies, Wiener (1992) presented the following criticisms of the DES: (1) scores of adolescents on this measure overlap with 50 percent of the scores of patients with multiple personality disorders; (2) many patients other than those diagnosed with dissociative disorders also score high on the DES; and (3) all the questions are scored in the same direction, which increases the risk of response bias (some individuals tend to answer questions the same way). These criticisms raised concern over the possibility that the Dissociative Experiences Scale may be measuring "something other than dissociation."

The questionnaire devised by Sanders and Giolas to measure child abuse and trauma did not appear to undergo validation procedures. In other words, we are not certain if the variable that they intended to measure (child abuse and trauma) is actually measured by the questionnaire. For example, consider what else might be assessed by the sample questions from their questionnaire:

> Do you feel safe living at home?
>
> Were your parents unwilling to attend any of your school-related activities?
>
> Were you physically mistreated as a child or teenager?
>
> When you didn't follow the rules of the house, how often were you severely punished?
>
> Did your parents ridicule you?
>
> Were there traumatic or upsetting sexual experiences when you were a child or teenager that you couldn't speak to adults about?
>
> As a child did you feel unwanted or emotionally neglected?
>
> Did you ever think you wanted to leave your family and live with another family?

As a reader, do you believe that these questions measure "child abuse and trauma?" How would you determine this? How might other groups of adolescents answer these questions? Might institutionalized adolescents describe their home situation inaccurately? As one individual pointed out, "One could undoubtedly question these adolescents about a good many things and produce interesting correlations and comparisons to others whose mind set is more objective" (Furlong, 1991, p. 1423). We would be more certain about the validity of the child abuse trauma questionnaire if we had some independent verification of the severity of actual abuse suffered by the adolescents. Unfortunately, in the Sanders and Giolas study, responses on their questionnaire were not even related to abuse ratings obtained by clinicians at the institution. Even if we accepted the operational definitions in this study, we could not say that child abuse is specifically related to dissociation. We would have to give both questionnaires to control groups and to other psychiatric populations to determine how they would respond.

In summary, correlations indicate the degree to which two variables are related. It is a very important method of scientific inquiry because we cannot control many variables such as genetic makeup, gender, and socioeconomic status. Variables that we might be able to control (exposing a child to trauma or abuse) are considered unethical. Correlations can tell us how likely it is that two variables can occur together. Even when the variables are highly related, however, caution must be exercised in interpreting causality. The two variables may not be causally related, or both may be influenced by a third variable. Even if they are causally related, the direction of causality may be unclear.

ANALOGUE STUDIES

For a variety of reasons, researchers may be unable to devise certain studies on mental disorders or on the effects of treatment. First, not enough subjects may be found for a particular study. For example, it may be difficult to find patients with a rare type of mental disorder. Second, ethical, moral, or legal standards may prevent certain studies from being conducted. For example, a researcher might be interested in the effects of intense stress such as the effects of torture on psychological adjustment, but it is unethical to torture people. Third, studying real-life situations is not only difficult but also frequently unmanageable because researchers have a hard time controlling extraneous variables.

In such cases, researchers may resort to **analogue studies**—research that attempts to replicate or simulate, under controlled conditions, a situation that occurs in real life. Here are some examples of analogue studies:

1. To study the possible effects of a new form of treatment on patients with anxiety disorders, the researcher may use students who have high test anxiety rather than patients with anxiety disorders.

2. To test the hypothesis that human depression is caused by continual encounters with events that one cannot control, the researcher may expose rats to uncontrollable aversive stimuli and examine the increase of depressive-like behaviors (such as lack of motivation, inability to learn, and general apathy) in these animals.

3. To test the hypothesis that sexual sadism is influenced by watching sexually violent films and television programs, an experimenter exposes normal subjects to either violent or nonviolent sexual programs. The subjects then complete a questionnaire assessing their attitudes and values toward women and their likelihood of engaging in violent behaviors with women.

Obviously, each example is only an approximation of real life. Students with high test anxiety may not be equivalent to individuals with anxiety disorders, findings based on rats may not be applicable to human beings, and exposure to one violent sexual film and the use of a questionnaire may not be sufficient to allow a researcher to draw the conclusion that sexual sadism is caused by long-term exposure to such films. To the extent that the research is not applicable to the population or phenomena of interest, it lacks external validity. However, analogue studies give researchers insight into the processes that might be involved in abnormal behaviors and treatment. Analogue studies are devised by the experimenter, who can thus control extraneous factors, which enhances the internal validity of such studies. Researchers use their judgment to try to balance the problems in internal and external validity.

FIELD STUDIES

In some cases, analogue studies would be too contrived to accurately represent the real-life situation. Investigators may then resort to the **field study,** in which behaviors and events are observed and recorded in the natural environment. The subjects of a field study are most often members of a given social unit—a group, institution, or community. However, the investigation may also be limited to a single individual; single-subject studies are discussed in the next section.

Data collection techniques such as questionnaires, interviews, and the analysis of existing records may be used in field studies, but the primary technique is observation. The observers must be highly trained and have enough self-discipline to avoid disrupting or modifying the behavior processes that they are observing and recording.

The field study may be used to examine mass behavior after events of major consequence, such as wars, floods, and earthquakes (see Focus 5.2). It may also be applied to the study of personal crises, as in military combat, major surgery, terminal disease, or the loss of loved ones. An example of a field study is the recordings made by mental health personnel of the emotional reactions of people in the aftermath of an earthquake. More than 50 percent of the victims

FOCUS 5.2

Field Study of a Natural Disaster: The Mt. St. Helens Eruption and Ashfall

Mt. St. Helens, a volcano located near Seattle, Washington, erupted on Sunday morning, May 18, 1980. Several local residents were killed, and the force of the explosion and the subsequent lava flow caused miles and miles of destruction to vegetation and wildlife. In addition, the disaster sent tons and tons of ashes throughout Washington, Oregon, and Idaho. In many communities, the ashfall was so heavy that it blotted out the sun, leaving residents in total darkness.

The Mt. St. Helens eruption and the people it affected provided a nat-ural setting for the study of stress reactions to catastrophic events. Two researchers conducted a field study of the disaster to evaluate what DSM-IV now calls posttraumatic stress disorder (Adams & Adams, 1984). Studies have generally supported the belief that severe stress

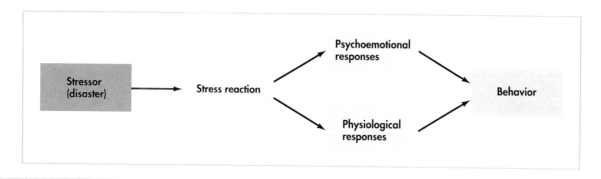

Homestead, Florida was severely damaged by Hurricane Andrew in 1992. Such a disaster provides a unique opportunity for social scientists to use field study techniques to study the psychological and social effects that a major disaster can have on a population.

can result in psychological disturbances, but the Mt. St. Helens disaster provided a unique opportunity to address two questions: does such stress cause long-term psychological disturbances in relatively normal people? Do the symptoms disappear as quickly as the environmental stressor? To answer these questions, the investigators used the following procedure:

1. They selected for study a single social unit—Othello, Washington, a town of approximately 5,000 persons. They identified the characteristics of its population and its community help-giving networks, from which data were collected.

2. They developed a conceptual model in which, according to theory, a stressor (here, the Mt. St. Helens disaster) was seen as creating a two-part stress reaction. One part is associated with physiological responses, and the second with psychoemotional responses; both are believed to be manifested in overt behavior.

3. They divided the observable behaviors and consequences into five categories and selected operational definitions for each.

4. They established postdisaster (experimental) and predisaster (control) time periods in which they could measure and compare behaviors. First, the researchers took the postdisaster period as the seven-month period after the disaster. Then, to eliminate (control) the effect of seasonal fluctuations on the measured behaviors, they took, as the predisaster period, the identical seven-month period of the preceding year.

The results revealed that cases of mental illness increased by nearly 236 percent, psychosomatic illness by 219 percent, and stress-aggravated illness by 198 percent. The researchers concluded that a disaster of this sort is likely to increase physical and psychosomatic illness, alcohol-related problems, aggression and violence, and family stress. They cautioned, however, that although they were able to control for seasonal variations, such variables as economic factors also need to be considered.

In any case, this particular field study is a prime example of the application of the scientific method: the formulation of hypotheses (here, as questions), identification of the unit of study, development of a conceptual scheme to guide the research, control of variables to the greatest extent possible, provision of an objective measurement scheme, reporting of the results, and critical analysis of the findings.

displayed generalized anxiety, agitation, trembling, and difficulty concentrating (De La Fuente, 1990).

Although field studies offer a more realistic investigative environment than other types of research, they suffer from certain limitations. First, as with other nonexperimental research, it is hard to determine the direction of causality because the data are correlational. Second, so many variables are at work in real-life situations that it is impossible to control—and sometimes even distinguish—them all. As a result, they may contaminate the findings. Third, observers can never be absolutely sure that their presence did not influence the interactions they observed.

SINGLE-SUBJECT STUDIES

Most scientists advocate the study of large groups of people to uncover the basic principles governing behavior. This approach, called the *nomothetic orientation,* is concerned with formulating general laws or principles while deemphasizing individual variations or differences. Experiments and correlational studies are nomothetic. Other scientists advocate the in-depth study of one person. This approach, exemplified by the single-subject study, has been called the *idiographic orientation.* Much debate has boiled over which method is more fruitful in studying psychopathology.

Although the idiographic method has many limitations, especially its lack of generality, it has proved very valuable in applied clinical work. Furthermore, the argument over which method is more fruitful is not productive because both approaches are needed to study abnormal behavior. The nomothetic approach seems appropriate for laboratory scientists, whereas the idiographic approach seems appropriate for their clinical counterparts, the psychotherapists, who daily face the pressures of treating disturbed individuals.

There are two types of single-subject studies: the

case study and the single-subject experiment. Both techniques may be used to examine a rare or unusual phenomenon, to demonstrate a novel diagnostic or treatment procedure, to test an assumption, to generate future hypotheses on which to base controlled research, and to collect comprehensive information for a better understanding of the individual. Only the single-subject experiment, however, can determine cause-effect relationships.

The Case Study

Physicians have used the case study extensively in describing and treating medical disease. In psychology, the **case study** is based on clinical data (observations, psychological tests, and historical and biographical information on the subject) and thus lacks the control and objectivity of many other methods. It serves as the primary source of data where systematic experimental procedures are not feasible. It is especially valuable for studying rare or unusual phenomena. For example, Hatcher (1989) reported a case in which a fourteen-year-old boy would "scream with terror" when seeing a doll with mobile eyes or with the roots of the hair showing. The origin of such a specific fear can be investigated by examining historical data. Case studies can also be helpful in determining diagnosis, characteristics, course, and outcome of a disorder. (They cannot, however, be used to demonstrate cause-and-effect relationships.) An example of a case study follows:

> Mr. P., a 28-year-old medical student, presented for treatment with a several-year history of recurrent and intrusive thoughts about losing his hair. He stated that he had been concerned with his appearance for as long as he could remember and had never been happy with the way his hair looked. In college, as his hair began to thin he began to use treatments to thicken his hair. During this time, he became a marathon runner, stating that "even if his hair wasn't right, he could make his body perfect." He began to have trouble looking in the mirror or at pictures of himself because of his defect. He developed a ritual way of fondling his hair in a certain way to relieve his anxiety over hair loss. At the time he entered treatment, the thoughts and ritualistic behaviors were interfering with his ability to perform in school. (Brady, Austin & Lydiard, 1991, p. 538)

The clinicians had observed certain patterns among their clients with body dysmorphic disorder (exaggerated preoccupation with an imagined defect in a normal-appearing individual). All of these clients showed behaviors that were consistent with obsessive-compulsive disorder (intrusive and recurrent thoughts, ritualistic behaviors, or both). The clinicians hypothesized that body dysmorphic disorder and obsessive-compulsive disorder may stem from the same biological cause. They based this view on the findings that both disorders show the same pharmacological response to the same medication.

Thus case studies can help a clinician formulate hypotheses that can be tested later in research. In another report, Goldman and Gutheil (1991) reported in the *American Journal of Psychiatry* that *bruxism* (clenching and grinding of teeth, especially during sleep) may be associated with sexual abuse. They base this preliminary observation on their work with five patients in whom this relationship was found. From their work with three patients, Coons and Bowman (1993) also believe that psychiatric patients who are unable to lose weight from dieting may suffer from dissociation. (Remember that these are hypothesized relationships that have to be verified in more rigorous studies.)

A number of new therapeutic procedures have also been reported in case study formats. Marquis (1991) reported success in working with individuals suffering from traumatic stress. His new approach is called eye movement desensitization. Clients visualize a disturbing situation and then are asked to follow with their eyes the therapist's moving finger. This procedure rapidly reduces the anxiety associated with the trauma. Of seventy-eight cases, sixty-eight were either "much improved" or "cured or almost cured."

Although the case study approach is not an experimental design, the degree of faith that we have in its findings can increase under certain conditions: (1) a number of clinicians report the same findings; (2) the clients are described in detail; (3) the concepts under study are operationally defined so we can all agree on what is being studied; (4) a description of the techniques is provided so that the study can be replicated by other clinicians; (5) if therapy is involved, premeasurements and postmeasurements are used to determine outcome; and (6) reports of the degree of successes and failures to find the relationship or in therapeutic outcome are provided.

One study involving the conditions just stated is the clinical series reported by Masters and Johnson (1970). A number of clinicians and researchers using the techniques described for sexual therapy have also reported similar success rates. Each of the disorders was operationally defined (premature ejaculation is the inability to delay ejaculation long enough during sexual intercourse to produce an orgasm in a female; a woman who has never achieved an orgasm through any means is diagnosed with primary orgasmic dysfunction). The outcome of the approach was assessed and reported. Although this is one of the better designed case studies, questions remain over some elements of the report (Barlow, Hayes & Nelson, 1984).

The Single-Subject Experiment

The **single-subject experiment** differs from the case study in that the former is actually an experiment in which some aspect of the person's own behavior is taken as the control or baseline from which to compare. Single-subject designs also use a **reversal design** (sometimes called an **ABAB design**) to demonstrate the effect of a treatment. In this design, a baseline for the frequency of a behavior is established. Then, a treatment is introduced. Next, the treatment is withdrawn and reinstated again. If the treatment affects the behavior, the behavior should vary according to the presence or absence of treatment.

An interesting type of single-subject experiment is the *multiple-baseline design,* which involves measuring changes (or the lack of change) in several related behaviors (for example, reading, writing, math) over a given period of time. The experimenter first makes a careful record of each behavior to establish the baselines. This allows the experimenter to determine responding before intervention. For example, reading proficiency might be 30 percent or accuracy in math problems 25 percent. Once this task is completed, the experimenter applies a modification such as a reward to one of the behaviors (reading proficiency) until a change occurs. Then the experimenter applies the same reward to the second behavior (math accuracy), and then to the third. If in all cases the behavior changes when the experimenter applies the modification, a strong inference of causal relationship can be made. A variation of this approach is to examine the impact of an intervention on the same behavior but in different settings (home, school,

church, community). Again a baseline is obtained in the different settings and the intervention applied to each.

Koegel and colleagues (1992a) used the multiple-baseline design to gauge success in treating an eleven-year-old autistic boy, Adam, who was largely unresponsive to verbalization from others. He would spin his entire body in circles while walking or standing, rapidly and repetitively tap his head with his hands, and scream and yell loudly. The experimenters wanted to determine if they could get Adam to respond appropriately to questions such as "What did you eat for lunch today?" Before treatment or during baseline, Adam rarely responded appropriately to questions in the clinic, community setting, and at home. The experimenters wanted to determine if they could get Adam to respond more appropriately by training him to evaluate his own answers to questions in terms of appropriateness (self-management). Small edibles were given to Adam when he learned to identify and record his correct responses. After the self-management training, in the clinic he responded appropriately 90 percent of the time to questions. Although Adam demonstrated improvement, the investigators were still not certain that the procedure itself had produced the change. They noticed that Adam was still responding inaccurately to questions in a community setting and at home. If the self-management procedure was responsible, they should also be able to improve Adam's performance by using it in these settings. They were able to demonstrate this relationship. When self-management was implemented in the community setting, Adam responded appropriately more than 80 percent of the time. At home he still responded inappropriately to questions. With self-management training, his accuracy improved to about 70 percent (see Figure 5.2).

Because the behavior changed successively with the introduction of the same technique in different settings, we can be fairly certain that self-management training caused the behavior changes. However, it is also possible that the food reinforcers rather than self-management were responsible for the change. To check this out, the experimenters used a withdrawal condition. Reinforcers were given but Adam no longer had to identify and record correct responses. Under this condition, correct responding dropped to one-half of what it was with self-management. This indicated that it was the self-

FIGURE 5.2   A Single-Subject Design

This experiment examines the impact of self-management training on appropriate verbal responses in three different settings.

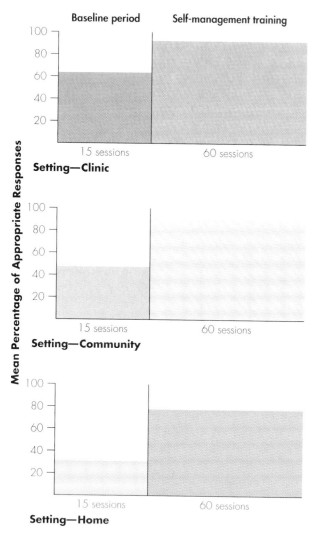

EPIDEMIOLOGICAL AND OTHER FORMS OF RESEARCH

In the field of abnormal and clinical psychology, different types of research are frequently employed, using experimental, correlational, case study, or field observation strategies. Some of these are listed here:

Survey research   Collecting data from all or part of a population to assess the relative prevalence, distribution, and interrelationships of naturally occurring phenomena. Surveys are frequently conducted by epidemiologists.

Longitudinal research   Observing and evaluating people's behaviors over a long period of time so that the course of a disorder or the effects of some factor such as a prevention program can be assessed over time.

Historical research   Reconstructing the past by reviewing and evaluating evidence available from historical documents (see Focus 5.3 for a revealing look at some of this research).

Twin studies   Focusing on twins as a population of interest because twins are genetically similar. Twin studies are often used to evaluate the influence of heredity and environment.

Historical researchers spend hours poring over original documents and records, systematically reconstructing some moment in the past in a detailed and accurate manner. Usually, the researcher is trying to prove some hypothesis, so any conclusions reached must be defensible.

management procedure rather than food given that was responsible for the change.

The Critical Thinking section in this chapter discusses a procedure called facilitated communication and presents various reports of its success. Applying what you've learned thus far in this chapter about the scientific method and the different experimental configurations, read the Critical Thinking section and try to answer the questions it asks.

Can Facilitated Communication Reach Autistic Individuals?

A few years ago, Douglas Biklen, a professor of special education at Syracuse university, developed an approach called "facilitated communication." The procedure is purported to help cognitively disabled individuals, such as those with autism, who may never have spoken, communicate their innermost thoughts. Amazing stories of its success have been reported.

One fourteen-year-old autistic male who spent his time rocking back and forth and moving his fingers in front of his eyes learned to quickly "talk" through a computer (Donaldson, 1992).

A seventeen-year-old girl with an estimated IQ score of 20 who had never learned to read, typed "I love you mommy and daddy." This occurred soon after she received training in facilitated communication (Whittenmore, 1992).

The training involved having the therapist "assist" the cognitively impaired individual by supporting the hand or arm of the client. The therapist also helps the client pull back the hand after each letter typed. Several programs have reported success in the use of facilitated communication. Biklen is so excited by the initial reports that he stated: "It's clear that facilitated communication could apply not only to the 350,000 persons in the U.S. with autism but also to those with other syndromes affecting speech or motor skills" (Whittenmore, 1992, p. 10).

Using the scientific method, how would you evaluate these reports? What type of scientific investigation do the reports involve? Are they case studies, field studies, or experiments? How might you examine the effectiveness of facilitated communication with a single individual? How could you guard against methodological problems such as expectancy effects? Can you think of any alternative explanations for the finding that "cognitive impaired" individuals can type out their "inner" thoughts? Design an experimental study to test the effectiveness of facilitated communication.

Treatment outcome studies   Evaluating the effectiveness of treatment in alleviating mental disorders. Outcome is concerned with answering the question of whether treatment is effective.

Treatment process studies   Analyzing how therapist, client, or situational factors influence each other during the course of treatment. Process research focuses on how or why treatment is effective.

Program evaluation   Analyzing the effectiveness of intervention or prevention programs.

These types of research frequently use experimental, correlational, and single-subject methods. For instance, survey researchers often collect data and then correlate certain variables such as social class and adjustment to discover the relationship between variables. Researchers may also combine elements in different types of research. For example, an investigator conducting treatment outcome studies may use surveys and longitudinal studies.

One of the more important types of research is **epidemiological research,** which examines the rate and distribution of mental disorders in the population. This type of research is used to determine the extent of mental disturbance that is found in a targeted population and the factors influencing the rate of mental disturbance. Two methods, prevalence and incidence, are used to describe the rates. First, the *prevalence rate* tells us how many individuals in a targeted population have a particular disorder. This figure is determined for a specified time period. Determining the prevalence rate is especially important for planning treatment services because mental health workers need to know the percentage of people who are likely to be afflicted with disorders.

FOCUS 5.3

Historical Research: Minorities and Pathology

When we seriously study the "scientific" literature of the past relating to people who are culturally different from the dominant social group, we are immediately impressed with how often minority groups and pathology are implicitly equated (Sue & Sue, 1990). For example, the historical use of science in the investigation of racial differences seems to be linked with white supremacist notions.

A. Thomas and Sillen (1972) referred to this as "scientific racism" and cited several historical examples to support their contention:

1. In 1840, fabricated census figures were used to support the notion that black people living under "unnatural" conditions

of freedom were prone to anxiety.

2. Mental health for blacks was taken to consist of contentment with subservience.

3. It was assumed that psychologically normal blacks were faithful to their "masters," and happy-go-lucky.

4. Influential medical journals presented as facts what were really fantasies supporting the belief that the anatomical, neurological, or endocrinological attributes of blacks were always inferior to those of whites.

5. The black person's brain was assumed to be smaller and less developed.

6. Blacks were thought to be less

prone to mental illness "because their minds were so simple."

7. The dreams of blacks were judged juvenile in character and not as complex as those of whites.

Furthermore, the belief that various human groups exist at different stages of biological evolution was accepted by the respected psychologist G. Stanley Hall (1904). He explicitly stated that Africans, Indians, and Chinese were members of "adolescent races" and in a stage of incomplete development. In most cases, the evidence used to support these conclusions was fabricated, extremely flimsy, or distorted to fit the belief in nonwhite inferiority

---

Second, the *incidence rate* tells us how many *new* cases of a disorder appear in an identified population within a specified time period. The incidence rate is likely to be lower than the prevalence rate because incidence involves only new cases, and prevalence includes new and existing cases during the specified time period. Incidence rates are important for examining etiologic hypotheses about the risk for a disorder. For example, if we find that new cases of a disorder are more likely to appear in a population that is exposed to a particular stressor than in another population not exposed to the stressor, we can hypothesize that the stress causes the disorder. Epidemiological research, then, is important not only in describing the distribution of disorders but also in analyzing the possible factors that contribute to disorders. Focus 5.4 compares the prevalence rates of disorders in the United States and China and some problems that must be considered in conducting epidemiological research.

Biological Research Strategies

More and more research is being performed in the biological area on the causes and treatment of mental disorders. We will present some of the research strategies involved. Some of them are also applicable to psychological research.

Genetic Linkage Studies Genetic linkage studies attempt to determine if a disorder follows a genetic pattern. That is, individuals closely related to a person with the disorder (called the *proband*) should be more likely to display the disorder or a related disorder if the disorder is genetically linked. Genetic studies of psychiatric disorders often follow this procedure (Alexander, Lerer & Baron, 1992):

1. The proband and his or her family members are identified.

2. The proband is asked for the psychiatric history of specific family members.

(A. Thomas & Sillen, 1972). For example, Gossett (1963) reported how, when one particular study in 1895 revealed that the sensory perception of Native Americans was superior to that of blacks, and that of blacks to that of whites, the results were used to support a belief in the mental superiority of whites. "Their reactions were slower because they belonged to a more deliberate and reflective race than did the members of the other two groups" (p. 364). The belief that blacks are "born athletes" (as opposed, for example, to being "born" scientists or heads of state) derives from this tradition. The fact that Hall was a well-respected psychologist often referred to as "the father of child study," and first president of the American Psychological Association (APA), did not prevent him from inheriting the racial biases of his times.

In psychological literature, the portrayal of the culturally different has generally taken the form of stereotyping them as "deficient" in certain "desirable" attributes. For example, de Gobineau's *Essay on the Inequality of the Human Races* (1915) and Darwin's *On The Origin of the Species by Means of Natural Selection* (1859) were used to support the genetic intellectual superiority of whites and the genetic inferiority of the "lower races." Galton (1869) wrote explicitly that African "Negroes" were "half-witted men" who made "childish, stupid and simpleton-like mistakes," and Jews were deemed inferior physically and mentally and fit only for a parasitical existence on other nations. Using the Binet scales in testing Spanish, Indian, Mexican American, and African American families, Terman (1916) concluded that these people were uneducable.

That the genetic deficiency model still exists can be seen in the writing of Shuey (1966), Jensen (1969), Hernstein (1982), and Shockley (1972). These writers adopted the position that genes play a predominant role in the determination of intelligence. While heredity plays a role in intelligence, the central issues are whether racial differences or IQ scores can be attributed to heredity and what policy implications are proposed. For example, Shockley (1972) expressed fears that the accumulation of genes for weak or low intelligence in the black population will seriously affect overall intelligence in the general population. Thus he advocated that people with low IQ scores should not be allowed to bear children; they should be sterilized. Such ideas have generated considerable anger and controversy.

3. These members are contacted and given some type of assessment to determine if they have the same or "related" disorder.

4. Assessment of the proband and family members may include psychological tests, brain scans, and neuropsychological examinations.

This research strategy depends on the accurate diagnosis of both the proband and the relatives. One complication is that the criteria for specific disorders have changed with each new edition of *Diagnostic and Statistical Manual of Mental Disorders* (DSM). Are the findings based on the DSM-IV categories applicable to the same ones in DSM-II, DSM-III, or DSM III-R? Another complication has been found in the family history interview method. In this procedure, the proband is asked if relatives also have the same disorder. Kendler and colleagues (1991) found that this method may be subject to error. Female twin pairs discordant (one twin has the disorder, the other

does not) for major depression, generalized anxiety disorder, and alcoholism were asked if their parents had the same disorder. The "sick" twin was more likely to report that her parents had the same disorder than the "well" twin. Caution must be used in employing the family history method in genetic linkage studies. An individual's psychiatric status ("sick" or "well") may influence the accuracy of his or her assessment of the mental health of relatives. This bias in reporting may be reduced by using multiple informants or assessing the family members directly.

Biological Markers   Genetic studies may attempt to identify **biological markers** (biological indicators of a disorder that may or may not be causal) for specific disorders. Thus differences in variables such as cerebral blood flow patterns, responses to specific medications, or brain structure differences have been noted. Some researchers believe that for schizophrenia, differences in eye movement pursuit, attention

Do Americans Have Higher Rates of Mental Disturbance than Chinese?

The prevalence rate of mental disorders in the mainland of China appears to be much lower than in the United States. A major epidemiological study of mental disorders in China was conducted with the assistance of U.S. investigators, including the director of mental health for the World Health Organization. The results revealed that the prevalence rate of most disorders was much lower in China than in the United States. For example, nearly 1 percent of the U.S. population was diagnosed as having schizophrenia (Myers et al., 1984), about two times the proportion in China. Americans were also far more likely than the Chinese to have other forms of mental disturbance. Do the findings mean that Americans are more disturbed?

Americans may in fact be more prone to mental illness, but an alternative explanation is that the different prevalence rates are the result of methodological and conceptual differences between the two studies that yielded the different results.

Bromet (1984) suggested that two major sources of error must be controlled, especially in cross-cultural comparisons: sample characteristics and case identification. If samples from the two populations were not comparable, that might account for the different rates. For example, the Chinese study included people fifteen years of age and older while the U.S. sample targeted people aged eighteen and older. Social class and rural-urban differences were also apparent. With respect to case identification, one requirement of an epidemiological study is that cases of a disorder be correctly identified. In cross-cultural or cross-national research, this task is extremely difficult. We do not know if the same procedures and assumptions were used in the two populations. The criteria used to define whether a person has a particular mental disorder may have varied from study to study. Furthermore, respondents might have differed in their willingness to report or show symptoms of mental disorders. Some studies have shown that Chinese may not as readily report psychological symptoms as Americans (Sue & Morishima, 1982).

Even more problematic is the possibility that different cultures express the same mental disorders in different ways. For example, Chinese are more likely than Americans to show somatic complaints when they are depressed. These factors are important to consider before the conclusion can be drawn that one population is more disturbed than another. Although it may be true that Chinese are less prone to mental disturbance, much more research needs to be conducted before this conclusion can be accepted.

---

and information-processing deficits, and reduced brain size are biological markers. Although some of these biological markers have been reported in close relatives of the patients, they have also been seen in nonschizophrenic populations. Several researchers concluded, "No definite 'biological marker' for schizophrenia or related spectrum conditions has been identified" (Szymanski, Kane & Lieberman, 1991, p. 106). They based their view on the criteria needed for a biological marker: (1) it is distributed differently in the patient group than in control populations; (2) it is stable over time; (3) it appears more frequently in relatives of the patients than in the general population; and (4) it is associated with and precedes the development of the disorder in high-risk children. It was hoped that biological markers could be included in DSM-IV's diagnostic criteria, but this has not been possible. Mass media constantly report that some biological marker has been found that either causes or is diagnostic of mental disorders. Unfortunately, most of these have not been supported with subsequent research.

Other Concepts in Biological Research Iatrogenic refers to the unintended results from the activity of the therapist. It includes any side effects of either biological or psychological therapy. One major source of error is not recognizing side effects of treatment and therefore erroneously treating the side effects as another disorder. Therapists have mistakenly diagnosed memory losses from antidepressant medication as Alzheimer's disease or other organic conditions (Heston & White, 1991). Psychological interventions or techniques may also produce unexpected results. Researchers and therapists believe that some cases of multiple personality disorder are the result of hypnotism or suggestion (Coons, 1988; Ofshe, 1992). Hypnotism has been used to retrieve memories, especially those of a traumatic nature, and clinicians often believe that the information obtained in this manner is accurate. The Council on Scientific Affairs (1985), however, concluded the following in its investigation of hypnosis: (1) traumatic memories retrieved may reflect an emotional reality rather than accurate recollection; (2) hypnosis produces a state in which an individual is more vulnerable to subtle cues and suggestions that often distort recollections; (3) hypnosis increases both accurate and inaccurate information; (4) without independent verification, neither the hypnotist nor the subject can distinguish between accurate and inaccurate information; (5) hypnosis can "increase the subject's confidence in his memories without affecting accuracy and . . . increase errors while also falsely increasing confidence" (p. 1921); and (6) in general, recollections obtained during nonhypnotic recall are more accurate than those obtained during hypnosis. These conclusions indicate the need to question material obtained during a hypnotic state. Investigators using hypnosis may obtain inaccurate information through unintended suggestion.

Penetrance refers to the degree to which a genetic characteristic is manifested by individuals carrying this gene. Complete penetrance occurs when a carrier always shows the characteristic associated with that gene. In mental disorders, incomplete penetrance is the rule. Even in cases of schizophrenia, only about half of the identical twins of the proband develop this disorder.

Pathognomonic refers to a symptom or characteristic on which a diagnosis can be made. A great deal of research has been directed to discovering a symptom that is specifically distinctive of a disorder.

Biological challenge tests are often used to determine the effect of a substance on behavior. If we believe that a specific additive or food is responsible for hyperactivity in a child, we might observe the child's behavior when given food with the additive

(the "challenge" phase) and behavior when given food without the additive. If the additive and disruptive behavior are linked, the behavior should be present during the challenge phase and absent during the other phase.

ETHICAL ISSUES IN RESEARCH

Although research is primarily a scientific endeavor, it has also raised ethical issues. Consider the following examples:

1. To study the effects of a new drug in treating schizophrenia, a researcher needs an experimental group that receives the drug treatment and a control group that receives no treatment. Is it ethical to withhold treatment from a control group of schizophrenics, who need treatment, to test the effectiveness of the drug?

2. To study the way depressed individuals respond to negative feedback, an investigator deceives depressed people into believing that they performed poorly on a task. Is the deception ethical?

3. A researcher is interested in developing a new assessment tool to uncover personal conflicts. The assessment tool asks people to disclose information about their sexual conduct and private thoughts and feelings—information that may cause embarrassment and discomfort. Does the assessment measure invade the subjects' privacy?

4. A researcher hypothesizes that alcoholics cannot stop drinking after having one alcoholic drink. He arranges for alcoholic patients to have one drink and then examines how strongly they are motivated to receive additional drinks. Is it ethical and detrimental for alcoholics to be given alcohol as a part of an experiment?

5. An investigator believes that people who are exposed to inescapable stress are likely to develop feelings of helplessness and depression. Because the investigator does not want to subject human beings to inescapable stress, the experiment is conducted with dogs, which are given painful

Research involving animals has yielded important information. The APA's 1992 ethical standards require that animals be treated "humanely" and that any procedure that subjects them to stress or pain be carefully evaluated.

and inescapable electric shocks. Is it ethical to cause pain to animals as part of a study?

These examples raise a number of ethical concerns about how research is conducted and whether it has, or should have, limits. How can the rights of human beings (or even of other animals) be protected without impeding valuable experimentation? There is no question that to understand psychopathology and to devise effective treatment and prevention interventions, experimenters may have to occasionally devise investigations that cause pain and involve deception. To study human behavior, pain may be inflicted (for example, surgical implants may cause pain or shocks may be used to induce stress), and deception is sometimes necessary to conceal the true nature of a study. The research must be consistent with certain principles of conduct, however, and intended to protect subjects as well as to enable researchers to contribute to the long-term welfare of human beings (and other animals).

The American Psychological Association (1992) has adopted the principle that the prospective scientific, applied, or educational value of the proposed research must outweigh the risk or discomfort to its subjects. Certain guidelines have been used to protect participants. Subjects should be fully informed of the procedures and risks involved in the research and should give their consent to participate. Deception may be used only when alternative means are not possible, and participants should be provided with a sufficient explanation of the study as soon as possible. They should be free to withdraw from a study at any time. Furthermore, all participants must be treated with dignity, and research procedures must minimize pain, discomfort, embarrassment, and so on. If undesirable consequences to participants are found, the researcher has the responsibility to detect and remedy these consequences. Finally, unless otherwise agreed on in advance, information obtained from participants is confidential.

Animal rights groups have also expressed recent concern over the use of animals in psychological research (Bales, 1988). The American Psychological Association's principles state that psychologists should make every effort to minimize discomfort, illness, and pain of animals. Only when alternative procedures are unavailable and the goal is justified by the potential value to human beings should researchers be allowed to consider subjecting animals to discomfort or pain. Animals should be treated humanely.

Researchers usually submit their research plans to review boards associated with their institutions (such as a university review board). If the review boards believe that the research is unethical, careless, or inhumane, the research is not approved. Although instances can be found of unethical or questionable conduct on the part of researchers, particularly in the past, the principles adopted by the American Psychological Association have now minimized such conduct.

The American Psychological Association (1993) has also published guidelines for those working with culturally diverse populations. The guidelines indicate the need for researchers to (1) consider the impact of sociopolitical factors, (2) become aware of how their own cultural background might affect their perception, and (3) consider the validity of instruments used in research in a cross-cultural context.

SUMMARY

1. The scientific method provides for the systematic and controlled collection of data and the formulation of objective hypotheses based on those data. The characteristics of the scientific method include self-correction, hypothesis testing, use of operational definitions, consideration of reliability and validity of instruments, and acknowledgment of base rates. Biological research strategies have involved genetic linkage studies and have attempted to identify biological markers or indications of a disorder. Iatrogenic effects are side effects resulting from the activity of the therapist.

2. The experiment is the most powerful research tool we have for determining and testing cause-and-effect relationships. In its simplest form, an experiment involves an experimental hypothesis, an independent variable, and a dependent variable. The independent variable is manipulated for the experimental group of subjects. Extraneous variables are typically controlled through the use of control groups, randomization procedures, or matching of subjects in experimental and control groups.

3. A correlation is a measure of the degree to which two variables are related. It is expressed as a correlation coefficient, a numerical value between −1 and +1, symbolized by r. Correlational techniques provide less precision, control, and generality than experiments, and they cannot be taken to imply cause-and-effect relationships.

4. In the study of abnormal behavior, an ana-

logue study is used to create a situation as close to real life as possible. It permits the study of phenomena under controlled conditions.

5. The field study relies primarily on naturalistic observations. In this technique, the psychologist enters a situation as unobtrusively as possible to observe and record behavior as it occurs naturally.

6. Rather than studying large groups of people, many scientists advocate the in-depth study of one individual. Two types of single-subject techniques are the case study and the single-subject experiment. The case study is especially appropriate when a phenomenon is so rare that it is impractical to try to study more than one instance of it. Single-subject experiments differ from case studies in that they rely on experimental procedures; some aspect of the person's own behavior is taken as the control.

7. A particularly important type of research in abnormal psychology is epidemiological research, which examines the rate and distribution of mental disorders in a population. It can also provide insight into what groups are at risk for mental disturbance and what factors may influence disturbance.

8. The scientific method has weaknesses and limitations. Like other tools, it is subject to misuse and misunderstanding, both of which can give rise to moral and ethical concerns. Such concerns have led to the development of guidelines from the American Psychological Association for ethical conduct and of ways to deal with violations within the mental health professions.

KEY TERMS

analogue study An investigation that attempts to replicate or simulate, as closely as possible, a situation under controlled conditions that occurs in real life

base rate The frequency of a behavior's natural occurrence in the population, used for comparison in research studies

biological markers Biological indicators such as eye movement dysfunctions that help identify a disorder

case study Intensive study of one individual that relies on observation, psychological tests, or historical and biological data

correlation The degree to which two variables covary or are associated with each other in a population

dependent variable Attitudes or behaviors that are expected to change as a result of the manipulation of the independent variable in a psychological experiment

epidemiological research The study of the rate and distribution of mental disorders in a population

experiment A technique of scientific inquiry in which an independent variable is manipulated, the changes in a dependent variable are measured, and extraneous variables are controlled to the extent possible

experimental hypothesis A prediction concerning how an independent variable affects a dependent variable in an experiment

field study An investigative technique in which behaviors are observed and recorded in the natural environment

genetic linkage studies Studies that examine whether a disorder follows a genetic pattern among family members

hypothesis A conjectural statement that describes a relationship between variables

iatrogenic Unintended side effects of therapy

independent variable The variable or condition that is manipulated by the experimenter and tested for its effects on the dependent variable

operational definitions Definitions of the variables under study

reliability The degree to which consistent results are obtained with the same procedure or measure

reversal (ABAB) design An experiment in which behaviors are measured at four times: (A) before the independent variable or treatment is introduced; (B) after the independent variable is introduced; (A) after the independent variable is withdrawn; and (B) after the reintroduction of the independent variable

scientific method A method of inquiry that provides for the systematic collection of data through controlled observation and for the testing of hypotheses based on those data

single-subject experiment An experiment performed on a single individual in which some aspect of that individual's own behavior is used as the control

theory A group of principles and hypotheses that together explain some aspect of a particular area of inquiry

CHAPTER 6

Anxiety Disorders

The disorders discussed in this chapter are all characterized by **anxiety,** or feelings of fear and apprehension. These disorders can produce seemingly illogical—and often restrictive—patterns of behavior, as illustrated in the following examples:

A woman reports, "All of a sudden, I felt a tremendous wave of fear for no reason at all. My heart was pounding, my chest hurt, and it was getting harder to breathe. I thought I was going to die." (National Institute of Mental Health, 1991, p. 1)

A male college student displayed extreme nervousness and anxiety in social situations with females. He would cross the street to avoid having to interact with female classmates. Thoughts of asking them out produced such anxiety that he had only tried once to ask a woman for a date. (Author's file)

The patient was a 35-yr-old woman who experienced a panic attack while driving to her home in a suburb of Albany, N.Y. during the first cold and snowy night of winter. She reported that her heart suddenly began to beat wildly as she struggled to breathe . . . she stopped her car in the middle of the road, got out, and started running down the highway . . . she felt that she was going to die. (Ley, 1992, pp. 349–350)

A 26-year-old man has an eleven-year history of obsessional thoughts involving similarities and differences. When reading, he often wonders if he has seen a particular word recently. To alleviate his anxiety over this, he spends hours going through newspapers and magazines in an attempt to locate the word. If two trees appear similar, he feels compelled to compare the texture and odor of their leaves, their bark, and the shape of their branches to find out if they are the same or different. (Junginger & Turner, 1987)

Anxiety is a fundamental human emotion that was recognized as long as 5,000 years ago. Everyone has experienced it, and we will continue to experience it throughout our lives. (Focus 6.1 examines the possible adaptive function that anxiety serves.) Many observers regard anxiety as a basic condition of modern

Anxiety and Fear: Do We Need Them?

It is clear that high levels of anxiety and fear can lead to psychomotor and intellectual errors, impair psychological functioning, and disturb concentration and memory. Yet some evidence exists that mild or moderate anxiety may serve a useful or adaptive function. In one study (Manyande et al., 1992), patients facing minor surgery (such as the removal of hemorrhoids or repair of an ulcer) listened to a tape describing relaxation training and mental strategies to help them deal with their concerns. A control group also facing surgery was exposed to a fifteen-minute informative tape that described the hospital and the staff. The patients listened to the tape at least twice before surgery and could also listen to the tape after the operation. Surprisingly, two of the hormones related to stress (adrenaline and cortisol) were much higher in the group exposed to the relaxation tape than the control group, both before and after the operation.

These results support the theory by Janis (1971), who believed that moderate anticipatory anxiety about realistic threats is necessary for the development of coping behavior. In his study of patients undergoing surgery, he found that moderately anxious patients did better postsurgically than individuals who were either highly anxious or expressed little or no anxiety. Moderate fear levels can enhance vigilance and aid in a realistic appraisal of what is to come, both of which help the individual develop appropriate coping responses.

existence. The British poet W. H. Auden called the twentieth century "the age of anxiety." Yet "reasonable doses" of anxiety act as a safeguard to keep us from ignoring danger, and anxiety appears to have an adaptive function. Something would be wrong if an individual did not feel some anxiety in facing day-to-day stressors. For example, many persons report anxiety in terms of overload at home, work, or school; family demands; financial concerns; and interpersonal conflicts (Bolger & Schilling, 1991). When facing these stressors, individuals without a disorder are likely to handle the situation by facing it. They use strategies such as relaxation and problem solving to reduce stress (Genest et al., 1990). A diagnosis of an anxiety disorder occurs only when overwhelming anxiety disrupts social or occupational functioning or produces significant distress, as illustrated in the following case.

> I've always been tense from as far back as I can remember. But lately it's getting worse. Sometimes I think I'm going crazy—especially at . . . night. I can't sleep for fear of what has to be done the next day. Should I go to my psych class tomorrow, or skip it and study for my stat exam? If I skip it, maybe the prof will throw a pop quiz. He's known for that, you know. These attacks are frightful. I had another one last week. It was horrible. I thought I would die. My roommate didn't know what to do. By the time it was over, my blouse was completely drenched. My roommate was so scared she called you. I was so embarrassed afterward. I think she [the roommate] wants to move out. I don't blame her. (Author's file)

MANIFESTATIONS OF ANXIETY

Anxiety is manifested in three ways: *cognitively* (in a person's thoughts), *behaviorally* (in a person's actions), and *somatically* (in physiological or biological reactions).

Cognitive manifestations of anxiety may range from mild worry to panic. Severe forms can bring a conviction of impending doom (the end of the world or death), a preoccupation with unknown dangers, or fears of losing control over bodily functions. Patients suffering from *panic disorder* often have terrifying cognitions such as dying of suffocation or physical catastrophe befalling a family member. Individuals with *generalized anxiety disorder (GAD)* tend to have milder anxiety-evoking thoughts dealing with themes such as misfortune, financial concerns, academic and social performance, and rejection (Lindsay

Evidence suggests that anxiety may serve an adaptive purpose and that moderate levels of fear about realistic threats may play a role in the development of coping behaviors. Functional fear appeals have been used in advertising campaigns to encourage people to use seat belts, to think about the effects of drinking and driving, and as shown in this photo, to stop smoking.

et al., 1987). These apprehensions are out of proportion to the actual situation.

Behavioral manifestations of anxiety involve avoiding anxiety-provoking situations. A student with an extreme fear of public speaking will avoid classes in which class presentations are necessary. Individuals who have panic attacks may stay at home rather than risk the possibility of experiencing anxiety in public.

Somatic changes include shallow breathing, mouth dryness, cold hands and feet, diarrhea, frequent urination, fainting, heart palpitations, elevated blood pressure, increased perspiration, muscular tenseness (especially in the head, neck, shoulders, and chest), and indigestion.

The anxiety disorders do not involve a loss of contact with reality: people suffering from them can usually go about most of the day-to-day business of living. Although these people are aware of the illogical and self-defeating nature of some of their behaviors, they seem incapable of controlling them. In severe cases, the disturbed individuals may spend great amounts of time dealing with their debilitating fears—but to no avail. This preoccupation may, in turn, lead to emotional stress and turmoil, maladaptive behaviors, and disruptions in interpersonal relationships.

Classification of the anxiety disorders is continuing and changes occur with each new edition of the *Diagnostic and Statistical Manual of Mental Disorders*. Although *panic disorder* appears to be a reliable and valid diagnosis, *generalized anxiety disorder* has proven less so, and the criteria for its diagnosis has changed in DSM-IV (for example, duration of one month has been changed to six months; Kendler, 1992a). In DSM-III-R, panic attacks (intense fear accompanied by symptoms such as a pounding heart, trembling, shortness of breath, fear of losing control or dying) were discussed only in the panic disorder section, and they were described as *unexpected*. This promoted the view that panic attacks only occurred in persons with panic disorder and that they were always unexpected. Panic attacks can occur with each anxiety disorder, however, and often they are not unexpected.

In DSM-IV three types of panic attacks can occur: (1) situationally bound (occurs before or during exposure to the feared stimulus); (2) situationally predisposed (occurs usually but not always in the presence of the feared stimulus); and (3) unexpected or uncued (occurs "spontaneously" and without warning). Persons with obsessive-compulsive disorder and social and specific phobias generally report that their panic attacks are triggered by specific situations (situationally bound). Individuals panicking when they face a feared situation is not considered unusual. What has generated much controversy and research is the question of unexpected or "spontaneous" panic

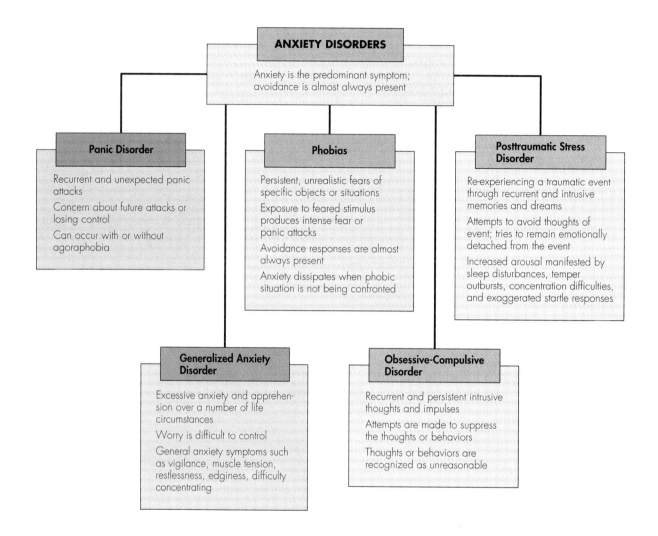

ANXIETY DISORDERS

Anxiety is the predominant symptom; avoidance is almost always present

Panic Disorder

Recurrent and unexpected panic attacks

Concern about future attacks or losing control

Can occur with or without agoraphobia

Phobias

Persistent, unrealistic fears of specific objects or situations

Exposure to feared stimulus produces intense fear or panic attacks

Avoidance responses are almost always present

Anxiety dissipates when phobic situation is not being confronted

Posttraumatic Stress Disorder

Re-experiencing a traumatic event through recurrent and intrusive memories and dreams

Attempts to avoid thoughts of event; tries to remain emotionally detached from the event

Increased arousal manifested by sleep disturbances, temper outbursts, concentration difficulties, and exaggerated startle responses

Generalized Anxiety Disorder

Excessive anxiety and apprehension over a number of life circumstances

Worry is difficult to control

General anxiety symptoms such as vigilance, muscle tension, restlessness, edginess, difficulty concentrating

Obsessive-Compulsive Disorder

Recurrent and persistent intrusive thoughts and impulses

Attempts are made to suppress the thoughts or behaviors

Thoughts or behaviors are recognized as unreasonable

attacks. Why is it that some persons experience panic when no identifiable fearful stimulus is present? Individuals with panic disorder can have both unexpected and situation-specific panic attacks (Rapee et al., 1992).

Certain controversies remain. Because obsessive-compulsive disorder is often accompanied by depression, some investigators believe that it should be considered a mood disorder (Tynes, White & Steketee, 1990). However, the finding that clients with obsessive-compulsive disorders show an increase in anxiety disorders seems to support the present categorization of the disorder. Questions have also been

raised about the appropriateness of classifying post-traumatic stress disorder (PTSD) as an anxiety disorder. In fact, Davidson and Foa (1991) recommended placing it in a new category that might be called "Disorders of Psychological Trauma." These controversies and conflicts, although confusing, are necessary to the development of more reliable and valid classifications.

Currently, to be included as an **anxiety disorder,** one of the following criteria must be met. The anxiety may itself be the major disturbance, as in *panic disorder* and *generalized anxiety disorder;* it may be manifested only when the affected individual encounters particular situations, as in the *phobias;* or the anxiety may result from an attempt to master other symptoms, as in *obsessive-compulsive disorder.* In this chapter, we discuss all four of these major groups of anxiety disorders, which are shown in the disorders chart on page 000. In addition, we discuss *posttraumatic stress disorder,* a disorder resulting from exposure to an extraordinary stressor.

PANIC DISORDER AND GENERALIZED ANXIETY DISORDER

The predominant characteristic of both panic disorder and generalized anxiety disorder is unfocused, or *free-floating,* anxiety. That is, the affected individual is fearful and apprehensive but often does not know exactly what he or she is afraid of.

Panic Disorder

Panic disorder is characterized by severe and frightening episodes of apprehension and feelings of impending doom. These attacks are often described as horrible and can last from a few minutes to several hours. The anxiety associated with this disorder is much greater than is found in generalized anxiety disorder. According to DSM-IV, a diagnosis of panic disorder includes recurrent panic attacks, some of which have to be unexpected, and at least one month of apprehension over having another attack or worrying about the consequences of an attack.

One 25-year-old woman described her feelings in the following way: "It could not be worse if I were hanging by my fingertips from the wing of an airplane in flight. The feeling of impending doom was just as real and frightening" (Fishman & Sheehan, 1985, p. 26). The attacks are especially feared because they often occur unpredictably and without warning. "They would start just out of nowhere with this explosive anxiety or panic, fast heartbeat—just uncontrollable shaking and wanting to clutch up and not move" (Pasnau, 1984, p. 7).

A variety of physical symptoms such as sweating, choking, and heart palpitations are reported during the panic attacks (Balon et al., 1988). In many such cases, people develop *agoraphobia,* or anxiety about leaving the home, which is caused by fear of having an attack in a public place. Such cases are diagnosed

The Scream, by Edvard Munch, depicts some of the symptoms that accompany anxiety. The swirling colors of the background evoke a feeling of uncontrollable disorder that cannot be escaped. The subject, clutching his head, seems terrorized by something, which must be in his own mind, for the scene is otherwise peaceful.

as panic disorder with agoraphobia. The following case seems typical:

Lois R. was sixteen when she had her first panic attack. She felt as if she were going to die. "My heart was beating so fast that I thought I was having a heart attack, my mouth was very dry, I couldn't think. . . ."

That was only the start. At school she began running to the nurse's office several times a week, in terror and asking for help. She lived in fear of attacks and of being where she could not cope with them. She stopped riding in elevators. She was afraid to go anywhere in a car. Open spaces seemed threatening, especially if she was alone.

For the next thirty-nine years fear plagued her. It sometimes waned but never left. She saw many doctors: a family physician who thought she was having a nervous breakdown and tried to cure her by making her sleep for a week; a psychiatrist who prescribed Valium and other tranquilizers, plus sleeping pills, over a ten-year period; a psychologist who hypnotized her to bring her back to her childhood. "It was expensive," she says, "and it didn't help." (*Novato* [California] *Independent Journal*, July 6, 1984, p. C3)

Individuals with panic disorder report periods of somewhat low anxiety alternating with intense panic attacks, although they may be apprehensive about having another panic attack. Many panic attack patients report a disturbed childhood environment; most indicate that they first experienced panic attacks after some form of separation, such as leaving home or the loss or threatened loss of a loved one (Raskin et al., 1982; Roy-Byrne et al., 1986).

The *lifetime prevalence rate* (proportion of individuals in the sample who ever had the disorder) for panic disorder is approximately 3.8 percent (Katerndahl & Realini, 1993). Women are three times more likely to be diagnosed with this disorder than are men. It is somewhat less prevalent a problem in Mexican Americans (Karno et al., 1987). Future studies will probably report a higher prevalence of the disorder because the category of panic disorder has been expanded to encompass most cases of agoraphobia.

Panic attacks appear to be fairly common. In one study of college students, one-fourth to one-third reported having had a panic attack during a one-year period (Asmundson & Norton, 1993; Brown & Cash, 1990). Approximately 43 percent of adolescents in one sample reported having had a panic attack (King et al., 1993). Most of these panic attacks are associated with an identifiable stimulus. However, more than 12 percent reported unexpected panic attacks (Telch, Lucas & Nelson, 1989). Although panic attacks appear common, few persons who have them will develop a panic disorder. The predisposing conditions that make some people more vulnerable to developing a panic disorder still need to be identified. Exposure to stressors may be a factor. Individuals who report having panic attacks report more major life events during the period when the attacks began than during the preceding six months (Pollard, Pollard & Corn, 1989).

Anxiety may arise suddenly and unexpectedly. In some cases, the increased arousal will result in a panic attack.

Generalized Anxiety Disorder

Generalized anxiety disorder (GAD) is characterized by persistent high levels of anxiety and excessive worry over many life circumstances. These concerns are accompanied by physiological responses such as heart palpitations, muscle tension, restlessness, trembling, sleep difficulties, poor concentration, and persistent apprehension and nervousness. Afflicted people are easily startled and are continually "on edge." Because they are unable to discover the "real" source of their fears, they remain anxious and occasionally experience even more acute attacks of anxiety.

Such people often feel apprehension or worry over life situations (such as the ability to do well in a job or in school, acceptance by others, or worry over misfortune befalling someone loved). As opposed to panic disorder, individuals with GAD are as likely to worry over minor events as they are over major events. Their physiological reactions are also less than those of people with panic disorder, but they tend to be more persistent (Gross & Eifert, 1990). Generalized anxiety disorder appears to be a cognitive problem involving worry or apprehension. As opposed to individuals without the disorder, those with GAD are more likely to engage in more thinking during relaxation and to engage in more negative thoughts during a period of induced worry (Pruzinsky & Borkovec, 1990). The following case illustrates a generalized anxiety disorder:

> Joanne W. was known by her college friends as a worrier. She was apprehensive about anything and everything: failing in school, making friends, eating the right foods, maintaining her health, and being liked. Because of her concerns, Joanne was constantly tense. She often felt short of breath, which was accompanied by a fast heart rate and trembling. Joanne also had difficulty making decisions. Her insecurity was so great that even the most common decisions—what clothes to wear, what to order at a restaurant, which movies to see—became major problems. At night Joanne reviewed and re-reviewed every real and imaginary mistake she had made during the day or might make in the future. This produced another problem, sleeplessness.

To meet DSM-IV's criteria for a diagnosis of generalized anxiety disorder, symptoms must be present for six months. The estimated lifetime prevalence of the disorder in the United States is 8.4 percent; it is the second most prevalent anxiety disorder after phobias (Compton et al., 1991).

Etiology of Panic Disorder and Generalized Anxiety Disorder

In our discussions of the causes and origins of mental disorders in this chapter and ensuing chapters, we must distinguish among the viewpoints that derive from the various models of psychopathology. Here we'll examine the etiology of unfocused anxiety disorders from the psychoanalytic, behavioral, and biological perspectives. Research has especially focused on explaining the reason for unexpected panic attacks.

Psychoanalytic Perspective The psychoanalytic view stresses the importance of internal conflicts (rather than external stimuli) in the origin of panic disorder and generalized anxiety disorder. Because the problem originates in sexual and aggressive impulses that are seeking expression, anxiety is always present. When a forbidden impulse threatens to disturb the ego's integrity, an intense anxiety reaction occurs. Because this conflict is unconscious, the individual does not know the source of the anxiety.

A person's defense against unfocused anxiety is generally considered poorly organized and less effective than defenses mounted against other anxiety disorders. In a phobia, for example, the conflict between id impulses and ego is displaced onto a specific external stimulus that can be controlled simply through avoidance. But the person with generalized anxiety disorder has only one defense—to try to repress the impulses. When that defense weakens, panic attacks may occur.

Behavioral Perspective The behavioral perspective encompasses both the classical conditioning and cognitive behavioral perspectives.

Classical conditioning The behaviorists believe that anxiety is a learned response to stimuli. Wolpe (1982) argued that so-called free-floating anxiety stems from classical conditioning to an omnipresent stimulus, such as light or shade contrasts, size, or the passage of time. Wolpe also preferred the term *pervasive* to *free-floating* because the latter implies the lack of an external source for the anxiety.

Wolpe suggested that two factors may be involved in producing pervasive anxiety. One is the intensity of the unconditioned stimulus (UCS); an intense UCS may produce conditioning to more of the stimulus elements present at the time of conditioning. The second factor is the lack of a distinct environmental stimulus during conditioning. Wolpe presented a case study involving a patient whose pervasive anxiety developed after a guilt-ridden sexual experience that took place in the dark and evoked much emotional turmoil. This person developed anxiety in many situations in which sexual cues and darkness were present.

Although classical conditioning to an often-present stimulus may account for some cases of panic and generalized anxiety disorder, it is difficult to believe that all cases develop in this manner. There is

FIGURE 6.1 Positive Feedback Loop Between Cognitions and Somatic Symptoms

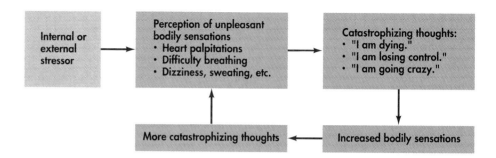

more support for the view that classical conditioning can increase the severity of panic disorder. Certain cues associated with the attacks can themselves bring on great anxiety. In a sample of clients with panic disorder, 83 percent had a panic attack in response to words describing symptoms that were paired to words describing catastrophes (breathlessness—suffocate; Clark et al., 1988). It is possible that conditioning to many situations, thoughts, and cues can increase the risk of having panic attacks.

Cognitive behavioral perspective Cognitive behavioral theorists emphasize that cognitions, not conditioning, are major factors in the development of anxiety disorders. Because an external source of anxiety often cannot be identified, it is possible that catastrophic thoughts and overattentiveness to internal bodily sensations may function as *internal triggers* for panic attacks (Belfer & Glass, 1992). Some theorists (Clark, 1986; Hibbert, 1984) believe that the cognitions and somatic symptoms can best be viewed as a positive feedback loop that results in increasingly higher levels of anxiety. In other words, after an external or internal stressor, a person may become aware of a bodily sensation, such as a racing heart. Anxiety develops when the sensation is interpreted as signaling a dreadful event. This belief produces even greater physical reactions. Figure 6.1 illustrates this pattern. If the positive feedback loop continues, a panic attack may follow. Twenty-eight subjects with panic disorder and twenty health controls wore portable ECGs so that heart rate during a 24-hour period could be recorded. Both groups noticed changes in cardiac activity. But only the clients with panic disorder showed an acceleration of their heart rate after observing these changes and reported feelings of anxiety (Pauli et al., 1991). Although this pattern begins with the perception of bodily sensations, some re-

search has also suggested that panic attacks may begin with anxiety-provoking thoughts.

To support this hypothesized relationship between cognitions and anxiety, a researcher must be able to (1) find that thoughts precede or contribute to panic attacks and (2) show that cognitions influence the severity of somatic symptoms. Some research supports the cognitive hypothesis. Cognitions preceding or accompanying panic attacks in patients have been reported by George and colleagues (1987) and by Rachman and colleagues (1988). The cognitions included thoughts of being "out of control," "passing out," or "acting foolish." These thoughts resulted in increased anxiety.

Cognitions or appraisal (interpretation) can have an influence on somatic symptoms. Significant increases in cardiovascular activity were found in a group of college students who were asked to focus on negative thoughts such as "My mind is racing," "I'm so worried. I can't concentrate on anything," or "It's frightening how tense I feel." In contrast, concentrating on neutral statements had little effect on somatic responses (York et al., 1987).

Although disturbing thoughts can increase cardiovascular activity, can they precipitate a panic attack? Sometimes, the answer is yes. A 25-year-old woman with a nine-year history of panic attacks received two types of feedback, accurate and false. When accurate feedback of her resting heart rate was given, no changes in physiological functioning were observed. Within 20 seconds of receiving inaccurate feedback showing an increase in heart rate, however, her heart rate increased fifty beats per minute over baseline. During this period, the patient reported having a severe panic attack (Margraf et al., 1987). Similar results were found in another group of patients with panic disorder. Of particular interest is the finding that false feedback suggesting arousal produced significantly greater increases in physiological measures in people who had histories of panic attacks than in people who lacked such a history (Ehlers et al., 1988).

Although the search for cognitive factors is promising, certain issues must be addressed. First, although most patients report that panic attacks are accompanied by cognitions, a substantial percentage report not being aware of any thoughts during these episodes (Rachman, Lopatka & Levitt, 1987). "Noncognitive" panic attacks present a problem for cognitive theorists. Second, it is unclear why individuals with GAD and panic disorder are so prone to having thoughts of catastrophe. It must be remembered that the cognitive approach does not preclude the possible impact of biological factors in the cause of panic disorders.

Biogenic Perspective   Biological factors associated with GAD have not been widely investigated. Panic disorder, however, has received much attention. Although the precise biologic mechanism triggering panic disorder has not been identified, several explanations have been offered. Papp and colleagues (1993) believe that people who experience panic have a specific biological dysfunction that predisposes them to this disorder. They hypothesized that the dysfunction involves the receptors that monitor the amount of oxygen in the blood. The receptors give the incorrect message that oxygen is insufficient, triggering fears of suffocation and resulting in hyperventilation.

George and Ballenger (1992) hypothesized that panic disorders may be associated with a dysfunction of the *locus ceruleus*, which is part of the central anxiety system in the brain. The increased sensitivity of the anxiety network can be activated by anything that increases anxiety such as thoughts or anxiogenic agents (such as cocaine and caffeine). To determine if some people have a predisposition to panic attacks, biological challenge tests have been used. This procedure involves administering a biological agent such as sodium lactate to people who have panic attacks and to others who do not have such attacks. It is expected that only people who are biologically susceptible will show a response.

Biological challenge tests   Most people with panic disorder will have a panic attack when given sodium lactate (Papp et al., 1993). It is assumed that a biological sensitivity to lactate produces feelings of alarm. In addition, antidepressants have been found to block both spontaneous and lactate-induced panic attacks (Aronson, 1987). Presumably medication raises the threshold for attacks in susceptible individuals.

Although these results support a biological model, some findings are contradictory. For example, some "normal" subjects infused with sodium lactate will also experience panic attacks (Balon et al., 1988). Individuals who have a panic attack after infusion of sodium lactate may no longer respond to the sodium lactate when treated with desensitization (Guttmacher & Nelles, 1984) or cognitive-behavioral therapy (Shear et al., 1991). Expectations may also affect the results of biological challenge tests. For example, instructions given before lactate infusion seem to influence the way subjects respond to the substance. Those who expect pleasant sensations show less anxiety than those who expect unpleasant bodily sensations (Van Der Molen et al., 1986). Psychological factors may influence panic attacks by changing the threshold for this response. Although the research seems to support a biological mechanism in panic disorder, cognitive factors also play a role.

Genetic studies   Adoption studies have not been reported for anxiety disorders, so environmental influences cannot be eliminated. We must be careful in interpreting studies because the possible impact of modeling has not been eliminated. Nevertheless, several studies do support a genetic influence. Higher concordance rates (percentages of relatives sharing the same disorder) for panic disorder have been found for monozygotic (MZ) twins versus dizygotic (DZ) twins (Torgersen, 1983). A lifetime risk of 41 percent has been found in first-degree relatives (parents and siblings) of individuals with panic disorder (Crowe et al., 1983). In general, available data support a genetic predisposition for panic disorder.

Fewer genetic studies have been done on generalized anxiety disorder than on panic disorder. The strategy used to study GAD has been to examine the distribution of anxiety disorders among family members of people with the disorder and compare it with control group members. There is less support for the role of genetic factors in generalized anxiety disorder than for panic disorder (Crowe et al., 1983; Last et al., 1991; Torgersen, 1983).

Treatment of Panic Disorder and Generalized Anxiety Disorder

Biochemical Treatment For Panic Disorder and GAD Treatments for panic disorder can generally be divided into two approaches: biological (via medication) and psychotherapeutic. Both antidepressants and tranquilizers have been used. Although there is considerable controversy about how antidepressants work against panic attacks, these drugs do seem to reduce not only depression but also extreme fears (Klein, 1984; Mavissakalian, 1987a). Success has been reported in treating panic disorder with a particular antidepressant, imipramine (Poling, Gadow & Cleary, 1991).

In a study of ten patients with panic disorder who were treated with imipramine, Garakani and his colleagues found that nearly all improved. Four patients discontinued the medication because of its side effects, however, and the researchers based their report of success on the self-reports of the patients. Moreover, with drug therapy, exposure to anxiety-producing situations may have affected the results. Antidepressants may be successful because they make it easier for patients to confront fearful stimuli. Aronson (1987) concluded that imipramine only blocks panic attacks and that patients still must learn to overcome avoidance responses through exposure.

Other medications, such as alprazolam (Fyer et al., 1987) and verapamil (Klein & Uhde, 1988), have also been effective in treating panic disorder. That so many different medications have been used successfully raises questions about the specificity of the biological nature of panic disorder. It is possible that there are several different forms of the disorder, which would help explain the success of so many different medications. In general, medications have been useful in treating anxiety disorders. But, relapse rates after ceasing drugs are high (Marks & O'Sullivan, 1988), and little follow-up data are available for the medical treatment of panic.

Although benzodiazepines (Valium and Librium) have been used to treat generalized anxiety disorder, tolerance and dependence are a problem (Committee on the Review of Medicines, 1980). Lindsay and associates (1987) compared the relative effectiveness of anxiety management training to treatment with benzodiazepines for a group of patients with GAD. At first, the benzodiazepines seemed more effective, but as the study progressed the anxiety management group began to show more improvement. In general, it appears that medication can help reduce anxiety in people who have GAD, but that psychological intervention is also necessary to reduce their avoidance responses.

Behavioral Treatment for Panic Disorder and GAD A review of cognitive behavior treatments for panic disorder found that 80 percent or more of clients achieve panic-free status. This is maintained according to follow-up studies. The reviewers (Margraf et al., 1993) concluded that "cognitive-behavioral treatments rest on firm experimental evidence that justifies their application in everyday practice" (p. 6). Michelson and Marchione (1991) found that behavioral approaches have had higher success rates and lower relapse rates than medications. Sometimes, clients who discontinued medication suffered rebound panic attacks that were worse than those they originally experienced.

Bourne (1990) suggested the following steps in dealing with panic disorder:

1. Provide cognitive explanations and strategies ("Maybe you are attributing danger to what is going on in your body," "A panic attack will not stop your breathing")
2. Help the client identify and change unrealistic thoughts
3. Encourage the client to face the symptoms ("Allow your body to have its reactions and let the reactions pass")
4. Provide coping statements ("This feeling is not pleasant but I can handle it")
5. Teach the client to identify the antecedents of the panic ("What stresses are you under?")
6. Help the client develop coping strategies such as relaxation and cognitive restructuring to handle stress

In general, psychological treatment for generalized anxiety disorder is similar to that for panic disorder. Treatment that deals with the three response systems (cognitive, physiological, and behavioral) is more effective in treating GAD than therapy relying on only a single technique such as relaxation training. Butler and colleagues (1987) reported a highly effective treatment that includes identifying and altering anxiety-evoking thoughts, developing coping strategies, teaching relaxation training, and gradually exposing the client to anxiety-evoking situations. Highly significant changes were reported in anxiety, depression, and avoidance responses. In a study that compared behavior therapy (relaxation and graded exposure) and cognitive behavior therapy (identification and examination of unrealistic thoughts and behavioral assignments), the researchers (Butler, Robson & Gelder, 1991) found that the latter was clearly superior. This makes sense if GAD is seen as primarily a cognitive disturbance.

PHOBIAS

The word *phobia* comes from the Greek word that means *fear*. A **phobia** is a strong, persistent, and unwarranted fear of some specific object or situation. Extreme anxiety or panic attacks often occur when the client encounters the phobic stimulus (Craske, 1991). Attempts to avoid the object or situation notably interfere with the individual's life. The person realizes that the fear is excessive (this feature may not be present in children). Nearly anything can become the focus of this intense fear. In fact, there is even a fear of phobias, called *phobophobia* (see Table 6.1). Phobias are the most common mental disorder in the United States. The estimated lifetime prevalence rate is 12.53 percent (Compton et al., 1991)

with more than 15 million individuals affected at any given time (National Institute of Mental Health, 1986).

DSM-IV includes three subcategories of phobias: agoraphobia, which is a single irrational fear of being trapped or helpless; the social phobias, which generally involve social situations; and the specific phobias, which include most of the fears listed in Table 6.1.

Agoraphobia

Agoraphobia is an intense fear of being in public places where escape or help may not be readily available. It often arises from a fear that frightening physical symptoms will incapacitate or cause the person to behave in an embarrassing manner (faint, lose control over bodily functions, display excessive fear in public). Anxiety over showing these symptoms can prevent people from leaving their homes. Agoraphobia has a lifetime prevalence rate of approximately 2.7 percent for males and 8.0 percent for females (Horwath, Johnson & Horning, 1993; Robins et al., 1984). Although this is not the most common phobia, people who have this disorder account for the majority of phobics who are seen for treatment (Michelson, 1987).

Many people report having panic attacks before developing agoraphobia (J. A. Franklin, 1987), as illustrated in the following case:

Table 6.1

Phobias and Their Objects

Acrophobia: fear of heights	*Microphobia:* fear of germs
Agoraphobia: fear of open spaces	*Monophobia:* fear of being alone
Ailurophobia: fear of cats	*Mysophobia:* fear of contamination or germs
Algophobia: fear of pain	*Nyctophobia:* fear of the dark
Arachnophobia: fear of spiders	*Ochlophobia:* fear of crowds
Astrapophobia: fear of storms, thunder, and lightning	*Pathophobia:* fear of disease
Aviophobia: fear of airplanes	*Phobophobia:* fear of phobias
Brontophobia: fear of thunder	*Pyrophobia:* fear of fire
Claustrophobia: fear of closed spaces	*Syphilophobia:* fear of syphilis
Dementophobia: fear of insanity	*Topophobia:* fear of performing
Genitophobia: fear of genitals	*Xenophobia:* fear of strangers
Hematophobia: fear of blood	*Zoophobia:* fear of animals or some particular animal

The anxiety over having a panic attack in public can cause individuals to become prisoners in their own home.

> The patient was a 28-year-old woman whose attacks of anxiety were triggered by the terrifying sensation of impending death. This feeling was so horrifying that she would clutch passers-by and beg them for help. These episodes were acutely embarrassing to her, because no physical illness could be found. In an interview, it was discovered that her anxiety attacks occurred in situations where she felt trapped, such as in a crowded restaurant. Finally, her fear of experiencing these symptoms in public reached the point where she was unwilling to leave her home unless accompanied by her husband.

The precise relationship between agoraphobia and panic disorder is not clear. One might be a variant of the other. If a person with agoraphobia meets the criteria for a panic disorder, the appropriate diagnosis is panic disorder with agoraphobia.

A nationwide survey of more than nine hundred persons with agoraphobia revealed that nearly 75 percent of those surveyed could recall an event that precipitated the disorder. In 38 percent of the per-

sons, this event was a traumatic experience; in 23 percent, it was the death of a family member or friend; in 13 percent, it was a personal illness; in 8 percent, it was giving birth; and in 4 percent, it was marital difficulties. The situations most likely to produce attacks involved being trapped, having to wait in line, being far away from home, and having domestic arguments. But most of those surveyed felt less anxious when they were accompanied by a spouse or friend or when they had easy access to an exit (Thorpe & Burns, 1983).

Interest in examining the role of cognitions in agoraphobia is increasing. Like depressed clients, people with panic disorders or agoraphobia display perception of personal helplessness (Ganellen, 1988). It is possible that agoraphobics misinterpret events or elevate them to catastrophes. In a study of sixty patients with agoraphobia, J. A. Franklin (1987) found the following pattern:

- *Some physical or psychological stressor*
- *Altered physical sensations* such as increased heart rate and overbreathing.
- *Faulty appraisal* Incorrectly interpreting the symptoms as representing a severe physical problem such as a heart attack or loss of control.
- *Avoidance* Although the attacks were described as highly aversive, believing that they represented a pathological outcome intensified the fear. This led to avoidance of the situation associated with the fear.

Not everyone who experiences altered physical sensations develops anxiety attacks. Reiss and co-workers (1986) contended that people react differently to physical symptoms or sensations. They developed the Anxiety Sensitivity Inventory (ASI) to investigate this phenomenon. The ASI measures a person's reaction to anxiety symptoms. People who score high on the test agreed with such statements as "When I notice that my heart is beating rapidly, I worry that I might be having a heart attack." People with low anxiety sensitivity interpreted the sensation as only being unpleasant. Reiss and colleagues did find that agoraphobics scored higher on the ASI than people who had other anxiety disorders. Similar results were obtained by Asmundson and Norton (1933). It is too early to tell whether anxiety sensitivity or faulty appraisal act as predisposing factors in the development of panic disorders and agoraphobia, or whether they are the result of having the disorders. However, there is increasing support for the role of cognitions in the cause of anxiety disorders.

Social Phobias

A **social phobia** is an intense, excessive fear of being scrutinized in one or more social situations. There is no fear when the person engages in any of these activities in private. The person's fear stems from anxiety that, in the company of others, he or she will perform one of these activities in a way that is embarrassing or humiliating, as indicated in the following case example:

> Mr. B. was a 37-year-old divorced male who reported being unable to urinate in the presence of other people since the age of 12. . . . Mr. B. would typically avoid restrooms if they were occupied and . . . had waited 4 to 5 hours for privacy. . . . He reported feeling very anxious when he had to urinate in the presence of others. (McCracken & Larkin, 1991, p. 58)

Like other phobics, socially phobic people usually realize that their behavior and fears are irrational, but this understanding does not reduce the distress they feel. Social phobias can be divided into three types: (1) performance (excessive anxiety over activities such as playing a musical instrument, public speaking, eating in a restaurant, using public restrooms); (2) limited interactional (excessive fear only in specific social situations such as going out on a date or interacting with an authority figure); and (3) generalized (extreme anxiety displayed in most social situations).

Although these distinctions are useful in conceptualizing differences in social phobias, the generalized type has come under much criticism. Several researchers (Herbert, Hope & Bellack, 1992; Turner, Beidel & Townsley, 1992) have reported a great overlap (100 percent in one study) between two diagnostic categories—generalized social phobia and avoidant personality disorder. Such an overlap between distinct categories raises the question about whether two separate disorders exist or whether they are variations of the same disorder. The six-month prevalence rate (whether the person had the disorder within the last six months) for social phobia is approximately 1.3 percent for males and 2.1 percent for females (Myers et al., 1984). Social phobias tend to begin during adolescence (Öst, 1987a). They are somewhat rare, except for public speaking and performance anxiety in music students (Cox & Kenardy, 1993), but anxiety in social situations is fairly common. Focus 6.2 explores the differences between the two.

One common type of social phobia is an irrational fear of public speaking. For some people, the anxiety felt before a public speaking engagement is so overwhelming that they are unable to deliver their prepared talk.

When Is a Fear a Phobia?

Social fears are common. In one study, 40 percent of college and high school students were found to suffer from social fears (Zimbardo, 1977). These students displayed excessive self-consciousness and concern about what others thought, along with such physiological reactions as increased pulse rate, blushing, and perspiration.

Social phobias, however, are considered to be relatively uncommon. But when is a fear extreme enough

to be considered a phobia? According to DSM-IV, several elements must be present for the diagnosis of phobia: (1) a persistent and irrational fear with a compelling desire to avoid the situation, (2) anxiety in the presence of the phobic stimulus, and (3) significant distress because the person recognizes that the fear is excessive.

Are these criteria fulfilled in the case of a student with public speaking anxiety who drops out of classes

where oral participation is required, or in the case of a student with heterosexual anxiety who will not talk to people of the opposite sex even when he or she strongly wants to do so? The subjective nature of the criteria makes that question difficult to answer. Exactly how "compelling" must the fear be, and how much distress is "significant"? When does a "normal" fear become "abnormal"?

Socially phobic (and anxious) people are concerned that their nervousness and anxiety will be detected by others. Researchers have found, however, that other people often do not detect behavioral signs of anxiety in highly socially anxious people (McEwan & Devins, 1983). Socially anxious persons apparently are more aware of their anxiety than are other people.

Specific Phobias

A **specific phobia** is an extreme fear of a specific object (such as snakes) or situation (such as being in an enclosed place). Exposure to the stimulus nearly always produces intense anxiety or a panic attack. The specific phobias provide a catchall category for irrational fears that are neither agoraphobia nor social phobias. The only similarity among the various specific phobias is the existence of an irrational fear. To produce some organizational framework, DSM-IV divides specific phobias into five types: (1) animal type; (2) natural environmental (such as animals, insects, earthquakes, thunder, water); (3) blood/injections or injury (as opposed to other phobias, individuals with this type of phobia are likely to have a history of fainting in the phobic situation; Öst, 1992); (4) situational (includes traveling in cars, planes, elevators, fear of heights, tunnels, and bridges); and (5) other (phobic avoidance of situations

that may lead to choking, vomiting, or contracting an illness).

The most common of the fears involve small animals, heights, the dark, and lightning; others involve death, exams, deep water, and being mentally ill (Kirkpatrick, 1984). Phobic reactions have also been

Over 25 million individuals fear flying. This photo shows a group of people who have successfully overcome this fear after participating in an anxiety reduction program.

described for animals such as slugs, cockroaches, and worms (Davey, Forster & Mayhew, 1993). Unusual and uncommon specific phobias have involved bath water running down the drain (after pulling out the plug, the affected person would dash out of the bathroom with great anxiety); snow (the fear developed after the man got stuck in a snowstorm and arrived too late to talk to his dying father); and three-legged stools (Adler et al., 1984). One boy who displayed a phobia of dolls reacted with greatest fear to plastic dolls with mobile eyes or dolls with the roots of their hair visible on the scalp (Hatcher, 1989).

The following is a report of a fairly common specific phobia:

> Ms. B, a 23-year-old woman, complained of a phobia of spiders that had not changed for as long as she could remember. She had no history of any other psychiatric symptoms. In treatment, when initially approached with a closed glass jar containing spiders, she breathed heavily, wept tears, and rated her subjective distress as 70 to 80. She suddenly began scratching the back of her hand, stating she felt as though spiders were crawling under her skin, although she knew this was not the case. The sensation lasted only a few seconds and did not recur. Her total treatment consisted of four 1-hour sessions distributed over the span of a month. At completion she had lost all fear of spiders and became able to let them crawl freely about her arms, legs, and face as well as inside her clothing with no distress whatever. She remained free of fear at one-year follow-up, expressing disbelief that she had allowed such a "silly fear" to dominate her life for so long. (Curtis, 1981, p. 1095)

Specific phobias are more prevalent in women than in men (see Critical Thinking) and are rarely incapacitating. The degree to which they interfere with daily life depends on how easy it is to avoid the feared object or situation. These phobias often begin during childhood. In a study of 370 patients with phobias (Öst, 1987a), retrospective data revealed that animal phobias tended to have the earliest onset age (seven years), followed by blood phobia (nine years), dental phobia (twelve years), and claustrophobia (twenty years).

Fears are common in children and involve themes such as injury and death, being in the dark, traffic accidents, not being able to breathe, and falling from high places (Ollendick & King, 1991). These fears very seldom remain to become phobias; most are lost as the child gets older. Most children with phobias recover without treatment, although phobias that begin during later adolescence or adulthood tend to persist if they are not treated.

Etiology of Phobias

How do such strong and "irrational" fears develop? Both psychological and biological explanations have been proposed. In this section, we will examine the psychoanalytic, behavioral, and biological views of the etiology of phobias.

Psychoanalytic Perspective   According to the psychoanalytic viewpoint, phobias are "expressions of wishes, fears and fantasies that are unacceptable to the patient" (Barber & Luborsky, 1991). These unconscious conflicts are displaced (or shifted) from their original internal source to an external object or situation. The phobia is less threatening to the person than is recognition of the underlying unconscious impulse. A fear of knives, for example, may represent castration fears produced by an unresolved Oedipus complex or aggressive conflicts. Agoraphobics may develop their fear of leaving home because they unconsciously fear that they may act out unacceptable sexual desires. The presence of a friend or spouse lowers anxiety because it provides some protection against the agoraphobic's impulses. In this sense, phobias represent a compromise between the ego and the impulses that seek gratification. The person blocks from consciousness the real source of anxiety and is able to avoid the dangerous impulse that the phobia represents.

Psychoanalysts believe that the level of phobic fear shows the strength of the underlying conflict. This formulation, presented by Freud in 1909, was based on his analysis of a fear of horses displayed by a five-year-old boy named Hans (Freud, [1909] 1959). Freud believed that the phobia represented a symptomatic or displaced fear arising from the Oedipus complex. The factors involved were the boy's incestuous attraction to his mother, hostility toward his father because of the father's sexual privileges, and castration fear (fear of retribution by his father). Freud became convinced that these elements were present in the phobic boy.

At the age of three, Hans had displayed an interest in his penis (which he called his "widdler"); he

Do Men Lie About Fear?

In general, men are thought to have fewer problems with specific fears and anxiety than women. Why this is the case is not clear. Several possible explanations to account for this difference have been offered.

1. Women are more predisposed to the development of fears. This might involve genetic or sociocultural factors. Women show more actual fears and phobias than men.

2. Women overreport and men underreport specific fears. This explanation focuses on responding in a socially desirable manner. Women may face less stigma in acknowledging fears than men.

3. Men are less likely to have specific fears because of extinction. This explanation indicates that because men are more likely to be expected to face phobic items such as snakes and other animals, fears become extinguished.

In a study titled "Do Men Lie on Fear Surveys?" Pierce and Kirkpatrick (1992) had thirty female and twenty-six male college students take a survey of specific fears. One month later, the same students took a shorter survey that contained fourteen items from the first survey. During the short survey, the students were hooked up to a heart rate sensor and told that it was often used in "a lie detector test." Under this condition, the male students rated the items of

would examine animate and inanimate objects for the presence of a penis. One day as he was fondling himself, his mother threatened to have a physician cut off his penis. "And then what will you widdle with?" (Freud 1909, p. 151). Hans enjoyed having his mother bathe him and especially wanted her to touch his penis. Freud interpreted these events to suggest that Hans was aware of pleasurable sensations in his penis and that he knew it could be "cut off" if he did not behave. Wanting his mother to handle his genitals showed Hans's increasing sexual interest in her.

Hans's fear that horses would bite him developed after he saw a horse-drawn van overturn. According to Freud, little Hans's sexual jealousy of his father and the hostility it aroused produced anxiety. He believed that his father could retaliate by castrating him. This unconscious threat was so unbearable that the fear was displaced to the idea that horses "will bite me." Freud concluded that phobias were adaptive because they prevented the surfacing of traumatic unconscious conflicts.

Although Freud's formulation has clinical appeal, it has problems. According to the psychoanalytic per-

spective, if the phobia is only a symptom of an underlying unconscious conflict, treatment directed to that symptom—the feared object or situation—should be ineffective, leave the patient defenseless and subject to overwhelming anxiety, or lead to the development of a new symptom. But the evidence does not support the view that eliminating the symptom is ineffective.

Classical Conditioning Perspective The behavioral position regarding the origin of phobias—that they are conditioned responses—is based primarily on Watson's conditioning experiment with Little Albert (see Chapter 3). The use of classical conditioning principles to produce intense fears in human beings was demonstrated more recently (Campbell, Sanderson & Laveny, 1964). This experiment, however, has been severely criticized on several ethical grounds. In the experiment, a traumatic conditioning procedure was used to establish fear of a tone in five alcoholic patients. The unconditioned stimulus was a drug (scoline) that paralyzes the skeletal musculature. The drug makes breathing very difficult, although the patient is still conscious and aware of what is happening. The experimenters sounded a tone at the first

specific fears significantly higher than they did during the earlier session. Females showed no change of ratings from the first to second session. Although the men acknowledged greater anxiety the second time around, they still showed significantly lower anxiety on the items than women.

From the results of the study, which one of the hypotheses do you believe has the greatest experimental support for the gender differences in ratings of specific fears? Is it possible that the men still underreport their fears in condition two? How might you set up an experiment to test this possibility? If you believe that gender

roles influence reports of anxiety, which fears do you think should be the most exaggerated between males and females?

Look at the table below. How would you account for the gender differences among the different anxiety disorders according to the different hypotheses?

Anxiety Disorder	Ratio Men/Women
Panic disorder	More females
Social phobias	More females
Specific phobias	More females
Obsessive-compulsive disorder	Equally common
Agoraphobia	More females

signs of paralysis. The paralysis produced an inability to breathe for 90 to 130 seconds, which resulted in feelings of utter terror for the subjects. All the subjects thought they were going to die. This conditioned emotional reaction was highly resistant to extinction.

Although some phobias may result from a traumatic event or from classical conditioning, the experimental data do not entirely support this view. English (1929) was unable to replicate the results of Watson and Rayner's experiment when he tried to establish a conditioned fear in a fourteen-month-old girl by presenting a painted wooden duck while banging a steel bar behind her. Conditioning did not take place (although the noise upset teachers and students throughout the building). Bregman (1934) was also unable to condition fifteen infants aged eight to sixteen months to be afraid of wooden blocks and triangles by using a loud electric bell as the unconditioned stimulus. Perhaps these experiments didn't replicate Watson and Rayner's experiment, however, because it may be more difficult to establish a fear response to inanimate objects than to animate stimuli.

Three possible pathways have been examined as causing phobias: classical conditioning, modeling,

and cognitive/negative information. Some combination of these factors may also cause phobias. It is also possible that different phobias are the result of different processes. In three studies (Öst, 1987a; Öst & Hugdahl, 1981; Rimm et al., 1977) on the acquisition of phobias, more clients attributed their disorders to direct (classical) conditioning experiences than to any other factor (see Table 6.2). Öst and Hugdahl (1981) found that agoraphobics were the most likely to attribute their disorder to direct conditioning experiences followed by claustrophobics and people with dental phobia. Phobias caused by indirect (or observational) conditioning experiences involved cognitive and subjective factors more than physiological ones. Among spider phobics, modeling was the most often reported cause (71 percent) followed by conditioning (57 percent). Negative information accounted for only 45 percent of the cases.

In general, retrospective reports seem to indicate that conditioning experiences play a major etiological influence in the development of phobias for most clients with this disorder and that this pathway might be more important for some types of phobias than for others. This finding, however, might only apply

Table 6.2

Means of Acquiring Phobias, as Reported by Patients (in percentages)

	Study		
Means of Acquisition	Öst and Hugdahl (1981)	Rimm et al. (1977)	Öst (1987a)
Direct conditioning	57.5	44.4	64
Indirect conditioning	17	8.3	14
Information/instruction	10.4	11.1	6
No recall	15.1	36.1	16

to phobias and not subclinical fears. In a study on the acquisition of childhood fears, Ollendick and King (1991) found that only 36 percent of the children reported a direct conditioning experience, whereas negative information accounted for 89 percent and modeling accounted for 56 percent of the source of their fears. It appears that strong fears can be produced through exposure to informational sources such as parents or television programs. But it is not clear if negative information is sufficient to produce a phobia.

There is some clinical and survey support for the behavioral perspective on phobias. However, a substantial percentage of surveyed patients report something other than a direct conditioning experience as the "key" to their phobias. And, according to Rimm and associates (1977), 36 percent could not recall how their fear was acquired. Besides, the classical conditioning perspective does not explain why only some people exposed to potential conditioning experiences actually develop phobias.

Observational Learning (Modeling) Perspective Emotional conditioning can be developed through modeling or observational learning. An observer who watched while a model exhibited pain cues in response to an auditory stimulus (a buzzer) gradually developed an emotional reaction to the sound (Bandura & Rosenthal, 1966). The buzzer, formerly a neutral stimulus, became a conditioned stimulus for the observer. In a clinical (rather than an experimental) example involving modeling, several people who had seen the horror film *The Exorcist* had to be treated for a variety of anxiety reactions (Bozzuto, 1975).

Table 6.2 shows that only a small proportion of surveyed patients indicated that they acquired phobias through observational (indirect) conditioning, or modeling. The data shown in Table 6.2, however, are based on patients' recollections of past events, and such data are subject to a variety of errors. The observational learning perspective seems to have the same problem as classical conditioning with regard to the cause of phobias. It's not enough by itself to explain why only some people develop phobias after exposure to a vicarious experience.

Cognitive and Information Perspective Some researchers believe that cognitions are associated with phobias. Negative thoughts such as "I will be trapped," "I will suffocate," or "I will lose control" have been reported by claustrophobic individuals. Removal of these thoughts was associated with dramatic decreases in their fear (Shafran, Booth & Rachman, 1993). The researchers believe their findings support the application of cognitive theory to fears other than panic. Information or instruction received is also considered as a cause of phobic reactions.

Operant Conditioning Perspective Some theorists have suggested that phobias may be learned through reinforcement (operant conditioning). For example, a child who is reinforced—perhaps by being held and comforted—after making statements about fears often increases such verbalizations of fears. Considering the aversive nature of phobias and the distress they produce, however, such reinforcement is not likely to be a major factor in their development.

Biogenic Perspective If a higher-than-average prevalence of a disorder is found in close relatives, or if identical twins (who share the same genetic makeup) show a higher concordance rate for the disorder than fraternal twins (who have different genetic makeups), a case can be made for the role of genetic factors in the disorder. Harris and her colleagues (1983) found that the prevalence of reported anxiety disorders for *first-degree relatives* (parents and siblings) of agoraphobic patients was more than twice that for first-degree relatives of a control group (32 percent versus 15 percent). Similar results were reported for the first-degree relatives of individuals with social phobia (8.7 percent versus 3.4 percent) and specific phobia (11.7 percent versus 4.3 percent; Last et al., 1991). These findings can be interpreted as supporting the view that agoraphobia is a familial disorder, although an alternative explanation for these results is that they are due to modeling.

Evidence for the direct genetic transmission of specific anxiety disorders is not strong. In a study of the influence of heredity on agoraphobia, social phobia, and specific phobias in women, Kendler and associates (1992b) concluded that genetic influences are modest and vary among the subtypes of phobias. Specific phobias appear to be a result of a modest genetic vulnerability and conditioning experiences, whereas agoraphobia has a slightly stronger genetic influence and involves an exposure to negative environmental experiences.

More support exists for the view that constitutional or physiological factors may *predispose* individuals to develop fear reactions. It is possible that a certain level of autonomic nervous system (ANS) reactivity is inherited; people born with high ANS reactivity respond more strongly to stimuli, and their chances of developing an anxiety disorder are increased. In support of this possibility, researchers found that people who had high resting arousal levels showed easier conditioning to certain stimuli than did people with low resting arousal levels (Hugdahl et al., 1977).

A different biological approach to the development of fear reactions is that of *preparedness* (Seligman, 1971). Proponents of this position argue that fears do not develop randomly. In particular, they believe that it is easier for human beings to learn fears to which we are physiologically predisposed. Such quickly aroused (or "prepared") fears may have been necessary to the survival of pretechnological humanity in the natural environment.

Several predictions can be made from the preparedness hypothesis:

1. Certain classes of stimuli (those dangerous to pretechnical humans such as snakes and other animals) should be more easily conditioned.
2. Onset of phobias should be sudden rather than gradual because the organism is biologically prepared to respond to certain stimuli.
3. The phobia should be resistant to extinction.

One proponent of this view noted that it is rare to encounter phobias about automobiles or electrical appliances, presumably because pretechnical human beings did not have an innate phobic response to these items (McConaghy, 1983). Ohman and Soares (1993) believe that the conditioning for prepared fears occurs at the subcortical level and is therefore not under conscious control. DeSilva (1988) wanted to see whether the preparedness theory applied to non-Western populations. Records of eighty-eight phobic patients treated in Sri Lanka were examined and rated in terms of "preparedness" (objects or situations dangerous to pretechnical humanity under most circumstances). Most of the phobias were rated as "prepared." In conflict with the preparedness theory, however, no association was found between the type of phobias and sudden or gradual onset. Matchett and Davey (1991) believe that Seligman's theory is incomplete and does not sufficiently explain phobias involving harmless animals such as cockroaches, maggots, and slugs. They believe that these fears are produced more by disgust and contamination concerns than being physically harmed.

The combination of classical conditioning and prepared learning is a promising area for further research. But it is difficult to believe that many (or even most) phobias stem from prepared fears, simply because they just do not fit into that model. It would be difficult, for example, to explain the survival value of social phobias as the fear of using public restrooms and of eating in public, of agoraphobia, and of many specific phobias. In addition, prepared fears appear to have variable age of onset and are among the most easy to eliminate.

Treatment of Phobias

Phobias are treated primarily by biochemical methods or behavioral methods. We focus mainly on agoraphobia, the disorder on which most treatment effort has been focused.

Biochemical Treatments Several studies have shown that antidepressants such as imipramine not only help reduce depression but also the extreme fear displayed by agoraphobics (Garakani et al., 1984; Mavissakalian et al., 1983). But less positive results were reported when imipramine was compared with a placebo and exposure to the feared object; these researchers concluded that the effective component was exposure (Lelliott et al., 1987; Marks et al., 1983). Significant improvement was also found in twenty agoraphobic patients who received a placebo rather than imipramine (Mavissakalian, 1987b).

Methodological flaws tend to hamper the evaluation of drugs in treating agoraphobia because (1) most studies rely only on self-reports as measures of success, (2) control groups are generally not employed, and (3) patients are often encouraged to expose themselves to the fear-producing situation while they are receiving medication. One study was designed specifically to separate and compare the contributions of drugs and exposure in the treatment of agoraphobics. The patients were randomly assigned to treatment with imipramine alone, imipramine plus exposure, or placebo plus exposure. An important element in the study was control of the possible effects of exposure on the drug-only group: patients in this group were told not to enter fear-arousing situations until the medication had a chance to build up (some six or eight weeks). Results were measured with self-reports and behavioral and physiological scales. Both exposure groups showed significant improvement according to all three measures. The imipramine-only patients showed no improvement on any of the measures, although they did show a significant reduction of depressed mood. Imipramine plus exposure showed a slight advantage over placebo plus exposure in reducing phobic anxiety (Telch, Tearnan & Taylor, 1983).

Behavioral Treatments Agoraphobics treated with imipramine appear to also require behavioral treatment to reduce anxiety and avoidance of the feared situation. Because 60 to 70 percent of agoraphobics can be successfully treated by exposure methods alone, medication is not necessary as a treatment for most individuals with this disorder (Mavissakalian et al., 1983).

The behavioral treatment of agoraphobia (and other phobias) has centered on **exposure therapy.** In this technique, the patient is gradually introduced to increasingly difficult encounters with the feared situation (Ghosh & Marks, 1987). An agoraphobic might, for example, be asked to take longer and longer walks outside the home with the therapist. The earliest of these encounters may often be only imagined or visualized by the patient, at the therapist's request. After the fear is reduced, relapse training is conducted to anticipate and deal with setbacks.

Exposure therapy has been successful in significantly reducing fears and panic attacks in agoraphobic patients. Exposure, especially with appropriate modifications, seems a viable treatment for agoraphobia. Follow-up studies at periods ranging from four to seven years after exposure treatment show little evidence of relapse (Marks, 1987). Though significant improvements occur, however, most patients retain mild to moderate symptoms (Michelson, Mavissakalian & Marchione, 1988).

To increase the effectiveness of behavioral treatment of agoraphobia, therapists increasingly emphasize multiple treatment methods. Exposure treatment usually ignores the cognitive aspects of phobias, although some studies show that cognitions and expectations are important in such treatment. Agoraphobics who have high expectancy (have been told that the procedure is an effective treatment) were able to travel about twice as far from home as those with low expectancy (being told that the procedure is merely for the purposes of assessment). Both groups had received ten *in vivo* exposure sessions. Thus expectancy may mediate exposure to feared situations.

Marchione and colleagues (1987) also contended that adding cognitive therapy to exposure therapy can increase the effectiveness of both. They assigned agoraphobic patients to (1) a gradual exposure-only group or (2) a gradual exposure plus cognitive therapy group. Cognitive therapy included the monitoring and recording of automatic thoughts, understanding their relationship to phobic behavior, generating alternative rational responses, developing problem-solving skills, and learning relapse prevention. Both approaches were successful in treating agoraphobia, but including cognitive therapy increased the potency of the exposure treatment. More researchers are stressing the importance of assessing and directly altering different response systems to increase the effectiveness of treating agoraphobia.

The treatment of choice for the social and specific phobias is also behavioral, but a number of different behavioral techniques appear to be beneficial. For example, **systematic desensitization** has been used as a treatment for phobias. Wolpe (1958, 1973), who introduced the treatment, taught phobics a response (relaxation) that is incompatible with fear by repeatedly pairing relaxation with visualizations of the feared stimulus. This procedure was adopted for Mr. B., who had a fear of urinating in restrooms when others were present. He was trained in muscle relaxation and, while relaxed, learned to urinate under the following conditions: no one in the bathroom, therapist in the stall, therapist washing hands, therapist at adjacent urinal, therapist waiting behind client. These conditions were arranged in ascending difficulty. The easier items were practiced first until anxiety was sufficiently reduced. Over a period of seventeen weeks, the anxiety diminished completely, and the gains have been maintained in a 7.5-month follow-up (McCracken & Larkin, 1991). Systematic desensitization has been shown to be effective with both specific and social phobias (Hekmat, Lubitz & Deal, 1984).

Modeling therapy procedures have also been highly effective in treating certain phobias. When modeling is used as therapy, the phobic person observes a model in the act of coping with, or responding appropriately in, the fear-producing situation. Some researchers believe that modeling is a unique therapeutic approach in its own right, whereas others believe that it is a type of exposure treatment.

Graduated exposure has been used successfully to treat a variety of phobias such as fear of heights (Marshall, 1988a), claustrophobia (Booth & Rachman, 1992), and flying (Walder et al., 1987). As with agoraphobia, it appears that graduated exposure is more effective if combined with other techniques such as coping skills and anxiety management (Butler et al., 1984). Interest is also increased in assessing cognitions and using cognitive treatment strategies. Walder and colleagues (1987) found that people with dental phobias had anxiety-provoking thoughts such as "The dentist is going to hit a nerve." Feelings of anxiety were related to thoughts of losing control. These researchers suggested that treatment procedures be developed to enhance control over both behavior and cognitions.

Modeling therapy has proven effective in treating both simple and social phobias. Watching a fear-producing act being successfully performed (like the act being performed by the man in this photo) can help a person overcome his or her own fear of the behavior.

The behavioral approaches just mentioned have all demonstrated reasonably good results in treating a variety of phobias. McCann and colleagues (1987) compared the effectiveness of systematic desensitization, behavioral rehearsal (exposure and practice), and cognitive restructuring in treating individuals with severe interpersonal anxiety. All the treatments successfully reduced social fears. Although few differences appeared among the three treatment groups, cognitive restructuring (identifying anxiety-inducing thoughts and replacing them with positive coping statements) had a more significant impact on the cognitive measures of anxiety, whereas behavioral re-

Fears of being contaminated trigger handwashing, which may last several hours a day. Unless this behavior is performed in a specific manner, intense anxiety occurs.

hearsal had greater impact on behavioral measures. The researchers believe that the results are consistent with the three-part model of anxiety, in which there is some overlap but also some independence among the three dimensions (cognitive, behavioral, and biological). A multimodal treatment strategy seems the most effective (Mattick & Peters, 1988).

Although cognitive-behavioral approaches are effective in treating phobias, interpersonal factors such as positive regard are also important. In one study, persons with phobias received treatment involving both exposure and cognitive intervention. Everyone improved, but those who rated their therapist more favorably during the initial session reported more improvement. Bennun and Schindler (1988) believe the effectiveness of behavior therapy could be improved by paying attention to interpersonal variables.

OBSESSIVE-COMPULSIVE DISORDER

Obsessive-compulsive disorder is characterized by **obsessions** (intrusive, repetitive thoughts or images that produce anxiety) or **compulsions** (the need to perform acts or thoughts to reduce anxiety). Obsessions and compulsions may occur together. One woman, for example, had the obsession that she might have thrown away important pieces of paper. These thoughts produced great anxiety, which was temporarily reduced when she repeatedly checked the contents of garbage cans and retrieved any paper she saw outside (Drummond & Mathews, 1988). The woman realized her concern was irrational but was unable to control the doubts or resist the compulsions.

The symptoms of obsessive-compulsive disorder are described as *ego-dystonic*—that is, they are considered alien and not voluntarily produced by the afflicted individual. Obsessive-compulsive disorder is highly distressing because it involves a lack of voluntary control over one's own thoughts and actions. The inability to resist or rid oneself of uncontrollable, alien, and often unacceptable thoughts or to keep from performing ritualistic acts over and over again arouses intense anxiety. These thoughts and impulses are recognized as being unreasonable (this latter characteristic may not apply to children). Failure to engage in ritual acts often results in mounting anxiety and tension.

Some features of obsessive-compulsive disorder are obvious in the following case:

A 24-year-old single man felt compelled to ruminate practically all his waking hours. He had a seven-year history of obsessional ruminations, had been out of work for three years, and was living with his parents. Ruminations usually involved worrying in case he had made a mistake in the course of performing some quite trivial action. Anxiety and doubt would be evoked by mundane activities, such as turning a light switch, changing direction when walking, or going from one room to another. For example, when driving his car and taking a right turn at a traffic light, he would start thinking, "What would happen if I had turned left?" His ruminations would only come to an end once he had gone through all the possible alternative routes in his head. The degree of doubt felt by this patient was so strong that at times, when switching on a light, he would not trust his perception, and wondering if he had made a mistake, he would attempt to trace the wiring behind the wall in order to try to follow where the current went back to the switch, thus convincing himself that the bulb was actually illuminated.

If necessary, his ruminations could be postponed for some hours but as long as they remained "unresolved" he would feel subjectively anxious. As a child, he remembered checking his schoolbooks and homework excessively. Later, mental checks replaced physical ones because they were quicker and unobtrusive. He reached university, but his obsessions had greatly multiplied by then. Yet he qualified as an engineer and started to work. The necessity to take responsibility and make decisions caused a significant deterioration and eventually forced him to abandon the job. His basic fear was that of making a mistake and appearing foolish in front of others. At the time of his admission to hospital, he was thinking of hypothetical solutions to hypothetical errors following almost every activity he did. (Robertson, Wendiggensen & Kaplan, 1983, p. 352)

Obsessive-compulsive disorder was once thought to be relatively rare. The prevalence of this disorder at a psychiatric hospital in 1969 was .2 percent and increased to more than 1 percent by 1983. The reason for the increased incidence of obsessive-compulsive disorder is not clear. Stoll, Tohen, and Baldessarini (1992) believe that the increase at the psychiatric hospital was "diagnostic vogue" in which "clinicians may more readily consider and diagnose a condition for which an innovative or effective treatment is available" (p. 638). Individuals with the disorder, however, may now be more willing to be identified as having the problem.

In an epidemiological study of obsessive-compulsive disorder, Karno and his colleagues (1988) reported that the lifetime prevalence rate for the disorder is between 2 and 3 percent. Of those who met the criteria for the disorder, 55.1 percent reported obsessions, 53.4 percent reported compulsions, and only 8.6 percent had both. The disorder was equally common in males and females, but less common in African Americans and Mexican Americans. It was more common among the young and among individuals who were divorced, separated, or unemployed.

Obsessions

As mentioned earlier, an *obsession* is an intrusive, uncontrollable, and persistent anxiety-arousing thought. The person may realize that the thought is irrational, but he or she can't keep it from arising over and over again. Among a sample of children and adolescents, the most common obsessions involved dirt or germs, disease and death, or danger to self or loved ones (Swedo et al., 1989). Obsessions common to adults involve bodily wastes or secretions, dirt or germs, and environmental contamination (George et al., 1993).

Sanavio (1988) found four factors associated with obsessional characteristics in both normal populations and in persons with obsessive-compulsive disorder:

1. *Impaired control over mental processes* This factor includes the inability to stop thinking of something such as thoughts of death of a loved one, catastrophic results from minor errors made, worry about hurting someone unintentionally, thoughts of obscene and dirty words or actions, or severe doubt over the correctness of a decision.

2. *Urges and worries over the possible loss of control over motor behaviors* Associated with this factor are impulses such as shouting obscene words in a church or classroom, throwing oneself in front of a car, killing or injuring others, performing inappropriate sexual acts in public, and feeling compelled to make stereotyped gestures or to perform activities in a certain way.

3. *Contamination* This factor involves worry, concern, and anxiety over being contaminated, including concern regarding contact with germs, diseases, dirty objects, animals, strangers, public lavatories, public telephones, library books, money, or bodily secretions. This factor was often associated with compulsions of washing and cleaning.

4. *Checking behaviors* Checking behaviors included worry that doors, windows, or drawers are not properly shut; that gas, water faucets, or lights have not been turned off; and subsequently feeling a need to "check" to determine that it had been "done properly."

Although most of us have experienced persistent thoughts—for instance, a song or tune that keeps running through one's mind—clinical forms are stronger and more intrusive. They create great distress or interfere with social or occupational activities. Many people who suffer from this disorder become partially incapacitated. Howard Hughes, a spectacularly successful businessman, pilot, and movie producer, withdrew so completely from the public that his only communication with the outside world was through telephones and intermediaries. His seclusiveness was connected to his obsessional fear of germ contamination.

> He took to refusing to shake hands with people and covering his hands with the ubiquitous sheets of Kleenex when he had to hold a glass or open a door. He forbade aides to eat onions, garlic, Roquefort dressing or other "breath destroyers." He considered air conditioners deadly germ collectors; he is said to have taken to sitting naked in darkened, sweltering hotel rooms, surrounded by crinkled Kleenex and covered only with a few sheets over his privates. (*Newsweek*, April 19, 1976, p. 31)

Covering his hands with Kleenex as a defense against germs suggests that Hughes had also developed compulsions. In addition, he was preoccupied with the care of women's breasts. If women were passengers in his car, he would instruct his chauffeur to slow down when going over bumps in the road. Otherwise, he felt, the stress on the breasts would cause tissue breakdown and sagging; he was very concerned about preventing this.

Do "normal" people have intrusive, unacceptable thoughts and impulses? Several studies (Edwards & Dickerson, 1987; Freeston & Ladouceur, 1993; Salkovskis & Harrison, 1984; Sanavio, 1988) have found that more than 80 percent of normal samples report the existence of unpleasant intrusive thoughts and impulses. Apparently, a considerable majority of the "normal" population have obsessive symptoms. But are obsessions reported by patients different from those reported by normal individuals?

Rachman and DeSilva (1987) printed the obsessions of individuals with and without obsessive-compulsive disorder on cards, mixed them up, and gave them to six expert judges to re-sort into normal and clinical obsessional thoughts. On the whole, the judges were not very accurate in identifying the clinical obsessions. They were somewhat more successful in identifying "normal" obsessions or impulses (such as the impulse to buy unwanted things). Obsessions reported by obsessive-compulsive patients and by normal populations overlap considerably. Rachman and DeSilva did find some differences, however. Obsessive patients reported that their obsessions lasted longer, were more intense, produced more discomfort, and were more difficult to dismiss. The mere existence of obsessive-compulsive symptoms for diagnostic purposes may not be very meaningful because these symptoms are also reported in "normal" populations.

Compulsions

A *compulsion* is a behavior performed in a stereotyped manner to reduce anxiety. Distress or anxiety occurs if the behavior is not performed or if it is not done "correctly." Compulsions are often, but not always, associated with obsessions. Mild forms include behaviors such as refusing to walk under a ladder or step on cracks in sidewalks, throwing salt over one's shoulder, and knocking on wood. The three most common compulsions among a sample of children and adolescents involved excessive or ritualized washing, repeating rituals (such as going in and out of a door, and getting up and down from a chair), and checking behaviors (doors, stove, appliances). Changes in patterns or type of compulsion were common (Swedo et al., 1989). In the severe compulsive state, the behaviors become stereotyped and rigid; if they are not performed in a certain manner or a specific number of times, the compulsive individual is flooded with anxiety. To the compulsive, these behaviors often seem to have magical qualities, as though their correct performance wards off danger. The following case, known to the authors, is fairly typical:

> A fifteen-year-old boy had a two-year history of compulsive behaviors involving sixteen repetitions of the following behaviors: opening and closing a door, touching glasses before drinking from them, walking around each tree in front of his house before going to school. These compulsive acts produced much discomfort in the boy. His schoolmates ridiculed him, and his parents were upset because his rituals prevented him from reaching school at the appropriate time. An interview with the boy revealed that his compulsive behaviors were associated with the onset of masturbation, an act that the boy considered "dirty," although he

Table 6.3

Clinical Examples of Obsessions and Compulsions

Patient		Duration of Obsession in Years	Content of Obsession
Age	**Sex**		
21	M	6	Teeth are decaying, particles between teeth
42	M	16	Women's buttocks, own eye movements
55	F	35	Fetuses lying in the street, killing babies, people buried alive
24	M	16	Worry about whether he has touched vomit
21	F	9	Strangling people
52	F	18	Contracting venereal disease

Patient		Duration of Compulsions in Years	Compulsive Rituals
Age	**Sex**		
47	F	23	Handwashing and housecleaning; contact with dirt, toilet, or floor triggers about 100 handwashings per day
20	F	13	Severe checking ritual; checks 160 times to see if window is closed; also compelled to read the license number of cars and the numbers on manhole covers
21	M	2	Intense fear of contamination after touching library books, money; washes hands 25 times a day and ruminates about how many people had handled the objects before him
7	M	4	Walking only on the edges of floor tiles
9	M	4	Going back and forth through doorways 500 times

Source: Compiled from Boersma et al., 1976; Rachman, Marks & Hodgson, 1973; Roper, Rachman & Marks, 1975; Shahar & Marks, 1980; Stern et al., 1973; and Swedo et al., 1989.

was unable to refrain from it. It was when he began to masturbate that the first of his compulsive behaviors (touching a glass sixteen times before drinking from it) developed.

Table 6.3 contains additional examples of obsessions and compulsions.

Etiology of Obsessive-Compulsive Disorder

The causes of obsessive-compulsive disorder remain speculative, although recently increased attention has been paid to biogenic explanations. We'll examine the cause of this disorder from the perspectives of the psychoanalytic, behavioral, and biogenic models.

Psychoanalytic Perspective Freud (1949) believed that obsessions represent the substitution or replacement of an original conflict (usually sexual in nature) with an associated idea that is less threatening. He found support for his notion in the case histories of some of his patients. One patient, a girl, had disturbing obsessions about stealing or counterfeiting money; these thoughts were absurd and untrue. During analysis, Freud discovered that these obsessions reflected anxiety that stemmed from guilt about masturbation. When the patient was kept under constant observation, which prevented her from masturbating, the obsessional thoughts (or perhaps, the reports of the thoughts) ceased.

The dynamics of obsession have been described as involving "the intrusion of the unwelcome thought [that] 'seeks' to prevent anxiety by serving as a more tolerable substitute for a subjectively less welcome thought or impulse" (Laughlin, 1967, p. 311). Freud's patient found thoughts involving stealing less disturbing than masturbation. Her displacement of that feeling to a *substitute* action prevented her ego defenses from being overwhelmed.

Several other psychoanalytic defense mechanisms are considered prominent in obsessive-compulsive behaviors. For example, *undoing* is canceling or atoning for forbidden impulses by engaging in repetitive, ritualistic activities. Washing one's hands may symbolically represent cleansing oneself of unconscious wishes. Because the original conflict remains, however, one is compelled to perform the act of atonement over and over again. *Reaction formation* provides a degree of comfort because it counterbalances forbidden desires with diametrically opposed behaviors. To negate problems stemming from the anal psychosexual stage (characteristic of obsessive-compulsives) such as the impulse to be messy, patients tend toward excessive cleanliness and orderliness. Obsessive-compulsives may also employ the defense of *isolation,* which allows the separation of a thought or action from its effect. Aloofness, intellectualization, and detachment reduce the anxiety produced by patently aggressive or sexual thoughts.

Behavioral Perspective Proponents of the behavioral perspective maintain that obsessive-compulsive behaviors develop because they reduce anxiety. A distracting thought or action recurs more often if it reduces anxiety. For example, many college students may develop mild forms of compulsive behavior during intense exam periods, such as final examinations. During this stressful and anxiety-filled time, students may find themselves engaging in escape activities such as daydreaming, straightening up their rooms, or eating five or more times a day, all of which serve to shield them from thoughts of the upcoming tests. If the stress lasts a long time, a compulsive behavior may develop.

Although the *anxiety reduction hypothesis* is popular among learning theorists, it has not been very helpful in explaining how a behavior, such as handwashing that goes on for hours, can originate. Maher (1966) suggested that a compulsion is acquired through operant conditioning. For example, a person who has developed a compulsion for handwashing might have been reinforced in the past by parents for cleanliness, and therefore he or she considers handwashing desirable. When a transgression occurs, performing a socially learned anxiety-reducing response

reduces the transgressor's feeling of guilt. Because this response is reinforcing, the person uses it whenever he or she feels anxiety or another negative emotion. Unfortunately, this formulation does not explain why anxiety-reducing behaviors are displayed by some adults and not by others. Neither does it explain why some compulsives perform acts that certainly were not endorsed by parents or otherwise socially reinforced—for example, walking around every tree in the back yard before performing a task.

Researchers have sought support for the anxiety reduction hypothesis with a specific sample of patients: obsessive washers and checkers. If the hypothesis is correct, touching a contaminated item should increase anxiety, and performing the compulsive act should reduce anxiety (Carr, 1974; Hodgson & Rachman, 1972; Roper & Rachman, 1976). Carr found that compulsive acts were performed when there were high levels of autonomic activity and that the performance of these acts reduced the person's arousal levels to those of a resting state.

Sometimes, it does appear that the compulsive acts may continue because they reduce anxiety. However, the anxiety reduction hypothesis does not explain how these behaviors originate. In addition, many obsessional ruminations involve disease, insanity, mutilation, or death—events that one would expect to elevate anxiety. Yet we can only speculate about the reinforcements associated with them.

Another behavioral explanation is the *superstition hypothesis.* This involves a chance association of a behavior with a reinforcer. Skinner's (1948) classic example of superstitious behavior involved reinforcing pigeons (with food) at regular intervals, despite their behavior. Each pigeon began to display unique head or body movements, presumably because these happened to be the behaviors the birds were engaged in when they were given food.

Many obsessive-compulsive rituals may be reinforced by chance when a positive outcome follows performance of a certain behavior (O'Leary & Wilson, 1975). A student may take exams with only one special pencil or pen that he or she associates with past success. Athletes have been reported to continue wearing the same dirty uniform as long as a winning streak lasts. Although no actual relationship exists between these behaviors and a favorable or unfavorable outcome, the obsessive-compulsive may behave as though such a relationship existed. Anxiety develops if these rituals are not observed because the person believes that they are necessary to produce a positive outcome.

Although the hypothesis that obsessive-compulsive disorders are produced by the chance association of a behavior with a reinforcer is plausible, the proponents of the hypothesis have not specified the conditions under which superstitious behavior develops. Furthermore, the hypothesis does not explain the development of powerful and intrusive thoughts or rituals.

Biogenic Models Biological explanations of obsessive-compulsive behaviors are based on data relating to brain structure, genetic studies, and biochemical abnormalities. Differences in brain activity have been found among people who have obsessive-compulsive disorder, severe depression, and those with no psychiatric disorders. Obsessive-compulsives show increased metabolic activity in the frontal lobe of the left hemisphere. Perhaps this area of the brain, the left orbital gyrus, is associated with obsessive-compulsive behaviors (Bower, 1987). Heightened glucose metabolism in the frontal lobes has also been found in individuals with obsessive-compulsive disorder. Of special interest is the fact that when these individuals were given fluoxetine, the cerebral blood flow to the frontal lobes was decreased to values found in individuals without the disorder and there was a reported reduction in symptoms (Hoehn-Saric et al., 1991). It is not clear, however, whether metabolic changes reflect the cause of obsessive-compulsive disorder or its effects, or a combination of the two.

Some researchers (Comings & Comings, 1987) believe that some obsessive-compulsive behaviors are caused by genetic factors. Family and twin studies offer some support for this theory. First-degree relatives of individuals with obsessive-compulsive disorder are more likely to have an anxiety disorder than first-degree relatives of psychiatrically normal controls (Black et al., 1992). In a carefully controlled study, McKeon and Murray (1987) found that the relatives of obsessive-compulsives were twice as likely to have a "neurotic" disorder than relatives of the matched control group. However, both groups had a similar number of relatives with obsessive-compulsive disorder. These studies seem to suggest that "neurotic tendency" or vulnerability to developing an anxiety disorder may be inherited, and that

whether an obsessive-compulsive disorder develops depends on life events or personality factors.

Because medications such as clomipramine and fluoxetine, which increase the amount of serotonin available in the brain, have been effective in treating individuals with obsessive-compulsive disorder, researchers have hypothesized that the disorder is the result of a serotonin deficiency (Jenike et al., 1989; Perse et al., 1987). Although most studies of medication have methodological flaws—including reliance on clinical reports, small sample size, failure to include control and placebo groups, and differences in dosage levels—a small body of methodologically sound literature supports serotonin involvement in obsessive-compulsive disorder (Turner et al., 1985).

Treatment of Obsessive-Compulsive Disorder

The primary modes of treatment for obsessive-compulsive disorder are either biological or behavioral in nature. Behavioral therapies have been used successfully for many years, but treatment with medication has recently enjoyed increased attention.

Biological Treatments Because obsessive-compulsive disorder is classified as an anxiety disorder, minor tranquilizers might be thought helpful. However, these drugs have not proven capable of decreasing to any extent the frequency of patients' obsessive thoughts or compulsive rituals.

Antidepressant drugs have also been tried with mixed results. A review of nineteen studies led to the conclusion that antidepressants were a beneficial part of the treatment for obsessive-compulsive disorder if the patient showed signs of depression. In these cases, the drugs not only alleviated depression but also decreased ritualistic behavior (Marks, 1983). Fluvoxamine and clomipramine, which increase the serotonin level in the brain, have been reported to successfully treat patients with obsessive-compulsive disorder (Jenike et al., 1989; Perse et al., 1987; Price et al., 1987). However, only 60 to 80 percent of persons with obsessive-compulsive disorder respond to these medications, and often the relief is only partial (Pigott & Murphy, 1991). Many clients also report adverse side reactions to medications and drop out of treatment (Clomipramine Collaborative Study Group, 1991). In addition, relapse is frequent within

FIRST PERSON

Beverly A. Brauer

When thinking of posttraumatic stress disorder, one generally does not first consider women. Yet, while studying anxiety disorders during my graduate program, it slowly occurred to me that I had experienced my own posttraumatic stress reaction. I had been a young, inexperienced Army nurse when I went to Vietnam in August 1972. I did not experience a combat situation, yet the tension of being in a war zone and the uncertainty of what could

and did happen around me (the beating of a corpsman within sight of the hospital compound, the windows being blown out of the hospital by the shelling of nearby headquarters, treatment of the sick and injured by the war) had a major impact. These experiences helped me understand that women are also damaged by the threat and the reality of violence. Although women may experience violence in a military setting as I did, violence most frequently takes place in the woman's own home.

When I first started working with battered women, I found it striking to see the psychological similarities between veterans and these women. The tension of never knowing when the abuse will occur, of being fearful for one's own life and of feeling responsible for every situation with no escape, is very similar to a war situation. There is no sense of safety anywhere—especially not at home.

When a woman first arrives at

the battered women's shelter where I did my pro-bono volunteer work, she usually has experienced quite a number of years of being traumatized by being on the "front line" and does not believe she can be safe. With the support of the staff, she is shown the shelter's security system and its homelike organization and appearance. The woman is then included in the shelter's groups, assigned a coordinator, and given whatever help she may need to establish a new home, an income, and a network of support. For example, Sally (not her real name), one of the women I worked with, came to the shelter in shock and with nothing but the clothes she was wearing. When Sally married, she considered her husband a caring, loving man. She was shocked when he began to abuse her after several years of marriage. She kept hoping things would get better, but her situation was bleak. She lived in another state, isolated from her family. Her husband toler-

months of stopping the medication (Marks & O'Sullivan, 1988).

Behavioral Treatments The treatment of choice for obsessive-compulsive disorder is the combination of flooding and response prevention. This approach typically requires fewer therapy sessions than systematic desensitization, and the results have been consistently impressive (Steketee & White, 1990). **Flooding** is a technique that involves continued *in vivo* (actual) or imagined exposure to a high fear-arousing situation. In the flooding segment, clients are repeatedly exposed to the anxiety-producing stimulus; in the response-prevention stage, the performance of rituals is prevented. As an example, consider a man who fears that he will develop a fatal infection from contact with germs. The flooding stage could involve exposing the patient to something that he perceives as containing deadly germs (perhaps dirt, a newspa-

per, or leftover food). The man would be required to touch the items at first, and later to smear them over his body. Once he was properly "contaminated," the client would not be allowed to cleanse himself by engaging in his compulsive ritual (such as repeated handwashing). Instead, in this response-prevention stage, he would be required to remain "contaminated" until his anxiety had been extinguished. Flooding is used to extinguish anxiety as a response to the conditioned stimulus, and the response prevention further extinguishes anxiety and helps eliminate the avoidance behavior (the ritual).

A promising approach is cognitive therapy that attempts to identify and modify clients' irrational thoughts. In one study, this technique was as effective as exposure in reducing symptoms of the disorder (Emmelkamp & Beens, 1991). To eliminate obsessive-compulsive disorder in a fourteen-year-old boy, both response prevention and cognitive therapy were

ated no social contacts and she would be beaten if he even thought she had talked to the neighbors. He demanded that she account for every minute of her commute to and from work. If she was late, she'd be beaten and tyrannized with a derogatory, demeaning lecture on her worthlessness.

Sally lived in constant terror that she would be killed if she made any efforts to leave. When her husband physically threatened her young son, she borrowed money to escape while her husband was not at home. She was able to utilize the support of the shelter to establish a safe home away from her abusive spouse.

When her basic needs (food, clothing, an apartment, and a job to support her son and herself) were met, Sally began to show increased symptoms of her PTSD. She felt very guilty at leaving her husband, yet highly fearful and anxious that he might find and hurt her as he had threatened to do. She was

hypervigilant to any stimulus that reminded her of the abuse and she experienced recurrent, intrusive dreams. Sally isolated herself to her home and had little interest in normal family or social activities. She became more depressed and suicidal. Sally tried to ignore the past and minimize the effect her abusive marriage had on her.

A concerned family member brought Sally in for an evaluation. Sally agreed to see a psychiatrist for antidepressant medication. When stable on the medication, Sally was referred to the educational support group of the outreach program of the battered women's shelter. There she learned she was not alone and that others understood what she had experienced. Sally also learned more about the abuse cycle and about herself.

In her individual therapy with me, Sally learned to tolerate addressing her memories, anger, feelings of helplessness, and fear. Sally worked cognitively to improve her

self-esteem and to recognize options open to her (that is, she was no longer trapped). She began to work on developing a network of support. Sally continues to work on building her self-esteem and confidence in her ability to make choices that will protect herself and her son.

As with all trauma survivors, Sally will have the memories—the "scars"—to live with the rest of her life. I find it very rewarding to work with these women to witness their courage to face their fears and to make a future for themselves despite the traumas they have experienced. It's a constant reminder for me of the human spirit's ability to survive in the face of adversity.

Beverly A. Brauer is a psychiatric nurse in group practice in Aurora, Colorado. She does pro-bono work at the Safehouse for Battered Women, Inc., in Denver, Colorado.

involved. The boy would continually check the windows for bats and check his body for saliva from bats. He had obsessions about contracting rabies, death and suicide, and harming others. The successful treatment involved severely reducing the checking behaviors (response prevention) and identifying each irrational thought ("I will die if I see a bat") and refuting them (Kearney & Silverman, 1990).

POSTTRAUMATIC STRESS DISORDER

Posttraumatic stress disorder (PTSD) is an anxiety disorder that develops in response to an extreme psychological or physical trauma. These events may involve a threat to one's life or to a spouse or family member. Examples include being abducted and threatened (Saigh, 1987), traumatic accidents and

natural disasters (Joseph et al., 1993), rape and incest (Kilpatrick et al., 1985), concentration camp experience (Kinzie et al., 1984), child abuse (Eth & Pynoos, 1985), and the battered woman syndrome (Walker, 1991). A large percentage of children exposed to a sniper attack at their school, the San Francisco earthquake, and hurricane Hugo exhibited symptoms of PTSD (Udwin, 1993). These events produce feelings of terror and helplessness (see the First Person narrative for an account of PTSD).

The following case illustrates the features and origin of posttraumatic stress disorder (PTSD).

Ms. A. is a 36-year-old woman who was admitted to the hospital for depression, suicidal ideation, anxiety attacks, dissociative episodes, hypervigilance, intrusive thoughts, and nightmares. These symptoms began after an experience seventeen years before admission, when she was picked up hitchhiking by a group of

The intense terror and fear associated with combat may result in posttraumatic stress disorder. Recurrent and disturbing recollections of the event may occur.

motorcyclists. For 3 days she was tortured, raped, beaten, burned, and threatened with sudden death by, for instance, Russian roulette. When she came home, she withdrew to her room, depressed and numbed, for 6 months. . . . Shortly thereafter, she began to reexperience the traumatic events through daytime flashbacks and nightmares. (Hudson et al., 1991, p. 572)

Diagnosis of Posttraumatic Stress Disorder

Not everyone who is exposed to an extreme stressor develops PTSD; the following additional symptoms are necessary for the diagnosis.

1. *Re-experiencing the event in dreams or intrusive memories* For Ms. A, these symptoms were displayed in flashbacks and nightmares of the event, "Different scenes came back, replays of exactly what happened, only the time is drawn out . . . it seems to take forever for the gun to reach my head (Hudson et al., 1991, p. 572). One veteran with PTSD reported continued disturb-

ing thoughts of a Viet Cong soldier whom he had taken prisoner. Later, he saw the prisoner pushed out of a helicopter in flight. Because Mr. B had captured the prisoner, he felt responsible for the death (Hendin et al., 1981) and continued to reexperience this episode. Many rape victims often report intrusive memories of the attack (Kilpatrick et al., 1985).

2. *Emotional numbing or avoiding stimuli associated with the trauma* As a defense against these thoughts, people who have this disorder may withdraw emotionally and may avoid anything that might remind them of the events. Ms. A reported emotional numbing and dissociative episodes. Concentration camp survivors who developed posttraumatic stress disorder often displayed emotional numbness and avoided talking about their experiences in the camp. One man said flatly, "What is there to say? There was just killing and death" (Kinzie et al., 1984, p. 646). Avoidance is only partially successful, however. Certain stimuli, such as the sound or sight of helicopters for combat veterans, would bring back the intrusive memories (Mooney, 1988).

3. *Heightened autonomic arousal* This reaction can include symptoms such as sleep disturbance, hypervigilance, and loss of control over aggression. Ms. A reported anxiety attacks and difficulty falling asleep or staying awake.

Although posttraumatic stress disorder clearly exists, many questions regarding diagnosis, etiology, and treatment remain. In diagnosing the disorder, subjective judgment still plays a big role. For example, what constitutes a "psychologically traumatic event"? Although examples are given in DSM-IV, it is not clear what specific situations can produce the disorder. Defining the criterion stressor is of vital importance in the diagnosis of PTSD because it acts as a gatekeeper. Unless a specific stressor occurs, the diagnosis is not given regardless of other symptoms that may be present such as reliving the experience, emotional numbing, and emotional reactivity.

Certainly the magnitude of the stressor may be very important in the development of PTSD. In a study of Cambodian refugees living in the United States for four to six years who had experienced multiple stressors such as the death of family members, torture, extreme fear, and deprivation during their escape, 86 percent met the criteria for PTSD (Carlson & Rosser-Hogan, 1991). Rape is also clearly a traumatic event. Immediately after a sexual assault, 94 percent of the victims met the criteria for PTSD and after three months, 47 percent of the sample still suffered from this disorder (Rothbaum et al., 1990). This supports the contention that some extreme stressors may produce PTSD in almost everyone (Carlson & Rosser-Hogan, 1991). Davidson and Foa (1991) raised additional questions about the criterion stressor. Whether a stressor is regarded as outside the range of normal human experience or "exceptional" may differ from person to person. In certain urban areas, killings and physical assault may occur frequently and may not be considered to be infrequent or unexpected. More work needs to be done to more clearly define the traumatic stressor in PTSD.

Little is also said about subjective perception of the event. The degree of trauma often depends on the way the individual views the event (Janoff-Bulman, 1985). There is little emphasis on individual differences in reaction to extreme stressors in DSM-IV. Figley (1985) posed the following questions that still have to be asked for PTSD: among people who are exposed to a psychologically traumatic event, which ones will develop posttraumatic stress disorder? Is this condition lifelong or curable? Among those who develop PTSD, how many will show the reaction immediately and how many after a period of time? Can we determine who has PTSD and who is malingering?

More research is necessary to answer questions about accurately diagnosing posttraumatic stress disorder. In one study (Sparr & Pankratz, 1983), five men who met the DSM-III criteria for PTSD (complained of reexperiencing the trauma, sleep disturbances, and concentration difficulties and were emotionally constricted) were later found to be feigning. Malloy and associates (1983) pointed out that diagnoses that are based on self-report measures are often unreliable and invalid. Instead, they recommended using a three-part assessment package that incorporates behavioral, physiological, and self-report measures. These three measures were used in a study of three groups of veterans: (1) those with PTSD, (2) those without PTSD, and (3) those with psychiatric disorders other than PTSD. These groups were exposed to both audiovisual combat stimuli (helicopters flying, soldiers disembarking from a helicopter,

and sounds of machine-gun fire) and neutral stimuli (couple departing from a house, people walking around a mall, and crowd sounds).

Veterans with posttraumatic stress disorder differed from the comparison groups only when exposed to the combat stimuli. To the latter, they displayed a greater physiological response (increased heart rate) and greater behavioral avoidance (pressed a button to terminate the stimuli); they also reported higher levels of fear and anxiety. Symptoms of PTSD appear to be specific to the traumatic situation and not merely increased arousal. The three-part assessment promises to increase diagnostic reliability and validity. Orr and his colleagues (1993) also found that reactions to combat stimuli discriminated between Korean and Vietnam veterans with PTSD versus Vietnam and Korean veterans without PTSD. These two studies showed that it is possible to find objective differences in the reactions of individuals with PTSD and that it is a mental disorder distinct from other anxiety disorders.

Breslau and associates (1991) studied PTSD in a random sample of 1,007 young adults living in Detroit, Michigan. They were specifically interested in the percentage of individuals exposed to extreme stressors using the DSM-III-R definitions. In this sample, the lifetime prevalence rate of exposure to one or more of the following stressors—sudden injury or serious accident, physical assault, seeing someone seriously hurt or killed, news of sudden death or injury of close relative or friend, narrow escape, threat to one's life, rape, robbery, childhood physical or sexual abuse, and natural disaster—was 39.1 percent. Of the individuals exposed to one of these conditions, 23.6 percent met the criteria for PTSD, showing a lifetime prevalence rate of 9.2 percent for the disorder.

Breslau and his colleagues also found that women were more likely to suffer from PTSD than men, even though men were more likely to be exposed to traumatic situations. As with men, most women did not develop PTSD after experiencing a trauma. The one exception was rape, in which 80 percent of the women developed PTSD. In an attempt to find differences between those who did or did not develop PTSD after being exposed to a stressor, these two groups were compared: 75.3 percent of those who developed PTSD had either a preexisting anxiety disorder or had a family history of anxiety symptoms

Posttraumatic stress is not isolated to combat situations. Any catastrophic event that is deeply traumatic, such as an earthquake or plane crash, can trigger a stress reaction in people experiencing or even observing the event.

as compared to 50 percent among the unaffected. Interestingly, the researchers only found one case of delayed-onset PTSD, so it may not be as common as many have thought.

Etiology and Treatment of Posttraumatic Stress Disorder

Because a traumatic event precipitates the disorder, several researchers (Keane et al., 1985; Kilpatrick et al., 1985; Kolb, 1987) believe that classical conditioning is involved. People who have PTSD often show reactions to stimuli present at the time of the trauma (darkness, time of day, smell of diesel fuel, propeller noises, and so on). Extinction does not oc-

cur because the individual avoids thinking about the situation. As we indicated in our discussion of phobias, however, the classical conditioning model is insufficient. Not everyone who is exposed to a traumatic event develops posttraumatic stress disorder. Other factors such as the person's individual characteristics, his or her perception of the event, and the existence of support groups also have an influence.

According to the model shown in Figure 6.2, the degree of trauma is one variable in developing PTSD but the person's own coping styles and a supportive recovery environment can reduce its effects. One study showed that war veterans who developed PTSD were more likely to have sustained injuries, came closer to their own death, felt more guilty about their role in the event, and perceived less support from their families (Solkoff et al., 1986). Negative childhood experiences (Bremner et al., 1993) and being more withdrawn and inhibited (Schnurr et al., 1993) are also associated with an increased risk of developing PTSD.

As was reported in the earlier study by Breslau and her colleagues (1991), individuals who develop PTSD were likely to have either a preexisting anxiety disorder or a family history of anxiety. Incest victims who were able to "make sense" of their victimization showed better adjustment than those who were unable to redefine the event (Janoff-Bulman, 1985). Victims of trauma whose experience leads them into developing a generalized perceived loss of control are likely to develop the most severe PTSD (Kushner et al., 1992). It appears that a variety of individual experiences or characteristics of a supportive environment can moderate the impact of a traumatic stressor.

Treatments for PTSD have varied from crisis intervention approaches for individuals who are suffering from the recent impact of a stressor to psychoanalytic and cognitive behavioral approaches for more chronic forms of PTSD. Because anxiety symptoms are reported, antianxiety medications are often given to individuals with this disorder. In working with Vietnam veterans with PTSD, Embry (1990) recommended the following steps: (1) build rapport by understanding the meaning of the trauma for the individual, (2) allow the individual to have "permission" to express his emotions, (3) help the individual learn to give up the "sick" role, and (4) focus on here-and-now problems as well as the earlier trauma.

FIGURE 6.2   Processing a Catastrophic Event: A Working Model

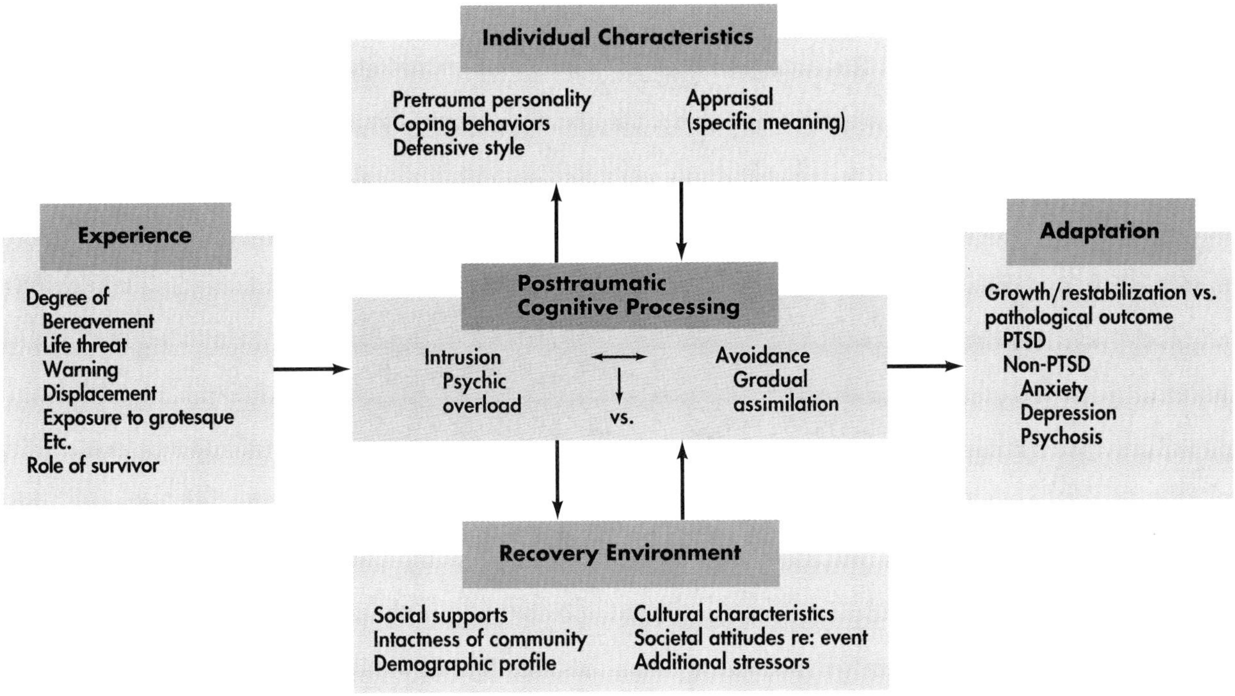

Individual Characteristics

Pretrauma personality
Coping behaviors
Defensive style

Appraisal
(specific meaning)

Experience

Degree of
  Bereavement
  Life threat
  Warning
  Displacement
  Exposure to grotesque
  Etc.
Role of survivor

**Posttraumatic
Cognitive Processing**

Intrusion
Psychic
overload

vs.

Avoidance
Gradual
assimilation

Adaptation

Growth/restabilization vs.
pathological outcome
  PTSD
  Non-PTSD
    Anxiety
    Depression
    Psychosis

Recovery Environment

Social supports
Intactness of community
Demographic profile

Cultural characteristics
Societal attitudes re: event
Additional stressors

Source: From Green, Wilson & Lindy, 1985.

Extinction procedures have also been successful. A six-year-old boy with PTSD that developed after being involved in a bomb blast and seeing injured people was successfully treated through relaxation techniques and imaginal flooding. The boy was asked to imagine scenes of injured people, the smell of smoke, and shouts of individuals. This procedure markedly reduced his symptoms (Saigh, 1986). Prolonged exposure (continued imagination of the rape scene) was more effective in reducing PTSD symptoms, rape-related distress, and general anxiety than stress inoculation training (learning coping skills, relaxation, and cognitive restructuring) or supportive counseling among rape victims. The authors (Foa et al., 1991) believe that a major therapeutic component in exposure was in confronting the anxiety situation directly so that a positive change in the rape memory occurs.

A recent and promising treatment for PTSD called *eye movement desensitization* has been developed by Shapiro (1989). It involves asking the client to visual-ize the disturbing imagery and then describe it using all sensory modalities. After the image is clear, the client visually tracks the lateral movements of the clinician's finger or pencil while holding his or her head immobile. These movements are repeated twenty to thirty times about one second apart. This procedure appears to result in a very rapid diminishing of distress and eliminates symptoms such as nightmares and flashbacks; few cases of relapse have been reported (Wolpe & Abrams, 1991). Although the initial findings are impressive, the reason that eye movements are effective is not clear. As Marquis (1991) pointed out in his review of this approach, "It is necessary to show beyond doubt that eye movements are essential to the deconditioning, and that not just any simultaneous activity will do—such as waving arms, repeating nonsense syllables, smelling roses, or sitting on a block of ice" (p. 192). Even if eye movements are shown to be essential to this procedure, we still need to find the mechanism that accounts for its success.

Cognitive behavioral approaches have also been developed for working with persons with posttraumatic stress disorder. Symptoms of PTSD are caused by the person seeing the world as an unpredictable or uncontrollable place in which to live. Treatment strategies include allowing the person to (1) redefine the event to gain a sense of consistency in the world (by comparing oneself with those who are less fortunate, considering possible benefits from the experience, and so on), (2) finding meaning and purpose in the experience, (3) changing behaviors to help prevent the event from recurring, and (4) seeking social support (Janoff-Bulman, 1985).

SUMMARY

1. Anxiety is an emotion that all of us experience. It appears in our cognitions or thoughts, in our behaviors, and in our physiological or biological reactions. The means of assessing anxiety include self-reports, observations of motor or behavioral reactions, and physiological measures.

2. The anxiety disorders are all characterized by anxiety—by feelings of fear and apprehension. The anxiety may be the major disturbance (as it is in panic disorder and generalized anxiety disorder), may arise when the individual confronts a feared object or situation (as in the phobias), may result from an attempt to master the symptoms (as in obsessive-compulsive disorder), or may occur during intrusive memories of a traumatic event (as in posttraumatic stress disorder).

3. Panic disorder and generalized anxiety disorder (GAD) are characterized by direct and unfocused anxiety. Panic disorder is marked by episodes of extreme anxiety and feelings of impending doom. Generalized anxiety disorder involves chronically high levels of anxiety, hypervigilance, and apprehension. Psychoanalysts feel that these disorders are unfocused because they stem from conflicts that remain in the person's unconscious. Behaviorists believe that these disorders are the result of conditioning to an omnipresent stimulus. Both drug therapy and behavioral therapies, as well as psychoanalysis, have been used to treat these disorders.

4. Phobias are strong fears that exceed the de-

mands of the situation. Agoraphobia is an intense fear of being in public places; it can keep afflicted people from leaving home because attempts to do so may produce panic attacks. Social phobias are irrational fears about situations in which the person can be observed by others. The anxiety generally stems from the possibility of appearing foolish or making mistakes in public. Specific phobias include all the irrational fears that are not classed as social phobias or agoraphobia. Commonly feared objects in specific phobias include small animals, heights, and the dark. In the psychoanalytic view, phobias represent unconscious conflicts that are displaced onto an external object. Behavioral explanations include the classical conditioning view, in which phobias are based on an association between some aversive event and a conditioned stimulus; conditioning through observation; the role of frightening thoughts; reinforcement for fear behaviors; and negative information. Biogenic explanations are based on genetic influences, biochemical, neurological, or on the idea of preparedness to develop certain fears. The most effective treatments for phobics seem to be medicinal (via antidepressants) and behavioral (via exposure and flooding, systematic desensitization, modeling, and graduated exposure).

5. Obsessive-compulsive disorder involves involuntary, intrusive, and uncontrollable thoughts or actions. Most persons with obsessive-compulsive disorder are aware that their distressing behaviors are irrational. Obsessions (which involve thoughts) and compulsions (which involve actions) may occur together or separately. Freud believed that this disorder represented the substitution of a threatening conflict with a behavior or thought that was less threatening. According to the anxiety reduction hypothesis, obsessions and compulsions develop because they reduce anxiety. The superstition hypothesis holds that the disorder stems from the chance association of a behavior with a reinforcer. The most commonly used treatments are behavioral: systematic desensitization or flooding plus response prevention.

6. Posttraumatic stress disorder involves exposure to a traumatic event resulting in intrusive memories of the occurrence, attempts to forget or repress the memories, emotional withdrawal, and increased arousal. Classical conditioning principles have been used to both explain and treat the condition.

KEY TERMS

agoraphobia An intense fear of being in public places or of being alone where help may not be available; in extreme cases, a fear of leaving one's home

anxiety Feelings of fear and apprehension

anxiety disorders Disorders (panic disorders, generalized anxiety disorders, phobias, obsessive-compulsive disorders and PTSD) whose major characteristics are irrational feelings of fear and apprehension

compulsion The need to perform acts to reduce anxiety

exposure therapy Exposure to a feared situation

flooding A therapeutic technique that involves continued *in vivo* (actual) or imagined exposure to a fear-arousing situation (always involves high anxiety)

generalized anxiety disorder (GAD) Disorder characterized by persistent high levels of anxiety in situations where no real danger is present

graduated exposure Gradual exposure to a feared situation

modeling therapy A therapeutic approach to phobias in which the phobic individual observes a fearless model coping with the fear-producing situation

obsession An intrusive, uncontrollable, and persistent thought

obsessive-compulsive disorder Anxiety disorder characterized by intrusive and uncontrollable thoughts, or the need to perform specific acts repeatedly, or both

panic disorder Anxiety disorder characterized by severe and frightening episodes of apprehension and feelings of impending doom

phobia A strong, persistent, and unwarranted fear of a specific object or situation

posttraumatic stress disorder (PTSD) An anxiety disorder that develops in response to an event that is "outside the range of normal human experience." It is characterized by intrusive memories of the traumatic event, emotional withdrawal, and increased arousal levels

social phobia An intense fear of being scrutinized

specific phobia An extreme fear of a specific object or situation; a phobia that is not classed as either agoraphobia or a social phobia

systematic desensitization A therapy in which relaxation is used to eliminate the anxiety associated with phobias and other fear-evoking situations

CHAPTER 7

Dissociative Disorders and Somatoform Disorders

A man was found severely dehydrated, wandering in the desert. It was estimated that he had been without water for at least three days. He claimed to have no memories of the past but retained many skills. For example, he demonstrated the ability to fly a plane. He appeared on the television program "Unsolved Mysteries" to ask the help of others to identify him.

A woman came in for therapy because of several puzzling events. She had been told that she had been dancing and flirting in a bar, an event she could not remember and that was against her moral standards. She had also awakened in a hospital after an overdose and had not remembered being suicidal. Under hypnosis 13 different personalities were revealed. (Shapiro, 1991)

T he first two cases illustrate characteristics found in the four dissociative disorders—mental disorders in which a person's identity, memory, and consciousness are altered or disrupted. These and the somatoform disorders, which involve physical symptoms or complaints that have no physiological basis, are the subjects of this chapter. Both groups of disorders occur because of some psychological conflict or need.

The symptoms of the dissociative disorders and the somatoform disorders, such as memory disturbance or hysterical blindness, generally become known through self-reports. There is, then, the possibility of faking. The man found wandering in the desert was identified as Arthur Beal after his appearance on television. But he was soon arrested by the

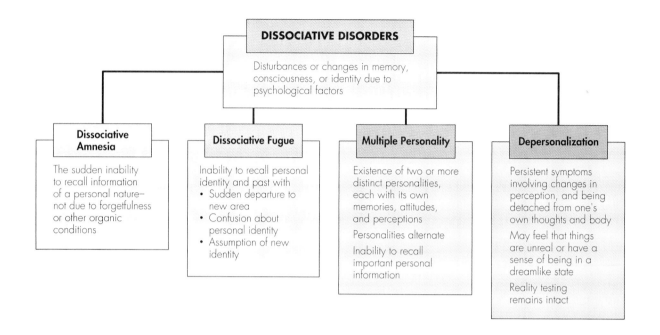

DISSOCIATIVE DISORDERS

Disturbances or changes in memory, consciousness, or identity due to psychological factors

Dissociative Amnesia

The sudden inability to recall information of a personal nature—not due to forgetfulness or other organic conditions

Dissociative Fugue

Inability to recall personal identity and past with
• Sudden departure to new area
• Confusion about personal identity
• Assumption of new identity

Multiple Personality

Existence of two or more distinct personalities, each with its own memories, attitudes, and perceptions

Personalities alternate

Inability to recall important personal information

Depersonalization

Persistent symptoms involving changes in perception, and being detached from one's own thoughts and body

May feel that things are unreal or have a sense of being in a dreamlike state

Reality testing remains intact

police for stealing a shipment of food just before his disappearance. The police believed that he was feigning the disorder. In addition, there are questions over the sudden increases in several dissociative disorders—multiple personality and dissociative amnesia. Some researchers believe that counselors and therapists or clients may be inadvertently "creating" these disorders.

Physical complaints from individuals with somatoform disorders are also difficult to evaluate when there appears to be no organic basis for the physical symptoms. Yet the fact remains that in genuine cases of dissociative and somatoform disorders, the symptoms are produced "involuntarily" or unconsciously. Affected individuals actually are puzzled by memory loss and behavioral changes or suffer from physical pain or disability. This situation leads to a paradox: A person *does* suffer memory disturbance in psychogenic amnesia, yet that memory must exist somewhere in the neurons and synapses of the brain. Similarly, a person *does* "lose" his or her sight in hysterical blindness, yet physiologically the eyes are perfectly capable of seeing. What exactly has happened? The dissociative disorders and the somatoform disorders are among the most puzzling of all disorders.

DISSOCIATIVE DISORDERS

The **dissociative disorders**—*dissociative amnesia, dissociative fugue, depersonalization disorder,* and *multiple personality*—are shown in the disorders chart above. Each disorder involves some sort of dissociation, or separation, of a part of the person's consciousness, memory, or identity. These disorders are highly publicized and sensationalized and, except for depersonalization disorder, were considered relatively rare. But reports of one dissociative disorder—multiple personality—have increased dramatically. It is now estimated that approximately 5 percent of patients on adult psychiatric units have this disorder (Ross et al., 1991). More than one thousand patients are currently being treated for this disorder (Kluft, 1985). (Reasons for this increase are discussed later in the chapter.) Interestingly, multiple-personality disorder is rarely diagnosed in Japan or Britain (Merskey, 1992).

Corresponding to this increase is a complex legal debate about acts that are committed and that the individual is amnesic for:

1. Billy Milligan was acquitted of the crime of rape because it was committed by another personality (Keyes, 1981).

2. A man was charged with the rape of a woman with multiple personalities when the nonconsenting personalities brought up the charge.

3. A woman with twenty-one personalities asked for alimony payments, claiming that she did not commit adultery and tried to stop the responsible personality "Rosie." (In South Carolina, adultery is grounds for barring alimony payments.)

These issues raise troubling questions regarding responsibility in these disorders. Do these conditions represent mitigating circumstances and constitute "diminished capacity"? (See Chapter 20 for a legal discussion.)

Dissociative Amnesia

Dissociative amnesia is the partial or total loss of important personal information. This disorder may occur suddenly after a stressful or traumatic event. The disturbed person may not be able to recall information such as his or her name, address, friends, and relatives but remembers the necessities of daily life—how to read, write, and drive.

There are four types of dissociative amnesia that vary in terms of the degree and type of memory loss reported. The most common, **localized amnesia,** involves the failure to recall all the events that happened in a particular short period of time. Most often, this "lost" period includes an event that was highly painful or disturbing to the afflicted individual, as illustrated in the following cases.

A 38-year-old mother had no memory of being molested by her father until the age of 33 after undergoing therapy.

An eighteen-year-old woman who survived a dramatic fire claimed not to remember it or the death of her child and husband in the fire. She claimed that her relatives were lying about there having been a fire. She became extremely agitated and emotional several hours later, when her memory abruptly returned.

A four-year-old boy whose mother was murdered in his presence was found mopping up her blood. During interviews with a psychiatrist, however, he denied any memory of the incident.

Selective amnesia involves the inability to remember certain details of an incident. For example, a man

Dissociative amnesia generally occurs after a traumatic event. People suffering from this disorder can usually perform the skills they've acquired over a lifetime, such as driving a car and reading, but they forget more personal information, such as who they are.

remembered having an automobile accident but could not recall that his child had died in the crash. Selective amnesia is often claimed by people who are involved in violent criminal offenses. Many murderers report remembering arguments but don't remember killing someone. In fact, 30 to 65 percent of individuals who are charged or convicted of homicide claim amnesia as a defense (Schacter, 1986).

In **generalized amnesia,** the person cannot remember anything about his or her past life. Arthur Beal, who appeared on the program "Unsolved Mysteries," was given this diagnosis. After talking to and meeting his mother, he still claimed not to remember her or who he was. The following case illustrates some of the psychological events associated with generalized amnesia:

Mr. X was brought to the admission ward of a psychiatric hospital at the end of February 1988. . . . He could not give any information about himself apart from vague recollections from the immediate past. He had no money or identification on him on admission . . . he mainly expressed concern that he might have left a wife who might be looking for him. . . . We contacted the pastor of the church mentioned in the leaflet Mr. X had had on him on admission. The pastor led us to a woman who recognised and identified Mr. X . . . he suddenly remembered that his wife had died and that he had promised her he would kill himself as he felt he could not live without her. . . . He explained in his own words: "I must have lost my memory because otherwise I might have killed myself." (Domb & Beaman, 1991, pp. 424–425)

Finally, **continuous amnesia,** the least common form of psychogenic amnesia, is the inability to recall any events that have occurred from a specific time in the past, up to the present time. The individual remains alert and attentive but forgets each successive event after it occurs (Aalpoel & Lewis, 1984).

Psychologists are uncertain about the processes involved in dissociative amnesia. They believe that it results from the person's repression of a traumatic event or from some process closely related to repression. For example, **posthypnotic amnesia,** in which the subject cannot recall events that occurred during hypnosis, is somewhat similar to dissociative amnesia. In both cases, the lost material can sometimes be retrieved with professional help. There is, however, one important difference. In posthypnotic amnesia, the hypnotist suggests what is to be forgotten, whereas in dissociative amnesia, both the source and the content of the amnesia are unknown (Sarbin & Cole, 1979). Because of this difference, experiments to study amnesia are difficult to design. Therefore, information on dissociative amnesia has been gathered primarily through case studies. Lately, an increasing number of cases of dissociative amnesia that involve sexual abuse have been reported (Shapiro et al., 1993). However, some researchers believe that the "memories" may be caused by therapists' suggestions and clients' attempts to explain their problems (see Critical Thinking).

Dissociative Fugue

Dissociative fugue (also called *fugue state*) involves confusion over personal identity (often involves the partial or complete assumption of a new identity) and unexpected travel away from home. Most cases involve only short periods away from home and an incomplete change of identity. However, there are exceptions:

A 38-year-old man who had been missing for a year was living in another state when relatives saw his pho-

Dissociative fugue and dissociative amnesia are similar disorders, except that a person experiencing a fugue literally walks away from his or her life and may assume an entirely different identity.

CRITICAL THINKING

How Valid Are Repressed Memories?

In May 1990, George Franklin was brought to trial for raping and killing a child twenty years previously. This case was one of the first to rely heavily on repressed memories. The man's daughter, twenty years after the incident, remembered the killing of her friend in flashes of memory. She was playing with her friend in the back of the family van when the attack took place. She also retrieved memories of being sexually abused by her father. Three of her sisters also related being sexually abused. George Franklin was convicted and is now in jail. Lately, many individuals have reported repressed memories. For example, Roseanne Arnold, the television celebrity, remembered being abused by her father thirty-six years ago after her husband related an instance of sexual abuse that he suffered as a child.

Although survey data show that childhood sexual abuse and incest are more prevalent than had been estimated earlier, controversy arises over the accuracy and validity of repressed

memories. Some clinicians would prefer to err on the side of the victim. Bass and Davis (1987), authors of the book *Courage to Heal*, which deals with sexual abuse, wrote, "If you are unable to remember any specific instances, but still have a feeling that something happened to you, it probably did." Psychologist Elizabeth Loftus, however, believes that for some individuals, the "memory" may be inaccurate and the result of imagination, suggestion, or a means of explaining unhappiness in life (Loftus, 1993). Determining the authenticity of the memories, especially ones at very early ages, is difficult. One therapist indicated that some of his patients remember incidents that occurred before speech had developed or even while in the womb (Laker, 1992).

Parents who believe that they have been falsely accused of child abuse have formed a nationwide support group called False Memory Syndrome Foundation. They claim that the "memories" are often a product of

the therapist's approach or perspective or their children's attempt to blame them for their problems. Although sexual abuse of children does exist and many victims repress the memory of the event, controversy remains over the accuracy and acceptability of the reports.

As a scientist, how could you determine if "repressed memories" are accurate representations of the past? How could you separate "true" from "false" memories, especially because information obtained through hypnosis may be unreliable? How might you interpret a statement from a client who says that she has no clear memory of her childhood before the age of five? In cases of suspected sexual abuse, clinicians often say that they will believe what the client says no matter how bad the details. What are the advantages and disadvantages of such an approach? Can counselors inadvertently "produce" false memories in their clients?

---

tograph printed in a newspaper. The man had established a new identity and was spearheading a charitable drive in his new home state; the newspaper article praised him for his energy and leadership. When confronted by his relatives, the man initially denied knowing them. The relatives were certain of their identification but also puzzled by his outgoing personality. The person they knew had always been shy and retiring.

Sometimes, a patient reports multiple fugue episodes, as here:

E. F. was a 46-year-old man who described twelve to fifteen episodes of "going blank" during the previous five years. He said that these episodes lasted 2 to 36 hours, and that, in "coming round," his feet were often sore, he was a long way from home, and he had no idea of the time or what had been happening during the previous hours. For example, he found himself on one occasion near the Thames, ten miles from his home, with his clothes sopping wet. Marital and legal difficulties were believed to be contributing factors in the episodes of fugue. (Kopelman, 1987, p. 438)

FIRST PERSON

Richard Reckman

How does a child bear the unbearable? What does a preschooler feel when her adoptive mother routinely threatens to return her to an orphanage and tells her that her birth mother did not want her? How does a seven-year-old cope with being taken to a motel every Saturday and subjected to sadistic sexual practices by her father? As I listen to these experiences, my stomach tightens. I feel nauseated, angry, and fearful. I have three children of my own. I can see how important it is to them to be able to rely on their mother and me. Children need to feel love for their parents and to feel loved by their parents. I have seen my own children's pain and fear when I have let them down in

some way. What happens then to a child when the parents he looks to for love and comfort respond with persistent, severe abuse? One way to survive the unbearable is to dissociate experiences into separate personalities. These multiple personalities or "alters" allow the child to continue to function.

One of my clients is a woman named Alice. Alice was referred to me by a counselor at a community crisis telephone hot line. Alice was calling the hot line several times a week. During some conversations, her voice would shift markedly and she would refer to herself as Betty. Betty would speak about Alice as if she was a different person.

When Alice came to see me, she told me she had a wonderful father and that she knew no one named Betty. My initial plan was to develop a trusting relationship with Alice and then use hypnosis to ask for Betty. In six months, we learned that Alice's father had sexually abused and tortured her from ages five to twelve. When Alice could no longer stand the abuse, an alter personality named Betty stepped in. When Betty could stand it no longer, she brought in Cathy, Diane, or Ellie.

The severe and persistent abuse

shaped each of the personalities. Alice has struggled with feelings of helplessness and depression her whole life. She has never felt safe and accepted. She has made numerous suicide attempts. From her early teens through her thirties, she blocked her memories of the abuse and remembered her father as the parent who loved her. But Alice is a survivor. She has worked throughout her adult life. She has raised a son. She has skillfully counseled other battered women.

Betty is the internal self-helper. Betty knows everyone in the internal family. She "created" the other alters, she assigned them roles, and she has often controlled who was "out." Betty feels a tremendous responsibility for protecting Alice and the others. Until entering therapy, Betty focused on making decisions to best manage the "family." She allowed herself to feel very little. Betty has grown to allow herself a full range of feelings.

Cathy was so angry about the abuse that Betty kept her locked in her "room" for many years. When Cathy forced her way "out" in my office for the first time, she threatened to kill me. I took her threat seriously but hoped I could count on Alice and Betty to stop her if need

---

As with dissociative amnesia, recovery from fugue state is often abrupt and complete, although the gradual return of bits of information has also been found.

Depersonalization Disorder

Depersonalization disorder is perhaps the most common dissociative disorder. It is characterized by feelings of unreality concerning the self and the environment. At one time or another, most young adults have experienced some symptoms typical of depersonalization disorder: perceptions that the body is distorted or the environment has somehow changed,

feelings of living out a dream, or minor losses of control (Aalpoel & Lewis, 1984). But episodes of depersonalization can be fairly intense, and they can produce great anxiety because the people who suffer from them consider them unnatural. This diagnosis is only given if the feeling of unreality and detachment cause major impairment in social or occupational functioning.

A twenty-year-old college student became alarmed when she suddenly perceived subtle changes in her appearance. The reflection she saw in mirrors did not seem to be hers. She became even more disturbed

be. Cathy punished Alice and Betty for the next few months by inflicting severe physical pain on them. Over time, Cathy has moved past her anger and developed into a compassionate, constructive adult.

Diane battled her father with her fists. He just hurt her even more. When I met her the first time she was as angry as Cathy. But she was also very fearful. Diane is still a child. She, too, has moved past her anger. She has extended her trust to me but still experiences the world as a scary, hurtful place.

Ellie responded to the abuse by identifying with the aggressor. When I met her, she said that she and her father were bonded as one. Alice's father had been dead for many years but Ellie insisted that he was in the room with us. Ellie said that she and her father would harm me. To add to my uneasiness, Betty told me that she had not known about Ellie and that Ellie didn't seem fully "human" to her. Feeling unsettled, I reminded myself that my clients have the means to heal themselves. I reminded myself of the duty to seek first to understand, and I tried to remember what I could of the movie *The Exorcist*. After a half-dozen encounters of this sort,

Ellie broke the bond with her father and joined the internal family.

Alice has about twenty other alters. Some are fully developed personalities; others are more fragmentary or one-dimensional. There are children, adolescents, and adults. One is male. When personalities are "out," they perceive themselves in ways that are consistent with their self-image. The children see and experience their bodies as children's bodies. The male who shares Alice's body sees and experiences his body as male.

My experience from the other chair is different and the same. When one of Alice's alters come out, I see the same body but at the same time, each alter "embodies" that body uniquely. I experience the children as children, not like an adult acting like a child. The transitions between personalities are transformations, not just a very good actor taking on a new role. It was amazing at first to see.

With Alice, as with other multiple-personality clients, her physiological processes change when she changes personalities. Alice wears eyeglasses with a 20/200 prescription. She has worn glasses since childhood. None of the alters wears

eyeglasses. Several years ago, Alice required surgery to remove a severely inflamed gall bladder. Hours before and the day after surgery, Betty moved about freely without pain.

Experiencing separate personalities within one person raises intriguing questions. I have always thought of myself as my (one) self, not my selves. But is it as simple as that? As I drift into sleep, sometimes visual images roll by with no conscious control or direction. I simply watch and enjoy. If my self is such a unitary thing, how is it that the characters in my dreams often do things that are surprising and even shocking to me? The farther I am removed from everyday consciousness, the less singular is my experience of self. Does the multiplicity of self that I experience while sleeping suggest a potential in all of us for the formation of separate personalities in our waking state? Through my experience with Alice and others, my notions of self are broadening.

Richard F. Reckman is a therapist in private practice in Cincinnati, Ohio.

---

when her room, her friends, and the campus also seemed to take on a slightly distorted appearance. The world around her felt unreal and was no longer predictable. During the day before the sudden appearance of the symptoms, the woman had been greatly distressed by the low grades she received on several important exams. When she finally sought help at the university clinic, her major concern was that she was going insane.

Like other dissociative disorders, depersonalization can be precipitated by physical or psychological stress.

Dissociative Identity Disorder (Multiple-Personality Disorder)

Multiple personality is a dramatic disorder in which two or more relatively independent personalities appear to exist in one person (see First Person). The relationship among the personalities is often complex. Only one personality is evident at any one time, and the alternation of personalities usually produces periods of amnesia in the personality that has been displaced. However, one or several personalities may be aware of the existence of the others. The personalities involved are usually different from one another;

sometimes, they are direct opposites. The following case illustrates the vast differences that can exist among personalities.

> A 28-year-old female has a total of sixteen personalities. Three major personalities are usually present sometime during each day.
>
> Margaret is the core personality and is described as having good social skills but tends not to be assertive. She has a good sense of humor and puts on a "good front" to prevent the detection of the other personalities. She is left-handed.
>
> Rachel is sixteen years old. She engages in antisocial behaviors involving activities such as prostitution and aggression. She has a sarcastic sense of humor and appears when there is a need to fight back. She is right-handed.
>
> Dee is eight years old. She speaks and behaves like a child. She appears to have "taken the pain" whenever the personalities have been abused. She holds the memories of sexual abuse. She is ambidextrous. (Dick-Barnes, Nelson & Aine, 1987)

In cases where one personality is that of a child (like Dee), that part of the personality may be aware only of events that took place at an early age. For example, one woman's "child" personality was confused about being in an adult body and had never heard of "Sesame Street," Burger King, or Sprite (they did not exist when she was a child). She wanted to see her childhood friends and return to elementary school (Davidson, Allen & Smith, 1987).

Multiple-personality disorder is much more prevalent in women, who often report having experienced childhood physical or sexual abuse (Boon & Draijer, 1993; Coons & Bradley, 1985; Kluft, 1987). No gender differences in the prevalence of the disorder, however, were found in Switzerland (Modestin, 1992). *Conversion symptoms* (loss of physical or sensory function with no physical basis), depression, and anxiety are common in people with the disorder (Bliss, 1980; Coons, 1986).

In the best-known case of multiple personality (discussed briefly in Chapter 4), Eve White—described as sad, conservative, dignified, and passive—alternated with Eve Black, who was flirtatious, lighthearted, and sexy (Thigpen & Cleckley, 1957). During therapy a third personality, Jane, emerged. And Jane was subsequently replaced by an even more mature personality, Evelyn.

Although it is widely reported that Eve was successfully treated, she later wrote a book indicating that during therapy she actually had more than the four personalities reported by her therapists, and that an additional eighteen personalities emerged after she completed psychotherapy. With further treatment and the support of her family, she feels that she became an integrated personality at the age of forty-eight (Sizemore & Pittillo, 1977). Kluft (1987) reported that a person with this disorder typically has thirteen or fourteen personalities.

Psychological and physiological tests have been used to try to confirm the existence of distinct personalities in dissociative identity disorders. Current attempts to identify this disorder through the use of electroencephalograms (EEGs), cerebral blood flow, galvanic skin response, and other physiological measures have produced contradictory and conflicting findings (Miller & Triggiano, 1992).

Diagnostic Controversy   We noted earlier that multiple personality is among the less common dissociative disorders, but there is some question about how rare it really is. Hundreds of cases of multiple personality have been reported in recent years (Fagan & McMahon, 1984); one clinician alone reported more than 130 cases (Kluft, 1982). The identification of multiple personality in children has also increased. Fagan and McMahon (1984) diagnosed eleven childhood cases in eighteen months and believe that thousands of children may have this disorder.

Fagan and McMahon believe that parents, teachers, and mental health professionals should be aware of the signs of multiple personality in children. These include trance states; confusion about time, place, or person; responding to more than one name; marked and rapid shifts in personality; forgetting recent events; extreme or odd variation in skills such as handwriting and differences in food preferences and artistic abilities; varying responses to discipline; self-injurious behavior; multiple physical complaints; hysteric symptoms such as sleepwalking, sudden blindness, or loss of sensation; and reports of hearing voices, losing track of time, or being innocent when punished. The more such symptoms the child displays, the more likely that the diagnosis of incipient multiple personality is appropriate.

Some clinicians believe that dissociative identity disorder is relatively common but that the condition is underreported because of misdiagnosis. For example, in a study of one hundred persons diagnosed with this disorder, Putnam and colleagues (1986) found that nearly seven years elapsed from the initial assessment of symptoms before an accurate diagnosis was made. The patients received an average of four prior psychiatric or neurological diagnoses.

Misdiagnosis is illustrated in the case of a 37-year-old man who reported having experienced symptoms of dissociation since age six. He reported a history of blackouts, amnesia for certain acts, and behavior and personality changes. He received several diagnoses, including undifferentiated schizophrenia, organic brain syndrome, schizoid personality, and seizure disorder (Salley, 1988). People with multiple personality have also been diagnosed as having bipolar disorder and major depression with psychotic features. They commonly complained about "hearing voices arguing," "hearing voices commenting on my actions," "experiencing feelings that don't seem to be coming from me," and feelings of depression (Kluft, 1987). Because changes in mood and memory and hearing voices are symptoms of multiple-personality disorder as well as schizophrenia, diagnosis may be difficult.

Of course, misdiagnosis works both ways: other disorders may be diagnosed as multiple-personality disorder. In addition, it is possible that some researchers and therapists, in their enthusiasm, are labeling people as having multiple personalities when they do not (*false positives*). For example, Bliss and coworkers (1983) reported that approximately 60 percent of a group of persons with schizophrenia who had auditory hallucinations showed evidence of multiple personality. It is difficult to believe that such a large percentage could be misdiagnosed, and the results of this study may reflect the researchers' bias. Other researchers have suggested that the sudden increase in reports of multiple-personality disorder may be an artifact of the procedures used in investigating this disorder (see Focus 7.1) and that it is a "fashionable" diagnosis.

In a study of multiple-personality disorder in Switzerland, Modestin (1992) concluded that the disorder is relatively rare and estimates its prevalence rate to be .05 percent to .1 percent of patients. He also found that three psychiatrists accounted for more than 50 percent of patients with this disorder. Why is it that some psychiatrists report treating many patients with multiple personalities whereas the majority do not? A prominent psychiatrist indicated that in forty years of practice he encountered only one "doubtful case" of the disorder and asks, "Why have my colleagues and I seen so few cases of multiple-personality disorder?" (Chodoff, 1987). The psychiatrists who treated Eve received tens of thousands of patients referred to them and only found one genuine case of multiple-personality disorder (Thigpen & Cleckley, 1984). One therapist characterized the disorder as a "psychiatric growth industry" (Weissberg, 1993).

In a careful study of patients with reported multiple-personality disorder, Merskey (1992) believes that the "personalities" represent differences in mood, memory, or attention and that "they" are developed by unwitting therapists through expectation, suggestion, and social reinforcement. Cases of dissociated states and multiple personality produced through hypnosis or suggestion have been reported (Coons, 1988; Ofshe, 1992). Dissociation experiences are common in the face of stress and are found in many different disorders. Many individuals developed dissociative symptoms in the aftermath of the San Francisco earthquake in 1989. They reported alterations in memory and thoughts, alterations of time perception, changes in reality, and depersonalization (feeling detached or numb). These symptoms abated over time (Cardena & Spiegel, 1993). Some clinicians may interpret these symptoms of stress as multiple personalities.

Because this disorder is difficult to diagnose, some clinicians have developed questionnaires to assess dissociation. The following are questions used to identify possible dissociation disorders in children (Shapiro, 1991):

"Do you ever kinda space out, and lose track of what's going on around you?" (decreased awareness of the environment)

"Do you have any problems with forgetting things?" (amnesia)

"Does it ever happen that time goes by, and then you can't really remember what you were doing during that time?" (fugue state)

"Does it ever seem like things aren't real, like everything is just a dream?" (feelings of unreality)

"Does it ever happen that you do things that sur-

Are Therapists Creating Multiple Personalities in Their Patients?

The term *iatrogenic* refers to conditions or disorders produced by a physician or therapist through mechanisms such as selective attention, reinforcement, and expectations (demand characteristics) that are placed on the patient. Could some or even most cases of multiple personality be the result of these factors? Is this a possible explanation for the sudden increase in the reported number of persons with this disorder? Many clinicians and researchers argue that this is indeed the case (Aldridge-Morris, 1989; Chodoff, 1987; Merskey, 1992; Modestin, 1992; Weissberg, 1993). Spanos and colleagues (1985) also believe that the methods used in investigating multiple-personality disorder may encourage the "appearance" of this phenomenon. Other elements, as outlined in the following list, may also be responsible for increased numbers of diagnosis of multiple personality.

1. *A well-known role* The characteristics of multiple personality are well known through the mass media. The disorder has been portrayed in newspapers, books, television, talk shows, and movies. The public is aware that symptoms of multiple personality include periods of amnesia and personality changes.

2. *A mechanism by which the disorder can be produced* In nearly all cases, hypnosis is used to investigate this phenomenon. Questions are often posed to "parts" of the person of which he or she might not be aware. Hypnosis then provides a vehicle for and "legitimizes" the appearance of another personality.

3. *Encouragement of the different "personalities"* Because the disorder is rare, people who report multiple personalities often achieve a "special patient" status. Therapists become highly attentive to the patients. Coons (1986) found this to be a major problem and warned against reinforcing a patient for having multiple personalities.

4. *Solidifying the roles* Hypnosis is used to contact the different personalities. Patients give names to the personalities. The history, feelings, and experiences of each personality are obtained.

Can characteristics of multiple personality be obtained based on these social psychological principles? Spanos and colleagues (1985) reasoned that whether symptoms of multiple personality were reported would depend on these factors. To test their hypothesis, a group of male and female college students were given the following information. "You are to play the role of an accused murderer who is to undergo an individual psychiatric evaluation." Men were given the name of Harry Hodgins, and women were named Betty Hodgins. They were told nothing about how to behave and there was no mention of multiple personality. All subjects were asked about the crime, their interpersonal relationships, their childhood, and their relationship with their parents. The subjects were assigned to one of three groups that varied in terms of the amount of suggestion for symptoms of multiple personality and whether hypnosis was employed.

Group A These subjects were hypnotized and then told the following: "I've talked a bit to Harry (used with male subjects and Betty with female subjects)

prise you, and afterwards you stop and say to yourself, 'Why did I do that'?" (multiple personality)

These questions direct the clinician to investigate possible dissociation disorders. Some researchers, however, doubt the validity of scales purporting to measure this phenomenon (Fischer & Elnitsky, 1990).

Many children, adolescents, and adults may answer "yes" to these questions without having a dissociative disorder. Interpretations are difficult to make without appropriate comparison groups. Whether the increase in cases of multiple personality is the result of more accurate diagnosis, false positives, an artifact, or an actual increase in the incidence of the disorder is still being debated.

but I think perhaps there might be another part of Harry (Betty) that I haven't talked to, another part that maybe feels somewhat differently from the part I've talked to. And I would like to communicate with that other part. Would you talk to me, Part, by saying, 'I'm here'?" After the subjects responded, the "psychiatrist" further asked, "Part, are you the same thing as Harry (or Betty) or are you different in any way?" The "part" was then asked questions regarding its name, identity, and other personal information.

Group B These subjects were also hypnotized but received less direct information about the hidden part. They were told that individuals often block certain feelings or thoughts from the conscious mind, and that under hypnosis it is possible to get behind the wall and to contact a different part. The subjects were told that when the "psychiatrist" placed his hand on a subject's shoulder, he would be in contact with that person's other part. After placing his hand on a subject's shoulder, the psychiatrist asked the part its name, identity, and other personal information.

Group C Subjects in Group C were not hypnotized but received the same information as in Group B. References to con-

tacting the part by placing the hand on the shoulder were not included.

During the second session, the subjects in Groups A and B were hypnotized again. Among those who exhibited a second personality, the "parts" were contacted and asked to complete the sentence completion and semantic differential tests. The individuals were then "awakened" and asked to complete the same tests again. Individuals in Group C and those not exhibiting a "second personality" completed the tests just once.

More than 80 percent of persons in Group A, which received the most specific cues for multiple personality, indicated having a different personality and referred to their primary identity in the third person. They demonstrated "spontaneous amnesia" for the other personality when they existed as Harry or Betty. The other personality made statements such as "I'm inside of Harry. I control Harry's outer feelings" or "I've always been with Betty since I can remember. She doesn't know I'm here, but I know I'm here." The psychological tests (often used in working with multiple personalities) revealed distinct personalities. Approximately one-third of the subjects in Group B displayed a different personality, while none in the control group did.

Spanos and his colleagues

showed that the ability to elicit a "different personality" depended on the number of suggestions made to the subjects and whether a means (hypnosis) was provided for the "emergence" of the personality. The subjects who reported "another personality" obviously knew the characteristics of a multiple personality (amnesia for the actions of the other personality, and so on). They were also able to respond on tests in a way that indicated different personality patterns. They knew the role and characteristics of multiple personality and displayed MPD when suggestions were given. Hypnosis gave the subjects a vehicle to express this disorder.

The results of this study raised several questions. Is the sudden increase in multiple personalities merely because of iatrogenic factors? In other words, is the therapist creating the disorder by use of suggestion or hypnosis? Additionally, how can we investigate this phenomenon without inducing reports of multiple personality? Certain therapists report having dealt with more than fifty persons with multiple personality (Allison & Schwartz, 1980; Bliss, 1980; Braun, 1984; Kluft, 1987). Are these therapists merely more accurate in diagnosing the disorder, or could their methods of investigation actually result in reports of these conditions in their patients?

Etiology of Dissociative Disorders

The diagnosis and cause of dissociative disorders are subject to much conjecture. Diagnosis is difficult because it depends heavily on patients' self-reports. Feigning or faking is always a possibility. One man charged with driving under the influence of alcohol said that he had been in a fugue state. In a study of accused murderers who claimed amnesia for the act,

almost all who submitted to polygraph tests or sodium amytal appeared to be lying (Bradford & Smith, 1979). Coons and Bradley (1985) also discovered that a person diagnosed as having multiple personalities was feigning the disorder. Differentiating between genuine cases of dissociative disorders and faked ones is difficult. Even expert judges cannot distinguish between genuine inability to recall and subjects who simulate amnesia (Schacter, 1986). Researchers have found that recollections obtained under hypnosis are often inaccurate and distorted and that the information retrieved can alter waking memories (Nash et al., 1986; Sheehan, Grigg & McCann, 1984).

It was hoped that objective measures such as EEG readings could show the presence of multiple personality. But the researchers concluded that EEG differences among the different personalities in individuals with multiple personality disorder reflected differences mainly in concentration, mood changes, and degree of muscle tension (Coons, Milstein & Marley, 1982). Although the clinical evidence supports the existence of dissociative disorders, reliable methods to determine their validity do not currently exist.

We will examine the cause of dissociative disorders from the psychoanalytic and learning perspectives, but it is important to realize that neither provides completely satisfactory explanations. As indicated earlier, the dissociative disorders are not well understood.

Psychoanalytic Perspective   In the psychoanalytic view, the dissociative disorders involve the person's use of repression to block from consciousness unpleasant or traumatic events (Kopelman, 1987). When complete repression of these impulses is not possible because of the strength of the impulses or the weakness of the ego, dissociation or separation of certain mental processes may occur. In dissociative amnesia and fugue, for example, large parts of the individual's personal identity are no longer available to conscious awareness. This process protects the individual from painful memories or conflicts (Paley, 1988).

A 27-year-old man found lying in the middle of a busy intersection was brought to a hospital. He appeared agitated and said, "I wanted to get run over." He claimed not to know his personal identity or anything about his past. He only remembered being brought to the hospital by the police. The inability to remember was highly distressful to him. Psychological tests using the TAT and the Rorschach inkblot test revealed primarily anxiety-arousing, violent, and sexual themes. The clinician hypothesized that a violent incident involving sex might underlie the amnesia. Under hypnosis the patient's memory returned, and he remembered being severely assaulted. He had repressed the painful experience. (Kaszniak et al., 1988)

The dissociation process is carried out to an extreme in multiple-personality disorder. Here, the splits in mental processes become so extreme that more or less independent identities are formed, each with its own unique set of memories. Conflicts within the personality structure are responsible for this process. Equally strong and opposing personality components (stemming from the superego and the id) render the ego incapable of controlling all incompatible elements. A compromise solution is then reached in which the different parts of the personality are alternately allowed expression and repressed. Because intense anxiety and disorganization would occur if these personality factions were allowed to coexist, each is sealed off from the other.

The split in personality may develop because of traumatic early experiences combined with an inability to escape them. Some researchers believe that one or more personalities take on the "pain" to shield the other personalities (Shapiro, 1991). From case histories, we have learned that some conditions may produce a dissociative reaction. In the case of Sybil, for example, Sybil's mother severely abused her. Dr. Wilbur, Sybil's psychiatrist, speculated that "by dividing into different selves [which were] defenses against an intolerable and dangerous reality, Sybil had found a [design] for survival" (Schreiber, 1973, p. 158).

Most people with multiple personalities do report a history of physical or sexual abuse during childhood (Boon & Draijer, 1993; Fagan & McMahon, 1984). Besides traumatic childhood events, however, the person must have the capacity to dissociate—or separate—certain memories or mental processes. A person's susceptibility to hypnotism may be a characteristic of the dissociation process, and, in fact, people who have multiple personalities appear to be very receptive to hypnotic suggestion (Frischholz, 1992). Those people might escape unpleasant experiences through self-hypnosis—by entering a hypnotic state. According to Kluft (1987), the four factors necessary in the development of multiple personality are

1. The capacity to dissociate (whether this is produced by traumatic events or is innate is not known)

2. Exposure to overwhelming stress, such as physical or sexual abuse

3. Walling off or encapsulating the experience

4. Developing different memory systems

If a supportive environment does not develop, multiple personality results from these factors.

Behavioral Perspective   Behavioral theorists suggest that the avoidance of stress by indirect means is the main factor to consider in explaining dissociative disorders. For example, patients with dissociative amnesia and fugue are often ill-equipped to handle emotional conflicts. Their way of fleeing stressful situations is to forget or block out disturbing thoughts. These people typically have much to gain and little to lose from their dissociative symptoms.

Behavioral explanations of multiple-personality disorder include the additional factors of role playing and selective attention. Each of us exhibits a variety of behaviors, moods, and emotions. For example, people wear different clothes, display different styles or mannerisms, and experience different emotional states depending on whether they are scrubbing a floor, thinking about something sad or happy, going shopping, working, or socializing. In persons with multiple-personality disorders, role playing may be combined with selective attention to certain cues. The person responds to only certain environmental stimuli and then behaves in a way that would be appropriate only if those stimuli were present. If that person seeks counseling, a clinician may mistake these changes in mood, attention, and behavior as different personalities and inadvertently create the disorder.

Treatment of Dissociative Disorders

A variety of treatments for the dissociative disorders have been developed, including supportive counseling and the use of hypnosis and personality reconstruction. Multiple personality has received the most attention by psychotherapists.

Dissociative Amnesia and Dissociative Fugue
The symptoms of dissociative amnesia and fugue tend to remit, or abate, spontaneously. Moreover, patients typically complain of psychological symptoms other than the amnesia, perhaps because the amnesia interferes only minimally with their day-to-day functioning. As a result, therapeutic intervention is often not directed specifically toward the amnesia. Instead, therapists provide supportive counseling for clients with amnesia.

It has been noted, however, that depression is often associated with the fugue state and that stress is often associated with both fugue and dissociative amnesia (Sackeim & Vingiano, 1984). A reasonable therapeutic approach is then to treat these dissociative disorders indirectly by alleviating the depression (with antidepressants or cognitive behavior therapy) and the stress (through stress management techniques).

Depersonalization Disorder   Depersonalization disorder is also subject to spontaneous remission, but at a much slower rate than dissociative amnesia and fugue. Treatment generally concentrates on alleviating the feelings of anxiety or depression or the fear of going insane. Occasionally a behavioral approach has been tried. For example, behavior therapy was successfully used to treat depersonalization disorder in a fifteen-year-old girl who had blackouts that she described as "floating in and out." These episodes were associated with headaches and feelings of detachment, but neurological and physical examinations revealed no organic cause. Treatment involved getting increased attention from her family and reinforcement from them when the frequency of blackouts was reduced, training in appropriate responses to stressful situations, and self-reinforcement (Dollinger, 1983).

Multiple Personality   The mental health literature contains more information on the treament of multiple personality than on the other three dissociative disorders combined. Treatment for multiple-personality disorder is not always successful. As discussed in Chapter 5, Chris Sizemore (of *The Three Faces of Eve*) developed additional personalities after therapy but has now recovered. She is a writer, lecturer, and artist. Sybil also had a positive outcome—she has become a college professor. Success, however, may be difficult to achieve. Coons (1986) conducted a follow-up study of twenty patients with multiple-personality disorder. Each patient was studied for about thirty-nine months after his or her initial assessment. Nine patients obtained partial or full recovery but this was maintained by only five patients—the others dissociated again. More than one-third were unable to work because of the disorder.

Patients with multiple-personality disorder are difficult to work with. Coons found that 75 percent of the therapists indicated that they had feelings of

The different personalities in multiple personality disorder often show contrasting interests. Here Chris Sizemore ("three faces of Eve") is surrounded by some of the paintings created by her personalities.

exasperation, 58 percent anger, and 50 percent emotional exhaustion during therapy. One or more of the personalities might resist treatment. A thirty-year-old physician abruptly got up in the middle of a session and remarked, "You can analyze HER, but I'm leaving" (p. 723). More positive outcomes have been reported when therapists are experienced in working with multiple personalities and when therapy continues even after the personality has become fused (Kluft, 1987).

The most widely reported approaches to treating multiple-personality disorder combine psychotherapy and hypnosis. One suggested procedure begins with hypnosis. With the patient in a hypnotic state, the different personalities are asked to emerge and introduce themselves to the patient, to make the patient aware of their existence. Then the personalities are asked to help the patient recall the traumatic experiences or memories that originally triggered the development of new personalities. An important part of this recalling step is to enable the patient to experience the emotions associated with the traumatic memories. The therapist then explains to the patient that these additional personalities used to serve a purpose, but that alternative coping strategies are available now. The final steps involve piecing together the events and memories of the personalities, integrating

them, and continuing therapy to help the patient adjust to the new self (Bliss, 1980; Sakheim, Hess & Chivas, 1988).

Behavioral therapy has also been used successfully in some cases of multiple personality. Here is an example:

A 51-year-old male, diagnosed as a schizophrenic with multiple personalities, was treated through selective reinforcement. The reinforcement consisted of material and social rewards; the patient received reinforcement only when he displayed his "healthiest" personality. Eventually his other two personalities were eliminated, and the patient was discharged. (Kohlenberg, 1973)

As illustrated in this case, reinforcement can dramatically increase the frequency with which a specific personality appears.

Some clinicians advocate the use of family therapy in treating multiple personalities. In one case, the therapist regarded a female client's symptoms as signifying an imbalanced family situation; he found an unusually strong, dependent, and emotional attachment between the client and her mother. He believed that the girl was part of an emotional triangle with her mother and father, and interpreted her transformations to different personalities as an at-

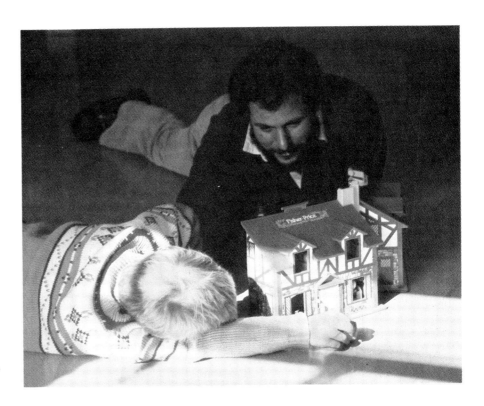

Family therapy and play therapy are two treatments advocated for children with multiple personality. The most important aspect of play therapy seems to be a supportive, nonthreatening environment in which the child can explore all of his or her personalities.

tempt to include the father in her family life. As the client gradually became somewhat detached from her mother, her relationship with her father improved, and the family system became more balanced. The multiple personalities appeared less frequently as the client accepted more responsibility for her actions (Beal, 1978).

Fagan and McMahon (1984) also recommended family therapy for children displaying multiple personalities. In addition, for the child client they suggested play therapy, in which games and fantasy are used to explore the child's other personalities in a nonthreatening manner. Particularly intriguing is their method of fusing the child's different personalities by having them hug each other repeatedly, a little harder each time, until they become one.

SOMATOFORM DISORDERS

The **somatoform disorders,** shown in the disorders chart on page 212, involve complaints of physical symptoms that closely mimic authentic medical conditions. Although no actual physiological basis exists

for the complaints, the symptoms are not considered voluntary or under conscious control. The patient believes that the symptoms are real and are indications of a physical problem. The somatoform disorders include the following:

◈ *Somatization disorder,* characterized by multiple physical complaints and an early onset of the condition

◈ *Conversion disorder,* characterized by the loss or alteration of physical functioning

◈ *Pain disorder,* or *psychalgia,* in which pain is the main complaint

◈ *Hypochondriasis,* characterized by fear of and complaints of bodily disease

◈ *Body dysmorphic disorder,* characterized by preoccupation with an imagined defect in a normal-appearing individual

Before we discuss the somatoform disorders individually, we should note that they are wholly different from the factitious disorders. **Factitious disorders** are mental disorders in which the symptoms of physical or mental illnesses are deliberately induced or

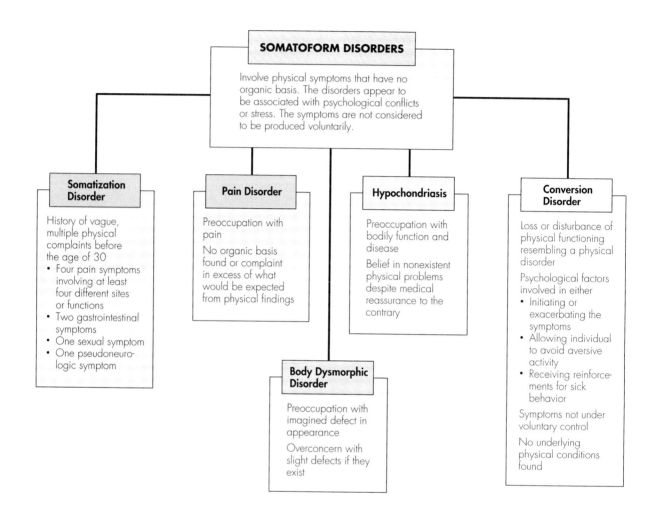

simulated (see Focus 7.2). Individuals with somatoform disorders believe that a physical condition actually exists. There are also cross-cultural differences in the frequency and interpretation of somatic complaints. Physical complaints often occur in reaction to stress among Asian Americans (Sue & Sue, 1990). In fact, Asian Indian children who were referred for psychiatric services had three times as many somatoform disorders compared with a control sample of white children (Jawed, 1991). These differences may reflect a difference in how cultures view the relation between mind and body. The dominant view in this culture is the *psychosomatic* perspective, in which psychological conflicts are expressed in physical complaints. But many other cultures have a *somatopsychic* perspective, in which physical problems produce psychological and emotional symptoms. Although we probably believe that our psychosomatic view is the "correct" one, the somatopsychic view may be the dominant perspective in most cultures. As White (1982) claimed, "It is rather the more psychological and psychosomatic mode of reasoning found in Western cultures which appears unusual among the world's popular and traditional system of belief" (p. 1520). Physical complaints in persons of ethnic minorities may have to be interpreted differently than physical complaints in members of the majority culture.

Factitious Disorders

A most remarkable type of mental disorder is illustrated in the following cases:

A Seattle Pacific University student was charged with assault in 1992 when it was discovered that she was giving her three-year-old son near-fatal doses of ipecac (a drug used to induce vomiting). No motive was found other than the attention she received from hospital staff for the "illness" of her child. (*Seattle Post-Intelligencer*, 1992)

The woman had an FUO (a fever of unknown origin) and nothing seemed to help. For two-and-a-half months, specialists at two hospitals studied her x-rays and blood tests, prescribed penicillin and a variety of other antibiotics, and had no success at all—until doctors at Massachusetts General tried a massive dose of skepticism. She was whisked off for x-rays and her belongings searched, and in her purse was found the source of her baffling sickness: three used syringes and a cup with traces of spittle. She had been injecting herself with traces of spittle. (Adler & Gosnell, 1979, p. 65)

A survey by the National Institute of Health suggests that the problem deserves more attention. Of 343 persons with FUO recorded over sixteen years, thirty-two patients (nearly 10 percent) were found to be faking their fevers. Among them was a 25-year-old practical nurse who underwent exploratory surgery four times before it was discovered that she was injecting herself with fecal matter (Adler & Gosnell, 1979). Others have "spit up blood from a rubber pouch hidden in the mouth, caused genital bleeding by use of sharp objects, [and] injected themselves with insulin, sputum, or bacteria" (Lipsitt, 1983).

These cases illustrate a group of mental disorders, termed *factitious disorders* in DSM-IV, in which people voluntarily simulate physical or mental conditions or voluntarily induce an actual physical condition. (This practice differs from **malingering**, which involves simulating a disorder to achieve some goal—such as feigning sickness to collect insurance.) In factitious disorders, the purpose of the simulated or induced illness is much less apparent, and complex psychological variables are assumed to be involved. Incentives such as monetary gain, avoiding legal responsibilities, or health improvement are not the reasons for the behavior. The person has a compulsive quality in the need to simulate illness. In the first case, the diagnosis would be factitious disorder by proxy. The mother produced a symptom in her child to indirectly assume the sick role. Because this diagnostic category is somewhat new, little information is available on prevalence, age at onset, or familial pattern.

Somatization Disorder

An individual with **somatization disorder** chronically complains of bodily symptoms that have no physical basis.

An internist was examining a woman who made jerky and contorted movements. She complained of seizures in her spine as well as nausea, abdominal cramps, and pain in her hands and feet. She's had these problems since the age of 17. The abdominal complaints were investigated during exploratory surgery, and no specific cause for the discomfort could be found. A hysterectomy was also performed to treat problems with a "tipped uterus." She's experienced "dizziness" and "blackouts" since the age of 40. In addition, symptoms involving weakness, blurred vision, and problems urinating were present. Medical assessments were made for the possibility of a hiatal hernia because of complaints of bloating and problems in digesting food. Exhaustive neurological, hypertensive and other workups were made. All examinations failed to reveal an organic basis for the physical complaints. The patient is divorced and lives with an adult son. She also indicated indifference to sex. The internist referred the client to a psychiatrist. (Spitzer et al., 1981)

This case illustrates several characteristics of somatization disorder. According to DSM-IV, the following are necessary for a diagnosis of somatization disorder: a history of complaints that involve at least four pain symptoms in different sites (back, head, extremities, etc.), two gastrointestinal symptoms (nausea, diarrhea, bloating, etc.), one sexual symptom (sexual indifference, irregular menses, erectile dysfunction, etc.), and one pseudoneurologic symptom (conversion symptoms, amnesia, breathing difficulties, etc.). People who have somatization disorder commonly report abdominal gas, nausea, diarrhea, feeling sickly, abdominal pain, dizziness, pain in the extremities, and vomiting (Swartz et al., 1986). They tend to constantly "shop around" for doctors and often have unnecessary operations. Psychiatric interviews typically reveal psychological conflicts that may be involved in the disorder. Anxiety and depression are common complications of somatization disorder (Gordon et al., 1986).

Historically, somatization disorder (or *hysteria*, as it was called) has been reported primarily in women; it is estimated that 1 percent of all women suffer from the disorder (Swartz et al., 1986). Accurate data on its prevalence are difficult to obtain, however, because until DSM-III was published, somatization disorder and conversion disorder were combined in prevalence studies. Although this disorder is rarely diagnosed in men, more than one-third of men who had been referred because of multiple unexplained somatic complaints met the criteria for somatization disorder (Golding, Smith & Kashner, 1991).

Conversion Disorder

Conversion disorder is one of the more puzzling disorders that we know about. The term *conversion neurosis* comes from Freud who believed that an unconscious sexual or aggressive conflict was "converted" into a physical problem. An individual with **conversion disorder** will complain of physical problems such as paralysis, loss of feeling, impairment in sight or hearing—all suggesting a neurological disorder without an underlying organic cause. The individual is not consciously faking the symptom as are those with factitious disorder or who are malingering; they actually believe, however, that there is a genuine physical impairment. The symptom produces notable distress or impairment in social or occupational functioning. As discussed in Chapter 1, it was known earlier as *hysteria*, and Mesmer was able to

effect cures of individuals with these complaints. A case of a visual conversion disorder follows:

DB was a 33-year-old, single white male who was employed in a clerical job and who lived with his parents. . . . DB's visual disorder began . . . when he was hit in the right eye with a rifle butt during military training. DB reported pain and impaired vision in his right eye and was hospitalized for 3 weeks. He reported seeing only "shapes and silhouettes of objects" and "cones of white rings" in his right eye. Toward the end of this period, DB reported that he could not see anything with his right eye. . . . DB then received intensive ophthalmological and neuropsychological assessment. None of these assessments revealed any apparent physical basis for his visual disorder. (Bryant & McConkey, 1989, pp. 326–327)

Although DB claimed to not be able to see, he did do better on tasks where visual cues were present than when they were absent. One intriguing factor in this case is DB's clear use of visual information. Yet he was not aware of this ability. This finding produces a contradiction between the belief that conversion disorders are involuntary and the evidence that on some level, DB could "see." The dynamic underlying this process is not clear. In addition, in conversion disorder, psychological factors are considered important in either the initiation or exacerbation of the problem, as illustrated in the following case:

The patient, a 42-year-old white, married male, was admitted in a wheelchair to the Psychiatry Service of the Veterans Administration Center, Jackson, Mississippi. When admitted, he was bent forward at the waist (45-degree angle) and unable to straighten his body or move his legs. For the past 15 years, he had consistently complained of lumbosacral [lower back] pain. On two occasions (12 and 5 years prior to admission) he underwent orthopedic surgery; however, complaints of pain persisted. In the last 5 years the patient had numerous episodes of being totally unable to walk. These episodes, referred to by the patient as "drawing over," typically lasted 10–14 days and occurred every 4–6 weeks. The patient was frequently hospitalized and treated with heat applications and muscle relaxants. Five years prior to this admission the patient had retired on Social Security benefits and assumed all household duties, as his wife was compelled to support the family.

Orthopedic and neurological examinations failed to reveal contributory causes. An assessment of the patient's family life revealed that there were numerous stresses coinciding with the onset of "drawing over" episodes. Included were the patient's recent discharge from the National Guard after twenty years of service, difficulties with his son and youngest daughter, and "guilt" feelings about the role reversal he and his wife had assumed. Moreover, it was clear that the patient received considerable social reinforcement from family members when he presented symptoms of "illness" (e.g., receiving breakfast in bed and being relieved of household chores). (Kallman, Hersen & O'Toole, 1975, pp. 411–412)

In a study of the prevalence and type of conversion symptoms in forty male patients at a Veterans Administration (VA) hospital, it was found that the most common symptoms were paresis (muscle paralysis), anesthesia (loss of bodily sensation), paresthesia (prickling or tingling sensations), and dizziness (Watson & Buranen, 1979). Conversion reactions were also diagnosed in fifteen children, of whom nine were girls. Their most common problems involved the function of the legs (paralysis and flexing or walking difficulties), whereas problems involving vision and speech were found in only three children. Twelve of the fifteen children had experienced psychological problems in the past (Regan & LaBarbera, 1984).

It is often difficult to distinguish between actual physical disorders and conversion reactions. Conversion disorder usually involves either the senses or motor functions that are controlled by the voluntary (rather than the autonomic) nervous system, however, and there is seldom any actual organic damage. For example, a person with hysterical paralysis of the legs rarely shows the atrophy of the lower limbs that occurs when there is an underlying organic cause (though in some persistent cases, disuse *can* result in atrophy).

Some symptoms, such as glove anesthesia (the loss of feeling in the hand, ending in a straight line at the wrist) are easily diagnosed as conversion disorder because the area of sensory loss does not correspond to the distribution of nerves in the body. Other symptoms may require extensive neurological and physical examinations to rule out a true medical disorder before a diagnosis of conversion disorder can be made. Discriminating between people who are faking and those with conversion disorder is difficult. For example, subjects asked to simulate a hearing loss can produce response patterns highly similar to individuals with hearing loss from conversion disorder (Aplin & Kane, 1985).

Pain Disorder

Pain disorder is characterized by reports of severe pain that may (1) have no physiological or neurological basis, (2) be greatly in excess of that expected with an existing physical condition, or (3) linger long after a physical injury has healed (Fordyce, 1988). The disorder occurs more frequently in women than in men. As with the other somatoform disorders, psychological conflicts are involved. People who have pain disorder make frequent visits to physicians and may become drug or medication abusers.

Pain is an extremely complex phenomenon involving both psychological and physiological factors (Elliot & Jay, 1987). Typically, pain results from *nocioception* (sensations from pain receptors) and cognitive factors such as the expectations of experiencing pain while engaging in certain activities such as exercising or working. If a painful experience is expected, fewer activities are attempted (Fordyce, 1988). Whether avoidance is exhibited depends on the following factors (Philips, 1987): (1) the current pain level, which fluctuates; (2) environmental rewards for avoidance; and (3) cognitions involving expectations, memories, and *self-efficacy beliefs* (the view that one can successfully perform a certain activity; see Figure 7.1). Avoidance reduces feelings of self-control and increases expectancies of pain. This "self-defeating cycle" between behavior and the cognitions may play the greatest role in maintaining avoidance.

Hypochondriasis

The primary characteristic of **hypochondriasis** is a persistent preoccupation with one's health and physical condition, even in the face of physical evaluations that reveal no organic problems. The disorder is a complex phenomenon that includes a fear of having a disease, fear of death or illness, a tendency of self-observation, and oversensitivity to bodily sensations (Kellner, Hernandez & Pathak, 1992). People with this disorder are hypersensitive to bodily functioning and processes. They regard symptoms such as chest pain or headaches as evidence of an underlying dis-

FIGURE 7.1   Avoidance Behavior and Its Role in Sustaining Chronic Pain

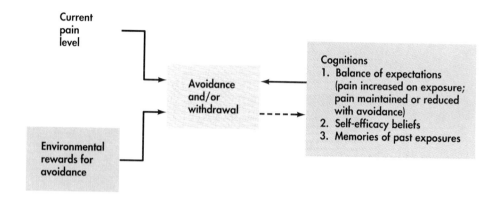

ease, and they seek repeated reassurance from medical professionals, friends, and family members. An estimated 4 to 5 percent of general medical patients have this disorder (Barsky, Wyshak & Klerman, 1992).

Hypochondriasis involves a preoccupation with physical symptoms and frequent visits to the doctor in an effort to identify a physical problem. If no readily discernible cause for the physical complaint can be found, a diagnosis of hypochondriasis may be made.

B. is a 26-year-old married manual worker. He developed headaches while on holiday abroad, probably due to excess exposure to direct sunlight. These persisted, and he also developed precordial [chest] pain associated with a range of other bodily symptoms, particularly dizziness, breathlessness, and weakness. Physical investigations by a number of physicians including cardiologists and neurologists revealed no physical basis for his symptoms, and he was referred to the department of clinical psychology after a further series of tests (including brain scans), which were carried out with the explicit purpose of reassuring him. He was on sick leave from work, spent much of his time in a prone position, and frequently called the emergency services. He also asked his wife constantly for reassurance, to take his pulse and not to leave him alone in the house. At referral he complained that the doctors were missing something and was eager for more tests to be carried out. The most probable causes of his symptoms were identified by the patient as heart disease, a brain tumour or some other cancer. (Salkovskis & Warwick, 1986, p. 599)

A study of forty-five hypochondriacs (twenty-eight females and seventeen males) found that fear, anxiety, and depression were common complaints. Each patient feared that he or she had an undetected physical illness; anxiety was increased by the expectation that the disorder was progressive and terminal. As a group, the patients also believed that previous physical examinations had been inaccurate (Kellner, 1982).

In his review of hypochondriacs, Kellner (1985) found several predisposing factors. These factors included a history of physical illness, parental attention to somatic symptoms, low pain threshold, or greater sensitivity to somatic cues. Hypochondriasis, therefore, might develop in predisposed people in the following manner: an anxiety- or stress-arousing event, the perception of somatic symptoms, and the fear that sensations reflect a disease process, resulting in even greater attention to somatic cues. Kellner believes that reassurance by physicians only temporarily reduces anxiety because the patients continue to experience bodily symptoms that they interpret as symptoms of an undiagnosed condition.

Body Dysmorphic Disorder

According to DSM-IV, **body dysmorphic disorder** involves a preoccupation with some imagined defect in appearance in a normal-appearing person or an excessive concern with a slight physical defect. The preoccupation produces marked clinical distress.

> Mr. F., a 27-year-old lawyer, was referred for treatment of severe anxiety and depression. At age 14, he developed a large acneform blemish on his face over which he developed tremendous concern. This blemish resolved in a rather natural fashion over the course of several weeks, but the patient remained convinced that it was visible and visited several physicians including a dermatologist, requesting help. Thirteen years later, he remained convinced that the blemish was visible, although he acknowledged that it was his perception and no one else's. (Brady, Austin & Lydiard, 1991, p. 539)

Concern over facial features such as spots, excessive hair, size or shape of the genitals, shape of the face, eyes, or nose are the most common. Individuals with this disorder often engage in frequent mirror checking, regard their "defect" with embarrassment and loathing, and are concerned that others may be looking at or thinking about their defect (Myers, 1992; Phillips, 1991; Phillips et al., 1993). People with body dysmorphic disorder show evidence of emotional problems, have a minimal degree of "disfig-

urement," and make frequent requests for additional operations despite the outcome of previous treatment. They may have a body image disorder similar to that found in anorexia. Most have more than one concern (Phillips et al., 1993). As with the other somatoform disorders, individuals with body dysmorphic disorder seek medical attention—often from dermatologists or plastic surgeons. They are also likely to undergo multiple medical procedures. One patient had surgery to increase the size of her breasts, later had them reduced because they were "too large," and then requested to change her breast size again (Turner, Jacob & Morrison, 1984).

Researchers have raised several issues regarding body dysmorphic disorder. First, the other somatoform disorders deal with physical disease or dysfunction. Does concern over appearance fit best in this category? Second, how easy is it to figure out where the boundary lies between those with the disorder and individuals who have "normal" concerns over their appearance or those who seek cosmetic surgery? In one study of college students, 70 percent indicated some dissatisfaction and 46 percent had some preoccupation with their appearance (Fitts et al., 1989). Third, what is the relationship between body dysmorphic disorder and obsessive-compulsive disorder or delusional disorder, somatic type (a psychotic disorder characterized by delusions that the person has a physical defect)? The preoccupation with the imagined defect is very similar to obsessive-compulsive disorder. The precise relationship between these disorders is still not known. Do imagined defects qualify as delusions? If so, delusional disorder, somatic type, may be an extreme form of body dysmorphic disorder.

Etiology of Somatoform Disorders

Most etiological theories tend to focus on what they consider to be the "primary" cause of somatoform disorders. In reading the theoretical perspectives that follow, consider how they might fit into the diathesis-stress model presented in Figure 7.2. For example, Barsky and colleagues (1988) believe that a predisposition involving (1) hypervigilance or exaggerated focus on bodily sensation, (2) increased sensitivity to weak bodily sensations, and (3) a disposition to react to somatic sensations with alarm may develop either through learning or may be "hard wired" into the

FIGURE 7.2 Diathesis-Stress Model for Somatoform Disorders

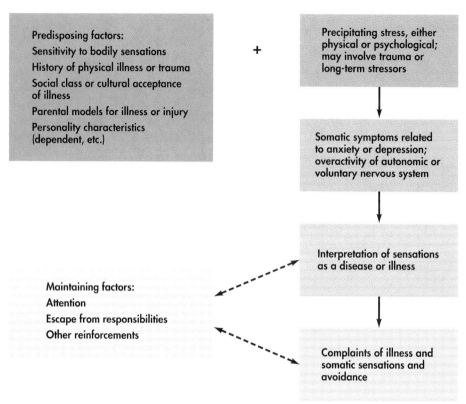

Source: Adapted from Kellner, 1985.

central nervous system. This predisposition only becomes a fully developed disorder when a trauma or stressor occurs that the individual cannot deal with. As you read the following etiological theories, consider what you believe are advantages of the diathesis-stress model over the single-focus explanations.

Psychoanalytic Perspective Sigmund Freud believed that hysterical reactions (psychogenic complaints of pain, illness, or loss of physical function) were caused by the repression of some type of conflict, usually sexual in nature. To protect the individual from intense anxiety, this conflict is converted into some physical symptom (Breuer & Freud, [1895] 1957). For example, in the case of a 31-year-old woman who developed visual problems with no physical basis, therapy revealed the woman had, as a child, witnessed her parents engaging in sexual intercourse. The severe anxiety associated with this traumatic scene was later converted into visual difficulties (Grinker & Robbins, 1954).

The psychoanalytic view suggests that two mechanisms produce and then sustain somatoform symptoms. The first provides a *primary gain* for the person by protecting him or her from the anxiety associated with the unacceptable desire or conflict; the need for protection gives rise to the physical symptoms. This focus on the body keeps the patient from an awareness of the underlying conflict (Simon & VonKorff, 1991). Then a *secondary gain* accrues when the person's dependency needs are fulfilled through attention and sympathy. Consider the case of an 82-year-old man who reported the sudden onset of diffuse right abdominal pain in March 1977. No abnormal signs were found at that time. In August 1977, he was rehospitalized for the same complaint. Again nothing physical was found. In an analysis of the case, Weddington (1979) noted that the patient's symptom first developed near the twelfth anniversary of his wife's death. His second hospitalization took place near the anniversary of his mother's death, which had occurred when he was twelve. Weddington hypothesized that the painful memories were converted to a physical symptom and that the care and attention bestowed by the hospital staff fulfilled the patient's dependency needs.

Behavioral Perspective Behavioral theorists generally contend that people with somatoform disorders assume the "sick role" because it is reinforcing and because it allows them to escape unpleasant circumstances or avoid responsibilities. Among 180 subjects, Moss (1986) found that parental modeling and reinforcement of illness behaviors were influential in determining people's current reactions to illness.

Fordyce (1982, 1988) analyzed psychogenic pain from the operant perspective. He pointed out that the only available data concerning the pain (or any other somatoform symptoms) are the subjective reports from the afflicted people. Physicians and nurses are trained to be attentive and responsive to reports of pain. Medication is given quickly to patients suffering pain. In addition, exercise and physical therapy programs are set up so that exertion continues only until pain or fatigue is felt. These practices serve to reinforce reports of pain.

Fordyce says that psychogenic pain is often under the influence of these and other external (or environmental) variables. He cited several studies that support his contention. For example, when patients with chronic pain were asked to perform physical therapy exercises until "the pain becomes too great," approximately half the time they stopped after multiples of five exercises! This led to the suspicion that something other than pain was controlling their behavior. When patients in pain exercised on bicycles arranged so that they received no feedback regarding their performance, their tolerance for exercise did not differ from that of patients not in pain. But when performance feedback was available, the pain patients performed significantly worse. Clearly, the pain patients' tolerance depended on more than their internal bodily sensations.

The importance of reinforcement was shown in a study of male pain patients. Men who had supportive wives (attentive to pain cues) reported significantly greater pain when their wives were present than when the wives were absent. The reverse was true of patients with wives who were nonsupportive. In this case, reports of pain were greater when the spouse was absent.

Sociocultural Perspective Hysteria (conversion disorder) was originally perceived as a problem that afflicted only women. (The word *hysteria* is derived from the ancient Greek word for *uterus*.) Hippocrates believed that a shift or movement of the uterus resulted in complaints involving breathing difficulties, anesthesia, and seizures. He presumed that the movement was due to the uterus "wanting a child." Although Freud was among the first to suggest that hysteria could also occur in men, most of his patients were women. Satow (1979) argued that hysteria was more prevalent in women when social mores did not provide them with appropriate channels for the expression of aggression or sexuality. Hollender (1980) also stressed the importance of societal restrictions in producing hysterical symptoms in women and suggested the case of Anna O. as an example:

Anna O., a patient of Freud and Breuer, was a 20-year-old woman who developed a variety of symptoms including dissociation, muscle rigidity, and insensitivity to feeling. Freud and Breuer both believed that these symptoms were the result of intrapsychic conflicts. They did not consider the impact of social roles on abnormal behavior.

According to Hollender, Anna O. was highly intelligent, but her educational and intellectual opportunities were severely restricted because she was a woman. She was described as "bubbling over with intellectual vitality" by Breuer. As Hollender pointed out, "Not only was Anna O., as a female, relegated to an inferior position in her family with future prospects limited to that of becoming a wife and mother, but at the age of 21 she was suddenly called on to assume the onerous chore of nursing her father" (Hollender, 1980, p. 798). He suggested that many of her symptoms were produced to relieve the guilt she felt because of her resentment of this duty—as well as to maintain her intellectually stimulating contact with Breuer. After treatment, Anna was supposedly cured. However, Anna O. remained severely disturbed and received additional treatment at an institution. Later, she headed a home for orphans, was involved in social work, and became recognized as a feminist leader. Interestingly, Ellenberger (1972) found that the cathartic treatment was unsuccessful and that Anna O. remained severely disturbed and required further treatment.

Satow believes that, as societal restrictions on women are loosened, the incidence of somatoform disorders among women should decline. Yet, the diagnostic criteria involved in some of these disorders tend to ensure the overrepresentation of women.

Biological Perspective   Some physical complaints may have more than a merely imaginary basis. Researchers have found that hypochondriac patients were more sensitive to bodily sensations than other people (Barsky et al., 1993); they were better at estimating their heart rates when exposed to short films than individuals with phobias (Tyrer, Lee & Alexander, 1980). It has been hypothesized that "people who continually report being bothered by pain and bodily sensations [hypochondriacs] may have a higher-than-normal arousal level, which results in increased perception of internal stimuli" (Hanback & Revelle, 1978, p. 523). College students who are predisposed to attending to somatic symptoms rate the sensations they experience more negatively than those who attend less to bodily symptoms (Ahles, Cassens & Stalling, 1987). Innate factors may account for greater sensitivity to pain and bodily functions.

Treatment of Somatoform Disorders

Somatoform disorders have been treated with psychoanalytic approaches, cognitive and operant techniques, and family therapy. The learning approaches have received the greatest amount of attention.

Psychoanalytic Treatment   The earliest treatment for somatoform disorders was psychoanalysis. Over the years Freud (1905) and Freud and Breuer (1895) reported many cases of "hysterical" patients who, like Anna O., would probably now be classified as showing a conversion reaction or a somatization disorder. Freud believed that the crucial element in treating hysterical patients with psychoanalysis was to help them *relive* the actual feelings associated with the repressed traumatic event—and not simply to help them remember the details of the experience. Once the emotions connected with the traumatic situation were experienced, the symptoms would disappear.

Although Freud eventually dropped hypnosis from his psychoanalytic repertoire, many of his disciples continued to find it beneficial, and variations of

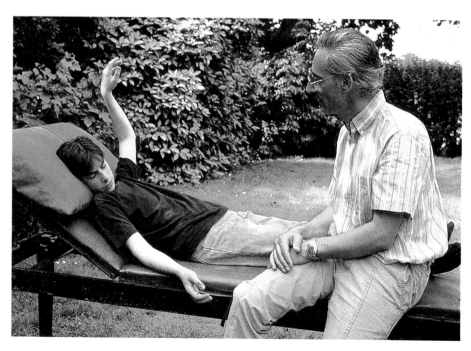

Freud dropped hypnosis as a treatment for hysteria because he believed the patient must re-experience the traumatic event; hypnosis actually prevented this reliving. Some modern treatments for somatization and conversion disorders are beginning to rely on hypnosis once again, based upon the belief that these disorders are induced by self-hypnosis.

it became known as *hypnotherapy*. Bliss (1984) was a modern advocate of hypnotherapy as treatment for somatization disorder and conversion symptoms. In essence, Bliss argued that people afflicted with a somatoform disorder engage in involuntary self-hypnosis as a defense, much as patients with multiple-personality disorders do. Hypnotherapy involves bringing repressed conflicts to consciousness, mastering these traumas, and developing coping skills that are more adaptive than self-hypnosis.

Behavioral Treatment Although psychoanalytic treatments are most often associated with certain somatoform disorders, several behavioral methods appear worth investigating. Individuals with hypochondriasis have been treated with a variety of approaches, including exposure and response prevention. The approach generally involves extinction and nonreinforcement of complaints of bodily symptoms. For example, in one study, seventeen patients were forced to confront their health fears by visiting hospitals, reading literature about their feared illness, and writing down extensive information about the illness. Some were asked to try to "bring forth a heart attack." Reassurance seeking was banned, and relatives were taught not to reinforce the behavior. If a patient said, "My heart has a pain. I think it might be a heart attack," relatives were instructed to ignore the statements. Under this program, the patients improved significantly. However, seven of the patients were found to still have concerns about illness or disease at a five-year follow-up (Warwick & Marks, 1988).

Some researchers have suggested that a cognitive-behavioral approach might be valuable in dealing with somatoform disorders. Salkovskis and Warwick (1986) compared the effectiveness of operant and cognitive treatments. Eighty-one patients with chronic low back pain were randomly assigned to one of three groups:

1. An operant-behavioral group that focused on changing social and environmental reinforcers (patients' spouses were instructed to reinforce exercising and well behaviors and to ignore complaints of pain)
2. A cognitive-behavioral group that focused on modifying patients' cognitions about pain (patients identified negative thoughts associated with pain and practiced more adaptive ones)

3. A waiting-list control group (a list of people to be treated at a later time)

Both the operant-behavioral and cognitive-behavioral treatments significantly reduced physical and psychosocial disability, although the operant-behavioral approach showed the greatest improvement. Interestingly, a twelve-month follow-up revealed that the cognitive-behavioral group eventually improved as much as the operant-behavioral group. Patients in the cognitive-behavioral group were more satisfied with their treatment. They rated the therapy as more helpful and the therapist as warmer (Turner & Clancy, 1988). A two-year follow-up of individuals with chronic pain treated with cognitive behavior therapy revealed that although important gains were maintained, the majority still reported notable levels of pain (Spence, 1991).

Future behavioral treatments probably will include more complete treatment packages. Most somatoform disorders are characterized by sensitivity to somatic symptoms, reinforcement for "sick" behaviors, and concern about disease and the inability to perform activities. Use of operant or cognitive approaches alone may not be enough. A combination of relaxation training to reduce somatic sensations, changing environmental rewards, and altering cognitions may be most successful in treating somatoform disorders.

Family Systems Treatment The role of the family in maintaining somatoform symptoms has also been recognized by promoters of family therapy for the disorder. Chronic pain is often used to gain rewards (such as attention) and to disclaim responsibility for certain behaviors (such as anger) within the family system. Thus family therapy is recommended as an important part of the treatment for somatoform disorders (Hudgens, 1979).

Research has indicated that, in families of patients with somatization disorder, a disproportionately high number of female relatives also have somatization disorder, and many male relatives are labeled either antisocial personalities or alcoholics (Arkonac & Guze, 1963; Bohman et al., 1984). It is certainly not necessary to have multiple cases of psychiatric disorders in a family before considering family therapy, but these research findings strongly suggest that the entire family be drawn into the treatment process. The therapy could then be used to place the identified patient's disorder in proper perspective, to teach the family adaptive ways of supporting each other, and to prepare family members to deal with anticipated and predicted problems.

SUMMARY

1. The dissociative disorders (which are considered relatively rare) involve a dissociation, or separation, of the person's memory, identity, or consciousness. Dissociative amnesia and dissociative fugue involve a selective form of forgetting in which the person loses memory of information that is of personal significance. Depersonalization disorder is characterized by feelings of unreality—distorted perceptions of oneself and one's environment. Multiple personality involves the alternation of two or more relatively independent personalities in one individual.

2. Psychoanalytic perspectives on the etiology of dissociative disorders attribute them to the repression of certain impulses that are seeking expression. Behavioral explanations suggest that avoiding stress by indirect means is the main causal factor. Dissociative amnesia and dissociative fugue tend to be short-lived and to remit spontaneously; behavioral therapy has also been used successfully. Multiple personality has most often been treated with a combination of psychotherapy and hypnosis, as well as with behavioral and family therapies. In most cases, the therapist attempts to fuse the several personalities.

3. Somatoform disorders involve complaints about physical symptoms that mimic actual medical conditions but for which no organic basis can be found. Instead, psychological factors are directly involved in the initiation and exacerbation of the problem. Somatization disorder is characterized by chronic multiple complaints and early onset. Conversion disorder involves such problems as the loss of sight, paralysis, or another physical impairment with no organic cause. Pain disorder is a condition in which reported severe pain has a psychological rather than a physical basis. Hypochondriasis involves a persistent preoccupation with bodily functioning and disease. Body dysmorphic disorder is preoccupation with an imagined bodily defect in a normal-appearing individual.

4. The psychoanalytic perspective holds that somatoform disorders are caused by the repression of sexual conflicts and their conversion into physical symptoms. Behavioral theorists contend that the role of "being sick" is reinforcing and allows the individual to escape from unpleasant circumstances or avoid responsibilities. Furthermore, psychogenic pain is often reinforced by the external environment. From the sociocultural perspective, the somatoform disorders are seen to result from the societal restrictions placed on women, who are affected to a much greater degree than men by these disorders. Psychoanalytic treatment emphasizes reliving the emotions associated with the repressed traumatic event. Other treatment approaches involve reinforcing only "healthy" behaviors rather than the pain or disability. If possible, treatment is administered within the family system.

KEY TERMS

body dysmorphic disorder A somatoform disorder that involves preoccupation with an imagined physical defect

continuous amnesia The inability to recall past and present events; each new event is forgotten after it occurs

conversion disorder A somatoform disorder in which there is significant impairment of sensory or motor function without an underlying physical cause (also known as *conversion reaction*)

depersonalization disorder A dissociative disorder in which there are feelings of unreality or distortion concerning the self or the environment

dissociative amnesia A dissociative disorder characterized by the inability to recall information of personal significance, usually after a traumatic event

dissociative disorders Mental disorders characterized by the alteration or disruption of the person's identity or consciousness; include dissociative amnesia, dissociative fugue, depersonalization disorder, and dissociative identity disorder (multiple-personality disorder)

dissociative fugue A dissociative disorder in which psychogenic amnesia is accompanied by flight from familiar surroundings; also called *fugue state*

factitious disorders Deliberately self-induced or simulated physical or mental condition

generalized amnesia The inability to recall the entire past, owing to some psychosocial stress

hypochondriasis A somatoform disorder characterized by a persistent and strong preoccupation with one's health and physical condition even in the face of physical evaluations that reveal no organic problems

localized amnesia The most common type of amnesia; the inability to recall all events during a specific period

malingering Faking an illness to obtain a goal

multiple personality A dissociative disorder in which two or more relatively distinct personalities exist in one individual

pain disorder A somatoform disorder characterized by pain that has primarily a psychological, rather than a physical, basis.

posthypnotic amnesia The inability to recall information as a result of a suggestion made during a hypnotic state

selective amnesia The inability to recall only some aspects of a situation owing to some psychosocial stress

somatization disorder A somatoform disorder in which the person chronically complains of a number of physical symptoms for which no physiological basis can be found; also called *Briquet's syndrome*

somatoform disorders Mental disorders that involve complaints of physical symptoms that closely mimic authentic medical conditions but have no physical basis; include somatization disorder, conversion disorder, pain disorder, and hypochondriasis

CHAPTER 8

Psychological Factors Affecting Medical Conditions

C an people "worry themselves to death"? Medical evidence suggests that they can. Stress and anxiety appear to have at least some role in what is called the **sudden death syndrome**—unexpected, abrupt death that often seems to have no specific physical basis.

A study of 170 cases of sudden death reported in newspaper articles indicated that most were preceded by an intense emotional event (such as the loss of significant others) or by the person's experience or perception of helplessness (Engel, 1971). One article reported the case of a 61-year-old woman who had taken her ailing 71-year-old sister to the hospital. After hearing that her sister had died, the younger woman developed an irregular heartbeat and died. Her sister's death seems to have created severe emotional distress, which in turn produced the physical symptoms that led to her death.

Emotional factors are also implicated in the following case:

A 22-year-old woman pleaded to be admitted to a hospital. She reported that she and her two sisters had been cursed by a midwife. The midwife said that one sister would die before her sixteenth birthday (one sister did die in an automobile accident before her sixteenth birthday); another would die before becoming twenty-one (the second sister died on the evening of her twenty-first birthday); and the last would die before her twenty-third birthday. This last, surviving sister was only a few days away from her birthday and was obviously frightened. She was admitted into the hospital but was found dead the next morning. (Seligman, 1975)

Each year, about half a million people in the United States wake up feeling fine, but later in the

CRITICAL THINKING

Should We Fear Our Birthdays?

An increasing number of studies are focusing on the impact of psychological states on disease and physical processes. Some are anecdotal or case studies, such as the example of the 22-year-old woman at the beginning of the chapter who died of a "curse." Such reports must be viewed with caution. Others are correlational or experimental in design. Consider the following study: Phillips, Van Voorhees, and Ruth (1992) believed that personally significant occasions can influence physical processes such as death.

They studied 2,745,149 persons who died of natural causes and found the following:

1. Women are slightly more likely to die the week after their birthday than any other week of the year.
2. For men, death is slightly more likely to occur the week before their birthday.

The investigators believe the patterns of death can be explained by psychological variables. If you adopt this per-

spective, what are some possible explanations for the gender differences in deaths around birthdays? What are other occasions with "personal significance" that might be related to week of death? Do you also expect to find the same gender differences associated with these other occasions? Scientists are also considering alternative explanations for a phenomenon. Instead of psychological factors, what are some possible physical reasons that may be associated with patterns of death?

day they collapse and die. Sudden death is the leading cause of death in industrialized countries. Most people who die this way are discovered to have coronary heart disease such as narrowing of the arteries or evidence of past heart attacks. Occasionally, some who succumb have normal hearts and cardiac vessels. Many persons appear to have had *ventricular fibrillation* (rapid, ineffective contractions of the heart) that may have been triggered by a strong emotional stress (Lane & Schwartz, 1987). Physiological response to stress may also take the form of *bradycardia* (slowing of the heartbeat), *tachycardia* (speeding up of the heartbeat), or *arrhythmia* (irregular heartbeat, as in the case of the 61-year-old woman described earlier).

Death from bradycardia in particular may result from feelings of helplessness. The following case shows the impact of this emotion on heart rate:

The patient was lying very stiffly in bed, staring at the ceiling. He was a 56-year-old man who had suffered an anterior myocardial infarction [heart attack] some 2½ days ago. He lay there with bloodshot eyes, unshaven, and as we walked into the room, he made eye

contact first with me and then with the intern who had just left his side. The terror in his eyes was reflected in those of the intern. The patient had a heart rate of forty-eight that was clearly a sinus bradycardia. I put my hands on his wrist, which had the effect of both confirming the pulse and making some physical contact with him, and I asked what was wrong. "I am very tired," he said. "I haven't slept in two and one-half days, because I'm sure that if I fall asleep, I won't wake up."

I discussed with him the fact that we had been at fault for not making it clear that he was being very carefully monitored, so that we would be aware of any problem that might develop. I informed him further that his prognosis was improving rapidly. As I spoke, his pulse became fuller. (Shine, 1984, p. 27)

Here, the patient's physiological response was counteracted by the physician's assurance that his situation was not hopeless—in essence, by removing the source of stress.

Certainly, the sudden death syndrome is an extreme example of the power of anxiety and stress to affect physiological processes. (See Critical Thinking on birthdays and death.) But the examples cited here

The Hmong Sudden Death Syndrome

Vang Xiong is a former Hmong (Laotian) soldier who, with his wife and child, was resettled in Chicago in 1980. The change from his familiar rural surroundings and farm life to an unfamiliar urban area must have produced a severe "culture shock." In addition, Vang vividly remembered seeing people killed during his escape from Laos, and he expressed feelings of guilt about having to leave his brothers and sisters behind in that country. He reported having problems almost immediately.

[He] could not sleep the first night in the apartment, nor the second, nor the third. After three nights of sleeping very little, Vang came to see his resettlement worker, a young bilingual Hmong man named Moua Lee. Vang told Moua that the first night he woke suddenly, short of breath, from a dream in which a cat was sitting on his chest. The second night, the room suddenly grew darker, and a figure, like a large black dog, came to his bed and sat on his chest. He could

not push the dog off, and he grew quickly and dangerously short of breath. The third night, a tall, white-skinned female spirit came into his bedroom from the kitchen and lay on top of him. Her weight made it increasingly difficult for him to breathe, and as he grew frantic and tried to call out he could manage but a whisper. He attempted to turn onto his side, but found he was pinned down. After fifteen minutes, the spirit left him, and he awoke, screaming. (Tobin & Friedman, 1983, p. 440)

About 117 of the SE Asian refugees who settled in the United States have died from the "Hmong sudden death syndrome." All the reports were the same: a person in apparently good health went to sleep and died in his or her sleep. Often, the victim displayed labored breathing, screams, and frantic movements just before death. The Centers for Disease Control investigated these mysterious deaths, but no medical cause has yet been found (Centers for Disease Control, 1988). Some consider

the deaths to represent an extreme and very specific example of the impact of psychological stress on physical health.

Vang was one of the lucky victims of the syndrome—he survived it. He went for treatment to a Hmong woman, Mrs. Thor, who is highly respected in Chicago's Hmong community as a shaman. She interpreted his problem as being caused by unhappy spirits and performed the ceremonies that are required to release them. After that, Vang reported, he had no more problems with nightmares or with his breathing during sleep.

As of 1993, 150 cases of sudden death among Southeast Asian refugees have been reported. All have involved men (possibly one or two have involved women), and most occur within the first two years of living in the United States. The number of cases, however, is declining. Autopsies have found no identifiable cause for the deaths. Some cases of sudden unexplained deaths have also been reported in Asian countries. This remains a most puzzling phenomenon (Gib Parrish, Center for Disease Control, personal communication, 1993).

and in Focus 8.1 are convincing proof that feelings and emotional states can have an impact on physical well-being. In DSM-I and II, physical disorders such as asthma, ulcers, hypertension, and headaches that stem from psychological problems were called *psychosomatic disorders*. This was to distinguish them from conditions that were considered strictly organic in nature. Mental health professionals now recognize, however, that almost any physical disorder can have a strong psychological component or basis.

Although the psychosomatic disorders were previously considered a separate class of disorders,

DSM-IV does not categorize them as such. Instead, it contains a category called psychological factors affecting medical condition. The physical disorders themselves are listed on Axis III. This classification method acknowledges the belief that both physical and psychological factors—both body and mind—are involved in all human processes. And the term *psychosomatic disorder* has been replaced with **psychophysiological disorder**, meaning any physical disorder that has a strong psychological basis or component.

The psychophysiological disorders should not be

confused with the conversion disorders discussed in Chapter 7. The conversion disorders do involve reported physical symptoms, such as loss of feeling, blindness, and paralysis, but they do not involve any physical disorder or process. They are considered essentially psychological in nature. By contrast, most psychophysiological disorders involve actual tissue damage (such as an ulcer) or physiological dysfunction (as in asthma or migraine headaches). Both medical treatment and psychotherapy are usually required.

In DSM-IV, a diagnosis of psychological factors affecting medical condition requires (1) the presence of a medical condition and (2) one of the following: temporal relationship between psychological factors and the onset, exacerbation, or delay in recovery with a medical condition; a psychological factor that interferes with treatment; or psychological factors that constitute additional health-risk factors in the individual. The relative contributions of physical and psychological factors in a physical disorder may vary greatly. Although psychological events are often difficult to detect, repeated association between stressors and the disorder or its symptoms should increase the suspicion that a psychological component is involved.

In this chapter, we first consider three models that help explain the impact of stress on physical health. Second, we examine the evidence suggesting a connection between stress and how decreased immunological function can contribute to the onset and course of cancer. Finally, we discuss several of the more prevalent psychophysiological disorders: coronary heart disease, hypertension (high blood pressure), ulcers, headaches, and asthma.

Before we turn to these disorders, we should emphasize that the change from the "psychosomatic" to the "psychophysiological" view is more than a change in terminology. It represents the enlarging and redirecting of efforts to control disease. The new field of behavioral medicine is an important product of this redirection, combining behavioral and biomedical sciences (Epstein, 1992). **Behavioral medicine** includes several disciplines concerned with illness and deals with the following factors (Gentry, 1984):

1. *Etiology,* involving the study of how stress, lifestyle, and personality characteristics interact to affect a person's susceptibility to illness

2. *Host resistance,* the study of the effects of factors such as social and economic support, cognitive style, and personality in reducing the impact of stress

3. *Disease mechanisms,* in particular, determining how stress changes physiology in such a way as to produce problems such as gastrointestinal disorders and cardiovascular disease

4. *Patient decision making,* the study of the process by which patients make decisions about their health practices

5. *Compliance,* the development of programs to increase patients' cooperation in taking medications, exercising, and participating in other therapies and preventive measures

6. *Intervention,* through educational and behavioral therapies aimed at altering unhealthy lifestyles and indirectly reducing illnesses or illness-inducing behavior

MODELS FOR UNDERSTANDING STRESS

Stress is an internal response to an external stimulus or situation (**stressor**). But something that disturbs one person doesn't necessarily disturb someone else. Moreover, different people react differently to the same stressors. Many people who are exposed to stressors, even traumatic ones, are eventually able to get on with their lives. Other people show intense and somewhat long-lasting psychological symptoms. What accounts for this difference?

The three stress models discussed in this section seek to explain (1) the development and differential effects of stress, (2) the apparent ability of relatively weak stressors to result in strong stress reactions, and (3) the ability some people have to cope more "easily" with stress.

The General Adaptation Model

Being alive means that you are constantly exposed to stressors: illness, marriage, divorce, the death of someone you love, hunting for and keeping a job, aging, retiring, even schoolwork. Most people can cope with most of the stressors they encounter, provided those stressors are not excessively severe and do not "gang up" on the individual. But when someone is confronted with excessive external demands—stressors—coping behaviors may fail, and he or she may resort to inappropriate means of dealing with them. The result may be psychophysiological symptoms, apathy, anxiety, panic, stupor, depression, violence, and even death.

There are, in general, three kinds of stressors:

◈ *Biological stressors* such as infection, physical trauma, disease, malnutrition, and fatigue

◈ *Psychological stressors* such as threats of physical harm, attacks on self-esteem, and guilt-inducing attacks on one's belief system

◈ *Social stressors* such as crowding, excessive noise, economic pressures, and war

A helpful model for understanding the body's physical reaction to biological stressors was proposed by Hans Selye (1956, 1982). He identified three stages in the **general adaptation syndrome (GAS)**, which is a model for understanding the body's physical and psychological reaction to biological stressors: (1) the alarm stage, (2) the stage of resistance, and (3) the stage of exhaustion.

Selye describes the first stage—the *alarm stage*—as a "call to arms" of the body's defenses when it is invaded or assaulted biologically. During this stage, the body reacts immediately to the assault (with rapid heartbeat, loss of muscle tone, and decreased temperature and blood pressure), followed by a rebound reaction in which the adrenal cortex enlarges and the adrenal glands secrete corticoid hormones. If exposure to the stressor continues, the *adaptation or resistance stage* follows. Now the body mobilizes itself to defend, destroy, or coexist with the injury or disease. The symptoms of illness may disappear. At the same time, however, there is a decrease in the body's resistance to most other assaults. That is, he or she may become susceptible to other infections or illnesses. If the stressor continues to tax the body's finite resistive resources, the symptoms may reappear as exhaustion sets in (therefore the name *exhaustion stage*). If stress continues unabated, death may result.

Biological Consequences of Stress Although Selye developed his model for describing physical responses to biological stressors, continuing research now suggests that psychological and social stressors have similar effects. In fact, sustained stress—resulting from psychological or social stressors—may not only make a person more susceptible to illness, but may actually alter the course of a disease. For example, it has been documented that recently be-

reaved widows are three to twelve times more likely to die than are married women; that tax accountants are most susceptible to heart attacks around April 15; that people living in high-noise areas near airports have more hypertension and medical complaints than other people; and that air traffic controllers suffer four times as much hypertension as the general population (Wilding, 1984). The common factor in these groups is *stress.*

For years scientists were skeptical about the supposed effects of stress on the body and dismissed any relationship between the two as folklore. We now know, however, that stress affects the immune system, heart function, hormone levels, the nervous system, and metabolic rates. Bodily "wear and tear" owing to stress can contribute to diseases such as hypertension, ulcers, chronic pain, heart attacks, cancer, and the common cold. For example, in cases of sudden death, Kamarck and Jennings (1991) have developed a model that involves the impact of stressors on the autonomic nervous system. Heart rate and blood pressure increase, nerve conduction changes in the muscles of the heart, and rapid blood clotting occurs in response to autonomic system activation. These processes can be dangerous for some individuals through the following sequence of events:

1. With stress, blood tends to clot more easily and may block the coronary arteries, especially if they have been narrowed through coronary arterial disease.

2. Higher blood pressure may tear loose fat deposits in arteries (atherosclerotic plaques).

3. The reduced amount of blood to the heart may interfere with and trigger lethal arrhythmias involving either ventricular tachycardia or bradyarrhythmias.

This sequence of events occurs in most cases of sudden death. However, psychological factors can also affect the threshold of arrhythmia in individuals without coronary heart disease. This may be the process involved in sudden death of healthy individuals.

Psychological Consequences of Stress Most of us maintain certain levels of psychological adjustment that vary little over time. When we encounter a crisis that cannot be resolved through our customary method of coping, our behaviors can become disorganized and ineffective in solving problems.

High-pressure jobs, such as that of a paramedic, are likely to be stressful and produce physical and psychological symptoms. But the amount of stress needed to negatively affect an individual varies from person to person. In fact, some people seem to deal efficiently with a great deal of stress, while others find it difficult to cope with even small amounts.

De La Fuente (1990) described stages in crisis **decompensation** that parallel the three stages of Selye's general adaptation syndrome after a study of survivors of the earthquake in Mexico City on September 19, 1985. Of the people interviewed, more than 90 percent had suffered either a total or partial loss of home, 28 percent had lost friends or family members, and 8 percent had been trapped under rubble. During the *impact* of the crisis (the first stage), the person experiences a sense of confusion and upset. He or she is bewildered and wonders what is happening, why it is happening, and how a situation so far beyond his or her experience can be resolved. Nearly 32 percent showed symptoms of posttraumatic stress disorder (PTSD), 19 percent generalized anxiety, and 13 percent depression. Many showed decompensated responses such as panic, weeping, hysteria, and dissociation. Guilt and anger were common. This disequilibrium is followed by a period of *attempted resolution* (the second stage), during which all resources are mobilized to deal with the situation. In the case of a disaster, the person may selectively perceive the situation in a more favorable light. ("We've lost our home and all our possessions, but we're lucky to be alive. We can always rebuild.") Within days or weeks, most of the victims were adapting. When people cope successfully, they are likely to resume func-

tioning again at the precrisis level and, in some cases, move into a growth adjustment phase. If coping is ineffective, the person is likely to move into a *decompensated adjustment phase* (the third stage). This phase may be characterized by withdrawal, depression, guilt, apathy, anxiety, anger, or any number of physical illnesses. As many as 20 percent of the victims required continued specialized help.

The Life Change Model

Holmes and Holmes (1970) accepted the GAS model for physical and psychological reactions to stressors. They noted, though, that the events that led to stress reactions need not be of crisis proportions; seemingly small, everyday events could also create stress. They hypothesized that any life change, even positive ones, can have a detrimental impact on health. Their work led to the formulation of the **life change model,** which assumes that all changes in a person's life—large or small, desirable or undesirable—can act as stressors. In addition, the accumulation of small changes is thought to be as powerful as a major stressor. Consider the following case:

Janet M., a college freshman, had always been a top-notch student in her small-town high school and had been valedictorian of her graduating class. Her SAT

Changes in a person's life can be stressful. Research has found, however, that undesirable life changes, such as loss of a spouse, are more likely to produce anxiety, depression, and physical symptoms in people than are positive life changes, such as graduating from college and beginning a new phase in life.

test scores placed her in the ninety-fifth percentile of all students taking the exam. Her social life was in high gear from the moment she arrived on the Berkeley campus. Yet Janet was suffering. It started with a cold that she seemed unable to shake. During her first quarter, she was hospitalized once with the "flu" and then three weeks later for "exhaustion." In high school Janet appeared vivacious, outgoing, and relaxed; at Berkeley she became increasingly tense, anxious, and depressed.

What was happening to Janet is often seen, to various degrees, among entering college students. Going to college is a major life change for students and may result in stress. Most students can cope with the demands, but others need direct help. In Janet's case, all the classic symptoms of stress were present. No single stressor was responsible; rather, a series of life changes had a cumulative impact. An examination of Janet's intake interview notes at the counseling center revealed the following stressors:

1. Change from a somewhat conservative small-town environment to a more permissive atmosphere on a liberal campus

2. Change from being the top student in her high school class to being slightly above average at Berkeley

3. Change in living accommodations, from a home with a private room to a dormitory with a roommate

4. Change from being completely dependent on family finances to having to work part-time for her education

5. Change from having a steady boyfriend in her home town to being unpaired

6. Change in family stability (her father recently lost his job, and her parents seem headed for divorce)

7. Change in food intake from home-cooked meals to dormitory food and quick snacks

Although each of these changes may seem small, their cumulative impact was anything but insignificant.

To measure the impact of life changes, Holmes and Rahe (1967) devised the *Social Readjustment Rating Scale (SRRS)*. People rated forty-three events in terms of the amount of readjustment required. For example, the death of a spouse was noted as requiring the greatest adjustment, whereas a minor law violation required the least. Each life event was given a numerical value that corresponded to its strength as a stressor (Wyler, Masuda & Holmes, 1971). These "stress potential" values are referred to as *life change units (LCUs)*. The investigators found that 93 percent of health problems (infections, allergies, bone and muscle injuries, and psychosomatic illness) affected patients who, during the previous year, had been exposed to events whose LCU values totaled 150 or more. Although a minor life change was not sufficient to constitute a serious stressor, the cumulative impact of many events could be considered a crisis. Particularly revealing was the finding that exposure to a greater number of LCUs increased the chances of illness. Of those exposed to mild crises (150 to 199 LCUs), 37 percent reported illness; to moderate crises (200 to 299 LCUs), 51 percent; and to major crises (more than 300 LCUs), 79 percent.

Although research supports the view that life changes have a cumulative effect on mental and physical health, it has not supported the hypothesis that any life change will increase stress. Only undesirable life changes were associated with negative emotions such as anxiety, depression, or physical symptoms (Sarason, Johnson & Siegel, 1978). Thus negative life changes seem to be more detrimental than positive life changes.

Clearly, stressful life events do play some part in producing physical and psychological illnesses for many people. Yet it is too soon to say these illnesses are caused by stress. Most studies that have been cited are retrospective and correlational in nature, so no cause-and-effect relationship can be inferred. In addition, the data used in the studies depend on (1) people's perceptions of health and illness, (2) their recollections and reports of illness (both psychological and physical; sick individuals may recall more events than healthy ones), and (3) their health histories over a defined period (Levenstein et al., 1993). Furthermore, the illnesses of many people do not seem to be preceded by identifiable stressors, and some who undergo stress don't seem to get sick. Finally, evidence now shows (1) that positive and negative life events do not have equal effects and (2) that personal interpretations or characteristics modify the impact of life changes (Lazarus, 1983; Kobasa, Hilker & Maddi, 1979; Sarason, Johnson & Siegel, 1978). Obviously, further investigation of the relationship between life changes and illness is needed.

The Transaction Model

The GAS model is concerned with the process by which the body reacts to stressors, and the life change model is concerned with external events that cause stress as a response. But neither model considers the person's subjective definition or interpretation of stressful events or life changes. Apparently, several processes intervene between the stressor and the development of stress. In particular, the thoughts that we have about impending threats (stressors), the emotions that we attach to them, and the actions that we take to avoid them can either increase or decrease the impact of stressors (Levenstein et al., 1993). In his classic book *Psychological Stress and the Coping Process* (1969), Lazarus formulated a **transaction model of stress.** He noted that stress resides neither in the person alone nor in the situation alone, but is a transaction between the two. Let us use an example to illustrate this point:

On the morning of August 16, 1992, Mrs. Mavis C. discovered a small lump on her left breast. She immediately contacted her doctor and made an appointment to see him. After examining her, the physician stated that the lump could be a cyst or tumor and recommended a biopsy. The results revealed that the tumor was malignant.

Mrs. C. accepted the news with some trepidation but went about her life with minimal disruption. When she was questioned about the way in which she was handling the situation, she replied that there was no denying that this was a serious problem, and there is great ambiguity about the prognosis, but people are successfully treated for cancer. She planned to undergo treatment and would not give up.

Unlike Mrs. C., many patients would have been horrified at even the thought of having cancer. The news that the tumor was malignant would have been viewed as a catastrophe. Thoughts of dying would have arisen; all hope might have been abandoned. This sort of reaction differs from Mrs. C.'s, who coped with the stressor through internal processes.

The impact of stressors can be reduced or increased depending on the way the situation is interpreted. A person who develops cognitive adaptation may reduce susceptibility to illness or limit its course. Individuals who deny any negative effects of a stressor or disease, however, do more poorly than those who attempt to cope (King et al., 1990).

One dominant theme threads its way through each of the models discussed: no one factor is enough to cause illness. Rather, illness results from a complex interaction of psychosocial, physiological, and cognitive stressors. Figure 8.1 illustrates this interaction.

FIGURE 8.1   Interaction Among Psychosocial, Physiological, and Cognitive Stressors

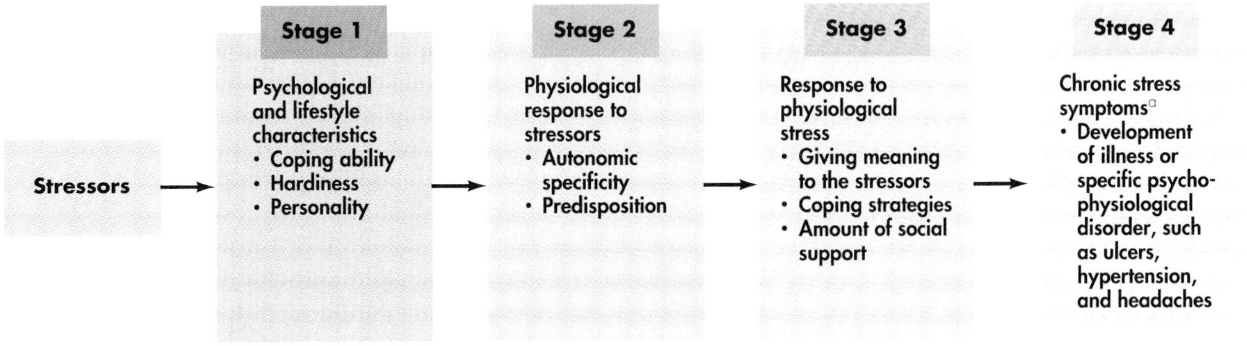

	Stage 1	Stage 2	Stage 3	Stage 4
Stressors →	Psychological and lifestyle characteristics • Coping ability • Hardiness • Personality	Physiological response to stressors • Autonomic specificity • Predisposition	Response to physiological stress • Giving meaning to the stressors • Coping strategies • Amount of social support	Chronic stress symptoms[a] • Development of illness or specific psycho-physiological disorder, such as ulcers, hypertension, and headaches

[a]This stage occurs only if the person has been unable to respond successfully to stressors.

Source: Adapted from Rahe & Arthur, 1978.

STRESS AND THE IMMUNE SYSTEM

We have already suggested a relationship between stress and illness. How do emotional and psychological states influence the disease process? Consider the following case:

> Anne was an unhappy and passive individual who always acceded to the wishes and demands of her husband. She had difficulty expressing strong emotions, especially anger, and often repressed her feelings. She had few friends and, other than her husband, had no one to talk to. She was also depressed and felt a pervasive sense of hopelessness. During a routine physical exam, her doctor discovered a lump in her breast. The results of a biopsy revealed that the tumor was malignant.

Could Anne's personality or emotional state have contributed to the formation or the growth of the malignant tumor? If so, how? Could she now alter the course of her disease by changing her emotional state? That such questions are being asked represents a profound change in the way in which physical illness is being conceptualized.

The view that diseases other than traditional psychophysiological disorders are strictly organic appears too simplistic. Many theorists now believe that most diseases are caused by an interaction of social, psychological, and biological factors. This relationship has been found in many diseases. King and Wilson (1991) found that interpersonal stress and depression were significantly related to dermatitis. The researchers pointed out, however, that although it is

possible to speculate that interpersonal stress caused the skin symptoms, it is also possible that increases in itchiness or unsightliness from the skin condition produced interpersonal stress. The recurrence of herpes symptoms also appears to be influenced by emotional factors. A study by McLarnon & Kaloupek (1988) appears to support the stress-causes-symptom view. People with herpes reported their moods and thoughts daily on a questionnaire. New lesions developed in participants who reported higher anxiety four days before lesions appeared. This held true even when physical symptoms such as tingling and itchiness were controlled. Here the emotional state clearly preceded the physical sensations. Stress has also been implicated in the cause and course of upper respiratory infections, and bacterial infections (Cohen & Williamson, 1991). Possible ways in which stress may increase susceptibility to infectious diseases involve (1) altering resistance to infections, (2) initiating or triggering a process that allows the expression of an already present pathogen, and (3) contributing to the maintenance of the disease process.

Even in a disease process such as acquired immune deficiency syndrome (AIDS), the great variations found in the clinical course may be due partly to psychological variables (Solano et al., 1993). Yet the evidence supporting the importance of psychosocial stressors on the development and progress of AIDS is mixed. In an ongoing five-year prospective study of 124 HIV-seropositive men who had not developed AIDS, Rabkin and her colleagues (1991) tried to determine answers to the following questions: (1) Do HIV-positive persons who are currently depressed have lower immune functioning than those who are not depressed? (2) Is psychological distress related to immune functioning? (3) Do men with depression have more symptoms of HIV infection than men without current depressive disorders? After examining the patients who participated in the study for six months, the researchers came up with some tentative findings. HIV-positive men who were depressed or reported more life stressors showed no more immunosuppression or advanced illness than the other men in the study. In a review of studies examining the impact of psychosocial variables such as depression on the immune function of individuals with HIV, Stein, Miller, and Trestman (1991) concluded that "psychosocial factors, such as depression or stress, do not have a measurable or substantial effect on the immune system in relation to physical disorders, such as AIDS" (p. 171).

It is possible that the studies reviewed involved too short a period for the impact of depression to be fully assessed. Burack and colleagues (1992) found that immune functioning tended to drop drastically after about three years for depressed men versus five years for nondepressed HIV-seropositive men. They believed that life can be prolonged by treating depression early in HIV-seropositive persons. In fact, Antoni and colleagues (1991) found that, compared with an assessment-only control group, a stress management group of HIV-seropositive men showed higher levels of immune functioning. At this point it is still unclear how much impact on immune function psychological factors have on a disease such as AIDS. Nevertheless, psychological treatments can at the very least improve the psychological well-being of clients.

The Immune System

We know that stress is related to illness, but what is the precise relationship between the two? How does stress affect health? Stress itself does not appear to cause infections, but it may decrease the immune system's efficiency, thereby increasing a person's susceptibility to disease. This connection has received the greatest amount of attention.

As mentioned earlier, stress results in physiological changes in the body. Part of the stress response involves the release of several neurohormones (catecholamines, corticosteroids, and endorphins). These substances impair immune functioning. *Corticoste-*

roids, for example, have very strong immunosuppressive actions and are often used to suppress immunity caused by allergic reactions. *Endorphins* also appear to decrease natural killer cells' tumor-fighting ability (Holland & Lewis, 1993).

The white blood cells in the immune system help maintain health by recognizing and destroying pathogens such as bacteria, viruses, fungi, and tumors. In an intact system, over a thousand billion white blood cells are based in the lymph system or circulate through the bloodstream. Two major classes of white blood cells are lymphocytes and phagocytes. *Lymphocytes* comprise B-cells (which produce antibodies against invaders), T-cells (which detect and destroy foreign cells), and natural killer (NK) cells (which act as an early detection system to prevent the growth of tumors). *Phagocytes* are also attracted to and destroy invaders (Kiecolt-Glaser & Glaser, 1993). A deficient immune system may fail to detect invaders or produce antibodies. Its killing ability may be impaired, or its blood cells may be unable to multiply. Because of the weakening in defenses, infections and diseases are more likely to develop or worsen.

Decreased Immunological Functioning as a Function of Stress Impaired immunological functioning has been associated with a variety of social and psychological stressors. The spouses of dementia victims showed lower immune functioning than controls, and those who reported lower levels of social support showed the greatest drop (Kiecolt-Glaser et al., 1991). Divorced or separated men tend to have poorer immunological functioning than do married men. And happily married men tend to have stronger immune systems than men who are experiencing marital problems (Kiecolt-Glaser et al., 1987). The quality of social relationships may affect our vulnerability to illnesses.

Bereavement (loss of a spouse) has also been found to weaken the immune system. The lymphocyte responsiveness of men who were married to women with terminal breast cancer was measured approximately one month before their wives' death and again afterward. The second measurement showed a drop in immune response. The decrease in efficiency continued for approximately two months, after which the immune functioning gradually increased (Schleifer et al., 1983). Similar results have also been reported in recently widowed women.

Women whose husbands had died showed lower NK cell responsiveness than a group of nonbereaved women (Irwin et al., 1987). Although these stressors are associated with a decrease in immune response, not everyone was equally affected. As indicated in our discussion of the transaction model, the person's perception or interpretation of the event is important. Separated and divorced men who were preoccupied with thoughts of their former partner showed a lower level of immune functioning (Kiecolt-Glaser et al., 1987). How a person interprets an event can influence its impact.

Although our discussion has focused on stress's direct impact on the immune system, indirect pathways must also be considered. For example, an individual who is depressed or facing many different stressors may deteriorate in health practices. He or she may sleep less, drink alcoholic beverages, neglect physical care, or eat fewer nutritious meals. These changes in health practices can also decrease immune functioning (Kiecolt-Glaser & Glaser, 1988). Thus decreased resistance to disease might be due to changes in behavioral or nutritional patterns as a function of being depressed or stressed. Research that attempts to link changes in immune functioning directly with stressors or psychological states must control for this variable. It is possible that bereaved persons may show lowered immune functioning because of a decrease in health care practices.

Mediating the Effects of Stressors

It is clear from the studies cited earlier that not everyone who faces stressful events develops an illness, which suggests that certain factors may mediate the effects of a stressor. In this section, we discuss certain factors that mitigate stress.

Helplessness or Control   Control and the perception of control over the environment and its stressors appear to mitigate the effects of stress. One study of nursing home residents examined the impact of control on the residents' health and emotional states. In the "responsibility induced" group, residents were allowed to make certain decisions, such as how to arrange their rooms, when to see movies, whether to accept visitors, and whether to have plants in their room. The "traditional" group was not offered these choices. Movies were seen when scheduled. Nurses

Control or the perception of control over one's environment and its stressors appears to lessen the effects of stress. People in low-stress, low-control jobs may experience greater levels of stress than do people in high-stress, high-control jobs.

arranged rooms and chose and cared for residents' plants.

Within a short period, the nurses rated 71 percent of the "traditional" group as more debilitated and 93 percent of the "responsibility induced" group as improved. Self-report questionnaires also revealed that the responsibility induced group rated themselves as more active and happier. Mortality rates also differed between the two groups. After eighteen months, 15 percent (7 of 47) of those in the responsibility induced group had died, versus 30 percent (13 of 44) in the traditional group. The reason for the differences in mortality rates is unclear. Some deaths, however, might be associated with a less-efficient immune system (Langer & Rodin, 1976; Rodin & Langer, 1977).

A direct relationship between control and the immune system has been found in several studies. In one study, ten subjects were placed in two stress situations—one they could control and one they couldn't. In the first situation, subjects could control the noise level by pressing buttons in a simple sequence. In the other, subjects could not control the noise level. Blood samples were obtained after each session and analyzed. Epinephrine (a hormone released during stress) levels in the uncontrollable stress situation were significantly higher than those in the controllable one. The subjects also reported a greater sense of helplessness, higher tension, anxiety, and depression while in the uncontrollable stress situation (Breier et al., 1987). Although changes in physical functioning occur with stress, can we show experimentally that lack of control is related to disease?

A study directly measured the ability to "control" on immune functioning. Rats were injected with cancer cells and assigned to one of three groups: (1) a controllable shock (pressing a bar would end the shock), (2) a yoked control (rats in this group would receive the same pattern of shocks as in the escapable condition, but would have no control over it), or (3) a no-shock control group. Sixty-five percent of the rats in the controllable shock group rejected the cancer cells, as opposed to only 27 percent in the yoked control group and 55 percent in the no-shock control group. The inability to control a stressor seems to decrease immune system efficiency (Laudenslager et al., 1983; Visintainer, Volpicelli & Seligman, 1982).

Hardiness: Personality Characteristics and Mood State Maddi (1972) believes that "hardy" people are more resistant to illnesses. Kobasa and her colleagues (1979) conducted large-scale research on highly stressed executives in various occupations, seeking to identify the traits that distinguish those who handle stress well from those who do not. They found that high-stress executives who reported few illnesses showed three kinds of **hardiness**, or ability to deal well with stress. In their attitudes toward life, these stress-resistant executives showed an *openness to change*, a feeling of *involvement* or *commitment*, and a *sense of control* over their lives. The most im-

portant protective factor correlated with health was attitude toward change (or *challenge*). Those who are open to change are more likely to interpret events to their advantage and to reduce their level of stress. Although the idea that hardiness may buffer the impact of stressors makes sense, the construct has been difficult to define and assess (Funk, 1992).

Suppose that two persons lost their jobs. The person who is open to change may view this situation as an opportunity to find a new career better suited to his or her abilities. The person who is not open to change is likely to see the job loss as a devastating event and to suffer the emotional and physical consequences of this perception.

What can we conclude about stress and its impact on the immune system? The results of many studies consistently show that both short-term stressors (exams, loss of sleep, emotional state) and long-term stressors (marital problems, divorce, bereavement, care for the chronically ill) impair immune system function. Although there is some evidence that certain psychological states such as depression can directly affect the immune system; changes in health practices also have an impact on immune functioning. Stress also aggravates and prolongs some viral or bacterial infections, but evidence has suggested that the reduction in immune system efficiency from psychological factors is often relatively small and may account for only about 10 percent of the variance in predicting disease occurrence (Rabkin et al., 1991). As Kiecolt-Glaser and Glaser (1992) pointed out, "It is sometimes erroneously assumed that changes in immune function translate directly into changes in health. In fact, whether interventions that produce relatively small immunological changes can actually affect the incidence, severity, or duration of infections or malignant disease is not known" (p. 573). And finally, attitudes and perceptions influence the impact of stress.

Personality, Mood States, and Cancer

Are certain emotions or personality characteristics involved in either the cause or the course of cancers? Certain researchers believe so. Demonstrating such a link would have important implications in treatment and prevention. In 1989, approximately 985,000 individuals were diagnosed with cancer and more than 494,000 died of this disease (Silberberg & Lubera, 1989).

Bahnson (1981) hypothesized that persons who were sad and depressed but coped by denial and repression of emotions were at greater risk for developing cancer. In the same vein, Simonton and colleagues (1978) believe that certain emotions can inhibit immune system functioning, allowing malignant cells to form. The inability to express emotions or to form lasting interpersonal relationships is hypothesized to be associated with cancer. According to Simonton and colleagues, positive emotions can enhance immune functioning. Meares (1979) agreed and said that physicians should take "the big step of attempting to influence cancer growth by psychological means" (p. 978). Many cancer patients also believe that they can control the course, outcome, and recurrence of the cancer. One patient put it this way: "I think that if you feel you are in control of it [cancer], you can control it up to a point. I absolutely refuse to have any more cancer" (Taylor, 1983, p. 1163). This patient clearly believed that her attitude would have an effect on her cancer. This interpretation, however, is still a subject of controversy (see Focus 8.2).

Several problems exist in research investigating the relationship between moods and personality on cancer. First, *cancer* is a general name for a variety of disease processes, each of which may have a varying susceptibility to emotions. Second, cancer develops over a relatively long period of time. Determining a temporal relationship between its occurrence and a specific mood or personality is not possible. Third, most studies examining the relationship between psychological variables and cancer have been retrospective—that is, personality or mood states were assessed after the cancer was diagnosed. The discovery that one has a life-threatening disease can produce a variety of emotional reactions. Women who received the life-threatening diagnosis of cancer responded with depression, anxiety, and confusion. Thus instead of being a cause, negative emotions may be a result of the knowledge of having a life-threatening disease. Fourth, although it has been shown that injected malignant cells are more likely to grow in stressed versus unstressed mice, the findings do not address the development of "spontaneous" cancers. Would the stressed mice be more likely to develop cancer anyway, without being injected with malignant cells?

The relationship between personality characteristics and cancer is difficult to demonstrate even with well-designed research. Consider the following study: one-hundred-and-sixty women with breast tumors were given a battery of personality tests before being told the results of their biopsies. This was done to control for effects that knowledge of the malignancy would create. Of the women, sixty-nine were found to have a malignant tumor. According to personality measures, the women in this group tended to display extremes in dealing with anger—some were very controlled, and others had frequent outbursts (Greer & Morris, 1975). Although this study appeared to control for the impact of knowledge of having a disease on the emotional state, perhaps it did not. Could some women in this study have guessed correctly about the results of their biopsies? And if so, how could they have guessed?

Schwartz and Geyer (1984) found that many patients are aware that they have cancer before a formal diagnosis is made. How do they know? Patients may be very attentive to their physicians' reactions during the examination; physicians may "unwittingly" convey cues that reflect their opinion. These cues may account for the fact that 75 percent of the women in the study were accurate in predicting whether they had the disease before the biopsy results were received. Schwartz and Geyer suggested that emotional expressions such as anger, depression, denial, and hopelessness may reflect the patient's reaction to the anticipated negative diagnosis. Because it is difficult to eliminate patient expectations, the precise relationship that exists between personality and cancer is still unclear.

Specific emotional states have been suspected of influencing the onset and course of cancer. Depression (measured by the MMPI) was positively associated with a twenty-year incidence of mortality from cancer (Persky et al., 1987). People with high depression scores were 1.38 times more likely to develop cancer and 1.96 times more likely to die of cancer as compared with those rated low in depression. This was true even when risk factors such as age, smoking, alcohol intake, occupational status, family history of cancer, and serum cholesterol levels were considered. Because the study was prospective (before cancer was diagnosed), the possibility that depression resulted from knowledge of having a cancer was eliminated. Depression was only assessed at the beginning of the study, however, and to demonstrate a relationship of this emotion with cancer, we would have to show that it was a long-term disorder in these people.

Do Psychological and Social Factors Contribute to the Development of Cancer?

Are cancers caused by psychological factors, and if so, can they be cured by psychological means? To examine the impact of social and psychological factors on patients' ability to fight their disease, Cassileth and colleagues (1985) studied a group of 204 men and women with advanced cancer and a group of 155 women with breast cancer. The variables they examined included social ties and marital history, job satisfaction, general life satisfaction, and degree of hopelessness and helplessness. These variables were selected because they were considered factors that might influence immune functioning. But no relationship was found between disease recurrence or length of survival and any of the social or psychological variables. Cassileth and colleagues concluded that in advanced cancer, "The inherent biology of the disease alone determines the prognosis" (p. 1555).

In an editorial accompanying the Cassileth study, deputy editor of the *New England Journal of Medicine* Marcia Angell (1985, p. 1570) asked, "Is cancer more likely in unhappy people? Can people who have cancer improve their chances of survival by learning to enjoy life and to think optimistically?" Angell answered these questions with a resounding "no!" She pointed out

that most reports suggesting the influence of psychological factors on diseases are anecdotal and that few of the studies are "scientifically sound." In addition, the view that psychological states can influence the development of cancer serves to blame the victim and to further burden them. She concluded by stating that "it is time to acknowledge that our belief in disease as a direct reflection of mental states is largely folklore" (p. 1572).

Angell's comments produced a flurry of letters to the *New England Journal of Medicine*. Williams, Benson, and Follick (1985), each of whom has served as the president of the Society of Behavioral Medicine, commented that the Cassileth study did not rule out the possibility that psychological factors were involved in the initiation of cancer and warned that accepting Angell's views could eliminate research into the biological correlates of mental states. Livnat and Felton (1985) pointed out that a growing body of scientific literature showed that psychological factors influence many physiologic functions. They argued that "Angell urges us to throw out the baby with the bath water" (p. 1357). The American Psychological Association sent a letter to the *New England Journal of Medicine*

characterizing Angell's editorial as "inaccurate" (Abeles, 1986).

This debate will continue. One study (Ramirez et al., 1989) reported a tentative relationship between severe life stressors and the recurrence of breast cancer in women. Another study (Dean & Surtees, 1989), however, reported that recurrence of breast cancer was less in women with a psychiatric illness prior to the mastectomy and those who used denial as a coping strategy after the operation. Psychosocial factors were not significantly related to survival among patients with hematologic or rectal cancers. These discrepant findings are confusing and represent the complexities in research in this area.

To make progress in determining the link between psychological state and cancer, first, we must decide what psychological or social variables may be important. Second, we need valid instruments to measure these dimensions. Third, we have to decide which one of the many types of cancer we are interested in studying and the stage of development. Fourth, even if we find a relationship, how can we be certain that the physiology of the cancer or knowledge of having cancer is not causing the psychological state rather than the other way around?

Do stress, emotional difficulties, or personality characteristics increase the chance that a person will develop cancer or increase the cancer's severity if it does occur? Certain emotions and stressors have been associated with a less-efficient immune system. Possibly under these conditions cancer might be more

likely to gain a foothold. Nevertheless, the connection between stress and naturally occurring cancers remains to be shown. Maybe only certain cancers, at a certain level of development, are influenced by emotional states. Researchers are currently investigating this possibility.

FIRST PERSON

Leslie Sue

Stress and police work go hand in hand. In fact, very few careers cause as much stress as law enforcement. Research shows that police officers spend more time maintaining order than making arrests. Nevertheless, at any moment in an otherwise routine day, an officer may confront a life-and-death situation. When an officer stops a vehicle for speeding, for example, he or she has no idea what to expect. The occupant could be a newly licensed teenager, a bank executive hurrying to get home, or a psychopath who has just robbed a local convenience store at gunpoint! It is the uncertainty of what lies ahead and the need to respond to it immediately that leads to stress and its symptoms.

I recall one incident that occurred in 1983. While assigned to the Selma resident agency of the Mobile, Alabama, FBI field office as a special agent, I was called to a scene where an armed robbery had just occurred. When I got there, the police had already cordoned off a heavily forested area where the suspect was thought to be hiding. We knew he was armed, but the area had to be searched anyway. It was a stressful situation, and I'm sure every officer there was as apprehensive as I was because we knew we could be wounded or killed. And in fact, during the early morning hours, the suspect was killed in an exchange of gunfire that began when he resisted arrest.

Police officers must always be mentally and physically prepared to respond quickly to threatening situations. Their lives and the lives of others often depend on quick response. It's not surprising, then, that the stress this causes often manifests itself in a high prevalence of cardiovascular disease, suicide, marital conflict and divorce, alcoholism and drug dependency, and stomach ailments.

There are also other reasons why police work tends to be very stressful. First, police departments are paramilitary organizations, which means they are patterned after military models. This type of organization reduces communication and decision making among the ranks; orders come from top to bottom.

Individualism is discouraged. Second, officers are expected to know what to do in every situation, to maintain order even during violent confrontations, to render first aid to the injured, and to use deadly force when appropriate. Third, they are also expected to have strong interpersonal skills, despite the fact that most officers don't receive any training in this area. Fourth, police are often undervalued by the communities they serve and criticized by people who don't fully appreciate or understand the nature of police work.

In recent years, researchers have identified stress as a major occupational hazard in the occupation. Some of the more progressive police agencies have even designed programs to help officers improve their diet and learn stress-reduction techniques such as meditation and relaxation. Many organizations also provide counseling services. These efforts have had a positive impact on reducing job stress and burnout, resulting in increased use of such programs. However, stress on the job continues to be a major debilitator in police work.

Leslie Sue is a professor at Truckee Community College, where he teaches in the law enforcement program. He is a former special agent with the FBI and police officer.

PSYCHOLOGICAL INVOLVEMENT IN SPECIFIC PHYSICAL DISORDERS

Although most research studying the impact of psychological factors on immune function is fairly recent, the mind-body connection between some physical disorders has been extensively studied. In many instances, a relationship has been found between psychological or social factors and the origin and exacerbation of these conditions. In addition, particularly stressful occupations have also been linked to the development of certain disorders. The First Person narrative in this chapter examines some of the more stressful aspects of police work.

Coronary Heart Disease

It is estimated that nearly 500,000 persons died of coronary heart disease (CHD) in 1990 in the United

States; of these, more than one-third are younger than 65 years of age (American Heart Association, 1993). But the incidence of this disorder has been diminishing in recent years because of changes in smoking, diet, exercise, and treatment of hypertension (Rothenberg & Aubert, 1990). **Coronary heart disease (CHD)** is a narrowing of the arteries in or to the heart, which results in the restriction or partial blockage of the flow of blood and oxygen to the heart. Its symptoms may include chest pain (*angina pectoris*), heart attack, or, in severe cases, cardiac arrest. Cigarette smoking, physical inactivity, obesity, hypertension, and elevated serum cholesterol have been found to increase the risk of CHD. These factors alone do not seem sufficient to cause the disease, however; studies suggest that other variables are involved as well.

Type A and Type B Personality Patterns Friedman and Rosenman (1974) identified a behavior pattern, called Type A behavior, that they believe is associated with increased risk of heart attack. The pattern involves aggressiveness, competitiveness, hostility, time pressure, and constant striving for achievement. In self-reports, Type A people indicate that they are easily aroused to anger and that they experience this emotion intensely and frequently (Levenkron et al., 1983; Stevens et al., 1984). A second behavior pattern, Type B, is characterized as relaxed and not subject to time pressure. These behavior patterns appear to be relatively stable.

In a 27-year follow-up of 1180 surviving participants who had been classified as either Type A or Type B, 61 percent maintained their original classification (Carmelli et al., 1991). Interestingly, in this group of men who were largely retired, 56 percent were now Type A personalities versus 46 percent twenty-seven years ago. Why retired men should show more Type A patterns is not known. Coronary heart disease is more likely in Type A than in Type B people. Among middle-aged men with coronary heart disease, 70 percent were type A; in healthy men, only 46 percent were Type A (Miller et al., 1991).

Questioning the Type A Hypothesis Although evidence initially suggested that the Type A personality was related to coronary heart disease, recent research has suggested something different. The picture of a

Although sensitivity to time pressure, hostility, competitiveness, and the inability to relax are some characteristics of type A personalities, only hostility has been directly related to coronary heart disease.

harried businessperson, under strict time constraints doing several things at once, competitive, and hostile is being reexamined. Julkunen and colleagues (1993) reviewed the qualities for CHD related to the Type A personality and found that the only significant risk factor was irritability and hostility (whether openly expressed or suppressed). Similar conclusions have been reached by Williams and associates (1988) and Wood (1986). The Type A behavior pattern apparently includes factors that are both benign and place individuals at risk. If hostility is the important element, programs to help people slow down and enjoy life may not be helpful.

Stress and Hypertension

On October 19, 1987 (or "Black Monday," the day the stock market dropped 508 points), a 48-year-old stockbroker was wearing a device that measured stress related to the work environment. The instrument measured his pulse every fifteen minutes. At the beginning of the day, his pulse was sixty-four beats per minute and blood pressure was 132/87 (both rates within the normal range). As stock prices fell dramatically, the man's physiological system surged in the other direction. His heart rate increased to eighty-four beats per minute and blood pressure hit a dangerous 181/105. His pulse was "pumping adrenalin, flooding his arteries, and maybe slowly killing himself in the process." (Tierney, 1988)

This case illustrates the impact of a stressor on blood pressure. Under what conditions will this physiological response, found in all of us, develop into a chronic condition? High blood pressure (the force of blood against the walls of the arteries and veins), or **essential hypertension,** is a common disorder that can lead to heart attacks or serious circulatory problems. In 90 percent of the persons with hypertension, no organic cause can be determined. More than 10 percent of the U.S. population suffers from this condition—which is defined as 140/90 mm Hg and higher. Chronic hypertension may lead to arteriosclerosis (narrowing of arteries) and increased risk of strokes and heart attacks (Waldstein et al., 1991).

A number of studies have suggested that stressors may be related to hypertension. Living in crowded neighborhoods and being in a stressful occupation are both associated with high blood pressure (Ely & Mostardi, 1986; Fleming et al., 1987). Increases in blood pressure have also been shown experimentally in persons exposed to stressors. Interestingly, people who indicated that they were feeling a great deal of stress before the experiment showed elevated blood pressure even after the stressor was eliminated, whereas the blood pressure of people reporting low stress quickly returned to their prestress levels (Pardine & Napoli, 1983). Reducing stress by relaxing, both at home and at work, significantly lowers blood pressure. Having social support also reduces the impact of stressors (Gerin et al., 1992). Such studies have shown that stress has a definite impact on blood pressure and supported the contention that people who suffer from chronic stress may be at risk for developing hypertension.

Along with exposure to stressors, emotional reactions may also contribute to hypertension. Blood pressure tends to be temporarily higher when people are angry or anxious than when they are relaxed and contented (James et al., 1986). Researchers are trying to identify emotional patterns that produce a chronic elevation. As with other disorders, there is evidence that angry cognitions or thoughts play a role in hypertension (Davison et al., 1991).

Environmental conditions, such as crowded neighborhoods, have been associated with elevated blood pressure.

Gender differences may also play a role in the development of hypertension. Gender differences in emotional expression and blood pressure were found in a study by Lai and Linden (1992). Men and women were classified as either "anger in" (suppressing anger) or "anger out" (expressing anger). They were then exposed to verbal harassment and either allowed or not to release their anger. Men displayed greater cardiovascular reactivity to the harassment than did women. The opportunity to release anger facilitated heart rate and diastolic recovery in men but not in women. Women with "anger in" tendencies showed better systolic recovery than women with "anger out" tendencies, regardless of whether they had an opportunity to express anger. As opposed to men, holding in anger did not have a negative physiological reaction for women. These differences in recovery patterns are hypothesized to be due to the differential socialization of males and females. Another study also found a significant relationship between suppressed anger and blood pressure in black and white men but not in women (Dimsdale et al., 1986).

Ethnic Factors in Hypertension   That blacks have higher mean blood pressure levels and higher rates of hypertension than whites has been taken as evidence of genetic influence. Findings that black men show greater increases in systolic and diastolic blood pressure in reaction to cold stimulation than white men have also been used to support the view that there may be differences in sympathetic nervous system activity between the two groups. Increased awareness and better treatment for the disorder has substantially reduced hypertension among blacks and has slightly reduced rates for white women (Foreyt, 1987). However, hypertension is still more prevalent among blacks than among whites (Treiber et al., 1993). Asian Americans show lower rates of hypertension than the general population (Stavig, Igra & Leonard, 1988).

Social factors are also involved. Dressler, Dos Santos, and Vitere (1986) found that the availability of psychosocial resources modified black-white differences in blood pressure. The highest blood pressure was found among blacks with the lowest psychosocial resources. This finding suggested the impact of environmental factors. The degree of genetic contribution to hypertension remains an open question.

Peptic Ulcers

Peptic ulcers, which are essentially open sores within the digestive system, cause 10,000 deaths each year in the United States. One of every ten persons is afflicted by this disorder at some point in his or her life (Weiner, 1991).

Tony L. is a hard-working and competitive student. For a period of about a year, he has felt a burning sensation in his stomach. On the day before he is to take his graduate record examinations, he feel an overwhelming pain in his abdomen. He collapses and is taken to a hospital where examination reveals that he has a duodenal ulcer.

The most common site for ulcers is the small intestine; ulcers located there are called *duodenal ulcers.* A somewhat less-common site is the stomach, where they are called *gastric ulcers.* (See Table 8.1 for differences between the two types.) Duodenal ulcers are associated with excessive hydrochloric acid secretion. The pain tends to be rhythmic, occurring when the stomach is empty and diminishing after eating. Gastric ulcers seem to be related to how well the mucous membrane protects the walls of the stomach. Ulcers may result from excessive secretion of stomach acid, insufficient secretion of the mucus that coats and protects the walls of the stomach, or slow or inadequate regeneration of the stomach lining (Whitehead, 1993). Under psychological stress, these conditions can lead to peptic ulcers.

Weiner and colleagues (1957) examine the proposition that a high level of *pepsinogen* (a digestive system secretion), along with stress, predisposes some-

Table 8.1

Some Differences Between Duodenal and Gastric Ulcers

Duodenal Ulcer	Gastric Ulcer
1. More frequent in young people	More frequent in older people
2. Associated with oversecretion of stomach acid	Associated with normal amounts of stomach acid
3. Occurs in members of higher social classes	Usually occurs in members of lower social classes
4. Associated with intellectually demanding jobs	Associated with jobs involving heavy manual labor
5. Eating relieves symptoms	Eating causes discomfort
6. Occurs mainly in males	Somewhat more common in males than in females

Source: Adapted from Eisenberg, 1989.

one to develop peptic ulcers. From 2073 newly inducted soldiers, a group of 63 oversecretors of pepsinogen and a group of 57 undersecretors were selected. None of the soldiers in these groups had ulcers at the beginning of their training period. After sixteen weeks of basic training, however, 9 of the oversecretors had developed ulcers, whereas none of the undersecretors displayed this disorder. Although the level of stomach acid is related to the development of peptic ulcers (and possibly to other gastrointestinal disorders), that certainly cannot be the only factor involved, because 86 percent of the oversecretors did not develop ulcers. In addition, in other studies, many individuals with peptic ulcers have not shown elevated levels of pepsinogen (Weiner, 1991).

Because physical factors cannot fully explain the cause of ulcers, psychological factors must be examined. Conflicts over dependency and subsequent feelings of guilt and hostility have been suggested as possible contributors. Magni and colleagues (1986) found three distinct personality profiles among seventy-nine patients: (1) dependent and anxious, (2) neurotic and anxious, and (3) "balanced personality." These ulcer patients, however, did not form a homogeneous group. Most attempts to find a specific personality type associated with this disorder have not been very successful. Instead of looking at personality as a cause, it may be more helpful to identify emotional states that lead to increased gastric activity and ulcer formation. Ulcer patients often report that emotional events preceded the onset of pain (Salim, 1987).

Migraine, Tension, and Cluster Headaches

Headaches are among the most common psychophysiological complaints. Approximately 45 million Americans suffer chronic or recurrent headaches that vary in intensity from dull to excruciating (Clark et al., 1988). It is unclear whether the different forms of headaches (migraine, tension, and cluster) are produced by different psychophysiological mechanisms or if they merely differ in severity. Individuals with headaches show greater sensitivity to pain in areas of the body other than the head than those who are headache free (Marlowe, 1992). One factor, stress, appears to contribute to the initiation of headaches (Gannon et al., 1987).

We discuss migraine, tension, and cluster headaches separately, although the same person can be susceptible to several types of headaches. Furthermore, Blanchard and Andrasik (1982), who analyzed well-designed research studies comparing the different forms of headaches, concluded that, in spite of some apparent differences, there is little support for the view that the forms can be easily distinguished from one another. (Figure 8.2 illustrates some differences among the three types of headaches.)

Migraine Headaches   Constriction of cranial arteries, followed by dilation of the cerebral blood vessels resulting in moderate to severe pain, are the distinguishing features of **migraine headache.** Anything that affects the size of these blood vessels, which are connected to sensitive nerves, can produce a headache. Thus certain chemicals, such as sodium nitrate (found in hot dogs), monosodium glutamate (used generously in restaurants that serve Asian food), and tyramine (found in red wines), can produce headaches by distending blood vessels in sensitive people (Goleman, 1976). Migraine headaches are usually severe, may last from a few hours to several days, and are often accompanied by nausea and vomiting. Women report more migraine episodes than do men (Clark et al., 1988).

Migraine headaches are of two general types: classic and common. The *classic* type begins with an intense constriction of the blood vessels in the brain, dramatically diminishing the supply of blood. Depending on which part of the brain is affected most, the person may show various neurological symptoms, such as distortion of vision, numbness of parts of the body, or speech and coordination problems. When the blood vessels then become distended to compensate for the diminished blood supply, severe pain occurs. The nerves become so sensitive that the blood, as it courses through the vessels with each heartbeat, produces a characteristic pulsating or throbbing pain (Goleman, 1976; Walen et al., 1977). With *common* migraine headaches, the first phase is less severe, and neurological symptoms may not be evident. The pain also is less intense than in classic migraine headaches.

Migraine sufferers have typically been described as moral, ambitious, perfectionistic, and possessing above-average intelligence and a tendency to repress emotions. But in a well-controlled study, migraine sufferers were

FIGURE 8.2   What to Do If Headaches Strike

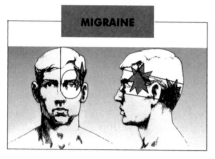
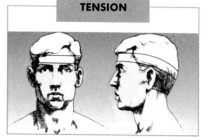
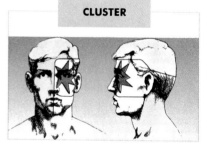

MIGRAINE	TENSION	CLUSTER

Symptoms

Throbbing pain (most severe in red) on one side of the head. Often preceded by an "aura," with glowing spots before the eyes. May cause nausea and aversion to lights, sounds. Often associated with menstruation. Lasts four hours to two days.

Symptoms

Dull, constricting ache on both sides of head rather than piercing pain. Often concentrated in "hatband" region or running into neck and shoulders. Can be intermittent or chronic.

Symptoms

Intense pain, always on the same side of the head. Eye often teary, nose clogged. Lasts 20 minutes to two hours. Occurs at least once a day for weeks or months, then stops for months or years before recurring.

Treatment

During attacks: rest in a quiet, dark place. Medications include ergot compounds and nonnarcotic and anti-inflammatory pain relievers. To prevent attacks: beta blockers, tricyclic antidepressants, and anti-inflammatories.

Treatment

During attacks: nonnarcotic pain relievers and muscle relaxants. To prevent attacks: biofeedback, relaxation exercises, and tricyclic antidepressants.

Treatment

During attacks: ergotlike compounds, oxygen. To prevent attacks: calcium channel blockers, ergotlike compounds, lithium, and steroids.

Source: From Newsweek on Health, Spring 1988.

not especially ambitious or highly desirous of perfection (Henryk-Gutt & Rees, 1973). Although their headaches were precipitated by emotional stress, the sufferers were not generally exposed to more stressors than the controls. It was concluded that migraine patients are congenitally predisposed to headaches. An extensive review of the migraine headache literature also indicated that this problem is probably hereditary, possibly represented by excessive cranial vascular responsiveness (Bakal, 1975).

Tension Headaches   Tension headaches were once thought to be produced by prolonged contraction of the scalp and neck muscles, resulting in vascular constriction and steady pain. Some studies, however, have found a lack of correspondence between reports of pain and muscle tension among people who have tension headaches. Many people showed no detectable muscle tension but still reported headaches (Philips, 1983). Friedman (1979) listed some complaints of 1420 persons who experienced tension headaches:

"Feeling as if my head is being squeezed in a vise"
"A tight headband that keeps getting tighter"
"Top of the head is blown off"

Psychological factors precipitated the headaches in 77 percent of the patients, most of whom were women. Tension headaches are generally not as severe as migraine headaches, and they can usually be relieved with aspirin or other analgesics.

Cluster Headaches   Little research has been conducted on **cluster headaches,** which are often described as excruciating. These headaches tend to occur on one side of the head near the eye, producing tears and a blocked nose. The pain is so great that sufferers may commit violent acts such as banging their heads against the wall (Clark et al., 1988).

Headaches appear to involve a biological predisposition such as greater reactivity of the blood vessels in the brain that respond to physical and psychological stressors. The precise mechanism involved, however, is not known. Headache pain is being perceived as more than a function of a physiological factor (muscle tension, dilation of cranial arteries). Cognitive-emotional and pain-motivated behaviors, such as verbal and nonverbal complaints and avoidance, are also being considered (Philips, 1983). Several psychological interventions such as relaxation, cognitive therapy, and biofeedback show promise in treating headaches (Blanchard, 1992).

Asthma

Asthma is a respiratory disorder that results from constriction of the airways in the lungs owing to muscle tone changes in the airways, excessive mucus secretion, edema, or inflammation. During asthma attacks, breathing becomes very difficult and produces a wheezing sound. The person struggles for breath and may develop acute anxiety, which aggravates the condition. For some unknown reason, there has been increased mortality for asthma during recent years (Lehrer, Sargunaraj & Hochron, 1992).

Asthma appears to have a diurnal variation, with symptoms often being worse during the night and early morning. Persons with asthma often report nightmares involving strangling or drowning (Monday, Montplaisir & Malo, 1987). The prevalence of asthma is estimated to be about 7 percent of the population, occurring mostly in persons younger than 17 years of age. As many as 80 percent show substantial or complete remission of symptoms as they grow older (Mrazek, 1993).

Pollens or other substances to which a person

with asthma is allergic can produce attacks, but sometimes psychological factors seem more important. Emotional arousal has been found to be associated with decreased size of the airways of the lung (Isenberg, Lehrer & Hochron, 1992). In one study (Fritz, Rubenstein & Lewiston, 1987), psychological factors such as depression and family conflicts were found to be the main causes in 18 percent of individuals with this disorder. Among children with asthma, deaths have been associated with family dysfunction, poor adherence to medication, and poor self-care (Lehrer, Sargunaraj & Hochron, 1992). Asthma attacks can also serve to influence family members, as indicated in the following case:

Kathy was a 15-year-old girl whose asthma was diagnosed at age six. . . . Early on, emotional reactions were identified as important triggers to her episodes, along with exercise and infections. . . . Her biologic parents had a stormy relationship that included the father's physical abuse of the mother during their frequent drinking bouts, numerous separations, and financial insecurity. . . . Her asthma also served to interrupt parental fights, and Kathy consciously used her asthma in her role as a peacemaker. . . . The asthmatic symptoms were . . . associated with helplessness and extreme anxiety. (Fritz, Rubenstein & Lewiston, 1987, pp. 253–254)

Although this case illustrates the interplay of psychological factors, physical factors such as infections can also play a major role in asthma. In most cases, however, physical and psychological causes interact. Self-management procedures can be effective in treating asthma. The program devised by Vazquez and Buceta (1993) involves giving the client and family members information about the disease, helping them identify and avoid situations associated with the attacks, and training in relaxation.

Perspectives on Etiology

Why does stress produce a physical disorder in some people but not in others? If a disorder does develop under emotional duress, what determines which psychophysiological illness it will be? Innate, developmental, and acquired characteristics certainly interact, but the nature and contribution of each are not well understood. In this section we discuss different perspectives on cause—none of which adequately accounts for all the factors involved.

Psychodynamic Perspective Psychoanalysts have developed several formulations to explain physical disorders associated with psychological factors. According to these formulations, each type of psychophysiological disorder is produced by a specific form of unconscious conflict.

Alexander (1950) believed that an early unresolved childhood conflict produces an emotional response that is reactivated in adulthood. For example, the inhibition of aggressive feelings may produce hypertension or other cardiovascular disorders. According to this hypothesis, aggression and dependency needs are the basis for most of the psychophysiological disorders. The expression of dependency needs increases activity of the parasympathetic division of the autonomic nervous system. Chronic activation of this division produces such disorders as peptic ulcers, diarrhea, and colitis. If feelings of anger predominate, the energy-expending sympathetic nervous system is activated, which may result in hypertension, migraine headaches, or arthritis.

A list of the unconscious complexes associated with certain disorders is given in Table 8.2. Although Alexander's theory is impressive in breadth and specificity, his propositions have not been experimentally supported.

Biological Perspective Some evidence points to a genetic base for the development of psychophysiological disorders. For example, ulcers are twice as common in siblings of ulcer patients as in siblings of nonpatients. Additionally, people with type O blood are more likely to develop duodenal ulcers than are people with type A, B, or AB blood (Eisenberg, 1978). A modest significant correlation on cardiovascular reactivity has been found between monozygotic (identical) twins. Presumably a greater reactivity could contribute to the development of hypertension and coronary heart disease (Smith et al., 1987). Children with one asthmatic parent have a 20 percent chance of developing asthma. The probability increases to 50 percent with two asthmatic parents (Mrazek, 1993).

In addition, three other biological explanations for psychophysiological disorders have been suggested: somatic weakness, autonomic response specificity, and general adaptation syndrome.

The *somatic weakness hypothesis* is a commonsense explanation for the development of particular

Table 8.2

A Psychodynamic Etiology: The Unconscious Correlates to Certain Physical Disorders

Disorder	Unconscious Correlates
Peptic ulcer	A conflict over dependency needs produces guilt and hostility. The person unsuccessfully attempts to sublimate these aggressive tendencies through achievement. Unsatisfied oral needs produce overactivity of gastrointestinal function, which produces an ulcer.
Asthma	The person has an unresolved dependency on his or her mother, who is perceived as cold; fears separation; or needs to be protected. The person feels guilty about the dependency needs. Instead of crying, he or she develops a wheeze that can develop into respiratory disorder.
Hypertension	The person experiences a struggle against unconscious hostile impulses and fluctuates from excessive control to outbursts of aggression. Repressing these hostile feelings leads to chronic blood pressure elevation.
Arthritis	The person inhibits hostile impulses or has experienced parental restrictions of freedom of movement. Developing arthritis allows the individual to avoid physically expressing aggression.

Source: Adapted from Alexander, 1950.

psychophysiological disorders. This view suggests that congenital factors or a vulnerability acquired through physical trauma or illness may predispose a particular organ to develop irregularities or become weakened structurally by stressors. Therefore, which particular physiological disorder develops is determined by which system is the "weakest link" in the body (Hovanitz & Wander, 1990). For example, 80 percent of the asthmatics in one study had previous respiratory infections, compared with only 30 percent of the nonasthmatic controls (Rees, 1964). The infection may have weakened the respiratory system and made it more vulnerable to the development of asthma. Logical as it seems, the somatic weakness hypothesis is difficult to validate because it is not yet possible to measure the relative strengths of the different physical systems in the human body before an organ weakness appears.

Closely related to the somatic weakness hypothesis is the concept of *autonomic response specificity:* each person has a unique physiological reaction to all types of stressful situations. This specific response is largely inherited, but it can be affected by a previously acquired vulnerability (Steptoe, 1991). Moreover, it has been demonstrated experimentally: college students subjected to a variety of stressors (from cold water to tough mathematics problems) tended to show stable and consistent idiosyncratic patterns of autonomic activity in the different stress-producing conditions. That is, a person who showed a rise in blood pressure when reacting to one type of stressor also showed a similar reaction to other types of stressors (Lacey, Bateman & Van Lehn, 1953). Similar consistency was found in people who suffered migraine headaches, but not in a control group of people who did not get migraines (Cohen, Richels & McArthur, 1978). The suggestion that these physiological responses are innate is supported by researchers who observed that distinctive autonomic behavior patterns in infants tended to persist throughout early childhood (Thomas, Chess & Birch, 1968).

The general adaptation syndrome, consisting of an alarm stage, a resistance stage, and an exhaustion stage, was discussed earlier in the chapter. According to Selye (1956), continued stress after the final stage may result in diseases of adaptation such as ulcers or hypertension. Unfortunately, this formulation is very general and does not explain why these diseases do not occur in all people experiencing long-term stress. Nor does it specify which psychophysiological disorder will develop. Combining this theory with the somatic weakness or autonomic response specificity hypotheses may be one way to deal with such conceptual problems.

The Behavioral Perspective   As noted, classical conditioning may be involved in the psychophysiological disorders. The conditioning of neutral stimuli can elicit or activate a physiological response through generalization, as discussed in Chapter 4. Probably, the greater the number of stimuli that can produce a

specific physical reaction, the more likely a chronic condition will develop. Psychophysiological reactions can generalize to words or thoughts. For example, the bronchial reactions of forty patients with asthma were compared with those of a normal control group. The patients were told that they were being exposed to different concentrations of substances to which they were allergic, when in fact they were exposed to only neutral saline solution. Nearly half (nineteen) of the patients with asthma displayed bronchial constriction (a symptom of asthmatic attacks), and twelve developed full-blown asthma attacks. None of the controls showed any of these symptoms (Luparello et al., 1968). The experimenters hypothesized that principles of classical conditioning could account for their finding. The thought of inhaling an allergic substance had become a conditioned stimulus capable of inducing asthmatic symptoms or attacks. In a review of twenty studies involving 427 persons with asthma, more than one-third of the persons with asthma were found to be "reactors," that is, they showed significant bronchial effects following suggestion (Isenberg, Lehrer & Hochron, 1992).

The classical conditioning position alone cannot, however, account for the cause of the disorders discussed in this section. Physiological reactions must occur before other stimuli can be conditioned to them, or before generalization can occur. Hence classical conditioning may explain the continuation or increased severity of a disorder, but not its origin.

Although theorists first believed that the autonomic nervous system is not under operant control, involuntary processes such as heart rate, blood pressure, and a variety of other functions can be influenced by reinforcement. These findings have important implications for the origin and the treatment of psychophysiological disorders.

Evidence that operant learning influences visceral (digestive tract) responses supports the possibility that disorders involving the autonomic nervous system can be learned (Miller, 1974). A child who fears school, for example, may show a variety of physiological responses (increase in heart rate, changes in blood pressure, constriction of the bronchioles, and increased gastrointestinal activity). The parents' attention to a particular physical symptom can reinforce the appearance of that symptom. Thus expressing sympathy or allowing a child to stay home to recover from a stomachache might contribute to the development of gastrointestinal disorders such as ulcers, colitis, or diarrhea.

The precise role of operant conditioning in the cause of the disorders discussed here is still not clear. There is support for the contention that autonomic processes can be altered through reinforcement. But there is also controversy about the magnitude of the changes that are possible.

Sociocultural Perspectives In a study of Japanese persons living in Japan, Hawaii, and California, researchers found that Japanese living in California had the highest mortality rate from coronary heart disease and that those living in Japan had the lowest. This difference was not accounted for by differences in the risk factors for CHD discussed earlier. In trying to decide what was responsible for the variation in mortality rates, the researchers compared Japanese immigrants who had maintained a traditional lifestyle with those who had acculturated (adopted the habits and attitudes prevalent in their new home). The CHD rate for acculturated Japanese was five times greater than that for Japanese who had retained their traditional values (Marmot & Syme, 1976). Perhaps breaking close social and community ties, which is part of the acculturation process, caused the acculturated Japanese to become more vulnerable to the disease.

TREATMENT OF PSYCHOPHYSIOLOGICAL DISORDERS

Treatment programs for psychophysiological disorders generally consist of both medical treatment for the physical symptoms and conditions and psychological therapy to eliminate stress and anxiety. Behavioral medicine has provided an array of psychological approaches to these disorders, with mainly positive results. Among these are stress management and anxiety management programs, which usually include either relaxation training or biofeedback. The concept of combined therapies is illustrated in the following case:

Jerry R. is a 33-year-old male who has always taken pride in the vigor with which he attacks everything he does. He worries about keeping slim, so he exercises at a health spa three nights a week. He was shocked to discover, during a routine physical exam, that he has borderline high blood pressure.

His physician recommends that he take steps to lower his blood pressure by reducing his intake of salt, caffeine, and alcohol. Because coronary heart disease runs in Jerry's family, the physician also recommends that Jerry decrease his cholesterol intake by reducing the amount of eggs, saturated fats, and whole milk in his diet. He commends Jerry for having given up smoking five months ago.

Finally, Jerry is urged to become active in a stress management program geared toward lowering his blood pressure and preventing coronary heart disease. Although the effectiveness of these programs is somewhat controversial, Jerry's physician feels that Jerry has more to gain than he has to lose by participating in a course of biofeedback and relaxation training.

The success of combined treatment programs has suggested that the psychological approach to the treatment of certain physical disorders is more than a passing fad (Bennett & Carroll, 1990; Bennett et al., 1991; Davison et al., 1991; Shahidi & Salmon, 1992).

In this section, we discuss relaxation training, biofeedback, and cognitive-behavioral interventions, which are emerging as the primary stress management techniques of behavioral medicine. They are used in treating all the psychophysiological disorders described in this chapter.

Relaxation Training

Current **relaxation training** programs are typically modeled after Jacobson's (1938, 1967) progressive relaxation training. Imagine that you are a patient who is beginning the training. You are instructed to concentrate on one set of muscles at a time—first tensing them and then relaxing them. First you clench your fists as tightly as possible for approximately ten seconds, and then release them. As you release your tightened muscles, you are asked to focus on the sensation of warmth and looseness in your hands. You practice this tightening and relaxing cycle several times before proceeding to the next muscle group in your lower arms. After each muscle group has received individual attention in tensing and relaxing, the trainer asks you to tighten and then relax your entire body. The emphasis throughout the procedure is on the contrast between the feelings produced dur-

In biofeedback training, clients can get instant-by-instant information about their heart rate, blood pressure, gastrointestinal activity, muscle tension, or other physical functions. Through operant conditioning techniques, they learn to control their physiological functions.

ing tensing and those produced during relaxing. For a novice, the entire exercise lasts about thirty minutes.

With practice, you eventually learn to relax the muscles without first having to tense them. You can then use the technique to relax at almost any time during the day, even when only a few moments are available for the exercise.

Biofeedback

In **biofeedback training,** the client is taught to *voluntarily* control a physiological function. During training, the client is provided with second-by-second information (feedback) regarding the activity of the organ or function of interest. For someone suffering from high blood pressure, for example, the biofeedback training would focus on developing the patient's ability to lower blood pressure. The feedback might be actual blood pressure readings presented visually on a screen or some auditory representation of blood pressure presented over a set of headphones. The biofeedback device enables the patient to learn his or her own idiosyncratic method for controlling the particular physiological function. Eventually the patient learns to use that method without benefit of the feedback device.

A 23-year-old male patient was found to have a resting heart rate that varied between 95 and 120 beats

per minute. He reported that his symptoms first appeared during his last year in high school, when his episodes of tachycardia were associated with apprehension over exams. The patient came into treatment concerned that his high heart rate might lead to a serious cardiac condition.

The treatment consisted of eight sessions of biofeedback training. The patient's heart rate was monitored, and he was provided with both a visual and an auditory feedback signal. After the treatment period, his heart rate had stabilized and was within normal limits. One year later, his heart rate averaged 73 beats per minute. The patient reported that he had learned to control his heart rate during stressful situations such as going for a job interview, both relaxing and concentrating on reducing the heart rate. (Janssen, 1983)

Biofeedback is essentially an operant conditioning technique in which the feedback serves as reinforcement. It has been used to help people lower their heart rate and decrease their blood pressure (Shahidi & Salmon, 1992), treat tension headaches (Hovanitz & Wander, 1990), reduce muscle tension (Gamble & Elder, 1983), and redirect blood flow (Reading & Mohr, 1976). Patients with duodenal ulcers have been taught to decrease the level of gastric acid secretion by providing feedback on stomach acidity (Welgan, 1974). Biofeedback and verbal reinforcement were used to help children with asthma control their respiratory functioning (Kahn, Staerk & Bonk, 1974). In an interesting marriage of operant and classical conditioning techniques, the children were also trained to control bronchial constriction by dilating their bronchi when exposed to previously conditioned stimuli.

Cognitive-Behavioral Interventions

More stress management programs are also including a cognitive-behavioral component that often involves self-instructional techniques and cognitive restructuring. In one study (Bennett et al., 1991), Type A persons with hypertension were taught how to evaluate and change the impact of stressors and to understand how their Type A behavior pattern contributes to the hypertension. They learned to change their thoughts to reduce their emotional reactions. This approach seems to augment the effectiveness of other components in stress management in dealing with hypertension (Davison et al., 1991).

Certainly both psychological and biological processes are involved in all diseases. In some disorders and in some people, biological factors have the primary influence, whereas in others, psychological factors predominate. Because so many variables are involved, the question of which person will develop a psychophysiological disorder and under what conditions is difficult to answer.

Although much is known about the psychophysiological disorders, a great deal is still to be learned. Psychologists involved in behavioral medicine are seeking to decrease a person's vulnerability to physical problems by suggesting changes in lifestyle, attitudes, and perceptions. Attention is also directed toward altering the course of an illness after it has occurred. The field of behavioral medicine will continue to receive greater attention from psychologists. We are only beginning to understand the relationship between psychological factors and physical illnesses.

SUMMARY

1. The sudden death syndrome is an extreme example of the effect of psychological factors on physical health. In sudden death, stress is thought to produce bradycardia, tachycardia, or arrhythmia and kill susceptible people.

2. Formerly, the term *psychosomatic* was used to categorize a number of specific physical disorders that stem from psychological problems. This usage fostered the incorrect view that only certain physical conditions have significant psychological components. Now, the DSM-IV category of psychological factors affecting medical condition recognizes the belief that both physical and psychological factors may be involved in any illness. The field of behavioral medicine represents this new direction in controlling disease.

3. Models explaining the impact of stress include the general adaptation syndrome, which examines the impact of stressors on physical functioning; the life change model which is based on the view that life changes have a detrimental impact on health; and the transaction model, which stresses the importance of subjective interpretation and stress.

4. Immunological functioning seems to be affected by physical and psychological stress. A variety of factors such as anxiety, divorce, and bereavement can produce poor immunological responses. Some research supports the suggestion that psychological stress can influence the initiation and course of certain infectious diseases. Although stress decreases the ability of animals to reject injected cancer cells, whether psychological variables influence the development of cancer in human beings is not known.

5. Coronary heart disease (CHD) and essential hypertension are the most pervasive cardiovascular disorders. The incidence of CHD is influenced by social factors, personality, and lifestyle as well as such risk factors as smoking and inactivity. Hypertension is related to the emotions and how they are expressed, especially anger.

6. Peptic ulcers—duodenal or gastric—afflict 10 percent of all people at some point in their lives. Along with stress, oversecretion of stomach acid and insufficient secretion of protective mucus apparently predispose people to ulcers.

7. Headaches are among the most common psychophysiological complaints. Migraine headaches involve the constriction and then the dilation of blood vessels in the brain. Tension headaches are thought to be caused by contraction of the neck and scalp muscles, which results in vascular constriction. These headaches can also occur in the absence of detectable tension. Cluster headaches are excruciating and occur on one side of the head near the eye.

8. Asthma attacks result from constriction of the airways in the lungs. Breathing is extremely difficult during the attacks, and acute anxiety may worsen the situation. Suppressed aggression and conditioning have been suggested as causes.

9. Etiological theories must be able to explain why some people develop a physical disorder under stress, whereas others do not, and what determines which psychophysiological illness develops. According to the psychodynamic perspective, the particular illness that is manifested depends on the stage of psychosexual development and the type of unresolved unconscious conflict involved. Biological explanations focus on somatic weakness and response specificity. The behavioral perspective emphasizes the importance of classical and operant conditioning in acquiring or maintaining these disorders.

10. Psychophysiological disorders are generally treated through stress management or anxiety management programs, combined with medical treatment for physical symptoms or conditions. Relaxation

training and biofeedback training, which help the client learn to control muscular or organic functioning, are usually a part of such programs. Cognitive-behavioral interventions, which involve changing anxiety-arousing thoughts, have also been useful.

KEY TERMS

asthma A respiratory disorder characterized by attacks in which breathing becomes extremely difficult due to constriction of the airways in the lungs

behavioral medicine A number of disciplines that study social, psychological, and lifestyle influences on health

biofeedback training A therapeutic technique in which the person is taught to voluntarily control a particular physiological function such as heart rate or blood pressure

cluster headache Excruciating headache that tends to occur on one side of the head near the eye

coronary heart disease (CHD) A cardiovascular disease in which the flow of blood and oxygen to the heart is restricted by a narrowing of the arteries in or near the heart

decompensation Loss of the ability to deal successfully with stress, resulting in more primitive means of coping

essential hypertension High blood pressure, usually with no known organic cause

general adaptation syndrome (GAS) A model for understanding the body's physical and psychological reaction to biological stressors

hardiness A concept developed by Kobasa and Maddi that refers to a person's ability to deal well with stress

life change model Hypothesis that all life changes can act as stressors

migraine headache Severe headache resulting from constriction and then dilation of the cerebral blood vessels

peptic ulcer An open sore within the digestive system

psychophysiological disorder A physical disorder that has a strong psychological basis or component

relaxation training A therapeutic technique in which the person acquires the ability to relax the muscles of the body in almost any circumstances

stress An internal response to an external stimulus (stressor)

stressor A physical or psychological demand placed on a person by some external event or situation

sudden death syndrome Unexpected abrupt death that may be brought on by stress. In most cases, there is an underlying coronary condition.

tension headache A headache that is thought to be produced by prolonged contraction of the scalp and neck muscles

transaction model of stress Hypothesis that a person's perception of a stressor mediates its impact

CHAPTER 9

Personality Disorders and Impulse Control Disorders

Although this chapter discusses personality disorders and impulse control disorders, the two are separate and distinct categories in DSM-IV. We are discussing them together because of convenience rather than because of any relationship between these two categories of disorders. As in other disorders, those involving personality or impulse control are associated with a person's subjective distress or impaired functioning. Some of these disorders (such as antisocial personality and pyromania) may have detrimental consequences for society.

THE PERSONALITY DISORDERS

Personality disorders are characterized by behavioral patterns that are inflexible and maladaptive. People with these disorders consistently show personality traits that cause personal and social difficulties, distress, or problems functioning. These people also have temperamental deficiencies or aberrations, rigidity in dealing with life problems, and defective perceptions of self and others.

In spite of all this, people with personality disorders often function well enough to get along without aid from others. For this reason, and because these people rarely seek help from mental health professionals, the incidence of personality disorders has been difficult to ascertain. Available statistics indicate that personality disorders account for about 5 to 15 percent of admissions to hospitals and outpatient clinics.

Diagnosing personality disorders is difficult for three primary reasons. First, many people show traits that characterize personality disorders—for example, suspiciousness, dependency, sensitivity to rejection, or compulsiveness. In fact, we all exhibit some of these traits to varying degrees and at various times. For this reason, many investigators (such as Wiggins & Pincus, 1989) prefer to see personality disorders as reflecting the extremes of underlying dimensions of normal personality traits. They argue that the dimensions of extraversion (dominance), agreeableness (nurturance), neuroticism, conscientiousness, and openness to experience may be used to describe personality disorders. Because people differ on the extent to which a trait is possessed, it is problematic for a clinician to know when a client exhibits enough of a trait to be considered as a symptom of a disorder. DSM-IV criteria for a diagnosis is based on a categorical model in which a disorder is present if "enough of" certain symptoms or traits are exhibited and is not present if "not enough of" the symptoms are demonstrated (Task Force on DSM-IV, 1991). Thus, according to DSM, people either have a personality disorder or they do not. In reality, people may "have" a personality disorder to varying degrees. In addition, personality patterns may not be stable. Many investigators have consistently argued that personality characteristics exhibited in one situation may vary or be unstable across situations (Mischel, 1968).

Second, because symptoms of one personality disorder may also be symptoms of other disorders, differential diagnosis is often a problem. Using DSM-III-R criteria, Morey (1988) found that many people diagnosed as having one type of personality disorder also met the criteria for other personality disorders. Moreover, people can have more than one type of personality disorder, so the problems in diagnosing these disorders are formidable. Investigators (Widiger & Shea, 1991) have also found that although the distinction between personality disorders and other disorders is valid, many individuals have symptoms that do not neatly fall into a particular disorder and that overlap with different disorders.

Third, clinicians rendering a diagnosis may not adhere to diagnostic criteria. In one study, clinicians were asked to indicate for their clients diagnosed with personality disorders the symptoms exhibited by these clients. In many cases, the diagnoses rendered by clinicians were incongruent with the symptom patterns required by the DSM criteria for diagnosing the personality disorders (Morey & Ochoa, 1989). For these reasons, the diagnosis of personality disorders has been especially problematic.

DSM-IV asserts that a number of traits, not just one, must be considered in determining whether a disorder exists. For example, to diagnose dependent personality disorder, the clinician must find a constellation of characteristics (such as the inability to make decisions independently and the subordination of one's own needs). Other criteria or factors must also be considered: the personality pattern (1) must characterize the person's current as well as long-term functioning, (2) must not be limited to episodes of illness, and (3) must either notably impair social or occupational functioning or cause subjective distress. Thus a person who is temporarily dependent because of an illness would not be diagnosed as having a dependent personality.

The signs of a personality disorder usually become evident during adolescence. In some cases, a person with a personality disorder may have had a similar childhood disorder. For example, it is common to find that a person diagnosed as having schizoid personality disorder was previously diagnosed as having schizoid disorder of childhood. When the features of certain childhood disorders persist into adulthood (that is, beyond age eighteen), the diagnosis may be changed to a personality disorder.

In the diagnostic scheme of DSM-IV, personality disorders are recorded on Axis II. A person may receive diagnoses on both Axis I and Axis II. For example, a person with a personality disorder may also be diagnosed as schizophrenic or as alcohol dependent (Axis I disorders). Usually, people with personality disorders are hospitalized only when a second, superimposed disorder so impairs social functioning that they require inpatient care. The rationale for having two axes for mental disorders is that Axis II disorders generally begin in childhood or adolescence and persist in a stable form into adulthood. Axis I disorders usually fail to show this early feature with stable characteristics.

DSM-IV lists ten specific personality disorders and groups them into three clusters, depending on whether they may be characterized by (1) odd or eccentric behaviors; (2) dramatic, emotional, or erratic behaviors; or (3) anxious or fearful behaviors. The clustering of these disorders is based more on convenience than on actual similarity of symptoms or cause. Clustering and categorizing the disorders also mask dimensional aspects. That is, the task of categorizing often fails to reveal differences in the degree to which people possess certain characteristics. In any event, first we shall discuss each of the ten personality disorders rather briefly. Then we will discuss one of them—the *antisocial personality disorder*—in more detail, primarily because more information is available about this disorder. Other proposed personality disorders are discussed in Focus 9.1.

Disorders Characterized by Odd or Eccentric Behaviors

Three personality disorders are included in this cluster: paranoid personality, schizoid personality, and schizotypal personality. These and two other clusters of personality disorders discussed in this chapter are shown in the disorders chart on page 258.

Paranoid Personality Disorder People with **paranoid personality disorder** show pervasive distrust and suspiciousness of others and interpret their motives as being malevolent. Many question the loyalty or trustworthiness of others, persistently bear grudges, or are suspicious of the fidelity of their spouse. They may demonstrate restricted affect (that is, aloofness and lack of emotion) and tend to be rigid and preoccupied with unfounded beliefs that stem from their suspicions and sensitivity. These beliefs are extremely resistant to change. Here is an example:

> Ralph and Ann married after knowing each other for two months. The first year of their marriage was relatively happy, although Ralph tended to be domineering and very protective of his wife. Ann had always known that Ralph was a jealous person who demanded a great deal of attention. She was initially pleased that her husband was concerned about how other men looked at her; she felt that it showed Ralph really cared for her. It soon became clear, however, that his jealousy was excessive. One day when she came home from shopping later than usual, Ralph exploded. He demanded an explanation but did not accept Ann's, which was that she stopped to talk with a neighbor. Ralph told her that he wanted her to be home when he returned from work—always. Believing him to be in a bad mood, Ann said nothing. Later, she found out that Ralph had called the neighbor to confirm her story.

The situation progressively worsened. Ralph began to leave work early to be with his wife. He said that business was slow, and they could spend more time together. Whenever the phone rang, Ralph insisted on answering it himself. Wrong numbers and male callers took on special significance for him; he felt they must be trying to call Ann. Ann found it difficult to discuss the matter with Ralph. He was always quick to take the offensive, and he expressed very little sympathy or understanding toward her.

Arguments between the two increased. Ann could not convince him that she had no interest in other men. At one point, she threatened to leave him; Ralph told her he would never let her go and threatened her with physical harm. He then produced a diary, which detailed his account of her behaviors. Ann was shocked to find out how many of her behaviors and the behaviors of others Ralph had interpreted as signs of infidelity. Her smiles or remarks to other men on the telephone or in stores were seen as secret messages inviting sexual contact; her neighbor was perceived as acting as a go-between for Ann and other men; dressing in a particularly attractive manner meant that she was going to see another man or that she was flirting with others. After reading the diary, which went back to the day they met, Ann realized that Ralph was disturbed, something she had not been willing to admit to herself before. Failing to convince her husband that he needed help, Ann went alone to a psychologist.

Ralph's suspicions regarding his wife's fidelity were obviously unjustified. Nothing that Ann did implicated her with other men. Yet Ralph persisted in his pathological jealousy and suspiciousness, and he took the offensive when she suggested that he was wrong in distrusting her. This behavior pattern, along with Ralph's absence of warmth and tenderness, indicates paranoid personality disorder.

As a follow-up to the case, it is interesting to note that after several weeks of treatment, Ann began to feel stronger in her relationship with Ralph. During one confrontation, in which Ralph objected to her seeing the therapist, Ann asserted that she would continue the treatment. She said that she had always been faithful to him and that his jealousy was driving their marriage apart. In a rare moment, Ralph broke down and started crying. He said that he needed her and begged her not to leave him. At this time, Ralph and Ann are each seeing a therapist for marital therapy.

Schizoid Personality Disorder **Schizoid personality disorder** is marked primarily by social isolation. People with this disorder have a long history of impairment of social functioning. They are often de-

New Personality Disorders That Have Been Proposed

From time to time, new personality disorders have been considered for inclusion in the DSM such as depressive personality disorder, negativistic personality disorder, self-defeating personality disorder, and sadistic personality disorder.

1. Depressive personality disorder involves a usual mood dominated by dejection, cheerlessness, worry, and unhappiness. The person with this disorder has low self-esteem and is pessimistic and prone to feelings of guilt. This disorder was officially considered for inclusion because depression appears to be a spectrum (wide-ranging) disorder that crosses Axis I and II.

2. Negativistic personality disorder is characterized by a pervasive pattern of passive resistance to demands for adequate social and occupational performance and of a negativistic attitude. Those with this disorder complain of being victimized or unappreciated, communicate a pervasive mix of anger and pessimism, and express envy and resentment toward those who are more fortunate. They often criticize authority and are personally discontent.

3. The essential feature of self-defeating personality disorder is a pervasive pattern of self-defeating behavior, in which the person chooses people and situations that lead to disappointment or mistreatment even when the person recognizes that other realistic options are available. The person may reject attempts of others to help; fails to accomplish tasks crucial to achieving personal objectives; and rejects opportunities for pleasure. These behaviors occur whether or not the person is depressed and do not occur only in response to, or anticipation of, being abused. Critics of this disorder question whether it should be considered as a disorder because of concern that the

scribed as being reclusive and withdrawn (Siever, 1981). Many live alone in apartments or furnished rooms and engage in solitary recreational activities such as watching television, reading, or taking walks. They tend to neither desire nor enjoy close relationships; they have few activities that provide pleasure. Because of a lack of capacity or desire to form social relationships, schizoid people are perceived by others as peculiar and aloof and therefore inadequate as dating or marital partners.

Schizoid people may have to relate to others in certain situations such as at work. But these relationships are superficial and frequently awkward. Such people tend to comply with the requests or feelings of others, perhaps in an attempt to avoid extensive involvements, conflicts, and expressions of hostility. Social isolation can be found even in their marital relationships. Spitzer and coworkers (1981) describe the case of a man who had married primarily to please his parents. After a while, his wife literally forced him to see a therapist because he was unaffectionate, lacked interest in sex, and was unwilling to participate in family activities. He was as emotionally unresponsive to members of his family as he was to his colleagues at work.

The relationship between this disorder and schizophrenia (which is described in Chapter 14) is unclear. One view is that schizoid personality is a beginning stage of schizophrenia. Another is that schizophrenia may develop as a complication of the schizoid personality disorder.

Schizotypal Personality Disorder People who have **schizotypal personality disorder** show marked social and interpersonal deficits in close relationships. They exhibit oddities in various aspects of their thinking and behavior. Many victims believe that they possess magical thinking abilities or special powers ("I can predict what people will say before they say it"), and some are subject to recurrent illusions ("I feel as if my dead father is watching me"). Speech oddities, such as frequent digression or vagueness in conversation, are often present.

The peculiarities seen in schizotypal personality

diagnosis of self-defeating personality disorder might unfairly be applied to battered women. The women could be diagnosed as having a mental disorder when they were actually victims of abuse. And women are often socialized into the roles of being more nurturant, deferential, and willing to delay gratification. These behaviors could be interpreted as being masochistic, a sign of a mental disorder (Caplan, 1984; Franklin, 1987).

4. Sadistic personality disorder is characterized by a pervasive pattern of cruel, demeaning, and aggressive behavior directed toward other people. The behavior is evident with family members, subordinates, and others but rarely with people in positions of authority or higher status. If the sadistic behavior is directed only toward one person (such as a spouse) or is exhibited for the purpose of sexual gratification (which would then be diagnosed as sexual sadism), the diagnosis would not be made. People with this disorder often come from families in which cruelty was evident or directed toward them as children. Feminists have charged that sadistic personality disorder, which mainly applies to men, was proposed in an attempt to counterbalance the creation of the category of self-defeating personality disorder, which applied primarily to women (Holden, 1986).

The fact that new disorders are being proposed and that some official disorders may be revised or eliminated is encouraging. It demonstrates that there are attempts to continually modify the classification scheme in accordance with new research findings. Nevertheless, it should also be noted that classification schemes are not simply objective systems, free from sociopolitical controversies. The allegations over sex bias, compromises made in trying to establish new categories of disorders, and concerns over the social implications of the categories illustrate this point. As noted in Chapter 4, other considerations also entered into the development of DSM, such as the ease of application and acceptability of the categories to practitioners. Thus classification schemes need continual revision and modification to respond to changing scientific and social issues involving validity, utility, and fairness.

disorder stem from distortions or difficulties in cognition (Siever, 1981). That is, these people seem to have problems in thinking and perceiving. People with this disorder often show social isolation, hypersensitivity, and inappropriate affect (emotions). It is believed that the disorder is defined primarily by cognitive distortions, however, and that affective and interpersonal problems are secondary.

The woman described in the following case was diagnosed as having schizotypal personality disorder:

The patient is a 32-year-old unmarried, unemployed woman on welfare who complains that she feels "spacey." Her feelings of detachment have gradually become stronger and more uncomfortable. For many hours each day she feels as if she were unreal. She feels especially strange when she looks into a mirror. For many years she has felt able to read people's minds by a "kind of clairvoyance I don't understand." According to her, several people in her family apparently also have this ability. She is preoccupied by the thought that she has some special mission in life, but is not sure what it is; she is not particularly religious.

She is very self-conscious in public, often feels that people are paying special attention to her, and sometimes thinks that strangers cross the street to avoid her. She is lonely and isolated and spends much of each day lost in fantasies or watching TV soap operas. She speaks in a vague, abstract, digressive manner, generally just missing the point, but she is never incoherent. She seems shy, suspicious, and afraid she will be criticized. She has no gross loss of reality testing, such as hallucinations or delusions. She has never had treatment for emotional problems. She has had occasional jobs, but drifts away from them because of lack of interest. (Spitzer et al., 1981, pp. 95–96)

As peculiar as this patient's behaviors may seem, they are not serious enough to warrant a diagnosis of schizophrenia. Her belief that she is clairvoyant does not appear to be delusional: it is not firmly held (she admits to being confused about it), and there is no gross loss of contact with reality. Moreover, she had no previous history of psychosis. All these factors point to a personality disorder.

As is true of schizoid personality, many charac-

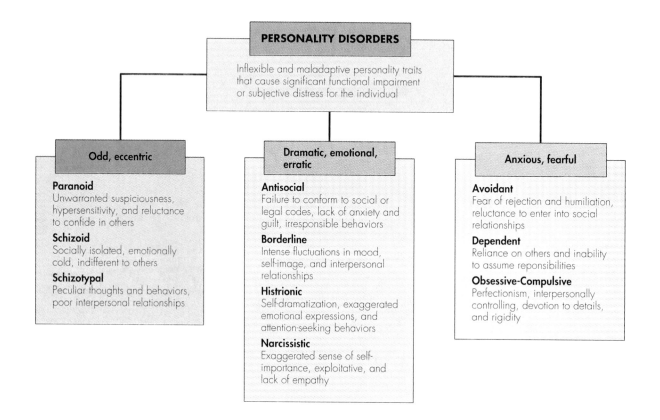

teristics of schizotypal personality disorder resemble those of schizophrenia (although in less serious form). For example, schizophrenics exhibit problems in personality characteristics, psychophysiological responses, and information-processing, and such deficits have also been observed among persons with schizotypal personality disorder (Grove et al., 1991; Lenzenweger, Cornblatt & Putnick, 1991). Some evidence is consistent with a genetic interpretation of the link between the two disorders. Kendler (1988) found a higher risk of schizotypal personality disorder among relatives of schizophrenics than among nonschizophrenic controls. In general, family, twin, and adoption studies support the genetic relationship between schizophrenia and schizotypal personality disorder.

Disorders Characterized by Dramatic, Emotional, or Erratic Behaviors

The group of disorders characterized by dramatic, emotional, or erratic bahaviors includes four person-

ality disorders: histrionic, narcissistic, antisocial, and borderline.

Histrionic Personality Disorder   The person who has **histrionic personality disorder** engages in self-dramatization, the exaggerated expression of emotions, and attention-seeking behaviors. Despite superficial warmth and charm, the histrionic person is typically shallow and egocentric. These behaviors were evident in a woman client seen by one of the authors of this book:

The woman was a 33-year-old real estate agent who entered treatment for problems involving severe depression. She had recently been told by her boyfriend that she was a self-centered and phony person. He found out that she had been dating other men, despite their understanding that neither would go out with others. The woman claimed that she never considered "going out with other men" as actual dating. Once their relationship was broken, her boyfriend refused to communicate with her. The woman then angrily called the boyfriend's employer and told him that unless the boy-

We all feel suspicious at one time or another—sometimes reasonably so and sometimes unreasonably. What differentiates normal suspiciousness from that which characterizes paranoid disorder is the degree and intensity of the belief and the rigidity with which it is held.

friend contacted her, she would commit suicide. He never did call, but instead of attempting suicide she decided to seek psychotherapy.

The woman was attractively dressed for her first therapy session. She wore a tight and clinging sweater. Several times during the session she raised her arms, supposedly to fix her hair, in a very seductive manner. Her conversation was animated and intense: when she was describing the breakup with her boyfriend, she was tearful; later, she raged over the boyfriend's failure to call her and, at one point, called him a "son of a bitch." Near the end of the session, she seemed to be upbeat and cheerful, commenting that the best therapy might be for the therapist to arrange a date for her.

None of the behaviors exhibited by this client by itself warrants a diagnosis of histrionic personality disorder. The combination of her self-dramatization, incessant drawing of attention to herself via seductive movements, angry outbursts, manipulative suicide gesture, and lack of genuineness, however, points to this disorder (which, in fact, is diagnosed far more frequently among women than among men, perhaps because of sex roles that have traditionally favored emotional expression among women). Millon and Everly (1985) believe that biogenic factors such as autonomic or emotional excitability and environmental factors such as parental reinforcement of attention-seeking behaviors among children and the existence of histrionic parental models are important in the disorder.

Narcissistic Personality Disorder The clinical characteristics of **narcissistic personality disorder** involve an exaggerated sense of self-importance and an excessive need for admiration. People with this disorder require attention and have difficulty accepting personal criticism. In conversations, they talk about themselves and show a lack of interest in others and a lack of empathy. Many have fantasies about power or influence, and they constantly overestimate their talents and importance. Owing to their sense of self-importance, narcissistic people expect to be the superior participants in all relationships. For example, they may be impatient and irate if others arrive late for a meeting, but they may frequently be late themselves and think nothing of it.

One narcissistic client reported, "I was denied promotion to chief executive by my board of directors, although my work was good, because they felt I had poor relations with my employees. When I complained to my wife, she agreed with the board, saying my relations with her and the children were equally bad. I don't understand. I know I'm more competent than all these people" (Masterson, 1981, p. ix). The client was depressed and angry about not being promoted and about the suggestion that he had difficulty in forming social relationships. His wife's confirmation of his problems further enraged him. During therapy, he was competitive and sought to devalue the observations of the therapist.

Narcissistic people may often use denial and devaluation of others to maintain an inflated self-concept (Kernberg, 1975). Denial is also used to ward off feelings of inferiority that may have devel-

Edward Spauster

FIRST PERSON

Growing up, I was always fascinated by the characters I encountered in literature, film, and television. Many seem to live exciting, enviable lives, and all were distinct individuals. Consider Scarlett O'Hara and *Dynasty*'s Alexis Carrington-Colby. Their dramatic, seductive, attention-seeking behaviors (*histrionic* is the clinical term) draw us to them; their lies, exploitation, and lack of true warmth or remorse (antisocial traits) arouse our dislike. Similarly, successful comedy often depends on humorous portrayals of personality extremes. Fonzie's narcissism, Felix Unger's compulsiveness, and Walter Mitty's flights into schizoidal fantasy are all enduring personality traits that actually define the characters who possess them.

As an adult, I continue to be intrigued by personality characteristics and, as a psychologist, I work with many patients who are considered personality disordered. They are usually quite distinct, occasionally exciting—but rarely enviable. Unable to change their behavior patterns, they repeatedly suffer the painful consequences that these patterns produce. This situation is most evident in borderline personality disorder, which is perhaps the most disturbing and most commonly treated character disorder. The following case is fairly typical.

Yolanda was transferred to the acute psychiatric unit after two days in intensive care, where she had been medically treated for an overdose of her antidepressant medication. The history gathered by the treatment team included several years of physical abuse by her parents; three prior suicide attempts; dozens of full- and part-time jobs; one marriage and three engagements; two abortions; and a cocaine habit that at times she supported through providing sex to dealers. Yolanda was twenty-four years old. During her hospitalization, Yolanda showed many sides of herself. Sometimes she was gregarious and quickly made friends with other patients. On other occasions, she grew

The symptoms of histrionic personality disorder include exaggerated emotional expression, attention-seeking or manipulative behavior, self-dramatization, egocentrism, and lack of genuineness. A person must exhibit a combination of these characteristics in order to be diagnosed as histrionic.

furious with staff and patients and sought solitude. Once, after a bitter phone conversation with her family, she was found in the bathroom scratching her wrists with an opened paper clip. Her emotions were so intense that she felt lost in them and unbearably empty. In this state, she found physical pain a relief because it reassured her of her existence.

Yolanda's constellation of symptoms, especially the mood instability, identity disturbance, uncontrolled anger, and self-destructive behaviors are typical of borderline personality disorder. It's often frightening. The reality of Yolanda's life is that she often considers suicide. Because she depends on others to provide boundaries for her emotions and behavior, she is extremely sensitive to the slightest shift in others, including me, her therapist. Her

anger, fueled by years of abuse, is always expressed as rage, and frightens both her and others. I've been its target more than once.

At other times, her attachment to me is so strong that she finds her own fragile boundaries breaking down. Soon after revealing to me that she had been sexually abused fifteen years earlier, Yolanda became afraid that I would be killed by her uncle, the abuser. He had silenced Yolanda by threatening to hurt her parents if she told anyone about the abuse. The fear produced by her disclosure was as real in our sessions as it was years ago. She found it very difficult to believe that my bout of flu was not some repercussion for her telling me about the abuse.

Although challenging and exciting, working with borderlines is also tiring. I function best when I

limit the number of borderline clients in my practice and have a colleague available for consultation. Maintaining an accepting and consistent therapeutic stance in the face of borderline chaos is not easy, but necessary. A therapeutic relationship that is stable, sets appropriate boundaries, survives in spite of intense emotions, and fosters hope becomes, in a very small way, a break in the pattern. And for disorders of personality, changing patterns is the only way out.

Edward Spauster is a staff psychologist on the Adult Services Unit at the Hollywood Hospital, a private psychiatric hospital in Queens, New York.

oped from early childhood (Marmar, 1988). These are the tools with which they take the offensive in response to criticism.

Antisocial Personality Disorder Chronic antisocial behavioral patterns such as irresponsibility, lying, using other people, and aggressive sexual behavior indicate **antisocial personality disorder**. People with this disorder fail to conform to social norms or legal prescriptions but show little guilt for their wrongdoing. Their relationships with others are superficial and fleeting, and little loyalty is involved. Antisocial personality disorder, which is far more prevalent among men than among women, is discussed in greater detail later in this chapter.

Borderline Personality Disorder Contrary to popular belief, **borderline personality disorder** is not a condition that is midway between, or that fluctuates between, neurotic and psychotic disturbances, as originally believed (Gallahorn, 1981). It is a disorder in and of itself, manifested by impulsiveness and by intense fluctuations in mood, self-image, and interpersonal relationships. Persons with this disorder often have chronic feelings of emptiness, recurrent suicidal behaviors or gestures, and unstable and intense interpersonal relationships. People with borderline personality disorder may be quite friendly one day and quite hostile the next day. Many perceived their early childhood as having malevolent others—others who were hostile or physically violent (Nigg et al., 1992). Although no single feature defines the disorder, its true essence can be captured in the capriciousness of behaviors and the lability of moods (Millon & Everly, 1985). The First Person narrative in this chapter and the following example illustrate the many facets of borderline personality disorder.

Bryan was a 23-year-old graduate student majoring in sociology at a prestigious university. He was active in student government and was viewed as charismatic, articulate, and sociable. When he met other students for the first time, he could often convince them to participate in the campus activities that interested him. Women were quite attracted to him because of his charm and self-disclosing nature. They described him as being exciting, intense, and different from other men. Bryan could form close relationships with others very quickly.

Bryan, however, could not maintain his social relationships. Sometimes he would have a brief but intense affair with a woman and then abruptly and angrily ask himself what he ever saw in her. At other times, the woman would reject him after a few dates, because she thought that Bryan was moody, self-centered, and demanding. He would often call his friends after midnight, because he felt lonesome, bored, and wanted to talk. He gave little thought to the inconvenience he was causing. Once he organized a group of students to protest the inadequate student parking the university provided. The morning of the planned protest demonstration, he announced that he no longer supported the effort. He said that he was not in the right mood for the protest, much to the consternation of his followers, who had spent weeks preparing for the event. Bryan's intense but brief relationships, the marked and continual shifts in moods, and boredom with others in spite of his need for social contacts all point to borderline personality.

Masterson (1981) believes that many clients with borderline personality disorder lack purposefulness. For example, one of his clients reported, "I have such a poor self-image and so little confidence in myself that I can't decide what I want, and when I do decide, I have even more difficulty doing it" (p. ix). Masterson sees this lack as a deficiency in the borderline personality–affected person's emotional investment in the self—a lack of directedness in long-term goals.

People who have borderline personality disorder may exhibit psychotic symptoms, such as auditory hallucinations (for example, hearing imaginary voices that tell them to commit suicide), but the symptoms are usually transient. Borderline people also usually have an ego-dystonic reaction to their hallucinations (Spitzer et al., 1981). That is, they recognize their imaginary voices or other hallucinations as being unacceptable, alien, and distressful. By contrast, a person with a psychotic disorder may not realize that his or her hallucinations are pathological.

Different explanatory views have been used to conceptualize borderline personality disorder. Most of the literature on the disorder comes from those with psychodynamic perspectives. For example, Kernberg (1976) proposed the concept of object splitting: borderline people perceive others as all good or all bad at different times. This split results in emotional fluctuations toward others. Conceptions of the

disorder from other perspectives have also been proposed. From a social learning viewpoint, Millon (1981) argued that borderline personality is caused by a faulty self-identity, which affects the development of consistent goals and accomplishments. As a result persons with this disorder have difficulty coping with their own emotions and with life in general. They then develop a conflict between the need to depend on others and a need to assert themselves. Fluctuations in emotions or dysfunctions in emotional regulation are at the core of the disorder, according to Linehan (1987), who adopted a behavioral perspective. Interestingly, she speculated that biological factors may be responsible for the emotional dysregulation among borderline persons.

Cognitive-oriented approaches have also been used to conceptualize the disorder. Westen (1991) defined two core aspects of borderline personality: difficulties in regulating emotions and unstable and intense interpersonal relationships. Because these two aspects are affected by distorted or inaccurate attributions (that is, explanations for others' behaviors or attitudes), Westen's cognitive-behavioral therapy for borderline personality disorders involves changing the way clients think about and approach interpersonal situations. Another cognitive theorist, Beck, assumed that an individual's basic assumptions (that is, thoughts) play a central role in influencing perceptions, interpretations, and behavioral and emotional responses (Beck et al., 1990). Borderline individuals seem to have three basic assumptions: (1) "The world is dangerous and malevolent," (2) "I am powerless and vulnerable," and (3) "I am inherently unacceptable." Belief in these assumptions makes borderline individuals fearful, vigilant, guarded, and defensive.

These diverse theoretical perspectives of the disorder reflect the current strong interest in borderline personality. In contrast to the theoretical contributions, empirical research is sparse. Some investigators have found that borderline individuals have come from chaotic family environments, including physical and sexual abuse (Clarkin, Marziali & Munroe-Blum, 1991). Such family experiences may affect perceptions of self and others.

Again, mood changes, intense and unstable interpersonal relationships, identity problems, and other characteristics associated with borderline personality disorder can be observed in all persons to a greater or lesser extent. For this reason, and as is the case with other personality disorders, diagnosis is difficult and formulations about the causes of the disorder must rely on what we know about personality development in general, as we discuss later.

Precise figures on the prevalence of the disorder are not available. Borderline personality disorder is apparently common (American Psychiatric Association, 1987), affecting from 1 percent to 4 percent of the general population (Farmer & Nelson-Gray, 1990). Some researchers believe that the prevalence of the disorder is increasing, because our society makes it difficult for people to maintain stable relationships and a sense of identity.

Disorders Characterized by Anxious or Fearful Behaviors

The cluster of personality disorders, characterized by anxious or fearful behaviors, includes the avoidant, dependent, and obsessive-compulsive personalities.

Avoidant Personality Disorder   The essential feature of **avoidant personality disorder** is a hypersensitivity to potential rejection, humiliation, and shame. Persons with avoidant personality disorder tend to have low self-esteem and are reluctant to enter into

People with avoidant personality disorder fear and avoid social contacts because they are hypersensitive to potential rejection. They often have few close friends or confidants.

social relationships without a guarantee of uncritical acceptance by others. Unlike persons with schizoid personalities who avoid others because they lack interest, avoidant personalities do not desire to be alone. On the contrary, people with this disorder crave affection and an active social life. They want—but fear—social contacts. Their ambivalence may be reflected in different ways: for example, many avoidants engage in intellectual pursuits, wear fine clothes, or are active in the artistic community (Millon, 1981). Their need for contact and relationships is often woven into their activities. Thus an avoidant person may write poems expressing the plight of the lonely or the need for human intimacy. A primary defense mechanism is fantasy whereby wishes are fulfilled to an excessive degree in the person's imagination (Millon & Everly, 1985).

People who have avoidant personality disorder are caught in a vicious cycle: because of their preoccupation with rejection, they are constantly alert to signs of derogation or ridicule. This concern, along with many perceived instances of rejection, causes them to avoid others. Their social skills may then become deficient and invite criticism from others. In other words, their very fear of criticism may lead to criticism. Avoidants often feel depressed, anxious, angry at themselves, inferior, and inadequate.

Jenny L., an unmarried 27-year-old bank teller, shows several features of avoidant personality disorder. Although she functions adequately at work, Jenny is extremely shy, sensitive, and quiet with fellow employees. She perceives others as being insensitive and gross. If the bank manager jokes with other tellers, she feels that the manager prefers them to her.

Jenny has very few hobbies. A great deal of her time is spent watching television and eating chocolates (as a result, she is about 40 pounds overweight). Television romances are her favorite programs; after watching one, she tends to daydream about having an intense romantic relationship. Jenny L. eventually sought treatment for her depression and loneliness.

Dependent Personality Disorder   People who are unwilling to assume responsibility because of an inability to function and to make decisions independently show **dependent personality disorder**. These people lack self-confidence, and they subordinate their needs to those of the people on whom they depend. Nevertheless, their dependency and inability to make decisions may go unrecognized or may be misinterpreted by casual observers. For example, a dependent personality may allow his or her spouse to be dominant or abusive for fear that the spouse will otherwise leave. Beck and associates (1990) believe that the dependency shown is not simply a matter of being passive and unassertive, which can be treated with assertiveness training. Rather, dependent personalities have two deeply ingrained assumptions about themselves that affect their thoughts, perceptions, and behaviors. First, they see themselves as inherently inadequate and unable to cope. Second, they conclude that their course of action should be to find someone who can take care of them.

Friends may perceive dependent personalities as understanding and tolerant, without realizing that they are fearful of taking the initiative because they are afraid of disrupting their relationships. Depression, helplessness, and suppressed anger are often a part of dependent personality disorder. All are evident in the following case.

Jim is 56, a single man who was living with his 78-year-old widowed mother. When his mother recently was hospitalized for cancer, Jim decided to see a therapist. He was distraught and depressed over his mother's condition. Jim indicated that he did not know what to do. His mother had always taken care of him, and, in his view, she always knew best. Even when he was young, his mother had "worn the pants" in the family. The only time that he was away from his family was during his six years of military service. He was wounded in the Korean War, was returned to the United States, and spent a few months in a Veterans' Administration hospital. He then went to live with his mother. Because of his service-connected injury, Jim was unable to work full-time. His mother welcomed him home, and she structured all his activities.

At one point, Jim met and fell in love with a woman, but his mother disapproved of her. During a confrontation between the mother and Jim's woman friend, each demanded that Jim make a commitment to her. This was quite traumatic for Jim. His mother finally grabbed him and yelled that he must tell the other woman to go. Jim tearfully told the woman that he was sorry but she must go, and the woman angrily left.

While Jim was relating his story, it was clear to the therapist that Jim harbored some anger toward his mother, though he overtly denied any feelings of hostility. Also clear were his dependency and his inability to take responsibility. His life had always been structured, first by his mother and then by the military. His mother's illness meant that his structured world might crumble.

Obsessive-Compulsive Personality Disorder The person with **obsessive-compulsive personality disorder** shows a limited ability to express warmth or warm feelings, coupled with excessive perfectionism, stubbornness, indecision, and devotion to details. Many of these traits are found in normal people. Unlike normal people, however, obsessive-compulsive personalities show marked impairment in occupational or social functioning. Furthermore, the extent of the character rigidity is greater among people who have this disorder (Weintraub, 1981). Unlike obsessive-compulsive disorder, in which there are specific recurrent thoughts or repetitive behaviors (see Chapter 6), obsessive-compulsive personality disorder involves general traits of perfectionism, inflexibility, and attention to details.

Coworkers may find the compulsive individual too demanding, inflexible, miserly, and perfectionistic. Compulsives may actually be ineffective on the job, despite long hours of devotion. Their preoccupation with details, rules, and possible errors leads to indecision and an inability to see "the big picture."

Cecil, a third-year medical student, was referred for therapy by his graduate adviser. The adviser told the therapist that Cecil was in danger of being expelled from medical school because of his inability to get along with patients and with other students. He often berated patients for failing to follow his advice. In one instance, Cecil told a patient with a lung condition to stop smoking. When the patient indicated that he was unable to stop, Cecil angrily told the patient to go for medical treatment elsewhere; the medical center had no place for such a "weak-willed fool." Cecil's relationships with others were similarly strained. He considered many members of the faculty to be "incompetent old deadwood," and he characterized fellow graduate students as "party-goers."

The graduate adviser told the therapist that Cecil had not been expelled only because several faculty members thought that he was brilliant. Cecil studied and worked sixteen hours a day. He was extremely well read and had an extensive knowledge of medical disorders. Although he was always able to provide a careful and detailed analysis of a patient's condition, it took him a great deal of time to do so. His diagnoses tended to cover every disorder that each patient could conceivably have, on the basis of all possible combinations of symptoms.

In the next section, the etiology and treatment of antisocial personality disorder are discussed in detail. Quite limited research has been conducted on the other personality disorders so that by discussing antisocial personality disorder, we hope that appreciation can be gained of the wide range of explanatory views that can exist for these disorders in general.

ANTISOCIAL PERSONALITY DISORDER

The following case presents an example of antisocial personality disorder:

Roy W. is a seventeen-year-old high school senior who was referred by juvenile court for diagnosis and evaluation. He was arrested for stealing an automobile, something he had also done on several other occasions. The court agreed with Roy's mother that he needed evaluation and perhaps psychotherapy.

During his interview with the psychologist, Roy was articulate, relaxed, and even witty. He said that stealing was wrong but that none of the cars he stole was ever damaged. The last theft occurred because he needed transportation to a beer party (which was located only a mile from his home) and his leg was sore from playing basketball.

When Roy was asked how he got along with girls, he grinned and said that he was very outgoing and could easily "hustle" girls. He then related the following incident: "Let me tell you what happened about three months ago. I was pulling out of the school parking lot real fast and accidentally sideswiped this other car. The girl who was driving it started to scream at me. God, there was only a small dent on her fender! Anyway, we exchanged names and addresses and I apologized for the accident. When I filled out the accident report later, I said that it was her car that pulled out from the other side and hit my car. How do you like that? Anyway, when she heard about my claim that it was her fault, she had her old man call me. He said that his daughter had witnesses to the accident and that I could be arrested. Bull, he was just trying to bluff me. But I gave him a sob story—about how my parents were ready to get a divorce, how poor we were, and the trouble I would get into if they found

out about the accident. I apologized for lying and told him I could fix the dent. Luckily he never checked with my folks for the real story. Anyway, I went over to look at the girl's car. I really didn't have any idea of how to fix that old heap so I said I had to wait a couple of weeks to get some tools for the repair job. Meanwhile, I started to talk to the girl. Gave her my sob story, told her how nice I thought her folks and home were. We started to date and I took her out three times. Then one night I laid her. The crummy thing was that she told her folks about it. Can you imagine that? Anyway, her old man called and told me never to get near his precious little thing again. She's actually a slut. At least I didn't have to fix her old heap. I know I shouldn't lie but can you blame me? People make such a big thing out of nothing."

The irresponsibility, disregard for others, and disregard for societal rules and morals evident in this interview indicated to the psychologist that Roy has antisocial personality disorder. Historically, the terms *moral insanity, moral imbecility, moral defect,* and *psychopathic inferiority* have been attached to this condition. An early nineteenth-century British psychiatrist, J. C. Prichard (1837), described it this way:

The moral and active principles of the mind are strongly perverted or depraved; the power of self-government is lost or greatly impaired; and the individual is found to be incapable, not of talking or reasoning upon any subject proposed to him . . . but of conducting himself with decency and propriety in the business of life. (p. 15)

Prichard believed that the disorder was reflected not in a loss of intellectual skills but in gross violations of moral and ethical standards.

The diagnosis of antisocial personality (also referred to as *sociopathic* or *psychopathic* personality) has now lost some of its original moral overtones. Nevertheless, people with antisocial personalities do show a disregard for conventional societal rules and morals.

Cleckley's (1976) classic description of the disorder included the following characteristics:

1. *Superficial charm and good intelligence* Persons with antisocial personalities are often capable in social activities and of manipulating others.

2. *Shallow emotions and lack of empathy, guilt, or*

Ted Bundy, who was responsible for the brutal deaths of many young women, seemed to exhibit certain characteristics that are associated with antisocial personality disorder: charm, intelligence, absence of remorse, deceitfulness, and a callous disregard for legal and social norms and rules.

remorse Absent are genuine feelings of love and loyalty toward others and of concern over the detrimental consequences of their behaviors.

3. *Behaviors are indicative of little life plan or order* The actions of antisocial personalities are not well planned and are often difficult to understand or predict.

4. *Failure to learn from experiences and absence of anxiety* Although the behaviors may be punished, people with antisocial personality may repeat the same behaviors and frequently show little anxiety.

5. *Unreliability, insincerity, and untruthfulness* Persons with antisocial personalities are irresponsible and may lie or feign emotional feelings to callously manipulate others; their social relationships are usually unstable and short-lived.

Some of these characteristics are apparent in Roy's case. For example, he felt no guilt for his actions or for manipulating the girl and her family. In fact, he was quite proud of his ability to seduce the girl and avoid responsibility for the automobile repair. The ease with which Roy related his story to the psychologist demonstrated his lack of concern for those who were hurt by his behaviors. Roy showed no anxiety during the interview.

DSM-IV criteria for the disorder differ somewhat from Cleckley's description, which is based on clinical observations of various cases. For example, DSM-IV criteria do not include lack of anxiety, shallow emotions, failure to learn from past experiences, and superficial charm, but do include a history before age fifteen of failing to conform to social norms with respect to lawful behaviors, irritability and aggressiveness, impulsivity, lack of remorse, and deceitfulness. For the diagnosis to be made, the individual must be at least eighteen years of age. DSM-IV criteria, however, fail to convey the conceptual sense of the disorder that was conveyed in Cleckley's original description. Hare and colleagues (Harpur, Hare & Hakstian, 1989; Hart & Hare, 1989) have constructed a measure, the *Psychopathy Checklist— Revised (PCL—R)*, that captured some of the elements of Cleckley's description as well as those of DSM-IV. In an analysis of the features of the PCL-R, Hare, Hart, and Harpur (1991) found two factors underlying the measure. The first factor reflects a set of interpersonal and affective characteristics such as egocentricity, lack of remorse, and callousness that are similar to those proposed by Cleckley. The second factor reflects characteristics that were found to be consistent with DSM-IV criteria—namely, impulsivity, antisocial and unstable lifestyle, and irresponsibility. The distinction between Cleckley's conceptualization and DSM-IV criteria is important because sole use of DSM-IV may not capture the "personality" aspect or the underlying construct of the disorder. DSM-IV may overemphasize behavioral manifestations and criminality (Task Force on DSM-IV, 1991). Therefore, whereas this emphasis makes it easier and more reliable to render a diagnosis, it may fail to capture the essence of the disorder.

The incidence of antisocial personality disorder is estimated to be 3 percent for American men and less than 1 percent for American women (American Psychiatric Association, 1987). Estimates, however, vary from study to study. The differences may be due to differences in the sampling, diagnostic, and methodological procedures used. Goodwin and Guze (1984) concluded that antisocial personality is fairly common, and probably increasingly so. It is much more frequent in urban than in rural environments and in lower socioeconomic groups.

A distinction should be made between the behavior patterns associated with antisocial personality disorder and behaviors involving social protest or criminal lifestyles. People who engage in civil disobedience or violate the conventions of society or its laws as a form of protest are not as a rule persons with antisocial personalities. Such people can be quite capable of forming meaningful interpersonal relationships and of experiencing guilt. They may perceive their violations of rules and norms as acts performed for the greater good. Similarly, engaging in delinquent or adult criminal behavior is not a necessary or sufficient condition for diagnosing antisocial personality. Although many convicted criminals have been found to have antisocial characteristics, many others do not. They may come from a subculture that encourages and reinforces criminal activity; hence, in perpetrating such acts they are adhering to group mores and codes of conduct. As just mentioned, DSM-IV criteria tend to emphasize criminality but the appropriateness of this emphasis is being questioned. Finally, a distinction is also made between primary and secondary psychopaths. A *primary psychopath* apparently lacks anxiety or guilt over antisocial behaviors but a *secondary psychopath* reports guilt over such behaviors.

People with antisocial personalities are a difficult population to study because they do not voluntarily seek treatment. Consequently, researchers often seek psychopathic subjects in prison populations, which presumably harbor a relatively large proportion of psychopaths. But now a different problem arises: researchers cannot know whether the psychopaths in prison are representative of the nonprison psychopathic population as well.

Using an ingenious research approach, Widom (1977) tried to find a number of noninstitutionalized psychopaths to discover whether their characteristics matched psychopaths typically found in prison groups. She placed the following advertisement in a major Boston counterculture newspaper:

> *Are You Adventurous?* Psychologist studying adventurous, carefree people who've led exciting, impulsive lives. If you're the kind of person who'd do almost anything for a dare and want to participate in a paid experiment, send name, address, phone, and short biography proving how interesting you are.

Widom reasoned that such an ad might appeal to individuals with antisocial personalities. Of the seventy-three people who responded, twenty-eight met her criteria for antisocial personality and were studied further. On the basis of psychological tests and interviews, Widom concluded that the noninstitutionalized people she studied did have characteristics similar to those associated with antisocial personality among prisoners. But her respondents tended to have a higher level of education and, although they were often arrested, they were convicted of crimes infrequently.

Explanations of Antisocial Personality Disorder

Antisocial people are apparently unable to learn from past experience. They continue to engage in antisocial behaviors despite criticism and scorn from others, the disruption of close personal relationships, and frequent encounters with legal authorities. They often sincerely promise to change their lives and make amends, only to return to antisocial behavior soon after. A variety of theories emphasize the inability of persons with antisocial personalities to learn appropriate social and ethical behaviors. The reasons given for this defect, however, are quite diverse.

Theories of the etiology of antisocial personality

vary with theoretical orientation and with the theorist's definition of antisocial personality. We will examine a number of the most frequently cited constructs from the psychoanalytic, family and socialization, biogenic, and learning perspectives.

Psychoanalytic Theory According to one psychoanalytic approach, the absence of guilt and the frequent violation of moral and ethical standards in psychopaths are the result of faulty superego development (Fenichel, 1945). Id impulses are more likely to be expressed when the weakened superego cannot exert very much influence. People exhibiting antisocial behavior patterns presumably did not adequately identify with their parents. Frustration, rejection, or inconsistent treatment resulted in fixation at an early stage of development.

Family and Socialization Theories Some theorists believe that relationships within the family—the primary agent of socialization—are paramount in the development of antisocial patterns (McCord & McCord, 1964). In a review of factors that predict delinquency and antisocial behaviors in children, Loeber (1990) found that socioeconomic status of the family was a weak predictor whereas family factors such as poor parental supervision and involvement were good predictors. Rejection or deprivation by one or both parents may provide little opportunity to learn socially appropriate behaviors or may diminish the value of people as socially reinforcing agents. Parental separation has been correlated with antisocial personality. Children may have been traumatized or subjected to a hostile environment during the parental separation (Vaillant & Perry, 1985). Millon and Everly (1985) believe that hostility in such families may result in interpersonal hostility among the children. Hence psychopaths may find little satisfaction in close or meaningful relationships with others. Psychopaths do show a significant amount of misperception about people in general (Widom, 1976). The inability to perceive another's viewpoint can create problems in personal interactions.

Note that antisocial personalities can learn and use social skills very effectively (Ullmann & Krasner, 1975), as shown in their adeptness at manipulation and at being charming and sociable. The difficulty is that, in many areas of learning, these people do not pay attention to social stimuli and have schedules of reinforcement that are different from most other people. Perhaps because they received negative or inconsistent reinforcement from parents or inadequate feedback for behaviors, persons with antisocial personalities find little reason to attend to social stimuli. Consequently, they feel no concern for others and easily use lying, cheating, and manipulation to their own advantage.

Another explanation is that the child may have modeled the behaviors of a parent who had antisocial tendencies. In one study, researchers examined the past records and statuses of nearly 500 adults who had been seen about thirty years earlier as children in a child guidance clinic. More than 90 of the adults exhibited antisocial tendencies. These persons were compared with a group of 100 adults who, as children, had lived in the same geographic area but had never been referred to the clinic. Results indicated that (1) there was little relationship between having antisocial personality as an adult and participation in gangs as a youth; (2) antisocial behavior (theft, aggression, juvenile delinquency, lying) in childhood was a predictor of antisocial behaviors in adults; (3) the adjustment level of fathers, but not that of mothers, was significant—having a father who was antisocial was related to adult antisocial characteristics; and (4) growing up in a single-parent home was not related to psychopathy (Robins, 1966).

The study seemed to indicate that antisocial behavior is probably influenced by the presence of an antisocial father who either serves as a model for such behavior or provides inadequate supervision, inconsistent discipline, or family conflict. The father's influence on antisocial behaviors in children may be a result of traditional sex role training. Males have traditionally received more encouragement to engage in aggressive behaviors than females, and antisocial patterns are more prevalent among men than among women. If traditional sex roles change, one might reasonably expect antisocial tendencies to increase among females and expect mothers to play a greater role in the development of antisocial behaviors in children. A more recent study also found that parental antisocial patterns, especially among fathers, was strongly associated with child conduct disorder (Lahey et al., 1988). Interestingly, results also indicated that divorce among parents was not related to having children with conduct disorder, once parental antisocial background was controlled. That is, although some researchers have speculated that divorce of parents is associated with antisocial conduct problems among children, this study found that the association was primarily caused by the fact that divorced, rather than married, parents were more likely to be antisocial. It is unclear, however, whether the effects of having a psychopathic parent are genetic (parents transmitting a certain genetic makeup to children) or environmental (parents providing an antisocial role model).

A disturbed family background or disturbed parental model is neither a necessary nor a sufficient condition for the development of antisocial personality. Indeed, antisocial personality probably has multiple causes.

Biogenic Perspectives Throughout history, many people have speculated that some individuals are "born to raise hell." These speculations are difficult to test because of the problems involved in distinguishing between the influences of environment and heredity on behavior. For example, antisocial personality disorder is five times more common among first-degree biologic relatives of males and ten times more common among first-degree biologic relatives of females with this disorder than among the general population (American Psychiatric Association, 1987). These findings can be used to support an environmental or genetic hypothesis. Within the last decade, however, some interesting research has been conducted on genetic influences in antisocial personality.

One strategy has been to compare concordance rates for identical, or monozygotic (MZ), twins with those for fraternal, or dizygotic (DZ), twins. Recall from Chapter 2 that MZ twins share exactly the same genes. But DZ twins share about 50 percent of the same genes; they are genetically no more alike than any two siblings. Most studies show that MZ twins do tend to have a higher concordance rate than DZ twins for antisocial tendencies, delinquency, and criminality (Mednick & Christiansen, 1977); this finding tends to support a genetic basis for these behavior patterns. Nevertheless, some caution must be exercised in drawing firm conclusions. Twin pairs can influence each other's behavior, and if MZ twins influence each other more than do DZ twins, the higher concordance rate may be caused at least in part by this influence. Carey (1992) found that twin interaction is important and believes that he-

redity and sibling interaction contribute to antisocial behavior.

Another strategy for studying genetic influence is to note the rate of antisocial personality among adopted people with antisocial biological parents. Because these adoptees were separated from their biological parents early in life, learning antisocial behaviors from their parents would have been difficult. Results have generally shown that adoptees whose biological parents exhibited antisocial behaviors have a higher rate of antisocial characteristics than adoptees whose biological parents did *not* exhibit antisocial behaviors (Cadoret & Cain, 1981). Even Robins's study (1966), in which the development of antisocial personality was associated with having antisocial fathers, revealed that the association existed even when the people were not raised in the presence of their fathers.

Do adoptive parents influence their psychopathic adoptees? (This influence would be environmental.) Results show that the rate of criminality or antisocial tendencies is higher among the biological parents than among the adoptive parents (Hutchings & Mednick, 1977; Mednick & Kandel, 1988; Schulsinger, 1972). Again the evidence suggests that antisocial personality patterns are influenced by heredity (Goodwin & Guze, 1984).

This evidence should be examined carefully, however, for several reasons. First, many of the studies do not clearly distinguish between antisocial personalities and criminals; or, as we noted earlier, they may draw subjects only from criminal populations. Truly representative samples of people with antisocial personality disorder should be investigated. Second, evidence that supports a genetic basis for antisocial tendencies does not preclude the environment as a factor. Antisocial personality is undoubtedly caused by environmental as well as genetic influences. The relative contribution of each factor, as well as the interaction between heredity and environment, should be investigated (Marmar, 1988). Third, studies indicating that genetic factors are important do not provide much insight into how antisocial personality is inherited (into what exactly is transmitted genetically). We need to understand more thoroughly the process that leads to the disorder.

Central Nervous System Abnormality Some early investigators suggested that antisocial personalities tend to have abnormal brain wave activity (Hill & Watterson, 1942; Knott et al., 1953). In these studies, the measurement of the brain waves, or electroencephalograms (EEGs), of psychopaths were sometimes found to be similar to those of normal young children. According to one survey, most studies revealed that between 31 and 58 percent of people with antisocial personality showed some EEG abnormality, frequently in the form of slow-wave, theta activity (Ellingson, 1954). Perhaps brain pathology inhibits the capacity of those with antisocial personalities to learn how to avoid punishment and therefore they are unable to learn from experience (Hare, 1970). This explanation is plausible, but simply not enough evidence supports its acceptance. Many persons diagnosed with antisocial personality do not show EEG abnormalities, and individuals who do not have antisocial personality may also exhibit theta-wave activity (Milstein, 1988). In addition, the EEG is an imprecise diagnostic device, and abnormal brain wave activity in people with antisocial personalities may be simply correlated with, rather than a cause of, disturbed behavior. For example, psychopathic personalities may simply be less anxious or more bored than are nonpsychopaths, which may account for slow-wave EEGs.

Autonomic Nervous System Abnormalities The inability to learn from experience, absence of anxiety, and thrill-seeking behaviors are prominent features of antisocial personality disorder. Some interesting and promising research has been conducted that points to the involvement of the autonomic nervous system (ANS) in the disorder. Two lines of investigation can be identified, both based on the assumption that antisocial personalities have ANS deficiencies or abnormalities. The first is based on the premise that ANS abnormalities make antisocial personalities less susceptible to anxiety, and therefore less likely to learn from experiences. People who lack anxiety may fail to learn in situations where aversive stimuli (or punishment) are involved. The second line of research focuses on ANS abnormalities that keep antisocial people emotionally underaroused. Underaroused individuals may then seek excitement and thrills, and fail to conform their behaviors to conventional standards, to achieve optimal level of arousal or to avoid boredom. The two concepts—lack of anxiety and underarousal—may, of course, be re-lated, because the underarousal may include underaroused anxiety.

Although Eysenck (Eysenck, 1957; Eysenck & Rachman, 1965) is considered a behaviorist, he was among the first to clearly argue the relevance of the ANS in antisocial personality. He believed that temperamental characteristics—or personality dimensions—could help explain why antisocial personalities fail to become adequately socialized to the rules and norms of society. Eysenck focused on two temperamental characteristics: neuroticism and introversion-extroversion. *Neuroticism* is autonomic instability or emotionality. Very neurotic people have an easily aroused and overactive autonomic nervous system. People who are not neurotic show the opposite characteristics—little anxiety or emotionality. The second personality dimension is *introversion-extroversion*. Introverts are inhibited, less sociable, and quick to learn. Extroverts tend to be impulsive, sociable, uninhibited, and slow to learn.

Eysenck hypothesized that temperamental characteristics are inherited and that primary psychopaths are neurotic and extroverted. The combination of these two temperaments result in impulsivity and a lack of inhibitions. They learn slowly, quickly develop reactive inhibition (fatigue in learning), and slowly dissipate that reactive inhibition. The difficulty in learning becomes a handicap in developing normal social patterns.

Eysenck argued that psychopaths can learn but they require more trials or repetitious experiences than others do. Hence antisocial patterns are seen primarily in youth or young adults who have not yet been exposed to enough experiences to learn to control their behaviors.

Fearlessness or Lack of Anxiety Lykken (1982) maintained that because of genetic predisposition, people vary in level of fearlessness. Antisocial personality develops because of fearlessness or low anxiety levels. People who have high levels of fear avoid risks, stress, and strong stimulation; relatively fearless people seek thrills and adventures. Fearlessness is associated with heroes (such as volunteering for dangerous military action or risking one's life to save others) as well as individuals with antisocial personalities, who may engage in risky criminal activities or impulsively violate norms and rules (see Focus 9.2). His classic research (Lykken, 1957) focused on behaviors of

Lykken theorized that people with low anxiety levels are often thrill seekers. The difference between the psychopath who takes risks and the adverturer may largely be a matter of whether the thrill-seeking behaviors are channeled into destructive or constructive acts.

prisoners judged to be primary psychopaths, of prisoners judged to be nonpsychopathic, and of students matched with the prisoners in socioeconomic background, age, and intelligence. He hypothesized that the psychopathic group would show less anxiety and greater deficiencies in avoidance learning. His results generally confirmed these hypotheses. In a classical conditioning procedure wherein a buzzer (conditioned stimulus or CS) was paired with a shock (unconditioned stimulus or US), psychopaths showed less galvanic skin response (GSR), or electrodermal, reactivity than the nonpsychopathic prisoners and the students. (GSR measures sweating, which is presumed to indicate emotional reaction or anxiety.) On the Activities Preference Questionnaire that Lykken devised, the psychopaths exhibited less aversion to frightening social and physical situations, perhaps reflecting their low anxiety in such situations. In an avoidance learning task, evidence showed that psychopaths were poorer at learning. Given a task in which errors could produce an electric shock, psychopaths made more errors than nonpsychopathic prisoners, who in turn made more errors than the students. Lykken's work suggested that, because psychopaths do not become conditioned to aversive stimuli as readily as nonpsychopaths, they fail to ac-

quire avoidance behaviors, experience little anticipatory anxiety, and consequently have fewer inhibitions about engaging in antisocial behavior.

Arousal, Sensation Seeking, and Behavioral Perspectives

Lykken's work suggested that antisocial personalities may have deficiencies in learning because of lower anxiety. As mentioned earlier, there is a second view—that antisocial personalities simply have lower levels of ANS reactivity and are underaroused. According to this view, the sensitivity of individuals' reticular cortical system varies, although there is an optimal level for each person. The system regulates the tonic level of arousal in the cortex, so that some people have high, and some have low, levels of arousal. Those with low sensitivity need more stimulation to reach an optimal level of arousal (Goma, Perez & Torrubia, 1988). It may take a more intense stimulus to elicit a reaction in psychopaths who are underaroused than in nonpsychopaths. The lowered levels of reactivity may cause psychopaths to show impulsive, stimulus-seeking behaviors to avoid boredom (Quay, 1965).

In a hypothesis similar to Lykken's concept of fearlessness, Farley (1986) proposed that people vary in their degree of thrill-seeking behaviors. Those at

Heroes and Psychopaths

Lykken (1982) argued that heroes and psychopaths are two sides of the same coin. For example, Lykken noted that Chuck Yeager, a heroic test pilot, once concealed broken ribs that he had suffered in a wild midnight horseback ride so that he could go aloft in the belly of a B-29, wedge himself in a tiny cockpit of the X-1 rocket plane, and let himself be jettisoned at an altitude of 26,000 feet to become the first person to travel faster than the speed of sound. And Ted Bundy was a charming, intelligent, and articulate psychopath who left a coast-to-coast trail of brutal and sadistic murders of young women. Lykken believes that heroes and psychopaths share one characteristic—namely, fearlessness. In an attempt to measure fearlessness, he developed the Activity Preference Questionnaire. The questionnaire instructs respondents to pretend that

one or the other situation described must occur, and asks respondents to choose the situation that is the lesser of two evils. Here are some of the items:

1.
   a. Cleaning up your house after floodwaters have left it filled with mud
   b. Making a parachute jump
2.
   a. Spending hours fixing a fancy barbecue for some guests, who then eat very little and seem not to like it
   b. Distributing 1,000 handbills in mailboxes from door to door
3.
   a. Having to walk around all day on a blistered foot
   b. Sleeping out on a camping trip in an area where rattlesnakes have been reported
4.
   a. Washing a car
   b. Driving a car at 95 miles an hour

The questionnaire items present a frightening or embarrassing situation paired with a situation that is merely onerous. People who are relatively fearless, such as heroes and psychopaths, may have a greater tendency to choose the frightening or embarrassing alternative than do fearful people.

What factors influence the probability of becoming a hero rather than a psychopath among those who are relatively fearless? Although very fearless children are difficult to bring up, circumstances and family environment may play crucial roles. Those who have the opportunity to channel their fearlessness into socially approved activities (such as being a test pilot) and who are socialized in families that emphasize warm and loving relationships rather than punishment techniques may be less likely to become psychopaths.

one end of the thrill-seeking continuum—the "Big T's"—are risk takers and adventurers who seek excitement and stimulation. Because of their low levels of CNS or ANS arousal, they need stimulation to maintain an optimal level of arousal. On the other end of the continuum, "Little t's" are people who have high arousal. They seek low levels of stimulation to calm their hyped-up nervous systems. In contrast to Big T's, Little t's prefer certainty, predictability, low risk, familiarity, clarity, simplicity, low conflict, and low intensity. Farley speculated that Big T characteristics can lead to both constructive or destructive behaviors in mental and physical domains. For constructive behaviors, artists, scientists, and entertainers are included in the mental domain because they channel their thrill-seeking tendencies into creative mental contributions. In the physical domain,

Big T's become adventurers and physical risk-takers. Big T characteristics can also result in antisocial, destructive tendencies. Criminal masterminds, schemers, and con artists are Big T's who make destructive mental contributions to society. In the physical domain, Big T destructive behaviors include violent delinquents and criminals. Farley (1986) reported that juvenile delinquents are more likely than nondelinquents to be Big T's. In a study of delinquents in prison, Big T's were more likely than Little t's to fight, disobey supervisors, and attempt to escape. Farley believes that we need to direct stimulation-hungry Big T's into constructive rather than destructive mental and physical activities.

Other researchers have found evidence of underarousal as well as lowered levels of anxiety among those with antisocial personality. In a study by Hare

FIGURE 9.1 Anxiety and Avoidance Learning Among Psychopaths and Others

Effects of anxiety-increasing (adrenalin) and placebo injections on the avoidance learning of psychopaths, of a group with mixed characteristics, and a control group.

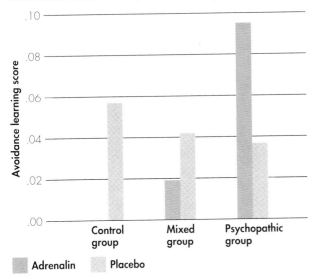

Source: 1964 Nebraska Symposium on Motivation.

FIGURE 9.2 Effect of Type of Punishment on Psychopaths and Others

Mean avoidance-learning scores plotted for three types of punishment among three subject groups.

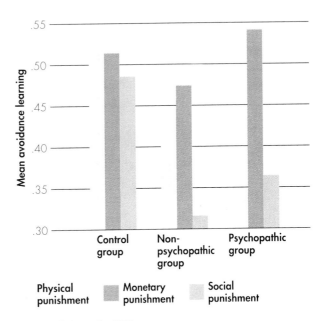

Source: Schmauk, 1970.

(1968), the resting state reactivity and the stress-produced reactivity of primary psychopaths, secondary psychopaths, and nonpsychopaths were determined through cardiac, electrodermal (GSR), and respiratory measures. Hare found that psychopaths demonstrated less autonomic reactivity in both the resting state and in response to stressors than did nonpsychopaths. In other words, a more intense stimulus is needed to elicit a reaction in psychopaths than in nonpsychopaths. Psychopaths' lowered levels of reactivity may cause them to engage in impulsive, stimulus-seeking behaviors to avoid boredom (Quay, 1965). In one study, antisocial preadolescent children did show stimulus-seeking behaviors, a finding that tends to support this hypothesis (Whitehill et al., 1976).

If learning deficiencies among individuals with antisocial personality are caused by the absence of anxiety and by lowered autonomic reactivity, is it possible to improve their learning by increasing their anxiety or arousal ability? Researchers tested the ability of psychopaths and nonpsychopaths to perform an avoidance learning task with electric shock

as the US, under two conditions. At different times, subjects were injected with adrenalin, which presumably increases arousal, and a placebo. Psychopaths receiving the placebo made more errors in avoiding the shocks than nonpsychopaths; psychopaths receiving adrenalin, however, tended to perform better than nonpsychopaths (see Figure 9.1). These findings imply that psychopaths do not react to the same amount of anxiety as do nonpsychopaths and that their learning improves when their anxiety is increased (Schachter & Latane, 1964).

The kind of punishment used in avoidance learning is also an important consideration in evaluating psychopaths' learning deficiencies (Schmauk, 1970). Whereas psychopaths may show learning deficits when faced with physical (electric shock) or social (verbal feedback) punishments, they learn as well as nonpsychopaths when the punishment is material (losing money for an incorrect response). Figure 9.2 charts the results of Schmauk's study of convicted psychopaths.

The certainty of punishment may also influence the responsiveness of antisocial personalities to punishment. Psychopaths and nonpsychopaths do not seem to differ in responding when punishment is a near certainty (Siegel, 1978). When the probability of punishment is highly uncertain, however, psychopaths do not suppress their behaviors. Threats of punishment alone do not seem to be sufficient to discourage psychopaths.

Normal people respond to physical, social, or material punishment, and they are influenced by uncertain as well as certain punishment. The work of Schmauk and Siegel suggested that psychopaths do not respond to the same range of aversive conditions. Hare (1975) proposed a psychophysiological model for this lack of responsiveness. He believes that psychopaths tend to lack anxiety, which makes learning difficult for them, and speculated that this lack of anxiety results from a defensive mechanism that reduces the aversiveness of painful stimuli. In other words, psychopaths may develop a psychophysiological ability to reduce the emotional impact (or anxiety-producing effect) of situations—a defense against anxiety and pain.

Hare's hypothesis is interesting but highly speculative. It, along with other hypotheses regarding anxiety, is based on a number of measures that do not always produce the same results. That is, a person may exhibit anxiety according to one measure but not according to another. Furthermore, some measures indicate not only anxiety but other states as well, such as general arousal. Obviously, an important goal in research on antisocial personality disorder is to develop a clearer concept of anxiety (and arousal) and a "pure" measure of this reaction.

Reid (1981) agreed that psychophysiological factors may be involved in the disorder. He viewed antisocial personality as a heterogeneous condition, however, caused by many factors. Diverse groups of factors (or correlates)—such as familial, biological, social, and developmental—may converge and provide a coherent picture in explaining the disorder.

Treatment of Antisocial Personality Disorder

As you have seen, there is growing evidence that low anxiety and low autonomic reactivity characterize antisocial personalities. But we still do not know whether the low anxiety and autonomic underreactivity are due to inherited temperament, an acquired

congenital defect, or social and environmental experiences that occur during childhood. The theory that psychopaths have developed a defense against anxiety is intriguing, but the factors behind the development of such a defense have not been pinpointed.

Because people with antisocial personalities feel little anxiety, they are poorly motivated to change themselves; they are also unlikely to see their behaviors as "bad." Thus traditional treatment approaches, which require the cooperation of the client, have not been very effective with antisocial personalities. For the same reason, relatively little research has been conducted on the efficacy of various treatment approaches. In some cases, drugs with tranquilizing effects (phenothiazines and Dilantin) have been helpful in reducing antisocial behavior (Meyer & Osborne, 1982). People with antisocial personalities, however, are not likely to follow through with the ritual of taking drugs; moreover, drug treatment is effective in only a few cases, and it can result in side effects such as blurred vision, lethargy, and neurological disorders.

It may be that successful treatment can occur only in a setting where behavior can be controlled (Vaillant, 1975). That is, treatment programs may need to provide enough control so that those with antisocial personalities cannot avoid confronting their inability to form close and intimate relationships and the effect of their behaviors on others. Such control is sometimes possible for psychopaths who are imprisoned for crimes or who, for one reason or another, are hospitalized. Intensive group therapy may then be initiated to help clients with antisocial personalities in the required confrontation.

Some behavior modification programs have been tried, especially with delinquents who behave in antisocial ways. Money and tokens that can be used to purchase items have been used as rewards for young people who show appropriate behaviors (discussion of personal problems, good study habits, punctuality, and prosocial and nondisruptive behaviors). This use of material rewards has been fairly effective in changing antisocial behaviors (Van Evra, 1983). Once the young people leave the treatment programs, however, they are likely to revert to antisocial behavior unless their families and peers help them maintain the appropriate behaviors. Cognitive approaches have also been used. Because individuals with antisocial personalities may be influenced by dysfunctional beliefs about themselves, the world, and the future, they vary in skills for anticipating and acting on possible negative outcomes for their behaviors. Rapport-building between the therapist and client and attempting to guide the patient from thinking only in terms of self-interest and immediate gratification to higher levels of thinking (for example, recognizing the effects of one's behaviors on others and developing a sense of responsibility) have been advocated by Beck and colleagues (1990).

Kazdin (1987) noted that because current treatment programs do not seem very effective, new strategies must be used. They include (1) focusing treatment on antisocial youth who seem amenable to treatment and (2) broadening the base of interventions so that youth and their families and peers are involved. Farley (1986) believes that because antisocial people may seek thrills (Big T's), they may respond to intervention programs that provide the physical and mental stimulation that they need.

ETIOLOGICAL AND TREATMENT CONSIDERATIONS FOR PERSONALITY DISORDERS IN GENERAL

Although personality disorders have generated rich clinical examples and speculations, not much empirical research has been conducted to provide definitive insight into the causes of the disorders. Indeed, the prevalence rates of the disorders are not clear. We do know that the sex distribution varies from disorder to disorder. Men are diagnosed as having paranoid, obsessive-compulsive, and antisocial personality disorders more often than women, whereas women receive a diagnosis of borderline, dependent, and histrionic personality disorder more frequently than men (Reich, 1987; Widiger & Spitzer, 1991). The existence of gender differences in the diagnosis of certain personality disorders is widely accepted. It raises some important issues, discussed in Critical Thinking. Are gender differences real or a product of biased diagnoses? Also see Focus 9.3 for a discussion of personality characteristics as disorders.

Research on personality disorders has been hindered by some of the problems discussed earlier. Diagnosis has been difficult, and many symptoms of

one disorder overlap with symptoms of other disorders. Personality characteristics are dimensional or continuous in nature—people have personality characteristics to different degrees. Yet, DSM-IV diagnosis is categorical—a person either has or does not have a personality disorder. To some clinicians, DSM-IV imposes artificial boundaries and promotes diagnostic errors in classification. Second, for a DSM-IV diagnosis to be reliable, symptoms associated with a diagnosis have to be specific and easily assessed. Such assessment, however, may reduce the validity of the diagnosis. For example, certain characteristics used to determine antisocial personality, such as armed robbery and truancy, may be relatively easy to assess; nevertheless, such characteristics may be more indicative of criminality than antisocial personality disorder in Cleckley's conceptualization of the disorder. Problems in rendering a valid diagnosis of personality disorders make it very difficult to conduct research studies. Third, researchers are still debating the importance of personality versus situational determinants in behaviors. Are symptoms or behaviors really reflections of one's personality or do they appear only in specific situations? Finally, while psychodynamic perspectives have guided the formulation of these disorders, many interpretations of the causes of the disorders are possible. Genetic, biological, learning, cognitive, humanistic, and family systems approaches have also been advanced as important frameworks for understanding these disorders.

As we have seen in antisocial personality disorder, biogenic, behavioral, and cognitive factors have been proposed to explain the development of the disorder. Although much less research has been conducted on the other personality disorders, we can well imagine that these factors can be used to explain the other disorders. The fact that the disorders deal with *personality* means that research on the determinants of personality characteristics is germane. Socialization and family upbringing, learning and modeling, development of cognitions, and culture all contribute to personality. Some interesting research has examined the role of heredity in personality development. In one study (Scarr et al., 1981), the personality characteristics of biologically related and adoptive families were studied. If heredity is important, biologically related parents, children, and siblings should show similar personality characteristics. If learning and environment are important, similarity should be shown

Are There Gender Differences in Diagnosed Mental Disorders?

Gender differences exist in the diagnosed prevalence of mental disorders such as depression, which has been found to be higher among women than men (see Chapter 12). In terms of personality disorders, men have been found to have a higher rate of antisocial, paranoid, and obsessive personality disorders, and women are more likely than men to be diagnosed with borderline, dependent, and histrionic personality disorders (Reich, 1987; Widiger & Spitzer, 1991), as mentioned in the text.

What is bias? Gender bias in the diagnostic system occurs when diagnostic categories are not valid and when they have a different impact on men and women. Note that the mere fact that men and women have different prevalence rates for a particular disorder is not sufficient to prove gender bias. Rates may differ because of actual biological (for example, genetic predisposition) or social conditions (stressors) that affect one gender more than another. For the diagnostic system itself to be biased, the differences must be attributable to errors or problems in the categories or diagnostic criteria. Widiger and Spitzer (1991) attempted to clarify the nature of bias in dealing with gender differences. They suggested that bias in the

diagnostic system is but one type of bias.

1. Clinicians themselves may be biased. For example, the behavior of an aggressive and manipulative person working in a business or corporation may be judged by the clinician as being appropriate if the person is a man but pathological if the person is a woman.

2. An assessment instrument or the diagnostic category may be biased. Items on an instrument or questionnaire may be constructed so that they define behaviors associated with males as being more

between the adoptive family and those who were adopted. Although the results indicated that genetic as well as environmental factors are important in personality traits, neither could fully explain the development of personality characteristics. Individual differences within families may be influential in personality. That is, certain genetic characteristics of individual children may determine much of the environment they experience, so that the contributions of heredity and environment may be quite complex. Tellegen and colleagues (1988) reported on an interesting study of the personality characteristics of monozygotic and dizygotic twins reared apart or together. MZ twins are genetically identical, and DZ twins share about 50 percent of each other's genes. Therefore, effects of genetic and environmental similarity on personality could be studied. Results indicated that heredity was important in personality development. Environment was also critical, although

the investigators found that a shared environment (that is, twin pairs coming from the same family environment) was not strongly related to personality similarity. Environmental influences can be shared or unshared. Although it is popularly believed that shared environmental influences explain personality similarity, it is possible that the unique, unshared experiences that a person has may be crucial. All of these studies indicate the complexities in trying to find determinants of personality in general and of personality disorders in particular.

Because of the many different theories about how personality characteristics develop and change, many varied treatment approaches have been used as illustrated in our discussion of antisocial personality. In general, however, treatment for personality disorders is not very effective. Many people with these disorders do not seek treatment, often because they don't believe they need it. Many can function in society

desirable and healthy than those associated with females.

3. Sampling bias occurs when one gender with a particular disorder is more likely than the other gender to be present in a particular setting. For example, if we collect data on mental disorders from clients at Veterans' Administration hospitals, we are likely to conclude that men have a higher rate of psychopathology than do women because the vast majority of psychiatric clients are male. The sampling bias exists because we are collecting data on a certain group of individuals (veterans) who happen to be primarily men.

These are the primary biases that can occur. Can you think of others?

Interestingly, the same behaviors exhibited by men and women may be judged differently. Take, for example, the characteristic of aggression. An aggressive woman may be perceived as being more deviant than a man who shows the very same characteristic. Wearing heavy facial makeup in public may be considered appropriate for women but not for men. Thus characteristics traditionally associated with a particular gender may be negatively evaluated when they occur in the opposite gender. Does this mean that inconsistencies in enacting one's gender roles are a sign of disturbance?

Tavris (1991) argued that characteristics associated with women rather than men are more likely to be considered as being deviant or undesirable. She attributed this to a male norm that tends to define characteristics found primarily in women as negative. For example, "premenstrual syndrome" (PMS) is viewed as a debilitating condition related to the menstrual cycle. Different versions of DSM had considered including PMS or "late luteal phase dysphoric disorder" because some women seemed to exhibit symptoms such as marked mood changes, decreased interest in usual activities, sleep problems, and conflicts, during certain phases of the menstrual cycle. Tavris believed that the very concept of PMS made women increasingly aware of their negative moods during the cycle—that is, the concept helped promote the belief that PMS was a real problem for women. She also asked why men do not have a disorder such as "excessive testosterone syndrome" when some researchers have found that unusually high levels of testosterone are associated with delinquency, drug use, and violence among men. Her concern is over the creation of labels or diagnostic categories that define characteristics or behaviors associated with women as being deviant or negative. What do you think?

despite their adjustment problems, so their motivation to change may be weak. Also, because the disorders are characterized by long-term and inflexible personality traits, modifying these traits is not easy.

DISORDERS OF IMPULSE CONTROL

The category that includes intermittent explosive disorder, kleptomania, pathological gambling, pyromania, and trichotillomania is a residual category for **impulse control disorders** (loss of control resulting in harm) that are not classified elsewhere. Impulse control behaviors related to sexual conduct or compulsive ingestion of drugs or alcohol, for example, are usually classified under the paraphilias and substance use disorders, respectively. Although not much is known about the cause of the disorders discussed here, most people have seen films and television programs that depict pathological gamblers, fire setters, or impulsive thieves. Impulse control disorders share three characteristics. First, such people fail to resist an impulse or temptation to perform some act. People with the disorder know that the act is considered wrong by society or is harmful to them. The impulse may or may not be consciously resisted, and its performance may or may not be premeditated. Second, tension or arousal is experienced before the act. Third, after committing the act, a sense of excitement, gratification, or release is felt. Guilt or regret may or may not follow. Let's briefly examine the five specified disorders, which are shown on the impulse disorders chart on page 279.

Intermittent Explosive Disorder

People with **intermittent explosive disorder** lose control over their aggressive impulses, which results in

Personality Patterns as Disorders: Questions for Thought

As noted in Focus 9.1, new personality disorders have been proposed in addition to the ten that have already been defined in DSM-IV. Isn't it possible to view almost any personality characteristic (or constellation of characteristics) as being a disorder if that characteristic is exhibited to an extreme degree? For example, can't chronically hostile and angry persons be diagnosed as having an angry personality disorder, overly trusting individuals as having a naive personality disorder, and extremely happy and idealistic persons as having a pollyanna personality disorder? What determines what personality characteristics constitute a disorder?

DSM-IV does have a personality disorder category for disorders "not otherwise specified." In other words, if disorders of personality functioning cannot be classified as ones identified by DSM, if they cause significant impairment in social or occupational functioning or subjective distress, and if they meet general guidelines for personality disorders (the traits are inflexible, maladaptive, generally recognizable by adolescence and are not a reflection

of another disorder such as schizophrenia), then they may be included in the category of a personality disorder not otherwise specified. Given the general guidelines, extreme happiness may not be a personality disorder unless the trait is maladaptive and causes significant impairment. But one can still ask why some personality disorders are included as specific disorders and why others are considered in the category of "not otherwise specified."

The creation of a specific personality disorder is probably influenced by many factors such as the observed frequency of the constellation of personality traits, the degree of impairment and distress, and the consequence for society. If one personality pattern affects relatively more people, causes greater impairment and distress, and has negative consequences for society than another personality pattern, the chances are increased that it will be listed as a specified disorder. Furthermore, characteristics having a "history" of being discussed in the theoretical, empirical, and clinical literature will stand a better chance of being specified as a disorder than

those without such a history.

The final question that we would like to raise is the cross-cultural validity of the DSM-IV personality disorders. Because people from different cultures and societies exhibit different personality characteristics and may disagree as to the traits that are considered maladaptive, are the DSM-defined personality disorders universally valid and applicable? DSM categories are highly similar with those in the *International Classification of Diseases,* a classification scheme developed for the World Health Organization by leading experts from different countries. Nevertheless, cross-cultural mental health researchers, such as Mezzich and Good (1991), have maintained that definitions of "normal" personality may vary across societies and ethnic groups and that behaviors considered highly deviant in one context (such as forms of drug use or sexual behavior or modes of expressing emotion) may fall within the norm of another. They also note that to date, little evidence either confirms or disconfirms the universality of specific personality disorders.

---

serious assaults on others or in the destruction of property. The aggressiveness is grossly out of proportion to any precipitating stress that may have occurred. People with this disorder show no signs of general aggressiveness between episodes and may genuinely feel remorse for their actions. However, some believe that individuals with this disorder harbor a good deal of suppressed anger (Meyer, 1989). The disorder is apparently rare and believed to be more common among males than females. A patient diagnosed with intermittent explosive disorder described the following incident:

I'm usually a good and safe driver. I'm married and a very successful businessman. My colleagues say that I am a kind and happy-go-lucky person. That's why it's so strange that I lose control of my temper while driving my car. Last week an elderly woman was driving her car very slowly in front of me. I wanted her to speed up so I honked at her. She kept on moving slowly. I became so irritated that I rammed the back of her car and then drove off. Her car was severely damaged—and so was mine—and I could have killed her. After driving for several miles, I was overwhelmed with guilt and disgust with myself. I tried to find the woman, to apologize and pay for damages.

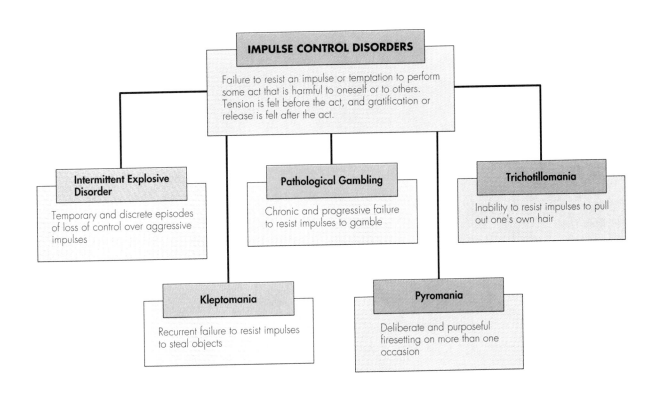

But I couldn't find her. There's something wrong with me. Why do I do these things? I've run several people off the road and tried to ram others if they honk or cut in front of my car. I get so overwhelmed with rage I become a different person. Maybe I should turn myself into the police.

Kleptomania

Kleptomania involves a recurrent failure to resist impulses to steal objects. The objects are not needed for personal use and are not stolen for their monetary value; indeed, people with this disorder usually have enough money to buy the objects, which are typically discarded, given away, or surreptitiously returned. They feel irresistible urges and tension before stealing or shoplifting and then an intense feeling of relief or gratification after the theft. The stealing is not committed to express anger or vengeance and is not in response to a delusion or hallucination. Although theft is common, only a small percentage of thieves fit the criteria for kleptomania, which is believed to be a rare disorder.

The patient . . . described a special problem that worried her and that she had never disclosed to her husband. Periodically she experienced the urge to walk into one of the more elegant department stores in the city and steal an article of clothing. Over the course of the previous three or four years, she had stolen several blouses, a couple of sweaters, and a skirt. Since her husband's income was over $150,000 a year and her investments worth many times that, she recognized the "absurdity" of her acts. She also indicated that what she stole was rarely very expensive and sometimes not even enough to her liking for her to wear. She would become aware of the desire to steal something several days before she actually did it. The thoughts would increasingly occupy her mind until, on impulse, she walked into the store, plucked an item off the rack, and stuffed it into a bag she happened to be carrying or under her coat. Once out the door she felt a sense of relaxation and satisfaction; but at home she experienced anxiety and guilt (Spitzer et al., 1981, p. 80)

Pathological gamblers cannot control their urge to gamble. They often go into debt, turn to illegal activities to support their gambling, and jeopardize their families' security. Even heavy losses cannot deter them from their self-destructive acts.

Pathological Gambling

The essential feature of **pathological gambling** is the inability to resist impulses to gamble, despite the detrimental consequences that often accompany the behavior, such as financial ruin, turning to illegal activities to support gambling, disruptions of family or interpersonal relationships, and sacrificing obligations and responsibilities. Gambling is big business. About $166.5 billion was legally wagered in 1986 and about 80 percent of the U.S. population gambles (Lesieur, 1989). Those afflicted with pathological gambling constitute about 2 to 3 percent of adults, with the disorder more common among men than women (American Psychiatric Association, 1987). Unlike social gamblers who may place limits on the amount of money that may be lost or who can avoid gambling, the pathological gambler is preoccupied with gambling for its own sake. There is a tendency to gamble with increasing amounts of money to achieve the desired excitement, and gambling may be used as a way to relieve dysphoric moods. He or she may constantly borrow money or engage in illegal activities (such as forgery or theft) to continue. The person usually feels tension or restlessness if he or she is unable to gamble. Although the person gambles and often shows manic behaviors and a heightened sense of excitement, especially during a winning streak, depression usually follows the frequent gambling losses. At such times, the person may try to borrow more money, rationalizing that the "big win" is about to happen, as in the following case:

Jason L. was a 29-year-old married salesman. His wife of two years came from a well-to-do family, and Jason increasingly asked his wife's family to help subsidize his business ventures. She was initially impressed with Jason's dreams to "make it big" in his business ventures. Unknown to his wife, however, Jason actually needed the money to continue his habit of gambling at a local card house. He was unable to stay away from gambling. When he won, he was ecstatic and would tell his wife that his business ventures were succeeding. Jason would then celebrate by taking her out to the finest restaurants. Unfortunately, he lost money most of the time. He would then beg his wife and her family for more money. After a while, she found out that Jason had no business ventures and that he was simply using the money to continue gambling. She threatened to divorce him if he did not stop gambling. At this point, Jason became infuriated. He claimed that her family looked down on him, so he was gambling in an attempt to get one big win that would let them live in luxury. He also said that he owed thousands of dollars in debts to the card house. Jason's wife indicated that she would take care of the debts but that he must stop gambling. After she gave him the money, Jason promptly lost the money playing cards. His wife then threatened to divorce him unless he entered psychotherapy and ceased his gambling habit. The therapist who saw Jason diagnosed him as a pathological gambler. Although Jason showed some antisocial behaviors, they were confined to his gambling and attempts to get money for gambling.

Pyromania

Pyromania is characterized by deliberate fire setting on more than one occasion. Pyromaniacs have a fascination with fire and with burning objects. They get intense pleasure or relief from setting the fires, watching things burn, or observing firefighters and their efforts to put out fires. Their impulses are driven by this fascination rather than by any motives involving revenge, sabotage, or financial gains for setting fires. Most pyromaniacs have a history of fire setting, beginning in childhood. Although many children may play with fire, they do so without the intense pleasure, lack of concern over the destruction caused by fires, and inability to control the impulse that is seen among pyromaniacs. Gaynor and Hatcher (1987) be-

lieve that many children first start fires out of curiosity, exploration, or accident. The persistence of fire-setting behavior is associated with individual characteristics (young male, experience of overwhelming anger, and conduct or personality disorder), social circumstances (poor family environment and interpersonal maladjustment), and environmental conditions (stressful life events). Others have also found that fire-setting children have higher levels of behavioral dysfunction, hostility, and impulsivity than non-fire-setting children (Kolko & Kazdin, 1991). The prevalence of the disorder is unknown, although it is diagnosed far more frequently among males than females. The case of Kevin, a fourteen-year-old boy, illustrates some of the characteristics associated with pyromania.

Kevin was arrested for the crime of arson in which he had allegedly set a fire that resulted in the destruction of some houses being constructed. Kevin was watching the fire when a witness told firefighters that she had seen Kevin with a gasoline can at the construction site just before the nighttime fire. After arson investigators found the gasoline can (which was later found to have Kevin's fingerprints) and questioned Kevin and his parents, he confessed to the crime. Kevin had a long history of fire setting. When he was about six

Pyromaniacs are fascinated with fire. In fact, it is this fascination with burning objects rather than any motives of revenge that drives them. To be diagnosed as a pyromaniac, a person must feel intense pleasure or relief when setting fires.

years of age, he used his father's lighter to burn his sister's doll, which then ignited the window curtain. At age eight, he burned some bushes while he was camping with his family. Kevin was always playing with matches and lighters. He was also caught setting off a fire alarm at an office building. Kevin's parents reported that he would always become quite excited when hearing the sirens of fire engines. He often asked his parents to follow the fire engines just to see the fires. Although the parents had punished Kevin for playing with fire, he would, without his parents' knowledge, continue burning items. Outside of the fire setting, Kevin had few problems. He was an average student who was quiet and fairly well behaved.

Trichotillomania

Trichotillomania is a disorder characterized by recurrent pulling out of one's own hair resulting in noticeable hair loss. The person usually feels a sense of tension before the hair pulling, and feels release or gratification after the act. Although trichotillomania principally involves the hairs in the scalp, hair from other parts of the body (such as eyelashes, beard, or eyebrows) may be pulled. The hair pulling is not provoked by skin inflammation, itch, or other physical conditions. Rather, the person simply cannot resist the impulse. Initially, the hair pulling may not disturb the follicles, and new hairs start to grow. In severe cases, new growth is compromised and permanent balding may occur. One 35-year-old woman entered therapy with one of the authors of this book. She said that she had a compulsion to pull the hairs from her head. When asked to reveal the extent of the hair pulling, the woman took off her wig. She was completely bald except for a few strands of hair at the back of her head. There is no information on the prevalence of the disorder, although it is probably more common than currently believed (American Psychological Association, 1987) and more common among women than men (Meyer, 1989).

Etiology and Treatment of Impulse Control Disorders

Although some of these disorders such as pathological gambling and pyromania have gained much public attention, not much is actually known about the specific causes. Furthermore, the characteristics of impulse control disorders seem to be similar to those found in other disorders. First, the disorders have an obsessive-compulsive quality in that the person feels a compulsion to perform certain acts. In obsessive-compulsive disorders, however, the repetitive behaviors seem more purposeful and serve to prevent or produce some future event or situation. Second, the impulse control disorders also have a compulsive feature that is found in substance abusers or addicts who must maintain their habits. Substance use, however, has more clear physiological involvement. Third, to some extent, the behaviors of people with impulse control disorders resemble those of people with sexual disorders (such as exhibitionism and fetishism) in that tension, fascination, and release may precede or follow the acts. Indeed, some psychoanalysts link pyromania to sexual release and gratification. The problem is that orgasm and many sexual activities are intrinsically pleasurable or reinforcing, whereas trichotillomania and fire setting are not.

Psychoanalytic explanations for impulse control disorders have been quite varied (see Booth, 1988). Pathological gambling has been likened to masturbation in that masturbation and gambling are both driven by built-up tension and a need to release the tension. Alternatively, it has been attributed to an unconscious need to lose because of underlying guilt. Kleptomania has been seen as an attempt to gain esteem, nourishment, or sexual gratification through stealing. Pyromania has been associated with sexual gratification, attempts to overcome feelings of impotence and inferiority, or unconscious anger toward a parental figure. And trichotillomania has been described as a response to unhealthy parent-child relationships. These psychoanalytic or psychodynamic formulations have been primarily based on clinical case studies rather than on empirical research.

Behaviorists tend to explain impulse control disorders through learning principles such as operant conditioning, classical conditioning, and modeling. For example, pathological gambling has been viewed as being influenced by reinforcement schedules. Researchers have shown that high rates of responding can occur because the positive reinforcement schedule is variable rather than continuous. That is, when people win only occasionally, they may strongly persist in gambling. Initial wins may attract the person to gamble. Then, as wins become less frequent and are quite variable, a high rate of responding is likely. Learning principles can also be used to conceptualize the other disorders. Some researchers have even speculated on the role of physiological factors. Roy and colleagues (1988) found that compulsive gamblers were more likely than nongamblers to have abnormalities in their noradrenergic system (affecting heart rate and blood pressure), which may indicate a greater sensation- or thrill-seeking drive among pathological gamblers.

Lesieur (1989) noted the existence of two explanatory "camps." (Although he applied his analysis to pathological gambling, the same analysis can be applied to other impulse control disorders.) The first is that impulse control problems range on a continuum from problem-free to troubled. Behavioral, cognitive, and sociological perspectives would probably be included in this first camp. The second explanatory orientation is that impulse control disorders are disease-like—one either has it or does not. Psychodynamic and physiologically based theories could, perhaps, fall into this orientation. The diversity of explanations and the lack of empirical research on impulse control disorders reflect the fact that these disorders have fascinated mental health professionals, and yet the prevalence of such disorders is sufficiently low so that researchers have difficulty studying the disorders. Furthermore, it's likely that impulse control disorders share similar symptoms (inability to resist an impulse) but lack a common specific cause. That is, different types of disorders, such as intermittent explosive disorder and kleptomania, may be influenced by quite different factors.

In terms of treatment, a wide variety of approaches has been used, as noted by Booth (1988) in his review of impulse control disorders. In many of the disorders, behavioral and cognitive behavioral methods have been moderately successful. Some patients have been taught to recognize tension states that lead to the behavior, to make self-statements (such as having a kleptomaniac say, "I feel like stealing the item but I'd better not"), rehearse alternative responses (such as having a person with intermittent explosive disorder take a deep breath and relax when tension exists), or associate their behavior with aversive consequences (such as through aversive conditioning). McCormick and Taber (1988) also believe that changing the cognitive styles of people with impulse control such as pathological gambling may be beneficial. They found that among pathological gamblers undergoing treatment, attributional style (that is, a way of thinking about the causes of negative experiences; see Chapter 12) was related to failure to abstain from gambling after treatment. The implication is that a cognitive approach in treatment may be beneficial in helping change the way gamblers think about events. Some insight-oriented approaches have been helpful in treating disorders such as kleptomania, especially with people who feel guilty over the theft. In treating intermittent explosive disorder, Meyer (1989) recommended awareness techniques, such as those found in gestalt therapy, which attempt to put clients in touch with their anger; teaching ways to deal with anger in a productive fashion is also recommended. Multimodal approaches (combining techniques) involving family and friends and even organizations (such as Gamblers Anonymous for pathological gamblers) may be beneficial.

SUMMARY

1. The personality disorders include a diversity of behavioral patterns in people who are typically perceived as being odd, overly sensitive and emotional, hot-tempered, suspicious, moody, or impulsive. DSM-IV lists ten specific personality disorders; each causes notable impairment of social or occupational functioning or subjective distress for the person. They are usually manifested in adolescence, continue into adulthood, and involve disturbances in personality characteristics.

2. The main characteristics of antisocial (or psychopathic) personality are selfishness, irresponsibility, lack of guilt and anxiety, failure to learn from experience, superficiality, and impulsiveness. People with antisocial personalities frequently violate the rules, conventions, or laws of society. Most explanations of antisocial personality attribute its development to family and socialization factors, heredity, or autonomic nervous system abnormalities that result in lowered anxiety or underarousal. Traditional treatment approaches are not particularly effective with antisocial personalities.

3. The impulse control disorders involve the person's failure to resist a temptation to perform an act. People with such disorders experience tension before the act and a sense of gratification or release afterward. DSM-IV lists five impulse control disorders: kleptomania, intermittent explosive disorder, patho-

logical gambling, pyromania, and trichotillomania. Although little is known about cause and effective treatment, the disorders have gained much public attention because of mass media dramatizations of kleptomania, pathological gambling, and pyromania.

KEY TERMS

antisocial personality disorder A personality disorder characterized by failure to conform to social and legal norms, superficial relationships with others, and lack of guilt feelings for wrongdoing

avoidant personality disorder A personality disorder characterized by hypersensitivity to rejection and humiliation and, as a result, reluctance to enter into social relationships

borderline personality disorder A personality disorder characterized by intense fluctuations in mood, self-image, and interpersonal relationships

dependent personality disorder A personality disorder characterized by extreme reliance on others and an unwillingness to assume responsibility

histrionic personality disorder A personality disorder characterized by self-dramatization, the exaggerated expression of emotions, and attention-seeking behaviors

impulse control disorder A disorder in which the person fails to resist an impulse or temptation to perform some act that is harmful to the person or to others

intermittent explosive disorder Loss of control over aggressive impulses, resulting in serious assaults or destruction

kleptomania An impulse control disorder in which the person recurrently fails to resist impulses to steal objects

narcissistic personality disorder A personality disorder characterized by an exaggerated sense of self-importance

obsessive-compulsive personality disorder A personality disorder characterized by inability to express warm feelings, perfectionism, indecision, devotion to details, and a lack of personal warmth

paranoid personality disorder A personality disorder characterized by unwarranted suspiciousness, hypersensitivity, a reluctance to confide in others, and preoccupation with unfounded beliefs

pathological gambling An impulse control disorder characterized by an inability to refrain from gambling

personality disorder A behavior pattern characterized by inflexible and maladaptive behaviors

pyromania An impulse control disorder having as its main feature deliberate fire setting on more than one occasion

schizoid personality disorder A personality disorder characterized by social isolation and emotional coldness

schizotypal personality disorder A personality disorder characterized by such oddities of thinking and behavior as recurrent illusions, belief in the possession of magical powers, and digression or vagueness of speech

trichotillomania An impulse control disorder in which the person cannot resist pulling out his or her own hair

CHAPTER 10

Substance-Related Disorders

The misuse of psychoactive substances is the nation's foremost public health challenge. The use and abuse of alcohol, cigarettes, illicit drugs (heroin, cocaine, marijuana, etc.), and licit drugs (sedatives and tranquilizers) are by far the largest cause of preventable and premature illness, disability, and death in our society. (Committee on Drug Abuse of the Council on Psychiatric Services, 1987, p. 698)

Throughout history, people have swallowed, sniffed, smoked, or otherwise taken into their bodies a variety of chemical substances for the purpose of altering their moods, levels of consciousness, or behaviors. The widespread use of drugs in our society today is readily apparent in our vast consumption of alcohol, cigarettes, coffee, medically prescribed tranquilizers, and illegal drugs such as cocaine, marijuana, and heroin. Our society is generally permissive (compared to other societies) with regard to the use of these substances. According to the 1990 U.S. Household Survey for those aged twelve and older, drug use is high. About 37 percent of the population has used illicit drugs, and more than 6 percent used them in the past month. Specifically, the survey found lifetime use (percentage of persons having used the substance at any time) to be as follows: marijuana, 33 percent; cocaine, 11 percent; inhalants, 5 percent; hallucinogens, 8 percent; heroin, 1 percent; and nonmedical use of psychotherapeutic drugs (stimulants, sedatives, tranquilizers, and analgesics), 12 percent. More than 83 percent had used alcohol and 73 percent had smoked cigarettes during their lifetime. More than one-half had consumed alcohol and more than one-quarter had smoked during the past month. Interestingly, use of most drugs declined from the late 1970s to the present (National Institute of Drug Abuse, 1991), perhaps because of public education and concern over drug abuse.

People and representatives of public institutions become concerned when the ingestion of drugs re-

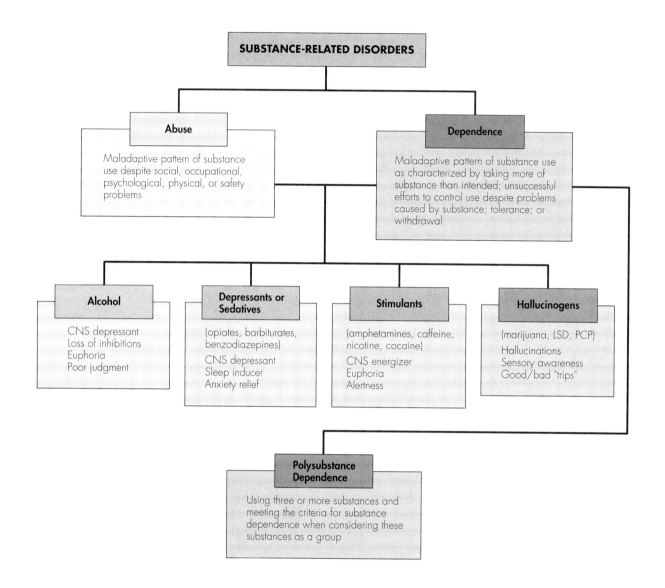

sults in (1) the impairment of a person's social or occupational functioning; (2) an inability to abstain from using the drug despite its harmful effects on the body; (3) the user becoming a danger to others; or (4) criminal activities, such as the sale of illegal drugs or robbery, to support a drug habit. The first two of these problems are directly involved in **substance-related disorders** (altering one's psychological state) or maladaptive behavior associated with the pathological use of a substance. The other problems arise as a concomitant of such use. Yet another problem is that use of one substance may lead to use of other substances. In a longitudinal study of drug use among youths, Ellickson, Hays, and Bell (1992) found that involvement with "legal" drugs such as alcohol and cigarettes tended to precede the use of illicit drugs such as marijuana and "hard" drugs.

DSM-IV distinguishes substance-related disorders from substance-induced cognitive disorders (see the substance-related disorders chart above). *Substance-related disorder* refers to the maladaptive behavior associated with substance use, and *substance-*

induced cognitive disorder describes the direct acute or chronic effects of such substances on the central nervous system. The distinction is maintained in this chapter. Substance-induced cognitive disorders are discussed in Chapter 16.

In DSM-IV, the substance-related disorders are differentiated from each other with regard to the actual substance used, as well as in terms of two disorder patterns—substance abuse and dependence—which have the same general characteristics regardless of the substance used. **Substance abuse** is a maladaptive pattern of excessive use leading to notable impairment or distress. The person cannot cease or reduce his or her intake of a substance, even though it may be causing physical damage or legal problems, jeopardizing safety (such as driving a car while intoxicated), or impairing ability to fulfill major role obligations at work, school, or home. Need for the substance may lead to a preoccupation with its acquisition and use.

To make the diagnosis of **substance dependence,** a therapist must find several of the following symptoms in the client:

1. An inability to cut down or control use, despite knowledge of the harmful physical, psychological, or interpersonal effects

2. A great deal of time spent in activities necessary to obtain the substance, even though important social, occupational, and recreational activities are sacrificed

3. **Tolerance** (needing increasing dosages of the substance to achieve the desired effect such as a "high")

4. **Withdrawal** (physical or emotional symptoms such as shaking, irritability, and inability to concentrate after reducing or ceasing intake)

In substance dependence, the clinician also specifies whether the dependence is physiological in nature. Evidence of either tolerance or withdrawal is a sign of physiological dependence.

In addition to substance dependence and abuse, intoxication and withdrawal are considered disorders with several primary symptoms. **Intoxication** refers to the ingestion of a substance affecting the central nervous system in which certain maladaptive behaviors or psychological changes (such as belligerence and impaired judgment and functioning) are evident.

The effects of intoxication and withdrawal vary according to the substance, but they generally cause significant distress or impairment in social, occupational, or other important areas of functioning.

As can be readily noted, criteria for substance dependence include those for abuse and withdrawal. People who meet the criteria for both substance dependence and abuse for a particular substance are diagnosed only as dependent and not as abusing because dependence is considered a more severe disorder. Although the two categories have some overlap in criteria, research has indicated that distinguishing between dependence and abuse is meaningful and can differentially predict severity of disorder and treatment outcome (Nathan, 1991). Diagnosis of withdrawal or intoxication may be made when the major symptoms of clients at the time of diagnosis involve withdrawal or intoxication. These clients may also be substance dependent. Finally, some clients may be substance dependent or an abuser but not show certain psychological characteristics such as intentional drug use. These persons may have substance-induced conditions as a result of unintentional exposure to substances or of side effects of medication.

In this chapter, we first examine alcohol- and drug-related disorders, including the effects of the abuse of alcohol and various drugs. Then we discuss the causes and treatments of substance-related disorders. Because alcohol abuse is a subject on which a great deal of research has been conducted (and is particularly prevalent among college students), we focus primarily on alcohol. We also comment on how different theories may be relevant to the abuse of substances other than alcohol.

ALCOHOL-RELATED DISORDERS

Jim is a 54-year-old alcoholic. He is well educated, having received a bachelors degree in engineering and a masters degree in management. Until recently, he was employed as a middle manager in an aerospace firm. Because of federal defense industry budget cuts and because of his absenteeism from work caused by drinking, Jim had lost his job. He decided to enter treatment.

His drinking history was long. Jim clearly recalled the first time that he drank. At age fifteen, he attended a party at his friend's house. Alcohol was freely served. Jim took a drink, and despite the fact that alcohol "tasted so bad," he forced himself to drink. Indeed, he became drunk and had a terrible hangover the next day. He swore that he would never drink again, but two weeks later he drank again at his friend's house. Over the next several years, Jim acquired the ability to consume large amounts of alcohol and was proud of his drinking capacity. At social gatherings, he was uninhibited and the "life of the party." His drinking continued during college, but it was confined primarily to his fraternity weekend parties. He was considered a very heavy drinker in the fraternity, but the drinking did not seem to affect his academic performance. He frequently drove his car during weekend binges, however, and was once caught and convicted of drunken driving.

After graduate school, he got married and took a position in an aerospace firm. Kattie, Jim's wife, also drank but never as heavily as Jim. Although his drinking had been largely confined to weekends, Jim started drinking throughout the week. He attributed his increased drinking to pressures at work, company-sponsored receptions in which alcohol was served, and a desire to feel "free and comfortable" in front of company executives during the receptions. The drinking continued despite frequent arguments with Kattie over his drinking and a physician's warning, after a routine physical examination, that alcohol had probably caused the abnormal results of Jim's liver functioning tests. He could not control his drinking.

Kattie noticed that Jim was getting more and more angry from his work. Jim felt that deadlines for him to complete assignments were unrealistic. She felt that he was increasingly difficult to be around. He drank now daily, usually in his office at the end of the work day. His colleagues knew that he had a drinking problem but because Jim was still functioning well at work, they kidded him about drinking rather than counseled him against consuming alcohol. They were, however, concerned about his absenteeism, frequent tardiness, and inability to get started in the morning, which were caused by his drinking.

Over the years, Kattie simply fell out of love with Jim. The arguments, Jim's drinking, and his unwillingness to communicate with her finally led to a divorce. He was quite bitter over the divorce, although Kattie could not see how he was getting anything out of the marriage.

When awards for defense contracts had diminished, Jim's company started to lay off workers. Jim was among the first to be asked to leave.

Problem drinking can develop in many different ways and can begin at almost any age. However,

Jim's history is typical in several respects. First, as is true of most people, he initially found the taste of alcohol unpleasant, and, after his first bout of drunkenness, he swore that he would never drink again. Nevertheless, he did return to drinking. Second, heavy drinking served a purpose: it reduced his anxiety, particularly at work. Third, consumption continued despite the obvious negative consequences. Finally, a preoccupation with alcohol consumption and the deterioration of social and occupational functioning are also characteristic of the problem drinker.

Alcohol Consumption in the United States

People drink considerable amounts of alcohol in the United States. About 11 percent of adults consume one ounce or more of alcohol a day, 55 percent drink fewer than three alcoholic drinks a week, and 35 percent abstain completely (American Psychiatric Association, 1987). Most of the alcohol is consumed by a small percentage of people; 50 percent of the total alcohol consumed is drunk by only 10 percent of drinkers. Men drink two to five times as much as women. It is estimated that 13 percent of the adult population has experienced problems with alcohol abuse or dependence at some time in their lives. Drinking is widespread among young people. According to the 1990 National Household Survey, heavy drinking was most common among those between 18 and 25 years of age (National Institute of Drug Abuse, 1991). In a national survey of high school seniors, Johnston, O'Malley, and Bachman (1991) found that 90 percent reported using alcohol at some time; 32 percent reported at least one instance of heavy consumption (five or more drinks) during the past two weeks.

Add to these statistics the estimates of the Office of Technical Assessment (1983) on the social, medical, and physical costs of drinking, and you can see how immense the problem really is:

1. An estimated 10 million to 15 million Americans have serious problems directly related to alcohol consumption, and about 35 million people are indirectly affected (family members and children of alcoholics).

2. Alcoholism may be responsible for up to 15 percent of the nation's health care costs and for

MADD (Mothers Against Drunk Driving)

On May 3, 1980, a thirteen-year-old girl was walking to a church carnival in Fair Oaks, California. A car suddenly swerved out of control and killed her. Police arrested the vehicle's driver, who was intoxicated. A check of the driver's record revealed that he had a long history of arrests for drunk driving. Only the week before, he had been bailed out of jail after being charged with hit-and-run drunk driving.

Candy Lightner, the mother of the girl, was furious over the death of her daughter and concerned that the driver might not be sent to prison for the crime. At that time the penalties for drunk driving were frequently light, even when someone was injured or killed. Lightner wanted to find ways to keep drunk people from driving and to help the victims of drunk drivers and victims' families. She decided to form an organization called Mothers Against Drunk Drivers (MADD).

Initially Lightner was unsuccessful. She wanted to meet with then California Governor Jerry Brown to find a means of dealing with drunk drivers, but the governor declined to see her. Finally, after Lightner began to show up at his office day after day and succeeded in obtaining newspaper publicity for her crusade, Brown took action. He appointed a task force to deal with drunk driving and named her a member.

As a result of the efforts of Lightner and the task force, California eventually passed tough new laws against drunk driving. Lightner's organization has grown as well; MADD now has 320 chapters nationwide and 600,000 volunteers and donors. They have succeeded in convincing most states to enact more severe penalties for drunk driving. In addition, MADD was the most aggressive group lobbying Congress for a law that would force every state to set its minimum drinking age at twenty-one or higher. Such a law was passed by Congress and signed by President Reagan in the summer of 1984. Now, any state that does not comply by a certain fixed date can lose millions of dollars in federal highway funds.

Incidentally, the driver responsible for the death of Lightner's daughter did eventually serve twenty-one months in jail (Friedrich, 1985).

In view of the dangers associated with drunken driving, every person should address several questions: have you ever driven after having several drinks? If so, did you feel that you were proficient as a driver? At a party where there is alcohol consumption, do you encourage others to drink to intoxication? What should you do if a friend who has driven to the party has had too much to drink? These questions are important to address ahead of time. After consuming alcohol, judgment may be impaired so that one may believe that safe driving is simply a matter of being careful. Safe driving is also a matter of being sober, and we must all plan strategies for handling situations in which we or others become intoxicated.

---

significantly lowering the worker productivity at all levels of the economic system. It is estimated that alcoholism costs our society almost $50 billion per year.

3. The life expectancy of an alcoholic is ten to twelve years shorter than average, and alcoholism is related to health problems such as organ damage, brain dysfunction, cardiovascular disease, and mental disorders. Specifically, alcohol abuse can lead to cirrhosis of the liver, high blood pressure, heart attacks, stomach ulcers, and premature aging (Office for Substance Abuse Prevention, 1990).

4. Alcoholics have a significantly higher suicide rate than nonalcoholics (up to 58 percent greater in some groups of alcoholics). In addition, alcohol is associated with nearly 55 percent of all automobile accidents (see Focus 10.1), with home and industrial accidents, and with crimes such as assault, rape, and spouse abuse.

5. Alcoholism is estimated to be a factor in up to 40 percent of all problems brought to family courts, is known to be a major factor in divorce, and has been associated with family destabilization. In other words, excessive alcohol consumption causes family problems (arguments,

Alcoholism is often an important factor in divorce and is associated with family destabilization. Women who drink during pregnancy pose a risk to their unborn children who may be born with physical deformities and mental retardation.

violence) and is not just the result of marital discord.

6. Despite the high cost of alcoholism and the wide range of problems associated with alcoholism, an estimated 85 percent of alcoholics never receive any treatment.

Concern has also developed over the children of alcoholic parents. Children who have an alcoholic parent are at risk for social maladjustment, self-depreciation, lower self-esteem, and alcoholism (Berkowitz & Perkins, 1988; Cooper & McCormack, 1992).

With such grim statistics, why do people continue to create serious problems for themselves, their families, their employers, and even total strangers on the highways through problem drinking? Before we can explore this question, we need to examine the effects of alcohol.

The Effects of Alcohol

Alcohol abuse and alcohol dependence are, of course, substance abuse and dependence in which the sub-

stance is alcohol. People who have either of these alcohol-related disorders are popularly referred to as **alcoholics,** and their disorder as **alcoholism.** Drinking problems can be exhibited in two major ways. First, the person may need to use alcohol daily to function; that is, he or she may be unable to abstain. Second, the person may be able to abstain from consuming alcohol for certain periods of time but then cannot control or moderate intake once he or she resumes drinking. This person is a "binge" drinker. Both patterns of drinking can result in deteriorating relationships, loss of job, family conflicts, and violence while intoxicated.

Short-Term Effects   Alcohol has both short-term and long-term effects and both physiological and psychological effects. Once swallowed, it is absorbed into the blood without digestion. When it reaches the brain, its short-term physiological effect is to depress central nervous system functioning. When the alcohol content in the bloodstream (the blood alcohol level) is about 0.1 percent (the equivalent of drinking 5 ounces of whiskey or 5 glasses of beer), muscular coordination is impaired. The drinker may have trouble walking a straight line or pronouncing certain words. At the 0.5 percent blood alcohol level, the person may lose consciousness or even die.

The short-term physiological effects of alcohol on a specific person are determined by the individual's body weight, the amount of food present in the stomach, the drinking rate over time, prior drinking experience, heredity, personality factors, and the environment and culture of the drinker. Table 10.1 shows the effect of alcohol intake on blood alcohol level as a function of body weight.

The short-term psychological effects of alcohol often include feelings of happiness, loss of inhibitions (because alcohol depresses the inhibitory brain centers), poor judgment, and reduced concentration. The precise effects also depend on the situation or context in which drinking occurs. For example, negative moods and anger may also be experienced. Reactions also depend on the expectancy that individuals have developed with respect to alcohol (Hull & Bond, 1986). Some people may behave differently in the presence of others, not because of alcohol's effects but because of their perception that they have been drinking (for example, individuals who have only a few sips of beer and then begin to act hostile). Heavy

Table 10.1

Blood Alcohol Level as a Function of Number of Drinks Consumed and Body Weight

Body Weight, pounds	Number of Drinks Consumed[a]						
	1	2	3	4	5	6	7
100	.020	.055	.095	.130	.165	.200	.245
120	.015	.045	.075	.105	.135	.165	.195
140	.010	.035	.060	.085	.115	.140	.165
160	.005	.030	.050	.075	.095	.120	.145
180	.0	.025	.045	.065	.085	.105	.125
200	.0	.020	.040	.055	.075	.095	.110
220	.0	.020	.035	.050	.065	.085	.100
240	.0	.015	.035	.045	.060	.075	.090

Source: Adapted from Vogler & Bartz, 1983.

[a]The given blood alcohol levels are those that would exist 1 hour after the start of drinking. Because alcohol is metabolized over time, subtract 0.015 from the given level for each additional hour. For example, a 100-pound person consuming 2 drinks would, after 2 hours, have a blood alcohol level of 0.055 − 0.015 = 0.040. One drink equals 12 ounces of beer, 4 ounces of wine, or 1.25 ounces of liquor.

and prolonged drinking often impairs sexual performance and produces a hangover.

Long-Term Effects The long-term psychological effects of heavy drinking are more serious. Although there is no single type of alcoholic, Jellinek (1971) observed certain patterns in the course of individuals who develop alcohol dependence. Most people begin to drink in social situations. Because the alcohol relieves tension, the drinkers tend to drink more and to drink more frequently. Tolerance levels may increase over a period of months or years.

Because of stress, inability to adequately cope, or biological predisposition to alcoholism, some drinkers become preoccupied with thoughts of alcohol. They may worry about whether there will be enough alcohol at a party; they may try to drink inconspicuously or even furtively. They begin to consume large amounts and may "gulp" their drinks. Such drinkers frequently feel guilty; they are somewhat aware that their drinking is excessive. Heavy, sustained drinking may lead to blackouts, periods of time for which drinkers have no memory of their activities. Jellinek believed that sustained drinking could then lead to a loss of control over alcoholic intake and to frequent periods of intoxication. Individuals may then drink only to become intoxicated.

It should also be noted that most investigators have formulated their ideas based on research with male alcoholics. Although relatively few studies have examined female alcoholics, the available evidence suggests that gender differences exist. For example, alcoholic women report more childhood problems such as alcoholic parents, unhappy childhoods, and broken homes than do alcoholic men. Furthermore, women become problem drinkers at a later age than men (Perodeau, 1984). These findings suggested that perspectives based on research with alcoholic men should be carefully scrutinized for their applicability to women.

The long-term physiological effects of alcohol consumption include an increase in tolerance as the person becomes used to alcohol, physical discomfort, anxiety, and hallucinations. Chronic alcoholism destroys brain cells and is often accompanied by poor nutritional habits and physical deterioration. Thus the left brain hemispheres of alcoholics have been found to be less dense than those of a control group of nonalcoholics (Golden et al., 1981). Other direct or indirect consequences generally attributed to

Alcohol reduces inhibitions and tension because it is a central nervous system depressant. In social situations, which can be anxiety provoking, a person may drink for its relaxing effect. Eventually, over a period of months or years, a person's tolerance level may increase, and alcoholism may develop.

chronic alcoholism are liver diseases such as *cirrhosis,* in which an excessive amount of fibrous tissue develops and impedes the circulation of blood; heart failure; hemorrhages of capillaries, particularly those on the sides of the nose; and cancers of the mouth and throat. Alcohol consumption in pregnant women may affect their unborn children: children who suffer fetal alcohol syndrome are born mentally retarded and physically deformed.

Interestingly, the moderate use of alcohol (one or two drinks a day) in adults has been associated in some studies with lowered risk of heart disease. The precise reasons for this effect are unknown. What is clear, though, is that chronic heavy consumption has serious negative consequences.

DRUG-RELATED DISORDERS

Miriam K. was a 44-year-old divorced pharmacist. She had been married for more than twenty years, but, during the last few years of the marriage, Miriam and her husband had talked about divorce. They had lost interest in each other and lived their own lives.

After their son and daughter left home to attend college, they obtained a divorce.

Although the divorce was relatively amicable, Miriam felt lonesome. With her children at college and her divorce completed, she was very much alone at home. Several of her friends took her along to "singles club" activities to establish some new social relationships. However, Miriam had mixed feelings about men. She was excited about meeting them, but she also felt anxious and inadequate. In addition, Miriam was facing additional responsibilities and demands at work, where a promotion now required that she supervise the operation of three pharmacies.

Although Miriam had occasionally used drugs to calm her nervousness, she now began taking Valium regularly to reduce tension and bring on sleep. Because she worked at pharmacies, she had no trouble in obtaining the drug secretly. Gradually she took more and more. Over the course of several years, her tolerance and intake increased to the point where she was consuming about 75 milligrams a day. This heavy consumption of Valium resulted in a general lethargy, and Miriam was absent from work a great deal. Her employer finally told her that she had to perform better or he would find someone else for her job. Immediately thereafter, Miriam sought help for her dependency on Valium.

Table 10.2

1990 Annual Prevalence of Thirteen Drugs Among Respondents Aged 19–28: Percentage Who Used Drugs in the Last Twelve Months

Substance	Percentage
Alcohol	87.4
Cigarettes	37.1
Marijuana	26.1
Cocaine	8.6
Stimulants (not under doctor's orders)	5.2
Tranquilizers (not under doctor's orders)	3.7
LSD	3.3
Other opiates	2.7
Barbiturates	1.9
"Crack"	1.6
Heroin	0.1

Source: Adapted from Johnston, O'Malley & Bachman, 1991.
Note: Number of respondents: 6,700.

In addition to alcohol, a number of other substances can result in abuse, dependence, intoxication, and withdrawal. The substances used include both prescription drugs such as Valium as well as cigarettes, narcotics, and LSD (lysergic acid diethylamine).

Substance-related disorders are most prevalent among youths and young adults. Comparing substance use among young adults, Johnston and colleagues (1991) found a decline in substance use during the past decade. Declines were noted for crack cocaine, cocaine, marijuana, stimulants (except for stay-awake pills, which showed an increase), PCP (phencyclidine), and tranquilizers. However, changes were slight for LSD, cigarettes, and heroin. Table 10.2 shows the 1990 annual prevalence rate of substance use for young adults (ages 19–28). About 87 percent reported the consumption of alcohol during the past twelve months; the prevalence rate was 26 percent for marijuana, 37 percent for cigarettes, and 9 percent for cocaine. These are the rates only for substance use over the past 12 months; lifetime prevalence rates (an estimate of the percentage of individ-

uals who use substances at any time during their lives) are obviously much higher than annual prevalence rates.

The drugs that we will discuss can all cause psychological or physical problems; many can cause legal problems as well. The use of certain substances, except under strict medical supervision, is expressly prohibited by law. Hence the user must obtain them illegally. We will specifically discuss a number of drugs or substances. Many have traditionally been considered depressants (or sedatives), stimulants, or hallucinogens. In practice, substances may not be easily classified into these three categories because they may have multiple effects (stimulating and depressing effects). Each of the drugs can result in an abuse disorder or a dependence disorder. Intoxication and withdrawal may also be diagnosed, although the precise criteria for these diagnoses depend on the specific drug. We shall discuss general categories of drugs as well as specific drugs such as opiates, barbiturates, benzodiazepines, amphetamines, caffeine and nicotine, cocaine and crack, hallucinogens, marijuana, LSD, and PCP.

Depressants or Sedatives

Depressants or sedatives cause generalized depression of the central nervous system and a slowing down of responses. People taking such substances feel calm and relaxed. They may also become sociable and open because of lowered interpersonal inhibitions.

Opiates (Narcotics)   The organic **narcotics**—opium and its derivatives morphine, heroin, and codeine—are drugs that depress the central nervous system. They act as sedatives to provide relief from pain, anxiety, and tension. Feelings of euphoria and well-being (and sometimes negative reactions such as nausea) often accompany narcotics use. Opium and its derivatives (especially heroin), however, result in dependency. Tolerance for narcotics builds rapidly, and withdrawal symptoms are severe. Opiates such as heroin are usually administered intravenously, spreading diseases such as AIDS, which can be transmitted through needle sharing (Smith & Landry, 1988).

Because dependency is likely to occur after repeated use, narcotics addicts are usually unable to maintain normal relationships with family and friends or to pursue legitimate careers. They live to

Heroin is a highly addictive narcotic that is generally taken through hypodermic injection. It acts as a sedative that relieves pain, tension, and anxiety and produces feelings of euphoria and well-being. The dependency is so strong that addicts are often unable to maintain normal social relationships or a legitimate career.

obtain the drug through any possible means. Nonmedical use of narcotics is illegal, and many addicts have little choice but to turn to criminal activities to obtain the drug and to support their expensive habits.

Barbiturates Synthetic **barbiturates,** or "downers," are powerful depressants of the central nervous system that are commonly used to induce relaxation and sleep. Next to the narcotics, they represent the largest category of illegal drugs, and they are quite dangerous for several reasons. First, dependence can develop. Second, although their legal use is severely restricted, widespread availability of the drugs makes it difficult to control misuse or abuse. More than 1 million persons—primarily the middle-aged and elderly—are now estimated to be barbiturate addicts. Third, users often experience harmful physical effects. Excessive use of either barbiturates or heroin can be fatal, but barbiturates are the more lethal. Constant heroin use increases the amount of the drug required for a lethal dosage. The lethal dosage of barbiturates does not increase with prolonged use, so accidental overdose and death can easily occur. And combining alcohol with barbiturates can be espe-

cially dangerous because alcohol compounds the depressant effects of the barbiturates.

Kelly M., a seventeen-year-old girl from an upper-middle-class background, lived with her divorced mother. Kelly was hospitalized after her mother found her unconscious from an overdose of barbiturates consumed together with alcohol. She survived the overdose and later told the therapist that she had regularly used barbiturates for the past year and a half. The overdose was apparently accidental and not suicidal.

For several weeks following the overdose, Kelly openly discussed her use of barbiturates with the therapist. She had been introduced to the drugs by a boy in school who told her they would help her relax. Kelly was apparently unhappy over her parents' divorce. She felt that her mother did not want her, especially because her mother spent a lot of time away from home building a real estate agency. And, although she enjoyed her occasional visits with her father, Kelly felt extremely uncomfortable in the presence of the woman who lived with him. The barbiturates helped her relax and relieved her tensions. Arguments with her mother would precipitate heavy use of the drugs. Eventually she became dependent on barbiturates and always spent her allowance to buy them. Her mother reported that she had no knowledge of her daughter's drug use. She did notice, though, that Kelly was increasingly isolated and sleepy.

The therapist informed Kelly of the dangers of barbiturates and of combining them with alcohol. Kelly agreed to undergo treatment, which included the gradual reduction of barbiturate use, and psychotherapy with her mother.

A hazardous practice illustrated in the case of Kelly M. is *polydrug use,* or the use of more than one chemical substance at the same time. This practice can be extremely dangerous. For example, heavy smokers who consume a great deal of alcohol run an increased risk of esophageal cancer. Chemicals may also exhibit a synergistic effect, in which drugs that are taken simultaneously interact to multiply each other's effects. For example, when a large dose of barbiturate is taken along with alcohol, death may occur because of a synergistic effect that depresses the central nervous system. Furthermore, one of the substances (such as alcohol) may reduce the person's judgment, resulting in excessive (or lethal) use of the other drug. Equally dangerous is the use of one drug to counteract the effect of another. For instance, a person who has taken a stimulant to feel euphoric may later take an excessive amount of a depressant (such as a barbiturate) in an attempt to get some sleep. The result can be an exceedingly harmful physiological reaction.

According to DSM-IV, polysubstance dependence may be diagnosed when a person has used at least three substances (not including nicotine and caffeine) for a period of six months, and, during this period, the person meets the criteria for substance dependence for the substances considered as a group but not for any single specific substance.

Benzodiazepines   One member of this category of drugs is Valium, which is one of the most widely prescribed drugs in the United States today. As in the case of Miriam K. (described at the beginning of this section), Valium is often used to reduce anxiety and muscle tension. People who take the drug seem less concerned with and less affected by their problems. Some side effects may occur, such as drowsiness, skin rash, nausea, and depression, but the greatest danger in using Valium is its abuse. Because life stressors are unavoidable, many people use Valium as their sole means of dealing with stress; then, as tolerance develops, dependence on the drug may also grow.

Stimulants

A **stimulant** is a substance that is a central nervous system energizer, inducing elation, grandiosity, hyperactivity, agitation, and appetite suppression.

Amphetamines   The **amphetamines,** also known as "uppers," speed up activity of the central nervous system and bestow on users increased alertness, energy, and sometimes feelings of euphoria and confidence. They increase the concentration of the neurotransmitter dopamine in the synapse, which exposes the postsynaptic cells to high levels of dopamine. Increased concentration of dopamine may amplify nerve impulses in the brain that are associated with pleasure (Wise, 1988). Amphetamines inhibit appetite and sleep. These stimulants may be physically addictive and become habit forming with a rapid increase in tolerance. "Speed freaks" inject amphetamines into their blood vessels and become extremely hyperactive and euphoric for days. Assaultive, homicidal, and suicidal behaviors can occur during this time. Heavy doses can also trigger delusions of persecution, similar to those seen among paranoid schizo-

phrenics. Overdoses are fatal, and brain damage has been observed among chronic abusers. Some people may use amphetamines to get "high" and then use barbiturates to "come down"—an extremely dangerous practice, as we have noted.

Caffeine and Nicotine   Two widely used and legal stimulants are caffeine and nicotine. *Caffeine* is ingested primarily in coffee, chocolate, tea, and cola drinks. It is considered intoxicating when, after the recent ingestion of 250 milligrams (about two cups of coffee) or more of caffeine, a person shows several of the following symptoms: restlessness, nervousness, excitement, insomnia, flushed face, gastrointestinal disturbance, rambling speech, and cardiac arrhythmia. The consequences of caffeine intoxication are usually transitory and relatively minor. In some cases, however, the intoxication is chronic and seriously affects the gastrointestinal or circulatory system.

Nicotine dependence is most commonly associated with cigarette smoking. The following problems are often seen among those who are nicotine dependent:

The person's attempts to stop or reduce tobacco use on a permanent basis are unsuccessful.

Attempts to stop smoking have led to withdrawal symptoms such as a craving for tobacco, irritability, difficulty in concentrating, and restlessness.

The person continues to use tobacco despite a serious physical disorder, such as emphysema, that he or she knows is exacerbated by tobacco use.

Focus 10.2 discusses two views on the development and maintenance of smoking behaviors.

Cocaine and Crack   A great deal of publicity and concern have been devoted to the use of **cocaine,** a substance extracted from the coca plant. A number of major-league baseball players, film stars, political figures, and other notables use this drug regularly. Indeed, its use is expanding, particularly among the young and the upwardly mobile. Because of its high cost and euphoria-inducing properties, cocaine is a fashionable drug, especially among middle-class and upper-class professionals. From one to three million cocaine abusers are in need of treatment, up to six times the number of heroin addicts (Gawin, 1991).

Smoking: Can the Body "Kick the Habit"?

Cigarette smoking is harmful to the body. A U.S. Surgeon General's report has indicated that cigarette smoking accounts for one-sixth of the deaths in the United States and is the single most preventable cause of death. It also noted that smoking among adults has declined from 50 percent in 1965 to 29 percent in 1988. The decline is especially evident among adults with higher levels of education (Toufexis, 1989).

Many people assume that sufficient will power and motivation on the part of smokers, or legal and social sanctions from nonsmokers (such as prohibiting smoking in public facilities), can reduce or eliminate the smoking habit. Judging from current statistics, however, efforts to motivate smokers to quit, to prohibit smoking in certain areas, and to regulate advertising by the tobacco industry have not been successful in achieving that goal. Why do smokers continue to smoke? The answer may lie in the physiological effects of smoking. Even though smokers report feeling more relaxed during smoking, cigarettes act as a stimulant. Heart rate, for instance, increases during smoking.

Stanley Schachter, a noted psychologist, argued that people smoke because they are physically addicted

to nicotine. In a series of experiments, Schachter (1977) drew two conclusions: first, chronic smokers need their "normal" constant intake of nicotine. When heavy smokers are given low-nicotine cigarettes, they smoke more cigarettes and puff more frequently. Withdrawal symptoms, such as irritability and increased eating, appear when smokers do not receive their "dose" of nicotine. Second, smoking does not reduce anxiety or calm the nerves. But not smoking increases anxiety and produces withdrawal reactions. Smokers can tolerate less stress when they are deprived of cigarettes than when they are able to smoke. Even with cigarettes, however, smokers do not perform better under stress than nonsmokers. Stress seems to deplete body nicotine, so that smoking is necessary to maintain the nicotine level.

If nicotine addiction maintains cigarette smoking, then supplying smokers with nicotine in a nontobacco product may reduce the need to smoke. Some researchers (Hall et al., 1987) found that giving smokers a nicotine gum was more effective than giving a placebo gum in a stop-smoking program, even if the smokers were not told what substance was in the gum. Gottlieb and

colleagues (1987), however, found that when smokers were led to believe that they had received nicotine gum (whether or not they actually had received it) in a treatment program, they reported fewer withdrawal symptoms and cigarette consumption in a two-week period than those who were told that they had received no nicotine. Smokers' *belief* about presence of nicotine was more important in treatment than actual *ingestion* of nicotine. This study seemed to negate the role of nicotine in treatment and, perhaps, in smoking. The study only followed the smokers for two weeks, however, so the long-term effects of nicotine versus expectancy are unclear.

In a review of the research on nicotine replacement therapy, Lichtenstein and Glasgow (1992) concluded that nicotine gum helps alleviate withdrawal and prevent short-term relapse. Behavioral treatment is most useful in warding off longer-term relapse. However, nicotine gum is not the most effective method of delivering nicotine. The levels of nicotine in the blood can vary considerably depending on the way the gum is chewed, the number of pieces of gum used, and the ingestion of drinks such as coffee that may alter the effects of nicotine.

In the late 1800s, cocaine was heralded as a wonder drug for remedying depression, indigestion, headaches, pain, and other ailments. It was often included in medicines, tonics, and wines; it was even used in cola drinks such as Coca-Cola. In the early 1900s, however, its use was controlled, and the possession of cocaine is now illegal.

Cocaine can be eaten, injected intravenously, or smoked, but it is usually "snorted" (inhaled). Eating

does not produce rapid effects, and intravenous use requires injection with a needle, which leaves needle marks and introduces the possibility of infection. When cocaine is inhaled into the nasal cavity, however, the person quickly begins to feel euphoric, stimulated, and confident. Heart rate and blood pressure increase, and (according to users) fatigue and appetite are reduced. As in the case of amphetamines, cocaine appears to increase synaptic dopamine levels

If the treatments involving nicotine gum are limited, are there more effective ways of delivering the nicotine? There has recently been a great deal of interest in nicotine transdermal patches. In this treatment, an adhesive patch, which delivers a standard dose of nicotine during the day, is placed on the upper arm. Problems in chewing and in achieving a consistent dosage level of nicotine are minimized. Studies comparing the nicotine patch with a placebo patch, in which neither the smokers nor the experimenters knew who had nicotine or placebo patches during treatment (a "double-blind" study), showed that the nicotine patch is more effective than the placebo patch in smoking cessation (Lichtenstein & Glasgow, 1992).

Without denying the role of nicotine in physical dependence, Lichtenstein (1982) sees the development and maintenance of smoking as a complex process involving a variety of factors. For example, factors such as the availability of cigarettes, curiosity, and smoking models influence the initial use of cigarettes. Then physiological and psychosocial factors such as nicotine addiction and positive consequences maintain smoking. For psychosocial reasons, including health and the expense of smoking materials, the person may try to stop smoking. Withdrawal symptoms and alcohol consumption (former smokers who drink are often tempted to smoke while consuming alcohol), however, are powerful factors motivating the resumption of smoking. Lichtenstein's analysis emphasized the value of multicomponent programs for the treatment and prevention of smoking. His factors are listed in the following table.

Factors Involved In Smoking Behaviors

Starting (psychosocial factors)	Continuing (psychological and psychosocial factors)	Stopping (psychosocial factors)	Resuming (psychosocial and physiological factors)
Availability	Nicotine	Health	Withdrawal symptoms
Curiosity	Immediate positive	Expense	Stress and frustration
Rebelliousness	consequences	Social support	Social pressure
Anticipation of	Signals (cues) in	Self-mastery	Alcohol consumption
adulthood	environs	Aesthetics	Abstinence violation
Social confidence	Avoiding negative	Example to others	effect
Social pressure/	effects (withdrawal)		
modeling: peers,			
siblings, parents,			
media			

Source: Lichtenstein, 1982.

in the brain by inhibiting the reuptake of the dopamine. Wise (1988) believes that these actions make the drug reinforcing and stimulating.

Users may become dependent on cocaine. That is, a user can develop an addiction and be unable to stop using it. Although users do not show gross physiological withdrawal symptoms, Gawin (1991) noted that the distinction between psychological and physical addiction is difficult to make and that chronic abuse of cocaine can produce neurophysiological changes in the central nervous system. The constant desire for cocaine can impair social and occupational functioning, and the high cost of the substance can cause users to resort to crime to feed their habit. In addition, side effects can occur. Feelings of depression and gloom may be produced when a cocaine high wears off. Heavy users sometimes report weight loss, paranoia, nervousness, fatigue, and hallucina-

Drug abuse on the job has become a national crisis. It affects worker productivity and safety. Cocaine abuse is particularly problematic. To combat the problem, many companies have initiated drug testing and treatment programs for their employees.

tions. The Committee on Drug Abuse of the Council on Psychiatric Services (1987) also noted that, because cocaine stimulates the sympathetic nervous system, premature ventricular heartbeats and death may occur.

Crack is one of the most talked-about drugs. It is a purified and potent form of cocaine produced by heating cocaine with ether ("freebasing"). Crack is sold as small, solid pieces or "rocks." When it is smoked in a pipe, euphoria is swift and marked, followed by depression. Johnston and colleagues (1991) found that 1.6 percent of young adults reported using crack during a twelve-month period.

Crack is a major concern to society for four reasons. First, it is inexpensive and readily obtainable, so large segments of the population can have easy access to the substance. Second, the euphoria of the high from crack is quite intense and immediate, compared with sniffing cocaine. Thus many people prefer crack. Third, users appear to develop relatively rapid addiction to crack, and they continually seek the substance. Fourth, because of the increasing popularity of the drug and the crimes associated with crack, law enforcement resources have been expanded trying to control its sale, distribution, and use.

Hallucinogens

Hallucinogens are not considered physiologically addictive. Use does not lead to physical dependence (that is, to increased tolerance or withdrawal reaction), although psychological dependency may occur. Many people use hallucinogens such as marijuana, LSD, and phencyclidine (PCP) to experience certain illusions, such as more vivid sensory awareness, heightened alertness, or increased insight.

Marijuana The mildest and most commonly used hallucinogen is **marijuana,** also known as "pot" or "grass." This substance is generally smoked in a cigarette, or "joint." More than 33 percent of the U.S. population (including youngsters) have used marijuana, although it is an illegal substance (National Institute of Drug Abuse, 1991).

The subjective effects of marijuana include feelings of euphoria, tranquility, and passivity. Once the drug has taken effect, subjective time passes slowly, and some users report increased sensory experiences as well as mild perceptual distortions. Prior experience with the drug, expectancy of its effects, and the setting in which marijuana is used influence the precise reactions.

In one experiment, marijuana smokers were given either a marijuana or a placebo cigarette to smoke. Some subjects were told to overcome the drug's effects in performing tasks; others were not told to do so. The researchers wanted to find out whether subjects could control their performance even after marijuana intoxication—that is, whether they could "come down" from a "high" at will. Their results indicated that marijuana intoxication influences the person's ability to estimate time and to remember lists of words. Moreover, motivating subjects to over-

Marijuana Smoking: Are There Harmful Effects?

There is growing concern over the potentially harmful physical effects of marijuana (Coates, 1980), especially because many Americans have tried the drug (National Institute of Drug Abuse, 1991). Smoking marijuana may cause more serious lung damage than smoking cigarettes. Indeed, smoking four joints a week may be as bad as smoking sixteen cigarettes a day. There is also some evidence that marijuana smoking may temporarily affect the reproductive systems of males and females: heavy marijuana use reduced sperm concentration and sperm motility in males and was associated with failure to ovulate in females. Because these findings are correlational in nature, it cannot be concluded that marijuana smoking causes problems in the reproductive system. The results do suggest, however, that much more caution should be exercised in the use of marijuana in view of the possible consequences.

Fears about marijuana have gone through various fluctuations. In the past (1920s) the physiological effects of marijuana smoking were greatly exaggerated. More recently (1970s) it was believed that these effects were insignificant. Now researchers are reexamining the latter belief.

The National Academy of Sciences (1982) has taken a dim view of marijuana use. Marijuana smoke can cause serious lung and respiratory problems and can increase the risk of cancer. Furthermore, because the drug affects short-term memory and causes intoxication, people who have recently smoked marijuana may pose a danger while driving a car, operating machinery, or working in occupations that require judgment and decision making (such as air traffic control). Other potential problems include confusion, flashbacks, and psychotic-like reactions (Committee on Drug Abuse of the Council on Psychiatric Services, 1987).

Coates (1980), however, pointed out the benefits of marijuana in treating certain physical ailments. For example, open-angle glaucoma, an eye disorder that can lead to blindness, temporarily responds to the drug; patients nauseated by chemotherapy for cancer often find relief with marijuana treatment. Researchers are now experimenting with the use of marijuana for victims of multiple sclerosis and for people afflicted by seizures. Such findings—and there seem to be new ones almost every week—show how little we know about marijuana and how much we still have to learn.

Should the use of marijuana be legalized? This is a question that has been periodically raised. There is evidence that use of one drug is associated with the use of other drugs and that health and safety issues are important to consider, as in the case of alcohol. Yet, alcohol consumption is not illegal among adults. Should marijuana use be legal but restricted in some manner?

---

come the effects of marijuana improved the subjects' performance at estimating time but not their ability to remember lists of words (Cappell & Pliner, 1973).

Although much controversy has raged over the effects of marijuana, many states have now decriminalized the possession of small quantities of this substance. Focus 10.3 is a brief report on some of the risks of marijuana smoking.

Lysergic Acid Diethylamide (LSD)   LSD or "acid" gained notoriety as a hallucinogen in the mid-1960s. Praised by users as a potent psychedelic, consciousness-expanding drug, LSD produces distortions of reality and hallucinations. "Good trips" are experiences of sharpened visual and auditory percep-

tion, heightened sensation, convictions that one has achieved profound philosophical insights, and feelings of ecstasy. "Bad trips" include fear and panic from distortions of sensory experiences, severe depression, marked confusion and disorientation, and delusions. Some users report "flashbacks" or the recurrence of hallucinations or other sensations days or weeks after taking LSD. Fatigue, stress, or the use of another drug may trigger a "flashback."

LSD is considered a *psychotomimetic* drug because, in some cases, it produces reactions that mimic those seen in acute psychotic reactions. It does not produce physical dependence, even in users who have taken the drug hundreds of times. Aside from its psychological effects, no substantial evidence supports the notion that LSD is dangerous in and of itself. Large doses do not cause death, although there are reports of people who have unwittingly committed suicide while under the influence of LSD. Initially researchers believed that LSD caused chromosomal damage and spontaneous abortions, but such events are probably attributable to impurities in the drug, the use of other drugs, or the unhealthy lifestyles of many users.

Phencyclidine (PCP) Phencyclidine, also known as PCP, "angel dust," "crystal," "superweed," and "rocket fuel," has emerged as one of the most dangerous of the so-called street drugs. Originally developed for its pain-killing properties, PCP is a hallucinatory drug that causes perceptual distortions, euphoria, nausea, confusion, delusions, and violent psychotic behavior. Reactions to the drug are influenced by dosage, the individual user, and the circumstances in which it is taken. One thing is clear: PCP has in many cases caused aggressive behaviors, violence, or deaths from the taker's recklessness or delusions of invincibility. The drug is illegal, but it is still widely used, often sprinkled on marijuana and smoked.

Spitzer and coworkers (1981, pp. 229–230) described the effects of PCP on a chronic user. As you will see, one long-term effect may have been a personality change.

> The patient is a 20-year-old male who was brought to the hospital, trussed in ropes, by his four brothers. This is his seventh hospitalization in the last two years, each for similar behavior. One of his brothers reports that he "came home crazy" late one night, threw a chair through a window, tore a gas heater off the wall, and ran into the street. The family called the police, who apprehended him shortly thereafter as he stood, naked, directing traffic at a busy intersection. He assaulted the arresting officers, escaped them, and ran home screaming threats at his family. There his brothers were able to subdue him.
>
> On admission the patient was observed to be agitated, his mood fluctuating between anger and fear. He had slurred speech and staggered when he walked. He remained extremely violent and disorganized for the first several days of his hospitalization, then began having longer and longer lucid intervals, still interspersed with sudden, unpredictable periods in which he displayed great suspiciousness, a fierce expression, slurred speech, and clenched fists.

After calming down, the patient denied ever having been violent or acting in an unusual way ("I'm a peaceable man") and said he could not remember how he got to the hospital. He admitted to using alcohol and marijuana socially, but denied phencyclidine (PCP) use except for once, experimentally, three years previously. Nevertheless, blood and urine tests were positive for phencyclidine, and his brother believes "he gets dusted every day."

According to his family, he was perfectly normal until about three years before. He made above-average grades in school, had a part-time job and a girlfriend, and was outgoing. Then, at age 17, he had his first episode of emotional disturbance. The onset was very sudden, with symptoms similar to the present episode. He quickly recovered from that first episode, went back to school, and graduated from high school. From subsequent episodes, however, his improvement was less and less encouraging.

After three weeks of the current hospitalization, he is sullen and watchful, quick to remark sarcastically on the smallest infringement of the respect due him. He is mostly quiet and isolated from others, but is easily provoked to fury. His family reports that "This is as good as he gets now." He lives and eats most of his meals at home, and keeps himself physically clean, but mostly lies around the house, will do no housework, and has not held a job for nearly two years. The family does not know how he gets his spending money, or how he spends his time outside the hospital.

DSM-IV includes a category for other substance-use disorders. Maladaptive use of substances such as anabolic steroids and nitrous oxide ("laughing gas") may be included in this category.

ETIOLOGY OF SUBSTANCE-RELATED DISORDERS

Why do people abuse substances, despite the knowledge that alcohol and drugs can have devastating consequences in their lives? The answer to this question is complicated by the number of different kinds of substances that are used and the number of factors that interact to account for the use of any one substance. Many theories have been proposed in the attempt to answer the question. Of these, the major types are either biogenic and physical in perspective (involving genetic or biological factors) or psychological and cultural (involving personality, sociocultural, or behavioral-cognitive factors). Both perspectives may have some validity in explaining addiction. The biogenic theories focus on dependence, or the bodily need for alcohol or drugs. The psychological-cultural theories attempt to explain how abuse patterns develop before actual dependence and why addicts who try to stop their habit may relapse and return to substance use. More recent theories have attempted to integrate psychological and biogenic approaches. In the past, investigators often assumed that the acquisition and maintenance of substances were largely distinct processes in which psychological factors influenced acquisition and biogenic factors were responsible for maintenance. For example, in the case of alcohol, drinking behavior was believed to be the result of psychological factors, whereas the maintenance of heavy drinking resulted from physical dependence on alcohol. That is, one first drinks because of curiosity; exposure to drinking models such as parents, peers, or television characters; and the tension-reducing properties of alcohol. After prolonged consumption, however, the person becomes physically dependent and drinks heavily to satisfy bodily needs. This assumption is overly simplistic. As you will see shortly, the acquisition and maintenance of drinking behavior are both influenced by the complex interaction of psychological and physical factors.

In our discussion, it is apparent that most research has been conducted on alcohol because of its widespread use, availability, and consequences to society. Most of our discussion therefore centers on alcohol, although we will comment on how different theories may be relevant to the use of substances other than alcohol.

Biogenic Explanations

Because alcohol affects metabolic processes and the central nervous system, investigators have explored the possibility that heredity or congenital factors increase susceptibility to addiction. The Research Task Force of the National Institute of Mental Health (1975) suggested that alcoholism "runs in families" and that 20 to 30 percent of the children of alcoholics eventually develop alcoholism. The challenge in these observations is to separate the contributions of genetic and environmental factors because children share both genetic and environmental influences with their parents. The role of in utero and neonatal influences must also be determined.

Several studies have indicated that children whose biological parents were alcoholics but who were adopted and raised by nonrelatives are more likely to develop drinking problems than adopted children whose biological parents were not alcoholics (Goodwin, 1979; Research Task Force of the National Institute of Mental Health, 1975). In their adoption study, Cadoret and Wesner (1990) found clear-cut evidence of a genetic factor operating from biologic parent to adoptee in the chance of alcohol abuse in the adoptee. They also found evidence of environmental influences in that having an alcoholic in the adoptive home also increases the risk of alcohol problems in the adoptee. Research comparing the concordance rates for alcoholism among identical (MZ) and fraternal (DZ) twins indicated that, although MZ twins have higher concordance rates, DZ twins also have high rates (Rosenthal, 1971). Concordance rates indicate the likelihood that *both* twins have the disorder. Collectively, these findings suggest that both heredity and environmental factors are important. Goodwin (1985) speculated that two types of alcoholism may exist: familial and nonfamilial. *Familial alcoholism* shows a family history of alcoholism, suggesting genetic predisposition. This type of alcoholism develops at an early age (usually by the late twenties), is severe, and increases the risk of alcoholism, but not other mental disorders, among blood relatives. *Nonfamilial alcoholism* does not show these characteristics and is presumably influenced more by environment. The consensus among experts in the field is that alcoholism has a genetic component, and new, sophisticated techniques are being used to localize the gene (or genes) responsible and to understand how the gene operates (Wijsman, 1990).

Other researchers have attempted to find risk factors or markers for alcoholism. The risk factors are variables that are related to, or etiologically significant in, alcoholism. Biological markers involving neurotransmitters in the brain have been found to be related to alcoholism (Tabakoff, Whelan & Hoffman, 1990). Another risk factor appears to be sensitivity or responsiveness to alcohol (Schuckit, 1990). Individuals who are not sensitive to alcohol may be able to consume large amounts of alcohol before feeling its effects and be more susceptible to alcoholism. Finally, being a child of an alcoholic and coming from a family with a history of alcoholism may be risk factors. Noble (1990) compared sons of alcoholic fathers with sons of social drinking fathers on central nervous system functioning (that is, behavioral, neuropsychological, and electrophysiological measures). The boys in the two groups were matched for demographic background, and none at the start of the study had drank alcohol or used drugs. The high-risk boys as well as their alcoholic fathers exhibited different central nervous system (CNS) functioning than the low-risk boys and their fathers. Furthermore, they were more likely than low-risk boys to begin drinking. Noble also studied the family environment of the boys to see if high-risk boys had disturbed family backgrounds. No differences in family background and environment were found. Noble concluded that hereditary factors may be important in alcoholism.

Finally, there have been attempts to implicate nutritional or vitamin deficiencies, hormonal imbalances, or abnormal bodily processes as causes of alcoholism. No clear-cut evidence has been found to indicate that these congenital factors are important in human alcoholism.

With respect to other substances such as opiates, cigarettes, and LSD, research on the hereditary basis for dependence has not been as extensive as it is for alcohol. Nevertheless, it is conceivable that genetic differences may be a factor in addiction. Some researchers have found racial (and presumably genetic) differences in responses to certain drugs (Rosenblat & Tang, 1987). Asian American, compared to white, clients appear to require smaller dosages of psychotropic medication to achieve the same clinical effects for mental disorders.

Psychodynamic and Personality Explanations

A number of psychoanalytic explanations have been proposed for alcoholism. Most hold that childhood traumas (such as an overprotecting mother, maternal neglect, or frustration of dependency needs), especially during the oral stage of development, result in the repression of painful conflicts involving dependency needs (Kanas, 1988). During stress or encounters with situations reminiscent of the original conflicts, symptoms such as anxiety, depression, and hostility begin to occur. Alcohol is seen as (1) releasing inhibitions and allowing the repressed conflicts

to be expressed or (2) enabling people to obtain oral gratification and to satisfy dependency needs. Most of the psychoanalytic formulations are based on retrospective clinical case studies rather than empirical data, so the validity of the formulations is open to question.

Some researchers believe that certain personality characteristics make people vulnerable to alcoholism. These characteristics may predispose people to use alcohol, rather than some other coping strategy, to deal with stressors. Low frustration tolerance, emotional immaturity, feelings of inadequacy, a need for power, and dependent personality characteristics have all been associated with alcoholism or heavy drinking (Jones, 1968, 1971; McClelland et al., 1972; Winokur et al., 1970).

Findings regarding a predisposition to drinking are mixed. In one long-term study, researchers found that adolescents reported increased drunkenness when they had (1) lower personal regard for academic achievement, (2) higher tolerance for deviance, (3) more positive reasons in relation to perceived drawbacks for drinking, and (4) more positive reasons for drug use (Jessor & Jessor, 1977). Although these four personality characteristics were significantly correlated with being drunk, the correlations were not strong. In another long-term study (of male drinkers only), evidence was found that an unhappy childhood does not cause alcohol abuse, as is popularly believed. Rather, the abuser is unhappy because of heavy drinking (Vaillant & Milofsky, 1982).

In a recent review of research on personality and alcoholism, Nathan (1988) concluded that only two personality characteristics—antisocial behavior and depression—have been associated with drinking problems. Particularly consistent is the relationship between a childhood or adolescent history of antisocial behavior (such as rejection of societal rules) and alcoholism. Nathan warned, however, that the role of personality characteristics, including antisocial tendencies and depression, as causal factors in alcoholism cannot be uncritically accepted. Many alcohol abusers do not show antisocial histories, and many antisocial people do not drink excessively. Furthermore, depression may well be a consequence rather than an antecedent of alcohol abuse (that is, problem drinking may cause people to feel depressed).

Nathan's points are also pertinent to research that has attempted to find a relationship between personality characteristics and the use of other drugs besides alcohol. In the 1960s and 1970s, some researchers had hoped that they could identify a cluster of personality traits that could account for addiction to substances. However, simple attempts to find a common pattern of personality traits that underlie addiction have failed (Platt, 1986). It is highly unlikely that addiction is caused by a single personality type (see Critical Thinking for a further discussion).

Sociocultural Explanations

Drinking varies according to sociocultural factors such as sex, age, socioeconomic status, ethnicity, religion, and country. As mentioned previously, males and young adults consume more alcohol than females and older adults, respectively. Interestingly, consumption tends to increase with increasing socioeconomic status, although alcoholism is more frequent in the middle socioeconomic classes (Kanas, 1988). Native Americans and Irish Americans are far more likely to become alcoholics than are Americans of Italian, Hispanic, and Asian backgrounds (Sue & Nakamura, 1984). In terms of religious affiliation, heavier drinking is found among Catholics than among Protestants or Jews. Finally, variations in drinking behavior are found in different countries. In wine countries, such as France and Italy, alcohol consumption is high (Goodwin, 1985). Consumption is low in Israel and mainland China, with the United States ranked in the middle, and Russia in the lower third of countries. Rates of alcoholism may not correspond to per capita consumption. For example, in Portugal and Italy where per capita consumption is high, the incidence of alcoholism is relatively low (Kanas, 1988). In the United States and the Soviet Union, where consumption is moderate, alcoholism is relatively high. France has high rates of both consumption and alcoholism. Drinking patterns in France are characterized by moderate alcoholic intake throughout the day, and drunkenness is more permissible there than in Italy. In Italy, drinking wine at mealtime is customary but drinking to become intoxicated is discouraged.

These findings suggest that cultural values play an important role in drinking patterns. The values affect not only the amount consumed and the occasions on which drinking takes place but also the given culture's tolerance of alcohol abuse.

Cultural values and behaviors are usually learned within the family and community. A review of the literature on adolescent drinking led researchers to conclude that teenage problem drinkers are exposed first to parents who are themselves heavy drinkers and then to peers who act as models for heavy consumption (Braucht, 1982). The parents not only consumed a great deal of alcohol but also showed inappropriate behaviors such as antisocial tendencies and rejection of their children. When such children loosened their parental ties, they tended to be strongly influenced by peers who were also heavy drinkers.

As in the case of alcohol, use of other substances shows great variation, as revealed by comparisons of different ethnic groups within the United States or of Americans versus citizens of other countries. For example, in the United States, although whites were found to be less likely to have used heroin than were African Americans or Latinos during their lifetimes, they were more likely to have used hallucinogens and PCP (National Institute of Drug Abuse, 1991). These variations are likely to reflect sociocultural influences.

Behavioral Explanations

Early behavioral explanations for alcohol abuse and dependence were based on two assumptions: (1) drinking behavior is learned and (2) alcohol temporarily serves to reduce anxiety and tension. In a classic experiment, an "experimental neurosis" was induced in cats. After the cats were trained to approach and eat food at a food box, they were given an aversive stimulus (an air blast to the face or an electric shock) whenever they approached the food. The cats stopped eating and exhibited "neurotic" symptoms—anxiety, psychophysiological disturbances, and peculiar behaviors. When the cats were given alcohol, however, their symptoms disappeared and they started to eat. As the effects of the alcohol wore off, the symptoms began to reappear (Masserman et al., 1944).

The experimenters also found that these cats now preferred "spiked" milk (milk mixed with alcohol) to milk alone. Once the stressful shocks were terminated and the fear responses extinguished, however, the cats no longer preferred spiked milk. Alcohol apparently reduced the cats' anxieties and was used as long as the anxieties were present. (Note that the cats

Is Drug Use an Indicator of Disturbance?

It has been difficult to establish that drug use and abuse are the result of a particular personality type, as mentioned in the text. Some of the difficulty stems from problems in establishing cause and effect. For example, if researchers find that having antisocial personality characteristics is associated with drug use, the results can be interpreted as indicating that antisocial traits lead to drug use or that drug use causes one to become antisocial. Furthermore, epidemiological studies of drug use patterns and user characteristics have primarily examined demographic variables associated with drug use and not in-depth psychological variables. Still, many clinicians have suspected that drug use is associated with maladjustment. How can these issues be addressed?

One way of examining these issues is to conduct a longitudinal study. As mentioned in Chapter 5, longitudinal research evaluates the behaviors of individuals over a period of time. If longitudinal research shows that antisocial behavior occurs *before* drug use, we are certain that drug use did not cause the antisocial behaviors. Can we conclude that antisocial behaviors caused the drug use? No, not necessarily. Let us imagine that individuals with antisocial tendencies tend to associate with other antisocial peers who may use and encourage drug use. In this case, the cause of drug use is peer pressure rather than antisocial tendencies.

In a longitudinal study, psychological evaluations (including personality, adjustment, and parent-child assessments) were made of boys and girls at different ages, beginning at age three and continuing to age eighteen.

were placed in an *approach-avoidance conflict*. That is, their desire to approach the food box and eat was in conflict with their desire to avoid the air blast or shock.)

An experimenter wanted to test the hypothesis that alcohol reduces the anxiety of conflict—that it resolves conflicts by increasing approach behaviors or by decreasing avoidance behaviors. He placed rats in a conflict situation and measured the strengths of approach behaviors and avoidance behaviors before and after the use of alcohol (Conger, 1951). He found that the main effect of alcohol was to reduce avoidance behaviors, and concluded that alcohol helps resolve conflicts by reducing fear of the unpleasant or aversive element. Many theorists believe that the anxiety-reducing properties of alcohol are reinforcing and therefore largely responsible for maintaining the drinking behavior of the alcoholic.

A group of researchers (Marlatt et al., 1973) provided evidence that learned expectations also affect consumption. In the process, they challenged the notion that alcoholism is a disease in which drinking small amounts of alcohol leads, in an alcoholic, to involuntary consumption to the point of intoxication. In their study, alcoholics and social drinkers were recruited to participate in what was described as a "tasting experiment." Both the alcoholics and the social drinkers were divided into four groups:

1. Members of the "told alcohol, given alcohol" group were told that they would be given a drink of alcohol and tonic, and they were actually given such a drink.

2. Members of the "told alcohol, given tonic" group were told that they would receive a drink of alcohol and tonic, but they were actually given only tonic.

3. Members of the "told tonic, given alcohol" group were told that they would receive a drink of tonic, but they were actually given an alcohol-and-tonic drink.

4. Members of the "told tonic, given tonic" group were told that they would be given tonic, and they were actually given tonic.

At age eighteen, they were interviewed about the frequency of drug use. The investigators, Shedler and Block (1990), wanted to see if certain psychological characteristics were associated with drug use—characteristics that were present before drug use and therefore could not be caused by drug use. The results were quite striking: those who frequently used marijuana and had tried at least one other drug were maladjusted, demonstrating alienation, poor control over impulses, and emotional distress. These psychological characteristics were present before and during drug use. Do the results also imply that adolescents who do not use drugs are better adjusted than those who do?

In addition to studying frequent users, the investigators also examined abstainers—those adolescents who had never tried marijuana or other drugs as well as experimenters or those who had used drugs only a few times. Interestingly, the abstainers were relatively anxious, emotionally constricted, and lacking in social skills. Those who had experimented with drugs occasionally were better adjusted than adolescents who used drugs frequently or had never used drugs! Parents of abstainers and frequent users exhibited greater personality problems.

Given the results that those who experiment with drugs are the best adjusted, should we advocate that adolescents occasionally try drugs? Such a position would be inconsistent with the results and very unwise for several reasons. First, recall from the data that adjustment patterns preceded drug use so that experimenting with drugs will not cause one to be better adjusted. Second, the study was not intended to test whether drug use can affect adjustment. To do that, one would have to find some way of testing adjustment before and after the use of drugs. Third, use of illicit drugs can have legal consequences. Finally, drug abuse and addiction can only come after one initially tries to use drugs. Shedler and Block also noted that drug use among youths is high. About three-quarters of youths have at some time smoked marijuana (Johnston, O'Malley & Bachman, 1991), and drug experimentation may be developmentally understandable in young people. To address drug abuse, Shedler and Block believe that personality development, family upbringing, and the characteristics of alienation, impulsivity, and distress in youths must be understood.

The experimenters used a mixture of five parts tonic and one part vodka for their alcohol-and-tonic drink; these proportions made it difficult to tell whether the drink contained alcohol. At the beginning of the experiment, the subjects were "primed" with an initial drink—either alcohol and tonic or tonic only, depending on which group they were in. (That is, the "given alcohol" groups were primed with alcohol, and the "given tonic" groups were primed with tonic.) After the primer drink, subjects were told what kind of drink they would next receive. They were free to sample as much of the drink as they wished, alone and uninterrupted.

If alcoholism is a condition in which alcoholics lose control of drinking (a disease model), then those given an alcohol primer should drink more alcohol. Alternatively, if alcoholics learn or expect that alcohol reduces anxiety or enhances feelings of well-being, then those told that they would receive alcohol (whether or not alcohol was actually given) would drink more because they expected alcohol. Subjects who were told that they would receive alcohol drank more than those who were told they would receive tonic; and those who actually consumed alcohol did not drink more than those who consumed tonic (Marlatt et al., 1973).

These results suggested that alcoholism is not simply a disease in which a person loses control over drinking. The subjects' expectancy had a stronger effect than the actual content of their drinks on how much they consumed. In fact, several subjects who were given tonic when they believed they were imbibing alcohol acted as though they were "tipsy" from the drinks!

These experiments on drinking behavior imply that psychological factors, such as tension reduction and expectancy, are important in maintaining drinking behavior. The *tension-reducing model,* which assumes that alcohol reduces tension and anxiety and that the relief of tension reinforces the drinking response, is difficult to test, and research with alcoholics has produced conflicting findings. In fact, prolonged drinking is often associated with increased anxiety and depression (McNamee, Mello & Mendelson, 1968). Although alcoholics who have high blood alcohol levels after drinking may show low muscular tension, they tend to report a high degree of distress (Steffen, Nathan & Taylor, 1974). Although alcohol is a sedative that can reduce anxiety, it is possible that the knowledge that one is drinking alcohol can increase one's level of anxiety (Polivy, Schueneman & Carlson, 1976).

Some evidence has suggested that the tension-reducing model is too simplistic. Several experiments have shown that other factors affect the relationship between the effects of alcohol and anxiety. Based on a theory in which alcohol is proposed to affect perception and thought, Steele and Josephs (1988, 1990) found that alcohol can either increase or decrease anxiety. When confronted with a stressful situation, people who drank alcohol in the experiment experienced anxiety reduction if they were allowed to engage in a distracting activity. When faced with a stressor, however, those who drank and did not have a distracting activity experienced an increase in anxiety. The investigators argued that the distracting activity allowed drinkers to divert attention from the stressor. Without the distraction, drinkers' attention may have focused on the anxiety, which served to magnify their anxiety.

Other studies also pointed to problems in the tension-reducing hypothesis. When a group of subjects expected to receive a painful shock, they did not consume any more alcohol than subjects who expected to receive a nonpainful shock. When a social, rather than a physical, source of tension or anxiety was anticipated (for example, when male subjects were told that they would be rated on their personal attractiveness by a group of females), however, subjects tended to consume more alcohol than a control group that did not expect to be evaluated by others. Thus different types of tension (electric shock versus social evaluation) produced different results (Marlatt, 1978). Cooper and associates (1992) also found that stress is related to drinking when individuals expect positive effects from drinking and have coping styles that avoid dealing with anger. However, stress and drinking were negatively correlated among those who had little positive expectancies for alcohol and tended to actively deal with their anger. Other investigators (Stacy, Newcomb & Bentler, 1991) have also found that expectancy is predictive of drug use. Marlatt (1978) suggested that the type of stressor, the

loss of a sense of personal control over situations, and the lack of alternative coping responses influence drinking, as indicated in his analysis of relapse.

Relapse is the resumption of drinking after a period of voluntary abstinence. Many alcoholics who try to stop drinking return to alcohol within a matter of weeks. Reviewing the circumstances leading to the relapse, Marlatt (1978) concluded that feelings of frustration or anger, social pressure to drink, or temptations (such as walking by a bar) are important preconditions for the resumption of drinking. Such "high-risk" situations make the person vulnerable. If the person has a coping response (a means of resisting social pressure—for instance, by insisting on a soft drink), that response provides an alternative to drinking. Coping responses include assertion (such as saying no when pressured by others to drink), avoidance (such as not walking near a favorite bar), and more satisfactory means of dealing with anger or anxiety. This, in turn, enables the person to feel control over drinking and to continue abstinence. If a person does not have a coping response to the high-risk situation, however, he or she takes that first drink. But why do these cues or preconditions (such as temptations) lead to drinking? One theory is that the cues, in the absence of drinking, lead to feelings of withdrawal. Relapse can occur, however, without acute withdrawal distress. Niaura and colleagues (1988) believe that relapse is caused more by anticipated positive feelings over alcohol use than by a motive to avoid withdrawal. Some support for this position was found in studies by Hall, Havassy, and Wasserman (1990, 1991). Their studies revealed that among alcoholics, opiate users, smokers, and cocaine users, relapse was not related to negative moods, physical symptoms, and stress. Rather, having the goal of absolute abstinence, greater expected success in quitting, and positive moods predicted a lower risk of initial relapse.

A person can obviously stop drinking after one drink. To explain the full-blown resumption of drinking that occurs with the alcoholic's first drink, Marlatt (1978) proposed the notion of an *abstinence violation effect*. That is, once drinking begins, the person senses a loss of personal control. He or she feels weak-willed and guilty and gives up trying to abstain. The abstinence violation effect may also apply to other relapse behaviors, such as overeating, masturbating, and smoking. Treatment to overcome the abstinence violation effect focuses on giving people coping responses for situations in which there is also a high risk of relapse.

Initially, it was believed that addiction to certain drugs, such as heroin, could be best explained by biogenic factors such as physical dependence and the attempt to avoid withdrawal symptoms. However, biogenic explanations do not appear sufficient. Withdrawal reactions have been characterized as being no more agonizing than a bad case of the flu (Ausubel, 1961). We also know that heroin addicts who enter the hospital and who do not receive any heroin while hospitalized stop having withdrawal symptoms in a week or two. Yet the vast majority who have lost their bodily need for the drug usually return to heroin after hospitalization. The role of learning, expectancy, and situational factors must be considered in drug dependence. For example, many Vietnam servicemen who were addicted to heroin when they returned to the United States discontinued its use on their return because of situational factors such as easier access to alcohol and the difficulty of procuring heroin (Pilisuk, 1975). Schafer and Brown (1991) also found that expectancies were related to marijuana and cocaine use. College students were surveyed as to the positive and negative expectancies (for example, relaxation, social facilitation, and cognitive impairment) they had over the use of marijuana and cocaine. Use of drugs was associated with stronger positive expectancies. Thus, as in the case of alcoholism, drug use is a complex phenomenon, and explanatory models must incorporate cognitive and behavioral as well as biogenic approaches.

Overall Theories of the Addiction Process

Thus far, we have cited biogenic, psychodynamic or personality, sociocultural, and behavioral approaches to explain alcohol consumption. In the process, we have briefly mentioned how these approaches also explain the development of drug dependence. Recently, some investigators have proposed broad theories that focus on the addiction process rather than on a particular substance. In this section, we will examine several of these theories.

Solomon (1977) argued that the conditions that cause a person to try a drug have not been identified. The best predictor of drug sampling is drug availability, but drug use is too widespread and drug addic-

tion too rare for the mere sampling of a drug to be a major cause of subsequent addiction. Solomon suggested that the initial reasons for using drugs are complex, varied, and obscure. Most drug use is probably reinforcing at the outset—an attempt to solve some social problem, to respond to peer group influences, to relieve unpleasant emotional states, or to become "high." Then, after continued use, the motivation for drug use changes. The user now must cope with drug craving, a fear of withdrawal, and other acquired motivations. The addict's desire to maintain social relationships and a certain lifestyle may also be a motivating factor.

In other words, Solomon believes that addiction is an acquired motivation, much like other acquired motivations such as love or attachment. To explain the process, Solomon (1980) proposed the *opponent process theory of acquired motivation*. Consider first the person who has used a drug only a few times. Before taking the drug again, that person, who is not yet addicted, is in a *resting* state. Then, while ingesting the drug the person experiences a *peak* state (the rush) and euphoria; in other words, the psychopharmacological properties of the drug make the user feel "high." After the effects subside, there may be mild discomfort ("coming down" from the drug). The person may start to crave the drug to combat the discomfort, but the discomfort soon subsides and the person returns to a resting state. The motivation for use is to achieve the high and to avoid the aversiveness of the craving.

For the chronic user, however, the process is somewhat different. During the period before the drug is consumed, this person experiences a *craving* for the drug. Then, during ingestion of the drug, the experienced user feels only *contentment* rather than a rush and intense euphoria. And, once the effects of the drug wear off, he or she experiences *withdrawal* reactions and intense physiological or psychological craving (or both), which do not subside until he or she again uses the drug. In essence, the motivation for drug use has changed with experience, from positive to aversive control. A new motivation for drug use has been acquired.

Wise (1988) also agreed that a single-factor explanation is insufficient. He believes that a two-factor model, involving positive and negative reinforcement, may explain addiction. He theorized that drugs have *positive* reinforcing effects (pleasure or euphoria) through a common biological mechanism. In addition, drugs can independently act as a *negative* reinforcer in that taking the drug can terminate distress or feelings of dysphoria. The theory suggested that either reinforcer results in cravings for the drug. Simply treating the withdrawal symptoms of a drug addict—the negative reinforcement component—is therefore inadequate because the positive reinforcing properties of drug use are not addressed. Wise's theory combines both a behavioral perspective involving learning and reinforcement and a biogenic approach in that the learning is rooted in neural mechanisms.

The theories posited by Solomon and Wise are considerably different. For Solomon, motivation for drugs changes with repeated consumption. In Wise's model, two separate processes help maintain addiction. Nevertheless, each theory points to the problems in conceptualizing addiction as simply one process with one main cause. Another common assumption is that addiction involves both psychological and biogenic components. Future research will probably shed more light on the adequacy of each.

Although Solomon and Wise agreed that the motivation and urge to use drugs are complex, Tiffany (1990) took issue with the role of urges and cravings in drug use. Most theories argued that urges, based on the positive aspects of drug use or on the avoidance of withdrawal, are important in drug-use behavior and in relapse. Research has, however, found only a modest relationship between self-reported urges to use drugs and actual drug use. This led Tiffany to reconceptualize the role of urges. In his view, drug-use behaviors are largely controlled by "automatic" processes. Over the course of drug use, addicts develop skills involving drug acquisition and use. The skills are invoked rather automatically so that drug-use behaviors tend to be relatively fast and efficient, repeated without much cognitive attention or effort, and initiated by the presence of certain stimuli. For example, a smoker can quickly and without thought or clumsiness pull out a cigarette, light it, and start smoking. These automatic processes are likely to occur in certain situations or in the presence of certain stimuli that have in the past been the occasions for smoking (for example, at a party with friends). Although drug-use behavior is an automatic cognitive process, urges are a nonautomatic process and may not be necessary to explain drug use. They may occur when drug-use plans are hindered (for example, an

alcoholic finds that his supply of alcohol has been depleted). To overcome this hindrance, the person must engage in nonautomatic processes that require attention, time, and effort (the alcoholic who no longer has any drinks must find ways of obtaining alcohol). The implications of Tiffany's theory are that urges are not necessary to explain consumption and that once drug-use behaviors become automated, they are highly resistant to change. Thus the theory emphasized the maintenance of behavior rather than the acquisition of drug use, before the development of automatic processes.

These three theories have general relevance for treatment: clinicians should attend to the course of addiction to understand the motives for addicts, according to Solomon's theory; from the perspective of Wise, clinicians should address the positive *and* negative reinforcement that addicts receive; and according to Tiffany's theory, automatic processes involving abstinence should be inculcated in addicts. Let us now turn to more specific treatment approaches to substance-use disorders.

TREATMENT OF SUBSTANCE-RELATED DISORDERS

Treatment of substance abusers and addicts depends on both the individual user and the type of drug being used. Most alcohol and drug treatment programs involve two phases: (1) removal of the abusive substance and (2) long-term maintenance without it. In the first phase, which is also referred to as **detoxification,** the addict or abuser is immediately or eventually not allowed to consume the substance. The removal of the substance may trigger withdrawal symptoms that are opposite in effect to the reactions produced by the drug. For instance, if a person is physically addicted to a CNS depressant such as a barbiturate, he or she experiences drowsiness, decreased respiration, and reduced anxiety when taking the drug. When the depressant is withdrawn, the user experiences symptoms that resemble the effects of a stimulant—agitation, restlessness, increased respiration, and insomnia. Helping someone successfully cope during withdrawal has been a concern of many treatment strategies dealing with various drugs, particularly in treating heroin addicts. Sometimes, addicts are given medication to alleviate some

Alcoholics Anonymous, a self-help group organized to help people deal with and overcome their addiction, has responded to more than a million people worldwide. Offshoot organizations, such as AlaTeen and AlAnon, provide support for teenagers and adults living with alcoholics.

of the withdrawal symptoms. For example, tranquilizers may be helpful to alcoholics experiencing withdrawal.

In the second phase, intervention programs attempt to keep the person from returning to the substance (in some rare cases, controlling or limiting the use of the substance). This may involve behavioral, cognitive, pharmacological, or community programs. Community programs include sending alcoholics or addicts to a hospital, residential treatment facility, or "halfway house," where support and guidance are available in a community setting. In this section, we discuss several approaches to the treatment of various substance-related disorders and review their effectiveness.

Self-Help Groups

Alcoholics Anonymous (AA) is a self-help organization composed of alcoholics who want to stop drinking. Perhaps a million or more alcoholics worldwide participate in the AA program, which is completely voluntary. There are no fees, and the only membership requirement is the desire to stop drinking. AA assumes that once a person is an alcoholic, he or she is always an alcoholic—an assumption based on the disease model of alcoholism. Members must recognize that they can never drink again and must con-

centrate on abstinence, one day at a time. As a means of helping members abstain, each may be assigned a sponsor who provides individual support, attention, and help. Fellowship, spiritual awareness, and public self-revelations about past wrongdoings because of alcohol are encouraged during group meetings.

Some people believe that membership in AA is one of the most effective treatments for alcoholism. Objective outcome studies, however, are difficult to find. Furthermore, it appears that the success rate of AA is not as high as AA members claim it is (Brandsma, 1979). Approximately one-half of the alcoholics who stay in the organization are still abstinent after two years (Alford, 1980). But many drop out of the program and are not counted as failures. Thus, although many people are helped by AA, its success rate has not been firmly established. Spinoffs of AA such as Al-Anon and AlaTeen have been helpful in providing support for adults and teenagers living with alcoholics (Kanas, 1988). There are similar self-help groups for drug abuse (Narcotics Anonymous), although they have not gained the widespread attention and participation seen in AA.

Use of Chemical Agents

To keep addicts from using certain substances, some treatment programs use other chemical substances.

For example, alcohol treatment programs may include the chemical *Antabuse* (disulfiram) to produce an aversion to alcohol. If a person consumes alcohol one to two days after taking Antabuse, he or she suffers a severe reaction, including nausea, vomiting, and discomfort. Antabuse has the effect of blocking the progressive breakdown of alcohol so that excessive acetaldehyde accumulates in the body; acetaldehyde causes dysphoria (depression or distress). Most alcoholics will not consume alcohol after ingesting Antabuse. Those who do risk not only discomfort but in some cases death.

While clients are taking Antabuse and are abstinent, psychotherapy and other forms of treatment may be used to help them develop coping skills or alternative life patterns. The families of patients may also be encouraged to work at solving the problems created by the drinking. Knowing that alcohol consumption is unlikely during Antabuse treatment, families do not have to rely solely on the alcoholic's promise to stop drinking—a promise that alcoholics often make but rarely are able to keep.

The problem with Antabuse treatment is that alcoholic patients may stop taking the drug once they leave the hospital or are no longer being monitored. And some may drink anyway because they believe that the effects of Antabuse have dissipated, because they have forgotten when they last took it, or because they are tempted to drink in spite of the Antabuse.

Chemical treatment may also be used to reduce the intensity of withdrawal symptoms in heroin addicts who are trying to break the drug habit. The drug methadone is prescribed to decrease the intensity of withdrawal symptoms. *Methadone* is a synthetic narcotic chemical that reduces the craving for heroin without producing euphoria (the "high"). It was originally believed that reformed heroin addicts could then quite easily discontinue the methadone at a later date. Methadone initially seemed to be a simple solution to a major problem, but it has an important drawback: it can itself become addicting. The following case illustrates this problem, as well as other facets of the typical two-phase heroin addiction treatment program.

After several months of denying the seriousness of his heroin habit, Gary B. finally enrolled in a residential treatment program that featured methadone maintenance, peer support, confrontational therapy, and job retraining. Although at first Gary responded well to the residential program, he soon began to feel depressed. He was reassured by the staff that recovering heroin addicts frequently experience depression and that several treatment options existed. A fairly low dose of tricyclic antidepressant medication was prescribed, and Gary also began supportive-expressive (psychodynamic) therapy.

Psychotherapy helped Gary identify the difficult relationships in his life. His dependence on these relationships and his dependence on drugs were examined for parallels. His tendency to deny problems and to turn to drugs as an escape was pointed out. The therapy then focused on the generation of suitable alternatives to drugs. He worked hard during his therapy sessions and made commendable progress.

For the next three months Gary enjoyed his life in a way that previously had been foreign to him. He was hired by a small restaurant to train as a cook. He was entirely satisfied with the direction in which his life was going until the day he realized that he was eagerly looking forward to his daily methadone dose. Gary knew of people who had become addicted to methadone, but it was still a shock when it happened to him. He decided almost immediately to terminate his methadone maintenance program. The withdrawal process was physically and mentally painful, and Gary often doubted his ability to function without methadone. But by joining a support group composed of others who were trying to discontinue methadone, he was eventually able to complete methadone withdrawal. Gary had never imagined that the most difficult part of his heroin treatment would be giving up methadone.

It is clear that the use of chemical substances, such as Antabuse or methadone, has not had a dramatic impact in the treatment of addiction. Side effects and potential addiction to chemical treatments are major problems that have to be considered. In smoking cessation programs, however, one very promising tactic has been the use of nicotine replacement strategy, especially in the application of transdermal nicotine patches, as discussed in Focus 10.2. A patch is applied to the arm, and the nicotine in the patch is absorbed through the skin. Researchers are also experimenting with the effectiveness of directly inhaling nicotine.

Cognitive and Behavioral Approaches

Cognitive and behavioral therapists have devised several strategies for treating alcoholism and other substance-related disorders. Aversion therapy, which is based on classical conditioning principles, has been used for many years. **Aversion therapy** is a process by which the sight, smell, or taste of alcohol is paired with a noxious stimulus. For example, alcoholics may be given painful electric shocks while drinking alcohol, or they may be given *emetics* (agents that induce vomiting) when they get the urge to drink or after smelling or tasting alcohol. After several sessions in which the emetic is used, alcoholics may vomit or feel nauseated whenever they smell, taste, or think about alcohol.

Imagery has been used as part of aversion conditioning in a technique that is also known as **covert sensitization**: alcoholic patients are trained to imagine nausea and vomiting in the presence of alcoholic beverages (Cautela, 1966). Covert sensitization has also been used for drug addicts. However, one difficulty with this technique is the inability of some patients to generalize the treatment—that is, to pair the learned aversive reaction (nausea and vomiting) with the stimulus (taking a particular drug) once they are outside the clinic or hospital.

Behavioral techniques have been used almost exclusively by people who wish to end their addiction to cigarette smoking. Most aversive procedures (such as covert sensitization and shock) have yielded rather disappointing results, but "rapid smoking" appears promising. This technique requires that the client puff a cigarette once every six seconds, until he or she absolutely cannot continue any longer. Its purpose is to pair a highly aversive situation (the feeling of illness that results from extremely rapid smoking) with the act of smoking. This is expected to eliminate or reduce the person's desire to smoke. Although the method has been reasonably effective over both the short and the long term, it is somewhat controversial. Early studies suggested that rapid smoking may increase heart rate and blood pressure (Lichtenstein & Glasgow, 1977; Lichtenstein & Rodrigues, 1977). A more recent study of smokers with cardiopulmonary disease who engaged in rapid smoking, however, showed that the treatment was effective and did not produce any cardiac complications (Hall et al., 1984).

Another treatment for cigarette smoking is *nicotine fading* (Foxx & Brown, 1979). In this method, the client attempts to gradually withdraw from nicotine by progressively smoking cigarette brands that

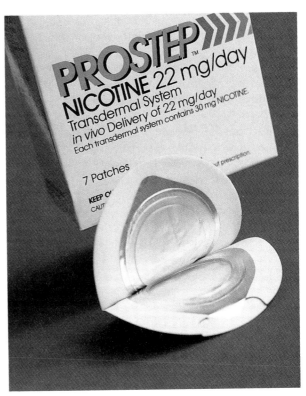

In trying to stop smoking, smokers often suffer from withdrawal symptoms and discomfort because they have become addicted to the nicotine in cigarettes. Many eventually relapse and go back to smoking. By using nicotine transdermal patches, which deliver nicotine through the arm, smokers can minimize the effects of nicotine withdrawal and decrease the chances of relapse.

contain less and less nicotine. When clients reach the stage where they are smoking cigarettes that contain only 0.1 milligram of nicotine, their reduced dependence should enable them to stop altogether (Lichtenstein & Danaher, 1976). See Focus 10.2 for a further analysis of smoking.

Relaxation and systematic desensitization may be used to reduce anxiety. Almost any aversive conditioning procedure may be effective in treating alcoholism if there is also a focus on enhanced social functioning, resistance to stress, and reduction of anxiety (Nathan, 1976). Social learning approaches to treatment have also been used. Cox and Klinger (1988) developed a motivational approach in which alcoholics set important and realistic goals that they would like to accomplish. The therapist helps alcoholics achieve these goals and develop a satisfying life without alcohol. Cooper, Russell, and George (1988) found that drinking to cope with emotional problems was a strong factor in alcohol abuse. They suggested that alcoholics should find more adaptive ways of coping with negative emotions and stress through techniques such as stress management and cognitive restructuring.

Other cognitive-behavioral treatments, based on analyses of why addicts experience relapse, have also been tried. Niaura and colleagues (1988) believe that certain cues are strongly associated with substance use (smoking while having coffee, drinking alcohol at a party, and so forth). They suggested that addicts be placed in these situations or in the presence of the cues and prevented from using the substance. In this way, the consumption response to these cues is extinguished. To prevent relapse, some treatment programs help addicts restructure their thoughts about the pleasant effects of drug use (Cooper, Russell & George, 1988). Addicts are taught to substitute negative thoughts for positive ones when tempted to drink. For example, instead of focusing on the euphoria felt from taking cocaine, a person might be taught to say, "I feel an urge to take the substance, but I know that I will feel depressed later on, many of my friends want me to stop taking it, and I may get arrested."

A great deal of controversy has been generated by the suggestion that it is possible for alcoholics to control their intake and learn to become social drinkers. Proponents of controlled drinking assume that, under the right conditions, alcoholics can learn to limit their drinking to appropriate levels. The finding that alcoholics tend to gulp drinks rather than sip them (as social or moderate drinkers do), to consume straight rather than mixed drinks, and to drink many rather than a few drinks gave investigators clues to behaviors that require modification. Alcoholics were then trained to drink appropriately. In a setting resembling a bar, they were permitted to order and drink alcohol, but they were administered an aversive stimulus for each inappropriate behavior. For example, if the alcoholics gulped drinks or ordered too many, they would be given painful electric shocks.

One problem with this technique is that patients need to receive periodic retraining or to learn alternative responses to drinking. Otherwise, they tend to revert to their old patterns of consumption on leaving the treatment program (Marlatt, 1983).

Opponents of controlled drinking generally believe that total abstinence should be the goal of treatment, that controlled drinking cannot be maintained over a period of time, and that alcoholism is a genetic-physiological problem. Furthermore, by trying to teach alcoholics that they can resume and control drinking, proponents are unwittingly contributing to the alcoholics' problems. There have even been questions about the validity of the findings in controlled drinking programs (see Focus 10.4).

Multimodal Treatment

In view of the many factors that maintain drug-related disorders, some treatment programs make systematic use of combinations of approaches. For example, alcoholics may be detoxified through Antabuse treatment and simultaneously receive behavioral training (via aversion therapy, biofeedback, or stress management) as well as other forms of therapy.

Other therapies may include combinations of Alcoholics Anonymous, educational training, family therapy, group therapy, and individual psychotherapy. Proponents of multimodal approaches recognize that no single kind of treatment is likely to be totally effective and that successful outcomes often require major changes in the lives of alcoholics. The combination of therapies that works best for a particular person in his or her particular circumstances is obviously the most effective treatment.

In the case of an amphetamine abuser, the individual may initially be admitted to an inpatient facility for approximately thirty days. There he or she receives individual and group therapy, takes part in occupational and recreational therapy, stress management counseling, and perhaps is introduced to a support group modeled after Alcoholics Anonymous. The patient's spouse may also be asked to participate in the group sessions.

Once the patient has successfully completed this inpatient phase, he or she is scheduled for outpatient treatment. As part of this treatment, the patient is asked to agree to unannounced urine screenings to test for the presence of drugs. The patient is encouraged to continue attending the support group, along with his or her spouse, and to become involved in

The Controlled-Drinking Controversy

In the 1970s, M. B. Sobell and L. C. Sobell (1978) conducted an experiment to determine whether alcoholics could learn to control their drinking. Up to this time, the goal of most treatment programs was total abstinence. The Sobells worked with forty hospitalized male alcoholics. (Other alcoholics in different treatment programs were also studied by the Sobells, but these studies were not part of the controlled-drinking controversy.) Half of the men (the control group) received conventional treatment designed to promote abstinence. The other half (the experimental group) received behavior therapy designed to train them to control, rather than abstain from, drinking. These men participated in therapy sessions in which they saw themselves drinking on videotapes, received electric shocks for inappropriate drinking behaviors

(such as ordering drinks too frequently), and learned to use alternative responses in drinking situations. After treatment and for about two additional years, the outcomes for the experimental and control groups were compared. In general, this comparison revealed that the controlled drinkers were functioning better and spent less time in hospitals than the abstaining group.

The controversy began when another group of investigators assessed the long-term effects of the treatment and conducted a follow-up investigation of the patients in the Sobells' experimental group. In addition to raising questions about some of the methods used by the Sobells, the later investigators came to very different conclusions about the success of the controlled-drinking subjects. Using hospital and arrest records and interviews of the subjects,

they found that the majority of the controlled drinkers had been hospitalized within one year of the experiment. Only one subject had maintained a pattern of controlled drinking. The majority showed drinking problems (Pendery, Maltzman & West, 1982).

The Sobells' work has been defended (Marlatt, 1983) as well as criticized (Blum & Payne, 1991). Much more research should be conducted on controlled drinking. Because some research suggests that relapse rates for drug users who intend to absolutely abstain are lower than those whose goals are less than total abstinence, at this time it may be wise to continue to emphasize abstinence in treatment programs (Hall, Havassy & Wasserman, 1990, 1991).

individual outpatient therapy. Family therapy is the treatment of choice for adolescent substance users (Haley, 1980; Reilly, 1984; Rueger & Liberman, 1984), and it is highly recommended for adults as well. The outpatient program typically continues for about two years.

Effectiveness of Treatment

With respect to the general effectiveness of the various treatment efforts for alcoholism (which again, has been studied more than any other substance-related disorder), Moos and Finney (1983) noted that they have helped a number of alcoholics to function normally. Estimates of the proportion of treated alcohol abusers who improve range from 32 to 53 percent, depending on the criteria used to measure improvement. In addition, 10 to 20 percent of alcohol

abusers recover "spontaneously" without formal treatment. Moos and Finney noted further that "treatment apparently facilitates the recovery process in that treated individuals show higher rates of improvement in many studies than do minimally treated or untreated comparison groups" (p. 1036).

But Moos and Finney (1983, p. 1037) also noted the following:

Relapse rates during the year after the completion of treatment may be as high as 60 or more. . . . Moreover, researchers have not been very successful in identifying superior treatment methods or in finding treatment approaches that are particularly effective for specific types of patients. Even the idea that more treatment (longer treatment of greater intensity) is better than less treatment has not received much support. . . . Finally, a large number of persons do not recover "spontaneously," but continue to drink heavily and to incur substantial personal and social costs by doing so.

Such apparently divergent findings indicate that intervention programs and life-context factors can have a powerful impact on the course of alcoholism. By suggesting that this impact can be for better or for worse, they highlight a set of important issues: why do some alcohol abusers respond positively to an intervention while others show little or no response and quickly resume problem drinking? In what ways do the characteristics of an individual's life context foster or inhibit the recovery process? How do patient, intervention, and life-context factors interrelate to affect recovery and relapse?

Such issues obviously need to be resolved as part of the effort to improve the effectiveness of alcohol treatment programs.

Research findings on the effectiveness of treatment for other substance-related disorders have been disappointing. In a review of the literature, Stark (1992) found that many drug abusers who entered treatment had high attrition rates, with approximately one-half prematurely terminating treatment. Those who prematurely terminated treatment had the same outcomes as drug abusers who never entered treatment. Stark also concluded that treatment programs with lower attrition rates compared with those having higher attrition rates tended to be conveniently located, smaller, and decentralized. They also had higher staff-client ratios and provided rapid initial response and individualized attention to clients. In other words, the treatment programs that were more successful in preventing dropouts from treatment were more user friendly and personalized.

SUMMARY

1. Substance abuse and dependence are widespread problems that can result in wasted lives, personal misery, crime, the inability to function socially or occupationally, and danger to the substance user and to others. Substance abuse is a maladaptive pattern of excessive and harmful use in which the person is unable to reduce or cease intake of a harmful substance, despite knowledge that its use causes social, occupational, psychological, medical, or safety problems. Substance dependence is a more serious disor-

der, involving not only excessive use but also tolerance and withdrawal in many cases.

2. Substance use is a major social problem in the United States. A large proportion of the population consumes alcohol. Alcohol is associated with traffic accidents, absenteeism from work, accidents, violence, and family problems. The consumption of alcohol results in both long-term and short-term psychological and physiological effects. Similarly, the use of other substances or drugs—depressants, stimulants, and hallucinogens—can result in psychological or physiological problems.

3. With respect to alcoholism, some research has indicated that heredity, along with environmental factors, plays an important role. Recent experiments have demonstrated the importance of cognitive factors in drinking behavior. The tension-reducing hypothesis alone is inadequate to account for alcoholism because alcohol consumption sometimes results in increased feelings of depression or anxiety. Rather, drinking and alcoholism may be closely related to the type of stress anticipated, the perceived benefits of alcohol, the availability of alternative coping responses in a particular situation, and the drinker's genetic or physiological makeup.

4. There appears to be no single factor that can account for drug abuse or dependence for other substances such as depressants, stimulants, hallucinogens, and opiates. In all likelihood, heredity and environmental factors are important, as in the case of alcoholism. For narcotic addiction, both physical and psychological factors are important. Interesting overall theories of addiction have been proposed that emphasize changes in motivation for drug use with chronic consumption, the positive and negative reinforcing effects of drugs, and cognitive factors in maintaining drug use.

5. A variety of treatment approaches have been used, including detoxification, drug therapies, psychotherapy, and behavior modification. Multimodal approaches (the use of several treatment techniques) are probably the most effective. Many alcoholics are helped by treatment, and some achieve abstinence by themselves. The treatment prescribed for other drug users depends on the type of drug and on the user. Heroin addicts usually undergo detoxification followed by methadone maintenance and forms of treatment such as residential treatment programs, psychotherapy, cognitive or behavior therapy, and

group therapy. Detoxification and occupational, recreational, and family therapies may be suggested for users of other drugs. For addiction to cigarette smoking, aversive procedures including "rapid smoking," nicotine fading (the use of brands containing less and less nicotine), and transdermal nicotine patches have had some success.

KEY TERMS

alcoholics People who abuse and depend on alcohol

alcoholism Substance abuse and dependence in which the substance used is alcohol

amphetamines Drugs that speed up central nervous system activity and produce increased alertness, energy, and euphoria; also called "uppers"

aversion therapy A conditioning procedure in which the response to a stimulus is decreased by pairing the stimulus with an aversive stimulus

barbiturate A substance that is a powerful depressant of the central nervous system, capable of inducing psychological and physical dependency

cocaine A drug that induces feelings of euphoria and self-confidence in users; usually inhaled into the nasal cavity

covert sensitization An aversive conditioning technique in which the individual imagines a noxious stimulus in the presence of a behavior

detoxification A treatment aimed at removing all alcohol (or other substance) from a user's body and ensuring that none is ingested

hallucinogen A substance that produces hallucinations, vivid sensory awareness, or increased insight

intoxication ingestion of a substance affecting the central nervous system and causing maladaptive behaviors or psychological changes (e.g., impairment of motor behaviors or feeling "high")

marijuana The mildest and most commonly used hallucinogen; pot

narcotic Opium and its derivatives, which depress the central nervous system, provide relief from pain and anxiety, and are addictive

stimulant A psychoactive substance that is a central nervous system energizer, inducing elation, grandiosity, hyperactivity, agitation, and appetite suppression

substance abuse A maladaptive pattern of excessive use of a substance, in which the person cannot reduce or cease intake despite physical harm or impaired social and occupational functioning

substance dependence A pathological pattern of inability to cut down or control use of a substance, despite knowledge of harmful effects; much time spent in obtaining the substance; frequent intoxication; tolerance and withdrawal symptoms

substance-related disorders Disorders resulting from the use of psychoactive substances that affect the central nervous system and cause significant social, occupational, psychological, or physical problems. The substances can result in abuse or dependence.

tolerance A condition in which the body requires increasing doses of a substance to achieve the desired effect, or a markedly diminished effect is experienced with regular use of the same dose

withdrawal Physical or emotional symptoms such as shaking or irritability that appear when the intake of a regularly used substance is reduced or halted

Sexual and Gender Identity Disorders

The following brief cases illustrate the major groups of sexual disorders described in DSM-IV:

As a child [although born a male], Murray/Mary had dressed like a girl, played like a girl, and fantasized about "really" being a girl. Her childhood playmates were girls, and she had no interest in boys' games like "ball or bat or dumb marbles." She always went to the ladies' restroom and never learned to urinate while standing. . . . She regrets that, despite sex-reassignment surgery, she will be unable to bear a child by the man she loves. (Sabalis et al., 1974, p. 907)

Mr. A., a 47-year-old man, complained of being unable to obtain sexual satisfaction unless he hurt his wife. His preoccupation with sadistic fantasies made it difficult for him to concentrate, even at work. . . . Every few weeks his cravings would build up to a point where he could not control them. During twenty-five years of marriage, he had frequently handcuffed his wife, shaved her head, stuck pins in her back and struck her. . . . Ejaculation could not be achieved unless he hurt her. (Berlin & Meinecke, 1981, p. 605)

I haven't had an orgasm during my marriage (twenty-seven years) or with the two other men with whom I had sex besides my husband. I remember an experience when I was fourteen or fifteen . . . I believe I had a mild orgasm. . . . That's the closest I've come to it. I have masturbated occasionally, but nothing happens. I have no idea what would cause me to respond. (Hite, 1976, p. 207)

As illustrated in these cases, sexual disorders encompass a wide range of behaviors. In this chapter the disorders we present include the following:

- The *gender-identity disorders* involve an incongruity or conflict between one's anatomical sex and gender identity (one's psychological feeling of being male or female). Included in this class is the transsexualism illustrated by Murray/Mary.

◆ The *paraphilias* involve sexual urges and fantasies about situations, objects, or people that are not part of the usual arousal pattern that leads to reciprocal and affectionate sexual activity. Included in this category is the sexual sadism Mr. A. shows.

◆ The *sexual dysfunctions* involve problems of inhibited sexual desire, arousal, and response such as the inhibited orgasm disorder of the married woman in the third description.

Of all the psychological or psychiatric disorders discussed in this text, sexual disorders (including gender identity disorders) present us with the greatest difficulty in distinguishing between "abnormal" (maladaptive) behavior and variances that are not harmful but reflect personal values and tastes that depart markedly from social norms. What constitutes normal sexual behavior varies widely, especially when one compares western and non-western cultures and different time periods, even within a particular culture. For example, sex with animals is fairly common among rural youths but rare among urban boys; in ancient Greece, homosexuality was encouraged (Arndt, 1991); and among the New Guinea Sambia, an aberrant bachelor is one who does not offer his penis to be sucked by young boys (Stoller, 1991). In many parts of Southeast Asia, a disorder called "Koro" has been identified in which afflicted individuals have a sudden and intense anxiety that the penis will recede into the body (Davis & Herdt, 1991). It seems to be a culture-bound syndrome that exists in some cultures and not in others.

Moreover, the definition of sexual disorders is influenced by both moral and legal judgments. For example, the laws of some states define oral-genital sex as a "crime against nature." This view is reflected in a California statute that was repealed as late as 1976:

> Oral Sex Perversion—Any person participating in an act of copulating the mouth of one person with the sexual organ of another is punishable by incarceration in the state prison for a period not exceeding 15 years, or by imprisonment in the county jail not to exceed one year.

Using a statistical model of normality, it would be difficult to justify the classification of oral sex as a "perversion." The pioneering work of Kinsey and colleagues revealed that oral sex is widespread, especially among the more highly educated part of the population (Kinsey et al., 1953). Surveys (McBride & Ender, 1977; Young, 1980) have found that most college men and women have engaged in this behavior.

Legal decisions on sexuality sometimes reflect past moods and morals or questionable and idiosyncratic views. In 1943, the Minnesota Supreme Court, in the case of *Dittrick v. Brown County*, upheld the conviction of a father of six as a sexual psychopath because he had an "uncontrollable craving for sexual intercourse with his wife." This "craving" amounted to three or four times a week (Kinsey et al., 1953). Conversely, today some researchers currently believe that not having sex often enough indicates a sexual desire disorder.

Ambiguities surround the legal and moral definitions of sexual disorders. Because the behaviors covered in this chapter are so heterogenous, any classification system will have its share of problems and conflicts. There would be no objection to our considering rape as deviant behavior; it includes the elements of nonconsent, force, and victimization. But sexual arousal to an inanimate object (fetishism), low sexual drive, or sexual identity issues are not threats to society. Moreover, these problems may not cause distress to people who experience them, and may not result in impaired social or occupational functioning. They are deviant simply because they do not fall within "normal arousal and activity patterns." And they are considered deviant even though what constitutes a normal sexual pattern is the subject of controversy.

Such controversies will become more obvious as we discuss the three groups of sexual disorders in the remainder of this chapter.

GENDER IDENTITY DISORDERS

The **gender identity disorders** (shown in the disorders chart on page 321) are characterized by conflict between the person's anatomical sex and his or her gender identity, or self-identification as male or female. These disorders are relatively rare, and they may appear in adults as well as in children.

In gender identity disorders—often called **transsexualism**—the person strongly and persistently identifies with the opposite sex. The person's own gender identity thus conflicts with his or her biological sex. The transsexual holds a lifelong conviction

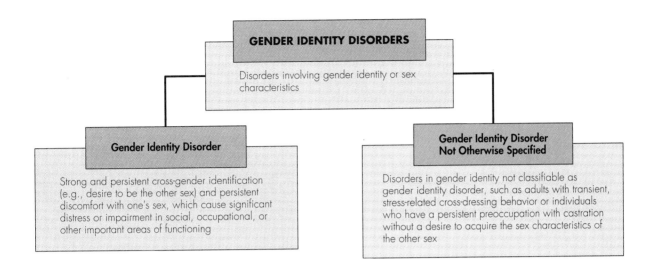

that nature has played a cruel hoax by placing that person in a body of the wrong gender. This feeling produces the person's preoccupation with eliminating the "natural" physical and behavioral sexual characteristics and acquiring those of the opposite sex. The cross-gender identification is accompanied by constant discomfort with one's assigned sex or sense of inappropriateness in that gender role. Major distress or impairment in social, occupational, or other areas of functioning is present. For girls, the gender identity disorder may involve the insistent claim of having a penis and an avid interest in rough-and-tumble play. A boy with this disorder may claim that he will grow up to be a woman, may demonstrate disgust with his penis, and may be exclusively preoccupied with activities considered "feminine." The disorder is much more common in boys than in girls.

Transsexuals tend to exhibit sex role conflicts at an early age and report transsexual feelings in childhood (Tsoi, 1990). Boys display early interests and characteristics that are considered feminine, and they are frequently labeled "sissies" by their male peers (see Table 11.1 for behaviors displayed by boys with opposite sex preferences). They prefer playing with girls and generally avoid the rough-and-tumble activities in which boys are traditionally encouraged to participate (Sabilis et al., 1974). Female transsexuals report being labeled "tomboys" during their childhood. Although it is not uncommon for girls to be considered tomboys, the strength, pervasiveness, and persistence of the cross-gender identification among those with a gender identity disorder are distinguishing features. Boys diagnosed as having gender identity disturbances are more likely than normal boys to play with "feminine" toys. They do not differ from girls in this respect (Bates et al., 1979; Rekers & Yates, 1976). Boys with gender disorder show general personality problems in addition to their adoption of opposite gender attitudes and behaviors (Bates et al., 1979).

Transsexuals may report little interest in homosexual, heterosexual, or bisexual activities before the diagnosis of transsexualism (Blanchard, 1988). Those who are attracted to members of the same sex do not consider themselves to be homosexuals because they believe that they are actually members of the opposite sex.

Transsexualism is more common in males than in females. According to various estimates, the prevalence rate of the disorder is from 1/100,000 to 1/37,000 among males and 1/400,000 to 1/100,000 among females (Arndt, 1991).

The gender identity category also includes disorders that are not classifiable as a specific gender identity disorder such as children with persistent cross-dressing behavior without the other criteria for gender identity disorder; adults with transient, stress-related cross-dressing behavior; and individuals who have a persistent preoccupation with castration with-

One of the treatments advocated for transsexuals is sex reassignment through surgery. Dr. Richard Raskin, a successful ophthalmologist and former top-rated tennis player (left) became Dr. Renee Richards (right).

out a desire to acquire the sex characteristics of the other sex.

Etiology of Gender Identity Disorders

The etiology of gender identity disorders is unclear. The disorder is quite rare (Zucker, 1990), so investigators have focused more attention on other sexual disorders. In all likelihood, an interaction between a number of variables is probably involved in gender identity disorders.

Psychoanalytic Perspective In psychoanalytic theory, all sexual deviations symbolically represent unconscious conflicts that began in early childhood (Meyers, 1991). They occur, say psychoanalysts, because the oedipal complex is not fully resolved. The male or female child has a basic conflict between the wish for and the dread of maternal reengulfment (Meyer & Keith, 1991). The conflict results from a failure to successfully deal with separation-individuation phases of life, which creates a gender identity problem. Although psychoanalysts have written more about other sexual disorders than about transsexualism, inability to resolve the oedipal complex is presumed by psychoanalysts as being important in gender identity disorder.

Behavioral Perspective Some researchers have hypothesized that childhood experiences have an influence on the development of gender identity disorders (Bernstein et al., 1981). Factors thought to contribute to these disorders in boys include parental encouragement of feminine behavior, discouragement of the development of autonomy, excessive attention and

Table 11.1

Frequency of Symptoms in 55 Boys with Opposite-Sex Preferences (elicited as part of a structured interview)

Symptom	Number of Boys			
	Present	Absent	Uncertain	No Data
Feminine dressing	50	2	2	1
Aversion to boys' games	50	1	3	1
Desire to be female	43	6	2	4
Girl playmate preference	42	5	3	5
Doll playing	41	5	4	5
Feminine gestures	40	5	5	5
Wearing lipstick	34	12	3	6

Source: Zuger, 1984.

overprotection by the mother, the absence of an older male as a model, a relatively powerless or absent father figure, a lack of exposure to male playmates, and being encouraged to cross-dress (Marantz & Coates, 1991; Rekers & Varni, 1977a; Stoller, 1969). A childhood background that results in other-sex behavior often leads to ostracism and rejection by one's peers; in that case, the only course available to the boy is complete adoption of the already familiar feminine role. Not all males with gender identity disorders describe their fathers as weak or passive, however, nor do they all have excessively attentive mothers (Sabalis et al., 1977).

Biogenic Perspective Are sexual orientation and sex-typed behaviors substantially determined by neurohormonal factors? Reviewing the research in this area, Ellis and Ames (1987) found some support for this view. For example, female-like gender behaviors are displayed by male rats who were castrated perinatally. In this situation, testosterone is reduced and is unable to effect appropriate neuro-organization. In human females, early exposure to male hormones has resulted in a more masculine behavior pattern. Thus it does appear that gender orientation can be influenced by the lack or excess of sex hormones, which appear to affect brain centers that govern sexual orientation. In a review of the research, Bancroft (1983) also noted other biologic differences in persons with gender identity disorder: female transsexuals have been found in some studies to show raised testosterone levels or menstrual irregularities. Arndt's (1991) review of the biological basis of transsexualism did

not yield clear support for the role of neuroendocrine or chromosomal involvement. Furthermore, not all studies have supported the biogenic perspective. In one study, children adopted the gender identity of their upbringing, even though it was opposite to their genetic and constitutional makeup (Money, Hampson & Hampson, 1957). The researchers concluded that gender identity is malleable. Because these children had normal hormone levels, their ability to adopt an opposite sex orientation raised doubt that biology alone determines male-female behaviors. Neurohormonal factors are important but their degree of influence on sexual orientation in human beings may be minor (Hurtig & Rosenthal, 1987).

Treatment of Gender Identity Disorders

Most treatment programs for children identified as having a gender identity disorder include separate components for the child and for his or her parents. For the child, treatment begins with sex education. The therapist highlights favorable aspects of the child's physical gender and discusses his or her reasons for avidly pursuing opposite-sex activities. The therapist attempts to correct stereotypes regarding certain roles that are "accepted" for one gender and not for the other. Young boys are always assigned to male therapists, which facilitates positive male identification. Meanwhile, the child's parents receive instruction in the behavior modification practice of reinforcing appropriate gender behavior and extinguishing "inappropriate" behavior (Roberto, 1983).

Some therapists help children deal with peer-group ostracism that frequently occurs with those who show strong cross-gender identities and behaviors (Zucker, 1990).

For transsexuals, there was considerable enthusiasm for sex conversion surgery in the 1960s and 1970s because such patients are so extremely resistant to psychotherapy. Most transsexuals regarded therapeutic exploration of their gender conflicts as an obstacle blocking the path to a sex change operation (Lothstein, 1977; Weitz, 1977).

Some success with behaviorally oriented therapy programs, however, has been reported. These behavioral programs consist of strategies for modifying sex-typed behavior through modeling and behavioral rehearsal. The therapist demonstrates appropriate masculine behavior and mannerisms (modeling) in a number of different situations, and then patients practice their own versions of these behaviors. This is followed by a behavioral procedure that reinforces heterosexual fantasies: electric shock is applied whenever the person reports transsexual fantasies (Barlow et al., 1979; Khanna, Desai & Channabasavanna, 1987).

In spite of such gains with psychotherapy and behavioral procedures, sex change operations are indicated for some transsexuals. Prior to surgery, patients may be required to pass the "real-life" test, in which they try to live as completely as possible as members of the opposite sex (Clemmensen, 1990). This requires changing names, clothing, roles, and so on. Almost all patients must deal with reactions from employers, coworkers, friends, and relatives. Successfully "passing" the test paves the way for actual surgical change. For men, the sex conversion operation begins with removal of the penis and testes. Then plastic surgery constructs female genitalia, including a vagina, cervix, and clitoris. The skin of the penis is used in this construction because the sensory nerve endings that are preserved enable some transsexuals to experience orgasm. The male-to-female operation is nearly perfected and sometimes even fools gynecologists (Stripling, 1986). Women who want to become men generally request operations to remove their breasts, uterus, and ovaries, and some ask for an artificial penis to be constructed. This procedure is much more complicated and expensive than the male-to-female conversion (Fleming et al., 1982). Hormonal treatments to accentuate desired physical and psychological effects can be used instead of, or in conjunction with, surgery (Dickey & Steiner, 1990).

Society often has difficulty in accepting and understanding people who undergo such extreme operations: a 21-year-old male transsexual who was charged with carrying a concealed weapon was placed in a maximum security prison with several thousand men. This person had already had breast implants and was taking hormones (Blank, 1981). The partners of transsexuals also go through self-doubt. One woman, married to a female transsexual scheduled to undergo the woman-to-man operation, wondered if she might be a lesbian and if her three-year-old son (through artificial insemination) would have gender confusion. Because others react negatively, few transsexuals make their condition public (Stripling, 1986).

Some studies of transsexuals have indicated positive outcomes (Fleming et al., 1982; Pauly, 1968). Most females who "changed" to males express satisfaction over the outcome of surgery, although males who "changed" to females are less likely to feel satisfied (Arndt, 1991). Perhaps adjusting to life as a man is easier than adjusting to life as a woman, or reactions of others may be less negative in the case of woman-to-man, rather than man-to-woman, changes. Nevertheless, many transsexuals remain depressed and suicidal after surgery (Hershkowitz & Dickes, 1978; Meyer & Peter, 1979). More than one-half of transsexuals in one study who were offered surgery later changed their minds or became ambivalent about having the operations (Kockott & Fahrner, 1987). Doubts about the benefits of sex conversion operations have resulted in a decrease in sex reassignment surgery. Psychotherapy is typically recommended for patients who discover that their problems have not disappeared as a result of the operation (McCauly & Ehrhardt, 1984).

PARAPHILIAS

Paraphilias are sexual disorders in which the person has persistent and strong sexual urges and sexual fantasies regarding (1) nonhuman objects, as in fetishism and transvestic fetishism; (2) real or simulated suffering, as in sadism and masochism; and (3) nonconsenting others, as in exhibitionism, voyeurism, and pedophilia (see the disorders chart on page 325).

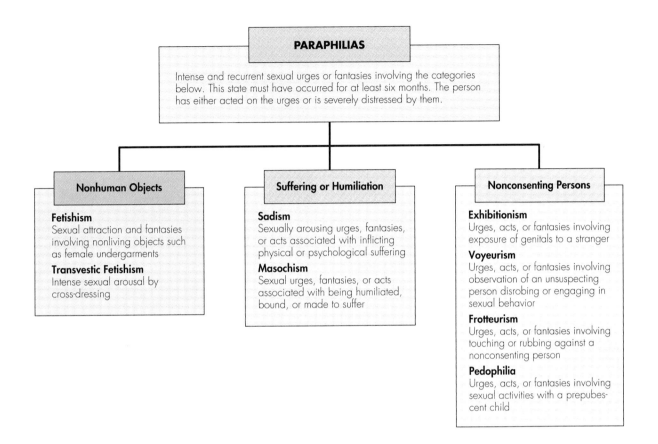

PARAPHILIAS

Intense and recurrent sexual urges or fantasies involving the categories below. This state must have occurred for at least six months. The person has either acted on the urges or is severely distressed by them.

Nonhuman Objects

Fetishism
Sexual attraction and fantasies involving nonliving objects such as female undergarments

Transvestic Fetishism
Intense sexual arousal by cross-dressing

Suffering or Humiliation

Sadism
Sexually arousing urges, fantasies, or acts associated with inflicting physical or psychological suffering

Masochism
Sexual urges, fantasies, or acts associated with being humiliated, bound, or made to suffer

Nonconsenting Persons

Exhibitionism
Urges, acts, or fantasies involving exposure of genitals to a stranger

Voyeurism
Urges, acts, or fantasies involving observation of an unsuspecting person disrobing or engaging in sexual behavior

Frotteurism
Urges, acts, or fantasies involving touching or rubbing against a nonconsenting person

Pedophilia
Urges, acts, or fantasies involving sexual activities with a prepubescent child

The diagnosis is made if the person has either acted on these urges or is severely distressed by them. A person who is highly distressed by paraphiliac urges or fantasies but has not acted on them would be diagnosed as having a mild case of the paraphilia. In addition, according to DSM-IV, the condition must have been present for at least six months.

People in this category often have more than one paraphilia. In one study of sex offenders, researchers found that nearly 50 percent had engaged in a variety of sexually deviant behaviors, averaging between three and four paraphilias, and had committed more than five hundred deviant acts. For example, of men who reported having committed incest, a substantial number also had molested nonrelatives, exposed themselves, raped adult women, and engaged in voyeurism and frotteurism (rubbing against others for sexual arousal; Rosenfield, 1985). Paraphilias are much more prevalent in males than females.

Paraphilias Involving Nonhuman Objects

Fetishism   Fetishism is an extremely strong sexual attraction for an inanimate object such as panties, bras, or shoes. The fetish is often employed as a sexual stimulus during masturbation or sexual intercourse. The disorder is rare among women, although milder forms, such as attraction to uniforms, beards, or tall men, are common.

Mr. M. met his wife at a local church. Some kissing and petting took place but never any other sexual contact. He had not masturbated before marriage. Although he and his wife loved each other very much, he was unable to have sexual intercourse with her since he could not obtain an erection. However, he had fantasies involving an apron and was able to get an erection while wearing an apron. His wife was described as upset over this discovery but was convinced to accept it. The apron was kept hanging somewhere in the bedroom and it allowed him to consummate the marriage. He remembers being forced to wear an apron by his mother during his childhood years. (Kohon, 1987)

The diagnosis of fetishism is not made if the fetishes only involve articles of clothing used in cross-dressing. Instead, the appropriate diagnosis would be transvestic fetishism. Most males find the sight of female undergarments sexually arousing and stimulating; again, this does not constitute a fetish. An interest in such inanimate objects as panties, stockings, bras, and shoes becomes a sexual disorder when the person is often sexually aroused to the point of erection in the presence of the fetish item, needs this item for sexual arousal during intercourse, chooses sexual partners on the basis of their having the item, or collects these items (Jones, Shainberg & Byer, 1977). In many cases, the fetish item is enough by itself for complete sexual satisfaction through masturbation, and the person does not seek contact with a partner. As a group, fetishists are not dangerous nor do they tend to commit serious crimes.

Transvestic Fetishism   Transvestic fetishism is a disorder among heterosexual males in which sexual arousal is obtained through cross-dressing or wearing clothes appropriate to the opposite sex. (This disorder should not be confused with transsexualism, which is a gender identity disorder in which one *identifies* with the opposite sex.) Several aspects of transvestism are illustrated in the following case study:

A 26-year-old graduate student referred himself for treatment following an examination failure. He had been cross-dressing since the age of 10 and attributed his exam failure to the excessive amount of time that he spent doing so (four times a week). When he was younger, his cross-dressing had taken the form of masturbating while wearing his mother's high-heeled shoes, but it had gradually expanded to the present stage in which he dressed completely as a woman, masturbating in front of a mirror. At no time had he experienced a desire to obtain a sex-change operation. He had neither homosexual experiences nor homosexual fantasies. Heterosexual contact had been restricted to heavy petting with occasional girlfriends. (Lambley, 1974, p. 101)

Not all people who cross-dress are transvestites; some homosexuals and transsexuals also cross-dress.

Transvestism is a disorder in which sexual gratification is obtained through cross-dressing. In some cases, makeup may be applied and the individual may attempt to pass as a woman. But in contrast to transsexuals, transvestites do not have a gender conflict.

In contrast to these latter two groups, however, the majority of transvestites are exclusively heterosexual, are married, and have fathered or borne children (Benjamin, 1967). Much latitude is given in our society to women who wear men's clothing (Arlow, 1991). This is not the case in many other countries such as those with strict Muslim customs. For males, our society has slowly changed in that men may now wear bracelets, necklaces, and earrings without drawing any attention; a man wearing a skirt, however, would draw much attention and frowns from others.

Sexual arousal while cross-dressing is an important criterion in the diagnosis. If arousal is not present or has disappeared over time, then the possibility of a gender identity disorder should be considered. This distinction, however, may be difficult to make. Some transsexuals show penile erections to descriptions of cross-dressing (Blanchard, Racansky & Steiner, 1986). Whether sexual arousal occurs in cross-dressing therefore may not serve as a valid distinction between transsexualism and transvestic fetishism. If the cross-dressing occurs only during the course of a gender identity disorder, the person is not considered in the category of transvestic fetishism.

Male transvestites often wear feminine garments or undergarments during sexual intercourse with their wives, as described by Newman and Stoller (1974, p. 438):

> He continued to have sexual intercourse (while clad in a woman's nightgown) with his wife, while imagining that they were no longer man and wife, but rather two women engaged in a lesbian relationship. He especially enjoyed it when she cooperated with his idea and referred to him by his chosen feminine name.

Many transvestites believe that they have alternating masculine and feminine personalities. In a feminine role, they can play out such behavior patterns as buying nightgowns and trying on fashionable clothes. Many transvestites introduce their wives to their female personalities and urge them to go on shopping trips together as women (Buckner, 1970). Other transvestites cross-dress only for the purposes of sexual arousal and masturbation and do not fantasize themselves as members of the opposite sex.

Paraphilias Involving Nonconsenting Others

Exhibitionism Exhibitionism involves sexual arousal by and intense urges or fantasies about the exposure of one's genitals to unsuspecting strangers. Often the person wants to shock the victim, as this case shows:

> A nineteen-year-old single white college man reported that he had daily fantasies of exposing and had exposed himself on three occasions. The first occurred when he masturbated in front of the window of his dormitory room, when women would be passing by. The other two acts occurred in his car; in each case he asked young women for directions, and then exposed his penis and masturbated when they approached. He felt a great deal of anxiety in the presence of women and dated infrequently. (Hayes, Brownell & Barlow, 1983)

Exhibitionism is relatively common. The exhibitionist is most often male and the victim female. Surveys of selected groups of young women in the United States have indicated that between one-third and one-half have been victims of exhibitionists (Cox & McMahon, 1978). Although the majority of women did not report any psychological traumas associated with the episodes, about 40 percent indicated being moderately to severely distressed, and 11 percent believed that the incident had negatively affected their attitude toward men (Cox, 1988).

Unlike normal (control) subjects, exhibitionists are sexually aroused by sexually neutral scenes such as women knitting, ironing, or sweeping (Kolarsky & Madlatfousek, 1983). Similar findings were obtained by Fedora, Reddon, and Yeudall (1986), who monitored sexual arousal in exhibitionists, normal controls, and nonexhibitionist sex offenders. Only the exhibitionists responded sexually to scenes of fully clothed erotically neutral women. Fedora hypothesized that exhibitionists may be aroused by female uncooperativeness or neutrality.

The main goal of the exhibitionist seems to be the sexual arousal he gets by exposing himself; most exhibitionists don't want any further contact. However, there may be two types of exhibitionists—those who have been involved with crime and those who have not. The former tend to be sociopathic and impulsive, and they may be more likely to show aggression (Forgac & Michaels, 1982; Forgac, Cassel & Michaels, 1984).

Exhibitionists may expect to produce surprise, sexual arousal, or disgust in the victim. The act may involve exposing a limp penis or masturbating an erect penis. In a study of ninety-six exhibitionists, only 50 percent reported that they "almost always" or "always" had erections when exposing, although a large percentage of the men wanted the women to be impressed with the size of their penis. Fantasies about being watched and admired by female observers were common among exhibitionists. More than two-thirds reported that they would not have sex with the victim even if she were receptive (Langevin et al., 1979).

Most exhibitionists are in their twenties—far from being the "dirty old men" of popular myth. Most are married. Their exhibiting has a compulsive quality to it, and they report that they feel a great deal of anxiety about the act. A typical exposure sequence involves the person first entertaining sexually

Many features of our society, such as topless bars, X-rated movies, or explicitly sexual magazines, are voyeuristic in nature and are accepted, if not approved of, by many people. When voyeurism includes serious risk, is done in socially unacceptable circumstances, or is preferred to coitus, the behavior is considered abnormal or deviant.

arousing memories of previous exposures and then returning to the area where previous exposures took place. Next, the person locates a suitable victim, rehearses the exposure mentally, and finally exposes himself. As the person moves through his sequence, his self-control weakens and disappears (Abel, Levis & Clancy, 1970). Alcohol use before the act of exhibiting occurs in many cases, perhaps to reduce inhibitions (Arndt, 1991).

Voyeurism Voyeurism is sexual gratification obtained by (1) observing the genitals and other body parts of unsuspecting people, or (2) watching couples engaging in sexual activity. The proliferation of sexually oriented television programs, "romance" paperbacks, explicit sexual magazines, and X-rated movies all point to the voyeuristic nature of our society. Note the growing number of "night clubs" featuring male exotic dancers and attended by women, which may indicate women's increasing interest in men's bodies and their acknowledgment that it is all right to be sexual.

"Peeping," as voyeurism is sometimes termed, is considered deviant when it includes serious risk, is done in socially unacceptable circumstances, or is preferred to coitus. The typical voyeur is not interested in looking at his wife or girlfriend (95 percent

of the cases of voyeurism involve strangers). Observation alone produces sexual arousal and excitement, and the voyeur often masturbates during this surreptitious activity (Katchadourian & Lunde, 1975).

The voyeur is like the exhibitionist in that sexual contact is not the goal; viewing an undressed body is the primary motive. However, a voyeur may also exhibit or use other indirect forms of sexual expression (Abel, Levis & Clancy, 1970). Because the act is repetitive, arrest is predictable. Usually an accidental witness or the victim notifies the police. It is also common for a potential rapist or burglar who is behaving suspiciously to be arrested as a voyeur.

Frotteurism Whereas physical contact is not the goal of voyeurism, contact is the primary motive in frotteurism. *Frotteurism* involves recurrent and intense sexual urges and fantasies of touching and rubbing against a nonconsenting person. The touching and not the coercive nature of the act is the sexually exciting feature. As in the case of the other paraphilias, the person has acted on the urges or is markedly distressed by them.

Pedophilia

Pedophilia is a disorder in which an adult obtains erotic gratification through fantasies or sexual contact with children. According to DSM-IV, to be diagnosed with this disorder, the person must be at least sixteen years of age and at least five years older than the victim. Pedophiliacs may victimize their own children (incest), stepchildren, or those outside the family. Most pedophiles prefer girls, although a few choose prepubertal boys. Child sexual abuse is common. Between 20 and 30 percent of women reported having had a childhood sexual encounter with an adult man (Herman & Hirschman, 1981; Zverina et al., 1987). And, contrary to the popular view of the pedophile (or child molester) as a stranger, most pedophiles were relatives, friends, or casual acquaintances of their victims (Alter-Reid, 1986).

In most cases of abuse, only one adult and one child are involved, but cases involving several adults or groups of children have recently been reported. For example, a 54-year-old man, a person who had won a community award for his work with youths, was arrested for child molestation involving boys as young as ten years old. The man would encourage and photograph sexual acts between the boys, including mutual masturbation and oral and anal sex. He then would have sex with one of them (Burgess et al., 1984).

A study of 229 convicted child molesters revealed the following information. Nearly one-fourth of their victims were younger than six years of age. Another 25 percent were ages six to ten, and about 50 percent were ages eleven to thirteen. Fondling the child was the most common sexual behavior, followed by vaginal and oral-genital contact. Bribery was often used to gain the cooperation of the victims (Erickson, Walbek & Seely, 1988). Pedophiliacs have a recidivism rate of approximately 35 percent, which is the highest among sex offenders (Erickson et al., 1987).

Child victims of sexual abuse show a variety of physical symptoms such as urinary tract infections, poor appetite, and headaches. Reported psychological symptoms include nightmares, difficulty in sleeping, a decline in school performance, acting-out behaviors, and sexually focused behavior. One boy was overheard asking another to take down his pants, which was the request made by the person who had molested him (Burgess, Groth & McCausland, 1981). Some child victims show the symptoms of posttraumatic stress disorder. In a sample of sixty-six victims, forty-five reported experiencing flashbacks of the molestation. They also demonstrated dimin-

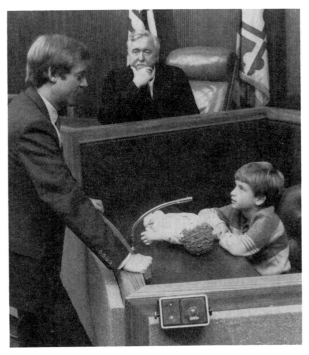

Young children who have been sexually abused often find it difficult to talk about the incident. Especially traumatic for them is having to testify in court against the person who abused them. Prosecutors often prepare their young witnesses by showing them the courtroom before they have to testify in order to make them feel more at ease about the upcoming trial.

ished responsiveness to their environment, hyperalertness, and jumpiness (Burgess et al., 1984). The First Person narrative in this chapter discusses child sexual abuse from a prosecutor's point of view.

On psychological tests such as the Minnesota Multiphasic Personality Inventory (MMPI), child molesters tend to have profiles indicating passive-dependent personality, discomfort in social situations, impulsiveness, and alcoholism (Erickson et al., 1987). Social skills deficits are found among child molesters when compared to control group members. They also display a significantly higher fear of negative evaluation (Overholser & Beck, 1986). Some studies found that pedophiles tend to score on the low end of normal on intelligence tests, and some show left hemispheric problems in brain functioning (Langevin, 1990), although brain dysfunction as a cause of the disorder is still speculative. Pedophiles display sexual arousal to slides of young children and

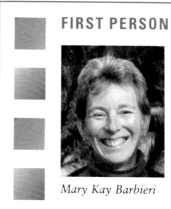

FIRST PERSON

Mary Kay Barbieri

When I first graduated from law school in 1975, I went to work for King County prosecutor's office in Seattle, Washington. Before that time, cases of child abuse—especially in-family child sexual abuse—were not handled in the criminal justice system. They were treated as "social problems" and handled by Child Protective Services. But around 1975 a movement was afoot to start treating these abuses of children as crimes. Most prosecutors didn't want to handle the cases—they didn't know how to talk to children, they didn't think children could testify in court, and they often didn't believe the children because they didn't understand why they would let the abuse go on so long without telling someone.

I volunteered for all the child sexual abuse cases I could get. I stocked my office with blocks and crayons and big floor cushions and spent hours sitting on the floor with children winning their trust and getting them to tell me about the terrible things that adults had done to them. I was appalled at what I heard from these children. People who were supposed to love or care for them—their parent or stepparent, grandpa or uncle, their teacher or Cub Scout leader or babysitter—these adults were performing every imaginable kind of sexual act with children. They usually started out by bribing the children and then invariably ended up threatening them to keep them from telling. The most common threats were "If you tell they'll think you're bad and they won't love you," or "If you tell I'll kill your mom." Kids always believed these threats, so usually they only disclosed the sexual abuse inadvertently. Fortunately, the school programs that now educate children will disclose abuse sooner.

I learned a lot about bravery from those children. Many of the offenders would plead guilty before trial, but many don't, and then the

report fantasies involving children during masturbation (Alford et al., 1987). More than 50 percent of one sample of child molesters reported using "hard core" pornography to excite themselves in preparing to commit an offense (Marshall, 1988b).

Paraphilias Involving Pain or Humiliation (Sadism and Masochism)

Pain and humiliation do not appear to be related to normal sexual arousal. In sadism and masochism, however, these factors play a prominent role.

The deviations of sadism and masochism involve the association of pain, humiliation, or both, with sexual gratification. In particular, **sadism** is obtaining sexual gratification by inflicting pain on others; **masochism** is obtaining sexual gratification by receiving pain, bondage, or humiliation. The word *sadism* was coined from the name of the Marquis de Sade (1740–1814), a French nobleman who wrote extensively about the sexual pleasure he received by inflicting pain on women. The marquis himself was so cruel to his sexual victims that he was declared insane and jailed for twenty-seven years. The word *masochism* is derived from the name of Leopold von Sacher-Masoch, a nineteenth-century Austrian novelist whose fictional characters obtained sexual satisfaction only when pain was inflicted on them.

Sadistic behavior may range from the pretended or fantasized infliction of pain, through mild to severe cruelty toward partners, to an extremely dangerous pathological form of sadism that may involve mutilation or murder. Because of their passive roles, masochists are not considered dangerous. For some sadists and masochists, coitus becomes unnecessary; pain or humiliation alone is sufficient to produce sexual pleasure. According to DSM-IV, to receive the diagnosis the person must have acted on the urges or is markedly distressed by them.

In a study of 178 sadomasochists (47 women and 131 men), most reported engaging and enjoying both submissive and dominant roles. Only 16 percent were exclusively dominant or submissive. Nearly all engaged in spanking, whippings, and bondage. Approximately 40 percent engaged in behaviors that caused minor pain using ice, hot wax, biting, or face slap-

children would have to go to court and testify. Courtrooms just aren't made for children: they're big and austere and intimidating even for adults. So, a few days before the trial, I would take a child to visit the courtroom when it was not in use. I'd have the child sit in the witness chair and swivel around and try out the microphone. I tell the child where the judge sat and what the court reporter did, and I'd prepare the child for the fact that the offender would be in court, too. That was always the hardest part, but by this time the child and I had spent a lot of time together and were friends and I'd say, "Don't worry, you don't have to look at him; just look at me instead." I put children as young as three years old on the witness stand. Yes, those children were brave.

I eventually set up a special unit in the prosecutor's office just to handle cases of child sexual abuse. The prosecutors were all trained to work with children and to understand the dynamics of child sexual abuse. As often happens when a program is set up to meet a perceived need, the caseload kept increasing and increasing. The unit became a national model, and my career benefited. Eventually I became the chief prosecutor in charge of the whole sixty-attorney prosecutor's office.

But I missed the kids. I'd always been a little envious of the therapists who worked with children. As a prosecutor my work ended with the trial while the therapists got to go on helping the children. A lot of the process of preparing children for trial is "doing therapy," but I wished that I could be the one to go

on working with the child, helping the child realize that it wasn't his or her fault, and doing the work that needed to be done to keep this experience from haunting the child on into adulthood. Finally I decided that if I wanted to be a therapist, I should become one. I left the practice of law and went to graduate school in clinical and counseling psychology. Now I still get to sit on the floor with blocks and crayons and pillows, and I don't have to stop doing it when the trial is over.

Mary Kay Barbieri was the former chief prosecutor for the King County prosecutor's office in Seattle, Washington. She is now a practicing therapist, specializing in cases involving child sexual abuse.

---

ping. Less than 18 percent engaged in more harmful procedures such as burning or piercing. Nearly all respondents reported sadomasochistic (S&M) activities to be more satisfying than "straight" sex (Moser & Levitt, 1987). Most sadomasochists studied don't seek harm or injury but report that they find the sensation of utter helplessness appealing (Baumeister, 1988). S&M activities are often carefully scripted and involve role playing and mutual consent to the activity by the participants (Weinberg, 1987). Sadomasochistic tendencies may exist to some extent in many people. In a national survey, 10.3 percent of single men reported having obtained sexual pleasure from inflicting or receiving pain (Hunt, 1974). In the same survey, single women were much more likely to report sexual pleasure when receiving pain (10 percent) than when inflicting pain (5.2 percent). In addition, fantasies involving sexual abuse, rejection, and forced sex are not uncommon among both male and female college students (Sue, 1979). Most of these cases involve very mild forms of pain (such as in biting or pinching) that are accepted in our society. Sadomasochistic behavior is considered deviant when

pain, either inflicted or received, is necessary for sexual arousal and orgasm.

Some cases of sadomasochism appear to be the result of an early experience associating sexual arousal with pain. One masochistic man reported that as a child he was often "caned" on the buttocks by a school headmaster as his "attractive" wife looked on. He reported, "I got sexual feelings from around the age of twelve, especially if she was watching" (p. 273). He and some of his schoolmates later hired prostitutes to spank them. Later yet, he engaged in self-whipping (Money, 1987). Although the association of pain and sexual arousal can account for some cases of sadomasochistic behaviors, 80 percent of a sample of sadomasochists did not remember a link between physical punishment during childhood and erotic sensations (Weinberg, 1987). Langevin (1990) and Langevin and associates (1988) found that sadists were more likely than nonsadistic but sexually aggressive men and nonsexual offenders (controls) to have anomalies in the right temporal portions of the brain—brain areas that are logically linked to sexual behavior. They speculate that

The association of pain and/or humiliation with sexual gratification is seen in sadism and masochism. The former involves inflicting pain on others, while the latter involves receiving pain. Instruments used in sadomasochistic activities include whips, chains, locks, and needles.

brain pathology and life experiences may underlie sadism.

DSM-IV has also listed many other paraphilias under the category of not otherwise specified that we will not discuss. They include *telephone scatalogia* (making obscene telephone calls) and sexual urges involving corpses (*necrophilia*), animals (*zoophilia*), or feces (*coprophilia*).

Etiology and Treatment of Paraphilias

All etiological theories for the paraphilias must answer three questions (Finkelhor & Araji, 1986). (1) What produced the deviant arousal pattern? (2) Why doesn't the person develop a more appropriate outlet for his or her sexual drive? (3) Why is the behavior not deterred by normative and legal prohibitions? So far, biogenic, psychoanalytic, and behavioral perspectives have provided satisfactory answers, and a number of behavioral strategies have emerged for treating the paraphilias.

Psychoanalytic Theory In psychoanalytic theory, all sexual deviations symbolically represent unconscious conflicts that began in early childhood. Castration anxiety is hypothesized to be an important etiological factor underlying transvestic fetishism and exhibitionism, sadism, and masochism. It occurs, say

psychoanalysts, when the oedipal complex is not fully resolved. Because the boy's incestuous desires are only partially repressed, he fears retribution from his father in the form of castration. Many sexual deviations are attempts to protect the person from castration anxiety. For example, in transvestic fetishism, acknowledging that women lack a penis raises the fear of castration. To refute this possibility, the male transvestite "restores" the penis to women through cross-dressing. In this manner, he unconsciously represents a "woman who has a penis" and therefore reduces the fear of castration (Shave, 1976). Clothes or a particular fetish is selected because it represents a phallic symbol (Arndt, 1991). Similarly, an exhibitionist exposes to reassure himself that castration has not occurred. The shock that registers on the faces of others assures him that he still has a penis. A sadist may protect himself from castration anxiety by inflicting pain (power equals penis), and a masochist engages in self-castration through the acceptance of pain. This acceptance limits the power of others to castrate him. Because castration anxiety stems from an unconscious source, the fear is never completely allayed, however, and so the person feels compelled to repeat deviant sexual acts.

The psychoanalytic treatment of sexual deviations involves helping the patient understand the relationship between the deviation and the unconscious conflict that produced it. To treat the man with a fetish who had to wear an apron before he could engage in sexual intercourse, the therapist used dream analysis and free association, which helped him and the patient understand the "roots" of his behavior. The following interpretation was made: the apron was made by his mother from a boiler suit that belonged to his father's mother. Because the patient's relationship with his mother produced castration anxiety, the fetish accomplished two purposes. First, it allowed him to reduce castration anxiety by denying that women do not have penises (the apron symbolized a "penis" that was cut out of the body of another woman). Second, a "penis" (the apron) was returned to him (Kohon, 1987). The psychoanalyst helped the patient bring the conflicts into conscious awareness through interpretation. After this, the patient gained insight into his behavior and was able to work through his problem.

Behavioral Perspective Learning theorists stress the importance of early conditioning experiences in the etiology of sexually deviant behaviors. Masturbating while engaged in sexually deviant fantasies combined with lack of social skills that hamper the development of normal sexual patterns is an example of such a conditioning experience. For example, one boy developed a fetish for women's panties at age twelve after he became sexually excited watching girls come down a slide with their underpants exposed. He began to masturbate to fantasies of girls with their panties showing and had this fetish for twenty-one years before seeking treatment (Kushner, 1965). In another example, two young men became sexually aroused while urinating in a semiprivate area after they were surprised by women passing by. The accidental association between sexual arousal and exposure resulted in exhibitionism (McGuire, Carlisle & Young, 1965). These reports must be interpreted carefully because they are extracted from case studies and do not originate from controlled research.

Experimental support for the possible role of conditioning in the development of a fetish was demonstrated by Rachman (1966). Three men were shown a picture of a pair of women's black boots and then were shown slides of nude women, which produced sexual arousal (as measured by penile volume). Initially, the picture of boots did not elicit any increases in penile volume. But after slides of boots and nude women were paired several times (classical conditioning), all three subjects developed conditioned sexual arousal at the sight of the boots alone. Although the conditioned responses were weak, they could have been strengthened by masturbating while the boots were shown. Laws and Marshall (1990) believe that the conditioning process may involve the concept of "preparedness." Unconditioned and conditioned stimuli, as well as responses and reinforcers, are not associated with equal ease. Organisms appear to be more prepared to learn to associate some stimuli with some reinforcers rather than others. For example, rats can learn to avoid the *taste* of a certain food if they experienced nausea after eating the food. However, they could not learn to associate the *sight* of food (but had not tasted it) with nausea, when the sight of food was paired with nausea (Garcia, McGowan & Green, 1972). Thus stimuli may vary in the extent to which they can be conditioned (that is, preparedness). Preparedness may depend on the survival value of the elements to be learned. Under this theory, human beings are less prepared to condition to, or find as sexually attractive, neutral objects (such as women's boots) than an opposite-sex person. Nevertheless, such conditioning may occur in some people.

Learning approaches to treating sexual deviations have generally involved one or more of the following elements: (1) weakening or eliminating the sexually inappropriate behaviors through processes such as extinction or aversive conditioning; (2) acquiring or strengthening sexually appropriate behaviors; and (3) developing appropriate social skills. The following case illustrates this multiple approach:

A 27-year-old man with a three-year history of pedophilic activities (fondling and cunnilingus) with four-to-seven-year-old girls was treated through the following procedure. The man first masturbated to orgasm while exposed to stimuli involving adult females. He then masturbated to orgasm while listening to a relaxation tape, and then masturbated (but not to orgasm) to deviant stimuli. The procedure allowed the strengthening of normal arousal patterns and lessened the ability to achieve an orgasm while exposed to deviant stimuli (extinction). Measurement of penile tumescence when exposed to the stimuli indicated a sharp decrease to pedophilic stimuli and high arousal to heterosexual stimuli. These changes were maintained over a twelve-month follow-up period. (Alford et al., 1987)

One of the more unique treatments for exhibitionism is the *aversive behavior rehearsal (ABR)* program developed by Wickramasekera (1976). This "shame aversion" technique uses shame or humiliation as the aversive stimulus. The technique requires that the patient exhibit himself in his usual manner to a preselected audience of women. During the exhibiting act, the patient must verbalize a conversation between himself and his penis. He must talk about what he is feeling emotionally and physically and must explain his fantasies regarding what he supposes the female observers are thinking about him.

The developer of ABR believes that exhibitionism often occurs when the person is in a hypnotic-like state. At that time, the exhibitionist's fantasies are extremely active and his judgment is impaired. The ABR method forces him to experience and examine his act while being fully aware of what he is doing (Kilmann et al., 1982).

The results of behavioral treatment have been generally positive, but the majority of the studies involved single-subject designs. Few control groups were included. Another problem in interpreting the results of these studies becomes apparent when we examine the approaches that were employed. For the most part, several different behavioral techniques were used within each study, so evaluation of a particular technique is impossible.

Biogenic Perspective Earlier, we noted that investigators have attempted to find genetic, neurohormonal, and brain anomalies that might be associated with sexual disorders. At this point, some of the research findings have been conflicting; others need replication and confirmation. In any event, researchers need to continue applying more advanced technological techniques in the study of the biogenic influences on sexual disorders. Even if biogenic factors are found to be important in the cause of these disorders, psychological contributions are also likely to play an important role.

OTHER DEVIATIONS INVOLVING SEX

Although certain other deviations are not included in DSM-IV, the magnitude and seriousness of the problems they present warrant discussion.

Rape

Considerable controversy exists on whether rape is primarily a crime of violence or sex (Marsh, 1988). Because it has sexual dimensions and implications, we will discuss rape in this chapter. **Rape** is defined by the Federal Bureau of Investigation (FBI) as "carnal knowledge of a female forcibly and against her consent." The criminal offense of statutory rape—sexual intercourse with a girl younger than a certain age, regardless of consent—is included in most states' laws. Furthermore, the FBI definition fails to include such behavior between individuals of the same sex and with males as victim, which certainly does occur.

FBI statistics show that more than 102,000 cases of rape were reported in 1990. However, in the past only about 16 percent of reported cases resulted in a conviction for this crime. Another 4 percent of those charged with rape were convicted of lesser offenses (Rabkin, 1979). The low conviction rate and the humiliation and shame involved in a rape trial keep many women from reporting rapes, so the actual incidence of the crime is probably much higher than reported. Some police officers still believe that the victims are partly to blame because of their manner of dress or behavior and endorse statements such as "Most charges of rape are unfounded" and "Nice women do not get raped" (LeDoux & Hazelwood, 1985). Estimates based on surveys indicate that as many as one of every five women will be a rape victim at some time during her life (Sorenson & Siegel, 1992). Most rape victims are young women in their teens or twenties, although victims as young as several years old and as old as seventy-three have been reported (Burgess & Holmstrom, 1979b). In approximately one-half of all rape cases, the victim is at least acquainted with the rapist and is attacked in the home or in an automobile (Kilpatrick, Veronen & Resick, 1979). One form of rape being reported with increasing frequency is "acquaintance" or "date" rape:

Colleen, twenty-seven, a San Francisco office manager, had been involved with her boyfriend for about a year when it happened. After a cozy dinner at her apartment, he suggested that she go to bed while he did the dishes. But a few moments later he stalked into Colleen's bedroom with a peculiar look on his face, brandishing a butcher knife and strips of cloth. After tying her, spread-eagled, to the bed, the formerly tender lover raped her brutally for three hours. When it was all over, he fell soundly asleep. (Seligman et al., 1984, p. 91)

Date rape may account for the majority of all rapes. Many victims may be reluctant to report such an attack; they feel responsible—at least in part—because they made a date with their attacker. Statistics vary as to the incidence of date rapes. Between 8 and 25 percent of female college students have reported that they had "unwanted sexual intercourse," and studies have generally found that most college women had experienced some unwanted sexual activity (Craig, 1990). Estimates vary from study to study because of different definitions of rape and intercourse as presented by the researchers, as well as the willingness or unwillingness of women to participate in surveys or to accurately report their experiences.

Craig (1990) argued that men who try to coerce women into intercourse have certain characteristics. They tend to (1) actively create the situation in which sexual encounters may occur; (2) interpret women's friendliness as provocation or their protests as being insincere; (3) try to manipulate women into sexual favors by using drugs or alcohol; and (4) attribute failures to succeed to perceived negative features of the woman, thereby protecting their egos. Many men who do not rape may also have these characteristics. Indeed, when asked to indicate the likelihood that they would rape if assured that they would not be caught and punished, about 35 percent of college males reported some likelihood and 20 percent indicated fairly high likelihood (Malamuth, 1981).

Should intercourse between a couple be considered rape if the woman did not want to engage in that activity? One police official, in reacting to the high number of rapes reported in his community, noted that "We definitely do not have a serious rape problem in this city. The problem is in the classification. If you took all our rapes one by one, you'd see that nine of ten are a girlfriend-boyfriend thing. These people are known to each other." (Girard, 1984, p. 12) The erroneous assumption made by that police official is that forced intercourse between acquaintances shouldn't be considered rape. Unfortunately, sexual aggression by men is quite common. Fifteen percent of a sample of college men reported that they did force intercourse at least once or twice. Only 39 percent of the men did not admit to any coerced sex (Rapaport & Burkhart, 1984). Of 6,159

male and female students enrolled in thirty-two universities in the United States, more than 50 percent of the women reported being the victims of sexual aggression, and 8 percent of men admitted to committing sexual acts that met the legal definition of rape. Women seldom reported episodes of date rape (Koss, Gidycz & Wisniewski, 1987). Many universities are conducting workshops for students to help them understand that intercourse without consent during a date or other social activity is rape.

Effects of Rape   Needless to say, rape is highly traumatic. Victims may experience psychological distress, phobic reactions, and sexual dysfunction. In one sample of victims, more than 50 percent reported one or more sexual dysfunctions as the result of the rape. Fear of sex and lack of desire or arousal were the most common complaints. Some women recovered quickly but others reported problems years after the episodes (Gilbert & Cunningham, 1986). A one-year follow-up of rape victims found that they were significantly more fearful than control groups. The fears were selective and involved things such as darkness and enclosed places—conditions likely to be associated with rape (Calhoun, Atkeson & Resick, 1982). Duration and intensity of fear were also found to be related to perceptions of dangerousness. Attacks in circumstances that the woman had defined as "safe" had a greater emotional impact than attacks in places that women felt were dangerous. Many women drastically changed their perception of how safe the environment really was (Scheppele & Bart, 1983).

In one survey, approximately two-thirds of rape victims reported that they couldn't resume sexual activity for at least six months (Burgess & Holmstrom, 1979b). Their sexual enjoyment was strongly affected. One victim described her attitude toward sex after the rape as follows:

It depends how I relate to the man. If I'm in a position to enjoy it—a 50-50 thing—then I'm ok. But if I'm feeling that I'm only doing this for him and not for my own enjoyment, then I feel like the incident again . . . then sex is bad. (p. 648)

Flashbacks were reported by 50 percent of the sexually active victims. These included fleeting memories that could not be repressed, reliving the experience, and associating the present sex partner with the rapist. Sympathetic understanding, nondemanding affection, and a positive attitude from the partner

Rape is an act of violence and aggression. Because rape victims are often stigmatized, many women fail to report it. When they do report it, victims are often subjected to an unsympathetic legal system that often seems to blame the victim for the crime. Rape crisis centers, and counselors like the women pictured here, counter this insensitivity by providing moral, emotional, and legal support to victims.

have been found beneficial. Hugging and gentle caressing are generally satisfying to the victim even if sexual approaches are aversive (Feldman-Summers, Gordon & Meagher, 1979).

In light of the severe sexual and psychological problems that a rape victim can experience, the availability of multiple support systems and counseling becomes very important. Most large cities now have rape crisis centers that provide counseling, as well as medical and legal information, to victims. Trained volunteers often accompany the victim to the hospital and to the police station. Women's organizations have made many hospital personnel and police offi-

cers more aware of the trauma of rape and have taught them to behave more sensitively when dealing with victims.

Etiology of Rape Rape is not specifically listed in DSM-IV as a mental disorder because the act can have a variety of motivations. In an analysis of 133 rapists, Groth, Burgess, and Holstrom (1977) distinguished the following three motivational types:

1. *Power rapist* This type of rapist (comprising 55 percent of those studied) is primarily attempting to compensate for feelings of personal or sexual inadequacy by trying to intimidate his victims.

2. *Anger rapist* The man in this category (40 percent of those studied) is angry at women in general; the victim is merely a convenient target.

3. *Sadistic rapist* This type (5 percent of those studied) derives satisfaction from inflicting pain on the rape victim and may torture or mutilate her.

These findings tend to support the contention that rape has more to do with power, aggression, and violence than with sex. In fact, a study of more than one hundred rapists indicated that 58 percent showed some sexual dysfunction, such as erectile difficulties, during the attack (Groth, Burgess & Holstrom, 1977).

Although these distinctions are of interest, little empirical research was done on the importance of aggressive cues in the sexual arousal of rapists until a study performed by Abel and colleagues (1977). These investigators recorded the degree of penile erection of rapists and nonrapists in response to two-minute audiotapes describing violent and nonviolent sexual scenes. The nonviolent tape described an incident of mutually enjoyable sexual intercourse. The violent tape described a rape in which the man forced himself on an unwilling woman. The rapists were aroused by both tape descriptions, whereas the nonrapists displayed a significantly lesser degree of erection in response to the portrayal of violent sex, preferring the scene involving mutually enjoyable sex. Some rapists also showed strong sexual arousal in response to another tape that was entirely aggressive in content.

Researchers initially thought that only sadists or rapists would show a sexual arousal pattern to aggressive sex. Later studies showed that certain groups of men who are not rapists also respond sexually to aggressive cues. In addition, whether the woman displays physical pleasure to the attack also increases sexual response in some men. Here are the results of some of these studies:

1. College men with sadistic tendencies rated slides of women displaying emotional distress (fear, anger, disgust, sadness) as more sexually arousing than did nonsadistic men (Heilbrum & Loftus, 1986).

2. Men who admitted to being more likely to commit rape showed more erections when listening to audiotapes of dramatized sex between nonconsenting participants than when listening to scenes between consenting participants. Men who reported that they weren't very likely to rape anyone showed the opposite pattern (Malamuth & Check, 1983).

3. When male students were exposed to a situation in which a woman is portrayed as being initially repelled but later responds sexually to rape, male students (but not females) became less sensitive to rape victims; viewed the rapist as being less responsible for the act and deserving less punishment; showed desensitization to violent sex; and were more likely to accept rape myths (Donnerstein & Linz, 1986).

Because of these findings, questions are being raised about the effects of media portrayals of violent sex, especially in pornography, on rape rates (see Focus 11.1). Exposure to such materials may affect attitudes and thoughts and influence patterns of sexual arousal (Malamuth & Briere, 1986). These media portrayals may reflect and affect societal values concerning violence and women.

Baron, Straus, and Jaffee (1988) proposed a "cultural spillover" theory—namely, that rape tends to be high in cultures or environments that encourage violence. The investigators studied the relationship between cultural support for violence, as well as demographic characteristics and rates of rapes in all fifty states. Rates of rape and cultural support for violence were measured in each state. The support for violence were determined by (1) the proportion of individuals who chose magazines and television programs involving violence; (2) the amount of legis-

lation permitting corporal punishment in schools, prisoners sentenced to death, and executions for crimes; (3) National Guard enrollments; and (4) public opinions such as favoring the death penalty, opposing the requirement that gun owners obtain mandatory gun permits, and approving punching a stranger under a variety of situations. Demographic variables that could be related to rates of rape in each state were also examined such as percentage of males who were divorced or single, percentage of women, age of individuals, social class, and percentage of African Americans. Results indicated that cultural support for violence was significantly related to the rate of rape, independent of the effects of demographic variables. Having a high proportion of divorced and single men was also related to increased rates of rape. The percentage of African Americans residing in the state was unrelated to rape. The results suggested that when violence is generally encouraged or condoned, there is a "spillover" effect on rape.

As illustrated in the study by Baron, Straus, and Jaffee (1988), researchers are turning their attention to variables other than personality characteristics of rapists. The role of sociocultural variables is gaining increasing attention, particularly by feminists who see rape as a manifestation of male dominance and control of women (Sorenson & White, 1992). Other researchers have proposed integrative models that incorporate many different factors (Barabee & Marshall, 1991; Hall & Hirschman, 1991; Malamuth et al., 1991). See Critical Thinking for a discussion of controversial explanations for rape.

Incest

Incest is sexual relations between close relatives. Estimates of the incidence of incest range from 48,000 to 250,000 cases per year (Stark, 1984). The most commonly reported incidents of incest to law enforcement agencies involve a father and his daughter or stepdaughter. In a survey in which 15 percent of the respondents reported sexual contacts with relatives, however, the most common incestuous relationship involved siblings (Hunt, 1974). Less than 0.5 percent of the women reported sexual contact with their fathers. Mother-son incest seems to be rare. In another study, sexual activities between siblings were again found to be relatively frequent: 15 percent of the women and 10 percent of the men

Is Pornography Harmful?

The Attorney General's Commission on Pornography (1986) concluded that a causal relationship exists between many forms of pornography and increased violence against women. The same conclusion was reached by the Surgeon General's Workshop on Pornography (Koop, 1987). The latter report indicated that pornography "increases beliefs that less common sexual practices are more common" and may lead men to believe that "coercion and violence are acceptable in sex relations." These views are very different from those of the Commission on Obscenity and Pornography (1970), which found no relationship between exposure to erotic materials and sex crimes. What accounts for the opposing findings? Part of the difference can be attributed to the types of materials that were examined by each committee. Unlike more recent studies, the 1970 report was based on nonviolent explicit sex. Perhaps not all forms of explicit sex are harmful.

The most important factor may not be the explicitness of the portrayal of sexual activity but the amount of violence and aggression directed toward women. Nonexplicit portrayals of sexual violence in the mass media have also been shown to increase men's negative attitudes toward women (Malamuth & Check, 1981). In fact, the Attorney General's Commission on Por-

reported that they had had sexual involvement with their siblings. In 75 percent of these cases, mutual consent was involved. About half considered the experience positive; the other half, negative (Finkelhor, 1980).

Most research has focused on father-daughter incest. This type of incestuous relationship generally begins when the daughter is between six and eleven years old, and it continues for at least two years (Stark, 1984). Unlike sex between siblings, father-daughter incest is always exploitative. The girl is especially vulnerable because she depends on her father for emotional support. As a result, the victims often feel guilty and powerless. Their problems continue into adulthood and are reflected in their high rates of drug abuse, sexual dysfunction, and psychiatric problems (Emslie & Rosenfeld, 1983; Gartner & Gartner, 1988). Incest victims often have difficulty establishing trusting relationships with men. Relationships that were forceful, intrusive, or of a long duration are more likely to result in long-lasting negative effects (Herman, Russell & Trocki, 1986).

Three types of incestuous fathers have been described (Rist, 1979). The first is a socially isolated man who is highly dependent on his family for interpersonal relationships. His emotional dependency gradually evolves (and expands) into a sexual relationship with his daughter. The second type of incestuous father has a psychopathic personality and is completely indiscriminate in choosing sexual partners. The third type has pedophilic tendencies and is sexually involved with several children, including his daughter. In addition, incest victims have reported family patterns in which the father is violent and the mother is unusually powerless (Herman & Hirschman, 1981). Williams and Finkelhor (1990) noted that some studies have shown that incestuous fathers were more likely than nonincestuous fathers to have experienced childhood sexual abuse themselves, although the phenomenon has not been found in many cases. They also found that incestuous fathers tend to have difficulties in empathy, nurturance, caretaking, social skills behaviors, and masculine identification.

Treatment for Incest Offenders and Rapists

Conventional Treatment   Imprisonment has been the main form of treatment for incest offenders and for rapists. In some cases of incest, an effort is usually made to keep the family intact for the benefit of the child. Behavioral treatment for sexual aggressors (rapists and pedophiliacs) generally involves the following steps:

1. Assessing sexual preferences through self-report and measuring erectile responses to different sexual stimuli

nography (1986) concluded that the "slasher films" in which violence is paired with sex are more harmful than other forms of pornography. One study examined the impact of violence or aggression toward women. Male subjects were first angered and then exposed to films showing (1) sexual aggression toward women, (2) explicit sex between mutually consenting adults, (3) nonsexual aggression toward women, and (4) nonsexual material. After this exposure, the men were given the opportunity to behave aggressively toward a woman (a confederate of the researcher). The films depicting sexual aggression toward women and nonsexual aggression were associated with high degrees of aggression in male subjects. The men who viewed the films depicting neutral scenes and nonviolent explicit sex displayed low degrees of aggression (Donnerstein, Berkowitz & Linz, 1986). The findings supported the belief that it is the violence depicted in pornographic material, and not the degree of sexual explicitness, that influences aggression in males. If violence is the culprit in pornography, why are the rates of rape so low in Japan where sexual violence is portrayed so often in the media (Abramson & Hayashi, 1984)? Murrin and Laws (1990) suggested that many variables may mediate the relationship between pornography and sexual crimes. They believe that exposure to pornography by itself does not influence sexual crimes. Rather certain individuals in certain cultures may be affected by pornography. In particular, they believe that when exposed to pornography, personality variables as well as the cultural milieu (for example, a society that overemphasizes male dominance, separation of sexes, and individuals as sexual objects) increase the likelihood of sexual crimes.

2. Reducing deviant interests through aversion therapy (the man receives electric shock when deviant stimuli are presented)

3. Orgasmic reconditioning or masturbating training to increase sexual arousal to appropriate stimuli

4. Social skills training to increase interpersonal competence

5. Assessing these men after treatment (Marshall et al., 1983)

Although treatment is becoming more sophisticated, questions remain about the effectiveness of these programs. In general, some treatment programs have been effective with child molesters and exhibitionists, although with rapists, treatment outcomes have often been poor (Marshall et al., 1991).

Public revulsion and outrage against incest offenders, pedophiles, and rapists have resulted in a call for severe punishment. A man who had an incestuous relationship with his stepdaughter for seven years was ordered by the judge to receive injections of the hormone progesterone to control his sex drive. This judicial ruling caused an uproar. Some groups believed that the punishment was inadequate, some believed that it would not work, and others indicated that it was "cruel and unusual."

Controversial Treatments   Surgical castration has been used to treat sexual offenders in many European countries, and results indicate that rates of recidivism have been low (Marshall et al., 1991). An investigation of sex offenders (rapists, heterosexual pedophiles, homosexual pedophiles, bisexual pedophiles, and a sexual murderer) who were surgically castrated reported a decrease in sexual intercourse, masturbation, and frequency of sexual fantasies. However, twelve of the thirty-nine were still able to engage in sexual intercourse several years after being castrated. The rapists constituted the group whose members were most likely to remain sexually active (Heim, 1981).

Chemical therapy, usually involving the hormone Depo-Provera, reduces self-reports of sexual urges in pedophiles but not the ability to show genital arousal. Drugs appear to reduce psychological desire more than actual erection capabilities (Wincze, Bansal & Malamud, 1986). The effectiveness of biological treatment such as surgery and chemotherapy is not known, and controversy obviously continues over the appropriate treatment for sexual offenders such as incest offenders, pedophiles, and rapists.

SEXUAL DYSFUNCTIONS

In contrast to the paraphilias, which are characterized by sexual arousal as a response to unusual situations, acts, or objects, a **sexual dysfunction** is a dis-

Why Does Rape Occur?

Because of survey results (Malamuth, 1981) indicating that a significant proportion of university men report some likelihood that they would rape if they could get away with it, and because of increased awareness over date rapes, students at colleges and universities have been discussing the causes of rape. Is rape a crime of sex or is it a crime of violence and dominance? Are men "oversexed" and more likely to seek multiple partners and "one-night stands" compared with women? Can rape be explained by natural selection and reproductive strategies? If biogenic factors are found to have a role in sexual aggression, do these factors mean that individuals are less responsible for their behaviors? These controversial issues have theoretical, social, political, and moral implications.

Sociocultural Perspectives A variety of views of the causes of rape have been proposed, as noted by Sorenson and White (1992). Some thought that rape was committed by mentally disturbed men, and studies were initiated to find personality characteristics that might be associated with rape. Malamuth's (1981) research, which indicated that a significant proportion of men would consider rape if they could get away with it, helped change the view that rapists were simply mentally disturbed. Socio-

cultural views then gained favor. Brownmiller (1975) argued that rape was a means of social control and dominance whereby men keep women in a perpetual state of intimidation. This view emphasized a "culture" of male dominance rather than a sexual motive as a primary reason for sexual assault. Also adopting sociocultural perspectives, others linked permissiveness toward violence (Baron, Straus & Jaffee, 1988) or rigid sex roles and societal dependency on men (Sanday, 1981) as factors in rape. What do you think? Can you give examples that support or disprove the sociocultural perspective?

ruption of any part of the normal sexual response cycle. Problems in sexual functioning such as premature ejaculation, low sexual desire, and difficulties in achieving orgasm are quite common in our society. Recently, fears associated with HIV infection and AIDS have increased our concerns and apprehensions about sex and sexual practices (see Focus 11.2). Because sexual behavior is such an important part of our lives and because so many taboos and myths surround it, people have great difficulty dealing with the topic in an open and direct manner. As a result, individuals and couples often suffer in silence, which often leads to feelings of failure, low self-esteem, frustrations, and divorces.

Although Freud made sex (libido) an important part of psychoanalytic theory, knowledge of sexual practices and behavior was largely confined to his clinical cases and his speculations from the understanding of social mores. It was not until the contributions of Alfred Kinsey and colleagues (1948, 1953)

that the scientific community and American public were given reliable information on sexual practices and customs. At the time they were published, Kinsey's findings were considered shocking, exciting, provocative, and at times controversial. Later "sex researchers" criticized Kinsey's self-report or questionnaire-interview approaches as being potentially biased (they dealt with intimate behavior, which might affect the respondent's answers). Nevertheless, the original Kinsey findings provided us with valuable baseline data concerning the incidence and prevalence of certain sexual practices.

The field of sex research took another major turn in the late 1960s when William Masters and Virginia Johnson published their seminal works *Human Sexual Response* (1966) and *Human Sexual Inadequacy* (1970). Instead of relying on interviews or self-report questionnaires, these researchers actually observed sexual behavior of volunteer subjects in the laboratory while their physiological responses were care-

Sociobiological Perspectives There are different sociobiological models for sexual aggression and rape. One is that sexual aggression has an evolutionary basis, although biochemical differences between sex offenders and non-sex offenders have not received unequivocal support (Hall & Hirschman, 1991). Ellis (1991) believes that sex differences have evolved as a means of maximizing the reproduction of the human species. Men have much more to gain in reproductive terms by being able to pass on their genes rapidly to a large number of women. This increases their chances of having offspring. On the other hand, because women must bear much more of the investment in each offspring before and after birth, they would be favored by natural selection to find mates who are likely to supply much investment for offsprings. Therefore, it would be advantageous for women to avoid multiple partners and to seek male commitment. Ellis argued that men have a stronger sex drive than do women: men in all societies have higher self-reported desires for copulation and other forms of sexual experiences; males (including males in other species of primates) masturbate more, expecially in the absence of sex partners; and women are more likely than men to report having sexual intercourse for reasons other than sexual gratification.

Ellis took issue with the view that rape is not a sexual crime: rapists often try to obtain sex by actions such as getting women drunk and falsely pledging love, and they use physical force only after these other tactics fail; fewer men than women believe that rape is motivated by power and anger. Nevertheless, sociobiological theories have difficulty explaining differences in rates of rape in different societies or changes in rates of rape over time, without references to cultural conditions or experiential factors. Ellis believes that the *motivation* for sexual assault is unlearned but that the *behavior* surrounding sexual assault is learned. Thus sexual motivation (including the drive to rape) is innate. If sexual aggression is reinforced (or not punished), forced copulatory attempts will persist. What do you think? Is punishment an effective deterrent to rape?

Because of the multitude of factors that may be important, isolating and testing different propositions concerning sexual assault has been difficult. Regardless of the theories taken to explain rape, no one—even those who believe that men have a stronger biological sexual drive—can excuse or condone such behavior. Research findings have suggested that changes in the way men and women relate to one another, attitudes toward violence, and cultural practices can reduce the incidence of rape. How has your school addressed this issue?

---

fully monitored. Although some in the American public objected to these studies on moral grounds (observing couples in intercourse, oral sex, and masturbation), Masters and Johnson did much to legitimize the scientific study of sexual behavior. They also dispelled many myths such as the belief that women were less sexual than men, that simultaneous orgasm between a man and woman was the ultimate in sex satisfaction, and the myth of vaginal versus clitoral orgasms. But perhaps Masters' and Johnson's most important contribution was to give us an understanding of what is now called the "normal" human sexual response cycle.

Recently, the Janus Report (Janus & Janus, 1993) was greeted enthusiastically by both sex researchers as well as other mental health professionals. A large-scale cross-sectional survey conducted over a nine-year period (1983–1992), the Januses gathered data concerning the sexual beliefs, thoughts, and behaviors of 1347 women and 1418 men. Among some of the findings destined to have an effect on our thoughts and behavior include the following:

1. Despite concerns of contracting sexually transmitted diseases (STD) and especially AIDS, frequency of sexual activity has not declined and may have increased.

2. Beliefs in declining and lower sexual satisfaction with the postmature population (those in their 50s, 60s, and 70s) are incorrect—people 65 and older report only slightly lower activity than those people in their 30s and 40s.

3. Education, regional differences, political beliefs, and economic level affect men and women's sexual attitudes and practices.

The Sexual Response Cycle

The contributions of Sigmund Freud, Alfred Kinsey, Masters and Johnson, and the Januses have given us

Sexual Behavior and the Era of AIDS

First identified between 1983 and 1984 in France and the United States, the human immunodeficiency virus (HIV) has been found to cause a chronic and progressive immune deficiency disease called AIDS (acquired immune deficiency syndrome). As of 1992, the Centers for Disease Control (1992) reported that more than 230,000 cases of AIDS have been diagnosed in the United States and estimated that one million persons are currently infected. Because of the long latency between infection and the onset of opportunistic infections, many people who are symptom-free unknowingly pass the HIV virus on through unsafe sex, unsafe needles, birth, and, until recently, blood transfusions (Douce, 1993).

How It Kills The AIDS virus kills white blood cells called T-helper lymphocytes, which are found in the immune system. These lymphocytes are involved in identifying patho-gens and instructing other white blood cells (B-lymphocytes) to make antibodies. As the AIDS virus progressively destroys the T-helpers, the body has a weakened ability to fight off "opportunistic diseases" like various kinds of cancer (Kaposi's sarcoma) and pneumonia. These diseases have very little chance of developing in persons with healthy and intact immune systems.

Public Concerns Although HIV infection has affected far fewer people than gonorrhea, syphilis, genital herpes, and other sexually transmitted diseases (STDs), it has become more of a public concern and obsession for several reasons. First, there is no known cure for full-blown AIDS. Approximately 92 to 96 percent of those diagnosed between 1978 and 1983 have died, suggesting that AIDS is inevitably fatal (Keeling, 1993). Equally disturbing is our lack of knowledge concerning what percentage of those with the HIV in-fection will develop AIDS. Medical consensus is lacking on this question, but many medical researchers believe that it is inevitable and estimate that it is a matter of a few short years.

Second, public perception of those infected with HIV are often negative, condemning, blaming, and stigmatizing (Dworkin & Pincu, 1993). Many people mistakenly assume that someone with an HIV infection is gay, uses drugs, is a prostitute, or engages in immoral sexual acts. Such misguided and phobic reactions often blame the victims and force them to hide their condition in shame and despair at a time when both medical and psychological help are sorely needed. Such beliefs have proved to be a major barrier in educating the public to facts concerning HIV and AIDS, and in instituting prevention practices. Although it is true that certain high-risk groups have been identified (gays, intravenous drug abusers, prostitutes, and

---

useful information and perspectives in viewing human sexuality. While we continue to grapple with questions regarding what is considered normal and abnormal sexual behavior, these individuals have allowed us to demystify many of our beliefs regarding sex and to understand how human sexual responsiveness occurs. For example, treating human sexual dysfunctions requires an understanding of the normal sexual response cycle. The works of Masters and Johnson are especially important in this regard.

This normal cycle consists of four stages as illustrated in Figure 11.1: appetitive, excitement, orgasm, and resolution. For accuracy, it is important to note that Masters and Johnson did not posit a separate appetitive stage; they included it with the excitement phase. The work of sex therapist Helen Kaplan

(1974) gave us an understanding of how important it is for a person to desire and be sexually ready, thus legitimizing a conceptually distinct state of sexual response.

1. The *appetitive phase* is characterized by the person's desire for sexual activity. The person begins to have thoughts or fantasies surrounding sex. He or she may begin to feel attracted to another person and to daydream increasingly about sex. The dysfunctions in which the person lacks sexual desire are called *sexual desire disorders.*

2. The *excitement phase* moves out of the appetitive phase when specific and direct sexual stimulation occurs (not necessarily physical). Heart

people receiving contaminated blood, for example), HIV infection is not a function of any group, but the practices that lead to the infection. For example, the belief that HIV is limited to only homosexual contact is a myth, as one-third of the women who have AIDS were infected via heterosexual contact (Douce, 1993). It is found in every region of the United States, all over the world, at all economic levels, across all races, and in men, women, and children.

What We Know About HIV Transmission The HIV virus is transmitted in body fluids: blood and blood derivatives, semen, vaginal and cervical secretions, and breast milk. Thus HIV spreads through acts or practices that expose the person to fluids and secretions.

Blood In general, HIV can be transmitted through needle-sharing, accidental injuries resulting in direct exposure to contaminated blood, and transfusion or transplantation of blood, blood derivatives, tissues, or organs in the infected donor. Again, precautions concerning the

use of clean needles, adequate screening and testing of blood and patients, and stringent safeguards in medical care to avoid accidents can do much to prevent contamination.

Mother to fetus or infant HIV can be transmitted by an infected mother to her infant during pregnancy and after birth during nursing. It is estimated that 10 to 40 percent of all infants born to HIV-positive mothers will be infected (Keeling, 1993).

Sexual practices HIV can be transmitted during insertive and receptive vaginal and anal intercourse. Among men who have unprotected anal intercourse with one another, the probability of transmission is higher for the receptive than the insertive partner (Darrow, Echenberg & Jaffee, 1987; Detels et al., 1989). There is greater risk of transmitting HIV from a man to a woman during anal than during vaginal intercourse (European Study Group, 1992), and the risk is higher for transmission of male to female than female to male during vaginal intercourse. Although the risk of transmission during fellatio is much

lower than intercourse, some infections have occurred as a result of exposure to semen or pre-ejaculatory fluid. Risk factors are uncertain regarding cunnilingus. No current evidence exists that HIV transmission occurs during kissing of any type, depth, or duration (United States Public Health Service, 1986); during oral-anal contact (rimming); during manual-anal contact (fisting); or by touching, massage, and other erotic behavior that does not involve contact with semen, pre-ejaculatory fluid, blood, or vaginal or cervical secretions.

It is clear that AIDS has affected our sexual behavior more than any other sexually transmitted disease. Apart from abstinence, there are few guarantees that one will not become infected when engaging in sex with others. Taking precautions by using condoms, carefully selecting your partner, and engaging in low-risk sexual practices may make sex safer but certainly not safe. As one sex educator put it, "There is no such thing as safe sex, only safer sex."

rate, blood pressure, and respiration rate increase. In the male, blood flow increases in the penis resulting in an erection. The ridge around the head of the penis turns deep purple and the testes enlarge and elevate in preparation for ejaculation. In the female, the breasts swell, nipples become erect, blood engorges the genital region, and the clitoris expands. Vaginal lubrication reflexively occurs, and a sex flush may appear on the skin (usually later in this phase). Psychologically based difficulties with these physiological changes are termed **sexual arousal disorders.**

3. The *orgasm phase* is characterized by involuntary muscular contractions throughout the body and the eventual release of sexual tension. In the

man, muscles at the base of the penis contract propelling semen through the penis. In the woman, the outer third of the vagina contracts rhythmically. Following orgasm, men enter a refractory period during which they are unresponsive to sexual stimulation for a period of time. However, women are capable of multiple orgasms with continued stimulation. The inability to achieve an orgasm after entering the excitement phase and receiving adequate sexual stimulation is called an *orgasm disorder.*

4. The *resolution phase* is characterized by relaxation of the body after orgasm. Heart rate, blood pressure, and respiration return to normal. Problems with this last stage are rare.

FIGURE 11.1   Human Sexual Response Cycle

The studies of Masters and Johnson reveal that the normal sexual response cycle for men and women are similar. Note that women may experience more than one orgasm. Sexual disorders may occur at any of the phases, but seldom at the resolution phase.

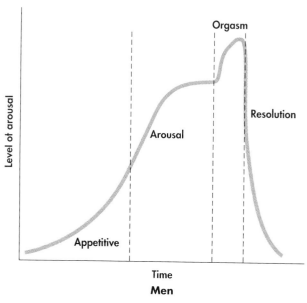

Men

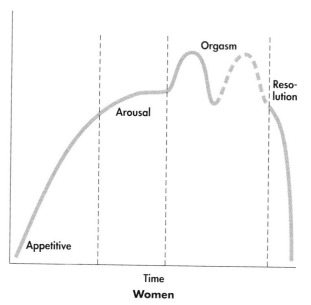

Women

Other problems that may be involved with the sexual response cycle include some form of a sexual pain disorder (*dyspareunia* and *vaginismus*) or pain associated with sexual intercourse owing primarily to psychological factors. DSM-IV also recognizes the diagnoses of sexual dysfunction due to a general medical condition and substance-induced sexual dysfunction. For example, a man may suffer from an erectile disorder caused by diabetes (general medical condition) or alcohol abuse (substance-induced).

As indicated earlier, problems occurring during the normal sexual response cycle are fairly common. To be diagnosed as a dysfunction, however, the problem must be recurrent and persistent. DSM-IV also requires that such factors as frequency, chronicity, subjective distress, and effect on other areas of functioning be considered in the diagnosis. The sexual dysfunctions are diagrammed in the disorders chart on page 345.

Sexual Desire Disorders

Sexual desire disorders involve (1) *hypoactive sexual desire disorder*, characterized by little or no interest in sexual activities either actual or fantasized, and (2) *sexual aversion disorder*, characterized by an avoidance and aversion to sexual intercourse. Both of these disorders can be lifelong or acquired and may be due to psychogenic or a combination of psychogenic and biogenic factors. In the following case, relationship problems contributed to the sexual dysfunction:

A 36-year-old woman and her 38-year-old husband were referred by her psychotherapist for sex therapy. The couple had little or no sexual contact over the preceding three years, and the sexual relationship had been troubled and unsatisfactory since the day they met. . . . Kissing and gentle fondling were enjoyable to both of them, but as their relationship progressed to genital caressing, she became more anxious, despite her being easily orgasmic. . . . She explained the difficulty as being due to conflict in the relationship. She saw him as angry, controlling and demanding, and very critical of her. Naturally, she did not feel loving or sexually receptive. Correspondingly, he felt angry, resentful, and cheated of a "normal sex life." (Golden, 1988, p. 304)

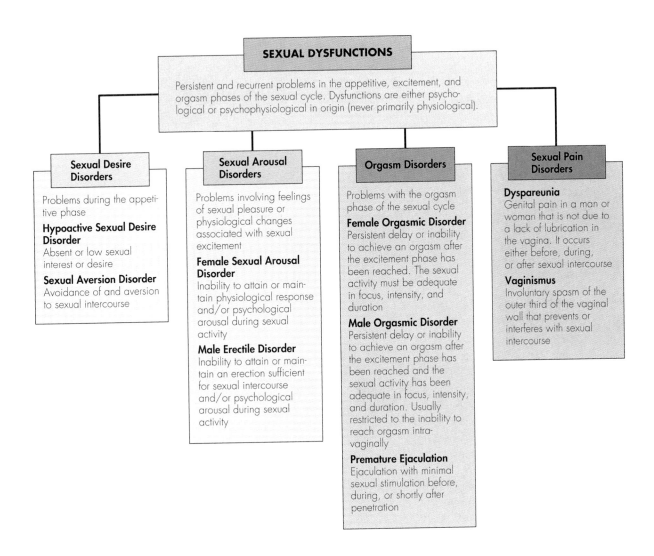

SEXUAL DYSFUNCTIONS

Persistent and recurrent problems in the appetitive, excitement, and orgasm phases of the sexual cycle. Dysfunctions are either psychological or psychophysiological in origin (never primarily physiological).

Sexual Desire Disorders

Problems during the appetitive phase

Hypoactive Sexual Desire Disorder
Absent or low sexual interest or desire

Sexual Aversion Disorder
Avoidance of and aversion to sexual intercourse

Sexual Arousal Disorders

Problems involving feelings of sexual pleasure or physiological changes associated with sexual excitement

Female Sexual Arousal Disorder
Inability to attain or maintain physiological response and/or psychological arousal during sexual activity

Male Erectile Disorder
Inability to attain or maintain an erection sufficient for sexual intercourse and/or psychological arousal during sexual activity

Orgasm Disorders

Problems with the orgasm phase of the sexual cycle

Female Orgasmic Disorder
Persistent delay or inability to achieve an orgasm after the excitement phase has been reached. The sexual activity must be adequate in focus, intensity, and duration

Male Orgasmic Disorder
Persistent delay or inability to achieve an orgasm after the excitement phase has been reached and the sexual activity has been adequate in focus, intensity, and duration. Usually restricted to the inability to reach orgasm intra-vaginally

Premature Ejaculation
Ejaculation with minimal sexual stimulation before, during, or shortly after penetration

Sexual Pain Disorders

Dyspareunia
Genital pain in a man or woman that is not due to a lack of lubrication in the vagina. It occurs either before, during, or after sexual intercourse

Vaginismus
Involuntary spasm of the outer third of the vaginal wall that prevents or interferes with sexual intercourse

In this case, the woman was diagnosed as having inhibited sexual desire. Controversy exists, however, over whether sexual desire disorders are labeled correctly. If the woman in the preceding case avoided sexual intercourse because of marital difficulties, is the diagnosis appropriate? And what about cases in which job stress or dual careers interfere with intimacy and sexual interest? According to DSM-IV, a sexual dysfunction should be diagnosed in such cases because the interpersonal problem is the primary cause of the disturbed functioning. Many people question the legitimacy of these criteria and the categories themselves, however, challenging the notion that sexual problems stemming from troubled relationships from job or academic stress are sufficient to indicate a disorder.

About 20 percent of the adult population are believed to be suffering from hypoactive sexual desire disorder (DSM-IV). Reports of diminished sexual desire or a lack of sexual desire are more common from women than from men. Some clinicians estimate that 40 to 50 percent of all sexual dysfunctions involve deficits in desire (Southern & Gayle, 1982; Stuart, Hammond & Pett, 1987). Although people with sexual desire disorders are often capable of experiencing orgasm, they claim to have little interest in, or to

Differences in sexual desire can have a negative impact on a couple's relationship. In this case the man feels pressure to perform sexually; the woman feels neglected because of the lack of sexual interest displayed by her husband.

derive no pleasure from, sexual activity. Some people may report low sexual desire because of inexperience. Many of these people may not have learned to label or identify their own arousal levels, may not know how to increase their arousal, and may have a limited expectation for their ability to be aroused (LoPiccolo, 1980).

Just as we do not really know what constitutes "normal" sexual desire, we know little about what frequency of sexual fantasies or activities is "normal." Kinsey, Pomeroy, and Martin (1948) found tremendous variation in reported total sexual outlet, or release. One man reported that he had ejaculated only once in thirty years; another claimed to have averaged thirty orgasms per week for thirty years. After analyzing mean frequencies of orgasm from sex surveys, a group of researchers noted that "a total orgasmic outlet of less than once every two weeks is considered one marker of low desire . . . unless extenuating circumstances such as a lack of privacy occur" (Schover et al., 1982, p. 616). However, using some average frequency of sexual activity doesn't seem appropriate for categorizing people as having inhibited sexual desire. Someone may have a high sex drive but not engage in sexual activities; someone else may not have sexual interest or fantasies but may engage in frequent sexual behaviors for the sake of

his or her partner (Rosen & Leiblum, 1987). Furthermore, using orgasms (intercourse or masturbation) or desire for orgasms may pose some gender bias. The Janus Report indicated that men as a group masturbate and experience orgasms more than women at all age groups (Janus & Janus, 1993). Does this mean that women have less sexual desire than men? Until we can decide on what a normal range of sexual desire is, we can hardly discover the causes of or develop treatments for sexual desire disorders.

Sexual Arousal Disorders

In men, inhibited sexual excitement takes the form of **erectile dysfunction,** a man's inability to reach or maintain a penile erection sufficient for sexual intercourse. The man may feel fully aroused but can't finish the sex act. Although Masters and Johnson (1970) estimated that only about 5 percent of erectile dysfunctions were due to physical conditions, recent studies have found that in more than 30 percent of men, biogenic factors may be involved (Segraves, Schoenberg & Ivanoff, 1983; Slag et al., 1981). That a man may have a minor organic impairment that "makes his erection more vulnerable to being disrupted by psychological, biological, and sexual technique factors" (LoPiccolo & Stock, 1986) is one of the primary reasons why DSM-IV includes general medical conditions as a factor in sexual dysfunctions. The technology does not yet exist, however, to accurately assess a "minor" organic impairment.

Distinguishing between erectile dysfunctions that are primarily biogenic and those that are psychogenic has been difficult. For example, one procedure involves recording nocturnal penile tumescence (NPT). The reasoning behind this is that men who do not display adequate spontaneous erections during sleep suffer from an organic impairment. Psychological causes are thought to predominate in men who show an adequate NPT response. Unfortunately, considerable overlap in NPT scores has been found between samples of diabetic men with erectile difficulties and normal functional controls (LoPiccolo & Stock, 1986). Therefore some people diagnosed as suffering from organic impotence actually have psychological factors as the cause. The reverse could also be true.

Primary erectile dysfunction is the diagnosis for a man who has never been able to successfully engage in sexual intercourse. This difficulty often clearly has a psychological origin because many men with this dysfunction can get an erection and reach orgasm during masturbation and can show erection during the REM (rapid eye movement) phase of sleep. The term *secondary erectile dysfunction* refers to a situation in which the man has had at least one successful instance of sexual intercourse but is currently having erectile difficulty. Failure to achieve an erection and penetration in 25 percent of sexual attempts is sufficient for this diagnosis (Masters & Johnson, 1970).

A twenty-year-old college student was suffering from secondary erectile dysfunction. His first episode of erectile difficulty occurred when he attempted sexual intercourse after drinking heavily. Although to a certain extent he attributed the failure to alcohol, he also began to have doubts about his sexual ability. During a subsequent sexual encounter, his anxiety and worry increased. When he failed in this next coital encounter, even though he had not been drinking, his anxiety level rose even more. The client sought therapy after the discovery that he was unable to have an erection even during petting.

The prevalence rate of erectile dysfunction is difficult to determine because it often goes unreported. Clinicians estimate that approximately 50 percent of men have experienced transient impotence (Kaplan, 1974). Of 448 men with sexual dysfunctions treated at the Masters and Johnson sex clinic, 32 were suffering from primary erectile dysfunction and 213 from secondary erectile dysfunction. The number of cases reported may be increasing now as people feel freer to talk about this problem and as it becomes more acceptable for women to expect greater satisfaction in sexual relationships.

In women, sexual arousal disorder is characterized by the lack of physical signs, such as vaginal lubrication or erection of the nipples, during sexual interactions. The individual may also complain that she derives no sexual pleasure. As with other sexual dysfunctions, this disorder may be lifelong or acquired and is often the result of negative attitudes about sex or early sexual experiences. Receiving negative information about sex, having been sexually assaulted or molested, and having conflicts with her sexual partner can contribute to the disorder.

A 38-year-old woman had a satisfying sexual relationship with her husband for many years. Then her husband developed a drinking problem, which created conflict between them. Sexual intercourse started to become aversive to her, and she eventually lost all interest in sex. After her divorce, the woman was disturbed to discover that she was unable to become sexually aroused with other men. A desensitization procedure was used to eliminate her conditioned anxiety toward sexual intercourse. (Wolpe, 1982)

Female Orgasmic Disorder (Inhibited Female Orgasm)

In **inhibited orgasm,** the woman is unable to achieve an orgasm with stimulation that is "adequate in focus, intensity, and duration" after entering the excitement phase. DSM-III-R includes an exception regarding female orgasm, however: "Some females are able to experience orgasm during noncoital clitoral stimulation, but are unable to experience it during coitus in the absence of manual clitoral stimulation. In most of these females, this represents a normal variation of the female sexual response" (DSM-III-R, p. 294). Whether the lack of orgasm is categorized as a dysfunction or as a "normal variant" is left to the judgment of the clinician. As is noted in Focus 11.3, the criteria that define adequate functioning during sexual intercourse are quite controversial.

Sexual Dysfunction or Normal Variant?

Should women who do not regularly have orgasms during coitus be considered sexually dysfunctional? This question is being debated more frequently as researchers and clinicians alike are discovering that coital orgasm is infrequent in women. Hite (1976) reported that only 30 percent of the women in her study could experience orgasm regularly during sexual intercourse. Similar findings have been reported by Hoch and associates (1981). Hite argued that the prevailing view of orgasm—that it "counts" only during sexual intercourse—is a reflection of our male-dominated society. Kaplan (1974) also denied that women who are otherwise sexually responsive are nonetheless "sick" because they do not have coital orgasms. She be-

lieves that "a woman who is otherwise orgasmic, but does not reach orgasm during coitus, is neither frigid nor sick. This pattern seems to be a normal variant of female sexuality for some women" (p. 83). Hoch went even further and suggested that the inability to achieve an orgasm without additional stimulation is "not a normal variation of female sexuality but rather normal sexuality for the majority of females" (p. 82).

This controversy has affected sexual therapy. Some sex therapists believe that orgasm during coitus is a justifiable goal for "normal" sexual functioning (Zeiss, Rosen & Zeiss, 1977). Others are satisfied when patients are able to achieve orgasm through manual stimulation

(Schneidman & McGuire, 1976). Regardless of the controversy, however, a reexamination of the "necessity" of coital orgasm for women (and for men?) seems to be in order. To require that women be able to achieve orgasm during sexual intercourse to be considered "normal" may be a disservice both to women and to their sex partners.

Male sexual dysfunction is also defined in terms of coital success. Does this mean that men who ejaculate rapidly or not at all during coitus, but who show the normal sexual cycle during masturbation and oral sex, are suffering from sexual problems? Perhaps. But many questions remain concerning the appropriate criteria for sexual dysfunction.

Inhibited female orgasm may be termed *primary*, to indicate that orgasm has never been experienced, or *secondary*, to show that orgasm has been experienced. Primary orgasmic dysfunction is considered relatively common in women: perhaps 8 to 10 percent of all women have never achieved an orgasm by any means (Hite, 1976; Kaplan, 1974; Kinsey et al., 1953). This disorder is not equivalent to primary orgasmic dysfunction in males, who often can achieve orgasm through masturbation or by some other means.

Nevertheless, Wakefield (1988) argued that inhibited female orgasm actually is rare and exists in less than 1 percent of women. He pointed out that many women do not reach orgasm during initial sexual encounters. In addition, they may not have engaged in masturbation. Wakefield believes that the diagnosis of inhibited orgasm should be made only if the woman has had experiences conducive to eliciting orgasmic responses but still has not had an orgasm.

Male Orgasmic Disorder (Inhibited Male Orgasm)

Inhibited male orgasm is the inability to ejaculate within the vagina, even with full arousal and penile erection. As noted, men who have this dysfunction can usually ejaculate when masturbating. Inhibited orgasm in males is relatively rare, and little is known about it (LoPiccolo & Stock, 1986). Treatment is often urged by the wife, who may want to conceive or who may feel (because of the husband's lack of orgasm) that she is not an exciting sexual partner (McCary, 1973).

An examination of the backgrounds of men who have this dysfunction may reveal either the occurrence of some traumatic event or a severely restrictive religious background in which sex is considered evil. Masters and Johnson (1970) gave an example of a man who discovered his wife engaged in sexual intercourse with another man. Although they remained married, he could no longer ejaculate during intercourse.

Premature Ejaculation

Premature ejaculation is a relatively common sexual problem in men, but sex researchers and therapists offer different definitions of it. Kaplan (1974) defined *prematurity* as the inability of a man to tolerate high (plateau) levels of sexual excitement without ejaculating reflexively. Kilmann and Auerbach (1979) suggested that ejaculation less than five minutes after coital entry is a suitable criterion of prematurity. Masters and Johnson (1970) contended that a man who is unable to delay ejaculation long enough during sexual intercourse to produce an orgasm in the woman 50 percent of the time is a premature ejaculator. The difficulty with the last definition is the possibility that a man may be "premature" with one partner but entirely adequate for another.

Some support has been found for Kaplan's definition. The sexual responsiveness of ten premature ejaculators was compared with that of fourteen normally functioning men, and no differences were found in rate of arousal, degree of arousal, or amount of arousal, either subjectively or physiologically. The premature ejaculators, however, did ejaculate at lower levels of arousal (Spiess, Geer & O'Donohue, 1984).

The inability to satisfy a sexual partner is a source of anguish for many men. In a campus newspaper column at a midwestern college, premature ejaculation was reported as the largest single source of concern in the realm of male sexual dysfunctions (Werner, 1975). In one sample of married men, 38 percent reported problems of too rapid ejaculation (Nettlebladt & Uddenberg, 1979). Additionally, of the sexually dysfunctional men seeking treatment at a clinic, 29 percent were diagnosed as having premature ejaculation (Hoch et al., 1981).

Sexual Pain Disorders

Vaginismus is the involuntary muscular constriction of the outer third of the vagina, severely restricting or preventing penile penetration. The incidence of this dysfunction is not known, but it is considered very rare.

Several causal factors have been identified in vaginismus. Masters and Johnson (1970) found one or more of the following conditions among many women with this dysfunction: (1) a husband or partner who was impotent; (2) rigid religious beliefs about sex; (3) prior sexual trauma, such as rape; (4) prior homosexual identification; and (5) *dyspareunia,* or painful intercourse. A history of incestuous molestation is often found in women with this disorder (LoPiccolo & Stock, 1986).

Sexual pain disorders can be manifested in both males and females in a condition termed **dyspareunia,** which is a recurrent or persistent pain in the genitals before, during, or after sexual intercourse. The condition is not caused by lack of lubrication or vaginismus.

Etiology and Treatment of Sexual Dysfunctions

Sexual dysfunctions may be due to psychogenic factors alone or a combination of psychological and biogenic factors. They may be mild and transient, or lifelong and chronic. Masters and Johnson (1970) identified some psychological elements in sexual dysfunctions, however, they deemphasized physical factors. Studies have now indicated that neurological,

William Masters and Virginia Johnson are pioneers in sex research and sex therapy. Their research has contributed much to our current understanding of normal sexual functioning. Many individuals suffering from various sexual dysfunctions have been successfully treated with therapy techniques developed at Masters' and Johnson's clinic.

vascular, and hormonal factors are important in many cases of sexual dysfunctions (Sakheim et al., 1987). It is now acknowledged that in some sexual disorders, organic factors may play a major role in the majority of cases (LoPiccolo, 1985, 1991). Although some of these physical problems may be relatively minor such as vaginal infections, which cause itching and burning, they may render sexual functioning more susceptible to psychological or social stresses.

Biological Factors and Treatment Lower levels of testosterone or higher levels of estrogens such as prolactin (or both) have been associated with lower sexual interest in both men and women and erectile difficulties in men (Bancroft, 1984; Segraves, 1988). Drugs that suppress testosterone levels appear to decrease sexual desire in men (Wincze, Bansal & Malamud, 1986).

In addition to the just-described conditions, certain drugs such as hypertensive medication (Rosen, Kostis & Jekelis, 1988), the consumption of alcohol (Malatesta et al., 1979), illnesses, and other physical conditions (Malatesta & Adams, 1984) are associated with sexual dysfunctions. Medications given to treat ulcers, glaucoma, allergies, and convulsions have also been found to affect the sex drive. Not everyone who takes hypertensive drugs, consumes alcohol, or is ill has a sexual dysfunction. In some people, however, these factors—in combination with a predisposing personal history or current stress—may be enough to produce problems in sexual function. A complete physical workup that includes the medical history, physical exam, and a laboratory evaluation is a necessary first step in assessment before treatment decisions are made.

In women, sexual desire is also influenced by male hormones. The administration of androgens is associated with reports of increased sexual desire in both men and women (Kaplan, 1974). However, the relationship between hormones and sexual behavior is complex and difficult to understand. People with sexual dysfunctions often have normal testosterone levels.

For some, a lack of sexual desire may be physiological. One group of women reported no feelings of anxiety about, or aversion to, sexual intercourse; but they showed significantly lower sexual arousal than did sexually active women during exposure to erotic stimuli. Moreover, participation in therapy did not increase their responsiveness (Wincze, Hoon & Hoon, 1978). The researchers concluded that the absence of sexual arousal in these women is biological and the appropriate treatment for this condition is unknown. Hypersensitivity to physical stimulation is another factor that may affect sexual functioning (Assalian, 1988). Men who ejaculate prematurely may have difficulty differentiating between ejaculation and its inevitability once the sympathetic nervous system is triggered.

The amount of blood flowing into the genital area is also associated with orgasmic potential in women and erectile functioning in men. In women, masturbation training and Kegel exercises (tightening muscles in the vagina) may increase vascularization of labia, clitoris, and vagina. Vascular problems may also hinder blood flow to the penis and result in erectile difficulties. Vascular surgery to increase blood flow has met with limited success because in most cases the problem is due to arteriosclerosis, which affects a number of the small blood vessels (LoPiccolo & Stock, 1986).

Men suffering from organic erectile dysfunction have received penile implants, especially if hormone replacement and sex therapy do not appear beneficial. The penile prosthesis is an inflatable or semirigid device that, once inflated, produces an erection sufficient for intercourse and ejaculation. One study of men with penile implants found 90 percent would choose it again (Steege, Stout, & Carson, 1986). As indicated in the following case, however, a significant number of men report dissatisfaction with the procedure and minimal improvement in their desire for sex:

Mr. F. was a 54-year-old recovered alcoholic who had received a surgical implant (Scott prosthesis) following a diagnosis of organic impotence. Despite the patient's new-found ability to perform intercourse at will, in the two years following surgery he made infrequent use of the prosthesis. His wife became increasingly distressed by his disinclination to either initiate or respond with any enthusiasm to her overtures for sexual contact. In reviewing the history, it became apparent that his loss of sexual desire had preceded the erectile failure and that the absence of desire appeared to be the primary problem for treatment. Unfortunately, both the urologist and the patient's wife had assumed that once the capacity for intercourse was restored, sexual interest would re-emerge unassisted. (Rosen & Leiblum, 1987, p. 153)

Another form of medical treatment for erectile problems is the injection of substances (papaverine and phentolamine) into the penis. Within a very short time the man will obtain a very stiff erection, which may last from one to four hours. Although men and their mates have reported general satisfaction with the method (Althof et al., 1987), there are some side effects. There is often bruising of the penis and the development of nodules. Some men find the prolonged erection disturbing in the absence of sexual stimulation.

Psychological Factors and Behavioral Therapy

Psychological causes for sexual dysfunctions can include historical or predisposing factors, sexual trauma, inadequate or inappropriate sexual experiences, and relationship conflicts.

Predisposing or Historical Factors Early experiences can interact with current problems to produce sexual dysfunctions. Traditional psychoanalysts have stressed the role of unconscious conflicts. For example, erectile difficulties and premature ejaculation represent male hostility to women due to unresolved early developmental conflicts involving the parents. Psychodynamic treatment is directed toward uncovering and resolving the unconscious hostility. The results of this approach have been disappointing (Kaplan, 1974; Kilmann & Auerbach, 1979). It seems plausible, however, that the attitudes parents display toward sex and affection and to each other can influence their children's attitudes. For example, women with sexual desire disorders rated their parents' attitude toward sex more negatively than did women without sexual desire disorders (Stuart, Hammond & Pett, 1987). Being raised in a strict religious environment is also associated with sexual dysfunctions in both men and women (Masters & Johnson, 1970). Traumatic sexual experiences involving incestuous molestations during childhood or adolescence or rape are also factors to consider (Burgess & Holmstrom, 1979b; LoPiccolo & Stock, 1986).

Current Factors Factors operating in the present may interact with predisposing factors to produce a sexual dysfunction. In other persons, current problems may be enough to interfere with sexual function.

A relationship problem is often a contributing factor. In a study of fifty-nine women with sexual desire disorders, only eleven had the problem before marriage; the other forty-eight developed it gradually after being married. The women voiced dissatisfaction about their relationship with their husbands, complaining that their spouses did not listen to them. Marital dissatisfaction may have caused them to lose their attraction toward their husbands (Stuart, Hammond & Pett, 1987).

Situational or coital anxiety can interrupt sexual functioning in both men and women. Anxieties over sexual overtures were reported by a group of men with psychogenic erectile dysfunction and included a fear of failing sexually, a fear of being seen as sexually inferior, and anxiety over the size of their genitals. These patients also reported marked increases in subjective anxiety and displayed somatic symptoms such as sweating, trembling, muscle tension, and heart palpitations when asked to imagine engaging in sexual intercourse (Cooper, 1969). In a sample of 275 college men, sexual pressure from a partner was associated with sexual dysfunction. The men most affected were those who identified most heavily with the traditional masculine role (Spencer & Zeiss, 1987).

Factors associated with orgasmic dysfunction in women include having a sexually inexperienced or dysfunctional partner; the crippling fear of performance failure, of never being able to attain orgasm, of pregnancy, or of venereal disease; an inability to accept the partner, either emotionally or physically; and misinformation or ignorance about sexuality or sexual techniques.

Many approaches have been used to treat sexual dysfunctions, including desensitization (Wolpe, 1973), graded exercises (Stravynski, 1986), masturbation (Kohlenberg, 1974; LoPiccolo & Stock, 1986; Sue, 1978), sex education training (Kilmann et al., 1986), and the modification of sexual expectations (Rosen & Leiblum, 1987). Most general treatment approaches include the following components:

- *Education* The therapist replaces sexual myths and misconceptions with accurate information. Discussion involving sexual anatomy and function are also presented.

- *Anxiety reduction* Therapists use procedures such as desensitization or graded approaches to keep anxiety at a minimum. Explanations are given of how constantly "observing and evaluating" one's performance can interfere with sexual functioning.

◆ *Structured behavioral exercises* The therapist gives a series of graded tasks that gradually increase the amount of sexual interaction that takes place. They generally involve having each partner take turns touching and being touched over different parts of the body except for the genital regions. Later the partners fondle the body and genital regions, without making demands for sexual arousal or orgasm. Successful sexual intercourse and orgasm is the final stage of the structured exercises.

◆ *Communication training* The partners are taught appropriate ways of communicating their sexual wishes to each other and are taught conflict resolution skills.

Specific treatments for the three dysfunctions are as follows:

1. *Orgasmic dysfunctions* Although the general approach just described has been successful in treating sexual arousal disorders in women and erectile disorders in men, masturbation appears to be the most effective way for orgasmically dysfunctional women to have an orgasm. The procedure involves education about sexual anatomy, visual and tactile self-exploration, using sexual fantasies and images, and masturbation both individually and with a partner. Success rates of 95 percent have been reported with this procedure for women with primary orgasmic dysfunction (LoPiccolo & Stock, 1986). This approach does not necessarily lead to the woman's ability to achieve orgasm during sexual intercourse.

2. *Premature ejaculation* In one technique, the partner stimulates the penis while it's outside the vagina until the man feels the sensation of impending ejaculation. At this point, stimulation is stopped for a short period of time, and then it is continued again. The pattern is repeated until the man can tolerate increasingly greater periods of stimulation before ejaculation (Semans, 1956). Masters and Johnson (1970) and Kaplan

(1974) used a similar procedure, called "the squeeze technique." They reported a success rate of nearly 100 percent. The treatment is easily learned.

Although the short-term success rate for treating premature ejaculation is very high, a follow-up period of up to six years found that relapses were very common (Hawton et al., 1986). More long-term follow-ups of all treatments for the sexual dysfunctions are necessary to judge treatment effectiveness.

3. *Vaginismus* The results of treatment for vaginismus have been uniformly positive (Kaplan, 1974; LoPiccolo, 1984; LoPiccolo & Stock, 1986). The involuntary spasms or closure of the vaginal muscle can be deconditioned by first training the woman to relax, and by then inserting successively larger dilators while she is relaxed, until insertion of the penis can occur.

Evaluation of Behavior Therapy Although the initial reports on behavioral treatment for the sexual dysfunctions have been highly positive, later studies have questioned the reports of high success rates (LoPiccolo & Stock, 1986; Malatesta & Adams, 1983). Lower reversal (success) rates than those reported by Masters and Johnson have been found by other researchers (LoPiccolo et al., 1985).

A long-term outcome study of the results of sexual therapy for 140 couples with a variety of sexual dysfunctions came to the following conclusions. Long-term outcome was very good for vaginismus, good for erectile dysfunction, surprisingly poor for premature ejaculation, and very poor for females with sexual desire disorders. Recurrence of the problem during the follow-up period was common (75 percent of the sample had relapses). Some couples were able to eliminate the problem themselves. Discussing the problem with one's partner, practicing exercises learned during therapy, and reading books on human sexuality were reported to be effective strategies. Ignoring the problem or not having sex were ineffective (Hawton et al., 1986). The results of this study indicated that relapse prevention procedures (strategies to be employed when problems recur) should be incorporated in sex therapy programs and that new treatment strategies, especially for the sexual desire disorders, should be developed.

FOCUS 11.4

Are Children Raised by Homosexuals Confused About Their Gender Identity?

In the face of strong objections, a growing number of homosexuals and transsexuals are asserting their right to raise children. The objectors argue that homosexuals and transsexuals follow deviant lifestyles and that children living with such parents will adopt their maladaptive orientation. In fact, both social learning and psychoanalytic theorists might predict that such children would be likely to have some form of gender identity problem or other serious confusion.

The development of twenty-one children (average age, eight years) living with homosexual parents was investigated by Green (1978). The children had lived in these households for an average of four and one-half years. Nearly all children were aware of their parents' atypical sexual orientation. For example, four girls were living in a transsex-

ual household while their mother underwent androgen hormone treatment and sex conversion surgery. This person became their "father," who then married their "stepmother."

Measures of sexual identity (toy and game preference, peer group composition preference, clothing preference, roles in fantasy games, vocational aspirations, reported romantic crushes, and fantasies) were obtained on all the children. All of them displayed heterosexual preferences that were appropriate for their gender. Green cautioned that this is a preliminary report and that no control group was present, nor are longer-term effects known. Given these limitations, Green (1978) tentatively suggested that "children being raised by transsexual or homosexual parents do not differ appreciably from children

raised in more conventional family settings on macroscopic measures of sexual identity" (pp. 696–697).

In another study, ten boys and ten girls between the ages of five and twelve who were living with their lesbian mothers were compared with children raised by heterosexual mothers. The two groups of children did not differ with respect to the sex of the first figure they drew, play and sexual preferences, and playroom behavior (Kirkpatrick, Smith & Roy, 1981). However, Green's comments regarding better control groups and longer-term studies apply to these results as well as to his own. We need more research before we can determine whether gender identity and sex-role development are influenced by homosexual or transsexual parentage.

HOMOSEXUALITY

Just two weeks into his term as president of the United States, Bill Clinton was met by a ferocious backlash from members of Congress, the armed forces and the American public over his stated intention to remove a ban on allowing homosexuals in the military. Although homosexuals have always served honorably and with distinction in the armed forces, they were subject to discharge if discovered. The controversy and public debate were unprecedented as the White House, Congress, and elected officials were flooded with letters and calls objecting to this action. The objections were not ameliorated when on January 28, 1993, a federal district judge ruled in the

highly publicized case of Navy Petty Officer Keith Meinhold (discharged because of declaring himself gay) that the ban against homosexuals serving in the military was unconstitutional and violated the Constitution's guarantee of equal protection under the law. Radio talk shows, television analysts, and political commentators raised issues such as the immorality of homosexuality and whether it is a sickness. It was clear from the tone of many statements that homophobia continues to be a major part of these objections.

We debated at length whether to include the topic of homosexuality in the fourth edition of this textbook. Given the level of public misunderstanding and misinformation (see Focus 11.4), however, we believe that it is important to discuss briefly what homosexuality is not. Is homosexuality a mental disorder? The answer is no. The American Psychiatric Association in DSM-III-R and DSM-IV does not include homosexuality. In earlier editions, homosexuality was classified as a disorder. The changing view of homosexuality has been influenced by many factors.

DSM-I and DSM-II classified homosexuality as sexual deviance because sexual behavior was considered normal only if it occurred between two consenting adults of the opposite sex. Two objections were made to this criterion. First, many clinicians felt that heterosexual sexuality shouldn't be the standard by which to judge other sexual behaviors. Second, many homosexual people argued that they are mentally healthy and that their sexual preference reflects a normal variant of sexual expression. For example, in one major study of homosexuality, researchers analyzed data obtained from four-hour interviews with 979 male and female homosexuals and 477 matched controls (Bell & Weinberg, 1978; Bell, Weinberg & Hammersmith, 1981). Most homosexuals (both male and female) indicated no regrets at being homosexual and accepted their sexual orientation.

In summary, these conclusions can be reached from the available studies on homosexuals and heterosexuals: (1) there are no physiological differences in sexual arousal and response between these two groups; (2) on measures of psychological disturbance, homosexuals and heterosexuals are not significantly different from one another; (3) homosexuals do not suffer from gender identity confusions; rather any conflicts are due to societal intolerance to their lifestyles (Bell & Weinberg, 1978; Green et al., 1986; Masters & Johnson, 1979; Paul et al., 1982; Wilson, 1984). Nothing more need be said. Homosexuality is not a psychological disorder.

AGING AND SEXUAL ACTIVITY

Sexuality during old age has been the subject of many myths and jokes. In our youth-oriented society, sexual activity is simply not associated with aging. Nevertheless, a large percentage of older Americans clearly have active sex lives.

In a study of sexual functioning in 60- to 79-year-old married men, a clear relationship was found between the reported frequency of intercourse at younger ages and at present. The most active respondents reported a present frequency that was 61 percent of their frequency between ages 40 and 59, whereas the least active reported a present frequency of only 6 percent of that between ages 40 and 59.

Contrary to the belief that the elderly lose their sexual desire, studies reveal that sexual activity remains high in the older population. The Janus Report found that post-mature men and women (65 and older) experience only a slight drop in sexual activity.

The most active also indicated that they became aroused on seeing women in public situations and in response to visual stimuli. The vast majority (69 percent) felt that sex was important for good health, and most (63 percent) looked on masturbation as an acceptable outlet. Sexual dysfunctions were also more prevalent in this population than in younger groups, and the prevalence was affected by the individuals' prior and present sexual activity levels. Of the least active, 21 percent suffered from premature ejaculation, and 75 percent were either impotent or had erectile difficulties. For the most active group, the corresponding percentages were 8 and 19 percent (Martin, 1981).

The most recent survey (Janus & Janus, 1993), however, suggested that sexual activity and enjoyment among the older population remains surprisingly high. The Januses survey found that (1) sexual activity of people age 65 and older declined little from their 30- to 40-year-old counterparts, (2) their ability to reach orgasm and have sex diminished very little from their early years, and (3) their desire to continue a relatively active sex life was unchanged.

Physiologically based changes in patterns of sexual arousal and orgasm have been found in people over age 65 (Masters & Johnson, 1966). For both men and women, sexual arousal takes longer. Erection and vaginal lubrication are slower to occur, and the urgency for orgasm is reduced. Both men and women are fully capable of sexual satisfaction if no organic conditions interfere. Many elderly individuals felt that such changes allowed them to experience sex more fully. They reported that they had more time to spend on a seductive buildup, felt positively about their ability to experience unhurried sex-for-joy, and experienced more warmth and intimacy after the sex act (Janus & Janus, 1993).

SUMMARY

1. Gender identity disorder involves a strong and persistent cross-gender identification. Transsexuals feel a severe psychological conflict between their sexual self-concept and their gender. Some transsexuals seek sex conversion surgery, although behavioral therapies are increasingly being used. Gender identity disorder can also occur in childhood. Children with this problem identify with members of the opposite sex, deny their own physical attributes, and often cross-dress. Treatment generally includes the parents and is behavioral in nature.

2. The paraphilias are of three types, characterized by (a) a preference for nonhuman objects for sexual arousal, (b) the association of real or simulated suffering with sexual activity, or (c) repetitive sexual activity with nonconsenting partners. Suggested causes of the paraphilias are unconscious conflicts (the psychodynamic perspective) and conditioning, generally during childhood. Biological factors such as hormonal or brain processes have also been studied, but the results have not been consistent enough to permit strong conclusions about the role of biogenic factors in the paraphilias. Treatments are usually behavioral and are aimed at eliminating the deviant behavior while teaching more appropriate behaviors.

3. Certain deviations involving sex, such as rape and incest, are not listed in DSM-IV but are serious problems. There appears to be no single cause for these deviations, and rapists seem to have different motivations and personalities. Some researchers feel that sociocultural factors can encourage rape and violence against women; others believe that biogenic factors coupled with sociocultural factors are important in explaining rape. In the case of incest, which involves sex relations between close relatives, most research has examined father-daughter incest. Several types of incestuous fathers have been identified, which points again to the likelihood that incest is caused by different factors.

4. Sexual dysfunctions are disruptions of the normal sexual response cycle. They are fairly common in the general population and may affect a person's ability to become sexually aroused or to engage in intercourse. Many result from fear or anxiety regarding sexual activities; the various treatment programs are generally successful.

5. Many myths and misunderstandings continue to surround homosexuality. The belief that homosexuality is deviant seems to reside more on homophobia than scientific findings. DSM-IV no longer considers homosexuality to be a psychological disorder.

6. Despite myths to the contrary, sexuality extends into old age. However, sexual dysfunction becomes increasingly prevalent with aging, and the frequency of sexual activity typically declines.

KEY TERMS

dyspareunia Recurrent or persistent pain in the genitals before, during, or after sexual intercourse

erectile dysfunction A man's inability to attain or maintain a penile erection sufficient for sexual intercourse

exhibitionism A disorder in which a person gets sexual gratification by exposing his genitals to strangers

fetishism A disorder characterized by an extremely strong sexual attraction for an inanimate object

gender identity disorder A psychological disorder characterized by conflict between a person's anatomical sex and his or her sexual identity

incest Sexual relations between close relatives

inhibited orgasm A sexual dysfunction in which the person is unable to achieve orgasm during coitus with adequate stimulation after entering the excitement phase of the sexual response cycle

masochism A sexual disorder in which erotic or sexual gratification is obtained by receiving pain or punishment

paraphilias Sexual disorders in which unusual or bizarre acts, images, or objects are required for sexual arousal

pedophilia A disorder in which an adult obtains erotic gratification through sexual contact with children

premature ejaculation Ejaculation before penile entry into the vagina or so soon after entry that an unsatisfactory sexual experience results

rape An act of intercourse that is accomplished through force or the threat of force

sadism A sexual disorder in which erotic or sexual gratification is obtained by inflicting pain or humiliation on others

sexual arousal disorder A sexual dysfunction characterized by erectile dysfunction in men, or by an inability to attain or sustain arousal in women

sexual desire disorders Sexual dysfunctions involving a lack of sexual interest as reflected in low levels of both sexual activity and fantasizing or an aversion to sexual intercourse

sexual dysfunction A disruption of any part of the normal sexual response cycle in a male or female

transsexualism A person's self-identification with the opposite sex

transvestic fetishism A disorder in which sexual arousal is obtained through cross-dressing

vaginismus Involuntary muscular constriction of the outer third of the vagina, which restricts or prevents penile insertion

voyeurism A disorder in which sexual gratification is obtained by surreptitiously observing nude people or couples engaged in coitus

Mood Disorders

All of us have experienced moods (or affect) involving depression or elation at some time during our lives. The loss of a job or the death of a loved one may result in depression: good news may make us manic (for example, ecstatic, hyperactive, and brazen). How do we know if these reactions are normal or manifestations of a serious mental disorder? In general, depression or mania that pervades every aspect of a person's life, that persists over a long period of time, or that occurs for no apparent reason may be symptomatic of a mood disorder.

Mood disorders are disturbances in emotions that cause subjective discomfort, hinder a person's ability to function, or both. Depression and mania are central to these disorders. **Depression** is characterized by intense sadness, feelings of futility and worthlessness, and withdrawal from others. **Mania** is characterized by elevated mood, expansiveness, or irritability, often resulting in hyperactivity. Depression is one of the most commonly diagnosed conditions among patients hospitalized for mental disorders and is also quite prevalent in the general population.

Depression is the most common complaint of individuals seeking mental health care (Gotlib, 1992; Strickland, 1992): during this year, some 10 million Americans, and more than 100 million people worldwide, will experience clinical depression. In a large-scale survey Myers and colleagues (1984) found that approximately 3 percent of the adult male population and 7 percent of the females in the U.S. had experienced a depressive mood disorder over a six-month period. Lifetime prevalence (the proportion of people who develop severe depression at some point in their lives) is more than 8 percent, with women having much higher rates than men (Regier et al., 1988). Some evidence also suggests that the frequency of depression has increased over the past 50 years (Robins et al., 1984).

Severe depression does not respect socioeconomic status, educational attainments, or personal qualities; it may afflict rich or poor, successful or unsuccessful, highly educated or uneducated. The prevalence of depression is much higher than for mania, which Myers and colleagues (1984) found to be about 0.6 percent for males and females. The following case illustrates one woman's experience with severe depression:

Amanda is a 39-year-old homemaker with three children, ages 9, 11, and 14. Her husband is the sales manager for an auto agency and the family does well financially and lives comfortably. For years, family life was stable and no serious problems existed between family members. The family could be described as cohesive and loving. However, Jim began to notice that his wife was becoming more and more unhappy and depressed. She constantly said that her life lacked purpose. Jim would try to reassure her, pointing out that they had a nice home and that she had no reason to be unhappy. He suggested that she find some hobbies or socialize more with their neighbors. But Amanda became progressively more absorbed in her belief that her life was meaningless.

After a while, Amanda no longer bothered to keep the house clean, to cook, or to take care of the children. At first Jim thought she was merely in a "bad mood" and that it would pass, but as her lethargy deepened, he became increasingly worried. He thought his wife was either sick or no longer loved him and the children. Amanda told him that she was tired, and that simple household chores took too much energy. She still loved Jim and the children, but said that she no longer had strong feelings for anything. Amanda did show some guilt about her inability to take care of the children and be a wife, but everything was simply too depressing. Life was no longer important, and she just wanted to be left alone. At that point she began to cry uncontrollably. Nothing Jim said could bring her out of the depression or stop her from crying. He decided that she had to see a physician, and he made an appointment.

The day of the appointment, Jim worked only until noon so that he could go with his wife to the physician's office. On arriving home, he found Amanda nearly unconscious; she had taken a lot of sleeping pills, apparently trying to commit suicide. She was rushed to a hospital where, fortunately, her life was saved. Both the timing of the suicide attempt (just before a scheduled appointment with the physician) and the large number of pills taken convinced hospital staff of her sense of hopelessness and of her need for intensive therapy. Amanda is currently receiving medication and psychotherapy to treat her depression.

In this chapter, we first describe the clinical symptoms of depression and mania, and the two major types of mental disorders—depressive disorders and bipolar disorders. Then we discuss their causes and treatment. In Chapter 13, we examine the very serious problem of suicide—a phenomenon that has been strongly linked to depression.

THE SYMPTOMS OF DEPRESSION AND MANIA

Depression and mania, the two extremes of mood or affect, can be considered the opposite ends of a continuum that extends from deep sadness to wild elation. Of the two, depression is much more prevalent. It appears in 90 percent of all diagnosed cases of mood disorders, and it would be expected to show up in the other 10 percent if they remained untreated.

Clinical Symptoms of Depression

Certain core characteristics are often seen among depressives. These characteristics may be organized within the four psychological domains used to describe anxiety: the affective domain, the cognitive domain, the behavioral domain, and the physiological domain. Table 12.1 shows this organization and the core group symptoms.

Affective Symptoms Depressed mood is the most striking symptom of depression. Depressives experience feelings of sadness, dejection, and an excessive and prolonged mourning. Feelings of worthlessness and having lost the joy of living are common. Wild weeping may occur as a general reaction to frustration or anger. Such crying spells do not seem to be directly correlated with a specific situation.

To illustrate these affective characteristics, the following statements were made by a severely depressed patient who had markedly improved after treatment:

It's hard to describe the state I was in several months ago. The depression was total—it was as if everything that happened to me passed through this filter which colored all experiences. Nothing was exciting to me. I felt I was no good, completely worthless and deserving of nothing. The people who tried to cheer me up were just living in a different world.

We should note here that severe depressive symptoms often occur as a normal reaction to the death of a loved one. This intensive mourning is thought

Table 12.1

Symptoms of Depression

Domain	Symptoms
Affective	Sadness, unhappiness, "blue" moods, apathy
Cognitive	Pessimism, ideas of guilt, self-denigration, loss of interest and motivation, decrease in efficiency and concentration, suicidal ideation
Behavioral	Neglect of personal appearance, psychomotor retardation, agitation, suicidal gestures
Physiological	Loss of or increase in appetite, loss of weight or weight gain, constipation, poor sleep, aches and pains, diminished sex drive

Source: Adapted from Mendels, 1970.

to have a positive psychological function in helping one to adjust. An excessively long period of bereavement accompanied by a preoccupation with feelings of worthlessness, marked functional impairment, and serious psychomotor retardation, however, can indicate a major mood disorder. Cultures vary in the normal duration of bereavement but severe, incapacitating depression rarely continues after the first three months.

Cognitive Symptoms Besides general feelings of futility, emptiness, and hopelessness, certain thoughts and ideas are clearly related to depressive reactions. For example, the person feels a profound pessimism about the future. Disinterest, decreased energy, and loss of motivation make it difficult for the depressed person to cope with everyday situations. Work responsibilities become monumental tasks, and the person avoids them. Self-accusation of incompetence and general self-denigration are common, as are thoughts of suicide. Other symptoms include difficulty in concentrating and in making decisions.

Depression may be considered to be reflected in a cognitive triad, which consists of negative views of the self, of the outside world, and of the future (Beck, 1974). The person has pessimistic beliefs about what he or she can do, about what others can do to help, and about his or her prospects for the future. Some of this triad can be seen in the following self-description of the thoughts and feelings of a severe depressive:

The single most striking symptom of depression is mood. Feelings of sadness, dejection, and excessive mourning are the predominant moods during depression. Also common are feelings of worthlessness and loss of the joy of living.

The gradual progression to this state of semicognizance and quiescence was steady; it is hard to trace. People and things counted less. I ceased to wonder. I asked a member of my family where I was and, having received an answer, accepted it. And usually I remembered it, when I was in a state to remember anything objective. The days dragged; there was no "motive," no drive of any kind. A dull acceptance settled upon me. Nothing interested me. I was very tired and heavy. I refused to do most of the things that were asked of me, and to avoid further disturbance I was put to bed again. (Hillyer, 1964, pp. 158–59)

Ezra Pound, one of the most brilliant poets of the twentieth century, suffered a severe depression when he was in his seventies. He told an interviewer bitterly, "I have lived all my life believing that I knew something. And then a strange day came and I realized that I knew nothing, nothing at all. And so words have become empty of meaning. Everything that I touch, I spoil. I have blundered always" (Darrach, 1976, p. 81). Pound stopped writing for years; for days on end, he ceased to speak. For both Hillyer and Pound, motivation, activity, vitality, and optimism had declined drastically.

Behavioral Symptoms The appearance and outward demeanor of a person is often a telltale sign of depression. The person's clothing may be sloppy or dirty; hair may be unkempt and personal cleanliness neglected. A dull, masklike facial expression may become characteristic. The depressed person moves his or her body slowly and does not initiate new activities. Speech is reduced and slow, and the person may respond with short phrases. This slowing down of all bodily movements, expressive gestures, and spontaneous responses is called *psychomotor retardation*. The person often shows social withdrawal and lowered work productivity.

By contrast to this typical retarded condition of depressives, however, some may manifest an agitated state and symptoms of restlessness.

Physiological Symptoms The following somatic and related symptoms are frequently found in persons with depression:

1. Depressed people often experience a *loss of appetite and weight*, although some may actually have increased appetite and gain weight. The loss of appetite often stems from the person's disinterest in eating; food seems tasteless. In severe depression, weight loss can become life threatening.

2. Depressives may become constipated and may not have bowel movements for days at a time.

3. *Sleep disturbance* is a common complaint. Difficulty in falling asleep, waking up early, waking up erratically during the night, insomnia, and nightmares leave the depressive exhausted and tired during the day. Many depressives dread the arrival of night because it represents a major fatigue-producing battle to fall asleep. (Some show hypersomnia or excessive sleep, however.)

4. In women, depression may *disrupt the normal menstrual cycle*. Usually, the cycle is prolonged, with possible skipping of one or several periods. The volume of menstrual flow may decrease.

5. Many depressives report an *aversion to sexual activity*. Their sexual arousal dramatically declines.

Clinical Symptoms of Mania

In mania, the person's mood is elevated, expansive, or irritable. Social and occupational functioning are impaired, as shown in the following case:

Alan was a 43-year-old unmarried computer programmer who had led a relatively quiet life until two weeks before, when he returned to work after a short absence for illness. Alan seemed to be in a particularly good mood. Others in the office noticed that he was unusually happy and energetic, greeting everyone at work. A few days later, during the lunch hour, Alan bought a huge cake and insisted that his fellow workers eat some of it. At first everyone was surprised and amused by his antics. But two colleagues working with him on a special project became increasingly irritated because Alan didn't put any time into their project. He just insisted that he would finish his part in a few days.

On the day that the manager had decided to tell Alan of his colleagues' concern, Alan behaved in a delirious, manic way. When he came to work, he immediately jumped on top of a desk and yelled, "Listen, listen! We aren't working on the most important aspects of our data! I know, since I've debugged my mind. Erase, reprogram, you know what I mean. We've got to examine the total picture based on the input!" Alan then spouted profanities and made obscene remarks to several of the secretaries. Onlookers thought that he must have taken drugs. Attempts to calm him down brought angry and vicious denunciations. The manager, who had been summoned, also couldn't calm him. Finally the manager threatened to fire Alan. At this point, Alan called the manager an incompetent fool and stated that he could not be fired. His speech was so rapid and disjointed that it was difficult to understand him. Alan then picked up a chair and said he was going to smash the computers. Several coworkers grabbed him and held him on the floor. Alan was yelling so loud that his voice was quite hoarse, but he continued to shout and struggle. Two police officers were called, and they had to hand-cuff him to restrain his movements. Within hours, he was taken to a psychiatric hospital for observation.

Manic people like Alan show boundless energy, enthusiasm, and self-assertion. Their mood or *affect* is one of elation or irritability, grandiosity, and exaggeration. Manic patients are often uninhibited, engaging impulsively in sexual activity or abusive discourse. The energy and excitement these patients show may cause them to lose weight or go without sleep for long periods. If frustrated, they may become profane and quite belligerent.

Cognitive symptoms are generally reflected in the verbal processes of manic patients. For example, their speech is usually quite accelerated and pressured. They may change topics in mid-sentence or utter irrelevant and idiosyncratic phrases. Although much of what they say is understandable to others, the accelerated and disjointed nature of their speech makes it difficult to follow their train of thought. They seem incapable of controlling their attention, as though they are constantly distracted by new and more exciting thoughts and ideas.

In the *behavioral* domain, two levels of manic intensity—hypomania and mania—have been recognized in DSM-IV. In the milder form, *hypomania,* affected people seem to be "high" in mood and over-active in behavior. Their judgment is usually poor, although delusions are rare. They start many projects, but few if any are completed. When they interact with coworkers, hypomanics dominate the conversation and are often grandiose.

Behaviors are more disruptive in people who suffer from *mania.* Overactivity, grandiosity, and irritability are pronounced; speech may be incoherent; and criticisms or restraints imposed by others aren't tolerated. In the more severe form, the person is wildly excited, rants, raves (the stereotype of a wild "maniac"), and is constantly agitated and on the move. Hallucinations and delusions may appear, and the person may be uncontrollable and frequently dangerous to himself or herself or to others. Physical restraint and medication are frequently necessary. The most prominent *physiological* or somatic characteristic is a decreased need for sleep accompanied by

high levels of arousal. Whereas hypomania is not severe enough to cause marked impairment or hospitalization, the mood disturbance in mania is sufficiently severe to cause marked impairment in social or occupational functioning.

CLASSIFICATION OF MOOD DISORDERS

Mood disorders are largely divided into two major categories in DSM-IV: depressive disorder (often referred to as **unipolar disorder**) and bipolar disorder (see the chart on page 364). Once a depressive or manic episode occurs, the disorder is classified into a category as well as a subcategory. Let us examine the major categories and subcategories as well as other aspects of the classification scheme.

Depressive Disorders

Depressive disorders in DSM-IV include major depressive disorders, dysthymic disorder, and depressive disorders not otherwise specified. In all of these disorders, there is no history of a manic episode. People who experience a major depressive episode are given the diagnosis of major depression disorder. Symptoms should be present for at least two weeks and represent a change from the individual's previous functioning. These symptoms include a depressed mood or a loss of interest or pleasure, including weight loss or gain, sleep difficulties, fatigue, feelings of worthlessness, inability to concentrate, and recurrent thoughts of death. If the episode is the first one, it is classified as a single episode. For people who have had previous episodes, the disorder is considered a recurrent one. About one-half of those who experience a depressive episode eventually have another episode. In general, the earlier the age of onset, the more likely is a recurrence (Reus, 1988).

Modifiers may be used to more precisely describe the major depressive episode. Severity, presence or absence of psychotic features, and remission status may be specified. For example, psychotic features include delusions, hallucinations, and gross impairment in reality testing (an inability to accurately perceive and deal with reality). Their presence tends to predict a relatively poor diagnosis, more chronicity, and impairment.

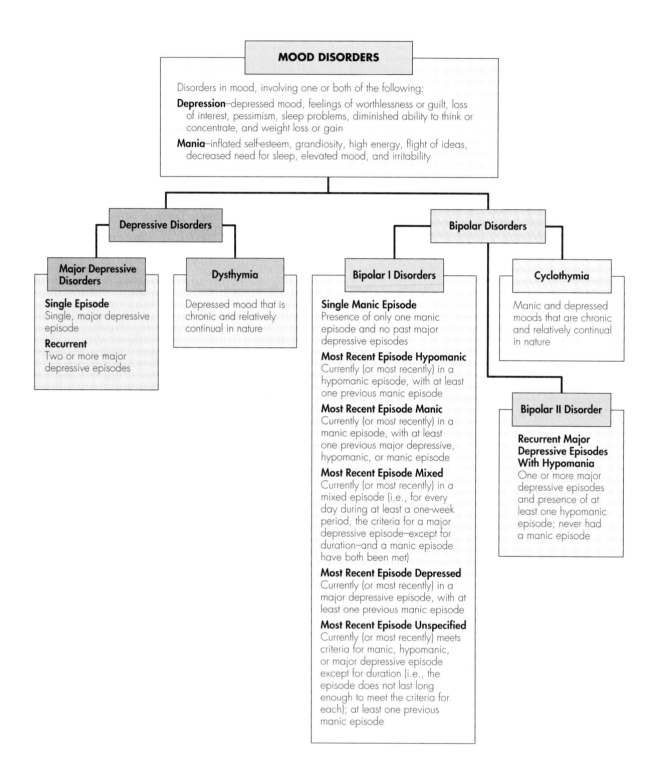

MOOD DISORDERS

Disorders in mood, involving one or both of the following:

Depression–depressed mood, feelings of worthlessness or guilt, loss of interest, pessimism, sleep problems, diminished ability to think or concentrate, and weight loss or gain

Mania–inflated self-esteem, grandiosity, high energy, flight of ideas, decreased need for sleep, elevated mood, and irritability

Depressive Disorders

Bipolar Disorders

Major Depressive Disorders

Single Episode
Single, major depressive episode

Recurrent
Two or more major depressive episodes

Dysthymia

Depressed mood that is chronic and relatively continual in nature

Bipolar I Disorders

Single Manic Episode
Presence of only one manic episode and no past major depressive episodes

Most Recent Episode Hypomanic
Currently (or most recently) in a hypomanic episode, with at least one previous manic episode

Most Recent Episode Manic
Currently (or most recently) in a manic episode, with at least one previous major depressive, hypomanic, or manic episode

Most Recent Episode Mixed
Currently (or most recently) in a mixed episode (i.e., for every day during at least a one-week period, the criteria for a major depressive episode–except for duration–and a manic episode have both been met)

Most Recent Episode Depressed
Currently (or most recently) in a major depressive episode, with at least one previous manic episode

Most Recent Episode Unspecified
Currently (or most recently) meets criteria for manic, hypomanic, or major depressive episode except for duration (i.e., the episode does not last long enough to meet the criteria for each); at least one previous manic episode

Cyclothymia

Manic and depressed moods that are chronic and relatively continual in nature

Bipolar II Disorder

Recurrent Major Depressive Episodes With Hypomania
One or more major depressive episodes and presence of at least one hypomanic episode; never had a manic episode

Dysthymic disorder is characterized by depressed mood, feelings of pessimism or guilt, loss of interest, poor appetite or overeating, low self-esteem, chronic fatigue, social withdrawal, or concentration difficulties. If the disorder does not meet the criteria for major depressive disorder and is chronic, dysthymic disorder is diagnosed. Unlike major depression, dysthymia is a chronic condition that may last for years. In dysthymia, the depressive symptoms are present most of the day and for more days than not during a two-year (or for children and adolescents, a one-year) period. One study (Myers et al., 1984) found the prevalence of dysthymia to be higher among women than men.

Bipolar Disorders

Bipolar disorders include a number of subcategories that describe the nature of the disorder: single manic episode, most recent episode hypomanic, most recent episode manic, most recent episode mixed, most recent episode depressed, most recent episode unspecified, and recurrent major depressive episodes with hypomania. The essential feature of **bipolar disorders** is the occurrence of one or more manic or hypomanic episodes. Symptoms for manic episodes include abnormally and persistently elevated, expansive, or irritable moods lasting at least one week in the case of mania and four days in the case of hypomania. Grandiosity, decreased need for sleep, flight of ideas, distractibility, and impairment in occupational or social functioning are often observed in persons with the disorder. The term *bipolar* is used because the disorders are usually accompanied by one or more depressive episodes. Persons in whom manic but not depressive episodes have occurred are extremely rare; in such cases, a depressive episode will presumably appear at some time.

Some people have hypomanic episodes and depressed moods that do not meet the criteria for major depressive episode. If the symptoms are present for at least two years, the individuals are diagnosed with cyclothymic disorder (for children and adolescents, one year rather than two years is the criterion). As in the case of dysthymia, **cyclothymia** is a persistent and chronic mood disorder, in which the person is never symptom free for more than two months. Cyclothymia is less common than dysthymia and more common than bipolar disorder.

This painting by Vincent van Gogh, *Portrait of Dr. Gachet,* suggests the extreme melancholy that can characterize the depressive side of manic-depressive disorders.

Other Mood Disorders

Mood disorder due to a general medical condition is a disturbance characterized by either (or both) depressed mood or elevated or irritable mood because of a general medical condition. For example, seriously, medically ill patients may exhibit insomnia, weight loss, and depression. It is diagnosed when the disorder is serious enough to cause significant impairment in social or occupational functioning or marked distress. *Substance-induced mood disorder* is a prominent and persistent disturbance of mood (depression, mania, or both) attributable to the use of a substance or to the cessation of the substance use. Again, it is diagnosed when notable distress and impairment occur.

Symptom Features and Course Specifiers

To be more precise about the nature of the mood disorders, DSM-IV has listed certain characteristics that may be associated with these disorders. They are important symptom features that may accompany the disorders but are not criteria used to determine diagnosis. For example, major depressive episodes for some of the mood disorders may include (1) *melancholia* (loss of pleasure, lack of reactivity to pleasurable stimuli, depression that is worse in the morning, early morning awakening, excessive guilt, weight loss) and (2) *catatonia*, which is motoric immobility (taking a posture and not moving), extreme agitation (excessive motor activity), negativism (resistance to changing positions), or mutism.

Course specifiers indicate the cyclic, seasonal, postpartum, or longitudinal pattern of the mood disorder. In *rapid cycling* type, which is applicable to bipolar disorders, the manic and depressive episodes are intermixed or rapidly alternate. The two phases may also appear with periods of relative normality in between. In some cases, there may be no intervening normal mood at all. One manic-depressive patient was reported to demonstrate manic behaviors for almost exactly 24 hours, immediately followed by depressive behaviors for 24 hours. At the manic extreme, the patient was agitated, demanding, and constantly shouting; the next day, he was almost mute and inactive. The alternating nature of the disorder lasted eleven years (Jenner et al., 1967). Typical manic episodes appear suddenly and last from a few days to months. Depressive episodes tend to last longer.

One of the more interesting course specifiers involves a *seasonal pattern*. For some people moods are accentuated during certain time periods. Lehmann (1985) noted that many depressed people find the morning more depressing than the evening. Many also find winter, when days are shorter and darker, more depressing than summer. In following DSM-IV, clinicians can indicate whether patients show a seasonal pattern. In some cases of recurrent major depression and bipolar disorder, the onset, end, or change of an episode coincides with a particular time of the year. For example, one man regularly became depressed after Christmas.

Other course specifiers include *postpartum onset* (if depression or mania in women occurs within four weeks of childbirth) and longitudinal course specifiers that indicate the nature of the recurrence and interepisode status of individuals.

Comparison Between Unipolar and Bipolar Disorders

Several types of evidence seem to support the distinction between unipolar and bipolar disorders (Goodwin & Guze, 1984; Research Task Force of the National Institute of Mental Health, 1975). First, genetic studies have revealed that blood relatives of patients with bipolar disorders have a higher incidence of manic disturbances than do relatives of patients with unipolar disorders. In addition, stronger evidence of genetic influences exists for bipolar disorders than for unipolar disorders. Second, the age of onset is typically earlier for bipolar disorders (the late twenties) than for unipolar disorders (the mid-thirties). Third, bipolars have retarded depressions (involving a slowing down of movements and speech) and a greater tendency to attempt suicide than unipolars, whose depressive symptoms often include anxiety. And fourth, bipolars respond to lithium, whereas the drug has little effect on unipolars.

Only about 0.4 to 1.2 percent of the adult population have experienced bipolar disorder, whereas about 7 to 18 percent have at some time experienced a major depressive episode (DSM-IV). Major depression seems to be more common in females than in males, but no apparent sex difference exists in the frequency of bipolar disorders (Weissman & Klerman, 1977).

THE ETIOLOGY OF MOOD DISORDERS

Despite increasing evidence for a unipolar-bipolar distinction, little is known about what causes the extreme mood changes in the bipolar disorders. Perhaps the regulatory mechanism for maintaining *homeostasis*, or stability of mood, no longer works. Maybe mania is a way of trying to deal with underlying depression. Maybe the apparent euphoria, irritability, and overactivity seen in mania are attempts to deny or ward off depression. In any event, much more is known about what causes depression than about what causes the bipolar disorders.

The Causes of Depression

Over the years, a number of different explanations have been proposed to account for depression. In this section, some of the major theories are discussed.

Sociocultural Explanations Cross-cultural studies of mood disorders have found that prevalence rates and manifestation of symptoms vary considerably among different cultural groups and societies (Goodwin & Guze, 1984). For example, American Indians and Southeast Asians in this country appear to have high rates of depression compared to other Americans (Chung & Okazaki, 1991; Vega & Rumbaut, 1991). In China, Chinese patients with depression commonly present somatic (bodily) complaints rather than dysphoria (depression, anxiety, or restlessness), which indicates that the expression of symptoms for a particular disorder may differ from culture to culture (Kleinman, 1991). These findings suggest that factors such as culture, social experiences, and psychosocial stressors play an important role in mood disorders. We focus on the role of stressors and resources in mood disorders and then address the issue of the apparent higher rates of depression among women than men.

Stress and Depression Conceptualizations of the role of stress in psychopathology in general and depression in particular have typically proposed that stress is one of three broad factors that are important to consider: diathesis, stress, and resources or social supports (see the discussion of stress in Chapter 8). *Diathesis* refers to the fact that because of genetic or constitutional or social conditions, certain individuals may have a predisposition or vulnerability to developing depression (Monroe & Simons, 1991). Stress may act as a trigger to activate this predisposition, especially when individuals lack resources to adjust to the stress. Presumably, individuals with low predisposition compared to those with high predisposition require greater levels of stress to become depressed.

The importance of stress in depression has been demonstrated. Studies have increasingly shown that severe psychosocial stress, such as the death of a loved one, life-threatening medical condition, and frustration of major life goals, often precedes the onset of major depression (Brown & Harris, 1989; Lewinsohn, Hoberman & Rosenbaum, 1988; Paykel, 1982). This finding has led investigators to ask what kinds of stress lead to depression. Brown and Harris

Stressors such as overwhelming demands and responsibilities can contribute to depression.

(1989) concluded that one severe stressor is more likely to cause depression than several minor stressors. In other words, several minor stressors do not seem to have the same effect as one very serious stressor. Moreover, in a survey of respondents in a study of stress and depressive symptoms, McGonagle and Kessler (1990) classified stress according to chronicity. Stress that was identified as beginning more than twelve months before the study was considered *chronic*. *Acute* stress was defined as stress beginning within twelve months of the study. The investigators found that chronic stress was more highly related to depression than was acute stress, even though respondents rated both types of stress as being equivalent in terms of severity. Perhaps stress that persists

FOCUS 12.1

Depression as a Cause of Depression?

Research has shown that stress can trigger a depressive episode. Now evidence is growing that depressed persons may seek or bring about conditions that tend to maintain their depression. Depressed college students have been found to choose interaction partners who perceived them unfavorably over those who perceive them favorably. Compared with nondepressed students, they also preferred friends and dating partners who had negative appraisals of them and were inclined to seek negative feedback from their roommates (Swann et al., 1992). Investigators raised the possibility that depressed individuals have negative views of themselves. By choosing others who give negative feedback, they verify, stabilize, and make predictable their unfavorable self-images.

In addition to seeking nega-

tive feedback, depressed persons may also create stress for themselves. Hammen (1991) conducted a one-year, longitudinal study of women with unipolar depression, bipolar disorder, chronic medical illness, and no illness or disorder. The purpose was to ascertain the relationship between stress and depression. Unipolar, bipolar, and medically ill women had similar levels of stress, which were greater than those encountered by normal women. The stressors were then evaluated as to the degree to which the occurrence of the stressors was certainly or almost certainly to be independent of the behaviors or characteristics of the women or was most likely caused by the women. In other words, some stressors were considered independent of the women's behaviors (such as being robbed), whereas other stressors

were judged to be dependent on the women's behaviors (such as initiating an argument with another person). Unipolar depressed women were more likely than other women to have experienced stressors in which they were contributors and to have stressors involving interpersonal interactions. Hammen speculated that depressed individuals may help contribute to the stress they encounter, which, in turn, provokes further depression!

The research should not be interpreted as demonstrating that depressed individuals purposely want to further their depressive states. Rather, depressive episodes and the associated negative self-images and cognitions may reduce coping skills, which then lead to situations (such as seeking negative feedback or creating stress for themselves) that lead to further depression.

---

for a long time is viewed as being uncontrollable and stable. Finally, stress also appears to be important in *relapse*—the recurrence of depression after treatment (Krantz & Moos, 1988; Lewinsohn, Zeiss & Duncan, 1989).

Why do some people who encounter stress develop depression while others do not? People may differ in the degree of vulnerability to depression. The vulnerability may be caused by biogenic factors (discussed later), psychosocial factors, or both. Hammen and colleagues (1992) argued that the relationship between stress and depression is complex and interactive. In a longitudinal study of unipolar depressed patients, the investigators found supporting evidence that vulnerability to stress may be influenced by having parents who are dysfunctional and who create stress conditions in the family. In turn, the individuals may fail to acquire adaptive skills and positive self-images, which brings on more stress and,

in the face of stress, leads to depression. Therefore, vulnerability may arise from early experiences in the family. (See Focus 12.1 for a further discussion of Hammen's ideas.)

Other investigators have examined social supports or resources as buffers against depression. The assumption is that persons who are exposed to stress may or may not develop depression, depending on whether they have adequate social supports. Holahan and Moos (1991) studied the role of social resources on stress and depression. They collected data on individuals at the beginning and end of a four-year period. Information included personality characteristics, family support (such as helpfulness of family members), stress, and depression. Persons with positive personality traits and family support, compared to those without these characteristics, had less depression four years later, even when initial level of depression (during year one) was controlled. The researchers speculated that personal or family resources help individuals cope and adjust to stress. The effects of social supports were also studied on gay men at risk for AIDS (Hays, Turner & Coates, 1992). The men were assessed as to their level of depression, social supports, and HIV-related symptoms over a one-year period. Results indicated that men who were more satisfied with their social supports were subsequently less likely to suffer from depression.

The research on stress and depression has been impressive. Longitudinal research designs and prospective studies (studies of individuals before their depressive episodes occur) have helped decipher cause and effect relationships between stress and depression. The work has also moved from the study of broad variables (for example, stress) to more specific ones (for example, types of stress).

Gender and Depression   Depression is far more common among women than among men. Regardless of region of the world, race and ethnicity, and social class, women are about twice as likely to suffer from depression as are men (Strickland, 1992). According to DSM-IV, 18 to 23 percent of females and 8 to 11 percent of males have at some time experienced a major depressive episode. Is this gender difference real, and, if so, what accounts for the difference?

Although women are more likely than men to be seen in treatment and to be diagnosed as depressed, this may not mean that women are more depressed, for several reasons. First, women may simply be more likely than men to seek treatment when depressed; this tendency would make the reported depression rate for women higher, even if the actual male and female rates were equal. Second, women may be more willing to report their depression to other people. That is, the gender differences may occur in self-report behaviors rather than in actual depression rates. Third, diagnosticians or the diagnostic system may be biased toward finding depression among women. And fourth, depression in men may take other forms and thus be given other diagnoses, such as substance dependency.

Some clinicians believe that these four possibilities account for only part of the sex difference in depression, and that women do have higher rates of depression (Radloff & Rae, 1981). The reasons for

these differences are unclear, however. Speculation has involved physiological or social psychological factors.

Genetic or hormonal differences between the sexes were once thought to influence depression. Although biogenic factors may account for the sex differences, relatively little research has been conducted on these factors, and available findings are inconsistent with respect to hormonal changes and depression. This has led researchers to propose social or psychological factors, one of which is the woman's traditional sex role. Women have been encouraged to present themselves as attractive, sensitive to other persons, and passive in relationships (Strickland, 1992). These roles, as well as subservience to men and a lack of occupational opportunities, may produce more depression in women (Bernard, 1976). For the same reason, women may be more likely than men to experience lack of control in life situations. They may then attribute their "helplessness" to an imagined lack of personal worth. Interestingly, women who are not employed outside the home and who are raising children are particularly vulnerable to depression (Gotlib, 1992). Finally, the traditional feminine sex role behaviors (gentleness, emotionality, and self-subordination) may not be so successful in eliciting reinforcement from others as the assertive and more forceful responses typically associated with males.

In a review of different explanations for the gender differences in depression, Nolen-Hoeksema (1987) concluded that none truly accounts for the observed sex differences in the rates of depression. She hypothesized that how a person responds to depressed moods contributes to the severity, chronicity, and recurrence of depressive episodes. In her view, women tend to ruminate and amplify their depressive moods, and men dampen or find means to minimize dysphoria. Nolen-Hoeksema (1991) found that when individuals tracked their depressed moods and responses to these moods for one month, women were more likely than men to ruminate in response to depressed moods. Those who tended to ruminate had longer periods of depressed moods, and when tendency to ruminate was statistically controlled, sex differences in duration of depressed moods disappeared.

Egeland and Hostetter (1983) also speculated that responses to depressive moods may affect observed rates of depression. In their study of the Amish, a religious community in Pennsylvania, they found that males and females have the same rates for depression. The researchers noted that because Amish men do not show alcoholism or antisocial behaviors, their depression cannot be masked. Additionally, Amish women, like the men, must work, so engaging in a sick (depressed) role is discouraged. Although role behavior may help explain some of the differences in rates of depression between men and women, it is not clear if the explanation is enough to account for the vast differences.

The work on sociocultural or psychosocial influences provides a perspective of how cultural, institutional, and environmental conditions affect depression. Now let us turn to theories that are primarily psychological or biogenic in nature.

Psychoanalytic Explanations The psychoanalytic explanation of depression focuses mainly on two concepts: separation and anger. Separation may occur when a spouse, lover, child, parent, or significant other person dies or leaves for one reason or another. But the loss (separation) need not be physical; it can also be symbolic. For example, the withdrawal of affection or support or a rejection (a symbolic loss) can induce depression.

Freud ([1917] 1924) believed that depressives are excessively dependent people because they are fixated in the oral stage. As we discussed in Chapter 2, he viewed the mouth as the primary mechanism by which infants relate to the world, so being fixated at this stage fosters dependency. Being passive and having others fill one's needs (being fed, bathed, clothed, cuddled, and so forth) results in emotional dependency that continues into adult life. Thus, for people fixated in the oral stage, self-esteem depends on other important people in the environment. When a significant loss occurs, the mourner's self-esteem plummets.

Freud also believed that the depressive shows a failure to follow through in the normal mourning process, which he called "grief or mourning work." In the normal course of mourning, the mourner consciously recalls and expresses memories about the lost person in an attempt to undo the loss. In addition, the mourner is flooded with two strong sets of feelings: anger and guilt. The anger, which arises

from the sense of being deserted, can be very strong. The mourner may also be flooded with guilt feelings about real or imagined sins committed against the lost person.

Because depression cannot always be correlated with the immediate loss of a loved one, Freud used the construct of "symbolic loss" to account for depression that did not result directly from a loss. That is to say, any form of rejection or reproach may be perceived by the depressive as symbolic of an earlier loss.

Psychoanalysis has strongly emphasized the dynamics of anger in explaining depression. Many depressed patients have strong hostile or angry feelings, and some clinicians believe that getting clients to express their anger reduces their depression. Such a belief has led some to speculate that depression is really anger turned against the self (Freud, [1917] 1924). Freud suggested that, when a person experiences a loss (symbolic or otherwise), he or she may harbor feelings of resentment and hostility toward the lost person in addition to feelings of love and affection. There have been relatively few empirical tests of psychoanalytic ideas. One study longitudinally examined whether persons whose spouses had died were less depressed if they directly confronted (that is, performed grief work) rather than avoided dealing with their loss (Stroebe & Stroebe, 1991). Results were equivocal in that performing grief work was inversely related to adjustment for widowers but not for widows.

Learning Explanations Behaviorists also see the separation or loss of a significant other as important in depression. However, behaviorists tend to see the cause as reduced reinforcement rather than as the untestable concept of fixation or symbolic grief. When a loved one is lost, an accustomed level of reinforcement (whether affection, companionship, pleasure, material goods, or services) is immediately withdrawn. No longer can one obtain the support or encouragement of the lost person. When this happens, one's level of activity (talking, expressing ideas, working, joking, engaging in sports, going out on the town) is markedly diminished because an important source of reinforcement has disappeared. Thus many behaviorists view depression as a product of inadequate or insufficient reinforcers in a person's life,

Learning theory suggests that depression may be a product of reduced reinforcement in a person's life. The reduced reinforcement leads to reduced activity levels. Unfortunately, consolation and sympathy from others may sometimes serve to reinforce and maintain depresive behaviors.

leading to a reduced frequency of behavior that previously was positively reinforced (Ferster, 1965; Lazarus, 1968; Lewinsohn, 1974a).

As the period of reduced activity (resulting from reduced reinforcement) continues, the person labels himself or herself "depressed." If the new lower level of activity causes others to show sympathy, the depressed person may remain inactive and chronically "depressed." By being sympathetic about the incident (loss), friends, relatives, and even strangers may be reinforcing the depressive's current state of inactivity. (This reinforcement for a lower activity level is known as *secondary gain*.) The depression tends to deepen, and the person disengages still further from the environment and further reduces the chance of obtaining positive reinforcement from normal activity. The result may be continually deepening depression.

Depression has been associated both with low levels of self-reinforcement and with reductions in environmental reinforcements (Heiby, 1983). In other words, when people get less reinforcement from the environment (such as after the death of a loved one) and do not give themselves reinforcement, they are prone to become depressed. Depressives may lack

the skills required to replace lost environmental reinforcements.

This behavioral concept of depression can be elaborated to cover many situations that may elicit depression (such as failure, loss, change in job status, rejection, and desertion). Lewinsohn's model of depression is perhaps the most comprehensive of the behavioral explanations (Lewinsohn, 1974a, 1974b; Lewinsohn & Graf, 1973; Lewinsohn & Libet, 1972; Lewinsohn, Weinstein & Alper, 1970). Along with the reinforcement view of depression, Lewinsohn suggested three sets of variables that may enhance or hinder a person's access to positive reinforcement.

First, *the number of events and activities that are potentially reinforcing to the person* is important. This number depends very much on individual differences and varies with the biological traits and experiential history of the person. For example, age, gender, or physical attributes may determine the availability of reinforcers. Handsome people are more likely to receive positive attention than those people who look nondescript. Young people are likely to have more social interaction than retirees. A task-oriented person who values intellectual pursuits may not be so responsive as other people to interpersonal or affiliative forms of reinforcement. To such a person, a compliment such as "I like you" may be less effective than "I see you as an extremely competent person."

Second, *the availability of reinforcements in the environment* can also affect the person. Harsh environments, such as regimented institutions or remote isolated places, reduce reinforcements.

Third, *the instrumental behavior of the person—* the number of social skills that can be exercised to bring about reinforcement—is important. Depressed patients lack social behaviors that can elicit positive reinforcements (Lewinsohn, Weinstein & Alper, 1970). They interact with fewer people, respond less, have very few positive reactions, and initiate less conversation. Depressed people also feel more uncomfortable in social situations (Youngren & Lewinsohn, 1980), and they elicit depression in others (Hammen & Peters, 1978). Further, depressed people seem to be preoccupied with themselves; they tend to talk about themselves (more so than nondepressed people) without being asked to do so (Jacobson & Anderson, 1982). For this reason or others, nondepressed people may not enjoy talking to those who are depressed and may provide little positive reinforcement to depressives during social interactions. Depressives may even create conditions that further their depression or drive others away and thus lose any social reinforcement that others could provide (Coyne, 1976).

A low rate of positive reinforcement in any of these three situations can lead to depression. A beautiful person who begins to age may notice declining interest from possible lovers. A person who has recently lost a loved one through divorce or death and has no other friends or family may receive little or no support. And a young student who lacks social skills in heterosexual relationships may be denied the pleasures of such interactions. Behavioral approaches to treating depression might attempt to intervene in any of these conditions.

Lewinsohn also recognized the important role of other factors in depression. For example, Lewinsohn, Hoberman, and Rosenbaum (1988) found that having a prior depressed mood, encountering stress, and being female (as mentioned previously, women are more likely than men to suffer depression) are associated with the occurrence of depressive episodes. Although a low rate of positive reinforcement is a critical feature of his theory, Lewinsohn and colleagues

(1985) adopted a more comprehensive view of depression. They believe that an antecedent event such as stress disrupts the predictable and well-established behavior patterns of people's lives. Such disruptions then reduce the rate of positive reinforcements or increase aversive experiences. If individuals are unable to reverse the impact of the stress, they begin to have a heightened state of self-awareness (for example, self-critical, negative expectancies and loss of self-confidence) and to experience depressed affect. With depressed moods, persons then have a more difficult time functioning appropriately, which makes them further vulnerable to depression. Thus Lewinsohn's model attempts to cover not only behavioral elements but also cognitive and emotional consequences.

It should be noted that although behaviorists have made major contributions to the understanding of depression, they and many other theorists have not really given much attention to mania. Acknowledging that biogenic factors may be important in bipolar disorders, Staats and Heiby (1985) believe that learning principles are also involved in mania. They believe that individuals may, because of some behavior (such as performing well using social or interpersonal skills), receive praise and admiration. The euphoria from receiving the praise may elicit further use of the skills, resulting in even more positive consequences. The behaviors then become accelerated and euphoria increases even more—as in a manic state. At some point, however, the behaviors may elicit negative reactions, which sets up conditions for depression.

Cognitive Explanations Some psychologists believe that low self-esteem is the key to depressive reactions. All of us have both negative and positive feelings about what we see as our "self." We like or value certain things about ourselves, and we dislike other things. Some people, especially those who are depressed, have a generally negative self-concept. Such people perceive themselves as inept, unworthy, and incompetent, regardless of reality. If they do succeed at anything, they are likely to dismiss it as pure luck or to forecast eventual failure. Hence a cognitive interpretation of oneself as unworthy may lead to a host of thinking patterns that reflect self-blame, self-criticism, and exaggerated ideas of duty and responsibility.

One major cognitive theory has been advanced by Beck (1976). According to this theory, depression is a primary disturbance in *thinking* rather than a basic disturbance in *mood*. How persons structure and interpret their experiences determines their affective states. If individuals see a situation as unpleasant, they will feel an unpleasant mood. Depressed patients are said to have schemas that set them up for depression. (A **schema** is a pattern of thinking or a cognitive set that determines a person's reactions and responses. In other words, schemas tend to modify, or color, interpretation of incoming information.)

According to this theory, depressives operate from a "primary triad" of negative self-views, present experiences, and the future. Four errors in logic typify this negative schema, which leads to depression and is characteristic of depressives:

1. *Arbitrary inference* The depressive tends to draw conclusions that are not supported by evidence. For example, a woman may conclude that "People dislike me" just because no one speaks to her on the bus or in the elevator. A man who invites a woman out to dinner and finds the restaurant closed that evening may see this as evidence of his own unworthiness. In both cases, these people draw erroneous conclusions from the available evidence. Depressives are apparently unwilling or unable to see other, more probable, explanations.

2. *Selected abstraction* The depressive takes a minor incident or detail out of context, and the incidents on which the depressive focuses tend to be trivial. The depressive who is corrected for a minor aspect of his or her work takes the correction as a sign of incompetence or inadequacy—even when the supervisor's overall feedback is highly positive.

3. *Overgeneralization* A depressive tends to draw a sweeping conclusion about his or her ability, performance, or worth from one single experience or incident. A person who is laid off from a job because of budgetary cuts may conclude that he or she is worthless. The comments of a student seen by one of the authors at a university psychology clinic provide another illustration of overgeneralization: when he missed breakfast at the dormitory because his alarm clock didn't ring, he concluded, "I don't deserve my own body because I don't take care of it." Later, when he showed up late for class through no fault of his own, he thought, "What a miserable excuse for a student I am." When a former classmate passed by and smiled, he thought, "I must look awful today or she wouldn't be laughing at me."

4. *Magnification and minimization* The depressive tends to exaggerate (magnify) limitations and difficulties and play down (minimize) accomplishments, achievements, and capabilities. Asked to evaluate personal strengths and weaknesses, the depressed person lists many shortcomings or unsuccessful efforts but finds it almost impossible to name any achievements.

All four of these cognitive processes can be seen as results or causes of low self-esteem, which makes the person expect failure and engage in self-criticism that is unrelated to reality. People with low self-esteem may have experienced much disapproval in the past from significant others, such as parents. Their parents or significant others may have responded to them by punishing failures and not rewarding successes or by holding unrealistically high expectations or standards. The following case is an example:

Paul was a twenty-year-old college senior majoring in chemistry. He first came to the student psychiatric clinic complaining of headaches and a vague assortment of somatic problems. Throughout the interview, Paul seemed severely depressed and unable to work up enough energy to talk with the therapist. Even though he had maintained a B+ average, he felt like a failure and was uncertain about his future.

His parents had always had high expectations for Paul, their eldest son, and had transmitted these feelings to him from his earliest childhood. His father, a successful thoracic surgeon, had his heart set on Paul's becoming a doctor. The parents saw academic success as very important, and Paul did exceptionally well in school. Although his teachers praised him for being an outstanding student, his parents seemed to take his successes for granted. In fact, they often made statements such as "You can do better." When he failed at something, his parents would make it obvious to him that they not only were disappointed but felt disgraced as well. This pattern of punishment for failures without recognition of successes, combined with his parents' high expectations, led to the development in Paul of an extremely negative self-concept.

Some studies have demonstrated a relationship between cognition and depression. Dent and Teasdale (1988) studied the depression levels and self-schemas (self-descriptions) of the same women at two different periods of time. Women who had negative self-descriptions tended to subsequently have higher levels of depression and to recover more slowly than women who had less negative self-descriptions. The investigator concluded that although two individuals may have equal levels of depression, the one who has negative self-cognitions may turn out to have a more serious and longer lasting depressive episode. Furthermore, depression is related to memory bias. When depressed individuals are given lists of words that vary in emotional content, they tend to recall negative words in contrast to nondepressives. This may indicate a tendency to attend to, and remember, negative and depressing events (Mineka & Sutton, 1992).

Refining his cognitive theory of depression, Beck (1983) raised the possibility that personality patterns—sociotropy and autonomy—may be important. *Sociotropy* is one's positive interchange with other people (resulting in intimacy, support, and guidance), and *autonomy* refers to independence, freedom of choice, and action and expression. Depressed individuals high in sociotropy will feel deprived and a sense of loss and attempt to gain social support and help. Depressed persons high in autonomy will feel defeated, avoid people, and have a sense of failure. Some research findings have shown that among unipolar depressed individuals, those with sociotropic and autonomy personality patterns do show different kinds of clinical symptoms, as predicted by Beck (Robins & Luten, 1991). The findings point to the importance of finding out why these personality patterns develop.

Although the cognitive explanation of depression has merit, it seems too simple. At times, negative cognitions may be the result of, rather than the cause of, depressed moods, as noted by Hammen (1985). That is, one may first feel depressed and then, as a result, have negative or pessimistic thoughts about the world. Hammen also found that a person's schema tends to mediate the relationship between stress and depression. Stress can lead to depression if a person has developed a predisposing schema. Another criticism of cognitive explanations is that many people get depressed, but they do not feel depressed all the time. Yet negative cognitive styles are often hypothesized to be stable or enduring.

Learned Helplessness A unique and interesting view of depression is that it is learned helplessness. This cognitive-learning theory was proposed by Seligman (1975). The basic assumption of **learned helplessness** is that cognitions and feelings of helplessness are learned. A person who sees that his or her actions continually have very little effect on the environment develops an expectation of being helpless. When this expectation is borne out in settings that may not be controllable, passivity and finally depression may result.

A person's susceptibility to depression, then, depends on his or her experience with controlling the environment. In his study of helplessness, Seligman discovered strong parallels between the symptoms, cause, and means of preventing helplessness and those for depression (see Table 12.2). He also noticed similarities in cure; one could say that depression is cured when the person no longer believes he or she is helpless.

Seligman described depression as a *belief in one's own helplessness*. Many other investigators have described depression in terms of hopelessness, powerlessness, and helplessness. For example, "The severely depressed patient believes that his skills and plans of action are no longer effective for reaching the goals he has set" (Melges & Bowlby, 1969, p. 693). And, according to Seligman (1975, pp. 55–56), "The expectation that an outcome is independent of responding (1) reduces the motivation to control the outcome; (2) interferes with learning that responding controls the outcome; (3) produces fear for as long as the subject is uncertain of the uncontrollability of the outcome, and then produces depression." In general, research has shown that depression is associated with an external locus of control—depressed persons tend to perceive events as being uncontrollable (Benassi, Sweeney & Dufour, 1988).

Attributional Style: A Learning and Cognitive Approach Seligman's theory of learned helplessness was first published in 1975. Three years later, he and his coworkers revised the model to include more cognitive elements (Abramson, Seligman & Teasdale, 1978). Essentially, they believe that human beings who encounter helplessness make *causal attributions*

Table 12.2

Similarities Between Learned Helplessness and Depression

Learned Helplessness		Depression
Symptoms	Passivity	Passivity
	Difficulty learning that response produces relief	Negative cognitive set
	Dissipates in time	Time course
	Lack of aggression	Introjected hostility
	Weight loss, appetite loss	Weight loss, appetite loss
	Social and sexual deficits	Social and sexual deficits
Cause	Learning that responding and reinforcement are independent	Feelings of helplessness
		Belief that responding is useless

Source: Adapted from Seligman, 1975.

(that is, they speculate as to why they are helpless). These attributions can be internal or external, stable or unstable, and global or specific. For instance, suppose that a student in a math course receives the same low grades regardless of how much he or she has studied. The student may attribute the low grades to internal or personal factors ("I don't do well in math because *I'm* scared of math") or to external factors ("The *teacher* doesn't like me, so I can't get a good grade"). The attribution can also be stable ("I'm the type of person who can never do well in math") or unstable ("My poor performance is due to my heavy work load"). Additionally, the attribution can be global or specific. A global attribution ("I'm a poor student") has broader implications for performance than a specific one ("I'm poor at math but good in

When individuals are provided with opportunities to control aspects of their lives, learned helplessness and depression can sometimes be prevented. With the aid of special equipment, this blind person can learn to manipulate and use a computer.

other subjects"). Abramson and coworkers believe that a person whose attributions for helplessness are internal, stable, and global is likely to have more pervasive feelings of depression than someone whose attributions are external, unstable, and specific. Attributions have been found to be associated with many aspects of life.

Some people tend to have a pessimistic attributional style, explaining bad events (such as failure to pass an examination) in global, stable, and internal terms (such as believing that "I fail in many courses, it always happens to me, and I am dumb"). The Attributional Style Questionnaire has been developed in which people are given hypothetical situations and are asked to indicate what the cause of each situation is. In this way, people can be rated as to their attributional style. Attributional style is related to a number of characteristics. People who have pessimistic attributional styles receive lower grades in universities, perform worse as sales agents, and have poorer health (Seligman, 1987).

Attributional style can also be reliably determined from a content analysis of verbatim explanations (CAVE), in which the content of an explanation is rated on attributional style. For example, a baseball player who says, "Once in a while I play poorly because of bad breaks, but I always know I'll get my good share of hits," is far more optimistic than one who says, "I'm getting old—my reactions to a pitch have slowed." In an analysis of newspaper quotes from Baseball Hall of Fame players who played between 1900 and 1950, Seligman found that players who had an optimistic attributional style outlived those who were more pessimistic. Zullow and his colleagues (1988) also noted that when President Lyndon Johnson's press conferences contained optimistic phrases, bold presidential actions were taken in the Vietnam War; when he used more pessimistic phrases, the actions were passive.

The implications are that (1) people vary in their attributional styles, (2) attributional style can be assessed, and (3) attributional style may be related to achievements, health, and other behaviors. Obviously, a causal relationship between attributional style and behavior hasn't been clearly established. But the research suggests that how we explain things may be quite important in our lives.

The learned helplessness model, as well as the attributional style idea, has generated a great deal of research. There is evidence that depressed people make "depressive" attributions and feel that their lives are less controllable than do nondepressives (Raps et al., 1982). As with cognitive theory, however, researchers question whether this model, even with its attributional components, can adequately explain depression and about whether attributions result from or are caused by depression. Cognitions and attributions may be important factors in depression, but the disorder is complex; current models tend to include or explain only particular facets of depression (Hammen, 1985). Helplessness theory (which some investigators have reformulated as the "hopelessness" theory) may explain only a certain type of depression (Abramson, Metalsky & Alloy, 1989; DeVellis & Blalock, 1992). For example, earlier it was mentioned that an external locus of control was associated with depression, yet Seligman believes that internal attributions are important in depression. Benassi, Sweeny, and Dufour (1988) raised the possibility that internality and externality may be related to different types of depression. Depression may be a heterogeneous disorder that can be caused by genetic, biochemical, or social factors.

Biological Perspectives on Mood Disorders

Biological approaches to the cause of mood or affective disorders generally focus on genetic predisposition, physiological dysfunction, or combinations of the two.

Genetic Factors Mood disorders tend to run in families, and the same type of disorder is generally found among members of the same family (American Psychiatric Association, 1987; Perris, 1966; Winokur, Clayton & Reich, 1969). One way to assess the role of heredity is to compare the incidence of mood disorders among the biological and adoptive families of people who were adopted early in life and who had the disorders. If heredity is more important, then biological families (which contributed the genetic makeup) should show a high incidence of the disorders. If environment is more important, then adoptive families (which provided the early environment) should show a high incidence. The results of such a comparison indicated that the incidence of mood disorders was higher among the biological families than among the adoptive families; the latter showed an incidence similar to that of the general population (Kety, 1979).

Another way to study the possible genetic transmission of mood disorders is to compare identical (MZ) and fraternal (DZ) twins. Nine such studies of twins have been reported. The concordance rate (the probability of one twin having the same disorder as the cotwin) for bipolar disorders was 72 percent for MZ twins and 14 percent for DZ twins. The rate suggests that the genetic component is extremely important, although nongenetic factors also appear important (Baron, 1991). By contrast, the concordance rate for unipolar mood disorders was only 40 percent for MZ twins and 11 percent for DZ twins (Goodwin & Guze, 1984).

Both of these research approaches (and others as well) consistently turn up evidence of genetic influence on mood disorders. Moreover, the bulk of the research has suggested that heredity is a stronger factor in bipolar mood disorders than in unipolar disorders (Reus, 1988).

Egeland and colleagues (1987) have also provided some evidence of genetic involvement in bipolar disorders. The investigators studied the Amish (a religious community in Pennsylvania). They found a number of people with bipolar disorders, many of whom had the same ancestors. Moreover, by using sophisticated techniques, they found that a gene located on a specific region of a chromosome was associated with mood disorders among the Amish. Gershon and colleagues (1989) could not replicate the findings in other populations, although the discrepancy in findings could be a result of the different populations studied. They noted that technological advancements in instrumentation, statistical genetic techniques, and molecular biology have allowed researchers to become increasingly sophisticated in the study of biological aspects of mood disorders. Although heredity appears to be important, especially in bipolar disorders, researchers show little consensus over the appropriate model for the transmission of affective disorders. Some researchers have proposed that depression is caused by one primary gene rather than many genes; most favor a polygenetic theory over a monogenetic theory (Gershon et al., 1989).

Biochemical Factors   But how is heredity involved in the major mood disorders? A growing number of researchers believe that genetic factors influence the amounts of certain substances (the *catecholamines*) found at specific sites in the brain. These substances, called **neurotransmitters**, help transmit nerve im-

Some fairly isolated groups, such as the Amish, avoid extensive contact with other groups. Under such circumstances, gene pools and cultural practices are likely to be relatively unique from other groups. Research on isolated groups can provide insight into the hereditary or cultural basis for mental disorders such as depression.

pulses from one neuron to another. They may mediate between active motor behavior and emotions (Becker, 1974; Weiss, Glazer & Pohorecky, 1975).

Nerve impulses are transmitted from neuron to neuron across *synapses*, which are junctions where the axon (or transmitting end) of one neuron is next to the dendrites (or receiving end) of the receptor neuron. According to the *catecholamine hypothesis*, or *biogenic amine theory of mood disorders*, depression is caused by a deficit of specific neurotransmitters (*norepinephrine, dopamine,* or *serotonin*) at brain synapses, whereas mania is caused by an oversupply of these substances (Bunney et al., 1979; Schildkraut, 1965).

Two lines of research implicate neurotransmitters in affective disorders: (1) findings that establish a relationship between levels of neurotransmitters and motor activity, and (2) studies of the effects of medication on these neurotransmitters and on mood changes. As noted earlier, depression is characterized by lower motor activity, and mania by overactivity. When rats are put in certain stressful situations—for example, a series of inescapable shocks—the level of norepinephrine in their brains is reduced. The animals then show ''depressive'' behaviors such as motor passivity and an inability to learn avoidance-escape responses. Giving rats a drug that depletes brain norepinephrine also results in motor passivity and an inability to learn. But if rats are given a drug that protects against the depletion of norepinephrine and if this drug is administered to rats before an experience with inescapable shock, they become immunized against passivity and poor learning (Weiss, Glazer & Pohorecky, 1975).

These findings not only suggest the importance of norepinephrine in depressive behaviors, but also show that environmental stressors produce biochemical and behavioral changes and, conversely, that biochemical changes can produce behavioral effects similar to those of environmental stressors. Even so, no matter how similar they may be in various respects, the behavior of animals is not the same as the behavior of human beings. Investigators obviously need a more direct link between the role of neurotransmitters and depressive behaviors in human beings.

Some evidence implicating neurotransmitters in human depression and mania has been obtained accidentally (Goodwin, 1974). For example, it was discovered that when the drug reserpine was used in treating hypertension, many patients became depressed. (*Reserpine* depletes the level of neutotransmitters in the brain.) Similarly, the drug iproniazid, given to tubercular patients, elevated the mood of those who were depressed. (*Iproniazid* inhibits the destruction of brain amines.) Thus mood levels in human beings were found to vary with the level of neurotransmitters in the brain. These variations are consistent with the catecholamine hypothesis.

Some researchers have suggested that the level, or amount, of neurotransmitters present is not the primary factor. They noted that, to travel from one neuron to another, an electrical impulse must release neurotransmitters that stimulate the receiving neuron. The problem may not be the amount of neurotransmitter produced or available, but rather a dysfunction in the reception of the neurotransmitter by the receiving neuron (Sulser, 1979). Whether mood disorders are caused by a deficiency in neurotransmitter substances, a blunted receptor response, or a more general dysregulation in neurotransmission cannot be resolved at this time; the distinct possibility also exists that depression is a heterogeneous collection of subtypes of disorders with differing biological and environmental precursors (Mann, 1989).

Findings of a different sort have also aroused interest in the biological or physiological processes of depression. For example, depressed adults differ from nondepressed persons in sleep patterns, particularly in rapid eye movement (REM) sleep. (There are several stages of sleep, and during REM sleep the eyes move rapidly and dreaming occurs.) Depression is linked with a relatively rapid onset of, and an increase in, REM sleep (Goodwin & Guze, 1984). Moreover, reducing the REM sleep of persons with depression seems to help (Vogel et al., 1980). Why sleep patterns are linked to depression is unclear. Monroe, Thase, and Simons (1992) found that some depressed patients experienced severe, acute life stress whereas others did not. REM latency (that is, the time before REM occurs during sleep) was short among those depressives who did not experience severe life stress. It may be that those with reduced REM latency have a lower threshold for the development of depression, in that less stress is needed to affect depression.

Considerable interest has also focused on possible abnormalities in neuroendocrine regulation in depressed people. Depressives tend to have high levels of *cortisol*, a hormone secreted by the adrenal cortex in the brain. Cortisol levels are measured by the *dexamethasone suppression test (DST)*. In this test, patients are given dexamethasone, which normally suppresses the cortisol secretion. Studies in different countries have shown that higher blood levels of cortisol are found in depressives than in normal people (World Health Organization, 1987) and that not suppressing these levels is linked to poorer prognosis for recovery (Reus, 1988). Whether cortisol helps cause depression or is produced by depression, however, is still unclear. Furthermore, measuring cortisol levels accurately has been difficult, and patients with other disorders often exhibit responses similar to depressives (Free & Oei, 1989), so questions remain over the value of using the DST as a tool for assessing depression and prognosis.

Evaluating the Causation Theories

Three developments have added to our understanding of mood disorders. First, longitudinal or prospective studies have allowed greater insights into the possible causal links between life experiences and depression. Second, technological advancements in psychophysiological tools have enabled researchers to more clearly identify biological markers and processes in mood disorders. Third, researchers are increasingly attentive to the possibility of viewing depression as a heterogeneous collection of disorders. In view of the fact that depression is so common and seemingly influenced by so many factors, the heterogeneous view of the disorder is not surprising. The three developments have, in turn, affected our theories of mood disorders.

The theories of depression presented in this chapter explain certain aspects of the disturbance, but all have weaknesses. According to the psychoanalytic perspective, loss and separation provoke a depressive reaction. But what determines the extent and severity of depression? Fixation at the oral stage, dependency, and symbolic loss are psychoanalytic concepts that are difficult to test. The psychoanalytic assumption that depression may simply be hostility turned inward on the self also seems open to question. When some depressed patients experienced success on experimental tasks, their self-esteem and optimism increased (Beck, 1974). If depression is hostility turned inward, why would success alleviate some of its symptoms?

As we have noted, Beck's idea is that the tendency to think in negative terms helps produce depression. His theory has, over time, become increasingly complex, and personality dimensions of sociotropy and autonomy have been added. How do these personality characteristics develop? To what extent is depression caused by depression or is the effect of it? Lewinsohn's behavioral theory and Seligman's learned helplessness theory are well grounded in research findings. Lewinsohn's work has mainly shown a relationship between depression and inadequate positive reinforcement. But do these low rates actually cause depression? Seligman has shown that learned helplessness and certain attributions can lead to depressive behaviors. However, this model explains only certain kinds of depression: reactions to stress. How can behavioral as well as cognitive theorists present a more convincing account of the development of manic behaviors?

Endogenous (congenital) factors seem to play a crucial role in mood disorders. Although genetic studies have not been extensive, evidence has shown that heredity is involved. The precise genetic mechanisms are not known, but research into biochemical factors or neurotransmitters seems quite promising.

One good way to think about mood disorders is to see them as resulting from an interaction between environmental and biological factors (Kraemer & McKinney, 1979). Thus they range from mild sadness, through normal grief and the specific affective disorders, to the major mood disorders. Milder instances of depression (or, for that matter, mania) may be more externally caused. In mood disorders in the middle of the spectrum both external and internal factors may be important. In severe disorders, including psychotic forms of the major mood disorders, endogenous factors may become more prominent (Goodwin, 1977).

THE TREATMENT OF MOOD DISORDERS

Biological approaches to the treatment of mood disorders are generally based on the catecholamine hypothesis. That is, treatment consists primarily of controlling the level of neurotransmitters at brain synapses. In addition, psychological treatment seems to offer promise for persons with depression.

Biomedical Treatments for Unipolar Disorders

Biomedical treatments are interventions that alter the physical or biochemical state of the patient. They include the use of medication and electroconvulsive therapy.

Medication The drugs that are primarily used to treat unipolar depression are of two general types; both were introduced in the mid-1950s. The *tricyclic antidepressants* (the first group) are still considered the more effective (Klein, Gittelman & Quitkin, 1980), and they seem to be especially effective in endogenous forms of depression (Georgotas, 1985). These drugs seem to block the re-uptake of norepinephrine. (*Re-uptake* is the process in which a neurotransmitter is taken back into the nerve cells.) When re-uptake is blocked, more norepinephrine is left at the synapses. These higher levels of residual norepinephrine seem to be linked with reduced depressive symptoms.

The *monoamine oxidase (MAO) inhibitors* (the second group of antidepressants) also work by increasing the level of norepinephrine at the brain synapses. Rather than blocking re-uptake as the tricyclics do, however, the MAO inhibitors prevent the MAO enzyme (which is normally found in the body) from breaking down norepinephrine that is already available at the synapse.

Although MAO inhibitors, as well as tricyclic antidepressants, affect levels of neurotransmitters, there is growing suspicion that the process is more complicated. The drugs may also affect the sensitivity of receptors on the receiving (postsynaptic) neurons.

Although MAO inhibitors are currently prescribed for depressed patients who have not responded well to treatment with tricyclics, MAO inhibitors have many side effects including insomnia, irritability, dizziness, constipation, and impotence. But the most serious side effect is the tyramine-cheese incompatibility. One normal function of the MAO enzyme is to break down tyramine, a substance found in many cheeses as well as in some beers, wines, pickled products, and chocolate. The MAO inhibitors interfere with this function, so someone who is using one of these drugs must severely restrict his or her intake of tyramine. Failure to do so triggers the tyramine-cheese reaction, which begins with increased blood pressure, vomiting, and muscle twitching and can, if untreated, result in intracranial bleeding followed by death.

Such side effects are a major drawback of the antidepressant drugs. (The tricyclics, too, may cause reactions such as drowsiness, insomnia, agitation, fine tremors, blurred vision, dry mouth, and reduced sexual ability.) Carefully monitoring the patient's reactions is thus absolutely necessary. Another drawback is that the antidepressant drugs are essentially ineffective during the first two weeks of use, which is a serious concern, particularly where suicide is a danger. As mentioned earlier, the effectiveness of antidepressant drugs may be caused by changes in the sensitivity of postsynaptic receptors. These changes in sensitivity seem to require a couple of weeks to develop.

Klein, Gittelman, and Quitkin (1980) noted that about 65 percent of moderately to severely depressed people improve while taking tricyclics. A recent review of the effects of selected antidepressant medication from rigorously designed studies, however, suggested that treatment outcomes have probably been overestimated (Greenberg et al., 1992). Although clinicians' ratings of outcome have been high, patients' ratings have been very similar to those patients who were given a placebo. Thus if researchers ask clinicians about the effects of antidepressant medication, they tend to give more favorable ratings than do patients. Another factor to consider is that drug effectiveness may be related to the "type" of depression. For example, Peselow and colleagues (1992) found that depressed patients who were considered high autonomous–low sociotropy personalities had more favorable response to antidepressant medication than did patients who were high sociotropic–low autonomy personalities.

More recently, fluoxetine (Prozac) has been widely used for depression because the effects are comparable to tricyclic antidepressants but there seems to be fewer unpleasant side effects (Strickland, 1992). As in the case of tricyclics, Prozac appears to block the re-uptake of transmitter substances such as norepinephrine and serotonin. As noted in Chapter 18, soon after its widespread use, Prozac was accused by some clients and client advocacy groups of precipitating suicides and violent behaviors. Research findings have not supported the accusations (U.S. Department of Health & Human Services, 1991).

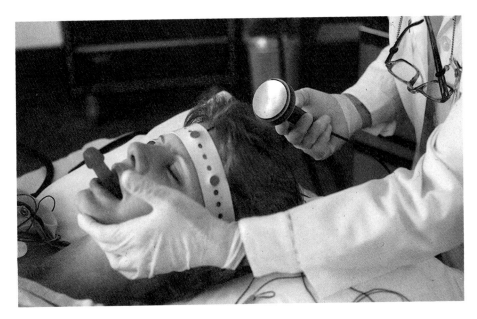

Severely depressed people whose depression cannot be relieved by tricyclics or MAO inhibitors are treated with electroconvulsive therapy. Although most seriously depressed patients show improvement after only a few treatments, negative side effects such as memory loss can result.

Electroconvulsive Therapy   Electroconvulsive therapy (ECT) is generally reserved for patients with severe unipolar depression who have not responded to tricyclics or MAO inhibitors. The procedure is described in Chapter 19; in essence, it consists of applying a moderate electrical voltage to the person's brain for up to half a second. The patient's response to the voltage is a convulsion (seizure) lasting 30 to 40 seconds followed by a 5- to 30-minute coma.

Most seriously depressed patients show at least a temporary improvement after about four ECT treatments (Campbell, 1981). The ECT mechanism is not fully understood; it may operate on neurotransmitters at the synapses, as do antidepressants. Some of the decrease in symptoms may also be due to the amnesia that develops for a short time after the treatment. One major advantage of ECT is that the response to treatment is relatively fast (Gangadhar, Kapur & Kalyanasundaram, 1982). However, common side effects include headaches, confusion, and memory loss. And many patients are terrified of ECT. In about 1 of 1,000 cases, serious medical complications occur (Goldman, 1988). ECT is controversial, and critics have urged that it be banned as a form of treatment. Focus 12.2 describes a case in which medication was used in combination with ECT to treat a bipolar affective disorder.

Cognitive-Behavioral Treatment for Unipolar Disorders

Because the use of antidepressant medication or ECT involves a number of disadvantages, clinicians have sought a therapeutic approach to depression to either supplement or replace medical treatment. A variety of psychological forms of treatment have been used—psychoanalysis, interpersonal therapies, and family therapies—all with some success (Hirschfeld & Shea, 1985). The most promising replacement is cognitive-behavioral therapy (Kovacs et al., 1981; Williams, 1984). (See the First Person narrative for one therapist's experience with a client.)

As its name implies, cognitive-behavioral therapy combines cognitive and behavioral strategies. The cognitive component involves teaching the patient (1) to identify negative, self-critical thoughts (cognitions) that occur automatically; (2) to note the connection between negative thoughts and the resulting depression; (3) to carefully examine each negative thought and decide whether it can be supported; and (4) to try to replace distorted negative thoughts with realistic interpretations of each situation (Beck et al., 1979). Cognitive therapists believe that distorted thoughts cause psychological problems such as depression and that changing the distorted thoughts can eliminate the depression.

I Am Suffering from Depression

I honestly felt subhuman, lower than the lowest vermin. Furthermore, I was self-deprecatory and could not understand why anyone would want to associate with me, let alone love me. . . . I was also positive that I was going to be fired from the university because of incompetence and that we could become destitute—that we would go broke. . . . I was positive that I was a fraud and phoney and that I didn't deserve my Ph.D. I didn't deserve to have tenure; I didn't deserve to be a full professor; I didn't deserve to be chairman of the psychology department. . . . I couldn't understand how I had written the books and journal articles that I had and how they had been accepted for publication. (Endler, 1982, pp. 45–48)

So wrote Dr. Norman Endler, a prominent psychologist, stable family man, and chairman of the psychology department at York University. In a poignant and very explicit book, Endler described his experiences with a bipolar disorder and his reactions to treatment.

Until the spring of 1977, Endler felt fine. He was at the height of his successful career. He was active in sports and was constantly on the move. In retrospect, Endler had realized that he was hypomanic in the fall of 1976, but not until the following April did he become aware that something was wrong. He had difficulty sleeping and had lost his sex drive. "I had gone from being a winner to feeling like a loser. Depression had turned it around for me. From being on top of the world in the fall, I suddenly felt useless, inept, sad, and anxious in the spring" (p. 11).

Endler sought treatment and was administered several drugs that did not prove effective. He was then given electroconvulsive therapy (ECT). Endler described his reaction to ECT as well as how the treatment was administered.

I was asked to lie down on a cot and was wheeled into the ECT room proper. It was about eight o'clock. A needle was injected into my arm and I was told to count back from 100. I got about as far as 91. The next thing I knew I was in the recov-

---

Patient: Not being loved leads automatically to unhappiness.

Therapist: Not being loved is a "nonevent." How can a nonevent lead automatically to something?

Patient: I just don't believe anyone could be happy without being loved.

Therapist: This is your belief. If you believe something, this belief will dictate your emotional reactions.

Patient: I don't understand that.

Therapist: If you believe something, you're going to act and feel as though it were true, whether it is or not.

Patient: You mean if I believe I'll be unhappy without love, it's only my belief causing my unhappiness?

Therapist: And when you feel unhappy, you probably say to yourself, "See, I was right. If I don't have love, I am bound to be unhappy."

Patient: How can I get out of this trap?

Therapist: You could experiment with your belief about having to be loved. Force yourself to suspend this belief and see what happens. Pay attention to the natural consequences of not being loved, not to the consequences created by your belief. For example, can you picture yourself on a tropical island with all the delicious fruits and other food available?

Patient: Yes, it looks pretty good.

Therapist: Now imagine that there are primitive people on the island. They are friendly and helpful, but they do not love you. None of them loves you.

Patient: I can picture that.

Therapist: How do you feel in your fantasy?

Patient: Relaxed and comfortable.

Therapist: So you can see that it does not necessarily follow that if you aren't loved, you will be unhappy. (Beck et al., 1979, p. 260)

At the outset of the cognitive therapy, the client is usually asked to begin monitoring his or her negative thoughts and listing them on a chart. It is important for the client to include all the thoughts and emotions that are associated with each distressing event that takes place each day (see Figure 12.1).

ery room and it was about eight-fifteen. I was slightly groggy and tired but not confused. (Endler, 1982, p. 81)

After about seven ECT sessions, his depression lifted dramatically: "My holiday of darkness was over and fall arrived with a bang!" (p. 83).

The next few months were free of depression, and Endler enjoyed everything he did. Later, he realized that he was actually hypomanic during this period also. He was a bit euphoric, energetic, and active; he talked incessantly. Then depression struck again. He recognized that he was experiencing the initial signs of depression and again underwent drug treatment and ECT. This time, however, the treatments were ineffective. Slowly, over the course of about two years, his depression dissipated with the aid of medication.

Endler concludes by offering some advice. First, when people think they are depressed, they should seek treatment immediately. Second, some combinations of treatments such as psychotherapy, antidepressant drugs, and ECT may be effective. Third, the depressive's family can have an important effect on recovery: when a family member becomes severely depressed, existing family conflicts may become exacerbated. A supportive and understanding family can help the depressive survive.

Depression is a common pervasive illness affecting all social classes, but it is eminently treatable. A great deal of heartbreak can be avoided by early detection and treatment. There is nothing to be ashamed of. There is no stigma attached to having an affective disorder. It is unwise to try to hide it and not seek help. I lived to tell and to write about it.

As of this writing . . . I have been symptom-free for almost three years. . . . I am not experiencing an emotional crisis and I hope I never do again. . . . I am reminded of a telephone conversation I had with my wife. . . . I mentioned that I had to do a lot of work to finish the first draft of Chapter 12, the last chapter in this book, before I left Stanford at the end of the month. Beatty said to me, "What's so terrible if you don't finish?" That put it all in perspective for me. I intend to live life to the fullest, but carefully. The sun will rise and shine whether or not I finish things today. But it's nice knowing that I did finish the first draft of this book before I left Stanford! (Endler, 1982, pp. 167–169)

Source: Endler, 1982.

The client brings the chart to the session each week, and the therapist uses it to demonstrate that the client's distress is being caused by his or her own unnecessarily negative thoughts. The client's own rational alternatives to these thoughts are discussed, and the client makes a conscious effort to adopt those alternatives that seem plausible. The goal of the cognitive part of the therapy is to train the client to automatically substitute logical interpretations for self-denigrating thoughts. Cognitive therapists maintain that when a patient's thoughts about himself or herself become more consistently positive, the emotions follow suit.

The second part of the cognitive-behavioral approach is behavior therapy, which is usually indicated in cases of severe depression in which the patient is virtually inactive. One primary assumption underlying this approach is that a depressed person is not doing enough pleasant, rewarding activities. Depressed people tend to withdraw from others when they belittle themselves; then they interpret their self-imposed social isolation as a sign of their being unpopular and inadequate (Lewinsohn, 1977).

To address this problem, depressed patients are asked to keep a daily activity schedule on which they list life events hour by hour and rate the "pleasantness" of each event. When a person is asked to monitor and rate events or activities, activities generally increase in frequency. This in itself is a worthwhile strategy for severely depressed patients; simply getting depressed people to engage in more activities increases the chance that they will become involved in some pleasant, reinforcing events. The patient's chart of this information also helps the therapist spot specific patterns. For instance, a client who insists that he or she does not enjoy anything may rate as "slightly pleasant" time spent outdoors. The therapist would point out this pattern and encourage the client to spend more time outdoors (Beck et al., 1979).

FIRST PERSON

Christopher Martell

As a cognitive-behavioral therapist, I look at how people's thought processes and behaviors contribute to mood disorders and help them to change these patterns of thinking and behaving to better cope with life. And, as a psychologist who works with persons whose sexual orientation is other than heterosexual, I must always take into account external stressors that affect my clients with mood disorders.

In my practice with adults in a city that encourages diversity, gay and lesbian persons (terms more accepted by these communities than "homosexual") seek psychotherapy for the same types of life issues as heterosexual people do. They are concerned with job stress, career choices, needs for intimacy, difficulty with relationships, childrearing issues, and especially with the AIDS epidemic bearing hard on the gay male community, death and dying issues.

Yet, because gay and lesbian people who have "come out" or openly acknowledged their orientation often face homophobia (the irrational fear of homosexuality) and heterosexism (the belief that heterosexuality is the only legitimate sexual orientation) throughout their lives, the social stigma associated with membership in a sexual minority complicates many life situations and psychological conditions that would be difficult to deal with even without such stigmatization. For those who already have a predisposition to a mood disorder (major depression, generalized anxiety disorder, and so forth), these societal pressures or real traumas make it harder to treat the basic psychological problem.

Joshua*, age 37, presented with

_____
* Joshua is a fictional character drawn from a composite of a number of clients I've seen.

complaints of depression and anxiety. He demonstrated all the symptoms of a major depressive episode—loss of pleasure in most activities, a decrease in sexual desire, difficulty sleeping, loss of appetite, fatigue, and blue mood. Because Joshua had also been diagnosed with AIDS, though, it was difficult at first to identify the depression as a separate condition. His fatigue and other depressive symptoms are also symptomatic of complications due to AIDS.

Joshua's recent history gave some insight into his depressed state, however. He had decided that he needed to cut back his work hours because of his illness, yet because his illness implied that he was gay he had waited longer than he may have otherwise to inform his employer of the situation. His hesitance was not unusual, given the frequent intolerance and prejudice that exists in the workplace. Joshua wanted to protect his dignity and his job. When he finally decided to approach his supervisor about his illness, he was met with a shocked reaction. Although his supervisor told him that the firm would support him in any way it could, Joshua

---

Once the severely depressed client becomes more active, he or she may be asked to attend a social skills training program. Improvements in social skills generally help clients become more socially involved and can make that involvement rewarding (Hersen, Bellack & Himmelhoch, 1980).

Cognitive-behavioral therapy seems very promising as a plausible treatment for depression (Kovacs, 1980; Williams, 1984). Hollon, DeRubeis, and Seligman (1992) even found that cognitive therapy may reduce the risk of depression episodes that occur after treatment. Depressed clients treated by cognitive therapy were less likely to develop subsequent symp-

toms of depression compared with those treated pharmacologically. Cognitive changes in explanatory styles and attributions among the clients in cognitive therapy may help prevent depressive symptoms. Some attempts have been made to combine both cognitive or cognitive-behavioral therapy with antidepressant medication. Early findings on such a treatment package have been positive (Goodwin & Guze, 1984; Roth et al., 1982; Wilson, 1982). Later research has questioned whether the combination is superior to using only one—cognitive therapy or antidepressant medication. A recent review of research has indicated that cognitive therapy is as effective as

soon began to notice that important assignments and accounts were being taken away from him. His request for a decrease in hours was becoming a loss of his job altogether. He had taken great pride in his work, had been a stellar employee, and was commended frequently by his superiors. Although it is hard to say that the response from his boss would have been different if Joshua had been heterosexual and suffering from leukemia, his belief that he was facing discrimination due to his sexual orientation and health status contributed to his depression.

Our therapy focused on his perception of being helpless, his need to confront his employer, and his very real concerns about his illness. As a cognitive therapist, I helped him see where he was distorting reality in a way that made his dysphoria greater. This was no easy task, as he was facing life situations that were truly frightening and traumatic. Joshua felt hopeless—a common aspect of depression. By helping him take control of confronting his employer, encouraging him to read about treatments for his illness, and to develop a plan for daily activities that would keep him from

slumping into lethargy, I began the behavioral task of breaking patterns of learned helplessness. We also discussed his beliefs that he was responsible for being sick; that life could have no meaning or joy because of his illness; and I helped him to disprove these notions.

Although it was very difficult for him to overcome his depression completely, he was better able to cope and we both felt the therapy was successful. We needed to be aware of our parameters, though: Joshua was not only dealing with depression or fears about his illness, but also with other peoples' fears and prejudice, his internalized homophobia, and multiple losses of friends and loved ones to AIDS.

All therapists need to be sensitive to cultural differences, and the gay and lesbian community is distinct from the heterosexual community socio-culturally as well as according to choice of sexual partners. It is as diverse as the heterosexual community. My clients' sexual orientations, for example, feel very normal to them. In terms of stress, however, they may be plagued by learned belief systems that challenge their comfort with their orientation or

decision to live according to that orientation.

Those of us who are gay or lesbian professionals and who work with this population of individuals can only do our small part to change society. We do, however, have an obligation to make sure that the issue of sexual orientation does not obscure the other issues that gay, lesbian, and bisexual persons face. All therapists are responsible for seeing that social and environmental pressures are accounted for in treatment strategies for mood disorders and other psychological problems.

Christopher Martell is a clinical and school psychologist in private practice in Seattle, WA. His clinical practice focuses primarily on psychotherapeutic interventions with individuals coping with disabilities or chronic illness, depression and anxiety disorders. He has worked extensively with the gay and lesbian community and is co-chair of the Committee on Lesbian and Gay Concerns for the Washington State Psychological Association.

using medication and that using both is not superior to using either form of treatment for patients with acute unipolar disorder (Hollon, Shelton & Loosen, 1991). Obviously, more research is needed to clarify the reasons for the discrepancy in findings. (See Critical Thinking for a discussion of the problems involved in evaluating the outcome of treatment.)

Biomedical Treatment for Bipolar Disorders

For bipolar disorders, drugs (especially lithium) are typically used together with psychosocial treatments.

Since it was introduced to the United States in 1969, lithium (in the form of lithium carbonate) has been the treatment of choice for bipolar and manic disorders (Fieve et al., 1976). It is also used as a maintenance drug to prevent or reduce future episodes of bipolar disorder (National Institute of Mental Health, 1985). As noted, the manic phase of bipolar disorder may be caused by too much neurotransmitter (primarily norepinephrine) at brain synapses or by neurotransmitter dysfunction. Lithium decreases the total level of neurotransmitters in the synaptic areas by increasing the re-uptake of norepinephrine into the nerve cells (Barchas et al., 1977).

How Are Treatment Outcomes Evaluated?

In general, various forms of treatment have been moderately effective in depression (Beckham, 1990). Nevertheless, drawing firm conclusions about treatment outcomes or about the relative advantage of one treatment over another has been difficult for a variety of reasons. Studies may differ in the measures used to assess treatment outcomes, in the kinds of individuals being studied, in the treatments provided, and in the attempts to control alternative explanations. Let us pose some questions and discuss some common problems involved in outcome research.

What measures should be used to assess treatment outcomes? The type of outcome measure used in studies has varied considerably. Researchers have used client self-reports, therapists' ratings, behavioral and symptom measures, and psychophysiological measures. Different measures may yield different results. For example, in the text we mentioned that Greenberg and colleagues (1992) found that therapists and clients differed on their evaluations of treatment, and that therapists were more likely than clients to rate treatment as having a favorable outcome. In general, multiple measures (such as therapists and client ratings, behavioral observations, psychophysiological measures) should be used whenever possible. Why might this be?

How should subjects for studies be selected? Studies differ in the kind of subjects being studied. The purpose of the study usually guides the selection of subjects. Sometimes, nonclients (students, community respondents, and so on) are used to investigate how moods or behaviors vary as a function of intervention. High-risk groups—for example, people exposed to major traumas or children of de-

FIGURE 12.1 Daily Cognition Chart for a Typical Depressive Client

Date	Situation	Automatic Thoughts	Emotions	Rational Alternative	Emotion
2/9	I sat home all alone on a Fri. night.	Nobody likes me or I would have been asked out.	Depressed	Most people know that I usually work Fri. nights. Maybe nobody knew I had the night off.	Relief, contentment
2/10	I had trouble understanding my reading assignment.	I must be an idiot. This should be an easy subject.	Depressed, anxious.	If I don't understand the material, I bet a number of others don't either.	Calm, determined

pressed parents—may be studied. Research on depression has most often used depressed clients. The type of depressed client may vary from study to study. What do you think might contribute to this variability? (Think back to Chapter 5, which deals with the scientific method. Then recall that earlier in this chapter, we noted that treatment outcomes differ for personality dimensions of sociotropy and autonomy. If some researchers unwittingly have many clients with one type of personality and other researchers unwittingly include clients with a different type of personality, outcomes from using the same treatment may vary not because of treatment but because of client-personality variables that go unnoticed. Other possible confounding variables include demographic characteristics, prior treatment experience, and willingness to participate in studies.) Researchers have increasingly attempted to de-

scribe their subjects in detail and to identify individual difference variables that may moderate or mediate the relationship between treatment and outcome. Specifying subject characteristics is also important in determining the external validity or generality of findings. For example, if one type of treatment is effective for depressed elderly women, we cannot assume that the treatment will be beneficial for depressed young men.

What kinds of problems occur in treatment? Treatment interventions may not be equivalent across studies. For example, some cognitive therapists may practice therapy strictly within cognitive therapy principles; others may be more "eclectic" and adopt noncognitive therapeutic techniques. Therapists in different studies may differ in experience and expertise. In psychopharmacology research, dosage levels for antidepressant medication may differ from study to study

or some studies may use other drugs in addition to the antidepressant medication being studied. How can researchers make sure that their results are presented so that others can use them to judge equivalence of interventions across studies?

How can we be sure that the outcomes are due to treatment? This is a question that has to do with internal validity, or the extent to which outcomes are actually caused by the specific treatment. Can you think of examples in which clients improve for reasons other than the treatment? What methods can be used to maximize the internal validity of the treatment study?

Given all of these considerations, it is not surprising that treatment outcome research must be viewed as a continuing enterprise in which researchers must conduct a large number of studies and develop increasingly sophisticated research designs.

The generally positive results achieved with lithium have been overshadowed somewhat by reports of distressing side effects (Dubovsky et al., 1982). The earliest danger signals are gastrointestinal complications (such as vomiting and diarrhea), fine tremors, muscular weakness, and frequent urination. The more serious side effects, associated with excessive lithium in the blood, are loss of bladder control, slurred speech, blurred vision, seizures, and abnormal heart rate. Fortunately, accurate measurements of lithium blood levels are easily obtained, and dosages can be adjusted accordingly.

Another problem associated with lithium is lack of patient compliance with the treatment program. For some reason, this problem is consistently worse with bipolar patients taking lithium than with any other group of patients taking any other drug. Bipolar patients often report that they have tried to adjust their lithium dosage by themselves so that they will experience the mania but not the depression of bipolar disorder. Unfortunately, lithium levels cannot be manipulated in this manner. When the dosage is de-

creased, the initial slightly manic state quickly develops into either a severe manic state or depression.

SUMMARY

1. Severe depression is a major component of the mood disorders; it involves affective, cognitive, behavioral, and physiological symptoms. Mania, which may accompany depression in these disorders, is characterized by elation, grandiosity, irritability, and almost boundless energy.

2. In bipolar mood disorders, manic episodes occur or alternate with depressive episodes. Depressive disorders (major depression and dysthymic disorder) involve only depression. Psychotic and other features may also appear in persons with severe mood disorders. The depressive disorders are the most common mood disorders; some evidence suggests that they are distinct from the bipolar disorders.

3. Sociocultural explanations have focused on cultural factors that influence the rates and symptoms

of mood disorders and the role of stress and of social supports. Even though stress often precipitates the occurrence of depression, some people may be more vulnerable to depression because of their greater vulnerability (perhaps because of biogenic or psychosocial factors). Furthermore, social supports may provide a buffer against depression. Sociocultural factors have also been used to explain the higher observed rates of depression among women. They include gender role differences that make women more likely than men to amplify depressive symptoms.

4. Psychological theories of depression have been proposed by adherents of the psychoanalytic, cognitive, and behavioral viewpoints, but each has certain weaknesses. According to the learned helplessness theory of depression, susceptibility to depression depends on the person's experience with controlling the environment. Genetic and biochemical research has demonstrated that heredity plays a role in depression and mania, probably by affecting neurotransmitter levels in the brain.

5. Biomedical approaches to treating depression focus on increasing the amounts of neurotransmitters available at brain synapses or by affecting the sensitivity of postsynaptic receptors through either medication or electroconvulsive therapy. A cognitive-behavioral treatment for depression seeks to replace negative thoughts with more realistic (or positive) cognitions. The most effective treatment for bipolar disorders is lithium, a drug that lowers the level of synaptic neurotransmitters.

KEY TERMS

bipolar disorder A major mood disorder in which both depression and mania are exhibited, or one in which only mania has been exhibited

cyclothymia A mild and chronic mood disorder characterized by nonpsychotic mood swings

depression An emotional state characterized by intense dysphoria, sadness, feelings of futility and worthlessness, and withdrawal from others

dysthymic disorder A mild and chronic mood disorder characterized by nonpsychotic depression

learned helplessness Acquiring the belief that one is helpless and cannot affect outcomes in one's life

mania An emotional state characterized by great elation, seemingly boundless energy, and irritability

mood disorders Severe disturbances of mood or affect that cause subjective discomfort, hinder a person's ability to function, or both; mood disorders involve depression, mania, or both

neurotransmitters Substances that contribute to the transmission of nerve impulses from one neuron to another

schema A pattern of thinking or a cognitive set that determines (or colors) an individual's reactions and responses

unipolar disorder A major mood disorder in which no mania has been exhibited, only depression

CHAPTER 13

Suicide

Late one evening Carl Johnson, M.D., left his downtown office, got into his Mercedes 500 SL, and drove toward his expensive suburban home. He was in no particular hurry because the house would be empty anyway; the year before, his wife had divorced him and with their two children had moved back east to her parents' home. Carl was deeply affected. Although he had been drinking heavily for two years before the divorce, he had always been able to function vocationally. For the past several months, however, his private practice had declined dramatically. He used to find his work rewarding, but now he found people boring and irritating. The future looked bleak and hopeless. Carl knew he had all the classic symptoms of depression—he was, after all, a psychiatrist. The garage door opened automatically as he rolled up the driveway. Carl parked carelessly, not even bothering to press the switch that closed the door. Once in the house, he headed directly for the bar in his den; there he got out a bottle of bourbon and three glasses, filled the glasses, and lined them up along the bar. He drank them down, one after the other, in rapid succession. For a good half hour, he stood at the window staring out into the night. Then Carl sat down at his mahogany desk and unlocked one of the drawers. Taking a loaded .38 caliber revolver from the desk drawer, Dr. Carl Johnson held it to his temple and fired.

Possible reasons for suicide: Recent divorce; loss of family life and subsequent depression.

Fifteen-year-old Eric Fadeley was an outstanding athlete in many sports, a top baseball player on both his Little League and high school teams, and a 3.8 grade-point-average student. In September 1992, he killed himself, in his bedroom, with a family handgun. At the funeral his father stated, "Through this whole thing, the main question to ask is 'Why?' Nobody will ever know for sure." The suicide was even more baffling because Eric had just pitched his team to victory at the Little League Senior Division U.S. championship, was honored the night before by the California Angels at an event called "Night of Champions," had expressed interest in playing for Michigan State and eventually turning pro, and was seen by classmates as tender, kind, and caring. This youngster, who appeared to have everything, revealed in a suicide note that he felt ugly and bad, and felt the intense burden of "making the grade." His mother said that Eric was a perfectionist in everything he did. His sister stated that Eric perhaps could not live up to his own standards.

Possible reasons for suicide: Could not live up to own high standards; felt pressured to excel; felt a failure.

In December 1983, Jenny Williams, a 62-year-old housewife, suffered a severe stroke that resulted in crippling paralysis, loss of speech, and an inability to control her basic eliminative functions. Although she had the full support of her husband, two sons, and a daughter, Mrs. Williams was distressed at having to rely on basic life support machinery. Although she couldn't speak, it was clear to her family that she didn't want to live this way and also didn't want to be a burden to others. Over several weeks Mrs. Williams's condition improved moderately, until she could move about, with great effort. But she still could not speak or attend to her own needs. She was discharged from the hospital and cared for at home by a part-time nurse and her devoted husband. Two weeks after her discharge, Mrs. Williams took her own life by swallowing a bottle of sleeping pills. Mr. Williams knew of his wife's intention, but he did nothing to prevent her suicide. He didn't have the heart to go against her wishes.

Possible reasons for suicide: Perceived that quality of life was poor; did not want to be a burden on others.

Ten-year-old Tammy Jimenez was the youngest of three children—a loner who had attempted suicide at least twice in the past two years. Tammy's parents always seemed to be bickering about one thing or another and threatening divorce. She and her sisters were constantly abused by their alcoholic father. Finally, in February 1986, Tammy was struck and killed by a truck when she darted out into the highway that passed by her home. The incident was listed as an accident, but her older sister said Tammy had deliberately killed herself. On the morning of her death, an argument with her father had upset and angered her. Her sister said that, seconds before Tammy ran out onto the highway, she had said that she was unwanted and would end her own life.

Possible reasons for suicide: Unhappy family life; child abuse; felt unwanted and unloved.

On October 23, 1983, a lone man in a truck containing six tons of explosives drove up to the U.S. Ma-

rine barracks in Beirut, Lebanon. The man, believed to be a Shi'ite Muslim terrorist, did not pause when Marine guards signaled him to stop. Instead he drove on through the entrance barricades and set off a blast that killed himself and 240 American soldiers.

Possible reason for suicide: Belief in killing oneself for a greater good or cause.

Not only is **suicide**—or the taking of one's own life—a tragic act, but it is a baffling and confusing one as well. Although we have provided reasons for why we believe that these individuals killed themselves, we can never be entirely certain. Why do people knowingly and deliberately end their own lives? The easy and most frequent explanation is that people who kill themselves are suffering from a mental disorder. For example, suicide is usually discussed in conjunction with mood disorders in most abnormal psychology texts. Yet our increasing understanding of suicide suggests that a single unitary explanation is simplistic. Suicide has many causes, and people kill themselves for many different reasons.

We have chosen to include a separate chapter on suicide for several reasons. First, although suicide is not classified as a mental disorder in DSM-IV, the suicidal person usually has clear psychiatric symptoms. Many persons who suffer from depression, alcohol dependence, and schizophrenia exhibit suicidal ideation or behavior. Yet suicide does not fall neatly into one of the recognized psychiatric disorders. There is evidence that suicide and suicide ideation may represent a separate clinical entity. Few, for example, would argue that it is not an important domain of the study of abnormal psychology. Second, interest in the topic of suicide is increasing, and it appears to deserve study in its own right. Throughout history, suicide has remained a hidden and mysterious act. People have traditionally avoided discussing it and have participated in a "conspiracy of silence" because of the societal shame and stigma involved in taking one's life. Mental health professionals as well have often found the topic an uncomfortable and personally disturbing one. Often abnormal psychology texts handle the topic of suicide in a small section along with mood disorders. Over the past several decades, we have learned much about suicide. Third, we are witnessing increased openness in discussing issues of death and dying, the meaning of suicide, and the right to take one's own life. Some prominent individuals have even gone so far as to advocate "the right to suicide." Last, we need to recognize that suicide is an irreversible act. There is no going back, no reconsideration of the action, and no reprieve.

Regardless of the moral stand one takes on this position, the decision to commit suicide is often an ambivalent one, clouded by many personal and social stressors. Many mental health professionals believe that the suicidal person, if taught how to deal with personal and social crisis, would not consciously take his or her own life. As a result, understanding the causes of suicide and what can be done to prevent such an act becomes extremely important to psychologists.

PROBLEMS IN THE STUDY OF SUICIDE

Someone once stated that "much is known about the facts surrounding suicide, but little about it is understood." Understanding why people commit suicide has haunted us for centuries. Although many of us freely offer explanations like those given in the chapter-opening cases, we can never know for sure the validity of our answers. These questions are difficult for two important reasons.

First, we can no longer ask people who commit suicide—who complete their suicide attempts—about their motives, frame of mind, and emotional state. We have only indirect information such as case records and reports by others to help us understand what led them to their tragic act. The systematic examination of such information, to understand and explain someone's behavior before his or her death, is called a **psychological autopsy** (Robbins & Kulbok, 1988; Shneidman, Farberow & Litman, 1970); a *medical autopsy* is an examination of a dead body to determine the cause or nature of the biological death. The psychological autopsy is patterned after the medical autopsy; it seeks to make psychological sense of a suicide or homicide. Case histories of victims, recollections of therapists, interviews with relatives and friends, information obtained from crisis phone calls, and suicide notes are compiled and analyzed in an attempt to uncover some underlying explanation for the act. Unfortunately, these sources are not always available or reliable. Only approximately 15 percent of victims leave suicide notes (Shneidman, 1979), many have never undergone psy-chotherapy (Fleer & Pasewark, 1982), and explanations from relatives or friends are often distorted because of the emotional impact caused by a loved one's death. Despite these weaknesses, the psychological autopsy continues to be used because it not only represents one of the few avenues open to us, but it has broader purposes as well. If psychologists can isolate the events and circumstances that lead to suicide and can identify the characteristics of potential suicide victims, they may be able to prevent other people from performing this irreversible act.

Another reason why we do not clearly understand suicide is that no single explanation is sufficient to account for all types of suicide. The examples given at the beginning of this chapter show the diversity of life situations that may result in suicide. Common sense alone should lead you to the conclusion that Jenny Williams's reasons for taking her own life differ from those of the terrorist, Eric Fadeley, or Tammy Jimenez. In seeking to understand suicide, researchers have focused on events, characteristics, and demographic variables that recur in psychological autopsies and are highly correlated with the act. Our first example, Dr. Carl Johnson, fits a particular profile. Higher suicide rates are associated with divorce (National Center for Health Statistics, 1988) and with certain professions (psychiatry in particular), alcohol is frequently implicated (Rogers, 1992), and men are more likely to kill themselves using firearms than by other means (Kranczer, 1986; NCHS, 1988). Focus 13.1 presents other research results. But the factors that are probably most closely linked with suicide are hopelessness and depression.

HOPELESSNESS, DEPRESSION, AND SUICIDE

Although it is dangerous to assume that depression causes suicide, a number of studies have indicated that the two are very highly correlated (McGuire, 1982; Shneidman, 1991). For example, researchers found that suicide wishes occurred in 74 percent of a group of severely depressed people, compared to only 12 percent in a nondepressed group (Beck, 1967). Of course, a suicide wish is very different from a suicide attempt; yet in another study, 80 percent of the patients admitted to a general hospital because of a suicide attempt were found to be depressed at the time of initial observation (Silver et al., 1971).

Some Facts About Suicide

1. Every 20 to 30 minutes, some-one in the United States takes his or her own life. More than 30,000 persons kill themselves each year. Suicide is among the top ten causes of death in the industrialized parts of the world; it is the second or third leading cause of death among young people. Some evidence shows that the number of actual suicides is probably 25 to 30 percent higher than that recorded. Many deaths that are officially recorded as accidental, such as single-auto crashes, drownings, or falls from great heights, are actually suicides. According to some estimates, for every person who completes a suicide, eight to ten persons make the attempt.

2. Recent reports have suggested that about 12,000 children aged five to fourteen are admitted to psychiatric hospitals for suicidal behavior

every year, and it is believed that twenty times as many actually try. Suicides among young people aged fifteen to twenty-four have increased by more than 40 percent in the past decade (50 percent for males and 12 percent for females); suicide is now the second leading cause of death for this group.

3. Suicide is the second or third leading cause of death among college students (more than 10,000 attempt it and more than 1000 succeed). The suicide rate for college students is twice as high as that for people not in college. One in five students possess suicidal thoughts sometime during their college career.

4. The completed suicide rate for men is about three times that for women (although recent findings suggest that many more women are now incurring a higher risk); among

the elderly, the rate for men is ten times that for women. However, women attempt suicide three times as often as men. The elderly, those older than 65 years of age, have the highest suicide rate of any age group, but men continue to lead in deaths.

5. In terms of marital status, the lowest incidence of suicide is found among people who are married, and the highest among those who are divorced. The suicide rates for single and widowed or divorced men are about twice those for women of similar marital status.

6. Physicians, lawyers, and dentists have higher than average rates of suicide. Among medical professionals, psychiatrists have the highest rate and pediatricians the lowest. Such marked differences raise the question of whether the specialty influences susceptibility or whether

And, again, a study of successful suicides by mental patients in Massachusetts showed that the suicide rate for depressives was thirty-six times higher than that for the general population (Temoche et al., 1964). More recent findings have continued to support these statistics (Hawton, 1987). Retrospective studies have also revealed that 80 percent of patients who committed suicide were depressed before they did so (Barraclough et al., 1969). Among children and adolescents as well, depression seems to be highly correlated with suicidal behavior (Garland & Zigler, 1993; Kosky, 1983; Rosenthal & Rosenthal, 1984).

Such data can lead to the conclusion that depression plays an important role in suicide. Yet other studies have indicated that this role is far from simple. For example, evidence has shown that patients

seldom commit suicide while severely depressed (Mendels, 1970). Such patients generally show motor retardation and low energy, which keep them from reaching the level of activity required for suicide. The danger period often comes after some treatment, when the depression begins to lift. Energy and motivation increase, and patients are more likely to carry out the act. Most suicide attempts occur during weekend furloughs from hospitals or soon after discharge, a fact that supports this contention (Wheat, 1960). The risk of suicide seems to be only about 1 percent during the year in which a depressive episode occurs, but it is about 15 percent in subsequent years (Klerman, 1982).

Although depression is undeniably correlated with suicidal thoughts and behavior, the relationship seems very complex. For example, why do some de-

suicide-prone people choose certain specialties.

7. Suicide is represented proportionately among all socioeconomic levels. Level of wealth does not seem to affect the suicide rate as much as do changes in that level. In the Great Depression of the 1930s, suicide was higher among the suddenly impoverished than among those who had always been poor.

8. Men most frequently choose firearms as the means of suicide; poisoning and asphyxiation via barbiturates are the preferred means for women. The violent means (which men are more likely to choose) are more certain to complete the act; this partially explains the disproportionately greater number of incomplete attempts by women. Recent studies, however, have indicated that women are increasingly choosing firearms and explosives as methods (55.9 percent increase). Some have speculated that this change may be related to a change in role definitions of women in society.

Among children younger than fifteen years, the most common suicide method tends to be jumping from buildings and running into traffic. Older children try hanging or drug overdoses. Younger children attempt suicide impulsively and thus use more readily available means.

9. Religious affiliation is correlated with suicide rates. Although the U.S. rate is 12.2 per 100,000, in countries where Catholic Church influences are strong—Latin America, Ireland, Spain, Italy—the suicide rate is relatively low (less than 10 per 100,000). Islam, too, condemns suicide, and the suicide rates in Arab countries are correspondingly low. Where church authority is weaker—as, for example, in Scandinavian countries, in Czechoslovakia, and in Hungary—higher rates are observed. Indeed, Hungary has the highest rate, 40.7 per 100,000, and Czechoslovakia has a rate of 22.4 per 100,000.

10. Suicide rates tend to decline during wars and natural disasters but increase during periods of shifting norms and values or social unrest, when traditional expectations no longer apply. Sociologists speculate that during wars, people "pull together" and are less concerned with their own difficulties.

11. More than two-thirds of the people who commit suicide communicate their intent to do so within three months of the fatal act. (The belief that people who threaten suicide are not serious about it, or will not actually make such an attempt, is ill-founded.) Most people who attempt suicide appear to have been ambivalent about death until the suicide. It has been estimated that fewer than 5 percent unequivocally wish to end their lives.

Sources: Berman & Jobes, 1991; Bongar, 1991; De Calazaro, 1981; Diekstra, 1990; Dublin, 1963; Kosky, 1983; McIntosh, 1991; Rogers, 1990; Rosenthal & Rosenthal, 1984; Shneidman, 1976; Shneidman, Farberow & Litman, 1970; U.S. Bureau of the Census, 1987; Wexler, Weissman & Kasl, 1978.

---

pressed people commit suicide while others do not? The answer may be found in the characteristics of depression and in the factors that contribute to it.

Beck, Emery, and Greenberg (1985) believe that hopelessness, or negative expectations about the future, may be the major catalyst in suicide and could be an even more important factor than depression. Beck conducted a ten-year study of 207 psychiatric patients who expressed suicidal thoughts but had no recent history of suicidal attempts. Within seventy-two hours after hospital admission, each patient was measured on three variables: hopelessness, depression, and **suicidal ideation** (thoughts about suicide). During the ten-year period, fourteen patients committed suicide, and the test scores of these people were compared with the others. The suicides did not differ from those who did not attempt suicide in terms of depression and suicidal ideation. But they did differ in terms of hopelessness. Those who died were more pessimistic about the future than those who survived. The analysis of the depression measure lent even greater support to the notion that hopelessness may be the greatest predictor of suicide. Although the overall results obtained by the scale did not predict suicidal risk, the hopelessness item within the measure did. These findings suggested that therapists should assess all depressed patients' attitudes toward their future to determine how hopeless they feel about it. Beck's work on suicide has resulted in the development of a number of depression and suicidality scales: Beck Depression Inventory (Beck et al., 1961), the Scale for Suicide Ideation (Beck, Kovacs & Weissman, 1979), the Suicide Intent Scale (Beck, Schuyler & Herman, 1974), and the Hope-

While depression is often correlated with suicide, it appears that hopelessness is a more powerful factor. When the future looks bleak and pessimism dominates a person's mood, suicide is more likely to be attempted. Fortunately, the man in this photo was saved when paramedics and relatives convinced him not to jump off the bridge.

lessness Scale (Beck et al., 1974). These assessment instruments have been employed in numerous outcome studies and routinely used in a clinical setting for monitoring and treating patients.

OTHER PSYCHOLOGICAL FACTORS AND SUICIDE

Although not as strong as the findings associated with hopelessness and depression, many other psychological factors have been found to be correlated with suicide. Findings have consistently revealed that many individuals who commit suicide suffer from a DSM-IV disorder (Litman, 1987; Roy, 1985); also, approximately 15 percent of individuals diagnosed as suffering from mood disorders, schizophrenia, and

substance abuse attempt to kill themselves (Brent et al., 1987). A review of the literature on suicide also reveals that separation and divorce (Garfinkel & Golumbek, 1983), academic pressures (Seiden, 1969), shame (Shreve & Kunkel, 1991), serious illness (Mackenzie & Popkin, 1987), loss of a job, and other life stresses may be contributing factors.

One of the most consistently reported correlates of suicidal behavior is alcohol consumption (Glavin et al., 1990; Hirschfield & Davidson, 1989; Schuckit & Schuckit, 1990). Indeed, some have even stated that a successful suicide is rare in which alcohol abuse is not a factor (Hatton & Valente, 1984). Alcohol-implicated suicide rates may be as high as 270 per 100,000, which is an astounding 27 times the rate in the general population (Stillion, McDowell & May, 1989). Many theorists have traditionally argued that alcohol may lower inhibitions related to the fear of death and make it easier to carry out the fatal act (Patel et al., 1972). Recent formulations, however, have suggested a cognitive interpretation of the relationship between alcohol use and suicide. Rogers (1992) argued that the strength of the relationship between alcohol and suicide is the result of *alcohol-induced myopia* (a constriction of cognitive and perceptual processes). This line of reasoning relies heavily on the cognitive characteristics of people who attempt suicide: they are more rigid in their line of thinking, less flexible in problem solving, and more prone to dichotomous thinking (Linehan et al., 1987; Neuringer, 1964; Shneidman, 1987). They generally perceive solutions as all-or-none (life or death) and are myopically incapable of coming up with alternative solutions. Alcohol use by an individual in psychological conflict may increase rather than decrease his or her distress. Steele and Josephs (1990) found that alcohol constricts cognitive and perceptual processes. Although it may relieve depression and anxiety by constricting thought (distracting the person from the problem), it is equally probable that alcohol-induced myopia may intensify the conflict and distress by narrowing the person's focus on his or her problems. Thus the link between alcohol and suicide may be the result of the myopic qualities of alcohol exaggerating a previously existing constrictive state. If this is true, alcohol is most likely to increase the probability of a suicide in an already suicidal person. Rogers (1992) stated, "The most efficacious and ethically sound intervention in this area would be to pro-

Ernest Hemingway, one of the great authors of the twentieth century (*The Old Man and the Sea* and *The Sun Also Rises* are two of his better-known works) committed suicide in 1961 by shooting himself. Although he did not leave a suicide note, many believe this avid sportsman ended his life because of illness and physical decline.

mote abstinence by providing information to clients regarding the potential dangers involved in alcohol consumption" (p. 542).

THE DYNAMICS OF SUICIDE

Some clinicians believe that everyone, at one time or another, has wished to end his or her life. Fortunately, most of us do not act on such wishes, even during extreme distress. But why do some people do so? Because suicide is closely linked to hopelessness and depression, many theories of depression apply to suicide as well. But still the question is not easy to answer. We have already discussed how difficult it is

to study this phenomenon. We can never know for certain what causes a person to take his or her life. Yet on a very general level such people do seem to share a common motive: to gain relief from a life situation that is unbearable.

Sociocultural Explanations

Early explanations of suicide emphasized its relationship to various social factors. Rates of suicide have been found to vary with occupation, the size of one's city of residence, socioeconomic status, age, gender, marital status, and race. Higher rates are associated with high- and low-status (as opposed to middle-status) occupations, urban living, middle-aged men, single or divorced people, and the upper and lower socioeconomic classes (Hall et al., 1970; Weile, 1960). In a pioneering work, the French sociologist Emile Durkheim related differences in suicide rates to the impact of social forces on the person (Durkheim, [1897] 1951). He proposed three categories of suicide: egoistic, altruistic, and anomic.

Egoistic suicide results from an inability to integrate oneself with society. Failing to maintain close ties with the community deprives the person of the support systems that are necessary for adaptive functioning. Without such support, and unable to function adaptively, the person becomes isolated and alienated from other people (Slater & Depue, 1981).

Altruistic suicide is motivated by the person's desire to further group goals or to achieve some greater good. Someone may give up his or her life for a higher cause (in a religious sacrifice or the ultimate political protest, for example). Group pressures may make such an act highly acceptable and honored. During World War II, Japanese kamikaze pilots voluntarily dove their airplanes into enemy warships "for the Emperor and the glory of Japan." The self-immolation of Buddhist monks during the Vietnam War and the terrorist truck bombing of the Marine barracks in Lebanon (described at the beginning of this chapter) are likewise in this category.

Anomic suicide results when a person's relationship to society is unbalanced in some dramatic fashion. When a person's horizons are suddenly broadened or constricted by unstable conditions, he or she may not be able to handle the change or cope with the new status and may choose suicide as an "out." The suicides of people who lost their personal wealth

Suicide Notes

Suicide notes represent one source of data used in a psychological autopsy. We have already reviewed one frequently cited study (Tuckman, Kleiner & Lavell, 1959), which gave us insights into the emotional state of the suicide victim. Additional studies have found that females are more likely to leave notes than males; that separated or divorced women left more notes than those who were single; whites left three times more notes than nonwhites; and many of the notes expressed intense feelings of self-blame, hatred, and vengeance (Cohen & Fiedler, 1974; Farberow & Simon, 1975; Shneidman & Farberow, 1957). One may conclude

from these findings that note-writing behavior in suicides is correlated with certain demographic variables and that the act of writing is apparently an attempt to influence the responses of survivors.

One suggested classification scheme for suicides is based in part on information gleaned from these suicide notes (Shneidman, 1957, 1961). Here are some of the categories, with illustrative suicide notes.

The *egoistic* suicide is the result of an intrapsychic debate, a struggle within the victim's mind. The victim's inner torment may be philosophical or religious in nature. An example:

Mr. Brown:

. . . It seems unnecessary to present a lengthy defense for my suicide, for if I have to be judged, it will not be on this earth. However, in brief, I find myself a misfit. To me, life is too painful for the meager occasional pleasure to compensate. It all seems so pointless, the daily struggle leading where? Several times I have done what, in retrospect, is seen to amount to running away from circumstances. I could do so now—travel, find a new job, even change vocation, but why? It is Myself that I have been trying to escape, and this I can do

---

during the Great Depression or who killed themselves after being freed from concentration camps at the end of World War II are of this type. Similarly, a person who suddenly and unexpectedly acquires great wealth may be prone to suicide.

Psychosocial explanations may be valid to an extent, but attributing suicide to a single sociological factor (economic depression, residence, or occupation) is too simplistic and mechanistic. As we have often noted, correlations do not imply cause-and-effect relationships. Thus Durkheim's three categories are more descriptive than explanatory. Moreover, purely sociological explanations that take into account only one psychosocial factor—group cohesion, for example—omit the intrapsychic dimension of the person's struggles. They don't explain why only certain members of any of the aforementioned groups commit suicide, and others do not.

Intrapsychic Explanations

Early psychological explanations of suicide tended to ignore social factors in favor of intrapsychic ones. In

the classical Freudian approach, for example, self-destruction was seen as the result of hostility that is directed inward against the *introjected love object* (the loved one with whom the person has identified). That is, people who kill themselves are really directing anger and the suicidal act against others whom they have incorporated within themselves. If the angry feelings (death instinct) reach murderous proportions, a suicide attempt is the result.

Unfortunately, these ideas aren't supported by evidence. Carefully analyzed psychological autopsies indicate that hate and revenge are not the only reasons for suicide; people kill themselves for a number of other psychological reasons such as shame, guilt, hopelessness, and pain (Pine, 1981; Shneidman, 1991). An analysis of 165 suicide notes conducted over a 25-year period showed that only 24 percent of the suicides expressed hostile or negative feelings toward themselves, whereas 51 percent expressed positive attitudes and another 25 percent were neutral. The investigators concluded that there isn't enough support for believing that hostility is the only cause of suicide (Tuckman, Kleiner & Lavall, 1959).

only as I am about to do! Goodbye!

Bill Smith

The *dyadic* suicide is interpersonal in nature and is influenced primarily by unfulfilled wishes or needs involving a significant other. Frustration, rage, manipulation, and attempts to elicit guilt are common. For example:

Bill,

You have killed me. I hope you are happy in your heart, if you have one which I doubt. Please leave Rover with Mike. Also leave my baby alone. If you don't I'll haunt you the rest of your life and I mean it and I'll do it.
    You have been mean and also

cruel. God doesn't forget those things and don't forget that. And please no flowers; it won't mean anything. Also keep your money. I want to be buried in Potter's Field in the same casket with Betty. You can do that for me. That's the way we want it. . . .

The *ageneratic* suicide is characteristic of the person who has lost the sense of participating in the transgenerational flow of human life—of belonging to "the scheme of things." Alienation, disengagement, and isolation are involved; the feeling and sense are existential.

To the authorities:

Excuse my inability to express myself in English and the trouble caused. I beg you not to lose

time in an inquest upon my body. Just simply record and file it because the name and address given on the register are fictitious and I wanted to disappear anonymously. No one expects me here nor will be looking for me. I have informed my relatives in America. Please do not bury me! I wish to be cremated and the ashes tossed to the winds. In that way I shall return to the nothingness from which I have come into this sad world. This is all I ask of the Americans for all that I have intended to give them with my coming into this country.

Many thanks,

José Marcia

———

Source: Shneidman, 1968, pp. 5–8.

Biochemical Factors in Suicide

Neither a purely sociological nor a purely psychological perspective seems to adequately explain the causes of suicide. Probably both sociological and psychological factors are involved; Focus 13.2 discusses a classification scheme that includes both.

It is also likely that other factors are involved. For example, consistent with the strong evidence that chemical neurotransmitters are associated with depression and mania, similar evidence shows that suicide is influenced by biochemistry. This evidence was discovered in the mid-1970s, when researchers identified a chemical called *5-hydroxyindoleacetic acid (5HIAA)*; Asberg, Traskman & Thoren, 1976, 1990; Stanley & Mann, 1983; Van Praag, 1983). The spinal fluid of some depressed patients had been found to contain abnormally low amounts of 5HIAA, which is produced when serotonin, a neurotransmitter that affects mood and emotions, is broken down in the body. Moreover, some evidence exists that the serotonin receptors in the brainstem and frontal cortex may be impaired (Mann et al., 1986). Preliminary

statistics on patients with low levels of 5HIAA indicated that they are more likely than others to commit suicide, more likely to select violent methods of killing themselves, and more likely to have a history of violence, aggression, and impulsiveness (Edman et al., 1986). Researchers believe that the tendency toward suicide is not a simple link to depression. We already know that depressed patients also exhibit low levels of 5HIAA. What is startling is that low levels of 5HIAA have been discovered in suicidal people without a history of depression, and in suicidal individuals suffering from other mental disorders (Brown et al., 1982; Ninan et al., 1984).

This discovery may lead to a chemical means of detecting people who are at high risk for attempting suicide. However, researchers in this area caution that social and psychological factors also play a role. If, in the future, cerebral serotonin can be detected easily in blood tests, it can be used as a biological marker (a warning sign) of suicide risk (Hawton, 1987). Researchers believe that low 5HIAA content does not cause suicide, but it may make people more vulnerable to environmental stressors (Pines, 1983).

And still another caution is in order: this evidence is correlational in nature; it does not indicate whether low levels of 5HIAA are a cause of or a result of particular moods and emotions—or even whether the two are directly related.

THE VICTIMS OF SUICIDE

In this section we briefly discuss four groups of people who are especially victimized by suicide: the very young, college students, the elderly, and those who are left behind by suicides.

Suicide Among Children and Adolescents

Suicide among the young is an unmentioned tragedy in our society. We have traditionally avoided the idea that some of our young people find life so painful that they consciously and deliberately take their own lives. As in the case of Tammy Jimenez, it may feel easier to call a suicide "an accident." Yet, as Focus 13.1 reports, as many as 250,000 children aged five to fourteen may attempt suicide each year (Rosenthal & Rosenthal, 1984); approximately 3000 teenagers successfully end their lives every year (Shaffer & Fisher, 1981). The suicide rate for children younger than fourteen is increasing at an alarming rate, and the rate for adolescents is rising even faster (Cosand, Bourque & Kraus, 1982; Kosky, 1983). Indeed, recent figures suggested that adolescent suicides rose by more than 200 percent between 1960 and 1988 compared to a general population increase of 17 percent (Garland & Zigler, 1993; National Center for Health Statistics, 1991). Suicide is now second only to automobile accidents as the leading cause of death among teenagers, and some automobile "accidents" may also really be suicides.

A recent Gallup poll of teenage respondents found that 6 percent admit to a suicide attempt and another 15 percent say they have come close to trying (Freiberg, 1991). Experts on adolescent suicide, however, believe these to be gross underestimations (Berman & Jobes, 1991). The Gallup Organization polled middle-class families (median family income of $41,500) and thus missed certain high-risk groups such as school dropouts. Their studies suggested that between 8 and 9 percent of teenagers have engaged in self-harm behavior. The latest available figures revealed that there were 4,924 officially recorded suicides for youngsters between the ages of fifteen and twenty-four, more than triple the rate in 1957 (Freiberg, 1991).

Suicide among high-school students is reaching epidemic proportions. One of the dangers parents and teachers need to guard against is copy-cat suicide, a phenomenon in which other students take their lives. To prevent more suicides, schools sometimes initiate programs that help students and faculty cope with their feelings of loss and anger.

A lack of research on childhood suicides has generally hindered our understanding of why such acts occur. Two studies, however, have helped identify characteristics of suicidal children.

In a retrospective study of admissions to a pediatric hospital emergency room over a seven-year period, researchers identified 505 children and adolescents who had attempted suicide (Garfinkel, Froese & Hood, 1982). This group was compared with a control group of children who were similar in age, sex, and date of admission. Children in the suicidal group had the following characteristics:

1. There were three times as many girls as boys, and the boys who attempted suicide were significantly younger than the girls. The gender rates are consistent with adult rates, but the younger age of the boys is not.

2. The clinical symptoms most often shown by both the children and the adolescents were fluctuating affect and aggressiveness, hostility, or both.

3. Most of the suicide attempts (73 percent) occurred at home; 12 percent occurred in public areas, 7 percent at school, and 5 percent at a friend's house. In 87 percent of the attempts, someone else was nearby—generally parents. The fact that most suicide attempts occur at home implies that parents are in the best position to recognize and prevent suicidal behavior.

4. Most of the attempts were made during the winter months, in the evening or afternoon.

5. Drug overdose was the primary means of attempted suicide, accounting for 88 percent of the attempts. Next, in order, were wrist laceration, hanging, and jumping from heights or in front of moving vehicles.

6. More than 77 percent of the attempts were judged to be of low lethality; 21 percent were moderately lethal; and slightly more than 1 percent were highly lethal. Most attempts were judged to have been made in a way that ensured a high likelihood of rescue. These figures lend credence to the belief that most children who attempt suicide do not really want to end their lives.

The researchers found that the families of the suicidal children were under greater economic stress than the families of the control group. The former had twice the rate of paternal unemployment. Maybe parents who are preoccupied with economic concerns are less readily available to support their children in time of need. Furthermore, fewer than half the families of those who attempted suicide were two-parent families. The families of suicide attempters also had higher rates of medical problems, psychiatric illness, and suicide than control group families. The dominant psychiatric problem was alcohol or drug abuse.

In the second study as well, family instability and stress and a chaotic family atmosphere were correlated with suicide attempts (Cosand, Borque & Kraus, 1982). Suicidal children seemed to have experienced unpredictable traumatic events and to have suffered the loss of a significant parenting figure before age twelve. Their parents tended to be alcohol or drug abusers who provided poor role models for coping with stress. As in the first study, the child's self-destructive behavior seemed to be a last-ditch attempt to influence or coerce those who threatened his or her psychological well-being. The suicidal children showed considerable anger.

Because such children are at great risk of committing suicide when their problems remain unrecognized and untreated, early detection of their distress signals is vital. Intensive family therapy, including the education of parents with regard to parenting roles, can help. Parents can be taught to recognize the signs of depression, to become aware of their children's after-school activities, and to be cognizant of the role and accessibility of drugs. In some cases the child may need to be removed from the family (Berman & Bernard, 1982). Finally, mental health professionals and the public need to be aware that the complexion of adolescent suicides is changing at a rapid pace. For example, since the publication of these two studies, it has been found that the ratio of male to female suicides in 1987 was about 5:1, a change from the previous decade's 3:1 ratio; youngsters are now selecting more lethal methods of killing themselves (Berman & Jobes, 1991).

More recently, considerable attention has been directed at multiple or so-called copycat suicides in which youngsters in a particular school or community seem to mimic a previous suicide. For example, within a three-month period in 1985, nine Native American youths ages fourteen to twenty-five killed themselves, all by hanging. They were members of the Shoshone tribe and lived in Wind River, Wyoming. In one high school in Omaha, Nebraska, seven students attempted suicide within a very short span of time; three were successful ("Suicide Belt," 1986). Likewise, the Bergenfield suicides, which grabbed headlines in 1987, involved the deaths of two male and two female students who killed themselves by inhaling fumes from their car. They had killed themselves after a friend had committed suicide. This event was unusual because the four signed a suicide pact on a brown paper bag. Tragically, their deaths were followed by two other young women who used the same method of death (*Newsweek*, 1987).

Although many factors may have led to these tragic deaths, suggestion and imitation seemed to have played an especially powerful role. Although young people may be especially vulnerable, studies have indicated that highly publicized suicides such as those of celebrities or suicides of a close friend, relative, coworker, or someone well known can increase the number of attempts (Bandura, 1985; Stack, 1987). For example, after Marilyn Monroe's death, suicides increased by some 12 percent in the ensuing months. Interestingly, media reports of natural deaths of celebrities are not followed by increases in suicide. Thus it appears that grief, depression, and mourning are not the culprits inducing copycat behaviors.

Although imitative suicides may not be as common as the media seem to suggest, research has indicated that publicizing the event may have the effect of glorifying and drawing attention to it. Thus depressed people may identify with a colorful portrayal, increasing the risk of even more suicides (Gould & Shaffer, 1986; Phillips & Carstensen, 1986). This pattern appears to be especially true for youngsters who may already be thinking about killing themselves. The stable, well-adjusted teenager does not seem to be at risk in these situations.

Adolescence is often a period of confusing emotions, identity formation, and questioning. It is a difficult and turbulent time for most teenagers, and suicide may seem to be a logical response to the pain and stress of growing up. A suicide occurring in school brings increased risk of other suicides because of its proximity to students' daily life. In such instances, a suicide prevention program should be implemented to let students vent their feelings in an environment equipped to respond appropriately and

perhaps even save their lives. Encouragingly, the Gallup survey (1991) reported that 41 percent of schools had programs aimed at suicide prevention (professional counseling services, peer counseling, and special seminars). It is no longer unusual to hear about school programs that are immediately implemented once a tragedy strikes (student suicide, violent death of a student or teacher, natural disaster, for example). One such program is discussed later.

College Student Suicides

As many as 20 percent of college students have entertained suicidal thoughts during their college careers, and college students represent the highest risk group for young people of this age (Carson & Johnson, 1985). When you consider how well-endowed college students as a group are—with youth, intelligence, and boundless opportunity—you might wonder whether something about the college situation fosters self-destructive acts among college students because suicide is such a high risk for them. Most studies that seek to answer this question have described the characteristics of suicidal students without controlling for the possibility that nonsuicidal students may share the same traits. What is needed is a clear understanding of the characteristics that differentiate suicidal from nonsuicidal students. These characteristics seem to have been pinpointed in several studies where comparison groups were included for controls (Klagsbrun, 1976; Seiden, 1966, 1984a, 1984b).

Characteristics of Student Suicides At the University of California at Berkeley, a ten-year study found that suicide ranked second only to accidents as the major cause of student deaths (Seiden, 1966, 1984a). Several characteristics of student suicides were distilled from this study. Compared to nonsuicidal students, students who committed suicide

- Tended to be older than the average student by almost four years
- Were significantly overrepresented among postgraduate students
- Were more likely to be men, although the proportion of women suicides was higher than among the general population
- Were more likely to be foreign students and language or literature majors

Many find it difficult to understand why members of such a privileged group as college students would commit suicide. Unrealistically high internal expectations, excessive pressure from family and friends to excel, and preexisting emotional problems may be some of the causes.

◆ As undergraduates, tended to have better academic records, but as postgraduate students, were below the graduate grade point average

In addition, more suicides occurred in February and October (near the beginning of a semester) than in the other months of the year. Thus the notion that suicides occur in response to anxiety over final examinations was not supported by the results. In fact, the danger period appeared to be the start, not the finish, of the school semester. Most of the students committed suicide at their campus residence. Suicides seemed more frequent at larger universities than at smaller ones such as community colleges and small liberal arts colleges. Firearms were the most common means of committing suicide; ingestion of drugs was next. In later studies on other campuses, however, drug overdose was found to be more frequently used than firearms (Klagsbrun, 1976).

Reasons for Student Suicides These findings suggest explanations for student suicides. First, whereas the ratio of male suicides to female suicides in the general population is 3 : 1, for college students it is 1.5 : 1. In the past, the greater risk of suicide among college women may have resulted from increased conflicting social pressures, which accompany the rapid shift of sex roles among women entering college. Whether this now holds true is certainly debatable. It may be that as women's roles and lifestyles become more similar to men's, so do their suicide rates.

Second, the fact that undergraduates who commit suicide have better scholastic records than the general college population reveals a painful paradox. By objective standards, suicidal students had done well. Friends and relatives report, however, that almost all these students were dissatisfied with their academic performance. They were filled with doubts about their own ability to succeed. One explanation for these feelings is that these students were highly motivated to achieve and had unrealistically high expectations for themselves. For example, at a large eastern university several years ago, an outstanding young woman student, who had consistently made the dean's list and had obtained nearly straight-A grades, leaped to her death from her dormitory room late one winter night. That a student with so much intellectual promise could commit such an act seemed inconceivable. Interviews with her friends, family, and fiancé indicated that she had been despondent over receiving a B in one of her courses, which spoiled her unbroken string of A's. Seiden (1966,

p. 391) described the psychological dynamics of this situation as follows:

> The internal standards these students applied to themselves were so Olympian, the demands they imposed upon themselves so exacting, that they were destined to suffer frustration and disappointments no matter how well they fared. . . . Whereas they had previously been crackerjack students in high school or junior college, excelling without much difficulty, the precipitous drop in grade points . . . threatened their feelings of self-esteem. Faced with a sudden loss of status, they may have suicided as a response to their egoistic conflict.

Third, and related to the previous explanation, many suicidal students feel overwhelming shame and disgrace because of their sense of failing others. On a particularly lovely June day, Patrick C. Do of Hong Kong, a graduate student at Florida State University, committed suicide after shooting his adviser, Professor James R. Fisher. Observers noted that Do had recently failed to pass a doctoral examination in chemistry (East-West, 1976). We might speculate that Patrick Do could no longer tolerate the experience of failure. He had indeed failed, and he partially blamed his adviser for the outcome. Death seemed the only avenue open.

Foreign students, especially, are under considerable pressure from families and friends to excel and achieve in this country. Their greatest fear is that they may not fulfill the expectations of their families, who may have sacrificed much to finance their educations. The pressures are even stronger for students from cultures in which it is important to bring honor to the family name (D. W. Sue & D. Sue, 1990). Academic achievement or occupational success reflects creditably on the whole family, not just on the individual. Conversely, unsatisfactory behaviors such as juvenile delinquency, mental illness, and failure in school shame the family. Faced with such pressures, some foreign students may report only successes to their families and cover up their failures. Needing to constantly reinforce the precariously fabricated image of continuous achievement, and knowing that a day of reckoning will eventually arrive, some students, like Patrick Do, choose suicide. Interestingly, Seiden's study revealed that 17 percent of the Berkeley suicides were Chinese students.

Finally, it is quite possible that the common denominator among suicidal students may simply be emotional disturbance. The other factors may all play a part, but psychopathology may predispose students to overreact to them. In fact, some people believe that suicide—any suicide—is simply not the act of a rational person. That is, some deviation within the person's personality causes or predisposes him or her to break with reality. Even the Japanese kamikaze pilots and the Shi'ite Muslim terrorists, who sacrificed their lives for a cause, are perceived in such western theories as mentally disturbed. Nevertheless, some psychologists hold firmly to the belief that some suicides may be culturally sanctioned and may represent rational responses to intolerable situations.

Suicide Among the Elderly

Aging inevitably results in generally unwelcome physical changes, such as wrinkling and thickening skin, graying hair, and diminishing physical strength. In addition, the elderly encounter a succession of stressful life changes as the years roll on. Friends and relatives die, social isolation may increase, and the prospect of death becomes more real (Goodstein, 1981; Kirsling, 1986; Osgood, 1987). Mandatory retirement rules may lead to the need for financial assistance and the difficulties of living on a fixed and inadequate income. Among the elderly, nearly 30 percent have an annual income of less than $3,200 (Baum & Boxley, 1983). Such conditions make depression one of the most common psychiatric complaints of the elderly. And their depression seems to be involved more with "feeling old" than with their actual age or poor physical health (Baum & Boxley, 1983).

Suicide seems to accompany depression for older people. Their suicide rates (especially for elderly European-American men) are higher than those for the general population (McIntosh & Santos, 1981; Pfeiffer, 1977); indeed, these rates are the highest for any age group (National Center for Health Statistics, 1989). In one study comparing rates of suicide among different racial groups, it was found that elderly European Americans committed almost 18 percent of all suicides but comprised only about 11 percent of the population. However, the suicide rate for elderly European Americans has been declining over the past twenty years (McIntosh & Santos, 1981). Suicide rates for Chinese Americans, Japanese Americans, and Filipino Americans are even higher than the rate for elderly European Americans. Native

Americans and African Americans show the lowest rates of suicide among older adults (although both groups are at high risk for suicide during young adulthood).

Of the Asian-American groups, first-generation immigrants were at greatest risk of suicide. One possible explanation for this finding is that the newly arrived Asian Americans had intended to earn money and then return to their native countries. When they found that they were unable to earn enough either to return home or to bring their families here, they developed feelings of isolation that increased their risk of suicide. This risk has decreased among subsequent generations of Asian Americans (and, probably, other immigrant groups as well) because of acculturation and the creation of strong family ties.

The Other Victims of Suicide

Relatives and Friends   When a suicide occurs, our thoughts immediately turn to the person who has taken his or her own life. What unbearable pain was he or she suffering to justify such an end? Yet the true victims of this tragedy are often the family, relatives, and friends who are left behind to face the meaning of this act.

The emotional processes that occur in suicide survivorship is a complex one. Lukas & Seiden (1990) made the point that death of a loved one is always painful and traumatic. However, family and friends of a suicide must not only cope with the death but a host of unanswered questions about the cause of the death. This is compounded by a society that does not sanction an open discussion of suicide; in many cases there is no funeral and a "conspiracy of silence" seems to prevail. Oftentimes, people who knew the suicide become "stuck"; they seem unable to move on with their own lives. Part of this is due to dysfunctional coping mechanisms used to protect oneself from devastating feelings, which aborts the normal grieving process (Lukas & Seiden, 1990).

Elisabeth Kübler-Ross (1983), a psychiatrist who has researched and written extensively about death and dying, has outlined a series of reactions people experience when a family member commits suicide. The first of three stages is characterized by shock, denial, and numbness. The act is often incomprehensible to loved ones, who find it difficult to talk about. They tend to avoid using the word *suicide*, and they

Elisabeth Kübler-Ross is a world-renowned psychiatrist, author, and lecturer, who has researched and written extensively about death and dying. Among her books are *Living with Death and Dying*, *On Children and Death*, and *AIDS: The Ultimate Challenge*.

go through the motions of arranging the funeral as though it had no personal meaning. The depths of pain are too great to be confronted, and family members close themselves off from their feelings. In this stage the bereaved person seems detached from others. Kübler-Ross suggested that friends can help most during this stage by making themselves available both day and night.

In the second stage, family members begin to experience grief. For the spouse especially, anguish is mixed with feelings of anger. He or she now tries to blame someone for something—himself or herself, for example: "Why didn't I see what was happening?" Although expressed as self-blame for the death of one's spouse or child, however, the true source of this anger is the person who committed suicide. And eventually that anger and rage toward the deceased is expressed: "How could you desert me and our children? How could you do this to us? Why didn't you have the courage to face life? Damn you, why didn't you tell me you were hurting?"

FIRST PERSON

Merryl Maleska Wilbur

When I think about it now, from the context of my normal life, what I did that day seems very odd. Wasn't I aware of the passing cars, the curious onlookers who surely must have stared? And what about my father, parked and waiting just up the road—didn't I worry about what he must be feeling and thinking?

But none of this troubled me at the time. All I knew was that my husband had been buried two days earlier and that this day, this Saturday in June, would have been our sixth wedding anniversary. I needed to be near him. If there was any place in the world that I belonged, it was with him. And so I had thrown myself on the upturned dirt that marked his grave and for one sweet, calming hour I had lain there, with my face in the ground, talking to him.

"Why did you do it, Carl? Why did it have to get that bad?" Over and over I asked him that question. "There would have been a way, if you could have only waited. You had no right to just get up and do this."

When my father came for me and I had to sit upright and face the blinding light of day, I felt a sudden paralyzing fear. It was as if I had unpeeled layers of my brain and was looking deep inside my own head: I am not going to make it through this. I will go crazy.

I could not know then that exactly one year hence, on the first anniversary of Carl's death, I would drive myself to that same cemetery, stand quietly in front of a newly placed gravestone, and read its inscription aloud to myself; that the tears would come but not in huge engulfing waves; and that when I now asked myself the question why, acknowledgement of a universe and a mystery larger than Carl or me would cause me a long moment of philosophical reflection.

Between those points would lie a year counted by its minutes. I got from one point to the other by something that did not feel at all like courage, although people often

---

Kübler-Ross believes that this stage is difficult for family and friends to handle. Most people stay away from the parents or spouse of a suicide, whose rage can often make them quite abusive to everyone. It is important, however, that someone listen, act as a sounding board, and bear the brunt of such anger, because it needs to be expressed and is preferable to denial. The family must be helped to experience the pain, rather than postpone or deny it. They need empathic and understanding people, not sedation. Kübler-Ross says that, in suicide, extreme and prolonged grief can be avoided by not fostering denial. The words *suicide, death,* and *dead* should be used directly, without attempts to soften or disguise them (as in "passed away"). Moreover, it is important for other members of the family to see the corpse, to identify it, and to touch it, so that they face the reality of death.

The third and last stage is letting go, or completing "unfinished business." In cases of suicide, there is usually much unfinished business to take care of. A husband may think, "I never told her I loved her" or "There's so much we haven't talked about or shared." It is often helpful for the family to say these things to the suicide victim, either at the funeral or in a role-playing situation. Letting go, saying goodbye, and accepting the feelings are important therapy for survivors. (The First Person narrative is a sensitive account of one survivor's experience.)

Mental Health Professionals We have discussed the tragic consequences of suicide from the perspective of suicide victims and their family and friends. Few of us would think that a mental health professional working with a client might also suffer intensely if that person took his or her own life. After all, aren't psychologists supposed to be able to handle such matters without becoming emotionally involved? Furthermore, aren't suicides rare and unlikely to happen to clients undergoing therapy?

Recently, a nationwide study of 365 psychologists listed in the *National Register of Health Service Providers* was conducted to (1) ascertain the prevalence of client suicides and (2) determine the impact of

called me courageous. Instead, it was a simple but pitiless formula that kept me going. I discovered soon enough that, despite that early panic, I really wasn't going to go crazy. Even after an hour of screaming aloud, I would always be there in my alertness and consciousness. Nor could I seem to do what Carl had done. Ending my life by any one of several specific plans was an idea I carried with me at all moments but could never act through. The formula had its own inexorable logic: if I wasn't going to fall apart and if I couldn't kill myself, then what I was left with was having to live.

The choice I made and the things I did that year also seemed to unfold naturally. Like other suicide survivors I met, I found that my guilt was unrelenting. Day after day I put myself on trial, reviewing the minutiae of my life with Carl, searching for ways in which I had hurt him. The feelings of loss, exaggerated not only by what he had meant to me but because of the suddenness with which he had disappeared, came in great swells. In public, I kept my head down, acted by my own laws and instincts, greeting and smiling at no one, and in private I screamed and cried aloud for hours at a time. The way Carl had died, the suicide itself, was so inconceivable that I had a great need to tell the story, to examine it and make it real. With my parents, a new friend who took me into her home, members of a self-help group for suicide survivors, a therapist, colleagues at work, Carl's family—over and over the story I went.

After many months of this, the grief began to change. Although there was no pivotal moment, a breakthrough occurred as I began to recognize that Carl had done something I could not control. He had acted out of who he was; neither my bad moods or nagging—nor my love—could make him be otherwise. Ironically, the fact that his death was a suicide gave me an unusual opportunity, for it helped me accept an essential human separateness. In giving up responsibility for his life, I also found it less and less astonishing that I had my own life and that I could go on without him.

Merryl Maleska Wilbur is a writer and editor. Her husband, Carl, committed suicide in 1982, after working eight years toward a doctorate degree. He was thirty-three.

---

client suicides on psychologists (Chemtob et al., 1988).

The findings revealed that 22 percent of psychologists had worked with a client who committed suicide. Those psychologists who experienced a client's suicide were asked a number of questions about how it affected their professional practice and personal lives. Many became more sensitive to suicide-related cues, consulted more with their colleagues, and became more aware of forensic-legal issues. Personally, suicides seemed to have a major emotional impact on the therapist; they reported increased concerns of death and dying, suffered from intrusive thoughts of suicide, and felt anger and guilt toward their client.

The investigators found that one in five psychologists can expect to have a patient kill himself or herself and that 39 percent of those who lost one patient can expect to lose another. They contended that client suicides should be acknowledged as an occupational hazard because of the impact they have on a therapist's professional and personal life. A large proportion of therapists reported symptoms typical of posttraumatic stress disorder lasting longer than six months.

These findings should not be surprising. After all, therapists are just as vulnerable as anyone else. What seems to be needed are resources for psychologists to work through their own experiences of suicide. In addition, training programs in mental health should be initiated to teach trainees and their supervisors how to cope with a client's suicide. The investigators hope that this study will motivate psychology training programs to deal with this issue directly, forcefully, and constructively.

PREVENTING SUICIDE

In almost every case of suicide, there are hints that the act is about to occur. Suicide is irreversible, of course, so preventing it depends very much on early detection and successful intervention (Bongar, 1992; Cantor, 1991; Maltsberger, 1991). Mental health professionals involved in suicide prevention operate under the assumption that potential victims are ambivalent about the act. That is, the wish to die is strong, but there is also a wish to live. Potential rescuers are trained to exert their efforts to preserve life.

Clues to Suicidal Intent

The prevention of suicide depends very much on the therapist's ability to recognize its signs, both demographic and specific. We have already discussed a number of demographic factors, such as the fact that men are three times more likely to kill themselves than are women and that increased age increases the probability of suicide. And, although the popular notion is that frequent suicidal gestures are associated with less serious intent, most suicides do have a history of making suicide threats; to ignore them is extremely dangerous.

General characteristics often help detect potential suicides, but individual cases vary from statistical norms. What does one look for in specific instances? Danto (1971) pointed out that the amount of detail involved in a suicide threat can indicate its seriousness. A person who provides specific details, such as method, time, and place, is more at risk than one who describes these factors vaguely. Suicidal potential increases if the person has direct access to the means of suicide, such as a loaded pistol. Also, sometimes a suicide may be preceded by a precipitating event. The loss of a loved one, family discord, or chronic or terminal illness may contribute to a person's decision to end his or her life.

A person contemplating suicide may verbally communicate the intent. Some people make very direct statements: "I'm going to kill myself," "I want to die," or "If such and such happens, I'll kill myself." Others make indirect threats: "Goodbye," "I've had it," "You'd be better off without me," and "It's too much to put up with." Cues are frequently very subtle:

> A patient says to Nurse Jones, who is leaving on vacation, "Goodbye, Miss Jones, I won't be here when you come back." If some time afterward Nurse Jones, knowing that the patient is not scheduled to be transferred or discharged prior to her return, thinks about that conversation, she may do well to telephone her hospital. (Danto, 1971, p. 20)

As this example illustrates, verbal expressions must be judged within the larger context of recent events and behavioral cues. We have all, at one time or another, made or heard such statements.

Behavioral clues can be communicated directly or indirectly. The most direct clue is a "practice run," an actual suicide attempt. Even if the act is not completed, *it should be taken seriously;* it often communicates deep suicidal intent that may be carried out in the future. Indirect behavioral clues can include actions such as putting one's affairs in order, taking a lengthy trip, giving away prized possessions, buying a casket, or making out a will, depending on the circumstances. In other words, the more unusual or peculiar the situation, the more likely it is that the action is a cue to suicide.

Crisis Intervention

Suicide prevention can occur at several levels, and the mental health profession has now begun to move in several coordinated directions to establish prevention efforts. At the clinical level, attempts are being made to educate staff at mental health institutions and even at schools to recognize conditions and symptoms that indicate potential suicides (Kneisel & Richards, 1988). For example, a single man older than fifty years of age, suffering from a sudden acute onset of depression and expressing hopelessness, should be recognized by mental health professionals as being at high risk.

When a psychiatric facility encounters someone who fits a particular risk profile for suicide, crisis intervention strategies will most likely be used to abort or ameliorate the processes that could lead to a suicide attempt. Crisis intervention is aimed at providing intensive short-term help to a patient in resolving an immediate life crisis. Unlike traditional psychotherapy, in which sessions are spaced out and treatment is provided on a more leisurely long-term basis, crisis intervention recognizes the immediacy of the patient's state of mind. The patient may be immediately hospitalized, given medical treatment, and seen by a psychiatric team for two to four hours every day until the person is stabilized and the immediate crisis has passed. In these sessions, the team is very active in not only working with the patient, but in taking charge of the person's personal, social, and professional life outside of the psychiatric facility. Much of suicide intervention strategies have been developed through clinical work rather than research because the nature of suicide demands immediate action. Waiting for empirical studies is not a luxury the clinician can afford (see Focus 13.3, a personal account of one of the authors).

After the patient returns to a more stable emotional state and the immediate risk of suicide has passed, the person is then given more traditional forms of treatment, either on an inpatient or outpatient basis. In addition to the intense therapy they receive from the psychiatric team, relatives and friends of the potential suicide will often be enlisted to help monitor the person outside of the hospital. In these cases, the responsible relatives or friends are provided with specific guidelines about how to deal with the patient between treatment team contacts, who to notify should problems arise outside of the hospital, and so forth.

Suicide Prevention Centers

Crisis intervention can be highly successful with potential suicidal patients because they are either already being treated by a therapist or have come to the attention of one through the efforts of concerned family or friends. Many people in acute distress, however, are not formally being treated. Although contact with a mental health agency may be highly desirable many are unaware of the services available to them. Recognizing that suicidal crises may occur at any time and that preventive assistance on a much larger scale may be needed, suicide prevention centers have been established in a number of communities.

The first suicide prevention center (SPC) was established in Los Angeles in 1958 by psychologists Norman L. Farberow and Edwin S. Shneidman. The center first sought patients from the wards of hospitals, but now, owing to its reputation, 99 percent of its contacts are by phone (Farberow, 1970). In the last thirty years, hundreds of suicide prevention centers patterned after the first one have sprung up throughout the United States. These centers are generally adapted to the particular needs of the communities they serve, but they all share certain operational procedures and goals.

Telephone Crisis Intervention   Suicide prevention centers typically operate twenty-four hours a day, seven days a week. Because most suicide contacts are by phone, a well-publicized telephone number is made available throughout the community for calls at any time of the day or night. Furthermore, many centers provide inpatient or outpatient crisis treatment. If they lack such resources, the centers develop cooperative programs with other community mental health facilities. Most telephone hotlines are staffed by paraprofessionals. All workers are trained in crisis intervention techniques and have been exposed to crisis situations under supervision. Among these techniques are the following (Heilig, 1970):

1. *Maintain contact and establish a relationship* The skilled worker who establishes a good relationship with the suicidal caller not only increases the caller's chances of working out an alternative solution but also can exert more influence. Thus it is important for the worker to show interest, concern, and self-assuredness.

2. *Obtain necessary information* The worker elicits demographic data and the caller's name and address. This information is very valuable in case an urgent need arises to locate the caller.

3. *Evaluate suicidal potential* The staff person must quickly determine the seriousness of the caller's self-destructive intent. Most centers use lethality rating scales to help the worker determine suicide potential. These usually contain questions on age, sex, onset of symptoms, situational plight, prior suicidal behavior, and the communication qualities of the caller. Staffers also elicit other demographic and specific information that might provide clues to lethality, such as the information discussed in the section on clues to suicidal intent.

4. *Clarify the nature of the stress and focal problem* The worker must help the caller clarify the exact nature of the stress, recognize that he or she may be under so much duress that his or her thinking may be confused and impaired, and realize that there are other solutions besides suicide. The caller is often disoriented, so the worker *must* be specific to help bring the caller back to reality.

5. *Assess strengths and resources* In working out a therapeutic plan, the worker can often mobilize the caller's strengths or available resources. In their agitation, suicidal people tend to forget their own strengths. Their feelings of helplessness are so overwhelming that helping them

A Clinical Approach to Suicide Intervention

As a practicing clinician, I have had the stressful experience of working with suicidal clients; indeed, one of my patients on a psychiatric ward committed suicide when I was serving my internship in 1968. Since that time I have had to deal with many feelings related to this tragic act, and have conscientiously kept up with both the literature and clinical work on suicide intervention. Notice that I prefer the term "intervention" rather than "prevention." I believe that, under certain conditions, individuals have a right to take their own lives. I may intervene in helping them understand their decision, but I do not necessarily view my role as one of prevention.

Despite this philosophical stand, my clinical experience has led me to conclude that, overwhelmingly, the majority of suicidal people do not wish to truly end their lives. When helped to understand the sources of their stress and the available resources and options open to them, they inevitably choose life over death. My purpose in discussing this topic is not to debate the ethical merits of suicide or to discuss how one arrives at such a conclusion,

but to explain how I, as a mental health professional, approach working with a potentially suicidal client. The setting I am most familiar with is our public schools where I train and supervise school counselors. Increasingly, many of my trainees are encountering students who express suicidal ideation and threats. Following are some of the clinical thoughts and suggestions that I attempt to impart to them. Interestingly, many of these suggestions are equally valid when applied to friends or relatives who may be contemplating suicide.

1. *Be comfortable discussing suicide* Many beginning counselors are not comfortable openly and directly discussing suicide with their clients or students. They are frightened that by opening the door to this topic, they will inadvertently encourage a suicidal gesture or their actions will result in the suicide of their clients. Nothing could be further from the truth. My experience has taught me that those who are serious about suicide have entertained those thoughts for some time. Indeed, not to discuss the topic or to indirectly allude to possible suicide can have a most devastating effect

on the suicidal student; it prevents the student from examining himself or herself objectively and reinforces the belief that "only crazy people" entertain these thoughts. Thus the psychological distress for the student may become even more heightened. Furthermore, it also prevents the mental health professional from quickly and accurately ascertaining suicidal risk. Thus asking direct questions like the following progression is a necessity:

"Are you feeling unhappy and down most of the time?"
    If yes . . .

"Do you feel so unhappy that you sometimes wish you were dead?"
    If yes . . .

"Have you ever thought about taking your own life?"
    If yes . . .

"What methods have you thought about using to kill yourself?"
    If the client specifies a method . . .

"When do you plan to do this?"

recognize what they can do about a situation is important. The worker explores the caller's personal resources (family, friends, coworkers), professional resources (doctors, clergy, therapists, lawyers), and community resources (clinics, hospitals, social agencies).

6. *Recommend and initiate an action plan* Besides being supportive, the worker is highly directive in recommending a course of action. Whether the recommendation entails immediately seeing

the person, calling the person's family, or referring the person to a social agency the next day, it is presented as a plan of action and outlined step by step.

This list implies a rigid sequence, but in fact the approach (as well as the order of the steps) is adjusted to fit the needs of the individual caller.

The Effectiveness of Suicide Prevention Centers

Today approximately two hundred SPCs function in the United States, as well as numerous "suicide hot-

Contrary to our fears that such an approach will adversely affect the student, I have found that directness diminishes the distress felt by the student. For many students it is a relief to be able to discuss a taboo topic openly and honestly.

2. *Use the natural barrier against suicide*   Studies reveal that almost all people who commit suicide have made attempts in the past. Most of us have a trained-in barrier against hurting ourselves or taking our own lives. Once we cross that barrier, it becomes easier for the person contemplating suicide to act against his or her moral, ethical, and religious upbringing. Even in students who have made a suicidal gesture, the barrier is never completely gone. In students who have never made an attempt to kill themselves, but have thought about ending their lives, it is important to immediately and forcefully reinforce the barrier or to prevent it from being crossed. This can be done in a number of different ways, but generally involves concrete actions on the part of the counselor.

3. *Take action to affect the client's immediate environment*   If your assessment leads you to believe that you are dealing with a high-risk student, no amount of talk or philosophical debate will help.

Although we may have hang-ups about acting in an autocratic manner, the counselor is often required to make decisions and take actions against the wishes of the student. High-risk students should not be allowed to leave the school office without a clear-cut treatment plan and the involvement of responsible parties. Parents may need to be immediately notified, and if they are not cooperative, the school should have specific procedures for involving civil authorities. I tell my students that it is always better to err on the conservative side than to gamble with a person's life.

If, however, our assessment leads us to conclude that we are dealing with a low-risk client, other more democratic and less severe actions may be taken. For example, involving the student in counseling (within the school) or referring the student to a private practitioner in the community are available options. If you decide to continue a counseling relationship with the student, you may use yourself to reinforce the barrier. I have found, for example, that obtaining an agreement with the student can be a powerful means of blocking suicidal attempts. It may be as simple as extracting a verbal promise from the student that he or she will not make any attempt at

suicide that week, to actually signing a behavioral contract. Such a contract may go something like this:

1. I agree not to attempt to kill myself or harm myself from

_____ to

_____ .

2. I agree to get rid of any or all things that may be used to kill myself such as knives, guns, or pills.

3. I agree to immediately call my counselor at

_____ or the Suicide Prevention Center should I feel like hurting myself.

4. I agree to these conditions as part of my counseling with _____ .

Signed _____

Witnessed _____

Dated _____

Suicide intervention, in some respects, goes against the traditional therapeutic training of most mental health professionals. A potential suicide crisis does not allow the mental health professional the luxury of time to explore the client's problems nor to simply sit back and behave in a passive, democratic manner. The actions we choose to take or not take can have major effects on the final outcome of our suicidal clients.

---

lines" in mental health clinics. Little research has been done on their effectiveness, however, and many clients of SPCs want to stay anonymous.

Nevertheless, some data are available. For example, it is known that 95 percent of callers to SPCs never use the service again (Speer, 1971). This finding may indicate that the service was so helpful that no further treatment was needed or, just as possibly, that callers do not find SPCs helpful and feel it is useless to call again. Worse yet, they may have killed themselves after the contact. Another study has shown

that potential suicides do not perceive contact with an SPC as more helpful than discussion with friends (Speer, 1972). And, if the justification for SPCs is based on their ability to offer services to a large number of clients, then the fact that only 2 percent of the people who kill themselves ever contact such a service is disturbing (Weiner, 1969). Furthermore, studies on cities with hotline services provide mixed findings (Lester, 1989). Some studies found that suicides decreased in a community with hotline services (Miller, Coombs & Leeper, 1984), some found no change

Suicide prevention centers (SPC) operate twenty-four hours a day, seven days a week and have well-publicized telephone numbers because most contacts are made by phone. Even though there is controversy about SPC effectiveness, the mental health profession continues to support these centers.

(Barraclough et al., 1977), and others found an increase (Weiner, 1969).

Before you jump to the conclusion that SPCs are ineffective, however, note that the studies cited could have been affected by several factors. For example, cities with and cities without SPCs may differ so much that they are not comparable. Additionally, clients may contact SPCs only when they are in such great distress that they despair of asking friends for help. They may later perceive their contacts with friends as being more beneficial relative to the distress they feel. Finally, despite the lack of convincing evidence, there is always the possibility that SPCs do help. Because life is precious, the mental health profession continues to support them.

Community Prevention Programs

Suicide prevention programs have recently begun to spring up at work sites and schools. Increasingly, community leaders have recognized that the suicide of a worker or student has dramatic and stressful emotional effects on fellow workers and students who may have known the victim (Calhoun, Atkeson & Resick, 1982). When a school experiences a suicide, the staff and students quickly learn of the event. This is often followed by emotional upheaval, anxiety, guilt, and severe grieving (Davis, 1985; Praeger & Bernhardt, 1985). Educational institutions now routinely consult mental health professionals after a suicide to help facilitate the natural grieving process; reduce the secrecy, confusion, and rumors surrounding a suicide; and prevent possible copycat suicides.

One interesting and effective form of intervention was developed in response to a particularly violent suicide (Kneisel & Richard, 1988). A fifth- and sixth-grade teacher took her own life by dousing herself with gasoline and igniting herself. Local media coverage was quite intense, and little else was discussed. In responding to this terrible event and the emotional needs of the students, the school assembled a mental health consulting team, comprising two child psychologists trained in crisis intervention and one representative each of the fire department and mayoral task force. The fire department representative was included because of concern about possible increased risk of fire setting among students. The team worked directly with the school psychologist, who already knew the students and staff. The primary goal of the program was to mitigate the effects of the tragedy by providing survivors with an opportunity to express and understand their reactions to the event. To accomplish this goal, the following activities were undertaken:

1. A faculty meeting was called to give teachers a forum in which they could share feelings and information with one another. This session was only partially successful. It gave the team insight into student concerns but it failed to meet the needs of the faculty.

2. In a classroom discussion, children were given an opportunity to express their feelings and concerns, especially those dealing with fears of

death, suicide, and fire. They were reassured that the teacher's decision to kill herself was not based on their behavior and her death was not their fault. All questions were answered truthfully and straightforwardly.

3. Throughout this period of intervention, the school psychologist was available for individual sessions with teachers, staff, and students. Some sought individual sessions because they had an especially close relationship to the victim; others sought help because they were already dealing with personal issues of loss, separation, and abandonment. Some students were referred because they were excessively tearful, withdrawn, or distraught; others were seen because they denied the suicide. Many of these individuals were referred for ongoing follow-up treatment.

After all of these meetings, the team met with the principal to plan follow-up actions. A memorial service was held. Parents were sent letters telling them about the suicide and informing them about mental health resources in the community. Written guidelines for suicide prevention were developed and distributed in the school.

Kneisel and Richards concluded that such an institutional response to a suicide minimizes mental health problems among the survivors, restores equilibrium in the school and community, and represents an effective suicide prevention program.

THE RIGHT TO SUICIDE: MORAL, ETHICAL, AND LEGAL IMPLICATIONS

The act of suicide seems to violate much of what we have been taught regarding the sanctity of life. Many segments of the population consider it immoral and provide strong religious sanctions against it (Redestam, 1977). Suicide is both a sin in the canonical law of the Catholic Church and an illegal act according to the secular laws of most countries. Many states have laws against suicide, and some consider it illegal. Of course, such laws are difficult to enforce because the victims are not around to prosecute. Many are beginning to question the legitimacy of such sanctions, however, and are openly advocating one's right to suicide.

One of the most outspoken critics of suicide prevention programs is Thomas Szasz (1986). He argued that suicide is an act of a moral agent who is ultimately responsible. Szasz opposed coercive methods used by mental health professionals (such as depriv-

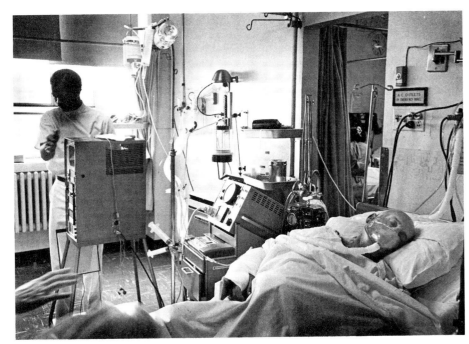

While modern medicine has made incredible advances in prolonging life, many of the procedures simply sustain life without regard to its quality. Many terminally ill or elderly patients, wishing to die with dignity, feel that they have a basic right to refuse treatment and end their own lives. The ethical and legal considerations are complex.

CRITICAL
THINKING

Do People Have a Right to Die?

In 1990 the psychological community was shocked by the suicide of one of their very own, Bruno Bettelheim. During an interview (Fremon, 1991), Bettelheim revealed some of his own thoughts regarding death and suicide. He stated that he did not fear death but was frightened at the prospect of suffering. At eighty-six years, he had lived a productive and enjoyable life and was fearful that he would be kept alive without a purpose. Bettelheim had recently suffered a stroke, was fearful that he would suffer another, and no longer could do many of the activities that had brought joy and meaning to his life. He believed that he was living on borrowed time and contemplated meeting with a doc-tor in the Netherlands who was willing to give him a lethal injection.

From 1989 to 1993, Dr. Jack Kevorkian, a physician, helped 16 persons (nearly all women) with chronic debilitating diseases commit suicide. He had invented a "suicide machine" composed of bottles containing chemicals that could be fed intravenously into the arm of the person. The solution could bring instantaneous unconsciousness and quick painless death. His first client, Mrs. J. Adkins, suffered from Alzheimer's disease. She did not want to put her family through the agony of the disease, believed that she had a right to choose death, stated that her act was of a rational mind, and had the consent of her husband. Two other women who committed suicide did not suffer from diseases that threatened to kill them in the immediate future. One suffered from multiple sclerosis and the other from a pelvic condition that caused severe and constant pain. Twice, charges of homicide were brought against Dr. Kevorkian, and in both cases they were ultimately dropped. In the last ruling, a Michigan judge dismissed the charges on grounds that suicide was not a crime in that state, and therefore assisting suicide cannot be a crime. The legal troubles for Dr. Kevorkian are not over, however. A new law in Michigan is scheduled to go into effect outlawing "physician-assisted suicides," and attempts are

ing clients of access to the means of suicide, involuntary hospitalization) to prevent suicide. The taking of one's own life is ultimately the responsibility of the person and not the mental health professional. By taking actions against a client's wishes, practitioners have allied themselves with the police power of the state, and have identified themselves as foes of individual liberty and responsibility. It should be noted that Szasz does not claim that suicide is always good or morally legitimate, but that we must abstain from empowering agents of the state to coercively prevent it.

Using another line of reasoning, Doris Portwood believes that elderly people have the right to end their own lives if their continued existence would result in psychological and physical deterioration:

The choice of suicide is ours to make. It is our life we are giving up, and our death we are arranging. The choice does not infringe on the rights of others. We do not need to explain and excuse. (Portwood, 1978, p. 68)

Portwood contended that these people should be allowed the choice of dying in a dignified manner, particularly if they suffer from a terminal illness or a severely incapacitating illness that would cause misery for their families and friends. Such was the case with Mrs. Jenny Williams (described at the beginning of this chapter), who chose death over life.

Since the debate over whether people have the right to end their own lives, another volatile and controversial issue has arisen. Do others have a right to aid a suicidal person in carrying out a suicide? Is it morally, ethically, and legally permissible to allow relatives, friends, or physicians to provide support, means, and actions to carry out a suicide (see Critical Thinking)? Two high-profile individuals have recently fueled the debate by virtue of their actions. Derek Humphrey, former director of the Hemlock

underway in California to suspend his medical license.

In November 1992, California citizens had the opportunity of voting on Proposition 161, the Death With Dignity Act. The statewide ballot initiative that would have made it legal for doctors to help their terminally ill patients die was narrowly defeated. If passed, California would have become the first state in the country to ever pass such an initiative. The bill would have required the dying patient to voluntarily sign a revocable directive in advance of the request for physician-assisted suicide. It had to be witnessed by two "disinterested adults," and could be revoked either verbally or in writing at any time. Other conditions in the bill make it clear that at least three physicians, including the attending doctor, must certify that the patient is terminally ill and will die within six months or less. This proposition was defeated for a number of different reasons, but popular surveys indicated that the majority of Californians believe that

physicians should be allowed to help terminally ill clients end their lives voluntarily.

What reactions do you have to these three events? Did Bruno Bettelheim have a right to end his own life? What reasons led you to your answer? Does a doctor, or anyone for that matter, have a right to help others terminate their lives? What would motivate someone like Dr. Kevorkian to risk censure and imprisonment in helping others to die? If you were a voting-age Californian, would you have voted for or against Proposition 161? Why or why not?

These questions do not have easy answers. Although we may pride ourselves as being social scientists concerned with objective facts in helping provide answers, the topic of suicide raises unavoidable moral, legal, and ethical issues. It is certainly possible for us to study suicide in an academic fashion, but what of the mental health professional who encounters clients who threaten to kill themselves? What if we encounter a

friend, classmate, neighbor, or relative who is contemplating suicide? In these situations we cannot be a mere observer. We are required to take action or make a decision that reflects our beliefs and values about suicide. Even more close to us is this question: "Might there ever come a time in your life when you would contemplate suicide?" Imagine yourself growing old, losing bodily functions, unable to move about, unable to read or feed yourself, and partially paralyzed by a stroke. Would you want to be kept alive?

We would like to have you, perhaps with other classmates, consider the three examples above. Can you build a case against suicide prevention? Can you build a case against the right to take one's own life? We hope that you and your classmates will be able to clarify your thoughts and values about suicide. Remember, allowing, respecting, and understanding the diversity of views on this controversial topic is important.

Society (an organization that advocates people's right to end their lives), published a best-selling book, *Final Exit* (1991). It is a manual that provides practical information such as drug dosages needed to end one's life; when published it created a national stir. Another individual who has become a household name is Dr. Jack Kervorkian, a physician who has helped sixteen persons (as of this writing) end their own lives using an invention of his called a "suicide machine."

Ironically, it is the success of medical science that has added fuel to the right-to-die movement. As a part of our remarkable successful efforts to prolong life, this society has also begun to prolong the process of dying. And this prolongation has caused many elderly or terminally ill people to fear the medical decision maker who is intent only on keeping them alive, giving no thought to their desires or dignity. They and many others find it abhorrent to impose on a dying patient a horrifying array of respirators,

breathing tubes, feeding tubes, and repeated violent-cardiopulmonary resuscitations—procedures that are often futile and against the wishes of the patient and his or her family. Humane and sensitive physicians, who believe that the resulting quality of life will not merit such heroic measures but whose training impels them to sustain life, are caught in the middle of this conflict. A civil or criminal lawsuit may be brought against the physician who agrees to allow a patient to die.

More and more people now believe that individuals ought to have the right to end their own lives, at least in certain circumstances. In cases of obvious terminal illness, when the patient has a short time to live and is suffering unbearable pain, the right-to-die argument seems sensible. In 1976 the California State Assembly became one of the first state legislatures to provide that right to people in such situations. Since then, many other states have passed "living will" laws that offer protection against dehumanized dying and confer immunity on physicians and hospital personnel who comply with a patient's wishes. And, in November 1992, California voters narrowly defeated Proposition 161, The Death With Dignity Act, which would have allowed physicians to legally help end the lives of terminally ill patients.

Advocates of such laws frequently use the terms *quality of life* and *quality of humanness* as the criteria for deciding between life and death. The meanings of these phrases are, however, somewhat indistinct and subjective. At what point do we consider the quality of life sufficiently poor to justify terminating it? Should people who have been severely injured or scarred (through loss of limbs, paralysis, blindness, or brain injury) be allowed to end their own lives? What about mentally retarded or emotionally disturbed people? It can be argued that their quality of life is equally poor. Moreover, who will decide that a person is or is not terminally ill? There are many recorded cases of "incurable" patients who recovered when new medical techniques arrested, remitted, or cured their illnesses. Such questions cannot be answered easily because they deal with ethics and human values.

Yet the mental health practitioner cannot avoid these questions. Like their medical counterparts, clinicians are trained to save people's lives. They have accepted the philosophical assumption that life is better than death, and that no one has a right to take his or her own life. Strong social, religious, and legal sanctions support this belief. Therapists work not only with terminally ill clients who wish to take their own lives but also with disturbed clients who may have suicidal tendencies. These latter clients are not terminally ill but may be suffering severe emotional or physical pain; their deaths would bring immense pain and suffering to their loved ones. Moreover, most people who attempt suicide do not want to die, are ambivalent about the act, or find that their suicidal urge passes when their life situation improves (Bongar, 1991, 1992; Murphy, 1973).

In working with clients who express suicidal wishes, the practicing therapist must confront the following questions (Corey, 1984):

1. Do therapists have a right and responsibility to forcefully protect people from the potential harm that their own decisions may cause?

2. Do therapists have an ethical right to prevent clients from committing suicide when they have clearly chosen death over life?

3. What ethical and legal considerations are involved in right-to-die decisions?

4. Once a therapist determines that a significant risk exists, must some course of action be taken? What are the consequences when a therapist fails to take steps to prevent a suicide?

Of course, these questions are answered differently by different people. We can, however, directly address one of the issues they raise—the legal implications. According to one observer, no clear constitutional or legal statement gives a person the right to choose death. But the Constitution does seem to provide a basis for the right to refuse treatment, even life-saving treatment (Powell, 1982). Therapists, however, have a responsibility to prevent suicide if they can reasonably anticipate the possibility of self-destruction. Failure to do so can result in legal liability (Schutz, 1982).

Clearly, suicide and suicide prevention involve a number of important social and legal issues, as well as the personal value systems of clients and their families, mental health professionals, and those who devise and enforce our laws. And just as clearly, we need to know much more about the causes of suicide and the detection of people who are at high risk for suicide, as well as the most effective means of intervention. Life is precious, and we need to do everything possible, within reason, to protect it.

SUMMARY

1. Suicide is both a tragic and puzzling act. In the past, it has represented an unspoken and hidden one. Recently, mental health professionals have begun to acknowledge that the study of suicide is extremely important. Much is known about the facts of suicide but little about it is understood. Although studies indicate that depression, hopelessness, and excessive alcohol consumption are highly correlated with suicide, the complex relationship between these variables and suicide is not simply one of cause and effect.

2. Early explanations of suicide were based on either a sociocultural or an intrapsychic view. Durk-

heim identified three categories of suicide on the basis of the nature of the person's relationship to a group: egoistic suicide results from an inability to integrate oneself with society; altruistic suicide is motivated by the need to further the goals of the group or to achieve a "higher good"; and anomic suicide results when a person's relationship to the group becomes unbalanced in some dramatic fashion. In the intrapsychic view, self-destruction results when hostility toward another person turns inward. More recent evidence has indicated that biochemical factors may be important, but no single explanation seems sufficient to clarify the many facets of suicide.

3. In recent years, childhood and adolescent suicides have increased at an alarming rate. A lack of research has limited our understanding of why children take their own lives. However, the available studies have indicated that those who attempt suicide come from families characterized by psychiatric illness (primarily drug and alcohol abuse), suicide, paternal unemployment, and the absence of one parent. Most childhood suicide attempts occur in the home, and drug overdose is the primary means.

4. Suicide among college students is particularly perplexing. Studies have indicated that students who commit suicide can be distinguished from their non-suicidal classmates: they are older and more likely to be postgraduate students, male, language or literature majors, and foreign students. As undergraduates, they have better academic records than their peers. Most college-student suicides occur at the beginning of a semester. They may be related to unrealistically high internal expectations, excessive pressures to excel from family and friends, or simply emotional disturbance.

5. Many people tend to become depressed about "feeling old" as they age, and depressed elderly people often think about suicide.

6. Suicide affects not only the person who commits the act but also the people left behind. Loved ones of the victim frequently respond with denial and shock, followed by grief and anger. The anger may be directed toward the self, but it is usually intended for the person who commits the act. The grief is resolved if and when he or she is able to "let go" of the deceased. Mental health professionals who treat a client who commits suicide also experience psychological distress.

7. Perhaps the best way to prevent suicide is to recognize its signs and intervene before it occurs. People are more likely to commit suicide if they are older, male, have a history of attempts, describe in detail how the act will be accomplished, and give verbal hints that they are planning self-destruction. Crisis intervention concepts and techniques have been used successfully to treat clients who contemplate suicide. Intensive short-term therapy is used to stabilize the immediate crisis. Suicide prevention centers operate twenty-four hours a day to provide intervention services to all potential suicides, especially those not undergoing treatment. Telephone hotlines are staffed by well-trained paraprofessionals who will work with anyone who is contemplating suicide. In addition, these centers provide preventive education to the public. More and more community intervention programs are directed at organizations that may have experienced a suicide. The focus is not only on preventing future suicides but also on helping friends, family, workers, and others affected by the tragedy.

8. The act of suicide raises moral, ethical, and legal concerns. Do people have a right to take their own lives? This question is difficult to answer in the case of the elderly or of people who are terminally ill and wish to end their suffering. Nevertheless, therapists, like physicians, have been trained to preserve life, and they have a legal obligation to do so.

KEY TERMS

altruistic suicide Suicide that is motivated by the need to further group goals or to achieve some greater good

anomic suicide Suicide that results when a person's relationship to society is unbalanced in some dramatic fashion

egoistic suicide Suicide that results from an inability to integrate oneself with society

psychological autopsy A systematic examination of existing information to understand and explain a person's behavior before his or her death

suicidal ideation Thoughts about suicide

suicide The taking of one's own life

CHAPTER 14

Schizophrenia: Diagnosis and Symptoms

Schizophrenia is a severely disabling disorder. At times, reality becomes so distorted people affected cannot trust their perceptions and thoughts. Zan Bockes, a woman who completed her undergraduate work between hospitalizations and eventually entered graduate school, gives a personal account of her struggles with schizophrenia.

I'd always been very quiet, somewhat of a "loner," usually energetic, and a good student with a particular interest in literature and creative writing, but the illness began disrupting my school work and job performance when I was 19 years old. . . . I increasingly heard voices (which I'd always called "loud thoughts" or "impulses with words") commanding me to take destructive action. I concluded that other people were putting these "loud thoughts" in my head and controlling my behavior in an effort to ruin my life. I smelled blood and decaying matter where no blood or decaying matter could be found (for example, in the classrooms at school). I had difficulty concentrating, I fantasized excessively, and I had trouble sleeping and eating. When I began responding to the voices' commands by breaking windows in my apartment and starting fires, I was committed with a diagnosis of "chronic hebephrenic schizophrenia." . . .

Over those 5 months, I had to deal with occasional hallucinations, recurrent illusions, increased energy . . . and periods during which I found myself indulging in various paranoid and grandiose thought patterns. Since I had learned to recognize these for what they were and had been able to appreciate the ultimate consequences of reacting to them, I was capable of preventing them from drastically affecting my behavior. . . . I recall one recent example of how I prevented further escalation of some irrational suspicions. In March, I became increasingly uneasy about something which I could not pinpoint, until I was quite fearful that some personal disaster was rapidly approaching. On my way to school one day, three large birds passed over me, stalling briefly in the air above my head. In my class, I noticed that a woman in front of me had a large black bag marked with white letters which read, among other things, "URGENT" and "CONFIDENTIAL." I heard a woman in the hallway say, "You won't go to jail." And my professor said during his lecture, "The choices you make are not inevitable," which angered and frightened me because I misunderstood him to mean, "The choices you make are inevitable." These events loomed in my head, and I interpreted them as warnings of impending disaster. With great difficulty, I suppressed my impulses to cry out and strike the nearby professor, and I tried to concentrate on the lecture. I managed to get through class and then hurried to my favorite isolated place on campus to get better control of myself. . . .

I acknowledge that although I have much control over my behavior, and some control over my thinking, and some control over my feelings, there remain a few things over which I have little or no control—for example, hallucinations. The trick is to realize when or if the hallucinations are truly disrupting my thoughts, feelings, and behaviors, and to take appropriate action before things get out of hand. Gradually I am learning where to draw the line—when medication is helpful and necessary and when I can manage safely without it. . . .

As of yet, I still have a long road ahead of me. There is much that I don't understand about schizophrenia, but I realize I am not alone in my lack of knowledge about the illness. . . . Life puts various limitations on each person, but within those limitations, there is always the freedom to make certain choices—an insight that I find relieving as well as revealing. (Bockes, 1987, pp. 40–42)

These few excerpts from Bockes's account illustrate many features of the schizophrenic disorders, which involve disorders of thought or cognition. More specifically, **cognition** consists of the processes of thinking, perceiving, judging, and recognizing. **Schizophrenia** is a group of disorders characterized by severely impaired cognitive processes, personality disintegration, and social withdrawal. The schizophrenic disorders are severe disturbances (psychoses) that always involve some disruption of thought processes. People thus affected may lose contact with reality, may see or hear things that are not actually occurring, or may develop false beliefs about themselves or others.

SCHIZOPHRENIA

Schizophrenia has received—and continues to receive—a great deal of attention for several reasons. First, the disorders are severely disabling and frequently require hospitalization. The financial costs of hospitalization and the psychological costs to patients, families, and friends can be enormous. Second, the lifetime prevalence rate of schizophrenia in the United States is about 1 percent, so it affects millions of people directly (it occurs equally among males and females; Bourdon et al; 1992). And third, the causes of these disorders are not well known, and it has been difficult to find effective treatments. Although DSM-IV tries to present schizophrenia as a distinct disorder, evidence has suggested that it is a heterogeneous clinical syndrome with different etiologies and outcomes (Heinrichs, 1993).

In this chapter we discuss the diagnosis and symptoms of schizophrenia, the different types of schizophrenic disorders, and the course of this disorder. Then, in Chapter 15, we examine the etiology and treatment of schizophrenia.

History of the Diagnostic Category

What is schizophrenia? Most clinicians agree that the symptoms shown by Zan Bockes (hearing disembodied voices, smelling nonexistent blood and decaying matter, and disturbed thought processes) are consistent with a diagnosis of schizophrenia. The criteria that define this disorder, however, have changed over time. Some who were diagnosed as schizophrenic under criteria used in the past might not be diagnosed as schizophrenic under the diagnostic system used today.

In 1896 Emil Kraepelin recognized that symptoms such as hallucinations, delusions, and intellectual deterioration were characteristic of a particular disorder whose onset began at an early age. He called this disorder *dementia praecox* (insanity at an early age). Because he believed that the disorder involved some form of organic deterioration, its outcome was considered to be poor. People who recovered from dementia praecox were thought to have been misdiagnosed.

A Swiss psychiatrist, Eugen Bleuler (1950), disagreed with Kraepelin's theory for several reasons. He did not believe that all or even most cases of

Universe Inversion (crayon), Joseph Schneller (pseudonym, Joseph Sell) (Note: This painting and the four others in this chapter were painted by people with schizophrenia)

schizophrenia developed at an early age. The symptoms of schizophrenia were believed to be the result of disordered thought processes affecting the four As: autism (complete self-focus), associations (unconnected ideas), affect (inappropriate emotions), and ambivalence (uncertainty over actions). He argued that the outcome of schizophrenia did not always involve progressive deterioration, and he believed that dementia praecox represented a group of disorders that have different causes. Bleuler also theorized that environmental factors interacting with a genetic predisposition produced the disorder.

Bleuler's definition of schizophrenia was broader than Kraepelin's in that age of onset and the course of the disorder was more variable. DSM-I and DSM-

II incorporated the broader definition of schizophrenia and focused on Bleuler's four As as the criteria. Several international studies (World Health Organization, Cooper et al., 1972) revealed that other countries used a stricter definition for schizophrenia. When schizophrenic patients in the United States were rediagnosed according to the international standards, approximately 50 percent were placed into other categories such as mood or personality disorders or other psychotic disorders.

This discrepancy with other diagnostic systems forced researchers to reexamine the criteria used to define schizophrenia and resulted in changes in DSM-III and DSM-III-R. "The DSM-III concept is more restrictive in order to identify a group that is more homogeneous in regard to differential response to somatic therapy, presence of a familial pattern, a tendency toward onset in early adult life, recurrence, and severe functional impairment (American Psychiatric Association, 1980, p. 373). But it appears that the pendulum swung too far in narrowing the definition of schizophrenia. The criteria in DSM-III-R (continued in DSM-IV) were considered to be some of the most restrictive among classification systems in the world (Andreasen & Falum, 1991; Carson, 1991). For example, the symptoms have to be present for at least six months for the diagnosis compared with only one month according to the tenth revision of the International Classification of Disease (ICD-10) developed by the World Health Organization. Individuals who would be classified as schizophrenic in other countries might not receive that diagnosis with DSM-IV. Although these changes are thought to increase diagnostic reliability and validity of research on schizophrenia, they also make comparing studies done in the United States under different diagnostic criteria difficult. Problems also occur in cross-cultural comparisons because different countries use ICD-10 instead of DSM-IV. How can you interpret studies on cause and treatment of schizophrenia using different diagnostic criteria? Why has it been so difficult to agree on a definition of such a severe mental disorder?

DSM-IV and the Diagnosis of Schizophrenia

Recall from Chapter 4 the Rosenhan (1973) study in which eight researchers, pretending to be mentally ill, gained admission to psychiatric hospitals. The eight experimenters all told the staff that they heard a voice saying "empty," "hollow," or "thud" and that the auditory hallucinations had occurred for three weeks. Except for their names, vocations, and occupations, all the other information they provided the hospital staff was true. All but one received a diagnosis of schizophrenia, and that one was labeled manic-depressive; all were admitted for treatment.

DSM-IV had not been published at the time of the Rosenhan study, so the pseudopatients were diagnosed according to DSM-II or another classification scheme. The obvious question is "Would these people have been diagnosed as schizophrenic under the DSM-III or DSM-IV criteria?" The answer is no, if the criteria were followed strictly. Among the requirements that would not have been fulfilled are (1) deterioration from a previous level of functioning and (2) two symptoms with a duration of six months or more. Actually, the symptoms reported by Rosenhan's pseudopatients do not fully meet the criteria for any of the psychotic disorders. (Any clinician would have a duty, however, to admit the pseudopatients for further observation based on their claims that they heard voices.)

The value of a diagnostic system such as DSM-IV depends on its consistent and appropriate use. Unfortunately, clinicians often do not follow classification guidelines. At a time when DSM-III criteria should have been applied, 301 psychiatrists were asked to "describe the clinical findings that would lead you to a diagnosis of schizophrenia" (Lipkowitz & Iduputganti, 1983). Only one respondent listed all findings necessary for such a diagnosis (symptoms, deterioration, six months' duration, and absence of major organic or affective disorder). Of further interest is that 49 percent said that they used only one diagnostic criterion, and some used idiosyncratic criteria that are obviously not in any of the accepted classification systems, such as the following:

The "smell of schizophrenia"

Patient "doesn't add up"

"Poor ego functions or boundaries"

"Poor eye contact"

"Rapid mood swings"

"Excess religiosity"

Table 14.1

DSM-IV Criteria for Schizophrenia

A. At least two of the following symptoms lasting for at least one month in the active phase (exception: only one symptom if it involves bizarre delusions or if hallucinations involve a running commentary on the person or two or more voices talking with each other).
   1. Delusions
   2. Hallucinations
   3. Disorganized speech (incoherence or frequent derailment)
   4. Grossly disorganized or catatonic behavior
   5. Negative symptoms (flat affect, avolition, alogia, or anhedonia)

B. During the course of the disturbance, functioning in one or more areas such as work, social relations, and self-care has deteriorated markedly from premorbid levels (in the case of a child or adolescent, failure to reach expected level of social or academic development).

C. Signs of the disorder must be present for at least six months.

D. Schizoaffective and mood disorders with psychotic features must be ruled out.

E. The disturbance is not substance-induced or caused by organic factors.

Source: Adapted from DSM-IV Draft Criteria.

According to the DSM-IV criteria, a diagnosis of schizophrenic disorder should be given only if delusions, auditory hallucinations, or marked disturbances in thinking, affect, or speech are shown. The patient must also have deteriorated from a previous level of functioning concerning work, interpersonal relationships, self-care, or the like. Evidence should show that the disorder has lasted at least six months at some point in the patient's history and has currently been present for at least one month. Organic mental disorders and affective disorders must be ruled out as causes of the patient's symptoms. (See Table 14.1 for DSM-IV criteria for schizophrenia.)

Schizophrenia is a severe and identifiable condition. Why has it been so difficult to define? What are the symptoms that are pathognomonic (specific) for this disorder? What are some pros and cons of adopting a broad or narrow definition of schizophrenia?

THE SYMPTOMS OF SCHIZOPHRENIA

Symptoms of schizophrenia involve delusions, hallucinations, thought disorder, and bizarre behavior. These are often described as **positive symptoms,** or symptoms that are present during the active phase of the disorder and tend to disappear with treatment. Schizophrenics with predominantly positive symptoms are often classified as Type I. **Negative symptoms** are associated with inferior premorbid social functioning and a poorer prognosis. They include flat affect, poverty of speech, anhedonia, apathy, and avolition. Individuals who have primarily negative symptoms are often classified as Type II. Some believe that the positive symptoms indicate a reversible condition and negative symptoms represent irreversible neuronal loss in a structurally abnormal brain (McGlashan & Fenton, 1992). We will discuss in more detail some symptoms associated with schizophrenia.

Delusions

The disordered thinking of schizophrenics may be exhibited in **delusions,** which are false personal beliefs that are firmly and consistently held despite disconfirming evidence or logic (Garety, 1991). Studies have suggested that delusions may differ in strength and their effect on the person's life. An example of a delusion follows:

> Ms. A., an 83-year-old widow who lived alone for fifteen years, complained that the occupant of an upstairs flat was excessively noisy and that he moved furniture around late at night to disturb her. Over a period of six months, she developed delusional persecutory ideas about this man. He wanted to frighten her from her home and had started to transmit "violet rays" through the ceiling to harm her and her ten-year-old female mongrel dog. . . . For protection, she placed her mattress under the kitchen table and slept there at night. She constructed what she called an "air raid shelter" for her dog from a small table and a pile of suitcases and insisted that the dog sleep in it. When I visited Ms. A. at her home, it was apparent that the dog's behavior had become so conditioned by that of

People with persecutory delusions may react with great fear over imagined threats and dangers.

> its owner that upon hearing any sound from the flat upstairs, such as a door closing, it would immediately go to the kitchen and enter the shelter. (Howard, 1992, p. 414)

Ms. A. absolutely believed in her delusion and had little insight into her behavior.

Several types of delusions are listed here.

- *Delusions of grandeur* A belief that one is a famous or powerful person (from the present or the past). Schizophrenics may assume the identities of these other people.

- *Delusions of control* A belief that other people, animals, or objects are trying to influence or take control of one.

◆ *Delusions of thought broadcasting* A belief that others can hear the thoughts of the individual.

◆ *Delusions of persecution* A belief that others are plotting against, mistreating, or even trying to kill one.

◆ *Delusions of reference* A belief that one is always the center of attention, or that all happenings revolve about oneself. Others are always whispering behind one's back, for example.

◆ *Thought withdrawal* A belief that one's thoughts are being removed from one's mind by other people.

A rare delusion is *Capgras's syndrome* (named after the person who first reported it). It is the belief in the existence of identical "doubles," who may coexist with or replace significant others or the patient. One fourteen-year-old girl, for example, believed that her mother was replaced by an imposter. She also questioned the identities of her brothers and sisters (Kouran & Williams, 1984).

Although it is believed that delusions are firmly held, the strengths actually varies from person to person and even within a single individual (from time to time). In a study of fifty-two delusional patients, researchers identified four qualities of delusions (Kendler, Glaser & Morgenstern, 1983).

1. The *conviction* with which a delusion is held is the degree to which the person is convinced of the delusion. In the study, a 48-year-old woman who was concerned about infecting others with a disease sometimes indicated that her concern could be due to her imagination. At the other extreme, a man who claimed to be in communication with aliens responded, "Absolutely not!" to the suggestion that his imagination was involved.

2. The *extension* of a delusion is the degree to which it involves other people. One 42-year-old woman complained about being poisoned by her boss, who was using radioactivity near her desk while she was at work. In another case, a 22-year-old man felt persecuted by friends and strangers alike.

3. *Disorganization* involves the degree of internal consistency of the delusional system. An example of a consistent belief involved a 48-year-old man who believed that a committee made up of members of his law school class were persecuting him. The persecution involved the committee's hiring of actors to jeer at and insult him. Cameras and monitors placed in his apartment alerted the committee about his movements so that actors could harass him whenever he left his home. In a case exhibiting inconsistency, a 24-year-old woman claimed that her parents had leukemia, that people were being killed, and that she was being poisoned and turned into a lesbian. She made no attempt to relate these delusional ideas to each other.

4. The *pressure* of a delusion is the degree to which the person is preoccupied with the belief. For example, one 28-year-old woman was convinced that she was the Virgin Mary. Asked how often she thought of herself in that way, she replied, "Oh, it comes to me now and then." At the other extreme, a 56-year-old man, convinced that he was a government double agent, spent all his waking hours trying to recall how and when he first became involved.

This individual variability suggests the need to reconceptualize delusions. Delusions may not always be held firmly or be disruptive. In a study of nine schizophrenic patients, Brett-Jones, Garety, and Hemsley (1987) found that most were not preoccupied with their delusions. They thought about them "only some of the time." In addition, most indicated that their delusions interfered very little with their daily activities. They responded to contradictory information by ignoring or denying it, and they didn't actively test out their beliefs. The researchers, however, warned that we should not automatically view the lack of reality testing as pathological. They pointed out that the responses shown by the schizophrenics are "little different from the way that most people deal with evidence concerning beliefs or theories that are important to them" (p. 265). Schizophrenic individuals do appear to manifest deficits in judgment and reasoning in dealing with their delusions. But normal persons have also been found to ignore alternative explanations of their strongly held beliefs (Butler & Braff, 1991).

One difference found between nonschizophrenic and schizophenic persons is that the latter were more likely to reach a conclusion on less information (Maher, 1988). This may be related to the development of unusual beliefs. One schizophrenic who was hospitalized developed the delusion that another patient was her grandmother from this short conversation:

"Where do I know you from?" I asked a hefty woman with a tiny face. The woman's short curly hair circled her pudgy face in ringlets. I thought I knew her.

"In the cottage by the sea," said the woman squinting austerely at me, "I was you and you were me."

This enigmatic message must be a piece to the puzzle. I pondered it. Grandma, before she died, had lived by the sea. Suddenly I knew the woman was my grandma. (Anonymous, 1990, p. 356)

In this example, the woman reached the conclusion that the older patient was her grandmother based on the word "sea." Schizophrenics may be attempting to search for a reason for their unusual experiences but are limited in considering different possibilities for their behavior.

Schizophrenics may be trained to challenge their delusions. One 51-year-old patient believed that she was younger than twenty years old and the daughter of Princess Anne. She expressed almost 100 percent belief in her delusions. The patient was asked to view her delusion as only one possible interpretation of the event. Then the evidence for the belief was discussed. Inconsistencies and the irrationality of the belief were presented as well as alternative explanations. After this procedure the patient reported a large drop in the conviction of her beliefs. She stated, "I look 50 and I tire more quickly than I use to; I must be 50"

(Lowe & Chadwick, 1990, p. 471). She also agreed that she was probably older than Princess Anne and therefore could not be her daughter. The patient also learned to react to a voice telling her that she was the mother of a different member of the royal family. She disputed the voice and said that it could not possibly be true. Belief modification appears to be a helpful procedure for some schizophrenics.

Perceptual Distortion

Schizophrenics often report **hallucinations,** which are sensory perceptions that are not directly attributable to environmental stimuli. They may claim to see people or objects, hear voices, or smell peculiar odors that are not really present. (Note the distinction between hallucinations and delusions: hallucinations are false sensory experiences, whereas delusions are false intellectual experiences.) Hallucinations are not **pathognomonic** (specifically distinctive) to schizophrenia. Persons with certain mood disorders, brief reactive psychosis, and schizophreniform disorders also report hallucinations. But it does appear that schizophrenics are more likely to report bizarre hallucinations than persons with other disorders (Goldman et al., 1992).

Auditory hallucinations may involve voices that make humiliating, blaming and insulting comments against an individual.

Hallucinations may involve a single sensory modality or combination of modalities: hearing (*auditory* hallucinations), seeing (*visual* hallucinations), smelling (*olfactory* hallucinations), feeling (*tactile* hallucinations), and tasting (*gustatory* hallucinations). Auditory hallucinations are the most common (Payne, 1992). Hallucinations sometimes accompany and are related to delusional beliefs. For example, a patient who believed that she had committed an unforgivable sin heard imaginary voices saying that she was evil and worthless. This woman became extremely guilt-ridden, distraught, and eventually suicidal in an attempt to atone for the imagined sin.

Hallucinations are puzzling because they do not seem to be produced by external stimuli. Researchers have therefore focused on the possible role of internal stimuli. Bick and Kinsbourne (1987) wanted to see if hallucinations are caused by a slight activity in the speech musculature (subvocal). Eighteen schizophrenics who had reported hearing voices every day for more than two years were asked to report the status of their hallucinations under three conditions: (1) eyes closed tightly, (2) mouth open, and (3) fists squeezed tightly. The conditions of eyes shut and tight fists were intended to control for variables such as distraction and facial involvement. Among the schizophrenics, most reported that under the "mouth open" condition hallucinations ceased. The other two conditions had little effect on the hallucinations. The researchers also found that nonschizophrenic controls who were hypnotized and told that they would hear voices reported that the "mouth open" condition eliminated their hallucinations. Bick and Kinsbourne (1987) concluded that hallucinations involve the following pattern: the patient subvocalizes, reacts to this activity, and then attributes it to another source. Although this hypothesis seemed promising, Green and Kinsbourne (1990) reported only partial support. They found that of three conditions designed to interfere with subvocalization (mouth open, biting the tongue, and humming a note), only humming was associated with a reduction in self-report of auditory hallucinations.

Delusions and hallucinations can be extremely distressing to schizophrenics as they respond to their internal realities. One college student who suffered auditory hallucinations involving messages from radio and television programs asked, "How can I tell when the radio is really on and when it is my imagi-nation?" This question obviously reflects an attempt to discriminate between reality and hallucinations. Some schizophrenics have developed ways of coping with their hallucinations. In a study of 186 schizophrenics who characterized their auditory hallucinations as being primarily negative (although approximately fifteen percent were positive), involving voices commenting on their action, and taking over their thinking processes, Romme and colleagues (1992) found that approximately one-third had developed coping strategies. The main groups of coping strategies were as follows:

1. *Distraction*   Taking a shower, jogging, watching a video, meditation, and so on.

2. *Ignoring*   One woman had auditory hallucinations telling her to injure herself. Her husband asked if she would harm herself if their neighbor told her to. She said no and has learned to ignore the voices.

3. *Selective listening*   A woman was able to select positive aspects from the voices.

4. *Setting limits*   One patient indicated that she had made a deal with the voices. After 8 P.M. they are allowed expression but not during the day. This was successful in removing the impact of the voices.

During acute stages (when the symptoms are most prominent), the person may be so involved in hallucinations that he or she cannot do anything but respond as though they were real. This may be true concerning delusions as well. As Focus 14.1 suggests, however, some schizophrenics can break into the process by which hallucinations or delusions are developed and ward them off.

Disorganized Speech and Thought Disturbances

According to the World Health Organization study cited in Focus 14.2, the most common symptom of schizophrenia is lack of insight. During the active phase of their disorder, schizophrenics often cannot recognize that their thinking is disturbed. For example, a psychology graduate student, David Zelt, who went through a schizophrenic episode, believed that the CIA was listening to his thoughts and would broadcast them. The student did not question these

Can Schizophenics Control Their Symptoms?

A 24-year-old man, diagnosed as paranoid schizophrenic, reported that he could sometimes stop or diminish both auditory hallucinations and the belief that he was being persecuted. Two researchers became intrigued by his report and began a study of twenty psychiatric patients to find out whether and how patients could control their symptoms (Breier & Strauss, 1983). Specifically, they tried to find out whether patients use self-control methods, the types of methods employed, and why some patients are unsuccessful in using these methods. They found that most of the patients (seventeen) did try to control their symptoms. The most important factor for success was identifying the feelings and thoughts that occurred before a psychotic episode. One man, for example, learned to be alert to a "high" sensation. If he took no action in response to that feeling, it evolved into psychotic symptoms.

Three general approaches were used by the patients to control their hallucinations or delusions. The first involved self-instruction. One woman would tell herself to "act like an adult" and to "be responsible." Others would actively compare their behavior with that of nearby people to determine if they were behaving normally. The second approach involved reducing activity when the symptoms began to appear. One woman found that she could reduce the severity of her symptoms by isolating herself in the bathroom. Others would stop what they were doing and take a walk or simply relax. The third approach involved increasing activity. For example, one patient found that her symptoms would get worse if she remained unoccupied, but she could reduce their severity by keeping busy. Similar results were reported by Tarrier (1987). Of those who were able to identify events that

precipitated psychotic episodes, 72 percent were able to use coping strategies. Those who used multiple strategies were the most successful at coping.

These studies showed that many psychotic patients are aware of the negative nature of their symptoms and take active steps to regulate their psychopathology. It was easier for patients to break the chain leading to a psychotic episode earlier than later in its development—and that the key may be identifying the antecedents to psychotic behavior. These findings have obvious implications for treating schizophrenia and other thought disorders. Based on the information from these studies, how would you design a program to help individuals with schizophrenia deal with psychotic symptoms?

beliefs. One of his therapists noted, "It was impressive to me to find someone with an exhaustive intellectual knowledge about psychosis and still unable to bring his critical faculties to bear upon the onslaught of ideation" (Zelt, 1981, p. 531). Another individual who obtained a Ph.D. could not understand the bizarre nature of her hallucinations and delusions, such as being controlled by the television station, having the power to make dogs bark by using mind rays, and receiving brain waves from alien creatures (Payne, 1992). Lack of insight itself is not enough to make a diagnosis of schizophrenia. This feature is also displayed in other disorders. Attempts are being made to identify pathognomonic symptoms—those that are specific only to schizophrenia. Thought disturbances are also exhibited in unusual patterns of speech or writing.

Loosening of Associations   The **loosening of associations,** or *cognitive slippage,* is the continual shifting of thoughts from topic to topic without any apparent logical or meaningful connection between them. It may be shown by incoherent speech and bizarre and idiosyncratic responses. One schizophrenic described the conflict in her thought processes:

I am often caught in guttural struggles with my own voice as I try to get the words out. These aborted thoughts, not lost, but taken over by a more powerful chaos, are among the things that cannot be said. . . . I battle to gain control over the unwieldy words that pour from my mouth, confusing me, frustrating me, and literally tying me down and making me prey once again to the whims of what my brain chooses to allow my lips to utter. (Ruocchio, 1991, pp. 367–368)

F O C U S 1 4 . 2

Symptoms of Schizophrenia

The World Health Organization (WHO) conducted a large-scale diagnostic study of schizophrenia to determine its characteristics. Patients from the United States, England, the Soviet Union, China, India, Denmark, Czechoslovakia, Colombia, and Nigeria were included in this International Pilot Study of Schizophrenia (World Health Organization, 1973b, 1981). The following symptoms were reported in 50 percent or more of schizophrenic individuals:

- Lack of insight   97 percent
- Auditory hallucinations 74 percent
- Verbal hallucinations 70 percent
- Ideas of reference   70 percent
- Suspiciousness   66 percent
- Flat affect   66 percent
- Voices speaking to patient 65 percent

- Delusional mood   64 percent
- Delusions of persecution 54 percent
- Thought alienation   52 percent
- Thoughts spoken aloud 50 percent

These are the symptoms most frequently seen in schizophrenics. For two reasons, however, they are not sufficient to ensure the accurate diagnosis of schizophrenia. First, many of these symptoms also occur in other disorders. Patients with major affective disorders, for example, may show delusions, hallucinations, and lack of insight (Harrow et al., 1982). Second, some of the most frequently observed symptoms, including lack of insight and flat affect, are defined in different ways by different clinicians, so that the symptoms themselves have low reliability in pinpointing schizophrenia.

What is needed for accurate diagnosis is a set of symptoms that are specific to schizophrenia. Unfortunately, these might not be the most common symptoms. An example is *neologisms*, or made-up words; their appearance in the speech of a patient almost guarantees a diagnosis of schizophrenia in any country in the world (Kaplan & Sadock, 1981). However, they are a fairly rare symptom. Of the common symptoms, the most discriminant— and therefore the most helpful in diagnosing schizophrenia—are auditory hallucinations, voices speaking to the patient, thought alienation, thoughts spoken aloud, and delusions of control.

Source: World Health Organization, 1973b, 1981.

In addition, communication may be vague or overly concrete (as opposed to abstract). Some of these characteristics are illustrated in the following patient responses to test questions:

Q: Why does a train have an engine?
A: To give it a fantasy of imagination that requires it useless until you produce it.
Q: [What is meant by] "One swallow doesn't make a summer"?
A: That's oriental. When the first bird in the summer swallows the first worm, then she can start to produce eggs. Which do you think comes first, the chicken or the egg? I think the egg, definitely. And it was fertilized with the sperm, so the sperm came first, too. Which came first, though, the egg or the sperm? (Harrow et al., 1982, p. 666)

Neologisms   As noted in Focus 14.2, the speech of some schizophrenics contains **neologisms,** which are

new words formed by combining words in common usage. For example, one psychologist asked a patient, "How do you feel today?" The patient responded,

Yes, sir, it's a good day. Full of rainbows you know. They go along on their merry way without concern for asphyxiation or impurities. Yes sir, like unconcerned flappers of the cosmoblue.

The patient's "cosmoblue" is a neologism, a combination of "cosmos" and "blue," the color of the sky. The response is also tangential; instead of answering the question directly, it seems to ramble though a series of asides.

Problems with Attention   Schizophrenics have trouble directing their attention to a particular aspect of their environment and keeping their attention focused on it. In other words, they find it difficult to concentrate and to organize incoming information

Untitled (pencil and watercolor), August Klett

(Penn et al., 1993): "Schizophrenia is frustrating when I can't hold onto my thoughts; when conversation is projected on my mind but won't come out of my mouth; . . . when my eyes and ears drown in a flood of sights and sounds (McGrath, 1987, p. 38). Although some schizophrenics appear to realize that they have problems with communication, others are unaware of their disturbance. Chaika (1985) videotaped a schizophrenic during the active phase of his illness. Later, when the man viewed the tape of himself, he said he never realized he spoke that way.

Disorganized Motoric Disturbances

The symptoms of schizophrenia that involve motor functions can be quite bizarre. The person may show extreme activity levels (either unusually high or unusually low), peculiar body movements or postures, strange gestures and grimaces, or a combination of these. Like hallucinations, a patient's motoric behav-

iors may be related to his or her delusions. For example, during a clinical interview one schizophrenic patient kept lowering his chin to his chest and then raising his head again. Asked why he lowered his head in that way, the patient replied that the atmospheric pressure often became too great to bear, and it forced his head down.

Schizophrenics who display extremely high levels of motor activity may move about quickly, swing their arms wildly, talk rapidly and unendingly, or pace constantly. At the other extreme, some patients hardly move at all, staring out into space (or perhaps into themselves) for long periods of time. The inactive patients also tend to show little interest in others, to respond only minimally, and to have few friends. During periods of withdrawal, they are frequently preoccupied with personal fantasies and daydreams.

The assumption and maintenance of an unusual (and often awkward) body position is characteristic of the *catatonic* type of schizophrenia (to be discussed shortly). A catatonic patient may stand for hours at a time, perhaps with one arm stretched out to the side, or may lie on the floor or sit awkwardly on a chair, staring, aware of what is going on around, but not responding or moving. If a hospital attendant tries to change the patient's position, the patient may either resist stubbornly or may simply assume and maintain the new position.

Negative Symptoms

Negative symptoms have been associated with a poor prognosis. Clinicians must be careful to distinguish between *primary symptoms* (symptoms that arise from the disease itself) and *secondary symptoms* (symptoms that may develop as a response to medication and institutionalization). It is the former that researchers are primarily interested in. The negative symptoms include **flat affect,** or little or no emotion in situations where strong reactions are expected. A delusional patient, for instance, might explain in detail how parts of his or her body are rotting away but show absolutely no concern or worry through voice tone or facial expression.

Beiser and colleagues (1988) reported that more than one-half the schizophrenic patients they studied showed restricted affect ("expressionless face and voice") whatever the topic of discussion. However,

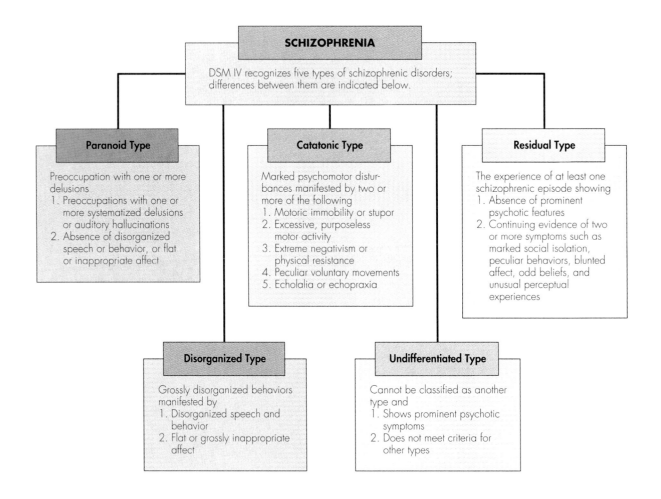

flat affect may not be a symptom of the disorder but the result of institutionalization or antipsychotic medications. Additional negative symptoms include *anhedonia* (the inability to feel pleasure), *avolition* (a lack of motivation or self-directed behavior), and *alogia* (a lack of meaningful speech).

Schizophrenics often show disturbances in their sense of self and are perplexed about their identity, as the following quotation shows:

> The reflection in the store window—it's me, isn't it? I know it is, but it's hard to tell. Glassy shadows, polished pastels, a jigsaw puzzle of my body, face, and clothes, with pieces disappearing whenever I move. And, if I want to reach out to touch me, I feel nothing but a slippery coldness. Yet I sense that it's me. I just know. (McGrath, 1987, p. 37)

TYPES OF SCHIZOPHRENIA

Five types of schizophrenic disorders are generally recognized: paranoid, disorganized, catatonic, undifferentiated, and residual. These are shown in the disorders chart shown above. Although some clinicians question the value and validity of attempting to identify different types of schizophrenia, research has found support for the paranoid type. The reliability and validity of the other types are not as clear. Little information exists about the catatonic type because it is rare (McGlashan & Fenton, 1991).

Paranoid Schizophrenia

The most common form of schizophrenia is the paranoid type. **Paranoid schizophrenia** is characterized by

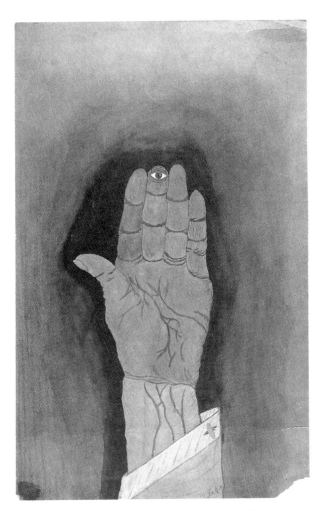

Untitled (pencil on cardboard), Berthold L. (or L. Berthold)

Mr. A., a 37-year-old Mexican-American Vietnam veteran previously treated at several Veterans Administration hospitals with the diagnosis of paranoid schizophrenia, came to the emergency room stating, "My life is in danger." . . . Mr. A. told a semicoherent story of international spy intrigue that was built around the release of soldiers still missing in action or held as prisoners of war in Vietnam. He believed he was hunted by Vietnamese agents. . . . Mr. A. reported hearing the voices of the men from his company who died. . . . These voices tended to severely criticize and chastise him. He had become so disturbed by these beliefs and auditory hallucinations that he made suicidal efforts to escape the torment. (Glassman et al., 1987, pp. 658–659)

Individuals with paranoid schizophrenia may be prone to anger since many feel persecuted. (A psychotic disorder involving delusions that is often confused with paranoid schizophrenia is described in Focus 14.3).

Disorganized Schizophrenia

Disorganized schizophrenia (formerly called *hebephrenic*) is characterized by severe disintegration and regressive behaviors beginning at an early age. The diagnostic criteria include frequent incoherence or disorganized speech, and flat or inappropriate affect (DSM-IV). People with this disorder act in an absurd, incoherent, or very odd manner that conforms to the stereotype of "crazy" behavior. Their emotional responses to real-life situations are typically flat, but a silly smile and childish giggle may be shown at inappropriate times. The hallucinations and delusions of disorganized schizophrenics tend to shift from theme to theme rather than remain centered on a single idea, such as persecution or sin. Because of the severity of the disorder, many people affected with disorganized schizophrenia are unable to care for themselves and are institutionalized.

Disorganized schizophrenics usually exhibit extremely bizarre and seemingly childish behaviors, such as masturbating in public or fantasizing aloud. An example appears in the following excerpt from a clinical interview with a young woman:

Therapist: Do you know why your mother brought you to this clinic?
Client: Well, Mom started yelling at me. She gets too excited about things. People are so excited nowadays. You know what I mean?
Therapist: What did she yell at you about?

delusions or frequent auditory hallucinations. No other symptoms such as disorganized speech and behavior or flat affect is apparent. Delusions of persecution are the most common. The deluded individuals believe that others are plotting against them, are talking about them, or are out to harm them in some way. They are constantly suspicious, and their interpretations of the behavior and motives of others are distorted: a friendly, smiling bus driver is seen as someone who is laughing at them derisively; a busy clerk who fails to offer help is part of a plot to mistreat them; a telephone call that was a wrong number is an act of harassment or an attempt to monitor their comings and goings.

Delusional Disorder

Delusional disorder is often confused with schizophrenia. In both, thought processes are disturbed. Nevertheless, some differences exist. Delusional disorder involves "non-bizarre" beliefs (situations that could actually occur) that have lasted for at least one month. Also, except for the delusion, the person's behavior is not odd. With schizophrenics, other disturbances in thoughts and perceptions are involved. People with delusional disorder behave normally when their delusional ideas are not being discussed. Common themes in delusional disorders involve:

- *Erotomania* (belief that someone is in love with you; usually romanticized rather than sexual love is involved)
- *Grandiosity* (conviction that you have great, unrecognized talent or have some special ability or relationship with an important individual)
- *Jealousy* (conviction that your spouse or partner is being unfaithful)
- *Persecution* (belief in being conspired or plotted against)
- *Somatic complaints* (convictions of having body odor, being malformed, or being infested by insects or parasites)

The following case illustrates some features of delusional disorders:

Mr. H. . . . was a 55-year-old man who was divorced, unemployed, and living on his own in a two-room flat. He had been referred by his general practitioner for treatment of a "phobia," after complaining that since he had laid an old carpet six weeks previously, he had become infested with minuscule insects, which lived under his skin and caused intense itching and burning sensations. He had visited the casualty and dermatology departments of his local hospital three times since then, with complaints of "gritty" sensations in his eyes, and skin rashes showing "samples" of insects for inspection. . . . To escape the insects, he had got rid of the carpet, had his flat fumigated, and got rid of virtually all his furnishings and clothing. (Macaskill, 1987, p. 262)

Lack of feedback may play a role in the development of delusional disorder. In a study of people with this disorder, most were characterized as socially isolated, and nearly half had a physical impairment such as deafness or visual problems (Holden, 1987). A decreased ability to obtain corrective feedback, combined with a preexisting personality type that tends toward suspiciousness, may increase the susceptibility of developing delusional beliefs.

Client: Just because I smeared some shit on a painting I was doing for school (silly giggle). See, the teacher in art class wanted us to do some finger painting at home. She said that we should be creative. I ran out of paint so I thought I would use some shit. After all, it is natural (giggle) and it feels like paint.

Catatonic Schizophrenia

Disturbance in motor activity—either extreme excitement or motoric immobility—is the prime characteristic of **catatonic schizophrenia**. The individual may show extreme negativism or peculiar voluntary posturing or movements. This disorder is quite rare.

Excited catatonics are agitated and hyperactive. People with this form of the disorder may talk and shout constantly, while moving or running until they drop from exhaustion. They sleep little and are continually "on the go." Their behavior can become dangerous, however, and violent acts are not uncommon. *Withdrawn catatonics* are extremely unresponsive with respect to motor activity. Such people show prolonged periods of stupor and mutism, despite their awareness of all that is going on around them. Some may adopt and maintain strange postures and refuse to move or change position. Others exhibit a *waxy flexibility*, allowing themselves to be "arranged" in almost any position and then remaining in that position for long periods of time. During periods of extreme withdrawal, catatonic schizophrenics may not eat or control their bladder or bowel functions.

People diagnosed with disorganized schizophrenia often display flat or inappropriate affect, such as giggling at the wrong time.

Catatonics may alternate between excited motor activity and withdrawal, as is illustrated in the following case:

A 43-year-old man was admitted to a hospital after his wife became alarmed over his complete inactivity. He had been unemployed for the last two months but had become progressively more uncommunicative during the last eight months. A few days before, he had stopped talking altogether, and he now sat in his chair all day with his eyes closed. After about a week in the hospital, a nurse reported that the patient had gotten out of bed and was standing in the hospital's recreation room, giving what appeared to be a lecture to other patients. The ward psychiatrist immediately asked the nurse to bring the patient to his office, where the following conversation took place:

Patient: You wanted to see me, Doctor?
Psychiatrist: Yes. You know you hardly said anything

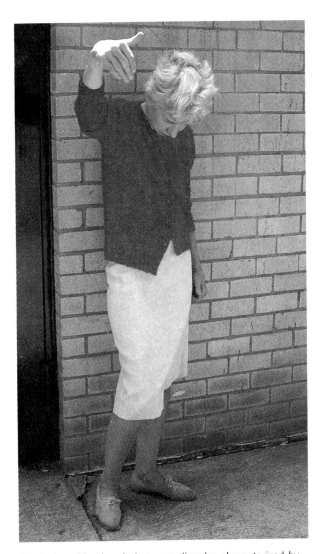

Catatonic schizophrenia is a rare disorder characterized by disturbances in motor activity. Excited catatonics exhibit great agitation and hyperactivity; withdrawn catatonics (like the woman shown in this picture) may exhibit extreme unresponsiveness or adopt strange postures.

for the past week, and now the nurse says you're interacting with other patients.
Patient: This past week, Doctor, I've been thinking and meditating.
Psychiatrist: About what?
Patient: You see, Doctor, the patient next door always has his television set on. I've been carefully listening to the kinds of programs on television—the walls in the hospital are thin. I'm appalled at the continual outpouring of filth, decadence, sin, immorality, sex, vio-

Church Light (watercolor), Konrad Zeuner

lence. My God! People are so numbed by the stuff that they don't realize the kind of brainwashing that goes on. No wonder we're a sick society. I've decided to counter this trend by informing others of the filth, but it's almost impossible for them to comprehend. If the hospital staff and patients fail to understand, I may start Phase Two of my efforts by breaking the television sets in this hospital!

A few days later the patient attempted to smash the television set in the next room but was restrained by several ward attendants.

Undifferentiated and Residual Schizophrenia

Undifferentiated schizophrenia is diagnosed when the person's symptoms are obviously schizophrenic

but are mixed or undifferentiated, so that they do not clearly fit into the disorganized, catatonic, or paranoid category. These symptoms may include thought disturbance, delusions, hallucinations, incoherence, and severely impaired behavior. Sometimes undifferentiated schizophrenia turns out to be an early stage of another subtype.

The diagnosis of **residual schizophrenia** is reserved for people who have experienced at least one episode of schizophrenia in the past but are presently exhibiting no prominent signs of the disorders (which may be in remission). These people may show some schizophrenic symptoms, but the symptoms are neither strong enough nor prominent enough to warrant classification as one of the other types of schizophrenia.

Psychotic Disorders Once Considered Schizophrenia

Brief psychotic episodes were considered to represent acute forms of schizophrenia in DSM-II. With DSM-III-R and DSM-IV, people who have "schizophrenic" episodes that last fewer than six months are now diagnosed as having either **brief psychotic disorder** (duration up to one month) or **schizophreniform disorder** (duration more than one month but less than six months). This distinction was made because "there is consistent evidence that people with symptoms similar to those of schizophrenia of less than six months' duration have a better outcome than those with a more prolonged disturbance" (American Psychiatric Association, 1987, p. 207). As we mentioned earlier, ICD-10 has a broader definition of schizophrenia in that it only requires that psychotic symptoms be present for one month.

Differences between these disorders and schizophrenia are shown in Table 14.2. Although there appear to be distinct differences, the disorders are often highly similar in characteristics. DSM-IV recommends that the diagnosis of brief psychotic disorder and schizophreniform disorder be "provisional." For example, an initial diagnosis of brief psychotic disorder should change to schizophreniform disorder if it lasts longer than one month and to schizophrenia if it lasts longer than six months. Because duration is the only accurate means of distinguishing among the disorders, questions about the validity of categories have been raised.

Table 14.2

Comparison of Brief Psychotic Disorder, Schizophreniform Disorders, and Schizophrenia

	Brief Psychotic Disorder	Schizophreniform Disorders	Schizophrenia
Duration	Less than one month	Less than six months	Six months or more
Psychosocial stressor	Always present	Usually present	May or may not be present
Symptoms	Emotional turmoil, psychotic symptoms	Emotional turmoil, vivid hallucinations	Emotional reactions variable; psychotic symptoms
Outcome	Return to premorbid level of functioning	Likely to return to earlier, higher level of functioning	Return to earlier, higher level of functioning is uncommon
Familial pattern	No information	Possible increased risk of schizophrenia among family members	Higher prevalence of schizophrenia among family members

THE COURSE OF SCHIZOPHRENIA

It is popularly believed that overwhelming stress can cause a well-adjusted and relatively normal person to experience a schizophrenic breakdown. There are, in fact, recorded instances of the sudden onset of psychotic behaviors in previously well-functioning people. Soldiers have been reported to develop auditory, visual, and tactile hallucinations under combat conditions (Spivak et al., 1992). In most cases, however, the person's *premorbid personality* (personality before the onset of major symptoms) shows some impairment. Similarly, most schizophrenics recover gradually rather than suddenly. The typical course of schizophrenia consists of three phases: prodromal, active, and residual.

The *prodromal phase* includes the onset and buildup of schizophrenic symptoms. Social withdrawal and isolation, peculiar behaviors, inappropriate affect, poor communication patterns, and neglect of personal grooming may become evident during this phase. Friends and relatives often consider the person's behavior as odd or peculiar.

Often, psychosocial stressors or excessive demands on a schizophrenic in the prodromal phase result in the onset of prominent psychotic symptoms, or the *active phase* of schizophrenia. The person now

Untitled (crayon) Franz Karl Bühler

FIGURE 14.1   Some Different Courses Found in Schizophrenia

This figure shows four of the many courses that people with schizophrenia may take. These courses were observed in a five-year follow-up study (Shepherd, Watt & Falloon, 1981). Some believe that long-term outcomes are even more positive.

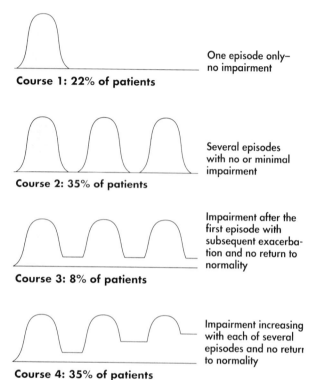

Course 1: 22% of patients
One episode only–no impairment

Course 2: 35% of patients
Several episodes with no or minimal impairment

Course 3: 8% of patients
Impairment after the first episode with subsequent exacerbation and no return to normality

Course 4: 35% of patients
Impairment increasing with each of several episodes and no return to normality

shows the full-blown symptoms of schizophrenia, including severe disturbances in thinking, deterioration in social relationships, and flat or markedly inappropriate affect.

At some later time, the person may enter the *residual phase*, in which the symptoms are no longer prominent. The severity of the symptoms declines, and the individual may show the milder impairment found in the prodromal phase. (At this point, the diagnosis would be residual schizophrenia.) Complete recovery is considered rare, although long-term studies have shown that many schizophrenics can lead productive lives (see Figure 14.1 for different courses of the disease). For whatever reason, recovery rates appear higher in developing countries. See Critical Thinking for a discussion of this phenomenon.

Long-Term Outcome Studies

What are the chances for recovery or improvement from schizophrenia? Kraepelin believed that the disorder follows a deteriorating course. He would have agreed with the following statement concerning the prognosis for schizophrenia. "A complete return to premorbid functioning is unusual—so rare, in fact, that some clinicians would question the diagnosis (American Psychiatric Association, 1980). The chances for improvement or recovery are difficult to evaluate because of the changing definitions for schizophrenia. Before DSM-III, the United States had a very broad definition of schizophrenia. DSM-III and DSM-IV provided a narrower definition. Symptoms of the disorder have to be present for six months for its diagnosis. It makes sense that an individual who does not recover within six months has a more severe condition than one who recovers sooner. We have, therefore, now defined schizophrenia as a chronic condition.

Even with the more restrictive definition for schizophrenia, differences remain in the interpretation of outcome data. Breier and colleagues (1991) pointed to a negative outcome with 78 percent of schizophrenics suffering a relapse and only 20 percent showing good improvement. Carone, Harrow, and Westermeyer (1992) also reported that more than 50 percent of schizophrenics had a poor outcome five years after hospitalization. But others believed that the conclusions of these studies "propagate an unduly pessimistic picture of schizophrenia" (Puryear et al., 1992, p. 74). Puryear and colleagues analyzed the data from the Carone study and reinterpreted the findings in the following manner: instead of stating that more than 50 percent had a poor outcome, it can be argued that nearly 50 percent had a good or moderately good outcome and that 17 percent of the patients had a complete remission of symptoms within five years. They also pointed out that of the fifty-one patients in the Breier study, thirty-eight were fully employed and sixteen were also working; 20 percent were described as having "good social functioning." Viewed this way, the outcome is seen to be more positive.

Some very long-term studies have also been performed. Ciompi (1980) conducted a 37-year follow-up of 289 schizophrenic patients and found that the long-term prognosis was favorable in 50 percent

CRITICAL THINKING

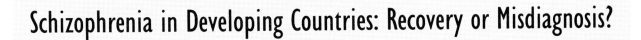

Schizophrenia in Developing Countries: Recovery or Misdiagnosis?

Do people in developing countries with schizophrenia recover more quickly and fully than those in developed countries? If so, why? These questions were examined in a cross-cultural study by the World Health Organization (Sartorius et al., 1986). Standardized and reliable sets of criteria were used to study schizophrenia in ten different countries. Similar prevalence rates for the disorder were found in the study. However, a follow-up of 1379 persons diagnosed as schizophrenic and described as "remarkably similar in their symptom profiles" in the nine countries revealed that patients in India, Colombia, and Nigeria showed more rapid and more complete recovery than those in London, Moscow, or Washington. Fifty-six percent of schizophrenics in developing countries had only one episode of the disorder as compared with 39 percent in developed countries. Severe chronic course was found in 40 percent of those from developed countries as opposed to 24 percent in developing countries. Sartorius and colleagues hypothesized

that some cultural factor might be responsible for the observed difference in outcome.

At the present time, reasons for the differences in outcome are unknown. Some have speculated that in developing countries recovered patients are quickly absorbed into the work force and do whatever tasks are available (Warner, 1986). Researchers in the follow-up study reported difficulty in interviewing recovered patients because they were in the fields. Returning to work may have helped prevent relapses.

Stevens (1987) believes that the higher recovery rate for schizophrenia found in developing countries is due to misdiagnosis. To support her view, she pointed out that in the WHO study, 36 percent of patients in Nigeria and 27 percent in India recovered in less than one month. She conjectured that the illnesses were really either brief psychotic disorder or schizophreniform disorders and not schizophrenia. Although this explanation is certainly plausible, the WHO investigation had found an approxi-

mately equal frequency of schizophrenia among the different countries. If misdiagnosis did occur, it must mean that brief psychotic disorder and schizophreniform disorders are more prevalent in developing countries and that schizophrenia occurs less frequently in these countries. Why this would be the case must be examined.

If further research does support the finding that schizophrenics in developing countries show a milder course and are more likely to recover fully, what do you believe are the implications for diagnosis and etiology? If we define schizophrenia as a "chronic" condition, how could we account for the fact that more than 50 percent of schizophrenics in developing countries recover after one episode? If schizophrenia is a brain disorder, why is the outcome so different between developing and developed countries? If "culture" is responsible for the more positive outcome in developing countries, how does it have an impact?

of patients. With advanced age, there was a "pronounced general tendency toward improvement and recovery." More than one-half the patients were in good physical condition and were employed either full- or part-time. Although the majority still showed evidence of problems with social relationships or independence, most indicated that they felt peaceful and free of conflicts. The findings prompted Ciompi to conclude that "quite contrary to the original—and today still popular—concepts of the nature of schizo-

phrenia, a good majority of definitely 'genuine' schizophrenias (from initial diagnoses) may develop favorably in the long run" (p. 611).

Similar results were obtained in a 22-year follow-up of 502 schizophrenic patients (Huber et al., 1980). Of this group, 22 percent were in complete remission, 43 percent showed only residual symptoms, and 35 percent remained unimproved; 87 percent lived in their homes. Two interesting findings were that the long-term prognosis is unrelated to the original dura-

Discrimination Against the Mentally Ill

Mental illnesses, especially psychoses such as schizophrenia, are still feared and misunderstood by the public. The resulting discrimination is illustrated by the experiences of a former schizophrenic patient. After he was released from a hospital psychiatric ward, he told his employer about his illness. This marked the beginning of a series of encounters with the general prejudice against former mental patients.

> I was at work only a few days when I was fired but "assured" that I would receive good references. The fact that I had been there for nearly 4 years and [was] a good worker did not matter. (Anonymous, 1981, p. 736)

In applying for a new job, he faced additional problems.

> I also noticed that many job applications would inquire about medical and psychological stability. . . . I learned that honesty is not always the best policy. . . . I am considering graduate school, and there too, questions about past and present psychiatric treatment confront me. . . . The admission forms often request a biographical sketch describing how the student became interested in the field and any personal experiences with psychiatry. This, too, obviously is a catch-22 position. To admit my personal experiences is to court possible and realistic rejection. I have spoken off the record with an instructor in a well-known school of social work about the situation, and his advice was: "I do not think discussing your hospital experiences would be a plus." [But if] I do not discuss it, I would in a way be compromising my principles. (pp. 736–737)

The former patient partly blames the media for this situation:

> Hardly a month goes by that we do not read a lurid news story of "man goes berserk and kills neighbor" or "former mental patient kills wife." . . . The evidence is overwhelming that the majority of mental patients are, as a class, less dangerous than the "average citizen." . . . Psychotherapy and psychotropic drugs have helped thousands of people to continue to go about their daily lives . . . but at times, I am sure they painfully wonder, for what? (p. 737)

What messages from the mass media have you received about the mentally ill? What do you believe are reasonable restrictions, if any, in hiring or working with persons with schizophrenia?

---

tion of the disorder and is more favorable for women than for men.

A criticism that can be leveled against these long-term outcome studies is that they involved patients that were diagnosed according to criteria that preceded DSM-III-R and probably included nonschizophrenic patients who might have a better prognosis. This issue was addressed in a study by Harding and associates (1987), who retrospectively applied DSM-III criteria to schizophrenics who were involved in a 32-year long-term follow-up. These patients from the "back wards" had been ill for an average of sixteen years and had been hospitalized continuously for about six years. Amazingly, the researchers found that "for one-half to two-thirds of these subjects who retrospectively met the DSM-III criteria for schizophrenia, long-term outcome was neither marginal but an evolution into various degrees of productivity, so-

cial involvement, wellness, and competent functioning" (p. 730).

The results of these studies indicated that the long-term outcome for schizophrenics may be more positive than portrayed by Kraepelin or by DSM-III and DSM-IV. One researcher who reviewed the prognosis of schizophrenia believes that there is a "wide spectrum of possible courses that patients follow," many of them being quite positive (Harding, Zubin & Strauss, 1992). Bleuler might have been more correct in indicating a variable outcome for the disorder. The increasing number of studies indicating positive long-term outcome for schizophrenia has prompted Zubin and Ludwig (1983) to comment that there is a "new optimism about this disorder." Unfortunately, this optimism has yet to spread to the general public. (See Focus 14.4.)

SUMMARY

1. Schizophrenia is a group of psychotic disorders characterized by impaired thinking. The criteria that differentiate schizophrenia, its subtypes, and other psychotic disorders are specified more precisely in DSM-IV than they have been in the past. However, the criteria must be applied consistently if they are to be effective.

2. The disorders are manifested in delusions; perceptual distortion as in hallucinations; disorganized speech and thought disturbances including loosening of associations, neologisms, and attention problems; disorganized motoric disturbances; and inappropriate affect.

3. DSM-IV distinguishes five types of schizophrenia. Paranoid schizophrenia is characterized by persecutory delusions or frequent auditory hallucinations. Disorganized schizophrenia is characterized by disorganized speech and behavior and inappropriate affect. Extreme social impairment and severe regressive behaviors are often seen. The major feature of catatonic schizophrenia is disturbance of motor activity. Patients show excessive excitement, agitation and hyperactivity, or withdrawn behavior patterns. The undifferentiated type includes schizophrenic behavior that cannot be classified as one of the other types, and residual schizophrenia is a category for people who have had at least one episode of schizophrenia but are not now showing prominent symptoms. In addition, other severe disorders may include schizophrenia-like symptoms.

4. The typical course of schizophrenia consists of three phases. In the prodromal phase, the symptoms first begin and build. In the active phase, they become quite prominent. And in the residual phase, they decline in severity. The degree of recovery from schizophrenia is conflicting; most schizophrenics recover enough to lead relatively productive lives.

KEY TERMS

brief psychotic disorder Psychotic disorder that lasts no longer than one month

catatonic schizophrenia A schizophrenic disorder characterized by disturbance in motor activity—extreme agitation and excitement or extreme withdrawal and unresponsiveness

cognition The processes of thinking, perceiving, judging, and recognizing

delusion A false belief that is firmly and consistently held despite disconfirming evidence or logic

delusional disorder A disorder characterized by persistent, nonbizarre delusions that are not accompanied by other unusual or odd behaviors

disorganized schizophrenia A schizophrenic disorder characterized by severe disintegration and absurd and incoherent behaviors beginning at an early age

flat affect Abnormal lack of emotional response

hallucinations Sensory perceptions that are not directly attributable to environmental stimuli

loosening of associations Continual shifting from topic to topic without logical or meaningful connection among topics

negative symptoms Symptoms that may represent an irreversible process in schizophrenia; they include flat affect, poverty of speech, anhedonia, apathy, and avolition

neologisms New words that are typically formed by combining words in common usage

paranoid schizophrenia A schizophrenic disorder characterized by persistent and systematized delusions

pathognomonic Symptoms specific to a disorder

positive symptoms Symptoms present only during the active phase of the illness

residual schizophrenia A category of schizophrenic disorder reserved for people who have experienced at least one schizophrenic episode but do not now show prominent signs of the disorder

schizophrenia A group of disorders characterized by severely impaired cognitive processes, personality disintegration, affective disturbances, and social withdrawal

schizophreniform disorder Psychotic disorder that lasts less than six months

undifferentiated schizophrenia A schizophrenic disorder characterized by mixed or undifferentiated symptoms that do not clearly fit any of the other types of schizophrenia

Schizophrenia: Etiology and Treatment

I know I'm a 37-year-old woman, a sculptor, a writer, a worker. I live alone. I know all of this, but, like the reflection in the glass my existence seems undefined—more a mirage that I keep reaching for, but never can touch.

I've been feeling this way for almost a year now, ever since I was diagnosed a paranoid schizophrenic. Sometimes, though, I wonder if I ever knew myself, or merely played the parts that were acceptable, just so that I could fit in somewhere. . . . There are still occasional episodes of hallucinations, delusions, and terrible fears, and I have medication for these times. It relieves my mental stress, but I hate my bodily responses to it and the dulling of my healthy emotions. Therefore, I stop using the drug as soon as the storms in my mind subside. . . .

I've searched, in library books and in articles about schizophrenia, hoping to find other solutions and answers to my whys, how longs, what's the cure. Some of the information is frightening. . . . Some of it is confusing. . . . Schizophrenia is genetic—no, no, it's surely biochemical—definitely nutritional—sorry, but it's caused by family interactions, maybe stress, etc. Now, with the worship of technological gods, the explanation is that schizophrenia is a brain disease colorfully mapped out by the PET scanner. I suddenly feel that my humanity has been sacrificed to a computer printout, that the researchers have dissected me without realizing that I'm still alive. I'm not comfortable or safe in all their certain uncertainties—I feel they're losing me, the person, more and more.

In the most recently published book I've read, a doctor writes that psychotherapy is useless with schizophrenia. How could he even suggest that, without knowing me, the one over here in this corner, who finds a lot of support, understanding, and acceptance by my therapist? Marianne is not afraid to travel with me in my fearful times. She listens when I need to release some of the "poisons" in my mind. She offers advice when I'm having difficulty with just daily living. She sees me as a human being and not only a body to shovel pills into or a cerebral mass in some laboratory. Psychotherapy is important to me, and it does help. . . .

I'm hopeful about the ongoing research to find an answer to schizophrenia. . . . But I know that I'm the schizophrenic living the experience, and I must look inside myself also for some ways to handle it. I have to be able to see me again as a real person and not a fading reflection. (McGrath, 1987, pp. 37–38)

Mary McGrath thus expressed her frustration in trying to discover the cause of her disorder. Researchers share her frustration. New theories are constantly being espoused. Some are more promising than others. But how do we know which theory, if any, is actually correct? In this chapter, we consider the different causal theories of schizophrenia, examining genetic, physiological, psychological, and environmental explanations. Unfortunately, although a great amount of work has been done, no one theory is universally accepted, and each fails to answer all the questions schizophrenia poses. As you will see in this chapter, methodological flaws and research design limitations restrict the kinds of conclusions that can be drawn about schizophrenia.

We also explore different forms of therapy for schizophrenia. Antipsychotic medications can help treat some symptoms of schizophrenia, but relapse rates remain unacceptably high, and undesirable side effects are reported. As McGrath remarked, her medication kept her "functional," but she also felt "drugged and unreal." Interest in psychotherapy for schizophrenia has revived because most people with this disorder now are only hospitalized temporarily and are then returned to their families. Some new promising approaches are discussed later.

ETIOLOGY OF SCHIZOPHRENIA

A thirteen-year-old boy who was having behavioral and academic problems in school was taking part in a series of family therapy sessions. Family communication was negative in tone with a great deal of blaming. Near the end of one session, the boy suddenly broke down and cried out, "I don't want to be like her." He was referring to his mother, who had been receiving treatment for schizophrenia and was taking antipsychotic medication. He had often been frightened by her bizarre behavior, and he was concerned that his friends would "find out" about her condition. But his greatest fear was that he would inherit the disorder. Sobbing, he turned to the therapist and asked, "Am I going to be crazy, too?"

If you were the therapist, how would you respond? We are constantly exposed to news articles indicating that schizophrenia is produced by an "unfortunate" combination of genes or is due to physical problems in the brain. Does this mean that schizophrenia is only a biological disorder? Some evidence also exists that family communication patterns can influence relapse in schizophrenic individuals. Can the way we interact in a family also precipitate a schizophrenic episode? If so, how? Researchers generally agree that this boy's chances of developing schizophrenia are greater than those of the average person. Why this is so is a subject of controversy. Researchers who favor a biological paradigm tend to favor genetic, brain structure, and biochemical explanations. Other researchers focus primarily on the impact of psychological and social factors in the development of the disorder. We will consider the strengths and weaknesses of the different approaches. At the end of the chapter, you should reach your own conclusion about what to tell the thirteen-year-old boy.

HEREDITY AND SCHIZOPHRENIA

Dr. Herbert Pardes, president of the American Psychiatric Association, stated, "We have been learning that the genetic factor plays a far greater role in some cases of schizophrenia than we'd ever thought before. . . . There is also evidence of physical or chemical disturbances in the brain" (Ubell, 1989). That genetic influences are important in the etiology of schizophrenia is no longer a subject of serious debate.

The following challenge posed by a researcher to his colleagues more than thirty years ago still stands:

You [are] required to write down a procedure for selecting an individual from the population who would be diagnosed as schizophrenic by a psychiatric staff; you have to wager $1,000 on being right. You may not include in your selection procedure any behavioral fact, such as a symptom or trait, manifested by the individual. (Meehl, 1962, p. 827)

In other words, what procedure would give you the greatest probability of selecting a schizophrenic from the general population when you *cannot* consider the person's symptoms or traits? According to Meehl, you should look for someone whose identical twin has already been diagnosed as schizophrenic. This solution reflects the belief that heredity is an important cause in the development of schizophrenia—a belief supported by research (Gottesman, 1991; Heinrichs, 1993; Roberts, 1991). However, the degree of influence is still quite controversial.

Problems in Interpreting Genetic Studies

Obtaining a clear picture of the genetic contribution in schizophrenia would seem to be a relatively easy task. Nevertheless, major complications exist. Some of them tend to inflate the degree of genetic influence. First, several types of schizophrenia may exist, each with a different cause or set of causes. For example, children with schizophrenic parents who do not respond to antipsychotic medication have a higher risk for developing schizophrenia and related disorders compared with children of parents who do respond. Thus the degree of genetic influence may vary among the different types of schizophrenia. Second, genetic researchers often do not consider the psychological condition of the nonschizophrenic parent. If the other parent had a similar or related disorder, this could increase the genetic risk. In one study (Parnas, 1987), the mates of schizophrenics were more likely to have functional psychoses and schizoid, paranoid, or borderline personality disorders before marriage than mates of nonschizophrenics. Because spousal contributions were not considered, genetic influences based only on the mother's diagnosis may be overestimated. Third, genetic studies are often based on severely and chronically ill schizophrenic patients, among whom genetic influence may be greater. The **concordance rate** (likelihood that both members of a twin pair will show the same characteristic) for schizophrenia was nearly three times higher among the monozygotic twins who were hospitalized for more than two years than for those hospitalized less than two years (Gottesman, 1991). Fourth, researchers differ in their definitions of "concordant." Some define schizophrenia very narrowly and use the same definition to determine concordance. This would result in lower estimates of genetic influence. Other investigators believe that a number of disorders (such as schizoid and borderline personality disorders and schizophreniform disorders) are genetically related to schizophrenia. They would consider as concordant not only a diagnosis of schizophrenia, but these other disorders as well. Researchers favoring this view tend to make higher estimates of genetic influence. In this section, we discuss several kinds of research that link heredity to the schizophrenic disorders. Many of them have some of the methodological problems that we have just discussed.

Studies Involving Blood Relatives

Close blood relatives are genetically more similar than distant blood relatives. For example, first-degree relatives (parents, siblings, child) of the schizophrenic individual share 50 percent of the genes and second-degree relatives (grandparents, uncles, aunts, nephews) share only 25 percent of the genes. If schizophrenia has a genetic basis, researchers should find more schizophrenia among close relatives of diagnosed schizophrenics than among more distant relatives.

Table 15.1 suggests that this situation is indeed the case. The data are summarized from several

Table 15.1

Risk of Schizophrenia Among Blood Relatives of Schizophrenics

Relationship to the Schizophrenic Person	Morbidity Risk (percent)
MZ twin	36–48
Child of two affected parents	36–46
Child of one affected parent	12–13
Sibling	8–9
Parents	4–6
Half-sibling	3–6
Grandchild	2–5
Cousin	2–3
Niece and nephew	2–4
Uncle and aunt	2–3
Grandparent	1–2
Spouse	2
No relationship	1

major studies on the prevalence of schizophrenia (Gottesman, 1978, 1991). They show that closer blood relatives of diagnosed schizophrenics run a greater risk of developing the disorder. Thus the boy described earlier has a 12 to 13 percent chance of being diagnosed as schizophrenic, but his mother's nieces or nephews have only a 2 to 3 percent chance. (Note that the risk for the general population is 1 percent.)

But the association between relatedness and risk is not as clear as Table 15.1 suggests. Other studies yield different results, showing that first-degree relatives—that is, parents and children—of schizophrenics have risks of 1.6 to 3.2 percent of developing the disorder (Abrams & Taylor, 1983; Guze et al., 1983; Tsuang, Winokur & Crowe, 1980). In fact, one study found no increased risk at all among first-degree relatives (Pope, Jonas & Cohen, 1982).

What could account for these discrepancies among the various study results? Methodological differences from the use of different diagnostic criteria and different research designs may produce these differing results (Abrams & Taylor, 1983; Levinson & Mowry, 1991). In evaluating genetic research, the following points should be considered:

1. Many studies, especially those performed before 1972, used very broad definitions that encompassed patients with disorders other than schizophrenia. This broadness obviously confounded conclusions on the inheritability of schizophrenia and tended to inflate genetic influence.

2. Each investigator has to determine what is a schizophrenia-related genotype. Should only a diagnosis of schizophrenia be included, or should schizophreniform, brief psychotic disorder, schizotypal personality disorders, and affective disorders be considered as well in determining concordance? The more disorders that are included, the greater is the likelihood that stronger genetic influence will be found.

3. Are the raters or interviewers blind to the diagnosis and status of the patients, controls, and their relatives? A rater who knows that he or she is interviewing relatives of a schizophrenic, for example, might be more likely to find pathology. Studies that do not use blind ratings report higher rates of psychopathology than studies that do (Gottesman & Shields, 1982).

Because many studies of schizophrenia differ in methodology, their findings must be interpreted very carefully.

Even if well-designed studies pointed to a relationship between degree of genetic relatedness and schizophrenia, however, they still do not clearly demonstrate the role of heredity. Why? Simply because closer blood relatives are more likely to share the same environmental factors or stressors as well as the same genes. To confirm a genetic basis for schizophrenia, research must separate genetic influences from environmental influences.

Twin Studies

We have already described the use of twin studies in seeking to differentiate between the effects of heredity and those of environment. The concept, in somewhat more detail, is this: identical, or monozygotic (MZ), twins are genetically identical, so differences between two MZ twins are presumably caused by differences in their environments. If reared together, MZ twins share the same general environment as well as the same hereditary makeup. But fraternal, or dizygotic (DZ) twins, though born at about the same time, are not more genetically similar than any other two siblings and may be of different sexes. If DZ twins are reared together, they share the same general environment, but their genetic makeup is, on the average, only 50 percent identical.

In a twin study, concordance rates for a particular disorder are measured among groups of MZ and DZ twins. (Recall that a concordance rate is the likelihood both members of a twin pair will exhibit the disorder being studied.) If environmental factors are of major importance, the concordance rates for MZ twins and for DZ twins should not differ much. If genetic factors are of prime importance, however, MZ twins should show a higher concordance rate than DZ twins.

In general, concordance rates for schizophrenia among MZ twins are two to four times higher than among DZ twins. This seems to point to a strong genetic basis for the disorders. One study of sixteen pairs of MZ twins found a concordance rate of zero, however; not one MZ twin of a schizophrenic had the disorder (Tienari, 1963). In fact, concordance rates among MZ twins vary from 0 to 86 percent

Identical and fraternal twins are studied to determine the relative importance of genetic factors in schizophrenia and other disorders. Identical twins share the same genes. Thus differences between identical twins can be attributed to differences in their environment rather than in their genetic makeup. Fraternal twins (shown in this photo) share some of the same genes, but no more so than any other pair of siblings.

(Weiner, 1975). How can some twin studies show little or no genetic influence while other studies indicate a strong genetic component in schizophrenia?

Again, methodological differences seem to be involved. Consider Table 15.2, which lists the results of several twin studies performed in Scandinavia. Two percentages are given for most entries in the concordance rate columns. The first percentage (not in parentheses) is the rate according to a narrow definition of schizophrenia. The second percentage (in parentheses) is the rate according to a broad definition that considers disorders such as "latent or borderline"

Table 15.2

Concordance Rates Found in Twin Studies in the Scandinavian Countries

		MZ Pairs		DZ Pairs	
Study	Country	Number of Pairs	Concordance Rate (percent)	Number of Pairs	Concordance Rate (percent)
Tienari (1963)	Finland	16	0 (19)[a]	21	5 (14)
Kringlin (1967)	Norway	55	25 (38)	90	10 (19)
Essen-Moller (1970)	Sweden	7	29 (75)	—	— —
Fischer (1973)	Denmark	21	24 (56)	41	10 (19)
Tienari (1975)	Finland	20	15 —	42	7.5 —

[a]The percentages not in parentheses are measured according to a narrow definition of schizophrenia. The percentages in parentheses are concordance rates for the wider schizophrenia spectrum; for example, if one twin has schizophrenia and the other twin has a borderline diagnosis, the pair is considered concordant according to this latter definition.
Source: Kringlen, 1980.

One of the problems with studying twins is the difficulty of separating heredity factors from environmental influences. Adoption studies are useful because heredity and environmental factors can be clearly differentiated.

schizophrenia, acute schizophrenic reactions, and schizoid and inadequate personality as concordant. These disorders are part of the schizophrenia spectrum—that is, they are considered to be genetically related to schizophrenia. Note that the Tienari (1963) MZ concordance rate of zero would rise to 19 percent if three twins who showed "borderline" psychotic features were counted. This is true, to varying degrees, of the other studies as well.

The broader definition of schizophrenia was used in most studies that reported high concordance rates. Unfortunately, this breadth decreases the diagnostic reliability and validity of twin studies as a whole. In one study, for example, 25 percent of a normal comparison control group received one of the schizophrenia spectrum diagnoses (Haier, Rosenthal & Wendler, 1978). That such a high percentage received this diagnosis is surprising and probably indicated problems in the validity of the assessment.

Even though the high concordance rates reported in many earlier studies have been inflated by using the broad definition of schizophrenia, we can conclude that there is clearly genetic influence in the disorders. This is so whether a strict definition is employed or the schizophrenia spectrum is included. Moreover, it appears that the spectrum disorders are

more likely to be found in "at-risk" groups: those whose families include diagnosed schizophrenics.

Adoption Studies

Even with twin studies, it is difficult to separate the effects of heredity from the effects of environment because twins are usually raised together. Thus when the child of a schizophrenic parent develops schizophrenia, three explanations are possible: (1) the schizophrenic mother or father may have genetically transmitted schizophrenia to the child; (2) the parent, being disturbed, may have provided a stressful environment for the child; or (3) the child's schizophrenia may have resulted from a combination of genetic factors and a stressful environment.

In an attempt to completely separate the effects of heredity and environment, the incidence of schizophrenia and other disorders was determined for a group of people who were born to schizophrenic mothers but who had no contact with their mothers and had left the maternity hospital within three days of birth (Heston, 1966; Heston & Denny, 1968). This condition eliminated the possibility that contact with the mother increased the chance of developing the disorder. The lives of these people were traced

Table 15.3

Comparison of Disorders in People Separated from Schizophrenic Mothers and from Normal Mothers Early in Life

Characteristic	At-Risk Children	Control
Number of individuals	47	50
Males	30	33
Mean age	35.8	36.3
Ratings of mental health/sickness[a]	65.2	80.1
Number diagnosed as schizophrenic	5	0
Number with mental deficiency (IQ less than 70)	4	0
Number with sociopathic personality	9	2
Number with neurotic personality	13	7
Number spending more than one year in a penal or psychiatric institution	11	2

[a] A lower score indicates greater severity.
Source: Heston, 1966.

through the records of child care institutions; all had been adopted by two-parent families. A control group, consisting of people born to normal mothers and adopted through the same child care institutions, was selected and matched. Information regarding both the at-risk and control groups was collected from many sources (including school records, court records, and interviews). The people themselves were interviewed and given psychological tests. The major results are shown in Table 15.3. Note that five children in the at-risk group were later diagnosed as schizophrenic, compared with none in the control group. These results are highly significant and support a genetic explanation for schizophrenia. The greater incidence of the other disorders such as sociopathic personality among the at-risk group is hard to explain because those disorders are not part of the schizophrenia spectrum.

The study seems to have been well designed. Its only weaknesses involve the diagnostic criteria, which were described as being based on "generally accepted standards" for schizophrenia, and the fact that the schizophrenic mothers "as a group were biased in the direction of severe, chronic disease." (As discussed earlier, genetic factors seem to play a greater role in the more severe cases of schizophrenia).

Two additional criticisms have been raised, however. First, the schizophrenic mothers received antipsychotic medication during pregnancy, and such drugs present a potential risk to the fetus (*Physician's Desk Reference*, 1992). Second, most families who adopted the child of a schizophrenic mother knew about the mother's disorder. This knowledge could have influenced the adoptive parents' attitude toward the child (Shean, 1987).

Of special interest is the finding that nearly one-half of the at-risk group were "notably successful adults."

> The twenty-one experimental subjects who exhibited no significant psychosocial impairment were not only successful adults but in comparison to the control group were more spontaneous when interviewed and had more colorful life histories. They held the more creative jobs: musician, teacher, home-designer; and followed the more imaginative hobbies: oil painting, music, antique aircraft. Within the experimental group there was much more variability of personality and behavior in all social dimensions. (Heston, 1966, p. 825)

Sohlberg (1985) reported similar findings that approximately 50 percent of "high-risk" children have "healthy personalities" and are "remarkably invulnerable" to schizophrenia. Being "at risk" doesn't necessarily (or even usually) lead to a negative outcome. Why do some children who have poor familial or environmental backgrounds develop so successfully? Perhaps studies of "stress resistant" children will one day answer this question (Luthar & Zigler, 1991).

In another study designed to separate hereditary and environmental influences, investigators identified adult schizophrenics who had been adopted in infancy. Then they located both the adoptive parents (the families that had raised the children who became schizophrenic) and the biological parents, who had minimal contact with their children. If environmental factors play the major role in schizophrenia, the adoptive families should be more disturbed than the biological parents. Conversely, if heredity is more important, biological families should show more disturbance than adoptive families. Interviews with both sets of families showed a greater incidence of the schizophrenia spectrum in the biological family (Kety et al., 1975).

Another group of researchers studied children who had normal biological parents but who were adopted and raised by a parent who later was diagnosed as schizophrenic. If environmental factors are of primary importance, these children should be more likely than others to develop schizophrenia, but no difference was found (Wender et al., 1977). Thus the various adoption studies do indicate that heredity plays a major role in the transmission of schizophrenia.

Studies of High-Risk Populations

Perhaps the most comprehensive way to study the etiology of schizophrenia is to monitor a large group of children over a long time to watch the differences between those who eventually develop schizophrenia and those who don't. This sort of developmental study allows the investigator to see how the disorders develop. But because the prevalence of schizophrenia in the general population is only 1 percent, a prohibitively large group would have to be monitored if a random sample of children were chosen. Instead, investigators have chosen subjects from "high-risk" populations; this increases the probability that a smaller group of subjects will include some who develop schizophrenia.

Mednick's Study   The best-known developmental studies are those by Mednick (1970) and Mednick and colleagues (1989), who are still studying about two hundred persons with schizophrenic mothers (the high-risk group) and about one hundred persons with nonschizophrenic mothers (the low-risk control group). The researchers have studied these same groups for more than twenty-seven years. On the basis of existing data, they have predicted the eventual outcome for both high-risk and low-risk persons. Their prediction is shown in Figure 15.1; approximately one-half of the high-risk group may eventually display some form of psychopathology, including but not limited to schizophrenia.

By the time of the first follow-up, twenty members of the high-risk group had already shown psychological problems ranging from theft to psychotic symptoms (Mednick, 1970). Thirteen of these persons had been admitted to psychiatric hospitals. Mednick believed that the subjects in this "sick group" were the most likely to have or to develop schizophrenia. But a later follow-up revealed that, of fifteen persons who had been diagnosed as schizophrenic, only four came from the sick group (Schulsinger, 1976). The high-risk subjects who became schizophrenic were compared with those who did not; the schizophrenics were more likely to

◈ Have mothers who displayed more severe symptoms of schizophrenia

◈ Have been separated from their parents and placed in children's homes early in their lives

◈ Have had mothers who had more serious pregnancy or birth complications

◈ Have been characterized by their teachers as extremely aggressive and disruptive

◈ Have a slower autonomic recovery rate (habituate more slowly when exposed to certain stimuli)

The Israeli Study   Are high-risk children more likely to develop schizophrenia or related disorders if they live with their schizophrenic parent or might they do better when raised in a "healthier" environment? An Israeli research team (Ayalon & Mercom, 1985; Marcus et al., 1987; Nagler et al., 1985; Shotten, 1985; Sohlberg, 1985) conducted a **prospective study** (a study of subjects before they begin to exhibit signs of illness) on fifty high-risk children (children

**FIGURE 15.1   Mednick's and Schulsinger's Predictions About the Development
of Deviance and Schizophrenia in High-Risk and Control Children**

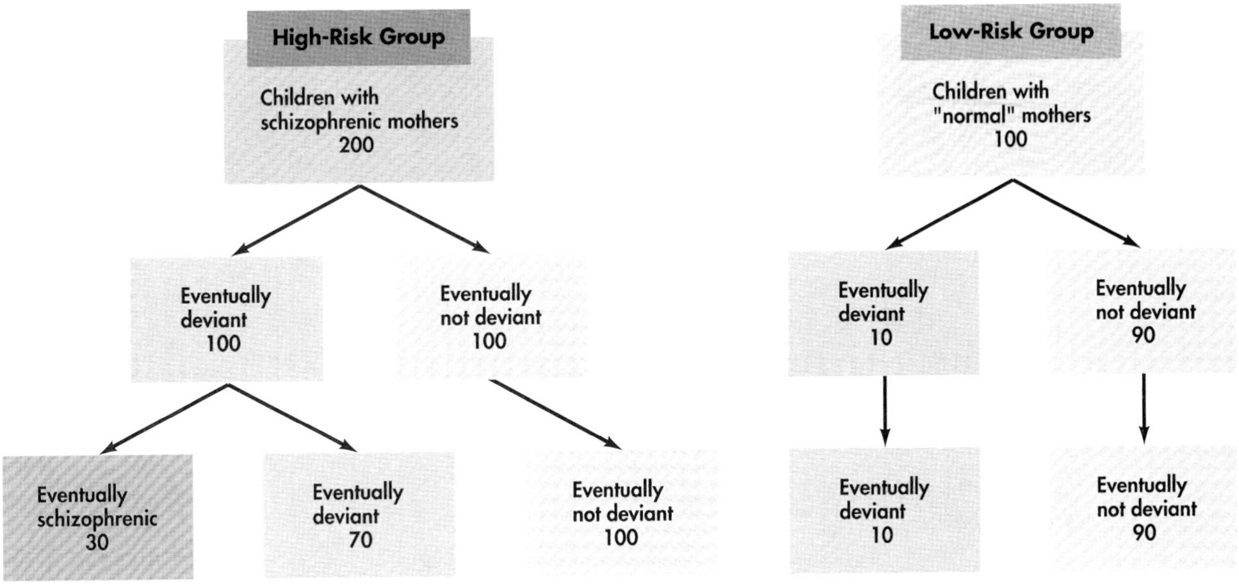

Source: Mednick, 1970.

who had schizophrenic parents). Twenty-five of the children were born and raised in a kibbutz (a collective farm), and the other twenty-five were living in a suburban area with their mentally ill parents. In the kibbutz, all the children lived together. They had regular contact with their parents, but were raised by child-care workers.

Researchers wanted to know whether a kibbutz environment would protect the high-risk children from developing schizophrenia. A control group comprising fifty low-risk children of mentally healthy parents—twenty-five living in the kibbutz and the other twenty-five living in town—were included in the study. Neurophysiological, observational, perceptual-motor, psychophysiological, and behavioral measures were regularly used. By the time the high-risk subjects reached their twenties, nine persons had been diagnosed with a disorder from the schizophrenic spectrum. Surprisingly, only three came from the group living in town with their parents. The other six came from the group raised in the kibbutz. None of the control group children was diagnosed as being schizophrenic, which again would indicate the importance of a genetic predisposition (see Table 15.4

for a breakdown of the different disorders). Is it possible that the kibbutz is more pathogenic (illness producing) than living with a schizophrenic parent? The finding is surprising and is yet to be explained.

The same researchers found a variety of differences between the high-risk and control children. High-risk children were more likely to be described as withdrawn, poorer in social relationships, behaving in antisocial ways, uncooperative and incapable of relating to the interviewers, poor at schoolwork, having problems with mood, accident prone, and functioning at lower perceptual-motor levels. Social withdrawal seemed to be the characteristic most related to risk of developing schizophrenia in the high-risk children (Hans et al., 1992). Nevertheless, the two groups of children overlapped considerably. Deficiencies were only shown by about one-half of the high-risk children. The other half appeared to show "healthy" development.

Could the mass of data be organized to help predict which children would most probably develop a schizophrenia spectrum disorder? Marcus and colleagues (1987, p. 431) believe it can: "Of the nine cases who received DSM-III diagnoses within the

Table 15.4

Diagnoses for Kibbutz and Town Subjects

Group	N	Schizophrenia	Other Schizophrenia Spectrum	Major Affective	Minor Affective	Other Diagnosis	No Diagnosis	Total DSM-III Diagnoses
Kibbutz								
High risk	23	3	3	5	4	1	7	16
Town								
High risk	23	2	1	1	0	3	16	7
Kibbutz								
Control	23	0	0	0	1	2	20	3
Town								
Control	21	0	0	0	0	1	20	1
Totals	90	5	4	6	5	7	63	27

Source: Marcus et al., 1987.

schizophrenia spectrum, seven followed the 'worst' developmental course: they had a schizophrenic parent, showed signs of neurobehavioral dysfunction, had stressful family environments, and showed premorbid signs of social maladjustment" (p. 431). Interestingly, none of the high-risk children who had received "adequate" parenting developed schizophrenia or one of the spectrum disorders. Approximately 60 percent of the schizophrenic parents provided adequate care for their children.

Conclusions and Methodological Problems What can we conclude from the high-risk studies? First, there is reasonably strong support for the involvement of heredity in schizophrenia and its associated spectrum disorders. Second, childhood and adolescence may be especially vulnerable periods. Third, schizophrenia seems to result from interaction between the predisposition and environmental factors. Fourth, most high-risk children don't develop the disorder.

Studies of high-risk subjects are a promising line of research. However, some methodological problems have already been pointed out. First, it may not be possible to generalize results of a study that takes as subjects the offspring of schizophrenic parents. The majority of diagnosed schizophrenics do not have a schizophrenic parent (Gottesman, 1991; Lewine, 1986). Additionally, differences have been found between patients with familial schizophrenia (those with a schizophrenic first-degree relative) and patients with no schizophrenia in the family (Kendler & Hays, 1982). Second, the studies do not include control groups with other psychopathologies; it's therefore hard to decide whether the characteristics found are specific to schizophrenia. For example, some characteristics listed by Mednick et al. (1989), such as pregnancy and birth complications, separation from parents, and problems in school, are also reported for other disorders. Third, there is uncertainty about whether the most relevant variables are being measured. Mednick believes that autonomic reactivity (measured by galvanic skin response) is an important factor in schizophrenia and has assessed this variable carefully. But parent-child interaction was not assessed because the investigators considered it less important. Fourth, the schizophrenic parents in both high-risk studies were diagnosed according to the criteria used at that time; they might not meet the DSM-IV criteria.

PHYSIOLOGICAL FACTORS IN SCHIZOPHRENIA

Two important areas of research into the causes of schizophrenia involve brain chemistry and brain pathology. Logically, either could serve as a vehicle for the genetic transmission of schizophrenia, but no substantive evidence to that effect has yet been found. Currently, no physiological pathognomonic (indicative of a specific disorder) sign or symptom has been found that leads to an invariant diagnosis of schizophrenia. Nonetheless, research in these areas has implications for treatment as well as etiology.

Biochemistry: The Dopamine Hypothesis

Biochemical explanations of schizophrenia have a long history. A century ago, for example, Émil Kraepelin suggested that these disorders result from a chemical imbalance caused by abnormal sex gland secretion. Since then, a number of researchers have tried to show that body chemistry is involved in schizophrenia. Most have failed to do so.

What generally happens is that a researcher finds a particular chemical substance in schizophrenic subjects and does not find it in "normal" controls, but other researchers cannot replicate those findings. In addition, schizophrenic patients differ from normal persons in lifestyle and in food and medication intake, all of which affect body chemistry and tend to confound research results.

One promising line of biochemical research has focused on the neurotransmitter dopamine and on its involvement in schizophrenia (Davis et al., 1991). According to the **dopamine hypothesis** (discussed briefly in Chapter 2), schizophrenia may result from excess dopamine activity at certain synaptic sites. This hyperactivity is caused by either (1) the release of excess dopamine by presynaptic neurons or (2) the oversensitivity of dopamine receptors.

Support for the dopamine hypothesis has come from research with three types of drugs. *Phenothiazines,* which are antipsychotic drugs that decrease the severity of thought disorders, alleviate withdrawal and hallucinations and improve the mood of schizophrenics. Their effectiveness is not due to a generalized sedating effect. (Phenobarbital, a depressant with sedative properties, is not nearly as effective against schizophrenic symptoms.) Rather, increasing evidence shows that the phenothiazines reduce dopamine activity in the brain by blocking dopamine receptor sites in postsynaptic neurons.

Another drug, *L-dopa,* is generally used to treat symptoms of Parkinson's disease such as muscle and limb rigidity and tremors. The body converts L-dopa to dopamine, and the drug sometimes produces schizophrenic-like symptoms. (By contrast, the phenothiazines, which reduce dopamine activity, can produce side effects that resemble Parkinson's disease.)

Finally, there is research on the effects of the *amphetamines,* stimulants that increase the availability of dopamine and norepinephrine (another neurotransmitter) in the brain. When nonschizophrenic subjects are given continual doses of amphetamines, they show symptoms very much like those of acute paranoid schizophrenia. Continual low dosages of these drugs also produce psychotic-like symptoms in monkeys (Nielsen, Lyon & Ellison, 1983). And very small doses may increase the severity of symptoms in diagnosed schizophrenics. Other stimulants, such as caffeine, do not produce these effects.

Thus a drug that is believed to block dopamine reception has the effect of reducing the severity of schizophrenic symptoms, whereas two drugs that increase dopamine availability either produce or worsen these symptoms. Such evidence obviously supports the idea that excess dopamine may cause schizophrenic symptoms.

The evidence is not all positive, however. For example, the dopamine hypothesis might lead us to expect that treating schizophrenia with phenothiazines would be effective in almost all cases. Yet about one-fourth of schizophrenic patients responded very little or not at all to antipsychotic medication. In fact, of sixty-five schizophrenics treated with antipsychotic medications, 25 percent reported negative effects (Van Putten et al., 1984). In addition, of a group of schizophrenics who were given amphetamines, one-third did not experience worse symptoms (Angrist, Rotrosen & Gershon, 1980). In another study, twenty-eight remitted schizophrenic patients were administered L-dopa. Only five relapsed within four weeks; the others did not meet the criteria for relapse until about three months (Davidson, Allen & Smith, 1987). In a review of studies on dopamine and schizophrenia, Davis and colleagues (1991) argued that the dopamine hypothesis has to be modified to explain the discrepant findings. They believe that specific brain areas have to be identified that may be sensitive to either an excess or deficiency of dopamine.

As noted earlier, schizophrenia may very well be a group of disorders with different causes; this explanation could account for the variable course of the disorders and the uneven responses to phenothiazines. Moreover, researchers may be looking for an oversimplified explanation by focusing on dopamine alone, without considering the interactive functioning of the brain and the biochemical system as a whole. Or perhaps dopamine blockers can influence the symptoms of schizophrenia but not the course of the illness. Obviously, much more remains to be discovered.

Neurological Findings

Abnormal Neurological Findings Do the symptoms of schizophrenia indicate neurological impairment? This is certainly a possibility. Anywhere from 20 to 65 percent of schizophrenics show some signs of neurological abnormalities (Buchsbaum, 1990; Heinrichs & Buchanan, 1988; Vitaetal, 1991). Again, the wide differences in estimates may indicate problems in the reliability of assessment techniques or may reflect the possibility that different subgroups of schizophrenics were assessed.

Some researchers (McGlashan & Fenton, 1992) believe that a group of schizophrenics with predominantly negative symptoms (Type II schizophrenics) such as flat affect, poverty of speech, and loss of drive display characteristics associated with neuronal loss or deterioration in a structurally abnormal brain. These schizophrenics would be expected to show less responsiveness to antipsychotic medication and have a poorer prognosis. In contrast, schizophrenics with positive symptoms (Type I schizophrenics) such as hallucinations and delusions do not show brain deterioration but reversible hyperactive neurological functioning. Some studies have found greater signs of neurological problems in Type II as compared to Type I schizophrenics (Pakkenberg, 1987).

The search for abnormal neurological factors in schizophrenia has intensified as increasingly sophisticated brain imaging techniques for studying the living brain have been developed. Using these procedures, researchers have found that, compared with controls, schizophrenics are more likely to show ventricular enlargement (enlarged spaces in areas of the brain) and cerebral atrophy or neuronal loss (Berman et al., 1987; Roberts, 1991; Vita et al., 1991; Zipursky, Lim & Pfefferbaum, 1991). They also show decreased functioning in the frontal lobes and other cerebral areas (Andreasen, 1988; Buchsbaum, 1990). Cerebral glucose metabolism is significantly lower in

The PET scan measures the metabolic level of different parts of the brain. Orange areas represent greater brain activity; green and blue areas indicate lower activity. Chronic schizophrenics show less activity in the frontal lobes (areas associated with higher intellectual functioning and fluent emotional expression) than normal subjects.

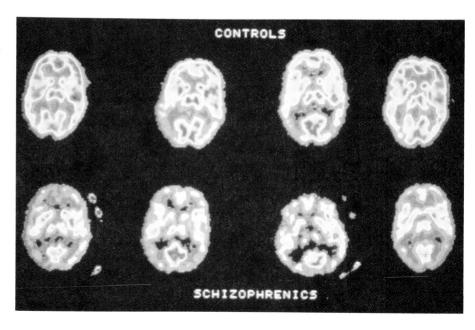

schizophrenic patients than in control subjects. This is especially true among patients with more negative symptoms—Type II (Volkow et al., 1987; Wolkin et al., 1988).

Cognitive Markers Schizophrenics appear to have information-processing deficits and problems in sustaining attention, recall memory, and visual processing. These characteristics are present during remission as well as during symptomatic periods (Brenner et al., 1992; Lieberman & Green, 1992). Researchers have hoped that these characteristics would function as "cognitive markers," that is, they would indicate a vulnerability for psychotic episodes. If these "markers" indicate genetic influence, they should also be present in a greater percentage of first-degree relatives than in comparison groups (Green, 1993).

To identify "markers" from transient symptoms, Nuechterlein and colleagues (1992) recommended that we distinguish between:

1. *Stable vulnerability indicators* These characteristics would be "enduring" or consistently different from nonschizophrenic individuals and would be evident before, during, and after schizophrenic episodes. They would not become "worse" during psychotic episodes, they would be genetically determined, and they would occur in much higher frequency in individuals with or at risk for schizophrenia.

2. *Mediating vulnerability factors* These characteristics would be present both during psychotic episodes and remission but become severely worse during manifestations of the disorder. These are also hypothesized to be genetically determined and occur at a higher frequency in schizophrenic populations.

3. *Episode indicators* These characteristics would be abnormal during psychotic episodes but return to normal levels during remission. These characteristics are short-term and a result of the disorder.

This strategy will allow us to separate characteristics that are causal or may function as cognitive markers rather than short-term symptoms due to the disorder. Several tests have been used to measure some of these deficits found in schizophrenics. In the *Visual Continuous Performance Test*, sustained attention to tasks

is measured. In one version, subjects monitor a series of letters or numbers and signal when a predetermined stimulus appears. Another test, *Eye Movement Dysfunction Measure*, analyzes how well the eye follows a target. On both tests, schizophrenics show greater impairment than control samples (Szymansk, Kane & Lieberman, 1991). These information-processing differences have been found consistently in schizophrenic samples. Researchers are not clear, however, on what these findings mean. Are they cognitive markers?

Problems with identified "markers" for schizophrenics have been found. Impairment on the tests has been associated with certain medications, fatigue, fluctuations in attention, and other physical and psychological disorders (Clementz & Sweeney, 1990). In addition, stable information-processing differences have also been found in other psychiatric patients (Penn et al., 1993). Another difficulty is that the course of schizophrenia is variable with peaks and valleys so that it is difficult to identify what phase of the disorder the individual is in. Because of this, it is difficult to know if we are looking at episode indicators, mediating factors, or stable indicators. Neuropsychological tests may also be unreliable for this population (Heinrichs, 1993).

Although the research strategy suggested by Nuechterlein and colleagues seems sound, the "enduring" characteristics pathognomonic to schizophrenia have been difficult to identify. As yet, none of the cognitive markers are specific enough to be included as a criterion in the diagnosis of schizophrenia (Szymanski, Kan & Lieberman, 1991).

Conclusions What can we conclude from studies of brain structure and functioning in schizophrenics? It appears that neurological abnormalities are reported more often in schizophrenics than in nonschizophrenics and more often in schizophrenics having negative symptoms. These observations are intriguing because they highlight the possibility that some subtypes of schizophrenia may be caused by structural brain pathology. Findings that abnormalities in the prefrontal cortex may be a factor are especially interesting because this area is involved with some of the intellectual symptoms associated with schizophrenia.

Problems in interpreting the findings exist, however. Neurological abnormalities do not seem to be specific to schizophrenia. They are also found in persons with mood disorders, alcohol and substance abuse, and organic impairment (Shelton et al., 1988; Wolkin et al., 1988). After a review of thirty-nine studies on ventricular size, Van Horn and McManus (1992) concluded, "It (the size difference) is probably too small to be of practical significance in diagnosis" (p. 6). Other problems in interpreting the results of neurophysiological studies include small sample sizes, old diagnostic criteria, unreliable assessment techniques, and the potential effects of medication (Heinrichs, 1993). However, the search for neurological abnormalities in people with schizophrenia is promising.

The research evidence has clearly indicated that schizophrenia is a brain disorder. However, the underlying structure(s) or neuropathological processes have not been identified. Heinrichs (1993) pointed out the many contradictions in the disorder:

1. The presentation of the disorder and its course is varied. Some patients have hallucinations; some have only delusions.

2. Some patients show poor premorbid adjustment in their history, and others seem fine until the disorder strikes.

3. Some patients respond positively to antipsychotic medications, whereas others do not.

4. Neuroanatomical abnormalities are found in some patients but not in others.

5. Genetic factors are important but do not seem sufficient for the expression of the disorder.

6. Information-processing deficits are found in most schizophrenics but also in other psychiatric patients.

7. Individuals with brain lesions in the areas of the brain associated with schizophrenia show different performance patterns than found in schizophrenics.

What does all this conflicting information mean? Heinrichs believes that "schizophrenia is a heterogeneous illness that, paradoxically, resists subdivision." We need to identify and subdivide the disorder so that the different etiological types can be studied. Unfortunately, attempts to do so have been largely unsuccessful.

ENVIRONMENTAL FACTORS IN SCHIZOPHRENIA

Obviously, genetic and biological research has not yet clarified the cause of the various schizophrenic disorders. If for no other reason then, psychologists must consider environmental factors as causes. Here we examine available information and theories concerning the role of family dynamics, social class, and cultural differences in the development of these disorders.

We should first note, however, that environmental factors become involved in psychopathology by acting as stressors. A logical question, then, is "Can stress produce schizophrenia?" Attempts to find an answer have not been successful, primarily because most rely on retrospective reports from people who have sought treatment. Such people don't comprise the entire population of schizophrenics, and their memories of past events may be inaccurate. There are reports of stress-induced hallucinations among individuals facing highly anxiety-arousing circumstances (Spivak et al., 1992). But these episodes were temporary and diagnoses of schizophrenia were not given.

Studies do show that a substantial minority of patients do experience a greater frequency of stressful events before receiving a diagnosis of schizophrenia. The number of stressful events is also correlated with the probability of relapse after treatment (Zubin, Steinhauer & Condray, 1992). In addition, a large minority reported a single precipitating factor: in a study of 502 schizophrenic individuals, 25 percent reported the death of a spouse or close relative as a precipitating event, 9 percent reported an illness or surgery, and 5 percent had borne a child shortly before diagnosis; the remaining 61 percent reported no precipitating factor (Huber et al., 1981). For some schizophrenics, stress appears to be related to the precipitation and relapse after recovery.

Family Influences

In 1978, a researcher in the field of schizophrenia concluded, "No environmental causes have been found that will invariably or even with moderate probability produce genuine schizophrenia in persons who are unrelated to a schizophrenic individual" (Gottesman, 1978, p. 67). Another researcher echoed this view: "There are no schizophrenogenic environments . . . environmental contributions have little or no specificity" (Fowler, 1984, p. 82). Both researchers believe that unless a person has a genetic predisposition toward schizophrenia, environmental stress has little impact on the development of the disorder. Others strongly disagree. In this section, we consider theories that support psychological factors as either the cause or a contributor to schizophrenia.

Theoretical Constructs   Theorists have suggested two ways in which family interaction can contribute to the development of schizophrenia. The first was proposed by psychodynamic theorists who believed that certain behavioral patterns of parents could inhibit appropriate ego development in the child. This, in turn, would make the child vulnerable to the severe regression characteristic of schizophrenia. Attention was focused mainly on the mother, who usually has a great deal of contact with the child; the **schizophrenogenic** (or schizophrenia-producing) mother was characterized as being simultaneously or alternately cold and overprotecting, rejecting and dominating. This behavior pattern led to the development of schizophrenia in the child.

The second theory involving family interaction is the communication **double-bind theory** mentioned in Chapter 3 (Bateson et al., 1956). Proponents suggested that the preschizophrenic child has repeated experiences with one or more family members (usually the mother and father) in which he or she receives two contradictory messages. The child cannot discern the parent's meaning and cannot escape the situation. This conflict eventually leads the person to develop difficulty in interpreting other people's communications and in accurately and appropriately conveying his or her own thoughts and feelings.

Assume, for example, that a mother harbors hostile feelings toward her daughter and yet wishes to be a good and loving mother. She might send her child to bed, saying, "You're tired and sleep will do you good." The overt message conveys the mother's concern for her child's health. Her tone of voice, however, is such that the child senses the mother's anger and her desire to be alone. The child then can interpret the contradictory messages in one of two ways (Bateson, 1978): she may correctly interpret her mother's hostility, in which case she is faced with the awful fact that she is not loved or wanted by her mother. Or she may accept the overt message—that

Family reactions may influence relapse in patients. Here a sister appears "cold" in response to a kiss from her schizophrenic sibling.

she is tired and that her mother cares for her—and then be forced to deny her real understanding of the message. The child is punished whether she discriminates the message correctly or incorrectly (the double bind).

To survive, the child may resort to self-deception, falsely interpreting her own thoughts as well as those communicated by others. She may develop a false concept of reality, an inability to communicate effectively, withdrawal, and other symptoms of schizophrenia.

Problems with Earlier Research Most studies conducted before the mid-1970s supported the view that communications were less clear and accurate in families with a schizophrenic member than in other families. Methodological shortcomings, however, kept researchers from generalizing these results to a relationship between schizophrenia and family dynamics. The most common flaws were the following: (1) a family's interactions were studied only after one of its members had been diagnosed as schizophrenic and (2) the lack of control groups. Thus even if difficult family interaction was correlated with schizophrenia, researchers could not tell which was the

cause and which the effect, or whether the correlation was unique to schizophrenia.

Expressed Emotion Current research is directed toward a specific behavior pattern called *expressed emotion (EE)* that is found among some relatives of schizophrenics. The expressed emotion index is determined by the number of critical comments by a relative (criticism), the number of statements of dislike or resentment toward the patient by family members (hostility), and a rating of statements reflecting emotional overinvolvement, overconcern, or overprotectiveness for the patient (Jenkins & Karno, 1992). For example, high-EE relatives are likely to make a greater number of statements such as "You have a bad attitude about work, Jim" (Miklowitz et al., 1984). The EE construct strongly predicts the course of the disorder (Karno et al., 1987; Mintz, Mintz & Goldstein, 1987). Patients living with high-EE relatives were three to four times more likely to relapse in the nine months after discharge than those living with low-EE relatives (Miklowitz et al., 1986). In fact, Leff (1976) reported that the amount of contact patients had with their high-EE relatives or spouses was related to relapse rates (see Figure 15.2).

FIGURE 15.2 Influence of Expressed Emotions on Relapse Rates

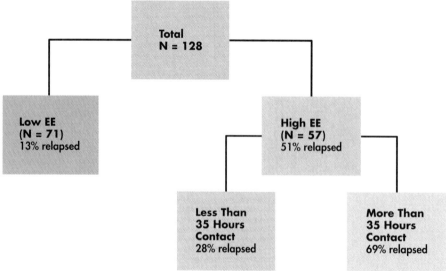

Source: Adapted from Leff, 1976.

Those who had more than thirty-five hours of direct contact were much more likely to suffer a relapse.

Medication seems to be especially important in preventing relapses in patients in high-EE families. Patients not taking medication who spent at least thirty-five hours with high-EE families relapsed at a rate of 92 percent, as opposed to 15 percent for patients on medication who had less than thirty-five hours of direct contact with their high-EE relatives. The importance of expressed emotions was also found among low-income, unacculturated Mexican Americans. High-EE levels in key relatives increased the risk of relapse among remitted schizophrenic patients who returned home after being discharged (Karno et al., 1987).

Although these studies are better designed than those discussed earlier, they are still correlational in nature. It is possible that living with a more severely ill schizophrenic patient is the cause, and not the result, of high-EE communication patterns in relatives. High-EE communication does not appear to be pathognomonic (specific) for schizophrenia. These patterns have also been found in the families of patients with depression, bipolar disorder, and eating disorders (Kavanagh, 1992). This communication pattern also appears to be more evident in western families. Studies of the families of patients living in India show much lower levels of high-EE than in American families (Leff et al., 1990). In addition, not all studies have supported the EE hypothesis and some researchers are expressing concern that EE may be used to blame families for the disorder. There is also a question about how EE is measured. The assessment of EE requires only one observation or interview, which might not be enough to give an accurate picture of family interaction patterns (Kavanagh, 1992).

Although it appears that environmental factors alone do not cause schizophrenia, researchers continue to find that the family environment may be involved in the onset and course of the disorder. Several prospective studies have found that high-risk children who develop schizophrenia, as opposed to those who do not, are more likely to have negative family relationships (Burman et al., 1987; Marcus et al., 1987).

The importance of parenting was indicated in the Israeli high-risk study. Among the high-risk group, none who had received "good parenting" from a schizophrenic parent developed schizophrenia or a spectrum disorder. Most investigators now accept the diathesis-stress model (discussed later in this chapter) in which a predisposition interacts with stressors to produce the onset of schizophrenia.

Effect of Social Class

Schizophrenia is most common at the lower socioeconomic levels, regardless of whether prevalence is measured relative to patient populations or to general populations. One of the most consistent findings in schizophrenia research is that the disorder is disproportionately concentrated among people in the poorest areas of large cities and in the occupations with the lowest status (Gottesman, 1991).

This correlation between social class and schizophrenia has two possible explanations. First, low socioeconomic status is itself stressful. Physical and psychological stressors associated with poverty, a lack of education, menial employment, and the like increase the chance that schizophrenia will develop (*breeder hypothesis*). Second, schizophrenic and preschizophrenic people tend to drift to the poorest urban areas and the lowest socioeconomic levels because they can't function effectively elsewhere in society (*downward drift theory*).

Although one way to test downward drift theory is to determine whether schizophrenics do actually move downward in occupational status, the results of such studies have been inconclusive. Some researchers have found evidence of downward mobility, but others have found none (Neale & Oltmanns, 1980).

Another research strategy is to compare the occupations of schizophrenics with their fathers' occupations. If the schizophrenics generally had lower-status jobs than their fathers, a downward drift interpretation would be supported. In several studies, schizophrenics were found to have lower-status occupations than their fathers (Gottesman, 1991). Overall, the evidence seemed to suggest that both interpretations apply. For some people, the stressors and limitations associated with membership in the lowest socioeconomic class facilitate the development of schizophrenia; for others, low socioeconomic status is a result of the disorders.

Cross-Cultural Comparisons

Schizophrenia appears to be present in the countries studied by the World Health Organization. The lowest prevalence of the disorder was found in Denmark (1.5 per 10,000) and the highest in India (4.2 per 10,000; Jablensky, 1988). A number of studies found various differences in symptomology, however, and these may result from environmental influences.

Third-world countries seem to have a greater percentage of "hysterical psychoses," "possession syndromes," and other brief psychotic disorders. These psychoses tend to be rapid in onset and short in duration; they have a good prognosis. These cases occur as a reaction to an extreme psychosocial stressor (Wig, 1983). The following case from Zimbabwe illustrates some of the characteristics:

> A young teacher was brought to the psychiatric hospital by the police after smashing several plate-glass windows in local shops and breaking the windows of cars parked on the street. . . . When captured, he was intensely aggressive, spoke incoherently, and claimed voices were talking to him and directing his actions. Following recovery, which required several weeks of treatment with high-dose, high-potency neuroleptics, he told the following story.
>
> Approximately one month prior to onset of his running amok, he consulted a local n'anga [healer] to determine whether the future of his job was secure. The n'anga told him his workmates were jealous of him and might try to harm him. A few weeks later he found a "flash card" in his office. It read, "To die." He knew at once that his colleagues planned to murder him, probably by bewitchment. This episode would not leave his mind. Hallucinated voices began to echo his thoughts, and his state of wild excitement ensued. (Stevens, 1987, p. 394)

Cases of psychotic reactions after hearing a negative prediction from a witch doctor have been reported in some third-world countries.

A comparison of the symptoms of hospitalized schizophrenic Americans of Irish and Italian descent found that Irish-Americans tended to show less hostility and acting out, but showed more fixed delusions, than did Italian-Americans. These differences have been attributed to cultural-familial backgrounds: in Irish families, mothers played a very dominant role, were quite strict, and prohibited strong emotional displays; in Italian families, mothers showed the opposite pattern (Opler, 1967). Similarly, Japanese hospitalized for schizophrenia are often described as rigid, compulsive, withdrawn, and passive—symptoms that reflect the Japanese cultural value of conformity within the community and reserve within the family (S. Sue & Morishima, 1982).

The content of delusions also seems to be influenced by culture and society. Since the social and political upheavals of the period known as the Cultural Revolution (during the 1960s), a number of new delusions have appeared among Chinese schizophrenic patients (Yu-Fen & Neng, 1981). These include the delusion of leadership lineage, in which patients insist that their parents are people in authority; the delusion of being tested, in which patients believe that their superiors are assessing them to determine whether they are suitable for promotion; the delusion of impending arrest, in which patients assume that they are about to be arrested by authorities; and the delusion of being married, in which a female patient insists that she has a husband even though she is unmarried. Each of these is associated with some facet of the new Chinese society.

Racial differences have also been observed. In a study of 273 schizophrenic patients admitted to hospitals and mental health centers in Missouri over a 3½-year period, researchers found that black patients exhibited more severe symptoms than white patients: angry outbursts, impulsiveness, and strongly antisocial behavior. Blacks also showed greater disorientation and confusion and more severe hallucinatory behaviors than whites (Abebimpe et al., 1982). These research findings may be interpreted as real differences in symptomology that may have environmental explanations. According to Abebimpe (1981), however, they may instead be produced by diagnostic errors. He noted that blacks are less likely than whites to be given a diagnosis of mood disorder and more likely to receive a diagnosis of schizophrenia, even when the two racial groups show similar symptoms. Also, cultural differences between patient and clinician tend to result in diagnostic errors—the greater the difference, the greater the likelihood of error. Finally, misdiagnosis can result from racial stereotyping or bias, or from applying diagnostic systems based on white middle-class norms to other racial groups.

FIGURE 15.3   The Diathesis-Stress Model of Nuechterlein and Dawson

The vulnerable individual overreacts to environmental stressors that are not buffered by his or her social support system. The feedback loop has the effect of "transforming" such overreaction into added stressors that eventually build up sufficiently to precipitate a schizophrenic episode.

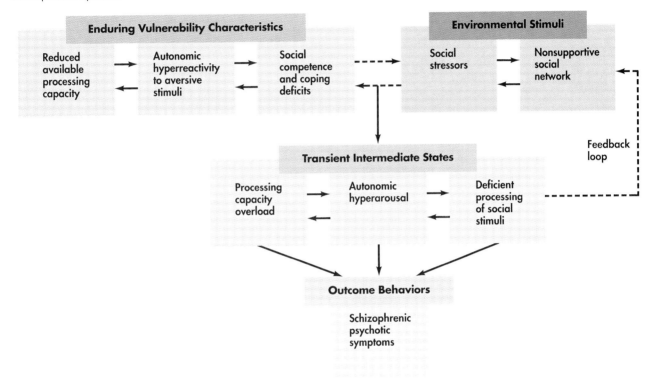

Source: Nuechterlein & Dawson, 1984.

THE DIATHESIS-STRESS MODEL OF SCHIZOPHRENIA

The lack of evidence pointing to a single etiology for the schizophrenic disorders has led Bleuler (1984, p. 8) to conclude that

> Today, it is certain that in their formation, unfavorable hereditary predispositions interact with unfavorable experiences in life.
>
> Neither a single, inherited predisposition specific only to schizophrenia nor a specific damaging experience in the life course has ever been found. Instead, there are multitudes of physical and mental, inherited and acquired dispositions that form predispositions for schizophrenia.

Researchers have thus developed a general model emphasizing the interaction between genetics and environmental stressors in schizophrenia (Zubin & Ludwig, 1983). This **diathesis-stress model** involves a vulnerability to the disorder, which may be inherited or acquired, combined with the impact of stressors. Schizophrenia develops when a vulnerable person encounters stress and lacks access to the resources or social support systems that he or she needs to cope with it.

A particularly elaborate version of the diathesis-stress model has been developed by Nuechterlein and Dawson (1984) and Neuchterlein (1987). As Figure 15.3 shows, these researchers believe that schizophrenics suffer from several "enduring vulnerability characteristics": (1) dysfunctions in dopaminergic neurochemistry; (2) a predisposition toward poor processing of information and difficulty in sustaining attention, brought on by various thought impairments; (3) overreaction to even mildly aversive stimuli; and (4) lack of adequate social competence and coping skills.

The vulnerable person may not experience psychotic episodes if he or she has good coping skills, takes antipsychotic medications, or is being raised in a supportive family and has good social supports. What might increase the chances of a schizophrenia episode are (1) family environment in which high EE is present, (2) an environment that is too stimulating, and (3) stressful life events. When the negative factors outweigh positive personal and protective environmental variables, the individual's cognitive functioning becomes overloaded and a feedback loop is created that continually compounds the stress. Eventually schizophrenic symptoms develop.

The diathesis-stress model is useful because it calls attention to the role both biological and psychological factors play in schizophrenia. The model also implies that intervention can take many forms. Therapy could involve increasing the "personal protectors" by teaching the individual coping skills and using antipsychotic medication. Family and social interventions can be used to provide a more supportive social environment. In the next section, we will discuss the variety of therapeutic approaches based on this model.

THE TREATMENT OF SCHIZOPHRENIA

Through the years, schizophrenia has been "treated" by a variety of means including "warehousing" severely disturbed patients in overcrowded asylums and prefrontal lobotomy, a surgical procedure in which the frontal lobes are disconnected from the remainder of the patient's brain. Such radical procedures were generally abandoned in the 1950s, when the beneficial effects of antipsychotic drugs were discovered. Today schizophrenia is typically treated with antipsychotic medication along with some type of psychosocial therapy. More severely disordered patients are still hospitalized until they are able to function adequately in society.

Antipsychotic Medication

> As a psychiatrist, I know that the best way in dealing with the biological basis of schizophrenia is by the well-adjusted intake of psychotropic medication (neuroleptics). I also know that the medication I prescribe has side effects at times quite troublesome, and I have to be sensitive to the patient's reports of side effects. (Seeman et al., 1982, p. 120)

Most mental health professionals consider the introduction of *Thorazine,* the first antipsychotic drug, the beginning of a new era in treating schizophrenia. For the first time, a medication was available that sufficiently relaxed even violent schizophrenics and helped organize their thoughts to the point where straitjackets were no longer needed to contain the individuals. Three decades later, the phenothiazines, which are variations of Thorazine, are still viewed as the most effective drug treatment for schizophrenia.

The antipsychotic medications (also called **neuroleptics**) are, however, far from perfect and can produce a number of extremely unwelcome side effects that resemble neurological conditions. They quite effectively reduce the severity of the positive symptoms of schizophrenia such as hallucinations, delusions, bizarre speech, and thought disorders. Most, however, offer little relief from the negative symptoms such as social withdrawal, apathy, and impaired personal hygiene (Christison, 1991), and many schizophrenics don't benefit at all from antipsychotic medication (Silverman et al., 1987). The First Person narrative discusses negative symptoms from an occupational therapist's viewpoint.

A new drug, *clozapine,* was released for use in the United States in 1990. It has several properties that have raised a great deal of interest. It seems to be effective with individuals who have not responded to other antipsychotic medications and seems to have fewer side effects (Kane, 1991). There is also some indication that clozapine may be able to treat negative symptoms in schizophrenia (Safferman et al., 1991). Its use is carefully monitored because one of the side effects, agranulocytosis, which involves lesions of the mucous membranes or gastrointestinal system, is potentially fatal.

Regulation and monitoring of antipsychotic drugs is especially important. Zito and colleagues (1987) found that many of 136 newly admitted schizophrenics were given doses in "excess of current guidelines." Women received higher doses of antipsychotic medications than men. In addition, medication was seldom reduced to a maintenance level once the acute stage passed. Segal and colleagues (1992) found that psychiatrists tended to administer higher and higher doses of antipsychotic medications to patients living in halfway houses and other sheltered care facilities. Nearly one-half received increases in medication during a twelve-year period, and 10 percent received "extreme doses." Equally disturbing, clinicians are often unaware of possible reactions to the drugs, which include tremors, motor restlessness, anxiety, agitation, extreme terror, and even impulsive suicide attempts (Drake & Ehrlich, 1985). In one study (Weiden et al., 1987) clinicians did not identify motor symptoms such as restlessness, rigidity, and tremors produced by medications. Only one of ten patients showing tardive dyskinesia (involuntary movement disorder) was identified by the clinicians. The inability to note these symptoms in medicated patients is disturbing. Critical Thinking discusses the issue of patients' rights in taking medication.

Because of the severity of some side effects, researchers are trying to determine which schizophrenic patients don't need maintenance medication. For example, twenty-three chronic schizophrenics who retrospectively met the DSM-III criteria were able to sustain good outcome for an average of fifteen years without maintenance doses of antipsychotic medication. This group had good premorbid and occupational adjustment as well as good social skills. This finding clearly indicated that not all schizophrenic patients require continuous medication. Nevertheless, researchers still need to address the inability to identify the groups of schizophrenic patients who do not require maintenance medication (Fenton & McGlashan, 1987).

One approach is to reduce medication and watch for a relapse. Those who function well on a lower dosage might later undergo a trial period in which medication is totally eliminated. In one study conducted over a twelve-month period, reducing dosage levels by 50 percent tripled the relapse rate (32 percent, as opposed to 10 percent on maintenance medication). A tradeoff, however, is that reduced-dose patients showed decreased risk of tardive dyskinesia (Johnson et al., 1987). Although a higher relapse rate

was associated with a lower level of medication (10 percent of the standard dose), the families of these patients expressed more satisfaction with their adjustment than the families of patients taking a standard dose. On the lower dose, patients showed greater social competence and adjustment. More than 50 percent remained stable. Researchers also found that negative family attitudes toward the patient were associated with relapse. So dosage reduction, together with careful monitoring, may be useful with some people, but standard dosage levels may be needed in nonsupportive families.

Psychosocial Therapy

Most clinicians today agree that the most beneficial treatment for schizophrenia is some combination of antipsychotic medication and therapy (Hogarty et al., 1991). This attitude is fairly new and was resisted for many years by strict advocates of a medical approach. But even as scientists continued to introduce drugs that effectively reduced or eliminated many symptoms of schizophrenia, it became clear that one vital fact was being ignored: medicated and adequately functioning schizophrenics who were discharged from the protective environment of hospitals were being returned to stressful home or work situations. The typical result was repeated rehospitalization; medication alone wasn't enough to help schizophrenics function in their natural environment. Clinicians soon realized that antipsychotic medication had to be supplemented with outpatient therapy. But which therapeutic strategy would yield the best results?

Institutional Approaches Traditional institutional treatments providing custodial care and medication for schizophrenics have yielded poor results, although milieu therapy and behavioral therapy were found to be more effective. In **milieu therapy**, patients exercise a wide range of responsibilities. They are involved in decision making and in managing the wards. This is in sharp contrast to the passive role that they have in traditional settings. Social learning programs focus on increasing appropriate self-care behaviors, conversational skills, and role skills (job training and ward activities). Undesirable behaviors such as "crazy talk" or social isolation are decreased through reinforcement and modeling techniques.

FIRST PERSON

Mary Ann Mayer

Schizophrenia—less a diagnosis than a human condition. Ten years ago I began practicing psychiatric occupational therapy because of my academic interest in the disease. I remain in practice today because of my respect for the people affiliated with it.

A few days after admission to the psychiatric unit, the psychotic storm that engulfs the schizophrenic quiets down and the person emerges, as if from a cocoon. The positive symptoms recede—the command hallucinations, the fear of being stalked or poisoned, hearing one's thoughts whispered by every passerby. But the negative symptoms linger—disturbances in attention, perception, psychomotor behavior, affect, and drive. These are the symptoms that most subtract from the quality of life.

People with schizophrenia are not "crazy"; they have a cognitive disability that robs them of choice and access to the everyday activities you and I take for granted, such as running a household, earning and spending money, and planning for the future. This is why meaningful activity is the treatment method used by occupational therapists; it uses people's assets while helping them cope with their limitations. For some, guided involvement in the activities of daily life can restore meaning, purpose, and identity.

I'm expected to help the schizophrenic person and his or her family understand and manage this disability, reduce environmental barriers to performance, and restore purpose and place in life. I act as an advocate for the schizophrenic, explaining to others why that person has difficulty doing certain things. I also assess the schizophrenic's environment and try to modify it in ways that optimize that person's performance. Not everything I do works, but anything can work—skills training, simplifying a work site, finding a compatible social group, instilling hope, and showing others alternatives to blaming the schizophrenic person for his or her disability.

The following statements are common misperceptions. One of my responsibilities as an occupational therapist is to interpret a schizophrenic's behavior in a way that can be understood by others, thereby en-

Supportive counseling or other forms of psychotherapy can supplement drug therapy for schizophrenic patients. Once the patient's psychotic symptoms are under control, a therapist can try to help the patient improve his or her social and coping skills.

Both approaches have been shown to be effective in helping many schizophrenics achieve independent living (Falloon, Boyd & McGill, 1984).

Cognitive-Behavioral Therapy Because schizophrenics typically lack social skills, a social skills training program is almost always included as part of behavior therapy. In many cases, it is the major part of the therapy. Therapy emphasizes communication skills and assertiveness training. The patient is repeatedly placed in social situations that he or she tends to avoid. Experience with such situations eventually decreases the patient's anxiety concerning them to the point where he or she will seek out, rather than avoid, these situations. This is a crucially important contribution of social skills training because social withdrawal is a major schizophrenic symptom that is untouched by antipsychotic medication. Social skills training has been found to be helpful for chronic schizophrenic patients (Lieberman & Green, 1992).

Cognitive approaches have also been used to

couraging their understanding and support.

Comment: "He just doesn't apply himself. He's always been lazy."
Response: Daily activities can represent an unachievable challenge. Perhaps he's had more experiences of failure than success. Maybe it's not that he won't perform the task, but that he can't manage it alone, yet. He might be too afraid to try.

Comment: "She seems easily distracted and her work is very disorganized."
Response: Is there a quieter place to work? Is supervision available? Let's analyze the job and work with her to find the easiest methods to perform the assigned tasks.

Comment: "When any medication is prescribed, she takes too much. She can be very uncooperative, you know."
Response: Consistent, familiar routines are important. She may not fully understand the cause and effect of certain actions, such as taking too many pills. A medication daily organizer might help.

Comment: "He has a hard time expressing himself and gets very frustrated when people don't understand. Then he withdraws from everyone, including me. That hurts."
Response: Perhaps he's scared of being rejected, which increases his anxiety, making it more difficult for him to express himself. Encouraging him to take his time when he speaks might help him relax and feel less self-conscious.

In addition to positive and negative symptoms, social stigma and exclusion have to be grappled with. All these factors contribute to the need for hospitalization, support, and stabilization. Symptoms can be reduced or compensated for. But social barriers are far more difficult to overcome. Fear and misunderstanding need to be replaced with compassion and acceptance. Schizophrenia is not just an illness, it's also a disability, and schizophrenic people deserve the same respect and support we accord other disabled people.

Mary Ann Mayer is a registered occupational therapist at Butler Hospital in Providence, Rhode Island. She evaluates the functional performance of patients, provides rehabilitative activities, and consults with families and caregivers in the community.

---

reduce the impact of delusions, hallucinations, and other thought disorders on the behavior of schizophrenics. In one program (Kingdon & Turkington, 1991) schizophrenics were furnished destigmatizing explanations for their symptoms and received training to question their psychotic symptoms. It was explained that stress often produces common reactions such as ideas of reference, paranoid ideas, and misinterpretation of events. The patients were taught to analyze their symptoms. For example, patients who heard voices were asked to determine if they were really coming from within their head. They were also asked to determine if stress was related to the appearance of the voices. One thirty-year-old man believed that his mind was more full of thoughts than others and that thoughts were transmitted like sound waves. After going through cognitive therapy, he admitted that his beliefs were theoretically interesting but not realistic. Kingdon and Turkington found that targeting the reduction of psychotic symptoms through the use of a destigmatizing explanation and providing patients with analytic skills were effective. The sixty-four schizophrenic patients treated with this procedure required minimal hospitalization and low levels of or no medication.

One recent cognitive-behavioral program that has shown promise is the *Integrated Psychological Therapy (IPT)* approach. This program identifies the specific cognitive deficits shown by schizophrenics and remediates them. Several subprograms are involved:

1. *Cognitive Differentiation* During this phase, patients are taught to discriminate stimulus categories by participating in perceptual tasks. They also learn to form concepts and to retrieve appropriate information.

2. *Social Perception* Patients learn to accurately recognize and respond to social cues. They are asked to describe individuals displayed on slides.

3. *Verbal Communication* The focus is on helping patients learn to understand, and evaluate

Should Patients Have the Right to Refuse Medication?

"There is no known effective treatment for tardive dyskinesia." This warning, contained in the *Physician's Desk Reference* (1992), represents a major source of concern for patients receiving antipsychotic medications. Perhaps even more alarming is that neuroleptics are being prescribed to treat anxiety, hyperactivity in children, aggression, and mood disorders.

Tardive dyskinesia is characterized by involuntary and rhythmic movements of the protruding tongue; chewing, lip smacking, and other facial movements; and jerking movements of the limbs. At risk are elderly patients, women, and people treated with neuroleptics over a long period of time. Women tend to have a higher prevalence and more severe tardive dyskinesia than men (Yassa & Jeste, 1992). However, this syndrome is becoming increasingly prevalent in younger patients and nonpsychotic patients. In one large prospective study, nearly 20 percent of the sample developed tardive dyskinesia after being on the medication for four years. After eight years, 40 percent had tardive dyskinesia (Kane et al., 1986). In the majority of cases, the symptoms persist and cannot be eliminated

(Glazer, Morgenstern & Douchette, 1991).

Although neuroleptics can produce Parkinson-like symptoms such as loss of facial expression, immobility, shuffling gait, tremors of the hand, rigidity of the body, and poor postural stability, these symptoms are usually reversible. *Akathisia* (motor restlessness) and *dystonia* (slow and continued contrasting movements of the limbs and tongue), which are also controllable, may appear as well. Patients described their reactions to the medication: "I feel restless; I cannot keep still; my nerves are jumpy; I feel like jumping out of my skin; my legs just want to keep moving; it's like having ants in my pants (Sachdev & Loneragan, 1991, p. 383). Other side effects include drowsiness, skin rashes, blurred vision, dry mouth, nausea, and tachycardia.

Should schizophrenics have the right to refuse antipsychotic medications that produce potentially hazardous side effects? Patients in many state hospitals do not have this right. Groups that support the concept of patients' rights argue that forced administration of drugs violates a person's basic freedoms. Yet hospital

staff members fear that violent patients may be dangerous to themselves, other patients, and staff if they are not medicated. One resident care aide said, "Those who refuse drugs may be those who need them most because they are dangerous. We don't have enough staff on the units to deal with that" (*Ann Arbor News*, June 6, 1984, pp. A1, A4). As the funding of state mental institutions has decreased, the use of medication has increased. According to the director of the Michigan Department of Mental Health, 98 percent of patients in state hospitals are on psychotropic drugs.

Should patients who admit themselves voluntarily for treatment be able to refuse antipsychotic medications? What about those who are involuntarily committed? Should the state, institution, or psychiatrist be liable for the development of permanent side effects among patients? Can an individual who is currently undergoing a psychotic episode give "consent" to being treated with antipsychotic medications? States and the mental health profession are wrestling with these treatment issues.

---

verbal statements. They are taught how to have conversations with others.

4. *Social Skills and Interpersonal Interventions*

During these last two subprograms, intensive practice and role-playing are used to develop social skills. IPT

has been shown to be more effective than placebo attention activities or routine care. Patients show improvement on tests measuring attention, have decreased scores on psychopathology, and lower hospitalization rates as compared with control groups at eighteen months follow-up (Brenner et al., 1992).

Interventions Focusing on Expressed Emotions

Because more than 50 percent of recovering patients return to live with their families, new psychological interventions have had to be developed (Goldman, 1980). Most of these approaches try to reduce the likelihood of relapse (rather than cure the disorder) and try to improve interaction between the patient and family members. This approach involves a two-pronged strategy: (1) disseminating information about the disorder to families of schizophrenics and (2) teaching families and the schizophrenic member how to alter their communication patterns. In one program, high-EE and low-EE family members of schizophrenics meet together in a group to talk about specific themes such as problems faced by families of recovering patients, methods of reducing guilt and responsibility for patients, and healthy ways of dealing with the stress and frustrations of living with a patient. Vaughn and Leff (1981) and Kavanagh (1992) found that this format successfully reduced EE levels and reduced relapse rates in patients.

A similar approach was developed by Falloon, Boyd, and McGill (1984) and is outlined in their book *Family Care of Schizophrenia*. Their intervention is much more comprehensive and includes a careful behavioral analysis of communication patterns in family members and patients. Stressful interactions are identified, and training in alternative methods of communicating is implemented. Specific skills such as listening, making requests clear, focusing on positive reinforcement, and reducing criticisms are stressed. These skills are then employed to help increase problem-solving abilities. Falloon (1992) has found these procedures to be even more useful when individuals first begin to show symptoms suggestive of a schizophrenic episode.

It is important that the patient also develop social skills to recognize the emotional responses from family members and learn to respond appropriately (Lieberman et al., 1986). Family communication patterns should be combined with skills development in individual patients. The positive gains reported from treatment packages that include educating family members, altering communication patterns, and developing social skills and competencies in the patient give an impetus to psychosocial treatments. Family approaches and social skills training have been shown to be much more effective in preventing relapse than drug treatment alone. Combining family and social skills approaches seems to produce the most positive result (Hogarty et al., 1991).

The combination of medication and the new psychological interventions has provided hope for many schizophrenic patients; continuing research points to an even more promising future. This optimism is reflected in the words of a young pharmacy student who is also a schizophrenic:

And even now in 1980, in a professional pharmacy school, it would probably shock many people to know that a schizophrenic was in their class, was going to be a pharmacist, and could do a good job. And knowledge of it could cause the loss of many friends and acquaintances. So even now I must write this article anonymously. But I want people to know that I have schizophrenia, that I need medicine and psychotherapy, and at times I have required hospitalization. . . . When you think about schizophrenia next time, try to remember me; there are more people like me out there trying to overcome a poorly understood disease. . . . And some of them are making it. (Anonymous, 1983)

SUMMARY

1. Much research and theorizing has focused on the etiology of schizophrenia. Using research strategies such as twin studies and adoption studies, investigators have shown that heredity does influence this group of disorders. The degree of influence is open to question, however; when methodological problems are taken into account, it appears lower than reported. Heredity alone is obviously not sufficient to cause schizophrenia; environmental factors are also involved.

2. The process by which genetic influences are transmitted has not been explained. Attempts to find specific biochemical or neurological differences between schizophrenics and nonschizophrenics have not yielded many positive findings. The most promising area of research involves the relationship between brain dopamine (a neurotransmitter) and schizophrenia.

3. The search for an environmental basis for schizophrenia has met with no more success than has the search for genetic influences. Certain negative

family patterns, involving parental characteristics or intrafamilial communication processes, seem correlated with schizophrenia. Recent studies have found that high expressed emotions (negative comments), or high EE, from family members are related to relapse in schizophrenics.

4. These disorders are most prevalent among people in low-status occupations who live in the poorest areas of large cities, and differences in symptomology seem to be loosely related to cultural variables. The effects of such sociocultural variables, however, are still open to speculation.

5. The research on the etiology of schizophrenia has thus suggested an interaction between genetic and environmental factors. The theoretical diathesis-stress model of schizophrenia considers personal vulnerability, which may be caused by hereditary, biological, or psychological factors. When the vulnerable person is exposed to strong environmental stressors but does not have the resources to cope with them, a schizophrenic episode may result.

6. Schizophrenia seems to involve both biological and physiological factors, and treatment programs that combine drugs with psychotherapy appear to hold the most promise. Drug therapy usually involves the phenothiazines, or antipsychotics, and the accompanying psychosocial therapy consists of either supportive counseling or behavior therapy, with an emphasis on social skills training and changing communication patterns among patients and family members.

KEY TERMS

concordance rate The likelihood that both members of a twin pair will show the same disorder

diathesis-stress model A theoretical model postulating that a predisposition (diathesis) and the effect of environmental stressors (stress) combine in producing mental disorders

dopamine hypothesis The suggestion that schizophrenia results from an excess of dopamine activity at certain brain synapses

double-bind theory The suggestion that schizophrenia develops in a person as a result of the continual reception of contradictory messages from parents during the person's upbringing

milieu therapy A therapy program in which the hospital environment operates as a community and patients have decision-making responsibilities

neuroleptics Antipsychotic drugs that can produce symptoms that mimic neurological disorders

prospective study A long-term study of a group of people, beginning before the onset of a disorder, to allow investigators to see how the disorder develops

schizophrenogenic Causing or producing schizophrenia; generally used to describe a parent who is simultaneously or alternately cold and overprotecting, rejecting and dominating

CHAPTER 16

Cognitive Disorders

Some individuals suffer from disorders in which the primary symptoms are cognitive in nature; these disorders are presumed to be caused by transient or permanent dysfunction of the brain. Disorders that affect thinking processes, memory, consciousness, perception, and so on and that are caused by brain dysfunction (for example, brain trauma, aging, substance abuse) are considered by DSM-IV as cognitive disorders. A psychiatric condition with associated cognitive symptoms (such as schizophrenia) is not considered in this category. In this chapter, we discuss cognitive disorders.

COGNITIVE DISORDERS

In the ring, Muhammad Ali was able to "float like a butterfly, sting like a bee" as he won, lost, and twice regained the world heavyweight boxing championship. Outside the ring he was known for his ego, his wit and rapid-fire speech, and his never-ending rhyming. But it was a different Muhammad Ali who, at age forty-two and retired from boxing, entered a New York City hospital for neurological testing. His speech was slurred and sometimes unintelligible, and he tended to shuffle when he walked; he often seemed remote and expressionless, constantly felt tired, and suffered occasional lapses of memory.

Ali's symptoms resembled those of Parkinson's disease, a brain disorder. But were they due to that disorder or to the poundings he must have taken in more than twenty years of boxing? His doctors reported that he did not have Parkinson's disease nor was he "punch-drunk." His disorder was diagnosed as Parkinson's syndrome, meaning that he has many symptoms of Parkinson's disease although he does not have the disorder.

Anti-Parkinson's medication has reduced the severity of some of Ali's symptoms, but the prognosis is vague. The former champion has made a few public appearances, but he is far from the old Ali. Five months after his disorder was diagnosed, he was an honored guest at the sixtieth annual Boxing Writers Association dinner. One writer described him thus:

> At times, Ali disappeared within himself, as if in a trance. A boxing annual from 1965—the cover headlined "Can Ali Beat Liston a Second Time?"—was deposited in front of him [by a fan]. Ali opened it to a picture of himself and Sonji, his first wife.
>
> "He kept staring at that page," said Schulian [who was sitting next to Ali]. "He put the magazine down in his shrimp and avocado salad and kept staring at it. Finally, José Torres lifted the magazine gently and asked him if he wanted his salad."
>
> Later, while somebody gave an award-acceptance speech, Ali allowed his eyelids to fall, and he slept for ten minutes. Only then did a faintly quizzical expression replace his usually benign and bemused countenance. (Marantz, 1985, p. 63)

Muhammad Ali's symptoms have not been tied specifically to the head blows he received as a boxer. Eliminating Parkinson's disease as the cause, however, seems to indicate that they are due to brain trauma.

As you will see in this chapter, it is often difficult to measure and assess, as well as to discern, the exact causes of the **cognitive disorders**, which are behavioral disturbances that result from pathology (or damage to the brain). Possible causes include aging, trauma, infection, loss of blood supply, substance abuse, and various biochemical imbalances. These may result in cognitive, emotional, and behavioral symptoms that can resemble the symptoms of the mental disorders discussed in preceding chapters.

Behavioral disturbance involving brain pathology is influenced by social and psychological factors as well as by the specific pathology. In other words, people with similar types of brain damage may behave quite differently, depending on their premorbid personalities, their coping skills, and the availability of such resources as family support systems. Furthermore, those with cognitive impairments often are treated insensitively by other people, so they experience a lot of stress. This stress may add to or modify the symptoms that stem from the disorder.

Physical, social, and psychological factors thus interact in complicated ways to produce the behaviors of people who have cognitive disorders (Binder,

1988). Treatment, too, often requires some combination of physical, medicinal, and psychological therapy; behavior modification; and skills training. For some patients who have severe and irreversible brain damage, the only available options may be rehabilitation, modified skills training, and the creation of a supportive environment.

The DSM-IV category of cognitive disorders is new in that the previous DSM manual (DSM-III-R) considered these disorders under categories such as organic mental syndromes and organic disorders. Because many disorders (such as schizophrenia) have organic involvement or brain dysfunction and because the DSM-III-R category was not well organized for diagnostic purposes, the disorders were renamed and categorized as cognitive disorders. In this category, DSM-IV distinguishes among (1) delirium, (2) dementia, (3) amnestic disorders, and (4) other cognitive disorders (see the disorder chart on p. 471). In each disorder, there is an attempt to specify the etiological agent.

In cognitive disorders, a pattern of psychological or behavioral signs and symptoms is associated with brain dysfunction. For example, delirium is a syndrome in which someone shows a disturbance of consciousness, inability to maintain attention, memory problems, disorientation, and so on. When the delirium cannot be attributed to another mental disorder (such as a mood disorder) and there is evidence that a general medical condition such as disease or brain trauma is related to the disturbance, it is considered a cognitive disorder. To some extent, the category of cognitive disorders is arbitrary because other mental disorders may be associated with cognitive dysfunctions and organic involvement.

Because the structure of the human brain was discussed in Chapter 2, this chapter focuses primarily on the major causes of cognitive disorders. We begin by discussing ways to assess brain damage, types of cognitive disorders, etiology, and treatment considerations.

THE ASSESSMENT OF BRAIN DAMAGE

The techniques used to assess brain damage were discussed in Chapter 4. There are two types: (1) neuropsychological tests that require behavioral responses from the patient and that assess functions such as

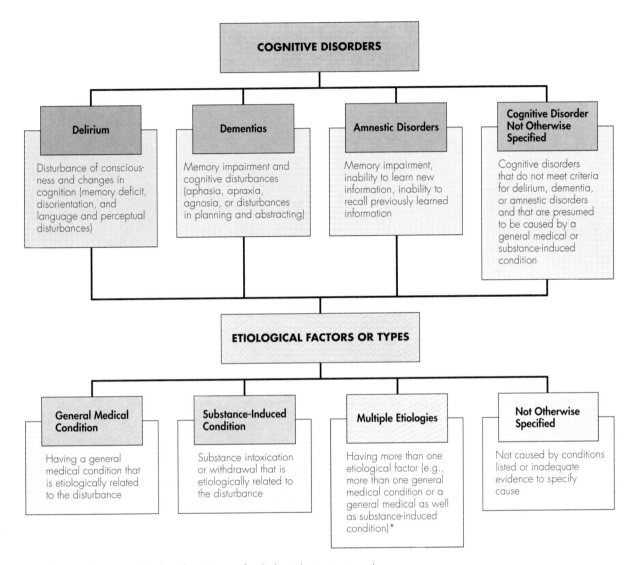

COGNITIVE DISORDERS

Delirium

Disturbance of consciousness and changes in cognition (memory deficit, disorientation, and language and perceptual disturbances)

Dementias

Memory impairment and cognitive disturbances (aphasia, apraxia, agnosia, or disturbances in planning and abstracting)

Amnestic Disorders

Memory impairment, inability to learn new information, inability to recall previously learned information

Cognitive Disorder Not Otherwise Specified

Cognitive disorders that do not meet criteria for delirium, dementia, or amnestic disorders and that are presumed to be caused by a general medical or substance-induced condition

ETIOLOGICAL FACTORS OR TYPES

General Medical Condition

Having a general medical condition that is etiologically related to the disturbance

Substance-Induced Condition

Substance intoxication or withdrawal that is etiologically related to the disturbance

Multiple Etiologies

Having more than one etiological factor (e.g., more than one general medical condition or a general medical as well as substance-induced condition)*

Not Otherwise Specified

Not caused by conditions listed or inadequate evidence to specify cause

* In the case of amnestic disorders, the category of multiple etiologies is not used.

memory and manual dexterity, and (2) neurological tests that allow one to "look into" the brain. Neuropsychological tests, which involve behavioral responses, are becoming quite sophisticated in that theories from neuropsychological science and quantitative methods are being applied to find a means to assess brain pathology (Meier, 1992). Neurological tests (discussed in Chapter 4), which permit more direct monitoring of brain functioning and structure, include the **electroencephalograph** (**EEG**), which measures electrical activity of brain cells, and **computerized axial tomography** (**CAT**) scanning.

Two additional techniques involve monitoring a radioactive substance as it moves through the brain (Boller, Kim & Detre, 1984). In **cerebral blood flow measurement,** the patient inhales a radioactive gas, which flows through the brain with the blood. The gas—and thus the flow of blood—is monitored with a gamma ray camera. In **positron emission tomography** (**PET**), the patient is injected with a radioactive

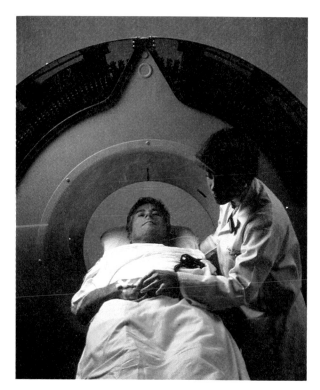

Computerized axial tomography (CAT) scanning uses x-rays to make a three-dimensional representation of the brain. A neurologist can study these computer-enhanced x-rays and locate abnormal tissues within the brain.

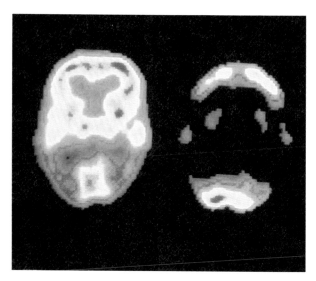

Positron emission tomography (PET) scanning uses a radioactive glucose substance to assess brain activity, which is represented in the photo by different color intensities. Red indicates areas of greatest brain activity. Yellow, blue, and green indicate decreasing levels of brain activity, with black representing the least. The photo on the left is of an Alzheimer's diseased brain, while the photo on the right is of a normal brain.

glucose substance. By monitoring the radioactivity, the physician can study the metabolism of glucose in the patient's brain, which provides a very accurate means of assessing brain function. A more recent development is **magnetic resonance imaging (MRI)**. MRI uses a magnetic field and radiowaves to produce snapshots of brain anatomy that have striking resolution, almost like a photograph with the skull removed—except that it is accomplished without surgery, exposure to X-rays (as in CAT scans), or ingesting radioactive materials (as in PET scans). The procedure involves placing the patient in a magnetic field and using radio waves to make pictures of the brain. Each technique has strengths and weaknesses in terms of costs, benefits, and possible side effects (Margolin, 1991). Collectively, these techniques increase diagnostic accuracy in cases of brain damage.

Equally important is an assessment of the patient's general cognitive functioning, personality characteristics, and coping skills, as well as his or her behaviors and emotional reactions—particularly when they differ from reported premorbid functioning. Such an assessment can provide crucial information about brain dysfunction and is of utmost importance in planning treatment and rehabilitation.

Localization of Brain Damage

Neurological techniques such as CAT and PET scans and MRI help determine the location and extent of brain damage. But can the location of a damaged or disrupted area of the brain be determined from the type of function loss the patient shows? Neuropsychologists have debated this question for a number of years and have made many attempts to relate functions to specific areas of the brain.

In one study, researchers used CAT scans to examine eighty-seven patients, each of whom had a brain lesion (brain damage) that was localized within one of eight areas of the brain (Golden et al., 1981). Each area was then matched with the particular functions affected. The brain areas (four in each hemisphere) are shown in Figure 16.1; the functions that they seemed to control are listed in Table 16.1.

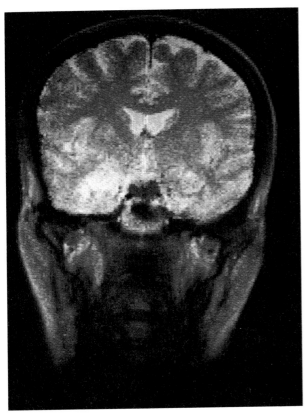

Magnetic resonance imaging (MRI) uses radio waves to produce striking "pictures" of the brain. MRI is more precise than computerized axial tomography, and images can be taken from different points of view.

Note the extensive overlapping of functions, which complicates the assessment of brain damage by determining functional losses. Moreover, "No two human brains are identical in appearance or in distribution of the functional organization of psychological skills. Although there are close approximations in most cases, it is not possible to find one-to-one correspondences for specific physical areas related to specific psychological functions from brain to brain" (Golden et al., 1981).

Two processes that may occur within the brain can further complicate the matching of function (or loss of function) with specific brain areas. The first, documented by many experimental and clinical studies, is **diaschisis,** in which a lesion in a specific area of the brain disrupts other intact areas, sometimes even in the other hemisphere (Smith, 1982).

A possible mechanism for diaschisis is the vast network of neurological pathways connecting the different areas and systems within the brain. These pathways, by which a "message" may be rerouted if it is blocked at a damaged area, may also explain the second process—the recovery of function after an area of the brain has been damaged. Other explanations for this recovery stress *redundancy*, in which an "unused" portion of the brain takes up the function of the damaged area, or *plasticity*, in which an undeveloped portion of the brain substitutes for the damaged portion. This plasticity would account for the development of language in young children who have left-hemisphere damage. For example, a five-year-old boy whose left hemisphere was removed (to stop his seizures) later developed superior language and intellectual abilities. Because the right hemisphere had not yet become fully specialized, it could develop the structure necessary to support language and intellectual ability (Smith & Sugar, 1975).

Nevertheless, some evidence shows that such a shift of function from one hemisphere to the other may decrease the functional space available for the

Table 16.1

Brain Areas and the Functions They Control

Left Frontal Area	*Right Frontal Area*
Expression via speech	Motor
Mathematics	Rhythm
Reception of speech	Mathematics
Left Sensorimotor Area	*Right Sensorimotor Area*
Expression via speech	Motor
Mathematics	Tactile
Left Parietal, Occipital Area	*Right Parietal, Occipital Area*
Mathematics	Tactile
Expression via speech	Motor
Writing	
Reading	
Left Temporal Lobe	*Right Temporal Lobe*
Reception of speech	Rhythm
Expression via speech	Motor
Memory	Tactile
Intelligence	

Source: Golden et al., 1981.

FIGURE 16.1 The Major Areas of the Brain

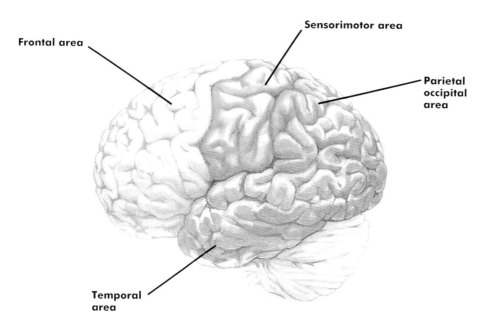

developing of other skills. One person who had left-hemisphere damage at birth did develop normal language ability, but his visual-spatial memory was impaired. The development of language may have required functional space normally devoted to visual-spatial ability (Bullard-Bates & Satz, 1983).

The Dimensions of Brain Damage

Brain damage can be evaluated along a continuum of degree, from mild to moderate to severe. In addition, clinicians often distinguish between endogenous and exogenous causes, between (1) diffuse, specific damage and (2) acute, chronic conditions.

Endogenous brain damage is caused by something within the person; for example, insufficient oxygen for neural tissue caused by loss of blood flow to the brain, for any reason. *Exogenous* brain damage is caused by an external factor such as a severe blow to the head or poisoning.

The diffuse-specific distinction helps indicate the extent of the brain damage. *Diffuse* damage is rather generalized; it typically involves widespread impairment of functioning, including disorientation, poor memory and judgment, and emotional instability.

Specific brain damage is fairly localized, usually causing impairment or behavioral consequences that correspond only to the psychological or physiological function of the injured area.

An *acute* brain disorder is not accompanied by significant and permanent brain damage. A high fever or a severe bout of alcoholic intoxication can result in acute brain changes that are reversible and thus temporary. (Note, however, that the ability of the central nervous system to repair itself when damaged is extremely limited.) A *chronic* disorder involves permanent and irreversible brain damage—for example, as a result of severe lead poisoning caused by a child eating paint that contains lead.

People with chronic brain disorders may display similar symptoms, but impaired memory is usually the first noticeable sign of a chronic condition. Over time, the person may learn to compensate for many of the other symptoms.

Diagnostic Problems

Problems exist in diagnosing cognitive disorders. People who have not suffered brain damage may be diagnosed as having a cognitive disorder. Deeply depressed people often show characteristics similar to those of individuals with cognitive disorders; in particular, the neuropsychological tests used to assess a wide range of functions (including language, cognition, motor functions, and visual-motor functions) were found to be subject to the effects of depression (Sweet, 1983). It is also difficult to distinguish brain-damaged from schizophrenic patients by using neuropsychological tests (Portnoff et al., 1983). If a client has symptoms of a mental disorder such as marked depression and if a general medical condition is related to the mood disturbance, the client may be classified as having a mood disorder due to a general medical condition.

The elderly are particularly vulnerable to being inaccurately diagnosed as brain-damaged. An aged adult is more likely to perform poorly during assessment testing because of reduced sensory acuity, performance anxiety, fatigue, or not understanding test instructions. For this reason, tests that differentiate between normal and brain-damaged young adults cannot be assumed to apply to older people. In a study of fifty retired teachers, many scored in the brain-damaged range on the Halstead-Reitan Neuropsychological Test Battery (discussed in Chapter 4), even though they scored in the superior range on the Wechsler Adult Intelligence Scale (WAIS) and functioned very well in their daily lives (Price, Fein & Feinberg, 1980).

To make sure that a particular set of symptoms is indicative of a cognitive disorder, clinicians usually try to determine whether the central nervous system has been damaged or whether a causal agent (such as a poison) is responsible for the symptoms. In some cases, support for a diagnosis of cognitive disorder can come from a patient's positive response to a treatment known to be effective against a particular disorder. For example, a diagnosis of Parkinson's disease is supported by the patient's response to treatment with L-dopa.

Another diagnostic problem is opposite in effect: people who have suffered brain damage may be diagnosed as having a psychological disorder. The following case is an example:

> Larry D., age thirty-eight, was an energetic community college teacher and athletic coach and the happily married father of four children. During a particularly busy period, he suffered an apparent seizure while at-

tending a professional conference. Just prior to the seizure, he reported smelling an unusual odor; he then temporarily lost consciousness. Medical evaluations following the episode revealed no obvious cause for Larry's loss of consciousness, and it was assumed to be due to a lack of sleep and general fatigue.

Although he did not pass out again, Larry began to show such symptoms as loss of appetite, difficulty in sleeping, fatigue, and some mental confusion. He became increasingly withdrawn both from his family and from his professional activities, and he mentioned suicide several times. His family and colleagues became extremely concerned about his behavior. A mental health professional was consulted, and psychiatric hospitalization was recommended. But Larry's condition continued to deteriorate.

At this point Larry's wife sought a second opinion from the neuropsychology clinic at a local university. The results of neuropsychological testing suggested brain dysfunction originating in the right temporal lobe of the brain. A CAT scan was performed, and a brain tumor was located.

In Larry's case, joint neuropsychological and medical assessment was able to pinpoint the cause of the disorder. Naturally, the course of treatment changed markedly once the brain tumor was discovered. In many cases, as here, the initial neuropsychological assessment or even the initial use of techniques such as CAT scanning may not yield information that clearly points to a brain impairment. For this reason, follow-up testing at regular intervals is often recommended. This also allows the clinician to monitor the patient's performance on succeeding neuropsychological tests to detect significant patterns of deterioration.

TYPES OF COGNITIVE DISORDERS

Four major cognitive disorder categories are listed in DSM-IV: dementia, delirium, amnestic disorders, and other cognitive disorders. In each, clinicians categorize the disorder according to its cause. In general, the causes are classified as being due to a general medical condition (e.g., a stroke, a blow to the head, or disease), substance-induced conditions, multiple etiologies, or not otherwise specified. For example, a client may be given the diagnosis of delirium. If the delirium is caused by the use of psychoactive substances, it is considered to be a case of substance-induced delirium. If the type of substance is identified, it is also specified. In some cases, individuals also have symptoms of other mental disorders (such as mood, psychotic, or anxiety) in which there is evidence that a general medical condition is judged to be etiologically related to the disorder. In this case, DSM-IV lists the disorder within the categories applicable to the symptom pattern. For example, a mood disorder due to a general medical condition is classified under mood disorders, and an anxiety disorder due to a general medical condition is found under the category of anxiety disorders, rather than in the cognitive disorder category.

Dementia

Dementia is characterized by multiple cognitive deficits, severe enough to hinder social and occupational activities and representing a significant decline from a previous level of functioning. The most prominent features are impaired memory and declining cognitive functioning as revealed by *aphasia* (language disturbance), *apraxia* (inability to carry out motor activities despite intact comprehension and motor function), *agnosia* (failure to recognize or identify objects despite intact sensory function), or disturbances in planning, organizing, and abstracting in thought processes. People with dementia may forget to finish tasks, the names of significant others, and past events. (Focus 16.1 presents the case of an individual with aphasia.) Some people who show this disorder also display impulse control problems. They may, for example, disrobe in public or make sexual advances to strangers. Dementia is characterized by gradual onset and continuing cognitive decline.

Dementia can occur for numerous reasons. DSM-IV lists the major etiological categories for dementia as (1) general medical conditions (such as Alzheimer's disease, cerebrovascular disease, Parkinson's disease, brain trauma); (2) substance-induced persisting dementia in which the symptoms are associated with substance use; (3) multiple etiologies where more than one factor has caused the disorder (such as a general medical condition and substance use); and (4) dementia not otherwise specified, in which there is insufficient evidence to establish a specific etiology.

About 1.5 million Americans suffer from severe dementia and an additional 1 million to 5 million have mild to moderate forms of the disorder (Read, 1991). Although dementia is most often encountered in the elderly, only a small proportion of elderly people actually develop this syndrome. Only 5 percent of older people have severe dementia, and 10 percent have mild or moderate dementia (National Institutes of Health, 1981). Dementia can also occur with delusions, hallucinations, disturbances in perception and communication, and delirium. If these features are predominant, they are noted in the DSM-IV classification.

Dementia is, in fact, associated with a range of disorders. Wells (1978) analyzed the records of 222 patients who displayed dementia as the primary sign, rather than a secondary sign, of a diagnosed disorder. The disorders associated with dementia and the percentage of the population suffering from them are as follows (data taken from Wells, 1978, p. 2):

- Atrophy of uncertain cause (probably Alzheimer's disease)—51 percent
- Vascular disease—8 percent
- Normal pressure hydrocephalus—6 percent
- Dementia in alcoholics—6 percent
- Intracranial masses—5 percent
- Huntington's chorea—5 percent
- Depression—4 percent
- Drug toxicity—3 percent
- Dementia uncertain—3 percent
- Others—9 percent

Note that Alzheimer's disease probably accounts for most cases of dementia among the elderly. These findings have important implications for diagnosis because such problems as depression, drug toxicity, normal pressure hydrocephalus, and benign intracranial masses can be corrected. Identifying noncorrectable causes of dementia is also important, because some may benefit from specific therapeutic intervention to reduce or limit symptoms.

Delirium

Delirium involves an impairment in consciousness with reduced ability to focus, sustain, or shift attention. Persons with delirium exhibit changes in cognition (memory deficit, disorientation, and language or perceptual disturbance) that are not attributable to

FOCUS 16.1

Aphasia

Aphasia is the loss of motor or sensory functions that are associated with language. Aphasic persons with motor disturbances may have trouble expressing themselves via verbal language (speech aphasia), be unable to recall the names of familiar objects (nominal aphasia), or have problems in writing words (manual aphasia). Sensory aphasias include the inability to understand spoken words (auditory aphasia) and the inability to understand written words (visual aphasia or alexia). Aphasic problems may be extremely specific. For example, persons with visual aphasia lose the ability to understand written words, although they have no difficulty in reading the words aloud or in understanding spoken words.

Two primary problems in aphasia are (1) loss of access to words and their meanings and (2) inability to retain words and their meanings (Schuell, 1974). Persons with aphasia may become quite emotional and frustrated over their deficits,

and this, in turn, can impede efforts at rehabilitation.

The following dialogue illustrates some of the problems involved in aphasia. Albert Harris is a 67-year-old man who suffered a stroke. In addition to physical therapy for his partially paralyzed right side, an effort was made to rehabilitate his speech. Mr. Harris was unable to fully communicate and expressed himself almost exclusively with the words "Mrs. Harris," his wife's name.

Psychologist: Hello, Mr. Harris.
Mr. Harris (responding to psychologist): Hello, Mrs. Harris. Hello, Mrs. Harris.
Psychologist: You look pretty cheerful today.
Mr. Harris: Yes, Mrs. Harris. Ah . . . Ah . . . Ah (apparently trying to elaborate on his response) . . . Yes, Mrs. Harris. Ah . . . Ah (looking disappointed and frustrated).

Psychologist: I know it's hard to say what you want to say.
Mr. Harris: Yes, Mrs. Harris, yes. Things will get better, Mrs. Harris.
Psychologist: You've already shown improvement, don't you think?
Mr. Harris: Mrs. Harris a little bit better, yes. Slow but sure, Mrs. Harris.

Speech therapy and skills training are frequently used to treat aphasia. Although many patients recover from the problem, the reasons for recovery are not well understood. It is possible that other areas of the brain can be trained to compensate for the damaged areas. A relatively new field, called *neurolinguistics,* is concerned with the relationship between language development and brain functioning and with the interrelationship among brain function, speech and language skills, cognitive capacities, and behavior (Blumstein, 1981).

---

dementia. The disorder develops rather rapidly over a course of hours or days. The patient often shows disorganized patterns of thinking, as manifested by rambling, irrelevant, or incoherent speech (Wells, 1985). Sometimes there is a reduced level of consciousness and disturbances in the cycle of sleep and waking. The following describes a case of a student who was treated for amphetamine-induced delirium:

An 18-year-old high-school senior was brought to the emergency room by police after being picked up wandering in traffic on the Triborough Bridge [in New York City]. He was angry, agitated, and aggressive and talked of various people who were deliberately trying to "confuse" him by giving him misleading direc-

tions. His story was rambling and disjointed, but he admitted to the police officer that he had been using "speed." In the emergency room he had difficulty focusing his attention and had to ask that questions be repeated. He was disoriented as to time and place and was unable to repeat the names of three objects after five minutes. The family gave a history of the patient's regular use of "pep pills" over the past two years, during which time he was frequently "high" and did very poorly in school. (Spitzer et al., 1981a, p. 36)

As in the case of dementia, delirium is classified according to its cause: general medical condition, substance-induced condition, multiple etiologies, and not otherwise specified.

Amnestic Disorders

Amnestic disorders are characterized by memory impairment as manifested by inability to learn new information and the inability to recall previously learned knowledge or past events. The memory disturbance causes major problems in social or occupational functioning and does not occur exclusively during the course of dementia or delirium. As in the case of dementia and delirium, the etiology is specified. The most common cause of amnestic disorders is Wernicke's encephalopathy, which is probably caused by thiamine deficiency (Conn, 1991).

All three conditions—dementia, delirium, and amnestic disorders—have overlapping symptoms, especially involving memory deficits. There are some important differences in the three. In dementia, there is not only memory impairment but also conditions such as aphasia, apraxia, or agnosia. On the other hand, the memory dysfunctions that occur in delirium happen relatively quickly in contrast to dementia, in which functioning gradually declines. In delirium, there is also an impairment of consciousness. In amnestic disorders, the primary symptom involves memory. Cognitive disorders that do not meet the criteria for dementia, delirium, or amnestic disorders would be classified under the other cognitive disorder category.

ETIOLOGY OF COGNITIVE DISORDERS

Cognitive disorders can be caused by many different factors, and the same factor can result in dementia, delirium, or amnestic disorder. The sources of cognitive disorders discussed here are brain trauma; processes associated with aging, disease, and infection; tumors; epilepsy; and psychoactive substance–induced disorders. In addition, toxic substances, malnutrition, and even brain surgery may produce cognitive disorders.

Brain Trauma

On September 13, 1848, at Cavendish, Vermont, Phineas Gage was working as foreman of a railroad excavation crew. A premature explosion of a blast sent a tamping iron—a 3½-foot rod about an inch in diameter—through the lower side of Gage's face and out of the top of his head. Exhibiting some convulsions and bleeding profusely, Gage soon regained speech. He was taken to his hotel, where he walked up a flight of stairs to get to his room. Remarkably, Gage survived the trauma, even though there must have been extensive damage to his brain tissue. Later, he appeared to have completely recovered from the accident with no physical aftereffects. However, Gage began to complain that he had a strange feeling, which he could not describe. Soon, his employers and others noticed a marked personality change in him. Although he had been a very capable employee prior to the accident and was known for his affable disposition, Gage now became moody, irritable, profane, impatient, and obstinate. So radically changed was Gage that his friends said that he was "no longer Gage." (Adapted from Harlow, 1868)

A **brain trauma** is a physical wound or injury to the brain, as in the case of Phineas Gage. The severity, duration, and symptoms may differ widely, depending on the person's premorbid personality and on the extent and location of the neural damage. Generally, the greater the tissue damage, the more impaired the functioning. In some cases, however, interactions among various parts of the brain, coupled with brain redundancy, in which different parts of the brain can control a specific function, may compensate for some loss of tissue.

Head injuries are usually classified as concussions, contusions, or lacerations. A *concussion* is a mild brain injury, typically caused by a blow to the head. Blood vessels in the brain are often ruptured, and circulatory and other brain functions may be disrupted temporarily. The person may become dazed or even lose consciousness and, on regaining consciousness, may experience postconcussion headaches, disorientation, confusion, and memory loss. The symptoms are usually temporary, lasting no longer than a few weeks. In some cases, symptoms may persist for months or years, for unknown reasons, without neurological signs of impairment (Binder, 1986).

In a *contusion*, the brain is forced to shift slightly and press against the side of the skull. The cortex of the brain may be bruised (that is, blood vessels may rupture) on impact with the skull. As in concussion, the person may lose consciousness for a few hours or even for days. Postcontusion symptoms often include headaches, nausea, an inability to concentrate, and irritability. Although the symptoms are similar to those of concussion, they are generally more severe and last longer.

> Thirteen-year-old Ron G. was catcher for his school baseball team. During a game, one of the players from the other school's team accidentally lost his grip on the bat as he swung at a pitch. The bat hit Ron on the forehead. Although his catcher's mask absorbed some of the blow, the blow knocked Ron out. An hour elapsed before he regained consciousness at a nearby hospital, where he was diagnosed as having a cerebral contusion. Headaches, muscle weakness, and nausea continued for two weeks.

Lacerations are brain traumas in which brain tissue is torn, pierced, or ruptured, usually by an object that has penetrated the skull. When an object also penetrates the brain, death may result. If the person survives and regains consciousness, a variety of temporary or permanent effects may be observed. Symptoms may be quite serious, depending on the extent of damage to the brain tissue and on the amount of hemorrhaging. Cognitive processes are frequently impaired, and the personality may change.

More than eight million Americans suffer head injuries each year, and about 20 percent of these result in serious brain trauma. The majority show deficits in attention and poor concentration, are easily fatigued, and tend to be irritable (Webster & Scott, 1983). Personality characteristics may change in the areas of motivation, subjective emotional experiences, or emotional expressions (Stuss, Gow & Hetherington, 1992). One study examined twenty-three patients with severe traumatic brain injuries (seventeen closed-head injuries, three penetrating missile wounds, two cerebral contusions, and one brainstem contusion) who had spent an average of twenty days in a coma. Every one displayed a distress syndrome characterized by depression, anxiety, tension, and nervousness—yet they all denied having these feelings (Sbordone & Jennison, 1983). It is, in fact, common for patients with severe traumatic injuries to deny emotional reactions and physical dysfunctions until they begin to recover from their injuries.

Closed-head injuries are the most common form of brain trauma and the most common reason why physicians refer patients younger than age forty to neurologists (Golden et al., 1983). They usually result from a blow that causes damage at the site of the impact and at the opposite side of the head. If the victim's head was in motion before the impact (as is generally the case in automobile accidents), the blow produces a forward-and-back movement of the brain, accompanied by tearing and hemorrhaging of brain tissue. Epilepsy develops in about 5 percent of closed-head injuries and in more than 30 percent of open-head injuries in which the brain tissue is penetrated. Damage to brain tissues in the left hemisphere often results in intellectual disorders, and affective problems more frequently result from damage to brain tissues in the right hemisphere (Lishman, 1978).

Severe brain trauma has long-term negative consequences. Many young adults who are comatose for at least twenty-four hours later experience residual cognitive deficits that interfere with employment and psychosocial adjustment. Recovery from the trauma often does not ensure a return to the victim's premorbid level of functioning. Along with any physical or mental disabilities produced by the brain damage, motivational and emotional disturbances result from the frustration of coping with these physical or mental deficits. As a consequence, only one-third of patients with severe closed-head injuries can return to gainful employment after traditional rehabilitative therapy (Prigatano et al., 1984).

New treatment techniques seem promising. In one approach, intensive cognitive retraining is combined with psychotherapeutic intervention. This program provides patients with increased awareness and acceptance of their injuries and residual deficits, cognitive retraining to counter selected residual deficits, a repertoire of compensatory skills, and understanding of their emotional and motivational disturbance. When patients in this program were compared with patients in a traditional rehabilitation program, the former showed better neuropsychological functioning, greater improvement in personality traits, and greater success at work (Prigatano et al., 1984).

Aging and Disorders Associated with Aging

Before discussing the cognitive disorders often associated with aging, it seems appropriate to describe the nature of the older population. A growing proportion of the population is sixty-five years of age or older. This group numbered over 31 million of the U.S. population in 1990 (U.S. Department of Commerce,

1991), and by 2010 nearly 15 percent of Americans will be sixty-five years or older and 25 percent will be fifty-five years or older (Warheit, Longino, & Bradsher, 1991). The increase is attributable to longer life expectancy and the relatively large numbers of people, who will then be elderly, from the "baby boomer" generation who were born in the 1940s.

In a report by the American Association of Retired Persons (1985), some other characteristics of the population are noteworthy. First, women outlive men. In 1990, there were 149 women for every 100 men in the older population as revealed in a 1991 report by the U.S. Department of Commerce. However, men were twice as likely to be married as were the women. Second, about one-fifth of the older population were poor or near-poor. Fully 89 percent were not working or seeking work. Third, statistics indicated that most older people have at least one chronic health condition and many have multiple conditions. The most frequent were arthritis (50 percent), hypertension (39 percent), hearing impairments (30 percent), heart conditions (26 percent), orthopedic impairments (17 percent), and cataracts and sinusitis (15 percent each). Although the report did not indicate mental disorders, Myers and colleagues (1984) found that cognitive impairment in people sixty-five years and older was the highest for any age group. Thus problems of the older population demand greater attention and research. (See Critical Thinking for a discussion of the effects of aging.)

The cognitive disorders most common among the elderly include stroke, memory loss, and Alzheimer's disease. Although these conditions are correlated with aging, they also occur among younger people.

Cerebrovascular Accidents or Strokes Although the brain represents only 2 percent of the body's weight, it requires 15 percent of the blood flow and 20 percent of the oxygen (Oliver et al., 1982). A *stroke* or **cerebrovascular accident** is a sudden stoppage of blood flow to a portion of the brain, which leads to a loss of brain function.

Strokes are the third major cause of death in the United States, afflicting more than 400,000 persons annually. Only about 50 to 60 percent of stroke victims survive, and they generally require long-term care while suffering from a variety of mental and sensory-motor disabilities (Oliver et al., 1982; see Focus 16.1). Stroke victims are often frustrated and depressed by their handicaps, and they show greater depression and interpersonal sensitivity than other groups of patients. At least one-fourth of stroke victims appear to develop major depression (Conn, 1991). Moreover, in many cases their depression seems to deepen with time (Magni & Schifano, 1984). Their anxiety about their disabilities occasionally leads to further disability.

The bursting of blood vessels (and the attendant intercranial hemorrhaging) causes 25 percent of all strokes and often occurs during exertion. Victims report feeling that something is wrong within the head, along with headaches and nausea. Confusion, paralysis, and loss of consciousness follow rapidly. Mortality rates for this type of stroke are extremely high.

Strokes may also be caused by the narrowing of blood vessels owing to a buildup of fatty material on interior walls (*atherosclerosis*) or by the blockage of blood vessels. In either case, the result is *infarction*, the death of brain tissue from a decrease in the supply of blood. These strokes often occur during sleep, and the person is paralyzed when he or she awakens. Approximately 20 percent die, 20 percent exhibit full to nearly full recovery, and 60 percent suffer residual disabilities (Lishman, 1978).

The residual loss of function after a stroke usually involves only one side of the body, most often the left. Interestingly, one residual symptom of stroke is a "lack of acknowledgment" of various stimuli to one particular side. For example, a patient who is asked to copy a pattern may draw half the pattern and may ignore the left side of his or her body (Golden et al., 1983).

Some functional reorganization of the brain may occur after a stroke to compensate for the loss of function. Three months after suffering a stroke owing to cerebral infarction, one patient showed significantly reduced cerebral blood flow in one area. An examination performed one year later showed no abnormalities. The pattern of blood flow, however, suggested increased activation in brain areas surrounding the affected area. It is possible that the patient's clinical improvement was due to brain reorganization in which the function of the destroyed area was taken over by other areas.

A series of infarctions may lead to a syndrome known as **multi-infarct dementia**, which is character-

CRITICAL THINKING

What Happens When We Become Older?

Losing cognitive and mental capabilities is the symptom of aging most feared by elderly people. One 82-year-old man commented, "It's not the physical decline I fear so much. It's becoming a mental vegetable inside of a healthy body. It is a shame that we can rehabilitate or treat so much of the physical ills, but when your mind goes, there's nothing you can do" (Gatz, Smyer & Lawton, 1980, p. 12). Indeed, can you think of elderly persons who appear to have reduced cognitive functioning? Are you afraid of becoming older?

Is mental deterioration the fate of the elderly? Reports of intellectual decline in aging have in fact been exaggerated. Although tests of intellectual functioning indicate that performance abilities generally start to decline with advancing age, verbal fluency and cognitive skills are usually quite stable over time (Gallagher et al., 1980). Intellectual performance on knowledge acquired over the course of the socialization process is fairly stable, whereas fluid abilities (e.g., those abilities involving solutions to novel pro-

blems or requiring creativity) tend to decline with age (Poon & Siegler, 1991). About 75 percent of older people retain sharp mental functioning, and an additional 10 to 15 percent experience only mild to moderate memory loss (Butler, 1984). Although the structures and biochemistry of the brain are affected in that brain cells and cerebral blood flow are reduced, many researchers now believe that the extent of brain atrophy has been overestimated (Duckett, 1991).

The vast majority of noninstitutionalized people aged sixty or older can live independently within the community. A statewide sample of 2146 Virginians, aged sixty to more than eighty-five and living in their own communities (rather than in institutions), was studied to determine the prevalence of mental disorders in the elderly population (Romaniuk, McAuley & Arling, 1983). Information from questionnaires, self-ratings, and interviews indicated relatively little psychopathology. Only 6.3 percent displayed mild cognitive impairment, and 2.1 percent showed

moderate to severe cognitive impairment. Only 15 percent displayed any signs of mental illness.

Are the elderly satisfied and happy? As we become older, stress levels may increase. The deaths of loved ones, declining health, functioning in a youth-oriented society, and facing retirement may be important life stressors. Yet many elderly find their lives enriched by their life accomplishments, retirement, opportunities to pursue interests, and their children and grandchildren. In the study of the elderly by Romaniuk, McAuley, and Arling (1983), most persons seemed satisfied with their health: 13 percent rated their health as excellent, 46 percent as good, 31 percent as fair, and only 9 percent as poor. About 90 percent of the sample displayed "common sense," "mental alertness," and "coping ability." More than 75 percent said that they enjoyed their lives. Given these findings, why do you think old age is often thought to be negative? Are there other cultures that consider old age as a positive event?

ized by the uneven deterioration of intellectual abilities (although some mental functions may remain intact). The specific symptoms of this disruption depend on the area and extent of the brain damage. Both physical and intellectual functioning are usually impaired. The patient may show gradual improvement in intellectual functioning, but repeated episodes of infarction can occur and produce additional disability.

Memory Loss in the Elderly   Memory loss is one of the most obvious symptoms of Alzheimer's disease. It is also a major symptom of **senile dementia,** a severe loss of intellectual functioning produced by brain cell deterioration as a result of aging—usually after age seventy-five. Loss of memory may also be shown by elderly people suffering multi-infarct dementia. And finally, occasional loss of memory is part of the normal aging process.

Because memory loss is associated with many disorders as well as normal aging, it is of concern to the elderly and yet difficult for clinicians to assess. Consider, for example, the following letter:

> Dear Dr. Smyer:
>
> I have toyed with the idea of writing you ever since I heard you speak at the Presbyterian Church a couple of years go. The occasion was one of the series of brown-bag lunches sponsored, I think, by the Area Agency on Aging. You may remember me, since I'm sure you were embarrassed when I substituted one word for another in trying to ask a question about the part inheritance plays in senility. My question made no sense, and you tactfully said, "I don't believe I understand your question," and I repeated it, correctly, saying, "You can see I'm senile already." (I was trying to be funny, but I was not amused.)
>
> The question I asked is one that has haunted me all my adult life (I've just turned 78), and I think I have always known the answer. My father's father, my father, and the three sisters who lived long enough were all senile. I am obviously following in their footsteps, and have discussed the matter with Dr. Klein, who became my physician last year. I have told him that I have never taken much medication and have been opposed to "painkillers," tranquilizers, etc., but that the day may come when I will accept medical help as the lesser of two evils. He assures me that there are new drugs that may help.
>
> My question, Dr. Smyer, is this: Since I'm sure there must be ongoing research into the problem of senility, would it be of any value to such research if I volunteered as a test subject? At this point, my memory is failing so rapidly, and I suffer such frequent agonies of confusion, that I am at the point of calling on Dr. Klein for the help he has promised. But I don't want to do so yet if my experience can be of value to someone else, and particularly to the nine daughters of my sisters, ranging in age from 58 to 70, and to my own daughter, 42, who must be wondering if they too are doomed.
>
> Is there any merit to this proposal? I will be most grateful for any advice you can give me. (Smyer, 1984, p. 20)

From her clear, lucid writing and her recall of events that took place several years ago, it is obvious that the writer is not suffering from senility. Yet her occasional lapses of memory are causing her to become worried. Smyer pointed out that complaints of memory loss must be examined in light of the person's perception of the event, concurrent factors such as depression or anxiety that might contribute to memory problems, and actual memory behavior. If the Halstead-Reitan Neuropsychological Battery were employed, Gallagher and Frankel (1980) believe that most normal elderly subjects would be incorrectly identified as brain damaged because no normative standards are established for their age group.

One of the most common reasons for memory loss and confusion in older patients is therapeutic drug intoxication. People may take several medications that can interact with one another to produce negative side effects (Butler, 1984). Medication often has a stronger effect on older people and takes longer to be cleared from their bodies, yet dosages are often determined by testing on young adults only. In addition, cardiac, metabolic, and endocrine disorders and nutritional deficiencies can produce symptoms resembling dementias.

Alzheimer's Disease

The disorder perhaps most often associated with aging is **Alzheimer's disease.** It is one of the most prevalent forms of dementia, accounting for almost 80 percent of dementia in older persons (Teri & Wagner, 1992).

Characteristics of Alzheimer's Disease In Alzheimer's disease, there is marked deterioration of intellectual and emotional functioning. Irritability, cognitive impairment, and memory loss are early symptoms that gradually become worse. Social withdrawal, depression, delusions, impulsive behaviors, neglect of personal hygiene, and other symptoms may eventually appear as well. Death usually occurs within five years of the onset of the disorder.

Elizabeth R., a forty-six-year-old woman diagnosed as suffering from Alzheimer's disease, is trying to cope with her increasing problems with memory. She writes notes to herself and tries to compensate for her difficulties by rehearsing conversations with herself, anticipating what might be said. However, she is gradually losing the battle and has had to retire from her job. She quickly forgets what she has just read, and she loses the meaning of an article after reading only a few sentences. She sometimes has to ask where the bathroom is in her own house and is depressed by the realization that she is a burden to her family. (Clark et al., 1984, p. 60)

The increasing deterioration of intellectual and emotional functioning, including memory loss, is perhaps the most debilitating aspect of Alzheimer's disease. Support groups try to help patients maintain their independence, sense of self-worth, and dignity by encouraging them to make personal decisions for themselves and to maintain social contacts.

The deterioration of memory seems to be the most poignant and disturbing symptom of Alzheimer's disease. The person may at first forget appointments, phone numbers, and addresses. As the disorder progresses, he or she may lose track of the time of day, have trouble remembering recent and past events, and forget who he or she is (Reisberg, Ferris & Crook, 1982). But even when memory is almost gone, contact with loved ones is still important.

> I believe the emotional memory of relationships is the last to go. You can see daughters or sons come to visit, for example, and the mother will respond. She doesn't know who they are, but you can tell by her expression that she knows they're persons to whom she is devoted. (Materka, 1984, p. 13)

Dorothy Coons, whom Materka quoted in the preceding lines, works at the University of Michigan Institute of Gerontology. She noted that Alzheimer's disease is the fourth leading cause of death in the United States, and she predicted that by the year 2000 as many as 4 million persons may be suffering from this disorder (Materka, 1984). The disease affects about 5 to 10 percent of those older than the age of sixty-five and about 20 percent of those older

than the age of eighty (Fisher & Carstensen, 1990; Teri & Wagner, 1992).

Alzheimer's Disease and the Brain Persons with this disease have an atrophy of cortical tissue within the brain, and there is currently no known cure. Autopsies performed on the brains of Alzheimer's victims reveal *neurofibrillary tangles* (abnormal fibers that appear to be tangles of brain tissue filaments) and *senile plaques* (patches of degenerated nerve endings). Both conditions are believed to disrupt the transmission of impulses among brain cells, thereby producing the symptoms of the disorder. Alzheimer's disease is generally considered a disease of the elderly, and its incidence does increase with increasing age. However, it also can attack people in their forties or fifties (see Focus 16.2 for a description of an early onset case of Alzheimer's). It occurs more frequently in women.

Etiology of Alzheimer's Disease The etiology of Alzheimer's disease is unknown. Many different explanations have been proposed. They include reduced levels of a neurotransmitter, acetylcholine, in the brain; exposure to aluminum; repeated head injuries; infections and viruses; decreased blood flow in the brain; and other neural and physiological abnormali-

Early Onset Alzheimer's Disease

We typically believe that Alzheimer's disease occurs among the elderly. Although the incidence of the disease is directly related to age, it does occur among middle-aged persons. Leon (1990) described a case of Lewis Edwards, a 53-year-old man, who developed Alzheimer's disease. The description is instructive because much data were collected on Mr. Edwards, and he was examined during a five-year period.

Mr. Edwards was on sick leave from his job as a post office supervisor and sought treatment for depression and memory problems. The memory problems were particularly evident. Mr. Edwards stated that at times he had difficulty filling out required forms and keeping track of the activities of those being supervised by him. His wife noted that he sometimes had problems finding his way around familiar streets and organizing and planning activities. At times, he would feel depressed. Although he drank alcohol, drinking did not appear to be excessive. Initially, he was given antidepressants for depression, but did not show much improvement from this treatment.

Mr. Edwards was administered neurological, mental status, and neuropsychological tests. Although conclusive confirmation of the diagnosis of Alzheimer's disease can only be made at autopsy when particular brain structures are examined, the neuropsychological tests can be helpful in ruling out other possible diseases or brain disorders. Computerized axial tomographic (CAT) brain scans and electroencephalogram (EEG) brain wave tests of Mr. Edwards did not reveal any abnormalities. His reflex functioning also appeared normal. Memory deficits were exhibited on the mental status examination, however, which is a structured interview that assesses a client's memory, thinking, general knowledge, background, and prob-

---

ties (Read, 1991). Some researchers do not consider Alzheimer's disease to be a genetic disorder because the majority of persons affected do not have a family history of Alzheimer's disease; nevertheless, for a small subgroup, heredity may be important (Johnson, 1990). Although abnormalities are found in the brains of affected individuals, it is not clear if the abnormalities are the cause, effect, or an accompanying condition of Alzheimer's disease. Of course, many different factors may be responsible for the disorder.

Other Diseases and Infections of the Brain

A variety of diseases and infections result in brain damage. As a consequence, behavioral, cognitive, and emotional changes occur (including the development of cognitive disorders).

Parkinson's Disease   Parkinson's disease is a progressively worsening disorder characterized by muscle tremors; a stiff, shuffling gait; a lack of facial expression; and social withdrawal. Dementia, and depression may develop. It affects about one person out of a thousand, and slightly more men than women have the disease (Rao, Huber & Bornstein, 1992). The disease is usually first diagnosed in people between the ages of fifty and sixty. In some persons the disorder stems from causes such as infections of the brain, cerebrovascular disorders, brain trauma, and poisoning with carbon monoxide; in other persons, a specific origin cannot be determined. Death generally follows within ten years of the onset of Parkinson's disease, although some patients have survived for twenty years or longer.

Parkinson's disease seems to be associated with lesions in the motor area of the brainstem and with a diminished level of dopamine in the brain. Treatment with L-dopa, which increases dopamine levels, relieves most of its symptoms (Lishman, 1978). Mohammad Ali's Parkinson-like condition has been treated with Sinemet and Symmetrel, which have the same effect.

AIDS (Acquired Immunodeficiency Syndrome)

It was frightening. It was terrifying. It was terrible headaches, months when I could only stand or lie down. I lost control of one side of my body. I

lems. On some interview questions, Mr. Edwards made mistakes such as specifying the current day of the week, the school he had attended, and remembering three words that he had been told to remember five minutes earlier. The neuropsychological exam revealed selective decline with verbal abilities relatively intact but nonverbal cognitive abilities showing deficits. Mild deficits were exhibited on tests of immediate or short-term memory and somewhat more serious impairment was shown on long-term memory. The mental health staff believed that the results were suggestive of early onset dementia of the Alzheimer's type. Mr. Edwards's memory impairment and difficulties in planning and organizing were consistent with Alzheimer's disease. Also consistent

with the disease was that Mr. Edwards's cognitive difficulties occurred gradually rather than suddenly and caused a significant impairment in occupational functioning, which was previously adequate. The cognitive deficits did not appear to be caused by identifiable conditions such as Parkinson's disease, systemic conditions known to cause dementia such as HIV infection or neurosyphilis, or substance-induced conditions. Finally, although depression was exhibited, the primary symptoms were cognitive in nature.

Over the course of five years, Mr. Edwards showed progressive cognitive deterioration. He could not remember the names of coworkers and perform tasks so he resigned. His functioning varied from day to day; for example, one morn-

ing he was unable to operate the toaster. Four years after he had sought help at the neurology clinic, he failed to recognize his daughter, although he consistently recognized his wife. He was unable to function; he got lost in his own house and could not get dressed by himself. His wife and relatives took care of him at home rather than send him to a nursing home. Mrs. Edwards vowed to take care of him at home as long as she could.

In cases such as Mr. Edwards, the outlook is bleak: deterioration to the point of muteness and immobility with a future life expectancy of several years (Leon, 1990). Fortunately, he had a very supportive and understanding wife during his last few years of life.

couldn't write. I had lost fine motor control. I also had memory lapses. One time I was in a supermarket and suddenly I couldn't remember how I got there. (Joyce, 1988, p. 38)

The person who made this statement suffered from AIDS, or acquired immunodeficiency syndrome. Although the general public knows about the disastrous consequences of AIDS—susceptibility to diseases, physical deterioration, and death, often within several years of infection—relatively few people know that dementia may be the first sign of AIDS. Joyce (1988) noted that the vast majority of AIDS victims may suffer from some form of dementia. The symptoms involve an inability to concentrate and to perform complex sequential mental tasks. The person may be unable to follow television or movie plots, may miss appointments, and may have hand tremors. Other symptoms include forgetfulness, impaired judgment, and personality disturbances such as anxiety and depression. After initial cognitive symptoms, progression to global cognitive impairment is rather rapid, usually within two months (Tross & Hirsch, 1988).

The dementia can be attributed to three factors. First, the AIDS virus itself reaches the brain at some phase of the infection and may lie dormant for a period of time (Baum & Nesselhof, 1988). When it becomes active, the virus can affect mental as well as physical processes. Second, because AIDS affects the immune system, AIDS-related infections may cause neuropsychological problems. A variety of chemical factors secreted during the course of an immune response may also cause changes in brain-controlled physiological processes (Hall, 1988). Third, depression, anxiety, and confusion can arise from simply knowing that one has AIDS, and experiencing negative reactions from others increases stress for AIDS victims (Kelly & Murphy, 1992). Thus people with AIDS are at high risk for cognitive disorders.

Neurosyphilis (General Paresis) Syphilis is caused by the spirochete *Treponema pallidum*, which enters the body through contact with an infected person. This microorganism is most commonly transmitted from infected to uninfected people through intercourse or oral-genital contact. A pregnant woman can also transmit the disease to her fetus, and the spirochete can enter the body through direct contact with mucous membranes or breaks in the skin. Within a few weeks, the exposed person develops a chancre, a small sore at the point of infection, as well as a copper-colored rash. If it is undetected or untreated, the infection spreads throughout the body. There may be no noticeable symptoms for ten to fifteen years after the initial infection, but eventually the body's organs are permanently damaged. In about 10 percent of persons with syphilis who are untreated, the spirochete directly damages the brain or nervous system, causing general paresis.

The most commonly described form of paresis, which includes approximately 18 percent of all cases, has grandiose characteristics: people display expansive and euphoric symptoms along with delusions of power or wealth. A depressive form has also been described, in which the affected person displays all the classic symptoms of depression.

The most frequent course for the illness begins with simple dementia, including memory impairment and early loss of insight. If the disorder remains untreated, the dementia increases, the occasional delusions fade, and the patient becomes quiet, apathetic, and incoherent. Paralysis, epileptic seizures, and death usually occur within five years of the onset of symptoms.

If syphilis is treated early, however, clinical remission occurs and the patient often can return to work. After five years of treatment, more than one-half of the patients with disorientation, convulsions, tremors, and euphoria generally lose their symptoms (Golden et al., 1983).

Encephalitis Encephalitis, or sleeping sickness, is a brain inflammation caused by a viral infection. Numerous different viruses can lead to encephalitis (Stacy & Roeltgen, 1991). It is not known whether the virus enters the central nervous system directly or whether the brain is hypersensitive to a viral infection at some other site in the body. One form, *epidemic encephalitis*, was widespread during World War I, but the disease is now very rare in the United States. It is still a problem, however, in certain areas of Africa and Asia.

Most cases follow a rapidly developing course that begins with headache, prostration (having to lie down), and diminished consciousness. Epileptic seizures are common in children with encephalitis, and

they may be the most obvious symptom. Acute symptoms include lethargy, fever, delirium, and long periods of sleep and stupor. When wakeful, the victim may show markedly different symptoms: hyperactivity, irritability, agitation, and seizures. In contrast to past behaviors, a child may become restless, irritable, cruel, and antisocial. A coma, if there is one, may end abruptly. Usually a long period of physical and mental recuperation is necessary, and the prognosis can vary from no residual effects to profound brain damage (Golden et al., 1983).

Meningitis Meningitis is an inflammation of the *meninges*, the membrane that surrounds the brain and spinal cord. Research on meningitis is complicated because the disorder has three major forms: bacterial, viral, and fungal. In the United States, approximately 400,000 persons develop *bacterial meningitis* annually (Wasserman & Gromisch, 1981). This form generally begins with a localized infection that spreads, via the bloodstream, first to the meninges and then into the cerebrospinal fluid. *Viral meningitis*, which involves symptoms much less serious than those of the bacterial type, is associated with a variety of diseases including mumps, herpes simplex, toxoplasmosis, syphilis, and rubella. *Fungal meningitis* usually occurs in children with such immunological deficiencies as leukemia.

The symptoms of meningitis vary with the age of the patient. In neonates and young infants, the symptoms are nonspecific (fever, lethargy, poor eating, and irritability), which makes diagnosis difficult (McCracken, 1976). In patients older than one year, symptoms may include stiffness of the neck, headache, and cognitive and sensory impairment. All three forms can produce cerebral infarction and seizures, but their incidence is much greater in the bacterial form than in the others (Edwards & Baker, 1981). The outcome is most serious when meningitis is contracted during the neonatal period.

Residual effects of the disorder may include partial or complete hearing loss as a result of cerebral infarction (Berlow et al., 1981), mental retardation, and seizures (Snyder et al., 1981). Meningitis also seems to attack the abstract thinking ability of some of its victims (Wright, 1978).

Huntington's Chorea Huntington's chorea is a rare, genetically transmitted disorder characterized by involuntary twitching movements and eventual dementia. Because it is transmitted from parent to child through an abnormal gene, approximately 50 percent of the offspring of an affected person develop this disorder. Recently, scientists have identified the gene that causes the disease, so they are now able to better detect whether a person has inherited the disorder (Saltus, 1993). At this time, Huntington's chorea can't be treated, so the genetic counseling of afflicted people is extremely important in preventing its transmission.

The first symptoms usually occur as behavioral disturbances when the person is between the ages of twenty-five and fifty, although some are afflicted before age twenty (Brooks et al., 1987). The first physical symptoms are generally twitches in the fingers or facial grimaces. As the disorder progresses, these symptoms become more widespread and abrupt, involving jerky, rapid, and repetitive movements. Changes in personality and emotional stability also occur. For example, the person may become moody and quarrelsome (Golden et al., 1983).

Woody Guthrie, a well-known folk singer and the father of Arlo Gurthrie, also a well-known singer, was a victim of Huntington's chorea. His first symptoms were increased moodiness and depression. Later he developed a peculiar manner of walking, and he found it difficult to speak normally. His inability to control his movements was often blamed on alcoholism. On one occasion, his apparent disorientation, walking problems, and disheveled appearance prompted police to arrest him. When his wife sought his release, she was met by a staff psychiatrist who said, "Your husband is a very disturbed man . . . with many hallucinations. He says that he has written a thousand songs." His wife responded by saying, "It is true." The psychiatrist went on: "He also says he has written a book." Guthrie's wife responded, "That is also true." Then the psychiatrist delivered the coup de grace: "He says that a record company has put out nine records of his songs!" The doctor's voice dripped disbelief. "That is also the truth," she replied (Yurchenco, 1970, pp. 147–148).

Huntington's chorea always ends in death, on the average from thirteen to sixteen years after the onset of symptoms. Early misdiagnoses are given in one-third to two-thirds of persons; schizophrenia is the most common misdiagnosis (Lishman, 1978).

Cerebral Tumors

A **cerebral tumor** is a mass of abnormal tissue growing within the brain. The symptoms depend on which particular area is affected and on the degree to which the tumor increases intracranial pressure. Fast-growing tumors generally produce severe mental symptoms, whereas slow growth may result in few symptoms. Unfortunately, in the latter case, the tumor is often not discovered until death has occurred in a psychiatric hospital (Lishman, 1978). Tumors that affect the temporal area produce the highest frequency of psychological symptoms (Golden et al., 1983).

The most common symptoms of cerebral tumors are disturbances of consciousness, which can range from diminished attention and drowsiness to coma. People with tumors may also show mild dementia and other problems of thinking. Mood changes may also occur from either the direct physical impact of the tumor or the patient's reaction to the problem. Removing a cerebral tumor can produce dramatic results.

The woman was admitted to a mental hospital, exhibiting dementia and confusion. She responded little to questioning by staff, or to attempts at therapy, even after twelve years of hospitalization. She would simply sit blindly, with her tongue protruding to the right, making repetitive movements of her right arm and leg. She also showed partial paralysis of the left side of her face.

This "left-side, right-side" pattern of symptoms suggested that her condition might be due to a physical problem. Surgery was performed, and a massive brain tumor was discovered and removed. After the operation, the patient improved remarkably. She regained her speech and sight and was able to recognize and converse with her relatives for the first time in twelve years. (Hunter, Blackwood & Bull, 1968).

Epilepsy

Epilepsy is a general term that refers to a set of symptoms rather than to a specific etiology. In particular, **epilepsy** includes any disorder characterized by intermittent and brief periods of altered consciousness, often accompanied by seizures, and excessive electrical discharge from brain cells. It is the most common of the neurological disorders; 1 to 2 percent of the population has epileptic seizures at some time during

Epilepsy refers to any disorder that is characterized by intermittent and brief periods of altered consciousness, often accompanied by seizures. It also seems to be one of the earliest recognized organic brain syndromes. Among those who suffered from the disease was Vincent van Gogh shown here in a self-portrait painted sometime after he had cut off his ear.

their lives. About 2.5 million children and adults in the U.S. live with epilepsy or other seizure disorders (McLin, 1992). It also seems to be one of the earliest recognized cognitive disorders: Julius Caesar, Napoleon, Dostoevsky, and van Gogh are among those who presumably were epileptic.

Epilepsy is most frequently diagnosed during childhood. It can be symptomatic of some primary disorder of the brain without apparent etiology, or it can arise from such causes as brain tumors, injury, degenerative diseases, and drugs (Lishman, 1978). Epileptic seizures and unconsciousness may last anywhere from a few seconds to several hours; they may occur only a few times during the patient's entire life or many times in one day. And they may involve only a momentary disturbance of consciousness or a

complete loss of consciousness—in which case they can be accompanied by violent convulsions and a coma lasting for hours. Alcohol, lack of sleep, fever, a low blood sugar level, hyperventilation, a brain lesion or injury, or general fatigue can all induce an epileptic seizure. Particular musical notes, flickering lights, and emotionally charged situations have also been known to provoke epileptic attacks. Even everyday stress can bring on a seizure (Laidlaw & Rickens, 1976).

Epilepsy can often be controlled but it cannot be cured. Although epileptics usually behave and function quite normally between attacks, their chronic, long-term illness is still regarded with suspicion and repugnance by much of society. An attack can be frightening to the afflicted person and observers alike. Epileptics face fear and anxiety resulting from the unpredictable nature of their seizures. They are embarrassed by their seeming lack of control over their illness and must deal with society's negative stereotypes concerning epilepsy (University of Minnesota, 1977). Perhaps as a result of these stereotypes concerning epilepsy, approximately 30 to 50 percent of epileptics have accompanying psychological problems (Golden et al., 1983). We shall discuss four types of epilepsy. Each type is associated with a different type of seizure—petit mal, Jacksonian, psychomotor, and grand mal. Although terms such as *tonic-clonic seizures* are increasingly used, the four types give the range of different behaviors that are exhibited during seizures.

Petit Mal Seizures *Petit mal* ("little illness") *seizures* involve a momentary dimming or loss of consciousness, sometimes with convulsive movements. During an attack, which usually lasts a few seconds, the epileptic stares blankly. Eyelids flutter, or slight jerking movements may be present, but in general there is little overall movement. After an attack, the epileptic may continue whatever he or she was doing, unaware that a seizure has occurred and that there was a momentary loss of consciousness.

Petit mal seizures are usually seen in children and adolescents; they rarely persist into adulthood. The following description highlights a common problem among petit mal epileptics.

Jack D. is a sixteen-year-old student who was admitted to the outpatient psychiatric service of a large hospital to receive treatment for petit mal epilepsy. Jack and his parents explained that the seizures lasted only a few seconds each but occurred twenty to thirty times a day. His parents were especially concerned because Jack was very eager to get a driver's license; driving a car would be quite dangerous if he were subject to momentary losses of consciousness. Jack was interviewed at a case conference where a group of mental health professionals, medical students, and paraprofessionals discussed his symptoms, the etiology of the disorder, the prognosis, and treatment. During the fifteen-minute interview, Jack experienced two petit mal seizures. The first occurred while he was answering a question. A psychiatrist had asked Jack whether his seizures significantly handicapped him in school. Jack replied, "It really hasn't been that bad. Sometimes I lose track of what the teacher is . . ." At that point, Jack paused. He had a blank stare on his face, and his mouth was slightly opened. After about four seconds, he resumed speaking and said, "Uh, writing on the blackboard." A psychologist then asked Jack if he had noticed that he had paused in midsentence. Jack answered that he was not aware of the pause or the brief seizure. Interestingly, several of those present at the case conference later admitted that they too were unaware that a seizure had occurred at that time. They thought Jack's pause was due to an attempt to find the right words.

Later Jack had another seizure that went unnoticed by most of the interviewers. While the resident psychiatrist was elaborating on a question, Jack appeared to be listening. But when the psychiatrist finished, Jack had a puzzled look on his face. He said, "It [a seizure] happened again. I was listening to what you were saying and suddenly you were all finished. I must have blanked out. Could you repeat the question?"

As you can see, such brief interruptions of consciousness may go unnoticed by people interacting with petit mal epileptics—and sometimes by the epileptics themselves. Fortunately the prognosis for Jack was good. Petit mal seizures usually disappear with age and can be controlled with proper medication and treatment.

Jacksonian Seizures   *Jacksonian seizures* typically begin in one part of the body and then spread to other parts. For example, the hands or feet may first begin to twitch, then the whole arm or leg, and then other parts of the body. Usually the person doesn't completely lose consciousness unless the seizure spreads to the entire body. At this point, the convulsions resemble those of grand mal epilepsy. Jacksonian seizures are frequently due to a localized and specific brain lesion; surgical removal of the affected area can bring about recovery.

Psychomotor Seizures   About 25 percent of epileptic seizures are psychomotor (Horowitz, 1970). *Psychomotor seizures* are characterized by a loss of consciousness during which the person engages in well-organized and normal-appearing behavioral sequences. For example, one psychomotor epileptic had an attack and lost consciousness while he was mowing his lawn. During the next hour, he went into his house, changed into swim trunks, and proceeded to take a swim in his pool. An hour later, when he came out of the "trance," he did not recall how he had gotten into the pool. His last memory was of mowing the lawn.

The disturbance in consciousness typically lasts for a brief period of time, usually just a few minutes; occasionally, however, it may affect someone for days. Although it was originally believed that many people were prone to violence during such seizures, violence is actually quite rare. It has been exaggerated because of some case reports in which violence was emphasized. This can be seen in the following report concerning a twenty-nine-year-old female psychomotor epileptic.

There was a dramatic change in her affect following the onset of spells. The patient developed deepening emotions and reported a marked tendency to become angry about trivial events. Over the past two years sounds of even normal volume had led to angry outbursts in which she had smashed furniture or struck her cat. During a recent examination, this highly intelligent woman had become tearful and anxious while attempting rapid serial seven subtraction. She then turned to the examiner and said in a menacing voice, "You're lucky I didn't punch you in the face for making me do that." (Devinsky & Bear, 1984, p. 651)

Some investigators have suggested that there is a relationship between psychomotor epilepsy and psychotic or schizophrenic behaviors (Glaser, Newman & Schafer, 1963; Stevens et al., 1969). The artist Van Gogh is supposed to have cut off his ear during a psychomotor attack. And the defense attorneys for Jack Ruby, who killed Lee Harvey Oswald (the alleged assassin of president John F. Kennedy), argued that Ruby had epileptic seizures and consequently was not responsible for his actions. But such accounts provide a misleading view of epilepsy. In only a very few cases have acts of violence been related to epileptic seizures (Gunn & Fenton, 1971; Turner & Merlis, 1962).

Grand Mal Seizures   The most common and dramatic type of epileptic seizure is the *grand mal* ("great illness") *seizure*. Although this type usually lasts no longer than a few minutes, it typically consists of four distinct phases. A majority of grand mal epileptics report that they experience an *aura* (an unusual sensory experience that provides a warning of an impending convulsion) before the loss of consciousness. The aura lasts only a few seconds and signals the onset of a seizure. During this first phase, the person feels physical or sensory sensations such as headaches, hallucinations, mood changes, dizziness, or feelings of unreality. During the *tonic* phase, the individual becomes unconscious and falls to the ground. The muscles become rigid and the eyes remain open. During the third or *clonic* phase, jerking movements result from the rapid contraction and relaxation of body muscles. These movements may be so violent that epileptics bruise their heads on the ground, bite their tongues, or vomit. Fourth and finally, the muscles relax and a *coma* ensues, lasting from a few minutes to several hours. When the epileptic awakens, he or she may feel exhausted, confused, and sore. Some people report that they awaken relieved and refreshed.

Grand mal attacks may occur daily or be limited to only once or twice during an entire lifetime. In rare cases, grand mal attacks may occur in rapid succession (a condition known as *status epilepticus*) and result in death if untreated.

Etiological Factors   As we have noted, the epilepsies have been attributed to a wide range of factors, including brain tumors, head injuries, biochemical imbalances, physical illness, and stress. Somehow these result in excessive neuronal discharge within the brain. Sometimes the discharge appears to be quite localized and results in focal seizures or twitching in isolated parts of the body. Generalized seizures are presumably caused by general cortical discharge, and the effects involve the whole body.

Some researchers have investigated the hypothesis that genetic or personality factors predispose people to epilepsy. Evidence has shown that the concordance rate for epilepsy is greater among identical than among fraternal twins, and that seizures are much more frequent among family members of an epileptic than among unrelated people (DeJong & Sugar, 1972; Jasper, Ward & Pope, 1969; Lennox & Lennox, 1960). However, heredity may not be a necessary or sufficient condition for the onset of epilepsy. With respect to personality factors, no single type of personality has been associated with epilepsy (Tizard, 1962). Although personality disturbances are correlated with some epileptics, it is unclear whether personality factors predispose people to epilepsy or whether epilepsy influences personality development. Another possibility is that epileptics are under great stress because of their condition and because of the stigma attached to the disorder. This stress, rather than either the disorder or its causes, may affect the personalities of epileptics.

Use of Psychoactive Substances

Using psychoactive substances (see Chapter 10) can result in cognitive disorders (dementia, delirium, or amnestic disorder). The substances have effects on the nervous system. Most people diagnosed as having a cognitive disorder involving psychoactive substances also have problems concerning substance use. The most common psychoactive substances that can lead to cognitive disorders are alcohol, amphetamines, caffeine, marijuana, cocaine, hallucinogens, inhalants, nicotine, opioids, PCP, and sedatives.

TREATMENT CONSIDERATIONS

Because cognitive disorders can be caused by many different factors and are associated with different symptoms and dysfunctions, a wide variety of treatment approaches have been used. The major approaches include surgery, medication, psychological treatments, and environmental intervention. Surgical procedures may be used to remove cerebral tumors, relieve the pressure caused by tumors, or restore ruptured blood vessels. Psychotherapy may help patients deal with the emotional aspects of these disorders. And some patients who have lost motor skills can be retrained to compensate for their deficiencies or can be retaught these skills. Sometimes, patients with cognitive disorders need complete hospital care.

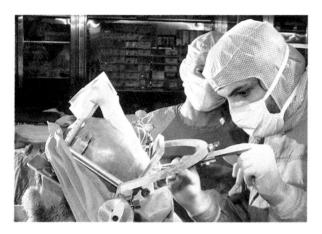

Brain surgery is often necessary to remove cerebral tumors or to restore ruptured blood vessels in the brain. Surgical procedures can be very complicated, requiring a great deal of preparation by the surgical team.

Medication

Drugs can prevent, control, or reduce the symptoms of brain disorders, such as in the use of L-dopa in Parkinson's disease. Medication is of the most benefit in controlling some symptoms of cognitive disorders. For example, more than 50 percent of all epileptics can control their seizures with medication such as Dilantin; another 30 percent can reduce the frequency of seizures. However, side effects, such as a decrease in the speed of motor responding, can occur (Dodrill & Matthews, 1992). Only 20 percent of epileptics do not find medications helpful (Epilepsy Foundation of America, 1982). Sometimes medication is used to control emotional problems that may accompany cognitive impairment. Teri and Wagner (1992) have shown that antidepressant drugs can alleviate the depression found in many patients with Alzheimer's disease.

Cognitive and Behavioral Approaches

The cognitive therapeutic approaches appear to be particularly promising. As an example, researchers have hypothesized that the impaired attention and concentration shown by head-injured people result from the disruption of private speech, which regulates behavior and thought processes (Luria, 1982). One therapeutic program uses self-instructional training to enhance the self-regulation of speech and behavior (Webster & Scott, 1983). The program was

used to treat a 24-year-old construction worker who had been in a coma for four days as a result of a car accident. Tests showed him to have poor recall, poor concentration, and attentional difficulties; he couldn't concentrate on any task for a long period of time. He also complained that intrusive nonsexual thoughts kept him from maintaining an erection during intercourse.

The patient was told to repeat the following self-instructions aloud before doing anything:

1. "To really concentrate, I must look at the person speaking to me."
2. "I also must focus on what is being said, not on other thoughts which want to intrude."
3. "I must concentrate on what I am hearing at any moment by repeating each word in my head as the person speaks."
4. "Although it is not horrible if I lose track of conversation, I must tell the person to repeat the information if I have not attended to it." (Webster & Scott, 1983, p. 71)

After he had learned to use these vocalized instructions (actually, he rephrased them in his own words), he was taught to repeat them subvocally before each task. His concentration and attention soon improved greatly, and he returned to his former job. He also successfully blocked intrusive thoughts during sexual intercourse by focusing on his partner. Such self-vocalizations often increase a person's effectiveness at the task at hand (Kohlenberg & Tsai, 1991).

A similar program was developed to eliminate the anger response brain-injured people sometimes display, either as a result of the brain damage or in reaction to their deficits. One 22-year-old patient had suffered a severe head trauma in a motorcycle accident at age sixteen. After two months of intensive medical treatment, he had returned home to live with his parents. There he showed outbursts of anger toward people and objects, a low frustration level, and impulsiveness. These behaviors led to many failures in a vocational rehabilitation program. Medication didn't help control his outbursts.

A stress inoculation program was developed for this patient. Twelve 30-minute sessions, spread over three weeks, trained him in the following areas:

1. *Cognitive preparation* The function and appropriateness of anger were explained, as were

alternatives to being destructive. The situations that produced anger were identified, and appropriate responses were demonstrated.

2. *Skills acquisition* The patient was taught to stop himself from becoming angry, to reevaluate anger-evoking situations, and to use self-verbalizations that were incompatible with the expression of anger.

3. *Application training* A hierarchy of situations evoking anger was developed. The patient role-played and practiced the use of cognitive and behavioral skills to cope with progressively greater anger-evoking stimuli. He also used these techniques in the hospital setting and received feedback about his performance.

Before treatment, the patient had averaged about three outbursts each week. No outbursts at all were recorded immediately after treatment, and a follow-up five months later indicated that the gain had been maintained. He found a part-time job as a clerk and was living independently.

An interesting seizure prevention program using classical conditioning was reported by Efron (1956, 1957). For example, one woman, suffering from grand mal seizures, learned to prevent the occurrence of the tonic (body extended and stiff) and clonic (rapid alternation of muscle contraction and relaxation) phases by sniffing an unpleasant odor during the initial stage of an attack. The odor was first presented to the woman while she stared at a bracelet. After the smell was paired with the bracelet over a period of several days, the bracelet alone was enough to elicit thoughts of the unpleasant odor. At that point the patient could stop a seizure by staring at her bracelet when she felt the attack starting. Eventually she could cut an attack short by just thinking about the bracelet. Other behavior modification and biofeedback techniques have also been helpful in reducing seizure activity (Mostofsky & Balaschak, 1979).

Environmental Interventions and Caregiver Support

The effects of many cognitive disorders are largely irreversible. This raises the issue of how family and friends can assist those with cognitive disorders.

There are a variety of means by which people with these disorders may be helped to live comfortably and with dignity while making use of those abilities that remain. The following interventions have been proposed by Butler (1984):

1. To preserve the patient's sense of independence and control over his or her life, the environment must be modified to make it safer. Rails can be installed to allow the patient to move freely in the house. A chair that is easy to get into and out of, a remote-control device for the television set, and guard rails for the bathtub will help the patient do things for himself or herself. The patient should be encouraged to make as many personal decisions as possible—to choose which clothing to wear and which activities to take part in—even if the choices are not always perfect.

2. Continued social contacts are important, but visits by friends and relatives should be kept short so that the patient does not feel pressured to continue the social interaction. Visits should not involve large groups of individuals, which could tend to overwhelm the patient.

3. Diversions, such as going out for a walk, are important. It is better to stroll through a calm and peaceful area than to visit a crowded shopping mall, where the environment tends to be unpredictable.

4. Tasks should be assigned to the patient to increase his or her sense of self-worth. These tasks may not be completed to perfection, but they will provide a very important sense of having contributed. In addition, the elderly can be taught the use of memory aids and other strategies to facilitate remembering.

The family and friends who provide care may, themselves, need support (see the First Person narrative). They often feel overwhelmed, helpless, frustrated, anxious, or even angry at having to take care of someone with a cognitive impairment. They may worry about how to take proper care of a loved one who has a cognitive disorder or feel guilty if the loved one gets injured or deteriorates under their care. In such circumstances, caregivers should learn as much as possible about the disorder and the means of taking care of loved ones, realize that the role of a caregiver is stressful, and receive personal support (such as through self-help groups composed of other caregivers).

SUMMARY

1. The effects of brain damage vary greatly. The most common symptoms include impaired consciousness and memory, impaired judgment, orientation difficulties, and attentional deficits. The effects can be acute (often temporary) or chronic (long term); the causes can be endogenous (internal) or exogenous (external); and the tissue damage can be diffuse or specific (localized). Assessing brain damage is complicated because its symptoms are often similar to those of functional disorders.

2. Four major types of cognitive disorders are listed by DSM-IV: dementia, delirium, amnestic disorders, and other cognitive disorders. In dementia, memory is impaired and cognitive functioning declines as revealed by aphasia (language disturbance), apraxia (inability to carry out motor activities despite intact comprehension and motor function), agnosia (failure to recognize or identify objects despite intact sensory function), or disturbances in planning, organizing, and abstracting in thought processes. Delirium is a condition in which there is an impairment in consciousness with reduced ability to focus, sustain, or shift attention. Changes in cognition (memory deficit, disorientation, and language or perceptual disturbance) are observed, and the disorder develops rather rapidly over a course of hours or days. Amnestic disorders are characterized by memory impairment as manifested by inability to learn new information and the inability to recall previously learned knowledge or past events. Finally, cognitive impairments that do not meet the criteria for the other three are classified as other cognitive disorders.

3. Many different agents can cause cognitive disorders; among these are physical wounds or injuries to the brain, processes of aging, diseases that destroy brain tissue (such as neurosyphilis and encephalitis), and brain tumors. Epilepsy is characterized by intermittent and brief periods of altered consciousness, frequently accompanied by seizures, and excessive electrical discharge by neurons. Psychoactive substances can also cause cognitive disorders.

4. Treatment strategies include corrective surgery and cognitive and behavioral training. Medication is often used, either alone or with other therapies, to decrease or control the symptoms of the various cognitive disorders. Caregivers can learn to provide assistance to loved ones with cognitive disorders.

KEY TERMS

Alzheimer's disease An organic brain disorder that involves the atrophy of brain tissue and leads to marked deterioration of intellectual and emotional functioning

amnestic disorders Disorders characterized by memory impairment as manifested by inability to learn new information and the inability to recall previously learned knowledge or past events

brain trauma A physical wound or injury to the brain

cerebral blood flow measurement A technique for assessing brain damage in which the patient inhales radioactive gas and the movement of the substance is followed throughout the brain

cerebral tumor A mass of abnormal tissue growing within the brain

cerebrovascular accident A sudden stoppage of blood flow to a portion of the brain, leading to a loss of brain function; also called *stroke*

cognitive disorders Behavioral disturbances that result from organic brain pathology—that is, damage to the brain

computerized axial tomography (CAT) A neurological test for the assessment of brain damage, which uses x-rays and computer technology

delirium A syndrome in which there is a reduced ability to attend to external stimuli, difficulty in shifting attention, and disorganized thinking

dementia A syndrome characterized by the deterioration of brain tissue resulting in decreased intellectual ability and impaired judgment, of sufficient severity to interfere with social and occupational functioning

diaschisis A process in which a lesion in a specific area of the brain disrupts other intact areas

electroencephalograph (EEG) A neurological test for the assessment of brain damage, which measures electrical activity of brain cells

FIRST PERSON

Marie Smart

I was fortunate to grow up in a multigenerational home and small village where I learned very early in my life to value and enjoy the elderly. In that environment I had the opportunity to know a number of elderly who were physically, intellectually, and emotionally active and involved into their eighties and some of them into their nineties. I also had opportunity to know and help care for less healthy elderly members of our community. Some of them had significant physical impairments and others had significant mental or emotional impairments. I believe that my career focus came at least partially from those childhood experiences.

I have been a social service pro-fessional for over twenty years; for the past eleven years I have specialized in the care of the elderly and their families. For the past five years I have worked almost exclusively with families afflicted with Alzheimer's disease or a related disorder. I am a Family Counselor with the Sanders-Brown Center on Aging at the Unviersity of Kentucky and am a member of the clinical care team of the Alzheimer's Disease Research Center there. We see patients and their families in the neurology clinic for the initial evaluation of a memory problem and then every six months for follow-up purposes. I am available on an as-needed basis to these families by telephone or in person in my office or their homes. My work with them involves helping accurately assess and evaluate the nature and extent of the dementia, educating the caregivers about their loved one's illness, and then providing ongoing counseling and support to these families as they live with Alzheimer's disease.

Challenging work to be sure, sometimes frustrating and discouraging, always interesting and demanding, frequently intellectually and emotionally satisfying. I want to share with you some of "my families" and their experiences living with and caring for a loved one with a cognitive disorder.

I have one family of nine children who are sharing in the care of their mother who has Alzheimer's disease. Some of the children live in the same town as their mother, some live in other areas of the state, others live out of state; all are involved. A son and daughter have joint durable power of attorney. One daughter who lives near her mother assists with personal care and routine household chores; another daughter in town does the shopping and other errands and helps with periodic heavy house cleaning. A son and daughter from a nearby town come home and take their mother for her routine medical care. The other children who live further away come home at regularly scheduled intervals to provide respite to the in-town caregivers and to have special time with their mother in the environment that is most comfortable for and supportive of her. They all meet at least twice a year to reassess their mother's needs and to make any necessary changes in their caregiving routines.

My role in counseling with these families is varied. For some of them, I am a "safe listener," the person to

---

encephalitis Inflammation of the brain caused by viral infection that produces symptoms of lethargy, fever, and long periods of stupor and sleep; sleeping sickness

epilepsy Any disorder characterized by intermittent and brief periods of altered consciousness, often accompanied by seizures, and excessive electrical discharge from brain cells

Huntington's chorea A genetically transmitted de-generative disease involving personality changes, depression, delusion, and a loss of control over bodily functions

magnetic resonance imaging (MRI) A technique to assess brain functioning, using a magnetic field and radio waves to produce pictures of the brain

meningitis Inflammation of the membrane surrounding the brain and spinal cord; can produce cerebral infarction and seizures

whom they can express their strongest feelings about the stresses of caregiving and know that it won't go beyond me. For these folks, often a good listener is the most they need. I have sessions with other family caregivers educating them about the disease itself and helping them identify different and hopefully more effective approaches to caring. With other families, I am the mediator who helps them consider and appreciate the caregiving strengths of each member of the family and then works with them to develop an acceptable care plan that can include all of them. My counseling frequently involves helping families make difficult decisions—whether to move their loved one out of a lifelong home, how to get them to stop driving, when and how to take over money management tasks, whether to place them in a nursing home and if so, which one to choose. My goal is not to make decisions for these families but to help them feel secure about their ability to make their own decisions.

I am involved with an elderly couple who have been married for over fifty years. She has Alzheimer's disease and frequently now doesn't recognize "that man" who spends so much time with her. She calls their daughter at bedtime each evening to ask her about the appropriateness of going to bed with "that man." The daughter has learned to offer reassurance in words and concepts that work for her mother. She tells her mother that she thinks it's okay for the man to be there: he's very nice and polite, "he's cute and he has money." With that reassurance, this wife of fifty-plus years is able to relax and let her husband help her prepare for bed.

Then there is the son and his wife and their three teenagers who are caring for his mother. She lives in the home with them; her granddaughter gave up her room so "Granny" would have a room of her own. Granny has reached the point in her disease where she no longer understands how to use the different eating utensils. She can manage only a spoon. When this family gathers at the table for their meals, there is only a spoon at each person's place. They refuse to do something that might make Granny feel different or inferior.

Another couple with whom I work are much younger and have been devoted square dancers for a number of years. Though he now has Alzheimer's disease and often does not recognize his home or his wife or daughter, the husband can still dance. At those times when he becomes very agitated, his wife has learned to play their favorite square dance music. With that he begins to dance and his agitation is relieved. He doesn't miss a step.

We say at our Center that "when you've worked with one Alzheimer family, you've worked with *one* Alzheimer family." Every family has different strengths and needs. Some of them have developed coping skills that help them meet their caregiving challenges without what they perceive to be any great difficulty. Others of these families quickly learn new and previously unthought of ways to care for a loved one with a cognitive disorder. Other families aren't ever able to make the adjustments in their lives to successfully cope with the trauma of their diseases.

It is my privilege to provide support and education and counseling to each of these families. From them I receive support and education and reinforcement of my valuing of the elderly and their families.

Marie Smart is a family therapist at the Sanders-Brown Center on Aging at the University of Kentucky.

multi-infarct dementia An organic brain syndrome characterized by uneven deterioration of intellectual abilities and resulting from a number of cerebral infarctions

Parkinson's disease A progressively worsening organic brain disorder characterized by muscle tremors; a stiff, shuffling gait; a lack of facial expression; and social withdrawal

positron emission tomography (PET) A technique for assessing brain damage in which the patient is injected with radioactive glucose and the metabolism of the glucose is monitored

senile dementia A severe loss of intellectual functioning produced by brain cell deterioration as a result of aging

CHAPTER 17

Disorders of Childhood and Adolescence and Mental Retardation

The disorders of childhood and adolescence encompass a wide variety of behavioral problems, ranging from severe disturbances affecting many aspects of behavior to the less-severe developmental disturbances that are typically confined to a given area. Between 11 to 14 percent of the 63 million children and adolescents in the United States have a serious emotional or behavioral problem. The annual cost for treatment is more than 1.5 billion dollars (Kazdin, 1993; Weisz et al., 1992). Fewer than 50 percent receive any form of treatment (Saxe, Cross & Silverman, 1988). Children and adolescents are, in fact, subject to many "adult" disorders discussed in previous chapters.

Changes have been made in the childhood disorders in DSM-IV. Two childhood anxiety disorders have been eliminated. Children or adolescents who meet the criteria for avoidant disorders are now diagnosed with social phobia disorder. Overanxious disorder has also been eliminated. Instead, the diagnosis of generalized anxiety disorder is used. These changes were made because the childhood disorders that were eliminated were highly similar to the adult disorders. To have the same disorder with different names would be confusing. Another change in DSM-IV concerns the presentation of the severe childhood disorders. In DSM-III-R, there was only one specific category (autistic disorder) under the pervasive developmental disorders. Cases that did not meet all the developmental criteria for this diagnosis were placed in pervasive developmental disorder not otherwise specified. In DSM-IV, this general category is divided into a group of specific disorders (Rett's disorder, childhood disintegrative disorder, and Asperger's disorder).

In this chapter, we discuss some of the problems that arise primarily during the earlier stages of life. We begin with severe disturbances that were formerly known as "childhood psychoses"; then we examine several less-disabling disorders of childhood and adolescence. Eating disorders tend to develop during adolescence and are also discussed in this chapter. We conclude the chapter with a discussion of mental retardation.

PERVASIVE DEVELOPMENTAL DISORDERS

In the past, severe disturbances that led to bizarre behaviors in children were given labels such as "childhood schizophrenia" and "childhood psychosis." But the pervasive developmental disorders distinctly differ from the psychotic conditions observed in adolescents and adults. For example, the childhood disorders don't include symptoms such as hallucinations, delusions, the loosening of associations, and incoherence. A child showing these symptoms probably would be diagnosed as schizophrenic.

The **pervasive developmental disorders** are severe childhood disorders that affect psychological functioning in such areas as language, social relationships, attention, perception, and affect. They include autistic disorder, Rett's disorder, childhood disintegrative disorder, Asperger's disorder, and pervasive developmental disorder not otherwise specified. The impairments shown in these disorders are not simply delays in development but are distortions that would not be normal at any developmental stage. Autistic disorder is quite rare—about four to seven cases in every 10,000 children. This disorder occurs three or four times more frequently in boys than in girls (Gillberg, 1992). About 22 in 10,000 do not show all the characteristics of autistic disorder but also show severe social impairment (Brook & Bowler, 1992). They would receive a diagnosis from one of the new categories of the pervasive developmental disorders. In the following section, we will first discuss autistic disorder and then the related disorders.

Autistic Disorder

Jim, currently twenty-nine years old, received a diagnosis of autism during his preschool years. His parents reported that Jim was not "cuddly." He would stiffen when touched and preferred being alone. Touching was not tolerated until the age of twenty-three. Jim found touching aversive because it produced soundlike sensations as well as tactile sensations. This was confusing to him. In talking about his reactions, Jim found it difficult to discuss sensations because he believed that his sensory and perceptual sensations were different from others. On responding to external stimuli he replied, "Sometimes the channels get confused, as when sounds come through as color. Sometimes I know that something is coming in somewhere, but I can't tell right away what sense it's coming through . . ." (Cesaroni & Garber, 1991, p. 305). Jim engaged in stereotyped movements involving rocking and twirling. He can now consciously control these behaviors but they still occur when he is tired and not consciously aware. Any environmental change was very distressing to him. He strongly responded to the sale of the family car as the "loss of a family member." Jim feels different from others and is unable to

Children suffering from autism are profoundly alone. Their unresponsiveness to adults, lack of bonding to parents and others, and language and speech deficits keep them locked in a socially isolated world.

understand social signals. He describes himself as "communication impaired." He is most comfortable when communication is concrete but not when different subjects or informal conversation occurs. Relationships are enormously difficult to form because of the communication problems. His inability to establish contact is reflected in his poem:

I built a bridge
out of nowhere, across nothingness
and wondered if there would be something on the
other side.
    I built a bridge
out of fog, across darkness
and hoped that there would be light on the other side.
    I built a bridge
out of despair, across oblivion
and knew that there would be hope on the other side.
    I built a bridge
out of helplessness, across chaos
and trusted that there would be strength on the other
side.
    I built a bridge
out of hell, across terror
and it was a good bridge, a strong bridge,
a beautiful bridge.
    It was a bridge I built myself
with only my hands for tools, my obstinacy for supports, my faith for spans, and my blood for rivets.
    I built a bridge, and crossed it,
but there was no one there to meet me on the other
side. (Cesaroni & Garber, 1991, p. 312)

In 1943 Leo Kanner, a child psychiatrist, described a group of children who shared certain symptoms with other psychotic children but who also displayed some unique behaviors. Kanner called the syndrome *infantile autism,* from the Greek *autos* ("self"), to reflect the profound aloneness and detachment of these children. A highly unusual symptom of autistic children is their extreme lack of responsiveness to adults: "The child is aware of people . . . but considers them not differently from the way he (or she) considers the desk, bookshelf, or filing cabinet" (Kanner & Lesser, 1958, p. 659).

The puzzling symptoms displayed by the children Kanner described fit the diagnostic criteria for **autistic disorder** in DSM-IV. Impairments are found in three major areas (American Psychiatric Association, 1993; Gillberg, 1992; Klin, Volkmar & Sparrow, 1992):

Social interactions Unusual lack of interest in others is a primary aspect of this disorder. As a result, children with autistic disorder fail to develop peer relationships. Disturbances may be displayed in body postures, gestures, facial expressions, and eye contact. They are impaired in their ability to understand emotions in others. Even when an autistic child looks at someone, that looking does not seem to be for finding out what the person is feeling. Autistic children appear to be unaware of other people's identity.

Frith (1991) hypothesized that autistic individuals lack a theory of mind. That is, they do not or cannot understand that others think and feel. It is this lack that produces their inability to empathize with others. They often do not need physical contact with or emotional response from their caretakers. In one study (Klin, 1991) autistic, mentally retarded, and normally developing children could choose to listen to their mothers' speech or the buzz of conversation in a cafeteria. The comparison group children all showed a strong preference for their mothers' voices. Autistic children were more likely to prefer the conversation tape or showed no preference for either audio selection. They interact with other people as if people were unimportant objects and show little interest in establishing friendships, imitating behaviors, or playing games (Stone & Lemanek, 1990). Autistic infants are usually content to be left alone and don't show an anticipatory response to being picked up.

Verbal and nonverbal communication About 50 percent of autistic children don't develop speech. Those who do generally show oddities such as *echolalia* (echoing what has previously been said). One child constantly repeated the words "How do you spell relief?" without any apparent reason. In addition, the child may reverse pronouns. For example, "you" might be used for "I," and "I" for "me." Even when they can speak, such children may be unable to, or unwilling to, initiate conversations. Autistic children also use more nonsensical and idiosyncratic language than matched controls (Volden & Lord, 1991).

Activities and interests Autistic children engage in few activities. They often have unusual repetitive habits such as spinning objects, whirling themselves, or fluttering or flapping their arms. They may show intense interest in self-induced sounds or in staring

The Original "Rain Man"

When screenwriter Barry Morrow first met Kim, his original model for the central character in *Rain Man*, Kim already knew Morrow's past and present phone numbers and the number of freeway exits to his house. They met in Texas where Kim and his father, Fran, were attending a 1984 meeting of the American Association of Retarded Citizens. Kim, thirty-seven, is an extremely rare prodigious savant, capable of recalling virtually anything his senses have ever told him.

But although Kim has a seemingly unlimited ability to absorb and recall facts and figures, he has limited reasoning power and his IQ score is a below-average 88. He has always lived with Fran in the Salt Lake City area, accompanying him on frequent business trips since Fran and Kim's mother divorced in 1981.

"I am Rain Man," Kim said in an interview. "This is an important time for me. I have many talents now."

Morrow, who calls Kim "an island of genius," believes the movie has changed Kim. "When I first met him, after he talked to me he dashed across the room and made low moaning sounds," Morrow said. "Now, he walks into a room and offers you his hand." Kim's father, who asked for privacy reasons that his and Kim's last name not be used, agrees that his son is changing. After a special screening of *Rain Man* for the Utah Legislature, Kim stood up and stressed the importance of understanding the needs of the handicapped.

"I had no idea he could talk to those guys that way," Fran said.

"He is really learning to put his thoughts together."

Coincidentally, Fran and Kim were rolling down the freeway when they heard the news that *Rain Man* had been nominated for eight Academy Awards, including best picture and best actor.

Kim has seen the movie three times, the first seated at the premiere between Morrow and Fran. Kim stared at his hands and the floor during most of the movie. When Morrow asked him why, Kim told him he had seen it with his heart.

Although there are behavioral similarities between Kim and Hoffman's film character, Kim is far more outgoing. Two years ago he spent an afternoon with Hoffman on a movie set, the actor mimicking his movements and his walk. When it was over, Kim recalls, Hoffman

---

at their hands and fingers. They may stare into space and be totally self-absorbed. Minor changes in the environment may produce rages and tantrums. Autistic children show a lack of imaginary activities. They rarely engage in behaviors such as caring for a doll, talking on a "telephone," or pretending to drink from an empty cup (Atlas & Lapidus, 1987).

Jerry, a high-functioning autistic person, showed many of these characteristics (Bemporad, 1979). During adolescence, for example, he couldn't understand the viewpoint of others. Once, during a trip to Mexico with his parents, Jerry "took off" by himself for most of a day without saying where he was going. When he returned, he simply could not understand the frantic search that his parents had conducted.

As an adult, Jerry still lacks social awareness. When he is with his parents (his only social contacts), he spends his time silently watching television in their presence. He has no ability to make "small talk."

Jerry's need for sameness also remains, although it has shifted to accommodate adult activities. Taking a shower requires about two hours because Jerry must first make sure that every item in the bathroom is in its "proper" place. He has to wash himself in a certain prescribed pattern.

Jerry reports having no daydreams, and he doesn't engage in leisure activities. He has a job completing fiscal efficiency reports and functions well when given explicit instructions. He cannot be relied on to use "common sense."

Bemporad (1979), who has described Jerry's behaviors in detail, concluded that "he remains an isolated, mechanical being, unable to intuit the social nuances of behavior and therefore forced to retreat from a world that is persistently surprising and lacking in regularity" (p. 195). The lack of social empathy was also evident in another autistic adult who complained that he could not "mind-read." He felt

said, "I may be the star, but you are the heavens."

Daniel Christensen, medical director of the Western Institute of Neuropsychiatry at the University of Utah, has made a thorough study of Kim. "He has a photographic memory, but has no way to minimize stimuli," Christensen said. "He's the closest I've seen to a human computer," unable to filter or forget information, or assign it relative importance. He can answer untold thousands of questions covering history, sports, maps, literature, mathematics, and other subjects.

Source: Abridged from Israelsen (1989).

that most people had this capacity because they seemed to know how others would respond. He could never predict how others would react until they actually did so (Rutter, 1983).

As many as three-fourths of autistic children have IQ scores less than 70. High-functioning autistic people such as Jim, Jerry, or the person played by Dustin Hoffman in the movie *Rain Man* account for only a minority of people with this disorder (see Focus 17.1). Only about 20 percent have average to above-average intelligence (Gillberg, 1988; Maltz, 1982). In the past, some theorists, including Kanner, believed that these children were unusually bright, primarily because some of them display *splinter skills*—that is, they often do well with drawings, puzzle construction, and rote memory but poorly with verbal tasks and tasks requiring language skills and symbolic thinking. Second, they often display unusual abilities. One Chinese autistic boy could identify the day of the week for different dates and convert the Gregorian calendar to the Chinese calendar. He also knew the lottery numbers and their drawing dates for the last three months; the titles of songs in the popular charts for the last ten years and their dates of release; and the numbers and routes of buses throughout the city (Ho, Tsang & Ho, 1991). Mentally retarded autistic children who score in the mentally retarded range on IQ tests but who have specific and unusual abilities have been described as "autistic savants."

Diagnosis Autism might seem to be easy to diagnose, given its unique characteristics. Yet questions have been raised about whether it is a distinct entity. Gillberg (1992) pointed out three problems in diagnosis: (1) many different medical conditions can produce the behavioral characteristics of autism, (2) the autistic symptom profile has been found in children with and without signs of neurological impairments, and (3) it shares several characteristics with other disorders that involve social and communication impairment. In addition, symptoms can vary widely among autistic children, especially with regard to developmental age and level of functioning. Some researchers (Brook & Bowler, 1992) believe that the degree of social impairment differentiates children with autistic disorder from children with other related disorders.

Because a specific etiological factor has not been identified and because symptoms of the disorder overlap with other pervasive developmental disorders, there is confusion over when to use the term *autism*.

Autistic children are often diagnosed as only mentally retarded. Autistic symptoms may not be recognized. The two disorders often coexist. Still, there are ways to distinguish children with both autism and mental retardation from children with just mental retardation. For example, children with autistic disorder exhibit splinter skills much more often than children with mental retardation. Also, children with mental retardation are more likely to relate to others and to be more socially aware than are autistic children with both autism and mental retardation.

Research on Autism   In this section we consider some recent research investigating social unresponsiveness and the unusual communication patterns of autistic children.

Hobson (1987) was interested in the social unresponsiveness of autistic children and wanted to find out if such children noticed people's age and gender. Even very young infants can distinguish between male and female and between child and adult, an ability that suggests responsiveness and attention to social cues. Autistic children, however, have been described as more interested in inanimate objects than in human beings. Seventeen autistic and seventeen nonautistic matched control children were exposed to videotapes of nonhuman stimuli (bird, dog, train, and car) and people (boy, girl, man, and woman). The stimuli were presented one at a time. Before, during, and after the videotaped presentations, the children were asked to match the object or person with five schematic drawings. Both the autistic and control children correctly matched videotapes of nonhuman stimuli with the schematic drawings at least 75 percent of the time. Yet on the videotapes

involving people, autistic children were highly inaccurate in choosing the correct face, whereas control children continued to achieve 75 percent accuracy. Autistic children do appear to be unattentive to human characteristics. Another study found similar results. Autistic children did a better job of discriminating between pictures of buildings than faces (Boucher & Lewis, 1992). They also had difficulty responding to people according to qualities such as age or sex. Hobson cited an example of a middle-aged autistic man who talked to babies, children, and elderly people with the same style of speech. This lack of social attentiveness has been shown experimentally but the reason for this has not been found.

Impaired communication is another characteristic of autistic children. They may have tantrums, engage in self-injurious behaviors, repeat what is said to them (echolalia), or repeat phrases that are out of context. Could these behavior patterns be primitive attempts at communication? Certain patterns were noticed by Carr and Durand (1987):

◆ A fourteen-year-old autistic boy has temper tantrums whenever his teacher attempts to give him a lesson. The tantrums are so severe that the teacher must wear gloves and a heavy coat to protect himself. After ten minutes, the teacher gives up. Then Bob, the autistic boy, begins to hum.

◆ An autistic child scratches himself badly. This occurs even when he is constantly nagged at by his parents. Interestingly, his scratching stops when his parents pay attention to something else.

Carr and Durand believe that these behaviors can be understood as a need for attention or the desire to avoid a task. The view that "unusual" behaviors may represent attempts to communicate was suggested by Durand and Crimmins (1987). A nine-year-old autistic child was referred by his teacher because of his nonsensical speech. Although the child could speak appropriately, he often repeated phrases that were out of context or did not make sense (such as "fried eggs on your head"). Attempts to control this behavior by ignoring and reinforcing appropriate speech were ineffective.

The researchers hypothesized that this behavior might represent an attempt to show stress from classroom tasks. An alternative means to escape was provided. The child was trained to say, "Help me," whenever the task demands were increased. This response was followed by teacher assistance. With this procedure, psychotic speech was greatly reduced during tasks. Understanding this mode of communication is important for successful treatment. If the misbehavior is a communication to avoid a task, a procedure using time out from a lesson may increase the problem behavior. If the communication is understood, children can be taught appropriate ways to elicit attention, such as asking, "Am I doing a good job?" or "See what I have done." If the task is difficult, the child can be taught to say, "Help me" or "I don't understand." Such research supports the view that some behavioral patterns in autistic children are attempts to communicate.

Although we are learning more about the symptoms of autism, many questions remain. What causes the bizarre and puzzling abnormalities that are seen in autistic children? Why do they occur so early in life? After a brief discussion of other pervasive developmental disorders, we consider the causes, prognosis, and treatment of autism.

Other Pervasive Developmental Disorders

The diagnosis of Rett's disorder, childhood disintegrative disorder, Asperger's disorder, or pervasive developmental disorders not otherwise specified is for people who don't meet the full criteria for autistic disorder but who show "severe and pervasive" impaired social interactions and verbal and nonverbal skills. Characteristics of the disorders in these categories often overlap with autistic disorder (see disorders chart, p. 504). Some question whether they should be considered distinctive disorders or are merely variants of autistic disorder. Little research exists on children with these diagnoses.

How would you diagnose the following case of a girl who was videotaped by her parents several times from birth to two years and seven months (Eriksson & de Chateau, 1992)?

> During the first year of her life the girl showed normal development (smiled, laughed, babbled, waved bye-bye to parents, and played peek-a-boo). During the second year she spoke few words. She sat on the floor and played with a book in a stereotyped manner and showed little response to her parents. After two years of age, she was withdrawn, spoke no words except

meaningless phrases from songs. She was preoccupied with rocking or spinning her mother's hair. Computerized axial tomography (CAT) scans, magnetic resonance imaging (MRI), and electroencephalogram (EEG) readings were normal. No physical condition was found to be associated with her condition.

Would you diagnose this child as suffering from autistic disorder or one of the following pervasive developmental disorders?

1. *Rett's disorder*   This disorder is characterized by normal development for at least six months, followed by deterioration and marked delay of language or social skills. Stereotyped hand movements, poor coordination, and deceleration of head growth occur.

2. *Childhood disintegrative disorders*   These disorders are characterized by normal development for at least two years in social relationships, verbal and nonverbal communication, and play followed by severe impairment and deterioration of these skills. Other symptoms of autistic disorder develop (impairment in social interaction and interest, and repetitive stereotyped behaviors).

3. *Asperger's disorder*   Children with this disorder have severe impairment in social interactions and skills, limited repetitive behaviors, and lack of emotional reciprocity. They have shown cognitive and language development.

4. *Pervasive developmental disorders not otherwise specified*   This category is for cases that are not typical in terms of age of onset or specific behavior pattern. There is pervasive and severe impairment in reciprocal social interactions, communication abnormalities, and limited interests and activities. These children do not, however, meet the full criteria for autistic disorder.

Etiology

Little research has been done on Rett's disorder, childhood disintegrative disorder, and Asperger's syndrome. They are new to DSM-IV. Because of this, the discussion on etiology will just deal with autistic disorder. One very puzzling aspect of autistic disorder is that different factors are associated with different cases (Folstein & Rutter, 1988; Gillberg, 1992; Volkmar et al., 1988). There are four major etiologi-

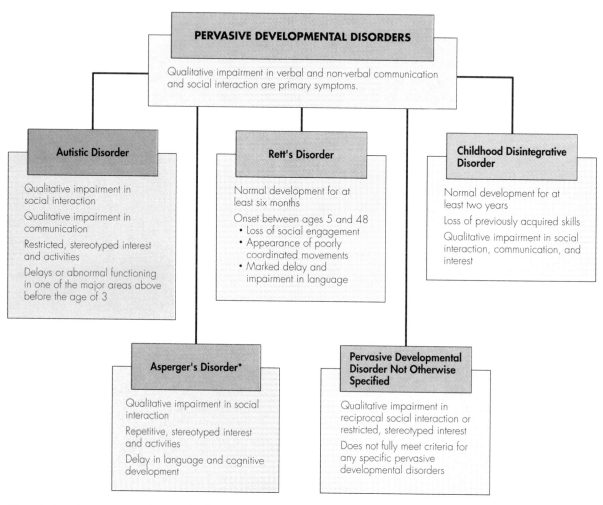

* Some believe there is not enough data to list this disorder as a specific PDD.

cal groupings in autism (Gillberg, 1992): (1) familial autism, (2) autism related to a medical condition, (3) autism associated with nonspecific brain dysfunction, and (4) autism without a family history or associated brain dysfunction. How the syndrome of autism can develop from these different conditions is not known. One important implication of the different groups is that a single cause for autism will not be found. Because of the early lack of normal development and distinct social and cognitive deficits, researchers increasingly believe that autism results from organic rather than psychosocial factors. However, the earli-

est explanations for autism involved parent-child relationships.

Psychoanalytic Theories Psychodynamic theories of autism stress the importance of deviant parent-child interactions in producing this condition. Kanner (1943), who named the syndrome, concluded that cold and unresponsive parenting is responsible for the development of autism. He described the parents as "successfully autistic," "cold, humorless perfectionists who preferred reading, writing, playing music, or thinking" (p. 663). These individuals "happened to defrost long enough to produce a child" (Steffenburg & Gillberg, 1989). Kanner has changed his position and now believes that the disorder is "innate."

Psychological factors are implicated in many disorders, but they don't seem involved in autism. Unfortunately, many mental health professionals continue to inflict guilt on parents who already bear the burden of raising an autistic child. Parents of autistic children show much stress and are particularly concerned about the well-being of their children after they can no longer take care of them (Koegel et al., 1992). In light of current research, no justification exists for allowing parents to think that they caused their child's autism.

Family and Genetic Studies Few family or genetic studies have been conducted on autism, and the studies that have been done are methodologically flawed. This is not surprising because the disorder is so rare.

About 2 to 9 percent of siblings of autistic children are also autistic, which is one to two hundred times greater than in the general population (Ritvo et al., 1989; Smalley & Asarnow, 1990). These findings are supportive of some genetic influences. A well-controlled twin study was performed by Folstein and Rutter (1977). They recruited fraternal (DZ) and identical (MZ) twins who were both discordant and concordant (that is, in some pairs both twins were autistic, in others only one twin was). Zygocity was determined through blood analysis, and diagnoses were made without knowing who the twins' siblings were or whether they were DZ or MZ. The concordance rate for twenty-one pairs of twins was 36 percent for MZ twins and 0 percent for DZ twins. An interesting finding of the Folstein and Rutter study is that seven of the disconcordant twins showed some language impairment—one characteristic of autism. Some type of inherited cognitive or semantic impairment may be associated with autism (Brook & Bowler, 1992). Folstein and Rutter also believe that the diathesis-stress model could account for some of their findings. Among the seventeen disconcordant twin pairs, twelve cases involved a birth complication for the autistic twin. So a predisposition interacting with an environmental stressor may result in the disorder.

Central Nervous System Impairment As mentioned earlier, autistic disorder seems to be associated with many organic conditions (Bolton et al., 1989; Ghaziuddin et al., 1992), none of which are pathognomonic (specific only to autism). Conditions such as the fragile X chromosome, tuberous sclerosis (a congenital hereditary disease associated with brain tumors), neurofibromatosis (tumors of the peripheral nerves), phenylketonuria (PKU), and intrauterine rubella (measles) have been reported among children with autistic disorder. These diseases affect the central nervous system, but most people with these conditions do not develop autism. Because cognitive and language deficits are a major characteristic of autism, attention has been directed to the left hemisphere, which is associated with these functions.

A plausible hypothesis is that autism develops only when the brain part responsible for the syndrome is affected. Attempts to identify brain structure or functioning differences associated with autism have produced mixed results. Some researchers have reported differences in brain structure between autistic and nonautistic individuals (Courchesne et al., 1988), whereas others have found no difference (Garber & Ritvo, 1992). An examination of the regional cerebral blood flow in autistic individuals also didn't reveal an abnormal pattern (Ghaziuddin et al., 1992). That so many organic conditions are associated with autism has suggested central nervous system impairment. No consistent pattern of impairment has yet been found, however, which is to be expected if different subgroups of autism exist.

Biochemical Studies Researchers are also interested in the role that neurotransmitters may play in autistic disorder. Elevated blood serotonin levels have been reported in a minority of autistic patients (Ritvo et al., 1984). The research on biochemical factors in autism is difficult to interpret. Studies often use different intellectual and behavioral measures and may study different subgroups of autistic people (DuVergals, Banks & Guyer, 1988). Some autistic children have elevated serotonin and dopamine levels. The significance of this elevation is still not clear, but it suggests a promising line of research.

Prognosis

The prognosis for children with pervasive developmental disorders is mixed. Those with severe mental retardation have a poorer outcome. The prognosis is somewhat better for those who are considered high functioning with good verbal skills. In a follow-up of twenty-two high-functioning persons aged eighteen or older, six were competitively employed, thirteen were in supervised employment or in special school programs, and three were unemployed and not in school (Venter, Lord & Schopler, 1992). In another study, researchers found that the symptoms in twenty patients diagnosed with autism or childhood psychosis had not changed. The behaviors of these patients—now adults—resembled those of mild schizophrenics, except that none displayed hallucinations or delusions (Howell & Guirguis, 1984). Some cases of highly significant improvement have been reported. Temple Grandlin overcame the symptoms of autistic disorder to earn a doctorate in animal science and is now a recognized leader in the field of livestock handling (Ratey, Grandlin & Miller, 1992).

Treatment

Because of the symptomatic lack of communication or social unresponsiveness, pervasive developmental disorders are very difficult to treat. Therapy with the parents, family therapy, drug therapy, and behavior modification techniques are all currently being used. Although they may improve social adjustment somewhat, overall success has been limited. Intensive behavior modification programs seem the most promising treatment.

Drug Therapy The antipsychotic medication, haloperidol, can produce modest reductions in withdrawal, stereotypical movements, and fidgetiness. However, long-term use can produce movement problems and other side effects in many children (Gadow, 1991). Recently, fenfluramine has been found to increase attention span and decrease hyperactivity in some autistic children. This medication inhibits the uptake of serotonin by nerve terminals and blocks dopamine receptors (Campbell, 1988). Other studies, however, have found few positive effects of fenfluramine compared with placebos (Campbell et al., 1987). Treatment with medication has produced mixed results.

Behavior Modification Behavior modification procedures have been used effectively to eliminate echolalia, self-mutilation, and self-stimulation. They also have effectively increased attending behaviors, verbalizations, and social play through social interaction

Behavior modification procedures have been effective in increasing attending behaviors and verbalizations in autistic children. A favorite food or drink is used to reinforce the desired behaviors. The autistic child in this photo must give the proper sign before he can get his drink.

training (Oke & Schreibman, 1990; Plienis et al., 1987). A follow-up study of autistic children treated by Lovaas (1987) using an intensive behavior modification program indicated that most of the children had improved and about one-half obtained intellectual test scores in the normal range. Harris and colleagues (1991) also found that a one-year behavioral language intensive educational program for preschool autistic children resulted in average IQ score gains of 19 points. It appears that young children with autism can make significant intellectual and language gains in early intervention programs. Nevertheless, certain symptoms of social impairment generally remain. Even high-functioning adults with autistic disorder display problem behaviors involving inappropriate communication and poor interpersonal skills. One group of high-functioning autistic adults had problems obtaining employment because of behaviors such as rudely terminating or interrupting conversations, walking sideways, or waving arms in a robot-like fashion. Through behavioral interventions, these adults were able to become competitively employed, although some oddities of be-havior remained (Burt, Fuller & Lewis, 1991).

OTHER DEVELOPMENTAL DISORDERS

The less-severe childhood and adolescent distur-bances cover a wide range of problems. In this chap-ter, we discuss some of the more common disorders, which include disruptive disorders and attention deficit hyperactive disorder, separation-anxiety disor-ders, tic disorders, eating disorders, and mental retar-dation. Decisions on what behaviors constitute a disorder are often based on vague and arbitrary inter-pretations of the extent to which a given child devi-ates from some "acceptable" norm.

How do we know whether a child has a child-hood disorder? The definition of a childhood disor-der frequently depends on the tolerance of the refer-ring agent. Kanner (1960) pointed out that many childhood problems are transient and that "a multi-tude of early breathholders, nose-pickers, and casual masturbators" develop into normal adults. If a child is brought to a mental health clinic, the difficulties will be interpreted as "far out of proportion to their role as everyday problems of the everyday child." Cultural factors also play a role in the types of prob-lems identified. In Thailand, where aggression is dis-couraged and values such as peacefulness, politeness, and deference are encouraged, clinic referrals are pri-marily for overcontrolled behaviors (fearfulness, sleep problems, somatization). In the United States, where independence and competitiveness are empha-sized, problems generally involve undercontrolled be-haviors (disobedience, fighting, arguing; Tharp, 1991). Differences in problem behaviors reported by teachers in different countries can be seen in Table 17.1.

Table 17.1

Comparisons Between Behavioral Symptoms Rated by Teachers of Children in China and Other Countries (in Percent)

Source	Rutter *et al.* (1974)				Minde (1977)	McGee *et al.* (1985)		Ekblad (1990)	
Year	1974				1977	1982		1984	
Place	England				Uganda	New Zealand		China	
Informant	Teacher				Teacher	Teacher		Teacher	
Age group (years)	10				7–15	7		11–13	
Population	Non-immigrant		West-Indian		Ugandan	New Zealand		Chinese	
Sex	Boys	Girls	Boys	Girls	Both	Boys	Girls	Boys	Girls
Number	873	816	172	182	577	491	449	139	127
Behavioral disturbances									
Hyperactivity	30.5	17.9	49.5	32.4	15.0	33.0	17.4	13.7	2.4
Tics, twitches	8.3	3.6	7.0	5.5	6.7	5.5	4.9	0.7	0.0
Nailbiting	17.5	14.7	13.9	10.4	7.2	3.9	6.4	7.9	1.6
Thumbsucking	5.1	6.4	2.9	8.2	3.8	4.9	7.4	7.9	0.0
Stuttering	8.2	2.4	10.5	1.1	5.8	5.3	2.7	2.9	2.4
Aggressiveness	24.3	13.9	51.7	34.1	12.8	22.4	14.9	19.4	3.9
Depression	18.5	15.5	26.2	31.8	19.4	11.8	15.6	6.5	2.4
Anxiety	32.5	30.0	32.0	25.3	17.2	36.0	31.6	5.0	0.8
Phobias	28.5	26.1	32.0	35.7	9.9	27.5	28.3	7.2	6.3
Lying	12.5	6.3	30.2	25.3	10.1	11.8	8.7	16.6	2.4
Theft	3.4	1.7	13.4	13.2	4.4	5.3	4.2	1.4	0.8
Truancy	5.6	1.9	5.2	1.6	7.3	1.2	0.4	4.3	0.0

Source: Ekblad, 1990.

Problems with Diagnosis

Has DSM-IV done much to improve the reliability and validity of the diagnosis of childhood disorders? Unfortunately, criticisms similar to those presented by Kanner remain. Guidelines about the type of behaviors and the degree of deviation necessary to make diagnostic decisions remain vague and depend on "clinical judgment." Controversy exists over where the threshold (how many behaviors or how excessive) are needed for the diagnosis. If the diagnosis is too easy to make, problems of false-positives and potential stigmatization will occur. If the diagnosis is too difficult to make, individuals who need help will not be identified. The correct balance has been difficult to determine for many childhood disorders.

In DSM-IV, childhood disorder diagnoses involve counting the number of symptoms displayed. For example, a diagnosis of attention-deficit hyperactive disorder requires the presence of at least six of nine listed symptoms dealing with inattention ("makes careless mistakes in schoolwork or other activities," "often has difficulty sustaining attention," "often does not finish tasks," "often avoids or strongly dislikes tasks," "often forgetful in daily activities," "often loses things necessary for a task," and is "often easily distracted"); or four of six symptoms reflecting hyperactivity ("often fidgets with hands or feet," "leaves seat in classroom without permission," "inappropriate running or climbing," "often has difficulty waiting in line," "often has difficulty playing quietly"). The clinician must first decide if these behaviors are present and then if they are "excessive," "maladaptive," or "inappropriate" for the developmental level. Because most children show varying amounts of these behaviors, discrimination among normal activity, boredom, and attention deficit hyperactive disorder may be difficult. This problem is found in all the childhood disorders discussed in this section. Even mental health professionals have difficulty making this judgment. Whether a problem exists is often "in the eye of the beholder." Ratings of children's problems by parents, teachers, mental health workers, and the children themselves have also produced only low to moderate correlations (Achenbach, McConaughty & Howell, 1987).

Can "normal" children be distinguished, in terms of severity or frequency of behaviors from those with childhood disorders? This may be difficult at best. In one study, many problems were noted in a group of three-year-old children (Jenkins et al., 1984). Eight percent were "frequently difficult to manage," and up to 46 percent displayed tantrum behaviors. In most of the children, however, the problems were short-lived and depended on variables such as parent-child interaction and environmental stressors. One wonders whether these children would be diagnosed as suffering from a childhood disorder if their parents or teachers were to refer them for psychiatric treatment. The diagnostic reliability and validity of the classification of childhood disorders discussed in this chapter remain in doubt.

DISRUPTIVE BEHAVIOR DISORDERS AND ATTENTION DEFICIT HYPERACTIVE DISORDER

These disorders involve symptoms that are often socially disruptive and distressing to others (see the disorders chart on page 509). They include attention deficit hyperactive disorders (ADHD), conduct disorder, and oppositional defiant disorder. These disorders often occur together and have overlapping symptoms. Without intervention, these disorders tend to persist (Esser, Schmidt & Woerner, 1990). In a longitudinal study of "hard to manage" preschoolers from age three until school entry and to age nine, 67 percent showed clinically significant problems at age six and met the criteria for one of the disorders in this category. The children displayed problem behaviors such as inattention, overactivity, aggression, and they required supervision (Campbell & Ewing, 1990). Early identification and intervention are necessary to interrupt the negative course of these disorders. Raising a child with a disruptive behavior disorder is difficult. Parents report more negative feelings about parenting, higher stress levels, and a more negative impact on their social life than parents of normally developing children (Donenberg & Baker, 1993).

Attention Deficit Hyperactive Disorders (ADHD)

Ron, an only child, was always on the go as a toddler and preschooler. He had many accidents because of his continual climbing and risk-taking. Temper out-

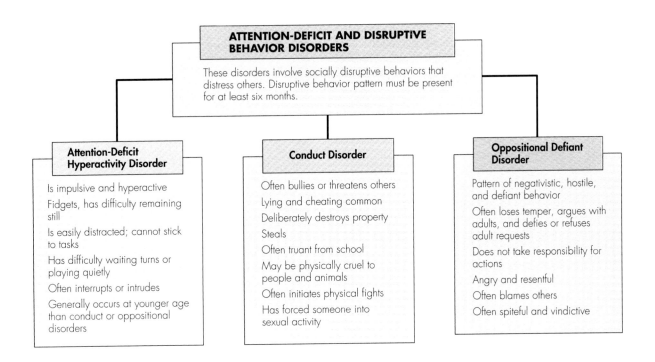

ATTENTION-DEFICIT AND DISRUPTIVE BEHAVIOR DISORDERS

These disorders involve socially disruptive behaviors that distress others. Disruptive behavior pattern must be present for at least six months.

Attention-Deficit Hyperactivity Disorder

Is impulsive and hyperactive

Fidgets, has difficulty remaining still

Is easily distracted; cannot stick to tasks

Has difficulty waiting turns or playing quietly

Often interrupts or intrudes

Generally occurs at younger age than conduct or oppositional disorders

Conduct Disorder

Often bullies or threatens others

Lying and cheating common

Deliberately destroys property

Steals

Often truant from school

May be physically cruel to people and animals

Often initiates physical fights

Has forced someone into sexual activity

Oppositional Defiant Disorder

Pattern of negativistic, hostile, and defiant behavior

Often loses temper, argues with adults, and defies or refuses adult requests

Does not take responsibility for actions

Angry and resentful

Often blames others

Often spiteful and vindictive

bursts were frequent. In kindergarten Ron had much difficulty staying seated for group work and in completing projects. The quality of his work was poor. In the first grade, Ron was referred to the school psychologist for evaluation. Although his high activity level and lack of concentration were not so pronounced in this one-on-one situation, his impulsive approach to tasks and short attention span were evident throughout the interview. Ron was referred to a local pediatrician who specializes in attention deficit disorders. The pediatrician prescribed Ritalin, which helped reduce Ron's activity level.

Two major types of **attention deficit hyperactive disorders (ADHD)** exist. One is characterized primarily by attentional problems and the other involves hyperactivity. Both of these problems may occur in the same individual. It is not clear if these types are different degrees of the same disorder or if they are unrelated disorders that should be listed separately. The most prevalent type of activity disorder is characterized by behaviors such as heightened motoric activity (fidgeting and squirming), short attention span, distractibility, impulsiveness, and lack of self-control. ADHD, often referred to as *hyperactivity,* is a confusing term because it refers to both a diagnostic category and behavioral characteristics. Children who are "overactive" or who have "short attention spans" are often referred to as "hyperactive" even though they may not meet the diagnostic criteria for this disorder (Gadow, 1986). Whether a child is merely overactive or has ADHD is often difficult to determine.

The second type of ADHD is characterized by children and adolescents who display problems such as distractibility, difficulty with sustained attention, inattention to detail, and difficulty completing tasks. Children with attentional deficits tend to have less-severe conduct problems and impulsivity than children with the hyperactive form of ADHD. Instead, they are more likely to be described as sluggish, daydreamers, anxious, and shy; they respond to lower doses of stimulants than do children with hyperactivity (Frick & Lahey, 1991). It is a much less common form of ADHD (Schachar, 1991).

A confusing aspect of attention deficit hyperactive disorders is their inconsistency. Attentional deficit or excessive motor activity are not necessarily always evident, nor are they displayed in all situations. In one study, ADHD boys showed greater motor activity during academic tasks but didn't differ from control boys during lunch, recess, and physical education activities (Porrino et al., 1983). Thus a child might be identified as hyperactive in one situation but not in others. To receive a diagnosis of ADHD, the individual must display these characteristics in two or more situations (DSM-IV). Some investigators (Luk, Lueng & Yuen, 1991; Schachar, 1991) believe that "pervasive" hyperactivity (displayed in different situations) may be a different form, a more severe type, or "true" ADHD.

ADHD is relatively common. Estimates of its prevalence range from 5 to 20 percent, with boys four times as likely to receive this diagnosis as girls (Lewinsohn et al., 1993; Shaywitz & Shaywitz, 1991). The wide range in its estimated prevalence shows the difficulty encountered in diagnosing the condition. It is a persistent disorder. Children with ADHD continue to show problems with impulsivity, family conflicts, and attention during adolescence. This is especially likely if a disruptive disorder is also present (Barkley et al., 1991). The prognosis in children with only attentional problems is more promising. Some 40 percent of the children display attentional problems at some point in their lives but in only about 5 percent does it persist (Palfney et al., 1985).

ADHD is associated with many behavioral and academic problems. Children with this disorder are more likely to need to attend special classes or schools, drop out of school, become delinquent, and have problems with the law (Lambert, 1988; Lambert et al., 1987). Hyperactive boys have fewer problems in structured situations where they are self-directed. They have more difficulty in less-structured situations or in activities demanding sustained attention. Because they tend to display coercive and critical styles, they are disliked by their peers (Buhrmester et al., 1992).

Does ADHD become less severe or disappear with age? The prognosis for this disorder is mixed. When 110 adolescent boys with ADHD were compared with 88 normal boys, researchers found that the delinquency rates for the ADHD boys ranged from 36 to 58 percent and were nineteen times higher than those for the comparison group. Relatively few of the ADHD boys became chronic offenders during their adult years, however, although most still showed

Some estimates indicate that as many as 10 percent of all elementary school children suffer from attention deficit hyperactivity disorder (ADHD). These children may show a variety of symptoms such as short attention span, impulsivity, constant activity, and lack of self-control.

symptoms such as impulsiveness, low educational achievement, poor social skills, and low self-esteem. Only a small percentage continued to have significant antisocial or psychiatric problems as adults (Hechtman & Weiss, 1983). Improvements seem to occur during the ages of sixteen to twenty-one. Those less likely to improve had a concurrent conduct disorder (Klein, 1987).

Several conclusions can be reached concerning the studies just cited. First, in most cases, ADHD does appear to persist until adolescence. Yet improvements do occur; during late adolescence, most no longer meet the criteria for the disorder. Second, the prognosis seems to depend on the presence or absence of other disruptive disorders. If conduct disorder or oppositional disorder occurs concurrently with ADHD, problems in adjustment are more likely to continue into adulthood. Third, the symptoms of ADHD seem to have the greatest impact on academic performance and peer relationships. Fourth, the prognosis for the attentional form of ADHD is relatively positive.

Etiology Many researchers believe that the symptoms of overactivity, short attention span, and impulsiveness suggest central nervous system involvement. In fact, many conditions thought to cause neurological impairment such as lead poisoning, chromosomal abnormalities, and fetal alcohol syndrome have been associated with ADHD (Hynd et al., 1991). Hynd and associates (1990) reported that compared with normal controls, children with ADHD did not show larger right frontal regions of the brain, which may indicate inadequate neurological development. The areas thought to be involved are the reticular activating system (attention), frontal lobes (voluntary control of attention), and the temporal-parietal regions (involuntary attention); (Schaughency & Hynd, 1989). Research, however, including attempts to identify brain impairment, has produced equivocal or negative findings. Part of the reason for conflicting findings is that ADHD appears to comprise several different types. Only those with pervasive hyperactivity may show neurological deficits (Luk, Lueng & Yuen, 1991; Schachar, 1991).

Some researchers believe that certain food or food additives produce physiological changes in the body or brain that result in hyperactive behaviors. This view was promoted by Feingold (1977), who developed a diet excluding these substances. Sugar is also suspected as a causal factor in ADHD (Chollar, 1988). Approximately 45 percent of physicians have recommended low-sugar diets for ADHD children (Bennett & Sherman, 1983). Many parents have tried the recommended diets on their children, and many claimed that their children's behavior improved. But parental expectations or treating the children differently (going shopping with them to buy only certain foods) might result in behavioral changes. To determine whether certain chemicals or sugars are implicated in· hyperactivity, carefully controlled double-blind studies were conducted. Some of these studies involved a "biological challenge test." In this design, the diets of the children were alternated so that some of the time they ate food with the additive and other times without. The parents were not aware of the type of food they were giving their children. Reviews of such studies showed that eliminating food additives or certain chemicals from the diets of hyperactive children had little effect on their behavior (Consensus Development Panel, 1982; Divorky, 1978; Milich & Pelham, 1986).

Family variables also seem related to ADHD, although it is not clear whether genetic or environmental factors or a combination are involved. Some evidence, including higher prevalence rates for the disorder in the first- and second-degree relatives of children with ADHD and higher concordance rates among monozygotic twins for this disorder, has supported the hypothesis of genetic transmission (Gillis et al., 1992; Knopf, 1984). Rutter and colleagues (1990) believe that a conclusion of genetic influences is premature and that environmental factors could be involved in ADHD.

Treatment Most children with ADHD have been treated with drug therapy. Stimulants in particular increase attention span and improve academic performance (Fischer & Newby, 1991; Gadow, 1991). However, only 70 percent of children with ADHD respond positively to stimulant medication; 30 percent do not show any response or become worse when taking medication. The drugs seem to treat the symptoms of ADHD rather than the causes, so that drug therapy alone does not produce any long-term benefits. Changes tend to be short-lived or only persist as long as medication continues, and only a subset of major problems is affected (Whalen & Henker, 1991). Medication has also been found to reduce prosocial behaviors in ADHD boys and did not markedly reduce aversive behaviors (Buhrmester et al., 1992). In fact, Satterfield, Hoppe, and Schell (1982) believe that using medication alone may be harmful because problems such as antisocial behavior, poor peer relationships, and learning difficulties are not addressed.

Drug therapy may tend to conceal a need for other types of therapies. Perhaps a combined approach is needed. In fact, some studies that compared medication and behavior therapy in treating ADHD have reported that combining the two treatments produced the most positive results (Carlson et al., 1992; DuPaul & Barkley, 1993). Other clinicians have suggested that both physicians and therapists should pay more attention to family dynamics and child management problems (Prior et al., 1983), rather than rely solely on pharmacological intervention. (Focus 17.2 elaborates some issues surrounding drug therapy.)

Self-instructional procedures, modeling, role playing, classroom contingency management programs,

Are We Overmedicating Children?

A large number of medications are being prescribed to treat childhood disorders. They include tranquilizers, stimulants, and antipsychotic medication. Researchers have been especially concerned regarding the use of stimulants for attention deficit hyperactivity disorder, or ADHD. Approximately 800,000 children receive Ritalin as treatment for this disorder. Opponents describe the use of medications as a "Band Aid" approach or a "chemical straitjacket" to ensure ease of management (Hutchens & Hynd, 1987).

In Georgia, a mother with an ADHD child filed suit against the Gwinnett County School District and the American Psychiatric Association. She charged that the school had insisted that her son be given Ritalin and that the medication made him suicidal and violent. The Ameican Psychiatric Association was included in the charge because the diagnosis was based on DSM-III. The mother's attorney claimed that the diagnostic criteria was too general, resulting in misidentification. In another case, involving a fifteen-year-old boy convicted of killing a classmate with a baseball bat, the defense attorney claimed that

Ritalin contributed to the boy's act. In addition, five other suits involving medical malpractice for prescribing Ritalin were filed in Massachusetts (Cowart, 1988).

Several questions are raised. Are medications such as Ritalin effective in treating the specific disorders? Are medications being prescribed too freely? Is there adequate assessment or evaluation to determine if medication is appropriate? Is there adequate monitoring of the effects of the drug and identification of possible side effects? A number of studies have indicated that stimulant medication such as Ritalin can help reduce some ADHD symptoms. However, nearly one-third of people with ADHD do not show positive results when given stimulant medication (Poling, Gadow & Cleary, 1990). Clinicians recommend that Ritalin be prescribed only after a comprehensive diagnostic and evaluation procedure. The particular symptom or symptoms to be treated should be identified and the dosage modified if necessary (Garfinkel, 1987; Shaywitz & Shaywitz, 1984). Unfortunately, a larger percentage of physicians and psychiatrists do not follow these guidelines (DuPaul, Barkley & McMurray, 1991). In the

case of the fifteen-year-old boy convicted of homicide, the pediatrician who prescribed the Ritalin was reported to have monitored the boy only through yearly physical exams.

Prescribing any medication also necessitates the communication of possible side effects and contraindications to the patient and parent. Stimulants, for example, should not be used for children with tics, glaucoma, or seizure disorders (Hutchens & Hynd, 1987). It is estimated that 15 percent of children with Tourette's syndrome (a severe tic disorder) might not have developed this disorder if stimulant medication had not been prescribed. If tics occur, the medication should be discontinued.

Medication has certainly been helpful in treating a variety of childhood disorders such as ADHD. However, medications should be employed only after carefully evaluating and monitoring their effects. Are we overmedicating our children? Barry Garfinkel, M.D., director of Child and Adolescent Psychiatry at the University of Minnesota, answers, "We just don't have a good way to judge that" (Cowart, 1988, p. 2521).

and parent training programs have been useful in dealing with the problems of ADHD and have been found as effective as drug therapy (Abramowitz & O'Leary, 1991; Whalen & Henker, 1991). In one approach, hyperactive children are trained to talk to themselves in a way that aids self-control. Here is an example of the kind of self-statements that a child learns to make, first overtly and then covertly:

Okay, what is it I have to do? You want me to copy the picture with the different lines. I have to go slowly and carefully. Okay, draw the line down, down, good; then to the right; that's it; now down some more and to the left. Good, I'm doing fine so far. Remember, go slowly. Now back up again. No, I was supposed to go down. That's okay. Just erase the line carefully. . . . Good. Even if I make an error I can go on slowly and carefully. Okay, I have to go down now. Finished, I did it! (Meichenbaum, 1974, p. 266)

Oppositional Defiant Disorder

Oppositional defiant disorder (ODD) is characterized by a negativistic, argumentative, and hostile behavior pattern. The child often loses his or her temper, defies rules, refuses to do chores, and blames others for his or her mistakes. The defiant behavior is primarily directed toward parents, teachers, and other people in authority. Although confrontation often occurs, it does not involve the more serious violations of the rights of others that are involved in conduct disorders (American Psychiatric Association, 1993).

Oppositional defiant disorder is a relatively new category and is certainly one of the more controversial childhood disorders. It is often difficult to separate this disorder from milder forms of conduct disorder and from normal developmental difficulties in children and adolescents. Most children and adolescents go through a period or several periods of defiant behaviors. ODD is not recognized or described as a separate disorder in the mental disorders section of the International Classification of Diseases, Tenth Revision (ICD-10), a classification system used by many other countries.

The symptoms of ODD can be found in several different childhood disorders. One study of preadolescent schoolchildren found that 15.8 percent met the criteria for oppositional defiant disorder (Pfeff et al., 1987). This percentage in a normal population seems high and may reflect the fact that many children and adolescents show some signs of oppositional defiant disorder. In DSM-IV, a criterion indicating that the problem causes "significant impairment in social or academic functioning" was added to try to discriminate between "normal" and "pathological" defiance. ODD is associated with parent-child conflict, the espousing of unreasonable beliefs, and negative family interactions (Barkley et al., 1992). Because DSM-IV has attempted to raise the threshold for the diagnosis of ODD, it is not clear how this will affect conclusions of studies using a lower threshold.

Conduct Disorders

Charles was well known to school officials for his many fights with peers. After a stabbing incident at

Conduct disorders, such as fighting, stealing, and assault, represent a serious societal problem. Estimates indicate that as many as 10 percent of adolescents (more males than females) have these disorders.

school, he was put on probation and then transferred to another junior high school. Two months later, at age fourteen, Charles was charged with armed robbery and placed in a juvenile detention facility. He had few positive peer contacts at the juvenile facility and seemed unwilling or unable to form close relationships. Some progress was achieved with a behavioral contract program that involved positive reinforcement from adults and praise for refraining from aggression in handling conflicts. He was transferred to a maximum-security juvenile facility when he seriously injured two of his peers, whose teasing had angered him. Charles completed a vocational training program in this second facility, but he couldn't hold a regular job. He was sent to prison following a conviction for armed robbery.

Conduct disorders involve a persistent pattern of antisocial behaviors that violate the rights of others. Many children and adolescents display isolated instances of antisocial behavior, but this diagnosis is only given when the behavior is repetitive and persistent. Conduct disorders include behaviors such as fighting, temper tantrums, stealing, lying, fire setting, assaults, rape, and truant behavior. The pattern of misconduct must last for at least six months for this diagnosis (DSM-IV). The prevalence of conduct disorders is estimated to range from 3 to 10 percent of children and adolescents and is four to five times more prevalent in males than in females (Kazdin, 1987; Lewinsohn et al., 1993).

Three subtypes of conduct disorders were recognized in DSM-III-R (group, solitary aggressive, and undifferentiated). This was done to attempt to form homogeneous groupings that had similar etiology and prognosis. Further research, however, did not support these divisions. Instead it was believed that subtyping according to the age of onset might be more valuable. In DSM-IV, the two types of conduct disorder are (1) childhood onset type (at least one conduct problem occurs before age ten) and (2) adolescent onset type (conduct problem occurs after age ten).

Conduct disorders in adolescence represent a serious societal problem. In the United States, approximately 83,000 juveniles are housed in correctional institutions for antisocial behaviors, and 1.75 million were arrested in 1990 (Zigler, Taussig & Black, 1992). Parents often report the following pattern in the development of the disorder: early argument, stubbornness, and tantrums, oppositional behaviors leading to fire setting and stealing and then truancy, vandalism, and substance abuse (Robins, 1991). Oppositional defiant disorder often precedes the development of conduct disorders and often exists concurrently with ADHD. Although many childhood disorders remit over time, children are unlikely to outgrow conduct disorders. Of concern is the increase in violence among young people. Homicide is the second leading cause of death among children and adolescents. Black males between the ages of fourteen and nineteen are especially at risk. They are ten times more likely to die of homicide than white males of the same age (Hammond & Yung, 1993).

Prognosis is poor; conduct disorders often lead to criminal behavior, antisocial personality, and problems in marital and occupational adjustment during adulthood (Kazdin, Siegel & Bass, 1992). A large percentage of offending delinquent adolescents later become adult criminals. Nearly all adult offenders have a history of repeated antisocial behavior as children, and about 25 percent develop an antisocial personality disorder (Robins, 1991). The key factor associated with negative outcome is aggression.

Highly aggressive children tend to remain aggressive over time, whereas other childhood adjustment problems show much less stability (Lerner et al., 1988). A particularly negative sign is sexually aggressive behaviors. Individuals who engage in sexual assaults are more likely to show subsequent violence (both sexual and nonsexual) than individuals who commit nonsexual violence (Rubenstein et al., 1993). People with higher IQ scores (Kandel et al., 1988) and females (Roff & Wirt, 1984) have a better prognosis.

Etiology *Psychoanalytic* Psychoanalysts interpret antisocial and delinquent behaviors in children as symptoms of an underlying anxiety conflict in the child. This conflict results from an inadequate relationship with the parents; the problem behaviors can be produced by either emotional deprivation or overindulgence. In the first case, the parents offer the child little affection or concern, so childhood conflicts are not resolved and the superego does not develop adequately. The lack of a strong conscience increases the likelihood of aggressive and antisocial behaviors. The child becomes unable to form close personal relationships with others.

Genetic Genetic factors may also be involved. Although boys with conduct disorders have a higher than predicted number of antisocial parents (Hinshaw, 1987), this could be the result of either genetic or social factors. Mednick (1985) tried to isolate influences by comparing the adult criminal records of children adopted early in life and the records of their biological and adoptive parents (sample comprised 14,427 adopted children). If genetic factors are important, the biological parents would have the greatest influence on subsequent criminal behavior on the adoptees. If environmental influences are the most important, the records of adoptive parents should have the greatest impact. As Table 17.2 shows, adopted sons whose biological parents have criminal records are more likely to also have criminal records. These results support the view of a genetic predisposition in criminality. However, social factors were also important. Children born to parents of low socioeconomic status had the highest rates of criminality no matter what type of adoptive family they lived with. More convictions were also found among children adopted into lower- versus higher-class families. As Mednick observed, "Regardless of genetic background, improved social conditions seem to reduce

Table 17.2

Effect of Parental Criminal Records on Adopted Sons

Parents with Criminal Records		Sons with Criminal Records (Percent)
Biological Parents	**Adoptive Parents**	
No criminal record	No criminal record	13.5
No criminal record	Criminal record	14.7
Criminal record	No criminal record	20
Criminal record	Criminal record	24.5

Source: Adapted from Mednick, 1985.

criminality" (1985, p. 60). But Rutter and colleagues (1990) cautioned that these studies are based on criminal acts and not on a diagnosis of conduct disorder. Very little is actually known about genetic influences for conduct disorder.

Behavioral Patterson (1986) believes that antisocial behaviors are the result of the parents' failure to effectively punish misbehavior. In his work with families of conduct-disordered children, he noticed that when a parent requested something from or criticized the child, the child would counterattack. This would result in the parents' withdrawal from the conflict. The child's failure to learn to respect authority generalizes to the school setting, resulting in academic failure and poor peer relations. Patterson concluded that the specific factors that contribute to the development of antisocial behaviors include (1) a lack of parental monitoring (increases in unsupervised street time were associated with increased rates of antisocial behaviors), (2) inconsistent disciplinary practices, (3) failure to use positive management techniques or to teach social process skills, and (4) failure to teach the skills necessary for academic success (listening, compliance, following directions, and so on). Although Patterson focused primarily on the learning aspects in the etiology of conduct disorders, he also supported the view that predisposing factors such as difficult child temperament may increase the need for parents to learn and consistently apply appropriate management skills.

Treatment Although conduct disorders and group delinquency have resisted traditional forms of psy-

chotherapy, social skills and cognitive training appears promising. One program (Kolko, Loar & Sturnick, 1990), for example, focused on helping aggressive boys develop verbal skills to enter groups, play cooperatively, and provide reinforcement for peers. The cognitive element included using problem-solving skills to identify behavior problems, generate solutions to them, and select alternative behaviors. In addition, the children learned positive social skills through viewing videotapes and role playing with therapists and peers. Role playing was continued until mastery was achieved. Each child would practice the skill learned in the classroom. Participants reported fewer feelings of loneliness, lower amounts of problem behaviors, and greater social competence. In a one-year follow-up, children involved in the program still engaged in more appropriate social behaviors than before treatment.

Even greater success has been found with parent management training (Patterson, 1986; Webster-Stratton, 1991). In these programs, specific skills are taught so that the parents learn how to appropriately establish rules for the child, implement consequences, and reward positive behaviors. The parents first practice their newly learned skills on simple problems and gradually work on the more difficult problems as they become more proficient in management techniques. Patterson's program has evolved over a period of twenty years of work with problem children. Success has been reported, and treatment changes have been maintained even for periods as long as four years after treatment (Kazdin, 1987). The combination of both cognitive social skills and parent management training appears to produce the most marked and durable changes in conduct disordered children (Kazdin, Siegel & Bass, 1992).

ANXIETY DISORDERS: SEPARATION ANXIETY DISORDER

Children and adolescents suffer from a variety of problems involving chronic anxiety—fears, nightmares, school phobia, shyness, timidity, and lack of self-confidence. Children with these disturbances display exaggerated autonomic responses and are apprehensive in new situations, preferring to stay at home or in other familiar environments. As opposed to the disruptive behavior disorders, which are socially disruptive and undercontrolled, the anxiety disorders are considered to be internalizing or overcontrolled. Higher distress scores are obtained from those with internalizing as opposed to externalizing disorders (McGee & Stanton, 1992).

The prognosis or course of internalizing disorders, even without treatment, is very promising (Esser, Schmidt & Woerner, 1990). The childhood disorders in which anxiety plays a prominent role include separation anxiety disorder, avoidant disor-

der of childhood and adolescence, and overanxious disorder. In DSM-IV, only separation anxiety disorder remains. Children or adolescents with avoidance disorder are now diagnosed with social phobia; overanxious disorder is now diagnosed as generalized anxiety disorder. Some researchers believe that specific personality patterns may predispose a child toward developing anxiety and other childhood disorders (see Focus 17.3).

Children who suffer from a **separation anxiety disorder** (SAD) show excessive anxiety when separated from parents or home. They constantly seek their parents' company and may worry too much about losing them. Separation may produce physical symptoms such as vomiting, diarrhea, and headaches. During separation, the child will often express negative emotions such as crying (Shouldice & Stevenson-Hinde, 1992). To receive a diagnosis of separation anxiety disorder, the child must display at least three of the following symptoms:

1. Excessive anxiety about separation from attachment figure.
2. Unrealistic fear that attachment figures will be harmed.
3. Reluctance to attend school.

Children with social phobia become extremely anxious in situations involving contact with peers or strangers and withdraw from these interactions. These children are very sensitive to rejection and criticism and have a difficult time forming friendships.

The Relationship Between Personality and Behavior: The Temperament-Environment Fit Model

For many childhood disorders, there is increasing interest in the temperament-environment fit model. Research continues to support the view that temperament is an important factor in adjustment. In a longitudinal study conducted by Chess and Thomas (1984), about 10 percent of the children studied showed a negative reaction to new situations and were emotionally reactive. These "difficult" children showed greater adjustment difficulties later in life. Tendencies toward "shyness" also appear early in development. Kagan (1987) found that some children showed behavioral inhibitions such as being cautious around strangers. In addition, they had high heart rates in response to mild mental stress. These early reactions persisted. Other differences in temperament may include characteristics such as depressive mood and need for stimulation. The child's temperament may predispose that individual to develop a specific disorder. For

example, a child with behavioral inhibition may develop an anxiety disorder, or a "difficult" child may develop a disruptive behavior. Three-year-old children identified as "hard to manage" were likely to display problems involving hyperactivity, defiance, or aggression at age nine (Campbell & Ewing, 1990). Whether a child develops a problem, however, also depends on environmental factors and parental skills. If parents are inexperienced, cannot adjust to the child's temperament, have personal difficulties and stresses that influence their parenting skills, or are inconsistent with the child, the chances of problem behaviors occurring greatly increase (Carey, 1986; Chess, 1986).

Temperament and the environment can affect one another. Difficult infants elicit more confrontation and conflict with their mothers (Lee & Bates, 1985). Environmental changes can also affect the child's temperament. Kagan (1987)

reported that 40 percent of the "inhibited" children became more outgoing. This change was associated with parental encouragement for the child to approach stressful situations.

What are the implications of the temperament-environment fit model? First, more research will be directed toward (1) individual differences in temperament, (2) the neurobiological bases for these differences, and (3) the interaction between temperament and environment. This would allow children who are at risk for developing a disorder and the type of disorder that they are most likely to develop to be identified. Psychotherapeutic interventions and parenting style may have to be altered to "fit" the child's temperament. For example, approaches that might be effective with a difficult child (being firm and consistent) may be inappropriate with an "inhibited" child.

---

4. Persistent refusal to go to sleep unless attachment figure is nearby.
5. Persistent avoidance of being alone.
6. Nightmares involving themes of separation.
7. Repeated physical complaints when separated.
8. Excessive distress when separation anticipated.

This pattern must last at least four weeks and occur before the age of eighteen (DSM-IV) to be diagnosed as a disorder. Children with this disorder tend to come from caring and close-knit families. During adolescence, the most frequent symptoms involve physi-

cal complaints on school days (Francis, Last & Strauss, 1987).

One type of separation anxiety disorder that has been studied extensively is *school phobia*. The physical symptoms may occur merely at the prospect of having to go to school. About 6 percent of females and 2.5 percent of males indicated having had this disorder sometime in their life (Lewinsohn et al., 1993). School refusal is common among children referred for treatment. It occurs more frequently in European-American children than African-American children and is more common in children from lower socioeconomic backgrounds (Last & Perrin, 1993).

Darcy's school phobias were first manifested while riding in the car with her mother on the second day of school. She began to cry and hold on to her mother, scream hysterically, and plead not to be taken to school. Once at school, Darcy screamed and kicked to avoid being taken into the building, and then to her classroom. Darcy's mother sat with the child in class and attempted to reassure her that school was pleasant and enjoyable. When the mother got up to leave the room, Darcy immediately began to cry, scream, and grab her mother's arm to prevent her from returning home. (Kolko, Ayllon & Torrence, 1987, p. 251)

Psychoanalytic explanations of school phobia stress the overdependence of the child on the mother. The reluctance to attend school is not seen as a fear of school but as anxiety over separation from the mother. If separation anxiety is the primary etiological factor in this disorder, however, it should occur in the early school history of the child. But many cases of school phobia do not develop until the third or fourth grade. Also, these children often do not display "separation anxiety" in other situations that require separation from their mothers.

School phobia has also been explained in terms of learning principles. Parents are important sources of reinforcement during a child's preschool period. Going to school requires that a child develop new skills and encounters with uncertain and anxiety-arousing situations. If a parent reinforces these fears (for example, by continually warning the child not to get lost), the child may seek refuge away from school, where the kind of reinforcement he or she received earlier in life is available.

For young children treated with most forms of psychotherapy, the prognosis for separation anxiety disorder is very good. But separation anxiety that develops during adolescence may be more resistant to change.

CHILDHOOD DEPRESSION

David had a history of depressive reactions to unpleasant events since infancy, which had become increasingly severe. Two events seemed to have produced affective pain and to have triggered the depressive acting out which led to his referral: one was a cerebral stroke suffered by his maternal grandmother with

Childhood depression can begin in infancy, although it is more common in children and adolescents. Symptoms include feelings of sadness, loss of appetite, sleep difficulties, and fatigue and are reported more by females than males.

whom he was very close, and the second was learning of his mother's fourth pregnancy. . . . His parents described him as fearful, socially isolated, and as making self-deprecating statements. His behavior at the time of referral was passive, quiet, and motorically slow, punctuated with occasional hostile outbursts. Suicidal ideation surfaced for several months—twice during the course of therapy (O'Connor, 1987, p. 106).

The five-year-old boy just described displays many symptoms of depression. Although DSM-IV does not list childhood depression in the childhood disorders (it would be diagnosed as a mood disorder), major depressive episodes can begin very early in life, even in infancy. Estimates of childhood depression range from 27 to 52 percent in clinical populations (Winnett et al., 1987). During a five-year longitudinal study of third-grade children, the percentage of children who scored at a "serious" level of depression ranged from 4.9 percent to 11.3 percent. Children who were depressed during the first year of the study tended to also be depressed throughout the five-year period. Correlated with depressive scores were stressful life events, high levels of helplessness in social and academic situations, and a more pessimistic explanatory style (Nolen-Hoeksema, Girgus & Seligman, 1992). Depression is also reported in adolescents, with girls reporting more depressive symptoms than boys (Weiss et al., 1992).

In a sample of 1000 preschool children who were referred to a child development center, only 0.9 percent evidenced a major depression. Symptoms of depression expressed by this group involved feelings of sadness, loss of appetite, sleep difficulties, fatigue, and other somatic complaints. Kashani and Carlson (1987) believe that a pattern of frequent somatic complaints may indicate depression in preschoolers. Environmental factors were also important. All children who were depressed had been abused or seriously neglected, as compared to 22 percent of control children. Depressed children were also more likely to live in a broken home (100 percent versus 33 percent).

Depressed mood is more prevalent during adolescence. Moderate to intense depressive symptoms were reported in 10 percent of adolescent boys and 40 percent of adolescent girls. Clinical depression is found in about 42 percent of psychiatric samples of adolescents and about 7 percent in nonclinical samples (Petersen et al., 1993).

Clearly, depression does occur in childhood and adolescence. Children are especially vulnerable to environmental factors because they lack the maturity and skills to deal with various stresses. Conditions such as poor or inconsistent parenting, parental illness, loss of an attachment figure, and neglect or abuse often produce lowered self-esteem and increased vulnerability to depression. Depressed children show many of the same characteristics as do depressed adults. They have more negative self-concepts and are more likely to engage in self-blame and self-criticism (Jaenicke et al., 1987). Programs involving social skills training, cognitive behavioral therapy (Winnett et al., 1987), and supportive therapy (O'Connor, 1987) have been effective in treating childhood depression.

TIC DISORDERS

Saul Lubaroff, a disc jockey in Iowa City, is able to deliver smooth news reports on the weather, news, and sports. However, whenever he turns off his microphone, an explosive, involuntary stream of obscenities follow. In high school, his classmates would mock and threaten him. Even today, his outbursts are highly embarrassing to him. He has shouted "HEY" and "I MASTURBATE" in a fancy restaurant. However, Saul does have control while he is on the air. He indicates that "I have no problem announcing. I can turn off my 'noises' for 20 to 25 seconds, sometimes up to two minutes." (Dutton, 1986, p. c1)

Saul Lubaroff has a chronic tic disorder. **Tics** are involuntary, repetitive, and nonrhythmic movements or vocalizations. Transient and chronic tic disorders and Tourette's syndrome comprise this group of disorders. Most individuals with tic disorders report bodily sensations or urges that precede the tic (Leckman, Walker & Cohen, 1993).

Most tics in children are *transient* and disappear without treatment. If a tic lasts longer than one year, it is diagnosed as a **chronic tic disorder.** Chronic tic disorders may persist into and through adulthood. According to DSM-IV, a diagnosis of Tourette's syndrome requires that "both multiple motor and one or more vocal tics have been present at some time during the illness, although not necessarily concurrently" (American Psychiatric Association, 1993, p. 80).

The most common tics are eye blinking and jerking movements of the face and head, although sometimes the extremities and larger muscle groups may be involved. In tic disorders, the movements, which are normally under voluntary control, occur automatically and involuntarily. Examples of tics reported in the literature include eye blinking, facial grimacing, throat clearing, head jerking, hiccoughing, foot tapping, flaring of the nostrils, flexing of the elbows and fingers, and contractions of the shoulders or abdominal muscles. Vocal tics can range from coughing, grunting, and sniffing to repeating words.

Approximately 15 to 23 percent of children have single, transient tics; their occurrence usually peaks at age seven. Diagnoses of tic disorders can only be made in retrospect because there is no way of determining if a tic will disappear or develop into a chronic tic disorder or Tourette's syndrome (Gadow, 1986; Golden, 1987).

Tourette's Syndrome

P. first exhibited features of GTS [Gilles de la Tourette's Syndrome] at the age of six years when she started to twitch her nose. She went on to develop a variety of motor and vocal tics as well as echolalia. Diagnosis of GTS was made when she was twelve, at which time it was noted that the tics could be triggered by coughing and sniffing. When she heard these noises she would experience an irresistible urge to tic. (Commander, Prendergast & Ridley, 1991, p. 877)

Tourette's syndrome usually begins in childhood, between the ages of two and thirteen. This puzzling disorder is characterized by facial and body tics, which increase in frequency and intensity as the person grows older, and by grunting and barking sounds that generally develop into explosive *coprolalia*, the compulsion to shout obscenities. Stress may increase the severity of these symptoms (Bornstein, King & Carroll, 1983). It occurs three to six times more frequently in males than in females.

Researchers have not yet determined whether Tourette's syndrome differs from the tic disorders. However, studies seem to have suggested that the two are quite similar. For example, Corbett (1971) studied data on groups of children and adults suffering from single or multiple tics, tics with vocalizations, and tics with coprolalia (Tourette's syndrome). These three groups displayed no significant differences in IQ scores, psychiatric symptoms, or EEG readings. The prognosis was more favorable for those with single or multiple tics (94 percent improved) than for those with Tourette's syndrome (approximately 60 percent improved). Corbett concluded that the different tic disorders may be different stages of the same syndrome.

Etiology and Treatment

Anxiety and stress seem to be primary factors in producing, maintaining, and exacerbating tic disorders. In the psychodynamic view, tics represent underlying aggressive or sexual conflicts. For example, eye blinking may represent attempts to block out thoughts of the "primal scene" (intercourse between the child's parents) or other anxiety-evoking stimuli. Although tics do appear early in life, when the fixation of sexual or aggressive impulses is most likely to occur, little support has been found for this explanation.

According to the learning theorists, tics are conditioned avoidance responses initially evoked by stress.

These responses become habit through reinforcement when they reduce anxiety. The therapeutic technique of negative practice or massed practice is based on this viewpoint. The technique requires that the person perform the tic intentionally, over and over again. This forced practice of the behavior produces fatigue, which inhibits the response. The tic gradually acquires aversive properties, so not performing the tic becomes reinforcing.

Only limited success was reported by researchers who used massed practice and relaxation training to treat three people with Tourette's syndrome (Turpin & Powell, 1984). The patients were required to reproduce their tics as frequently as possible for five minutes; they were also taught to relax on cue. The massed practice didn't reduce tic frequency at all, and the cue-controlled relaxation resulted in only a moderate decrease in one tic in one patient.

Both multiple tics and Tourette's syndrome appear to be transmitted in families. If a parent has a tic disorder, there is an increased risk for the children to also have the disorder (Rutter et al., 1991). This relationship may be due to either genetic or environmental factors—or perhaps to both. Some also believe that tic disorders are related genetically to obsessive-compulsive disorder (George et al., 1993; Leonard et al., 1992). Other researchers, however, have not found a relationship between these disorders (Black et al., 1992).

Interestingly, as many as 50 percent of children with Tourette's syndrome also meet the criteria for ADHD, which might reflect a genetic link between the two disorders (Golden, 1987). Treating ADHD with stimulants may precipitate Tourette's syndrome: it should not be done if a familial history of tic disorder is present and should be discontinued if tics appear in the patient (Gadow, 1991).

Several investigators believe that Tourette's syndrome may stem from an impairment of the central nervous system (Bauer & Shea, 1984). Reported therapeutic success with the drug haloperidol has supported this view (Gadow, 1991). However, there have also been reports that drug treatment has had unfavorable results (Bauer & Shea, 1984). In addition, haloperidol results in some negative side effects in children and could lead to motor dysfunctions such as tardive dyskinesia.

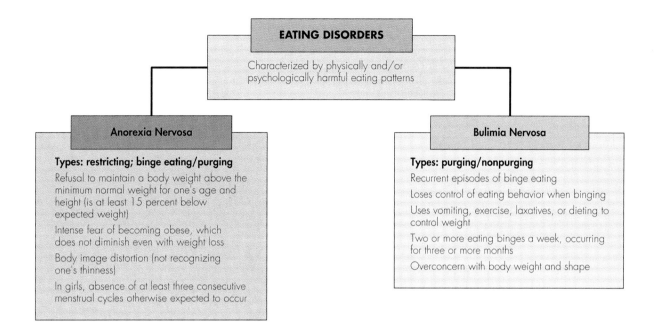

EATING DISORDERS

Eating problems are becoming more prevalent in the United States, especially among younger people. It is estimated that 35 percent of women engage in binge eating, 8 percent attempt to control their weight through self-induced vomiting, and nearly 6 percent abuse laxatives (Kendler et al., 1991). Eating problems may be a result of both the availability of many attractive high-calorie foods and the American pursuit of thinness. Preoccupation with weight and body dimensions may become so extreme that it develops into one of the eating disorders—anorexia nervosa or bulimia (see the disorders chart for anorexia nervosa and bulimia nervosa above).

There is often a confusion between eating behaviors and an eating disorder. For example, binge eating occurs in a large number of individuals but in itself is not enough for a diagnosis of bulimia. Only when all the criteria are met does it meet the criteria for an eating disorder. A change in eating disorders from DSM-III-R is that anorexia nervosa in DSM-IV is subtyped to include a binge eating/purging type

and a restricting type. This is to acknowledge the finding that anorexia can be a result of strict dieting or purging.

Anorexia Nervosa

The patient was a 25-year-old woman who had a diagnosis of anorexia nervosa since she was 12 years old. She came in for therapy because of complaints of "having her whole life revolve around her eating symptoms." Her highest weight has been 110 pounds and her lowest, 56 pounds. To control her weight, she uses laxatives, exercises excessively, and induces vomiting. Her prognosis is "extremely guarded." (Baker & Webb, 1987)

Although anorexia has been known for more than one hundred years, it is receiving increased attention, owing to greater public knowledge of the disorder and the apparent increase in its incidence. The disorder occurs primarily in adolescent girls and young women, and only rarely in males. Estimates of its prevalence range from 0.4 to 0.7 percent of the female population (Lewinsohn et al., 1993; Pope, Hudson & Yurgelun-Todd, 1984). One disturbing finding is an increase in early onset (between ages of eight and thirteen) anorexia in girls (Lask & Bryant-Waugh, 1992). The causes for this condition are similar to those in women and include the pursuit of thinness, preoccupation with body weight and shape, disparagement of body shape, low self-esteem, and perfectionism.

Anorexia nervosa is a bizarre and puzzling disorder. A person with the disorder is intensely afraid of becoming fat and literally engages in self-starvation. Even when skeletal in appearance, such patients deny the seriousness of their physical condition. As Bruch (1978, p. 209) noted, anorexics "vigorously defend their often gruesome emaciation as not being too thin . . . they identify with the skeleton-like appearance, actively maintain it, and deny its abnormality." The inability to objectively assess one's physical condition is characteristic of this disorder. Because they believe that they are overweight, anorexic patients deny that their weight loss is a problem. Their concern about weight is reflected in frequent thoughts such as "I'm getting fatter and fatter" (Cooper & Fairburn, 1992). Some controversy exists over whether a disturbance in body image perception is necessary for the diagnosis. Although about 75 percent of anorexics did show a distorted body image, the remainder did not (Horne, Van Vactor & Emerson, 1991).

Self-starvation produces a variety of physical complications along with weight loss. Anorexic patients often exhibit cardiac arrhythmias because of electrolyte imbalance; about 80 percent display bradycardia and hypotension (low blood pressure). Heart rates as low as 25 beats per minute have been reported (Zwaan & Mitchell, 1993). In addition, the heart muscle is often damaged and weakened because the body may use it as a source of protein during starvation. One result of such complications is a mortality rate of approximately 5 percent (American Psychiatric Association, 1993).

There are two subgroups of patients with anorexia. Of 105 patients hospitalized with this disorder, 53 percent had lost weight through constant fasting (*restricting type*); the remainder had periodically resorted to binge eating by purging or vomiting (*binge eating/purging type*). Although both groups displayed a vigorous pursuit of thinness, some differ-

Anorexia nervosa is a devastating eating disorder that involves self-starvation. It is most prevalent in adolescent and young adult women. Approximately 5 percent of anorexics die from the disorder.

ences were found. The restricting anorexics were more introverted and tended to deny that they suffered hunger and psychological distress. The binge/purging type were more extroverted; reported more anxiety, depression, and guilt; admitted more frequently to having a strong appetite; and tended to be older.

Bulimia Nervosa

The 22-year-old single female had uncontrollable binge eating episodes for 7 years. She made herself vomit after binging. Binge eating episodes were followed by strict dieting during which she would only eat "healthy" foods such as fruits. She showed excessive preoccupation with weight and appearance. Specific foods were chosen for the binge and included ice cream, chocolate candy, cookies, shortbread, licorice, bananas, milk, diet 7-up, and tea. She would dress in comfortable clothing, arrange the food on a tray, and eat while reading. The food was consumed in about fifteen minutes. (Jansen et al., 1989)

Sandy, a singer-actress who appeared in Broadway musicals such as *Grease* and *Nine*, would secretly gorge herself with enormous amounts of food and then stick her fingers down her throat to induce vomiting. She describes a typical dinner as composed of one large pizza, spaghetti and meat sauce, two veal parmesan sandwiches, two pecan pies, and one cherry pie. Her late night "snack" included a club sandwich, two grilled cheese sandwiches with bacon, an order of onion rings and french fries, three cartons of milk, two root beers and one glazed donut. (Bartlett, 1984)

Bulimia nervosa is an eating disorder characterized by binge eating (the rapid consumption of large quantities of food) at least twice a week for three months. The patient senses a loss of control over eating and uses inappropriate means to control weight such as vomiting, taking laxatives, and exercising to excess. Eating episodes may be stopped when abdominal pain develops or by self-induced vomiting. Frequent weight fluctuations of more than 10 pounds often are caused by alternating binges and fasts. A persistent overconcern with body image and weight also characterizes this disorder.

Bulimic subjects overestimate their body size (Williamson, Cubic & Gleaves, 1993) and are afraid to gain weight. When asked to imagine gaining five pounds, a group of bulimic subjects showed pronounced motoric, heart rate, and muscle tension changes (Cutts & Barrios, 1986). Compared with nonbulimic women at similar weight levels, bulimic women exhibited greater psychopathology, more external locus of control, lower self-esteem, and a lower sense of personal effectiveness on questionnaires (Shisslak, Pazda & Crago, 1990).

Bulimic people realize that their eating patterns are not normal and are frustrated by that fact. They become disgusted and ashamed of their eating and hide it from others. Some don't eat during the day but lose control and binge in late afternoon or evening. The loss of self-control over eating is typical of bulimics (Cooper & Fairburn, 1992). Weight is controlled through vomiting or the use of laxatives. The vomiting, or purging, produces feelings of relief and, often, a commitment to a severely restrictive diet—one that ultimately fails.

Bulimia is much more prevalent than anorexia, although prevalence estimates depend on the sample being described. These estimates range from 2 to 4 percent of the general population (Kendler et al., 1991). An additional 10 percent of women reported some symptoms but didn't meet all the criteria for the diagnosis (Drewnowski, Yee & Krahn, 1988). Few males exhibit the disorder, presumably because there is less cultural pressure for them to remain thin.

A person's weight seems to have little to do with whether he or she develops bulimia. Of a sample of forty women with the disorder, twenty-five were of normal weight, two were overweight, one was obese, and twelve were underweight. The average number of bingeing episodes for these women was twelve per week, and the estimated number of calories consumed in a binge could be as high as 11,500. Typical binge foods included ice cream, candy, bread or toast, and donuts.

A variety of measures are used to control the weight gain accompanying binge eating. These include fasting, self-induced vomiting, diet pills, laxatives, and exercise (Kendler et al., 1991). Side effects and complications occur in bulimics because of self-induced vomiting or the excessive use of laxatives. The effects of vomiting include swollen parotid glands, which produces a puffy facial appearance. Vomited stomach acid can erode tooth enamel. Possible gastrointestinal disturbances include esophagitis (inflammation of esophagus) and gastric and rectal irritation. Vomiting also results in a loss of potassium, which can weaken the heart and cause arrhythmia and cardiac arrest.

Some evidence has shown that bulimics eat not only out of hunger but also as an emotionally soothing response to distressing thoughts or stress. Women with this disorder have a negative self-image, feelings of inadequacy, dissatisfaction with their bodies, and

Is Our Society Creating Eating Disorders?

There appears to be a dramatic increase in eating disorders during the last twenty years, which is correlated with our society's emphasis on thinness and attractiveness. We spent close to $30 billion in the 1980s on diet foods, programs, and books. Liposuction is the leading cosmetic surgical procedure (Brownell, 1991). Equating thinness with success and attractiveness has taken a toll, however, especially among women. As many as 64 percent of college women exhibit symptoms of eating disorders and even more are dissatisfied with their body shape (Mintz & Betz, 1988).

What role has society played in eating disorders and why do they appear primarily in western societies?

Eating disorders are rare in China, Singapore, Malaysia, and Hong Kong (Lee, Hsu & Wing, 1992) and other nonwestern cultures (Bhadrinath, 1990). Root (1990) believes that thinness represents success and control in western societies. Other societies do not place such emphasis on thinness. Is it possible that eating disorders are culture-bound syndromes and are attempts by women to resolve identity issues?

As psychologists, we are interested in the etiology or causes of problems. What do you think about the position that the "pursuit of thinness" is a culture-bound phenomenon? Do contemporary women gain status or identity through their physical appear-

ance? Why have western cultures been so susceptible to eating disorders and do you foresee this problem increasing in the future in other societies? The women's movement was one that stressed the importance of ability over appearance. Why, with the greater freedom and power that women have gained, is there an increase in the importance of appearance? We are also beginning to see more physically attractive men in the mass media. Will this cause a dramatic increase in eating disorders in men? If society continues to equate desirable characteristics with thinness, how can we change its message? How did this standard arise in the first place?

a tendency to perceive events as more stressful than most people would (Vanderlinden, Norre & Vandereycken, 1992). Stress and emotional difficulties may lead them to consume food for gratification. Sandy, the bulimic actress-singer, reported, "I would stuff down my feelings with the food. . . . I used the food as a catalyst to flush my feelings down the toilet and watch them go away. It was numbing" (Bartlett, 1984, p. 1). We should note that these characteristics of diagnosed bulimics may be a result of their loss of control over eating patterns, however, rather than causes of the disorder.

Etiology of Eating Disorders

Both social and psychological factors are probably important in the etiology of eating disorders. Yager, Landsverk, and Edelstein (1987) believe that the

eating disorders result from the sociocultural demand for thinness in females, which produces a preoccupation with weight. Some believe that eating disorders are a culture-bound syndrome that is only found in western cultures (see Critical Thinking). Society's increasing emphasis on thinness over the last twenty years is related to the increasing incidence of eating disorders (Ruderman & Besbeas, 1992).

We will first discuss evidence for preoccupation over weight in females and then the social or psychological factors. One question researchers have looked at is whether body dissatisfaction is pathognomonic (specific or distinctive) to eating disorders. The answer appears to be no. Young women without eating disorders display a high degree of body dissatisfaction that is "striking and disturbing" (Klemchuk, Hutchinson & Frank, 1990). Many women have a distorted body image. They overestimate the size of their waist, thighs, and hips to a much greater extent than men do (Thompson, 1986). They see themselves as heavier than they are and have as an ideal body image a picture of a much thinner woman. A study of more than 2000 women found that they wanted to weigh about 9 pounds less than their current weight (Drewnowski, Yee & Krahn, 1988). Most men seem to equate their current body shape with their ideal shape (Fallon & Rozin, 1985).

A preoccupation with thinness appears to develop by early adolescence. A study of 288 girls between the ages of ten and fifteen found that girls wanted thinner bodies than they thought boys found attractive. They did not consider themselves overweight, however, and displayed less body dissatisfaction than older women (Cohn et al., 1987).

Women in their twenties have a much higher standard of thinness than girls do. This might indicate that a need to be increasingly thin begins to develop in adolescence and becomes deeply ingrained when the young woman reaches full adulthood. Especially intriguing is the finding by Cohn and colleagues (1987) that adolescent girls were aware that their "ideal" body shape was thinner than the body shape they thought boys found attractive.

Variables other than being attractive to men must be involved. An independent standard of thinness might be one factor. Some support for this view was found by Silverstein and Perdue (1988). They found that women equated thinness with attractiveness. In addition, being slim was also associated with professional success and intelligence.

Although preoccupation with weight and evidence of a distorted body image appear in most women, other factors must also be involved because only a small percentage of women develop eating disorders. Females with eating disorders appear to suffer from poor self-esteem (Mallick, Whipple & Huerta, 1987). Bulimics and repeating dieters also believe that they have little control over environmental factors (Dyken & Gerrard, 1986). Immaturity, passive-aggression, and a self-defeating behavior pattern were found in patients with anorexia nervosa and bulimia nervosa. They tended to displace their emotional conflicts onto somatic concerns (Scott & Baroffio, 1986). Although it is widely believed that sexual abuse is a causal factor in eating disorders, two reviews (Conners & Morse, 1993; Pope & Hudson, 1992) have found no such connection.

Because rates of affective disorders were higher in the relatives of individuals with eating disorders than in control relatives, some investigators believe that eating disorders represent an expression of an affective disorder (Rutter et al., 1990). Depression often accompanies eating disorders. One interesting finding is that binge eating, purging, and mood varied seasonally among patients with bulimia nervosa (Blouin et al., 1992). The researchers hypothesize that for some bulimics, a relationship with seasonal affective disorder may exist. The cycle of bingeing and purging may be associated with light availability. At this point, we still do not know the precise relationship between affective disorders and eating disorders. Some therapists believe that depression is the result and not the cause of anorexia or bulimia (Vanderlinden, 1992). Kendler and associates (1991) examined monozygotic and dizygotic twins to estimate the role of genetics in bulimia nervosa. They reported concordance rates of 22.9 percent and 8.7 percent respectively, which suggested a modest genetic influence.

Treatment of Eating Disorders

First and foremost the anorexic patient has to gain weight; the goal is to ensure that the body is not endangered by electrolyte imbalance and weakened muscles caused by starvation (American Psychiatric Association, 1993). Either a medical or a behavioral inpatient weight gain program can be implemented. The medical approach generally involves complete bed rest and either intravenous or nasogastric (tube through the nose) feeding. The behavioral approach is designed to positively reinforce weight gain. Among the reinforcers that may be earned through weight gain are television or telephone privileges, visits from family and friends, mail, and access to street clothes. The particular reinforcers that are used, of course, depend on the likes and dislikes of the patient. Weight gain plans are generally aimed at increases of up to 1 pound per day (see First Person for an account of a treatment program).

Cognitive-behavioral treatments have also been successful. They involve encouraging the consumption of three or more balanced meals, reducing rigid food rules and body image concerns, and developing cognitive and behavioral strategies. This approach was as successful as antidepressant medication in

FIRST PERSON

Karen J. Shaw

"Why in the world would you want to work in that unit?" This was the response I received from many of my friends when I informed them that I would be leaving the medical-surgical unit to work on the Eating Disorder Program (EDP) within my hospital. It became apparent to me that many nurses view psychiatric nursing as an uncomplicated job.

However, my experience is entirely different. I had never worked as intensely as I do now, and I have never had a more rewarding and enjoyable job.

The EDP is located on the north wing of the medical-surgical floor, giving it a definite hospital atmosphere. Patients have regular beds rather than hospital beds, though, so the room resembles a dormitory. Most of our patients' time is spent in the large group room, which looks like a combined living room and dining room. We follow a fairly rigid daily structure. Most meals are eaten in the group room and are supervised by a staff person. We ask that patients refrain from using the bathroom for one hour after meals. During the one-hour post-meal supervision, staff people on the unit run various groups. The EDP also provides individual and family-therapy.

Every staff person on the unit is responsible for running groups. The first group of the day is a goals group, where the staff works with patients to identify three attainable goals that address their individual issues. Other groups include a community meeting, here and now, women's issues, journal writing, self-assertive techniques, relaxation, and a daily walk when the patient has eaten 100 percent for twenty-four hours. Every evening ends with a wrap-up group, which is a time for patients to "put things away" for the night.

It has been spiritually and professionally uplifting for me to watch many young women grow within our unit. For many, it is their first time as an inpatient. Although patients admit themselves voluntarily, their reactions to the fairly rigid structure of the EDP vary. Some may be slightly anxious; others may

treating bulimia nervosa, although combined treatment was the most effective (Agras et al., 1992).

Once the anorexic patient has gained sufficient weight to become an outpatient, family therapy sessions may be implemented. Experience has shown that this approach helps maintain the treatment gains achieved in the hospital. In one case, the struggle over eating served to distract from family conflicts. After issues involving the marital relationship of her parents were resolved, one female patient showed a dramatic weight gain (Lane & Kern, 1987). The patient also continued with a weight gain program and the option of additional psychotherapy.

Approximately 50 percent of treated anorexics recover completely (remain within the normal weight range), and another 30 to 40 percent show some weight gain but remain underweight (American Psychiatric Association, 1993; Anderson, Hedblom & Hubbard, 1983; Lask & Bryant-Waugh, 1992). For the most part, these percentages do not include pa-

tients who were treated with the family therapy approach; expectations are that it will improve overall therapeutic results.

Bulimia has been successfully treated through psychotherapy and through antidepressant medication (American Psychiatric Association, 1993). A somewhat novel treatment is the psychoeducational group approach, which combines behavioral and educational techniques. Clients are told that to eliminate binges they must eat regularly. They are taught how to anticipate the urge to binge and how to either prevent or delay binges. Clients also learn to delay purging for as long as possible after an eating binge (in which case they may not require purging at all) and then to go back to eating regularly. Each binge is considered an isolated incident, rather than part of a pattern. Cognitive-behavior approaches have been effective in increasing self-efficacy in bulimics developing a sense of self-control. Bulimics learn to replace urges to binge with exercise, relaxation, or other al-

feel motivated, ambivalent, or in denial.

Sara (not her real name) was admitted to the EDP during her summer break from college. She was anxious and frightened, as evidenced by her words and tears. Sara shared with the staff and other patients that she felt she could not deal with her eating disorder any longer; that it was "controlling her." Sara said that she felt overwhelmed with guilt after any meal or snack, and would excuse herself to the bathroom to purge. She complained of many physical symptoms: cold hands and feet, heart palpitations, amenorrhea, dental deterioration, fatigue, and extreme labile emotions.

One of the first goals on the EDP is to enable a patient like Sara to complete 100 percent of her meals and snacks. Once a patient's nutrition is improved, he or she is less food-oriented and more able to focus closely on personal behavior. For example, once Sara began to eat all her portioned food, she was able to explore how she had felt growing up in her family as the youngest child. Sara reported that her older sister was very difficult, causing the family much concern and worry. Consequently, Sara always tried to identify how her parents would like her to behave, and then do so. As a result, Sara had difficulty understanding her own needs and wants.

Therapy enabled Sara to identify her feelings and begin to communicate them in a more appropriate manner. She learned to recognize factors that would trigger a binge/purge cycle and to develop new coping strategies. Sara was very pleased with herself because within the last five years this was the longest period of time she had refrained from purging.

Sara was discharged from the EDP after one month of therapy. She was not totally cured, but she had gained insight and had learned a myriad of coping strategies to confront life's difficulties. One year after Sara's discharge, she sent a letter to the unit expressing that she has had some slips, but she is "getting on with her life" by identifying her feelings and using the various strategies that she had learned on the unit. Enclosed was a photograph of Sara and another former patient. I saw two beautiful women smiling at me appearing ready to deal with life. I ask you, "Wouldn't you like a job like mine?"

Karen J. Shaw is a psychiatric nurse at Hahnemann Hospital in Brighton, Massachusetts.

---

ternative behaviors (Fairburn et al., 1991; Garner et al., 1993).

MENTAL RETARDATION

A teenager with mental retardation told his fellow students, during a high school assembly, how he felt about his handicap:

My name is Tim Frederick . . . I would like to tell you what it is like to be retarded. . . . I am doing this so that you might be able to understand people like me. I do chores at home. I have to take care of all the animals—twelve chickens, three cats, a dog, three goldfish, and a horse. That's a lot of mouths to feed. . . . After I graduate from school, I hope to live in an apartment. . . . The hardest thing is when people make fun of me. I went to a dance a few weeks ago, and no girl would dance with me. Can you guys imagine how you would feel if that happened to you? Well, I feel the same way. (Smith, 1988, pp. 118–119)

How mental retardation is perceived is undergoing a fundamental change. Until recently, it was considered a hopeless condition that required institutionalization. Tim Frederick's mother was told that her son's development would be delayed and he might never be able to walk or talk. We now know that the effects of mental retardation are variable and that with training, even people who are severely handicapped can make intellectual and social gains.

The Association for Retarded Citizens, an advocacy organization, has estimated that 75 percent of children with mental retardation can become completely self-supporting adults if given appropriate education and training. Another 10 to 15 percent have the potential to be self-supporting. The challenge is to develop appropriate programs to ensure the greatest success. The movement away from institutional-

In contrast to common misconceptions about mental retardation, most research shows that people with mental retardation can successfully perform many tasks necessary for daily living. They can control their own lives and have a remarkably clear picture of their own situation and capabilities.

ization will continue to create greater contact between people with mental retardation and the general population. In 1967, more than 200,000 people with mental handicaps lived in public institutions. By 1984, this number had decreased to 110,000 (Landesman & Butterfield, 1987). It is now widely accepted that mentally retarded people should have the opportunity to live, work, learn, and develop relationships with nonretarded people in integrated settings. People are beginning to question assumptions about what individuals with mental retardation can do. A dance troupe called "Images in Motion," comprised of individuals with IQs between 30 and 60, has won rave reviews (Walker, 1991). The next frontier will be fuller integration of people into the social fabric (Wolfensberger, 1988).

Diagnosing Mental Retardation

About 7 million or more persons in the United States are mentally retarded, with IQ scores of about 70 or less (Madle, 1990). The definition of **mental retardation** in DSM-IV includes the following criteria:

1. *Significant subaverage general intellectual functioning* (this ordinarily means an IQ score of 70 or less on an individually administered IQ test).

2. *Concurrent deficiencies in adaptive behavior* (social and daily living skills, degree of independ-

ence lower than would be expected by his or her age or cultural group).

3. *Onset before age eighteen* (subaverage intellectual functioning arising after age eighteen is typically categorized as dementia).

Common characteristics that accompany mental retardation are dependency, passivity, low self-esteem, low frustration tolerance, depression, and self-injurious behavior (American Psychiatric Association, 1987). The more severe levels of mental retardation are associated with speech difficulties, neurological disorders, cerebral palsy, and vision and hearing problems (McQueen et al., 1987).

Issues Involved in Diagnosing Mental Retardation Arguments have been raised against the use of IQ scores to determine mental retardation, especially among members of ethnic minority groups. The validity of IQ scores is questionable especially when they are used to test members of minority groups. Although IQ tests are increasingly standardized on representative samples, questions regarding their validity remain. IQ tests also may measure familiarity with mainstream middle-class culture, not intelligence. Jane Mercer (1988) argued that the IQ test has been inappropriately used and that it is unfair to attempt to "measure" the intelligence by using items from one culture in a different cultural group. In ad-

Table 17.3

Estimated Number of Mentally Retarded People by Level

Level	Range Wechsler IQ	Percentage of All Mentally Retarded	Number
Mild	50–70	85	6,075,000
Moderate	35–49	10	715,475
Severe	20–34	3–4	250,400
Profound	0–19	1–2	107,300

Source: Reprinted with permission from *Psychology Today Magazine.* Copyright © 1985 Sussex Publishers, Inc.
Note: Estimates based on percentages from the American Psychiatric Association (1993) and applied to the normal probability distribution of intelligence based on a U.S. population of 210 million.

dition, IQ tests do not acknowledge the positive coping characteristics of the disadvantaged.

In 1979 Judge Peckham in the *Larry P. v. Riles* case held that IQ tests were culturally biased and were not to be used in decisions regarding the placement of African-American children in classes for the educable mentally retarded. He broadened his decision in 1986 by saying that IQ tests could not be used to determine the educational needs of African-American children as part of a comprehensive educational program—even with parental consent. Judge Peckham's decision was challenged by the mother of an African-American child who requested IQ testing. She argued that this was a case of reverse discrimination since IQ tests can be administered to European American, Hispanic American, Asian American, and Native Americans for special education services. On September 1, 1992, Judge Peckham reversed his 1986 ruling. IQ tests can again be used with African-American children as part of a special education assessment. However, the 1979 ruling still holds. They cannot be used to place African-American children in classes for the mentally retarded.

Levels of Retardation DSM-IV specifies four different levels of mental retardation, which are based only on IQ scores. The four levels and IQ ranges, as measured on the revised Wechsler scales (WISC-R and WAIS-R), are (1) mild (IQ score 50–55 to 70), (2) moderate (IQ score 35–40 to 50–55), (3) severe (IQ score 20–25 to 35–40), and (4) profound (IQ score below 20 or 25). Social and vocational skills and degree of adaptability may vary greatly for peo-

ple within each category. Table 17.3 contains estimates of the number of people within each level in the United States.

It should be noted that the American Association on Mental Retardation (AAMR), unlike the American Psychiatric Association and DSM-IV, no longer uses a classification of mental retardation that is based on levels of intellectual functioning as revealed in IQ scores. Instead, AAMR classifies the intensity of needed support (how much support the person needs to function in the environment) rather than assesses the level of intellectual deficit (Dawson, 1992). However, the AAMR accepts an IQ cutoff point of 75, which is higher than the 70 in DSM-IV. Unfortunately the higher IQ accepted by AAMR may lead a greater number of persons of different cultural or social backgrounds to be labeled mentally retarded.

Etiology of Mental Retardation

Mental retardation is thought to be produced by environmental factors (such as poor living conditions), by genetic or biogenic factors, or by a combination of the two. Biogenic factors in mental retardation include genetic variations, genetic abnormalities, metabolic disorders, malnutrition, infection, or prematurity. Environmental conditions such as a blow to the head causing brain trauma can also directly affect the brain.

Environmental Factors Certain features of the environment may contribute to retardation. Among these are the absence of stimulating factors or situations, a lack of attention and reinforcement from parents or significant others, and chronic stress and frustration. In addition, poverty, lack of adequate health care, poor nutrition, and inadequate education place children at a disadvantage. A lower socioeconomic status generally implies a lower mean group IQ score (Ardizzone & Scholl, 1985).

Genetic Factors   Genetic factors in mental retardation include genetic variations and genetic abnormalities. As noted earlier, mental retardation may be caused by the normal genetic variation. In a normal distribution of traits, it is assumed that some individuals have lower intelligence than others. No organic or physiological anomaly associated with mental retardation is found in this type of retardation. Researchers have suggested that the normal range of intelligence lies between the IQ scores of 50 and 150, and that some individuals simply lie on the lower end of this normal range (Zigler, 1967). In any case, the majority of people classified as mildly retarded have normal health, appearance, and physical abilities.

In contrast to normal genetic variation, mental retardation can be caused by genetic anomalies. These conditions are rare and generally result in the more severe forms of mental retardation. Those who are profoundly retarded (about 1 to 2 percent of those who are retarded) may be so intellectually deficient that constant and total care and supervision are necessary. Many also have significant sensorimotor impairment (Irwin & Gross, 1990) and are confined to a bed or wheelchair by the congenital defects that produced the retardation; even with teaching, there is minimal, if any, acquisition of self-help skills. Their mortality rate during childhood is extremely high with more than one-half dying before age twenty (Ramer & Miller, 1992). Associated physical problems such as neuromuscular disorders, impairment of vision or hearing, and seizures may coexist (Irwin & Gross, 1990). Therefore, mental retardation associated with genetic anomalies may result in quite serious retardation.

Down syndrome, which is due to an autosomal (nonsex chromosome) abnormality, is one of the most common clinically defined forms of mental retardation; it may occur as often as twice per 1000 live births. About 10 percent of children with severe or moderate retardation show this genetic anomaly. Down syndrome is caused by the presence of one or more than the normal complement of forty-six chromosomes (twenty-three from the mother and twenty-three from the father).

Down syndrome is the most common form of mental retardation. It appears in approximately 10 percent of children with moderate to severe retardation. Although these children have below normal intellectual functioning, they can acquire academic skills in highly structured learning environments, geared to their needs.

The well-known physical characteristics of Down syndrome are short in-curving fingers, short broad hands, slanted eyes, furrowed protruding tongue, flat and broad face, harsh voice, and incomplete or delayed sexual development. Cosmetic surgery (consisting mostly of modifying tongue size) is being used with some Down syndrome children in an effort to make their physical appearance more nearly normal and to allow them to speak more clearly and to eat more normally. The procedure is intended to allow Down syndrome people to fit in as much as possible with their peers to enhance their social interactions and communication abilities (May & Turnbull, 1992). People with Down syndrome who live past age forty are at high risk for developing Alzheimer's disease. The gene responsible for the conditions of *amyloid plaques* (patches of degenerated nerve endings) and neurofibrillary tangles (fibers that appear to be tangles of brain tissue filaments) found in Alzheimer's disease, is located on chromosome 21, indicating a possible relationship between Down syndrome and Alzheimer's disease (Clarke & Clarke, 1987). People who have Down syndrome show a greater intellectual decline after the age of 35 than do other individuals with mental retardation (Young & Kramer, 1991). Congenital heart abnormalities are also common in people with Down syndrome, causing a high mortality rate. Recent surgical procedures have improved the probability of surviving these heart defects but have given rise to legal and ethical issues.

The incidence of this disorder increases with the age at which the mother gives birth, from 1 in 15,000 live births for mothers younger than age thirty to 1 in 65 births for mothers older than age forty-five. One-third of all Down syndrome children are born to mothers older than age thirty-eight. Although much is made of the fact that older women are more likely than younger women to conceive children with Down syndrome, it must also be remembered that approximately two-thirds of all children with this disorder are born to women younger than thirty-seven. There has also been increased interest in the effect of the father's age on the incidence of Down syndrome.

Prenatal detection of Down syndrome is possible through **amniocentesis,** which is performed during the fourteenth or fifteenth week of pregnancy. In this procedure, a hollow needle is inserted through the abdominal wall into the amniotic fluid sac. Some of the fluid is withdrawn, and the fetal cells are cultivated. Within three weeks, these cells can be tested to determine whether Down syndrome is present. This procedure involves some risk for both mother and fetus, so it is employed only when the chance of finding Down syndrome is high—as, for example, with women older than age thirty-five. Remember, however, that the greater percentage of babies with Down syndrome are born to younger mothers, and yet testing for Down syndrome through amniocentesis occurs primarily among older women.

A procedure that allows earlier detection of Down syndrome is *chorionic villus sampling.* Tests are made of cells on the hairlike projections (villi) on the sac that surrounds the fetus and can be performed after the ninth week of pregnancy (Pueschel, 1991).

Other, less-common genetic anomalies include Turner's syndrome, Klinefelter's syndrome, phenylketonuria (PKU), Tay-Sachs disease, and cretinism.

Nongenetic Biogenic Factors Mental retardation may be caused by a variety of environmental mishaps that can occur during the prenatal period (from conception to birth), the perinatal period (during the birth process), and the postnatal period (after birth). During the prenatal period, the developing organism is susceptible to viruses and infections (such as German measles), drugs, radiation, poor nutrition, and other nongenetic influences.

Increasing attention is being focused on the problem of mental deficits related to alcohol consumption during pregnancy. Some children born to alcoholic mothers show, to varying degrees, a group of congenital physical and mental defects known as **fetal alcohol syndrome (FAS).** Children with this syndrome tend to be small and to suffer from *microcephaly,* an anomaly whose most distinguishing feature is an unusually small brain. Usually such children are generally mildly retarded, but neither moderate retardation nor average intelligence is uncommon. Those with normal intelligence seem to have significant academic and attentional difficulties, however, as well as a history of hyperactivity and behavioral deficits (Shaywitz, 1980; Streissguth, 1993). Smoking and poor nutrition may increase the likelihood that an alcoholic mother will have FAS offspring. Available information suggests that 1 case of FAS occurs in each 750 live births, which places alcohol among the

Although most forms of mental retardation now have decreasing prevalence rates, the incidence of postnatal retardation is rising, due to severe brain injury. Some of these injuries are accidental, but many are the result of child abuse, which is a worsening social problem in this country.

most common causes of retardation for which an etiology can be determined (Streissguth et al., 1980).

During the perinatal period, mental retardation can result from birth trauma, prematurity, or asphyxiation. After birth or during the postnatal period, head injuries, infections, tumors, malnutrition, and ingesting toxic substances such as lead can cause brain damage and consequent mental retardation. Compared with prenatal factors, however, these hazards account for only a small proportion of organically caused mental retardation. The most common birth condition associated with mental retardation is prematurity and low birth weight. Although most premature infants develop normally, approximately 20 percent show signs of neurological problems reflected in learning disabilities and mental retardation (Pound, 1987). In a study of more than 53,000 U.S. women and their children, researchers found that low birth weight was generally associated with low IQ scores. The average IQ score of children who had birth weights between 26 ounces and 52.5 ounces was 86, whereas those with birth weights between 122 ounces and 140 ounces had an average IQ score of 105 (Broman, Nichols & Kennedy, 1975).

Although most types of mental retardation now have decreasing incidence rates, mental retardation owing to postnatal causes is on the increase. For example, direct trauma to the head produces hemorrhaging and tearing of the brain tissue, often as the result of an injury sustained in an automobile accident or from child abuse. Depending on the definition of child abuse, estimates of the number of cases of child abuse per year range from 35,000 to 1.9 million. Of this group, a large percentage are subjected to violent abuse that could cause serious injury (Gelard & Janford, 1987). The authors of a British study of child abuse go so far as to argue that violence-induced handicaps should be recognized as a major cause of retardation: "Children rendered mentally handicapped as a result of abuse may account for more cases than PKU. The consequences are frequently more severe than those of Down syndrome" (Buchanan & Oliver, 1977, p. 465).

Programs for People with Mental Retardation

Early Intervention Programs such as Head Start have not produced dramatic increases in intellectual ability among at-risk children (those from low-income families). But long-term follow-up studies have found that they do produce positive results

There are a number of programs designed to develop the capabilities of people with mental retardation. Among the better known is the Special Olympics, which provides the opportunity for special athletes to compete against their peers.

(Royce, Lazar & Darlington, 1983; Zigler & Berman, 1983). Children who participated in early intervention programs were found to perform better in school than nonparticipants, and the difference between the two groups continued to widen until the twelfth grade. In addition, a greater proportion of the participants in early intervention finished high school, which no doubt helped them obtain and hold better jobs.

The families of participants were also positively influenced by the programs. They rated the programs as personally helpful, spent more time working with their children on school tasks, and perceived their children as becoming happier and healthier. There is continuing optimism about the efficacy of such pro-

grams, even though two well-known studies that reported large increases in IQ scores (the studies of Heber & Garber, 1975, and Skeels, 1966) were found to have serious methodological flaws (Longstreth, 1981; Page, 1972).

Employment Programs   People with mental handicaps can achieve more than was previously thought. The parents of a teenage boy, for example, were told that he would always be childlike and the only job he would ever be fit for was stringing beads. Another person with moderate retardation, who spent most of his time staring at his hands and rubbing his face, also appeared to have a dismal future. Both of these men now have paying jobs, one as a janitor and the other as a dishwasher. Programs designed to help people with mental handicaps learn occupational skills are largely responsible for the improved outcome of these men and others like them (McLeod, 1985). Social and vocational skills gained appear to be maintained or increased in follow-up studies (Foxx & Faw, 1992).

One such program is the Structured Training and Employmnent Transitional Services (STETS) project funded by the U.S. Department of Labor (Kerachsky & Thornton, 1987). The program, designed for people between the ages of eighteen and twenty-four who have moderate to mild levels of mental retardation, has three phases. The first involves initial training and work in a low-stress environment. After a suitable skill level is attained, the second phase begins. This phase involves on-the-job training during which participants are expected to meet the same requirements as nonretarded workers doing the same job. Phase three involves a six-month follow-up of the workers who are employed in unsolicited, competitive jobs.

Participants in this training program were compared with a control group who used other community services, but not STETS services. At the end of the six-month follow-up period, 31 percent of the people in the STETS program were regularly employed in competitive jobs versus 19 percent of the control group. About 45 percent of the people in both groups had paid employment that involved noncompetitive jobs (sheltered workshops and activity centers). People in the STETS program also received better pay than those in the control group. Interestingly, the most successful participants were those with lower IQ scores and whose mental handicaps were associated with organic causes. Such training allows people to become self-sufficient members of the community.

Living Arrangements There has been an increase in the deinstitutionalization of people with mental retardation. More of them are being placed in group homes or in situations where they can live independently or semi-independently within the community. The idea is to provide the "least restrictive environment" that is consistent with their condition and that will give them the opportunity to develop more fully. Although the implication seems to be that institutions are bad places, they do not have uniformly negative effects. Nor do group homes always provide positive experiences. What seems to be most important are the goals; programs that promote social interaction and the development of competence have positive effects on the residents of either institutions or group homes (Tjosvold & Tjosvold, 1983).

Nontraditional group arrangements, in which a small number of people live together in a home, sharing meals and chores, provide increased opportunity for social interactions. These "normalized" living arrangements were found to produce benefits such as increased adaptive functioning, improved language development, and socialization (Kleinberg & Galligan, 1983; MacEachron, 1983). Many of these positive behaviors, however, were already part of the residents' repertoires; what they need are systematic programs that will teach them additional living skills (Kleinberg & Galligan, 1983). Merely moving retarded people from one environment to another does not alone guarantee that they will be taught the skills that they need. Nonetheless, properly planned and supported deinstitutionalization does provide persons with mental retardation the opportunity to experience a more "normal" life.

SUMMARY

1. Pervasive developmental disorders include autistic disorder, Rett's disorder, Childhood Disintegrative disorder, Asperger's disorder, and pervasive developmental disorder not otherwise specified.

2. Autistic disorder is characterized by an extreme lack of responsiveness and by language and speech deficits. It appears early in life and seems to

be inherited. Psychological causes do not seem to be involved in autism. The prognosis for the pervasive development disorders is poor. Behavior modification procedures have yielded promising results, but evidence has suggested that long-term (if not lifelong) treatment is needed.

3. Developmental problems are reported in both "normal" children and children who are clinic patients. Attention deficit hyperactivity disorder, or ADHD (characterized by overactivity, restlessness, distractibility, short attention span, and impulsiveness) is a somewhat common problem. Although this disorder may be produced by organic problems, many children diagnosed as "hyperactive" do not show pathological neurological signs. Drugs have been used extensively to treat this disorder, but the use of behavior modification and self-control methods is increasing. Oppositional defiant disorder is characterized by a pattern of hostile, defiant behavior toward authority figures.

4. Conduct disorders (or antisocial behaviors) constitute one of the few childhood conditions that show a clear continuity with adult problems. Unfortunately, the prognosis is poor. Possible causes include emotional deprivation or overindulgence; genetic factors; the learning, reinforcement, and modeling of aggression; and the influence of the family.

5. Children may also suffer from a variety of problems related to anxiety and depression. Separation-anxiety disorder involves physical symptoms that appear when the child is separated from parents and home. Children's anxiety reactions are usually transitory and disappear with age. Depression also occurs in childhood and becomes more prevalent during adolescence.

6. Tics and other stereotyped movements often occur in children and adolescents. In most cases, the disorder is transient and disappears with or without treatment. Tics that last longer than a year are diagnosed as chronic tic disorders. A more severe problem is Tourette's syndrome, which may involve organic problems and last into adulthood. Drugs and behavior therapy have been only partially successful in treating tic disorders.

7. The eating disorders, anorexia nervosa and bulimia, are becoming more prevalent in the United States. Anorexia involves a loss of body weight through self-starvation, body image distortion, and

an intense fear of becoming obese that does not diminish with weight loss. Anorexics have poor self-esteem and may use their bizarre behavior as a way to control others. Bulimia is characterized by episodes of binge eating followed by self-induced vomiting or purging. The excessive weight consciousness of bulimics may be a result of societal emphasis on thinness, especially for women. The disorders are treated primarily by reinforcing desirable behaviors.

8. The vast majority of those with mental retardation can become completely self-supporting with appropriate education and training. Causes of retardation include environmental factors, normal genetic processes, genetic anomalies, and other biogenic abnormalities such as physiological or anatomical defects.

9. DSM-IV identifies four different levels of retardation, which are based only on IQ scores: mild (IQ score 50 to 70), moderate (IQ score 40 to 50), severe (IQ score 20 to 40), and profound (IQ score below 20).

10. Most mental retardation does not have an identifiable organic cause and is associated with only mild intellectual impairment.

11. Public schools provide special programs for children and adolescents; even people who are severely retarded are given instruction and training in practical self-help skills. Various approaches—behavioral therapy in particular—are being used successfully to help retarded people acquire needed "living" skills.

KEY TERMS

amniocentesis A screening procedure performed during the fourteenth or fifteenth week of pregnancy, used to determine the presence of Down syndrome

anorexia nervosa An eating disorder in which the person is intensely fearful of becoming obese and engages in self-starvation

attention deficit hyperactivity disorder (ADHD) A disorder of childhood and adolescence characterized by short attention span, impulsiveness, constant activity, and lack of self-control

autistic disorder A severe childhood disorder that is characterized by early onset and an extreme lack of interest in interpersonal relationships, and impairment in verbal and nonverbal communication

bulimia nervosa An eating disorder characterized by the rapid consumption of large quantities of food, usually followed by self-induced vomiting

conduct disorders Disorders of childhood and adolescence that involve a persistent pattern of antisocial behaviors that violate the rights of others

Down syndrome A condition produced by the presence of an extra chromosome (trisomy 21) and resulting in mental retardation and distinctive physical characteristics

fetal alcohol syndrome (FAS) A group of symptoms, including mental retardation and physical defects, that are produced in the infant by the ingestion of alcohol by a pregnant woman

mental retardation Substandard intellectual functioning accompanied by deficiencies in adaptive behavior, with onset before age eighteen

oppositional defiant disorder (ODD) A childhood disorder characterized by negativistic, argumentative, and hostile behavior

pervasive developmental disorders Severe disorders of childhood that affect language, social relationships, attention, perception, and affect; include autistic disorder, Rett's disorder, childhood disintegrative disorder, Asperger's disorder, and pervasive developmental disorder not otherwise specified

separation anxiety disorder A childhood disorder characterized by excessive anxiety concerning separation from parents and home

tic disorders Disorders with onset in childhood and characterized by involuntary and repetitive movements and/or vocalizations, including transient and chronic tic disorders and Tourette's syndrome

tics Stereotyped and repetitive but involuntary twitchings or spasms of the voluntary muscles

Tourette's syndrome A childhood disorder characterized by multiple motor and verbal tics that may develop into coprolalia (compulsion to shout obscenities)

Individual and Group Therapy

At some time in our lives, all of us have experienced personal, social, and emotionally distressing problems. Although many of us have been fortunate enough to handle these difficulties on our own, others have been greatly helped by discussing their difficulties with someone who could reassure and advise. People have always relied on friends, relatives, members of the clergy, teachers, and even strangers for advice, emotional and social support, approval, and validation. Recently, however, this function has been increasingly taken over by professionals who practice psychotherapy (Zilbergeld, 1983). In fact, psychotherapists have even been called the "secular priests" of our society (London, 1964a, 1984).

In preceding chapters, we have examined a wide variety of disorders, ranging from personality disturbances to schizophrenia. We have also examined the treatment approaches that seem to help people suffering from these disorders. In this chapter, we provide a more rounded view of the various techniques used to treat psychopathology: biologically based approaches, individual psychotherapy (both insight and action approaches), and group and family therapies. To close the chapter, we examine one possible integrative (eclectic) approach to the treatment of Steven V., whose psychological history was discussed in Part 1.

BIOLOGY-BASED TREATMENT TECHNIQUES

Biological or somatic treatment techniques use physical means to alter the patient's physiological state and hence psychological state (Andreasen, 1984; Lickey & Gordon, 1991). Such treatment philosophy can be traced to ancient times beginning with the practices of trephining (see Chapter 1) and bleeding and purging (laxatives and emetics) unwanted substances from the body. These primitive and barbaric methods of treatment have given way to more enlightened and benign forms. As our understanding of human physiology and brain functioning has increased, so has our ability to provide more effective biologically based therapies for the mentally ill. Three biology-based techniques are examined here: electroconvulsive therapy, psychosurgery, and psychopharmacology, or drug therapy.

Electroconvulsive Therapy

Many people consider physically shocking the patient's body an abhorrent form of treatment. But such treatment can be used to successfully treat certain mental disorders. This is especially true for severe depressive reactions in which quite dramatic improvements occur (Fink, 1979; National Institute of Mental Health, 1985; Scovern & Killman, 1980).

The first therapeutic use of shock was *insulin shock treatment*, introduced in the 1930s by psychiatrist Manfred Sakel. Insulin was injected into the patient's body, drastically reducing the blood sugar level. The patient then went into convulsions and coma. The behavior of some schizophrenic patients improved after they awakened from this shock treatment.

Also in the 1930s, another psychiatrist, Lazlo von Meduna, hypothesized that schizophrenia and epileptic seizures are antagonistic (seizures seem to prevent schizophrenic symptoms) and that by inducing convulsions in schizophrenics he could eliminate their bizarre behaviors. Meduna injected patients with the drug *metrazol* to induce the seizures. Neither insulin nor metrazol shock treatment was very effective, however, and their use declined with the advent of electroconvulsive therapy.

Two Italian psychiatrists, Ugo Cerletti and Lucio Bini, introduced **electroconvulsive therapy** (**ECT**), or electroshock treatment, in 1938. In ECT, the patient lies on a padded bed or couch and is first injected with a muscle relaxant to minimize the chance of self-injury during the later convulsions. Then 65 to 140 volts of electricity are applied to the temporal region of the patient's skull (refer to Figure 16.1), through electrodes, for 0.1 to 0.5 seconds. This treatment induces convulsions followed by coma. On regaining consciousness, the patient is often confused and suffers a memory loss for events immediately before and after the ECT. Recent findings show that unilateral shock (applying shock to one hemisphere

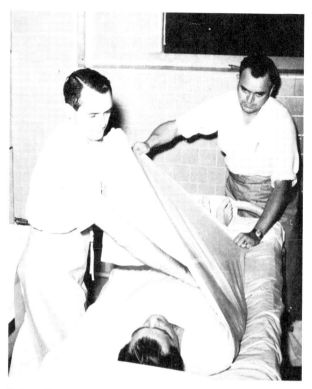

Before the 1950s and the development of effective drugs to treat mental illness, a number of seemingly bizarre treatment methods, such as wrapping people in cold wet sheets to offset some of the negative effects of ECT treatment, were routinely used.

only) causes less confusion and memory loss, and studies have indicated that it is just as effective as bilateral shock (Abrams & Essman, 1982; Horne et al., 1985; Squire & Slater, 1978).

ECT is much more useful in treating depression than in treating schizophrenia, against which it provides at most temporary relief (Berkwitz, 1974). But how ECT acts to improve depression is still unclear (Alexander & Selesnick, 1966). Some ECT researchers believe that it alters brain chemistry through suppressing the hormone cortisol (Fink, 1982; Grunhaus et al., 1987). As you recall from Chapter 12, failure to suppress cortisol functioning has been associated with some forms of depression. Other investigators have suggested that ECT is so aversive that some patients get better simply to avoid treatment. Or perhaps shocks stimulate the amines in the brain, leading to increased activity and improved mood. Another possibility is that depressed patients feel better after experiencing ECT because they see the shocks as punishment for perceived sins. Whatever the mechanism, ECT seems to be effective against severe depression (Abrams, 1988; Fink, 1979). Indeed, psychologist Norman Endler (1990) wrote a biography about his own struggle with depression and how ECT greatly helped his recovery.

For several reasons, the use of ECT declined in the 1960s and 1970s, despite its success. First, there is concern that ECT might cause permanent damage to important parts of the brain. Indeed, animals who have undergone ECT treatment show brain damage. Would it be unreasonable to expect similar damage in human beings? Second, a small percentage of patients fracture or dislocate bones during treatment. Although modern techniques have reduced pain and side effects (the convulsions are now almost unnoticeable), many patients anticipate a very unpleasant experience. Third, clinicians often argue that the "beneficial changes" initially observed in patients after ECT do not persist over the long term. Fourth, the abuses and side effects of ECT have been dramatized—often sensationally—in the mass media. In the movie *One Flew Over the Cuckoo's Nest,* for instance, ECT was administered repeatedly to the hero because he would not conform to regulations while in a mental hospital (such use of ECT is now illegal and probably nonexistent). Fifth, and most important, recent advances in drug therapy have diminished the need for ECT, except for profoundly depressed patients for whom drugs act too slowly. Objections to ECT were so strong that citizens in Berkeley, California, in 1982 voted to ban its use in the city. This ban was, however, subsequently overturned by the courts. Because the procedure is so controversial and so little is known about how and why it works, ECT should be used only as a last resort.

The 1980s have seen a slight increase in the use of ECT for carefully selected patients. Currently, about 33,000 psychiatric patients undergo ECT each year (National Institute of Mental Health, 1985). Severe depression in old age and the depressed stages of bipolar disorders are most responsive to shock therapy.

Psychosurgery

As noted in Chapter 16, damage to brain tissue can dramatically alter the person's emotional characteristics and intellectual functioning. In the 1930s, the Portuguese neurologist Egas Moniz theorized that destroying certain connections in the brain, particularly in the frontal lobes, could disrupt psychotic thought patterns and behaviors. During the 1940s and 1950s, **psychosurgery** became increasingly popular. The treatment was applied most often to schizophrenic and severely depressed patients, although many patients with personality and anxiety disorders also underwent psychosurgery.

Several procedures or techniques may be used. *Prefrontal lobotomy* involves drilling holes in the skull. A leukotome (a hollow tube that extrudes a cutting wire) is inserted through the holes to cut nerve fibers between the frontal lobes and the thalamus or hypothalamus. In *transorbital lobotomy*, the instrument is inserted through the eye socket, eliminating the need to drill holes in the skull. In a *lobectomy*, some or all of the frontal lobe is removed (to treat such disorders as brain tumors). Parts of the brain may also be subjected to electrical *cauterization* (searing or burning), which destroys selected brain tissue.

Psychosurgical techniques have been refined to the point where it is possible to operate on extremely small and contained areas of the brain. For example, videolaserscopy allows the surgeon to use a video camera in making extremely small incisions with a laser (Cowley, 1990). However, both scientific and ethical objections to these procedures have been raised. Initial reports of results were enthusiastic, but later evaluations seemed to indicate that lobotomies have little therapeutic effect. Whether patients improved or failed to improve was independent of psychosurgical treatment. In addition, serious negative and irreversible side effects were frequently observed (Valenstein, 1986). Although postlobotomy patients often became quite manageable, calm, and less anxious, many emerged from surgery with impaired cognitive and intellectual functioning, listless (even vegetative), or showing uninhibitable impulsive behavior. Some such patients were described as "robots" or "zombies." A small number suffer from continuing seizures and, in rare cases, psychosurgery resulted in death. Finally, because permanent brain damage is always involved, some critics called for a halt to this form of treatment on humanitarian grounds.

Although surgery is widely accepted to treat some organic brain disorders such as tumors, its use to

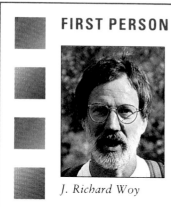

FIRST PERSON

J. Richard Woy

I will never forget my first exposure to people suffering from severe mental disorders, nor will I forget my first involvement in the care and treatment of mental illness. Those first experiences had a strong effect on me, and I was both horrified and fascinated by what I saw.

These experiences occurred just after my graduation from college in 1964. In order to get some firsthand experience in the field before starting a doctoral program in clinical psychology, I worked for several months as a "psychiatric attendant" at a private mental hospital.

The mental health field in 1964 was in the middle of a major transition. Some mental hospitals were already relying heavily on the recently introduced and powerful new psychotropic medications. Others were more cautious and continued a primary reliance on traditional treatment methods—some of which have disappeared entirely since then.

The mental hospital where I worked was old and very conservative in its practices, and I realized later that I had witnessed a kind of living museum, the last vestiges of an earlier era in the treatment of mental illness. Wearing a starched white jacket and carrying an impressive set of very large keys, I escorted patients from one locked portion of the hospital to another, supervised patients on the ward, and assisted the doctors and nurses in their various treatments.

Three treatment practices made particular impressions on me. The first was the practice of doing "cold wet packs" in conjunction with electroconvulsive shock therapy. "Shock therapy" was done early every Tuesday and Thursday morning.

Each patient first was asked to take off all of his clothes and lie down on a padded rolling cart. We then tightly wrapped each patient from head to foot in wet sheets that had been soaked in cold water. Each patient then lay in the "cold wet pack" for a period of fifteen minutes to a half hour. During this time the room looked like it was filled with mummies. Then I and three other attendants rolled each patient individually into the treatment room where we removed the sheets wrapped around the patient's arms and legs. While each of the four of us held one of the patient's limbs, the doctor placed an electrode on each side of the patient's head and then administered the electrical charge, producing an immediate and violent seizure and physical convulsions. We held onto the patient's arms and legs so that the powerful muscular spasms would not cause injury. After the treatment, we rolled patients back to the recovery room, where they gradually returned to a waking condition. The electroconvulsive shock therapy was intended to reduce both manic and depres-

treat functional mental disorders has declined drastically since the late 1960s. Along with the problems cited, increased reliance on drug therapy has contributed to its demise. Nowadays, psychosurgery is considered only as a last resort, in the most intractable cases of dangerous pathological behavior. On the whole, this severe restriction and regulation of its use seems wise. The First Person narrative in this chapter discusses some experiences one therapist had with other treatment methods that are no longer used to combat the effects of mental illness.

Psychopharmacology

As we have said, **psychopharmacology** approaches (**drug therapy**) have generally replaced shock treat-

ment and psychosurgery for treating serious behavior disorders. Since the 1950s drug therapy has been a major factor in allowing the early discharge of hospitalized mental patients and permitting them to function in the community. Drug treatment is now widely used throughout the United States: more mental patients receive medication than receive all other forms of therapy combined (Kovel, 1976), and it is estimated that we spend more than $500 million annually on antianxiety drugs alone (Baldessarini & Cole, 1988). The alarming rise in the use of minor tranquilizers has become a major concern to society because of possible abuses and their addictive qualities. Some researchers have also noted that sexual bias may operate in the prescription of them to women. Studies have revealed that twice as many women are pre-

sive symptoms, and the cold wet packs were believed to enhance the effectiveness of the shock treatments.

The second treatment method was called "hydrotherapy." This treatment was administered in a specially constructed room that was tiled from floor to ceiling and looked much like a shower room. However, the only fixtures in the room were sets of metal and leather fasteners on one wall and a powerful adjustable nozzle like those on a fire engine on the opposite wall. Treatment consisted of shackling one or more nude patients spread-eagled on one wall and pummeling them with powerful jets of water from the large nozzle. The physical assault of the water jets was intended to shock depressed patients out of their depression.

I don't recall what the third treatment was called. It also occurred in a specially constructed room that was tiled from floor to ceiling. The only thing in the room was a very large bathtub that was constructed so that warm water would continually circulate through it, much like

a jacuzzi. However, the tub had a heavy canvas cover on top of it with a single hole at one end, and the cover could be securely fastened down with straps and buckles. An agitated patient was confined in the tub for several hours at a time with only his head sticking out through the hole in the top. The purpose of the treatment was to reduce the patient's agitation through the soothing effects of immersion in the warm water. I or another attendant remained with the patient to be sure he was safe and was instructed to record everything the patient said and to say nothing.

This hospital was not a backwater or a snake pit. Located in a suburb of a major city, it had an excellent facility on an attractive and spacious campus, had competent and caring staff, was affiliated with a major university medical school, and drew its patients primarily from the wealthy and well to do. Furthermore, in retrospect it is clear to me that the patients I met suffered from the most serious and profound of the mental disorders, including schizophrenia, major depression,

manic-depressive disorders, and the like.

Nevertheless, I was disturbed by the methods just described even at the time. The emphasis on physically controlling and constraining patients against their will, even to the extent of tying them up, seemed excessive to me and made me very uncomfortable. These methods seemed to me to be demeaning and to involve a loss of personal dignity that left me feeling guilty and embarrassed. I'm glad that I have never seen those three treatment methods used again in all the years since 1964.

J. Richard Woy spent ten years as a researcher and administrator at the National Institute of Mental Health. He is currently head of JRW Associates, a management consulting firm in Boston that serves health and human service organizations. In addition, Dr. Woy publishes, teaches, and maintains a clinical practice.

---

scribed antianxiety drugs; that although they compose only slightly more than one-half of the patients seen by psychiatrists, they receive 73 percent of the prescriptions; and that male psychiatrists prescribe medication twice as often as their female counterparts (Cypress, 1980; Hohmann et al., 1988; Rossiter, 1983).

Four major categories of drugs, already mentioned in previous chapters, are discussed in this section. These are the antianxiety drugs (or minor tranquilizers), the antipsychotic drugs (or major tranquilizers), the antidepressant drugs (which relieve depression by elevating one's mood), and antimanic drugs such as lithium. Table 18.1 lists the generic and brand names of the drugs most frequently prescribed to treat psychological disorders.

Antianxiety Drugs (Minor Tranquilizers) Before the 1950s barbiturates were often prescribed to relieve anxiety. *Barbiturates* are sedatives that have a calming effect, but they are also highly addictive. Many people who take barbiturates develop a physical tolerance to these drugs and require increasing doses to obtain the same effects. An overdose can result in death, and discontinuing the drug can produce agonizing withdrawal symptoms. Moreover, physical and mental disturbances such as muscular incoordination and mental confusion can result even from normal dosages. For these reasons, the barbiturates were replaced with antianxiety drugs almost as soon as the latter became available.

During the 1940s and 1950s, the propanediols (meprobamate compounds) and benzodiazepines

Table 18.1

The Drugs Most Commonly Used in Drug Therapy

Category	Generic Name	Brand Name
Antianxiety drugs	Meprobamate	Miltown, Equanil
	Chlordiazepoxide	Librium
	Diazepam	Valium
Antipsychotic drugs	Alprozolam	Xanac
	Chlorpromazine	Thorazine
	Trifluoperazine	Stelazine
	Thioxanthene	Haldol, Prolixin
	Clozapine	Clozaril
Antidepressants	Phenelzine	Nardil
	Isocarboxazid	Marplan
	Tranylcypromine	Parnate
	Imipramine	Tofranil
	Doxepin	Sinequan
	Amitriptyline	Elavil
	Fluoxetine	Prozac
Antimanic drugs	Lithium	Eskalith

took over as the preferred medications. Researchers first developed *meprobamate* (the generic name of Miltown and Equanil) for use as a muscle relaxant and anxiety reducer. Within a few years, it was being prescribed for patients who showed neurotic symptoms, complained of anxiety and nervousness, or had psychosomatic problems. Soon other antianxiety drugs, the benzodiazepines (Librium and Valium) also entered the market. Because of its ability to selectively diminish anxiety and leave adaptive behavior intact, Valium has become the most often-prescribed drug in all medicine. Studies have suggested that the benzodiapines work by binding to specific receptor sites at the synapses and blocking transmission, which is another piece of evidence that supports the hypothesis that anxiety, like many other mental conditions, is linked to brain structure and physiology (Hayward, Wardle & Higgitt, 1989).

The antianxiety drugs can be addictive and can impair psychomotor skills; discontinuing these drugs after prolonged usage at high doses can result in withdrawal symptoms (Bassuk, Schoonover & Gelenberg, 1983; Levenson, 1981). But they are considered safer than barbiturates, and there is little doubt that they effectively reduce anxiety and the behavioral symptoms of anxiety disorder (Rickels, 1966).

The major problem of the minor tranquilizers is the great potential for overuse and overreliance. For example, about one in ten adults uses antianxiety drugs at least once a year (Uhlenhuth et al., 1983), and people are becoming more receptive to their use in relieving psychological problems (Clinthorne et al., 1986). Almost everyone feels anxious at one time or another, and the antianxiety drugs are effective, readily available, low in cost, and easy to administer. They are a quick, easy alternative to developing personal coping skills. As a result, people tend to choose the short-term relief offered by these drugs, over the long-term but slower gains of developing the ability to manage stress and solve one's own problems.

Antipsychotic Drugs (Major Tranquilizers) Although the antianxiety drugs seem to relax and reduce anxiety in patients, they have minimal impact on the hallucinations and distorted thinking of schizophrenic and highly agitated patients. In 1950 a synthetic sedative was developed in France. This drug, *chlorpromazine* (the generic name of Thora-

In the 1950s drug therapy began to have a major impact on the prognosis and course of many mental disorders. Many patients with severe psychological problems once thought to be incurable can now live relatively normal lives.

zine), had an unexpected tranquilizing effect, which decreased patients' interest in the events taking place around them. Some two million patients used Thorazine in less than a year after its introduction. Chlorpromazine also seemed to reduce psychotic symptoms (believed to be a biochemical effect of blocking dopamine receptors). Thereafter, a number of other major tranquilizers were developed, mainly for administration to schizophrenics.

Many schizophrenic patients who use these drugs become calm and manageable; show fewer inappropriate behaviors, disturbed associations, and delusional and hallucinatory symptoms; and are more amenable to other forms of treatment such as psychotherapy. Several experimental studies have demonstrated the efficacy of antipsychotic drugs in treating schizophrenia (NIMH Pharmacology Study Group, 1964; Hymovitz & Spohn, 1980; Kane & Lieberman, 1987). A review of many large-scale controlled studies has indicated that the beneficial effects of Thorazine, Stelazine, Prolixin, and other antipsychotic drugs have allowed institutions to release thousands of chronic "incurable" mental patients throughout the country (Lickey & Gordon, 1991; Wender & Klein, 1981). When hospitalized schizophrenics were given *phenothiazines* (a class of major tranquilizers), they showed more social interaction with others, better self-management, and less agitation and excitement than when they were given *placebos* (chemically inert or inactive substances). The placebos were used to rule out the possibility that the gains might be due to patients' expectations of improvement or to the attention staff gave patients in administering the drugs (Cole, 1964).

Outcome research on drug treatment (and, for that matter, on psychotherapy) must control **placebo effects.** These are positive responses to a drug that result from the patient's understanding of the drug's action, from faith in the doctor, or from other psychological factors unrelated to the drug's specific physiological action (Korchin, 1976). Similarly, in evaluating any form of treatment or psychotherapy, the patient's expectancy of improvement and the attention received from the doctor may influence improvement rates. A particular treatment is usually considered effective if it results in greater improvement than would result giving a patient a placebo, as it did in the Cole (1964) research.

May (1968) assessed the relative effectiveness of phenothiazine treatment, individual psychotherapy, phenothiazine treatment combined with individual psychotherapy, ECT, and milieu therapy (in which a hospital is organized to provide a total therapeutic community). The use of phenothiazine alone was as effective as phenothiazine plus individual psychotherapy. And both forms of treatment were superior to individual psychotherapy alone, ECT, and milieu therapy on measures of improvement that included staff ratings of patients and discharge rates from the hospital. All patients in the experimental groups were given some sort of therapy, so placebo effects presumably had no bearing on the results.

Despite their recognized effectiveness, antipsychotic drugs do not always reduce anxiety, and they can produce side effects. Patients may develop psychomotor symptoms resembling those of Parkinson's disease, sensitivity to light, dryness of the mouth, drowsiness, or liver disease. After at least six months of continuous treatment with antipsychotic drugs, some patients (usually patients older than forty years of age) develop tardive dyskinesia (Kane & Smith, 1982).

Patients discharged from hospitals typically show only marginal adjustments to community life, and psychotic symptoms usually return when the medication is discontinued. As a result, the rehospitalization rate is high. Nevertheless, drug therapy is very important in treating schizophrenia, and nearly all psychiatric institutions use it. Antipsychotic drugs have dramatically increased the proportion of schizophrenic patients who can return and function in the community, even though such patients may show residual symptoms (Lehmann, 1974).

Antidepressant Drugs   As in the case of antipsychotic drugs, the development of antidepressants was aided by a fortunate coincidence. During the 1950s, clinicians noticed that patients treated with the antituberculosis drug *iproniazid* became happier and more optimistic. When tested on depressed patients, the drug was found to be effective as an antidepressant. Unfortunately, liver damage and fatalities caused by the drug were relatively high. Continued interest in antidepressants has led to the identification of two large classes of the compounds: the **monoamine oxidase (MAO) inhibitors,** and the **tricyclics.**

A number of the MAO inhibitors such as *phenelzine* were found to be less dangerous but similar in effect to iproniazid. It is hypothesized that the MAO inhibitors work primarily to correct a deficiency in concentrations of neurotransmitters in the brain. They block the action of monoamine oxidase, thereby preventing the breakdown of norepinephrine and serotonin. As you recall from Chapters 1 and 12, the lack of these neurotransmitters at pertinent

synaptic sites has been implicated in depression. Although these compounds did relieve depression (Davis, Klerman & Schildkraut, 1967), they produced certain toxic effects and required careful dietary monitoring (certain foods and other drugs when taken with an MAO inhibitor could cause severe illness).

More frequently used in cases of depression are the tricyclics, which seem to work like the MAO inhibitors, but produce fewer of the side effects associated with prolonged drug use. The drug *imipramine*, a tricyclic, has been valuable in relieving the symptoms of depression (Klerman, 1988). Up until the present tricyclics were the most widely used medication in treating depression.

A recent addition to antidepressant medication that may become the preferred drug of treatment is fluoxetine hydrochloride (better known as Prozac). It works by inhibiting the CNS neuronal uptake of serotonin and nonepinephrine, although it appears to be a much more potent inhibitor of serotonin. When originally introduced, it was thought to be a relatively safe drug with minimal addictive characteristics and dangers associated with high overdoses. Its side effects were reported to be relatively mild and included nervousness, insomnia, and nausea (Cole & Bodkin, 1990). Recently, however, Prozac has become the center of a controversy because of its association with suicide and violent behavior (Cole & Bodkin, 1990; Food and Drug Administration, 1991; Papp & Gorman, 1990; Teicher, 1990). Claims that it increases suicidal and violent acting out behavior quickly brought Prozac to the attention of the public ("20/20" [television program], 1992); that a patient took Prozac has even been used as a defense in homicide trials.

The bad press received by Prozac and concerns for the safety of individuals prompted a special FDA Psychopharmacological Drug Advisor Committee meeting in 1991 (U.S. Department of Health & Human Services, 1991). Testimony from patients, advocacy groups, and other interested parties was taken, and selected studies were reanalyzed. The Committee concluded that there was no credible link showing an increase in suicidality or violent behavior in patients who use Prozac. They noted that suicidality is often a manifestation of depression and that reports of increased violent behaviors after taking Prozac were the result of a difference in reporting practices.

Despite these conclusions, it is safe to say that controversy surrounding the effects of Prozac will continue. The positive outcome from this may be a closer monitoring of drug usage by researchers and mental health practitioners.

Antimanic Drugs *Lithium* is another mood-controlling drug (antimanic) that has been very effective in treating bipolar disorders, especially mania (Bassuk, Schoonover & Gelenberg, 1983; Berger, 1978). It also controls depressive episodes. About 70 to 80 percent of manic states can be controlled by lithium. How it works remains highly speculative. One hypothesis is that it somehow limits the availability of serotonin and norepinephrine at the synapses and produces the opposite effect as the antidepressants. Yet lithium can also relieve depression, which appears contradictory to this explanation. Other speculations involve electrolyte changes in the body, which alters neurotransmission in some manner.

Strangely enough, lithium, which is administered as a salt, has no known physiological function (Berger, 1978). Yet when properly administered, patients' manic and depressive cycles can be modulated and prevented by simply taking a single tablet in the morning and in the evening. However, cautions limit the use of lithium in treating bipolar disorders. First, it is largely preventive and must be taken before symptoms appear. Once a manic or depressive state occurs, lithium has minimal effect on these conditions. Second, it is often extremely difficult to determine a patient's appropriate dosage. Often, the effective dosage level borders on toxicity (can cause convulsions, delirium, and so forth). So it is important to carefully and constantly monitor the lithium level in a patient's blood.

Psychopharmacological Considerations Deciding which drug to use with which kind of patient under what circumstances is a major issue in **psychopharmacology**—the study of the effects of drugs on the mind and on behavior. For example, imipramine is more effective with long-standing depressions without specific situational causes, and it is particularly indicated for people older than age forty and for people who show psychomotor retardation or psychotic symptoms (Research Task Force of the National Institute of Mental Health, 1975). But antidepressants often do not begin to help patients until two to three weeks after treatment begins. As a last resort, ECT is used to treat severely depressed or suicidal patients when rapid improvement is necessary.

The use of antidepressants, antianxiety drugs, and antipsychotics has greatly changed therapy. Patients who take them report that they feel better, that symptoms decline, and that overall functioning improves. Long hospitalization is no longer needed in most cases, and patients are more amenable to other forms of treatment, such as psychotherapy. Remember, however, that drugs do not cure mental disorders. Some would characterize their use as "control measures"; somewhat better than traditional hospitalization, "straightjackets," or "padded cells." Furthermore, it appears that drugs are effective with primarily "active" symptoms such as delusions, hallucinations, and aggression and much less effective with "passive" symptoms like withdrawal, poor interpersonal relationships, and feelings of alienation. Medication does not help the patient improve living skills. Many patients discharged from hospitals require continuing medication to function even minimally in the community. Unfortunately, many patients do not continue taking their medication once they leave the mental hospital. For example, many may not realize the importance of continued and timely medication, their ability to obtain medication financially may be impaired, or their lifestyles may not be conducive to taking it. Once this happens, patients may again experience the same disorder that led to their hospitalization.

PSYCHOTHERAPY

In most cases, biological treatments such as drug therapy are used as an adjunct to psychotherapy. But beyond general agreement that psychotherapy is an internal approach to treating psychopathology, involving interaction between one or more clients and a therapist, there is little consensus on exactly what else it is. Psychotherapy has been called "a conversation with a therapeutic purpose" (Korchin, 1976); it has also been called "the talking cure" or the "purchase of friendship" (Schofield, 1964). One observer has suggested that psychotherapy can be variously defined by goals, procedures, and methods; practitioners; or the relationship formed (Reisman, 1971).

The practice of therapy is both a science and an art. Based upon a conceptual framework, a trained professional must select the appropriate therapy techniques that will be beneficial to a particular client. Moreover, the therapist must establish a rapport with the client in order for the therapeutic process to be successful.

For our purposes, **psychotherapy** may be defined as the systematic application of techniques derived from psychological principles by a trained and experienced professional therapist, for the purpose of helping psychologically troubled people. We can't be more succinct or precise without getting involved in specific types of therapy. Depending on their perspective and theoretical orientation, therapists may seek to modify attitudes, thoughts, feelings, or behaviors; to facilitate the patient's self-insight and rational control of his or her own life; to cure mental illness; to enhance mental health and self-actualization; to make clients "feel better"; to remove a cause; to change a self-concept; or to encourage adaptation. Psychotherapy is practiced by many different kinds of people in many different ways—a fact that seems to preclude establishing a single set of standard therapeutic procedures. And—despite our emphasis on the scientific basis of therapy—in practice it is often more art than science.

Diverse psychotherapies do seem to share some common therapeutic factors. In a study of fifty publications on psychotherapy, the investigators found the most consensual commonalities to be (1) development of a therapeutic alliance, (2) opportunity for

catharsis, (3) acquisition and practice of new behaviors, and (4) the clients' positive expectancies (Grencavage & Norcross, 1990). These characteristics are very consistent with those proposed by Korchin (1976). First, psychotherapy is a chance for the client to *relearn*. Many people say to their psychotherapists, "I know I shouldn't feel or act this way, but I just can't help it." Psychotherapy provides a chance to unlearn, relearn, develop, or change certain behaviors or levels of functioning.

Second, psychotherapy helps generate the development of new, emotionally important experiences. A person questioning the value of psychotherapy may ask, "If I talk about my problems, how will that cause me to change, even though I may understand myself better? I talk things over now, with friends." But psychotherapy is not merely a "talking cure." It involves the reexperiencing of emotions that clients may have avoided, along with the painful and helpless feelings fostered by these emotions. This *experiencing* allows relearning as well as emotional and intellectual insight into problems and conflicts.

Third, there is a *therapeutic relationship*. Therapists have been trained to listen, show sympathetic concern, be objective, value the client's integrity, communicate understanding, and use their professional knowledge and skills. Therapists may provide reassurance, interpretations, self-disclosures, reflections of the client's feelings, or information, each at appropriate times. As a team, therapist and client are better prepared to venture into frightening areas that the client would not have faced alone.

Finally, clients in psychotherapy have certain *motivations* and *expectations*. Most people enter therapy with both anxiety and hope. They are frightened by their emotional difficulties and by the prospect of treatment, but they expect or hope that therapy will be helpful.

The goals and general characteristics of psychotherapy as described seem admirable, and most people consider them so. Nevertheless, psychotherapy itself has been criticized as being biased and inappropriate to the lifestyles of many clients such as members of minority groups. A few of its more specific characteristics, and their potential effects on culturally different clients, are outlined in Focus 18.1.

First we will discuss individual psychotherapy, in which one therapist treats one client at any one time, and then group and family therapy. We will also distinguish between insight- and action-oriented approaches to individual therapy. This distinction separates (1) approaches that stress awareness, understanding, and consciousness of one's own motivations (that is, insight) from (2) approaches that stress actions such as changing one's behavior or thoughts (London, 1964a). The first set includes the psychoanalytic and humanistic-existential therapies, whereas the second set involves mainly behavioral therapies. Despite this variety of approaches, many therapists use similar treatment strategies (Weiner, 1976). And, as noted in Chapter 1, many therapists choose relevant techniques from all the various "pure" approaches to develop the most effective integrative approach for each particular client.

INSIGHT-ORIENTED APPROACHES TO INDIVIDUAL PSYCHOTHERAPY

The theoretical bases of the major insight-oriented psychotherapies were discussed in Chapter 2. Here we briefly review these theoretical bases, and then discuss most common treatment techniques.

Psychoanalysis

According to Freud's theory of personality, people are born with certain instinctual drives, urges that constantly seek to discharge or express themselves. As the personality structure develops, conflicts occur among the id, ego, and superego. If conflicts remain unresolved, they will resurface during adulthood. The relative importance of such an unresolved conflict depends on the psychosexual stage (oral, anal, phallic, latency, or genital) in which it occurs. The earlier the stage in which an unresolved conflict arises, the greater the conflict's effect on subsequent behaviors. Repressing unacceptable thoughts and impulses (within the unconscious) is the primary way that people defend themselves against such thoughts.

Psychoanalytic therapy, or psychoanalysis, seeks to overcome defenses so that (1) repressed material can be uncovered, (2) the client can achieve insight into his or her inner motivations and desires, and (3) unresolved childhood conflicts can be controlled. Psychoanalysis requires many sessions of therapy over a long period of time. It may not be appropriate for certain types of people, such as nonverbal adults, young children who cannot be verbally articulate or reasonable, shizoid people, those with urgent problems requiring immediate reduction of symptoms, and the mentally retarded (Fenichel, 1945).

Psychoanalysts traditionally use four methods to achieve their therapeutic goals: free association and dream analysis, analysis of resistance, transference, and interpretation.

Free Association and Dream Analysis In free association the patient just talks, saying whatever comes to mind, regardless of how illogical or embarrassing it may seem. Psychoanalysts believe the material that surfaces in this process is determined by the patient's psychic makeup and that it can provide some understanding of the patient's conflicts, unconscious processes, and personality dynamics. Simply asking the patient to talk about his or her conflicts is fruitless because the patient has repressed the really important material from his or her consciousness. Instead, reports of dreams, feelings, thoughts, and fantasies reflect the patient's psychodynamics; the therapist's tasks are to encourage continuous free association of thoughts and to interpret the results.

Similarly, dream analysis is a very important therapeutic tool that depends on psychoanalytic interpre-

Psychotherapy and Cultural Bias

Racial and ethnic minorities have frequently criticized psychotherapy as being a "handmaiden of the status quo," a "transmitter of society's values," and an "instrument of oppression." Rather than helping people reach their full potential, critics say, it has often been used to subjugate the very people it was meant to free. The meaning of such statements is clear: the process and goals of psychotherapy are culture bound and thus culturally biased against people whose values differ from those of western societies. The following "generic characteristics of therapy," which seem to be common to most schools of thought, often conflict with clients' cultural values (D. W. Sue, 1981; D. W. Sue & D. Sue, 1990):

1. *Focus on the individual* Most forms of counseling and psychotherapy stress the importance and uniqueness of the individual, as reflected in the I-thou relationship, the one-to-one encounter, and the belief that the client must take responsibility for himself or herself. In many cultural groups, however, the basic psychosocial unit is not the individual but the family, the group, or the collective society. For example, many Asians and Hispanics define their identities within the family constellation. Whatever a person does reflects not only on that person, but on the entire family as

well. Important decisions are thus made by the entire family rather than by the individual.

Therapists who work with people from such cultures may see their clients as "dependent," "lacking in maturity," or "avoiding responsibility." These negative labels do much harm to the self-esteem of minority-group members, especially when they become part of a diagnosis.

2. *Verbal expression of emotions* The psychotherapeutic process works best for clients who are verbal, articulate, and able to express their feelings and be assertive. The major medium of communication is the spoken word (in standard English). Those who tend to be less

tation of hidden meanings in dreams. Freud is often credited with referring to dreams as "the royal road to the unconscious." According to psychoanalytic theory, when people sleep, defenses and inhibitions of the ego weaken, allowing unacceptable motives and feelings to surface. This material comes out in the disguised and symbolic form of a dream. The portion we remember is called the *manifest content,* and the deeper, unacceptable impulse is the *latent content.* The therapist's job is to uncover the disguised symbolic meanings and let the patient achieve insight into the anxiety-provoking implications.

Analysis of Resistance Throughout the course of psychoanalytic therapy, the patient's unconscious may try to block the process—to prevent the exposure of repressed material. In free association, for example, the patient may suddenly change the subject, lose the train of thought, go blank, or become silent. As noted in Chapter 2, such **resistance** may also show up in a patient's late arrival or failure to keep an appointment. A trained analyst is alert to telltale signs of resistance because they indicate that a sensitive area is being approached. The therapist

can make therapeutic use of properly interpreted instances of resistance to show the patient that repressed material is coming close to the surface and to suggest means of uncovering it.

Transference When a patient begins to perceive, or behave toward, the therapist as though the therapist were an important person in the patient's past, the process of transference is occurring. In **transference** the patient reenacts early conflicts by carrying over and applying to the therapist feelings and attitudes that the patient had toward significant others—primarily parents—in the past. These feelings and attitudes then become accessible to understanding. They may be positive, involve feelings of love for the analyst, or negative, involving feelings of anger and hostility.

Part of the psychoanalyst's strategy is to remain "unknown" or ambiguous, so that the client can freely develop whatever kind of transference is required. The patient is allowed, even encouraged, to develop unrealistic expectations and attitudes regarding the therapist. These expectations and attitudes are used as a basis for helping the patient deal realisti-

verbal, who speak with an accent, or who do not use standard English are placed at a disadvantage. In addition, many cultural groups (including Asians and Native Americans) are brought up to conceal rather than verbalize their feelings; therapists often perceived them as "inhibited," "lacking in spontaneity," or "repressed." Thus the therapeutic process, by valuing expressiveness, may not only force minority clients to violate their cultural norms but also label them as having negative personality traits.

3. *Openness and intimacy* Self-disclosure and discussion of the most intimate and personal aspects of one's life are hallmarks of therapy. Cultural and sociopolitical factors, however, may make some clients unwilling or unable to engage in such self-disclosure. For example,

in Focus 1.1 we discussed the "cultural paranoia" that many African-Americans have developed as a defense against discrimination and oppression—a healthy distrust that would make them reluctant to disclose their innermost thoughts and feelings to a European-American therapist. Unfortunately, therapists who encountered this reluctance might perceive their clients as suspicious, guarded, and paranoid. Likewise, many therapists don't understand the cultural implications of disclosure among Asians, who discuss intimate matters with only close acquaintances, and not with strangers (which therapists may well be).

4. *Insight* Most closely associated with the psychodynamic approach but valued in many theoretical orientations, *insight* is the ability to

understand the basis of one's motivations, perceptions, and behavior. But many cultural groups do not value insight. In China, for example, when a person becomes depressed or anxious, he or she may be advised to avoid the thoughts that are causing the distress. This contrasts abruptly with the western belief that insight is always helpful in therapy.

The solution to this "culture gap" is obvious: therapists need to (1) become aware of their own cultural values, biases, and assumptions; (2) learn and understand the cultural values of other groups; and (3) develop more appropriate culture-specific intervention strategies for use with minority-group clients (Sue, 1990).

Source: D. W. Sue, 1981; D. W. Sue & D. Sue, 1990.

---

cally with painful early experiences. In essence, a miniature neurosis is re-created; its resolution is crucial to the therapy.

At the same time, the therapist must be careful to recognize and control any instances of *countertransference*. In this process, the therapist—who is also a human being with feelings and fears—transfers those feelings to the patient. This is one reason why Freud believed so strongly that all psychoanalysts need to undergo psychoanalysis themselves.

Interpretation Through interpretation—the explanation of a patient's free associations, reports of dreams, and the like—a sensitive analyst can help the patient gain insight (both intellectual and emotional) into his or her repressed conflicts. By pointing out the symbolic attributes of a transference relationship or by noting the peculiar timing of symptoms, the therapist can direct the patient toward conscious control of unconscious conflicts.

The following example shows the timely interpretation of an important instance of transference:

Sandy (the patient): John [her ex-husband] was just like my father. Always condemning me, always making

me feel like an idiot! Strange, the two of them—the most important men in my life—they did the most to screw me up. When I would have fun with my friends and come home at night, he would be sitting there—waiting—to disapprove.
Therapist (male): Who would be waiting for you?
Sandy: Huh?
Therapist: Who's the "he" who'd be waiting?
Sandy: John—I mean, my father—you're confusing me now. . . . My father would sit there—smoking his pipe. I knew what he was thinking, though—he didn't have to say it—he was thinking I was a slut! Someone—who, who was a slut! So what if I stayed up late and had some fun? What business was it of his? He never took any interest in any of us. (Begins to weep.) It was my mother—rest her soul—who loved us, not our father. He worked her to death. Lord, I miss her. (Weeps uncontrollably.)—I must sound angry at my father. Don't you think I have a right to be angry?
Therapist: Do you think you have a right to be angry?
Sandy: Of course, I do! Why are you questioning me? You don't believe me, do you?
Therapist: You want me to believe you.
Sandy: I don't care whether you believe me or not. As far as I'm concerned, you're just a wall that I'm talking to—I don't know why I pay for this rotten ther-

Freud often referred to dreams as "the royal road to the unconscious." Dream analysis is based upon the premise that during sleep the ego's defenses weaken, allowing repressed and unacceptable feelings to surface in the form of images and symbols. The therapist's task is to help the client understand the meaning of those images.

apy.—Don't you have any thoughts or feelings at all? I know what you're thinking—you think I'm crazy—you must be laughing at me—I'll probably be a case in your next book! You're just sitting there—smirking—making me feel like a bad person—thinking I'm wrong for being mad, that I have no right to be mad.
Therapist: Just like your father.
Sandy: Yes, you're just like my father.—Oh my God! Just now—I—I—thought I was talking to him.
Therapist: You mean your father.
Sandy: Yes—I'm really scared now—how could I have—can this really be happening to me?
Therapist: I know it must be awfully scary to realize what just happened—but don't run away now, Sandy. Could it be that your relationship with your father has affected many of the relationships you've had with

other men? It seems that your reaction to me just now, and your tendency to sometimes refer to your ex-husband as your father—
Sandy: God!—I don't know—what should I do about it?—Is it real?

Modern Psychoanalysis In Chapter 2, we noted the contemporary changes in theoretical formulations of psychoanalytic theory, especially the increased importance of the ego (ego autonomy theorists) and past interpersonal relationships (object relations theorists). Among the ego autonomy theorists were people such as Anna Freud, Heinz Hartmann, and Erik Erikson, who believed that cognitive processes of the ego were often constructive, creative, and productive (independent from the id). Likewise, object relations theorists such as Melanie Klein, Margaret Mahler, Otto Kernberg, and Heinz Kohut stressed the importance of interpersonal relationships and the child's separation from the mother as important in one's psychological growth. The contributions of these theorists and practitioners expanded and loosened the rigid therapeutic techniques of traditional psychoanalysis. Today, very few psychodynamic therapists practice traditional psychoanalysis. Most are more active in their sessions, restrict the number of sessions they have with clients, place greater emphasis on current rather than past factors, and seem to have adopted a number of client-centered techniques in their practice.

The Effectiveness of Psychoanalysis The theoretical validity of psychoanalysis has come under attack, as have its lack of research support and its methods. The impossibility of providing operational definitions for such constructs as the unconscious and the libido makes it extremely difficult to confirm the various aspects of the theory. For example, psychoanalytic theory suggests that neurotic symptoms are caused by underlying emotional conflicts. When these symptoms are eliminated without removing the conflict, the person merely expresses the neurosis in other ways and shows other symptoms—a phenomenon known as *symptom substitution.* Many researchers, particularly behavior therapists, assert that it is possible to eliminate neurotic symptoms without symptom substitution occurring (Rachman, 1971). Furthermore, they contend that when the symptoms are eliminated the neurosis is cured.

Table 18.2

Results of Three Treatments for Interpersonal Performance Anxiety

	Results Found at 2-Year Follow-up		
Treatment	Significantly Improved (%)	No Change (%)	Significantly Worse
Desensitization	85	15	—
Attention-placebo	50	50	—
Insight	50	50	—
Control	22	78	—

Source: Adapted from Paul, 1967.

In a classic study, the effectiveness of various treatment approaches was examined, and possible substitution was assessed in a follow-up performed two years later (Paul, 1967). Students who were very afraid of public speaking were assigned to one of four treatment groups:

1. A systematic desensitization group with which a behavior modification approach involving relaxation was used (this technique is discussed later in this chapter)

2. An attention placebo group that was given placebo pills and told that the pills would reduce anxiety

3. An insight therapy group conducted by experienced psychotherapists to help the subjects gain insight into their anxieties

4. A control group that received no treatment

Anxiety was measured in several ways, both before and after the treatments, which were conducted over a five-week period. As Table 18.2 shows, the systematic desensitization treatment was the most effective approach, although insight therapy and attention placebo treatment also reduced more anxiety than did no treatment at all. These results persisted over two years; symptom substitution did not occur.

Proponents of psychoanalysis might argue, however, that a five-week treatment is too short to provide full benefit and that the student subjects did not have the kinds of problems typically seen in treatment. Furthermore, in clinical practice it is often evident that *the symptom is not the disorder*. For exam-

ple, a child who shows antisocial behavior and aggression may really be suffering from neglect. If the symptoms are removed but the neglect remains, symptom substitution may occur. Some behavior therapists acknowledge this potential problem (O'Leary & Wilson, 1975). Meanwhile, psychoanalysis continues to have strong supporters (Silverman, 1976).

Humanistic-Existential Therapies

In contrast to the psychic determinism implicit in psychoanalysis, the humanistic-existential therapies stress the importance of self-actualization, self-concept, free will, responsibility, and the understanding of the client's phenomenological world. The focus is on qualities of "humanness"; human beings cannot be understood without reference to their personal uniqueness and wholeness. Among the several humanistic-existential therapies are person-centered therapy, existential analysis, and gestalt therapy.

Person-Centered Therapy Carl Rogers, the founder of person-centered therapy, believed that people can develop better self-concepts and move toward self-actualization if the therapist provides certain therapeutic conditions. These are the conditions in which clients use their own innate tendencies to grow, to actively negotiate with their environment, and to realize their potential. Thus therapists must accept clients as people, show empathy and respect, and provide unconditional positive regard for clients. A therapist should not control, inhibit, threaten, or interpret a client's behaviors. These actions are manip-

Some Types of Therapy Groups

1. *Human relations training groups* The goal of sensitivity training is to help people increase their sensitivity to others and improve their human relations skills so that they can be more efficient and responsive in their relationships with others—particularly in schools or business organizations. The group leader focuses on group processes (such as how members are relating to one another and what is happening in the group) and encourages members to be open, honest, and flexible. Rather than dominating the sessions, the leader helps members develop their own ideas (Korchin, 1976).

2. *Encounter groups* Drawing on certain principles of sensitivity training, Carl Rogers conceived of encounter groups to facilitate human growth and development (greater effectiveness, openness, spontaneity, and flexibility) through encounter experiences. Freedom of expression and the reduction of defensiveness are encouraged. The group leader acts as a facilitator, refusing to direct the group authoritatively or to manipulate group activities. Merely by providing a climate of respect and freedom, the group helps members develop trust and become less defensive and allows greater freedom to grow and use positive experiences. Although Rogers observed that group members are initially frustrated and anxious over the lack of group structure and direction, they later begin to feel freedom and trust.

3. *Transactional analysis* Transactional analysis (TA) is a group therapy technique based on the assumption that people play certain "games" that hinder development of genuine and deep interpersonal relationships. These games have disguised goals, which are usually related to the need for recognition. The game of "one-up-manship" is an example: person A may approach person B to get help with a problem. B sincerely attempts to help A by offering advice and sympathy, taking on the role of therapist. A rejects the advice and points out its flaws. B offers alternative advice, only to have it rejected again.

ulative, and they undermine the client's ability to find his or her own direction.

Person-centered therapy thus emphasizes the kind of person the therapist should be in the therapeutic relationship rather than the precise techniques to use in therapy. Particular details of this therapeutic approach were discussed in Chapter 2.

Existential Analysis

Existential analysis follows no single theory or group of therapeutic techniques. Instead, it is concerned with the person's experience and involvement in the world as a being with consciousness and self-consciousness. Existential therapists believe that the inability to accept death or nonbeing as a reality restricts self-actualization. In contemporary society, many people feel lonely and alienated; they lose a sense of the meaning of life, of self-responsibility, and of free will. This state of mind is popularly called "existential crisis." The task of the therapist is to engage clients in an encounter in which they can experience their own existence as being real. The encounter should involve genuine sharing between partners, in which the therapist, too, may grow and be influenced. (The encounter group, described in Focus 18.2, owes much to Rogerian and existential analysis.) When clients can experience their existence and nonexistence, then feelings of responsibility, choice, and meaning re-emerge. (Again, see Chapter 2 for additional details.)

Existential approaches to therapy are strongly philosophical in nature. They have not received any research scrutiny because many existential concepts and methods are difficult to define operationally for research purposes. Furthermore, existential therapists point out that therapist and client are engaged in a complex encounter that can't be broken down into components for empirical observation, so research studies are incapable of assessing the impact of therapy. Although impressive case histories indicate its effectiveness, little empirical support exists.

Gestalt Therapy

The German word gestalt means "whole." As conceptualized by Fritz Perls in 1969, **gestalt therapy** emphasizes the importance of a per-

B then feels helpless and perhaps guilty for letting A down. A is "one up" over B, who has been "put down" and has become apologetic. A transactional role reversal has been accomplished by person A.

Underlying TA is the idea that people adopt certain roles (child, adult, and parent) that reflect their ego states (Berne, 1972). "Spoiled brat" behavior or excessive dependency indicates the child role; the adult role is characterized by mature and rational behavior; and the parent role is a controlling one, in which the person treats others like children. In many marriages, one spouse often acts as parent (dominating, commanding), while the other adopts the role of child (incapable, immature). Berne felt that such interpersonal transactions hinder the development of authentic relationships. The purpose of TA ther-

apy is first to make the client aware of the games he or she is playing and then to eliminate them and allow more authentic means of expression, more meaningful relationships with others, and better life adjustment. Transactional analysis may be used for families or for unrelated people in group therapy.

4. Assertiveness training groups Assertiveness training groups use behavior therapy techniques to help people who want to assert or express themselves better. Many people feel unable to express hostility, criticism, or warmth. In assertiveness training, people are constantly reminded of the negative consequences of nonassertive behaviors and are encouraged to act out and practice assertive skills (both in the group sessions and outside of the sessions).

Assertiveness training has been

unfairly characterized as a breeding ground for the development of overly critical and hostile people. The actual intent is to train people to express themselves appropriately.

5. Psychodrama Jacob Moreno (1946) was among the first to use the term *group therapy* in his writings. He developed psychodrama, a form of group therapy in which patients and other people role-play situations. When clients act out current or anticipated situations, they become aware of their feelings, and they can rehearse techniques for working out their problems. Others may play supporting roles, so that the client can fully act out the situation and interact with them. At times the client and another person may exchange roles, so that the client can understand the motives and behaviors of others with whom he or she interacts.

son's totality of experience, which should not be fragmented or separated. Perls believed that when affective and cognitive experiences are isolated, people lack full awareness of their complete experience.

In gestalt therapy, clients are asked to discuss the totality of the here-and-now. Only experiences, feelings, and behaviors occurring in the present are stressed. Past experiences or anticipated future experiences are brought up only in relation to current feelings. Interestingly, Perls was originally trained as a psychoanalyst, but he later rejected Freudian theory. He did, however, incorporate dream analysis in his work. Dreams too are interpreted in relation to the here-and-now. As a means of opening clients to their experiences, therapists encourage clients to

1. Make personalized and unqualified statements that help them "act out" their emotions. For example, instead of hedging by saying, "It is sometimes upsetting when your boss yells at you," a client is encouraged to say "I get scared when my boss yells at me."

2. Exaggerate the feelings associated with behaviors to gain greater awareness of their experiences and to eliminate intellectual explanations for them.

3. Role-play situations and then focus on what was experienced during the role playing.

As in the case of existential analysis, gestalt therapy has generated little research. Thus it is difficult to evaluate its effectiveness. Proponents of gestalt therapy are convinced that clients are helped, but sufficient empirical support has never emerged. (You might be interested in reading Perls's remarkable book *Gestalt Therapy Verbatim* [1969] for a fuller explanation of this approach.)

ACTION-ORIENTED APPROACHES TO INDIVIDUAL PSYCHOTHERAPY

The principles underlying the action-oriented or behaviorist approaches to abnormal behavior were dis-

Fritz Perls (1893–1970) developed gestalt therapy to help troubled clients become aware of themselves as whole individuals. He believed this awareness to be therapeutic in and of itself. Experiencing, feeling, and being in the here-and-now were the goals of his therapeutic approach.

cussed in Chapter 3. Treatment based on classical conditioning, operant conditioning, observational learning, and cognitive-behavioral processes has gained widespread popularity, and behavior therapists typically use a variety of techniques (Kazdin & Wilson, 1978). Many of these techniques have been discussed in preceding chapters; this section presents selected important behavioral techniques.

Classical Conditioning Techniques

Using classical conditioning principles described in Chapter 3, Joseph Wolpe (1973) used systematic desensitization as treatment for anxiety (discussed in Chapter 6). Its objective is to reduce anxiety that is a response to a stimulus situation by eliciting—in the given situation—a response that is incompatible with anxiety. For example, if a woman is afraid of flying

in a jet plane, her anxiety response could be reduced by training her to relax while in airplanes.

Systematic desensitization typically includes training in relaxation, the construction of a fear hierarchy, and the combination of relaxation and imagined scenes from the fear hierarchy. To illustrate the process, we can use the example of the person who wants to overcome her fear of flying. The therapist would first train her to relax, probably employing a progressive relaxation method in which the muscles are alternately tensed and relaxed (Jacobson, 1964). The client would be asked to list situations involved in flying that make her anxious and to rank them from least upsetting to most anxiety producing. For example, making airline reservations might arouse a little anxiety; taking a taxi to the airport could result in more anxiety; entering the plane, fastening the seatbelt, taking off, flying 35,000 feet above sea level, and so on all would probably involve increasing anxiety levels.

In systematic desensitization, the client is asked to *imagine* herself in each of these situations. It is obviously more convenient to imagine situations than to actually go through them, and most clients experience anxiety when they imagine such situations. (*In vivo* approaches, in which clients are actually present in the fear-provoking situations, have also been used.)

Once the person is able to relax, the therapist asks the client first to imagine a low-anxiety scene (such as making flight reservations) and to relax at the same time. The client then proceeds up the fear hierarchy, imagining each situation in order. If a particular situation elicits too much anxiety, the client is told to return to a less anxiety-provoking one. This procedure is repeated until the client can imagine the entire hierarchy without anxiety.

Behavior therapists believe that systematic desensitization is more effective than psychotherapy; it certainly requires fewer sessions to achieve desired results (Paul, 1967; Wolpe, 1973). Systematic desensitization has stimulated a great deal of research, and its efficacy in reducing fears has been well documented (Rachman & Hodgeson, 1980). Some researchers question the need for certain procedural aspects of the treatment approach. For example, Wolpe's rather rigid format for desensitization may be unnecessary, and alternatives to relaxation, such as talking about the fear or listening to soothing music, may be used in the process (Nathan & Jackson, 1976; Sue, 1972).

Flooding and Implosion Two other techniques that use the classical conditioning principles of extinction are flooding and implosion (Levis, 1985; Stampfl & Levis, 1967). The two are very similar to one another: **flooding** involves placing the client in a real-life anxiety-provoking situation, and **implosion** relies on the client's ability to imagine the anxiety-arousing scene. The difference between systematic desensitization and flooding and implosion lies in the speed with which the fearful situation is introduced to the client. Systematic desensitization introduces it more slowly. Flooding and implosion require the client to immediately confront the feared situation in its full intensity. The belief is that the client's fears will be extinguished if he or she is not allowed to avoid or escape the situation. In flooding, for example, a client who's afraid of heights may be taken to the top of a tall building, mountain, or bridge and physically prevented from leaving. Some studies have indicated that flooding effectively eliminates specific fears such as phobias (Emmelkamp & Wessels, 1975; Foa & Kozak, 1986). In implosion therapy, the client is forced to imagine a feared situation. For example, a therapist might ask a client who is afraid of flying to close her eyes and imagine the following:

> You are flying in an airplane. Suddenly the plane hits an air pocket and begins to shake violently from side to side. Meal trays fly around, and passengers who do not have their seatbelts fastened are thrown from their seats. People start to scream. As you look out the window, the plane's wing is flying by. The pilot's frantic voice over the loudspeaker is shouting: "Prepare to crash, prepare to crash!" Your seatbelt breaks and you must hang on for dear life, while the plane is spinning around and careening. You can tell that the plane is falling rapidly. The ground is coming toward you. The situation is hopeless—all will die.

Presumably the client feels intense anxiety, after which she is told to "wake up." Repeated exposure to such a high level of anxiety eventually causes the stimulus to lose its power to elicit anxiety and leads to extinction.

The developers of implosion and flooding believe that they can be effective, though some clients find the procedures too traumatic and discontinue treatment (Emmelkamp & Wessels, 1975). In general,

these methods have not been scrutinized as carefully as systematic desensitization, but they have been used successfully with some clients (Barrett, 1969; Baum, 1970).

Aversive Conditioning In aversive conditioning, a widely used classical conditioning technique, the undesirable behavior is paired with an unpleasant stimulus. For example, it was used in an attempt to modify the smoking behaviors of heavy smokers (Franks, Fried & Ashem, 1966). The smokers were asked to sit in front of an apparatus that delivers either smoke or fresh air to the face. They were told to smoke their favorite cigarettes; as long as they continued puffing, smoke was blown into their faces. When the smoke became unbearable, they could put out their cigarettes and have fresh air delivered. The program showed limited positive results: of twenty-three volunteer smokers, fourteen did not complete the four-week program because of low motivation, dislike of the method, or unavailability. Of the remaining nine who completed the project, four stopped smoking, one smoked less, one changed to a pipe, and two showed no change.

Aversive conditioning has also been applied to alcoholics, drug addicts, and people with sexual disorders, again with varying degrees of success. The noxious stimuli have included electric shock, drugs, odors, verbal censure, and reprimands. Some aversive conditioning programs also provide positive reinforcement for alternative behaviors that are deemed appropriate.

Several problems have been encountered in the use of aversive conditioning. First, because noxious stimuli are used, many people in treatment discontinue therapy, as in the smoking-reduction program just described. Second, aversive methods often suppress the undesirable behavior only temporarily, especially when punishment for those behaviors is applied solely in a laboratory situation that bears little resemblance to real life. Third, the client may become anxious and hostile. And some critics argue that punishment is unethical or has potential for misuse and abuse (Silverstein, 1972). Partially as a response to these criticisms, as well as for practical reasons, some therapists advocate the use of *covert sensitization*. Like implosion, it requires imagining the aversive situation along with the behavior one is trying to eliminate (Cautela, 1966, 1967). A person who wants to stop smoking may be asked to imagine a smoke-filled room, becoming nauseous, suffocating, and dying of lung cancer and emphysema.

Operant Conditioning Techniques

Behavior modification using operant methods has flourished, and many ingenious programs have been developed. As in the case of classical conditioning, only a few important examples are presented here.

Token Economies   Treatment programs that reward patients with tokens for appropriate behaviors are known as **token economies** (Kazdin, 1980). The tokens may be exchanged for hospital privileges, food, or weekend passes. The goal is to modify patient behaviors using a secondary reinforcer (the tokens). In much the same way, money operates as a secondary reinforcer for people who work.

Three elements are necessary to a token economy: (1) the designation by hospital staff of certain patient behaviors as desirable and reinforceable; (2) a medium of exchange, such as coinlike tokens or tallies on a piece of paper; and (3) goods, services, or privileges that the tokens can buy. It is up to the hospital staff to dispense the tokens for desirable patient behaviors (Ullman & Krasner, 1975). In one psychiatric hospital ward, tokens could be exchanged for hospital passes, cigarettes, food, television viewing, and the choice of dining room tablemates. Patients were given tokens for good grooming and neat physical appearance, and for washing dishes and performing other chores. Although the program markedly improved the behavior of schizophrenic patients, when tokens were no longer given, patient involvement in the previously reinforced activities decreased (Ayllon & Azrin, 1968). This finding supported the conclusion that tokens were responsible for the success. Other studies have also indicated that token economy systems are effective with chronic hospitalized patients who are considered resistant to treatment (Paul, 1982). Token economies also tend to raise staff morale (Ullman & Krasner, 1975).

Token economy programs are used in a variety of settings, with such different types of people as juvenile delinquents, schoolchildren, the retarded, and patients in residential community homes. Although such programs have been extremely successful in modifying behaviors in institutional settings, problems remain. Some patients don't respond to token economies; complex behaviors, such as those involving language, are difficult to modify with this technique; and desirable patient behaviors that are exhibited in a hospital may not be continued outside the hospital setting.

Punishment   When less drastic methods are ineffective, punishment is sometimes used in treating autistic and schizophrenic children (Lovaas, 1977; Lovaas, Schaeffer & Simmons, 1965). In an early study, Lovaas and colleagues attempted to modify the behaviors of two 5-year-old identical twins who were diagnosed as schizophrenics. The children had shown no response to conventional treatment and were largely unresponsive in everyday interpersonal situations. They showed no reaction to speech and did not themselves speak; they did not recognize adults or each other; and they engaged in temper tantrums, self-destructive behaviors, and inappropriate handling of objects. The experimenters decided to use electric shock as a punishment for the purpose of modifying the children's behaviors. A floor gridded with metal tape was constructed so that a painful but not physically damaging shock could be administered to their bare feet. By turning the shock on and off, the experimenters found it possible to condition approach (social) behaviors in the children. Affectionate responses (kissing and hugging) were developed and tantrum behaviors were eliminated—all via the use of shock as an aversive stimulus.

Lovaas's work has shown that operant conditioning is a powerful technique for changing the behavior of autistic children who have failed to respond to other forms of treatment. For many years, researchers have stressed that autism and childhood schizophrenia are learned disorders and that autistic behaviors can be modified with behavioral techniques (Ferster, 1961). Because of the ethical issues raised by the use of electric shocks, however, use of this punishment technique has declined in recent years (Harris & Ersner-Hershfield, 1978; Russo, Carr & Lovaas, 1980).

Observational Learning Techniques

As discussed in Chapter 3, *observational learning* is the acquisition of new behaviors by watching them. The process of demonstrating these behaviors to a person or audiences is called *modeling*. Modeling has been shown to be effective in helping people acquire more appropriate behaviors. In one experiment, young adults who showed an intense fear of snakes were assigned to four groups:

1. The *live modeling with participation* group watched a live model who initiated progressively more fear-evoking activities with the snake. Subjects were then guided to imitate the model and encouraged to touch the snake, first with a gloved hand and then with a bare hand.

2. The *symbolic modeling* group underwent relaxation training and then viewed a film in which children and adults were seen handling snakes in progressively more fear-evoking circumstances.

3. The *systematic desensitization* group received systematic desensitization treatment for snake phobias.

4. The *control* group received no treatment.

Before treatment, the approach behaviors of all the subjects toward snakes were equally low. After treatment, the ability to approach and touch snakes had increased for all treated subjects (the first three groups), who performed better than the control group. The live modeling with participation group showed the greatest change: nearly all the subjects voluntarily touched the snake (Bandura, Blanchard & Ritter, 1969).

In a different kind of application, modeling was used to effect changes in institutionalized delinquent boys. The boys were asked to observe the behavior of a model and then to imitate that behavior. The model demonstrated how to behave appropriately in situations that the boys were likely to encounter: job situations, school settings, and interactions with parents and authority figures. The results were encouraging. The boys behaved more maturely than an untreated control group, and a follow-up study found them less likely to be institutionalized (Sarason & Ganzer, 1973).

The modeling of behaviors shown in films has been successfully used in medical and dental practices to reduce fears of medical procedures (Wilson & O'Leary, 1980), in teaching social skills (Bellack, Hersen & Himmelnoch, 1983), and in reducing compulsions and phobias (Rachman & Hodgeson, 1980).

Aaron Beck (b.1921) is probably best known for his cognitive-behavioral approach to the treatment of depression. His theory, however, has wider applications. Believing that many disorders are cognitively produced, Beck attempts to recognize what the client is thinking, help that person recognize faulty or ineffective thinking patterns, and effect change via feedback.

Cognitive-Behavioral Therapy

In Chapter 3, we discussed in some detail how cognitive-behavioral approaches believe that psychopathology stems from irrational, faulty, negative, and distorted thinking or self-statements that a person makes to himself or herself. As a result, most cognitive approaches share several elements. First, cognitive restructuring is used to change a client's irrational, self-defeating, and distorted thoughts and attitudes to more rational, positive, and appropriate ones (Beck, 1976, 1985; Ellis, 1973; Meichenbaum, 1977). Second, skills training is used to help clients

CRITICAL THINKING

Is "Healthy Denial" Healthy?

While taking a shower one morning, Patricia N. discovered a lump on her right breast. Although it was neither sore nor itchy, she believed it to be an insect bite. After several weeks when it did not disappear, she became concerned but put off seeing her doctor. Indeed, during her showers she avoided touching her right breast and seemed to operate on the belief "out of sight, out of mind."

Fred was an avid hiker and mountain climber who worked part-time as a guide at Yosemite National Forests. He had recently begun exploring unknown caves and abandoned mines. During one of these forays into a former California gold mine, he became trapped when part of the opening collapsed. Heavy boulders blocked the opening and there appeared to be no other entrance out. With only a two-day supply of water and food, Fred showed no outward signs of panic. Indeed, he found a comfortable spot in the cave, rested for the remainder of the day, and fell asleep.

Are these healthy responses on the part of Patricia and Fred? Shouldn't Patricia be seeking medical advice in case the lump turns out to be cancer?

Shouldn't Fred be doing something productive to get out of his predicament? Both of these individuals seem to be denying the possible danger that they are in. According to traditional psychotherapeutic thinking, denial is an unhealthy defense mechanism that not only distorts reality, but prevents us from taking corrective actions to solve our problems. Although this belief may be more true than false (as in the case of Patricia), a number of researchers have begun to question this premise.

According to Lazarus (1983) and Lazarus and Launier (1979), denial and illusions may not always be pathological. This line of thought

learn to manage and overcome stress. Third, problem solving provides clients with strategies for dealing with specific problems in living.

Initially, Albert Ellis's rational-emotive therapy, or RET (1962) was not well received by therapists. Attitudes soon changed, however, when the behaviorists became increasingly interested in mediating cognitive processes. In addition, RET and the behavioral strategies are similar in a number of ways. For example, RET incorporates cognitive restructuring, skills training, and problem-solving skills. Cognitive restructuring specifically is used to help clients deal with their irrational thoughts and beliefs. For example, a client's belief that he or she should be loved by everyone is attacked directly by the therapist: "What is so awful about not being loved by everyone? If your father doesn't love you, that's his problem!" Once the client begins to restructure his or her thoughts, the therapist begins the task of helping the client learn new ways to appraise and evaluate situa-

tions. Last, homework assignments (behavioral rehearsal) are given to help the client learn new strategies to deal with situations.

Aaron Beck (1976, 1985; Beck & Weishaar, 1989) has also been a major contributor to cognitive behavioral therapy. Originally using this approach to treat depression, he has extended his treatment to other disorders such as anxiety and phobias (Beck, 1985; Beck & Emery, 1985). Beck has held that emotional disorders are primarily caused by negative patterns of thought, which he labeled the "cognitive triad"—errors in how we think about ourselves (such as "I'm worthless"), our world ("Everything bad happens to me"), and our future ("Nothing is ever going to change"). Whereas RET engages the client in a rational or socratic "debate," Beck's approach emphasizes the client's capacity for self-discovery. Less hurried and confrontive, the therapist and client work as a team to uncover underlying assumptions, to test them in the client's everyday life situations,

runs counter to the belief that a healthy person accurately recognizes what is real in the world. Lazarus (1979) pointed out that collective illusions ("Government always deals fairly with citizens") and individual illusions ("I am superior to most people in intelligence") add richness and meaning to our lives. This does not negate the fact that denial *is* often pathological.

Lazarus distinguished between two different coping responses to stress: problem-solving responses and emotion-focused responses. A problem-solving response is an attempt to change the troublesome situation. For example, a person trapped in a house that has just collapsed during an earthquake may handle anxiety by sizing up the situation and deciding to systematically shout loudly while trying to crawl out. A woman who finds a lump on her breast may become anxious but seek additional information through medical examination and advice. In these cases, the circum-

stances may be changed by means of problem-solving responses.

Some realities, however, cannot be changed. For example, it is possible that Fred, being an expert outdoorsman, has accurately appraised his situation realistically. There is little that he can do to extricate himself from the collapsed mine (the boulders blocking the cave entrance are too heavy to move and no other possible exits exist). In such cases, emotion-focused responses may be used.

Emotion-focused responses do not change the relationship between the person and the environment, but they can make the person feel better. The most common of these responses are thinking of something else, distancing, minimizing, and making light of the situation. These defenses are frequently referred to as *intra* or *cognitive* means of coping.

Traditionally, psychologists have contended that "healthy" people use problem-solving responses, whereas

"sick" people use emotion-focused responses. The proponents of "healthy denial" believe that serious sources of stress in life—circumstances for which very little can be done to alleviate the stress—require emotion-focused modes of coping. The healthy person in this case is one who handles his or her feelings through denial. For example, a patient with a terminal illness may choose to deny his or her ultimate fate and sustain hope. According to Lazarus, the competent coper is one who can use problem-solving strategies when something can be done to change the environmental factors that brought on stress, and one who can use denial to soothe feelings when nothing can be done. Have you experienced healthy denial? What aspects of the situation made denial an appropriate strategy? When would it be unhealthy?

and to determine by logical means whether they are valid. As in systematic desensitization, smaller challenges are assigned first and more difficult ones are tackled as successes are experienced.

Other variations of cognitive-behavioral methods have been developed, and all are based on similar assumptions. One of the newer approaches, discussed in Chapter 3, is stress inoculation therapy, developed by Meichenbaum (Meichenbaum, 1985; Meichenbaum & Cameron, 1982). The assumption behind stress inoculation training is that people can be taught to better handle life stresses. Meichenbaum uses cognitive preparation and skill acquisition, rehearsal, application, and practice. An interesting twist in the use of cognitions is discussed in Critical Thinking.

Cognitive-behavioral therapy shows much promise. Studies have indicated that RET (Lipsky, Kassinove & Miller, 1980), Beck's approach (Kovacs et al., 1981), and stress inoculation therapy (Denicola

& Sandler, 1980; Meichenbaum, 1986) have been used successfully. Furthermore, some evidence has suggested that the approaches may be better than drug therapy for certain situational and specific depressions (Lipman & Kendall, 1992; Simons et al., 1986).

Behavioral Medicine

Behavioral medicine integrates behavioral and biomedical science. The two fields merged because people realized that psychological factors were often related to the cause and treatment of physical illnesses (Brownell, 1982). The term *psychobiology* has also been used to address the importance of viewing the totality of the human condition (both biology and experience) in explaining and understanding behavior (Dewsbury, 1991). The goal of behavioral medicine is to help people change their lifestyles to prevent illness or to enhance the quality of their lives. As

Behavioral medicine and studies in stress coping have taught us much about how to deal with life's traumas. The women in this breast cancer self-help group are using sound psychological principles to help reduce stress. Among these principles are social support and taking control of their lives.

discussed in Chapter 8, heart disease, strokes, and cancer have been correlated with lack of exercise, diet, smoking, alcohol consumption, and other behaviors of a particular lifestyle. Behavioral medicine makes people aware of the effects of these behaviors and helps them develop healthier patterns.

One way to do this is through **biofeedback therapy,** which combines physiological and behavioral approaches. A patient receives information, or feedback, regarding particular autonomic functions such as heart rate, blood pressure, and brain wave activity and is rewarded for returning these functions to normal levels. Monitoring devices supply the information; the rewards vary, depending on the patient and the situation. Studies have found that biofeedback therapy can reduce high blood pressure (Benson et al., 1971) and alter brain wave activity (Kamiya, 1962; Nowlis & Kamiya, 1970). The applicability of biofeedback therapy to the treatment of behavioral disorders is still being investigated.

In one particular study, researchers attempted to help patients with essential hypertension (elevated blood pressure) lower their systolic pressure. They used an operant conditioning feedback system in which patients saw a flash of light and heard a tone whenever their systolic blood pressure decreased. They were told that the light and tone were desirable

and were given rewards—slides of pleasant scenes and money—for achieving a certain number of light flashes and tones. The patients gradually reduced their blood pressure at succeeding biofeedback sessions. When they reached the point where they were unable to reduce their pressure further for five consecutive sessions, the experiment was discontinued (Benson et al., 1971).

Meyer Friedman and colleagues in 1984 reported a study of 591 coronary patients in which they found that those patients who changed their lifestyles drastically reduced their recurrence of heart attacks. They discovered that 95 percent of patients who suffer heart attacks exhibit what is called "Type A" behavior (discussed in Chapter 8), which is characterized by time urgency (the compulsion to finish tasks early, be early for appointments, and always race against the clock), attempts to perform several tasks at once, the propensity to anger quickly when others don't perform as expected, and rapid speech and body movements (Friedman & Rosenman, 1974). The patients in Friedman's Recurrent Coronary Prevention Project learned, through counseling and practice drills, to control and change their Type A behaviors.

As pointed out in Chapter 8, the Type A hypothesis proved to have a number of shortcomings (Friedman & Booth-Kewley, 1988), but behavioral medicine techniques, which focus on lifestyle changes, have proven very beneficial. Some of these are listed here:

1. *Establish priorities* It is important for each of us to determine where to put our time and energies. Establishing a daily or weekly priority list, including everything that must be done, is a helpful strategy. If time is limited, learn to postpone the low-priority items without feeling guilty.

2. *Avoid stressful situations* Don't put yourself in situations that involve unnecessary stress. For example, if you know that a particular traffic route involves constant tie-ups, consider another time for your commuting or take another route. Remember, we can and do have control over much of our lives.

3. *Take time out for yourself* We all need to engage in activities that bring pleasure and gratification. Whether they involve going fishing, playing cards, talking to friends, or taking a vacation, they are necessary for physical and mental health. And they give the body time to recover from the stresses of everyday life.

4. *Exercise regularly* Exercise is effective in reducing anxiety and increasing tolerance for stress. Furthermore, a healthy body gives us greater energy to cope with stress and greater ability to recover from a stressful situation.

5. *Eat right* You've heard this advice before, but it happens to be excellent advice: eat well-balanced meals that are high in fiber and protein but low in fat and cholesterol. Nutritional deficiencies can lower our resistance to stress.

6. *Make friends* Good friends share our problems, accept us as we are, and laugh and cry with us. Their very presence enables us to reduce or eliminate much of the stress we may be experiencing.

7. *Learn to relax* A major finding of stress management research is that tense, "up-tight" people are more likely to react negatively to stress than are relaxed people. Relaxation can do much to combat the autonomic effects of anxiety and stress; thus the various relaxation techniques are helpful in eliminating stress.

Resisting Stress: Guiding Principles

Just as behavioral medicine has given us some helpful suggestions in which to improve our psychological and physical health, some very promising stress research (Lazarus, 1966, 1983; Matheny et al., 1986) has given us ideas on how we can resist the buildup of stress or reduce the severity of stressful situations and events. Stress research and suggestions that arise from it represent a combination of behavioral, cognitive, and social psychology. A review of the literature indicates four major techniques or methods: *practice, preparation, the reduction of ambiguity,* and *reliance on social support and reassurance.*

Practice Victims of civilian disasters, combat, and imprisonment are survivors of situations that they may never have encountered before and usually don't know how to deal with. Coping behaviors used to mitigate ordinary stress are insufficient to deal with extraordinary stress. Furthermore, considerable confusion and disorientation may occur in a disaster. Unless a coping behavior has been well learned and rehearsed, the victim is likely to be in such a state of shock that he or she can become immobilized.

Practice tends to increase coping skills, to reduce uncertainty, and to enhance a person's confidence that he or she can deal with a situation successfully. For example, fire drills in public schools reflect the importance of practice in reducing panic and stress. The armed forces have also instituted programs that prepare people for survival as prisoners of war. Simulated capture and interrogation prepare the soldier for what to expect and *what to do* if captured.

Preparation Against Harm When people know the type of threat they encounter and the probability of its occurrence, they can take specific actions to reduce or eliminate the danger. For example, storm shelters can be built against tornadoes, dams can be used against floods, increased studying can guard against the possibility of failing an exam, and so on. About one-third of the residents of San Angelo, Texas, built storm shelters after a major tornado struck. Interviews indicated that these families showed less fear during subsequent storms.

Reduction of Ambiguity Before people can prepare against harm, they need to know what to expect. Human beings (and animals) prefer predictable aversive events (Seligman, 1975); high anxiety is likely to result when the situation is ambiguous.

People placed in confusing or disorienting situations have a strong need to clarify those situations by actively seeking information. Sometimes the unknown is much more frightening than a known threat.

Preparatory information can give people a feeling of cognitive control by allowing them to classify events and situations by expectations. Researchers tested the value of providing surgical patients with preparatory explanations about the expected type and duration of postoperative pain. Approximately one-half of a large group of patients were given detailed information, while the other half received only minimal information. The fully prepared patients recovered more quickly and experienced less pain and discomfort. Their mental rehearsal of the aftereffects of surgery acted to reduce novelty and surprise (Egbert et al., 1964).

Social Reassurance and Support To a large extent, people depend on others for social support, reassurance, and confirmation. Their resources against a threat are drawn largely from those people on whom they have learned to depend. Reactions to the death of a loved one, for example, vary depending on the supports provided by each culture (Lindemann, 1960). In Italy, severe mourning reactions are less likely because of Italy's extended kinship system. Social reassurance also lets a person know that others have experienced similar difficulties and survived—and thus reduces the perceived magnitude of the crisis.

In short, the easiest way for people to withstand or reduce the stress they feel is to prepare for it. Together, the techniques we have discussed can inoculate individuals against the potentially damaging consequences of excessive stress. They are preventive, not remedial, mental health measures.

EVALUATING INDIVIDUAL PSYCHOTHERAPY

Both insight- and action-oriented approaches have attracted firm followers and loud critics. Behavioral therapists, for example, believe that this approach has solid theoretical support and empirical justification; that it provides a rapid means of changing be-

haviors; and that (unlike the insight-oriented approaches) it includes specific goals, procedures, and means of assessing its effectiveness. Critics have argued that behavioral therapy is dehumanizing, mechanical, and manipulative; that its relationship to learning theory is more apparent than real; and that it is applicable only to a narrow range of problems.

Whether one argues for either insight- or action-oriented therapies depends largely on whether the person believes that human behavior is determined primarily by internal or external factors. There are also psychologists who argue against psychotherapy of every sort.

More than forty years ago, Hans Eysenck (1952) concluded that there was *no evidence that psychotherapy facilitates recovery* from what were then classified as neurotic disorders. According to the criteria he used, patients receiving no formal psychotherapy recovered at least as well as those who were treated! Since that time, others have also claimed that psychotherapy's success has been oversold and that both practitioners and clients are wasting time, money, and effort in psychotherapy. Some opponents feel so strongly that they advocate a "truth in packaging" policy: prospective clients should be warned that "Psychotherapy will probably not help you very much."

Critics of the Eysenck study raise several objections. First, it's not clear that the groups of treated and untreated patients were comparable in demographic variables such as age, socioeconomic class, and race—factors associated with prognosis. Second, the improvement criteria applied to the untreated patients (discharge rate, return to work, lack of complaints) are not the same as those used by many psychotherapists, who aim for far more substantial personality changes. Furthermore, Eysenck's criteria used to calculate improvement for patients in psychoanalysis were such that he underestimated the rate. In fact, one critic has shown that it is possible to come up with an improvement rate of more than 80 percent for psychoanalysis—using Eysenck's data (Bergin, 1971). Finally, was the "untreated" group really untreated? We know that disturbed people often seek help from relatives, friends, or members of the clergy during times of stress. A form of psychotherapy may have been rendered by these other sources. In addition, more recent studies have revealed that Eysenck's high spontaneous remission rates have not held up and may be closer to 40 to 45 percent rather than 70 percent (Bergin & Lambert, 1978).

In a thought-provoking article, Persons (1991) pointed out that past outcome studies showing no positive effects from psychotherapy or no difference in outcome in the use of different therapies may have suffered from a major methodological flaw. She argued that psychotherapy outcome studies do not accurately represent current models of psychotherapy. Her argument is based on three lines of reasoning.

First, outcome studies fail to carry out a theory-driven psychological assessment of clients. Instead, assessment of the disorders are based on narrow criteria in an attempt to meet a single diagnostic category like dysthymia (depression). This is accomplished by using a particular standard or inventory. Patients are assumed to possess the same problem differing only in severity. Real psychotherapy, in contrast, is highly idiographic and attempts to understand the comprehensive multitude of problems encountered by patients. For example, depressed patients typically manifest problems associated with aspects of their lives such as family, work, and social isolation. These difficulties are frequently ignored in favor of a single descriptor. In addition, outcome studies are characterized by an atheoretical approach emphasizing diagnosis. In actual clinical practice, assessment strategies are determined by the theoretical model used and its constructs. The psychodynamic model collects information about the patient's core conflicts; the behavioral model collects information about antecedents and consequences related to the behavioral problem; and the cognitive model collects information concerning dysfunctional cognitive processes. Treatment is based not so much on a diagnostic category but on the underlying mechanisms described in the theory.

Second, Persons (1991) argued that assessment and treatment in outcome studies are separate whereas in actual therapy they are inseparable. Clinicians believe that assessment is intimately and inextricably linked to treatment. The process of therapy involves assessing the patient's problems, designing a therapy program, assessing the progress, and using the information to revise the treatment. This interplay is continual and requires ongoing assessment and change in treatment. This leads us to Persons' third criticism. One of the major weaknesses in outcome studies is that treatment is standardized whereas actual clinical practice requires treatment to be individualized. Studies aimed at comparing or determining the effectiveness of therapy make every effort to see that the treatment received by patients in a given treatment condition is the same (standardized). Such manipulations do not reflect clinical reality and lead Persons to conclude that contemporary outcome studies do not accurately represent psychotherapy.

Recently, a new form of statistical analysis (*meta-analysis*) has been found to be a useful tool in analyzing therapy outcome studies. Meta-analysis allows us to analyze a large number of different studies by looking at treatment-produced change called the effect size (ES). The method involves calculating the ES through subtracting the mean of the control group from the mean of the treatment group. The difference is then divided by the standard deviation of the control group. The larger the numerical figure obtained, the larger is the effect of the treatment. Such a method allows us to compare the ESs from many studies in an attempt to determine the effectiveness of different treatment approaches. It is important to note that meta-analysis is controversial with staunch supporters (Shapiro & Shapiro, 1983; Smith, Glass & Miller, 1980) and detractors (Erwin, 1986; Paul, 1985).

One such study using meta-analysis examined hundreds of studies on the outcome of psychoanalysis and behavior therapy. The adequacy of research design, outcome measures, and therapist and client factors were all considered, and the investigators systematically weighed and compared variables. They concluded that treated patients show far more improvement than untreated people (Smith & Glass, 1977). Other important findings were that (1) psychodynamically treated clients showed greater well being than 70 to 75 percent of those untreated; (2) 75 percent of person-centered–treated clients were better off than the untreated group; and (3) Gestalt therapy–treated individuals were 60 percent better off than untreated persons. In general, the higher the quality of the research, the more the results support psychotherapy.

Reviews of outcome research have indicated that psychotherapy is effective and that people who are treated show more and larger desirable changes than those who don't receive formal psychotherapy (Bergin, 1971; Lambert, Shapiro & Bergin, 1986; Meltzoff & Kornreich, 1970; Sloane et al., 1975; Smith & Glass, 1977; Smith, Glass & Miller, 1980). In addition, it appeared that the largest gains in treatment tend to occur within the first few months and are lasting (Lambert, Shapiro & Bergin, 1986; Nicholson & Berman, 1983; Smith, Glass & Miller, 1980).

Controversy over the effectiveness of the various approaches to psychotherapy—and of psychotherapy itself—is likely to continue. We believe that psychotherapy *is* valuable and that it's not productive to unreservedly accept or reject a whole group of treatments, either behavioral or insight-oriented. A more meaningful issue is how best to match therapist, client, and situational variables.

GROUP, FAMILY, AND MARITAL THERAPY

The classic form of psychotherapy involves a one-to-one relationship between one therapist and one client. In **group therapy,** the therapeutic experience always involves more than one client and may involve more than one therapist. The increasing popularity of group therapy stems from certain economic and therapeutic advantages: because the therapist sees several clients at each session, he or she can provide much more mental health service to the community. And, because several clients participate in the sessions, the cost of each is noticeably reduced. Saving time and money is important, but the increasing use of group therapy seems to be related to the fact that many psychological difficulties are basically interpersonal in nature; that is, they involve relationships with others. These problems are best treated within a group rather than individually.

Most of the techniques of individual psychotherapy are also used in group therapy. Rather than repeat them here, we will first discuss some general features of group therapy and family and marital therapy.

Group Therapy

Group Member 1: What you just said really makes me angry, Frank. You're blaming me for something you should be responsible for.
Frank: I was just pointing out that you never contribute to the decision-making process. I wasn't blaming you! What's your problem anyway?
Group Member 1: There you go again! I don't have a problem with the group exercises. When they go wrong, I try to see what happened and why. If it's my fault, I'll try to correct it—okay?
Frank: If the shoe fits, wear it!

Group therapy is a technique well-suited for treating psychological difficulties that are basically interpersonal in nature. One of the most powerful mechanisms of group therapy is that groups provide an environment in which an individual can develop new communication skills, social skills, and insights.

Group Member 1: Damn! It's no use trying to talk to you. Why do you always blame others?

Frank (angrily): Piss on you! It seems like you're the only one who thinks that way. I totally reject your accusations!

Group Member 2 (hesitantly): Frank, you do blame others a lot—

Frank: Shit! Do I have to put up with another conspirator?

Group Member 3: I don't think he's the only one in the group who sees you that way. For the past few times I've been angry at you too. You make me and the others feel incompetent and anxious. Last week you made fun of me when I talked about my problems with Janice.

Frank (somewhat bewildered): I wasn't making fun of you. Why are you so defensive?

Therapist: Frank, we have at least three members in this group who are giving you feedback about your behavior and how it affects them. Maybe you should check out how the others feel and think about your behavior.

Frank: Well—I don't want to waste our time—there are more important things—

Therapist: It's important for us to give and ask for feedback from one another. I know it's hard sometimes, but that's one part of learning about ourselves. —If it's OK with you I'd like to start—

Frank (quietly): It's okay.

There are now a great variety of group therapies, reflecting the many dimensions along which a therapeutic group may be characterized. (Focus 18.2 presents several examples.) One obvious dimension is the type of people who comprise the group. In marital and family therapy, they are related; in most other groups, they are initially strangers. Group members may share various characteristics. Groups may be formed to treat elderly clients, unemployed workers, or pregnant women; to treat clients with similar psychological disturbances; or to treat people with similar therapeutic goals.

Therapeutic groups also differ with regard to psychological orientation and treatment techniques, size, frequency of and duration of meetings, and the role of the therapist or group leader. Some groups work without a leader. Others have leaders who play active or passive roles within the group. Moreover, the group may focus either on interrelationships and the dynamics of interaction or on the individual members. And groups may be organized to *prevent* problems as well as to solve them; for example, group

therapy has been suggested for divorced people who are likely to encounter stress (Bloom, Asher & White, 1978).

Commonalities of Group Therapy   Despite their wide diversity, successful groups and group approaches share several features that promote beneficial change in clients (Kottler & Brown, 1992; Yalom, 1970).

First, the group experience allows each client to become involved in a social situation and to see how his or her behavior affects others. In the group dialogue that begins this section, Frank is slowly and painfully being asked to examine the impact of his behavior on others. He may easily dismiss unpleasant feedback about his behavior from one member as inaccurate, but it is much more difficult to do so when others reinforce the feedback (agreeing that Frank externalizes his problems and avoids responsibility for his own behavior). Once the group member can view his or her interactions realistically, problems can be identified and then resolved.

Second, in group therapy the therapist can see how clients respond in a real-life social and interpersonal context. In individual therapy, the therapist either must rely on what clients say about their social relationships or must assess those relationships on the basis of client-therapist interactions. But data gathered thus are often unrepresentative or inaccurate. In the group context, response patterns are observed rather than communicated or inferred. For example, Frank's therapist could see and hear him try to blame his fellow group members with such statements as

"What's your problem anyway?"

"I totally reject your accusations!"

"Why are you so defensive?"

Third, group members can develop new communication skills, social skills, and insights. (This is one of the most powerful mechanisms of group therapy.) The group provides an environment for imitative learning and practice. Frank's group members can show him that his statements and behaviors indicate defensiveness and that they affect others negatively. He may then be able to change his interpersonal behavior by imitating other group members and practicing better social and communication skills with them.

Fourth, groups often help their members feel less isolated and fearful about their problems. Many clients enter therapy because they believe that their problems are unique: no one else could possibly be burdened with such awful impulses, evil or frightening thoughts, and unacceptable ways. The fear of having others find out how "sick" they are may be as problematic to clients as their actual disorders. But when they suddenly realize that their problems are common, that others also experience them, and that others have similar fears, their sense of isolation is eased. This realization allows group members to be more open about their thoughts and feelings.

Finally, groups can provide their members with strong social and emotional support. The feelings of intimacy, belonging, protection, and trust (which members may not be able to experience outside the group) can be a powerful motivation to confront one's problems and actively seek to overcome them. The group can be a safe environment in which to share one's innermost thoughts and to try new adaptive behaviors without fear of ridicule or rejection.

Evaluating Group Therapy Clients are sometimes treated in group and individual psychotherapy simultaneously. There are no simple rules for determining when one or the other, or both, should be employed. The decision is usually based on the therapist's judgment, the client's wishes, and the availability (or unavailability) of one treatment or the other. Of course, people who are likely to be disruptive are generally excluded from group therapy.

As desirable as it would be to base decisions regarding treatment techniques on the observed effectiveness of group therapy, little substantial research has been done on that topic. Much of the debate has generally dealt with its safety as well. Proponents (Bergin & Garfield, 1978; Ohlsen, Horne & Lawe, 1988) believe that it holds the future of our field although opponents (Corazzini & Anderson, 1980; Lieberman, Yalom & Miles, 1973) believe that it is potentially detrimental and "faddish." Reviews of studies have suggested that group therapy results in improvement, compared to no treatment or placebo treatment (Bednar & Kaul, 1978; Kaul & Bednar, 1986). The problems encountered in evaluating the success of group therapy include all those problems involved in assessing individual therapy, compounded by group variables and the behaviors of

group members. Indeed, some have even questioned whether group therapy is really any different from individual therapy because the same therapeutic variables are used (Hill, 1990).

Some disadvantages of group therapy have been pointed out. For example, groups cannot give intensive and sustained attention to the problems of individual clients (Korchin, 1976). Moreover, clients may not want to share some of their problems with a large group, and the sense of intimacy with one's therapist is often lost in a group. Group pressures may prove too strong for some members, or the group may adopt values or behaviors that are themselves deviant. And, in leaderless groups, the group members may not recognize or be able to treat psychotic or potentially suicidal people.

Family Therapy

Johnny is a seven-year-old boy, attractive and energetic, who came to the attention of the school psychologist midway through his third year in grade school. He had been a good student in the first and second grades, but his schoolwork and attention span deteriorated dramatically at the beginning of the third year. Among the symptoms noticed by his teacher were multiple fears, tardiness, and failure to complete school assignments.

Johnny's mother, Mrs. B., was contacted by his teacher several times in the three months before Johnny was referred to the psychologist. Mrs. B. reported that her son had become school-phobic only this year, and that she had tried unsuccessfully to reassure Johnny that there was nothing to fear. Nevertheless, getting Johnny to school was a daily struggle; he overslept, ate breakfast at a snail's pace, and took what seemed like hours to wash and get dressed. When she dropped him off at school, he would cry and beg to be taken back home. Mr. B. noted that Johnny was younger than his classmates and wondered whether his son was simply finding the work too demanding.

Both parents were obviously concerned about their son. They were subsequently referred to a reputable child psychologist, who saw the family together several times. After their third session, both parents reported a marked improvement in Johnny's behavior. The therapist suggested that Johnny be seen individually for a period of time but also recommended marital counseling for the parents. Mr. B. vigorously objected to that suggestion and stated that there was

In family therapy the focus is on the family unit, which is considered the client. If one family member has been identified as the patient, family therapy considers his or her problems as symptoms of a deeper problem in the family itself.

nothing wrong with their marriage; the problem was helping Johnny overcome his school phobia and helping him cope with the pressures of school. At the urging of the wife, however, they did seek marital counseling, attending four sessions before Mr. B. abruptly terminated treatment. His reason was that the counseling was not helping with the family relationships and that, in fact, he and his wife had begun to argue and express anger at one another. In addition, shortly after Mr. and Mrs. B. had sought counseling, Johnny had reverted to his earlier fears and behaviors. The husband felt that the marital therapy had diverted their attention from the real problem—Johnny.

Family therapy may be broadly defined as group therapy that seeks to modify relationships within a family to achieve harmony (Foley, 1989). We'll use this definition to include all forms of therapy that involve more than one family member in joint sessions, including marital therapy and parent-child therapy. The important point is that the focus is not on an individual, but rather on the family as a whole. Family therapy is based on three assumptions: (1) it is logical and economical to treat together all those who exist and operate within a system of relationships (here, the primary nuclear family); (2) the problems of the "identified patient" are only symptoms, and the family itself is the client; and (3) the task of the therapist is to modify the relationships within the family system.

These basic tenets have arisen from the repeated observations of therapists who have worked with individuals and families. They are illustrated nicely by Johnny's case. Both parents saw their son as the "identified patient" and the problem. Even the teacher and school psychologist saw the problem as one of adjustment for Johnny. Attempts to treat Johnny individually had to fail, because the problem lay in the family system. For example, marital therapy revealed basic antagonisms and conflicts between Mr. and Mrs. B., but as long as Johnny was the identified patient, the parental problems could be covered up. When Johnny improved with therapy and the focus shifted to the marital relationship, many of the husband-wife problems were uncovered. To maintain the family's stability, Johnny, who sensed that the relationship was getting worse, became phobic again.

Johnny's return to phobic behavior is typical of family dynamics, and actually serves several functions for the entire family. First, Johnny again becomes the center of attention and helps ward off a possible divorce. Second, the husband and wife can avoid examining their own relationship and its problems. Third, the status quo of the system is maintained.

Obviously, as long as the family members are treated as individuals, little progress will be made. The family is a social system that needs to be treated as a whole. Mr. and Mrs. B. would probably benefit not only from therapy involving the entire family but from marital therapy as well.

Two general classes of family therapy have been identified: the *communications approach* and the *systems approach* (Foley, 1989). Let us look briefly at each of them.

The Communications Approach The communications approach to family therapy is based on the assumption that family problems are communication difficulties. Many family communication problems are both subtle and complex. Family therapists may have to concentrate on improving not only faulty communications but also interactions and relationships among family members (Satir, 1967). The way in which rules, agreements, and perceptions are communicated among members may also be important (Haley, 1963).

The therapist's role in repairing faulty family communications is active but not dominating. He or she must seek to show family members how they are now communicating with one another; prod them into revealing what they feel and think about themselves and other family members and what they want from the family relationship; and convince them to practice new ways of responding.

The Systems Approach People who favor the systems approach to family therapy also consider communication important, but they especially emphasize the interlocking roles of family members (Minuchin, 1974). Their basic assumption is that the family system itself contributes to pathological behavior in the family. As in Johnny's case, a family member becomes "sick" because the family system requires a sick member. Treating that person outside the system may result in transitory improvement, but once the client returns to the family system, he or she will be forced into the "sick role" again. Thus family systems therapy is directed at the organization of the family. It stresses accurate assessment of family roles and dynamics and intervention strategies to create more flexible or changed roles that foster positive interrelationships.

Marital Therapy

Marital therapy has become increasingly popular treatment for couples who find that the quality of their relationship needs improvement. Typically, the married couple is seen together and the session focuses on communications, role relationships, unfulfilled needs, and unrealistic or unmet expectations. Indeed, seeing only one partner has proven less effective in resolving interpersonal problems than seeing both together (Gurman & Kniskern, 1978). Marital therapists work on the assumption that it is normal for any couple in an intense long-term relationship to experience conflicts. For example, the husband may find it difficult to express affectionate feelings toward his wife, who may have a strong need to be nurtured and loved. Or the couple may be locked in a power struggle involving financial decisions. Or the wife may resent a husband who shows any sign of weakness because the man she married was supposed to be "strong and invulnerable." In all these cases, marital therapy attempts to clarify and improve the communications, interactions, and role relationships between the couple. Note that it is not the purpose of marital therapy to "save a marriage," as many couples believe when they first enter treatment. The decision to remain together, separate, or divorce is a decision that must be made by the couple. The role of the therapist is to help the couple understand the nature of their relationship, how it may be contributing to conflicts and unhappiness, their available options, and, if they want, how to work toward a healthier and happier marriage.

Here is an example of how a marital therapy session might run:

Therapist: Betty [the wife], I wonder if the last two sessions have been helpful to you in saying more openly what you think and feel.

Husband: Well, I think she's feeling better about the sessions, but there's been no big change in how she relates to the kids.

Therapist: Is that right, Betty?

Husband: Of course it is. She's always been afraid of—

Therapist (interrupting): I'd like to hear from Betty.

Wife: Well—Leonard [the husband]—he's not exactly right—I have—.

Husband: She tried, but nothing's happened.

Therapist (to Leonard): Do you realize that several times now you've spoken for your wife and cut her off when I've directed questions to her? I wonder if this is something that frequently happens with you and your wife?

Husband: I wasn't doing that. I was just trying to help my wife clarify her thoughts and feelings.

Wife: But—you don't—you only make me feel worse.

Husband: Betty does need a lot of—.

Therapist: What did your wife just say to you?

Husband: Huh! Uh—she said something about—about not feeling well—I think—isn't that right?

Wife: I said you make me feel like a child who can't think or feel for myself.

Therapist (after a long silence): What do you think your wife is saying to you? Can you paraphrase it?

Husband: She's saying that I make her feel incompetent—or dumb.

Therapist: I wonder, Betty, if you could turn to Leonard now, and tell him exactly how you feel. —Did he hear what you said?

Wife: You do make me feel stupid and incompetent, when—when you always speak for me. Don't you realize that I'm my own person with my own feelings and thoughts!

Husband (to therapist): I didn't realize—that my wife or that—I was doing that—I'm sorry if—if—.

Therapist: Don't tell me, tell your wife.

Husband (to wife): I'm sorry—for—for—I didn't know that's what I was doing.

SYSTEMATIC INTEGRATION AND ECLECTICISM

The therapies discussed in this chapter share the common goal of relieving human suffering. Yet as we have seen, they differ considerably in their basic conception of psychopathology and in the methods used to treat mental disorders. Many theories and techniques seem almost diametrically opposed to one another. For example, early criticisms of psychoanalysis concentrated on the mystical and unscientific nature of its explanation and treatment of behavioral pathology. Most of these criticisms came from behaviorists, who were likewise attacked by psychoanalysts as being superficial and concerned with "symptom removal" rather than with the cure of "deeper conflicts in the psyche." Recently there have been attempts at rapprochement between psychoanalysis and behavior therapy (Davis, 1983; Goldfried, Greenberg & Marmar, 1990; Marmor & Woods, 1980; Murray, 1983; Wachtel, 1982). But even these sophisticated attempts have come under fire as being empirically and theoretically inconsistent (Yates, 1983).

As we mentioned in Chapter 1, most practicing clinicians consider themselves eclectics. It appears that relying on a single theory and a few techniques is correlated with inexperience; the more experienced the clinician, the greater the diversity and resourcefulness used in a session (Norcross & Prochaska, 1988). *Therapeutic eclecticism* has been defined as the "process of selecting concepts, methods, and strategies from a variety of current theories which work" (Brammer & Shostrom, 1982, p. 35). An example is the early "technical eclecticism" of Lazarus (1967). This approach has now been refined into a theoretical model called *multimodal behavior therapy* (Lazarus 1976, 1984). Although behavioral in basis, it embraces many cognitive and affective concepts as well.

Although the eclectic model calls for openness and flexibility, it can also encourage the indiscriminate, haphazard, and inconsistent use of therapeutic techniques and concepts. As a result, therapists who call themselves eclectic have been severely criticized as confused, inconsistent, contradictory, lazy, and unsystematic (Goldfried & Safran, 1986; Patterson, 1980). The resulting negative reception of the term *eclecticism* has led to other terms (including *creative synthesis*, *masterful integration*, and *systematic eclecticism*) that are more positively associated with attempts to integrate, to be consistent, to validate, and to create a unique and personalized theoretical position. Indeed, evidence has indicated that practitioners prefer the term *integrative* to *eclectic* (Norcross & Prochaska, 1988).

There is, of course, no single integrative theory or position. Rather, an integrative approach recognizes that no one theory or approach is sufficient to explain and treat the complex human organism. All the therapies that we have discussed have both strengths and weaknesses; no one of them can claim to tell "the whole truth." The goal of the eclectic approach is to integrate those therapies that work best with specific clients who show specific problems under specific conditions. Thus in one sense, all therapists are eclectics—that is, each has his or her own personal and unique approach to therapy.

In the remainder of this chapter, we present one systematic eclectic approach to the treatment of Steven V. Before you read it, we encourage you to review the discussions of Steve's case in Chapters 1, 2, and 3 to reacquaint yourself with his background and history. And, as you read, remember that what follows represents one therapist's integrative attempt to work with Steve as a feeling, thinking, behaving, social, and biological being.

A SYSTEMATIC ECLECTIC APPROACH TO THE CASE OF STEVEN V.

I am the therapist who has worked with Steve throughout his college career. I've been asked to comment on our sessions and to give you insights into Steve's progress, but before I do so, it is important that I explain my therapeutic approach and goals.

I believe strongly that therapy should involve a blend of techniques aimed at recognizing that each client is a whole human being. Many current schools of psychotherapy are one-dimensional; they concentrate only on feelings, or only on cognitions, or only on behaviors. It is important to realize that each of us comprises all these and more. I also believe that no single theory or approach to therapy is appropriate for all populations and all problems. People are similar in many respects, but each is also different and unique. To recognize this difference means to use different strategies and techniques for each individual.

I have tried to organize my comments topically. This may give you the impression that I worked with isolated parts of Steve's makeup, but that impression would be wrong. I try always to work in an integrated fashion and to deal with all aspects of the client's cognitive, affective, and behavioral makeup.

Meeting Steve: The Initial Session Steven V. first came to my attention during the early part of his junior year. A very "unstable" relationship with Linda, his woman friend, had just ended, and he seemed quite disturbed by it. As I found out later, his own private therapist was on vacation, and he did not like the therapist who was on call. As a result, he contacted the university psychological services center and was assigned to me.

During our initial contact, Steve appeared extremely suspicious, withdrawn, and reluctant to disclose his thoughts or feelings. I can recall the long periods of silence following my questions and his short but sarcastic responses. It was almost as though he were testing me to see what kind of therapist I was, to see whether he could trust me. Usually I try to be less active at first and to encourage the client to tell his or her own story. I employ almost a person-centered approach, listening and mirroring the client's thoughts, feelings, and perceptions. It was obvious, however, that this was not having the desired effect with Steve. It seemed to be alienating him and to be compounding a relationship problem.

Here is a portion of our first conversation.

Therapist: My name is Dr. S., Steve.—I wonder if we could begin by having you tell me what brought you here. (Long silence; Steve looks down, looks up at the therapist, looks down again, crosses his arms in front of his chest, and turns away.)
Therapist: It's hard for you to tell me what's on your mind.
Steve: Yeah (sarcastic tone, but does not change body posture). I'm not sure you can help me. —My therapist is on vacation, otherwise I would be seeing him. He's a psychiatrist, you know.
Therapist: It must be hard to begin a new therapy relationship again—to start all over.
Steve: Great, that's real perceptive.
Therapist: You sound angry right now.—Where is your anger coming from?
(Silence from Steve)

This type of interaction—or lack of interaction—was characteristic of nearly the entire first half of our first session. My attempts to get Steve to open up and to trust me didn't seem to work. It was at this point that I felt a change in approach was necessary. I took on an active and directive manner characteristic of the behavioral therapies.

Therapist: We don't seem to be connecting, Steve; something is blocking us from working together.
Steve: You're the therapist, so you tell me what it is!
Therapist: You want me to tell you what the answer is.
Steve: I don't need a damned parrot for a therapist!
Therapist (raising voice): Look, Steve! If you want to waste this session in a tug-of-war, let's just end it now. I'm not going to sit here and be insulted by you. You respect me, and I'll respect you! —I know it must be difficult to trust a stranger. You'd rather be seeing your own therapist, but the fact is, he's not available. You're hurting enough to come for help. If you want to waste the session playing games, go ahead!
Steve (looking up and obviously surprised): I didn't mean to be disrespectful—I was only—only—
Therapist: Testing me—to see if you could trust

me, to see where I'm coming from—to see if you could manipulate me.

Steve: Yeah, it was nothing personal.

Therapist: I know. Now suppose we start over again.—What brings you here, Steve?

As I look back, I believe this brief but heated exchange represented the beginning of our relationship. I think Steve realized that I was an authentic person who could get angry but would not let the anger become destructive. Clients like Steve often test the therapist with attempts at manipulation. They are ambivalent about this ploy because they want it to succeed (so they can "win"), but they also want it to fail (which means the therapist is perceptive and competent enough to see through their manipulations and thus to give them the help they need). In any event, this tactic changed the entire tone of our session. Steve became much more cooperative and open, and he lost the conscious antagonism and resistance of the early part of our meeting. It also became much easier for me to use a nondirective approach.

Gathering Information   Gathering biographical information is very important to my understanding of clients, and I do much of it during the actual therapy sessions. I needed to know Steve V. Who is he? How does he see things? What are the important events and relationships of his past and present? What type of medical history does he have? Are there any biological conditions that have a major impact on his psychological or social life? What type of therapy has Steve had in the past, and how successful was it? The more information I have about a client, the better I can identify his or her problems and formulate treatment strategies.

In some of our early sessions, Steve briefly mentioned how much he had hated physical education classes in high school. When I asked why, he referred to the "jocks" who were always exhibiting themselves in the shower rooms.

> *Steve:* They strut around like Greek Gods, showing off their bodies. —They don't seem to have any shame at all.
>
> *Therapist:* Shame of what?
>
> *Steve:* I mean, I don't exactly mean shame.—Yes—they're trying to make the others feel ashamed of their own—well, you know.

Therapist: Tell me what you mean.

Steve: Just because they have bigger genitals, they're trying to show off and make the others feel bad.

Therapist: When they did that, how did it make you feel?

Steve: I didn't pay any attention to them. They're not worth it.—Let them strut around, I got bigger grades than all of them.

Therapist: But how did that make you feel?

Steve: I know what you're trying to imply. (Raising voice) You're trying to get me to say I felt inadequate!

(Silence)

Steve: The size of a penis is no measure of a man! Those dumb pricks—most of them barely made it out of high school. —I could outthink all of them.

Therapist: You sound very angry at them. What exactly did they do?

Steve: When I had to take a shower, they—they made fun of me.

Therapist: How did they make fun of you?

Steve: Nothing in particular—but I knew what they were thinking.

Therapist: What were they thinking?

Steve: I don't want to talk about it.

Therapist: I know it's difficult to talk about these things, Steve. —Maybe when you feel ready.

Steve: You'd laugh at me.

Therapist: Is that what you really think?

Steve (after a silence): I had this operation when I was young; they removed my left—I mean, I've only got one. And those bastards never let me forget it. They wanted to humiliate me.

When Steve was six years old, his left testicle was surgically removed because of a malignant growth. Apparently this incident and Steve's self-consciousness about it had haunted him throughout his life. I am not particularly psychoanalytic in orientation, but I believe that Steve did relate his sexual potency and his own masculinity to the absence of a testicle. His feelings of inferiority, low self-esteem, and periodic impotence may have evolved from his erroneous interpretation of this relationship. In this discussion Steve also made what might be labeled a Freudian slip (or a slip of the tongue) in describing his grades as *bigger* (unconscious equation of penis size?) when he probably meant *better*. (Steve's Rorschach responses also led the therapist who originally administered the test to infer a severe castration anxiety related to his surgery.)

Our discussions also revealed some potential areas for treatment. For example, cognitive strategies might be used to directly attack Steve's implicit equating of the size and intactness of his genitals with the idea of masculinity. Perhaps strategies aimed at helping Steve get in touch with his feelings would be helpful; he continually avoided "feeling" statements in our conversations.

Using Tests and Formal Assessment To gather information about my clients, I sometimes resort to more structured, formal assessment means. I may use homework assignments (asking the client to keep a diary of important events or to write an autobiography) or actual psychological tests. I rarely use projective testing but rely more on objective personality measures. (The use of tests is consistent with the behavioral, the cognitive, and even the psychoanalytic approaches. It is inconsistent, however, with the humanistic-existential school.) When I do use tests, I consider them mainly as a source of corroborating data. I try to demystify testing for the client by explaining what testing is, what its limitations are, and how we will use the results.

The computer interpretation of Steve's MMPI responses, for example, seems to reinforce what I have learned during our interviews. The interpretation suggests that Steve is moderately to severely disturbed. It indicates that he is defensive, is hostile, and has a tendency to blame others. (I saw many of these tendencies in our first interview.) The MMPI suggests that a more confrontive, direct approach might work best with Steve. Other problems that are noted, like Steve's poor perception of his social impact on others, difficulty in getting close to people, confusion of aggression with sexuality, and depression and suicidal tendencies, seem right on target. The MMPI interpretation does note, however, that patients with Steve's profile are typically poor academic achievers. But Steve is an exception to this. He has consistently performed well in school, despite his emotional problems.

Steve keeps a diary, so I asked him to write a brief autobiography, emphasizing important childhood experiences, relationships with peers, relationships with his parents, current struggles, and future goals and aspirations. My intent was, first, to help Steve actively sort out his life experiences, away from our therapy sessions, and second, to help me understand his subjective world. The following portion reveals his reactions to our first therapy session; I believe Steve copied it out of his diary.

> My first time with Dr. S. was very confusing. I thought I was in complete control. I'm still not sure what really happened. I know I was angry and resentful the moment I saw him. He was sitting there sipping a cup of coffee without offering me one. When I called the center, they told me I could only come in for an 8 A.M. appointment. I'm not even alive at that time of the morning. Usually Dr. J., the psychiatrist I've been seeing, sees me in the afternoons. I guess I was angry at Dr. J. for going on vacation and making me see another therapist who isn't even a psychiatrist.
>
> I really wanted to talk to somebody about Linda. I guess I was pretty bad with Dr. S. I wasn't sure I could trust him, and I took out my anger on him. I tried to put him down and make him uncomfortable. I tried to make him feel defensive by saying he was only a psychologist and not a psychiatrist. It scared the shit out of me when he got angry back at me. I never had a therapist do that to me. It was like he knew what I was doing. He thinks I do it with other people too. Maybe he's right. He seems to be able to see through me, and I don't like that. I'm afraid to have someone really know what's going on inside. What is going on inside? I don't know! Why should I be afraid? Strange, I really don't like Dr. S. Or do I? Why am I seeing him now instead of my therapist? Mom and Dad are angry at me because I won't go back to Dr. J.

There are some very revealing elements in this passage. First, it supports my previous impression that Steve finds it difficult to trust people and behaves so as to push others away. Second, he is beginning to gain some insight into his behaviors—how he attributes his feelings to others and blames them for his troubles. Third, he has a long way to go. There is something that he is afraid to reveal to himself and others. When he expresses the fear that I can "see through" him, his writing becomes disjointed and fragmented. Obviously, this "dark secret" is deeply frightening to him. It affects not only his emotional state but his cognitive state as well.

What was encouraging was that, despite his discomfort with me, Steve decided to continue in therapy—and with me rather than with his previous therapist. A part of him didn't want to look at himself, but another part seemed to know that this was the only way he could ever get better.

Overall Objectives in Therapy   As I got to know Steve better and better, I was able to identify some treatment objectives that would benefit him. Again, let me emphasize that I saw Steve as I see each of my clients—as a complex individual who feels, thinks, experiences emotions, behaves, and is a social being. I had to deal with each of these aspects during the two years I worked with him. Here, though, I'll discuss only a few facets of Steve's self to illustrate my therapeutic approaches.

Dealing with Steve's Feelings   One theme that persisted throughout my work with Steve was his inability to get in touch with his feelings. He found it difficult to experience feelings or to make "feeling" statements. The autobiographical passage suggests that there is something he was afraid to acknowledge. He was ambivalent about therapy because it was forcing him to face frightening parts of his existence; he could no longer be safe and avoid taking risks.

It would have been a mistake to directly reassure Steve that he could trust me and that things would turn out well. Such reassurance would have been transitory at best, unless Steve ventured out on his own to take the risk and to confront his own fears. I saw myself as a guide who would use various strategies to help Steve confront himself. In this respect I relied on existential psychology, which places choice and responsibility clearly in the hands of the client. Here is an example, from one of our sessions.

Steve: My parents are upset with me for terminating with Dr. J. They think I should continue because he's a psychiatrist, and I've been with him for years.—I like him—and he really understands me. I feel comfortable with him.
Therapist: What made you decide to continue seeing me instead of Dr. J.?
Steve: I don't know, I mean—I'm not sure I even like you. Maybe it's just so much more convenient to go to a campus shrink than to travel across town.

Therapist: I don't believe that's the reason. You're hiding from yourself again! When are you finally going to start facing yourself?
Steve (angrily): That's what I mean. I don't know if I like you—you're always picking on me.—Shit!
Therapist: Say it again.
Steve: Shit! (Pounds the table.)
Therapist: Again and louder!
Steve: Shit! Shit!
Therapist: What are you feeling?
Steve: I'm pissed off at you!
Therapist: That's not a feeling!
Steve: I'm angry! (Yells at the top of his lungs.) Are you satisfied now?
Therapist (after a silence): That was real.
Steve: Yeah. (Exhales.) Funny how I felt like an overcooked artichoke crumbling just then.
Therapist: I want you to close your eyes and become that artichoke. What are you feeling now?
Steve: I want to keep all the leaves from falling away so that no one will see my artichoke heart. I want to strike out at whoever tries to peel the leaves off.
Therapist: Imagine the leaves being peeled away—
Steve: No, I can't do it!
Therapist: You don't want to do it.—What are you afraid of?
Steve: I'm afraid you'll see me—what's really wrong with me.
Therapist: Become that fear and tell me what's going on now.
Steve: I've got to hide.—All the artichoke leaves help me hide, so others won't see.
Therapist: Can you peel off just a few of the leaves?
Steve: Yes, but it doesn't feel good.
Therapist: For each leaf you peel off, say what it is.
Steve: I'm peeling off my phony self—I'm peeling off my mask—I'm peeling off my rationalizations—I'm peeling off my anger.
Therapist: Okay, open your eyes. What's happening now?
Steve: I feel naked, I feel everyone can see how inadequate I really am. I don't like myself either.—I feel scared—scared you won't like me anymore. I feel ashamed because you saw a part of me that no one else did.
Therapist: I know. It's scary to let others see the real you.—But look at you. Before we began this session you were very uptight and defensive. Your fists were clenched; you were sitting bolt upright on the edge of your chair; you had a strained expression on your face; your voice was tight. Now your body looks more relaxed.—Can you feel it?

Steve: Yeah—

Therapist: Get into your body.—What is it telling you?

Steve: It's funny—I don't like what I see in myself, but—but—I hate myself but I feel relieved. I don't have to always hide from you.

Therapist: You mean you don't have to always hide from yourself.

Steve: Yeah.

Dealing with Irrational Thoughts I had to discover how Steve's feelings and many of his self-defeating behaviors were related to his cognitions. I had enough evidence to indicate that Steve created his own miseries through the thoughts and beliefs he held. My work with him in this vein tended to parallel cognitive behavior modification and rational-emotive therapy: in some way, Steve was feeding himself irrational and unrealistic assumptions. My task was to identify these irrational beliefs, show Steve that he was constantly reindoctrinating himself with these messages, and teach him how to challenge or dispute them.

Some of Steve's irrational beliefs are evident in these words of his, taken from another session:

> I just feel like I'm a miserable failure. I've disappointed my parents. I know Dad wanted someone who was more athletic. I tried, but I'm not a jock. I did well in school and Mom is proud of that—but—I thought when I went to college and could do well at the university, Dad would come around. So far I have a 3.75 GPA, but I should have a 4.0. In several classes I missed an A by just a few points. When I told him [Steve's father] my grade point average last night, he told me Jeff, my cousin, has a 3.9 GPA. I guess I let him down again. I was so bummed out last night—I couldn't sleep—maybe it's not worth going on. Life just isn't worth it. Why should I keep trying? Maybe I should just take courses I know I'll do well in.

Several themes in this paragraph appear to form the basis for Steve's feelings of worthlessness and his low self-esteem. These absolutist themes are often punctuated with must, should, and ought:

1. "I must do what is necessary to please my parents, especially Dad. I must get my parents' approval, love, and recognition. If I fail to do this, I will never be able to value myself or feel I have succeeded. If they don't love me, I can't love myself. And life would not

be worth living without their love and approval."

2. "I must be at the top of my class. I must live up to the expectations of my professors, peers, and parents. I must be perfect. If I fail to attain straight A's, it means I've failed again and am basically stupid."

3. "I must be thoroughly competent in everything I do. If I can't, I'll avoid trying anything new. I cannot make mistakes because they will prove how deficient I really am."

After identifying these themes with Steve, I discussed with him how these thoughts and self-indoctrinations lie at the root of many of his problems. For example, he thinks his parents' lack of approval has caused him to feel unloved and unappreciated. I tried to show Steve that it is his belief about a real or imagined situation, rather than an actual situation, that is causing his difficulties. In therapy sessions, I confronted his belief system by having him respond to these following questions:

1. Who is telling you that you are worthless unless your parents approve of you?

2. Do you need to be loved and liked by everyone?

3. Do you want to spend the rest of your life in a futile attempt to win over your father?

This line of questioning was helpful in getting Steve to think, to challenge himself, and to decide—for himself—how he would live.

Learning New Behaviors One thing that I have discovered is that a client's insight into or understanding of a problem doesn't necessarily lead to a behavior change. The understanding that he feared rejection by members of the opposite sex because he equated rejection with his "worthlessness" would not have made it easier for Steve to interact with women. And from my work with Steve, it had become clear that he suffered from immense interpersonal anxiety, especially with women. Not only did he not know how to interact with others or to "make small talk," but he also engaged in inappropriate behaviors that put people off. When Steve was with his friend Linda, he had constantly tried to make her prove she "cared for him." He had accused her of not being faithful to him, of not caring for him, and of not including him in her extracurricular school activities. This continual "prove you love me" testing of their relationship never ended because no amount of reassurance seemed to be enough. In fact, it pushed Linda away from him.

This mode of interaction was characteristic of nearly all Steve's relationships. While he worked to combat this irrational belief ("I am worthless; therefore no one can like me"), I felt it was important to help Steve become more comfortable in interpersonal and heterosexual relationships. I attempted to help Steve subtract anxiety from his interpersonal encounters by using a behavioral technique: assertiveness training.

Here is Steve talking to me again:

> The truth is I'm always afraid. I panic when I think about being in a group of people and having to talk to them. What am I going to say? Even if I could say something, who would listen? Last month I went to a party with Linda—it was thrown by her friends.—When she introduced me all I could say was "hi." I stuttered when I said anything else. It was like in class—I really felt inadequate. And one of the guys was trying to hustle Linda. He knew Linda came with me, but he ignored me completely. He asked her to dance, and I spent the whole evening sitting in the corner. I was really angry at him and Linda too, but I couldn't do anything about it. Then he came over and asked if I would mind if he took her home. I could only say, "Sure, go ahead." What I really wanted to say was "Go to hell." I feel like I'm a doormat for the world.

Obviously we had to work on Steve's assertive behaviors. What I intended to do was, briefly, the following:

1. Identify Steve's unassertive behaviors that were linked to specific situations (for example, withdrawing and sitting in a corner by himself and not being able to say no).

2. Determine the specific skills he needed for assertion (saying no, introducing himself to strangers, asking Linda to dance, and so on). Then try to grade these skills from least to most assertive.

3. Recreate the problem situations, as vividly as possible, in the consultation room. Engage Steve in role playing and behavioral rehearsal with me or volunteers.

4. Get Steve to practice the assertive behaviors in actual situations, under my guidance and monitoring.

Our first use of the procedure will illustrate how we implemented it. Steve and I identified an upcoming event that was causing him considerable apprehension—a class assignment. He was to give an oral critical analysis of an assigned novel in his English class and then lead a discussion of the novel.

Steve needed to practice the assertive skills related to the oral presentation. First, to desensitize him, I had him practice very low-level assertive skills in front of groups. For example, he practiced raising his hand in class in situations where he was sure he would not be called on—for example, when many other students raised their hands or while he was out of sight of the professor. To Steve, this act was an assertive one. After he became comfortable with that, I asked him to raise his hand and ask a simple question (a safe assertive skill), such as "Could you repeat that last point?" After his anxiety regarding this act was conquered, he proceeded to paraphrase what the instructor had said and finally to state an opinion. Each succeeding act represented an increase in assertiveness.

While he was practicing these classroom acts, Steve was finishing his book report. I then asked him to do his oral report for me. Next I asked another counselor and the two clerical staff members to be present while he repeated the report. After a second repetition, we simulated a question-and-answer session and then repeated that several times.

This systematic training helped Steve greatly when he finally presented his report to his English class. Although he was anxious throughout the presentation, he felt that he had the anxiety under control.

A similar program, which I developed for his heterosexual anxiety, proved only moderately successful.

Steve's Threat Against Linda   "She doesn't deserve to live—I swear, I'm going to kill her." Given the conduct in which it occurred, Steve's threat to kill Linda placed me in a dilemma. My conflicting feelings and apprehension were, no doubt, similar to those experienced by any therapist whose client threatens to kill someone or to commit suicide. Today more than ever, we as therapists must recognize that our work does not occur in a social vacuum. What we do or don't do in therapy has not only clinical implications but ethical, moral, and legal ramifications as well.

In that particular session Steve was becoming increasingly agitated about his breakup with Linda; his expressions of anger were stronger and stronger. He was quite depressed at the time, and in my therapeutic judgment, his venting of feelings was healthy. I had been working on that with him when he blurted out his threat. The first thoughts that came to my mind were questions: "Does he really mean what he's saying?" "How likely is he to carry out the threat?" "Is this just an empty threat characteristic of his anger and hostility?" "What should I do?" "Should I inform the proper authorities, breaking confidentiality, and risk losing Steve's trust?"

I chose to go along with my clinical judgment to let Steve continue to express his feelings without cutting him off, while constantly assessing the strength of his anger and the likelihood of his acting impulsively. I made that decision for several reasons. First, in the time I had known Steve, he had made several suicide threats. In each case, when he was allowed to express his feelings, the suicidal ideation and threats diminished. I felt that his threat to kill Linda would follow a similar course. Second, despite his often bizarre thoughts and behaviors, I had never considered Steve to be a danger to others. He was more a danger to himself than to anyone else. Third, I felt that some other perspective was needed. There was still time to consult with colleagues about the case and to get their input. And last, I was prepared to cancel other appointments and extend our session if that became necessary. I felt that I could monitor Steve closely, and I even made an appointment for him to return the following day. In other words, after pondering all the issues, including the need to protect myself by informing the proper authorities or even Linda, I decided that the likelihood of his carrying out the threat was very low. Luckily this did prove to be the case.

The dilemma for me as a therapist was not whether I should inform a potential victim or the appropriate authorities about a homicide that I deemed likely. I have no doubt that I would have taken that action if it were necessary. I was disturbed that I lacked the ability to precisely assess dangerousness and—even more—was unable to inform a client about the legal limits of confidentiality without adversely affecting our therapist-client relationship.

An Epilogue to the Case Several years have passed since my sessions with Steve came to an end. He graduated from the university with a degree in English literature and went to a graduate school in the east. I did get the chance to see some changes in Steve that are definitely for the better. He relates reasonably well to people now, though I still consider him a loner. His bizarre behavior and ideation have eased off, but he still suffers from periodic bouts of depression. Whereas most clients need only brief periodic therapy to help them cope with life's problems, I'm afraid Steve is one of those people who will need some form of therapy for the rest of his life. He has chosen to work toward a doctorate degree and to become a teacher, doing research and writing. I think this is as good a vocational choice as any. Not only does it play to his strengths (writing, reading, and research), but the college environment seems to be one of the few in which Steve has done well and has felt sufficiently secure. Perhaps this is a statement about academic life as well as about Steve. Some perceive it as a protected environment that is structured and, in some ways, undemanding.

I don't know what has happened to Steve since he left this university. I am aware that he signed a release of information form so that his case records could be transferred to the university he now attends. I can only assume that he has chosen to continue therapy, and I wish him well.

SUMMARY

1. A variety of psychotherapeutic or treatment procedures are used to change behaviors, modify attitudes, and facilitate self-insight. Biological (or so-

matic) treatments use physical means to alter the bodily and psychological states of patients. The use of electroconvulsive therapy (ECT), or electroshock, has diminished but is still the preferred treatment for some severely depressed patients. Because psychosurgery permanently destroys brain tissue, it too is now rarely used and strictly regulated. One reason for the declining use of ECT and psychosurgery is a correspondingly greater reliance on drug therapy. Antianxiety drugs reduce anxiety, antipsychotic drugs help control or eliminate psychotic symptoms, and antidepressants effectively reduce depression. Drug therapy has enabled very many patients to function in the community and to be more amenable to other forms of treatment, particularly insight-oriented and behavioral therapy.

2. The insight-oriented therapeutic approaches include psychoanalytic therapy, person-centered therapy, existential analysis, and gestalt therapy. These approaches provide the patient with an opportunity to develop better levels of functioning, to undergo new and emotionally important experiences, to develop a therapeutic relationship with a professional, and to relate personal and private thoughts and feelings.

3. Action-oriented or behavior therapies (based on classical conditioning, operant conditioning, modeling, and cognitive restructuring) have been applied to a variety of disorders. Behavioral assessment, procedures, goals, and outcome measures are more clearly defined and more easily subjected to empirical investigation than are insight-oriented approaches. Two promising approaches are behavioral medicine and stress resistance training, which combine behavioral, cognitive, medical, and social knowledge.

4. Some critics claim that the effectiveness of psychotherapy—of whatever orientation—has not been demonstrated. Others have refuted that claim. The real issue, however, may be one of finding the best combination of therapies and situational variables for each client.

5. Although critics argue that behavior therapy is dehumanizing, limited to a narrow range of human problems, and mechanical, proponents consider behavior modification both effective and efficient.

6. Group therapy involves the simultaneous treatment of more than one person. Many psychological difficulties are interpersonal in nature, and the group format allows the therapist and clients to work

in an interpersonal context. Family and marital therapy consider psychological problems as residing within the family rather than in one individual. The communications approach to family therapy concentrates on improving family communications, whereas the systems approach stresses the understanding and restructuring of family roles and dynamics.

7. Most practicing therapists are eclectic in perspective. They try to select therapeutic methods, concepts, and strategies from a variety of current theories that work. Being eclectic is sometimes criticized as being haphazard and inconsistent, but every therapist who fits the therapy to the client is, in fact, eclectic.

KEY TERMS

aversive conditioning A classical conditioning technique in which an undesirable behavior is paired with a noxious stimulus to suppress the undesirable behavior

biofeedback therapy A therapeutic approach in which a patient receives information regarding particular autonomic functions and is rewarded for influencing those functions in a desired direction

drug therapy The treatment of mental disorders with drugs

electroconvulsive therapy (ECT) The application of an electric voltage to the brain to induce convulsions and reduce depression; also called *electroshock therapy*

existential analysis A therapeutic approach that is concerned mainly with the person's experience and involvement in the world and that involves a complex encounter between client and therapist

family therapy Group therapy that seeks to modify relationships within the family in such a way as to achieve harmony

flooding A behavioral treatment aimed at extinguishing fear by having the client confront the real-life feared situation at full intensity

free association A psychoanalytic method during which the patient says whatever comes to mind, regardless of how illogical or embarrassing it may seem; the material is thought to represent the contents of the patient's unconscious

gestalt therapy A humanistic-existential approach to therapy that emphasizes the client's awareness of the "here and now" and his or her totality of experience in the present

group therapy A form of therapy that involves the simultaneous treatment of two or more clients

implosion A behavioral treatment aimed at extinguishing a fear by having the client imagine the feared situation in its full intensity

marital therapy A treatment aimed at helping couples understand and clarify their communications, role relationships, unfulfilled needs, and unrealistic expectations

monoamine oxidase (MAO) inhibitor An antidepressant compound believed to correct balance of neurotransmitters in the brain

person-centered therapy A humanistic therapy that emphasizes the kind of person the therapist should be in the therapeutic process, rather than the techniques that should be used

placebo effects Positive responses to a drug that result from the patient's understanding of the drug's effect, faith in the doctor, or other psychological factors unrelated to the specific physiological action of the drug

psychopharmacology The study of the effects of drugs on the mind and on behavior

psychosurgery Brain surgery performed for the purpose of correcting a severe mental disorder

psychotherapy The systematic application, by a trained therapist, of techniques derived from psychological principles, for the purpose of helping psychologically troubled people; includes both insight-oriented and action-oriented therapies

resistance The process during psychoanalysis in which the patient unconsciously attempts to impede the psychoanalysis by preventing the exposure of repressed material; tactics include silence, late arrival, or failure to keep an appointment

token economy A treatment program, based on principles of operant conditioning, that rewards patients for appropriate behaviors with tokens, which can then be exchanged for hospital passes, special privileges, or food

tricyclics An antidepressant compound that relieves symptoms of depression

transference A process during psychotherapy in which the patient reenacts early conflicts by carrying over and applying to the therapist feelings and attitudes that the patient had toward significant others (primarily parents) in the past

Community Psychology

Can treatment ever meet the needs of the great numbers of people who are mentally disturbed? According to George Albee, past president of the American Psychological Association,

> The number and distribution of persons with serious emotional problems in our society were far beyond what our resources, in terms of both personnel and institutions, could deal with on a one-to-one basis. The gap was so wide as to be impossible even to bridge. This reality forced me to look for alternatives to the "early treatment." . . . I became convinced of the logic of the public health dictum that holds that no mass disorder afflicting humankind is ever eliminated or brought under control by attempting to treat affected individuals, or by attempting to train individual practitioners in large numbers. . . . Every assessment of the distribution of disturbance in the society arrives at an estimate of approximately 15 percent of the population. In addition to this number of "hard-core cases," each year there is a much larger number of people experiencing intense life crises. And when we realize that in any given year only about 7 million separate persons are seen throughout the entire mental health system, both public and private, we can appreciate the hopelessness of our present efforts. (Albee, 1983, p. xi)

In fact, the situation may be worse than Albee suggested: according to the largest prevalence survey in the United States, about 19 percent of adult Americans (more than 29 million persons) suffer from a mental disorder or have suffered from one in the previous six months (Myers et al., 1984). That only a small proportion of these people actually seek treatment within the mental health system has caused great concern among many mental health professionals (Shapiro et al., 1984). Other troubled people may find help in clergy, teachers, physicians, friends, relatives, and folk or indigenous healers (for example, spiritualists, medicine men, and shaman). Furthermore, Albee has pointed to the fact that there is a severe shortage of mental health workers—therapists and clinicians—especially if more emotionally-disturbed individuals seek treatment. But his major concern is that the entire concept—that of treating mental disturbances *after* they have appeared—may not be powerful enough to do any good. Many psychologists are seeking alternatives to treatment, such as the community psychology approach.

In this chapter we examine some factors that led to the development of community psychology, as well as to the various activities of community psychologists. For the sake of completeness, we discuss a fairly wide range of activities—not everyone considers that all of these activities fall within the domain of community psychology.

WHY COMMUNITY PSYCHOLOGY?

Community psychology is an approach to mental health that takes into account the influence of environmental factors and encourages the use of community resources and agencies to eliminate conditions that produce psychological problems. To many, its ecological focus and emphasis on competence and prevention represent a sharp departure from the practices of clinical psychology. This difference is especially apparent in the following major areas of concentration:

- *Social ecological focus* Clinical psychology emphasizes the diagnosis and treatment of individuals; community psychology is interested in **human ecology**—the interaction between human beings and their environments (Kelly, 1966; Kingry-Westergaard & Kelly, 1990). Clinical psychology seeks to alter client's behaviors and personality, whereas community psychology seeks to understand and modify contextual factors such as social settings, institutions, and ecological systems. Thus broad social factors are targeted for intervention rather than simply focusing on the individual (Knight, Kelly & Gatz, 1992).

- *"Doing" as well as studying* Community psychologists attempt not only to understand and study contextual factors but also to apply research to real-life problems and issues, such as crime and juvenile delinquency, homelessness,

prejudice, and discrimination (Tolan et al., 1990). Theory and practice are emphasized.

- *Emphasis on psychological strengths and competencies* Clinical psychology has traditionally focused on deviance and disorders. In contrast, community psychology often seeks to foster competencies and to enhance the coping potential of people who may or may not exhibit mental disorders.

- *Prevention activities* Rather than treating people with disorders, community psychologists advocate programs to prevent the development of new cases of emotional and behavioral problems (Heller et al., 1984).

Community psychology has evolved primarily in reaction to a growing dissatisfaction with traditional approaches to mental health (Goodstein & Sandler, 1978). A major source of this dissatisfaction is the perceived inability of the one-to-one treatment approach to provide for the mental health needs of the nation. Another is the emphasis of traditional approaches—primarily the medical model but others as well—on the concept that mental problems are *illnesses* that result from *individual dynamics*. Interest in community psychology grew in part because psychologists became more concerned with the role of environmental forces than with the dynamics of the individual's psyche. Klein (1968) suggested that a person's adjustment depends on the nature and extent of environmental stressors, on the person's competencies and skills, and on the kinds of resources available in the community to help people deal with stress. According to this view, one could expect that the healthiest people would come from communities in which stressors were minimized and resources were readily available. Klein's notion reflects the focus of community psychologists on promoting prevention programs (to reduce stress) and on increasing the availability of mental health resources.

In the next section we discuss some other problems that have led to the search for new approaches and to the growth of community psychology.

The Ineffectiveness of Mental Institutions

The system of psychiatric hospitals has been another source of dissatisfaction. As early as the eighteenth

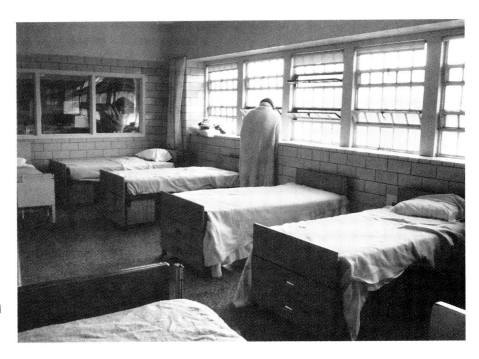

Prolonged hospitalization, while necessary for some patients, often reduces opportunities to learn skills required for living in the community. In addition, many patients receive minimal care and attention from hospital staff, so that hospital treatment often has little value.

century, many hospitals freed psychiatric patients from chains and encouraged respect for patients' rights, but hospitalization seemed increasingly unsatisfactory for treating more and more patients. First, it is expensive financially. Second, psychiatric hospitals are frequently understaffed and lack the resources to provide more than custodial care. Third, state mental hospitals tend to be located in rural areas, making them somewhat inaccessible. Fourth, and most important, hospitalization often keeps the patient from developing the coping behaviors needed for life in the community. When institutionalized mental patients are dehumanized and degraded, they learn to adjust to a role that is inconsistent with community demands for responsibility and competence (Goffman, 1961).

Patient Treatment   According to one view of institutionalization, hospitalized mental patients are sometimes treated as powerless and irresponsible. Many patients receive only minimal care and attention from hospital staff, so that hospital treatment has little value (Rosenhan, 1973).

An opposing view of the powerlessness just described has suggested that patients in mental hospitals often manipulate the image that others have of

them in such a way as to control their own fate (Braginsky, Grosse & Ring, 1966). In so doing, these patients may regard the hospital as a vacation resort and may see themselves as free of responsibilities and worries. But again, the problem is that these patients may not learn the skills needed to survive in the community. In fact, a review of the effectiveness of individualized supportive care, which involves the administration of specific biomedical and psychosocial treatments to each inpatient, demonstrated that widely used, traditional hospital care had limited effectiveness. Programs based on social learning principles and therapeutic communities appear to achieve better outcomes (Paul & Menditto, 1992).

Therapeutic Communities   The important issue is whether there is a better way to facilitate the patient's early return to, and functioning in, the community. In the early 1900s, psychiatrist Adolph Meyers suggested that the mental patient's recovery was enhanced when hospital treatment could be integrated into the patient's family and community living situations. Involving the family and community would help smooth the transition between the hospital setting and community life. Along the same lines, Maxwell Jones (1953) conceived of a **therapeutic commu-**

nity, a hospital environment in which all the hospital activities are structured to have a therapeutic function and in which patients participate to the greatest extent possible. The environment, or *milieu*, would be crucial to the therapy. Patients would be free to interact with staff, who would relinquish much of their traditional authority. Patients would be encouraged to make constructive criticisms during "gripe" sessions and to become more involved in decisions about their own treatment. Patients would receive training in social, recreational, and job skills and would participate in role-playing activities to facilitate the formation of adaptive behaviors.

Patient alumni clubs, halfway houses, and day treatment would also be available as bridges to community life. In a halfway house, patients who are discharged from a hospital live together in a house. The halfway house helps residents make a transition from hospital life to more independent functioning in the community. Residents have an opportunity to help each other develop social skills, gain emotional support, and learn better ways of coping in the community. Mental health workers may also reside in the house to provide some guidance.

One group of investigators carried the idea of patient autonomy a step further. Noting that adjustment to hospital life often hinders adjustment to community life, they developed an innovative program through which chronic mental patients could be placed in "lodges" located in the community. These lodges were set up so that patients could gain a sense of autonomy, manage their own lives, and develop a small business (janitorial services). At the same time, patients could also be learning skills necessary to function in the community. Comparing the patients in the lodge program with a matched group of discharged patients who received traditional outpatient mental health care, the investigators found that lodge patients were better able to remain in the community and to work productively. On other measures of adjustment, the two groups showed few differences (Fairweather et al., 1969).

Reviews of such programs, in which patients are given autonomy and an alternative to hospitalization, have been favorable. Alternative programs cost less and result in lower rates of rehospitalization than does treatment in mental institutions (Kiesler, 1982). Given such findings, it is unfortunate that alternative programs have not gained a stronger foothold in the

mental health field. Three reasons have been cited for this slow growth. First, the public often resists the idea of housing mental patients in the community rather than in the hospital. Fears about having mental patients in one's neighborhood have caused the public to frown on alternative treatment programs. Second, hospitalization for mental disorders is strongly affected by public and private insurance plans. It is the only treatment for which insurance programs provide full payment, and treatment in alternative programs may not qualify for any payment at all. Third, the mental health staff of a hospital may oppose alternative programs. Accustomed to the roles, procedures, and responsibilities of the hospital system, staff members may be interested in maintaining that system (Kiesler, 1982).

Rising costs and the potential negative side-effects of hospitalization have given added impetus to the current trend toward deinstitutionalization. Admissions to hospitals are discouraged, and hospital stays are briefer. Clinicians have hoped that community resources (such as halfway houses and outpatient clinics) can be used as alternatives to hospitalization. Deinstitutionalization has reduced the dominance of mental hospitals in long-term mental health care, but some former patients are now living only marginally in communities because alternative resources are not available. (Some effects of deinstitutionalization are more fully discussed in Chapter 20.) There is now an increasingly large population of disturbed people who receive minimal service from the mental health system (Levine & Perkins, 1987).

Inequities in the Delivery of Services

Another important factor in stimulating the community psychology movement was the discriminatory or unresponsive quality of mental health services available to members of minority groups and the poor. An analysis of the community mental health system based on nearly 14,000 patients indicated that minority group patients tended to drop out of therapy after one session at almost twice the rate for white patients (Sue, 1977). A number of studies have indicated the difficulties in establishing trust, rapport, and a working relationship between patients and therapists who differ in race, socioeconomic class, and lifestyle (Lorion & Felner, 1986; Tyler, Brome & Williams, 1991). Therapists who differ from pa-

Culturally Appropriate Mental Health Services

The United States is one of the most ethnically diverse societies in the world (Comas-Diaz & Griffith, 1988). Although this diversity is enriching, it has also challenged our mental health system. Many ethnic minorities find mainstream mental health services alien to their cultural values and traditions. Consequently, they avoid using services, prematurely terminate services, or find treatment unhelpful. To decrease the disparity between the cultural backgrounds of clients and treatment practices, some therapists provide orientation sessions to explain to clients what they can expect from therapy (Acosta, 1984). Another strategy is to tailor treatment to the cultural background of clients, so that the services are less strange or alien to clients.

In San Francisco, which has a large Asian American population, an effort was made to develop services that would be appropriate to this population. San Francisco Gen-

eral Hospital created a special psychiatric ward for severely disturbed Asian clients (Lee, 1985). Mental health staff who were knowledgeable about Asian cultures and who could speak different Asian languages were hired. The ward had oriental decor and served Asian diets (such as rice and tea). Information was provided in English and Asian languages. The treatment programs were modified so that they would be more consistent with the cultural backgrounds of clients. For example, because Asian cultural values emphasize the role of family, members of clients' families were encouraged to visit the clients and to participate in treatment. These strategies seem to be successful, at least in terms of service utilization. Whereas Asians represented only 10 percent of the client population in 1981, this figure had increased to 34 percent by 1984.

Culturally consistent forms of treatment were also provided by a

mental health program designed to serve a multiethnic population (primarily African Americans, African Caribbeans, Cubans, and Puerto Ricans) in an inner-city area of Miami (Bestman, 1986). Clients were treated by a team of mental health workers that included staff knowledgeable and familiar with the culture of the clients. For those clients who believed in folk or indigenous healers, the mental health team asked such folk healers to collaborate in the treatment process.

In addition to these programs, a variety of other innovative service programs have been created in other cities to more adequately treat the mental health problems of a diverse ethnic population. There is evidence that culturally responsive treatment programs have an effect in lowering treatment dropout rates and in facilitating positive treatment outcomes (Sue et al., 1991).

---

tients in these characteristics may be insensitive to their clients' needs or may fail to adequately consider the influence of the social environment in which their clients live. As a result, minority or lower-class patients often prematurely terminate therapy at mental health facilities. (See First Person narrative as well as Focus 19.1 for a discussion of innovative treatment programs to serve ethnic minority groups.)

In addition, therapists themselves select clients on the basis of characteristics that place people from low socioeconomic levels at a severe disadvantage. One researcher found that therapists often prefer patients who are young, attractive, verbal, intelligent, and successful—the "YAVIS" syndrome in patient selection (Schofield, 1964). This observation led others to urge that greater attention be given to "HOUND"

patients—those who are homely, old, unattractive, nonverbal, and dumb (Goldstein & Simonson, 1971). The problem is twofold: minority and poor patients find therapists unresponsive, and therapists prefer not to work with lower-class or less articulate patients. This problem has led to a call for an appreciation of cultural diversity and the search for mental health practices that respond to different cultural groups (Snowden, 1987).

The search for alternative approaches to mental health care has thus been stimulated by the lack of sufficient professional personnel to meet needs on a one-to-one basis, by dissatisfaction with the present approach, by the high cost and ineffectiveness of psychiatric hospitalization, and by inequities in the delivery of mental health services. Many mental

FIRST PERSON

Patricia Arredondo

Over the years, I have had many op-portunities to work with persons from different ethnic, linguistic, and racial backgrounds. Some of my first experiences were as a novice high school counselor. There were many new arrivals from Iran, Viet-nam, the Soviet Union, Hong Kong, and South America. I speak Span-ish, which was helpful with students and their families from South America, but with others I had to use gestures, drawings, and a few basic English words. I can honestly say that there were many times that

both the students and I felt frus-trated and helpless. We wanted to communicate but were limited by language differences.

These experiences made me real-ize the importance of cultural and linguistic similarity between a coun-selor and a client. Even though I es-tablished good relationships with students from non-Latino back-grounds, they expressed real com-fort with the resource persons who were more similar to them cultur-ally. I also believe that my knowl-edge of issues of loss and grief typically experienced by immi-grants enabled me to demonstrate understanding.

Currently, I am a licensed psy-chologist whose small clinical prac-tice focuses on women. My work is twofold: providing seminars and psychoeducational groups on topics such as career transitions, enhancing personal empowerment, and man-aging stress; and providing psycho-therapy. Most clients have weekly sessions.

I remember one client who was sent to me by an employee assis-

tance program of a local hospital. Elsa, a woman in her fifties, was originally from Ecuador but had been in the United States for ten years. Elsa's supervisor was con-cerned about her withdrawn behav-ior. She thought it might indicate a personality problem with her co-workers, although Elsa had had no previous work problems.

Elsa came in looking very de-jected. When I greeted her in Span-ish, she broke into tears, saying that she was glad she could finally speak with someone who might under-stand her. Elsa continued to cry as she shared her story. Her husband had died two years after coming to Boston. Although her work at the hospital was not a problem, only one of her coworkers spoke Span-ish. She could make small talk with others but could not share anything very personal.

Elsa's current sadness involved her son who had stayed in Ecuador with an aunt and uncle, hoping to join her and her husband after they had settled economically. The years had passed and with her husband's

---

health professionals have turned to a model in which psychologists draw on community resources to de-liver mental health care. Programs based in the com-munity are quite diverse. Several features are, how-ever, particularly characteristic of the community approach to psychology. These include establishing a community mental health center system, emphasizing prevention, training paraprofessionals, becoming so-cially and politically active, and making increased use of social supports.

COMMUNITY MENTAL HEALTH CENTERS

The community mental health center system, estab-lished by Congress in 1963, was created in recogni-tion of the following facts: psychiatric hospitals were

overcrowded, short-term treatment appeared to be effective, medication could be used to control grossly bizarre behaviors, and the social stigma attached to the mental patient was declining (Levenson, 1972). The goal of the program was to make services more accessible to the community. **Community mental health centers** were planned to be centrally located and physically harmonious with medium-sized com-munities (of 75,000 to 200,000 persons) and to provide short-term inpatient care, outpatient care, partial hospitalization, emergency services, and com-munity consultation and education (Smith & Hobbs, 1966).

From the beginning of the program, many centers had difficulty fulfilling their goals. First, few centers were opened; only about one-third of the originally planned 2000 centers received funding (Bellack &

death the reunion had never taken place. Now, her son was about to graduate from dental school and Elsa was unable to make a visit to Ecuador for the special occasion. As a result, she was experiencing profound loss and grief. She talked about her dreams for her children and how sad and angry she felt at not being able to be with them. I listened to her story, empathizing with her separation from her family and the loneliness of living in a foreign culture. We spoke entirely in Spanish.

Elsa and I met on a weekly basis. I saw my role as helping Elsa clarify her feelings and develop coping strategies to deal with her situation. We talked about her options, and she kept a journal during this time. Since she had few people to speak with after work, I suggested that she transfer some of her thoughts and feelings to paper. She did so and reported this to be a very comforting activity.

Within a few weeks, Elsa reported feeling better and was making arrangements for her son to

visit Boston. Elsa seemed to have relieved herself of many sad thoughts and loneliness, enabling her to be resourceful and involved with her job. She told me how much she appreciated my listening and communicating with her in Spanish.

I have thought about what might have happened to Elsa if the EAP had not sought out a Spanish speaking, Latina therapist. It is possible that Elsa may have had difficulty describing her grief in English. Most persons, I have found, prefer to use their native language when expressing feelings. A non-Latina therapist may also have inferred a culturally inappropriate explanation for Elsa's sadness. She may have been seen as overinvolved with her grown son and in a dependent relationship. Her emotional crying in the first session might have been interpreted as the behavior of a helpless, passive woman unable to deal with disappointment.

A person familiar with Latino culture, on the other hand, would appreciate the great emphasis placed on family interdependence and close-

ness, a mother's wish to be with her child at special events, and a child's wish to have his or her success be recognized by the family. A culturally aware therapist would likely recognize Elsa's case as situational rather than chronic depression, and avoid administering American-normed tests or prescribing drugs as the first step in treatment.

Based on my experiences, I believe that knowledge of culture is key to providing appropriate and relevant interventions. Learned cultural, linguistic, and counseling competencies are essential, but cultural and linguistic similarity between counselor and client are equally desirable.

Patricia Arredondo is director of Empowerment Workshops, a women-oriented private practice in Brookline, Massachusetts.

Hersen, 1980). More important, many community mental health centers were criticized for being unresponsive to their communities and for lacking community participation. Critics charged that many centers were structured in a rigid, authoritarian manner and that decisions were made by administrators who took little account of the attitudes and opinions of staff members and consumers. Critics also expressed concern about the system's continued adherence to the biogenic model, which stresses intrapsychic therapy (that is, treatment focusing on the personality dynamics of an individual) rather than on environmental intervention and prevention (Chu & Trotter, 1974; Goldenberg, 1973). Because patients become the passive recipients of treatment, this model discourages the active participation of consumers and of the community.

These criticisms have some validity. Some community mental health centers have failed to form strong enough roots in the communities they serve. And funding problems have indeed limited the system's development (Bloom, 1977). Of necessity, most professional personnel in these centers had been trained traditionally, with emphasis on the biogenic model. The growth of training programs in community psychology should help alleviate this problem (Heller et al., 1984).

Although community mental health centers continue to play a critical role in the provision of services, another important development has been the inclusion of psychotherapy in health maintenance organizations (HMOs). Increasingly, HMOs such as Kaiser-Permanente are including psychotherapy in their coverage of services (Vandenbos, Cummings &

As a primary prevention program, Head Start was designed to help deprived children develop social, emotional, and intellectual skills. By fostering these competencies in children, the program hoped to prevent possible future mental health problems.

DeLeon, 1992), which means that individuals enrolled in the HMO can receive mental health treatment as well as preventive and educational programs intended to promote mental health.

PREVENTION PROGRAMS

Preventing psychopathology is one of the most innovative functions of community psychology. Prevention programs are attempts to maintain health rather than to treat sickness. The main emphasis is on reducing the number of new cases of mental disorders, the duration of disorders among afflicted people, and the disabling effects of disorders. These three areas of prevention have been called *primary, secondary,* and *tertiary* prevention (Cowen, 1983).

Primary Prevention

Primary prevention is an effort to lower the incidence of new cases of behavioral disorders by strengthening or adding to resources that promote mental health and by eliminating features of a community that threaten mental health. As an example of the former,

Project Head Start was initiated in 1964 with the goal of setting up a new and massive preschool program to help neglected or deprived children develop social, emotional, and intellectual skills. Examples of the latter are efforts to eliminate discrimination against members of minority groups to help them fulfill their potential. Both techniques—introducing new resources and eliminating causal factors—can be directed toward specific groups of people or toward the community as a whole.

In one primary prevention program, researchers demonstrated that mothers can be trained to facilitate the development of interpersonal cognitive problem-solving skills in their children. Children of trained mothers demonstrated greater ability to think of alternative solutions to interpersonal problems and to exhibit less impulsive or inhibited behaviors than a control group of children (Shure & Spivack, 1979). The same researchers also examined the feasibility of having teachers implement an interpersonal, problem-solving, skills-training program with young children. When the children learned coping and problem-solving skills, they showed fewer behavioral disturbances and fewer other problems than a control group of untrained children (Shure & Spivack, 1982).

Emotional Support   Marital separation or divorce is a major stressor that is likely to produce emotional distress. One group of investigators reasoned that, by providing emotional support and enhancing the competencies of separated people, they could reduce the likelihood of disturbance. To test this supposition, they gathered a group of newly separated people found through media advertisements and by reference from agencies and practitioners, and divided them into an experimental group and a control group. Both groups were given intensive interviews and were reassessed six months later. In addition, the experimental group participated in a prevention program that consisted of one-to-one consultation with a representative who provided emotional support and served as the link between the individual member and the program. People in the experimental group were also offered the chance to participate in study groups that focused on skills and tasks such as job hunting and career planning; legal, financial, and child custody issues; child-rearing and single-parenting problems; housing and homemaking issues; and socialization and self-esteem building. Results indicated that, after participating in the program, the experimental group (1) favorably evaluated the program, (2) exhibited significantly fewer problems and better adjustment than the control group, and (3) showed a decrease in adjustment problems on a questionnaire of psychological distress and a symptom checklist (Bloom, Hodges & Caldwell, 1982).

Community-Wide Prevention   A community-wide project to prevent depression was initiated by Munoz and coworkers (1982). During a two-week period, nine 4-minute programs intended to prevent depression were televised in San Francisco. They showed viewers coping skills such as how to think positively, engage in rewarding activities, and deal with depression. Telephone interviews were conducted with 294 San Francisco residents. Some respondents were interviewed one week before the television segments were shown; others were interviewed one week after; and still others were interviewed before and after the segments. Information about respondents' depression levels was collected during the interviews (for those who were interviewed before and after the segments, the depression measure was administered twice). Respondents interviewed after the televised segments

People in communities need a variety of different social services. Here, a crisis intervention telephone service (help line) is located at a social service center that offers a variety of programs to the community.

were also asked to indicate whether they had watched any of the segments. Results indicated that those who saw the segments exhibited a significantly lower level of depression than nonviewers. The results, however, held only for respondents who had some depressive symptoms to begin with. Watching the television programs did not change the depression levels of those who initially (before the segments) reported little depression.

The results indicated that a community-wide prevention program can be beneficial. A large proportion (approximately one-third) of the viewers had some depressive symptoms, and this group showed fewer symptoms. The long-term effects of the programs were not assessed. Another problem in the study was that those who benefitted from the television programs exhibited some initial symptoms. If they were clinically diagnosable as being depressed, the intervention might be considered secondary rather than primary prevention. Nevertheless, the San Francisco study demonstrated the effects of large-scale interventions that may help disorders.

Evidence also exists that early, primary prevention efforts can be successful in reducing the incidence of juvenile delinquency. Zigler, Taussig, and Black (1992) noted that few treatment and rehabilitation programs for juvenile delinquents have had much effect. In their review of early intervention programs aimed at children, they found evidence that these programs, intended to promote social and intellectual competence, have had an expected positive effect on preventing delinquency. The investigators speculated that gaining competence may snowball to generate further success in other aspects of life and prevent delinquency.

Types of Primary Prevention Programs The goals of primary prevention programs cover an immense range. They include promoting social and intellectual competence in low-income, Mexican-American children (Johnson & Walker, 1987); preventing teenage pregnancy and sexually transmitted diseases such as AIDS (Fisher, 1990); preventing child abuse (Garbarino, 1980); enhancing competence in older adults (Gatz et al., 1982); encouraging car seat belt use and discouraging alcohol consumption (Geller, 1990); reducing domestic violence (Carlson & Davis, 1980); and preventing substance use among high-risk youths (Bruce & Emshoff, 1992). Such programs can have an enormous impact. Consider, for example, an analogous success in the field of public health: the development of the polio vaccines cost less than $40 million. Since they were first used, these vaccines have prevented 2000 deaths and 2500 permanently crippling cases of polio and have saved more than $1 billion each year in hospital costs and lost income (Jason et al., 1983). Preventing mental disorders can yield similar benefits.

Although interest in primary prevention continues to grow, resistance to prevention is also strong (see Focus 19.2). Problems have been noted by a number of researchers (Cowen, 1983; Felner et al., 1983; Glidewell, 1983). First, only through prospective and longitudinal research can developmental processes in primary prevention be uncovered (Lorion, 1990). Primary prevention is future oriented in that the benefits of the effort are not immediately apparent. Second, primary prevention competes with traditional programs aimed at treating people who already show emotional disturbances. Third, prevention may require social and environmental changes so that stressors can be reduced or resources can be enhanced. Most mental health workers are either unable or unwilling to initiate such changes; many others doubt that people have the ability to modify social structures. Fourth, funding for mental health programs has traditionally been earmarked for treatment. Prevention efforts constitute a new demand on the funding system. And fifth, primary prevention requires a great deal of planning, work, and long-term evaluation. This effort alone discourages many from becoming involved.

Secondary Prevention

Secondary prevention is an attempt to shorten the duration of mental disorders and to reduce their impact. If the presence of a disorder can be detected early and an effective treatment found, it is possible to minimize the impact of the disorder or to prevent its developing into a more serious and debilitating form. For example, classroom teachers can play an important role in secondary prevention by identifying children who are not adjusting to the school environment. Once identified, such children can be helped by teachers, parents, or school counselors.

In practice, secondary prevention has encountered a number of problems. First, traditional diagnostic methods are often unreliable and provide little insight into which treatment procedures to use. It has been suggested that more specialized diagnostic techniques be used, perhaps focusing on certain behaviors or on demographic characteristics that may

The goal of secondary prevention programs, such as the alcohol abuse program shown in this photo, is the early detection and prompt treatment of abusers. The idea is to minimize the impact of a disorder or to prevent it from developing into a more serious problem.

Prevention Versus Psychotherapy: Who's Wasting the Public's Time and Money?

With all the lip service paid to prevention these days, it might not sound like it wants for support. But when the bureaucracy doesn't want to do something [prevention programs], including something urgently recommended by the White House, it stalls. . . . Resistance is coming from the mental health industry, from psychotherapists, and from the organicists-geneticists who disparage social causation. . . . Prevention is bad for business. . . . [Mental health] centers simply can't spare staff for activities that are not reimbursable, and the immediate problems of the mentally distressed leave little time free for prevention efforts that might show results only after many years. (Albee, 1979b, p. 2)

Prevention has remained largely an unrealized hope rather than a technological reality for most health conditions. . . . Albee's assertion . . . that greedy psychotherapists, in collusion with other profit-oriented groups, have conspired to prevent preven-

tion because it is bad for business is a falsehood. (Wiggins, 1979, p. 2)

I hereby request a debate with Jack Wiggins at a time and place to be chosen by him and his seconds. . . . Anyone with the most elementary knowledge of health care in the western world knows that practically every significant advance in health maintenance has resulted from primary prevention efforts. (Albee, 1979a, p. 31)

This exchange between advocates of prevention and psychotherapy in the *APA Monitor* set the stage for a debate on the controversy at a meeting of the Division of Psychotherapy of the American Psychological Association at its 1980 convention in San Diego, California. The debate pitted against each other two past presidents of the American Psychological Association as well as two other prominent psychologists. The prevention advocates acknowledged the importance of psychotherapy in mental health efforts but emphasized the potential benefits of pri-

mary prevention. They argued that substantial opposition to primary prevention was based on (1) mental health professionals' lack of training in prevention, (2) the personal satisfaction and economic benefits of conducting psychotherapy, (3) the "newness" of systematic prevention efforts in the mental health field, (4) numerous misconceptions about the concept of primary prevention, and (5) a reluctance to initiate the social reforms that are needed to reduce stress.

The psychotherapy advocates acknowledged the value of prevention but denied that therapists resist prevention because of their own economic interests. They believed that, whereas psychotherapy has demonstrated its value, the field of prevention suffers from disunity and a lack of consensus regarding priorities, goals, and procedures.

The issues discussed in this classic debate are still being discussed. Although proponents and opponents of prevention can still be found, there is growing consensus that prevention programs are valuable, effective, and wise (Price 1987).

---

be related to psychopathology (Zax & Spector, 1974). Second, once a disorder is detected, it is often difficult to decide what form of treatment will be most effective with a particular patient. Third, prompt treatment is frequently unavailable because of the shortage of mental health personnel and the inaccessibility of services. Indeed, many mental health facilities have long lists of would-be patients who must wait months before receiving treatment. "Walk-in" clinics, crisis intervention facilities, and

emergency telephone lines have been established in an attempt to provide immediate treatment.

One of the most elaborate secondary prevention programs focused on first-grade public school children in Rochester, New York. It sought to answer the following questions:

1. Is it possible to identify "high-risk" first-grade children—those who are likely to become emotionally disturbed later on?

2. Can special efforts be made to help high-risk children adjust and to prevent later emotional disturbance?

In the first, or early detection, phase of the study, the investigators used interviews with mothers, teachers' ratings, and psychological tests to determine which children had (or could potentially have) emotional problems; these children were given a "red tag." The remaining children—about 70 percent of the total—were designated "non-red-tag" children. All the students in this school, whether red-tagged or not, were compared with control students from two demographically comparable schools.

The second, or prevention, phase was initiated in the experimental school but not in the control schools. It consisted of special meetings during and after school for teachers, parents, and mental health specialists. These meetings were designed to help teachers understand child development and focus on the needs of individual children. During the prevention phase, teachers gave special after-school attention to particular children who needed it.

In the final, or assessment, phase of the study, the investigators used academic scores and peer and teacher ratings to measure the children's adjustment.

In answer to question 1, results showed that children given a red tag in the first grade were more likely to show problems in the third and seventh grades than non-red-tag children. Findings about the effectiveness of prevention efforts (question 2), however, were less consistent. After third grade, children in the experimental group did not do consistently better than control group children on the various adjustment measures. Furthermore, by the seventh grade it was no longer possible to demonstrate positive effects of the prevention program. One benefit of the program was the finding that it resulted in a more positive attitude toward mental health personnel on the part of parents and teachers (Cowen et al., 1963; Zax & Cowen, 1972; Zax & Spector, 1974).

Cowen and colleagues have continued to modify the program and to increase the number of children in the project. More than 2000 children have been studied so far. A summary of the overall results has suggested that, despite methodological problems (such as the lack of more varied outcome measures and of more comparable, untreated control groups), the findings are quite consistent across a large population (Weissberg et al., 1983). The series of studies showed that intervention reduced problems involving shyness, learning difficulties, and (to some extent) acting out and aggressive behaviors. In addition, adaptive assertiveness, peer sociability, and frustration tolerance improved.

Suicide Prevention   Secondary prevention programs have also been initiated in suicide control. It has been estimated that more than 20,000 self-inflicted deaths occur per year and that there are ten suicide attempts for every suicidal death (Levy, 1988). These alarming statistics have initiated major efforts to prevent suicide (Farberow & Shneidman, 1961). Hundreds of suicide prevention centers, functioning autonomously or within mental health centers or hospitals, have been organized. These centers try to identify potentially suicidal people and to prevent suicides. Once a person is identified as running a high risk, attempts can be made to intervene directly.

Suicide prevention centers vary a great deal in complexity, from simple twenty-four-hour telephone "hot lines" to comprehensive therapeutic services. Many have publicized their availability or have established working relationships with police, hospitals, churches, and other organizations to more quickly identify, reach, and serve potentially suicidal people. Although the research evidence for the overall effectiveness of suicide prevention is equivocal (see Chapter 13), these programs represent a major effort in the attempt to prevent suicides. Crisis intervention services are also available for alcoholics, compulsive gamblers, and drug addicts. Some communities have also initiated services to help rape victims handle the emotional trauma and stress of their experience.

Tertiary Prevention

The goal of **tertiary prevention** is to facilitate the readjustment of the person to community life after hospital treatment for a mental disorder (Felner et al., 1983). Tertiary prevention focuses on reversing the effects of institutionalization and providing a smooth transition to a productive life in the community. Several programs have been developed to accomplish this goal. One involves the use of "passes," whereby hospitalized patients are encouraged to leave the hospital for short periods of time. By spending gradually increasing periods of time in the community (and then returning each time to the hospital), the patient can slowly readjust to life away from the hospital while still benefiting from therapy.

Psychologists can also ease readjustment to the community by educating the public about mental disorders. Public attitudes toward mental patients are often based on fears and stereotypes. Factual information can help modify these attitudes so that patients will be more graciously accepted. This help is especially important for the family, friends, and business associates of patients, who must interact frequently with them.

A more difficult problem to deal with is the growing backlash against the discharge of former mental patients into nursing homes or rooming houses in the community. Many community members feel threatened when such patients live in their neighborhoods. Again, education programs may help dispel community members' fears and stereotypes.

Halfway house programs can provide patients with a support system while they learn or redevelop skills they will need if they are to function in the community. In *outpatient* (patients live in the community and visit mental health clinics) and *night hospital* (patients are treated and stay in a hospital at night while working daily in the community) programs, patients can receive therapy and still hold down jobs or spend time with their families. Such programs help smooth the transition from the hospital to the community environment by offering exposure to both settings.

Evaluating Prevention

The concept of prevention has obvious appeal. It adds a proactive component to community psychology. In other words, rather than waiting for people to exhibit disorders before treating them, community psychologists actively seek to eliminate the causes or the antecedents of disorders and use community resources to prevent disorders. But the goals of prevention—to reduce the incidence and severity of mental disorders and to foster mental health—are difficult to attain for several reasons. We have noted some of them; others also should be mentioned. First, attempts to identify people at high risk of exhibiting juvenile delinquency or behavioral disorders have come under attack for fear that certain members of political or minority groups may be falsely identified and unwillingly assigned to a prevention program.

Second, doubts still remain about whether community psychologists have enough knowledge and power to implement effective programs. Third, prevention programs often require massive funding, and results are difficult to obtain in a short period of time. Because intensive evaluations of program effectiveness are generally rare, people are reluctant to invest in prevention (Bloom, 1972). And, fourth, some people fear that prevention efforts constitute an invasion of personal privacy. Continuing efforts are needed to reorganize priorities and to educate people about the benefits of prevention.

PARAPROFESSIONALS

If you had a serious marital problem or a personal adjustment difficulty, where would you seek help? Many factors obviously enter into such a choice. In an analysis of help-seeking behavior, it was found that disturbed people turn first to relatives, friends, and coworkers for assistance. Other helpers within their social networks, such as clergy or teachers, are also used. Relief agencies and professional mental health services are often used as a last resort (Gourash, 1978).

Clearly, then, a substantial proportion of disturbed individuals are helped by people who are not mental health professionals (Gottlieb, 1981). In an attempt to expand the availability of mental health services and at the same time take advantage of resources outside the mental health profession, community psychologists are training paraprofessional therapists and are themselves becoming more involved in consultation (helping paraprofessionals).

Paraprofessional therapists are people who are taught by professionals to provide some mental health services but do not have extensive formal mental health training. The training of more paraprofessionals would help solve the personnel shortage. In addition, many paraprofessionals have intimate knowledge of and experience in the community, which can help them understand clients and their environment. And paraprofessionals do not typically trigger the reluctance of many patients to enter therapy, a reluctance stemming from distrust or suspicion of mental health professionals.

The role of paraprofessionals in caring for others is not new. For many years Alcoholics Anonymous

A particularly effective form of paraprofessional assistance is to pair therapists and clients with similar backgrounds, problems, or disabilities. Such paraprofessional therapists are a valuable community mental health resource.

has used alcoholics who are no longer drinking as therapeutic agents for other alcoholics who are trying to stop drinking. The central issue is whether paraprofessionals are as effective as professionals, and ample evidence has suggested that they are effective (Cowen, 1982; Durlak, 1979).

In general, the nature and extent of training paraprofessionals has varied considerably from program to program. Some programs have selected paraprofessionals on the basis of personality test results (Holzberg, Knapp & Turner, 1967); others are chosen on the basis of performance in small-group interaction (Goodman, 1972). People from many different groups have also been used as paraprofessionals, including ghetto youths, many of whom were high-school dropouts (Klein, 1967); college students

(Gruver, 1971; Mitchell, 1983); mothers (Shah, 1969); teachers (Harris, Wolf & Baer, 1964); grandparents (Johnston, 1967); foster parents (Cobb, Leitenberg & Burchard, 1982); and members of minority groups (Sue, 1973). People who are not mental health professionals, yet who frequently offer help in the course of their work, have also been studied as possible paraprofessionals: hairdressers, divorce lawyers, industrial supervisors, and bartenders (Cowen, 1982; Toro, 1986). Rhodes, Ebert, and Fischer (1992) found that young African American women who had mentors (older, supportive individuals other than those who raised the women) were less depressed and made better use of social networks than women without mentors. Furthermore, paraprofessionals have acted as therapists (Rioch, 1967), companions (Goodman, 1972), advocates for abused women (Sullivan & Davidson, 1991), and foster grandparents (Johnston, 1967) and have used a wide variety of therapeutic orientations, including person-centered therapy, behavior modification, and filial therapy (that is, parents working with their child in client-oriented play therapy). One review of forty-two studies of paraprofessional helpers led to the conclusion that paraprofessionals are effective as therapeutic agents (Durlak, 1979). Little information was presented about the reason for this effectiveness, however.

The roles of professionals, paraprofessionals, and nonprofessionals have been conceptualized as a "mental health pyramid" (Seidman & Rappaport, 1974). At the narrow top of the pyramid are experienced mental health professionals who serve as teachers, consultants, and supervisors. As one moves down toward the base of the pyramid, one finds more people with less intensive mental health training. For example, in a university setting, psychology faculty (at the pyramid's top) might train graduate students (in the middle of the pyramid), who, in turn, would train undergraduates (near the pyramid's base) to act as therapeutic agents. The influence of this training expands progressively because a small number of professionals can train a larger number of paraprofessionals, who can train an even larger number of nonprofessionals.

The wide range of programs for training paraprofessionals indicates the growing involvement of lay workers in the mental health field. The community psychology approach gives nonprofessional mental health workers major responsibility in taking care of others—a role formerly considered exclusively the domain of professionals.

SOCIAL AND POLITICAL ACTION

The development of community psychology has led to a deeper appreciation of the massive influence of environmental forces and resources on mental health. This appreciation, however, has led to a serious conflict among psychologists about the wisdom of political activism: should psychologists become active in the social and political arena, or should they stay out of politics and remain within their traditional professional roles? Advocates of social and political activism argue that if psychologists are to effect major improvements in mental health, they must be able to influence political decisions and policies regarding environmental resources; that mental health services are already politicized; and that to separate one's professional role from one's social and political concerns is to refuse responsibility for society's future (Altrocchi, 1972). In other words, activists believe that mental health professionals should use their knowledge of human behavior to make positive changes in the policies that affect people. Opponents of this view contend that it is unprofessional for psychologists to become social activists. They fear that politically active psychologists may start imposing their own community-action programs and social policies.

In another sense, it is impossible to avoid social and political implications for creating or changing programs. For example, community psychologists may participate in activities such as helping to create citizen advisory boards to community agencies, helping to organize programs for the homeless, advocating changes in mental health programs, acting as consultants or experts to the legal system, and helping powerless groups to gain political clout. In all these activities, there are social and political repercussions because change in one aspect of a social system affects other parts of the social system (Levine & Perkins, 1987). Earlier we mentioned that mental health patients, when given autonomy and alternatives to mental hospitals, seem to have favorable outcomes. Such alternatives to hospitalization affect the entire mental health system: will programs that provide health insurance extend coverage to patients who now enter alternative programs? If alternatives to

hospitalization grow, will mental health workers in hospitals feel threatened by the possible loss of jobs in hospital care? In other words, when social change is initiated, many other segments of the system are affected and often these segments are in conflict with each other.

Psychologists within the American Psychological Association have long been addressing four kinds of policy issues. The first deals with Association "housekeeping" concerns, such as devising accreditation criteria for psychology programs. The second issue affects professional interests; for example, seeing that congressional appropriations are sufficient for psychological research and training. The third involves matters of public interest such as effective programs for children, the elderly, and minority groups. The fourth involves moral and ethical stances concerning controversial and emotional issues such as gun control, abortion, and a nuclear freeze (Kimmel, 1984). The involvement of psychologists in the last two areas has created the greatest controversy.

Is it possible for community psychologists to facilitate social action without directly imposing their own values on others? The answer is "yes and no." Rappaport (1981) advocated an empowerment model whereby community psychologists enhance the ability of people to control their own lives. Rappaport's model is based on three principles: (1) the resources to affect change already exist in communities, (2) people already know what is best for their communities, and (3) no single solution is applicable to all communities. The term *empowerment* implies that the program is aimed at helping people become able to participate in decisions that affect their lives (Rappaport, 1987). The task of psychologists is to help others find better means to use already existing skills and strengths to solve their own problems. Benefits of empowerment strategies have been found in numerous studies of community agencies and community residents (Florin & Wandersman, 1990; Pestby et al., 1990). If in trying to help others, psychologists use research findings to guide their actions, then some safeguards exist against the imposition of personal values that have no research justification (Sue, 1992).

Rappaport's model has value implications. Advocating the empowerment of people as a preferred model for social action is itself a value decision, and choosing which community groups to empower may also have political implications. The model represents

FOCUS 19.3

Increasing Social Supports: Use of Community Self-Help Groups

Self-help groups bring people together so that they can help each other more effectively cope with some personal or life-disrupting problems by exchanging psychological support, information, and resources. In this sense, group members are "prosumers"—that is, both providers and consumers of services (Borkman, 1990). Informal self-help groups have always existed. Alcoholics Anonymous is one self-help group with which most people are familiar.

Community psychologists have been interested in facilitating the development of self-help groups. Indeed, as former U.S. Surgeon Gen-

eral C. Everett Koop and others recognized, such groups are a community resource that can provide immense social supports. The rapid growth of self-help groups reflects the growing belief that people can help themselves and others (Levine & Perkins, 1987).

The task of community psychologists is to help organize these groups, facilitate their development, and conduct research on their effectiveness. In California, a self-help center was established to enhance the growth and development of thousands of self-help groups (see Eisman, 1988). Headed by Gerald Goodman and Marion Jacobs, the

center monitors a diverse range of self-help groups such as parents of high-risk infants (those born prematurely), victims of AIDS, single parents, widowed or divorced men and women, parents of drug abusers, Vietnam War veterans, relatives of people with Alzheimer's disease, survivors of rape or incest, child abusers, and parents of runaway children. People who face common problems, because of health or psychological disturbances, and people who are the relatives or friends of those facing such problems, can help each other in these groups.

Elderly people often lack social contact with others. Senior citizen programs, such as the one shown in this photo, provide the elderly with social supports and the opportunity to interact with their peers.

Should People Engage in Do-It-Yourself Psychology?

The success of paraprofessionals and self-help groups (see Focus 19.3) points to the role that others can play in helping people adjust and deal with personal problems. Recently, the public has been bombarded with media-oriented means of self-help: examples include advice columns ("Dear Abby" features in newspapers); television counseling programs that give callers personal advice; and audiotapes, videotapes, and books that focus on parenting, personal adjustment, and interpersonal skills. Literally hundreds of books deal with stress management, weight loss, assertiveness, handling anger and depression, eating and sleeping disorders, improving self-esteem and personal growth, communication skills, and sexual concerns (Quackenbush, 1991). Have you seen or heard of them? Do they appeal to you?

What advantages do you see in these media aids? Media aids reach a large segment of the population. As mentioned in the text, many people

with personal problems do not seek the assistance of professional mental health services. Thus they are unlikely to receive individualized professional care. Media aids can make available professional advice for those who do not seek the services of psychologists, psychiatrists, or other mental health personnel. Media aids such as books are also inexpensive and allow people to work on problems in the privacy of their home without coming to the attention of others. Finally, by being able to purchase books or videotapes, some people feel a degree of personal control in being able to work on problems by themselves. What other advantages do you see?

What kinds of problems can you see in these media aids? Do self-help books and materials really help people? Little research has been conducted on these questions. Most of the research is pertinent to self-help books. Rosen (1987) has discussed several questions that need to be addressed. First, are people likely to use

and continue to use successfully self-administered forms of treatment? Second, can self-help efforts lead to a worsening of problems? How can this happen? Third, what do you think of specific claims such as: "In just a few weeks, learn how to master your fears"; "instantly achieve weight loss—and how to keep it off"?

What can be done? Self-help materials can be of great use. In the course of treatment, many psychologists recommend that their clients use self-help books (Starker, 1988). Assuming that their use will continue, what kind of safeguards can be implemented to avoid exaggerated claims? Some research also suggests that individuals who use self-help books find them useful (Halliday, 1991). Why do some people find them useful while others do not? What kind of research should be conducted in order to test the effectiveness of self-administered treatments? These are important questions to think about and discuss.

a shift away from the position that mental health professionals are the sole experts, the group that must decide what is best for mental health. It recognizes, appreciates, and makes use of existing competencies in laypeople.

SOCIAL SUPPORTS

As noted, people often turn to others for help and guidance during emotional stress. They first seek support from family members, friends, coworkers, or clergy, and then perhaps from mental health profes-

sionals. By **social supports,** we mean the availability and quality of interpersonal resources that people can call on during emotional stress. Social supports can provide guidance, feedback, material aid, behavioral assistance, intimate relationships, and positive social interactions (Barrera & Ainlay, 1983). Community psychologists are particularly interested in social supports as resources that already exist and are available within communities (Rappaport, 1981). Focus 19.3 discusses one form of community support, self-help groups, and Critical Thinking discusses the use of self-help materials. Of particular interest is their potential for preventing emotional problems.

People with effective support networks tend to show fewer symptoms of both physical and mental disorders in the face of stress than do people without such support (Heller et al., 1984; Hirsch & DuBois, 1992). The relationship between social supports, stressors, and psychiatric symptoms was examined in a study in which social supports were measured in terms of interactions and involvement with, as well as feelings toward, friends, neighbors, community organizations, and the like (Lin et al., 1979). Measures of life event stressors and self-reported psychiatric symptoms were also obtained. The results indicated that more severe stressors were related to increased numbers and severity of symptoms, but stronger social supports reduced the number of symptoms. The researchers speculated that social supports mediate the relationship between stress and emotional disturbance. That is, social supports may help decrease the impact of stress on mental health. Other researchers have also recognized the possibility that social supports cushion the impact of stress (Cassel, 1974; Cobb, 1976; Digman, Barrera & West, 1986).

Some researchers have tried to identify the helpfulness of different social supports. Cauce and Srebnik (1990) found that supports can be characterized by degree of *intimacy* in the relationship (for example, between family members) and by *relevance* of the support to daily life. Interestingly, students rate the family as being high in intimacy but low in terms of relevance, and friends were rated high on both. Faculty members were low in intimacy but high on relevance, and dentists and physicians were rated low on both. This means that the people with whom we have intimate relations may not be the most relevant to our daily support, especially among college students who may be living away from family members.

If social supports are important in mental health, then we may enable more people to cope better with stress by improving the number, range, and quality of these supports. Many of the studies cited earlier have shown that increasing interpersonal resources can, in fact, reduce or prevent emotional distress. This function is especially important because it is impossible to eliminate all the stressors that human beings may face.

Although a great deal of research has recently been done on social support, much is still unknown (Gottlieb, 1983). Precisely how do social supports enable one to cope? What aspects of social supports are beneficial? What kinds of people, with what kinds of support, exposed to what kinds of stressors, can adjust and adapt? What are the most effective means for enhancing social supports? These and many more questions have yet to be addressed.

RACISM AND SEXISM: TWO PROBLEMS FOR COMMUNITY PSYCHOLOGISTS

Because of its ecological perspective, community psychology must be involved in modifying or altering social and environmental conditions that give rise to and maintain stress. Such conditions can have a tremendous impact on the mental well-being of large groups of people. One of the most malignant is the personal and institutional practices of prejudice, discrimination, and stereotyping—which have been directed against women, the elderly, ethnic and religious minorities, people with physical handicaps, and homosexuals. Here we examine the psychological consequences of racism and sexism.

Racism

African Americans, Hispanic Americans, Native Americans, and Asian Americans share many of the experiences of oppression that are manifested through **racism,** discrimination, and prejudice. These attitudes and behaviors are often aimed at specific groups out of hatred, misunderstanding, and fear of people whose values and culture differ in some ways from that of the dominant cultural group. The standard of living of many minority group members is much lower than that of European Americans, and rather than identifying this standard as a by-product of racism, it is often used as "evidence" of the supposed inferiority of minority groups.

Because of a history of discrimination in housing, employment, income, and education, many members of ethnic minorities experience high unemployment, less desirable jobs, and low income as well as higher suicide and juvenile delinquency rates and poorer health. Although African Americans comprise about 12 percent of the American population, they represent more than 20 percent of the officially unemployed and as much as 40 percent of the discouraged workers who have dropped out of the labor force (Bowman, 1991). Historically, African Americans have suffered from segregated and inferior education—larger class size, lower teacher qualifications, poorer physical facilities, and fewer funds for extracurricular activities.

Native Americans have experienced a succession of massacres of genocidal proportions (Wrightsman, 1972). Today, the median family income of the Native American family ($13,680) is much less than that of the nation as a whole ($19,920), and the poverty rate of 28 percent is much higher than the 12 percent for the U.S. population (Trimble, 1991).

Effects on Self-Esteem Many scholars have written about the psychological costs of racism for members of ethnic minority groups (Jones & Korchin, 1982; Ruiz & Padilla, 1977; Sue, 1978). Exposure to mainstream American values and to ethnic stereotypes has caused some members of minority groups to behave in ways that confirm the stereotypes—a self-fulfilling prophecy (Jones, 1991)—or to question whether they themselves are to blame for being different and whether segregation is justified. A sense of confused self-identity among African American children, to which racism may contribute, was first brought to the attention of social scientists by Clark and Clark (1947). In a study of racial awareness and preference among African American and white children, they found that African American children preferred to play with a white doll rather than a black one; that the black doll was perceived as being somehow "bad"; and that about one-third of the African American children, when asked to pick the doll that looked like them, picked the white one.

Malcolm X was an African American activist leader who advocated revolutionary change. In the *Autobiography of Malcolm X* (Haley, 1966), he relates how, as a young man, he tried desperately to appear as white as possible. He went to painful lengths to straighten and dye his hair so that he would look more like white males.

The development of a negative self-image and the fostering of racial self-hatred are not unique to African Americans. Many minority groups come to accept white standards for physical attractiveness, personality characteristics, and social relationships (Kardiner & Ovesey, 1962). That such an orientation may lead to racial self-hatred is evident in the following clinical description of Janet, a Chinese-American girl:

Janet, a 21-year-old senior majoring in sociology, was born and raised in Portland, Oregon, where she had limited contact with members of her own race. Her father, a second-generation Chinese-American, is a doctor. Her mother is a homemaker. Janet is the middle sibling; she has an older brother in medical school and a younger brother, age 17.

Janet entered therapy suffering from a severe depressive reaction manifested by feelings of worthlessness, by suicidal ideation, and by an inability to concentrate. She was unable to recognize the cause of her depression throughout the initial interviews. However, much light was shed on the problem when the therapist, also a Chinese-American, noticed an inordinate amount of hostility; it became apparent that Janet really resented being seen by a psychologist of her own race. She suspected that she had been deliberately assigned a Chinese-American therapist. When asked about this, Janet openly expressed scorn for "anything that reminds me of Chinese." She expressed hostility toward Chinese customs and especially Chinese males, whom she described as introverted, passive, and sexually unattractive.

Further exploration revealed that all through school she had associated only with Caucasians. When she was in high school, Janet would frequently bring home white boyfriends, greatly upsetting her parents. It was as though she blamed her parents for having been born Chinese and used this method to hurt them.

During her college years, Janet became involved in two love affairs with Caucasians, both ending unsatisfactorily and abruptly. The last breakup had occurred four months earlier, when the boy's parents had threatened to cut off financial support for their son unless he ended the relationship. Apparently, objections had arisen because of Janet's race.

Although not completely conscious of it, Janet was having increasing difficulty denying her racial heritage. The breakup of her last love affair brought home to her the fact that she was a member of a group that was not fully accepted by all segments of society. At first she vehemently and bitterly denounced the Chinese for her present dilemma. Later, much of her hostility was turned inward against herself. Feeling alienated from her own subculture and not fully accepted by white society, she experienced an identity crisis. This resulted in feelings of worthlessness and depression. It was at this point that Janet had come for therapy. (Sue & Sue, 1971, p. 41)

Although some African Americans and other ethnic group members show self-hatred, most researchers question how widespread the phenomenon is.

Rodney King being beaten by L.A. police officers, March 3, 1991. This beating of an African-American man was captured in a videotape and heightened racial tensions. It began a series of events that eventually culminated in rioting, looting, violence, and arson in the city.

First, as pointed out by Banks (1982) and Powell (1983), many studies demonstrating low self-esteem among ethnic minorities contain methodological or conceptual flaws. This may be particularly true of early research studies that were relatively unsophisticated. Second, some African Americans may exhibit racial self-hatred, and focusing on these individuals may result in overgeneralizations concerning all African Americans. Third, being socialized in this country, African Americans may adopt some white patterns and standards but not others. Undue emphasis on the adoption of white behaviors and styles may lead to a misconception that African Americans have low self-esteem. (It should also be noted that the adoption of behavioral patterns and standards is a two-way process. For example, many non–African American athletes have adopted handshakes, gestures, mannerisms, and expressions that were initiated by African American athletes.) Fourth, times have changed. During the 1960s and 1970s, we witnessed a movement to redefine the minority group's existence by raising consciousness of, and pride in, racial and cultural heritage. Positive aspects of ethnic cultures were emphasized, and many ethnic groups (African Americans, Hispanic Americans, Native Americans, Asian Americans, and others) joined in the fight against racism.

Racism and Mental Health   We have indicated that oppression, racism, prejudice, and discrimination have deleterious effects. If racism is viewed as a stressor, it would seem reasonable to assume that rates of mental disorders would be greater among oppressed groups. Indeed, the authors of one report on the distribution of mental disorders have gone so far as to state that "Racist practices undoubtedly are key factors—perhaps the most important ones—in producing mental disorders in African Americans and other underprivileged groups" (Kramer, Rosen & Willis, 1973, p. 355). But is there any evidence to indicate that African Americans, for example, experience higher rates of psychopathology than European Americans?

Two methods are used to assess the incidence of mental disorders in a population (Dohrenwend & Dohrenwend, 1974). In the first, the rate of disorders in a population is estimated by noting how many people from that population are *treated* for psychological disorders in mental institutions and clinics and by practitioners. (The assumption is that the greater the number of treated cases, the greater the psychological disturbance in that group or population.) In the second method, the rate of disorders is obtained for a *sample* of the population through interviewing, testing, or the like; the rate for the sam-

1. Treatment rates may not accurately indicate disorder rates, especially in cross-cultural comparisons.

2. Many studies comparing African American and white treatment patterns have failed to control for such variables as age, socioeconomic status, or marital status that may confound the effects of race.

3. Because of difficulties in diagnosing people who differ culturally, many African Americans may be misdiagnosed by European American therapists.

4. Stress may result in increased maladjustment or in adjustment, depending on coping skills, resources, and the ability to learn from negative experiences (Myers & King, 1983).

The second method of assessing disorder rates—sampling the population—has not been used to any great degree in comparing African Americans and whites. This may be due to a lack of adequate data and valid measures of psychopathology for use in comparing ethnic groups. In any case, the question of whether African Americans and whites have different rates of psychopathology cannot be fully answered on the basis of the currently available data (Dohrenwend & Dohrenwend, 1974; Jones & Thorne, 1987).

Evidence exists that ethnic minority groups are experiencing significant mental health problems. The available data suggest that prevalence rates for these groups are at least as high as those in the general population (Vega & Rumbaut, 1991). Some groups, such as immigrants and Southeast Asian refugees, appear to be at risk for mental disorder. Immigrant or refugee background, encounters with prejudice and discrimination, cultural differences, and other experiences associated with minority group status may act as stressors that influence mental health. In a survey of psychological distress among 1000 African Americans and European Americans, African Americans were found to be more likely than European Americans to report psychological symptoms (Neff, 1984). After the effects of age and social class were removed, however, the racial differences were largely negligible. This finding suggests that African Americans may not have higher rates of mental disorder. Because African Americans are overrepresented among

Positive aspects of ethnic cultures are emphasized to combat racism and its harmful effects. Raising consciousness and fostering pride in racial and cultural heritages can be used to change prejudicial attitudes and racial stereotypes.

ple is then used to estimate the rate for the whole population.

The results of such assessments have so far been conflicting. Most studies of treated cases support the notion that African Americans have higher rates of mental disorders than European Americans. That is, most studies have found that higher relative proportions of African Americans than European Americans are admitted to mental institutions (Bulhan, 1985; Sue et al., 1991). A few investigators have found no difference or have found lower rates among African Americans (Snowden, Collinge & Runkle, 1982). These contradictory results may be due to the following conceptual and methodological problems:

the lower socioeconomic classes (which do have higher rates for certain disorders), effects of race and social class may often be confounded. Above and beyond social class, the stress experienced by African Americans and other ethnic minority groups may result in problems involving alienation, autonomy, and achievement rather than mental disorders.

Reducing Racism Nearly three decades ago, the National Advisory Commission on Civil Disorders (1968) noted,

> Of the basic causes [of urban riots of the 1960s], the most fundamental is the racial attitude and behavior of European Americans toward African Americans. Race prejudice has shaped our history decisively; it now threatens our future. White racism is essentially responsible for the explosive mixture that has been accumulating in our cities. (p. 10)

The commission recognized that the history of the United States is intertwined with racial prejudice and racism.

Much has been written about eliminating racism through legislative, judicial, economic, political, and social changes of one kind or another. Various community or national strategies include the following (Katz, 1976):

1. The widespread use of educational programs and the mass media to correct racial stereotypes and to provide accurate information on minority groups
2. Increasing the quality of interpersonal and interracial contacts
3. Changing the way people view violence
4. Rewarding nonaggressive responses
5. Legal remedies

Psychological approaches to the reduction of prejudice have included self-insight, cooperative interactions among various groups, socialization practices that are helpful in rearing unbiased children, and role modeling (see Katz & Taylor, 1988). A current trend in schools, universities, corporations, police departments, social service facilities, and governmental agencies is to engage in some form of **diversity training,** or training intended to increase awareness of ethnic-related attitudes and behaviors, discourage prejudice and discriminatory behaviors, and promote effective and cooperative human relationships

(Smith, 1990). It is possible to change attitudes and behaviors, but the main problem has been in achieving changes that are long-lasting and meaningful rather than superficial and comprehensive.

Sexism

Sexism is prejudice and discrimination directed against people of either sex, because of their sex. On the basis of employment, income, and education statistics, women qualify as an oppressed group in our society (Grefe, 1980). In the field of mental health, studies have indicated that a significant number of mental health professionals have allowed sex role biases, stereotypes, and a double standard of mental health to influence their practice with female clients (American Psychological Association Task Force on Sex Bias, 1975). Understanding these biases may be the first step toward eliminating them.

Sex Role Stereotyping The values of this society have traditionally been male oriented. In an industrial, highly technological society such as ours, great value is placed on a person's role in the labor force. Although there has been a great increase in the number of women in the labor force, especially in the last two decades, this increase has mainly affected the jobs that have customarily been held by women—secretarial, retail sales, and elementary school teaching. Some people believe that inborn differences in competencies between men and women justify differential sex roles. Yet substantial evidence shows that sex differences in cognitive abilities are actually quite small (Deaux, 1984) or nonexistent (Caplan, MacPherson & Tobin, 1985). In the Soviet Union, one-third of the engineers and three-fourths of the physicians are women.

Children are usually reared in accordance with sex role stereotypes from birth. A sex role preference can be observed by age three and is well established by age five (Williams, 1977). Boys are socialized to be aggressive, competitive, and independent; girls are encouraged to be passive and dependent (Russo & Denmark, 1984). Sex-role standards usually stress that women should be nurturing and desirable to men; standards for men emphasize independence and control.

The effectiveness of such socialization practices was illustrated in a national survey in which eight personality characteristics had to be attributed to either males or females. Eighty percent of the respondents said that four of the traits (aggressiveness, independence, objectivity, and mathematical reasoning) were typically male and that the other four traits (nurturance, empathy, monogamy, and emotionality) were typically female (Tavris, 1972). In another study, aging men were seen as becoming more mature, distinguished, and respected. Older women, however, were seen as becoming sexually undesirable, unattractive, powerless, and old (Nutt, 1979). Differences in the standards and interpretations used to evaluate the behaviors of men and women were highlighted by Tavris (1991). Take, for example, the following contrasting statements: "women have lower self-esteem" versus "men are more conceited than women"; women are more likely to say they are 'hurt' than to admit they are 'angry'" versus "men are more likely than women to accuse and attack others when they are unhappy, instead of stating that they feel hurt and inviting sympathy." By contrasting the statements, Tavris pointed out that similar behaviors can be evaluated quite differently and that male standards have in the past been used to the disadvantage of women.

Men are thought to be more influential than women, and women more easily influenced. In one experiment, subjects were given written scenarios describing two employees (male and female), one of whom was trying to persuade the other on a policy issue. Subjects rated the female as more likely than the male to be influenced by the attempt to persuade. They also inferred that the man in the scenario had a higher-status job than the woman, although no information was provided about job statuses. When job titles (a high-status and a low-status title) were assigned to the hypothetical employees, however, subjects felt that the low-status person would be more compliant than the high-status person, regardless of sex (Eagly, 1983). This finding emphasized the importance of status and implied an effect on behavior: the stereotypes that convey a low-status image for women also create expectations about how women should perform. Men and women then may perform in accordance with these expectations. Such expectations, however, are more likely to affect performance on interactive and interpersonal tasks than on less social and more individualistic tasks (Deaux, 1984).

Like many others, mental health professionals have been found to engage in sex role stereotyping. However, that practice has decreased over time (Hare-Mustin, 1983). It seems to be due, at least in part, to a lack of knowledge or misinformation that therapists have about women's problems. If this is

Women are increasingly assuming roles and positions that were previously limited to men. Thirty years ago, an all-women fire department would have been inconceivable. Today, more and more women are holding key jobs in both the private and public sectors of our society.

indeed the case, more accurate information, along with education and training, may eventually eliminate it altogether. Meanwhile, as we are about to see, sex role stereotyping in the mental health professions does have implications for the mental health of women.

Sexism and Mental Health   Many studies have shown that most patients in therapy are women (Chesler, 1976; Gove & Tudor, 1973; Kulka, 1982; Sue, Fujino, Hu, Takeuchi, & Zane, 1991). The role of patient is highly consistent with a female sex role characterized by weakness, dependency, irrationality, and acceptance of care (Williams, 1977).

Relative to the incidence of physical and medical illnesses among women and men, women are more likely to seek medical and psychiatric help (Chesler, 1971; Shapiro et al., 1984). This tendency again may be explained in terms of socialization; a woman's sex role permits her to seek help, whereas men may consider it "unmasculine" to do so. As a group, women are not more prone to mental disorders than men, except for some specific disorders such as depression. They are also less prone to some disorders, including antisocial personality (Myers et al., 1984).

Especially crucial to an understanding of the mental health of women is recognizing the value that society (including mental health professionals) places on the different behaviors that are approved for the sexes (Tavris, 1991). An early study suggested that many clinicians view their patients in a very traditional manner (Broverman & Broverman, 1970). Therapists were asked to complete a questionnaire on sex role stereotypes in which a healthy male, a healthy female, and a healthy adult were rated in terms of 122 antonymous (opposite) pairs of traits. There was high agreement among the clinicians on their ratings, and there were no major differences between male and female clinicians. The results indicated that there is a double standard of mental health for males and females. A healthy male was described and rated in the same terms as a healthy adult. The healthy female was described differently from both, with such terms as *submissive, emotional, easily influenced, sensitive to hurt, excitable, conceited about appearance, dependent, less competitive, unaggressive,* and *unobjective.* This study has powerful implications. When the traits that are said to characterize

a healthy woman are considered socially undesirable for a healthy adult, it is not the least bit surprising that women are more likely to seek therapy!

The study by the Brovermans served to alert the mental health profession to the possible sex role bias that therapists may have toward women. Furthermore, because the study by the Brovermans focused on therapists, little is known about the perceptions of clients. A study by Sesan (1988) examined the attitudes and perceptions of women clients toward their therapists who were male or female. Women who had completed treatment were asked to respond to a survey that was intended to assess sex bias among their therapists. Several interesting results emerged. First, the majority of women clients experienced a sex-fair therapy process. Second, the clients did not perceive differences on the basis of the therapist's gender. That is, clients with a male therapist reported no more bias than those with a female therapist. Third, bias varied somewhat according to educational level and the presence of children, in that women with the least amount of formal education and those with children reported more bias than women with higher levels of education and with no children. When therapist bias did occur, it tended to be in the areas of the therapist projecting a traditional sex role onto the clients and not accepting anger on the part of the women clients. The findings suggest that although bias exists, it is not as pervasive as it was in 1970, when the Brovermans' study was conducted. Further studies are necessary to provide more definitive answers.

The DSM diagnostic system has been criticized as being biased in that women may be diagnosed as being disturbed for acting "out of line"—that is, for not acting "like women" (Kaplan, 1983). Yet DSM also has been defended by others as being unbiased (Williams & Spitzer, 1983). At this point there is no evidence that DSM should be considered a sex-biased system. This does not mean, however, that every category within the diagnostic system is unbiased and accurate.

Reducing Sexism   As is true for racism, eliminating sexism requires ambitious psychological, educational, and legal efforts—in this case aimed at correcting sex biases, sexual stereotypes, and inequities. To change the image of women conveyed through the mass media alone is a massive undertaking, fortunately already underway. Making the educational system more responsive to the concerns and needs of women is another primary goal. For victims of sexual harassment, legal redress is possible; many employers have now developed guidelines for determining and eliminating harassment (Livingston, 1982). In the mental health field, counselors and therapists have available a publication of the American Psychological Association outlining "Principles Concerning the Counseling and Therapy of Women" (Ad Hoc Committee on Women, 1979). It includes specific recommendations to help therapists confront their own sexism in a way that will enhance their ability to help women clients.

SUMMARY

1. Community psychology is concerned with the influence of community and environmental forces on human behavior and with using these resources to alleviate human problems. The community psychology approach grew out of dissatisfaction with the inability of the treatment approach to care for the large number of disturbed people, with the biogenic or disease model of psychopathology, with the ineffectiveness of psychiatric hospitals, and with inequities in the delivery of mental health services.

2. As a result of this dissatisfaction, community mental health centers were initiated in the 1960s. These centers are located in many communities and are accessible to the surrounding population. They offer a wide range of services including outpatient and short-term inpatient care, consultation, emergency services, and partial hospitalization. Despite the lack of adequate financial support and community involvement in some centers, they are a major mental health resource.

3. One goal of community psychology is to prevent mental disorders. This prevention takes three forms. Primary prevention (reducing the incidence of new cases) seeks to introduce new resources and reduce stressors. Secondary prevention seeks to reduce the duration or severity of a disorder through early detection and prompt treatment. Tertiary prevention seeks to reduce the disabling effects of a disorder by

facilitating the adjustment and early return to the community of those who have experienced mental disorders.

4. To alleviate the shortage of professional mental health personnel, psychologists have begun to train paraprofessionals or laypeople to act as therapeutic agents. Psychologists can thus take advantage of the knowledge and experience of community members and can combat the reluctance of some people to enter therapy with unfamiliar mental health professionals.

5. Some believe that the prevention and treatment of mental disorders in the community require control or modification of environmental forces and resources. This approach, however, raises the controversial question of whether mental health professionals should become active in the social or political arena to effect major changes in mental health. Most psychologists believe that social and political implications of their work cannot be avoided.

6. Social supports, too, have been explored as a tool for fostering adjustment and for preventing disorders. They may act as a buffer against stress.

7. Racism and sexism are community problems that affect mental health. Racism is manifested in a lower standard of living for racial minorities (Asian Americans, African Americans, Hispanics, and American Indians). It can cause some people to believe that they are inferior and to feel racial self-hatred. The development of feelings of racial pride and identity is necessary to reverse this negative attitude. Women, like members of racial minorities, represent an oppressed group in our society. Historically, women have been subordinated and controlled through sex role stereotyping. Studies have shown that some therapists allow sex role biases, stereotypes, and a double standard of mental health to influence their practice with women clients. Eliminating racism and sexism will not be easy. Proposed strategies include using educational programs to correct stereotyping, increasing the quality of interracial contacts, changing perceptual processes, using the mass media for change, using rewards, and instituting legal remedies. Currently, many individuals in business and industry, governmental agencies, and other institutions are receiving diversity training. As part of the training program, they become more aware of the backgrounds of culturally diverse

groups, the effects of prejudice and discrimination, and means to work effectively with all groups.

KEY TERMS

community mental health centers Centrally located mental health facilities (for medium-sized communities) that provide a number of services such as short-term inpatient care, outpatient care, partial hospitalization, emergency services, and community consultation and education

community psychology An approach to mental health that takes into account the influence of environmental factors and stresses the use of community resources to eliminate various conditions that produce psychological problems

diversity training Training intended to increase awareness of ethnic-related attitudes and behaviors, discourage prejudice and discriminatory behaviors, and promote effective and cooperative human relationships

human ecology The interaction between human beings and their environments

paraprofessional therapists People who are taught by professionals to provide some mental health services but who do not have formal mental health training

primary prevention An effort to lower the incidence of new cases of behavioral disorders by strengthening or adding to resources that promote mental health and by eliminating features of a community that threaten mental health

racism Discrimination and prejudice that are aimed at a specific group because it is considered inferior in some way

secondary prevention An attempt to shorten the duration of mental disorders and to reduce their impact

sexism Prejudice and discrimination directed against people of either sex because of their sex

social supports The availability and quality of interpersonal resources that people can call on during emotional stress

tertiary prevention Efforts to facilitate the readjustment of the person to community life after hospital treatment for a mental disorder

therapeutic community A hospital environment in which all activities are structured to have a therapeutic function and in which patients participate to the greatest extent possible

CHAPTER 20

Legal and Ethical Issues in Abnormal Psychology

For five months between 1977 and 1978 Los Angeles was terrorized by a series of murders of young women whose bodies were left on hillsides. All the women had been raped and strangled; some had been brutally tortured. The public and press dubbed the culprit the Hillside Strangler, and a massive hunt for the killer or killers ensued. A major break occurred one year after the Los Angeles murders when 27-year-old Kenneth Bianchi was arrested for two unrelated murders of college students in Bellingham, Washington. His fingerprints matched those found at the scene of the Hillside murders.

Bianchi was an unlikely murder suspect because many who knew him described him as dependable and conscientious—"the boy next door." Furthermore, despite the strong evidence against Bianchi, he insisted that he was innocent. Police noticed that he was unable to remember much of his past life. During interviews in which hypnosis was used, a startling development occurred: Bianchi exhibited another personality (Steve). Steve freely admitted to killing the women, called Ken a "turkey," and laughed at Ken's ignorance of his existence.

She was a well-known "bag lady" in the downtown Oakland area who by night slept on any number of park benches and in store fronts. By day she could be seen pushing her Safeway shopping cart full of boxes, extra clothing, and garbage, which she collected from numerous trash containers. According to her only surviving sister, the Bag Lady had lived this way for nearly ten years and had been tolerated by local merchants. Over the past six months, however, Bag Lady's behavior had become progressively intolerable. She had always talked to herself, but recently began shouting and screaming at anyone who approached her. Her use of profanity was graphic, and she often urinated and defecated in front of the stores. Bag Lady was occasionally arrested and detained for a short period of time by local law enforcement officials, but she always returned to her familiar haunts. Finally, her sister and several merchants requested that the city take action to commit her to a mental institution.

In 1968, Prosenjit Poddar, a graduate student from India studying at the University of California at Berkeley, sought therapy from the student health services for depression. Apparently Poddar was upset over what he perceived to be a rebuff from a female student, Tatiana Tarasoff, whom he claimed to love. During the course of treatment, Poddar informed his therapist that he intended to purchase a gun and kill the woman. Judging Poddar to be dangerous, the psychologist breached the confidentiality of the professional relationship by informing the campus police. The police detained Poddar briefly, but freed him because he agreed to stay away from Tarasoff. On October 27, Poddar went to Tarasoff's home, wounded her with a gun, and repeatedly stabbed her to death with a knife. This much-celebrated case elicited the court response that came to be known as the *Tarasoff* decision, regarding the therapist's duty to warn the victim directly and not just the authorities (police).

A male therapist said, "I remember the incident quite clearly. I was seeing a female student for a therapy session at the university counseling center. Jennifer, the student, was in extreme distress as she mourned the loss of her younger sister. She was not only grieving about her sister's death, but she was also attempting to cope with her own feelings of guilt. Jennifer had been the driver when she was broadsided by another car on the passenger side. Both her sister and the driver of the other car were killed instantaneously. Jennifer had lost consciousness and had no recollection of the incident. Fault could not be determined definitively, but it was obvious that Jennifer blamed herself (even though police reports suggested that the other driver had probably entered the intersection illegally).

"During this particular session, Jennifer's pain seemed especially intense. I could feel the depths of her grief and sorrow. Without thinking, I pulled my chair next to her, placed my arms around her, and pulled her to my chest, where she wept uncontrollably."

In Chapter 1, we defined abnormal psychology as the scientific and objective approach to describing,

explaining, predicting, and treating behaviors that are considered strange and unusual. All four of the preceding examples of behavior fit this definition well, and we can clearly see their clinical implications. What is less clear to many is that clinical or mental health issues can often become legal and ethical ones as well. This is most evident in the Kenneth Bianchi (Hillside Strangler) case. If his attorneys could prove that he was insane, Bianchi could be judged "not guilty by reason of insanity." Yet how do we determine whether a person is insane or sane? What criteria do we use? If we call on experts as in the Bianchi case, we find that professionals often disagree with one another. Might defendants in criminal trials attempt to fake mental disturbances to escape guilty verdicts? When defendants are mentally ill and found to be insane, what should the state do with them? These questions lead us into the area of criminal commitment. Furthermore, finding a person insane is a legal ruling that forces mental health practitioners to go beyond clinical concepts defined in DSM-IV.

The example of the homeless woman raises issues of civil commitment. When should a person who has committed no crime, but appears severely disturbed, be institutionalized? Certainly, defecating and urinating in public are disgusting to most people and are truly unusual behaviors, but are they enough to deprive someone of her civil liberties? What are the procedures for civil commitment? What happens to people once they are committed?

In the first two examples, the focus of legal and ethical issues tends to be on the individual or defendant. Mental health issues become legal ones (1) when decisions must be made about involuntary commitment to mental hospitals, (2) when competence to stand trial is in doubt, (3) when an accused person bases his or her criminal defense on insanity or diminished mental capacity, and (4) when the rights of mental patients are legally tested.

In the *Tarasoff* case, the focus of legal and ethical concern shifts to the therapist. When is the therapist legally and ethically obligated to breach patient-therapist confidentiality? In this case, had the therapist done enough to prevent a potentially dangerous situation from occurring? According to all previous codes of conduct issued by professional organizations such as the American Psychological Association and according to accepted practice in the field, many would answer yes. Yet in 1976 the California Supreme Court ruled that the therapist should have warned not only the police but also the likely victim!

The ruling has major implications for therapists in the conduct of therapy. One implication is also related to the two earlier cases. How does a therapist predict dangerousness (to self, to others, or to society)? To protect himself or herself from being sued, does the therapist report all threats of homicide or suicide? Should a psychologist warn clients that not everything they say is privileged or confidential? How will this affect the clinical relationship?

Last, but not least, we come to ethical issues related to treatment itself. The male therapist who put his arms around his client, Jennifer, apparently did so as an act of human compassion. Yet although he may have been comforting the client, the act involves some serious controversial questions with respect to the therapeutic value of "touching." The incident may appear insignificant, but it has broad implications. Some people believe that touching is professionally unethical because of its possible erotic implications, especially with opposite-sex clients. Others argue that nonerotic touch is therapeutic for many clients. How does a therapist determine if a touch is erotic or nonerotic? What about hugging or kissing? The point is that therapeutic techniques and strategies have moral and ethical implications. For example, should psychoactive drugs be given to patients against their will? Should painful techniques, such as electroshock therapy (ECT), be used to treat clients?

We address some of these questions and issues in greater depth in this chapter. First we look at the issues of criminal and civil commitment, and then discuss patient rights and deinstitutionalization. Last, we explore the legal and ethical parameters of the therapist-client relationship.

CRIMINAL COMMITMENT

Basic to the premise of criminal law is the assumption that all of us are responsible beings who exercise free will and are capable of choices (Stone, 1974). If we do something wrong, we are responsible for our actions and should suffer the consequences. **Criminal commitment** is the incarceration of an individual for having committed a crime. Abnormal psychology accepts different perspectives on free will; criminal law

does not. Yet criminal law does recognize that some people lack the ability to discern the ramifications of their actions because they are mentally disturbed. Although they may be technically guilty of a crime, their mental state at the time of the offense exempts them from legal responsibility. Let us explore the landmark cases that have influenced this concept's evolution and application.

The Insanity Defense

The concept of "innocent by reason of insanity" has provoked much controversy among legal scholars, mental health practitioners, and the general public (Shapiro, 1984). The **insanity defense** is a plea used by defendants who admit they committed a crime but believe that they should not be held responsible for the action because they were mentally disturbed at the time it was committed. The insanity plea recognizes that under specific circumstances people may not be held accountable for their behavior. One of the public's greatest fears is that such a plea might be used by a guilty individual to escape criminal responsibility. This fear is further reinforced by findings that people acquitted of crimes because of insanity spend less time in psychiatric hospitals than convicted people spend in prison (Kahn & Raufman, 1981; Pasework, Pantel & Steadman, 1982). Some point to the Kenneth Bianchi case as a prime example of this tendency. The question confronting the state prosecutors, defense attorney, and mental health experts was whether the defendant was a shrewd, calculating, cold-blooded murderer or a true multiple personality. It is important to note, however, that any number of psychiatric conditions may be used in an insanity plea.

Psychologist Martin Orne, an internationally recognized expert on hypnosis, was asked by the prosecution to examine Bianchi. Orne knew that Bianchi was either a multiple personality or a clever liar. He reasoned that if Bianchi was pretending, he would be highly motivated to convince others that he was a multiple personality. Orne thought that if he told Bianchi that multiple personalities rarely show just two distinct personalities, Bianchi might show still another personality to convince Orne that his was a true case. After hinting to Bianchi in the waking state that two personalities are rare, Orne placed Bianchi under hypnosis. Bianchi took the bait. Another per-

For five months between 1977 and 1978, Kenneth Bianchi and his cousin Angelo Buono raped, tortured, and murdered a number of young Los Angeles women. To try to escape what would inevitably be a life imprisonment sentence, Bianchi tried to convince psychiatrists that he was a multiple personality; he thought this would enhance his chances of being found not guilty by reason of insanity. Fortunately, he was unable to pull off his scheme and will now spend the rest of his life in jail.

sonality—Billy—emerged. (Other experts were unable to draw out more than two personalities.)

Orne also noticed that Bianchi's behaviors were unusual for someone under hypnosis. For example, during one session Orne wanted Bianchi to hallucinate the presence of his attorney, so he suggested to Bianchi that his attorney was sitting in the room. Bianchi immediately got up and shook hands with his (hallucinated) attorney. Orne then asked whether his attorney was shaven. Bianchi responded, "Oh,

no. Beard. God, you can see him. You must be able to see him" (*Frontline,* "The Mind of a Murderer," Part II, 1984, p. 11). These behaviors are unusual for the following reasons: first, multiple personalities almost never shake hands spontaneously because that requires a tactile hallucination. Bianchi would have to imagine not only seeing his attorney but also feeling the touch of his hand. Second, the statement, "You can see him. You must be able to see him" seemed to be excessive and to be aimed at convincing Orne that Bianchi really saw his attorney. Orne believed that Bianchi was faking. His work, coupled with other evidence, forced a change in Bianchi's plea from "not guilty by reason of insanity" to "guilty." Unfortunately, it is the rare but highly publicized cases such as the Hillside Strangler and Hinckley (attempted assassination of Ronald Reagan) cases that seem to have the greatest impact and provoke public outrage and suspicion (Quen, 1978, 1981; Robitscher, 1966; Rogers, 1987).

Legal Precedents In this country, a number of different standards are used as legal tests of insanity. One of the earliest is the *M'Naghten Rule.* In 1843, Daniel M'Naghten, a grossly disturbed woodcutter from Glasgow, Scotland, claimed that he was com-

The insanity defense has evolved over the last hundred years in recognition of the fact that some people are so mentally disturbed at the time they commit their crimes that under specific circumstances they should not be held responsible for their behavior.

manded by God to kill the English prime minister, Sir Robert Peel. He killed a lesser minister by mistake and was placed on trial, where it became obvious that M'Naghten was quite delusional. Out of this incident emerged the M'Naghten Rule, which has popularly been referred to as the "right-wrong" test. The ruling held that people could be acquitted of a crime if it could be shown that, at the time of the act, they (1) had such defective reasoning that they didn't know what they were doing or (2) were unable to comprehend that the act was wrong. The first part of the standard refers to a person being unaware of the *nature* (for example, strangling a person, but believing that he or she was squeezing a lemon) or *quality* (a disturbed person's belief that it would be amusing to cut off someone's head to watch him or her search for it in the morning) of the act due to mental impairment (Shapiro, 1984). The M'Naghten Rule has come under tremendous criticism from some who regard it as being exclusively a cognitive test (knowledge of right or wrong), which does not consider volition, emotion, and other mental activity (Rogers, 1987; Shapiro, 1984). Furthermore, it is not often easy to evaluate the defendant's awareness or comprehension.

The second major precedent that strengthened the insanity defense was the **irresistible impulse test.** In essence, the doctrine says that a defendant is not criminally responsible if he or she lacked the will power to control his or her behavior. Combined with the M'Naghten Rule, this rule broadened the criteria for using the insanity defense. In other words, a verdict of not guilty by reason of insanity could be obtained if it was shown that the defendant was unaware of or did not comprehend the act (M'Naghten Rule) or was irresistibly impelled to commit the act. Criticisms of the irresistible impulse defense revolve around what constitutes an irresistible impulse. Shapiro (1984) asked the question, "What is the difference between an *irresistible* impulse (*unable* to exert control) and an *unresisted* impulse (*choosing* not to exert control)?" For example, is a person with a history of antisocial behavior unable to resist his or her impulses, or is he or she choosing not to exert control? Neither the mental health profession nor the legal profession has answered this question satisfactorily.

In the case of *Durham v. United States* (1954), the U.S. Court of Appeals broadened the M'Naghten

Rule with the so-called products test. An accused person was not considered criminally responsible if his or her unlawful act was the *product* of mental disease or defect. It was Judge David Bazelon's intent to (1) give the greatest possible weight to expert evaluation and testimony and (2) allow mental health professionals to define mental illness. The *Durham* standard, unfortunately, also has its drawbacks. The term "product" is vague and difficult to define because almost anything can cause anything (as you've learned by studying the many theoretical viewpoints in this text). Leaving the task of defining mental illness to mental health professionals often results in having to define mental illness in every case. In many situations, relying on psychiatric testimony only serves to confuse the issues because both the prosecution and defense present psychiatric experts, who often present conflicting testimony (Otto, 1989). Interestingly, Judge Bazelon eventually recognized these problems and withdrew support for it.

In 1962, the American Law Institute (ALI), in its Model Penal Code, produced guidelines to help jurors determine the validity of the insanity defense on a case-by-case basis. The guidelines combined features from the previous standards.

1. A person is not responsible for criminal conduct if at the time of such conduct as a result of mental disease or defect he lacks substantial capacity either to appreciate the criminality of his conduct or to conform his conduct to the requirements of the law.
2. As used in the Article, the terms "mental disease or defect" do not include an abnormality manifested by repeated criminal or otherwise antisocial conduct. (Sec. 401, p. 66)

It is interesting to note that the second part of this guideline was intended to eliminate the insanity defense for people diagnosed as antisocial personalities.

With the attempt to be more specific and precise, the ALI guidelines moved the burden of determining criminal responsibility back to the jurors. As we have seen, previous standards, particularly the *Durham* standard, gave great weight to expert testimony, and many feared that it would usurp the jury's responsibilities (Simon, 1967; Walker, 1968; Weiner, 1985). By using phrases such as "substantial capacity," "appreciate the criminality of his conduct," and "conform his conduct to the requirements of the law," the ALI standard was intended to allow the jurors the greatest possible flexibility in ascribing criminal responsibility.

In some jurisdictions, the concept of *diminished capacity* has also been incorporated into the ALI standard. As a result of a mental disease or defect, a person may lack the *specific intent* to commit the offense. For example, a person under the influence of drugs or alcohol may commit a crime without premeditation or intent; a person who is grief-stricken over the death of a loved one may harm the one responsible for the death. Although diminished capacity has been used primarily to guide the sentencing and disposition of the defendant, Shapiro (1984) noted that it is being used more frequently in the trial phase as well.

Such was the trial of Dan White, a San Francisco supervisor who killed Mayor George Moscone and Supervisor Harvey Milk on November 27, 1978. White blamed both individuals for his political demise. During the trial, his attorney used the now famous "Twinkies defense" (White gorged himself on junk food such as Twinkies, chips, and soda) as partial explanation for his client's actions. White's attorney attempted to convince the jury that the high sugar content of the junk food affected his cognitive and emotional state and was partially to blame for his actions. Because of the unusual defense (the junk food diminished his judgment), White was convicted only of voluntary manslaughter and sentenced to less than eight years in jail. Of course, the citizens of San Francisco were outraged by the verdict and never forgave Dan White. Facing constant public condemnation, he eventually committed suicide after his release.

Guilty, but Mentally Ill Perhaps no other trial has more greatly challenged the use of the insanity plea than the case of the *United States v. Hinckley* (1982). John W. Hinckley, Jr.'s attempt to assassinate President Ronald Reagan, and Hinckley's subsequent acquittal by reason of insanity outraged the public as well as legal and mental health professionals (Dix, 1984; Simon & Aaronson, 1988; Weiner, 1985). The increasingly successful use of the insanity defense had been a growing concern in both legal circles and the public arena. Many had begun to believe that the criteria for the defense were being too broadly interpreted, even though it had been shown that the insan-

ity defense was used in less than 2 percent of cases and that its use was rarely successful (Fersch, 1980; Morris, 1968; Morse, 1982; Steadman, 1979). For some time, the *Hinckley* case aroused such strong emotional reactions that calls for reform were rampant. The American Psychiatric Association (1983), the American Medical Association (Kerlitz & Fulton, 1984), and the American Bar Association (1984) all advocated a more stringent interpretation of insanity. As a result, Congress passed the Insanity Reform Act of 1984, which based the definition of insanity totally on the individual's ability to understand what he or she did. The American Psychological Association's position on the insanity defense ran counter to these immediate changes (Rogers, 1987). Its position is that even though a given verdict might be wrong, the standard is not necessarily wrong.

Nevertheless, in the wake of the *Hinckley* verdict, some states have begun to adopt alternative pleas such as "culpable and mentally disabled," "mentally disabled, but neither culpable nor innocent," and "guilty, but mentally ill." These pleas are attempts to (1) separate mental illness from insanity and (2) hold people responsible for their acts.

One noted psychiatrist, Thomas S. Szasz, not only argued against the insanity defense, but against involuntary commitment as well (Szasz, 1963, 1986). Szasz made the case that mental illness is a myth, that the label has been used throughout history to deprive people of their civil liberties, and that the behaviors of people are ultimately their own responsibility. To label a criminal act as "mental illness" is to take responsibility away from them (a violation of their civil liberties) and to act on behalf of the state. Such actions are a threat to individual liberty and responsibility. Szasz also argued that labeling a person insane potentially masks the social ills of a society that may have led to the so-called insane act. Very concerned with the use of psychiatry in political oppression, Szasz believes that psychiatric labels allow "the state" to discredit dissenting opinions or behaviors.

Competency to Stand Trial

The term **competency to stand trial** refers to the defendant's mental state at the time he or she is being examined by a practitioner. It has nothing to do with the issue of criminal responsibility, which refers to an individual's behavior at the time of the offense (insanity defense). Three criteria are usually used to judge whether a person is competent to stand trial. First, does the defendant have a factual understanding of the proceedings? Second, does a client have a rational understanding of the proceedings? Third, can the defendant rationally consult with counsel in presenting his or her own defense (Shapiro, 1984)?

The final criteria for competency involves the ability to consult with counsel. If the defendant is suffering from a paranoid delusion and believes that his or her attorney is conspiring with the prosecution, a serious impairment exists.

It is clear that many more people are committed to prison hospitals because of incompetency determinations than are acquitted on insanity pleas (Steadman, 1979). Competency to stand trial is important to ensure that a person understands the nature of the proceedings and is able to help in his or her own defense. After all, it would be unfair to try a person incapable of self-defense. Although determination of competency is meant to protect mentally disturbed people and to guarantee preservation of criminal and civil rights, being judged incompetent to stand trial may have unfair negative consequences as well. A person may be committed for a long period of time, denied the chance to post bail, and isolated from friends and family, all without having been found guilty of a crime.

Such a miscarriage of justice was the focus of a U.S. Supreme Court ruling in 1972 (*Jackson v. Indiana*). In the *Jackson* case, a severely retarded, brain-damaged deaf-mute was charged with robbery, but was determined incompetent to stand trial. He was committed indefinitely, which in his case probably meant for life, because it was apparent by the severity of his disorders that he would never be competent. His lawyers filed a petition to have him released on the basis of deprivation of **due process** (legal checks and balances guaranteed to everyone: right to a fair trial, right to face accusers, right to present our evidence, right to counsel, and so on). The U.S. Supreme Court ruled that a defendant cannot be confined indefinitely solely on the grounds of incompetency. After a reasonable time, a determination must be made as to whether the person is likely or unlikely to regain competency in the foreseeable future. If, in the hospital's opinion, the person is unlikely to do

so, the hospital must either release the individual or initiate civil commitment procedures.

CIVIL COMMITMENT

When people are severely disturbed and exhibit bizarre behaviors that can pose a threat to themselves or others, **civil commitment** may be necessary, even though the person has not committed a crime. The commitment of a person in acute distress may be viewed as a form of protective confinement (Bednar et al., 1991; Ponterotto, 1987) and a concern for the psychological and physical well-being of that person or others (Everstine & Everstine, 1983). Hospitalization is considered in the case of potential suicide or assault, bizarre behavior, destruction of property, and severe anxiety leading to loss of impulse control (Hipple & Hipple, 1983). Involuntary hospitalization, however, should be avoided, if at all possible, because it has many potentially negative consequences. Ponterotto (1987) summarized these consequences as the lifelong social stigma associated with psychiatric hospitalization, major interruption in the person's life, losing control of his or her life and being dependent on others, and loss of self-esteem and self-concept. To this we would add a possible loss or restriction of civil liberties—a point that becomes even more glaring when we consider that the person has actually committed no crime at all!

Criteria for Commitment

States vary in the criteria used to commit a person, but there do appear to be certain general standards. It is not enough that a person be mentally ill: additional conditions need to exist before hospitalization is considered (Everstine & Everstine, 1983; Hipple & Hipple, 1983; Schwitzgebel & Schwitzgebel, 1980; Turkheimer & Parry, 1992; Warren, 1982).

1. *The person presents a clear and imminent danger to self or others.* An example is someone who is displaying suicidal or bizarre behavior that places him or her in immediate danger (walking out on a busy freeway). Threats to harm someone or behavior viewed to be assaultive or destructive are also grounds for commitment.

2. *The person is unable to care for himself or herself or does not have the social network to*

Should this homeless man be considered mentally disturbed and committed to an institution? Is he a danger to himself or to others? Residents in the neighborhood where Larry Hogue lives claim that he has been frightening people for years. He has been arrested numerous times for threatening people and damaging property but he has never been permanently confined.

provide for such care. These criteria vary. This generally involves insufficient (a) food (being malnourished, food is unavailable, and the individual has no feasible plan to obtain it); (b) clothing (not appropriate for climate, dirty or torn, has no plans for obtaining it); and (c) shelter (no permanent residence, insufficient protection from climatic conditions, and no logical plans for obtaining adequate housing). Most civil commitments are based primarily on this criterion (Turkheimer & Parry, 1992).

3. *The person is unable to make responsible decisions about appropriate treatment and hospitalization.* As a result, there is a strong chance for deterioration.

4. *The person is in an unmanageable state of fright or panic.* Such people may believe and feel that they are on the brink of losing control.

Certainly the example of the homeless lady in the beginning of the chapter would seem to fulfill the second and possibly third criteria. In the past, commitments could be obtained solely on the basis of

mental illness and a person's need for treatment, which was often determined arbitrarily. Increasingly, the courts have tightened up civil commitment procedures and have begun to rely more on a determination of **dangerousness** to self or others. How do we define dangerousness? Many people would not consider the homeless woman a danger to herself or others. Some, however, might believe that she could be assaultive to others and injurious to herself. Disagreements among the public may be understandable, but are trained mental health professionals more accurate in their predictions? Let's turn to that question.

Assessing Dangerousness   Most studies have indicated that mental health professionals have difficulty predicting whether their clients will commit dangerous acts (Monahan, 1976; Stone, 1975) and that they often overpredict violence (Megargee, 1970; Monahan, 1981). The fact that civil commitments are often based on a determination of dangerousness makes this conclusion even more disturbing. The difficulty in predicting dangerousness seems linked to four factors.

1. It is quite apparent that the rarer something is, the more difficult it is to predict. As a group, psychiatric patients are not dangerous! A frequent misconception shared not only by the public, but the courts as well, is that mental illnesses are in and of themselves dangerous. Studies have indicated that few psychotic patients are assaultive: estimates range from 10 percent of hospitalized patients to about 3 percent in outpatient clinics (Tardiff, 1984; Tardiff & Koenigsburg, 1985; Tardiff & Sweillam, 1982). Homicide is even rarer, and psychiatric patients are no more likely to commit a homicide than the population at large (Monaham, 1981).

2. It appears that violence is as much a function of the context in which it occurs as it is of the person's characteristics. Although it is theoretically possible for a psychologist to accurately assess an individual's personality, one has little idea about the situations in which people will find themselves. Shapiro (1984) advocated that the mental health professional needs to help the court define the term "dangerous" so that testimony can be restricted to a description of the patient's personality and kinds of situations in which personality may deteriorate, lead to assaultive behavior, or both (see Focus 20.1).

3. Probably the best predictor of dangerousness is past criminal conduct or a history of violence or aggression. Such a record, however, is frequently ruled irrelevant or inadmissible by mental health commissions and the courts.

4. The definition of dangerousness is itself unclear. Most of us would agree that murder, rape, torture, and physical assaults are dangerous. Are we confining our definition to physical harm only? What about psychological abuse or even harm to property?

Procedures in Civil Commitment

Despite the difficulties in defining dangerousness, once someone believes that a person is a threat to himself or herself or to others, civil commitment procedures may be instituted. The rationale for this action is that it (1) prevents harm to the person or to others, (2) provides appropriate treatment and care, and (3) ensures due process of law (that is, legal hearing). In most cases, people deemed in need of pro-

tective confinement can be convinced to *voluntarily* commit themselves to a period of hospitalization. This process is fairly straightforward, and many believe that it is the preferred one (Ponterotto, 1987). *Involuntary* commitment occurs when the client does not consent to hospitalization.

Involuntary commitment can be a temporary emergency action or a longer period of detention that is determined at a formal hearing. All states recognize that cases arise in which a person is so grossly disturbed that immediate detention is required. Because formal hearings may take a long time, delaying commitment might prove adverse to the person or to others.

Formal and civil commitment usually follows a similar process. First, a concerned person such as a family member, therapist, or family physician petitions the court for an examination of the person. If the judge believes that there is responsible cause for this action, he or she will order an examination. Second, the judge appoints two professionals with no connection to each other to examine the person. In most cases, the examiners are physicians or mental health professionals. Third, a formal hearing is held in which the examiners testify to the person's mental state and potential danger. Others, such as family members, friends, or therapists, may also testify. The person is also allowed to speak on his or her behalf and is represented by counsel. Last, if it is determined that the person must enter treatment, a finite period (periods of six months to one year are common) may be specified. Some states have indefinite periods subject to periodic review and assessment.

Protection Against Involuntary Commitment   We have said that involuntary commitment can lead to a violation of civil rights. Some have even argued that criminals have more rights than the mentally ill. For example, a person accused of a crime is considered innocent until proven guilty in a court of law. Usually, he or she is incarcerated only after a jury trial, and only if a crime is committed (not if there is only the possibility or even high probability of crime). Yet, a mentally ill person may be confined without a jury trial and without having committed a crime if it is thought possible that he or she might do harm to self or others. In other words, the criminal justice system will not incarcerate a person because he or she *might* harm someone (they must already have done it), but

Predicting Dangerousness: The Case of Serial Killers and Mass Murderers

Jeffrey L. Dahmer admits to killing his first victim in 1978 near his boyhood home. After killing his second victim, Dahmer states that he began to lose control of his necrophilia, a desire to have sex with the dead. Over a period of years until 1991 when he was arrested, he killed fifteen other men or young boys. Not only did he murder them, but he often killed them in hideous and torturous fashion. Once dead he would have sex with them, dismember their bodies, and feed upon them in cannabalistic fashion. As of this writing, Dahmer has pleaded "not guilty by reason of mental disease or defect."

In the worst mass shooting in U.S. history, 35-year-old George

Hennard smashed his pickup truck through a restaurant window, leaped out of the truck, and opened fire on a lunch-time crowd with a high-powered pistol. On that sunny afternoon in October 1991, Hennard killed twenty-two innocent patrons and workers in Killeen, Texas. Shortly after the slaughter, he put a bullet through his head and killed himself.

These examples of serial killers and mass murderers often make us wonder why such people were never identified as being potentially dangerous. Jeffrey Dahmer, for example, tortured animals as a small boy and was arrested in 1988 for molesting a child. Even though his father suspected Dahmer to be dangerous,

he was released. And there appears to be sufficient evidence to suggest that mass murderer Hennard was a feared man who acted in paranoid fashion. In both cases, aberrant thoughts and behaviors appeared to go unrecognized or ignored.

Lest we be too harsh on psychologists and law enforcement officials, it is important to realize that few serial killers or mass murderers will willingly share their deviant sexual or asocial fantasies. Furthermore, many of the problems in predicting dangerousness lie in (1) limited knowledge concerning the characteristics associated with violence, (2) lack of a one-to-one correspondence between danger signs and possible violence, (3) increasing knowledge that violent behavior is most often the result of many variables, and

---

civil commitment *is* based on possible future harm! It can be argued that in the former case, confinement is punishment, while in the latter case it is treatment (for the individual's benefit). Stone (1975), for example, argued that mentally ill people may be incapable of determining their own treatment, and that once treated, will be grateful for the treatment they received! If people resist hospitalization, they are thus being irrational, which is a symptom of their mental disorder.

Critics do not accept this reasoning. They point out that civil commitment is for the benefit of those initiating commitment procedures (society), and not for the individual. Even after treatment, people rarely appreciate it (Ennis & Emery, 1978). These concerns have raised and heightened sensitivity toward patient welfare and rights, resulting in a trend toward restricting the powers of the state over the individual.

Rights of Mental Patients Many people in the United States are concerned about the balance of power among the state, our mental institutions, and our citizens. The U.S. Constitution guarantees certain "inalienable rights" such as trial by jury, legal representation, and protection against self-incrimination. As indicated in Chapter 1, the mental health profession has great power, which may be used wittingly or unwittingly to abridge individual freedom. In recent decisions, some courts have ruled that commitment for any purpose constitutes a major deprivation of liberty that requires due process protection.

Until 1979, the level of proof required for civil commitments varied from state to state. In a case that set legal precedent, a Texas man claimed that he was denied due process because the jury that committed him was instructed to use a lower standard than "beyond a reasonable doubt" (more than 90 percent

(4) recognition that incarceration—both criminal and civil—cannot occur on the basis of "potential danger" alone. Nevertheless, our limited experiences with mass murderers and serial killers have produced patterns and profiles of interest to mental health practitioners and law enforcement officials. It is important to note, however, that the profiles of mass murders and serial killers contain some major differences and similarities. Some of these are discussed as follows:

Profile of Serial Killers   Serial killers are usually white males and often suffer from some recognized psychiatric disorder such as sexual sadism, antisocial personality, extreme narcissism, and borderline personality disorder. Few are psychotic, and psychoses does not appear to be the cause of their compulsion to kill. Almost all, however, entertain violent sexual fantasies and have experienced traumatic sex at a young age. Their past lives are troubled with family histories of abuse, alcoholism, and criminal activity. Dahmer, for example, was sexually molested as a youngster. Most serial killers seem to exhibit little remorse for their victims, have little incentive to change, and seem to lack a value system. The compulsion to kill is often associated with what has been described as "morbid prognostic signs" (Schlesinger, 1989): breaking and entering for nonmonetary purposes; unprovoked assaults and mistreatment of women; a fetish for female undergarments and destruction of them; showing hatred, contempt, or fear of women; violence against animals, especially cats; sexual identity confusion, including underlying homosexual feelings; a "violent and primitive fantasy life"; and sexual inhibitions and preoccupation with rigid standards of morality (Youngstrom, 1991, p. 32).

Profile of Mass Murderers   Mass murderers are usually men who are social isolates and seem to exhibit inadequate social and interpersonal skills. They have been found to be quite angry and to be filled with rage. The anger appears to be cumulative and is triggered by some type of event, usually a loss. For example, it may be the loss of a job or a relationship that is seen as being catastrophic to the person. Most have strong mistrust of people and entertain paranoid fantasies such as a wide-ranging conspiracy against them. They tend to be rootless and have few support systems such as family, friends, or church or fraternal groups. Many researchers believe that the number of mass murders will increase as firearms proliferate in our society. Other social correlates affecting mass murders are an increasing sense of rootlessness in the country, general disenchantment, and loneliness. The more random the killings the more disturbed, delusional, and paranoid the person is likely to be.

---

sure). The appellate court agreed with the man, but when the case finally reached the Supreme Court in April 1979 (*Addington v. Texas*), the court ruled that the state must only provide "clear and convincing evidence" (approximately 75 percent sure) that a person is mentally ill and potentially dangerous before that person can be committed. Although it is important to note that confinement requires a higher standard than advocated by most mental health organizations, this ruling represented the first time that the Supreme Court considered any aspect of the civil commitment process (Shapiro, 1984).

Due to decisions in several other cases (*Lessard v. Schmidt*, 1972, Wisconsin Federal Court; and *Dixon v. Weinberger*, 1975), states must provide the **least restrictive environment** for people. This means that people have a right to the least restrictive alternative to freedom that is appropriate to their condition. Only patients who cannot adequately care for themselves are confined to hospitals. Those who can function acceptably should be given alternative choices, such as boarding homes and other shelter.

Right to Treatment   One of the primary justifications for commitment is that treatment will improve a person's mental condition and increase the likelihood that he or she will be able to return to the community. If we confine a person involuntarily and do not provide the means for release (therapy), isn't this deprivation of due process? Several cases have raised this problem as a constitutional issue. In 1966, in a suit brought against St. Elizabeth's Hospital in Washington, D.C. (*Rouse v. Cameron*), the court held that (1) **right to treatment** is a constitutional right and (2) failure to provide treatment cannot be justified by lack of resources. In other words, a men-

The Constitution guarantees legal representation and due process to everyone, including mental patients who have often been deprived of their rights. In recent years court decisions have more clearly defined the criteria under which individuals can be committed and how they must be treated once confined to a mental facility.

tal institution or the state could not use lack of funding facilities or labor power as reasons for not providing treatment. Although this decision represented a major advance in patient rights, the ruling provided no guidelines for what constitutes treatment.

This issue was finally addressed in 1972 by U.S. District Court Judge Frank Johnson in the Alabama Federal Court. The case (*Wyatt v. Stickney*) involved a mentally retarded boy who not only did not receive treatment, but had to live in an institution that was unable to meet even minimum standards of care. Indeed, the living conditions in two of the hospital buildings resembled those found in early asylums of the eighteenth century. Less than 50 cents a day was spent on food for each patient; the toilet facilities were totally inadequate and filthy; patients were crowded in group rooms with minimal or no privacy; and personnel (one physician per 2000 patients) and patient care were practically nonexistent.

Judge Johnson not only ruled in favor of the right to treatment, but also specified standards of adequate treatment such as staff-patient ratios, therapeutic environment conditions, and professional consensus about appropriate treatment. The court also made it clear that mental patients could not be forced to

work (scrub floors, cook, serve food, wash laundry, and so on) or engage in work-related activities aimed at maintaining the institution in which they lived. This practice, widely used in institutions, was declared unconstitutional. Moreover, patients who volunteered to perform tasks had to be paid at least the minimum wage to do them instead of merely be given token allowances or special privileges. This landmark decision ensures treatment beyond custodial care and protection against neglect and abuse (right to human environment and right to treatment).

Another important case (tried in the U.S. District Court in Florida), *O'Connor v. Donaldson* (1975), has also had a major impact on the right-to-treatment issue. It involved Kenneth Donaldson, who at age forty-nine was committed for twenty years to the Chattahoochee State Hospital on petition by his father. He was found to be mentally ill and dangerous. Throughout his confinement, Donaldson petitioned for release, but Dr. O'Connor, the hospital superintendent, determined that the patient was too dangerous. Finally, Donaldson threatened a lawsuit and was reluctantly discharged by the hospital after fourteen years of confinement. He then sued both O'Connor and the hospital, winning an award of $20,000. The monetary award is insignificant compared to the significance of the ruling. Again, the court reaffirmed the client's right to treatment (the court ruled that Donaldson did not receive appropriate treatment), said that the state cannot constitutionally confine a nondangerous person who is capable of caring for himself or herself outside of an institution or who has willing friends or family to help, and that physicians as well as institutions are liable for improper confinements.

One major dilemma facing the courts in all cases of court-ordered treatment is what constitutes treatment. As discussed in earlier chapters, treatment can range from rest and relaxation to psychosurgery, medication, and aversion therapy. Mental health professionals believe that they are in the best position to evaluate the type and efficacy of treatment, a position supported by the case of *Youngberg v. Romeo* (1982). The court ruled that a mentally retarded boy, Nicholas Romeo, had a constitutional right to "reasonable care and safety," and it deferred judgment to the mental health professional as to what constitutes therapy. Whether this marks a subtle shift away from patient rights is still to be seen.

Right to Refuse Treatment   Patients frequently refuse medical treatment on religious grounds or because the treatment would only prolong a terminal illness. In many cases, physicians are inclined to honor such refusals, especially if they seem based on reasonable grounds. But should mental patients have a right to refuse treatment? At first glance, it may appear that the question doesn't make sense. After all, patients are committed for treatment, aren't they? Why commit them for treatment and allow them to refuse it? Furthermore, isn't it possible that mental patients may be incapable of deciding what is best for themselves? For example, a man with a paranoid delusion may refuse treatment because he believes that the hospital staff is plotting against him. If he is allowed to refuse medication or other forms of therapy, his condition may deteriorate more. The result is that the client becomes even more dangerous or incapable of caring for himself outside of hospital confinement (Stone, 1975).

Proponents of the right to refuse treatment argue, however, that many forms of treatment, such as medication or ECT may have long-term side effects (discussed in earlier chapters). They also point out that involuntary treatment is generally much less effective than treatment accepted voluntarily (Shaprio, 1984). People forced into treatment seem to resist it, thereby nullifying the beneficial effects.

The case of *Rennie v. Klein* (1978) involved several state hospitals in New Jersey that were forcibly medicating patients in nonemergency situations. The court ruled that people had a constitutional right to refuse treatment (psychotropic medication) and to be given due process. In another related case, *Rogers v. Okin* (1979), a Massachusetts court supported these guidelines. Both cases made the point that psychotropic medication was often used only to control behavior or as a substitute for treatment. Furthermore, the decisions noted that drugs might actually inhibit recovery.

In these cases, the courts supported the right to refuse treatment under certain conditions and have extended the least restrictive alternative principle to include *least intrusive forms of treatment*. Generally, psychotherapy is considered less intrusive than somatic or physical therapies (ECT and medication). Although this compromise may appear reasonable, other problems present themselves. First, how do we define an intrusive treatment? Are insight therapies equally intrusive as behavioral techniques (punishment and aversion procedures)? Second, if patients are allowed to refuse certain forms of treatment and if the hospital does not have alternatives for them, can clients sue the institution? These questions are still unanswered.

DEINSTITUTIONALIZATION

Deinstitutionalization is the shifting of responsibility for the care of mental patients from large central institutions to agencies within local communities. When originally formulated in the 1960s and 1970s, the concept excited many mental health professionals. Since its inception, many state-run hospitals have experienced a greater than 50 percent reduction in the hospital population and a 75 percent decrease in the average daily number of committed patients (Mechanic, 1987; Turkheimer & Parry, 1992). The impetus behind deinstitutionalization came from several quarters.

Deinstitutionalization was originally conceived of as a way to provide better and more effective community-based care to hospitalized patients who were seen to be languishing in state institutions. Unfortunately, due to lack of funds and community support, many patients were released to the streets and were left there to wander, uncared for and homeless.

First, there has been (and still is) a feeling that large hospitals provide mainly custodial care, produce little benefit for the patient, and may even impede improvement. Court cases discussed earlier (*Wyatt v. Stickney* and *O'Connor v. Donaldson*) exposed the fact that many mental hospitals are no better than "warehouses for the insane." Institutionalization was accused of fostering dependency, promoting helplessness, and lowering self-sufficiency in patients. The longer patients were hospitalized, the more likely they were to remain hospitalized, even if they had improved (Wing, 1980). Furthermore, symptoms such as flat affect and nonresponsiveness, which were generally thought to be clinical signs of schizophrenia, may actually result from hospitalization.

Second, the issue of patient rights has received increasing attention. As already discussed, recent legal decisions have mandated that patients live in the least restrictive environments. Mental health professionals became very concerned about keeping patients confined against their will and began to discharge patients whenever they approached minimal competencies. It was believed that **mainstreaming** (integrating) patients back into the community could be accomplished by providing local outpatient or transitory services (such as board-and-care facilities, halfway houses, churches). In addition, advances in tranquilizers and other drug treatment techniques made it possible to medicate patients, which made them manageable once discharged.

Third, insufficient funds for state hospitals have almost forced these institutions to release patients back into communities. Overcrowded conditions made mental health administrators view the movement favorably; state legislative branches encouraged the trend, especially because it reduced state costs and funding.

What has been the impact of deinstitutionalization on patients? Critics of deinstitutionalization believe that it is a policy that allows states to relinquish their responsibility to care for patients unable to care for themselves. There are alarming indications that deinstitutionalization has been responsible for placing or "dumping" up to one million former patients on the street who should have remained institutionalized (Cordes, 1984). The majority appear severely disabled, have difficulty coping with daily living, suffer from schizophrenia, and are alcoholic (Goleman, 1986a, 1986b; Jones, 1983; Lamb, 1984; see Focus 20.2). Recently, two federal reports (*Outcasts on Mainstreet* and *Caring for People: Conclusions for Research*) have examined the issue of the homeless mentally ill and painted a distressing picture of the fragmented nature of existing programs to assist millions of mentally ill citizens (Observer, 1992).

Some criminalization of the mentally ill also seems to be a byproduct of deinstitutionalization. Lamb and Grant (1982, 1983) studied male and female county jail inmates who were referred for psychiatric evaluation. They found that more than 85 percent had a history of psychiatric hospitalizations and more than 50 percent met the current criteria for involuntary hospitalization (either dangerous to oneself or others or gravely disabled). More than one-third were living on the streets or in missions, and fewer than 12 percent were employed. On the basis of their findings, Lamb and Grant have supported the position that these people should be hospitalized and not imprisoned. In contrast, however, another study produced only modest evidence of such criminalization (Teplin, 1983).

Nonetheless, it is becoming apparent that many mentally ill people are not receiving treatment. Approximately 750,000 mentally ill now live in nursing homes, board-and-care homes, or group residences (Appelbaum, 1987). The quality of care in these places is marginal, forcing continuing and periodic rehospitalization of the mentally ill (Turkheimer & Parry, 1992). The mentally ill constitute a substantial portion of the homeless population (Fischer & Breakey, 1991; Levine & Rog, 1990).

Much of the problem with deinstitutionalization appears to be the community's lack of preparation and resources to care for the chronically mentally ill. Many patients lack family or friends who can help them make the transition back into the community; many state hospitals do not provide patients with adequate skills training; many discharged patients have difficulty finding jobs; many find substandard housing worse than the institutions from which they came; many are not adequately monitored and receive no psychiatric treatment; and many become homeless (Westermeyer, 1987). It is difficult to estimate how many discharged mental patients comprise the burgeoning ranks of the homeless. We do know

Deinstitutionalization: Treatment or Dumping?

Mary Jean Willis, founder and president of Families and Friends of the Adult Mentally Ill and the mother of a schizophrenic son, wrote the following comment on current policies regarding the mentally ill:

> Now we have deinstitutionalization—release of the mentally ill from hospitals as soon as they are stabilized (and sometimes even sooner).

> We think that our son was prematurely discharged from hospitals at least twice. At one time he was sent home on a weekend pass from a state hospital. When the family, including our oldest son, daughter-in-law, and their infant daughter, was gathered around to celebrate his homecoming, he suddenly disappeared into his room, where he proceeded to smash a glass and slash at his throat. Another time, when he was hospitalized in San Francisco after throwing himself in front of a car, he refused medication and

demanded to be released. The hospital would not keep him against his will, so he was discharged after a few days, whereupon he jumped in front of a truck and was severely injured.

> Deinstitutionalization has meant not only early discharge, but also inaccessibility of hospitals. Because our son is suicidal, we have not had any great difficulty getting him into a hospital. However, I know of a mother who has not been able to gain hospital admission for her son, even though he is violent and a danger to society when he is in his manic phase. . . .

> Another common problem for family members is the feeling of being tied down and not able to live one's own life. Families of a chronic mentally ill person find it difficult to travel or to maintain much of a social life.

> Our own social life has become practically nonexistent, not necessarily because our friends

have deserted us due to the stigma of mental illness, but because of the unpredictability of our son's illness, and because, after coping with the many problems it causes, we have little energy left over for entertaining.

> The financial burden of mental illness is another big problem which families must face. When insurance (if there is any) runs out as it eventually does in most cases, not even well-to-do families can handle the frequent hospitalizations at exorbitant rates. . . .

> When all of the above problems are considered, it can be seen that deinstitutionalization has in some ways made life for the families of the chronic mentally ill more difficult than it was for my mother-in-law back in the days when lifelong hospitalization was the fate of most of the mentally ill. (Willis, 1982, pp. 617–619)

that homelessness in the United States, especially in large, urban areas, is increasing at an alarming pace (Kondratas, 1991; Toro et al., 1991). Certainly, it is not difficult to see the number of people who live in transport terminals, parks, flophouses, homeless shelters, cars, and storefronts. It is hard to determine how many of the homeless, like the woman discussed at the beginning of this chapter, have been deinstitutionalized before adequate support services were present in a community. We do know, however, that the homeless have significantly poorer psychological adjustment and higher arrests and conviction records

(Regier et al., 1984). The solution is complex but probably does not call for the return to the old institutions of the 1950s, but rather the provision of more and better community-based treatment facilities and alternatives (Kiesler, 1991).

For patients involved in alternative community programs, the picture appears somewhat more positive. After reviewing reports of experimental studies on alternative treatment, a group of researchers concluded that such patients fared at least as well as those in institutions. Where differences were found, they favored the alternative programs (Braun et al.,

1981). Such studies are few, however, and much remains to be done if deinstitutionalized patients are to be provided with the best supportive treatment.

THE THERAPIST-CLIENT RELATIONSHIP

Confidentiality and Privileged Communication

Basic to the therapist-patient relationship is the premise that therapy involves a deeply personal association in which clients have a right to expect that whatever they say will be kept private. Therapists believe that genuine therapy cannot occur unless clients trust their therapists and believe they will not divulge confidential communications. Without this guarantee, clients may not be completely open with their thoughts and may thereby lose the benefits of therapy. This raises several questions. First, what professional ethics and legal statutes govern the therapist-client relationship? Under what conditions can one breach the confidentiality of the relationship? Second, what if, in a conflict between clinical issues (need for trust) and legal ones (need to disclose), the therapist chooses trust? What are the consequences? Third, if a therapist decides to disclose information to a third party, what effects can the disclosure have on the therapist-client relationship? Last, how can a therapist discuss the limits of confidentiality in a way that would be least likely to disrupt the therapeutic relationship?

Siegel (1979) has defined **confidentiality** as an ethical standard that protects clients from disclosure of information without their consent. Generally, mental health organizations publish codes of ethics endorsing confidentiality in the therapist-client relationship. The American Psychological Association (1991) ethics code specifies:

> Psychologists disclose confidential information only as required by law, or where permitted by law, for a valid purpose such as: (1) to provide needed professional services to the patient or client, (2) to obtain appropriate professional consultations, (3) to protect the patient or client or others from harm, or (4) to obtain payment for services, in which instance, disclosure is limited to the minimum that is necessary to achieve the purpose (1991).

Furthermore, the public also seems to believe in the importance of confidentiality in the therapeutic relationship. In one study, it was found that 74 percent of respondents thought everything told to a therapist should be confidential; indeed, 69 percent believed that whatever they discussed was never disclosed (Miller & Thelen, 1986).

Confidentiality is an ethical, not a legal obligation. **Privileged communication,** a narrower legal concept, protects privacy and prevents the disclosure of confidential communications without a client's permission (Corey, Corey & Callanan, 1993; Herlicky & Sheeley, 1988). It must be kept in mind that the "holder of the privilege" is not the therapist, but the client. In other words, if a client waives this privilege, the therapist has no grounds for withholding information. Shapiro (1984) pointed out that our society recognizes how important certain confidential relationships are, and protects them by law. These relationships are the husband-wife, attorney-client, pastor-congregant, and therapist-client relationships. Psychiatric practices are regulated in all fifty states, including the District of Columbia, and forty-two states have privileged communication statutes (Herlicky & Sheeley, 1988).

Exemptions from Privileged Communication
Although states vary considerably, all states recognize certain situations in which communications can be divulged. Corey and associates (1984, 1993) summarized these conditions:

1. In situations that deal with civil or criminal commitment or competency to stand trial, the client's right to privilege can be waived. For example, a court-appointed therapist who determines that the client needs hospitalization for a psychological disorder may disclose the results of his examination to an appropriate third party.

2. Disclosure can also be made when a client sees a therapist or in any civil action when the client introduces mental condition as a claim or defense.

3. When the client is younger than sixteen years of age and information leads the therapist to believe that the child has been a victim of crime (incest, rape, or child abuse), the therapist must provide that information.

4. When criminal action is involved, the therapist

is again obligated to disclose related information to that action. The therapist who feared his client would confess his participation in the bank bombings clearly did not want to be placed in a conflict between therapeutic concerns and legal obligations.

5. When the therapist has reason to believe that a client presents a danger to himself or herself (possible injury or suicide) or may potentially harm someone else, the therapist must act to ward off the danger.

Clearly privilege in communication is not absolute. It involves the delicate balance between the individual's right to privacy and the public's need to know certain information (Leslie, 1991). Problems arise when we try to determine what the balance should be and how important various events and facts are. Originally, Max Siegel (a former president of the American Psychological Association) argued that under no circumstances should the confidential nature of the therapeutic relationship ever be breached. Clinical concerns are paramount and should be given greatest weight (Siegel, 1979). Others have challenged the position that confidentiality is necessary for effective treatment (Denkowski & Denkowski, 1982). Clearly, the issues are complex. The rights of both clients and the general public must be protected, and the courts must decide when the rights of one group conflict with those of the other.

The Duty-to-Warn Principle

At the beginning of the chapter, we briefly described the case of Prosenjit Poddar (*Tarasoff v. Board of Regents of the University of California*, 1976), a graduate student who killed Tatiana Tarasoff after notifying his therapist that he intended to take her life. Before the homicide, the therapist had decided that Poddar was dangerous and likely to carry out his threat, and had notified the director of the Cowell Psychiatric Clinic that the client was dangerous. He also informed the campus police, hoping that they would detain the student. Surely the therapist had done all that could be reasonably expected. Not so, ruled the California Supreme Court. When a therapist determines, according to the standards of the mental health profession, that a patient presents a serious danger to another, the therapist is obligated to warn the intended victim. The court went on to say that the protective privilege ends where public peril begins.

In another case, *Hedlund v. Superior Court of Orange County* (1983), the duty-to-warn ruling

Tatiana Tarasoff, a college student at a local community college, was brutally stabbed to death in 1969 by Prosenjit Poddar, a graduate student at the University of California at Berkeley. Although Poddar's therapist notified the university that he thought Poddar was dangerous, the California Supreme Court ruled that the therapist should have warned the victim as well. The duty-to-warn principle is controversial in that it puts the burden on therapists to balance the rights of their clients to privileged communications and the right of society to be protected from violent behavior.

Does the Duty-to-Warn Principle Apply to AIDS?

George, a 24-year-old graduate student, had known for some time that he was HIV-infected. He entered counseling at the university psychiatric services center because of extreme feelings of guilt associated with his dishonesty in not disclosing his infection to a woman-student he had recently become intimate with. He had hid his medical condition from family, friends, and past lovers because of the social stigma involved and the fear that others would find out that he had often engaged in bisexual relationships. On numerous occasions, George had unprotected sex with past partners, but had started to use condoms with his current woman-friend. However, she did not enjoy George's use of a condom and had encouraged him to avoid their use in lovemaking. Several times, George had complied with her request.

If you were George's therapist, what would you do? What ethical or legal obligations do you have toward George and toward the larger society? Should you maintain the confidentiality of the therapeutic relationship or inform others about George's HIV condition? If you choose to disclose this information, just who would you tell? From reading the section on the *Tarasoff* decision, are there any guidelines that can help you decide? Before reading further, take a few minutes to contemplate your answers to these questions.

Under the Family Education Rights and Privacy Act (McGowan, 1991), student records are confidential and prohibitions are strong in not releasing information. HIV- and AIDS-positive students are guaranteed confidentiality because of their rights to privacy. In addition, a public diagnosis of HIV or AIDS may stigmatize the student and subject him or her to social ostracism and discrimination. Proponents of maintaining confidentiality believe that any violation of the therapeutic trust would endanger students' likelihood of discussing their health status with a counselor. They believe that it would be more beneficial in the long run to have the counselor explore with students the

seems to have been broadened even further. A woman was killed by a shotgun blast while seated in a car next to her seven-year-old son. Advocates for the boy later sued the therapist who had treated the killer (before the shooting) for emotional trauma. The court contended that the therapist should have known the child was likely to be with his mother and should have warned him as well.

Criticism of the Duty-to-Warn Principle These rulings seem to place the therapist in the unenviable role of being a double agent (Bednar et al., 1991). Therapists have an ethical and legal obligation to their clients, but they also have legal obligations to society. Not only can these dual obligations conflict with one another, but they can be quite ambiguous. Many situations exist in which state courts must rule to clarify the implications and uncertainties of the "duty-to-warn" rule (Fulero, 1988; see Critical Thinking).

Siegel (1979) has loudly criticized the *Tarasoff* ruling, stating that it was a "day in court for the law and not for the mental health professions." He reasoned that if confidentiality had been an absolute policy, Poddar might have been kept in treatment, thus ultimately saving Tarasoff's life. Other mental health professionals have echoed this theme in one form or another. A hostile client with pent-up feelings and emotions may be less likely to act out or become violent when allowed to ventilate his thoughts. The irony, according to critics, is that the duty-to-warn principle may actually be counterproductive to its intent to protect the potential victim.

Another controversial issue surrounding the duty-to-warn principle relates not just to determining danger but to when that determination should be made. Stimulated mainly by the *Tarasoff* ruling, mental health professionals and government and private institutions have begun to develop guidelines to use in dealing with dangerous clients. These guidelines seem

motives for concealing their condition and encourage them to inform their sexual partners.

Others, however, have less faith in the counselor's ability to convince infected students about being honest with their partners (Hoffman, 1991). Studies have revealed that dishonesty about one's sexual history and infectious state is quite common (Kegeles, Catania & Coates, 1988): 12 percent of gay or bisexual men who are diagnosed as HIV positive did not plan to tell their primary sexual partners; 27 percent would not tell their nonprimary partners. For heterosexual men, 20 percent said they would lie about being seropositive, and 35 percent said they had lied to female partners about their past sexual behavior (Elias, 1988). Some counselors would argue that breaking confidentiality is a small price to pay when an unknowing partner may be receiving a "death sentence."

Thus far there have been no legal tests of the *Tarasoff* decision and its relationship to HIV infection (Cohen,

1990; Knapp & VandeCreek, 1990). The decision, however, does have important ramifications for a therapist's decision to breach confidentiality. Hoffman (1991) outlined three criteria important in that decision:

1. A (fiduciary) special relationship of trust must exist between the counselor and client. A therapeutic relationship fulfills this criteria.

2. There must be an identifiable potential victim. Remember, the duty to warn extends only to identifiable victims rather than all persons whom the client could conceivably infect. Anonymous partners or casual partners who are unknown to the counselor would not fall within the duty to protect principle. Partners who live with the person under a monogamous or exclusive relationship would most likely meet this criterion.

3. The assessment of dangerousness must be made. Three factors

need to be clarified under this criteria: (a) the certainty of an HIV infection in the client, (b) the extent to which the client engages in behaviors that carry a high risk of HIV transmission, and (c) the use or nonuse of safer sex techniques.

In light of the above criteria, how would you apply these to the case of George? Perhaps it would be helpful to divide yourselves into smaller groups to discuss these issues and come to a decision. Remember, even with these criteria, many gray areas exist. For example, not all sexual practices are high risk with regard to transmission. Thus not all sexual practice necessitates a legal obligation to report. As mentioned, there have been no legal tests of the *Tarasoff* criteria in HIV-infected persons, and the APA Ethical Guidelines make no mention of confidentiality and HIV (Melton, 1988).

to have several common elements. First, there is a recognition that the therapist's principal duty is to the client and that confidentiality is a crucial aspect of the therapeutic relationship. Second, therapy necessarily encourages people to engage in open dialogue with the therapist and to share their innermost thoughts and feelings. It is not unusual for clients to voice thoughts about ending their own lives or harming others. Relatively few of these threats are actually carried out, and therapists are not expected to routinely report all of them. Third, only in the most extraordinary circumstances can the duty-to-warn principle be invoked. During the therapy session, however, the therapist should continue to treat the client and, if therapeutically appropriate, attempt to dissuade the client from the threatened violence. Last, somewhere in the therapy process, the therapist must discuss the limits of confidentiality and inform the client about the possible actions he or she must take to protect a third party. In other words, professionals

are obligated to inform their clients that they have a duty to warn others about the threatened actions of their clients. Although some therapists fear that such actions might prevent the client from being open and honest, one study seemed to suggest that informing clients about the limits of confidentiality had little impact in inhibiting clients' disclosures (Muehleman, Pickens & Robinson, 1985).

CULTURAL PLURALISM AND THE MENTAL HEALTH PROFESSION

Increasingly, mental health providers are coming into contact with clients who differ from them in terms of race, culture and ethnicity (Sue, Arredondo & McDavis, 1992). The 1990 U.S. Census reveals that the United States is fast undergoing some very radical demographic changes. It is estimated that by the year 2000, over one-third of the population will be composed of racial/ethnic minorities with an even higher proportion (45 percent) in our public schools; within several decades, racial minorities will become the majority (Sue, 1991; Johnston & Packer, 1987). These estimates are based upon two observed trends: (a) different birthrates between European Americans (1.7 children per mother) and racial/ethnic minorities (for example, African Americans = 2.4, Mexican Americans = 2.9, Vietnamese = 3.4, Hmongs = 11.9) and (b) immigration patterns from Asian and Latin American countries.

Many mental health professionals assert that the prevailing concepts of mental health and mental disorders are culture bound, and that the prevailing theories of therapy are based on a middle-class, European-American, highly individualistic, and ethnocentric ethic (Ivey, 1990; Special Populations Task Force of the President's Commission on Mental Health, 1978; D. W. Sue & D. Sue, 1990). As a result, misdiagnosis and inappropriate treatments often victimize racial/ethnic minority clients (see Focus 18.1). Underutilization of traditional mental health facilities and premature termination by culturally different clients have been well documented (Sue, Allen & Conaway, 1975; Sue & McKinney, 1975; Sue, McKinney, Allen & Hall, 1974). Sue & Sue (1990) state "the services offered are frequently antagonistic or inappropriate to the life experiences of the culturally different client; they lack sensitivity and understanding, and they are oppressive and discriminating toward minority clients" (p. 7).

These ethical and professional concerns are reflected in the most recent *Ethical Principles of Psychologists and Code of Conduct of The American Psychological Association* (APA, 1992). Below are some of the more pertinent principles:

> Psychologists are aware of cultural, individual, and role differences, including those due to age, gender, race, ethnicity, national origin, religion, sexual orientation, disability, language, and socioeconomic status. Psychologists try to eliminate the effect on their work of biases based on those factors, and they do not knowingly participate in or condone unfair discriminatory practices (*Principle D: Respect for People's Rights and Dignity*, pp. 1599–1600).
>
> Where differences of age, gender, race, ethnicity, national origin, religion, sexual orientation, disability, language, or socioeconomic status significantly affect psychologists' work concerning particular individuals

or groups, psychologists obtain the training, experience, consultation or supervision necessary to ensure the competence of their services, or they make appropriate referrals (*General Standards: Human Differences*, p. 1601).

> Psychologists attempt to identify situations in which particular interventions or assessment techniques or norms may not be applicable or may require adjustment in administration or interpretation because of factors such as individuals' gender, age, race, ethnicity, national origin, religion, sexual orientation, disability, language, or socioeconomic status (*Evaluation, Assessment, or Intervention: Use of Assessment in General and with Special Populations*, p. 1603).

These ethical principles make it clear that working with culturally different clients is unethical unless the mental health professional has adequate training and expertise in multicultural psychology. From an ethical perspective, Sue and Sue (1990) maintain that mental health professionals have a moral and professional responsibility to (a) become aware of and deal with the biases, stereotypes, and assumptions that support their practice; (b) become aware of the culturally different client's values and world view; and (c) develop appropriate intervention strategies that take into account the social, cultural, historical, and environmental influences of culturally different clients.

The increased awareness of multicultural influences in our understanding of abnormal psychology is reflected in the most recent version of the *Diagnostic and Statistical Manual of the American Psychiatric Association* (DSM-IV). For the first time since its publication in 1952, DSM is acknowledging the importance of culture in diagnosis and treatment of mental disorders. A new section on culturally related features describes culture-specific symptom patterns, preferred idioms for describing distress, and prevalence information. The clinician is given specific guidance on how clinical presentation of disorders among various racial and cultural groups may vary. Also, DSM-IV contains a section dealing with culture-bound syndromes unique to particular groups, cultures, or societies. Appendix I in DSM-IV will present many of these culture-bound syndromes, the cultures in which they were first described, and, possibly, related DSM-IV categories. The inclusion of cultural issues is intended to enhance the cross-cultural applicability of DSM-IV, and reduce clinicians' possible bias stemming from their own cultural backgrounds.

In further recognition of the importance of cultural differences in psychotherapy, the Office of Minority Affairs of the American Psychological Association (APA, 1991) has published *Guidelines for Providers of Psychological Services to Ethnic, Linguistic, and Culturally Diverse Populations*. This document makes it clear that service providers need to become aware of how their own culture, life experiences, attitudes, values, and biases have influenced them. It also emphasizes the importance of culture and environmental factors in diagnosis and treatment, and insists that therapists respect and consider using traditional healing approaches intrinsic to a client's culture. Finally, it suggests that therapists learn more about cultural issues and seek consultation when confronted with cultural-specific problems.

SOCIAL AND PERSONAL RELATIONSHIPS IN THERAPY

Traditionally, mental health practitioners have emphasized the importance of separating their personal and professional lives. They reasoned that therapists need to be objective and removed from their clients because becoming emotionally involved with them was nontherapeutic. Having a personal relationship with a client may make the therapist less confrontive, allow the therapist to fulfill his or her own needs at the expense of the client, and unintentionally allow the therapist to exploit the client because of his or her position (Corey et al., 1984, 1993). Some people question the belief that a social or personal relationship is necessarily antitherapeutic (Burton, 1972). Although it is not within the scope of this section for us to debate the issue, matters of personal relations with clients are being increasingly raised, especially when they deal with erotic and sexual intimacies with clients.

Sexual Relationships with Clients

Sexual misconduct of therapists is considered to be one of the most serious of all ethical violations. Indeed, virtually all professional organizations condemn sexual intimacies in the therapist-client relationship.

According to the American Psychological Association (1992),

> Psychologists do not engage in sexual intimacies with current patients or clients.
> Psychologists do not accept as patients or clients persons with whom they have previously engaged in sexual intimacies.
> Psychologists do not engage in sexual intimacies with a former therapy patient or client for at least two years after cessation or termination of professional services.

According to the American Psychiatric Association (1989),

> The necessary intensity of the therapeutic relationship may tend to activate sexual and other needs and fantasies on the part of both patient and therapist, while weakening the objectivity necessary for control. Sexual activity with a patient is unethical. Sexual involvement with one's former patients generally exploits emotions deriving from treatment and therefore almost always is unethical.

The American Association for Counseling & Development (1988) stated,

> The member will avoid any type of sexual intimacies with clients. Sexual intimacies with clients are unethical.

According to the National Association of Social Workers (1990),

> The social worker should under no circumstances engage in sexual activities with clients.

The American Association for Marriage and Family Therapy (1991) guidelines are that

> Sexual intimacy with clients is prohibited. Sexual intimacy with former clients for two years following the termination of therapy is prohibited.

And, according to the American Psychoanalytic Association (1983),

> Sexual relationships between analyst and patient are antithetical to treatment and unacceptable under any circumstances. Any sexual activity with a patient constitutes a violation of this principle of ethics.

But what are the practitioners' thoughts about sexual intimacies with clients? How often does it really occur? Who does what to whom? In one nationwide study of 500 male and 500 female psychologists, Holroyd and Brodsky (1977) reported that 5.5 percent of male therapists and 0.6 percent of female therapists have had sexual intercourse with clients. Sexual intimacy is almost always between male therapists and female clients. Of those who had sexual intercourse with clients, 80 percent were likely to repeat the practice. Of those responding, 88 percent of female and 70 percent of male therapists believed that erotic contact is never beneficial to clients. However, 4 percent of the respondents thought that erotic contact with clients was beneficial. Although in the minority, these therapists took the position that sexual intimacy may be beneficial to clients because it validates the clients as sexual beings, frees them from inhibitions and guilt, and allows them to enjoy their sexuality.

Critics of these arguments find them weak and self-serving. First, sexual intimacy represents an abuse of the therapist's power. Clients who discuss the most intimate aspects of their lives (sexual desires and struggles) are very vulnerable, and it is extremely easy for therapists to take advantage of their clients' trust and to exploit it. Second, sexual intimacy fosters dependency in clients, who look toward the therapist as an "ideal" and as someone who has "the answers." An individual's personal therapeutic goals become subordinate to a desire to please the therapist or to live up to his or her standards. Third, objectivity may also be lost. When therapists become sex partners, they cease to be therapists (Bouhoutsos et al., 1983; Corlis & Rabe, 1969). Fourth, clients often feel exploited, used, embittered, and angry. Their self-esteem is also harmed.

Statistics on the harmful effects of sexual intimacy on clients have supported these conclusions. In a survey of 559 clients who became sexually involved with their therapists, ninety percent were deemed adversely affected (Bouhoutsos et al., 1983). The harm included mistrust of opposite-sex relationships, hospitalizations, deterioration of their relationships with primary partners, and suicide. Many victims of therapist-client sexual contact had responses that seemed similar to the rape syndrome, the battered-spouse syndrome, and victims of child abuse (Pope, 1988). The Committee on Women in Psychology of the American Psychological Association (1989) took the position that sexual relationships between therapists and clients are never the fault of the client and that

the therapist can never be excused for sexual misconduct.

Most professional organizations and states have procedures for filing and processing ethical complaints related to sexual intimacies between therapist and client. In the state of California, the Board of Medical Quality Assurance—the parent organization of the Psychology Examining Committee—has power to suspend or revoke the licenses of therapists who engage in sexual misconduct with their clients. Furthermore, clients always have legal recourse to sue their therapists for malpractice. Therapists who engage in sex with clients have few arguments they can use in court (Austin, Moline & Williams, 1990) because the courts have generally rejected claims of consent. Many cases of misconduct, however, probably go unreported because of the client's shame and guilt over their "complicity." In any case, the consensus is that sexual intimacy with clients is unethical, antitherapeutic, and detrimental.

Touching Clients

Most of us would agree that sexual relations with clients is clearly unethical and improper. Yet we need to recognize that physical contacts with clients may or may not contain sexual or erotic intent and connotations. Fondling of the breasts or genital areas, kissing, and other sexual actions such as intercourse can easily be classified as sexual in nature. However, what about hugging, touching someone on the arm, or even shaking hands?

At the beginning of the chapter, we presented the case of a male therapist who placed his arms around a young female client as an obvious act of compassion. In this instance, the contact was nonerotic and a spontaneous act of compassion that may have comforted the client in her grief. Some therapists make the point that "touch" as a means of communication is as old as the human species itself. Touch in therapy can enhance communication and be therapeutic (Willison & Masson, 1986).

In therapy, however, touching or any other physical contact is taboo, and many therapists hold back when they feel like touching clients compassionately or affectionately. Many therapists fear that touching a client may be misrepresented, especially in a male-female relationship (Brodsky, 1985). Research has

Physical contact with clients is another controversial issue dividing the therapeutic community. Is it ever appropriate to touch a client or to be sexually intimate with that person? It is difficult not to respond to a person's pain with a simple gesture of compassion—a touched shoulder, a held hand. It is equally difficult to deal with the consequences that any misperception of that gesture might produce. The issue is complex, and a clear consensus on it will be hard to reach. Sexual intimacy is another matter, with most of the therapeutic community opposing any such contact.

found that 27 percent of therapists occasionally engaged in nonerotic hugging, kissing, or touching of opposite-sex clients, and 7 percent said they did so frequently (Holroyd & Brodsky, 1977, 1980). Nearly one-half of the therapists surveyed believe that nonerotic touch could be therapeutic. Whether therapists used nonerotic touch seemed to depend on their theoretical orientation: 25 percent of humanistic therapists did it frequently or always; 10 percent of the eclectics; and fewer than 5 percent of psychoanalytic, behavioral, or rational-cognitive therapists. In addition, therapists who advocated nonerotic touching believe it to be appropriate in the following situations: (1) relationships with socially or emotionally immature clients (such as those having a history of maternal deprivation), (2) relationships with people suffering acute distress (grief), (3) providing emotional support, and (4) greeting or termination (handshakes).

Opponents of therapeutic touch claim that, at best, it is often misinterpreted by clients, and that, at worst, it represents a clear-cut case of sexual exploi-

tation. This is especially true in male therapist–female client relationships. Their objections are based on the following grounds. First, the definition of erotic and nonerotic touch is vague. *Erotic contact* can be defined as the *intent* to arouse or satisfy sexual desire (Holroyd & Brodsky, 1977). Often the therapist may not be truly aware of his or her intent, and the client is placed in a conflicting situation as well. The patient may wonder what the therapist's intent really is. Female patients often interpret the meaning of a male therapist's touch as sexual. Furthermore, many female clients have reported that many male therapists have stated that the purpose of rubbing, stroking, and touching their female clients was to calm or relax them. Yet some touching frequently progressed to more erotic fondling of their bodies (Brodsky, 1985).

Second, some raise the issue that touch has political implications in the male-female relationship (Alyn, 1988). Sex and status in our society determines who touches whom (women are touched more often) and where (Henley, 1977). Even those who advocate therapeutic touch (Willison & Masson, 1986) have admitted that touch has power implications. Different touching patterns reflect the different status of men and women in western culture. The danger, according to critics, is that this power structure is brought into the therapist-client relationship (Alyn, 1988). We have already discussed in a previous chapter how the psychological distress of women in our society is often attributed to their second-class status and sex role stereotypes (Chesler, 1972; Eichenbaum & Orbach, 1983). Critics of physical contact believe that the prevailing power structure in a therapeutic relationship mirrors the power relationships in our society (male-female). Erotic touch in therapy is unethical; nonerotic touch even if ethical may blur the boundaries of the therapeutic relationship.

SUMMARY

1. Legal interpretations of insanity are always changing. Historically, several interpretations have been applied. The M'Naghten Rule holds that people could be acquitted of a crime if it could be shown that their reasoning was so defective that they were

unaware of their actions, or if aware of their actions, were unable to comprehend the wrongness of them. The irresistible impulse test holds that people are innocent if they are unable to control their behavior. The *Durham* decision acquits people if their criminal actions were products of mental disease or defects. The American Law Institute guidelines state that people are not responsible for a crime if they lack substantial capacity to appreciate the criminality of their conduct or to conform their conduct to the requirements of the law. Weaknesses in the standards and public outrage with the acquittal of some highly publicized people (such as John Hinckley, Jr.) have resulted in movements to restrict use of the defense. The "guilty, but mentally ill" plea is an attempt to separate mental illness from insanity and to hold people responsible for their actions.

2. The phrase, "competency to stand trial," refers to defendants' mental state at the time they are being examined. It is a separate issue from criminal responsibility, which refers to past behavior at the time of the offense. Accused people are considered incompetent if they have difficulty understanding the trial proceedings or cannot rationally consult with attorneys in their defense. Although competency to stand trial is important in ensuring fair trials, being judged incompetent can have negative consequences, such as unfair and prolonged denial of civil liberties.

3. Concern with denial of civil liberties is also present in civil commitment cases. People who have committed no crime can be confined against their will if it can be shown that (a) they present a clear and imminent danger to themselves or others, (b) they are unable to care for themselves, (c) they are unable to make responsible decisions about appropriate treatment and hospitalization, and (d) they are in an unmanageable state of fright or panic. Courts have tightened criteria and rely more than ever on the concept of dangerousness. Mental health professionals have great difficulty in predicting dangerousness because dangerous acts depend as much on social situations as personal attributes, and because the definition is unclear.

4. Concern with patient rights has become an issue because many practices and procedures seem to violate constitutional guarantees. As a result, court rulings have established several important precedents. First, the standard of proof for commitment is "clear and convicing evidence." Second, commitment

laws are now designed to provide patients with the "least restrictive environment," which does not necessarily involve hospitalization. Third, patients have a right to treatment (as opposed to custodial care) and a right to a humane environment (this latter ruling was a reaction to inhumane and abhorrent conditions that existed in some hospitals). Last, patients also have a right to refuse treatment in certain situations. The courts have used the "less intrusive forms of treatment" concept in applying their rulings.

5. During the 1960s and 1970s, the policy of deinstitutionalization became popular: the shifting of responsibility for the care of mental patients from large central institutions to agencies within the local community. Deinstitutionalization was considered a promising answer to the "least restrictive environment" ruling and to monetary problems experienced by state governments. Critics, however, have accused the states of "dumping" former patients and avoiding their responsibilities under the guise of mental health innovations.

6. Most mental health professionals believe that confidentiality is crucial to the therapist-client relationship. Exceptions to this privilege include situations that involve (a) civil or criminal commitment and competency to stand trial, (b) a client's initiation of a lawsuit for malpractice or a civil action where the client's mental condition is introduced, (c) the belief that child abuse has occurred to a client younger than sixteen, (d) a criminal action, or (e) the danger of a client to himself or herself or to others. Although psychologists have always known that privileged communication is not an absolute right, the *Tarasoff* decision makes therapists responsible for warning a potential victim to avoid liability.

7. Major demographic changes are forcing mental health professionals to consider race, culture, and ethnicity as powerful variables in (a) the manifestation of mental disorders and (b) the need to provide culturally appropriate intervention strategies for minority groups. Increasingly, mental health organizations are taking the position that it is unethical to treat members of minority groups without adequate training and expertise in cross-cultural psychology.

8. Mental health professionals are beginning to recognize that ethical and moral values permeate the therapeutic process. The most controversial issues involve erotic and sexual intimacy. Sexual intimacy with clients is almost universally condemned by ther-

apists as immoral, unethical, and antitherapeutic. It is more difficult to make a judgment in the case of "touch." Nonerotic touch as an adjunct to therapy is acceptable to many, but erotic touch is seen as antitherapeutic. It is difficult, however, to determine when a touch is erotic or nonerotic. Furthermore, touch in male-female relationships may reflect status differences in our society and may thus have political implications.

KEY TERMS

civil commitment A form of protective confinement when the person is judged to be a danger to himself or herself or to others even though he or she has not committed a crime

competency to stand trial The defendant's mental state at the time he or she is being examined by a practitioner

confidentiality An ethical standard that protects clients from disclosure of information without their consent

criminal commitment Incarceration of a person on the basis of committing a crime

dangerousness A person's potential for doing harm to himself or herself or to others

deinstitutionalization The shifting of responsibility for the care of mental patients from large central institutions to agencies within local communities

due process Legal checks and balances guaranteed to everyone (right to a fair trial, right to face accusers, right to present own evidence, right to counsel, and so on)

insanity defense The legal argument used by defendants who have committed a crime, but plead not guilty because of a mental disturbance

irresistible impulse test One of the tests of insanity, which states that a defendant is not criminally responsible if he or she lacked the will power to control his or her behavior

least restrictive environment A patient's right to the least restrictive alternative to freedom that is appropriate to his or her condition

mainstreaming Integrating mental patients as soon as possible back into the community

privileged communication In therapy, it regulates privacy protection and prevents clients from having their confidential communications disclosed without their permission

right to treatment A mental patient's right to receive therapy that would improve his or her emotional state

Glossary

abnormal behavior Behavior that departs from some norm and that harms the affected individual or others

abnormal psychology The scientific study whose objectives are to describe, explain, predict, and control behaviors that are considered strange or unusual

action-oriented therapy Therapy that bases treatment on classical conditioning, operant conditioning, observational learning, and cognitive-behavioral process

affect Emotion or mood

agoraphobia An intense fear of being in public places or of being alone where help may not be available; in extreme cases, a fear of leaving one's home

alcoholics People who abuse and depend on alcohol

alcoholism Substance dependence in which the substance used is alcohol

altruistic suicide Suicide that is motivated by the need to further group goals or to achieve some greater good

Alzheimer's disease An organic brain disorder that involves the atrophy of brain tissue and leads to marked deterioration of intellectual and emotional functioning

amnestic disorders Disorders characterized by memory impairment as manifested by inability to learn new information and inability to recall previously learned knowledge or past events

amniocentesis A screening procedure performed during the fourteenth or fifteenth week of pregnancy in which a hollow needle is inserted through the abdominal wall and into the amniotic sac to draw out fluid containing fetal cells

amphetamines Drugs that speed up central nervous system activity and produce increased alertness, energy, and euphoria; also called "uppers"

analogue study An investigation that attempts to replicate or simulate, as closely as possible, under controlled conditions, a situation that occurs in real life

anal retentive personality In Freudian theory, a stubborn, stingy, and constantly procrastinating character, caused by childhood conflict with parents over toilet training

anal stage In Freudian theory, the stage during the second year of life in which the anal region becomes the focus of pleasurable sensations

anomic suicide Suicide that results when a person's relationship to society is unbalanced in some dramatic fashion

anorexia nervosa An eating disorder in which the person is intensely fearful of becoming obese and engages in self-starvation

Antabuse Drug that produces an aversion to alcohol

antidepressant drugs Drugs that relieve depression by elevating mood; include iproniazid, phenelzine, and imipramine

antisocial personality A type of delinquency characterized by impulsivity, inability to delay gratification, inability to profit from punishment or experience, and lack of guilt

antisocial personality disorder A personality disorder characterized by failure to conform to social and legal norms, superficial relationships with others, and lack of guilt feelings for wrongdoing

anxiety Feelings of fear and apprehension

anxiety disorders Disorders (panic disorder, generalized anxiety disorders, phobias, and obsessive-compulsive disorders) whose major characteristic is irrational feelings of fear and apprehension

aphasia The loss of motor or sensory functioning associated with language; results from damage to the brain

arrhythmia Irregular heartbeat

assessment With regard to psychopathology, the process of gathering information and drawing conclusions about the traits, skills, abilities, emotional functioning, and psychological problems of an individual

asthma A respiratory disorder characterized by attacks in which breathing becomes extremely difficult because of constriction of the airways in the lungs

attention deficit hyperactivity disorder A disorder of childhood and adolescence characterized by short attention span, impulsiveness, constant activity, and lack of self-control

autistic disorder A severe childhood disorder that is characterized by early onset and an extreme lack of interest in interpersonal relationships, and impairment in verbal and nonverbal communication

autonomic nervous system The system responsible for regulating the body's internal environment, such as the heart, intestines, and endocrine glands; composed of the sympathetic and parasympathetic systems

autonomic response specificity The concept that each individual has a unique physiological reaction to all types of stressful situations

aversion therapy A conditioning procedure in which the attractiveness of a stimulus is decreased by pairing the stimulus with an aversive stimulus

aversive behavior rehearsal (ABR) An aversive conditioning treatment for exhibitionism that uses shame or humiliation as the aversive stimulus

aversive conditioning A classical conditioning technique in which an undesirable behavior is paired with a noxious stimulus to suppress the undesirable behavior

avoidant personality disorder A personality disorder characterized by hypersensitivity to rejection and humiliation, and, as a result, reluctance to enter into social relationships

axon A long, thin extension attached to a neuron that transmits impulses to other neurons

barbiturate A substance that is a powerful depressant of the central nervous system, capable of inducing psychological and physical dependency

baseline In behavior therapy, the initial level of responses emitted by the individual

base rate The frequency of a behavior's occurrence in the general population, used for comparison in research studies

behavioral medicine A number of disciplines that study social, psychological, and lifestyle influences on health

behavioral models Theories of psychopathology that are concerned with the role of learning in abnormal behavior

behavioral repertoire The range of responses an individual has learned to make in each given situation

being An existential concept referring to the awareness that human beings have of their own existence; this awareness makes people responsible for choosing their own direction in life

being-in-the-world An existential concept referring to the awareness that human beings exist in the context of a "world" of meaningful relationships with other human beings and with nature

Bender-Gestalt Visual-Motor Test A test used to assess visual-motor integration skills; can detect neurological impairment

biofeedback therapy A therapeutic approach in which a patient receives information about particular autonomic functions and is rewarded for influencing those functions in a desired direction

biofeedback training A therapeutic technique in which the person is taught to voluntarily control a particular physiological function, such as heart rate or blood pressure

biogenic model The theory or expectation that every mental disorder has an organic basis and cure

biogenic view The belief or theory that mental disorders have a physical or physiological basis

biological markers Biological indicators of a disorder such as responses to medication

biological stressors Physical conditions such as infections, trauma, malnutrition, and fatigue that can produce stress

biopsychosocial model An approach to understanding and explaining human behavior by recognizing the influence of biological, psychological, and social factors

bipolar disorder A major mood disorder in which both depression and mania are exhibited, or one in which only mania has been exhibited

body dysmorphic disorder A somatoform disorder that involves preoccupation with an imagined physical defect

borderline personality disorder A personality disorder characterized by intense fluctuations in mood, self-image, and interpersonal relationships

bradycardia Slowing-down of the heartbeat

brain pathology Dysfunction or disease of the brain

brain trauma A physical wound or injury to the brain

brief psychotic disorder A psychotic disorder that lasts less than one month

bulimia An eating disorder characterized by the rapid consumption of large quantities of food, usually followed by self-induced vomiting

caffeine Stimulant found in coffee, tea, and cola drinks

case study Intensive study of one individual that relies on observation, psychological tests, or historical and biographical data

castration anxiety In Freudian theory, the fear in males that they will be punished for their forbidden oedipal desires by suffering the loss of their penis

catatonic schizophrenia A schizophrenic disorder characterized by disturbance in motor activity—extreme agitation and excitement or extreme withdrawal and lack of responsiveness

catecholamines Neurotransmitter substances that are implicated in states of arousal and mood states

cathartic method The therapeutic use of verbal expression to release pent-up unconscious conflicts

central nervous system The brain and the spinal cord, which coordinate all activities of the nervous system of vertebrates

cerebral blood flow measurement A technique for assessing brain function in which the patient inhales a radioactive gas and the movement of the substance is followed throughout the brain

cerebral cortex The outermost layer of the cerebrum, which is involved in higher mental processes

cerebral tumor A mass of abnormal tissue growing within the brain

cerebrovascular accident A sudden stoppage of blood flow to a portion of the brain, leading to loss of brain function; also called *stroke*

cerebrum The largest structure in the brain; the seat of human consciousness and of all learning, speech, thought, and memory

child abuse Physical or psychological mistreatment of a child, carried out by parents, adult relatives, or other adult caretakers and resulting in physical or psychological trauma that can produce a variety of disorders, among them mental retardation

chromosomal anomaly Abnormality or irregularity that produces inherited defects or vulnerabilities such as Down syndrome

civil commitment A form of protective confinement when the person is judged to be a danger to himself or herself or to others even when he or she has not committed a crime

classical or **respondent conditioning** A principle of learning, involving involuntary behaviors, in which responses to new stimuli are learned through association

classification system With regard to psychopathology, a system of distinct categories, indicators, and nomenclature for different patterns of behavior, thought processes, and emotional disturbances

clinical psychology The professional field concerned with the study, assessment, treatment, and prevention of abnormal behavior in disturbed individuals

cluster headache A severe headache that tends to occur on one side of the head near the eye

cocaine A drug that induces feelings of euphoria and self-confidence in users; usually inhaled into the nasal cavity

cognition The process of thinking, perceiving, judging, and recognizing

cognitive behavioral therapy A therapy approach directed toward helping clients restructure their thoughts and reinterpret environmental inputs and internal stimulation

cognitive disorders Behavioral disturbances that result from organic brain pathology—that is, damage to the brain

cognitive mode A principle of learning holding that conscious thoughts mediate, or modify, an individual's behavior in response to a stimulus

cognitive restructuring An attempt to alter problematic cognitions by replacing them with more rational and positive thoughts

collective unconscious A term devised by Jung that refers to ancient, primordial memories common to all humanity

community mental health centers Centrally located mental health facilities (for medium-sized communities) that provide a number of services such as short-term inpatient care, outpatient care, partial hospitalization, emergency services, and community consultation and education

community psychology An approach to mental health that takes into account the influence of environmental factors and stresses the use of community resources to eliminate various conditions that produce psychological problems

competency to stand trial The defendant's mental state at the time he or she is being examined by a practitioner

compulsion The need to perform acts or thoughts to reduce anxiety

computerized axial tomography (CAT) Neurological test for the assessment of brain damage

concordance rate The likelihood that family members will exhibit the disorder that is being studied

concussion A mild brain injury often involving the rupture of blood vessels, typically caused by a blow to the head

conditioned response (CR) In classical conditioning, the response made to a previously neutral stimulus

conditioned stimulus (CS) In classical conditioning, a previously neutral stimulus

conduct disorders Disorders of childhood and adolescence that involve a persistent pattern of antisocial behaviors that violate the rights of others

confidentiality An ethical standard that protects clients from disclosure of information without their consent

congenital Present from birth but not inherited

conjoint family therapy A type of family therapy in which family members are taught message-sending and message-receiving skills

conscience In Freudian theory, the component of the superego that inculcates guilt feelings about engaging in immoral or unethical behavior

consultation Working with and through community institutions such as police, schools, the courts, or corporations to help individuals in the community

contingency Relationship, usually causal, between two events in which one is usually followed by the other

continuous amnesia The inability to recall past and present events; each new event is forgotten after it occurs

control group A group exposed to the same conditions as the experimental group with the exception of the independent variable

controlled drinking A treatment for alcoholism whose goal is to teach alcoholics to control their intake and become social drinkers, rather than to abstain entirely

contusion   A brain injury in which the brain shifts slightly and presses against the skull

conversion disorder   A somatoform disorder in which there is significant impairment of sensory or motor function without an underlying physical cause (also known as *conversion reaction*)

coping skills training   A form of cognitive behavioral therapy aimed at helping clients learn to manage or overcome stress

coping strategies   Cognitive and behavioral skills used in stressful situations to reduce stress

coprolalia   A compulsion to shout obscenities; a symptom of Tourette's syndrome

coronary heart disease (CHD)   A cardiovascular disease in which the flow of blood and oxygen to the heart is restricted by a narrowing of the arteries in or near the heart

corpus callosum   A collection of nerve fibers that connects the two hemispheres of the cerebrum

correlation   The degree to which two variables covary or are associated with each other in a population

counseling psychology   A professional field similar to clinical psychology, but usually more concerned with the study of life problems in relatively normal people

counterconditioning   A therapeutic means of eliminating anxiety by gradually pairing the fear-producing stimulus with a pleasant stimulus

countertransference   A process during psychotherapy in which feelings that the therapist had toward significant others (primarily parents) in the past are transferred to the patient; therapist must recognize and control this process

covert sensitization   An aversive conditioning technique in which the individual imagines a noxious stimulus occurring in the presence of a behavior

criminal commitment   Incarceration of a person on the basis of committing a crime

criminal insanity   A legal term referring either to a criminal's unawareness that he had committed a crime or incomprehension that it was wrong to do so because of a mental disturbance

cultural-familial retardation   Generally mild mental retardation thought to be produced through normal genetic processes, by environmental factors, or both

cultural relativism   The belief that lifestyles, cultural values, and world views affect the expression and determination of deviant behavior

cultural universality   The belief that many behavior disorders cut across lifestyles, cultural norms, and world views

cyclothymia   A mild and chronic mood disorder characterized by nonpsychotic mood swings

dangerousness   A person's potential for doing harm to himself or herself or to others

death instincts   In Freudian theory, the drive for the biological death of the organism, used to explain phenomena such as war and suicide; Thanatos

decompensation   Loss of the ability to deal successfully with stress, resulting in more primitive means of coping

defense mechanism   In psychoanalytic theory, the unconscious and automatic means by which the ego is protected from anxiety-provoking conflicts

deinstitutionalization   The shifting of responsibility for the care of mental patients from large institutions to agencies within local communities

delirium   Inability to maintain attention; disorganized thinking, confusion, and disorientation

delusion   A false belief steadfastly held by the individual despite contradictory objective evidence

delusional disorder   A disorder characterized by persistent, nonbizarre delusions that are not accompanied by other unusual or odd behavior

delusion system   An internally coherent, systematized pattern of delusions

dementia   A syndrome characterized by the brain tissue deterioration resulting in decreased intellectual ability and impaired judgment, of sufficient severity to interfere with social and occupational functioning

demonology   The belief, commonly held by ancient peoples, that both mental and physical disorders are caused by the influence of supernatural forces

dendrite   Rootlike structure attached to the body of the neuron that receives impulses from other neurons

dependent personality disorder   A personality disorder characterized by extreme reliance on others and unwillingness to assume responsibility

dependent variable   Attitudes or behaviors that are expected to change as a result of the manipulation of the independent variable in a psychological experiment

depersonalization disorder   A dissociative disorder in which there are feelings of unreality or distortion concerning the self or the environment

depression   An emotional state characterized by intense dysphoria, sadness, feelings of futility and worthlessness, and withdrawal from others

detoxification   A treatment aimed at removing all alcohol (or other substance) from a user's body and ensuring that none is ingested

developmental study   A long-term study of a group of people, beginning before the onset of a disorder, to allow investigators to see how the disorder develops

diaschisis   A process in which a lesion in one specific area of the brain disrupts other anatomically intact areas

diathesis-stress model   A theoretical model postulating that a predisposition (diathesis) and the effect of environmental stressors combine in producing mental disorders

diathesis-stress theory The theory that a predisposition to develop mental illness is inherited and that this predisposition may or may not be activated by environmental factors

disaster syndrome A hypothesized series of phases an individual goes through when exposed to disaster

discriminative stimulus A cue that is usually present when reinforcement occurs

disorganized schizophrenia A schizophrenic disorder characterized by severe disintegration and absurd and incoherent behaviors beginning at an early age

disorientation Confusion with regard to identity, place, or time

displacement A defense mechanism in which an individual's negative emotions are expressed toward a substitute target

dissociative amnesia A dissociative disorder characterized by the inability to recall information of personal significance, usually after a traumatic event

dissociative disorders Mental disorders characterized by the alteration or disruption of the individual's identity or consciousness; includes dissociative amnesia, dissociative fugue, depersonalization disorder, and dissociative identity disorder (multiple personality disorder)

dissociative fugue A dissociative disorder in which dissociative amnesia is accompanied by flight from familiar surroundings (also called *fugue state*)

diversity training Training intended to increase awareness of ethnic-related attitudes and behaviors, discourage prejudice and discriminatory behaviors, and promote effective and cooperative human relationships

dizygotic (DZ) or fraternal twins Twins from two separate eggs; such twins share about 50 percent of the same genes

dopamine A catecholamine neurotransmitter substance

dopamine hypothesis The theory that schizophrenia results from an excess of dopamine activity at certain brain synapses

double-bind theory The suggestion that schizophrenia develops in an individual as a result of the continual reception of contradictory messages from parents during the person's upbringing

Down syndrome A condition produced by the presence of an extra chromosome (trisomy 21), resulting in mental retardation and distinctive physical characteristics

drug therapy The treatment of mental disorders with drugs

DSM I, II, III, III-R, IV The diagnostic and statistical manuals of mental disorders published by the American Psychiatric Association; contain the diagnostic categories and criteria for differential diagnosis of abnormal behavior

due process Legal checks and balances guaranteed to everyone (right to a fair trial, right to face accusers, right to present own evidence, right to counsel, and so)

dyspareunia Painful coitus in males or females

dysthymic disorder A mild and chronic mood disorder characterized by nonpsychotic depression

echolalia Echoing what has previously been said; a symptom of autism and other disorders

eclectic approach An openness to all models of abnormal behavior, along with a willingness to borrow and integrate techniques from all approaches and to use them selectively with clients

eclecticism In treatment and diagnosis, selection of concepts, methods, and strategies from a variety of current theories in a systematic fashion

ego In Freudian theory, the part of the personality that mediates between instinctual urges and the environment

ego-dystonic Unacceptable to the ego

ego ideal In Freudian theory, the part of the superego that rewards altruistic or moral behavior with feelings of pride

egoistic suicide Suicide that results from an inability to integrate oneself with society

ego psychologists Followers of Anna Freud and Erik Erikson who accept Freud's three-part division of the personality, but believe that the ego is independent of the sexual and aggressive drives

ego weakness In Freudian theory, a state during sleep or times of excessive fatigue when the ego's guard over repressed desires is relaxed and unconscious impulses often seep out

ejaculation In males, the expulsion of semen during orgasm

electroconvulsive therapy (ECT) The application of an electric voltage to the brain to induce convulsions and thereby reduce depression; also called *electroshock therapy*

electroencephalograph (EEG) A neurological test for the assessment of brain damage

encephalitis Inflammation of the brain caused by viral infection that produces symptoms of lethargy, fever, and long periods of stupor and sleep; sleeping sickness

encounter groups Group therapy designed to facilitate human growth and development by encouraging freedom of expression and reduction of defensiveness

endogenous depression A depression that is caused largely by internal, chemical imbalances

epidemiological research The study of the rate and distribution of mental disorders in a population

epilepsy Any disorder characterized by intermittent and brief periods of altered consciousness, often accompanied by seizures, and excessive electrical discharge from brain cells

erectile dysfunction Inability of a male to attain or maintain a penile erection sufficient for sexual intercourse

essential hypertension High blood pressure, usually with no known organic cause

etiology The causes or origins of a disorder

eustress Any kind of stress that is good for people; a concept developed by Hans Selye

exhibitionism A disorder in which a person gets sexual gratification by exposing his or her genitals to strangers

existential analysis A therapeutic approach that is concerned mainly with the person's experience and involvement in the world

existential approach The belief that contemporary society has a dehumanizing effect and that mental disorders result from a conflict between essential human nature and the demands made on people by themselves and others

existential crisis A state in which individuals feel lonely and alienated and lose a sense of the meaning of life, of self-responsibility, and of free will

exogenous depression A depression that is due largely to environmental or external causes

exorcism Ritual in which prayer, noise, emetics, and extreme measures such as starvation or flogging were used to cast evil spirits out of an afflicted person's body

experiment A technique of scientific inquiry in which an independent variable is manipulated, the changes in a dependent variable are measured, and extraneous variables are controlled to the extent possible

experimental group In an experiment, a group that is exposed to the independent variable

experimental hypothesis A prediction that is made concerning how an independent variable affects a dependent variable in an experiment

exposure therapy Gradual exposure to a feared situation

extinction In classical and operant conditioning, the process by which a response is gradually eliminated by not being reinforced

extraneous variable A variable not being tested or controlled that influences the outcome of a study; a source of error in an experiment

factitious disorders Deliberately self-induced or simulated physical or mental condition

family counseling A professional field of psychology focusing on relationships within the family

family dynamics The day-to-day "operation" of the family system

family systems model A model of psychopathology that emphasizes the influence of the family on individual behavior

family therapy Group therapy that seeks to modify relationships within the family in such a way as to achieve harmony

fetal alcohol syndrome (FAS) A group of symptoms, including mental retardation and physical defects, that are produced in the infant by the ingestion of alcohol by a pregnant woman

fetishism A disorder characterized by an extremely strong sexual attraction for a particular nongenital part of the anatomy or for an inanimate object

field study An investigative technique in which behaviors are observed and recorded in the natural environment

fixation In Freudian theory, the arresting of emotional development at a particular psychosexual stage due to either overgratification or insufficient gratification at that developmental level

flat affect Abnormal lack of emotional response

flooding A behavioral treatment aimed at extinguishing a fear by having the client confront the feared situation

free association A psychoanalytic method during which the patient says whatever comes to mind, regardless of how illogical or embarrassing it may seem; the material is thought to represent the contents of the patient's unconscious

free-floating anxiety Pervasive anxiety without an identifiable external source

gender identity disorders A psychological disorder characterized by conflict between an individual's anatomical sex and his or her sexual identity

general adaptation syndrome (GAS) A model for understanding the body's physical and psychological reactions to biological stressors

generalization Responding in a similar manner to different stimuli that share common characteristics

generalized amnesia The inability to recall the entire past, owing to some psychosocial stress

generalized anxiety disorder (GAD) Disorder characterized by persistent high levels of anxiety in situations where no real danger is present

genetic linkage studies Studies that examine whether a disorder appears more often in persons related to the person with the disorder

genital stage In Freudian theory, the psychosexual stage beginning at puberty during which true heterosexual rather than narcissistic love can develop

genotype The genetic component of a trait or characteristic

gestalt therapy A humanistic-existential approach to therapy that emphasizes the client's awareness of the "here and now" and his or her totality of experience in the present

graduated exposure Gradual exposure to a feared situation

grand mal seizure The most severe and dramatic form of epilepsy; involves violent contractions, relaxation of body muscles, and loss of consciousness

group therapy A form of therapy that involves the simultaneous treatment of two or more clients

halfway house A program that provides deinstitutionalized patients with a support system while they learn or redevelop skills they will need if they are to function in the community

hallucinations Sensory perceptions not directly attributable to environmental stimuli

hallucinogen A substance that produces hallucinations, vivid sensory awareness, or increased insight

Halstead-Reitan Neuropsychological Test Battery A series of tests used to differentiate brain-damaged from non-brain-damaged patients and to locate areas of damage

hardiness A concept developed by Kobasa and Maddi that refers to a person's ability to deal well with stress

historical research The systematic and objective reconstruction of some aspect of the past by use of the evidence available in historical documents

histrionic personality disorder A personality disorder characterized by self-dramatization, the exaggerated expression of emotion, and attention-seeking behaviors

homeostasis A state of physiological, psychological, or emotional equilibrium produced by a balance of functions and chemical composition within the individual

homosexuality Sexual preference for members of one's own sex

human ecology The study of the interaction between human beings and their environments

humanism An emphasis on human welfare and on the worth and uniqueness of the individual

humanistic-existential therapy A therapy that stresses the importance of self-growth, self-concept, free will, and responsibility; includes person-centered therapy, existential analysis, and gestalt therapy

humanistic perspective The optimistic viewpoint that people are born with the ability to fulfill their potential and that abnormal behavior results from disharmony between the person's potential and self-concept

Huntington's chorea A genetically transmitted degenerative disease involving personality changes, depression, delusion, and a loss of control over bodily functions

hyperactive Restless, distractable, and having a short attention span (with reference to a childhood syndrome); sometimes accompanied by attention deficit disorder

hypervigilance Overalertness and arousal; often a characteristic of the anxiety disorders

hypnotherapy The use of hypnosis as an adjunct to psychotherapy to help patients seeking relief from psychological problems and wishing to change

hypnotism An induced state of narrowed perception in which the individual becomes highly suggestible

hypochondriasis A somatoform disorder characterized by persistent and strong preoccupation with one's health and physical condition even in the face of physical evaluations that reveal no organic problems

hypomania Mild form of manic reaction in which affected individuals seem to be high-spirited and are overactive in their behaviors

hypotension Low blood pressure

hypothalamus Part of the brain in the subcortex concerned with the regulation of bodily activities such as hunger, sex, temperature, and hormone balance

hypothesis A conjectural statement that describes a relationship between variables

hysteria The appearance of physical symptoms that seem to have no organic basis

id In Freudian theory, the part of the personality that is subjective, impulsive, selfish, and pleasure-seeking

identification In Freudian theory, resolution of the oedipal conflict through adoption of the values or mannerisms of the same-sex parent

implosion A behavioral treatment aimed at extinguishing a fear by having the client imagine the feared situation in its full intensity

impulse control disorder A disorder in which the person fails to resist an impulse or temptation to perform some act that is harmful to the person or to others

incest Sexual relations between close relatives

independent variable The variable or condition that is manipulated and tested for its effect on the dependent variable

infarction Death of brain tissue owing to a decrease in the blood supply

inhibited male orgasm The inability to ejaculate in the vagina, even with full arousal and penile erection

inhibited orgasm A sexual dysfunction in which the person is unable to achieve orgasm during coitus with adequate stimulation after entering the excitement phase of the sexual response cycle

inhibited sexual excitement A sexual dysfunction characterized by erectile dysfunction in men, or by an inability to attain or sustain arousal in women

insanity defense The legal argument used by defendants who have committed a crime, but plead not guilty because of a mental disturbance

insight The ability to understand the basis of one's motivations, perceptions, and behavior

instinct An unlearned behavior pattern

insulin shock treatment An early treatment for schizophrenia in which insulin was injected into the patient, causing convulsions and a coma

intelligence quotient (IQ) A number used to express a person's relative intelligence as assessed by a standardized test, such as the Stanford-Binet or Wechsler scales

intermittent explosive disorder Loss of control over aggressive impulses, resulting in serious assaults or destruction

introjection In Freudian theory, the process by which a depressed person identifies with the faults of the loved one he or she has lost

introversion-extroversion A personality dimension; introverts are inhibited, less sociable, and quick to learn; extroverts are more sociable, impulsive, and slow to learn

in vivo Taking place in actuality, rather than in the imagination

involuntary commitment The hospitalization of persons judged to be mentally disturbed and dangerous or incapacitated, without their consent

irresistible impulse test One of the tests of insanity, which states that a defendant is not criminally responsible if he or she lacked the willpower to control his or her behavior

Jacksonian seizures A form of epileptic seizure in which a twitch develops in one part of the body and spreads; loss of consciousness does not usually occur

kleptomania An impulse control disorder in which the person recurrently fails to resist impulses to steal objects

lacerations Brain traumas in which brain tissue is torn, pierced, or ruptured, usually by an object that has penetrated the skull

latency stage In Freudian theory, the psychosexual stage that occurs between six and twelve years of age and is generally devoid of sexual motivation

law of effect An increase in behaviors associated with positive consequences and a reduction when associated with unpleasant consequences

lead poisoning A postnatal cause of retardation produced by an infant's ingestion of lead-based or lead-containing substances

learned helplessness Acquiring the belief that one is helpless and cannot affect outcomes in one's life

least intrusive form of treatment A concept recognizing that patients may have a right to more benign forms of treatment (psychotherapy) before more severe measures (ECT, medication, etc.) are considered

least restrictive environment A patient's right to the least restrictive alternative to freedom that is appropriate to his or her condition

libido In Freudian theory, the energy of the id, often associated with the sexual drive

life change model Hypothesis that all life changes can act as stressors

life instincts In Freudian theory, the drives associated with sex and self-preservation; Eros

limbic system The part of the brain involved with experiencing and expressing emotions

lobotomy Severing of the fibers between the frontal lobes and the thalamus or hypothalamus

localized amnesia The most common type of amnesia; the inability to recall all events during a specific period

loosening of associations Continual shifting from topic to topic without logical or meaningful connection among topics

Luria-Nebraska Neuropsychological Battery An inexpensive standardized test used in screening for brain damage and in pinpointing damaged areas

lysergic acid diethylamide (LSD) A strong hallucinogen

magnetic resonance imaging (MRI) A technique to assess brain functioning, using a magnetic field and radio waves to produce pictures of the brain

mainstreaming Integrating mental patients back into the community as soon as possible

major depression A major affective disorder in which only depression and not mania has been exhibited (see also *unipolar disorders*)

malingering Faking an illness to obtain a goal

mania An emotional state characterized by great elation, seemingly boundless energy, and irritability

marijuana The mildest and most commonly used hallucinogen; pot

marital therapy A treatment aimed at helping couples understand and clarify their communications, role relationships, unfulfilled needs, and unrealistic expectations

marriage counseling A professional field of psychology concerned with improving interaction and communication between husband and wife

masochism A sexual disorder in which erotic or sexual gratification is obtained by receiving pain or punishment

mass madness Group hysteria

medical model A model of psychopathology that conceptualizes abnormal behavior in the same way as physical disorder

melancholia Biologically caused depression characterized by loss of pleasure in all activities, weight loss, and guilt

meningitis Inflammation of the membrane surrounding the brain and spinal cord; can produce cerebral infarction and seizures

mental disorder (or **mental disturbance**) Any of a range of recognizable patterns of abnormal behavior

mental retardation Substandard intellectual functioning accompanied by deficiencies in adaptive behavior, with onset before age eighteen

mesmerism A treatment developed by Anton Mesmer that induced a sleeplike state; considered to be the forerunner of modern hypnotism

methadone A drug prescribed during heroin detoxification to decrease the intensity of withdrawal symptoms

microcephaly An anomaly characterized by an unusually small brain; found in children with fetal alcohol syndrome

migraine headache Severe headache resulting from constriction and then dilation of the cerebral blood vessels

milieu therapy A therapy program in which the hospital environment operates as a community and patients have decision-making responsibilities

Minnesota Multiphasic Personality Inventory (**MMPI**) An objective personality inventory used widely in clinical settings to assess psychological disturbances

model An analogy most often used to describe or explain something that cannot be directly observed

modeling The process of learning by observing models

modeling therapy A therapeutic approach to phobias in which the phobic individual observes a fearless model coping with the fear-producing situation

monoamine oxidase (**MAO**) **inhibitor** An antidepressant compound believed to correct the balance of neurotransmitters in the brain

monozygotic (**MZ**) or **identical twins** Genetically identical twins who developed from one fertilized egg

mood disorders Severe disturbances of mood or affect that cause subjective discomfort, hinder a person's ability to function, or both; mood disorders involve depression, mania, or both

moral treatment movement A shift to more humane treatment of the mentally disturbed; its initiation is generally attributed to Philippe Pinel

multi-infarct dementia An organic brain syndrome characterized by uneven deterioration of intellectual abilities and resulting from a number of cerebral infarctions

multimodal behavior therapy A model of psychotherapy that advocates using a variety of concepts, methods, and strategies from behavioral as well as cognitive and affective theories

multiple-baseline design A type of single-subject experiment that involves recording multiple behaviors, serially applying the same modification to each behavior, and measuring any changes that occur

multiple personality A disorder in which two or more relatively distinct personalities exist in one individual

narcissistic personality disorder A personality disorder characterized by an exaggerated sense of self-importance

narcotic Opium and its derivatives, which depress the central nervous system, provide relief from pain and anxiety, and are addictive

negative reinforcer Increases the frequency of a behavior by removing an aversive event

negative symptoms Symptoms that may represent an irreversible process in schizophrenia; they include flat affect, poverty of speech, anhedonia, apathy, and avolution

neo-Freudians Psychologists whose ideas are strongly influenced by Freud's psychoanalytic model but who have modified that model in various ways

neologisms New words typically formed by combining words in common usage; often invented by schizophrenics

neurasthenia A disorder characterized by complaints of extreme mental and physical weariness

neuroleptics Antipsychotic drugs that can produce symptoms resembling neurological conditions

neurons Nerve cells that transmit messages throughout the body

neurosis Formerly a category of mental disorders including what are presently called the "anxiety, dissociative, and somatoform disorders"; now generally used to denote any less severe mental disorder

neurotic anxiety In Freudian theory, anxiety produced when the ego loses control over the id's wild impulses

neurotransmitter Chemical substances involved in the transmission of nerve impulses between neurons

nicotine A stimulant found in tobacco

night hospital program A program that allows patients to carry on their normal activities during the day while remaining institutionalized at night

nomothetic orientation The scientific approach taken by experimenters who study large groups of individuals to find common laws and principles

nonbeing An existential concept referring to the awareness that human beings have of their impending death; this awareness is the source of existential anxiety

norepinephrine A catecholamine neurotransmitter substance

objective personality test   An inventory of personality attributes in which the test taker either agrees or disagrees with specific self-descriptive statements; administration, scoring, and interpretation are largely independent of the test giver's subjectivity

object relations   Past interpersonal relations that shape and affect the individual's current interactions with people

observational learning   Acquisition of new behaviors by watching someone perform them

observational learning theory   A theory of learning that holds that people can learn new behaviors by observing other people perform those behaviors and then imitating them

obsession   An intrusive, uncontrollable, and persistent thought

obsessive-compulsive disorder   Anxiety disorder characterized by intrusive and uncontrollable thoughts, or the need to perform specific acts repeatedly, or both

obsessive-compulsive personality disorder   A personality disorder characterized by inability to express warm feelings, perfectionism, indecision, devotion to details, and a lack of personal warmth

oedipal complex   In Freudian theory, a process during which a male child desires sexual possession of his mother and wants to eliminate his father; eventually resolved by identification with the father

operant behavior   A voluntary and controllable behavior that effects a change in the individual's environment

operant conditioning   A theory of learning, applying primarily to voluntary behaviors, that holds that these behaviors are controlled by the consequences that follow them

operational definition   Definitions of the variables under study

oppositional defiant disorder (ODD)   A childhood disorder characterized by negativistic, argumentative, and hostile behavior

oral stage   In Freudian theory, the stage during the first year of life in which the primary source of pleasure involves the mouth and lips

organicity   Brain damage or deterioration

orgasm   The pleasurable culmination of sexual arousal that is usually accompanied by ejaculation in males and vaginal contractions in females

orgasmic reconditioning   A behavioral technique aimed at increasing appropriate heterosexual arousal

outpatient program   A program that allows patients to return to their homes in the community while still receiving therapeutic services from the hospital

overselective attention   The tendency of an autistic child to focus on only one kind of stimulus or cue, such as either auditory or visual cues but not both

panic disorder   Anxiety disorder characterized by severe and frightening episodes of apprehension and feelings of impending doom

paranoid personality disorder   A personality disorder characterized by unwarranted suspiciousness, hypersensitivity, a reluctance to confide in others, and preoccupation with unfounded beliefs

paranoid schizophrenia   A schizophrenic disorder characterized by persistent and systematized delusion

paraphilias   Sexual disorders in which unusual or bizarre acts, images, or objects are required for sexual arousal

paraprofessional therapists   People who are taught by a professional to provide some mental health services but who do not have formal mental health training

parasympathetic nervous system   The division of the nervous system that controls metabolic function and conserves energy when the organism is at rest

parental management techniques   Ways in which a parent can relate to a child, such as a means of supervision or discipline

Parkinson's disease   A progressively worsening organic brain disorder characterized by muscle tremors; a stiff, shuffling gait; lack of facial expression; and social withdrawal

pathognomonic   A characteristic that is specific to a disorder

pathological gambling   An impulse control disorder characterized by an inability to refrain from gambling

pedophilia   A disorder in which an adult obtains erotic gratification through sexual contact with children

penis envy   In Freudian theory, a condition in which females desire to possess a penis or demonstrate masculine characteristics

peptic ulcer   An open sore within the digestive system

personality disorder   A behavior pattern characterized by inflexible and maladaptive behaviors

person-centered therapy   A humanistic therapy that emphasizes the kind of person the therapist should be in the therapeutic process, rather than the techniques that should be used

pervasive developmental disorders   Severe disorders of childhood that affect language, social relationships, attention, perception, and affect; include autistic disorder, Rett's disorder, childhood disintegrative disorder, Asperger's disorder, and pervasive developmental disorder not otherwise specified

petit mal seizure   A mild form of epileptic seizure in which there is a momentary dimming or loss of consciousness, sometimes with convulsive movements

phallic stage   In Freudian theory, the third stage of life, during which the genital region becomes the focus of pleasurable sensations

phencyclidine (PCP)   Hallucinogen that produces perceptual distortions, euphoria, nausea, confusion, delusions, and violent psychotic behavior; also known as *angel dust*

phenothiazines Drugs used to control thought disorders, affect, and hallucinations in schizophrenics

phenotype The observable results of the interaction of the genotype and the environment

phobia A strong, persistent, and unwarranted fear of a specific object or situation

placebo A chemically inert or inactive substance, administered to a patient who believes it is an active medication

placebo effects Positive responses to a drug that result from the patient's belief in the drug's action, faith in the doctor, or other psychological factors unrelated to the specific physiological action of the drug

pleasure principle The impulsive, pleasure-seeking aspect of our being usually associated with the id, which seeks immediate gratification regardless of moral and realistic concerns

positive reinforcer Increases the frequency of the behavior it follows by providing a positive, wanted, or pleasant consequence

positive symptoms Symptoms present only during the active phase of the illness

positron emission tomography (PET) A technique for assessing brain damage in which the patient is injected with radioactive glucose and the metabolism of the glucose is monitored

posthypnotic amnesia The inability to recall information as a result of a suggestion made during a hypnotic state

posttraumatic stress disorder (PTSD) An anxiety disorder that develops in response to an event that is "outside the range of normal human experience"; characterized by intrusive memories of the traumatic incident, emotional withdrawal, and increased arousal levels

predisposition An inherited characteristic that favors the development of a certain condition, especially a disease

premature ejaculation Ejaculation before penile entry into the vagina, or so soon after entry that an unsatisfactory sexual experience results

premorbid Existing prior to the onset of mental disorder

preparedness A theory that humans are physiologically predisposed to fears that were necessary for the survival of pretechnological human beings

primal therapy A therapy intended to help patients reexperience early psychological and physical hurts in their original form by encouraging them to express emotions through violent thrashing, screams, and convulsions

primary prevention An effort to lower the incidence of new cases of behavioral disorders by strengthening resources that promote mental health and eliminating features that threaten mental health

privileged communication In therapy, it regulates privacy protection and prevents clients from having their confidential communications disclosed without their permission

proband In genetic study, an individual with the trait that is being investigated

problem-solving therapy A form of cognitive-behavioral therapy aimed at providing clients with strategies for dealing with specific problems encountered in life

prognosis A prediction of the future course of an untreated disorder

projection A defense mechanism in which unacceptable impulses are handled by attributing them to others

projective personality test A personality assessment technique in which the test taker is presented with ambiguous stimuli and is asked to respond to them in some way

prospective study A long-term study that is performed before the symptoms of an illness have been identified to allow investigators to see how the disorder develops

psychiatric epidemiology The study of relationships between immediate environmental stressors and psychopathological reactions

psychiatric social worker A social worker trained to work with clients who have mental disorders and with their families

psychiatry A medical specialty dealing with the prevention, diagnosis, treatment, and cure of mental disorders

psychoanalysis Therapy based on the Freudian view that unconscious conflicts must be aired and understood by the patient if abnormal behavior is to be eliminated

psychoanalytic model The view that adult disorders arise from the unconscious operation of repressed anxieties originally experienced during childhood

psychodiagnosis An attempt to describe, assess, and systematically draw inferences about an individual's psychological disorder

psychodrama Group therapy in which patients and other persons role-play situations

psychogenic view The belief or theory that mental disorders are caused by psychological and emotional factors

psychological autopsy A systematic examination of existing information to understand and explain the behavior exhibited by an individual prior to his or her death

psychological test Any test instrument used to assess personality, maladaptive behavior, development of social skills, intellectual abilities, vocational interest, and brain damage

psychometrics   Mental measurement, including its study and techniques

psychomotor seizures   A form of epilepsy characterized by loss of contact with the environment during which the individual may engage in well-organized and normal-appearing behavioral sequences

psychopath   An individual with an antisocial personality

psychopathology   Abnormal behavior

psychopharmacology   The study of the effects of drugs on the mind and on behavior

psychophysiological disorder   A physical disorder that has a strong psychological basis or component

psychosexual dysfunction   A disruption of any part of the normal sexual response cycle, in a male or female

psychosexual stages   In psychoanalytic theory, the sequence of stages—oral, anal, phallic, latency, and genital—through which human personality develops

psychosurgery   Brain surgery performed for the purpose of correcting severe mental disorder

psychotherapy   The systematic application, by a trained therapist, of techniques derived from psychological principles, for the purpose of helping psychologically troubled people; includes both insight-oriented and action-oriented therapies

punishment   In operant conditioning, either the removal of a positive reinforcer or the presentation of an aversive stimulus

pyromania   An impulse control disorder having as its main feature deliberate fire setting on more than one occasion

racism   Discrimination and prejudice that are aimed at a specific group because its members are considered inferior in some way

rape   An act of intercourse that is accomplished through force or the threat of force

rational-emotive therapy (RET)   The system of therapy developed by Albert Ellis that stresses that psychological problems are produced by irrational thought patterns

rationalization   A defense mechanism in which individuals justify their behavior through explanation

reaction formation   A defense mechanism in which a dangerous impulse is repressed and converted to its direct opposite

reactive disorders   Unusual or bizarre behaviors exhibited under stress-producing conditions

reactivity   A situation in which people who know they are being observed or assessed change the way they respond

realistic anxiety   In Freudian theory, anxiety that occurs when there is a potential danger from the external environment

reality principle   In Freudian theory, awareness of the demands of the environment and adjustment of behavior to meet these demands; acts to modify the pleasure principle and is part of the ego structure

regression   A defense mechanism involving a retreat to an earlier developmental level in the face of stress

reinforcer   In operant conditioning, a consequence that increases the frequency or magnitude of the behavior it follows; may be either positive or negative

relaxation training   A therapeutic technique in which the person acquires the ability to relax the muscles of the body in almost any circumstances

relearning   A characteristic of psychotherapy that refers to the client's opportunity to unlearn, develop, or change certain behaviors or levels of functioning

reliability   The degree to which a procedure or test will yield the same result repeatedly, under the same circumstances

replication   Repetition of an experiment to ensure that the results obtained in the original experiment are valid

repression   A defense mechanism that prevents unacceptable desires from reaching consciousness and expels painful experiences from consciousness

residual schizophrenia   A category of schizophrenic disorder reserved for people who have experienced at least one schizophrenic episode but do not now show prominent signs of schizophrenia

resistance   The process during psychoanalysis in which the patient unconsciously attempts to impede psychoanalysis by preventing the exposure of repressed material; tactics include silence, late arrival, or failure to keep an appointment

reticular activating system   Bundle of nerve fibers connected to the higher brain centers; controls sleep, attention, and memory

reuptake   The process by which a neurotransmitter is reabsorbed by the nerve cells

reversal (ABAB) design   An experiment in which behaviors are measured at four times: (A) before the independent variable or treatment is introduced; (B) after the independent variable is introduced; (A) after the independent variable is withdrawn; and (B) after the independent variable is reintroduced

right to treatment   A mental patient's right to receive therapy that would improve his or her emotional state

Rorschach technique   A projective technique employing symmetrical inkblots

sadism   A sexual disorder in which erotic gratification is obtained by inflicting pain or punishment on others

schema   The underlying assumptions held by a person that are influenced by experiences, values, and perceived capabilities and by how he or she interprets events

schizoid personality disorder A personality disorder characterized by social isolation and emotional coldness

schizophrenia A group of disorders characterized by severe impairment of cognitive processes, personality disintegration, and social withdrawal

schizophreniform disorder Disorder similar to the schizophrenic disorders but shorter in duration, lasting less than six months

schizophrenogenic Causing or producing schizophrenia; generally used to describe a parent who is simultaneously or alternately cold and overprotecting, rejecting and dominating

schizotypal personality disorder A personality disorder characterized by such oddities of thinking and behavior as recurrent illusions, belief in the possession of magical powers, and digression or vagueness of speech

school phobia A type of separation anxiety whose symptoms may occur merely at the prospect of having to go to school

scientific method A method of inquiry that provides for the systematic collection of data through controlled observation and for the testing of hypotheses based on those data

secondary gain Indirect benefits from neurotic or other symptoms

secondary prevention An attempt to shorten the duration of mental disorders and reduce their impact

selective amnesia The inability to recall only some aspects of a situation owing to some psychosocial stress

self The individual's sense of personal identity

self-actualization An inherent tendency in people to strive toward the realization of their full potential

self concept An individual's assessment of his or her own value and worth

self-control therapy A therapy approach that assumes people can actively modify their own behaviors by managing behavioral contingencies

senile dementia A severe loss of intellectual functioning that is produced by a deterioration of brain cells

separation-anxiety disorder (SAD) A childhood disorder characterized by excessive anxiety over separating from parents and home

serotonin A catecholamine neurotransmitter substance

sexism Prejudice and discrimination directed against people of either sex because of their sex

sexual desire disorder A sexual dysfunction involving a lack of sexual interest as reflected in low levels of sexual activity and fantasizing

sexual dysfunction A disruption of any part of the normal sexual response cycle, in a male or female

shaping The process of developing a new or complex behavior by reinforcing successive behaviors that increasingly approximate the final goal desired by the experimenter

simulation An investigative technique in which a real-life situation is recreated under controlled conditions

single-subject experiment An experiment performed on a single individual in which some aspect of that individual's own behavior is used as the control

social phobia An intense fear of being scrutinized

social supports The availability and quality of interpersonal resources that people can call on during emotional distress

somatization disorder A somatoform disorder in which the person chronically complains of a number of physical symptoms for which no physiological basis can be found; also called *Briquet's syndrome*

somatoform disorders Mental disorders that involve complaints of physical symptoms that closely mimic authentic medical conditions but have no physical basis; include somatization disorder, conversion disorder, somatoform pain disorder, and hypochondriasis

somatoform pain disorder A somatoform disorder characterized by pain that primarily has a psychological, rather than a physical, basis; also called *psychalgia*

specific phobia An extreme fear of a specific object or situation; a phobia not classified as either agoraphobia or a social phobia

splinter skills Characteristics of some autistic children who show deficits in verbal tasks, language skills, and symbolic thinking, but who have a facility for drawing, puzzle construction, and rote memory

Stanford-Binet Intelligence Scale An individual intelligence test used to assess cognitive development and functioning

statutory rape The seduction of a girl who has not yet reached the legal age of consent

stimulant A psychoactive substance that is a central nervous system energizer inducing elation, grandiosity, hyperactivity, agitation, and appetite suppression

stimulus control In classical and operant conditioning, the situation in which the occurrence or nonoccurrence of a particular behavior is influenced by a preceding stimulus

stimulus discrimination Being able to differentiate between similar stimuli

stress An internal response to an external stimulus (stressor)

stressor A physical or psychological demand placed on a person by some external event or situation

stroke See *cerebrovascular accident*

structural family therapy A treatment in which the therapist helps clients restructure the roles and relationships within a pathogenic family system

substance abuse A maladaptive pattern of excessive use

of a substance, in which the person cannot reduce or cease intake despite physical harm or impaired social and occupational functioning

substance dependence   A pathological pattern of inability to cut down or control use of a substance, despite knowledge of harmful effects; much time spent in obtaining the substance; frequent intoxication; and tolerance or withdrawal

sudden death syndrome   Unexpected abrupt death that may be brought on by stress; in most cases, there is an underlying coronary condition

suicidal ideation   Thoughts about taking one's own life

suicide   The taking of one's own life

superego   In Freudian theory, the purely moral facet of the personality, whose goals are idealistic rather than realistic

sympathetic nervous system   A division of the nervous system that prepares the body for emergency action

symptom substitution   The concept that if neurotic symptoms are eliminated without resolving or removing the underlying conflict, then the individual will merely express the neurosis in other ways and exhibit other symptoms

synapse   A small gap between the axon terminal of the transmitting neuron and the dendrites of the receiving neuron

syndrome   A cluster of symptoms that tend to occur together and are believed to indicate a particular disorder

systematic desensitization   A therapy in which relaxation is used to eliminate the anxiety associated with phobias and other fear-evoking situations

tachycardia   Speeding up of the heartbeat

tarantism   A hysterical reaction, common in the thirteenth century and attributed to the sting of the tarantula, in which people raved, danced, and had convulsions

tardive dyskinesia   A syndrome characterized by involuntary and rhythmic movements of the protruding tongue, chewing, lip smacking, other facial movements, and sidewise jaw movements; a possible side effect of antipsychotic drugs

tension headache   A headache that is thought to be produced by prolonged contraction of the scalp and neck muscles

tertiary prevention   Efforts to facilitate the readjustment of the person to community life after hospital treatment for a mental disorder

thalamus   The part of the brain stem that serves as a relay station, transmitting nerve impulses to other regions of the brain

Thematic Apperception Test (TAT)   A projective test involving a series of pictures, most portraying scenes of two or more persons; subjects make up a story about the pictures

theory   A group of principles and hypotheses that together explain some aspect of a particular area of inquiry

therapeutic community   A hospital environment in which all activities are structured to have a therapeutic function and in which patients participate to the fullest extent possible

therapeutic relationship   The interaction between therapist and client in which the therapist may provide reassurance, interpretations, self-disclosures, reflections of the client's feelings, or information, each at the appropriate time

therapy   A program of systematic intervention whose purpose is to modify a client's behavioral, affective, or cognitive state

tic disorders   Disorders with onset in childhood characterized by involuntary and repetitive movements, vocalizations, or both, including transient and chronic tic disorders and Tourette's syndrome

tics   Stereotyped and repetitive but involuntary twitchings or spasms of the voluntary muscles

token economy   A treatment program, based on principles of operant conditioning, that rewards patients for appropriate behaviors with tokens, which can then be exchanged for hospital passes, special privileges, or food

tolerance   A condition in which the body requires increasing doses of a substance to achieve the desired effect, or a markedly diminished effect is experienced with regular use of the same dose

Tourette's syndrome   A childhood disorder characterized by multiple motor and verbal tics that generally develop into coprolalia (compulsion to shout obscenities)

transactional analysis (TA)   A technique of group therapy based on the assumption that people play certain games that hinder the development of genuine and deep interpersonal relationships

transaction model of stress   Hypothesis that a person's perception of a stressor mediates its impact

transference   A process during psychotherapy in which the patient reenacts early conflicts by carrying over and applying to the therapist feelings and attitudes that the patient had toward significant others (primarily parents) in the past

transsexualism   A person's self-identification with the opposite sex

transvestite fetishism   A disorder in which the person feels intense sexual interest and urges to cross-dress. The person is highly distressed with these urges or has acted on them

trephining   An ancient surgical technique in which part of the skull was chipped away to provide an opening through which evil spirits could escape

trichotillomania   An impulse control disorder in which the person cannot resist pulling out his or her own hair

tricyclics   Antidepressant compounds that relieve symptoms of depression

unconditional positive regard   A humanistic concept referring to love and acceptance of an individual, regardless of his or her behavior

unconditioned response (UCR)   In classical conditioning, the response first made to the unconditioned stimulus

unconditioned stimulus (UCS)   In classical conditioning, the stimulus that elicits an unconditioned response

unconscious   In Freudian theory, an area of unawareness into which repressed desires and memories are forced

undifferentiated schizophrenia   A schizophrenic disorder characterized by mixed or undifferentiated symptoms that do not clearly fit the other types of schizophrenia

undoing   A defense mechanism involving ritualistic and repetitive behaviors performed in an attempt to atone for misdeeds

unipolar disorder   A major mood disorder in which no mania has been exhibited, only depression

vaginismus   Involuntary contraction of the outer part of the vagina, so as to restrict or prevent penile insertion

validity   The degree to which a procedure or test actually performs the function that it was designed to perform

vicarious conditioning   The development of an emotional response by observing reactions in others

voyeurism   A disorder in which sexual gratification is obtained by surreptitiously observing nude people or couples engaging in coitus

vulnerability/stress model   A theoretical model that combines an innate vulnerability and the effect of environmental stressors in the production of mental disorders

Wechsler Adult Intelligence Scale   The most widely used individual intelligence test

withdrawal symptoms   Physical or emotional symptoms such as shaking or irritability that appear when the intake of a regularly used substance is reduced or halted

References

Aalpoel, P. N., & Lewis, D. J. (1984). Dissociative disorders. In H. E. Adams & P. B. Sutker (Eds.), *Comprehensive handbook of psychopathology*, (pp. 223–249). New York: Plenum Press.

Abebimpe, V. R. (1981). Overview: White norms and psychiatric diagnosis of black patients. *American Journal of Psychiatry, 138,* 279–285.

Abebimpe, V. R., Chu, C. C., Klein, H. E., & Lange, M. H. (1982). Racial and geographic differences in the psychopathology of schizophrenia. *American Journal of Psychiatry, 139,* 888–891.

Abel, G. G., Barlow, D. H., Blanchard, E. B., & Guild, D. (1977). The components of rapists' sexual arousal. *Archives of General Psychiatry, 34,* 895–903.

Abel, G. G., Levis, D. J., & Clancy, J. (1970). Aversion therapy applied to taped sequences of deviant behavior in exhibitionism and other sexual deviations: A preliminary report. *Journal of Behavior Therapy and Experimental Psychiatry, 1,* 59–66.

Abels, G. (1975). *The double bind: Paradox in relationships.* Unpublished doctoral dissertation, Boston University.

Abels, G. (1976). Researching the unresearchable: Experimentation on the double bind. In C. E. Sluzki & D. C. Ransom (Eds.), *Double bind: The foundation of the communication approach to the family.* New York: Grune & Stratton.

Abels, N. (1986). Proceedings of the American Psychological Association, Incorporated, for the year 1985: Minutes of the Annual Meeting of the Council of Representatives. *American Psychologist, 41,* 631–663.

Abramowitz, A. J., & O'Leary, S. G. (1991). Behavioral interventions for the classroom: Implications for students with ADHD. *School Psychology Review, 20,* 220–234.

Abrams, R. (1988). *Electroconvulsive treatment: It apparently works, but how and at what risks are not yet clear.* New York: Oxford University Press.

Abrams, R., & Essman, W. B. (1982). *Electroconvulsive therapy.* Jamaica, NY: Medical & Scientific Books.

Abrams, R., & Taylor, M. A. (1983). The genetics of schizophrenia: A reassessment using modern criteria. *American Journal of Psychiatry, 140,* 171–175.

Abramson, L. Y., Metalsky, G. I., & Alloy, L. B. (1989). Hopelessness in depression: A theory-based subtype of depression. *Psychological Review, 96*(2), 358–372.

Abramson, L. Y., Seligman, M. E. P., & Teasdale, J. D. (1978). Learned helplessness in humans: Critique and reformulation. *Journal of Abnormal Psychology, 87,* 49–74.

Abramson, P., & Hayashi, H. (1984). Pornography in Japan: Cross-cultural and theoretical considerations. In N. M. Malamuth & E. Donnerstein (Eds.), *Pornography and sexual aggression* (pp. 173–183). Orlando, FL: Academic Press.

Achenbach, T. M., McConaughty, S. H., & Howell, C. T. (1987). Child/adolescent behavioral and emotional problems: Implications of cross-informant correlations for situational specificity. *Psychological Bulletin, 101,* 213–232.

Acosta, F. X. (1984). Psychotherapy with Mexican Americans: Clinical and empirical gains. In J. L. Martinez & R. H. Mendoza (Eds.), *Chicano psychology* (pp. 163–189). New York: Academic Press.

Ad Hoc Committee on Women (1979). Principles concerning the counseling and therapy of women. *Counseling Psychologist, 8,* 21.

Adams, P. R., & Adams, G. R. (1984). Mount St. Helen's ashfall: Evidence for a disaster stress reaction. *American Psychologist, 39,* 252–260.

Adler, J., & Gosnell, M. (1979, December 31). A question of fraudulent fever. *Newsweek,* p. 65.

Adler, J., Hager, M., Zabarsky, M., Jackson, T., Friendly, D. T., & Abramson, P. (1984, April 23). The fight to conquer fear. *Newsweek,* pp. 66–72.

Agras, W. S., Rossiter, E. M., Arnow, B., Schneider, J. A., Telch, C. F., Raeburn, S. D., Bruce, B., Perl, M. & Koran, L. M. (1992). Pharmacologic and cognitive-behavioral treatment for bulimia nervosa: A controlled comparison. *American Journal of Psychiatry, 149,* 82–87.

Ahles, T. A., Cassens, H. L., & Stalling, R. B. (1987). Private body consciousness, anxiety and the perception of pain. *Journal of Behavior Therapy and Experimental Psychiatry, 18,* 215–222.

Albee, G. W. (1979a). Anytime, anyplace. *APA Monitor, 10,* 31.

Albee, G. W. (1979b). Preventing prevention. *APA Monitor, 10,* 2.

Albee, G. W. (1983). Foreword. In R. D. Felner, L. A. Jason, J. N. Moritsugu, & S. S. Farber (Eds.), *Preventive psychology: Theory, research and practice.* New York: Pergamon Press.

Aldridge-Morris, R. (1989). *Multiple personality. An exercise in deception.* Hove, United Kingdom: Erlbaum.

Alexander, A. B. (1981). Asthma. In S. N. Haynes & L. Gannon (Eds.), *Psychosomatic disorders* (pp. 320–358). New York: Praeger.

Alexander, F. (1950). *Psychosomatic medicine.* New York: Norton.

Alexander, F. G., & Selesnick, S. T. (1966). *The history of psychiatry.* New York: Harper & Row.

Alexander, P. C. (1992). Introduction to the special section on survivors of childhood sexual abuse. *Journal of Consulting and Clinical Psychology, 60,* 160–166.

Alford, G. S., Morin, C., Atkins M., & Schuen, L. (1987). Masturbatory extinction of deviant sexual arousal: A case study. *Behavior Therapy, 18,* 265–271.

Allison, R. B., & Schwartz, T. (1980). *Minds in many pieces: The making of a very special doctor.* New York: Rawson, Wade.

Alter-Reid, K., Gibbs, M. S., Lachenmeyer, J. R., Sigal, J., & Massoth, N. A. (1986). Sexual abuse of children: A review of the empirical findings. *Clinical Psychology Review, 6,* 249–266.

Althof, S. E., Turner, L. A., Levine, S. B., Risen, C., Kursch, E. D., Bodner, D., & Resnick, M. (1987). Intracavernosal injection in the treatment of impotence: A prospective study of sexual, psychological, and marital functioning. *Journal of Sex and Marital Therapy, 13,* 155–167.

Altrocchi, J. (1972). Mental health consultation. In S. E. Golann & C. Eisdorfer (Eds.), *Handbook of community mental health.* New York: Appleton-Century-Crofts.

Alyn, J. H. (1988). The politics of touch in therapy: A response to Willison and Masson. *Journal of Counseling and Development, 65,* 432–433.

American Association for Counseling and Development. (1988). *Ethical Standards* (rev. ed.). Alexandria, VA: Author.

American Association for Marriage and Family Therapy. (1991). *AAMFT code of ethics.* Washington, DC: Author.

American Association of Retired Persons. (1985). *A profile of older Americans: 1985.* Washington, DC: American Association of Retired Persons.

American Bar Association. Standing Committee on Association Standards for Criminal Justice. (1984). *Criminal justice and mental health standards.* Chicago: American Bar Association.

American Medical Association. (1985). Scientific status of refreshing recollection by the use of hypnosis. *Journal of the American Medical Association, 253,* 1918–1923.

American Psychiatric Association. (1952). *Diagnostic and statistical manual of mental disorders* (1st ed.). [DSM-I]. Washington, DC: American Psychiatric Association.

American Psychiatric Association. (1968). *Diagnostic and statistical manual of mental disorders* (2nd ed.). [DSM-II]. Washington, DC: American Psychiatric Association.

American Psychiatric Association (1980). *Diagnostic and statistical manual of mental disorders* (3rd ed.). [DSM-III]. Washington, DC: American Psychiatric Association.

American Psychiatric Association. (1987). *Diagnostic and statistical manual of mental disorders* (3rd ed.). [DSM-III-R]. Washington, DC: American Psychiatric Association.

American Psychiatric Association. (1983). American Psychiatric Association statement on the insanity defense. *American Journal of Psychiatry, 140,* 681–688.

American Psychiatric Association. (1989). *The principles of medical ethics, with annotations especially applicable to psychiatry.* Washington, DC: American Psychiatric Association.

American Psychiatric Association. (1993). *DSM-IV Draft Criteria.* Washington, DC: American Psychiatric Association.

American Psychiatric Association. (1993). Practice guideline for eating disorders. *American Journal of Psychiatry, 150,* 212–228.

American Psychoanalytic Association. (1983). *Principles of ethics for psychoanalysts and provisions for implementation of the principles of ethics for psychoanalysts.* New York: Author.

American Psychological Association (1989). *Ethical principles of psychologists.* Washington DC: Author.

American Psychological Association. (1991). Draft of APA ethics code. *APA Monitor, 22,* 30–35.

American Psychological Association. (1992). Ethical principles of psychologists and code of conduct. *American Psychologist, 47,* 1597–1611.

American Psychological Association. (1993). Guidelines for providers of psychological services to ethnic, linguistic, and culturally diverse populations. *American Psychologist, 48,* 45–48.

Anastasi, A. (1982). *Psychological testing.* New York: Macmillan.

Andersen, B. L., Anderson, B., & de Prosse, C. (1989). Controlled prospective longitudinal study of women with cancer: II. Psychological outcomes. *Journal of Consulting and Clinical Psychology, 57,* 692–697.

Anderson, A., Hedblom, J., & Hubbard, F. (1983). A multidisciplinary team treatment for patients with anorexia nervosa and their families. *International Journal of Eating Disorders, 2,* 181–192.

Anderson, C. G., Ruth, D., Ayllon, T., & Kandel, H. (1987). Training and generalization of social skills with problem children. *Journal of Child and Adolescent Psychotherapy, 4,* 294–298.

Anderson, N. B., Lane, J. D., Muranaka, M., Williams, L. R. B., & Hoseworth, S. J. (1988). Racial differences in blood pressure and forearm vascular responses to the cold face stimulus. *Psychosomatic Medicine, 50,* 57–63.

Andreasen, N. C. (1984). *The broken brain.* New York: Harper & Row.

Andreasen, N. C. (1988). Brain imaging: Applications in psychiatry. *Science, 239,* 1381–1388.

Andreasen, N. C. (1989). Nuclear magnetic resonance imaging. In N. C. Andreasen (Ed.), *Brain imaging: Applications in psychiatry* (pp. 67–121). Washington, DC: American Psychiatric Press.

Andreason, N. C., & Flaum, M. (1991). Schizophrenia: The characteristic symptoms. *Schizophrenia Bulletin, 17,* 27–48.

Angell, M. (1985). Disease as a reflection of the psyche. *New England Journal of Medicine, 312,* 1570–1572.

Angrist, B., Rotrosen, J., & Gershon, S. (1980). Responses to apomorphine and amphetamine, and neuroleptics in schizophrenia subjects. *Psychopharmacology, 67,* 31–38.

Anonymous (1981). First person account: The quiet discrimination. *Schizophrenia Bulletin, 7,* 739.

Anonymous. (1983). First person account: Schizophrenia—a pharmacy student's view. *Schizophrenia Bulletin, 9,* 152–155.

Anonymous (1990). First person account: A pit of confusion. *Schizophrenia Bulletin, 16,* 355–359.

Antoni, M. H., Baggett, L., Ironson, G. I., La Perriere, A., August, S., Klimas, N., Schneiderman, N., & Fletcher, M. A. (1991). Cognitive-behavioral stress management intervention buffers distress responses and immunologic changes following notification of HIV-I seroposity. *Journal of Consulting and Clinical Psychology, 59,* 906–915.

Aplin, D. Y., & Kane, J. M. (1985). Variables affecting pure tone and speech audiometry in experimentally simulated hearing loss. *British Journal of Audiology, 19,* 219–228.

Applebaum, P. S. (1987). The right to refuse treatment with antipsychotic medications: Retrospect and prospect. *American Journal of Psychiatry, 145,* 413–419.

Ardizzone, J., & Scholl, G. T. (1985). Mental retardation. In G. T. Scholl (Ed.), *The school psychologist and the exceptional child.* Reston, VA: Council for Exceptional Children.

Arkonac, O., & Guze, S. (1963). A family study of hysteria. *New England Journal of Medicine, 268,* 239–242.

Arlow, J. A. (1991). Derivative manifestations of perversions. In G. I. Fogel & W. A. Myers (Eds.), *Perversions and near-perversions in clinical practice* (pp. 59–74). New Haven, CT: Yale University Press.

Arndt, W. B. Jr. (1991). *Gender disorders and the paraphilias.* Madison, CT: International Universities Press.

Aronson, T. A. (1987). A naturalistic study of imipramine in panic disorder and agoraphobia. *American Journal of Psychiatry, 144,* 1014–1019.

Asberg, M., Traskman, L., & Thoren, P. (1976). 5HIAA in the cerebrospinal fluid: A biochemical suicide predictor? *Archives of General Psychiatry, 33,* 297–309.

Ash, P. (1949). The reliability of psychiatric diagnosis. *Journal of Abnormal and Social Psychology, 44,* 272–276.

Asmundson, G. J. G., & Norton, G. R. (1993). Anxiety sensitivity and its relationship to spontaneous and cued panic attacks in college students. *Behaviour Research and Therapy, 31,* 199–201.

Assalian, P. (1988). Clomipramine in the treatment of premature ejaculation. *Journal of Sex Research, 24,* 213–215.

Atkinson, D. R., Morten, G., & Sue, D. W. (1993). *Counseling American minorities.* Dubuque, IA: Brown & Benchmark.

Atlas, J. A., & Lapidus, L. B. (1987). Patterns of symbolic expression in subgroups of the childhood psychoses. *Journal of Clinical Psychology, 43,* 177–188.

Attorney General's Commission on Pornography. *Final reports. (1986).* Washington, DC: U.S. Department of Justice.

Austin, K. M., Moline, M. M., & Williams, G. T. (1990). *Confronting malpractice: Legal and ethical dilemmas in psychotherapy.* Newbury Park, CA: Sage.

Ausubel, D. P. (1961). Causes and types of narcotic addiction: A psychosocial view. *Psychiatric Quarterly, 35,* 523–531.

Ayalon, M., & Mercom, H. (1985). The teacher interview. *Schizophrenia Bulletin, 11,* 117–120.

Ayllon, T., & Azrin, N. H. (1968). *The token economy: A motivational system for therapy and rehabilitation.* New York: Appleton-Century-Crofts.

Bahnson, C. B. (1981). Stress and cancer: The state of the art. *Psychosomatics, 22,* 207–209.

Bakal, D. A. (1975). Headache: A biopsychological perspective. *Psychological Bulletin, 82,* 369–382.

Baker, L. A., & Clark, R. (1990). Introduction to special feature on genetic origins of behavior: Implications for counselors. *Journal of Counseling and Development, 68,* 597–605.

Baldessarini, R. J., & Cole, J. O. (1988). Chemotherapy. In A. M. Nicholi, Jr. (Ed.), *The new Harvard guide to psychiatry.* Cambridge, MA: Harvard University Press.

Bales, J. (1988). New laws limiting duty to protect. *APA Monitor, 19,* 18.

Ball, J. D., Archer, R. P., Gordon, R. A., & French, J. (1991). Rorschach depression indices with children and adolescents: Concurrent validity findings. *Journal of Personality Assessment, 57,* 465–476.

Ballenger, J. C. (1989). Toward an integrated model of panic disorder. *American Journal of Orthopsychiatry, 59,* 204–293.

Balon, R., Pohl, R., Yeragani, V. K., Rainey, J. M., & Berchou, R. (1988). Follow-up study of control subjects with lactate- and isoproterenol-induced panic attacks. *American Journal of Psychiatry, 145,* 238–241.

Bancroft, J. (1984). Testosterone therapy for low sexual interest and erectile dysfunctions in men: A controlled study. *British Journal of Psychiatry, 14,* 146–151.

Bancroft, J. (1989). *Human sexuality and its problems.* New York: Churchill-Livingstone.

Bandler, R., & Grinder, J. (1979). *The structure of magic.* Palo Alto, CA: Science and Behavior Books.

Bandura, A. (1969). *Principles of behavior modification.* New York: Holt, Rinehart & Winston.

Bandura, A., Blanchard, E., & Ritter, B. (1969). Relative efficacy of desensitization and modeling approaches for inducing behavioral, affective, and attitudinal changes. *Journal of Personality and Social Psychology, 13,* 173–199.

Bandura, A., & Rosenthal, T. L. (1966). Vicarious classical conditioning as a function of arousal level. *Journal of Personality and Social Psychology, 3,* 54–62.

Bandura, A., & Walters, R. H. (1963). *Social learning and personality development.* New York: Holt, Rinehart & Winston.

Banks, W. C. (1982). Deconstructive falsification: Foundations of a critical method in black psychology. In E. E. Jones & S. J. Korchin (Eds.), *Minority mental health.* New York: Praeger.

Barbaree, H. E., & Marshall, W. L. (1991). The role of male sexual arousal in rape: Six models. *Journal of Consulting and Clinical Psychology, 59,* 621–630.

Barber, J. (1990). Invited discussion of Watkins & Watkin's paper "Dissociation and displacement: Where goes the ouch?" *American Journal of Clinical Hypnosis, 33,* 11–12.

Barber, J. P., & Luborsky, L. (1991). A psychodynamic view of simple phobias and prescriptive matching: A commentary. *Psychotherapy, 28,* 469–472.

Barchas, J., Berger, P., Ciaranello, R., & Elliott, G. (1977). *Psychopharmacology: From theory to practice.* New York: Oxford University Press.

Barker, J., & Webb, W. L. (1987). The difficult-to-treat eating-disordered patient. *Bulletin of the Menninger Clinic, 51,* 383–390.

Barkley, R. A., Anastopoulous, A. D., Guevremont, D. C., & Fletcher, K. E. (1992). Adolescents with attention deficit hyperactivity disorder: Mother-child-adolescent interactions, family beliefs and conflicts, and psychopathology. *Journal of Abnormal Child Psychology, 20,* 263–288.

Barkley, R. A., Fischer, M., Edelbrock, C., & Smallish, L. (1991). The adolescent outcome of hyperactive children diagnosed by research criteria—III. Mother-child interactions, family conflicts and maternal psychopathology. *Journal of Child Psychology and Psychiatry, 32,* 233–255.

Barlow, D. H. (1991). Introduction to the special issue on diagnoses, dimensions, and DSM-IV: The science of classification. *Journal of Abnormal Psychology, 100,* 243–244.

Barlow, D. H., Abel, G., & Blanchard, E. (1979). Gender identity change in transsexuals. *Archives of General Psychiatry, 36,* 1001–1007.

Baron, M. (1991). Genetics of manic depressive illness: Current status and evolving concepts. In P. R. McHugh & V. A. McKusick (Eds.), *Genes, brain, and behavior* (pp. 153–164). New York: Raven Press.

Baron, L., Straus, M. A., & Jaffee, D. (1988). Legitimate violence, violent attitudes, and rape: A test of the cultural spillover theory. In R. A. Prentky and V. L. Quisey (Eds.), *Human sexual aggression: Current perspectives. Annals of the New York Academy of Sciences, 528* (pp. 79–110). Salem, MA: New York Academy of Sciences.

Barraclough, B. M., Nelson, B., Bunch, J., & Sainsbury, P. (1969). The diagnostic classification and psychiatric treatment of 180 suicides. *Proceedings of the Fifth International Conference for Suicide Prevention,* London.

Barrera, M., & Ainlay, S. L. (1983). The structure of social support: A conceptual and empirical analysis. *Journal of Community Psychology, 11,* 133–143.

Barrett, C. L. (1969). Systematic desensitization versus implosive therapy. *Journal of Abnormal Psychology, 74,* 587–592.

Barrett, G. V., & Depinet, R. L. (1991). A reconsideration of testing for competence rather than for intelligence. *American Psychologist, 46,* 1012–1024.

Barron, F. (1963). *Creativity and psychological health.* Princeton, NJ: Van Nostrand.

Barsky, A. J., Cleary, P. D., Wyshak, G., Spitzer, R. L., Williams, J. B. W., & Klerman, G. L. (1992). A structured diagnostic interview for hypochondriasis. *Journal of Nervous and Mental Disease, 180,* 20–27.

Barsky, A. J., Cleary, P. D., Sarnie, M. K., & Klerman, G. L. (1993). The course of transient hypochondriasis. *American Journal of Psychiatry, 150,* 484–488.

Barsky, A. J., Wyshak, G., & Klerman, G. L. (1991). In reply. *Archives of General Psychiatry, 48,* 955–956.

Barsky, A. J., Wyshak, G., & Klerman, G. L. (1992). Psychiatric comorbidity in DSM-III-R hypochondriasis. *Archives of General Psychiatry, 49,* 101–108.

Bartlett, K. (1984, August 26). Bulimia: The secret that becomes a compulsion. *Ann Arbor News*, p. F1.

Bass, E., & Davis, L. (1988). *The courage to heal.* New York: Harper & Row.

Bassuk, E. L., Schoonover, S. C., & Gelenberg, A. J. (1983). *The practitioner's guide to psychiatric drugs* (2nd ed.). New York: Plenum.

Bates, J. E., Bentler, P. N., & Thompson, S. K. (1979). Gender-deviant boys compared with normal and clinical control boys. *Journal of Abnormal Child Psychology, 7*, 243–259.

Bateson, G. (1978). The birth of a matrix or double-bind and epistemology. In M. M. Berger (Ed.), *Beyond the double bind.* New York: Brunner/Mazel.

Bateson, G., Jackson, D., Haley, J., & Weakland, J. (1956). Toward a theory of schizophrenia. *Behavioral Science, 1*, 251–264.

Bauer, A. M., & Shea, T. M. (1984). Tourette's syndrome: A review and educational implications. *Journal of Autism and Developmental Disorders, 14*, 69–80.

Baum, A., & Nesselhof, S. E. A. (1988). Psychological research and the prevention, etiology, and treatment of AIDS. *American Psychologist, 43*(11), 900–906.

Baum, M. (1970). Extinction of avoidance responding through response prevention (flooding). *Psychological Bulletin, 74*, 276–284.

Baum, S. K., & Boxley, R. L. (1983). Depression and old age identification. *Journal of Clinical Psychology, 39*, 584–590.

Baumeister, A. A. (1987). Mental retardation. *American Psychologist, 42*, 796–800.

Baumeister, R. F. (1988). Masochism as escape from self. *Journal of Sex Research, 25*, 28–59.

Beal, E. (1978). Use of the extended family in the treatment of multiple personality. *American Journal of Psychiatry, 135*, 539–543.

Beck, A. T. (1962). Reliability of psychiatric diagnosis: A critique of systematic studies. *American Journal of Psychiatry, 119*, 210–216.

Beck, A. T. (1963). Thinking and depression. *Archives of General Psychiatry, 9*, 324–333.

Beck, A. T. (1967). *Depression: Causes and treatment.* Philadelphia: University of Pennsylvania Press.

Beck, A. T. (1970). Cognitive therapy: Nature and relationship to behavior therapy. *Behavior Therapy, 1*, 184–200.

Beck, A. T. (1974). The development of depression: A cognitive model. In R. J. Friedman & M. M. Katz (Eds.), *The psychology of depression: Contemporary theory and research.* New York: Wiley.

Beck, A. T. (1976). *Cognitive therapy and emotional disorders.* New York: International Universities Press.

Beck, A. T. (1983). Cognitive therapy of depression: New perspectives. In P. Clayton & J. Barrett (Eds.), *Treat-ment of depression: Old controversies and new approaches* (pp. 265–290). New York: Raven.

Beck, A. T. (1985). Cognitive therapy, behavior therapy, psychoanalysis, and pharmacotherapy: A cognitive continuum. In M. Mahoney & A. Freeman (Eds.), *Cognition and psychotherapy.* New York: Plenum Press.

Beck, A. T. (1991). Cognitive therapy. *American Psychologist, 46*, 368–375.

Beck, A. T., Emery, G., & Greenberg, R. L. (1985). *Anxiety disorders and phobias: A cognitive perspective.* New York: Basic Books.

Beck, A. T., Freeman, A., & Associates. (1990). *Cognitive therapy of personality disorders.* New York: Guilford Press.

Beck, A. T., Kovacs, M., & Weissman, A. (1979). Assessment of suicidal ideation: The Scale for Suicide Ideation. *Journal of Consulting and Clinical Psychology, 47*, 343–352.

Beck, A. T., Laude, R., & Bohnert, M. (1974). Ideational components of anxiety neurosis. *Archives of General Psychiatry, 31*, 319–325.

Beck, A. T., Rush, A., Shaw, B., & Emery, G. (1979). *Cognitive therapy of depression.* New York: Guilford Press.

Beck, A. T., Schuyler, D., & Herman, I. (1974). Development of suicidal intent scales. In A. T. Beck, H. L. P. Resnik, & D. J. Lettieri (Eds.), *The prediction of suicide.* Bowie, MD.: Charles Press.

Beck, A. T., & Ward, C. H. (1961). Dreams of depressed patients: Characteristic themes in manifest content. *Archives of General Psychiatry, 5*, 462–467.

Beck, A. T., & Weishaar, M.E. (1989). Cognitive therapy. In R. J. Corsini & D. Wedding (Eds.), *Current psychotherapies* (pp. 285–320). Itasca, IL: Peacock.

Beck, S. J. (1953). The science of personality: Nomothetic or idiographic? *Psychological Review, 60*, 353–359.

Becker, J. (1974). *Depression: Theory and research.* Washington, DC: Winston-Wiley.

Becker, W. M., & Becker, P. (1983, May 30). Mourning the loss of a son. *Newsweek*, p. 17.

Beckham, E. E. (1990). Psychotherapy of depression research at a crossroads: Directions for the 1990s. *Clinical Psychology Review, 10*, 207–228.

Bednar, R. L., Bednar, S. C., Lambert, M. J., & Waite, D. R. (1991). *Psychotherapy with high-risk clients: Legal and professional standards.* Pacific Grove, CA: Brooks/Cole.

Bednar, R. L., & Kaul, T. J. (1978). Experiential group research: Current perspectives. In S. L. Garfield & A. E. Bergin (Eds.), *Handbook of psychotherapy and behavior change: An empirical analysis* (2nd ed.). New York: Wiley.

Beiser, M., Fleming, J. A. E., Iacono, W. G., & Lin, T-Y. (1988). Redefining the diagnosis of schizophreniform disorder. *American Journal of Psychiatry, 145,* 695–700.

Belfer, P. L., & Glass, C. R. (1992). Agoraphobic anxiety and fear of fear: Test of a cognitive-attentional model. *Journal of Anxiety Disorder, 6,* 133–146.

Bell, A. P., & Weinberg, M. S. (1978). *Homosexualities: A study of diversity among men and women.* New York: Simon & Schuster.

Bell, A. P., Weinberg, M. S., & Hammersmith, S. K. (1981). *Sexual preference: Its development in men and women.* Bloomington: Indiana University Press.

Bellack. A. S. (1992). Cognitive rehabilitation for schizophrenia: Is it possible? Is it necessary? *Schizophrenia Bulletin, 18,* 43–49.

Bellack, A. S., & Hersen, M. (1980). *Introduction to clinical psychology.* New York: Oxford University Press.

Bellack, A. S., Hersen, M., & Himmelhoch, J. M. (1983). A comparison of social skills training. *Behavior Research & Therapy, 21,* 101–108.

Bellack, A. S., Hersen, M., & Turner, S. M. (1976). Generalization effects of social skills training in chronic schizophrenics: An experimental analysis. *Behavior Research and Therapy, 14,* 391–398.

Bellack, A. S., Mueser, K. T., Wade, J., Sayers, S., & Morrison, R. L. (1992). The ability of schizophrenia to perceive and cope with negative affect. *British Journal of Psychiatry, 160,* 473–480.

Bellack, A. S., Turner, S. M., Hersen, M., & Luber, R. F. (1984). An examination of the efficacy of social skills training for chronic schizophrenic patients. *Hospital and Community Psychiatry, 35,* 1169–1177.

Bemporad, J. R. (1979). Adult recollections of a formerly autistic child. *Journal of Autism and Developmental Disorders, 9,* 179–197.

Benassi, V. A., Sweeney, P. D., & Dufour, C. L. (1988). Is there a relation between locus of control orientation and depression? *Journal of Abnormal Psychology, 97*(3), 357–367.

Bender, L. (1938). A visual-motor Gestalt test and its clinical use. *American Orthopsychiatric Association Research Monographs,* No. 3.

Benjamin, H. (1967). Transvestism and transsexualism in the male and female. *Journal of Sex Research, 3,* 107–127.

Bennett, L. F. C., & Sherman, R. (1983). Management of childhood "hyperactivity" by primary care physicians. *Journal of Developmental and Behavioral Pediatrics, 4,* 88–93.

Bennett, P., & Carroll, D. (1990). Stress management approaches to the prevention of coronary heart disease. *British Journal of Clinical Psychology, 29,* 1–12.

Bennett, P., Wallace, L., Carroll, D., & Smith, N. (1991). Treating type A behaviours and mild hypertension in middle-aged men. *Journal of Psychosomatic Research, 35,* 209–223.

Bennun, I., & Schindler, L. (1988). Therapist and patient factors in the behavioural treatment of phobic patients. *British Journal of Clinical Psychology, 27,* 145–150.

Benson, H., Shapiro, D., Tursky, B., & Schwartz, G. (1971). Decreased systolic blood pressure through operant conditioning techniques in patients with essential hypertension. *Science, 173,* 740–742.

Benson, D. F., & Stuss, D. T. (1990). Frontal lobe influences on delusions: A clinical perspective. *Schizophrenia Bulletin, 16,* 403–411.

Berger, P. A. (1978). Medical treatment of mental illness. *Science, 200,* 974–981.

Berger, S. M. (1962). Conditioning through vicarious instigation. *Psychological Review, 69,* 450–466.

Bergin, A. E. (1971). The evaluation of therapeutic outcomes. In A. E. Bergin & S. L. Garfield (Eds.), *Handbook of psychotherapy and behavior change: An empirical analysis.* New York: Wiley.

Bergin, A. E. (1980). Psychotherapy and religious values. *Journal of Consulting and Clinical Psychology, 48,* 95–105.

Bergin, A. E., & Garfield, S. L. (Eds). (1978). *Handbook of psychotherapy and behavior change.* New York: Wiley.

Bergin, A. E., & Lambert, M. J. (1978). The evaluation of therapeutic outcomes. In S. L. Garfield & A. E. Bergin (Eds.), *Handbook of psychotherapy and behavior change: An empirical analysis* (2nd ed.). New York: Wiley.

Berkowitz, A., & Perkins, H. W. (1988). Personality characteristics of children of alcoholics. *Journal of Consulting and Clinical Psychology, 56,* 206–209.

Berkowitz, N. J. (1974). Up-to-date review of theories of shock therapies. *Diseases of the Nervous System, 35,* 523–527.

Berlin, F. S., & Meinecke, C. F. (1981). Treatment of sex offenders with antiandrogenetic medication: Conceptualization, review of treatment modalities, and preliminary findings. *American Journal of Psychiatry, 138,* 601–607.

Berlow, S. J., Caldarelli, D. D., Matz, G. J., Meyer, D. H., & Harsch, G. G. (1981). Bacterial meningitis and SHL. *Laryngoscope, 4,* 1445–1452.

Berman, A. L., & Jobes, D. A. (1991). *Adolescent suicide: Assessment and intervention.* Washington, DC: American Psychological Association.

Berman, J., & Bernard, M. L. (1982). Factors related to suicidal behavior. *Journal of College Student Personnel, 23,* 409–413.

Berman, K. F., Weinberger, D. R., Shelton, R. C., Zec, R. F. (1987). A relationship between anatomical and physiological brain pathology in schizophrenia: Lateral cerebral ventricular size predicts cortical blood flow. *American Journal of Psychiatry, 144*, 1277–1282.

Bernard, J. (1976). Homosociality and female depression. *Journal of Social Issues, 32*, 213–238.

Bernardi, G., Carpenter, M. B., Di Chiara, G., Morelli, M., & Stanzione, P. (Eds.). (1991). *The basal ganglia III.* New York: Plenum Press.

Berne, E. (1972). *What do you say after you say hello?* New York: Grove Press.

Bernstein, S. M., Steiner, B. W., Glaisler, J. T. D., & Muir, C. F. (1981). Changes in patients with gender identity problems after parental death. *American Journal of Psychiatry, 138*, 41–45.

Berrios, G. E. (1991). Delusions as "wrong beliefs": A conceptual history. *British Journal of Psychiatry, 159*, 6–13.

Bersoff, D. N. (1981). Testing and the law. *American Psychologist, 36*, 1047–1057.

Bestman, E. W. (1986). Cross-cultural approaches to service delivery to ethnic minorities: The Miami model. In M. R. Miranda & H. H. Kitano (Eds.), *Mental health research and practice in minority communities: Development of culturally sensitive training programs* (pp. 199–226). Washington, DC: U.S. Government Printing Office.

Bettelheim, B. (1967). *The empty fortress.* New York: Free Press.

Beutler, L. E., & Hill, C. E. (1992). Process and outcome research in the treatment of adult victims of childhood sexual abuse: Methodological issues. *Journal of Consulting and Clinical Psychology, 60*, 204–212.

Bhadrinath, B. R. (1990). Anorexia nervosa in adolescents of Asian extraction. *British Journal of Psychiatry, 156*, 565–568.

Bhatia, M. S., Nigam, V. R., Bohra, N., & Malik, S. C. (1991). Attention deficit disorder with hyperactivity among pediatric outpatients. *Journal of Child Psychology and Psychiatry, 32*, 297–306.

Bick, P. A., & Kinsbourne, M. (1987). Auditory hallucinations and subvocal speech in schizophrenic patients. *American Journal of Psychiatry, 144*, 222–225.

Bild, R., & Adams, H. E. (1980). Modification of migraine headaches by cephalic blood volume pulse and EMG biofeedback. *Journal of Consulting and Clinical Psychology, 48*, 51–57.

Binder, L. M. (1986). Persisting symptoms after mild head injury: A review of the postconcussive syndrome. *Journal of Clinical and Experimental Neuropsychology, 8*, 323–346.

Binder, R. L. (1988). Organic mental disorders. In H. H. Goldman (Ed.), *Review of general psychiatry* (pp. 252–265). Norwalk, CT: Appleton & Lange.

Black, D. W., Noyes, R., Goldstein, R. B., & Blum, N.

(1992). A family study of obsessive-compulsive disorder. *Archives of General Psychiatry, 49*, 362–368.

Blanchard, E. B. (1992). Psychological treatment of benign headache disorders. *Journal of Consulting and Clinical Psychology, 60*, 537–551.

Blanchard, E. B., & Andrasik, F. (1982). Psychological assessment and treatment of headache: Recent developments and emerging issues. *Journal of Consulting and Clinical Psychology, 50*, 859–879.

Blanchard, R. (1988). Nonhomosexual gender dysphoria. *Journal of Sex Research, 24*, 188–193.

Blanchard, R., Racansky, I. G., & Steiner, B. W. (1986). Phallometric detection of fetishistic arousal. *Journal of Sex Research, 22*, 452–462.

Blank, R. J. (1981). The partial transsexual. *American Journal of Psychiatry, 35*, 107–112.

Blaska, B. (1991). First person account: What it is like to be treated like a CMI. *Schizophrenia Bulletin, 17*, 173–176.

Bleecker, E. R., & Engel, B. T. (1973). Application of operant conditioning techniques to the control of cardiac arrhythmias. In P. Obrist, A. Black, J. Brener, & L. DiCara (Eds.), *Contemporary trends in cardiovascular psychophysiology.* Chicago: Aldine-Atherton.

Bleuler, E. (1911). *Dementia Praecox or the group of schizophrenias.* (Translated 1950 by J. Zinkin.) New York: International Universities Press.

Bleuler, M. (1984). What is schizophrenia? *Schizophrenia Bulletin, 10*, 8–10.

Bliss, E. L. (1980). Multiple personalities: A report of 14 cases with implications for schizophrenia and hysteria. *Archives of General Psychiatry, 39*, 823–825.

Bliss, E. L. (1984). Hysteria and hypnosis. *Journal of Nervous and Mental Disease, 172*, 203–208.

Bliss, E. L., Larson, E. M., & Nakashima, S. R. (1983). Auditory hallucinations and schizophrenia. *Journal of Nervous and Mental Disease, 171*, 30–33.

Bloom, B. L. (1972). Mental health program evaluation. In S. E. Golann & C. Eisdorfer (Eds.), *Handbook of community mental health.* New York: Appleton-Century-Crofts.

Bloom, B. L. (1977). *Community mental health: A general introduction.* Monterey, CA: Brooks/Cole.

Bloom, B. L., Asher, S. J., & White, S. W. (1978). Marital disruption as a stressor: A review and analysis. *Psychological Bulletin, 85*, 867–894.

Bloom, B. L., Hodges, W. F., & Caldwell, R. A. (1982). A preventive program for the newly separated: Initial evaluation. *American Journal of Community Psychology, 10*, 251–264.

Blouin, A., Blouin, J., Aubin, P., Carter, J., Goldstein, C., Boyer, H., & Perez, E. (1992). Seasonal patterns of bulimia nervosa. *American Journal of Psychiatry, 149*, 73–81.

Blum, K., & Payne, J. E. (1991). *Alcohol and the addictive brain: New hope for alcoholics from biogenetic research.* New York: The Free Press.

Blumstein, S. (1981). Neurolinguistic disorders: Language-brain relationships. In S. Filskov & T. Boll (Eds.), *Handbook of Clinical Neuropsychology.* New York: Wiley.

Bockes, Z. (1987). "Freedom" means knowing you have a choice. In *Schizophrenia: The experiences of patients and families* (pp. 40–42). Rockville, MD: National Institute of Mental Health.

Boersma, K., Den Hengst, S., Dekker, J., & Emmelkamp, P. M. G. (1976). Exposure and response prevention in the natural environment: A comparison with obsessive-compulsive patients. *Behaviour Research and Therapy, 14,* 12–24.

Bogdan, R., & Taylor, S. (1976). The judged, not the judges: An insider's view of mental retardation. *American Psychologist, 31,* 47–52.

Bohman, M., Cloninger, R., von Knorring, A., & Sigvardsson, S. (1984). An adoption study of somatoform disorders. *Archives of General Psychiatry, 41,* 872–878.

Bohnen, N., Nicolson, N., Sulson, J., & Jolles, J. (1991). Coping style, trait anxiety and cortisol reactivity during mental stress. *Journal of Psychosomatic Research, 35,* 141–147.

Bolger, N., & Schilling, E. A. (1991). Personality and the problems of everyday life: The role of neuroticism in exposure and reactivity to daily stress. *Journal of Personality, 59,* 355–386.

Bolgrad, M. (1984). Family systems approaches to wife battering: A feminist critique. *American Journal of Orthopsychiatry, 54,* 558–568.

Bolgrad, M. (1986) A feminist examination of family systems models of violence against women in the family. In J. C. Hansen & M. Ault-Riche (Eds.), *Women and family therapy* (pp. 34–50). Rockville, MD: Aspen Systems.

Boll, T. J. (1983). Neuropsychological assessment. In I. B. Weiner (Ed.), *Clinical methods in psychology.* New York: Wiley.

Boller, F., Kim, Y., & Detre, T. (1984). Assessment of temporal lobe disorder. In P. E. Logue & J. M. Schear (Eds.), *Clinical neuropsychology.* Springfield, IL: Thomas.

Bolton, P., Rutter, M., Butler, L., & Summers, D. (1989). Females with autism and the fragile x. *Journal of Autism and Developmental Disorders, 19,* 473–476.

Bongar, B. (1991). *The suicidal patient: Clinical and legal standards of care.* Washington, DC: American Psychological Association.

Bongar, B. (1992). Effective risk management and the suicidal patient. *Register Report, 18,* 1–3, 21–27.

Boon, S., & Draijer, N. (1993). Multiple personality disorder in the Netherlands: A clinical investigation of 71 patients. *American Journal of Psychiatry, 150,* 489–494.

Booth, G. K. (1988). Disorders of impulse control. In H. H. Goldman (Ed.), *Review of general psychiatry* (pp. 381–390). Norwalk, CT: Appleton & Lange.

Booth, R., & Rachman, S. (1992). The reduction of claustrophobia I. *Behaviour Research and Therapy, 30,* 207–221.

Borkman, T. (1990). Self-help groups at the turning point: Emerging egalitarian alliances with the formal health care system? *American Journal of Community Psychology, 18*(2), 321–332.

Bornstein, R. A., King, G., & Carroll, A. (1983). Neuropsychological abnormalities in Gilles de la Tourette's syndrome. *Journal of Nervous and Mental Disorders, 171,* 497–502.

Boucher, J., & Lewis, Y. (1992). Unfamiliar face recognition in relatively able autistic children. *Journal of Child Psychology and Psychiatry, 33,* 843–859.

Bouhoutsos, J., Holroyd, J., Lerman, H., Forer, B. R., & Greenberg, M. (1983). Sexual intimacy between psychotherapists and patients. *Professional Psychology: Research and Practice, 14,* 185–196.

Bourdon, K. H. (1992). Estimating the prevalence of mental disorders in U.S. adults from the epidemiologic catchment area survey. *Public Health Reports,* pp. 663–667.

Bourne, E. J. (1990). *The anxiety and phobia workbook.* Oakland, CA.: New Harbinger Publications.

Bower, B. (1987). Images of obsession. *Science News, 131,* 236–237.

Bowers, M. B. (1981). Biochemical processes in schizophrenia: An update. In S. J. Keith & L. R. Mosher (Eds.), *Special report: Schizophrenia 1981* (pp. 27–37). Washington, DC: U.S. Government Printing Office.

Bowler, D. M. (1992). "Theory of mind" in Asperger's syndrome. *Journal of Child Psychology and Psychiatry, 33,* 877–893.

Bowman, E. S., & Coons, P. M. (1990). The use of hypnosis in a deaf patient with multiple personality disorder: A case report. *American Journal of Clinical Hypnosis, 33,* 99–104.

Bowman, P. J. (1991). Joblessness. In J. S. Jackson (Ed.), *Life in black America* (pp. 156–178). Newbury Park, CA: Sage Publications.

Bozzuto, J. C. (1975). Cinematic neurosis following *The Exorcist. Journal of Nervous and Mental Disease, 161,* 43–48.

Bradford, J. W., & Smith, S. M. (1979). Amnesia and homicide: The Padula case and a study of thirty cases. *Bulletin of the American Academy of Psychiatry and Law, 7,* 219–231.

Brady, K. T., Austin, L., & Lydiard, R. B. (1991). Body dysmorphic disorder: The relationship to obsessive-compulsive disorder. *Journal of Nervous and Mental Disease, 178,* 538–539.

Brady, R. J. (1975). *Emergency psychiatric care: Management of mental health crises.* Bowie, MD: Charles Press.

Braginsky, B. M., & Braginsky, D. D. (1973). The mentally retarded: Society's Hansels and Gretels. *Psychology Today, 7,* 18–20.

Braginsky, B. M., Grosse, M., & Ring, K. (1966). Controlling outcomes through impression management: An experiential study of the manipulative tactics of mental patients. *Journal of Consulting Psychology, 30,* 295–300.

Brammer, L. M., & Shostrom, E. (1984). *Therapeutic psychology.* Englewood Cliffs, NJ: Prentice-Hall.

Brandsma, J. (1979). *Outpatient treatment of alcoholism.* Baltimore: University Park Press.

Bratter, T. (1973). Treating alienated, unmotivated, drug-abusing adolescents. *American Journal of Psychotherapy,* 585–599.

Braucht, G. (1982). Problem drinking among adolescents: A review and analysis of psychosocial research. In National Institute on Alcohol Abuse and Alcoholism, *Alcohol Monograph 4: Special Population Issues.* Washington, DC: U.S. Government Printing Office.

Braucht, G., Follingstad, D., Brakarsh, D., & Berry, K. (1973). A review of goals, approaches, and effectiveness, and a paradigm for evaluation. *Quarterly Journal on the Study of Alcoholism, 34,* 1279–1292.

Braun, B. G. (1984). Hypnosis creates multiple personality: Myth or reality? *International Journal of Clinical and Experimental Hypnosis, 32,* 191–197.

Braun, P., Kochonsky, G., Shapiro, R., Greenberg, S., Gudeman, J. E., Johnson, S., & Shore, M. F. (1981). Overview: Deinstitutionalization of psychiatric patients: A critical review of outcome studies. *American Journal of Psychiatry, 138,* 736–749.

Bregman, E. D. (1934). An attempt to modify the emotional attitudes of infants by the conditioned response technique. *Journal of Genetic Psychology, 45,* 169–198.

Breier, A., Albus, M., Pickar, D., Zahn, T. P., Wolkowitz, O. M., & Paul, S. M. (1987). Controllable and uncontrollable stress in humans: Alterations in mood and neuroendocrine and psychophysiological function. *American Journal of Psychiatry, 144,* 1419–1425.

Breier, A., Schreiber, J. L., Dyer, J., & Pickard, D. (1991). National Institute longitudinal study of chronic schizophrenia. *Archives of General Psychiatry, 48,* 239–246.

Breier, A., & Strauss, J. S. (1983). Self-control in psychotic disorders. *Archives of General Psychiatry, 40,* 1141–1145.

Bremner, J. D., Southwick, S. M., Johnson, D. R., Yehuda, R., & Charney, D. S. (1993). Childhood physical abuse and combat-related posttraumatic stress disorder in Vietnam veterans. *American Journal of Psychiatry, 150,* 235–239.

Brenner, H. D., Hodel, B., Roder, V., & Corrigan, P. (1992). Treatment of cognitive dysfunctions and behavioral deficits in schizophrenia. *Schizophrenia Bulletin, 18,* 21–26.

Brent, D. A., Perper, J. A., & Allman, C. J. (1987). Alcohol, firearms, and suicide among youth. *JAMA: The Journal of the American Medical Association, 257,* 3369–3372.

Breslau, N., Davis, G. C., Andreski, P., & Peterson, E. (1991). Traumatic events and posttraumatic stress disorder in an urban population of young adults. *Archives of General Psychiatry, 48,* 216–222.

Brett-Jones, J., Garety, P., & Hemsley, D. (1987). Measuring delusional experiences: A method and its application. *British Journal of Clinical Psychology, 26,* 257–265.

Breuer, J., & Freud, S. (1957). *Studies in hysteria.* New York: Basic Books. (Originally published 1895.)

Briere, J. (1992). Methodological issues in the study of sexual abuse effects. *Journal of Consulting and Clinical Psychology, 60,* 196–203.

Brislin, R. (1993). *Understanding culture's influence on behavior.* New York: Harcourt Brace Jovanovich.

Brodsky, A. (1985). Sex between therapists and patients: Ethical gray areas. *Psychotherapy in Private Practice, 3,* 57–62.

Broman, S. H., Nichols, P. L., & Kennedy, W. A. (1975). *Preschool IQ: Prenatal and early developmental correlates.* Hillsdale, NJ: Erlbaum.

Bromet, E. J. (1984). Epidemiology. In A. S. Bellack & M. Hersen (Eds.), *Research methods in clinical psychology* (pp. 266–282). New York: Pergamon Press.

Brook, S. L., & Bowler, D. M. (1992). Autism by another name? Semantic and pragmatic impairments in children. *Journal of Autism and Developmental Disorders, 22,* 61–81.

Brooks, D. S., Murphy, D., Janota, I., & Lishman, W. A. (1987). Early-onset Huntington's chorea. *British Journal of Psychiatry, 151,* 850–852.

Brotman, A. W., & Stern, T. A. (1983). Case study of cardiovascular abnormalities in anorexia nervosa. *American Journal of Psychiatry, 140,* 1227–1228.

Broverman, I. K., & Broverman, D. (1970). Sex role stereotypes and clinical judgments of mental health. *Journal of Consulting and Clinical Psychology, 34,* 1–7.

Broverman, I. K., Vogel, S. R., Broverman, D. M., Clarkson, F. E., & Rosenkrantz, P. S. (1972). Sex-role stereotypes: A current reappraisal. *Journal of Social Issues, 28,* 59–78.

Brown, G. R., & Anderson, B. (1991). Psychiatric morbidity in adult inpatients with childhood histories of sexual and physical abuse. *American Journal of Psychiatry, 148*, 55–61.

Brown, G. W., & Harris, T. O. (1989). Depression. In G. W. Brown & T. O. Harris (Eds.), *Life events and illness* (pp. 49–93). New York: Guilford Press.

Brown, T. A., & Cash, T. F. (1990). The phenomenon of nonclinical panic: Parameters of panic fear, and avoidance. *Journal of Anxiety Disorders, 4*, 15–29.

Brownell, K. D. (1982). Behavioral medicine. In C. M. Franks, G. T. Wilson, P. C. Kendall, & K. D. Brownell (Eds.), *Annual Review of Behavior Therapy: Theory and Practice* (Vol. 8). New York: Guilford Press.

Brownell, K. D. (1991). Dieting and the search for the perfect body: Where physiology and culture collide. *Behavior Therapy, 22*, 1–12.

Brownmiller, S. (1975). *Against our will: Men, women, and rape.* New York: Simon & Schuster.

Bruce, C., & Emshoff, J. (1992). The SUPER II program: An early intervention program. *Journal of Community Psychology, OSAP Special Issue*, 10–21.

Bruch, H. (1978). Obesity and anorexia nervosa. *Psychosomatics, 19*, 208–221.

Bryant, R. A., & McConkey, K. M. (1989). Visual conversion disorder: A case analysis of the influence of visual information. *Journal of Abnormal Psychology, 98*, 326–329.

Buchanan, A., & Oliver, J. E. (1977). Abuse and neglect as a cause of mental retardation. *British Journal of Psychiatry, 131*, 458–467.

Buchsbaum, M. S. (1990). The frontal lobes, basal ganglia, and the temporal lobes as sites for schizophrenia. *Schizophrenia Bulletin, 16*, 379–389.

Buckner, H. T. (1970). The transvestic career path. *Psychiatry, 33*, 381–389.

Buhrmester, D., Whalen, C. K., Henker, B., McDonald, V., & Hinshaw, S. P. (1992). Prosocial behavior in hyperactive boys: Effects of stimulant medication and comparison with normal boys. *Journal of Abnormal Child Psychology, 20*, 103–121.

Bulhan, H. A. (1985). Black Americans and psychotherapy: The dilemma. *Psychotherapy, 22*, 370–378.

Bullard-Bates, P. C., & Satz, P. (1983). A case of pathological left-handedness. *Clinical Neuropsychology, 5*, 128–135.

Bunney, W. E., Pert, A., Rosenblatt, J., Pert, C. B., & Gallaper, D. (1979). Mode of action of lithium: Some biological considerations. *Archives of General Psychiatry, 36*, 898–901.

Burack, J. H. (1992, July). *Depression and early death in HIV cases.* Paper presented at the VIII International Conference on AIDS, Amsterdam.

Burgess, A. W., Groth, A. N., & McCausland, M. P. (1981). *American Journal of Orthopsychiatry, 51*, 110–119.

Burgess, A. W., Hartman, C. R., McCausland, M. P., Powers, P. (1984). Response pattern in children and adolescents exploited through sex rings and pornography. *American Journal of Psychiatry, 141*, 656–662.

Burgess, A. W., & Holmstrom, L. L. (1979). Rape: Sex disruption and recovery. *American Journal of Orthopsychiatry, 49*, 648–657.

Burman, B., Mednick, S. A., Machon, R. A., Parnas, J., & Schulsinger, F. (1987). Children at high risk for schizophrenia: Parents and offspring perceptions of family relationships. *Journal of Abnormal Psychology, 96*, 364–366.

Burt, D. B., Fuller, S. P., & Lewis, K. R. (1991). Brief report: Competitive employment of adults with autism. *Journal of Autism and Developmental Disorders, 21*, 237–242.

Burton, A. (1972). *Interpersonal psychotherapy.* Englewood Cliffs, NJ: Prentice-Hall.

Buss, A. H. (1966). *Psychopathology.* New York: Wiley.

Butcher, J. N. (1990). *The MMPI-2 in psychological treatment.* New York: Oxford University Press.

Buss, A. H., & Plonin, R. (1986). The EAS approach to temperament. In R. Plonin & J. Dunn (Eds.), *The study of temperament: Changes, continuities and challenges* (pp. 67–79). Hillsdale, NJ: Erlbaum.

Butler, G., Cullington, A., Munby, M., Amies, P., & Gelder, M. (1984). Exposure and anxiety management in the treatment of social phobia. *Journal of Consulting and Clinical Psychology, 52*, 642–650.

Butler, G., Fennell, M., Robson, P., & Gelder, M. (1991). Comparison of behavior therapy and cognitive behavior therapy in the treatment of generalized anxiety disorder. *Journal of Consulting and Clinical Psychology, 59*, 167–175.

Butler, G., Gelder, M., Hibbert, G., Cullington, A., & Klimes, I. (1987). Anxiety management: Developing effective strategies. *Behaviour Research and Therapy, 25*, 517–522.

Butler, R. N. (1984). Senile dementia: Reversible and irreversible. *Counseling Psychologist, 12*, 75–79.

Butler, R. W., & Braff, D. L. (1991). Delusions: A review and integration. *Schizophrenia Bulletin, 17*, 633–645.

Cadoret, R. J., & Cain, C. (1981). Environmental and genetic factors in predicting adolescent antisocial behavior in adoptees. *Psychiatric Journal of the University of Ottawa, 6*, 220–225.

Cadoret, R. J., & Wesner, R. B. (1990). Use of the adoption paradigm to elucidate the role of genes and environment and their interaction in the genesis of alcoholism. In C. R. Cloninger & H. Begleiter (Eds.), *Genetics and biology of alcoholism* (pp. 31–42). Cold Spring Harbor, NY: Cold Spring Harbor Laboratory Press.

Calhoun, K. S., Atkeson, B. M., & Resick, P. A. (1982). A longitudinal examination of fear reactions in victims of rape. *Journal of Counseling Psychology, 29,* 655–661.

Campbell, S. B., & Ewings, L. J. (1990). Follow-up of hard-to-manage preschoolers: Adjustment at age 9 and predictors of continuing symptoms. *Journal of Child Psychology and Psychiatry, 31,* 871–889.

Campbell, M. K. (1988). Fenfluramine treatment of autism. *Journal of Child Psychology and Psychiatry, 29,* 1–10.

Campbell, M. K., Small, A. M., Palij, M., Perry, R., Polonsky, B. B., Lukashok, D., & Anderson, L. T. (1987). The efficacy and safety of fenfluramine in autistic children: Preliminary analysis of a double-blind study. *Psychopharmacology Bulletin, 23,* 123–127.

Campbell, R. J. (1981). *Psychiatric dictionary* (5th ed.). New York: Oxford University Press.

Camus, A. (1946). *The stranger.* New York: Random House.

Caplan, P. J. (1984). The myth of a woman's masochism. *American Psychologist, 39,* 130–139.

Caplan, P. J., MacPherson, G. M., & Tobin, P. (1985). Do sex-related differences in spatial abilities exist? A multilevel critique with new data. *American Psychologist, 40,* 786–799.

Cappell, H., & Pliner, P. (1973). Volitional control of marijuana intoxication: A study of the ability to "come down" on command. *Journal of Abnormal Psychology, 82,* 428–434.

Cardena, E., & Spiegel, D. (1993). Dissociative reactions to the San Francisco Bay Area earthquake of 1989. *American Journal of Psychiatry, 150,* 474–478.

Carey, G. (1992). Twin imitation for antisocial behavior: Implications for genetic and family environment research. *Journal of Abnormal Psychology, 101,* 18–25.

Carey, W. B. (1986). Interactions of temperament and clinical conditions. In M. Wolraich & D. Routh (Eds.), *Advances in developmental and behavioral pediatrics.* Greenwich, CT: JAI Press.

Carlson, B. E., & Davis, L. V. (1980). Prevention of domestic violence. In R. H. Price, R. F. Ketterer, B. C. Bader, & J. Monahan (Eds.), *Prevention in mental health: Research, policy, and practice.* Beverly Hills, CA: Sage.

Carlson, C. L., Pelham, W. E. Jr., Milich, R., & Dixon, J. (1992). Single and combined effects of methylphenidate and behavior therapy on the classroom performance of children with attention-deficit hyperactivity disorder. *Journal of Abnormal Child Psychology, 20,* 213–232.

Carlson, E. B., & Rosser-Hogan, R. (1991). Trauma experiences, posttraumatic stress, dissociation, and depression in Cambodian refugees. *American Journal of Psychiatry, 148,* 1548–1551.

Carmelli, D., Dame, A., Swan, G., & Rosenman, R. (1991). Long-term changes in Type A behavior: A 27-year follow-up of the Western Collaborative Study. *Journal of Behavioral Medicine, 14,* 593–606.

Carone, B. J., Harrow, M., & Westermeyer, J. F. (1991). Post-hospital course and outcome in schizophrenia. *Archives of General Psychiatry, 48,* 247–253.

Carr, A. T. (1974). Compulsive neurosis: A review of the literature. *Psychological Bulletin, 81,* 311–318.

Carr, E. G. (1977). The motivation of self-injurious behavior: A review of some hypotheses. *Psychological Bulletin, 84,* 800–816.

Carr, E. G., & Durand, V. M. (1987). See me, help me. *Psychology Today, 21,* 62–64.

Carson, N. D., & Johnson, R. E. (1985). Suicidal thoughts and problem-solving preparation among college students. *Journal of College Student Personnel, 26,* 484–487.

Carson, R. C. (1991). Dilemmas in the pathway of the DSM-IV. *Journal of Abnormal Psychology, 100,* 302–307.

Casper, R. C., Eckert, E. D., Halmi, K. A., Goldberg, S. C., & Davis, J. M. (1980). Bulimia: Its incidence and clinical importance in patients with anorexia nervosa. *Archives of General Psychiatry, 37,* 1030–1035.

Cassel, J. (1974). Psychosocial processes and "stress": Theoretical formulations. *International Journal of Health Services, 4,* 471–482.

Cassileth, B. R., Lusk, E. J., Miller, D. S., Brown, L. L., & Miller, C. (1985). Psychosocial correlates of survival in advanced malignant disease? *New England Journal of Medicine, 312,* 1551–1555.

Cauce, A. M., & Srebnik, D. S. (1990). Returning to social support systems: A morphological analysis of social network. *American Journal of Community Psychology, 18,* 609–616.

Cautela, J. R. (1966). Treatment of compulsive behavior by covert sensitization. *Psychological Record, 16,* 33–41.

Cautela, J. R. (1967). Covert sensitization. *Psychological Reports, 20,* 459–468.

Centers for Disease Control (1981). *Morbidity and Mortality Weekly Report, 30,* 582.

Centers for Disease Control (1992, June 30). *HIV AIDS survey report.* Atlanta, GA: Author.

Cesaroni, L., & Garber, M. (1991). Exploring the experience of autism through firsthand accounts. *Journal of Autism and Developmental Disorders, 21,* 303–313.

Chaika, E. (1985). Crazy talk. *Psychology Today, 19,* 30–35.

Chance, P. (1987). Saving grace. *Psychology Today, 21,* 42–44.

Chapman, L. J., & Chapman, J. P. (1967). Genesis of popular but erroneous psychodiagnostic observations. *Journal of Abnormal Psychology, 72,* 193–204.

Chemtob, C. M., Hamada, R. S., Bauer, G., Torrigue, R. Y., & Kinney, B. (1988). Patient suicide: Frequency and impact on psychologists. *Professional Psychology: Research and Practice, 19*(4), 416–420.

Chesler, P. (1971). Men drive women crazy. *Psychology Today, 5,* 22–28.

Chesler, P. (1972). *Women and madness.* Garden City, NY: Doubleday.

Chesler, P. (1976). Patient and patriarch: Women in the psychotherapeutic relationship. In S. Cox (Ed.), *Female psychology: The emerging self.* Chicago: Science Research Associates.

Chess, S. (1986). Commentary on the difficult child. *Pediatrics in Review, 8,* 35–37.

Chess, S., & Thomas, A. (1984). *Origins and evolution of behavior disorders.* New York: Brunner/Mazel.

Chistison, G. W., Kirch, D. G., & Wyatt, R. J. (1991). When symptoms persist: Choosing among alternative somatic treatments for schizophrenia. *Schizophrenia Bulletin, 17,* 217–245.

Chodoff, P. (1987). Letters to the editor. *American Journal of Psychiatry, 144,* 124.

Chodorow, N. (1978). *The reproduction of mothering: Psychoanalysis and the sociology of gender.* Berkeley: University of California Press.

Chollar, S. (1988). Food for thought. *Psychology Today, 22,* 30–34.

Chu, F. D., & Trotter, S. (1974). *The madness establishment.* New York: Grossman.

Chung, R., & Okazaki, S. (1991). Counseling Americans of Southeast Asian descent: The impact of the refugee experience. In C. C. Lee & B. L. Richardson (Eds.), *Multicultural issues in counseling: New approaches to diversity* (pp. 107–126). Alexandria, VA: American Association for Counseling and Development.

Ciompi, L. (1980). Long-term study on the course of life and aging of schizophrenics. *Schizophrenia Bulletin, 6,* 606–618.

Clark, D. M. (1986). A cognitive approach to panic. *Behaviour Research and Therapy, 24,* 461–476.

Clark, K. B., & Clark, M. K. (1947). Racial identification and preference in Negro children. In T. M. Newcomb & E. L. Hartley (Eds.), *Readings in social psychology.* New York: Holt, Rinehart & Winston.

Clark, M., Gosnell, M., Hager, M., Shapiro, D., Norris, E., & Gordon, J. (1988, Spring). Headaches: How to ease the pain. *Newsweek on Health,* pp. 12–21.

Clark, M., Gosnell, M., Witherspoon, J., Huck, J., Hager, M., Junkin, D., King, P., Wallace, A., & Robinson, T. (1984, December 3). A slow death of the mind. *Newsweek,* pp. 56–62.

Clarke, A. D. B., & Clarke, A. M. (1987). Research on mental handicap, 1957–1958: A selective review. *Journal of Mental Deficiency Research, 31,* 317–328.

Clarkin, J. F., Marziali, E., & Munroe-Blum, H. (1991). Group and family treatments for borderline personality disorder. *Hospital and Community Psychiatry, 42,* 1038–1043.

Cleckley, J. (1976). *The mask of sanity* (5th ed.). St. Louis, MO: Mosby.

Clementz, B. A., & Sweeney, J. A. (1990). Is eye movement dysfunction a biological marker for schizophrenia? A methodological review. *Psychological Bulletin, 108,* 77–92.

Clemmensen, L. H. (1990). The "real-life test" for surgical candidates. In R. Blanchard & B. W. Steiner (Eds.), *Clinical management of gender identity disorders in children and adults* (pp. 119–136). Washington, DC: American Psychiatric Press.

Clinthorne, J. K., Cisin, I. H., Balter, M. B., Mellinger, G. D., Uhlenhuth, E. H. (1986). Changes in popular attitudes and beliefs about tranquilizers: 1970–1979. *Archives of General Psychiatry, 43,* 527–532.

Clomipramine Collaborative Study Group (1991). Clomipramine in the treatment of patients with obsessive-compulsive disorder. *Archives of General Psychiatry, 48,* 730–738.

Cloninger, C. R., Reich, T., Sigvardsson, S., Von Knorring, A. L., & Bohman, M. (1986). The effects of changes in alcohol use between generations or the inheritance of alcohol abuse. In American Psychological Association (Ed.), *Alcoholism: A medical disorder: Proceedings of the 76th Annual Meeting of the American Psychological Association.*

Coates, J. (1980, March 26). Pot more perilous than we thought. *Chicago Tribune,* pp. 1, 14.

Cobb, E. J., Leitenberg, H., & Burchard, J. D. (1982). Foster parents teaching foster parents: Communication and conflict resolution skills training. *Journal of Community Psychology, 10,* 240–249.

Cobb, S. (1976). Support as a moderator of life stress. *Psychosomatic Medicine, 38,* 300–314.

Coelho, G. V., Hamburg, D. A., & Murphy, E. G. (1963). Coping strategies in a new learning environment: A study of American college freshman. *Archives of General Psychiatry, 9,* 433–443.

Coffman, J. A. (1989). Computed tomography in psychiatry. In N. C. Andreasen (Ed.), *Brain imaging: Applications in psychiatry* (pp. 1–65). Washington, DC: American Psychiatric Press.

Cohen, E. D. (1990). Confidentiality, counseling, and clients who have AIDS: Ethical foundations of a model rule. *Journal of counseling and development, 68,* 282–286.

Cohen, M. J., Rickles, W. H., & McArthur, D. L. (1978).

Evidence for physiological response stereotypy in migraine headaches. *Psychosomatic Medicine, 40,* 344–354.

Cohen, S., & Williamson, G. M. (1991). Stress and infectious disease in humans. *Psychological Bulletin, 109,* 5–24.

Cohen, S. L., & Fiedler, J. E. (1974). Content analyses of multiple messages in suicide notes. *Life-Threatening Behavior, 4,* 75–95.

Cohn, L. D., Adler, N. E., Irwin, C. E. Jr., Millstein, S. G., Kegeles, S. M., & Stone, G. (1987). Body-figure preferences in male and female adolescents. *Journal of Abnormal Psychology, 96,* 276–279.

Cole, J. O. (1964). Phenothiazine treatment in acute schizophrenia: Effectiveness. *Archives of General Psychiatry, 10,* 246–261.

Cole, J. O., & Bodkin, J. A. (1990). Antidepressant drug side effects. *Journal of Clinical Psychiatry, 51,* 21–26.

Comas-Diaz, L., & Griffith, E. E. (Eds.). (1988). *Clinical guidelines in cross-cultural mental health.* New York: Wiley.

Comings, D. E., & Comings, B. G. (1987). Hereditary agoraphobia and obsessive-compulsive behaviour in relatives of patients with Gilles de la Tourette's syndrome. *British Journal of Psychiatry, 151,* 195–199.

Commander, M., Corbett, J., & Ridley, C. (1991). Reflect tics in two patients with Gilles de la Tourette syndrome. *British Journal of Psychiatry, 159,* 877–879.

Commission on Obscenity and Pornography. (1970). *The report of the commission on obscenity and pornography.* New York: Bantam.

Committee on Drug Abuse of the Council on Psychiatric Services. (1987). Position statement on psychoactive substance use and dependence: Update on marijuana and cocaine. *American Journal of Psychiatry, 144,* 698–702.

Committee on the Review of Medicines (1980). Systematic review of the benzodiazepines. *British Medical Journal, 280,* 910–912.

Compton W. M. III, Helzer, J. E., Hwu, H-G., Yeh, E-K., McEvoy, L., Tipp, J. E., & Sptiznagel, E. L. (1991). New methods in cross-cultural psychology: Psychiatric illness in Taiwan and the United States. *American Journal of Psychiatry, 148,* 1697–1704.

Conger, J. J. (1951). The effects of alcohol on conflict behavior in the albino rat. *Quarterly Journal of Studies on Alcohol, 12,* 1–30.

Conn, D. K. (1991). Delirium and other organic mental disorders. In J. Sadavoy, L. W. Lazarus, & L. F. Jarvik (Eds.), *Comprehensive review of geriatric psychiatry* (pp. 11–336). Washington, DC: American Psychiatric Press.

Conners, M. E., & Morse, W. (1993). Sexual abuse and eating disorders: A review. *International Journal of Eating Disorders, 13,* 1–11.

Consensus Development Panel. (1982). Defined diets and childhood hyperactivity. *Clinical Pediatrics, 21,* 627–630.

Cook, E. W. III, Hodes, R. L., & Lang, P. J. (1986). Preparedness and phobia: Effects of stimulus content on human visceral conditioning. *Journal of Abnormal Psychology, 95,* 195–207.

Coons, P. M. (1986). Treatment progress in 20 patients with multiple personality disorder. *Journal of Nervous Mental Disease, 174,* 715–721.

Coons, P. M. (1988). Misuse of forensic hypnosis: A hypnotically elicited false confession with the apparent creation of a multiple personality. *International Journal of Clinical and Experimental Hypnosis, 36,* 1–11.

Coons, P. M., & Bowman, E. S. (1993). Dissociation and eating. *American Journal of Psychiatry, 150,* 171–172.

Coons, P. M., & Bradley, K. (1985). Group psychotherapy with multiple personality patients. *Journal of Nervous and Mental Diseases, 173,* 515–521.

Cooper, A., & McCormack, W. A. (1992). Short-term group treatment for adult children of alcoholics. *Journal of Counseling Psychology, 39,* 350–355.

Cooper, A. J. (1969). A clinical study of coital anxiety in male potency disorders. *Journal of Psychosomatic Research, 13,* 143–147.

Cooper, J. E., Kendell, R. E., Gurland, B. J., Sharp, L., Copeland, J. R. M., & Simon, R. (1972). *Psychiatric diagnosis in New York and London.* Maudsley Monograph Series No. 20. London: Oxford University Press.

Cooper, J. R., Bloom, F. E., & Roth, R. H. (1986). *The biochemical basis of neuropharmacology* (5th ed.) New York: Oxford University Press.

Cooper, M. J., & Fairburn, C. G. (1992). Thoughts about eating, weight and shape in anorexia nervosa and bulimia nervosa. *Behaviour Research and Therapy, 30,* 501–511.

Cooper, M. L., Russell, M., & George, W. H. (1988). Coping, expectancies, and alcohol abuse: A test of social learning formulations. *Journal of Abnormal Psychology, 97,* 218–230.

Corazzini, J. G., & Anderson, S. M. (1980). An apprentice model for training group leaders: Revitalizing group treatment. *Journal for Specialists in Group Work, 5,* 29–35.

Corbett, J. A. (1971). The nature of tics and Gilles de la Tourette's syndrome. *Journal of Psychosomatic Research, 15,* 32.

Corey, G. (1991). *Theory and practice of counseling and psychotherapy.* Pacific Grove, CA: Brooks/Cole.

Corey, G., Corey, M. S., & Callanan, P. (1984). *Issues and ethics in the helping professions* (2nd ed.). Pacific Grove, CA.: Brooks/Cole.

Corlis, R., & Rabe, P. (1969). *Psychotherapy from the center: A humanistic view of change and of growth.* Scranton, PA: International Textbook.

Cosand, B. J., Bourque, L. B., & Kraus, J. F. (1982). Suicide among adolescents in Sacramento County, California 1950–1979. *Adolescence, 17,* 917–930.

Cottone, R. R. (1992). *Theories and paradigms of counseling and psychotherapy.* Boston: Allyn & Bacon.

Council on Scientific Affairs (1986). Scientific status of refreshing recollection by the use of hypnosis. *Journal of the American Medical Association, 253,* 1918–1923.

Courchesne, I., Yeung-Courchesne, R., Press, G. A., Hesselink, J. R., & Jernigan, T. L. (1988). Hypoplasia of cerebellar vermal lobules VI and VII in autism. *New England Journal of Medicine, 318,* 1349–1354.

Cowart, V. S. (1988). The ritalin controversy: What made this drug's opponents hyperactive. *Journal of the American Medical Association, 259,* 2521–2523.

Cowen, E. L. (1982). Help is where you find it: Four informal helping groups. *American Psychologist, 37,* 385–395.

Cowen, E. L. (1983). Primary prevention in mental health: Past, present, and future. In R. D. Felner, L. A. Jason, J. N. Moritsugu, & S. S. Farber (Eds.), *Preventive psychology: Theory research and practice.* New York: Pergamon Press.

Cowen, E. L., Izzo, L. D., Miles, H. C., Teleschow, E. F., Trost, M. A., & Zax, M. (1963). A preventive mental health program in the school setting: Description and evaluation. *Journal of Psychology, 56,* 307–356.

Cowley, G. (1990, February 12). Hanging up the knife. *Newsweek,* pp. 58–59.

Cox, D. J., & McMahon, B. (1978). Incidence of male exhibitionism in the United States as reported by victimized college students. *International Journal of Law and Psychiatry, 1,* 453–457.

Cox, W. J., & Kenardy, J. (1993). Performance anxiety, social phobia, and setting effects in instrumental music students. *Journal of Anxiety Disorders, 7,* 49–60.

Cox, W. M., & Klinger, E. (1988). A motivational model of alcohol use. *Journal of Abnormal Psychology, 97,* 168–180.

Coyne, J. C. (1976). Depression and the response of others. *Journal of Abnormal Psychology, 85,* 186–193.

Craig, M. E. (1990). Coercive sexuality in dating relationships: A situational model. *Clinical Psychology Review, 10,* 395–424.

Craske, M. G. (1991). Phobic fear and panic attacks: The same emotional states triggered by different cues? *Clinical Psychology Review, 11,* 599–620.

Crowe, R. R., Noyes, R. Jr., Pauls, D. L., & Slymen, D. (1983). A family study of panic disorder. *Archives of General Psychiatry, 40,* 1065–1069.

Cummings, N. A. (1984). The future of clinical psychology in the United States. *Clinical Psychologist, 37,* 19–20.

Curtis, G. C. (1981). Sensory experiences during treatment of phobias by in vivo exposure. *American Journal of Psychiatry, 138,* 1095–1097.

Cutts, T. F., & Barrios, B. A. (1986). Fear of weight gain among bulimic and nondisturbed females. *Behavior Therapy, 17,* 626–636.

Cypress, B. K. (1980). *Characteristics of visits to female and male physicians: The national ambulatory medical care survey, 1977.* Hyattsville, MD: National Center for Health Statistics.

Dahlstrom, W. G., & Welch, G. S. (1965). *An MMPI handbook.* Minneapolis: University of Minnesota Press.

Danto, B. L. (1971, Fall). Assessment of the suicidal person in the telephone interview. *Bulletin of Suicidology,* 48–56.

Darrach, D. (1976, March 8). Poetry and poison. *Time.*

Darrow, W. W., Echenberg, D. F., Jaffe, H. W. (1987). Risk factors for human immunodeficiency virus infections in homosexual men. *American Journal of public health, 77,* 479–483.

Darwin, C. (1859). *On the origin of the species by means of natural selection.* London: Murray.

Davey, G. C. (1989). UCS reevaluation and conditioning models of acquired fears. *Behaviour Research and Therapy, 27,* 521–528.

Davey, G. C. L., Forster, L., & Mayhew, G. (1993). Familial resemblances in disgust sensitivity and animal phobias. *Behaviour Research and Therapy, 31,* 41–50.

Davidson, J., Allen, J. G., & Smith W. H. (1987). Complexities in the hospital treatment of a patient with multiple personality disorder. *Bulletin of the Menninger Clinic, 51,* 561–568.

Davidson, J. R. T., & Foa, E. B. (1991). Diagnostic issues in the posttraumatic stress disorder: Considerations for DSM-IV. *Journal of Abnormal Psychology, 100,* 346–355.

Davis, J. D. (1983). Slaying the psychoanalytic dragon: An integrationist's commentary on Yates. *British Journal of Clinical Psychology, 22,* 133–134.

Davis, J. M. (1985). Suicidal crisis in schools. *School Psychology Review, 14,* 313–324.

Davis, J. M., Klerman, G., & Schildkraut, J. (1967). Drugs used in the treatment of depression. In L. Efron, J. O. Cole, D. Levine, & J. R. Wittenborn (Eds.), *Psychopharmacology: A review of progress.* Washington, DC: U.S. Clearinghouse of Mental Health Information.

Davis, J. M., Schaffer, C. B., Killian, G. A., Kinard, C., & Chan, C. (1980). Important issues in the drug treatment of schizophrenia. In S. J. Keith and L. R. Mosher (Eds.),

Special report: Schizophrenia 1981 (pp. 109–126). Washington, DC: U.S. Government Printing Office.

de Calazaro, D. (1981). *Suicide and self-damaging behavior: A sociobiologic perspective.* New York: Academic Press.

de Gobineau, A. (1915). *The inequality of human races.* New York: Putnam.

De La Fuente, R. (1990). The mental health consequences of the 1985 earthquakes in Mexico. *International Journal of Mental Health, 19,* 21–29.

de Zwann, M., & Mitchell, J. E. (1993). Medical complications of anorexia nervosa and bulimia nervosa. In A. S. Kaplan & P. E. Garfinkel (Eds.), *Medical issues and the eating disorders.* New York: Brunner/Mazel.

Dean, C., & Surtees, P. B. (1989). Do psychological factors predict survival in breast cancer? *Journal of Psychosomatic Research, 33,* 561–569.

Deaux, K. (1984). From individual differences to social categories: Analysis of a decade's research on gender. *American Psychologist, 39,* 105–116.

DeJong, R. N., & Sugar, O. (1972). *The yearbook of neurology and neurosurgery.* Chicago: Year Book Medical Publishers.

Denicola, J., & Sandler, J. (1980). Training abusive parents in child management and self-control skills. *Behavior Therapy, 11,* 263–270.

Denkowski, K. M., & Denkowski, G. C. (1982). Client-counselor confidentiality: An update of rationale, legal status, and implications. *Personnel and Guidance Journal, 60,* 371–375.

Dent, J., & Teasdale, J. D. (1988). Negative cognition and the persistence of depression. *Journal of Abnormal Psychology, 97*(1), 29–34.

DeRuiter, C., Garssen, B., Rijken, H., & Kraaimaat, F. (1989). The hyperventilation syndrome in panic disorder, agoraphobia and generalized anxiety disorder. *Behaviour Research and Therapy, 27,* 447–452.

DeSilva, P. (1988). Phobias and preparedness: Replication and extension. *Behaviour Research and Therapy, 26,* 97–98.

Detels, R., English, P., Visscher, B. R., (1989). Seroconversion, sexual activity, and condom use among 2915 seronegative men followed for up to 2 years. *Journal of AIDS, 2,* 77–83.

Deutsch, A. (1949). *The mentally ill in America* (2nd ed.). New York: Columbia University Press.

DeVellis, B. M., & Blalock, S. J. (1992). Illness attributions and hopelessness depression: The role of hopelessness expectancy. *Journal of Abnormal Psychology, 101*(2), 257–264.

Devinsky, O., & Bear, D. (1984). Varieties of aggressive behavior in temporal lobe epilepsy. *American Journal of Psychiatry, 141,* 651–656.

Dewsbury, D. A. (1991). Psychobiology. *American Psychologist, 46,* 198–205.

Dick-Barnes, M., Nelson, R. O., & Aine, C. J. (1987). Behavioral measure of multiple personality: The case of Margaret. *Journal of Behavior Therapy and Experimental Psychiatry, 18,* 229–239.

Dickey, R., & Steiner, B. (1990). Hormone treatment and surgery. In R. Blanchard & B. W. Steiner (Eds.), *Clinical management of gender identity disorders in children and adults* (pp. 137–158). Washington, DC: American Psychiatric Press.

Diekstra, R. F. (1990). Suicidal behavior in adolescents and young adults: The international picture. *Crisis, 10,* 16–35.

Digman, J. T., Barrera, M., & West, S. G. (1986). Occupational stress, social support, and burnout among correctional officers. *American Journal of Community Psychology, 14,* 177–194.

Dimsdale, J. E., Pierce, C., Shoenfeld, D., Brown, A., Zusman, R., & Graham, R. (1986). Suppressed anger and blood pressure: The effects of race, sex, social class, obesity, and age. *Psychosomatic Medicine, 48,* 430–436.

Divorky, D. (1978, December). Behavior and food coloring: Lessons of a diet fad. *Psychology Today,* pp. 145–148.

Dix, G. E. (1984). Criminal responsibility and mental impairment in American criminal law: Response to the Hinckley acquittal in historical perspective. In D. N. Weissstub (Ed.), *Law and mental health: International perspectives* (pp. 1–44). New York: Pergamon Press.

Dodrill, C. B., & Matthews, C. G. (1992). The role of neuropsychology in the assessment and treatment of persons with epilepsy. *American Psychologist, 47,* 1139–1142.

Dohrenwend, B. P., & Dohrenwend, B. S. (1982). Perspectives on the past and future of psychiatric epidemiology: The 1981 Rema Lapouse Lecture. *American Journal of Public Health, 72,* 1271–1279.

Dohrenwend, B. P., Dohrenwend, B. S., Gould, M. S., Link, B., Neugebauer, R., & Wunsch-Hitzig, R. (1980). *Mental illness in the United States: Epidemiological estimates.* New York: Praeger.

Dohrenwend, B. S., & Dohrenwend, B. P. (1974). An approach to the problem of valid comparison of psychiatric disorders in contrasting class and ethnic groups from the general population. In M. Hammer, K. Salzinger, & S. Sutton (Eds.), *Psychopathology: Contributions from social, behavioral, and biological sciences.* New York: Wiley.

Doll, E. A. (1953). *Measurement of social competence: A manual for the Vineland Social Maturity Scale.* Circle Pines, MN: American Guidance Service.

Dollinger, S. J. (1983). A case of dissociative neurosis (depersonalization disorder) in an adolescent treated with family therapy and behavior modification. *Journal of Consulting and Clinical Psychology, 15,* 479–484.

Donenberg, G., & Baker, B. L. (1993). The impact of young children with externalizing behaviors on their families. *Journal of Abnormal Child Psychology, 21,* 179–198.

Donnerstein, E., Berkowitz, L., & Linz, D. (1986). *Role of aggressive and sexual images in violent pornography.* Unpublished manuscript, University of Wisconsin—Madison.

Donnerstein, E., & Linz, D. (1986). Mass media sexual violence and male viewers. *American Behavioral Scientist, 29,* 601–618.

Dorfman, D. D. (1978). The Cyril Burt question: New findings. *Science, 201,* 1177–1186.

Dorken, H., Stapp, J., & VandenBos, G. (1986). Licensed psychologists: A decade of major growth. In H. Dorken & Associates (Eds.), *Professional psychology in transition: Meeting today's challenge* (pp. 3–19). San Francisco: Jossey-Bass.

Douce, L. A. (1993). AIDS and HIV: Hopes and challenges for the 1990s. *Journal for Counseling and Development, 71,* 259–260.

Draguns, J. G. (1985). Psychological disorders across cultures. In P. Pedersen (Ed.), *Handbook of cross-cultural counseling and therapy.* Westport, CT: Greenwood Press.

Drake, R. E., & Ehrlich, J. (1985). Suicide attempts associated with akathisia. *American Journal of Psychiatry, 142,* 499–501.

Dressler, W. W., Dos Santos, J. E., & Viteri, F. E. (1986). Blood pressure, ethnicity, and psychosocial resources. *Psychosomatic Medicine, 48,* 509–519.

Drewnowski, A., Yee, D. K., & Krahn, D. D. (1988). Bulimia in college women: Incidence and recovery rates. *American Journal of Psychiatry, 145,* 753–755.

Drummond, L. M., & Matthews, H. P. (1988). Obsessive-compulsive disorder occurring as a complication in benzodiazepine withdrawal. *Journal of Nervous and Mental Disease, 176,* 688–691.

Dryden, W. (1989). Albert Ellis: An efficient and passionate life (an interview with Albert Ellis). *Journal of Counseling and Development, 67,* 539–546.

Dublin, L. I. (1963). *Suicide: A sociological and statistical study.* New York: Ronald Press.

Dubovsky, S., Franks, R., Lifschitz, M., & Coen, R. (1982). Effectiveness of verapamil in the treatment of a manic patient. *American Journal of Psychiatry, 139,* 502–504.

Dubow, E. F., Huesmann, L. R., & Eron, L. D. (1987). Mitigating aggression and promoting prosocial behav-ior in aggressive elementary school boys. *Behavior Research and Therapy, 25,* 527–531.

Duckett, S. (1991). The normal aging human brain. In S. Duckett (Ed.), *The pathology of the aging human nervous system* (pp. 1–19). Philadelphia: Lea & Febiger.

DuPaul, G. J., & Barkley, R. A. (1993). Behavioral contributions to pharmacotherapy: The utility of behavioral methodology in medication treatment of children with attention deficit hyperactivity disorder. *Behavior Therapy, 24,* 47–65.

Durand, V. M., & Crimmins, D. B. (1987). Assessment and treatment of psychotic speech in an autistic child. *Journal of Autism and Developmental Disorders, 17,* 17–28.

Durkheim, E. (1951). *Suicide.* New York: Free Press. (Originally published 1897.)

Durlak, J. A. (1979). Comparative effectiveness of paraprofessional and professional helpers. *Psychological Bulletin, 86,* 80–92.

Dutton, J. (1986, September 30). Doctors seek reason for bizarre syndrome. *Bellingham Herald,* p. C1.

Du Verglas, G., Banks, S. R., & Guyer, K. E. (1988). Clinical effects of fenfluramine on children with autism: A review of the research. *Journal of Autism and Developmental Disorders, 18,* 297–308.

Dworkin, S. H., & Pincu, L. (1993). Counseling in the era of AIDS. *Journal of Counseling and Development, 71,* 275–281.

Dykens, E., Volkmar, F., & Glick, M. (1991). Thought disorder in high-functioning autistic adults. *Journal of Autism and Developmental Disorders, 21,* 291–301.

Dykens, E. M., & Gerrard, M. (1986). Psychological profiles of purging bulimics, repeat dieters, and controls. *Journal of Consulting and Clinical Psychology, 54,* 283–288.

Eagly, A. H. (1983). Gender and social influence: A social psychological analysis. *American Psychologist, 38,* 971–981.

Eaton, W. W., Holzer, C. E. III, Von Korff, M., Anthony, J. C., Helzer, J. E., George, L., Brunam, A., Boyd, J. H., Kessler, L. G., & Locker, B. Z. (1984). The design of the Epidemiologic Catchment Area surveys. *Archives of General Psychiatry, 41,* 942–948.

Edelson, J. L., Miller, D. M., Stone, G. W., & Chappan, D. G. (1985). Group treatment for men who batter. *Social Work Research and Abstracts, 21,* 18–21.

Edman, G., Asberg, M., Levander, S., & Schalling, D. (1986). Skin conductance habituation and cerebrospinal fluid 5-hydroxyindoleactic acid in suicidal patients. *Archives of General Psychiatry, 43,* 586–592.

Edwards, M. S., & Baker, C. J. (1981). Meningitis infections in children. *Journal of Pediatrics, 99,* 540–545.

Edwards, S., & Kickerson, M. (1987). On the similarity of positive and negative intrusions. *Behaviour Research and Therapy, 25,* 207–211.

Efron, R. (1956). The effect of olfactory stimuli in arresting uncinate fits. *Brain, 79,* 267–281.

Efron, R. (1957). The conditioned inhibitions of uncinate fits. *Brain, 80,* 251–262.

Egbert, L., Battit, G., Welch, C., & Bartlett, M. (1964). Reduction of postoperative pain. *New England Journal of Medicine, 270,* 835–837.

Egeland, J. A., Berhard, D. S., Pauls, D. L., Sussex, J. N., Kidd, K. K., Allen, C. R., Hostetter, A. M., & Housman, D. E. (1987). Bipolar affective disorders linked to DNA markers on chromosome 11. *Nature, 325,* 783–787.

Egeland, J. A., & Hostetter, A. M. (1983). Amish study, I: Affective disorders among the Amish. *American Journal of Psychiatry, 140,* 56–61.

Ehlers, A., Margraf, J., Roth, W. T., Taylor, C. G., & Birbaumer, N. (1988). Anxiety induced by false heart rate feedback in patients with panic disorder. *Behaviour Research and Therapy, 26,* 1–11.

Eichenbaum, L., & Orbach, S. (1983). *Understanding women: A feminist psychoanalytic approach.* New York: Basic Books.

Eisenberg, M. M. (1978). *Ulcers.* New York: Random House.

Eisman, C. (1988). *California self-helper.* Los Angeles: California Self-Help Center.

Ekblad, S. (1990). The children's behaviour questionnaire for completion by parents and teachers in a Chinese sample. *Journal of Child Psychology and Psychiatry, 31,* 775–791.

Elias, M. (1988, August 15). Many lie about AIDS risk. *USA Today,* p. D-1.

Ellenberger, H. F. (1972). The story of "Anna O.": A critical review with new data. *Journal of the History of the Behavior Sciences, 8,* 267–279.

Ellickson, P. L., Hays, R. D., & Bell, R. M. (1992). Stepping through the drug use sequence: Longitudinal scalogram analysis of initiation and regular use. *Journal of Abnormal Psychology, 101,* 441–451.

Ellingson, R. (1954). Incidence of EEG abnormality among patients with mental disorders of apparently nonorganic origin: A critical review. *American Journal of Psychiatry, 111,* 363–375.

Elliott, C. H., & Jay, S. M. (1987). Chronic pain in children. *Behaviour Research and Therapy, 25,* 263–271.

Ellis, A. (1962). *Reason and emotion in psychotherapy.* New York: Stuart.

Ellis, A. (1971). *Growth through reason.* Palo Alto, CA: Science and Behavior Books.

Ellis, A. (1973). Are cognitive behavior therapy and rational therapy synonymous? *Rational Living, 8,* 8–11.

Ellis, A. (1979). Rational-emotive therapy: Research data that support the clinical and personality hypotheses of RET and other modes of cognitive-behavior therapy. In A. Ellis & J. M. Whiteley (Eds.), *Theoretical and empirical foundations of rational-emotive therapy* (pp. 101–173). Monterey, CA: Brooks/Cole.

Ellis, A. (1984). Rational-emotive therapy. In R. J. Corsini (Ed.), *Current psychotherapies.* Itasca, IL: Peacock.

Ellis, A. (1987). A sadly neglected cognitive element in depression. *Cognitive Therapy and Research, 11,* 121–146.

Ellis, A. (1989). Rational-emotive therapy. In R. J. Corsini & D. Wedding (Eds.), *Current psychotherapies* (pp. 197–238). Itasca, IL: Peacock.

Ellis, A. (1991). Rational-emotive treatment of simple phobias. *Psychotherapy, 28,* 452–456.

Ellis, L. (1991). A synthesized (biosocial) theory of rape. *Journal of Consulting and Clinical Psychology, 59,* 631–642.

Ellis, L., & Ames, M. A. (1987). Neurohormonal functioning and sexual orientation: A theory of homosexuality-heterosexuality. *Psychological Bulletin, 101,* 233–258.

Ely, D. L., & Mostardi, R. A. (1986). The effects of recent life events stress, life assets, and temperament pattern on cardiovascular risk factors for Akron city police officers. *Journal of Human Stress, 12,* 77–91.

Embry, C. (1990). Psychotherapeutic interventions in chronic posttraumatic stress disorder. In M. E. Wolf & A. D. Mosmain (Eds.), *Post traumatic stress disorder: Etiology, phenomenology and treatment.* Washington, DC: American Psychiatric Press.

Emmelkamp, P. M. G., and Beens, H. (1991). Cognitive therapy with obsessive-compulsive disorder: A comparative evaluation. *Behaviour Research and Therapy, 29,* 293–300.

Emmelkamp, P. M. G., & Wessels, H. (1975). Flooding in imagination vs. flooding in vivo: A comparison with agoraphobics. *Behavior Research & Therapy, 13,* 7–15.

Emslie, G. J., & Rosenfeld, A. (1983). Incest reported by children and adolescents hospitalized for severe psychiatric problems. *American Journal of Psychiatry, 140,* 108–111.

Endler, N. (1982). *Holiday of darkness.* New York: Wiley.

Endler, N. (1990). *Holiday of darkness: A psychologist's journey out of his depression* (rev. ed.). Toronto: Wall & Thompson.

Engel, G. (1971). Sudden and rapid death during psychological stress. *Annals of Internal Medicine, 74,* 771.

English, H. B. (1929). Three cases of the conditioned fear response. *Journal of Abnormal and Social Psychology, 24,* 221–225.

Ennis, B., & Emery, R. (1978). *The rights of mental patients: An American Civil Liberties Union Handbook.* New York: Avon.

Enright, M. F., Welch, B. L., Newman, R., & Perry, B. M. (1990). The hospital: Psychology's challenge in the 1990s. *American Psychologist, 45,* 1057–1058.

Erickson, W. D., Walbek, N. H., & Seely, R. K. (1988). Behavior patterns of child molesters. *Archives of Sexual Behavior, 17,* 77–86.

Erickson, W. D., Luxenberg, M. G., Walbek, N. H., & Seely, R. K. (1987). Frequency of MMPI two-point code types among sex offenders. *Journal of Consulting and Clinical Psychology, 55,* 566–570.

Ericksson, A. S., & Chateau, P. (1992). Brief report: A girl aged two years and seven months with autistic disorder videotaped from birth. *Journal of Autism and Developmental Disorders, 22,* 127–129.

Erikson, E. H. (1968). *Identity: Youth and crisis.* New York: Norton.

Eron, L. D., Lefkowitz, M. M., Huesmann, L. R., & Walder, L. O. (1972). Does television violence cause aggression? *American Psychologist, 27,* 253–263.

Erwin, E. (1986). Establishing causal connections: Meta-analysis and psychotherapy. *Midwest Studies in Philosophy, 9,* 421–436.

Esser, G., Schmidt, M. H., & Woerner, W. (1990). Epidemiology and course of psychiatric disorders in school-age children: Results of a longitudinal study. *Journal of Child Psychology and Psychiatry, 31,* 243–263.

Eth, S., & Pynoos, R. S. (1985). Developmental perspective on psychic trauma in childhood. In C. R. Figley (Ed.), *Trauma and its wake* (pp. 36–52). New York: Brunner/Mazel.

European Study Group on Heterosexual Transmission of HIV. (1992). Comparison of female to male and male to female transmission of HIV in 563 stable couples. *British Medical Journal, 304,* 809–813.

Evans, F. J. (1990). Will the real pain say, "yes." *American Journal of Clinical Hypnosis, 33,* 12–13.

Everstine, D. S., & Everstine, L. (1983). *People in crisis: Strategic therapeutic interventions.* New York: Brunner/Mazel.

Exner, J. E. (1983). Rorschach assessment. In I. B. Weiner (Ed.), *Clinical methods in psychology.* New York: Wiley.

Exner, J. E. (1990). *A Rorschach workbook for the Comprehensive System* (2nd ed.). Asheville, NC: Rorschach Workshops.

Eysenck, H. J. (1952). The effects of psychotherapy: An evaluation. *Journal of Consulting Psychology, 16,* 319–324.

Eysenck, H. J., & Rachman, S. (1965). *The causes and cures of neurosis.* San Diego: Knapp.

Fagan, J., & McMahon, P. P. (1984). Incipient multiple personality in children: Four cases. *Journal of Nervous and Mental Disease, 172,* 26–36.

Fahy, T. A., Abas, M., & Brown, J. C. (1989). Multiple personality: A symptom of psychiatric disorder. *British Journal of Psychiatry, 154,* 99–101.

Fairburn, C. G., Jones, R., Peveler, R. C., Carr, S. J., Solomon, R. A., O'Connor, M. E., Burton, J., & Hope, R. A. (1991). Three psychological treatments for bulimia nervosa: A comparative trial. *Archives of General Psychiatry, 48,* 463–469.

Fairweather, G. W., Sanders, D. H., Cressler, D. L., & Maynard, H. (1969). *Community life for the mentally ill: An alternative to institutional care.* Chicago: Aldine.

Fallon, A. E., & Rozin, P. (1985). Sex differences in perceptions of desirable body shape. *Journal of Abnormal Psychology, 94,* 102–105.

Falloon, I. R. H. (1992). Early intervention for first episodes of schizophrenia: A preliminary exploration. *Psychiatry, 55,* 4–15.

Falloon, I. R. J., Boyd, J. L., & McGill, C. W. (1984). *Family care of schizophrenia.* New York: Guilford Press.

Farberow, N. L. (1970). Ten years of suicide prevention—past and future. *Bulletin of Suicidology, 6,* 5–11.

Farberow, N. L., & Shneidman, E. S. (Eds.). (1961). *The cry for help.* New York: McGraw-Hill.

Farberow, N. L., & Simon, M. D. (1975). Suicide in Los Angeles and Vienna. In N. L. Farberow (Ed.), *Suicide in different cultures* (pp. 185–204). Baltimore: University Park Press.

Farley, F. (1986). World of the type T personality. *Psychology Today, 20,* 45–52.

Farmer, R., and Nelson-Gray, R. O. (1990). Personality disorders and depression: A review of the research. *Clinical Psychology Review, 100,* 453–476.

Farrell, A. D., Stiles-Camplair, P., & McCullough, L. (1987). Identification of target complaints by computer interview: Evaluation of the computerized assessment system for psychotherapy evaluation research. *Journal of Consulting and Clinical Psychology, 55,* 691–700.

Fedora, O., Reddon, J. R., & Yeudall, L. T. (1986). Stimuli eliciting sexual arousal in genital exhibitionists as possible clinical application. *Archives of Sexual Behavior, 15,* 417–427.

Feinberg, S. S., Kay, S. R., Elijovich, L. R., Fiszbein, A., & Opler, L. A. (1988). Pimozide treatment of the negative schizophrenic syndrome: An open trial. *Journal of Clinical Psychiatry, 49,* 235–238.

Feingold, B. F. (1977). Behavioral disturbances linked to the ingestion of food additives. *Delaware Medical Journal, 49,* 89–94.

Feldman-Summers, S., Gordon, P. E., & Meagher, J. R. (1979). The impact of rape on sexual satisfaction. *Journal of Abnormal Psychology, 88,* 101–105.

Felner, R. D., Jason, L. A., Moritsugu, J., & Farber, S. S.

(1983). Preventive psychology: Evolution and current status. In R. D. Felner & L. A. Jason (Eds.), *Preventive psychology: Theory, research and practice.* New York: Pergamon Press.

Fenichel, O. (1945). *The psychoanalytic theory of neuroses.* New York: Norton.

Fenton, W. S., & McGlashan, T. H. (1987). Sustained remission in drug-free schizophrenic patients. *American Journal of Psychiatry, 144,* 1306–1309.

Ferrari, C. (1993, January). Are you burying your past? *Redbook,* p. 86.

Fersch, E. A. Jr. (1980). *Psychology and psychiatry in courts and corrections.* New York: Wiley.

Ferster, C. B. (1961). Positive reinforcement and behavior deficits of autistic children. *Child Development, 32,* 437–456.

Ferster, C. B. (1965). Classification of behavior pathology. In L. Krasner & L. P. Ullmann (Eds.), *Research in behavior modification.* New York: Holt, Rinehart & Winston.

Fieve, R., Dunner, D., Kumbaraci, et al. (1976). Lithium carbonate prophylaxis in three subtypes of primary affective disorder. *Pharmakopsychiatri Neuropsychopharmakol, 9,* 100–107.

Figley, C. R. (Ed.). (1985). *Trauma and its wake* (pp. 53–69). New York: Brunner/Mazel.

Fink, M. (1979). *Convulsive therapy: Theory and practice.* New York: Raven Press.

Fink, M. (1982). ECT in anxiety: An appraisal. *American Journal of Psychotherapy, 36,* 371–378.

Finkelhor, D. (1980). Sex among siblings: A survey on prevalence, variety, and effects. *Archives of Sexual Behavior, 9,* 171–194.

Finkelhor, D., & Araji, S. (1986). Explanations of pedophilia: A four-factor model. *Journal of Sex Research, 22,* 145–161.

Fischer, D. G., & Elnitsky, S. (1990). A factor analytic study of two scales measuring dissociation. *American Journal of Clinical Hypnosis, 32,* 201–207.

Fischer, M., & Newby, R. F. (1991). Assessment of stimulant response in ADHD children using a refined multimethod clinical protocol. *Journal of Clinical Child Psychology, 20,* 232–244.

Fischer, P. J., & Breakey, W. R. (1991). The epidemiology of alcohol, drug, and mental disorders among homeless persons. *American Psychologist, 46,* 1115–1128.

Fisher, J. E., & Carstensen, L. L. (1990). Behavior management of the dementias. *Clinical Psychology Review, 10,* 611–629.

Fisher, W. A. (1990). Understanding and preventing teenage pregnancy and sexually transmitted disease/AIDS. In J. Edwards, R. S. Tindale, L. Heath, & E. J. Posavac (Eds.), *Social influence processes and prevention* (pp. 71–102). New York: Plenum.

Fishman, A. (1982). *Arteriosclerosis 1981.* Washington, DC: U.S. Department of Health and Human Services.

Fishman, S. M., & Sheehan, D. V. (1985). Anxiety and panic: Their cause and treatment. *Psychology Today, 19,* 26–32.

Fitts, S. N., Gibson, P., Redding, C. A., & Deiter, P. J. (1989). Body dysmorphic disorder: Implications for its validity as a DSM-III-R clinical syndrome. *Psychological Reports, 64,* 655–658.

Fleer, J., & Pasewark, R. A. (1982). Prior public health agency contacts of individuals committing suicide. *Psychological Reports, 50,* 1319–1324.

Fleming, I., Baum, A., Davidson, L. M., Rectanus, E., & McArdle, S. (1987). Chronic stress as a factor in physiologic reactivity to challenge. *Health Psychology, 6,* 221–237.

Fleming, M. Z., MacGowan, B. R., Robinson, L., Spitz, J., & Salt, P. (1982). The body image of the post-operative female-to-male transsexual. *Journal of Consulting and Clinical Psychology, 50,* 461–462.

Florin, P., & Wandersman, A. (1990). An introduction to citizen participation, voluntary organizations, and community development: Insights for empowerment through research. *American Journal of Community Psychology, 18,* 41–54.

Flynn, M. C., & Saleem, J. K. (1986). Adults who are mentally handicapped and living with their parents: Satisfaction and perceptions regarding their lives and circumstances. *Journal of Mental Deficiency, 30,* 379–387.

Foa, E., Steketee, G., Turner, R., & Fischer, S. (1980). Effects of imaginal exposure to feared disasters in obsessive compulsive checkers. *Behaviour Research and Therapy, 18,* 449–455.

Foa, E., & Tillmanns, A. (1980). The treatment of obsessive-compulsive neurosis. In A. Goldstein & E. Foa (Eds.), *Handbook of behavioral interventions.* New York: Wiley.

Foa, E. B., & Kozak, M. J. (1986). Emotional processing of fear: Exposure to corrective information. *Psychological Bulletin, 99,* 20–35.

Foa, E. B., Rothbaum, B. O., Riggs, D. S., & Murdock, T. B. (1991). Treatment of posttraumatic stress disorder in rape victims: A comparison between cognitive-behavioral procedures and counseling. *Journal of Consulting and Clinical Psychology, 59,* 715–723.

Foley, V. (1989). Family therapy. In R. J. Corsini & D. Wedding (Eds.), *Current psychotherapies* (pp. 455–500). Itasca, IL: Peacock.

Folstein, S., & Rutter, M. (1977). Infantile autism: A genetic study of 21 twin pairs. *Journal of Child Psychology, 18,* 297–321.

Folstein, S., & Rutter, M. (1988). Autism: Familial aggregation and genetic implications. *Journal of Autism and Developmental Disorders, 18,* 3–30.

Food and Drug Administration. (1991, October 18). *Talk Paper: Antidepressants Update*. Rockville, MD: United States Department of Health and Human Services.

Fordyce, W. E. (1982). A behavioral perspective on chronic pain. *British Journal of Clinical Psychiatry, 21*, 313–320.

Fordyce, W. E. (1988). Pain and suffering: A reappraisal. *American Psychologist, 43*, 276–283.

Forehand, R., & Wierson, M. (1993). The role of developmental factors in planning behavioral interventions for children: Disruptive behavior as an example. *Behavior Therapy, 24*, 117–141.

Forehand, R., Wierson, M., Frame, C., Kempton, T., & Armistead, L. (1991). Juvenile delinquency entry and persistence: Do attention problems contribute to conduct problems? *Journal of Behavior Therapy and Experimental Psychiatry, 22*, 261–264.

Foreyt, J. P. (1987). Behavioral medicine. In G. T. Wilson, C. M. Franks, P. C. Kendall, & J. P. Foreyt (Eds.), *Review of behavior therapy: Theory and practice* (Vol. 2) (pp. 154–176). New York: Guilford Press.

Forgac, G. E., Cassel, C. A., & Michaels, E. J. (1984). Chronicity of criminal behavior and psychopathology in male exhibitionists. *Journal of Clinical Psychology, 40*, 827–832.

Forgac, G. E., & Michaels, E. J. (1982). Personality characteristics of two types of male exhibitionism. *Journal of Abnormal Psychology, 91*, 287–293.

Forgays, D. K., & Forgays, D. G. (1991). Type A behavior within families: Parents and older adolescent children. *Journal of Behavioral Medicine, 14*, 325–339.

Fowles, D. C. (1984). Biological variables in psychopathology. In H. E. Adams & P. B. Sutker (Eds.), *Comprehensive handbook of psychopathology* (pp. 77–110). New York: Plenum Press.

Foxx, R. M., & Faw, G. D. (1992). An eight-year follow-up of three social skills training studies. *Mental Retardation, 30*, 63–66.

Frances, A. J., First, M. B., Widiger, T. A., Miele, G. M., Tilly, S. M., Davis, W. W., & Pincus, H. A. (1991). An A to Z guide to DSM-IV conundrums. *Journal of Abnormal Psychology, 100*, 407–412.

Francis, G., Last, C. G., Strauss, C. C. (1987). Expression of separation anxiety disorder: The roles of age and gender. *Child Psychiatry and Human Development, 18*, 82–89.

Franklin, D. (1987). The politics of masochism. *Psychology Today, 21*, 51–57.

Franklin, J. A. (1987). The changing nature of agoraphobic fears. *British Journal of Clinical Psychology, 26*, 127–133.

Franks, C., Fried, R., & Ashem, B. (1966). An improved apparatus for the aversive conditioning of cigarette smokers. *Behaviour Research and Therapy, 4*, 301–308.

Free, M. L., & Oei, T. P. S. (1989). Biological and psychological processes in the treatment and maintenance of depression. *Clinical Psychology Review, 9*, 653–688.

Freedman, D. X. (1984). Psychiatric epidemiology counts. *Archives of General Psychiatry, 41*, 931–933.

Freeman, S. J. (1991). Group facilitation of the grieving process with those bereaved by suicide. *Journal of Counseling and Development, 69*, 328–331.

Freeston, M. H., & Ladouceur, R. (1993). Appraisal of cognitive intrusions and response style: Replication and extension. *Behaviour Research and Therapy, 31*, 185–191.

Freeston, M. H., Ladouceur, R., Thibodeau, N., & Gagnon, F. (1991). Cognitive intrusions in a non-clinical population: Response style, subjective experience, and appraisal. *Behaviour Research and Therapy, 29*, 585–597.

Freiberg, P. (1991). Suicide in family, friends is familiar to too many teens. *APA Monitor. 22*, 36–37.

Fremon, C. (1991, January 27). Love and death. *Los Angeles Times Magazine*, pp. 17–35.

French, O. (1987). Letters to the editor. *American Journal of Psychiatry, 144*, 123–124.

Freud, S. (1924). Mourning and melancholia. In J. Riviere (Trans.), *Collected papers* (Vol. 4). London: Hogarth Press. (Original work published 1917.)

Freud, S. (1938). The psychopathology of everyday life. In A. B. Brill (Ed.), *The basic writings of Sigmund Freud*. New York: Modern Library.

Freud, S. (1949). *An outline of psychoanalysis*. New York: Norton.

Freud, S. (1959). *Beyond the pleasure principle*. New York: Bantam.

Frick, P. J., & Lahey, B. B. (1991). Nature and characteristics of attention-deficit hyperactivity disorder. *School Psychology Review, 20*, 163–173.

Friedman, A. P. (1979). Characteristics of tension headache: Profile of 1,420 cases. *Psychosomatics, 20*, 451–461.

Friedman, H. S., & Booth-Kewley, S. (1988). The "disease prone" personality: A meta-analytic view of the construct. *American Psychologist, 42*, 539–555.

Friedman, M. (1984). *Treating Type A Behavior and your heart*. New York: Knopf.

Friedman, M., & Rosenman, R. H. (1974). *Type A Behavior*. New York: Knopf.

Friedrich, J. (1985, January 7). Seven who have succeeded. *Time*, pp. 41–45.

Frischholz, E. J., Braun, B. G., Lipman, L. S., & Sachs, R. (1992). Suggested posthypnotic amnesia in psychiatric patients and normals. *American Journal of Clinical Hypnosis, 35*, 29–39.

Frith, U. (1991). *Autism and Asperger syndrome*. Cambridge: Cambridge University Press.

Fritz, G. K., Rubenstein, S., & Lewiston, N. J. (1987).

Psychological factors in fatal childhood asthma. *American Journal of Orthopsychiatry, 57,* 253–257.

Fromm, E. (1941). *Escape from freedom.* New York: Holt, Rinehart & Winston.

Frost, R. O., & Sher, K. J. (1989). Checking behavior in a threatening situation. *Behaviour Research and Therapy, 27,* 385–389.

Fulero, S. M. (1988). Tarasoff: 10 years later. *Professional Psychology: Research and Practice, 19,* 184–190.

Funk, S. C. (1992). Hardiness: A review of theory and research. *Health Psychology, 11,* 335–345.

Furlong, F. W. (1991). Credibility of patients in psychiatric research. *American Journal of Psychiatry, 148,* 1423.

Fyer, A. J., Liebowitz, M. R., Gorman, J. M., Campeas, R., Levin, A., Davies, S. O., Goetz, D., & Klein, D. (1987). Discontinuation of Alprazolam treatment in panic patients. *American Journal of Psychiatry, 144,* 303–308.

Gadow, K. D. (1986). *Children on medication* (Vol. 1). San Diego: College-Hill Press.

Gadow, K. D. (1991). Clinical issues in child and adolescent psychopharmacology. *Journal of Consulting and Clinical Psychology, 59,* 842–852.

Gallagher, D., & Frankel, A. S. (1980). Depression in (an) older adult(s): A moderate structuralist viewpoint. *Psychotherapy: Theory, Research, and Practice, 17,* 101–104.

Gallahorn, G. E. (1981). Borderline personality disorders. In J. R. Lion (Ed.), *Personality disorders: Diagnosis and management.* Baltimore: Williams & Wilkins.

Galton, F. (1869). *Hereditary genius: An inquiry into its laws and consequences.* London: Macmillan.

Gamble, E., & Elder, S. (1983). Multimodal biofeedback in the treatment of migraine. *Biofeedback and Self-Regulation, 8,* 383–392.

Ganellen, R. J. (1988). Specificity of attributions and over-generalization in depression and anxiety. *Journal of Abnormal Psychology, 97,* 83–86.

Gangadhar, B., Kapur, R., & Kalyanasundaram, S. (1982). Comparison of electroconvulsive therapy with imipramine in endogenous depression: A double blind study. *British Journal of Psychiatry, 141,* 367–371.

Gannon, L. R., Haynes, S. N., Cuevas, V., & Chavez, R. (1987). Psychophysical correlates of induced headaches. *Journal of Behavioral Medicine, 10,* 411–423.

Garakani, H., Zitrin, C. M., & Klein, D. F. (1984). Treatment of panic disorder with imipramine alone. *American Journal of Psychiatry, 141,* 446–448.

Garbarino, J. (1980). Preventing child maltreatment. In R. H. Price, R. F. Ketterer, B. C. Bader, & J. Monahan (Eds.), *Prevention in mental health: Research, policy, and practice.* Beverly Hills, CA: Sage.

Garber, H. J., Ananth, J. V., Chiu, L. C., Griswold, V. J., &

Oldendorf, W. H. (1989). Nuclear magnetic resonance study of obsessive-compulsive disorder. *American Journal of Psychiatry, 146,* 1001–1005.

Garber, H. J., & Ritvo, E. R. (1992). Magnetic resonance imaging of the posterior fossa in autistic adults. *American Journal of Psychiatry, 149,* 245–247.

Garcia, J. (1981). The logic and limits of mental aptitude testing. *American Psychologist, 36,* 1172–1180.

Garcia, J., McGowan, B. K., & Green, K. F. (1972) Biological constraints on conditioning. In A. H. Black & W. F. Prokasy (Eds.), *Classical conditioning II: Current research and theory.* New York: Appleton-Century-Crofts.

Garety, P. (1991). Reasoning and delusions. *British Journal of Psychiatry, 159,* 14–18.

Garfield, S. L., & Kurtz, R. (1977). A study of eclectic views. *Journal of Consulting and Clinical Psychology, 45,* 78–83.

Garfield, S. L., & Kurtz, R. (1976). Clinical psychologists in the 1970s. *American Psychologist, 31,* 1–9.

Garfinkel, B., Froese, M., & Hood, J. (1982). Suicide attempts in children and adolescents. *American Journal of Psychiatry, 139,* 1257–1261.

Garfinkel, B. D., & Golumbek, H. (1983). Suicidal behavior in adolescence. In H. Golumbek & B. D. Garfinkel (Eds.), *The adolescent and mood disturbance.* New York: International Universities Press.

Garland, A. F., & Zigler, E. (1993). Adolescent suicide prevention: Current research and social policy implications. *American Psychologist, 48,* 169–182.

Garmezy, N. (1987). Stress, competence, and development: Continuities in the study of schizophrenic adults, children vulnerable to psychopathology, and the search for stress-resistant children. *American Journal of Orthopsychiatry, 57,* 159–173.

Garner, D. M., Olmstead, M. P., Polivy, J., & Garfinkel, P. E. (1984). Comparison between weight-preoccupied women and anorexia nervosa. *Psychosomatic Medicine, 46,* 255–266.

Gartner, A. F., & Gartner, J. (1988). Borderline pathology in post-incest female adolescents. *Bulletin of the Menninger Clinic, 52,* 101–113.

Gatz, M. (1990). Interpreting behavioral genetic results: Suggestions for counselors and clients. *Journal of Counseling and Development, 68,* 601–605.

Gatz, M., Barbarin, O. A., Tyler, F. B., Mitchell, R. E., Moran, J. A., Wirzbicki, P. J., Crawford, J., & Engelman, A. (1982). Enhancement of individual and community competence: The older adult as community worker. *American Journal of Community Psychology, 10,* 291–304.

Gatz, M., Smyer, M. A., & Lawton, M. P. (1980). The mental health system and the older adult. In L. W. Poon (Ed.), *Aging in the 1980s.* Washington, DC: American Psychological Association.

Gawin, F. H. (1991). Cocaine addiction: Psychology and neurophysiology. *Science, 251,* 1580–1586.

Gaynor, J., & Hatcher, C. (1987). *The psychology of child firesetting.* New York: Brunner/Mazel.

Gelard, M. S., & Sanford, E. E. (1987). Child abuse and neglect: A review of the literature. *School Psychology Review, 16,* 137–155.

Gelernter, C. S., Uhde, T. W., Cimbolic, P., Arnkoff, D. B., Vittone, B. J., Tancer, M. E., & Bartko, J. J. (1991). Cognitive-behavioral and pharmacological treatments of social phobia. *Archives of General Psychiatry, 48,* 938–945.

Geller, E. S. (1990). Preventing injuries and deaths from vehicle crashes: Encouraging belts and discouraging booze. In J. Edwards, R. S. Tindale, L. Heath, & E. J. Posavac (Eds.), *Social influence processes and prevention* (pp. 249–278). New York: Plenum.

Genest, M., Bowen, R. C., Dudley, J., & Keegan, D. (1990). Assessment of strategies for coping with anxiety: Preliminary investigations. *Journal of Anxiety Disorders, 4,* 1–14.

Gentry, W. D. (Ed.). (1984). *Handbook of behavioral medicine.* New York: Guilford Press.

George, D. T., Ladenheim, J. A., & Nutt, D. J. (1987). Effect of pregnancy on panic attacks. *American Journal of Psychiatry, 144,* 1078–1079.

George, M. S., & Ballenger, J. C. (1992). The neuroanatomy of panic disorder: The emerging role of the right parahippocampal region. *Journal of Anxiety Disorder, 6,* 181–188.

George, M. S., Trimble, M. R., Ring, H. A., Sallee, F. R., & Robertson, M. M. (1993). Obsessions in obsessive-compulsive disorder with and without Gilles de la Tourette's syndrome. *American Journal of Psychiatry, 150,* 93–97.

Georgotas, A. (1985). Affective disorders: Pharmacotherapy. In H. I. Kaplan & B. J. Sadock (Eds.), *Comprehensive textbook of psychiatry* (4th ed., pp. 821–833). Baltimore: Williams & Wilkins.

Gerin, W., Pieper, C., Levy, R., & Pickering, T. G. (1992). Social support in social interaction: A moderator of cardiovascular reactivity. *Psychosomatic Medicine, 54,* 324–336.

Geronimus, A. T. (1991). Differences in hypertension prevalence among U.S. Black and White women of childbearing age. *Public Health Reports, 106,* 393–399.

Gershon, E. S., Berrettini, W. H., Nurnberger, J. I. Jr., & Goldin, L. R. (1989). Genetic studies of affective illness. In J. J. Mann (Ed.), *Models of depressive disorders: Psychological, biological, and genetic perspectives* (pp. 109–142). New York: Plenum.

Geyer, S. (1992). Artifacts in "limited prospective" designs? Testing confonding effects on responsive behaviour of women prior to breast surgery. *Journal of Psychosomatic Research, 36,* 107–116.

Ghaziuddin, M., Tsai, L., Eilers, L., & Ghaziuddin, N. (1992). Brief report: Autism and herpes simplex encephalitis. *Journal of Autism and Developmental Disorders, 22,* 107–113.

Ghaziuddin, M., Tsai, L., & Ghaziuddin, N. (1991). Brief report: Violence in Asperger syndrome, a critique. *Journal of Autism and Developmental Disorders, 21,* 349–354.

Ghosh, A., & Marks, I. M. (1987). Self-treatment of agoraphobia by exposure. *Behavior Therapy, 18,* 3–16.

Gilbert, B., & Cunningham, J. (1986). Women's post-rape sexual functioning: Review and implications for counseling. *Journal of Counseling and Development, 65,* 71–73.

Gillberg, C. (1988). The neurobiology of infantile autism. *Journal of Child Psychology and Psychiatry, 29,* 257–266.

Gillberg, C. (1992). Autism and autistic-like conditions: Subclasses among disorders of empathy. *Journal of Child Psychology and Psychiatry, 33,* 813–842.

Gillberg, I. C., & Gillberg, C. (1989). Asperger syndrome—some epidemiological considerations: A research note. *Journal of Child Psychology and Psychiatry, 30,* 631–638.

Gillberg, I. C., Gillberg, C., & Kapp, S. (1992). Hypothyroidism and autism spectrum disorders. *Journal of Child Psychology and Psychiatry, 33,* 531–542.

Gillie, D. (1977). The IQ issue. *Phi Delta Kappan, 58,* 469.

Gilligan, C. (1982). *In a different voice: Psychological theory and women's development.* Cambridge, MA: Harvard University Press.

Gillis, J. J., Gilger, J. W., Pennington, B. F., & DeFries, J. C. (1992). Attention deficit in reading-disabled twins: Evidence for a genetic etiology. *Journal of Abnormal Child Psychology, 20,* 303–315.

Girard, F. (1984, August 5). State crime data called flawed, late. *Detroit News,* pp. 1, 12.

Glaser, G. H., Newman, R. J., & Schafer, R. (1963). Interictal psychosis in psychomotor-temporal lobe epilepsy: An EEG psychological study. In G. H. Glaser (Ed.), *EEG and behavior.* New York: Basic Books.

Glassman, J. N. S., Magulac, M., & Darko, D. F. (1987). Folie a famille: Shared paranoid disorder in a Vietnam veteran and his family. *American Journal of Psychiatry, 144,* 658–660.

Glavin, D. K., Franklin, J., & Francis, R. J. (1990). Substance abuse and suicidal behavior. In S. Blumenthal & D. Kupfer (Eds.), *Suicide over the life cycle: Risk factors, assessment, and treatment of suicidal patients* (pp. 177–204). Washington, DC: American Psychiatric Press.

Glazer, W. M., Morgenstern, H., & Doucette, J. T. (1991). The prediction of chronic persistent versus intermittent tardive dyskinesia. *British Journal of Psychiatry, 158,* 822–828.

Glidewell, J. C. (1983). Prevention: The threat and the promise. In R. D. Felner, L. A. Jason, J. Moritsugu, & S. S. Farber (Eds.), *Preventive psychology: Theory, research, and practice.* New York: Pergamon Press.

Goff, D. C., Brotman, A. W., Kindlon, D., Waites, M., & Amico, E. (1991). The delusion of possession in chronically psychotic patients. *Journal of Nervous and Mental Disease, 179,* 567–571.

Goffman, E. (1961). *Asylums.* Garden City, NY: Doubleday.

Golden, C. J. (1981). A standardized version of Luria's neuropsychological tests: A quantitative and qualitative approach to neuropsychological evaluation. In S. Filskov & T. J. Boll (Eds.), *Handbook of clinical neuropsychology.* New York: Wiley.

Golden, C. J. (1989). The Nebraska Neuropsychological Children's Battery. In C. R. Reynolds & E. Fletcher-Janzen (Eds.), *Handbook of clinical child neuropsychology* (pp. 193–204). New York: Plenum Press.

Golden, C. J., Graber, B., Blose, I., Berg, R., Coffman, J., & Bloch, S. (1981). Differences in brain densities between chronic alcoholic and normal control patients. *Science, 211,* 508–510.

Golden, C. J., Moses, J. A., Coffman, J. A., Miller, W. R., & Strider, F. D. (1983). *Clinical neuropsychology.* New York: Grune & Stratton.

Golden, C. J., Moses, J. A., Fishburne, F. J., Engum, E., Lewis, G. P., Wisniewski, A. M., Conley, F. K., Berg, R. A., & Graber, B. (1981). Cross-validation of the Luria-Nebraska Neuropsychological Battery for the presence, lateralization, and location of brain damage. *Journal of Consulting and Clinical Psychology, 49,* 491–507.

Golden, C. J., & Vincente, P. J. (Eds.). (1983). *Foundation of clinical neuropsychology.* New York: Plenum Press.

Golden, G. S. (1987). Tic disorders in childhood. *Pediatrics in Review, 8,* 229–234.

Golden, J. (1988). A second look at a case of inhibited sexual desire. *Journal of Sex Research, 25,* 304–306.

Goldenberg, H. (1973). *Contemporary clinical psychology.* Monterey, CA: Brooks/Cole.

Goldfried, M. R., & Davison, G. C. (1976). *Clinical behavior therapy.* San Francisco: Holt, Rinehart & Winston.

Goldfried, M. R., Greenberg, L. S., & Marmar, C. (1990). Individual psychotherapy: Process and outcome. *Annual Review of Psychology* (Vol. 41, pp. 659–88). Palo Alto CA.: Annual Reviews.

Goldfried, M. R., & Safran, J. D. (1986). Future directions in psychotherapy integration. In J. C. Norcross (Ed.), *Handbook of eclectic psychotherapy* (pp. 463–483). New York: Brunner/Mazel.

Golding, J. M., Smith, G. R., & Kashner, T. M. (1991). Does somatization disorder occur in men? *Archives of General Psychiatry, 48,* 231–235.

Goldman, D., Brown, G. L., Bolos, A. M., Lucas-Derse, S.,

& Dean, M. (1991). The dopamine D2 receptor gene and alcoholism. *Journal of the American Medical Association, 265,* 2668.

Goldman, D., Hien, D. A., Haas, G. L, Sweeney, J. A., & Frances, A. J. (1992). Bizarre delusions and DSM-III-R schizophrenia. *American Journal of Psychiatry, 149,* 494–499.

Goldman, H. H. (1980). The post-hospital mental patient and family therapy: Prospects and populations. *Journal of Marriage and Family Therapy, 6,* 447–452.

Goldman, H. H. (1988). Psychiatric epidemiology and mental health services research. In H. H. Goldman (Ed.), *Review of general psychiatry* (pp. 143–156). Norwalk, CT: Appleton & Lange.

Goldman, H. H., & Foreman, S. A. (1988). Psychiatric diagnosis and psychosocial formulation. In H. H. Goldman (Ed.), *Review of general psychiatry* (pp. 136–142). Norwalk, CT: Appleton & Lange.

Goldman, M. J., & Gutheil, T. G. (1991). Bruxism and sexual abuse. *American Journal of Psychiatry, 148,* 1089.

Goldman, R. D., & Hartig, L. K. (1976). The WISC may not be a valid predictor of school performance for primary grade minority children. *American Journal of Mental Deficiency, 80,* 583–587.

Goldstein, A. P., & Simonson, N. (1971). Social psychological approaches to psychotherapy research. In A. Bergin & S. Garfield (Eds.), *Psychotherapy and behavior change.* New York: Wiley.

Goldstein, J. M., & Tsuang, M. T. (1990). Gender and schizophrenia: An introduction and synthesis of findings. *Schizophrenia Bulletin, 16,* 179–183.

Goleman, D. (1976). Why your temples pound. *Psychology Today, 10,* 41–47.

Goleman, D. (1986a, November 4). To expert eyes, city streets are open mental wards. *New York Times,* pp. C1, C3.

Goleman, D. (1986b, November 11). For mentally ill on the street, a new approach shines. *New York Times,* pp. C1, C3.

Goma, M., Perez, J., & Torrubia, R. (1988). Personality variables in antisocial and prosocial disinhibitory behavior. In T. E. Moffitt & S. A. Mednick (Eds.), *Biological contributions to crime causation* (pp. 211–222). Boston: Martinus Nijhoff Publishers.

Goodman, G. (1972). Systematic selection of psychotherapeutic talent: Group assessment of interpersonal traits. In S. E. Golann & C. Eisdorfer (Eds.), *Handbook of community mental health.* New York: Appleton-Century-Crofts.

Goodman, R. (1989). Infantile autism: A syndrome of multiple primary deficits? *Journal of Autism and Developmental Disorders, 19,* 409–424.

Goodstein, L. D., & Sandler, I. (1978). Using psychology to promote human welfare: A conceptual analysis of the role of community psychology. *American Psychologist, 33*, 882–892.

Goodstein, R. K. (1981). Inextricable interaction: Social, psychologic and biologic stresses facing the elderly. *American Journal of Orthopsychiatry, 51*, 219–229.

Goodwin, D. W. (1979). Alcoholism and heredity. *Archives of General Psychiatry, 36*, 57–61.

Goodwin, D. W. (1985). Alcoholism and alcoholic psychoses. In H. I. Kaplan & B. J. Sadock (Eds.), *Comprehensive textbook of psychiatry/IV* (pp. 1016–1025). Baltimore: Williams & Wilkins.

Goodwin, D. W., & Guze, S. B. (1984). *Psychiatric diagnosis* (3rd ed.). New York: Oxford University Press.

Goodwin, D. W., Schulsinger, F., Knop, J., Mednick, S., & Goodwin, F. (1974). On the biology of depression. In R. J. Friedman & M. M. Katz (Eds.), *The psychology of depression: Contemporary theory and research*. New York: Wiley.

Goodwin, F. K. (1977). Diagnosis of affective disorders. In M. Jarvik (Ed.), *Psychopharmacology in the practice of medicine*. New York: Appleton-Century-Crofts.

Gordon, E., Kraiuhin, C., Meares, R., & Howson, A. (1986). Auditory evoked response potentials in somatization disorder. *Journal of Psychiatric Research, 20*, 237–248.

Gossett, T. F. (1963). *The history of an idea in America*. Dallas: Southern Methodist University Press.

Gotlib, I. H. (1992). Interpersonal and cognitive aspects of depression. *Current Directions in Psychological Science, 1*(5), 149–154.

Gottesman, I. I. (1978). Schizophrenia and genetics: Where are we? Are you sure? In L. C. Wynne, R. L. Cromwell, & S. Matthysse (Eds.), *The nature of schizophrenia: New approaches to research and treatment* (pp. 59–69). New York: Wiley.

Gottesman, I. I. (1991). *Schizophrenia genesis*. New York: W. H. Freeman & Co.

Gottesman, I. I., & Shields, J. (1982). *Schizophrenia: The epigenetic puzzle*. New York: Cambridge University Press.

Gottlieb, A. M., Killen, J. D., Marlatt, G. A., & Taylor, C. B. (1987). Psychological and pharmacological influences in cigarette smoking withdrawal: Effects of nicotine gum and expectancy on smoking withdrawal symptoms and relapse. *Journal of Consulting and Clinical Psychology, 55*, 606–608.

Gottlieb, B. H. (Ed.). (1981). *Social networks and social support*. Beverly Hills, CA: Sage.

Gottlieb, B. H. (1983). Social support as a focus for integrative research in psychology. *American Psychologist, 38*, 278–287.

Gould, M. S., & Schaffer, D. (1986). The impact of suicide in television movies: Evidence of imitation. *New England Journal of Medicine, 315*, 690–693.

Gourash, N. (1978). Help-seeking: A review of the literature. *American Journal of Community Psychology, 6*, 413–424.

Gove, W. R., & Tudor, J. F. (1973). Adult sex roles and mental illness. *American Journal of Sociology, 78*, 812–835.

Graham, J. R. (1990). *MMPI-2: Assessing personality and psychopathology*. New York: Oxford University Press.

Gray, S. H. (1977). Social aspects of body image: Perception of normalcy of weight and affect on college undergraduates. *Perceptual and Motor Skills, 45*, 1035–1040.

Green, B. L., Wilson, J. P., & Lindy, J. D. (1985). Conceptualizing PTSD: A psychosocial framework. In C. R. Figley (Ed.), *Trauma and its wake* (pp. 53–69). New York: Brunner/Mazel.

Green, M. F. (1993). Cognitive remediation in schizophrenia: Is it time yet? *American Journal of Psychiatry, 150*, 178–187.

Green, M. F., & Kinsbourne, M. (1990). Subvocal activity and auditory hallucinations: Clues for behavioral treatments? *Schizophrenia Bulletin, 16*, 617–625.

Green, R. (1978). Sexual identity of 37 children raised by homosexual or transsexual parents. *American Journal of Psychiatry, 135*, 692–697.

Green, R., Mandel, J. B., Hotvedt, M. E., Gray, J., & Smith, L. (1986). Lesbian mothers and their children: A comparison with solo parent heterosexual mothers and their children. *Archives of Sexual Behavior, 15*, 167–184.

Green, R. L. (1991). *The MMPI-2/MMPI: An interpretive manual*. Boston: Allyn & Bacon.

Greenberg, R. P., Bornstein, R. F., Greenberg, M. D., & Fisher, S. (1992). A meta-analysis of antidepressant outcome under "blinder" conditions. *Journal of Consulting and Clinical Psychology, 60*(5), 664–669.

Greer, S., & Morris, T. (1975). Psychological attributes of women who develop breast cancer: A controlled study. *Journal of Psychosomatic Research, 19*, 147–153.

Grefe, M. A. (1980, March/April). Equity—a cause for every woman. *Graduate Woman*, pp. 11–17.

Grencavage, L. M., & Norcross, J. C. (1990). Where are the commonalities among the therapeutic common factors? *Professional Psychology: Research and Practice. 21*, 372–378.

Grier, W., & Cobbs, P. (1968). *Black rage*. New York: Basic Books.

Grinker, R. R., & Robbins, F. P. (1954). *Psychosomatic case book*. New York: Blakiston.

Gross, P. R., & Eifert, G. H. (1990). Components of generalized anxiety: The role of intrusive thoughts vs worry. *Behaviour Research and Therapy, 28*, 421–428.

Groth, A. N., Burgess, A. W., & Holstrom, L. (1977).

Rape: Power, anger, and sexuality. *American Journal of Psychiatry, 134,* 1239–1243.

Grove, M. W., Lebow, B. S., Clementz, B. A., Cerri, A., Medus, C., & Iacono, W. G. (1991). Familial prevalence and coaggregation of schizotypy indicators: A multitrait family study. *Journal of Abnormal Psychology, 100,* 115–121.

Grunhaus, L., Zelnick, T., Albala, A., Rabin, D., Haskett, R. F., Zis, A. P., & Greden, F. Jr. (1987). Serial dexamethasone suppression tests in depressed patients treated only with electroconvulsive therapy. *Journal of Affective Disorders, 13,* 233–240.

Gruver, G. G. (1971). College students as therapeutic agents. *Psychological Bulletin, 76,* 111–127.

Guerin, P. J. Jr., & Chabot, D. R. (1992). Development of family systems theory. In D. K. Freedheim (Ed.), *History of psychotherapy* (pp. 225–260). Washington, DC: American Psychological Association.

Gunn, J., & Fenton, G. (1971, June 5). Epilepsy, *Lancet,* pp. 1173–1176.

Guntrip, H. (1968). *Schizoid phenomena, object relations, and the self.* New York: International Universities Press.

Gurman, A. S., & Razin, M. (Eds) (1977). *Effective psychotherapy: A handbook of research.* New York: Pergamon Press.

Gurman, A. S., & Kniskern, D. P. (1978). Research on marital and family therapy: Progress, perspective, and prospect. In S. L. Carfield & A. E. Bergin (Eds.), *Handbook of psychotherapy and behavior change: An empirical analysis* (2nd ed.). New York: Wiley.

Guttmacher, L. B., & Nelles, C. (1984). In vivo desensitization alteration of lactate-induced panic: A case study. *Behavior Therapy, 15,* 369–372.

Guze, S. B., Cloninger, C. R., Martin, R. L., & Clayton, P. J. (1983). A follow-up and family study of schizophrenia. *Archives of General Psychiatry, 40,* 1273–1276.

Haier, R. J., Rosenthal, D., & Wendler, P. H. (1978). MMPI assessment of psychopathology in the adopted-away offspring of schizophrenics. *Archives of General Psychiatry, 35,* 171–175.

Haley, A. (1966). *The autobiography of Malcolm X.* New York: Grove.

Haley, J. (1963). *Strategies of psychotherapy.* New York: Grune & Stratton.

Haley, J. (1977). *Problem-solving therapy.* San Francisco: Jossey-Bass.

Haley, J. (1980). *Leaving home.* New York: McGraw-Hill.

Haley, J. (1987). *Problem-solving therapy* (2nd edition). New York: Jossey-Bass.

Hall, C. S., & Lindzey, G. (1970). *Theories of personality.* New York: Wiley.

Hall, G. C. N., & Hirschman, R. (1991). Toward a theory of sexual aggression: A quadripartite model. *Journal of Consulting and Clinical Psychology, 59,* 662–669.

Hall, G. S. (1904). *Adolescence: Its psychology and its relation to physiology, anthropology, sociology, sex, crime, religion and education.* New York: Appleton.

Hall, J. C., Bliss, M., Smith, K., & Bradley, A. (1970, July 1). Suicide gestures, attempts found high among poor. *Psychiatric News,* p. 20.

Hall, N. R. S. (1988). The virology of AIDS. *American Psychologist, 43*(11), 907–913.

Hall, R. G., Sachs, D. P. L., Hall, S. M., & Benowitz, N. L. (1984). Two-year efficacy and safety of rapid smoking therapy in patients with cardiac and pulmonary disease. *Journal of Consulting and Clinical Psychology, 52,* 574–581.

Hall, S. M., Havassy, B. E., & Wasserman, D. A. (1990). Commitment to abstinence and acute stress in relapse to alcohol, opiates, and nicotine. *Journal of Consulting and Clinical Psychology, 58,* 175–181.

Hall, S. M., Havassy, B. E., & Wasserman, D. A. (1991). Effects of commitment to abstinence, positive moods, stress, and coping on relapse to cocaine use. *Journal of Consulting and Clinical Psychology, 59,* 526–532.

Hall, S. M., Tunstall, C. D., Ginsberg, D., Benowitz, N. L., & Jones, R. T. (1987). Nicotine gum and behavioral treatment: A placebo controlled trial. *Journal of Consulting and Clinical Psychology, 55,* 603–605.

Halliday, G. (1991). Psychological self-help books—How dangerous are they? *Psychotherapy, 28,* 678–680.

Hammen, C. (1991). Generation of stress in the course of unipolar depression. *Journal of Abnormal Psychology, 100*(4), 555–561.

Hammen, C., Davilla, J., Brown, G., Ellicott, A., & Gitlin, M. (1992). Psychiatric history and stress: Predictors of severity of unipolar depression. *Journal of Abnormal Psychology, 101*(1), 45–52.

Hammen, C., & Peters, S. (1978). Interpersonal consequences of depression: Responses to men and women enacting a depressed role. *Journal of Abnormal Psychology, 87,* 322–332.

Hammen, C. L. (1985). Predicting depression: A cognitive-behavioral perspective. In P. Kendall (Ed.), *Advances in cognitive-behavioral research and therapy* (Vol. 4). New York: Academic Press.

Hammond, W. R., & Yung, B. (1993). Psychology's role in the public health—response to assaultive violence among young African-American men. *American Psychologist, 48,* 142–154.

Hanback, J. W., & Revelle, W. (1978). Arousal and perceptual sensitivity in hypochondriacs. *Journal of Abnormal Psychology, 87,* 523–530.

Hans, S. L., Marcus, J., Henson, L., Auerbach, J. G., & Mirsky, A. F. (1992). Interpersonal behavior of children at risk for schizophrenia. *Psychiatry, 55,* 314–335.

Harburg, E., Gleiberman, L., Russell, M., & Cooper, M. L. (1991). Anger-coping styles and blood pressure in black and white males: Buffalo, New York. *Psychosomatic Medicine, 53,* 153–164.

Harding, C. M., Zubin, J., & Strauss, J. S. (1992). Chronicity in schizophrenia: Revisited. *British Journal of Psychiatry, 161,* 27–37.

Hare, R. D. (1968). Psychopathy, autonomic functioning and the orienting responses. *Journal of Abnormal Psychology, 73,* 1–24.

Hare, R. D. (1970). *Psychopathy: Theory and research.* New York: Wiley.

Hare, R. D. (1975). Anxiety, stress, and psychopathy. In I. Sarason & C. Spielberger (Eds.), *Stress and anxiety* (Vol. 2). Washington, DC: Hemisphere Publishing.

Hare, R. D., Hart, S. D., & Harpur, T. J. (1991). Psychopathology and the DSM-IV criteria for antisocial personality disorder. *Journal of Abnormal Psychology, 100,* 391–398.

Hare-Mustin, R. T. (1983). An appraisal of the relationship between women and psychotherapy: 80 years after the case of Dora. *American Psychologist, 38,* 593–601.

Harlow, J. M. (1868). Recovery from the passage of an iron bar through the head. *Publication of the Massachusetts Medical Society, 2,* 327.

Harpur, T. J., Hare, R. D., and Hakstian, A. R. (1989). Two-factor conceptualization of psychopathology: Construct validity and assessment implications. *Psychological Assessment: A Journal of Consulting and Clinical Psychology, 1,* 6–17.

Harris, P. R. (1980). *Promoting health—preventing disease: Objectives for the nation.* Washington, DC: U.S. Government Printing Office.

Harris, R. R., Wolf, M. M., & Baer, D. M. (1964). Effects of adult social reinforcement of child behavior. *Young Children, 20,* 8–17.

Harris, S. L. (1980). *Psychopathology and society.* New York: McGraw-Hill.

Harris, S. L., & Ersner-Hershfield, R. (1978). Behavioral suppression of seriously disruptive behavior in psychotic and retarded patients: A review of punishment and its alternatives. *Psychological Bulletin, 85,* 1352–1375.

Harris, S. L., Handleman, J. S., Gordon, R., Kristoff, B., & Fuentes, F. (1991). Changes in cognitive and language functioning of preschool children with autism. *Journal of Autism and Developmental Disorders, 21,* 281–290.

Harrow, M., Grossman, L. S., Silverstein, M. L., & Meltzer, H. Y. (1982). Thought pathology in manic and schizophrenic patients. *Archives of General Psychiatry, 39,* 665–671.

Hart, S. D., & Hare, R. D. (1989). Discriminant validity of the psychopathology checklist in a forensic psychiatric population. *Psychological Assessment: A Journal of Consulting and Clinical Psychology, 1,* 211–218.

Hartmann, H. (1958). *Ego psychology and the problems of adaptation.* New York: International Universities Press.

Hatcher, S. (1989). A case of doll phobia. *British Journal of Psychiatry, 155,* 255–257.

Hathaway, S. R., & McKinley, J. C. (1943). *Manual for the Minnesota Multiphasic Personality Inventory.* New York: Psychological Corporation.

Hatton, C. L., & Valente, S. M. (1984). *Suicide assessment and intervention* (2nd ed.). Norwalk, CT: Appleton-Century-Crofts.

Hawton, K. (1987). Assessment of suicide risk. *British Journal of Psychiatry, 150,* 145–153.

Hawton, K., Catalan, J., Martin, P., & Fagg, J. (1986). Long-term outcome of sex therapy. *Behaviour Research and Therapy, 24,* 665–675.

Hayes, S. C., Brownell, K. D., & Barlow, D. H. (1983). Heterosexual skills training and covert sensitization: Effects on social skills and sexual arousal in sexual deviants. *Behaviour Research and Therapy, 21,* 383–392.

Hayes, S. C., & Zettle, R. D. (1979). The mythology of behavioral training. *Behavior Therapist, 2,* 5–6.

Hays, R. B., Turner, H., & Coates, T. J. (1992). Social support, AIDS-related symptoms, and depression among gay men. *Journal of Consulting and Clinical Psychology, 60*(3), 463–469.

Hayward, P., Wardie, J., & Higgitt, A. (1989). Benzodiazepine research: Current findings and practical consequences. *British Journal of Psychiatry, 28,* 307–327.

Heber, R., & Garber, H. (1975). The Milwaukee project: A study of the use of familial retardation to prevent cultural-familial retardation. In B. Z. Friedlander, G. M. Sterrit, & G. E. Kirk (Eds.), *Exceptional infant, Vol. 3: Assessment and intervention.* New York: Brunner/Mazel.

Hechtman, L., & Weiss, G. (1983). Long-term outcome of hyperactive children. *American Journal of Orthopsychiatry, 53,* 532–541.

Heiby, E. M. (1983). Depression as a function of the interaction of self- and environmentally controlled reinforcement. *Behavior Therapy, 14,* 430–433.

Heilbrun, A. B. Jr., & Loftus, M. P. (1986). The role of sadism and peer pressure in the sexual aggression of male college students. *Journal of Sex Research, 22,* 320–332.

Heilig, S. M. (1970). Training in suicide prevention. *Bulletin of Suicidology, 6,* 41–44.

Heim, N. (1981). Sexual behavior of castrated sex offenders. *Archives of Sexual Behavior, 10,* 11–19.

Heinrich, D. W., & Buchanann, R. W. (1988). Significance and meaning of neurological signs in schizophrenia. *American Journal of Psychiatry, 145,* 11–18.

Heinrichs, R. W. (1993). Schizophrenia and the brain. *American Psychologist, 48,* 221–233.

Hekmat, H., Lubitz, R., & Deal, R. (1984). Semantic desensitization: A paradigmatic intervention approach to anxiety disorders. *Journal of Clinical Psychology, 40,* 463–466.

Heller, K., Price, R. H., Reinharz, S., Riger, S., & Wandersman, A. (1984). *Psychology and community change: Challenge of the future.* Homewood, IL: Dorsey.

Helms, J. E. (1992). Why is there no study of cultural equivalence in standardized cognitive ability testing? *American Psychologist, 47,* 1083–1101.

Hendin, H., Pollenger, A., Singer, P., & Ulman, R. (1981). Meanings of combat and the development of posttraumatic stress disorder. *American Journal of Psychiatry, 131,* 1490–1493.

Henley, N. (1977). *Body politics.* Englewood Cliffs, NJ: Prentice-Hall.

Henryk-Gutt, R., & Rees, L. W. (1973). Psychological aspects of migraine. *Journal of Psychosomatic Research, 17,* 141–153.

Herbert, J. D., Hope, D. A., & Bellack, A. S. (1992). Validity of the distinction between generalized social phobia and avoidant personality disorder. *Journal of Abnormal Psychology, 101,* 332–339.

Herlicky, B., & Sheeley, V. L. (1988). Privileged communication in selected helping professions: A comparison among statutes. *Journal of Counseling & Development, 65,* 479–483.

Herman, J., & Hirschman, L. (1981). Families at risk for father-daughter incest. *American Journal of Psychiatry, 38,* 967–970.

Herman, S., Russell, D., & Trocki, K. (1986). Long-term effects of incestuous abuse in childhood. *American Journal of Psychiatry, 154,* 1293–1296.

Hernstein, R. (1982). IQ. *Atlantic Monthly,* pp. 43–64.

Herschkowitz, S., & Dickes, R. (1978). Suicide attempts in a female-to-male transsexual. *American Journal of Psychiatry, 135,* 368–369.

Hersen, M., Bellack, A., & Himmelhoch, J. (1980). Treatment for unipolar depression with social skills training. *Behavior Modification, 4,* 547–556.

Hersen, M., & Van Hasselt, V. B. (1992). Behavioral assessment and treatment of anxiety in the elderly. *Clinical Psychology Review, 12,* 619–640.

Hertzog, D. B. (1982). Anorexia nervosa: A treatment challenge. *Drug Therapy, 7,* 3.

Heston, L. L. (1966). Psychiatric disorders in foster-home–reared children of schizophrenic mothers. *British Journal of Psychiatry, 122,* 819–825.

Heston, L. L., & Denny, D. (1968). Interactions between early life experience and biological factors in schizophrenia. In D. Rosenthal & S. Kety (Eds.), *The transmission of schizophrenia.* New York: Pergamon Press.

Hetherington, M. M., Spalter, A. R., Bernat, A. S., Nelson, M. L. & Gold, P. W. (1993). Eating pathology in bu-

limia nervosa. *International Journal of Eating Disorders, 13,* 13–24.

Hibbert, G. (1984). Ideational components of anxiety: Their origin and content. *British Journal of Psychiatry, 144,* 618–624.

Hill, D., & Watterson, D. (1942). Electroencephalographic studies of the psychopathic personality. *Journal of Neurology and Psychiatry, 5,* 47–64.

Hills, C. E. (1990). Is individual therapy process really different from group therapy process: The jury is still out. *Counseling Psychologist, 18,* 126–130.

Hillyer, J. (1964). Reluctantly told. In B. Kaplan (Ed.), *The inner world of mental illness.* New York: Harper & Row.

Hinshaw, S. (1987). On the distinction between attentional deficits/hyperactivity and conduct problems/aggression in child psychopathology. *Psychological Bulletin, 101,* 443–463.

Hipple, J. L., & Hipple, L. B. (1983). *Diagnosis and management of psychological emergencies.* Springfield, IL: Thomas.

Hirsch, B. J., & DuBois, D. L. (1992). The relation of peer social support and psychological symptomatology during the transition to junior high school: A two-year longitudinal analysis. *American Journal of Community Psychology, 20,* 333–347.

Hirschfeld, R. M., & Davidson, L. (1989). Clinical risk factors for suicide. *Psychiatric Annals, 18,* 628–635.

Hirschfeld, R. M., & Shea, T. (1985). Affective disorders: Psychosocial treatment. In H. I. Kaplan & B. J. Sadock (Eds.), *Comprehensive textbook of psychiatry* (4th ed., pp. 786–810). Baltimore: Williams & Wilkins.

Hite, S. (1976). *The Hite report.* Chicago: Dell.

Ho, E. D. F., Tsang, A. K. T., & Ho, D. Y. F. (1991). An investigation of the calendar calculation ability of a Chinese calendar savant. *Journal of Autism and Developmental Disorders, 21,* 315–327.

Ho, M. K. (1987). *Family therapy with ethnic minorities.* Newbury Park, CA: Sage Publications.

Hobson, R. P. (1987). The autistic child's recognition of age- and sex-related characteristics of people. *Journal of Autism and Developmental Disorders, 17,* 63–79.

Hoch, Z., Safir, M. P., Peres, Y., & Stepler, J. (1981). An evaluation of sexual performance—comparison between sexually dysfunctional and functional couples. *Journal of Sex and Marital Therapy, 7,* 195–206.

Hodgson, R. J., & Rachman, S. (1972). The effects of contamination and washing in obsessional patients. *Behavior Research and Therapy, 10,* 111–117.

Hoehn-Saric, R., Pearlson, G. D., Harris, G. J., Machlin, S. R., & Camargo, E. E. (1991). Effects of fluoxetine on regional cerebral blood flow in obsessive-compulsive patients. *American Journal of Psychiatry, 148,* 1243–1245.

Hoff, A. L., Riordan, H., O'Donnell, D. W., Morris, L., & Delisi, L. E. (1992). Neuropsychological functioning of first-episode schizophreniform patients. *American Journal of Psychiatry, 149,* 898–903.

Hoffart, A. (1993). Cognitive treatments of agoraphobia: A critical evaluation of theoretical basis and outcome evidence. *Journal of Anxiety Disorders, 7,* 75–91.

Hoffman, M. A. (1991). Counseling the HIV-infected client: A psychosocial model for assessment and intervention. *The Counseling Psychologist, 19,* 467–542.

Hogarty, G. E., Anderson, C. M., Reiss, D. J., Kornblith, S. J., Greenwald, D. P., Ulrich, R. F., & Carter, M. (1991). Family psychoeducation, social skills training, and maintenance chemotherapy in the aftercare treatment of schizophrenia. *Archives of General Psychiatry, 48,* 340–347.

Hohmann, A. A., Larson, D. B., Thompson, J. W., & Beardsley, R. S. (1988, November). *Psychotropic medication prescription in U.S. ambulatory medical care.* Paper presented at the American Public Health Association Annual Meeting, Boston, Massachusetts.

Holahan, C. J., & Moos, R. H. (1991). Life stressors, personal and social resources, and depression: A 4-year structure model. *Journal of Abnormal Psychology, 100*(1), 31–38.

Holcomb, H. H., Links, J., Smith, C., & Wong, D. (1989). Positron emission tomography: Measuring the metabolic and neurochemical characteristics of the living human nervous system. In N. C. Andreasen (Ed.), *Brain imaging: Applications in psychiatry* (pp. 235–370). Washington, DC: American Psychiatric Press.

Holden, C. (1986). Proposed new psychiatric diagnoses raise charges of gender bias. *Science, 231,* 327–328.

Holden, N. L. (1987). Late paraphrenia or the paraphrenias? A descriptive study with a 10-year follow-up. *British Journal of Psychiatry, 150,* 635–639.

Hollender, M. H. (1980). The case of Anna O.: A reformulation. *American Journal of Psychiatry, 137,* 797–800.

Hollon, S. D., Shelton, R. C, & Loosen, P. T. (1991). Cognitive therapy and pharmacotherapy for depression. *Journal of Consulting and Clinical Psychology, 59*(1), 88–99.

Hollon, S. D., DeRubeis, R. J., & Seligman, M. E. P. (1992). Cognitive therapy and the prevention of depression. *Applied and Preventive Psychology. 1,* 89–95.

Holmes, T. H., & Rahe, R. H. (1967). The social readjustment rating scale. *Journal of Psychosomatic Research, 11,* 213–218.

Holmes, T. S., & Holmes, T. H. (1970). Short-term intrusion into the life style routine. *Journal of Psychosomatic Research, 14,* 121–132.

Holroyd, J. (1980). Psychotherapy and women's liberation. *Counseling Psychologist, 6,* 22–28.

Holroyd, J., & Brodsky, A. (1977). Psychologists' attitudes and practices regarding erotic and nonerotic physical contact with patients. *American Psychologist, 32,* 839–843.

Holroyd, J., & Brodsky, A. (1980). Does touching patients lead to sexual intercourse? *Professional Psychology, 11,* 807–811.

Holt, C. S., Heimberg, R. G., & Hope, D. A. (1992). Avoidant personality and the generalized subtype of social phobia. *Journal of Abnormal Psychology, 101,* 318–325.

Holt, C. S., Heimerg, R. G., Hope, D. A., & Liebowitz, M. R. (1992). Situational domains of social phobia. *Journal of Anxiety Disorders, 6,* 63–77.

Holt, R. R. (1962). The logic of the romantic point of view in personology. *Journal of Psychoanalysis, 38,* 377–402.

Holzberg, J. D., Knapp, R. H., & Turner, J. L. (1967). College students as companions to the mentally ill. In E. L. Cowen, E. A. Gardner, & M. Zax (Eds.), *Emergent approaches to mental health problems.* New York: Appleton-Century-Crofts.

Horne, R. L., Pettinati, H. M., Sugerman, A. A., & Varga, E. (1985). Comparing bilateral to unilateral electroconvulsive therapy in randomized study with EEG monitoring. *Archives of General Psychiatry, 42,* 1087–1092.

Horne, R. L., Van Vactor, C., & Emerson, S. (1991). Disturbed body image in patients with eating disorders. *American Journal of Psychiatry, 148,* 211–215.

Horney, K. (1965). *Feminine psychology.* New York: Norton.

Horowitz, M. J. (1970). *Psychosocial function in epilepsy.* Springfield, IL: Thomas.

Horwath, E., Johnson, J., & Horning, C. D. (1993). Epidemiology of panic disorder in African-Americans. *American Journal of Psychiatry, 150,* 465–469.

Horwitz, A. V., & White, H. R. (1987). Gender role orientations and styles of pathology among adolescents. *Journal of Health and Human Behavior, 28,* 158–170.

Hovanitz, C. A., & Wander, M. R. (1990). Tension headache: Disregulation at some levels of stress. *Journal of Behavioral Medicine, 13,* 539–560.

Howard, R. (1992). Folie a deux involving a dog. *American Journal of Psychiatry, 149,* 414.

Howells, J. G., & Guirgis, W. R. (1984). Childhood schizophrenia 20 years later. *Archives of General Psychiatry, 41,* 123–128.

Hsiao, J. K., & Potter, W. Z. (1990). Mechanisms of action of antipsychotic drugs. In J. C. Ballenger (Ed.), *Clinical aspects of panic disorder* (pp. 297–317). New York: Wiley-Liss.

Huber, G., Gross, G., Schuttler, R., & Linz, M. (1980). Longitudinal studies of schizophrenic patients. *Schizophrenia Bulletin, 6,* 592–605.

Hudgens, A. (1979). Family-oriented treatment of chronic pain. *Journal of Marital and Family Therapy, 5,* 67–78.

Hudson, J. I., Manoach, D. S., Sabo, A. N., & Sternbach, S. E. (1991). Recurrent nightmares in posttraumatic stress disorder: Association with sleep paralysis, hypnopompic hallucinations, and REM sleep. *Journal of Nervous and Mental Disease, 179,* 572–573.

Hull, J. C., & Bond, C. F. (1986). Social and behavioral consequences of alcohol consumption and expectancy: A meta-analysis. *Psychological Bulletin, 99,* 347–360.

Hulsey, T. L. (1991). Traumas and dissociation. *American Journal of Psychiatry, 148,* 1422.

Hunt, M. M. (1974). *Sexual behavior in the 1970s.* Chicago: Playboy Press.

Hunter, R., Blackwood, W., & Bull, J. (1968). Three cases of frontal meningiomas presenting psychiatrically. *British Medical Journal, 3,* 9–16.

Hunter, R., & Macalpine, I. (1963). *Three hundred years of psychiatry, 1535–1860.* London: Oxford University Press.

Hurtig, A. L., & Rosenthal, I. M. (1987). Psychological findings in early treated cases of female pseudohermaphroditism caused by virilizing congenital adrenal hyperplasia. *Archives of Sexual Behavior, 16,* 209–223.

Hutchens, T. A., & Hynd, G. W. (1987). Medications and the school-age child and adolescent: A review. *School Psychology Bulletin, 16,* 527–542.

Hutchings, B., & Mednick, S. A. (1977). Criminality in adoptees and their adoptive and biological parents: A pilot study. In S. A. Mednick & K. L. Christianson (Eds.), *Biosocial bases of criminal behavior.* New York: Garden Press.

Hymowitz, P., & Spohn, H. (1980). The effects of antipsychotic medication on the linguistic ability of schizophrenics. *Journal of Nervous and Mental Disease, 168,* 287–296.

Hynd, G. W., Semrud-Clikeman, M., Lorys, A., Novey, E. S., & Eliopulos, D. (1990). Brain morphology in developmental dyslexia and attention deficit disorder/hyperactivity. *Archives of Neurology, 47,* 919–926.

Hynd, G. W., Hern, K. L., Voeller, K. K., & Marshall, R. M. (1991). Neurobiological basis of attention-deficit hyperactivity disorder. *School Psychology Review, 20,* 174–186.

Irwin, A., & Gross, A. M. (1990). Mental retardation in childhood. In M. Hersen & C. G. Last (Eds.), *Handbook of child and adult psychopathology* (pp. 325–336). New York: Pergamon Press.

Irwin, M., Daniels, M., Smith, T. L., Bloom, E., & Weiner, H. (1987). Impaired natural killer cell activity during bereavement. *Brain, Behavior, and Immunity, 1,* 98–104.

Isenberg, S. A., Lehrer, P. M., & Hochron, S. (1992). The effects of suggestion and emotional arousal on pulmonary function in asthma: A review and a hypothesis regarding vagal medication. *Psychosomatic Medicine, 54,* 192–216.

Israelson, H. (1989, February 19). "Original 'Rain Man' proud to be movie's inspiration." *Bellingham Herald.*

Jackson, M., & Calridge, G. (1991). Reliability and validity of a psychotic traits questionnaire (STQ). *British Journal of Psychiatry, 30,* 311–323.

Jacobson, E. (1938). *Progressive relaxation.* Chicago: University of Chicago Press.

Jacobson, E. (1964). *Self-operations control.* New York: Lippincott.

Jacobson, E. (1967). *Tension in medicine.* Springfield, IL: Thomas.

Jacobson, N. S., & Anderson, E. A. (1982). Interpersonal skill and depression in college students: An analysis of the timing of self-disclosures. *Behavior Therapy, 13,* 271–282.

Jaenicke, C., Hammen, C., Zupan, B., Hiroto, D., Gordon, D., Adrian, C., & Burge, D. (1987). Cognitive vulnerability in children at risk for depression. *Journal of Abnormal Child Psychology, 15,* 559–572.

Jahoda, M. (1958). *Current concepts of positive mental health.* New York: Basic Books.

James, G. D., Yee, L. S., Harshfield, G. A., Blank, S. G., & Pickering, T. G. (1986). The influence of happiness, anger, and anxiety on the blood pressure of borderline hypertensives. *Psychosomatic Medicine, 48,* 502–508.

Janoff-Bulman, R. (1985). Aftermath of victimization: Rebuilding shattered assumptions (pp. 15–31). In C. R. Figley (Ed.), *Trauma and its wake.* New York: Brunner/Mazel.

Jansen, A., Van Den Hout, M. A., De Loof, C., Zandbergen, J., & Griez, E. (1989). A case of bulimia successfully treated by cue exposure. *Journal of Behavior Therapy and Experimental Psychiatry, 20,* 327–332.

Janssen, K. (1983). Treatment of sinus tachycardia with heart-rate feedback. *Psychiatry and Human Development, 17,* 166–176.

Janus, S. S., & Janus, C. L. (1993). *The Janus report on sexual behavior.* New York: John Wiley & Sons.

Jason, L. A., Felner, R. D., Moritsugu, J., & Farber, S. S. (1983). Future directions for preventive psychology. In R. D. Felner, L. A. Jason, J. Moritsugu, & S. S. Farber (Eds.), *Preventive psychology: Theory, research, and practice.* New York: Pergamon Press.

Jasper, H. H., Ward, A., & Pope, A. (Eds.). (1969). *Basic mechanisms of the epilepsies.* Boston: Little, Brown.

Jawed, S. Y. (1991). A survey of psychiatrically ill Asian children. *British Journal of Psychiatry, 158,* 268–270.

Jellinek, E. M. (1971). Phases of alcohol addiction. In G. Shean (Ed.), *Studies in abnormal behavior*. Chicago: Rand McNally.

Jemmott, III, J. B., & Locke, S. E. (1984). Psychosocial factors, immunologic mediation, and human susceptibility to infectious diseases: How much do we know? *Psychological Bulletin, 95,* 78–108.

Jenike, M. A., Baer, L., Summergrad, P., Weilburg, J. B., Holland, A., & Seymour, R. (1989). Obsessive-compulsive disorder: A double-blind, placebo controlled trial of clomipramine in 27 patients. *American Journal of Psychiatry, 146,* 1328–1330.

Jenkins, J. H, & Karno, M. (1992). The meaning of expressed emotion: Theoretical issues raised by cross-cultural research. *American Journal of Psychiatry, 149,* 9–21.

Jenkins, S., Owen, C., Bax, M., & Hart, H. (1984). Continuities of common behavior problems in preschool children. *Journal of Child Psychology and Psychiatry, 25,* 75–89.

Jenner, F. A., Gjessing, L. R., Cox, J. R., Davies-Jones, A., Hullin, R. R., & Hanna, S. M. (1967). A manic-depressive psychotic with a persistent forty-eight-hour cycle. *British Journal of Psychiatry, 113,* 895–910.

Jensen, A. (1969). How much can we boost IQ and school achievements? *Harvard Educational Review, 39,* 1–123.

Jerome, L. (1992). Body dysmorphic disorder: A controlled study of patients requesting cosmetic rhinoplasty. *American Journal of Psychiatry, 149,* 577.

Jessor, R., & Jessor, S. L. (1977). *Problem behavior and psycho-social development: A longitudinal study of youth.* New York: Academic Press.

Johnson, C., & Berndt, D. J. (1983). Preliminary investigation of bulimia and life adjustment. *American Journal of Psychiatry, 140,* 774–777.

Johnson, D. A. W., Ludlow, J. M., Street, K., & Taylor, R. D. W. (1987). Double-blind comparison of half-dose and standard-dose flupenthixol decanoate in the maintenance treatment of stabilized out-patients with schizophrenia. *British Journal of Psychiatry, 151,* 634–638.

Johnson, D. L., & Walker, T. (1987). Primary prevention of behavior problems in Mexican-American children. *American Journal of Community Psychology, 15,* 375–385.

Johnson, W. G. (1990). Multifactorial diseases and other disorders with non-Mendelian inheritance. In H. E. Hendrie, L. G. Mendelsohn, & C. Readhead (Eds.), *Brain aging: Molecular biology, the aging process and neurodegenerative disease* (pp. 5–19). Bern, Germany: Hans Huber Publishers.

Johnston, L. D., O'Malley, P. M., & Bachman, J. G. (1991). *Drug use among American high school seniors, college students and young adults, 1975–1990* (Vols. 1 & 2). Rockville, MD: National Institute on Drug Abuse.

Johnston, R. (1967). Some casework aspects of using foster grandparents for emotionally disturbed children. *Children, 14,* 46–52.

Johnston, W. B., & Packer, A. H. (1987). *Workforce 2000: Work and workers for the twenty-first century.* Indianapolis, IN: Hudson Institute.

Jones, E. E., & Korchin, S. J. (Eds.). (1982). *Minority mental health.* New York: Praeger.

Jones, E. E., & Thorne, A. (1987). Rediscovery of the subject: Intercultural approaches to clinical assessment. *Journal of Consulting and Clinical Psychology, 55,* 488–496.

Jones, J. M. (1991). Psychological models of race: What have they been and what should they be? In J. D. Goodchilds (Ed.), *Psychological perspectives on human diversity in America* (pp. 7–46). Washington, DC: American Psychological Association.

Jones, K. L., Shainberg, L. W., & Byer, C. O. (1977). *Sex and people.* New York: Harper & Row.

Jones, M. (1953). *The therapeutic community: A new treatment method in psychiatry.* New York: Basic Books.

Jones, M. C. (1924). A laboratory study of fear: The case of Peter. *Pedagogical Seminary, 31,* 308–315.

Jones, M. C. (1968). Personality correlates and antecedents of drinking patterns in adult males. *Journal of Consulting and Clinical Psychology, 32,* 2–12.

Jones, R. E. (1983). Street people and psychiatry: An introduction. *Hospital Community Psychiatry, 34,* 899–907.

Jordan, B. K., Schlenger, W. E., Hough, R., Kulka, R. A., Weiss, D., Fairbank, J. A., & Marmar, C. R. (1991). Lifetime and current prevalence of specific psychiatric disorders among Vietnam veterans and controls. *Archives of General Psychiatry, 48,* 207–215.

Joseph, E. (1991). Psychodynamic personality theory. In K. Davis, H. Klar, & J. J. Coyle (Eds.), *Foundations of psychiatry.* Philadelphia: Saunders.

Joseph, S. A., Brewin, C. R., Yule, W., & Williams, R. (1993). Causal attributions in posttraumatic stress in adolescents. *Journal of Child Psychology and Psychiatry, 34,* 247–253.

Joyce, C. (1988). Assault on the brain. *Psychology Today, 22,* 38–44.

Judd, F. K., Burrows, G. D., & Norman, T. R. (1991). Follow-up study of patients with panic disorder. *Archives of General Psychiatry, 48,* 860–861.

Julkunen, J., Idanpaan-Heikkila, U., & Saarinen, T. (1993). Components of type A behavior and the first-year prognosis of a myocardial infarction. *Journal of Psychosomatic Research, 37,* 11–18.

Junginger, J., Barker, S., & Coe, D. (1992). Mood theme

and bizarreness of delusions in schizophrenia and mood psychosis. *Journal of Abnormal Psychology, 101,* 287–292.

Junginger, J., & Turner, S. M. (1987). Spontaneous exposure and "self-control" in the treatment of obsessive checking. *Journal of Behavior Therapy and Experimental Psychiatry, 18,* 115–119.

Kagan, D. M., & Squires, R. L. (1984). Eating disorders among adolescents: Patterns and prevalence. *Adolescence, 19,* 15–29.

Kagan, J., Reznick, J. S., & Snidman, N. (1987). The physiology and psychology of behavioral inhibition in children. *Child Development, 58,* 1459–1473.

Kahn, A. U., Staerk, M., & Bonk, C. (1974). Role of counterconditioning in the treatment of asthma. *Journal of Psychosomatic Research, 18,* 88–92.

Kahn, M. W., & Raufman, L. (1981). Hospitalization versus imprisonment and the insanity plea. *Criminal Justice and Behavior, 8*(4), 483–490.

Kallman, W. M., Hersen, M., & O'Toole, D. H. (1975). The use of social reinforcement in a case of conversion reaction. *Behavior Therapy, 6,* 411–413.

Kamarck, T., & Jennings, J. R. (1991). Biobehavioral factors in sudden cardiac death. *Psychological Bulletin, 109,* 42–75.

Kamiya, J. (1962, April). *Conditioning discrimination of the EEG alpha rhythm in humans.* Paper presented at the meeting of the Western Psychological Association.

Kanas, N. (1988). Psychoactive substance use disorders: Alcohol. In H. H. Goldman (Ed.), *Review of general psychiatry* (pp. 286–298). Norwalk, CT: Appleton & Lange.

Kandel, E., Mednick, S. A., Kirkegaard-Sorenson, L., Hutchings, B., Knop, J., Rosenberg, R., & Schulsinger, F. (1988). IQ as a protective factor for subjects at high risk for antisocial behavior. *Journal of Consulting and Clinical Psychology, 56,* 224–226.

Kane, J. M. (1991). New developments in the pharmacologic treatment of schizophrenia: Editor's introduction. *Schizophrenia Bulletin, 17,* 193–195.

Kane, J. M., & Lieberman, J. A. (1987). Maintenance pharmacotherapy in schizophrenia. In H. Y. Meltzer (Ed.), *Psychopharmacology: The third generation of progress* (pp. 1103–1109). New York: Raven Press.

Kane, J. M., & Smith, J. M. (1982). Tardive dyskinesia: prevalence and risk factors, 1959–1979. *Archives of General Psychiatry, 39,* 473–481.

Kane, J. M., Woerner, M., Borenstein, M., Wegner, J., & Lieberman, J. (1986). Investigating the incidence and prevalence of tardive dyskinesia. *Psychopharmacology Bulletin, 22,* 254–258.

Kanfer, F. H., & Phillips, J. S. (1969). A survey of current behavior therapies and a proposal for classification. In C. M. Franks (Ed.), *Behavior therapy: Appraisal and status.* New York: Wiley.

Kanner, L. (1943). Autistic disturbances of affective content. *Nervous Child, 2,* 217–240.

Kanner, L. (1960). Do behavior symptoms always indicate psychopathology? *Journal of Child Psychological Psychiatry, 1,* 17–25.

Kanner, L., & Lesser, L. I. (1958). Early infantile autism. *Pediatrics Clinic of North America, 5,* 711–730.

Kanter, J., Lamb, H. R., & Loeper, R. (1987). Expressed emotion in families: A critical review. *Hospital and Community Psychiatry, 38,* 374–380.

Kaplan, H. I., & Sadock, B. J. (1981). *Modern synopsis of comprehensive textbook of psychiatry* (3rd ed.). Baltimore: Williams & Wilkins.

Kaplan, H. S. (1974). No nonsense therapy for six sexual malfunctions. *Psychology Today, 8,* 76–80, 83, 86.

Kaplan, M. (1983). A woman's view of DSM-III. *American Psychologist, 38,* 786–792.

Kardiner, A., & Ovesey, L. (1962). *The mark of oppression.* New York: Norton.

Karno, M., Golding, J. M., Sorenson, S. B., & Burnam, M. A. (1988). The epidemiology of obsessive-compulsive disorder in five U. S. communities. *Archives of General Psychiatry, 45,* 1094–1099.

Karno, M., Hough, R. L., Burnam, A., Escobar, J. I., Timbers, D. M., Santana, F., & Boyd, J. H. (1987). Lifetime prevalence of specific psychiatric disorders among Mexican Americans and non-Hispanic whites in Los Angeles. *Archives of General Psychiatry, 44,* 695–701.

Karno, M., Jenkins, J. H., De la Selva, A., Santana, F., Telles, C., Lopez, S., & Mintz, J. (1987). Expressed emotion and schizophrenic outcome among Mexican-American families. *Journal of Nervous and Mental Disease, 175,* 143–151.

Kashani, J. H., & Carlson, G. A. (1987). Seriously depressed preschoolers. *American Journal of Psychiatry, 144,* 348–350.

Kaszniak, A. W., Nussbaum, P. D., Berren, M. R., & Santiago, J. (1988). Amnesia as a consequence of male rape: A case report. *Journal of Abnormal Psychology, 97,* 100–104.

Katchadourian, H. A., & Lunde, D. T. (1975). *Fundamentals of human sexuality* (2nd ed.). New York: Holt, Rinehart & Winston.

Katerndahl, D. A., & Realini, J. P. (1993). Lifetime prevalence of panic states. *American Journal of Psychiatry, 150,* 246–249.

Katz, J. (1985). The sociopolitical nature of counseling. *The Counseling Psychologist, 13,* 615–624.

Katz, P. A. (Ed.). (1976). *Toward the elimination of racism.* New York: Pergamon Press.

Katz, P. A., & Taylor, D. A. (Eds.). (1988). *Eliminating racism: Profiles in controversy.* New York: Plenum.

Katz, S., & Kravetz, S. (1989). Facial plastic surgery for persons with Down syndrome: Research findings and their professional and societal implications. *American Journal on Mental Retardation, 94,* 101–110.

Kaufman, A. S., Kamphaus, R. W., & Kaufman, N. L. (1985). The Kaufman Assessment Battery for Children (K-ABC). In C. S. Newmark (Ed.), *Major psychological assessment instruments* (pp. 249–276). Boston: Allyn & Bacon.

Kaufman, A. S., & Kaufman, N. L. (1983). *Kaufman Assessment Battery for Children.* Circle Pines, MN: American Guidance Services.

Kaul, T. J., & Bednar, R. L. (1986). Experiential group research: Results, questions, and suggestions. In S. L. Garfield and A. E. Bergin (Eds.), *Handbook of psychotherapy and behavior change: An evaluative analysis.* New York: Wiley.

Kavanagh, D. J. (1992). Recent developments in expressed emotions and schizophrenia. *British Journal of Psychiatry, 160,* 601–620.

Kazdin, A. E. (1980). *Behavior modification in applied settings* (2nd ed.). Homewood, IL: Dorsey.

Kazdin, A. E. (1987). Treatment of antisocial behavior in children: Current status and future directions. *Psychological Bulletin, 102,* 187–203.

Kazdin, A. E. (1993). Adolescent mental health: Prevention and treatment programs. *American Psychologist, 48,* 127–141.

Kazdin, A. E., Siegel, T. C., & Bass, D. (1992). Cognitive problem- solving skills training and parent management training in the treatment of antisocial behavior in children. *Journal of Consulting and Clinical Psychology, 60,* 733–747.

Kazdin, A. E., & Wilson, G. T. (1978). *Evaluation of behavior therapy: Issues, evidence and research strategies.* Cambridge, MA: Ballinger.

Keane, T. M., Fairbank, J. A., Caddell, J. M., Zimering, R. T., & Bender, M. E. (1985). A behavioral approach to assessing and treatment of posttraumatic stress disorder in Vietnam veterans (pp. 257–294). In C. R. Figley (Ed.), *Trauma and its wake.* New York: Brunner/Mazel.

Kearney, C. A., & Silverman, W. K. (1990). Treatment of an adolescent with obsessive-compulsive disorder by alternating response prevention and cognitive therapy: An empirical analysis. *Journal of Behavior Therapy and Experimental Psychiatry, 21,* 39–47.

Keeling, R. P. (1993). HIV disease: Current concepts. *Journal of Counseling and Development, 71,* 261–274.

Kegeles, T., Catania, J., & Coates, T. (1988). Intentions to communicate positive HIV status to sex partners (letters to the editor). *Journal of the American Medical Association, 259,* 216–217.

Keith, S. J., & Matthews, S. M. (1991). The diagnosis of schizophrenia: A review of onset and duration issues. *Schizophrenia Bulletin, 17,* 51–59.

Kellner, R. (1982). Psychotherapeutic strategies in hypochondriasis: A clinical study. *American Journal of Psychotherapy, 36,* 146–157.

Kellner, R. (1985). Functional somatic symptoms and hypochondriasis. *Archives of General Psychiatry, 42,* 821–833.

Kellner, R., Hernandez, J., & Pathak, D. (1992). Hypochondriacal fears and beliefs, anxiety, and somatization. *British Journal of Psychiatry, 160,* 525–532.

Kelly, G. A. (1955). *The psychology of personal constructs.* New York: Norton.

Kelly, J. A., & Murphy, D. A. (1992). Psychological interventions with AIDS and HIV: Prevention and treatment. *Journal of Consulting and Clinical Psychology, 60*(4), 576–585.

Kelly, J. G. (1966). Ecological constraints on mental health services. *American Psychologist, 21,* 535–539.

Kendall, P. C., & Chansky, T. E. (1991). Considering cognition in anxiety-disordered children. *Journal of Anxiety Disorders, 5,* 167–185.

Kendler, K. S. (1988). Familial aggregation of schizophrenia and schizophrenic spectrum disorders. *Archives of General Psychiatry, 45,* 377–383.

Kendler, K. S., Glaser, W. M., & Morgenstern, H. (1983). Dimensions of delusional experience. *American Journal of Psychiatry, 140,* 466–469.

Kendler, K. S., & Hays, P. (1982). Familial and sporadic schizophrenia: A symptomatic, prognostic, and EEG comparison. *American Journal of Psychiatry, 139,* 1557–1562.

Kendler, K. S., MacLean, C., Neale, M., Kessler, R., Heath, A., & Eaves, L. (1991). The genetic epidemiology of bulimia nervosa. *American Journal of Psychiatry, 148,* 1627–1637.

Kendler, K. S., Neale, M. C., Kessler, R. C., Heath, A. C., & Eaves, L. J. (1992a). Generalized anxiety disorder in women. *Archives of General Psychiatry, 49,* 267–271.

Kendler, K. S., Neale, M. C., Kessler, R. C., Heath, A. C., & Eaves, L. J. (1992b). The genetic epidemiology of phobias in women. *Archives of General Psychiatry, 49,* 273–281.

Kendler, K. S., Silberg, J. L., Neale, M. C., Kessler, R. C., Heath, A. C., & Eaves, L. J. (1991). The family history method: Whose psychiatric history is being measured? *American Journal of Psychiatry, 148,* 1501–1504.

Kerachsky, S., & Thornton, C. (1987). Findings from the STETs transitional employment demonstration. *Exceptional Children, 53,* 515–521.

Kerlitz, I., & Fulton, J. P. (1984). *The insanity defense and its alternatives: A guide to policy makers.* Williamsburg, VA: National Center for State Courts.

Kernberg, O. (1976). Technical considerations in the treatment of borderline personality organization. *Journal of the American Psychoanalytic Association, 24,* 795–829.

Kernberg, O. (1980). Developmental theory, structural organization, and psychoanalytic technique. In *Reapproachment.* New York: Aronson.

Kernberg, O. F. (1975). *Borderline conditions and pathological narcissism.* New York: Jason Aronson.

Kety, S. S. (1979). Disorders of the human brain. *Scientific American, 241,* 202–214.

Kety, S. S., Rosenthal, D., Wender, P. H., Schulsinger, F., & Jacobsen, B. (1975). Mental illness in the biological and adoptive families of adopted individuals who have become schizophrenic: A preliminary report based on psychiatric interviews. In R. R. Fieve, D. Rosenthal, & H. Brill (Eds.), *Genetic research in psychiatry.* Baltimore: Johns Hopkins University Press.

Khanna, S., Desai, N. G., & Channabasavanna, S. M. (1987). A treatment package for transsexualism. *Behavior Therapy, 2,* 193–199.

Kiecolt-Glaser, J. K., Dura, J. R., Speicher, C. E., Trask, O. J. & Glaser, R. (1991). Spousal caregivers of dementia victims: Longitudinal changes in immunity and health. *Psychosomatic Medicine, 53,* 345–362.

Kiecolt-Glaser, J. K., & Glaser, R. (1988). Psychological influences on immunity: Implications for AIDS. *American Psychologist, 43,* 892–898.

Kiecolt-Glaser, J. K., & Glaser, R. (1992). Psychoneuroimmunology: Can psychological interventions modulate immunity? *Journal of Consulting and Clinical Psychology, 60,* 569–575.

Kiecolt-Glaser, J. K., & Glaser, R. (1993). Mind and immunity. In D. Goleman & J. Gurin (Eds.), *Mind/body medicine* (pp. 39–64). New York: Consumer Reports Books.

Kiecolt-Glaser, J. K., Glaser, R., Dyer, C., Shuttleworth, E. C., Ogrocki, P., & Speicher, C. E. (1987). Chronic stress and immune function in family care-givers of Alzheimer's disease victims. *Psychosomatic Medicine, 49,* 523–535.

Kiesler, C. A. (1982). Mental hospitals and alternative care: Noninstitutionalization as potential public policy for mental patients. *American Psychologist, 37,* 349–360.

Kiesler, C. A. (1991). Homelessness and public policy priorities. *American Psychologist, 46,* 1245–1252.

Kilmann, P. R., & Auerbach, R. (1979). Treatments of premature ejaculation and psychogenic impotence: A critical review of the literature. *Archives of Sexual Behavior, 8,* 81–100.

Kilmann, P. R., Mills, K. H., Caid, C., Davidson, E., Bella, B., Milan, R., Drose, G., Boland, J., Follingstad, D., Montgomery, B., & Wanlass, R. (1986). Treatment of secondary orgasmic dysfunction: An outcome study. *Archives of Sexual Behavior, 15,* 211–229.

Kilmann, P., Sabalis, R., Gearing, M., Bukstel, L., & Scovern, A. (1982). The treatment of sexual paraphilias: A review of the outcome research. *Journal of Sex Research, 18,* 193–252.

Kilpatrick, D. G., Veronen, L. J., & Best, C. L. (1985). Factors predicting psychological distress among rape victims (pp. 113–141). In C. R. Figley (Ed.), *Trauma and its wake.* New York: Brunner/Mazel.

Kilpatrick, D. G., Veronen, L. J., & Resick, P. A. (1979). The aftermath of rape: Recent empirical findings. *American Journal of Orthopsychiatry, 49,* 658–669.

Kimmel, P. (1984). Information and action. *Division of Community Psychology Newsletter, 18,* 13.

King, A. C., Taylor, C. B., Albright, C. A., & Haskells, W. L. (1990). The relationship between repressive and defensive coping styles and blood pressure responses in healthy, middle-aged men and women. *Journal of Psychosomatic Research, 34,* 461–471.

King, D. W., & King, L. A. (1991). Validity issues in research on Vietnam veteran adjustment. *Psychological Bulletin, 109,* 107–124.

King, N. J., Gullione, E., Tonge, B. J., & Ollendick, T. H. (1993). Self-reports of panic attacks and manifest anxiety in adolescents. *Behaviour Research and Therapy, 31,* 11–116.

King, R. M., & Wilson, G. V. (1991). Use of a diary technique to investigate psychosomatic relations in atopic dermatitis. *Journal of Psychosomatic Research, 35,* 697–706.

Kingdon, D. G., & Turkington, D. (1991). The use of cognitive behavior therapy with a normalizing rationale in schizophrenia. *Journal of Nervous and Mental Disease, 179,* 207–211.

Kingry-Westergaard, C., & Kelly, J.G. (1990). A contextualist epistemology for ecological research. In P. Tolan, C. Keys, F. Chertok, & L. Jason (Eds.), *Researching community psychology* (pp. 23–31). Washington, DC: American Psychological Association.

Kinsey, A. C., Pomeroy, W. B., Martin, C. E., & Gebhard, P. H. (1953). *Sexual behavior in the human female.* Philadelphia: Saunders.

Kinzie, J. D., Frederickson, R. H., Ben, R., Fleck, J., & Karls, W. (1984). Posttraumatic stress disorder. *American Journal of Psychiatry, 141,* 645–650.

Kinzl, J., Biebl, W., & Herold, M. (1993). Significance of vomiting for hyperamylasemia and sialadenosis in patients with eating disorders. *International Journal of Eating Disorders, 13,* 117–124.

Kirkpatrick, D. R. (1984). Age, gender and patterns of common intense fears among adults. *Behavior Research and Therapy, 22,* 141–150.

Kirkpatrick, M., Smith, D., & Roy, R. (1981). Lesbian

mothers and their children: A comparative survey. *American Journal of Orthopsychiatry, 5,* 545–551.

Kirsling, R. A. (1986). Review of suicide among elderly persons. *Psychological Reports, 59,* 359–366.

Kiser, L., Heston, J., Hickerson, S., Millsap, P., Nunn, W., & Pruitt, D. (1993). Anticipatory stress in children and adolescents. *American Journal of Psychiatry, 150,* 87–92.

Klagsbrun, F. (1976). *Too young to die: Youth and suicide.* Boston: Houghton Mifflin.

Klein, D., Gittelman, R., & Quitkin, F., et al. (1980). *Diagnosis and drug treatment of psychiatric disorders: Adults and children* (pp. 268–404). Baltimore: Williams & Wilkins.

Klein, D. C. (1968). *Community dynamics and mental health.* New York: Wiley.

Klein, D. F. (1984). Psychopharmacologic treatment of panic disorder. *Psychosomatics, 25,* 32–36.

Klein, D. F., & Klein, H. M. (1989). The substantive effect of variations in panic measurement and agoraphobia definition. *Journal of Anxiety Disorders, 3,* 45–56.

Klein, E., & Uhde, T. W. (1988). Controlled study of Verapamil for treatment of panic disorder. *American Journal of Psychiatry, 145,* 431–434.

Klein, M. (1975). *Envy and gratitude and other works, 1946–1963.* London: Hogarth.

Klein, R. G. (1987). Prognosis of attention deficit disorder and its management in adolescence. *Pediatrics in Review, 8,* 216–222.

Klein, W. L. (1967). The training of human service aides. In E. L. Cowen, E. A. Gardner, & M. Zax (Eds.), *Emergent approaches to mental health problems.* New York: Appleton-Century-Crofts.

Kleinberg, J., & Galligan, B. (1983). Effects of deinstitutionalization on adaptive behavior of mentally retarded adults. *American Journal of Mental Deficiency, 88,* 21–27.

Kleinknecht, R. A., Lenz, J., Ford, G., & DeBerard, S. (1990). Types and correlates of blood/injury–related vasovagal syncope. *Behaviour Research and Therapy, 28,* 289–295.

Kleinman, A. (1991, April). *Culture and DSM-IV: Recommendations for the introduction and for the overall structure.* Paper presented at the Conference on Culture and DSM-IV, Pittsburgh.

Kleinmutz, B. (1967). *Personality measurement: An introduction.* Homewood, IL: Dorsey.

Klemchuk, H. P., Hutchins, C. B., & Frank, R. I. (1990). Body dissatisfaction and eating-related problems on the college campus. *Journal of Counseling Psychology, 37,* 297–305.

Klerman, G. L. (1982). Practical issues in the treatment of depression and mania. In E. S. Paykel (Ed.), *Handbook of affective disorders.* New York: Guilford Press.

Klerman, G. L. (1988). Depression and related disorders of mood (affective disorders). In A. M. Nocholi Jr. (Ed.), *The new Harvard guide to psychiatry.* Cambridge, MA: Harvard University Press.

Klin, A. (1991). Young autistic children's listening preferences in regard to speech: A possible characterization of the symptom of social withdrawal. *Journal of Autism and Developmental Disorders, 21,* 29–42.

Klin, A., Volkmar, F. R., & Sparrow, S. S. (1992). Autistic social dysfunction: Some limitations of the theory of mind hypothesis. *Journal of Child Psychology and Psychiatry, 33,* 861–876.

Kline, M., Frances, A., Davis, W. W., Pincus, H. A., & Comer, R. J. (1993). *DSM-IV: 1993 update.* New York: W. H. Freeman and Company.

Klopfer, B., & Davidson, H. (1962). *The Rorschach technique.* New York: Harcourt, Brace, & World.

Klosko, J. S., Barlow, D. H., Tassinari, R., & Cerny, J. A. (1990). A comparison of Alprazolam and behavior therapy in the treatment of panic disorder. *Journal of Consulting and Clinical Psychology, 58,* 77–84.

Kluft, R. P. (1982). Varieties of hypnotic interventions in the treatment of multiple personality. *American Journal of Clinical Hypnosis, 24,* 230–240.

Kluft, R. P. (1985). Using hypnotic inquiry protocols to monitor treatment progress and stability in multiple personality disorder. *American Journal of Clinical Hypnosis, 28,* 63–74.

Kluft, R. P. (1987). First-rank symptoms as a diagnostic clue to multiple personality disorder. *American Journal of Psychiatry, 144,* 293–298.

Kluft, R. P. (1987). Dr. Kluft replies. *American Journal of Psychiatry, 144,* 125.

Knapp, S., & VandeCreek, L. (1990). Application of the duty to protect to HIV-positive patients. *Professional Psychology: Research and Practice, 21,* 161–166.

Kneisel, P. J., & Richards, G. P. (1988). Crisis intervention after the suicide of a teacher. *Professional Psychology: Research and Practice, 19,* 165–169.

Knight, B. G., Kelly, M., & Gatz, M. (1992). Psychotherapy and the older adult. In D. K. Freedheim (Ed.), *History of psychotherapy* (pp. 528–551). Washington, DC: American Psychological Association.

Knopf, I. J. (1984). *Childhood psychopathology* (2nd ed.). Englewood Cliffs, NJ: Prentice-Hall.

Knott, J., Platt, E., Ashley, M., & Gottlieb, J. (1953). A familial evaluation of the electroencephalogram of patients with primary behavior disorder and psychopathic personality. *EEG and Clinical Neurophysiology, 5,* 363–370.

Kobasa, S. C., Hilker, R. J., & Maddi, S. R. (1979). Psychological hardiness. *Journal of Occupational Medicine, 21,* 595–598.

Kockott, G., & Fahrner, E.-M. (1987). Transsexuals who have not undergone surgery: A follow-up study. *Archives of Sexual Behavior, 16,* 511–522.

Koegel, R. L., Screibman, L., Loos, L. M., Dirlich-Wilheim, H., Dunlap, G., Robbins, F. R., & Plienis, A. J. (1992). Consistent stress profiles in mothers of children with autism. *Journal of Autism and Developmental Disorders, 22*, 205–216.

Kohlenberg, R. J. (1973). Behavioristic approach to multiple personality: A case study. *Behavior Therapy, 4*, 137– 140.

Kohlenberg, R. J. (1974). Directed masturbation and the treatment of primary orgasmic dysfunction. *Archives of Sexual Behavior, 3*, 349–356.

Kohlenberg, R. J., & Tsai, M. (1991). *Functional analytic psychotherapy*. New York: Plenum.

Kohler, T., & Haimerl, C. (1990). Daily stress as a trigger of migraine attacks: Results of thirteen single-subject studies. *Journal of Consulting and Clinical Psychology, 58*, 870–872.

Kohon, G. (1987). Fetishism revisited. *International Journal of Psycho-Analysis, 68*, 213–228.

Kohut, H., & Wolf, E. S. (1978). The disorders of the self and treatment: An outline. *International Journal of Psychoanalysis, 59*, 413–425.

Kolarsky, A., & Madlatfousek, J. (1983). The inverse rule of preparatory erotic stimulation in exhibitionists: Phallometric studies. *Archives of Sexual Behavior, 12*, 123–148.

Kolb, L. C. (1987). A neuropsychological hypothesis explaining posttraumatic stress disorder. *American Journal of Psychiatry, 144*, 989–995.

Kolko, D. J., Ayllon, T., & Torrance, C. (1987). Positive practice routines in overcoming resistance to the treatment of school phobia: A case study with follow-up. *Journal of Behavior Therapy and Experimental Psychiatry, 18*, 249–257.

Kolko, D. J., and Kazdin, A. E. (1991). Children who set fires. *Journal Clinical Child Psychology, 20*, 191–201.

Kolko, D. J., Loar, L. L., & Sturnick, D. (1990). Inpatient social–cognitive skills training groups with conduct disordered and attention deficit disordered children. *Journal of Child Psychology and Psychiatry, 31*, 734–748.

Kondratas, A. (1991). Ending homelessness. *American Psychologist, 46*, 1226–1231.

Koop, C. E. (1987). Report of the Surgeon General's Workshop on pornography and public health. *American Psychologist, 42*, 944–945.

Kopelman, M. D. (1987). Amnesia: Organic and psychogenic. *British Journal of Psychiatry, 144*, 293–298.

Korchin, S. J. (1976). *Modern clinical psychology*. New York: Basic Books.

Korchin, S. J., & Ruff, G. E. (1964). Personality characteristics of the Mercury astronauts. In G. H. Grosser, H. Wechsler, & M. Greenblatt (Eds.), *The threat of impending disaster*. Cambridge, MA: M.I.T. Press.

Kosky, R. (1983). Childhood suicidal behavior. *Journal of Child Psychology and Psychiatry, 24*, 457–468.

Koss, M. P., Gidycz, C. A., & Wisniewski, N. (1987). The scope of rape: Incidence and prevalence of sexual aggression and victimization in a national sample of higher education students. *Journal of Consulting and Clinical Psychology, 55*, 162–170.

Kottler, J. A., & Brown, R. W. (1992). *Introduction to therapeutic counseling*. Belmont, CA: Brooks/Cole.

Kourany, R. F. C., & Williams, B. V. (1984). Capgras' syndrome with dysmorphic delusion in an adolescent. *Psychosomatics, 25*, 715–717.

Kovacs, M. (1980). The efficacy of cognitive and behavior therapies for depression. *American Journal of Psychiatry, 137*, 1495–1501.

Kovacs, M., Rush, A., Beck, A., & Hollon, S. (1981). Depressed outpatients treated with cognitive therapy or pharmacotherapy. *Archives of General Psychiatry, 38*, 33–39.

Kovel, J. (1976). *A complete guide to therapy*. New York: Crown.

Kraemer, G. W., & McKinney, W. T. (1979). Interactions of pharmacological agents which alter biogenic amine metabolism and depression: An analysis of contributing factors within a primate model of depression. *Journal of Affective Disorders, 1*, 33–54.

Kraepelin, E. (1923). *Textbook of psychiatry* (8th ed.). New York: Macmillan. (Originally published 1883.)

Kramer, B. (1973, November 16). Mass hysteria: An age-old illness still crops up in modern times. *Wall Street Journal*, p. 36b.

Kramer, M., Robins, L. N., George, L. K., Karno, M., & Locke, B. Z. (1988). One-month prevalence of mental disorders in the U.S.: Based on five epidemiologic catchment area (ECA) sites. *Archives of General Psychiatry, 45*, 977.

Kramer, M., Rosen, B. M., & Willis, E. M. (1973). Definitions and distributions of mental disorders in a racist society. In C. V. Willie, B. M. Kramer, & B. S. Brown (Eds.), *Racism and mental health*. Pittsburgh: University of Pittsburgh Press.

Krantz, S. E., & Moos, R. H. (1988). Risk factors at intake predict nonremission among depressed patients. *Journal of Consulting and Clinical Psychology, 56*(6), 863–869.

Kringlen, E. (1980). Schizophrenia: Research in Nordic countries. *Schizophrenia Bulletin, 6*, 566–578.

Kringlen, E., & Cramer, G. (1989). Offspring of monozygotic twins disconcordant for schizophrenia. *Archives of General Psychiatry, 46*, 873–888.

Kulka, R. A. (1982). Monitoring social change via survey replication: Prospects and pitfalls from a replication survey of social roles and mental health. *Journal of Social Issues, 38*, 17–38.

Kushner, M. (1965). The reduction of a long-standing fetish by means of aversive conditioning. In L. P. Ullmann & L. Krasner (Eds.), *Case studies in behavior modification*. New York: Holt, Rhinehart & Winston.

Kushner, M. G., Riggs, D. S., Foa, E. B., & Miller, S. M. (1992). Perceived controllability and the development of posttraumatic stress disorder (PTSD) in crime victims. *Behaviour Research and Therapy, 31*, 105–110.

LaGreca, A. M., & Stringer, S. A. (1985). The Wechsler Intelligence Scale for Children—Revised. In C. S. Newmark (Ed.), *Major psychological assessment instruments* (pp. 277–322). Boston: Allyn & Bacon.

Lacey, J. I., Bateman, D. E., & Van Lehn, R. (1953). Autonomic response specificity. *Psychosomatic Medicine, 15*, 8–21.

Lahey, B., Hartdagen S. E., Frick, P. J., McBurnett, K., Connor, R., & Hynd, G. W. (1988). Conduct disorder: Parsing the confounded relation to parental divorce and antisocial personality. *Journal of Abnormal Psychology, 97*, 334–337.

Lai, J. Y., & Linden, W. (1992). Gender anger expression style, and opportunity for anger release determine cardiovascular reaction to and recovery from anger provocation. *Psychosomatic Medicine, 54*, 297–310.

Laidlaw, J., & Rickens, A. (Eds.). (1976). *A textbook of epilepsy.* Edinburgh, Scotland: Churchill & Livingston.

Laing, R. D. (1965). Mystification, confusion and conflict. In I. Boszormenyi-Nagy & J. Framo (Eds.), *Intensive family therapy.* New York: Harper & Row.

Laker, B. (1992, April 14). A nightmare of memories. *Seattle Post-Intelligencer*, pp. C1–C2.

Lamb, H. R., & Grant, R. W. (1982). The mentally ill in an urban county jail. *Archives of General Psychiatry, 39*, 17–22.

Lamb, H. R., & Grant, R. W. (1983). Mentally ill women in a county jail. *Archives of General Psychiatry, 40*, 363–368.

Lamb, H. R. (1984). Deinstitutionalization and the homeless mentally ill. *Hospital Community Psychiatry, 35*, 899–907.

Lambert, M. J., Shapiro, D. A., & Bergin, A. E. (1986). The effectiveness of psychotherapy. In S. L. Garfield & A. E. Bergin (Eds.), *Handbook of psychotherapy and behavior change* (3rd ed., pp. 157–212). New York: Wiley.

Lambert, N. M., Hartsough, C. S., Sassone, D., & Sandoval, J. (1987). Persistence of hyperactivity symptoms from childhood to adolescence and associated outcomes. *American Journal of Orthopsychiatry, 57*, 22–23.

Lambert, N. M. (1988). Adolescent outcomes for hyperactive children. *American Psychologist, 43*, 786–799.

Lambley, P. (1974). Treatment of transvestism and subsequent coital problems. *Journal of Behavior Therapy and Experimental Psychiatry, 5*, 101–102.

Landesman S., & Butterfield, E. C. (1987). Normalization and deinstitutionalization of mentally retarded individuals. *American Psychologist, 42*, 809–816.

Lane, R. D., & Schwartz, G. E. (1987). Induction of lateralized sympathetic input to the heart by the CNS during emotional arousal: A possible neurophysiologic trigger of sudden cardiac death. *Psychosomatic Medicine, 49*, 274–284.

Lane, W. D., & Kern, R. M. (1987). Multidimensional treatment of a 14-year-old anorexia nervosa patient. *Journal of Child and Adolescent Psychotherapy, 4*, 211–215.

Langer, E. J., & Rodin, J. (1976). The effects of choice and enhanced personal responsibility for the aged: A field experiment in an institutional setting. *Journal of Personality and Social Psychology, 34*, 191–198.

Langevin, R. (1990). Sexual anomalies and the brain. In W. L. Marshall, D. R. Laws, & H. E. Barbaree (Eds.), *Handbook of sexual assault: Issues, theories, and treatment of the offender* (pp. 103–114). New York: Plenum Press.

Langevin, R., Bain, J., Wortzman, G., Hucker, S., Dickey, R., & Wright, P. (1988). Sexual sadism: Brain, blood, and behavior. In R. A. Prentky and V. L. Quisey (Eds.), *Human sexual aggression: Current perspectives. Annals of the New York Academy of Sciences, 528*, 79–110. Salem, MA: New York Academy of Sciences.

Langevin, R., Paitich, D., Ramsay, G., Anderson, C., Kamrad, J., Pope, S., Geller, G., Pearl, L., & Newman, S. (1979). Experimental studies of exhibitionism. *Archives of Sexual Behavior, 8*, 307–331.

Lask, B., & Bryant-Waugh, R. (1992). Early-onset anorexia nervosa and related eating disorders. *Journal of Child Psychology and Psychiatry, 33*, 281–300.

Last, C. G., Francis, G., Hersen, M., Kazdin, A. E., & Strauss, C. C. (1987). Separation anxiety and school phobia: A comparison using DSM-III criteria. *American Journal of Psychiatry, 144*, 653–657.

Last, C. G., Hersen, M., Kazdin, A., Orvaschel, H., & Perrin, S. (1991). Anxiety disorders in children and their families. *Archives of General Psychiatry, 48*, 928–934.

Last, C. G., & Perrin, S. (1993). Anxiety disorders in African-American and white children. *Journal of Abnormal Child Psychology, 21*, 153–162.

Last, C. G., Phillips, J. E., & Statfeld, A. (1987). Childhood anxiety disorders in mothers and their children. *Child Psychiatry and Human Development, 18*, 103–109.

Laudenslager, M. L., Ryan, S. M., Drugan, R. C., Hyson, R. L., & Maier, S. F. (1983). Coping and immunosuppression: Inescapable but not escapable shock suppresses lymphocyte proliferation. *Science, 220*, 568–570.

Laughlin, H. P. (1967). *The neuroses.* Washington, DC: Butterworth.

Lavy, E., Van Den Hout, M., & Arnitz, A. (1993). Attentional bias and spider phobia: Conceptual and clinical issues. *Behaviour Research and Therapy, 31,* 17–24.

Laws, D. R., & Marshall, W. L. (1990). A conditioning theory of the etiology and maintenance of deviant sexual preference and behavior. In W. L. Marshall, D. R. Laws, & H. E. Barbaree (Eds.), *Handbook of sexual assault: Issues, theories, and treatment of the offender* (pp. 209–230). New York: Plenum Press.

Lazarus, A. A. (1967). In support of technical eclecticism. *Psychological Reports, 21,* 415–416.

Lazarus, A. A. (1968). Learning theory and the treatment of depression. *Behavior Research and Therapy, 6,* 83–90.

Lazarus, A. A. (1977). Has behavior therapy outlived its usefulness? *American Psychologist, 32,* 550–554.

Lazarus, A. A. (1984). Multimodel therapy. In R. J. Corsini (Ed.), *Current psychotherapies.* Itasca, IL: Peacock.

Lazarus, R. S. (1966). *Patterns of adjustment and human effectiveness.* New York: McGraw-Hill.

Lazarus, R. S. (1969). *Psychological stress and the coping process.* New York: McGraw-Hill.

Lazarus, R. S. (1979, November). Positive denial: The case for not facing reality. *Psychology Today,* pp. 44–60.

Lazarus, R. S. (1983). *Psychological stress.* New York: McGraw-Hill.

Lazarus, R. S., & Launier, R. (1979). Stress-related transactions between person and environment. In L. A. Pervin & M. Lewis (Eds.), *Internal and external determinants.* New York: Plenum.

Leckman, J. F., Walker, D. E., & Cohen, D. J. (1993). Premonitory urges in Tourette's syndrome. *American Journal of Psychiatry, 150,* 98–102.

LeDoux, J. C., & Hazelwood, R. R. (1985). Police attitude and beliefs toward rape. *Journal of Police Science Administration, 13,* 211–220.

Lee, C. L., & Bates, J. E. (1985). Mother-child interaction at age two years and perceived difficult temperament. *Child Development, 56,* 1314–1325.

Lee, E. (1985). Inpatient psychiatric services for Southeast Asian refugees. In T. C. Owan (Ed.), *Southeast Asian mental health: Treatment, prevention, services, training, and research* (pp. 307–328). Washington, DC: U.S. Government Printing Office.

Lee, S., Hsu, L. K., & Wing, Y. K. (1992). Bulimia nervosa in Hong Kong Chinese patients. *British Journal of Psychiatry, 161,* 545–551.

Leff, J., Wig, N. N., Bedi, H., Menon, D. K., Kuipers, L., Korten, A., Ernberg, G., Day, R., Sartorius, N., & Jablenski, A. (1990). Relatives' expressed emotion and the course of schizophrenia in Chandigarh. *British Journal of Psychiatry, 156,* 351–356.

Leff, J. P. (1976). Schizophrenia and sensitivity to the family environment. *Schizophrenia Bulletin, 2,* 566–574.

Lehmann, H. E. (1974). Physical therapies of schizophre-

nia. In S. Arieti (Ed.), *American handbook of psychiatry* (2nd ed., Vol. 2). New York: Basic Books.

Lehmann, H. E. (1985). Affective disorders: Clinical features. In H. I. Kaplan & B. J. Sadock (Eds.), *Comprehensive textbook of psychiatry/IV* (pp. 786–810). Baltimore: Williams & Wilkins.

Leitenberg, H., Gross, J., Peterson, J., & Rosen, J. (1984). Analysis of an anxiety model and the process of change during exposure plus response prevention treatment of bulimia nervosa. *Behavior Therapy, 15,* 3–20.

Lelliott, P. T., Marks, I. M., Monteiro, W. O., Tsakiris, L. F., & Noshirvani, H. (1987). Agoraphobics 5 years after imipramine and exposure. *Journal of Nervous and Mental Disease, 175,* 599–605.

Lennox, W. J., & Lennox, M. A. (1960). *Epilepsy and related disorders.* Boston: Little, Brown.

Lenzenweger, M. F., Cornblatt, B. A., and Putnick, M. (1991). Schizotypy and sustained attention. *Journal of Abnormal Psychology, 100,* 84–89.

Leon, G. R. (1990). *Case histories of psychopathology.* Boston: Allyn & Bacon.

Leonard, H. L., Lenane, M. C., Swedo, S. E., Rettew, D. C., Gershon, E. S., & Rapoport, J. L. (1992). Tics and Tourette's disorder: A 2- to 7-year follow-up of 54 obsessive-compulsive children. *American Journal of Psychiatry, 149,* 1244–1251.

Leong, F. (1986). Counseling and psychotherapy with Asian-Americans: Review of the literature. *Journal of Counseling Psychology, 33,* 196–206.

Lerner, J. V., Hertzog, C., Hooker, K. A., Hassibi, M., & Thomas, A. (1988). A longitudinal study of negative emotional states.

Lesieur, H. R. (1989). Current research into pathological gambling and gaps in the literature. In H. J. Shaffer, S. A. Stein, B. Gambino, & T. N. Cummings (Eds.), *Compulsive gambling: Theory, research, and practice* (pp. 223–248). Lexington, MA: Lexington Books.

Leslie, R. (1991, July/August). Psychotherapist-patient privilege clarified. *The California Therapist,* 11–19.

Lesser, I. M. (1985). *Current concepts in psychiatry. New England Journal of Medicine, 312,* 690–692.

Levenkron, J. C., Cohen, J. D., Mueller, H. S., & Fisher, E. B. (1983). Modifying the type A coronary-prone behavior pattern. *Journal of Consulting and Clinical Psychology, 51,* 192–204.

Levenson, A. I. (1972). The community mental health centers program. In S. E. Golann & C. Eisdorfer (Eds.), *Handbook of community mental health.* New York: Appleton-Century-Crofts.

Levenson, A. J. (1981). *Basic psychopharmacology.* New York: Springer.

Levenstein, C., Prantera, C., Varvo, V., Scribano, M. L., Berto, E., Luzi, C., & Andreoli, A. (1993). Development of the Perceived Stress Questionnaire: A new tool for psychosomatic research. *Journal of Psychosomatic Research, 37,* 19–32.

Levine, D. S., & Willner, S. G. (1976, February). The cost of mental illness, 1974. *Mental Health Statistical Note No. 125* (pp. 1–7). Washington, DC: National Institute of Mental Health.

Levine, I. S., & Rog, D. J. (1990). Mental health services for homeless mentally ill persons: Federal initiatives and current service trends. *American Psychologist, 45,* 963–968.

Levine, M., & Perkins, D. V. (1987). *Principles of community psychology: Perspectives and applications.* New York: Oxford University Press.

Levine, S. V. (1984). *Radical departures: Desperate detours to growing up.* New York: Harcourt, Brace, Jovanovich.

Levinson, D. F., & Mowry, B. J. (1991). Defining the schizophrenia spectrum: Issues for genetic linkage studies. *Schizophrenia Bulletin, 17,* 491–514.

Levis, D. J. (1985). Implosive therapy: A comprehensive extension of conditioning theory of fear/anxiety to psychology. In S. Reiss & R. R. Bootzin (Eds.), *Theoretical issues in behavior therapy.* New York: Academic Press.

Levy, R. (1988). Suicide, homicide, and psychiatric emergencies. In H. H. Goldman (Ed.), *Review of general psychiatry* (pp. 651–657). Norwalk, CT: Appleton & Lange.

Lewine, R. (1986). Familial and nonfamilial schizophrenia? *American Journal of Psychiatry, 143,* 1064–1065.

Lewinsohn, P. M. (1974a). A behavioral approach to depression. In R. J. Friedman & M. M. Katz (Eds.), *The psychology of depression: Contemporary theory and research.* New York: Wiley.

Lewinsohn, P. M. (1974b). Clinical and theoretical aspects of depression. In K. S. Calhoun, H. C. Adams, & K. M. Mitchell (Eds.), *Innovative treatment methods of psychopathology.* New York: Wiley.

Lewinsohn, P. M. (1977). The behavioral study and treatment of depression. In M. Hersen, R. M. Eisler, & P. M. Miller (Eds.), *Progress in behavior modification.* New York: Academic Press.

Lewinsohn, P. M., & Graf, M. (1973). Pleasant activities and depression. *Journal of Consulting and Clinical Psychology, 41,* 261–268.

Lewinson, P. M., Hoberman, H. M., & Rosenbaum, M. (1988). A prospective study of risk factors for unipolar depression. *Journal of Abnormal Psychology, 97*(3), 251–264.

Lewinson, P. M., Hoberman, H. M., Teri, L., & Hautzinger, M. (1985). An integrative theory of depression. In S. Reiss & R. R. Bootzin (Eds.), *Theoretical issues in behavioral therapy* (pp. 331–359). Orlando, FL: Academic Press.

Lewinsohn, P. M., Hopps, H., Roberts, R. E., Seeley, J. R., & Andrews, J. A. (1993). Adolescent psychopathology: I. Prevalence and incidence of depression and other DSM-III-R disorders in high school students. *Journal of Abnormal Psychology, 102,* 133–144.

Lewinsohn, P. M., & Libet, J. (1972). Pleasant events, activity schedules, and depression. *Journal of Abnormal Psychology, 79,* 291–295.

Lewinsohn, P. M., Weinstein, M. S., & Alper, T. (1970). A behavioral approach to the group treatment of depressed persons: A methodological contribution. *Journal of Chemical Psychology, 26,* 525–532.

Lewinson, P. M., Zeiss, A. M., & Duncan, E. M. (1989). Probability of relapse after recovery from an episode of depression. *Journal of Abnormal Psychology, 97,* 387–398.

Ley, R. (1989). Dyspneic-fear and catastrophic cognitions in hyperventilatory panic attacks. *Behaviour Research and Therapy, 27,* 549–555.

Ley, R. (1992). The many faces of Pan: Psychological and physiological differences among three types of panic attacks. *Behaviour Research and Therapy, 30,* 347–357.

Li-Repac, D. (1980). Cultural influences on clinical perceptions: A comparison between Caucasian and Chinese-American therapists. *Journal of Cross-Cultural Psychology, 11*(3), 327–342.

Liberman, R. P., & Green, M. F. (1992). Whither cognitive-behavioral therapy for schizophrenia. *Schizophrenia Bulletin, 18,* 27–35.

Liberman, R. P., Mueser, K. T., & DeRisi, W. J. (1989). *Social skills training for psychiatric patients.* Elmsford, NY: Pergamon Press.

Liberman, R. P., Mueser, K. T., & Wallace, C. J. (1986). Social skills training for schizophrenic individuals at risk for relapse. *American Journal of Psychiatry, 143,* 523–526.

Lichtenstein, E. (1982). The smoking problem: A behavioral perspective. *Journal of Consulting and Clinical Psychology, 50,* 804–819.

Lichtenstein, E., & Danaher, B. (1976). Modification of smoking behavior: A critical analysis of theory, research, and practice. In M. Hersen, R. Eisler, & P. Miller (Eds.), *Progress in behavior modification: 3.* New York: Academic Press.

Lichtenstein, E., & Glasgow, R. (1977). Rapid smoking: Side effects and safeguards. *Journal of Consulting and Clinical Psychology, 45,* 815–821.

Lichtenstein, E., & Glasgow, R. E. (1992). Smoking cessation: What have we learned over the past decade? *Journal of Consulting and Clinical Psychology, 60,* 518–527.

Lichtenstein, E., & Rodrigues, M. (1977). Long-term effects of rapid smoking treatment for dependent cigarette smokers. *Addictive Behaviors, 2,* 109–112.

Lickey, M. E., & Gordon, B. (1991). *Medicine and mental illness.* New York: W.H. Freeman & Co.

Lieberman, M., Yalom, I., & Miles, M. (1973). *Encounter groups: First facts.* New York: Basic Books.

Liebert, R. M., & Baron, R. A. (1972). Some immediate effects of television violence on children's behavior. *Developmental Psychology, 6,* 469–475.

Lin, K-M., Miller, M. H., Poland, R. E., Nuccio, I., & Yamaguchi, M. (1991). Ethnicity and family involvement in the treatment of schizophrenia patients. *Journal of Nervous and Mental Disease, 179,* 631–633.

Lin, N., Simeone, R. S., Ensel, W. M., & Kuo, W. (1979). Social support, stressful life events, and illness: A model and an empirical test. *Journal of Health and Social Behavior, 20,* 108–119.

Lindemann, E. (1960). Psychosocial factors as stressor agents. In I. H. Tanner (Ed.), *Stress and psychiatric disorder.* Oxford, England: Basil, Blockwell & Mott.

Lindsay, W. R., Gamisu, C. V., McLaughlin, E., Hood, E. M., & Espie, C. A. (1987). A controlled trial of treatments for generalized anxiety. *British Journal of Clinical Psychology, 26,* 3–15.

Linehan, M. M. (1987). Dialectical behavior therapy for borderline personality disorder. Theory and method. *Bulletin of the Menninger Clinic, 51,* 261–276.

Linehan, M. M., & Nielsen, S. L., (1987). Assessment of suicide ideation and parasuicide: Hopelessness and social desirability. *Journal of Consulting and Clinical Psychology, 49,* 773–775.

Lipkowitz, M. H., & Idupuganti, S. (1983). Diagnosing schizophrenia in 1980: A survey of U.S. psychiatrists. *American Journal of Psychiatry, 140,* 52–55.

Lipman, A. J., & Kendall, P. C. (1992). Drugs and psychotherapy: Comparison, contrasts, and conclusions. *Applied and Preventive Psychology, 1,* 141–148.

Lipsitt, D. R. (1974). Psychodynamic considerations of hypochondriasis. *Psychosomatic Medicine, 23,* 132–141.

Lipsitt, D. R. (1983). The Munchausen mystery. *Psychology Today, 17,* 78–79.

Lipsky, M. J., Kassinove, H., & Miller, N. J. (1980). Effects of rational-emotive therapy, rational role reversal and rational-emotive imagery on the emotional adjustment of community mental health center patients. *Journal of Consulting & Clinical Psychology, 48,* 366–374.

Lishman, W. A. (1978). *The psychological consequences of cerebral disorder.* Oxford, England: Blackwell.

Litman, R. E. (1987). Hospital suicides: Lawsuits and standards. *Suicide and Life-Threatening Behavior, 12,* 212–220.

Livingston, J. A. (1982). Responses to sexual harassment on the job: Legal, organizational, and individual actions. *Journal of Social Issues, 38,* 5–22.

Livnat, S., & Felton, D. L. (1985). To the editor. *New England Journal of Medicine, 313,* 1357.

Lobel, B., & Hirschfeld, R. M. A. (1984). *Depression: What we know.* Washington, DC: U.S. Department of Health and Human Services, National Institute of Men-

tal Health.

Loeber, R. (1990). Development and risk factors of juvenile antisocial behavior and delinquency. *Clinical Psychology Review, 10,* 1–42.

Loftus, E. F. (1993). The reality of repressed memories. *American Psychologist, 48,* 518–537.

London, P. (1964a). *Modes and morals of psychotherapy.* New York: Holt, Rinehart & Winston.

London, P. (1964b). Subject characteristics in hypnosis research: Part 1. A survey of experience, interest, and opinion. *International Journal of Experimental Hypnosis, 9,* 151–161.

London, P. (1986). *The modes and morals of psychotherapy* (2nd ed.). New York: Hemisphere Publishing.

Longstreth, L. E. (1981). Revisiting Skeels's final study: A critique. *Developmental Psychology, 17,* 620–625.

Lopez, S. R. (1989). Patient variable biases in clinical judgment: Conceptual overview and methodological considerations. *Psychological Bulletin, 106,* 1–20.

Lopez, S. R., & Hernandez, P. (1987). When culture is considered in the evaluation and treatment of Hispanic patients. *Psychotherapy, 24,* 120–126.

Lopez, S. R., & Hernandez, P. (1986). How culture is considered in evaluations of psychotherapy. *The Journal of Nervous and Mental Disease, 176,* 598–606.

LoPiccolo, J. (1985). Advances in diagnosis and treatment of male sexual dysfunction. *Journal of Sex and Marital Therapy, 11,* 215–232.

LoPiccolo, J. (1991). Post-modern sex therapy for erectile failure. In R. C. Rosen & S. R. Leiblum (Eds.), *Erectile failure: diagnosis and treatment.* New York: Guilford.

LoPiccolo, J., Heiman, J. R., Hogan, D. R., & Roberts, C. W. (1985). Effectiveness of single therapists versus cotherapy teams in sex therapy. *Journal of Consulting and Clinical Psychology, 53,* 287–294.

LoPiccolo, J., & Stock, W. E. (1986). Treatment of sexual dysfunction. *Journal of Consulting and Clinical Psychology, 54,* 158–167.

LoPiccolo, L. (1980). Low sexual desire. In S. R. Leiblum & L. A. Pervin (Eds.), *Principles and practice of sex therapy.* New York: Guilford Press.

Lord, C., & Ward, M. J. (1984). Autism and childhood psychosis. In H. E. Adams & P. B. Sutker (Eds.), *Comprehensive handbook of psychopathology* (pp. 973–1000). New York: Plenum Press.

Lorion, R. P. (1990). Developmental analyses of community phenomena. In P. Tolan, C. Keys, F. Chertok, & L. Jason (Eds.), *Researching community psychology* (pp. 32–41). Washington, DC: American Psychological Association.

Lorion, R. P., & Felner, R. D. (1986). Research on psychotherapy with the disadvantaged. In A. E. Bergin & S. L. Garfield (Eds.), *Handbook of psychotherapy and behavior change* (pp. 739–776). New York: Wiley.

Losche, G. (1990). Sensorimotor and action development

in autistic children from infancy to early childhood. *Journal of Child Psychology and Psychiatry, 31,* 749–761.

Lothstein, L. (1977). Psychotherapy with patients with gender dysphoria syndromes. *Bulletin of Menninger Clinic, 41,* 563–582.

Lovaas, O. I. (1977). *The autistic child: Language development through behavior modification.* New York: Halsted Press.

Lovaas, O. I. (1987). Behavioral treatment and normal educational and intellectual functioning in young autistic children. *Journal of Consulting and Clinical Psychology, 55,* 3–9.

Lovaas, O. I., Schaeffer, B., & Simmons, J. Q. (1965). Building social behavior in autistic children by use of electric shock. *Journal of Experimental Research in Personality, 1,* 99–109.

Lowe, C. F., & Chadwick (1990). Verbal control of delusions. *Behavior Therapy, 21,* 461–479.

Ludwig, A. M., Brandsma, J. M., Wilbur, C. B., Bendfeldt, F., & Jameson, D. H. (1972). The objective study of multiple personality. *Archives of General Psychiatry, 26,* 298–310.

Luk, S. L., Leung, P. W. L., & Yuen, J. (1991). Clinical observations in the assessment of pervasiveness of childhood hyperactivity. *Journal of Child Psychology and Psychiatry, 32,* 833–850.

Lukas, C., & Seiden, H. M. (1990). *Silent grief: Living in the wake of suicide.* New York: Bantam Books.

Luparello, T., Lyons, H. A., Bleecker, E. R., & McFadden, E. R. (1968). Influences of suggestion on airway reactivity in asthmatic subjects. *Psychosomatic Medicine, 30,* 819–825.

Luria, A. R. (1982). *Language and cognition.* New York: Oxford University Press.

Lykken, D. F. (1957). A study of anxiety in the sociopathic personality. *Journal of Abnormal and Social Psychology, 55,* 6–10.

Lykken, D. T. (1982). Fearlessness: Its carefree charm and deadly risks. *Psychology Today, 16,* 20–28.

Macaskill, N. D. (1987). Delusion and parasitosis: Successful nonpharmacological treatment of Folie-a-deux. *British Journal of Psychiatry, 150,* 261–263.

MacEachron, A. E. (1983). Institutional reform and adaptive functioning of mentally retarded persons: A field experiment. *American Journal of Mental Deficiency, 88,* 2–12.

Machover, K. (1949). *Personality projection in the drawing of the human figure: A method of personality investigation.* Springfield, IL: Thomas.

Mackenzie, T. B., & Popkin, M. K. (1987). Suicide in the medical patient. *International Journal of Psychiatry in Medicine, 17,* 3–22.

Maddi, S. R. (1972). *Personality theories.* Homewood, IL: Dorsey.

Madle, R. A. (1990). Mental retardation in adulthood. In M. Hersen & C. G. Last (Eds.), *Handbook of child and adult psychopathology* (pp. 337–352). New York: Pergamon Press.

Madsen, C. H., Becker, W. C., Thomas, D. R., Koser, L., & Plager, E. (1970). An analysis of the reinforcing function of "sit-down" commands. In R. K. Parker (Ed.), *Readings in educational psychology.* Boston: Allyn & Bacon.

Magni, G., DiMario, F., Rizzardo, R., Pulin, S., & Naccarato, R. (1986). Personality profiles of patients with duodenal ulcer. *American Journal of Psychiatry, 143,* 1297–1300.

Magni, G., & Schifano, F. (1984). Psychological distress after stroke. *Journal of Neurology, Neurosurgery and Psychiatry, 47,* 567–568.

Maher, B. A. (1966). *Principles of psychopathology.* New York: McGraw-Hill.

Maher, B. A. (1988). Anomalous experiences and delusional thinking: The logic of explanations. In T. F. Oltmanns & B. A. Maher (Eds.), *Delusional beliefs.* New York: Wiley.

Maher, W. B., & Maher, B. A. (1985). Psychopathology: I. From ancient times to the eighteenth century. In G. A. Kimble & K. Schlesinger (Eds.), *Topics in the history of psychology* (Vol. 2). Hillsdale, NJ: Erlbaum.

Mahler, M. S. (1979). *The selected papers of Margaret S. Mahler* (Vol. 2). New York: Aronson.

Mahler, M. S., Pine, F., & Bergman, A. (1975). *The psychological birth of the human infant.* New York: Basic Books.

Mahoney, M. J. (1977). Reflections on the cognitive-learning trend in psychotherapy. *American Psychologist, 32,* 5–13.

Mahoney, M. J., & Lyddon, W. J. (1988). Recent developments in cognitive approaches to counseling and psychotherapy. *Counseling Psychologist, 16,* 190–234.

Malamuth, N. M. (1981). Rape proclivity among males. *Journal of Social Issues, 37,* 138–157.

Malamuth, N. M., & Briere, J. (1986). Sexual violence in the media: Indirect effects on aggression against women. *Journal of Social Issues, 42,* 75–92.

Malamuth, N. M., & Check, J. V. P. (1981). The effects of mass media exposure on acceptance of violence against women: A field experiment. *Journal of Research in Personality, 15,* 436–446.

Malamuth, N. M., & Check, J. V. P. (1983). Sexual arousal to rape depictions: Individual differences. *Journal of Abnormal Psychology, 92,* 55–67.

Malamuth, N. M., Sockloskie, R. J., Koss, M. P., & Tanaka, J. S. (1991). Characteristics of aggressors against women: Testing a model using a national sample of college students. *Journal of Consulting and Clinical Psychology, 59,* 670–681.

Malatesta, V. J., & Adams, H. E. (1984). The sexual dysfunctions. In H. E. Adams & P. B. Sutker (Eds.), *Comprehensive handbook of psychopathology* (pp. 725–776). New York: Plenum Press.

Malatesta, V. J., Pollack, R. H., Wilbanks, W. A., & Adams, H. E. (1979). Alcohol effects on the orgasmic-ejaculatory response in human males. *Journal of Sex Research, 15,* 101–107.

Mallick, M. J., Whipple, T. W., & Huerta, E. (1987). Behavioral and psychological traits of weight conscious teenagers: A comparison of eating disordered patients and high- and low-risk groups. *Adolescence, 22,* 157–168.

Malloy, P. F., Fairbank, J. A., & Keane, T. M. (1983). Validation of a multi-method assessment of posttraumatic stress disorders in Vietnam veterans. *Journal of Consulting and Clinical Psychology, 51,* 488–494.

Maltz, A. (1982). *Autism: Diagnostic and placement consideration.* Michigan State Planning Council for Developmental Disabilities.

Mann, J. J. (1989). Neurobiological models. In J. J. Mann (Ed.), *Models of depressive disorders: Psychological, biological, and genetic perspectives* (pp. 143–177). New York: Plenum Press.

Mann, J. J., Stanley, J. M., McBride, P. A., & McEwen, B. S. (1986). Increased serotonin Z and B-adrenergic receptor binding in the frontal cortices of suicide victims. *Archives of General Psychiatry, 43,* 954–956.

Manyande, A., Chayen, S., Priyakumar, P., Smith, C. C. T., Hayes, M., Higgins, D., Kee, S., Phillips, S., & Salmon, P. (1992). Anxiety and endocrine responses to surgery: Paradoxical effects of preoperative relaxation training. *Psychosomatic Medicine, 54,* 275–287.

Marantz, S. (1985, May 12). In the eyes of his public Ali is still the greatest. *Boston Globe,* p. 63.

Marantz, S., & Coates, S. (1991). Mothers of boys with gender identity disorder: A comparison of matched controls. *Journal of the American Academy of Child and Adolescent Psychiatry, 30,* 310–315.

Marchione, K., Michelson, L., Greenwald, M., & Dancu, C. (1987). Cognitive behavioral treatment of agoraphobia. *Behaviour Research and Therapy, 25,* 319–328.

Marcus, J., Hans, S. L., Nagler, S., Auerbach, J. G., Mirsky, A. F., & Aubrey, A. (1987). Review of the NIMH Israeli kibbutz–city study and the Jerusalem Infant Developmental study. *Schizophrenia Bulletin, 13,* 425–437.

Margolin, R. (1991). Neuroimaging. In J. Sadavoy, L. W. Lazarus, & L. F. Jarvik (Eds.), *Comprehensive review of geriatric psychiatry* (pp. 245–271). Washington, DC: American Psychiatric Press.

Margraf, J., Barlow, D. H., Clark, D. M., & Telch, M. J. (1993). Psychological treatment of panic: Work in progress on outcome, active ingredients, and follow-up. *Behaviour Research and Therapy, 31,* 1–8.

Margraf, J., Ehlers, A., & Roth, W. T. (1987). Panic attacks associated with perceived heart rate acceleration: A case report. *Behavior Therapy, 18,* 84–89.

Margraf, J., Ehlers, A., Roth, W. T., Clark, D. B., Sheikh, J., Agras, W. S., & Taylor, C. B. (1991). How "blind" are double-blind studies? *Journal of Consulting and Clinical Psychology, 59,* 184–187.

Marks, I. M. (1983). Are there anticompulsive or antiphobic drugs? Review of the evidence. *British Journal of Psychiatry, 143,* 338–347.

Marks, I. M. (1987). *Fears, phobias, and rituals.* New York: Oxford University Press.

Marks, I., & O'Sullivan, G. (1989). Drug and psychological treatments for agoraphobia, panic and obsessive-compulsive disorders: A review. *British Journal of Psychiatry, 153,* 650–658.

Marlatt, G. A. (1978). Craving for alcohol, loss of control and relapse: A cognitive-behavioral analysis. In P. E. Nathan & G. A. Marlatt (Eds.), *Experimental and behavioral approaches to alcoholism.* New York: Plenum.

Marlatt, G. A. (1983). The controlled-drinking controversy: A commentary. *American Psychologist, 38,* 1097–1110.

Marlatt, G. A., Demming, B., & Reid, J. (1973). Loss-of-control drinking in alcoholics: An experimental analogue. *Journal of Abnormal Psychology, 81,* 233–241.

Marlowe, N. I. (1992). Pain sensitivity and headache: An examination of the central theory. *Journal of Psychosomatic Research, 36,* 17–24.

Marmar, C. R. (1988). Personality disorders. In H. H. Goldman (Ed.), *Review of general psychiatry* (pp. 401–424). Norwalk, CT: Appleton & Lange.

Marmor, J., & Woods, S. M. (1980). *The interface between the psychodynamic and behavioral therapies.* New York: Plenum Medical.

Marmot, M. G., & Syme, S. L. (1976). Acculturation and coronary heart disease in Japanese-Americans. *American Journal of Epidemiology, 104,* 225–247.

Marquis, J. N. (1991). A report on seventy-eight cases treated by eye movement desensitization. *Journal of Behavior Therapy and Experimental Psychiatry, 22,* 187–192.

Marsh, J. C. (1988). What have we learned about legislative remedies for rape? In R. A. Prentky and V. L. Quisey (Eds.), *Human sexual aggression: Current perspectives. Annals of the New York Academy of Sciences, 528,* 79–110. Salem, MA: New York Academy of Sciences.

Marshall, W. L. (1988). Behavioral indices of habituation and sensitization during exposure to phobic stimuli. *Behaviour Research and Therapy, 26,* 67–77.

Marshall, W. L., Earls, C. M., Segal, Z., & Durke, J.

(1983). A behavioral program for the assessment and treatment of sexual aggressors. In K. D. Craig & R. J. McMahon (Eds.), *Advances in clinical behavior therapy* (pp. 148–174). New York: Brunner/Mazel.

Marshall, W. L., Jones, R., Ward, T., Johnston, P., & Barbaree, H. E. (1991). Treatment outcome with sex offenders. *Clinical Psychology Review, 11,* 465–486.

Martin, C. E. (1981). Factors affecting sexual functioning in 60–79-year-old married males. *Archives of Sexual Behavior, 10,* 399–420.

Maser, J. D., Kaelber, C., & Weise, R. E. (1991). International use and attitudes toward DSM-III and DSM-III-R: Growing consensus in psychiatric classification. *Journal of Abnormal Psychology, 100,* 271–279.

Maslow, A. H. (1954). *Motivation and personality.* New York: Harper & Row.

Masserman, J., Yum, K., Nicholson, J., & Lee, S. (1944). Neurosis and alcohol: An experimental study. *American Journal of Psychiatry, 101,* 389–395.

Masters, W. H., & Johnson, V. E. (1966). *Human sexual response.* Boston: Little, Brown.

Masters, W. H., & Johnson, V. E. (1970). *Human sexual inadequacy.* London: Churchill.

Masters, W. H., & Johnson, V. E. (1979). *Homosexuality in perspective.* Boston: Little, Brown.

Masterson, J. F. (1981). *The narcissistic and borderline disorders: An integrated developmental approach.* New York: Brunner/Mazel.

Masuda, M., & Holmes, T. H. (1976). The social readjustment rating scale: A cross-cultural study of Japanese and Americans. *Journal of Psychosomatic Research, 11,* 227–237.

Matarazzo, J. D. (1984). Behavioral health: A 1990 challenge for the health profession. In J. D. Matarazzo, S. M. Weiss, J. A. Herd, & N. E. Miller (Eds.), *Behavioral health: A handbook of health enhancement and disease prevention* (pp. 3–40). New York: Wiley.

Matarazzo, J. D. (1986). Computerized clinical psychological test interpretations. Unvalidated plus all mean and no sigma. *American Psychologist, 41,* 14–41.

Matarazzo, J. D. (1992). Psychological testing and assessment in the 21st century. *American Psychologist, 47,* 1007–1018.

Matchett, G., & Davey, G. C. L. (1991). A test of a disease-avoidance model of animal phobias. *Behaviour Research and Therapy, 29,* 91–94.

Matheny, K. B., Aycock, D. W., Pugh, J. L., Curlette, W. L., & Silva Cannella, K. P. (1986). Stress coping. *Counseling Psychologist, 14,* 499–549.

Mattick, R. P., & Peters, L. (1988). Treatment of severe social phobia: Effects of guided exposure with and without cognitive restructuring. *Journal of Consulting and Clinical Psychology, 56,* 251–260.

Mavissakalian, M. (1987a). Initial depression and response to imipramine in agoraphobia. *Journal of Nervous and Mental Disease, 175,* 358–361.

Mavissakalian, M. (1987b). The placebo effect in agoraphobia. *Journal of Nervous and Mental Disease, 175,* 95–99.

Mavissakalian, M., Michelson, L., & Dealy, R. S. (1983). Pharmacological treatment of agoraphobia: Imipramine with programmed practice. *British Journal of Psychiatry, 143,* 348–355.

May, D. C., & Turnbull, N. (1992). Plastic surgeons' opinions of facial surgery for individuals with Down syndrome. *Mental Retardation, 30,* 29–33.

May, P. R. (1968). *Treatment of schizophrenia: A comparative study of five treatment methods.* New York: Science House.

May, R. (1958). *Existence: A new dimension in psychiatry and psychology.* New York: Basic Books.

May, R. (Ed.). (1961). *Existential psychology.* New York: Random House.

May, R. (1967). *Psychology and the human dilemma.* New York: Van Nostrand.

May, R. (1983). *The discovery of being: Writings in existential psychology.* New York: Norton.

May, R. (1985). *My quest for beauty.* New York: Norton.

May, R., Angel, E., & Ellenberger, H. F. (Eds.). (1958). *Existence.* New York: Basic Books.

McBride, A. B. (1990). Mental health effects of women's multiple roles. *American Psychologist, 45,* 381–384.

McBride, M. C. (1990). Autonomy and the struggle for female identity: Implications for counseling women. *Journal of Counseling and Development, 69,* 22–26.

McBride, M. C., & Ender, K. L. (1977). Sexual attitudes and behavior among college students. *Journal of College Student Personnel, 18,* 183–187.

McCann, B. S., Woofolk, R. L., & Lehrer, P. M. (1987). Specificity in response to treatment: A study of interpersonal anxiety. *Behaviour Research and Therapy, 25,* 129–136.

McCary, J. L. (1973). *Human sexuality.* New York: Van Nostrand.

McCauley, E., & Ehrhardt, A. A. (1984). Follow-up of females with gender identity disorders. *Journal of Nervous and Mental Disease, 172,* 353–358.

McClelland, D., Davis, W., Kalin, R., & Wanner, E. (1972). *The drinking man.* New York: Free Press.

McConaghy, N. (1983). Agoraphobia, compulsive behaviours, and behaviour completion mechanisms. *Australian and New England Journal of Psychiatry, 17,* 170–179.

McCord, W., & McCord, J. (1964). *The psychopath: An essay on the criminal mind.* Princeton, NJ: Van Nostrand.

McCormick, R. A., and Taber, J. I. (1988). Attributional style in pathological gamblers in treatment. *Journal of Abnormal Psychology, 97,* 368–370.

McCracken, G. H. (1976). Neonatal septicemia and meningitis. *Hospital Practice, 11,* 89–97.

McCracken, L. M., & Larkin, K. T. (1991). Treatment of paruresis with in vivo desensitization: A case report. *Journal of Behavior Therapy and Experimental Psychiatry, 22,* 57–62.

McEwan, K. L., & Devins, G. M. (1983). Is increased arousal in social anxiety noticed by others? *Journal of Abnormal Psychology, 92,* 417–421.

McGee, R., Williams, S., Bradshaw, J., Chapel, J. L., Robins, A., & Silva, P. A. (1985). The Rutter scale for completion by teachers: Factor structure and relationships with cognitive abilities and family adversity for a sample of New Zealand children. *Journal of Child Psychology and Psychiatry, 26,* 727–739.

McGee, R., & Stanton, W. R. (1992). Sources of distress among New England adolescents. *Journal of Child Psychology and Psychiatry, 33,* 999–1010.

McGeer, P. L., & McGeer, E. G. (1980). Chemistry of mood and emotions. *Annual Review of Psychology, 31,* 273–307.

McGlashan, T. H., & Fenton, W. S. (1991). Classical subtypes for schizophrenia: Literature review for DSM III. *Schizophrenia Bulletin, 17,* 609–622.

McGoldrick, M., Pearce, J., & Giordano, J. (Eds.). (1982). *Ethnicity and family therapy.* New York: Guilford Press.

McGonagle, K. A., & Kessler, R. C. (1990). Chronic stress, acute stress, and depressive symptoms. *American Journal of Community Psychology, 18*(5), 681–706.

McGowan, S. (1991, November). Confidentiality and the ethical dilemma. *Guidepost, 34,* 1, 6, 10.

McGrath, M. E. (1987). *Where did I go? Schizophrenia: The experiences of patients and families.* Rockville, MD: National Institutes of Health.

McGuire, D. (1982). The problem of children's suicide: Ages 5–14. *International Journal of Offender Therapy and Comparative Criminology, 26,* 10–17.

McGuire, R. J., Carlisle, J. M., & Young, B. G. (1965). Sexual deviations as conditioned behavior: A hypothesis. *Behavior Research and Therapy, 2,* 185–190.

McInnis, M., & Mark, I. (1990). Audiotape therapy for persistent auditory hallucinations. *British Journal of Psychiatry, 157,* 913–914.

McIntosh, J. L., & Santos, J. F. (1981). Suicide among Native Americans: A compilation of findings. *Omega: Journal of Death and Dying, 11,* 303–316.

McKeon, P., & Murray, R. (1987). Familial aspects of obsessive-compulsive neurosis. *British Journal of Psychiatry, 151,* 528–534.

McLarnon, L. D., & Kaloupek, D. G. (1988). Psychological investigation of genital herpes recurrence: Prospective assessment and cognitive-behavioral intervention for a chronic physical disorder. *Health Psychology, 1,* 231–249.

McLeod, B. (1985). Real work for real pay. *Psychology Today, 19,* 42–50.

McLeod, J. D., Kessler, R. C., & Landis, K. R. (1992). Speed of recovery from major depressive episodes in a community sample of married men and women. *Journal of Abnormal Psychology, 101*(2), 277–286.

Mannuzza, S., Klein, R. G., Bonagura, N., Malloy, P., Giampino, T. L., & Addalli, K. A. (1991). Hyperactive boys almost grown up. *Archives of General Psychiatry, 48,* 77–83.

McLin, W. M. (1992). Introduction to issues in psychology and epilepsy. *American Psychologist, 47*(9), 1124–1125.

McNamee, H. B., Mello, N. K., & Mendelson, J. H. (1968). Experimental analysis of drinking patterns of alcoholics: Concurrent psychiatric observations. *American Journal of Psychiatry, 124,* 1063–1069.

McQueen, P. C., Spence, M. W., Garner, J. B., Pereira, L. H., & Winson, E. J. T. (1987). Prevalence of major mental retardation and associated disabilities in the Canadian Maritime Provinces. *American Journal of Mental Deficiency, 91,* 460–466.

McReynolds, R. (1989). Diagnosis and clinical assessment: Current status and major issues. *Annual Review in Psychology, 40,* 83–108.

Mead, M. (1949). *Male and female.* New York: Morrow.

Meares, A. (1979). Mind and cancer. *Lancet, 22,* 978.

Mechanic, D. (Coordinator). (1978). Report of the task panel on the nature and scope of the problems. In *President's Commission on Mental Health* (Vol. 2, pp. 1–138). Washington, DC: U.S. Government Printing Office.

Mednick, S. A. (1985). Crime in the family tree. *Psychology Today, 19,* 58–61.

Mednick, S. A., Cannon, T., Parnas, J., & Schulsinger, F. (1989). 27 year follow-up of the Copenhagen high-risk for schizophrenia project: Why did some of the high-risk offspring become schizophrenic? *Schizophrenia Research, 2,* 14.

Mednick, S. A., & Christiansen, K. O. (Eds.). (1977). *Biosocial bases of criminal behavior.* New York: Gardner Press.

Mednick, S. A., & Kandel, E. (1988). Genetic and perinatal factors in violence. In T. E. Moffitt & S. A. Mednick (Eds.), *Biological contributions to crime causation* (pp. 40–54). Boston: Martinus Nijhoff Publishers.

Mednick, S. A., & Schulsinger, F. (1968). Some premorbid characteristics related to breakdown in children with schizophrenic mothers. In D. Rosenthal & S. Kety (Eds.), *The transmission of schizophrenia.* New York: Pergamon Press.

Meehl, P. E. (1962). Schizotaxia, schizotypia, schizophrenia. *American Psychologist, 17,* 827–838.

Megargee, E. I. (1970). The prediction of violence with psychological tests. In C. D. Speilberger (Ed.), *Current topics in clinical and community psychology* (Vol. 2). New York: Academic Press.

Meichenbaum, D. H. (1974). The clinical potential of modifying what clients say to themselves. In M. J. Mahoney & C. E. Thoresen (Eds.), *Self-control: Power to the person.* Monterey, CA: Brooks/Cole.

Meichenbaum, D. H. (1976). Cognitive behavior modification. In J. T. Spence, R. C. Carson, & J. W. Thibaut (Eds.), *Behavioral approaches to therapy.* Morristown, NJ: General Learning Press.

Meichenbaum, D. H. (1977). *Cognitive-behavior modification: An integrative approach.* New York: Plenum.

Meichenbaum, D. H. (1985). *Stress-inoculation training.* New York: Pergamon Press.

Meichenbaum, D. H., & Cameron, R. (1982). Cognitive behavior therapy. In G. T. Wilson & C. M. Franks (Eds.), *Contemporary behavior therapy: Conceptual and empirical foundations.* New York: Guilford Press.

Meichenbaum, D. H., Gilmore, J., & Fedoravicius, A. (1971). Group insight versus group desensitization in treating speech anxiety. *Journal of Consulting and Clinical Psychology, 36,* 410–421.

Meier, M. J. (1992). Modern clinical neuropsychology in historical perspective. *American Psychologist, 47*(4), 550–558.

Melges, F., & Bowlby, J. (1969). Types of hopelessness in psychopathological process. *Archives of General Psychiatry, 20,* 690–699.

Melton, G. B. (1988). Ethical and legal issues in AIDS-related practice. *American Psychologist, 43,* 941–947.

Meltzoff, J., & Kornreich, M. (1970). *Research in psychotherapy.* New York: Atherton.

Mendels, J. (1970). *Concepts of depression* (p. 6). New York: Wiley.

Mercer, J. R. (1979). *System of Multicultural Pluralistic Assessment (SOMPA): Technical manual.* New York: Psychological Corporation.

Mercer, J. R. (1988). Death of the IQ paradigm: Where do we go from here? In W. J. Lonner & V. O. Tyler (Eds.), *Cultural and ethnic factors in learning and motivation: Implications for education.* Bellingham, WA: Western Washington University.

Mersky, H. (1992). The manufacture of personalities: The production of multiple personality disorder. *British Journal of Psychiatry, 160,* 327–340.

Meyer, J., & Peter, D. (1979). Sex reassignment: Follow-up. *Archives of General Psychiatry, 36,* 1010–1015.

Meyer, R. G. (1989). *The clinician's handbook.* Needham Heights, MA: Allyn & Bacon.

Meyer, R. G., & Osborne, Y. V. H. (1982). *Case studies in abnormal behavior.* Boston: Allyn & Bacon.

Meyer, W. S., & Keith, C. R. (1991). Homosexual and preoedipal issues in the psychoanalytic psychotherapy of a female-to-male transsexual. In C. W. Socarides & V. D. Volkan (Eds.), *The homosexualities and the therapeutic process* (pp. 75–96). Adison, CT: International Universities Press.

Meyers, W. A. (1991). A case history of a man who made obscene telephone calls and practiced frotteurism. In G. I. Fogel & W. A. Myers (Eds.), *Perversions and near-perversions in clinical practice* (pp. 109–126). New Haven, CT: Yale University Press.

Mezzich, J. E., & Good, B. (1991, April 11). *Cultural proposals for the DSM-IV multiaxial formulation.* Paper presented at the Conference on Culture and DSM-IV, Pittsburgh.

Michelson, L. (1987). Cognitive-behavioral assessment and treatment of agoraphobia. In L. Michelson & M. Ascher (Eds.), *Anxiety and stress disorders: Cognitive behavioral assessment and treatment.* New York: Guilford Press.

Michelson, L. K., & Marchione, K. (1991). Behavioral, cognitive, and pharmacological treatments of panic disorder with agoraphobia: Critique and synthesis. *Journal of Consulting and Clinical Psychology, 59,* 100–114.

Miklowitz, D. J., Goldstein, M. J., Falloon, I. R. H., & Doaner, J. A. (1984). Interactional correlates of expressed emotion in the families of schizophrenics. *British Journal of Psychiatry, 144,* 482–487.

Miklowitz, D. J., Strachan, A. M., Goldstein, M. J., Doane, J. A., Snyder, K. S., Hogarty, G. E., & Falloon, I. R. H. (1986). Expressed emotion and communication deviance in the families of schizophrenics. *Journal of Abnormal Psychology, 95,* 60–66.

Milich, R., & Pelham, W. E. (1986). Effects of sugar ingestion on the classroom and playground behavior of attention deficit disordered boys. *Journal of Consulting and Clinical Psychology, 54,* 714–718.

Miller, D. J., & Thelen, M. H. (1986). Knowledge and beliefs about confidentiality in psychotherapy. *Professional Psychology, 17,* 15–19.

Miller, H. L., Coombs, D. W., & Leeper, J. D. (1984). An analysis of the effects of suicide prevention facilities on suicide rates in the United States. *American Journal of Public Health, 74,* 340–343.

Miller, J. B. (1976). *Toward a new psychology of women.* Boston: Beacon Press.

Miller, N. E. (1974). Applications of learning and biofeedback to psychiatry and medicine. In A. M. Freedman, H. I. Kaplan, & B. J. Sadock (Eds.), *Comprehensive textbook of psychiatry* (2nd ed.). Baltimore: Williams & Wilkins.

Miller, S. D., & Triggiano, P. J. (1992). The psychophysiological investigation of multiple personality disorder: Review and update. *American Journal of Clinical Hypnosis, 35,* 47–61.

Miller, T. Q., Turner, C. W., Tinsdale, R. S., Posavac, E. J., & Dugoni, B. L. (1991). Reasons for the trend toward null findings in research on Type A behavior. *Psychological Bulletin, 110,* 469–485.

Millon, T. (1973). *Theories of psychopathology and personality.* Philadelphia: Saunders.

Millon, T. (1975). Reflections on Rosenhan's "On being sane in insane places." *Journal of Abnormal Psychology, 84,* 456–461.

Millon, T. (1983). The DSM-III: An insider's perspective. *American Psychologist, 38,* 804–814.

Millon, T., & Everly, G. S. (1985). *Personality and its disorders.* New York: Wiley.

Mills, C. J., & Noyes, H. L. (1984). Patterns and correlates of initial and subsequent drug use among adolescents. *Journal of Consulting and Clinical Psychology, 52,* 231–243.

Milstein, V. (1988). EEG topography in patients with aggressive violent behavior. In T. E. Moffitt & S. A. Mednick (Eds.), *Biological contributions to crime causation* (pp. 121–134). Boston: Martinus Nijhoff Publishers.

The mind of a murderer (1984). *Frontline: Part I.*

Minde, K. K. (1977). Children in Uganda: Rates of behavioural deviations and psychiatric disorders in various school and clinic populations. *Journal of Child Psychology and Psychiatry, 18,* 23–27.

Mineka, S., & Sutton, S. K. (1992). Cognitive biases and the emotional disorders. *Psychological Science, 3*(1), 65–69.

Miniszek, N. A. (1983). Development of Alzheimer's disease in Down syndrome individuals. *American Journal of Mental Deficiency, 87,* 377–385.

Mintz, J., Mintz, L., & Goldstein, M. (1987). Expressed emotion and relapse in first episodes of schizophrenia. *British Journal of Psychiatry, 151,* 314–320.

Mintz, L. B., & Betz, N. E. (1988). Prevalence and correlates of eating disordered behaviors among undergraduate women. *Journal of Counseling Psychology, 35,* 463–471.

Minuchin, S. (1974). *Families and family therapy.* Cambridge, MA: Harvard University Press.

Mischel, W. (1968). *Personality and assessment.* New York: Wiley.

Mitchell, C. M. (1983). The dissemination of a social intervention: Process and effectiveness of two types of para-

professional change agents. *American Journal of Community Psychology, 11,* 723–740.

Modestin, J. (1992). Multiple personality disorder in Switzerland. *American Journal of Psychiatry, 149,* 88–92.

Monahan, J. (1981). *The clinical prediction of violent behavior.* Rockville, MD: National Institute of Mental Health.

Monahan, J. (1976). The prevention of violence. In J. Monahan (Ed.), *Community mental health and the criminal justice system.* Elmsford, NY: Pergamon Press.

Monday, J., Montplaisir, J., & Malo, J-L. (1987). Dream process in asthmatic subjects with nocturnal attacks. *American Journal of Psychiatry, 144,* 638–640.

Money, J. (1987). Masochism: On the childhood origin of paraphilia, opponent-process theory, and antiandrogen therapy. *Journal of Sex Research, 23,* 273–275.

Money, J., Hampson, J. G., & Hampson, J. L. (1957). Imprinting and establishing gender role. *Archives of Neurological Psychiatry, 77,* 333–336.

Monroe, M., & Simons, A. D. (1991). Diathesis-stress theories in the context of life stress research: Implications for the depressive disorders. *Psychological Bulletin, 110*(3), 406–425.

Monroe, S. M., Simons, A. D., & Thase, M. E. (1991). Onset of depression and time to treatment entry: Roles of life stress. *Journal of Consulting and Clinical Psychology, 59*(4), 566–573.

Monroe, S. M., Thase, M. E., & Simons, A. D. (1992). Social factors and the psychobiology of depression: Relations between life stress and rapid eye movement sleep latency. *Journal of Abnormal Psychology, 101*(3), 528–537.

Mooney, J. (1988, November 18). A flight from pain for Vietnam veterans. *Seattle Post-Intelligencer,* p. B2.

Moos, R. H., & Finney, J. W. (1983). The expanding scope of alcoholism treatment evaluation. *American Psychologist, 38,* 1036–1044.

Moreno, J. L. (1946). *Psychodrama.* New York: Beacon.

Morey, L. C. (1988). Personality disorders in DSM-III and DSM-III-R: Convergence, coverage, and internal consistency. *American Journal of Psychiatry, 145,* 573–577.

Morey, L. C., & Ochoa, E. S. (1989). An investigation of adherence to diagnostic criteria: Clinical diagnosis of the DSM-III personality disorders. *Journal of Personality Disorders, 3,* 180–192.

Morgan, S. B., & Brown, T. L. (1988). Luria-Nebraska Neuropsychological Battery—Children's Revision: Concurrent validity with three learning disability subtypes. *Journal of Consulting and Clinical Psychology, 56,* 463–466.

Morris, N. (1968). Psychiatry and the dangerous criminal. *Southern California Law Review, 41,* 514–547.

Morse, S. J. (1982). Failed explanation and criminal responsibility: Experts and the unconscious. *Virginia Law Review, 68*, 971–1084.

Moser, C., & Levitt, E. E. (1987). An exploratory-descriptive study of a sadomasochistically oriented sample. *Journal of Sex Research, 23*, 322–337.

Mostofsky, D. I., & Balaschak, B. A. (1979). Psychological control of seizures. *Psychological Bulletin, 84*, 723–750.

Mrazek, D. A. (1993). Asthma: Stress, allergies, and the genes. In D. Goleman & J. Gurin (Eds.), *Mind/body medicine* (pp. 193–205). New York: Consumer Reports Books.

Muehleman, T., Pickens, B. K., & Robinson, F. (1985). Informing clients about the limits to confidentiality, risks, and their rights: Is self-disclosure inhibited? *Professional Psychology: Research and Practice, 16*, 385–397.

Mukherjee, S., Shukla, S., Woodle, J., Rosen, A. M., & Olarte, S. (1983). Misdiagnosis of schizophrenia in bipolar patients: A multiethnic comparison. *American Journal of Psychiatry, 140*, 1571–1574.

Murphree, O. D., & Dykman, R. A. (1965). Litter patterns in the offspring of nervous and stable dogs: I. Behavioral tests. *Journal of Nervous and Mental Disorders, 141*, 321–332.

Murphy, C. E. (1973). Suicide and the right to die. *American Journal of Psychiatry, 130*, 472–473.

Murphy, J. (1987, March 16). Tracing fragile X syndrome. *Time*, p. 78.

Murray, E. J. (1983). Beyond behavioral and dynamic therapy. *British Journal of Clinical Psychology, 22*, 127–128.

Murray, H. A., & Morgan, H. (1938). *Explorations in personality*. New York: Oxford University Press.

Murrey, G. J., Cross, H. J., & Whipple, J. (1992). Hypnotically created pseudomemories: Further investigation into "memory distortion or response bias" question. *Journal of Abnormal Psychology, 101*, 75–77.

Murrin, M. R., & Laws, D. R. (1990). The influence of pornography on sexual crimes. In W. L. Marshall, D. R. Laws, & H. E. Barbaree (Eds.), *Handbook of sexual assault. Issues, theories, and treatment of the offender* (pp. 73–92). New York: Plenum Press.

Myers, H. F., & King, L. M. (1983). Mental health issues in the development of the black American child. In G. J. Powell (Ed.), *The psychosocial development of minority group children*. New York: Brunner/Mazel.

Myers, J. K., Weissman, M. M., Tischler, G. L., Holzer, C. E., Leaf, P. J., Orvaschel, H., Anthony, J. C., Boyd, J. H., Burke, J. D., Kramer, M., & Stoltzman, R. (1984). Six-month prevalence of psychiatric disorders in three communities. *Archives of General Psychiatry, 41*, 959–967.

Myers, W. A. (1992). Body dysmorphic disorder. *American Journal of Psychiatry, 149*, 718.

Nagler, S., Marcus, J., Sohlberg, S. C., Lifshitz, M., & Silberman, E. K. (1985). Clinical observation of high-risk children. *Schizophrenia Bulletin, 11*, 107–111.

Nash, M. R., Drake, S. D., Wiley, S., & Khalsa, S. (1986). Accuracy of recall by hypnotically age-regressed subjects. *Journal of Abnormal Psychology, 95*, 298–300.

Nathan, P. E. (1976). Alcoholism. In H. Leitenberg (Ed.), *Handbook of behavior modification and behavior therapy*. Englewood Cliffs, NJ: Prentice-Hall.

Nathan, P. E. (1988). The addictive personality is the behavior of the addict. *Journal of Consulting and Clinical Psychology, 56*, 183–188.

Nathan, P. E. (1991). Substance use disorders in the DSM-IV. *Journal of Abnormal Psychology, 100*, 356–361.

Nathan, P., & Jackson, A. (1976). Behavior modification. In I. Weiner (Ed.), *Clinical methods in psychology*. New York: Wiley.

National Association of Social Workers. (1990). *Code of ethics* (rev. ed.). Silver Springs, MD: Author.

National Center for Health Statistics. (1988). Advance report of final mortality statistics, 1986, *NCHS Monthly Vital Statistics Report, 37* (Supp. 6).

National Center for Health Statistics. (1990). Washington, DC: U.S. Government Printing Office.

National Institute on Drug Abuse. (1991). *National household survey on drug abuse: Main findings 1990*. Washington, DC: U.S. Government Printing Office.

National Institute of Mental Health. (1975). *Report of research task force: Research in the service of mental health*. DHEW Pub. 75–236. Rockville, MD: National Institute of Mental Health.

National Institute of Mental Health. (1985). *Mental Health: United States, 1985*. Washington, DC: U.S. Government Printing Office.

National Institute of Mental Health. (1986). *Phobias and panic*. Rockville, MD: U.S. Department of Health and Human Services.

National Institute of Mental Health. (1991). *Panic disorder*. Washington, DC: U.S. Government Printing Office.

National Institutes of Health. (1981). *The dementias: Hope through research*. Bethesda, MD: National Institutes of Health.

Neale, J. M., & Oltmanns, T. F. (1980). *Schizophrenia*. New York: Wiley.

Neff, J. A. (1984). Race differences in psychological distress: The effects of SES, urbanicity, and measurement strategy. *American Journal of Community Psychology, 12*, 337–352.

Nelson-Gray, R. O. (1991). DSM-IV: Empirical guidelines

from psychometrics. *Journal of Abnormal Psychology, 100*, 308–315.

Nettlebladt, P., & Uddenberg, N. (1979). Sexual dysfunction and sexual satisfaction in 58 married Swedish men. *Journal of Psychosomatic Research, 23*, 141–148.

Neugebauer, R. (1979). Medieval and early modern theories of mental illness. *Archives of General Psychiatry, 36*, 477–483.

Neuringer, C. (1964). Rigid thinking in suicidal individuals. *Journal of Consulting Psychology, 28*, 54–58.

Neuringer, C. (1976). Current developments in the study of suicidal thinking. In E. S. Schneidman (Ed.), *Suicidology: Contemporary developments.* New York: Grune & Stratton.

Newman, L. E., & Stoller, R. J. (1974). Nontranssexual men who seek sex reassignment. *American Journal of Psychiatry, 131*, 437–441.

Newmark, C. S. (1985). The MMPI. In C. S. Newmark (Ed.), *Major psychological assessment instruments* (pp. 11–64). Boston: Allyn & Bacon.

Niaura, R. S., Rohsenow, D. J., Binkoff, J. A., Monti, P. M., Pedraza, M., & Abrams, D. B. (1988). Relevance of cue reactivity to understanding alcohol and smoking relapse. *Journal of Abnormal Psychology, 97*, 133–152.

Nichols, M. (1984). *Family therapy.* New York: Gardner Press.

Nicholson, R. A., & Berman, J. S. (1983). Is follow-up necessary in evaluating psychotherapy? *Psychological Bulletin, 93*, 261–278.

Nielsen, E. B., Lyon, M., & Ellison, G. (1983). Apparent hallucinations in monkeys during the around-the-clock amphetamine for seven to fourteen days. *Journal of Nervous and Mental Disease, 171*, 222–233.

Nigg, J. T., Lohr, N. E., Westen, D., Gold, L. J., & Silk, K. R. (1992). Malevolent object representations in borderline personality disorder and major depression. *Journal of Abnormal Psychology, 101*, 61–67.

NIMH Pharmacology Study Group. (1964). Phenothiazine treatment in acute schizophrenics. *Archives of General Psychiatry, 10*, 246–261.

Noble, E. P. (1990). Alcoholic fathers and their sons: Neuropsychological, electrophysiological, personality, and family correlates. In C. R. Cloninger & H. Begleiter (Eds.), *Genetics and biology of alcoholism* (pp. 159–170). Cold Spring Harbor, NY: Cold Spring Harbor Laboratory Press.

Nolen-Hoeksema, S. (1987). Sex differences in unipolar depression: Evidence and theory. *Psychological Bulletin, 101*, 259–282.

Nolen-Hoeksema, S. (1991). Responses to depression and their effects on the duration of depressive episodes. *Journal of Abnormal Psychology, 100*(4), 569–582.

Nolen-Hoeksema, S., Girgus, J. S., & Seligman, M. E. (1992). Predictors and consequences of childhood depressive symptoms: A 5-year longitudinal study. *Journal of Abnormal Psychology, 101*, 405–422.

Norcross, J. C., & Prochaska, J. O. (1988). A study of eclectic (and integrative) views revisited. *Professional Psychology: Research and Practice, 19*, 170–174.

Nowlis, D., & Kamiya, J. (1970). The control of EEG algorithm through auditory feedback and the associated mental activity. *Psychophysiology, 6*, 476–484.

Nuechterlein, K. H. (1987). Vulnerability models for schizophrenia: State of the art. In H. Hafner, W. F. Gattaz, & W. Janzarik (Eds.) *Search for the causes of schizophrenia.* Heidelberg: Springer-Verlag, 1987.

Nuechterlein, K. H., & Dawson, M. E. (1984). A heuristic vulnerability/stress model of schizophrenic episodes. *Schizophrenic Bulletin, 10*, 300–311.

Nuechterlein, K. H., Dawson, M. E., Gitlin, M., Ventura, J., Goldstein, M. J., Snyder, K. S., Yee, C. M., & Mintz, J. (1992). Developmental processes in schizophrenic disorders: Longitudinal studies of vulnerability and stress. *Schizophrenia Bulletin, 18*, 387–425.

Nussbaum, N. L., & Bigler, E. D. (1989). Halstead-Reitan neuropsychological test batteries for children. In C. R. Reynolds & E. Fletcher-Janzen (Eds.), *Handbook of clinical child neuropsychology* (pp. 181–191). New York: Plenum Press.

Nutt, R. L. (1979). Review and preview of attitudes and values of counselors of women. *Counseling Psychologist, 8*, 18–20.

O'Connor, K. (1987). The interaction of hostile and depressive behaviors: A case study of a depressed boy. *Journal of Child and Adolescent Psychotherapy, 3*, 105–108.

O'Leary, K. D., & Wilson, G. T. (1975). *Behavior therapy: Application and outcome.* Englewood Cliffs, NJ: Prentice-Hall.

Observer. (1992, July). *The severely mentally ill and the homeless mentally ill.* Washington, DC: American Psychological Society, 14–15.

Office of Technical Assessment. (1983). *The effectiveness of costs of alcoholism treatment.* Washington, DC: U.S. Congress.

Ofshe, R. J. (1992). Inadvertent hypnosis during interrogation: False confession due to dissociative state; misidentified multiple personality and the satanic cult hypothesis. *International Journal of Clinical and Experimental Hypnosis, XL*, 125–156.

Ohlsen, M. M., Horne, A. M., & Lawe, C. F. (1988). *Group counseling.* New York: Holt, Rinehart & Winston.

Ohman, A., & Soares, J. J. F. (1993). On the autonomic nature of phobic fear: Conditioned electrodermal responses to masked fear-relevant stimuli. *Journal of Abnormal Psychology, 102,* 121–132.

Oke, N. J., & Schreibman, L. (1990). Training social imitations to a high-functioning autistic child: Assessment of collateral behavior change and generalization in a case study. *Journal of Autism and Developmental Disorders, 20,* 479–497.

Oliver, J., Shaller, C. A., Majovski, L. V., & Jacques, S. (1982). Stroke mechanisms: Neuropsychological implications. *Clinical Neuropsychology, 4,* 81–84.

Ollendick, T. H., & King, N. J. (1991). Origins of childhood fears: An evaluation of Rachman's theory of fear acquisition. *Behaviour Research and Therapy, 29,* 117–123.

Olmsted, M. P., Davis, R., Rockert, W., Irvine, M. J., Eagle, M., & Garner, D. M. (1991). Efficacy of a brief group psychoeducational intervention for bulimia nervosa. *Behaviour Research and Therapy, 29,* 71–83.

Opler, M. K. (1967). *Culture and social psychiatry.* New York: Atherton Press.

Ornstein, R., & Sobel, D. (1987). The healing brain. *Psychology Today, 21,* 48–52.

Orr, S. P., Pitman, R. K., Lasko, N. B., & Herz, L. R. (1993). Psychophysiological assessment of posttraumatic stress disorder imagery in World War II and Korean combat veterans. *Journal of Abnormal Psychology, 102,* 152–159.

Osgood, M. J. (1985). *Suicide in the elderly: A practitioner's guide to diagnosis and mental health intervention.* Rockville, MD: Aspen.

Öst, L. G. (1987a). Age of onset in different phobias. *Journal of Abnormal Psychology, 96,* 223–229.

Öst, L. G. (1987b). Applied relaxation: Description of a coping technique and review of controlled studies. *Behavior Research and Therapy, 25,* 397–409.

Öst, L. G. (1992). Blood and injection phobia: Background and cognitive, physiological, and behavioral variables. *Journal of Abnormal Psychology, 101,* 68–74.

Öst, L. G., & Hugdahl, K. (1981). Acquisition of phobias and anxiety response patterns in clinical patients. *Behaviour Research and Therapy, 19,* 439–447.

Ottenbacher, K. H., & Cooper, H. M. (1983). Drug treatment of hyperactivity in children. *Developmental Medicine in Child Neurology, 25,* 358–366.

Otto, M. W., Pollack, M. H., Sachs, G. S., & Rosenbaum, J. F. (1992). Hypochondriacal concerns, anxiety sensitivity, and panic disorder. *Journal of Anxiety Disorders, 6,* 93–104.

Otto, R. K. (1989). Bias and expert testimony of mental health professionals in adversarial proceedings: A preliminary investigation. *Behavioral Science and Law, 7,* 267–273.

Overholser, J. C., & Beck, S. (1986). Multimethod assessment of rapists, child molesters, and three control groups in behavioral and psychological measures. *Journal of Consulting and Clinical Psychology, 54,* 682–687.

Ozonoff, S., Pennington, B. F., & Rogers, S. J. (1991). Executive function deficits in high-functioning autistic individuals: Relationship to theory of mind. *Journal of Child Psychology and Psychiatry, 32,* 1085–1105.

Ozonoff, S., Rogers, S. J., & Pennington, B. F. (1991). Asperger's syndrome: Evidence of an empirical distinction from high-functioning autism. *Journal of Child Psychology and Psychiatry, 32,* 1107–1122.

Page, E. B. (1972). Miracle in Milwaukee: Raising the IQ. *Educational Researcher, 1,* 3–16.

Pakkenberg, B. (1987). Post-mortem study of chronic schizophrenic brains. *British Journal of Psychiatry, 151,* 744–752.

Paley, A-M. (1988). Growing up in chaos: The dissociative response. *American Journal of Psychoanalysis, 48,* 72–83.

Palfrey, J. S., Levine, M. D., Walker, D. K., & Sullivan, M. (1985). The emergence of attention deficits in early childhood: A prospective study. *Developmental and Behavioral Pediatrics, 6,* 339–348.

Papp, L., & Gorman, J. M. (1990). Suicidal preoccupation during fluoxetine treatment. *American Journal of Psychiatry, 147,* 1380.

Papp, L. A., Klein, D. F., Martinez, J., Schneier, F., Cole, R., Liebowitz, M. R., Hollander, E., Fyer, A. J., Jordan, F., & Gorman, J. M. (1993). Diagnostic and substance specificity of carbon-dioxide-induced panic. *American Journal of Psychiatry, 150,* 250–257.

Pardine, P., & Napoli, A. (1983). Physiological reactivity and recent life-stress experience. *Journal of Consulting and Clinical Psychology, 51,* 467–469.

Parnas, J. (1987). Assortative mating in schizophrenia: Results from the Copenhagen high-risk study. *Psychiatry, 50,* 58–64.

Pasework, R. A., Pantel, M. L., & Steadman, H. J. (1982). Detention and rearrest rates of persons found not guilty by reason of insanity and convicted felons. *American Journal of Psychiatry, 139(7),* 892–897.

Pasnau, R. O. (1984). Clinical presentations of panic and anxiety. *Psychosomatics, 25,* 4–9.

Patterson, C. H. (1980). *Theories of counseling and psychotherapy.* New York: Harper & Row.

Patterson, G. (1982). *Coercive family process.* Eugene, OR: Cascalia Press.

Patterson, G. R. (1986). Performance models for antisocial boys. *American Psychologist, 41,* 432–444.

Paul, G. L. (1967). Insight versus desensitization in psychotherapy two years after termination. *Journal of Consulting Psychology, 31,* 333–348.

Paul, G. L. (1985). Can pregnancy be a placebo effect:

Terminology, designs, and conclusions in the study of psychosocial and pharmacological treatments of behavioral disorders. In L. White, B. Tursky, & G. Schwartz (Eds.), *Placebo: Clinical phenomenon and new insights.* New York: Guilford Press.

Paul, G. L., & Lentz, R. J. (1977). *Psychosocial treatment of chronic mental patients: Milieu versus social-learning programs.* Cambridge, MA: Harvard University Press.

Paul, G. L., & Menditto, A. A. (1992). Effectiveness of inpatient treatment programs for mentally ill adults in public psychiatric facilities. *Applied and Preventive Psychology, 1*, 41–63.

Pauli, P., Marquardt, C., Hartl, L., Nutzinger, D. O., Holzl, R., & Strian, F. (1991). Anxiety induced by cardiac perceptions in patients with panic attacks: A field study. *Behaviour Research and Therapy, 29*, 137–145.

Pelletier, K. R. (1993). Between mind and body: Stress, emotions, and health. In D. Goleman & J. Gurin (Eds.), *Mind/body medicine* (pp. 19–38). New York: Consumer Reports Books.

Pauly, I. B. (1968). The current status of the change of sex operation. *Journal of Nervous and Mental Diseases, 147*, 460–471.

Paykel, E. S. (Ed.). (1982). *Handbook of affective disorders.* New York: Guilford Press.

Payne, R. L. (1992). First person account: My schizophrenia. *Schizophrenia Bulletin, 18*, 725–728.

Pearl, D., Bouthilet, L., & Lazar, J. (Eds.). (1982). *Television and behavior: Ten years of scientific progress and implications for the eighties* (Vols. 1 and 2). Washington, DC: U.S. Government Printing Office.

Pearlson, G. D., Barta, P. E., Schraml, F. V., Chase, G. A., & Tune, L. A. (1991). In reply. *Archives of General Psychiatry, 48*, 180–181.

Pendery, M. L., Maltzman, I. M., & West, L. J. (1982). Controlled drinking by alcoholics? New findings and a reevaluation of a major affirmative study. *Science, 217*, 169–175.

Penn, D. L., Van Der Does, W., Spaulding, W. D., Garbin, C. P., Linszen, D., & Dingemans, P. (1993). Information processing and social cognitive problem solving in schizophrenia. *Journal of Nervous and Mental Disease, 181*, 13–20.

Perls, F. (1969). *Gestalt therapy verbatim.* Moab, UT: Real People Press.

Perodeau, G. M. (1984). Married alcoholic women: A review. *Journal of Drug Issues, 14*, 703–720.

Perris, C. (1966). A study of bipolar (manic-depressive) and unipolar recurrent depressive psychosis. *Acta Psychiatrica Scandinavica* (Suppl. 194).

Perse, T. L., Greist, J. H., Jefferson, J. W., Rosenfeld, R., & Dar, R. (1987). Fluvoxamine treatment of obsessive-compulsive disorder. *American Journal of Psychiatry, 144*, 1543–1548.

Persky, V. W., Kempthorne-Rawson, J., & Shekelle, R. B. (1987). Personality and the risk of cancer: 20 years follow-up of the Western Electric Company. *Psychosomatic Medicine, 49*, 435–449.

Persons, J. B. (1986). The advantages of studying psychological phenomena rather than psychiatric diagnosis. *American Psychologist, 41*, 1252–1260.

Persons, J. B. (1991). Psychotherapy outcome studies do not accurately represent current models of psychotherapy: A proposed remedy. *American Psychologist. 46*, 99–106.

Peselow, E. D., Robins, C. J., Sanfilipo, M. P., Block, P., & Fieve, R. R. (1992). Sociotropy and autonomy: Relationship to antidepressant drug treatment response and endogenous-nonendogenous dichotomy. *Journal of Abnormal Psychology, 101*(3), 479–486.

Petersen, A. C., Compas, B. E., Brooks-Gunn, J., Stemmler, M., Ey, S., & Grant, K. E. (1993). Depression in adolescence. *American Psychologist, 48*, 155–168.

Pfeffer, C. R., Zuckerman, S., & Plutchik, R., & Mizruchi, M. S. (1987). Assaultive behavior in normal school children. *Child Psychiatry and Human Development, 17*, 166–176.

Pfeiffer, E. (1977). Psychopathology and social pathology. In J. E. Birren & K. W. Schaie (Eds.), *Handbook of psychology and aging.* New York: Van Nostrand Reinhold.

Phares, E. J. (1984). *Clinical psychology: Concepts, methods, and professions.* Homewood, IL: Dorsey.

Philips, H. C. (1983). Assessment of chronic tension headache behavior. In R. Melzack (Ed.), *Pain measurement and assessment* (pp. 155–165). New York: Raven Press.

Philips, H. C. (1987). Avoidance behavior and its role in sustaining chronic pain. *Behaviour Research and Therapy, 25*, 273–279.

Phillips, D. P., & Carstensen, L. L. (1986). Clustering of teenage suicides after television news stories about suicide. *New England Journal of Medicine, 315*, 685–689.

Phillips, D. P., Van Voorhees, C. A., & Ruth, T. E. (1992). The birthday: Lifeline or deadline? *Psychosomatic Medicine, 54*, 532–542.

Phillips, K. A. (1991). Body dysmorphic disorder: The distress of imagined ugliness. *American Journal of Psychiatry, 148*, 1138–1149.

Phillips, K. A. (1992). Dr. Phillips replies. *American Journal of Psychiatry, 149*, 719.

Phillips, K. A., McElroy, S. L., Keck, P. E., Pope, H. G. Jr., & Hudson, J. I. (1993). Body dysmorphic disorder: 30 cases of imagined ugliness. *American Journal of Psychiatry, 150*, 302–308.

Pickering, P. G., Harshfield, G. A., Kleinert, H. D., Blank, S., & Laragh, J. L. (1982). Blood pressure during normal daily activities, sleep, and exercise: Comparison of values in normal and hypertensive subjects. *Journal of the American Medical Association, 247,* 992–996.

Pierce, K. A., & Kirkpatrick, D. R. (1992). Do men lie on fear surveys? *Behaviour Research and Therapy, 30,* 415–418.

Pigott, T. A., & Murphy, D. L. (1991). In reply. *Archives of General Psychiatry, 48,* 858–859.

Pilisuk, M. (1975). The legacy of the Vietnam veteran. *Journal of Social Issues, 31*(4), 3–12.

Pine, C. J. (1981). Suicide in American Indian and Alaskan native tradition. *White Cloud Journal, 2,* 3–8.

Pines, M. (1983, October). *Science,* pp. 55–58.

Pitman, R. K., Orr, S. P., Forgue, D. F., Altman, B., Dejong, J. B., & Herz, L. R. (1990). Psychophysiologic responses to combat imagery of Vietnam veterans with posttraumatic stress disorder versus other anxiety disorders. *Journal of Abnormal Psychology, 99,* 49–54.

Platt, J. J. (1986). *Heroin addiction: Theory, research, and treatment.* New York: Wiley.

Plienis, A. J., Hansen, D. J., Ford, F., Smith, S. Jr., Stark, L. J., & Kelly, J. A. (1987). Behavioral small group training to improve the social skills of emotionally-disordered adolescents. *Behavior Therapy, 18,* 17–32.

Plonin, R. (1989). Environment and genes: Determinant of behavior. *American Psychologist, 44,* 105–111.

Plonin, R., DeFries, J. C., & Fulker, D. W. (1988). *Nature and nurture during infancy and early childhood.* New York: Cambridge University Press.

Plonin, R., DeFries, J. C., & McClearn, G. E. (1988). *Behavioral genetics: A primer.* New York: Freeman.

Pogue-Geile, M. F., & Rose, R. J. (1985). Developmental genetic studies of adult personality. *Developmental Psychology, 21,* 547–557.

Poling, A., Gadow, K. D., & Cleary, J. (1991). *Drug therapy for behavior disorders.* New York: Pergamon Press.

Polivy, J., Schueneman, A. L., & Carlson, K. (1976). Alcohol and tension reduction: Cognitive and physiological effects. *Journal of Abnormal Psychology, 85,* 595–600.

Pollard, C. A., Pollard, H. J., & Corn, K. J. (1989). Panic onset and major events in the lives of agoraphobics: A test of continuity. *Journal of Abnormal Psychology, 98,* 318–321.

Ponterotto, J. G. (1987). Client hospitalization: Issues and considerations for the counselor. *Journal of Counseling and Development, 65,* 542–546.

Ponterotto, J. G., & Casas, J. M. (1991). *Handbook of racial/ethnic minority counseling research.* Springfield, IL: Thomas.

Poon, L. W., & Siegler, I. C. (1991). Psychological aspects of normal aging. In J. Sadavoy, L. W. Lazarus, & L. F. Jarvik (Eds.), *Comprehensive review of geriatric psychiatry* (pp. 117–145). Washington, DC: American Psychiatric Press.

Pope, H. G. Jr., & Hudson, J. I. (1992). Is childhood sexual abuse a risk factor for bulimia nervosa? *American Journal of Psychiatry, 149,* 455–463.

Pope, H. G., Hudson, J. I., Jonas, J., & Yurgelun-Todd, D. (1983). Bulimia treated with imipramine: A placebo-controlled, double-blind study. *American Journal of Psychiatry, 140,* 554–558.

Pope, H. G., Hudson, J. I., & Yurgelun-Todd, D. (1984). Anorexia nervosa and bulimia among 300 suburban women shoppers. *American Journal of Psychiatry, 141,* 292–294.

Pope, H. G., Jonas, J. M., & Cohen, B. M. (1982). Failure to find evidence of schizophrenic probands. *American Journal of Psychiatry, 139,* 826–828.

Pope, K. S. (1988). How clients are harmed by sexual contact with mental health professionals: The syndrome and its prevalence. *Journal of Counseling and Development, 67,* 222–226.

Pope, K. S., Tabachnick, B. G., & Keith-Spiegel, P. (1988). Good and poor practices in psychotherapy: National survey of beliefs of psychologists. *Professional Psychology: Research and Practice, 19,* 547–552.

Porrino, L. J., Rapoport, J. L., Behar, D., Sceery, W., Ismond, D. R., & Bunney, W. E. (1983). A naturalistic assessment of the motor activity of hyperactive boys. *Archives of General Psychiatry, 40,* 681–687.

Portnoff, L. A., Golden, C. J., Wood, R. E., & Gustavson, J. L. (1983). Discrimination between schizophrenic and parietal lesion patients with neurological tests of parietal involvement. *Clinical Neuropsychology, 5,* 175–178.

Portwood, D. (1978, January). A right to suicide. *Psychology Today, 2,* pp. 66–74.

Pound, E. J. (1987). Children and prematurity. In A. Thomas & J. Grimes (Eds.), *Children's needs: Psychological perspectives* (pp. 441–450). Washington, DC: National Association of School Psychologists.

Powell, C. J. (1982, August). *Adolescence and the right to die: Issues of autonomy, competence, and paternalism.* Paper presented at the meeting of the American Psychological Association, Washington, DC.

Powell, G. J. (1983). Coping with adversity: The psychosocial development of Afro-American children. In G. J. Powell (Ed.), *The psychosocial development of minority group children.* New York: Brunner/Mazel.

Powers, P. S., Schulman, R. G., Gleghorn, A. A., & Prange, M. E. (1987). Perceptual and cognitive abnormalities in bulimia. *American Journal of Psychiatry, 144,* 1456–1460.

Praeger, S. G., & Bernhardt, G. R. (1985). Survivors of suicide: A community in need. *Family and Community Health, 3,* 62–72.

President's Commission on Mental Health. (1978). *Report from the President's Commission on Mental Health.* Washington, DC: U.S. Government Printing Office.

Prestby, J. E., Wandersman, A., Florin, P., Rich, R., & Chavis, D. (1990). Benefits, costs, incentive management and participation in voluntary organizations: A means to understanding and promoting empowerment. *American Journal of Community Psychology, 18,* 117–149.

Pribor, E. F., & Dinwiddie, S. H. (1992). Psychiatric correlates of incest in childhood. *American Journal of Psychiatry, 149,* 52–56.

Price, L. H., Goodman, W. K., Charney, D. S., Rasmussen, S. A., & Heninger, G. R. (1987). Treatment of severe obsessive-compulsive disorder with fluvoxamine. *American Journal of Psychiatry, 144,* 1059–1061.

Price, L. J., Fein, G., & Feinberg, I. (1980). Neurological assessment of cognitive function in the elderly. In L. W. Poon (Ed.), *Aging in the 1980's.* Washington, DC: American Psychological Association.

Price, R. (1987). Series Editor's preface. In J. Hermalin & J. A. Morell (Eds.), *Prevention planning in mental health.* Beverly Hills, CA: Sage.

Prichard, J. C. (1837). *Treatise on insanity and other disorders affecting the mind.* Philadelphia: Haswell, Barrington, & Haswell.

Prigatano, G. P., Fordyce, D. J., Zeiner, H. K., Roueche, J. R., Pepping, M., & Wood, B. C. (1984). *Journal of Neurology and Neuropsychology, 47,* 505–513.

Prior, M. (1984). Developing concepts of childhood autism: The influence of experimental cognitive research. *Journal of Consulting and Clinical Psychology, 52,* 4–16.

Prior, M., Leonard, A., & Wood, G. (1983). A comparison study of preschool children diagnosed as hyperactive. *Journal of Pediatric Psychology, 8,* 191–207.

Pruzinsky, T., & Borkovec, T. D. (1991). Cognitive and personality characteristic of worriers. *Behaviour Research and Therapy, 28,* 507–512.

Pueschel, S. M. (1991). Ethical considerations relating to prenatal diagnosis of fetuses with Down syndrome. *Mental Retardation, 29,* 185–190.

Puryear, D. A., Carson, C., Fuentes, R., & Valls, T. (1992). Subjective conclusions about schizophrenia. *Archives of General Psychiatry, 49,* 74.

Quackenbush, R. L. (1991). The prescription of self-help books by psychologists: A bibliography of selected resources. *Psychotherapy, 28,* 671–677.

Quay, H. C. (1965). Psychopathic personality as pathological stimulation seeking. *American Journal of Psychiatry, 122,* 180–183.

Quen, J. M. (1978). Isaac Ray and Charles Doe: Responsibility and justice. In W. E. Barton & C. J. Sanborn (Eds.), *Law and the mental health professions* (pp. 235–250). New York: International Universities Press.

Quen, J. M. (1981). Anglo American concepts of criminal responsibility. In S. J. Hucker, C. D. Webster, & M. H. Ben-Aron (Eds.), *Mental disorder and criminal responsibility* (pp. 1–10). Toronto: Butterworths.

Rabkin, J. G. (1979). The epidemiology of forcible rape. *American Journal of Orthopsychiatry, 49,* 634–647.

Rabkin, J. G., McGrath, P. J., Quitkin, F. M., Tricamo, E., Stewart, J. W., & Klein, D. F. (1990). Effects of pill-giving on maintenance of placebo response in patients with chronic depression. *American Journal of Psychiatry, 147,* 1622–1626.

Rabkin, J. G., Williams, J. B. W., Remien, R. H., Goetz, R., Kertzner, R., & Gorman, J. M. (1991). Depression, distress, lymphocyte subsets, and human immunodeficiency virus symptoms on two occasions in HIV-positive homosexual men. *Archives of General Psychiatry, 48,* 11–119.

Rachman, S. (1966). Sexual fetishism: An experimental analogue. *Psychological Record, 16,* 293–296.

Rachman, S. (1971). *The effects of psychotherapy.* New York: Pergamon.

Rachman, S. (1993). Obsessions, responsibility and guilt. *Behaviour Research and Therapy, 31,* 149–154.

Rachman, S., & Hodgson, R. (1980). *Obsessions and compulsions.* Englewood Cliffs, NJ: Prentice-Hall.

Rachman, S., Lopatka, C., & Levitt, K. (1987). Panic: The link between cognitions and bodily symptoms—I. *Behavior Research and Therapy, 25,* 411–423.

Rachman, S., Lopatka, C., & Levitt, K. (1988). Experimental analysis of panic—II. Panic patients. *Behaviour Research and Therapy, 26,* 33–40.

Rachman, S., Marks, I. M., & Hodgson, R. (1973). The treatment of obsessive-compulsive neurotics by modeling and flooding in vivo. *Behaviour Research and Therapy, 13,* 271–279.

Rachman, S. J., & Wilson, G. I. (1980). *The effects of psychological therapy* (2nd ed.). New York: Pergamon Press.

Radojevic, V., & Nicassio, P. M. (1992). Behavioral intervention for rheumatoid arthritis with and without family support. *Behavior Therapy, 23,* 13–30.

Rahe, R. H. (1968). Life change measurement as a predictor of illness. *Proceedings of the Royal Society of Medicine, 61,* 1124–1126.

Rahe, R. H., & Arthur, R. J. (1978). Life change and illness studies: Past history and future directions. *Journal of Human Stress, 4,* 3–15.

Ramer, J. C., & Miller, G. (1992). Overview of mental retardation. In G. Miller & J. C. Ramer (Eds.), *Static encephalopathies of infancy and childhood* (pp. 1–10). New York: Raven Press.

Ramirez, A. J., Craig, T. K. J., Watson, J. P., Fentiman, I. S., North, W. R. S., & Rubens, R. D. (1989). Stress and relapse in breast cancer. *British Medical Journal, 298,* 291–293.

Rao, S. M., Huber, S. J., & Bornstein, R. A. (1992). Emotional changes with multiple sclerosis and Parkinson's disease. *Journal of Consulting and Clinical Psychology, 60*(3), 369–378.

Rapaport, K., & Burkhart, B. R. (1984). Personality attitudinal characteristics of sexually coercive college males. *Journal of Abnormal Psychology, 93,* 216–221.

Rapee, R. M., Sanderson, W. C., McCauley, P. A., & DiNardo, P. A. (1992). Differences between panic disorder and other DSM-III-R anxiety disorders. *Behaviour Research and Therapy, 30,* 45–52.

Rappaport, J. (1981). In praise of paradox: A social policy of empowerment over prevention. *American Journal of Community Psychology, 9,* 1–26.

Rappaport, J. (1987). Terms of empowerment/exemplars of prevention: Toward a theory for community psychology. *American Journal of Community Psychology, 15,* 121–148.

Rappaport, J., & Cleary, C. P. (1980). Labeling theory and the social psychology of experts and helpers. In M. S. Gibbs, J. R. Lachenmyer, & J. Sigal (Eds.), *Community psychology: Theoretical and empirical approaches.* New York: Gardner Press.

Raps, C. S., Peterson, C., Reinhard, K. E., Abramson, L. Y., & Seligman, M. E. P. (1982). Attributional styles among depressed patients. *Journal of Abnormal Psychology, 91,* 102–108.

Raskin, M., Pecke, H. V. S., Dickman, W., & Pinsker, H. (1982). Panic and generalized anxiety disorders. *Archives of General Psychiatry, 39,* 687–689.

Ratey, J. J., Grandin, T., & Miller, A. (1992). Defense behavior and coping in an autistic savant: The story of Temple Grandin, PhD. *Psychiatry, 55,* 382–391.

Ratican, K. L. (1992). Sexual abuse survivors: Identifying symptoms and special treatment considerations. *Journal of Counseling and Development, 71,* 33–38.

Read, S. (1991). The dementias. In J. Sadavoy, L. W. Lazarus, & L. F. Jarvik (Eds.), *Comprehensive review of geriatric psychiatry* (pp. 287–309). Washington, DC: American Psychiatric Press.

Reading, C., & Mohr, P. (1976). Biofeedback control of migraine: A pilot study. *British Journal of Social and Clinical Psychology, 15,* 429–433.

Red Horse, Y. (1982). A cultural network model: Perspectives for adolescent services and paraprofessional training. In S. M. Manson (Ed.), *New directions in prevention among American Indian and Alaska Native communities* (pp. 173–184). Portland, OR: Oregon Health Sciences University.

Redestam, K. E. (1977). Physical and psychological response to suicide in the family. *Journal of Consulting and Clinical Psychology, 45,* 162–170.

Rees, L. (1964). The importance of psychological, allergic, and infective factors in childhood asthma. *Journal of Psychosomatic Research, 1,* 253–262.

Regan, J., & LaBarbera, J. D. (1984). Lateralization of conversion symptoms. *American Journal of Psychiatry, 141,* 1279–1280.

Regier, D. A., Goldberg, I. O., & Taube, C. A. (1978). The de facto U.S. mental health services systems: A public health perspective. *Archives of General Psychiatry, 35,* 685–693.

Regier, D. A., Boyd, J. H., Burke, J. D., Rae, D. S., Myers, J. K., Kramer, M., Robins, L. N., George, L. K., Karno, M., & Locke, B. Z. (1988). One-month prevalence of mental disorders in the U.S.: Based on five epidemiologic catchment area (ECA) sites. *Archives of General Psychiatry, 45,* 977–1986.

Reich, J. (1987). Sex distribution of DSM-III personality disorders in psychiatric outpatients. *American Journal of Psychiatry, 144,* 485–488.

Reich, J., Noyes, R., & Yates, W. (1988). Anxiety symptoms distinguishing social phobia from panic and generalized anxiety disorder. *Journal of Nervous and Mental Disease, 176,* 510–513.

Reid, W. H. (1981). The antisocial personality and related symptoms. In J. R. Lion (Ed.), *Personality disorders: Diagnosis and management.* Baltimore: Williams & Wilkins.

Reilly, D. (1984). Family therapy with adolescent drug abusers and their families: Defying gravity and achieving escape velocity. *Journal of Drug Issues, 14,* 381–389.

Reisberg, B., Ferris, S. H., Crook, T. (1982). Signs, symptoms, and course of age-associated cognitive decline. In S. Corkin, K. L. Davis, J. H. Growdon, E. Usdin, & R. J. Wurtman (Eds.), *Alzheimer's disease: A report of progress.* New York: Raven Press.

Reiser, D. E. (1988). The psychiatric interview. In H. H. Goldman (Ed.), *Review of general psychiatry* (pp. 184–192). Norwalk, CT: Appleton & Lange.

Reisman, J. (1971). *Toward the integration of psychotherapy.* New York: Wiley.

Reiss, S., Levitan, G. W., & Szyszko, J. (1982). Emotional disturbance and mental retardation: Diagnostic overshadowing. *American Journal of Mental Deficiency, 86,* 567–574.

Reiss, S., Peterson, R. A., Gursky, D. M., & McNally, R. J. (1986). Anxiety sensitivity, anxiety frequency, and the prediction of fearfulness. *Behaviour Research and Therapy, 24,* 1–8.

Reissman, F. (1962). *The culturally deprived child.* New York: Harper & Row.

Rekers, G. A., & Varni, J. W. (1977a). Self-monitoring and self-reinforcement processes in a pre-transsexual boy. *Behaviour Research and Therapy, 15,* 177–180.

Rekers, G. A., & Varni, J. W. (1977b). Self-regulation of gender-role behaviors: A case study. *Journal of Behavior Therapy and Experimental Psychiatry, 8,* 427–432.

Rekers, G. A., & Yates, C. E. (1976). Sex-typed play in feminoid boys versus normal boys and girls. *Journal of Abnormal Child Psychology, 4,* 1–8.

Reschly, D. J. (1992). Mental retardation: Conceptual foundations, definitional criteria, and diagnostic operations. In S. R. Hooper, G. W. Hynd, & R. E. Mattison (Eds.), *Developmental disorders: Diagnostic criteria and clinical assessment* (pp. 23–67). Hillsdale, NJ: Lawrence Earlbaum Associates.

Research Task Force of the National Institute of Mental Health. (1975). *Research in the service of mental health* (DHEW Publication No. ADM 75–236). Washington, DC: U.S. Government Printing Office.

Resick, P. A. (1983). The rape reaction: Research findings and implications for intervention. *Behavior Therapist, 6,* 129–132.

Reus, V. I. (1988). Affective disorders. In H. H. Goldman (Ed.), *Review of general psychiatry* (pp. 332–348). Norwalk, CT: Appleton & Lange.

Reynolds, C. R., Kamphaus, R. W., & Rosenthal, B. L. (1989). Applications of the Kaufman Assessment Battery for Children (K-ABC) in neuropsychological assessment. In C. R. Reynolds & E. Fletcher-Janzen (Eds.), *Handbook of clinical child neuropsychology* (pp. 181–191). New York: Plenum Press.

Rhodes, J. E., Ebert, L., & Fischer, K. (1992). Natural mentors: An overlooked resource in the social networks of young, African-American mothers. *American Journal of Community Psychology, 20,* 445–461.

Richardson, J. L., Zarnegar, Z., Bisno, B., & Levine, A. (1990). Psychosocial status at initiation of cancer treatment and survival. *Journal of Psychosomatic Research, 34,* 189–201.

Rickarby, G., Carruthers, A., & Mitchell, M. (1991). Brief report: Biological factors associated with Asperger syndrome. *Journal of Autism and Developmental Disorders, 21,* 341–354.

Rickels, K. (1966). Drugs in the treatment of neurotic anxiety. In P. Solomon (Ed.), *Psychiatric drugs.* New York: Grune & Stratton.

Rimland, B. (1978). Inside the mind of the autistic savant. *Psychology Today, 12,* 69–80.

Rimm, D. C., Janda, L. H., Lancaster, D. W., Nahl, M., & Dittmar, K. (1977). An exploratory investigation of the origin and maintenance of phobias. *Behaviour Research and Therapy, 15,* 231–238.

Rimm, D. C., & Masters, J. C. (1979). *Behavior therapy: Techniques and empirical findings* (2nd ed.). New York: Academic Press.

Rioch, M. J. (1967). Pilot projects in training mental health counselors. In E. L. Cowen, E. A. Gardner, & M. Zax (Eds.), *Emergent approaches to mental health problems.* New York: Appleton-Century-Crofts.

Rist, K. (1979). Incest: Theoretical and clinical views. *American Journal of Orthopsychiatry, 49,* 680–691.

Ritvo, E. R., Freeman, B. J., Yuwiler, A., Geller, E., Yokota, A., Schroth, P., & Novak, P. (1984). Study of fenfluramine in outpatients with the syndrome of autism. *Journal of Pediatrics, 105,* 823–828.

Ritvo, E. R., Jorde, L. B., Mason-Brothers, A., Freeman, B. J., Pingree, C., Jones, M. B., McMahon, W. M., Petersen, B., Jenson, W. R. & Mo, A. (1989). The UCLA–University of Utah epidemiologic survey of autism: Recurrent risk estimates and genetic counseling. *American Journal of Psychiatry, 146,* 1032–1036.

Roberto, L. (1983). Issues in diagnosis and treatment of transsexualism. *Archives of Sexual Behavior, 12,* 445–473.

Roberts, G. W. (1991). Schizophrenia: A neuropathological perspective. *British Journal of Psychiatry, 158,* 8–17.

Robertson, J., Wendiggensen, P., & Kaplan, I. (1983). Toward a comprehensive treatment for obsessional thoughts. *Behaviour Research and Therapy, 21,* 347–356.

Robins, C. J., & Luten, A. G. (1991). Sociotropy and autonomy: Differential patterns of clinical presentation in unipolar depression. *Journal of Abnormal Psychology, 100*(1), 74–77.

Robins, L. N. (1966). *Deviant children growing up: A sociological and psychiatric study of sociopathic personality.* Baltimore: Williams & Wilkins.

Robins, L. N. (1991). Conduct disorder. *Journal of Child Psychology and Psychiatry, 32,* 193–212.

Robins, L. N., Helzer, J. E., Weisinann, M. M., Orvaschel, H., Gruenberg, E., Burke, J. D., & Regier, D. A. (1984). Lifetime prevalence of specific psychiatric disorders in three sites. *Archives of General Psychiatry, 41,* 949–958.

Robins, L. N., & Kulbok, P. (1988). Epidemiological studies in suicide. *Psychiatric Annual, 18,* 619–627.

Robinson, J. P., Shaver, P. R., & Wrightsman, L. S. (Eds.). (1991). *Measures of personality and social psychological attitudes.* San Diego, CA: Academic Press.

Robinson, L. R. (1975). Basic concepts in family therapy: A differential comparison with individual treatment. *American Journal of Psychiatry, 132*(10), 1045–1048.

Robitscher, J. B. (1966). *Pursuit of agreement: Psychiatry and the law.* Philadelphia: Lippincott.

Rodin, J., & Langer, E. J. (1977). Long-term effects of a control-relevant intervention with the institutionalized aged. *Journal of Personality and Social Psychology, 35,* 897–902.

Roff, J. D., & Wirt, R. D. (1984). Childhood aggression and social adjustment as antecedents of delinquency. *Journal of Abnormal Child Psychology, 12,* 111–126.

Rogers, C. (1980). *A way of being.* Boston: Houghton Mifflin.

Rogers, C. (1987). The underlying theory: Drawn from experiences with individuals and groups. *Counseling and Values, 32,* 38–45.

Rogers, C. R. (1951). *Client-centered therapy.* Boston: Houghton Mifflin.

Rogers, C. R. (1959). A theory of therapy, personality, and interpersonal relationships, as developed in client-centered framework. In S. Koch (Ed.), *Psychology: A study of science* (Vol. 3). New York: McGraw-Hill.

Rogers, C. R. (1961). *On becoming a person.* Boston: Houghton Mifflin.

Rogers, J. R. (1990). Female suicide: The trend toward increased lethality in method of choice and its implications. *Journal of Counseling and Development, 69,* 37–41.

Rogers, J. R. (1992). Suicide and alcohol: Conceptualizing the relationship from a cognitive-social paradigm. *Journal of Counseling and Development, 70,* 540–543.

Rogers, R. (1987). APA's position on the insanity defense. *American Psychologist, 42,* 840–848.

Rogers, R., Bagby, M., & Rector, N. (1989). Diagnostic legitimacy of factitious disorder with psychological symptoms. *American Journal of Psychiatry, 146,* 1312–1314.

Romaniuk, M., McAuley, W. J., & Arling, G. (1983). An examination of the prevalence of mental disorders among the elderly in the community. *Journal of Abnormal Psychology, 92,* 458–467.

Romme, M. A., Honig, A., Noorthoorn, E. O., & Escher, A. D. M. A. C. (1992). Coping with hearing voices: An emancipatory approach. *British Journal of Psychiatry, 161,* 99–103.

Root, M. P. (1990). Disordered eating in women of color. *Sex Roles, 22,* 525–536.

Roper, G., & Rachman, S. (1976). Obsessive-compulsive checking: Experimental replication and development. *Behaviour Research and Therapy, 14,* 25–32.

Roper Organization (1992). *Unusual personal experiences.* Las Vegas: Bigelow Holding Company

Rosen, G. M. (1987). Self-help treatment books and the commercialization of psychotherapy. *American Psychologist, 42,* 46–51.

Rosen, J., & Leitenberg, H. (1982). Bulimia nervosa: Treatment with exposure and response prevention. *Behavior Therapy, 13,* 117–124.

Rosen, R. C., Kostis, J. B., & Jekelis, A. W. (1988). Beta-blocker effects on sexual function in normal males. *Archives of Sexual Behavior, 17,* 241–255.

Rosen, R. C., & Leiblum, S. R. (1987). Current approaches to the evaluation of sexual desire disorders. *Journal of Sex Research, 23,* 141–162.

Rosenblat, R., & Tang, S. W. (1987). Do Oriental psychiatric patients receive different dosages of psychotropic medication when compared with Occidentals? *Canadian Journal of Psychiatry, 32,* 270–274.

Rosenfield, A. H. (1985). Discovering and dealing with deviant sex. *Psychology Today, 19,* 8–10.

Rosenhan, D. L. (1973). On being sane in insane places. *Science, 179,* 250–258.

Rosenthal, D. (1970). *Genetic theory and abnormal behavior.* New York: McGraw-Hill.

Rosenthal, D. (1971). *Genetics of psychopathology.* New York: McGraw-Hill.

Rosenthal, J., & Jacobson, L. (1968). *Pygmalion in the classroom.* New York: Holt, Rinehart & Winston.

Rosenthal, P., & Rosenthal, S. (1984). Suicidal behavior by preschool children. *American Journal of Psychiatry, 141,* 520–525.

Ross, A. O. (1982). *Psychological disorders of children.* New York: McGraw-Hill.

Ross, C. A., Anderson, C., Fleisher, W. P., & Norton, G. R. (1991). The frequency of multiple personality disorder among psychiatric inpatients. *American Journal of Psychiatry, 148,* 1717–1720.

Rossiter, L. F. (1983). Prescribed medicines: Findings from the National Medical Care Expenditure Survey. *American Journal of Public Health, 73,* 1312–1315.

Roth, D., Bielski, R., Jones, M., Parker, W., & Osborn, G. (1982). A comparison of self-control therapy and combined self-control therapy and antidepressant medication in the treatment of depression. *Behavior Therapy, 13,* 133–144.

Rothenberg, R. B., & Aubert, R. E. (1990). Ischemic heart disease and hypertension: Effects of disease coding on epidemiologic assessment. *Public Health Reports, 105,* 47–52.

Roy-Byrne, P. P., Geraci, M., & Uhde, T. W. (1986). Life events and course of illness in patients with panic disorder. *American Journal of Psychiatry, 143,* 1033–1035.

Roy, A. (1985). Suicide in doctors. *Psychiatric Clinics of North America, 8,* 377–387.

Roy, A., Adinoff, B., Roehrich, L., Lamparski, D., Custer, R., Lorenz, V., Barbaccia, M., Guidotti, A., Cost, E., & Linnoila, M. (1988). Pathological gambling: A psychobiological study. *Archives of General Psychiatry, 45,* 369–373.

Royce, J. M., Lazar, I., & Darlington, R. B. (1983). Minority families, early education, and later life changes. *American Journal of Orthopsychiatry, 53,* 706–720.

Rubinstein, E. A. (1983). Television and behavior. *American Psychologist, 38,* 7.

Rubinstein, M., Yaeger, C. A., Goodstein, C., & Lewis, D. O. (1993). Sexually assaultive male juveniles: A follow-up. *American Journal of Psychiatry, 150,* 262–265.

Ruderman, A. J., & Besbeas, M. (1992). Psychological characteristics of dieters and bulimics. *Journal of Abnormal Psychology, 101,* 383–390.

Rueger, D., & Liberman, R. (1984). Behavioral family therapy for delinquent and substance-abusing adolescents. *Journal of Drug Issues, 14,* 403–417.

Ruff, G. E., & Korchin, S. J. (1964). Psychological responses of Mercury astronauts to stress. In G. H. Grosser, H. Wechsler, & M. Greenblatt (Eds.), *The threat of impending disaster*. Cambridge, MA: M.I.T. Press.

Ruiz, R. A., & Padilla, A. M. (1977). Counseling Latinos. *Personnel and Guidance Journal, 55,* 401–408.

Ruocchio, P. J. (1991). First person account: The schizophrenic inside. *Schizophrenia Bulletin, 17,* 357–360.

Russo, D. C., Carr, E. G., & Lovaas, O. I. (1980). Self injury in pediatric populations. In J. Ferguson & C. R. Taylor (Eds.), *Comprehensive handbook of behavioral medicine. Vol. 3: Extended applications and issues.* Holliswood, NY: Spectrum Publications.

Russo, N. F., & Denmark, F. L. (1984). Women, psychology, and public policy: Selected issues. *American Psychologist, 39,* 1161–1165.

Rutter, M. (1983). Cognitive deficits in the pathogenesis of autism. *Journal of Child Psychology and Psychiatry, 24,* 513–531.

Rutter, M., MacDonald, H., LeCouteur, A., Harrington, R., Bolton, P., & Bailey, A. (1990). Genetic factors in child psychiatric disorders—II. Empirical findings. *Journal of Child Psychology and Psychiatry, 31,* 39–83.

Rutter, M., Yule, W., Berger, M., Yule, B., Morton, J., & Bagley, C. (1974). Children of West Indian immigrants: Rates of behavioural deviance and psychiatric disorders. *Journal of Child Psychology and Psychiatry, 15,* 241–262.

Sabalis, R. F., Frances, A., Appenzeller, S. N., & Moseley, W. B. (1974). The three sisters: Transsexual male siblings. *American Journal of Psychiatry, 131,* 907–909.

Sabalis, R. F., Staton, M. A., & Appenzeller, S. N. (1977). Transsexualism: Alternative diagnostic etiological considerations. *American Journal of Psychoanalysis, 37,* 223–228.

Sachdev, P., & Loeragan, C. (1991). The present status of akathisia. *Journal of Nervous and Mental Disease, 179,* 381–391.

Sackeim, H. A., & Vingiano, W. (1984). Dissociative disorders. In S. Turner & M. Hersen (Eds.), *Adult psychopathology and diagnosis.* New York: Wiley.

Safferman, A., Lieberman, J. A., Kane, J. M., Szymanski, S., & Kinon, B. (1991). Update on the clinical efficacy and side effects of clozapine. *Schizophrenia Bulletin, 17,* 247–261.

Sakheim, D. K., Barlow, D. H., Abrahamson, D. J., & Beck, J. G. (1987). Distinguishing between organogenic and psychogenic erectile dysfunction. *Behavior Research and Therapy, 25,* 379–390.

Sakheim, D. K., Hess, E. P., & Chivas, A. (1988). General principles for short-term inpatient work with multiple personality disorder patients. *Psychotherapy, 25,* 117–124.

Salim, A. S. (1987). Stress, the adrenergic hypothalamovagal pathway, and the aetiology of chronic duodenal ulceration. *Journal of Psychosomatic Research, 31,* 231–237.

Salkovskis, P. M., & Harrison, J. (1984). Abnormal and normal obsessions—A replication. *Behaviour Research and Therapy, 22,* 549–552.

Salkovskis, P. M., & Warwick, H. M. C. (1986). Morbid preoccupations, health anxiety and reassurance: A cognitive-behavioral approach to hypochondriasis. *Behavior Research and Therapy, 24,* 597–602.

Salley, R. D. (1988). Subpersonalities with dreaming functions in a patient with multiple personalities. *Journal of Nervous and Mental Disease, 176,* 112–115.

Saltus, R. (1993, March 24). Huntington's disease gene is identified. *Boston Globe.* p. 1, 20.

Sanavio, E. (1988). Obsessions and compulsions: The Padua Inventory. *Behaviour Research and Therapy, 26,* 169–177.

Sanday, P. R. (1981). The socio-cultural context of rape: A cross-cultural study. *Journal of Social Issues, 37,* 5–27.

Sanders, B. (1991). Dr. Sanders replies. *American Journal of Psychiatry, 148,* 1422–1423.

Sanders, B. (1991). Letter to the editor. *American Journal of Psychiatry, 148,* 1424.

Sanders, B., & Giolas, M. H. (1991). Dissociation and childhood trauma in psychologically disturbed adolescents. *American Journal of Psychiatry, 148,* 50–54.

Sanderson, W. C., & Beck, A. T. (1989). Classical conditioning model of panic disorder: Response to Wolpe and Rowan. *Behaviour Research and Therapy, 27,* 581–582.

Sandler, L. S., Wilson, K. G., Asmundson, G. J. G., Larsen, D. K., & Ediger, J. M. (1992). Cardiovascular reactivity in nonclinical subjects with infrequent panic attacks. *Journal of Anxiety Disorders, 6,* 27–39.

Santos, A. B., Hawkins, G. D., Julius, G., Deci, P. A., Hiers, T. H., & Burns, B. J. (1993). A pilot study of assertive community treatment for patients with chronic psychotic disorders. *American Journal of Psychiatry, 150,* 501–504.

Sarason, I. G., & Ganzer, V. (1973). Modeling and group discussion in the rehabilitation of delinquents. *Journal of Counseling Psychology, 20,* 442–449.

Sarason, I. G., Johnson, J. H., & Siegel, J. M. (1978). Assessing the impact of life changes: Development of the Life Experiences Survey. *Journal of Consulting and Clinical Psychology, 46,* 932–946.

Sarbin, P. R., & Cole, W. C. (1979). Hypnosis and psychopathology: Replacing old myths with fresh metaphors. *Journal of Abnormal Psychology, 88,* 506–526.

Sartorius, N., Jablensky, A., Korten, A., Ernberg, G., Anker, M., Cooper, J. E., & Day, R. (1986). Early manifestations and first-contact incidence of schizophrenia in different cultures. *Psychological Medicine, 16,* 909–928.

Satir, V. (1967). A family of angels. In J. Haley & L. Hoffman (Eds.), *Techniques of family therapy*. New York: Basic Books.

Satterfield, J. H., Hoppe, C. M., & Schell, A. M. (1982). A prospective study of delinquency in 110 adolescent boys with attention deficit disorder and 88 normal adolescent boys. *American Journal of Psychiatry, 139,* 795–798.

Saxe, L., Cross, T., & Silverman, N. (1988). Children's mental health. *American Psychologist, 43,* 800–807.

Sbordone, R. J., & Jennison, J. H. (1983). A comparison of the OBD-168 and MMPI to assess the emotional adjustment of traumatic brain-injured inpatients to their cognitive deficits. *Clinical Neuropsychology, 5,* 87–88.

Scarr, S., Webber, P. L., Weinberg, R. A., and Wittig, M. A. (1981). Personality resemblance among adolescents and their parents in biologically related and adoptive families. *Journal of Personality and Social Psychology, 40,* 885–898.

Scarr, S., & Weinberg, R. A. (1976). IQ test performance of black children adopted by white families. *American Psychologist, 31,* 726–739.

Schachar, R. (1991). Childhood hyperactivity. *Journal of Child Psychology and Psychiatry, 32,* 155–191.

Schacht, T. E. (1985). DSM-III and the politics of truth. *American Psychologist, 40,* 513–521.

Schacht, T. E., & Nathan, P. E. (1977). But is it good for the psychologists? Appraisal and status of DSM-III. *American Psychologist, 32,* 1017–1025.

Schachter, S. (1977). Nicotine regulation in heavy and light smokers. *Journal of Experimental Psychology (General), 106,* 5–12.

Schachter, S., & Latane, B. (1964). Crime, cognition, and the autonomic nervous system. *Nebraska Symposium on Motivation, 12,* 221–274.

Schacter, D. L. (1986). Amnesia and crime. *American Psychologist, 41,* 186–295.

Schaef, A. W. (1981). *Women's reality: An emerging female system in the white male society*. Minneapolis: Winton Press.

Schaefer, H. H. (1970). Self-injurious behavior: Shaping "head banging" in monkeys. *Journal of Applied Behavior Analysis, 3,* 111–116.

Schaefer, H. H., & Martin, P. L. (1969). *Behavioral therapy*. New York: McGraw-Hill.

Schafer, J., & Brown, S. A. (1991). Marijuana and cocaine effect expectancies and drug use patterns. *Journal of Consulting and Clinical Psychology, 59,* 558–565.

Schaughency, E. A., & Hynd, G. W. (1989). Attention and impulse control in attention deficit disorders (ADD). *Learning and Individual Differences, 1,* 423–449.

Scheppele, K. L., & Bart, P. B. (1983). Through women's eyes: Defining danger in the wake of sexual assault. *Journal of Social Issues, 39,* 63–80.

Schildkraut, J. J. (1965). The catecholamine hypothesis of affective disorders: A review of supporting evidence. *American Journal of Psychiatry, 122,* 509–522.

Schleifer, S. J., Keller, S. E., Camerino, M., Thornton, J. C., & Stein, M. (1983). Suppression of lymphocyte stimulation following bereavement. *Journal of the American Medical Association, 250,* 374–377.

Schlesinger, L. (1989). *Sex murder and sex aggression*. New York: Wiley.

Schmauk, F. J. (1970). Punishment, arousal, and avoidance learning. *Journal of Abnormal Psychology, 76,* 325–335.

Schmidt, H. O., & Fonda, C. P. (1956). The reliability of psychiatric diagnosis: A new look. *Journal of Abnormal and Social Psychology, 52,* 262–267.

Schmidt, J. A. (1974). Research techniques for counselors: The multiple baseline. *Personnel and Guidance Journal, 53,* 200–206.

Schneidman, B., & McGuire, L. (1976). Group therapy for nonorgasmic women: Two age levels. *Archives of Sexual Behavior, 5,* 239–247.

Schnurr, P. P., Friedman, M. J., & Rosenberg, S. D. (1993). Premilitary MMPI scores as predictors of combat-related PTSD symptoms. *American Journal of Psychiatry, 150,* 479–483.

Schoeneman, T. J. (1984). The mentally ill witch in textbooks of abnormal psychology: Current status and implications of a fallacy. *Professional Psychology, 15,* 299–314.

Schofield, W. (1964). *Psychotherapy: The purchase of friendship*. Englewood Cliffs, NJ: Prentice-Hall.

Schopler, E., Rutter, M., & Chess, S. (1979). Editorial: Change of journal scope and title. *Journal of Autism and Developmental Disorders, 9,* 1–10.

Schover, L. R., Friedman, J. M., Weiler, S. J., Heiman, J. R., & LoPiccolo, J. (1982). Multiaxial problem-oriented system for sexual dysfunctions. *Archives of General Psychiatry, 39,* 614–619.

Schreiber, F. R. (1973). *Sybil*. Chicago: Regnery.

Schreibman, L., & Koegel, R. L. (1975). Autism: A defeatable horror. *Psychology Today, 8,* 61–67.

Schroth, M. L., & Sue, D. W. (1975). *Introductory psychology*. Homewood, IL: Dorsey.

Schuckit, M. A. (1990). A prospective study of children of alcoholics. In C. R. Cloninger & H. Begleiter (Eds.), *Genetics and biology of alcoholism* (pp. 183–194). Cold Spring Harbor, NY: Cold Spring Harbor Laboratory Press.

Schuell, H. (1974). *Aphasia theory and therapy: Selected lectures and papers of Hildred Schuell*. Baltimore: University Park Press.

Schulsinger, F. (1972). Psychopathy: Heredity and environment. *International Journal of Mental Health, 1,* 190–206.

Schulsinger, H. (1976). A ten-year follow-up of children of schizophrenic mothers: Clinical assessment. *Acta Psychiatrica Scandinavica, 53*, 371–386.

Schultz, B. (1982). *Legal liability and psychotherapy.* San Francisco: Jossey-Bass.

Schwartz, D. M., & Thompson, M. G. (1981). Do anorectics get well? Future research and current needs. *American Journal of Psychiatry, 138*, 319–323.

Schwartz, R., & Geyer, S. (1984). Social and psychological differences between cancer and noncancer patients: Cause or consequence of the disease? *Psychotherapy and Psychomatics, 41*, 195–199.

Schwitzgebel, R. L., & Schwitzgebel, R. K. (1980). *Law and psychological practice.* New York: Wiley.

Scott, R. L., & Baroffio, J. R. (1986). An MMPI analysis of similarities and differences in three classifications of eating disorders: Anorexia nervosa, bulimia, and morbid obesity. *Journal of Clinical Psychology, 42*, 708–713.

Scovern, A. W., & Kilmann, P. R. (1980). Status of electroconvulsive therapy: A review of the outcome literature. *Psychological Bulletin, 87*, 260–303.

Seattle Post-Intelligencer (1992, January 17), p. C2.

Seeman, M. V., Littman, S. K., Thornton, J. F., Jeffries, J. J., & Plummer, E. (1982). *Living and Working with Schizophrenia.* Toronto: University of Toronto Press.

Segal, N. L. (1990). The importance of twin studies for individual differences research. *Journal of Counseling and Development, 68*, 612–622.

Segal, S. P., Cohen, D., & Marder, S. R. (1992). Use of antipsychotic medication in sheltered-care facilities. *American Journal of Public Health, 47*, 39–46.

Segal, S. P., Cohen, D., & Marder, S. R. (1992). Neuroleptic medication and prescription practices with sheltered-care residents: A 12-year perspective. *American Journal of Public Health, 82*, 846–852.

Segraves, R. T., Schoenberg, H. W., & Ivanoff, J. (1983). Serum testosterone and prolactin levels in erectile dysfunction. *Journal of Sex and Marital Therapy, 9*, 19–26.

Segraves, R. T. (1988). Hormones and libido. In R. C. Rosen & S. R. Leiblum (Eds.), *Sexual desire disorders.* New York: Guilford.

Seiden, R. H. (1966). Campus tragedy: A study of student suicide. *Journal of Abnormal and Social Psychology, 71*, 389–399.

Seiden, R. H. (1969). *Suicide among youth: A review of the literature, 1900–1967.* Department of Health, Education & Welfare. Washington, DC: U.S. Government Printing Office.

Seiden, R. H. (1984a). Death in the West—a regional analysis of the youthful suicide rate. *Western Journal of Medicine, 140*, 969–973.

Seiden, R. H. (1984b). The youthful suicide epidemic. *Public Affairs Report, 25*, 1.

Seidman, E., & Rappaport, J. (1974). The educational pyramid: A paradigm for research, training, and manpower utilization in community psychology. *American Journal of Community Psychology, 2*, 119–130.

Seligman, J., Huck, J., Joseph, N., Namuth, T., Prout, L. R., Robinson, T. L., & McDaniel, A. L. (1984, April 9). The date who rapes. *Newsweek*, pp. 91–92.

Seligmann, J., Zabarsky, M., Witherspoon, D., Rotenberk, L., & Schmidt, M. (1983, March 7). A deadly feast and famine. *Newsweek*, pp. 59–60.

Seligman, M. E. P. (1971). Phobias and preparedness. *Behavior Therapy, 2*, 307–320.

Seligman, M. E. P. (1975). *Helplessness.* San Francisco: Freeman.

Seligman, M. E. P. (1987). Stop blaming yourself. *Psychology Today, 21*, 30–32, 34, 36–39.

Seligman, M. E. P., & Maier, S. F. (1967). Failure to escape traumatic shock. *Journal of Experimental Psychology, 74*, 1–9.

Selye, H. (1956). *The stress of life.* New York: McGraw-Hill.

Selye, H. (1982). Stress: Eustress, distress, and human perspectives. In S. B. Day (Ed.), *Life stress* (pp. 3–13). New York: Van Nostrand Reinhold.

Semans, J. H. (1956). Premature ejaculation: A new approach. *Southern Medical Journal, 49*, 353–357.

Sesan, R. (1988). Sex bias and sex-role stereotyping in psychotherapy with women: Survey results. *Psychotherapy, 25*, 107–116.

Shaffer, D., & Fisher, P. (1981). The epidemiology of suicide in children and young adolescents. *Journal of the American Academy of Child Psychiatry, 21*, 545–565.

Shafran, R., Booth, R., & Rachman, S. (1993). The reduction of claustrophobia—II: Cognitive analysis. *Behaviour Research and Therapy, 31*, 75–85.

Shah, S. (1969). Training and utilizing a mother as a therapist for her child. In B. G. Guemey (Ed.), *Psychotherapeutic agents: New roles for nonprofessionals, parents, and teachers.* New York: Holt, Rinehart & Winston.

Shahar, A., & Marks, I. (1980). Habituation during exposure treatment of compulsive rituals. *Behavior Therapy, 11*, 397–401.

Shahidi, S., & Salmon, P. (1992). Contingent and non-contingent biofeedback training for type A and B health adults: Can type As relax by competing? *Journal of Psychosomatic Research, 36*, 477–483.

Shapiro, D. A., & Shapiro, D. (1983). Meta-analysis of comparative therapy outcome studies: A replication and refinement. *Psychological Bulletin, 92*, 581–594.

Shapiro, D. L. (1984). *Psychological evaluation and expert testimony.* New York: Van Nostrand Reinhold.

Shapiro, J. P. (1991). Interviewing children about psychological issues associated with sexual abuse. *Psychotherapy, 28*, 55–65.

Shapiro, L., Rosenberg, D., Lauerman, J. F., & Sparkman, R. (1993, April 19). Rush to judgment. *Newsweek,* pp. 54–60.

Shapiro, M. K. (1991). Bandaging a "broken heart:" Hypnoplay therapy in the treatment of multiple personality disorder. *American Journal of Clinical Hypnosis, 34,* 1–9.

Shapiro, S., Skinner, E. A., Kessler, L. G., Von Korff, M., German, P. S., Tischler, G. L., Leaf, P. J., Benham, L., Cottler, L., & Regier, D. A. (1984). Utilization of health and mental health services. *Archives of General Psychiatry, 41,* 971–978.

Shave, D. (1976). Transsexualism as a manifestation of orality. *American Journal of Psychoanalysis, 36,* 57–66.

Shaywitz, S. E., & Shaywitz, B. A. (1984). Evaluation and treatment of children with attention deficit disorders. *Pediatrics in Review, 6,* 99–109.

Shaywitz, S. E., & Shaywitz, B. A. (1991). Introduction to the special series on attention deficit disorder. *Journal of Learning Disabilities, 24,* 68–71.

Shean, G. (1987) *Schizophrenia.* Cambridge, MA: Winthrop Publishers.

Shear, M. K., Ball, G., Fitzpatrick, M., Josephson, S., Klosko, J., & Frances, A. (1991). Cognitive-behavioral therapy for panic: An open study. *Journal of Nervous and Mental Disease, 179,* 468–472.

Shedler, J., & Block, J. (1990). Adolescent drug use and psychological health: A longitudinal inquiry. *American Psychologist, 45,* 612–630.

Sheehan, D. V. (1982). Panic attacks and phobias. *New England Journal of Medicine, 307,* 156–158.

Sheehan, P. W., Grigg, L., & McCann, T. (1984). Memory distortion following exposure to false information in hypnosis. *Journal of Abnormal Psychology, 93,* 259–265.

Shelton, R. C., Karson, C. N., Doran, A. R., Pickar, D., Bigelow, L. B., & Weinberger, D. R. (1988). Cerebral structural pathology in schizophrenia: Evidence for a selective prefrontal cortical defect. *American Journal of Psychiatry, 145,* 154–163.

Shepherd, M., Watt, D., Falloon, I. R. F., & Smeeton, N. (1989). The natural history of schizophrenia: A five-year follow-up study of outcome and prediction in a representative sample of schizophrenics. *Psychological Medicine, 15,* 1–46.

Shine, K. I. (1984). Anxiety in patients with heart disease. *Psychosomatics, 25,* 27–31.

Shisslak, C. M., Pazda, S. L., & Crago, M. (1990). Body weight and bulimia as discriminators of psychological characteristics among anoretic, bulimic, and obese women. *Journal of Abnormal Psychology, 99,* 380–384.

Shneidman, E. S. (1968). *Classifications of suicide phenomena: Bulletin of suicidology.* For the National Institute of Mental Health, Alcohol, Drug Abuse, and Mental Retardation, U.S. Department of Health, Education, and Welfare. Washington, DC: U.S. Government Printing Office.

Shneidman, E. S. (1976). Introduction: Contemporary overview of suicide. In E. S. Shneidman (Ed.), *Suicidology: Contemporary developments.* New York: Grune & Stratton.

Shneidman, E. S. (1987). A psychological approach to suicide. In G. VandenBos & B. Bryant (Eds.), *Cataclysms, crises, and catastrophes: Psychology in action* (pp. 151–183). Washington, DC: American Psychological Association.

Shneidman, E. S. (1989). Overview: A multidimensional approach to suicide. In D. G. Jacobs & H. N. Brown (Eds.), *Suicide: Understanding and responding: Harvard Medical School perspectives on suicide* (pp. 1-30). Madison, CT: International Universities Press.

Shneidman, E. S., & Farberow, N. L. (Eds.). (1957). *Clues to suicide.* New York: McGraw-Hill.

Shneidman, E. S., Farberow, N. L., & Litman, R. E. (Eds.). (1970). *The psychology of suicide.* New York: Aronson.

Shockley, W. (1972). Negro IQ deficit. *Journal of Criminal Law and Criminology, 7,* 530–543.

Shore, J. H. (1988). *American Indian and Alaskan native mental health research, 1,* 3–4.

Shotten, J. H. (1985). The family interview. *Schizophrenia Bulletin, 11,* 112–116.

Shouldice, A., & Stevenson-Hinde, J. (1992). Coping with security distress: The Separation Anxiety Test and attachment classification at 4.5 years. *Journal of Child Psychology and Psychiatry, 33,* 331–348.

Shreve, B. W., & Kunkel, M. A. (1991). Self-psychology, shame, and adolescent suicide: Theoretical and practical considerations. *Journal of Counseling and Development, 69,* 305–311.

Shuey, A. (1966). *The testing of Negro intelligence.* New York: Social Science Press.

Shure, M. B., & Spivack, G. (1979). Interpersonal problem-solving thinking and adjustment in the mother-child dyad. In M. W. Kent & J. E. Rolf (Eds.), *Primary prevention of psychopathology* (Vol. 3). Hanover, NH: University Press of New England.

Shure, M. B., & Spivack, G. (1982). Interpersonal problem-solving in young children: A cognitive approach to prevention. *American Journal of Community Psychology, 10,* 341–356.

Sibler, E., Hamburg, D. A., Coelho, G. V., Murphy, E. B., Rosenberg, M., & Perle, L. I. (1961). Adaptive behavior in competent adolescents. *Archives of General Psychiatry, 5,* 354–365.

Siegel, M. (1979). Privacy, ethics, and confidentiality. *Professional Psychology, 10,* 249–258.

Siegel, R. A. (1978). Probability of punishment and suppression of behavior in psychopathic and nonpsychopathic offenders. *Journal of Abnormal Psychology, 87,* 514–522.

Siever, L. J. (1981). Schizoid and schizotypal personality disorders. In J. R. Lion (Ed.), *Personality disorders: Diagnosis and management.* Baltimore: Williams & Wilkins.

Siever, L. J., Davis, K. L., & Gorman, L. K. (1991). Pathogenesis of mood disorders. In K. Davis, H. Klar, & J. T. Coyle (Eds.), *Foundations of psychiatry.* Philadelphia: Saunders.

Silver, M. A., Bohnert, M., Beck, A. T., & Marcus, D. (1971). Relation of depression of attempted suicide and seriousness of intent. *Archives of General Psychiatry, 25,* 573–576.

Silverman, J. M., Mohs, R. C., Davidson, M., Losonczy, M. F., Keefe, R. S. E., Breitner, J. C. S., Sorokin, J. E., & Davis, K. L. (1987). Familial schizophrenia and treatment response. *American Journal of Psychiatry, 144,* 1271–1276.

Silverman, L. H. (1976). Psychoanalytic theory: "The reports of my death are greatly exaggerated." *American Psychologist, 31,* 621–637.

Silverstein, B., & Perdue, L. (1988). The relationship between role concerns, preference of slimness, and symptoms of eating problems among college women. *Sex Roles, 18,* 101–160.

Silverstein, C. (1972). *Behavior modification and the gay community.* Paper presented at the annual convention of the Association for Advancement of Behavior Therapy, New York.

Simon, G. E., & Vonkorff, M. (1991). Somatization and psychiatric disorder in the NIMH epidemiologic catchment area study. *American Journal of Psychiatry, 148,* 1494–1500.

Simon, R. A. (1967). *The jury and the defense of insanity.* Boston: Little, Brown.

Simon, R. J., & Aaronson, D. E. (1988). *The insanity defense: A critical assessment of law and policy in the post-Hinckley era.* New York: Praeger.

Simons, A. D., Murphy, G. E., Levine, J. L., & Wetzel, R. D. (1986). Cognitive therapy and pharmacotherapy for depression: Sustained improvement over one year. *Archives of General Psychiatry, 43,* 43–48.

Simonton, O. C., Mathews-Simonton, S., & Creighton, J. (1978). *Getting well again: A step-by-step, self-help guide to overcoming cancer for patients and their families.* Los Angeles: Tarcher.

Singer, J. L., & Singer, D. G. (1983). Psychologists look at television: Cognitive developmental, personality, and social policy implications. *American Psychologist, 38,* 826–834.

Sizemore, C., & Pittillo, E. (1977). *I'm Eve.* New York: Doubleday.

Skeels, H. M. (1966). Adult status of children with contrasting early life experiences. *Monographs of the Society for Research in Child Development, 31.*

Skinner, B. F. (1948). "Superstition" in the pigeon. *Journal of Experimental Psychology, 38,* 168–172.

Skinner, B. F. (1990). Can psychology be a science of mind? *American Psychologist, 45,* 1206–1210.

Slater, J., & Depue, R. A. (1981). The contribution of environmental events and social support to serious suicide attempts in primary depressive disorder. *Journal of Abnormal Psychology, 90,* 275–285.

Sloane, R. B., Staples, F. R., Cristol, A. H., Yorkston, N. J., & Whipple, K. (1975). *Psychotherapy versus behavior therapy.* Cambridge, MA: Harvard University Press.

Small, G. W., Propper, M. W., Randolph, E. T., & Eth, S. (1991). Mass hysteria among student performers: Social relationships as a symptom predictor. *American Journal of Psychiatry, 148,* 1200–1205.

Smalley, S. L., & Asarnow, R. F. (1990). Brief report: Cognitive subclinical markers in autism. *Journal of Autism and Developmental Disorders, 20,* 271–278.

Smith, A. (1990). Social influence and antiprejudice training programs. In J. Edwards, R. S. Tindale, L. Heath, & E. J. Posavac, *Social influence processes and prevention* (pp. 183–196). New York: Plenum Press.

Smith, A., & Sugar, O. (1975). Development of above normal language and intelligence 21 years after left hemispherectomy. *Neurology, 25,* 813–818.

Smith, D. (1982). Trends in counseling and psychotherapy. *American Psychologist, 37,* 802–809.

Smith, D., & Kraft, W. A. (1983). DSM-III: Do psychologists really want an alternative? *American Psychologist, 38,* 777–785.

Smith, D. E., & Landry, M. J. (1988). Psychoactive substance use disorders: Drugs and alcohol. In H. H. Goldman (Ed.), *Review of general psychiatry* (pp. 266–285). Norwalk, CT: Appleton & Lange.

Smith, E. (1991). First person account: Living with schizophrenia. *Schizophrenia Bulletin, 17,* 689–691.

Smith, E. K. (1972). *The effect of double-bind communications upon the state of anxiety of normals.* Unpublished doctoral dissertation, University of New Mexico, Albuquerque.

Smith, K. (1988, May). Loving him was easy. *Reader's Digest,* pp. 115–119.

Smith, M. B. (1950). The phenomenological approach in personality theory: Some critical remarks. *Journal of Abnormal and Social Psychology, 45,* 516–522.

Smith, M. B., & Hobbs, N. (1966). The community and the community mental health center. *American Psychologist, 21,* 299–309.

Smith, M. L., & Glass, G. V. (1977). Meta-analysis of psychotherapy outcome studies. *American Psychologist, 32,* 752–760.

Smith, M. L., Glass, G. V., & Miller, T. I. (1980). *The benefits of psychotherapy.* Baltimore, MD: The Johns Hopkins University Press.

Smith, T. W., Turner, C. W., Ford, M. H., Hunt, S. C., Barlow, G. K., Stults, B. M., & Williams, R. R. (1987). Blood pressure reactivity in adult male twins. *Health Psychology, 6,* 209–220.

Smyer, M. A. (1984). Life transitions and aging: Implications for counseling older adults. *Counseling Psychologist, 12,* 17–28.

Snowden, L. R. (1987). The peculiar successes of community psychology: Service delivery to ethnic minorities and the poor. *American Journal of Community Psychology, 15,* 575–586.

Snowden, L. R., Collinge, W. B., & Runkle, M. C. (1982). Help seeking and underservice. In L. R. Snowden (Ed.), *Reaching the underserved: Mental health needs of neglected populations* (pp. 281–298). Beverly Hills: Sage Publications.

Snyder, R. D., Stovring, J., Cushing, A. H., Davis, L. E., & Hardy, T. L. (1981). Cerebral infarction in childhood bacterial meningitis. *Journal of Neurology, Neurosurgery, and Psychiatry, 44,* 581–585.

Snyder, S. (1986). *Drugs and the brain.* New York: Scientific American Library.

Sobell, M. B., & Sobell, L. C. (1978). *Behavioral treatment of alcohol problems.* New York: Plenum.

Sobell, M. B., & Sobell, L. C. (1984). The aftermath of Heresy: A response to Pendery et al.'s (1982) critique of "Individualized behavior therapy for alcoholics." *Behaviour Research and Therapy, 22,* 413–440.

Sohlberg, S. C. (1985). Personality and neuropsychological performance of high-risk children. *Schizophrenia Bulletin, 11,* 48–65.

Solano, L., Costa, M., Salvati, S., Coda, R., Aiuti, F., Mezzaroma, I., & Bertini, M. (1993). Psychosocial factors and clinical evolution in HIV-1 infection: A longitudinal study. *Journal of Psychosomatic Research, 37,* 39–51.

Solkoff, N., Gray, P., & Keill, S. (1986). Which Vietnam veterans develop posttraumatic stress disorders? *Journal of Clinical Psychology, 42,* 687–698.

Solomon, R. L. (1977). An opponent-process theory of motivation: The affective dynamics of drug addiction. In J. D. Maser & M. E. Seligman (Eds.), *Psychopathology: Experimental models.* San Francisco: Freeman.

Solomon, R. L. (1980). The opponent-process theory of acquired motivation: The costs of pleasure and the benefits of pain. *American Psychologist, 35,* 691–712.

Sorenson, S. B., & Siegel, J. M. (1992). Gender, ethnicity, and sexual assault: Findings from a Los Angeles study. *Journal of Social Issues, 48,* 93–104.

Sorenson, S. B., & White, J. W. (1992). Adult sexual assault: Overview of research. *Journal of Social Issues, 48,* 1–8.

Southern, S., & Gayle, R. (1982). A cognitive behavioral model of hypoactive sexual desire. *Behavioral Counselor, 2,* 31–48.

Spanos, N. P. (1978). Witchcraft in histories of psychiatry: A critical analysis and an alternative conceptualization. *Psychological Bulletin, 85,* 417–439.

Spanos, N. P., Weekes, J. R., & Bertrand, L. D. (1985). Multiple personality: A social psychological perspective. *Journal of Abnormal Psychology, 94,* 362–376.

Sparr, L., & Pankratz, L. D. (1983). Factitious posttraumatic stress disorder. *American Journal of Psychiatry, 140,* 1016–1019.

Speer, D. C. (1971). Rate of caller re-use of a telephone crisis service. *Crisis Intervention, 3,* 83–86.

Speer, D. C. (1972). *An evaluation of a telephone crisis service.* Paper presented at the meeting of the Midwestern Psychological Association, Cleveland, Ohio.

Spence, S. H. (1991). Cognitive-behavioral therapy in the treatment of chronic occupational pain in the upper limbs: A 2 year follow-up. *British Journal of Psychiatry, 29,* 503–509.

Spencer, S. L., & Zeiss, A. M. (1987). Sex roles and sexual dysfunction in college students. *Journal of Sex Research, 23,* 338–347.

Spiegel, D., & Cardena, E. (1991). Disintegrated experience: The dissociative disorders revisited. *Journal of Abnormal Psychology, 100,* 366–378.

Spiegler, M. D. (1983). *Contemporary behavioral therapy.* Palo Alto, CA: Mayfield Publishing.

Spiess, W. F., Geer, J. H., & O'Donohue, W. T. (1984). Premature ejaculation: Investigation of factors in ejaculatory latency. *Journal of Abnormal Psychology, 93,* 242–245.

Spinhoven, P., & Van Wijk, J. (1992). Hypnotic age regression in an experimental and clinical context. *American Journal of Clinical Hypnosis, 35,* 40–45.

Spitzer, R. L. (1975). On pseudoscience in science, logic in remission, and psychiatric diagnosis: A critique of Rosenhan's "On being sane in insane places." *Journal of Abnormal Psychology, 84,* 442–452.

Spitzer, R. L. (1981a). The diagnostic status of homosexuality in DSM-III: A reformation of the issues. *American Journal of Psychiatry, 138,* 210–215.

Spitzer, R. L. (1981b). Nonmedical myths and the DSM-III. *APA Monitor, 12*(3), 33.

Spitzer, R. L., Skodol, A. E., Gibbon, M., & Williams, J. B. W. (1981). *DSM-III casebook.* Washington, DC: American Psychiatric Association.

Spitzer, R. L., & Williams, J. B. (1987). Introduction. In American Psychiatric Association *Diagnostic and statistical manual of mental disorders* (3rd ed. [DSM-III]). Washington, DC: American Psychiatric Association.

Spivak, B., Trottern, S. F., Mark, M., Bleich, A., & Weizman, A. (1992). Acute transient stress-induced hallucinations in soldiers. *British Journal of Psychiatry, 160,* 412–414.

Spotnitz, H. (1963). The toxoid response. *Psychoanalytic Review, 50*(4), 81–94.

Spotnitz, H. (1968). *Modern psychoanalysis and the schizophrenic patient.* New York: Grune & Stratton.

Spotnitz, H. (1976). *Psychotherapy of preoedipal conditions.* New York: Aronson.

Sprafka, J. M., Folsom, A. R., Burke, G. L., Hahn, L. P., & Pirio, P. (1990). Type A behavior and its association with cardiovascular disease prevalence in blacks and whites: The Minnesota Heart Survey. *Journal of Behavioral Medicine, 13,* 1–13.

Squire, L. R., & Slater, P. C. (1978). Bilateral and unilateral ECT: Effects on verbal and nonverbal memory. *American Journal of Psychiatry, 135,* 89–95.

Srole, L., & Fischer, A. K. (1980). The midtown Manhattan longitudinal study vs. "the mental paradise lost" doctrine: A controversy joined. *Archives of General Psychiatry 37*(2), 209–221.

Srole, L., Langer, T. S., Michael, S. T., Opler, M. K., & Rennie, T. A. (1962). *Mental health in the metropolis: The midtown Manhattan study.* New York: McGraw-Hill.

St. Clair, D. (1987). Chromosome 21, Down's syndrome and Alzheimer's disease. *Journal of Mental Deficiency Research, 31,* 213–214.

Staats, A. W., & Heiby, E. M. (1985). Paradigmatic behaviorism's theory of depression: Unified, explanatory, and heuristic. In S. Reiss & R. R. Bootzin (Eds.), *Theoretical issues in behavioral therapy* (pp. 279–330). Orlando, FL: Academic Press.

Stack, S. (1987). Celebrities and suicide: A taxonomy and analysis, 1948–1983. *American Sociological Review, 52,* 401–412.

Stacy, A. W., Newcomb, M. D., & Bentler, P. M. (1991). Cognitive motivation and drug use: A 9-year longitudinal study. *Journal of Abnormal Psychology, 100,* 502–515.

Stacy, M., & Roeltgen, D. (1991). Infection of the central nervous system in the elderly. In S. Duckett (Ed.), *The pathology of the aging human nervous system* (pp. 374–392). Philadelphia: Lea & Febiger.

Stampfl, T., & Levis, D. (1967). Essentials of implosive therapy: A learning-theory-based psychodynamic behavioral therapy. *Journal of Abnormal Psychology, 72,* 496–503.

Stanley, M., & Mann, J. J. (1983). Increased serotonin-z binding sites in frontal cortex of suicide victims. *Lancet, 2,* 214–216.

Stark, E. (1984). The unspeakable family secret. *Psychology Today, 18,* 38–46.

Stark, M. J. (1992). Dropping out of substance abuse treatment: A clinically oriented review. *Clinical Psychology Review, 12,* 93–116.

Starker, S. (1988). Do-it-yourself therapy: The prescription of self-help books by psychologists. *Psychotherapy, 25,* 142–146.

Stavig, G. R., Igra, A., & Leonard, A. R. (1988). Hypertension and related health issues among Asian and Pacific Islanders in California. *Public Health Report, 103,* 28–37.

Steadman, H. J. (1979). *Beating a rap: Defendants found incompetent to stand trial.* Chicago: University of Chicago Press.

Steege, J. F., Stout, A. L., & Carson, C. C. (1986). Patient satisfaction in Scott and small-Carrion penile implant recipients: A study of 52 patients. *Archives of Sexual Behavior, 15,* 171–177.

Steele, C. M., & Josephs, R. A. (1988). Drinking your troubles away II: An attention-allocation model of alcohol's effect on psychological stress. *Journal of Abnormal Psychology, 97,* 196–205.

Steele, C. M., & Josephs, R. A. (1990). Alcohol myopia: Its prized and dangerous effects. *American Psychologist, 45,* 921–933.

Steffen, J. J., Nathan, P. E., & Taylor, H. A. (1974). Tension-reducing effects of alcohol: Further evidence and methodological considerations. *Journal of Abnormal Psychology, 83,* 542–547.

Steffenburg, S., & Gillberg, C. (1989). The etiology of autism. In C. Gillberg (Ed.), *Diagnosis and treatment of autism* (pp. 63–82). New York: Plenum Press.

Stein, J. (1993). Vocal alterations in schizophrenic speech. *Journal of Nervous and Mental Disease, 181,* 59–62.

Stein, M., Miller, A. H., & Trestman, R. L. (1991). Depression, the immune system, and health and illness. *Archives of General Psychiatry, 48,* 171–177.

Steinhausen, H. C., & Erdin, A. (1992). Abnormal psychosocial situations and ICD-10 diagnoses in children and adolescents attending a psychiatric service. *Journal of Child Psychology and Psychiatry, 33,* 731–740.

Steketee, G., & White, K. (1990). *When once is not enough.* Oakland, CA.: New Harbinger Publications.

Steptoe, A. (1991). Invited review: The links between stress and illness. *Journal of Psychosomatic Research, 35,* 633–644.

Stern, R. S., Lipsedge, M. A., & Marks, I. M. (1973). Thought-stopping of neutral and obsessive thoughts: A controlled trial. *Behavior Research and Therapy, 11,* 659–662.

Stevens, E. V., & Salisbury, J. D. (1984). Group therapy for bulimic adults. *Archives of Orthopsychiatry, 54,* 156–161.

Stevens, J. (1987). Brief psychoses: Do they contribute to the good prognosis and equal prevalence of schizophrenia in developing countries? *British Journal of Psychiatry, 151,* 393–396.

Stevens, J., Mark, B., Erwin, F., Pacheco, P., & Suematsu,

K. (1969). Deep temporal stimulation in man. *Archives of Neurology, 21,* 157–169.

Stevens, J. H., Turner, C. W., Rhodewalt, F., & Talbot, S. (1984). The type A behavior pattern and carotid artery atherosclerosis. *Psychosomatic Medicine, 46,* 105–113.

Stillion, M. J., McDowell, E. E., & May, J. H. (1989). *Suicide across the life span: Premature exits.* Washington, DC: Hemisphere Publishing.

Stoll, A. L., Tohen, M., & Baldessarini, R. J. (1992). Increasing frequency of the diagnosis of obsessive-compulsive disorder. *American Journal of Psychiatry, 149,* 638–640.

Stoller, R. J. (1969). Parental influences on male transsexualism. In R. Green & J. Money (Eds.), *Transsexualism and sex reassignment.* Baltimore: Johns Hopkins University Press.

Stoller, R. J. (1991). The term *perversion.* In G. I. Fogel & W. A. Myers (Eds.), *Perversions and near-perversions in clinical practice* (pp. 36–58). New Haven, CT: Yale University Press.

Stone, A. A. (1974). *Law, psychiatry, and morality.* Washington, DC: American Psychiatric Press.

Stone, A. A. (1975). *Mental health and law: A system in transition.* Rockville, MD: National Institute of Mental Health.

Stone, W. L., & Lemanek, K. L. (1990). Parental report of social behaviors in autistic preschoolers. *Journal of Autism and Developmental Disorders, 20,* 513–522.

Stravynski, A. (1986). Indirect behavioral treatment of erectile failure and premature ejaculation in a man without a partner. *Archives of Sexual Behavior, 15,* 355–360.

Streissguth, A. P., Barr, H. M., & Sampson, P. D. (1990). Moderate prenatal alcohol exposure: Effects on child IQ and learning problems at age 7½ years. *Alcoholism: Clinical and Experimental Research, 14,* 662–669.

Streissguth, A. P., LaDue, R. A., & Randels, S. P. (1988). *A manual on adolescents and adults with fetal alcohol syndrome with special reference to American Indians.* Rockville, MD: Indian Health Service.

Streissguth, A. P., Landesman-Dwyer, S., Martin, J. C., & Smith, D. W. (1980). Teratogenic effects of alcohol in humans and laboratory animals. *Science, 209,* 353–361.

Strickland, B. R. (1992). Women and depression. *Current Directions in Psychological Science, 1*(4), 132–135.

Stripling, S. (1986, August 3). Crossing over. *Seattle Post Intelligencer,* pp. K1–K2.

Stroebe, M., & Stroebe, W. (1991). Does "grief work" work? *Journal of Consulting and Clinical Psychology, 59*(3), 479–482.

Strupp, H. H., & Hadley, S. W. (1977). *Psychotherapy for better or worse: An analysis of the problem of negative effects.* New York: Jason Aronson.

Stuart, F. M., Hammond, D. C., & Pett, M. A. (1987). Inhibited sexual desire in women. *Archives of Sexual Behavior, 16,* 91–106.

Stubbe, D. E., Zahner, G. E. P., Goldstein, M. J., & Leckman, J. F. (1993). Diagnostic specificity of a brief measure of expressed emotion: A community study of children. *Journal of Child Psychology and Psychiatry, 34,* 139–154.

Stuss, D. T., Gow, C. A., & Hetherington, C. R. (1992). "No longer Gage": Frontal lobe dysfunction and emotional changes. *Journal of Consulting and Clinical Psychology, 60*(3), 349–359.

Sue, D. (1972). The role of relaxation in systematic desensitization. *Behaviour Research and Therapy, 10,* 153–158.

Sue, D. (1978). The use of masturbation in the in vivo treatment of impotence. *Journal of Behavior Therapy and Experimental Psychiatry, 9,* 75–76.

Sue, D. (1979). Erotic fantasies of college students during coitus. *Journal of Sex Research, 15,* 299–305.

Sue, D. W. (1981). *Counseling the culturally different: Theory and practice.* New York: Wiley.

Sue, D. W. (1990). Culture-specific strategies in counseling: A conceptual framework. *Professional Psychology: Research and Practice, 21,* 424–433.

Sue, D. W., Arredondo, P., & McDavis, R. J. (1992). Multicultural competencies/standards: A pressing need. *Journal of Counseling and Development, 70*(4), 477–

Sue, D. W., & Sue, D. (1990). *Counseling the culturally different* (2nd ed.). New York: John Wiley.

Sue, S. (1973). The training of third world students to function as counselors. *Journal of Counseling Psychology, 20,* 73–78.

Sue, S. (1977). Community mental health services to minority groups: Some optimism, some pessimism. *American Psychologist, 32,* 616–624.

Sue, S. (1992). Ethnicity and mental health: Research and policy issues. *Journal of Social Issues, 48,* 187–205.

Sue, S., & Abe, J. (1988). *Predictors of academic achievement among Asian American and white students.* New York: The College Board.

Sue, S., Fujino, D., Hu, L., Takeuchi, D. T., & Zane, N. (1991). Community mental health services for ethnic minority groups: A test of the cultural responsiveness hypothesis. *Journal of Consulting and Clinical Psychology, 59,* 533–540.

Sue, S., & Morishima, J. K. (1982). *The mental health of Asian Americans.* San Francisco: Jossey-Bass.

Sue, S., & Nakamura, C. Y. (1984). An integrative model of physiological and social/psychological factors in alcohol consumption among Chinese and Japanese Americans. *Journal of Drug Issues, 14,* 349–364.

Sue, S., & Sue, D. W. (1971). Chinese-American personality and mental health. *Amerasia Journal, 1,* 36–49.

Sugarman, J. R., Gilbert, T. J., Percy, C. A., & Peter, D. G. (1992). Serum cholesterol concentrations among Navajo Indians. *Public Health Reports, 107*, 92–99.

Suicide belt. (1986, February 24). *Time, 116*(9), 56.

Sullivan, C. M., & Davidson, W. S. II (1991). The provision of advocacy services to women leaving abusive partners: An examination of short-term effects. *American Journal of Community Psychology, 19*, 953–960.

Sullivan, H. S. (1953). In H. S. Perry & M. L. Gawel (Eds.), *The interpersonal theory of psychiatry.* New York: Norton.

Sulser, F. (1979). Pharmacology: New cellular mechanisms of antidepressant drugs. In S. Fielding & R. C. Effland (Eds.), *New frontiers in psychotropic drug research.* Mount Kisco, NY: Futura.

Sundberg, N. D., Taplin, J. R., & Tyler, L. E. (1983). *Introduction to clinical psychology.* Englewood Cliffs, NJ: Prentice-Hall.

Swann, W. B. Jr., Wenzlaff, R. M., Krull, D. S., & Pelham, B. W. (1992). Allure of negative feedback: Self-verification strivings among depressed persons. *Journal of Abnormal Psychology, 101*(2), 193–306.

Swartz, M., Hughes, D., George, L., Blazer, D., Landerman, R., & Bucholz, K. (1986). Developing a screening index for community studies of somatization disorder. *Journal of Consulting and Clinical Psychology, 56*, 233–238.

Swedo, S. E., Rapoport, J. L., Leonard, H., Lenane, M., & Cheslow, D. (1989). Obsessive-compulsive disorder in children and adolescents. *Archives of General Psychiatry, 46*, 335–341.

Sweet, J. J. (1983). Confounding effects of depression on neuropsychological testing: Five illustrative cases. *Clinical Neuropsychology, 5*, 103–108.

Szasz, T. S. (1963). *Law, liberty, and psychiatry.* New York: Macmillan.

Szasz, T. (1986). The case against suicide prevention. *American Psychologist, 41*, 806–812.

Szymanski, S., Kane, J. M., & Lieberman, J. A. (1991). A selective review of biological markers in schizophrenia. *Schizophrenia Bulletin, 17*, 99–111.

Tabakoff, B., Whelan, J. P., & Hoffman, P. L. (1990). Two biological markers of alcoholism. In C. R. Cloninger & H. Begleiter (Eds.), *Genetics and biology of alcoholism* (pp. 195–204). Cold Spring Harbor, NY: Cold Spring Harbor Laboratory Press.

Taras, M. E., & Matese, M. (1990). Acquisition of self-help skills. In J. L. Matson (Ed.), *Handbook of behavior modification with the mentally retarded* (2nd ed., pp. 273–303). New York: Plenum Press.

Tarasoff vs. The Regents of the University of California, 17 Cal. 3d 435, 551 P.2d, 334, 131 Cal. Rptr. 14, 83 Ad. L. 3d 1166 (1976).

Tardiff, K. (1984). Characteristics of assaultive patients in private psychiatric hospitals. *American Journal of Psychiatry, 141*, 1232–1235.

Tardiff, K., & Koenigsberg, H. W. (1985). Assaultive behavior among psychiatric outpatients. *American Journal of Psychiatry, 142*, 960–963.

Tardiff, K., & Sweillam, A. (1982). Assaultive behavior among chronic inpatients. *American Journal of Psychiatry, 139*, 212–215.

Tarrier, N. (1987). An investigation of residual psychotic symptoms in discharged schizophrenic patients. *British Journal of Clinical Psychology, 26*, 141–143.

Task Force on DSM-IV, American Psychiatric Association. (1991). *DSM-IV Options Book: Work In Progress (9/1/91).* Washington, DC: American Psychiatric Press.

Tavris, C. (1972, March). Woman and man. *Psychology Today,* pp. 57–64.

Tavris, C. (1991). The mismeasure of woman: Paradoxes and perspectives in the study of gender. In J. D. Goodchilds (Ed.), *Psychological perspectives on human diversity in America* (pp. 91–136). Washington, DC: American Psychological Association.

Taylor, E. H. (1990). The assessment of social intelligence. *Psychotherapy, 27*, 445–457.

Taylor, S. E. (1983). Adjustments to threatening events: A theory of cognitive adaptation. *American Psychologist, 38*, 1161–1173.

Teicher, M. H., Glod, C., & Cole, J. O. (1990). Emergence of intense suicidal preoccupation during fluoxetine treatment. *American Journal of Psychiatry, 147*, 207–

Telch, M. J., Brouillard, M., Telch, C. F., Agras, W. S., & Taylor, C. B. (1989). Role of cognitive appraisal in panic related avoidance. *Behaviour Research and Therapy, 27*, 373–383.

Telch, M. J., Lucas, J. A., & Nelson, P. (1989). Nonclinical panic in college students: An investigation of prevalence and symptomatology. *Journal of Abnormal Psychology, 98*, 300–306.

Tellegen, A., Lykken, D. T., Bouchard, T. J. Jr., Wilcox, K. J., Segal, N. L., and Rich, S. (1988). Personality similarity in twins reared apart and together. *Journal of Personality and Social Psychology, 54*, 1031–1039.

Teplin, L. A. (1983). The criminalization of the mentally ill: Speculation in search of data. *Psychological Bulletin, 94*, 54–67.

Teri, L., & Wagner, A. (1992). Alzheimer's disease and depression. *Journal of Consulting and Clinical Psychology, 60*(3), 379–391.

Terman, L. M. (1916). *The measurement of intelligence.* Boston: Houghton Mifflin.

Terman, L. M., & Merrill, M. A. (1960). *Stanford-Binet intelligence scale.* Boston: Houghton Mifflin.

Terr, L. C. (1991). Childhood traumas: An outline and overview. *American Journal of Psychiatry, 148*, 10–20.

Tharp, R. G. (1991). Cultural diversity and treatment of children. *Journal of Consulting and Clinical Psychology, 59,* 799–812.

Thiers, N. (1988, August 1). Murder rampant in America: Professionals respond. *Guidepost, 51,* 1, 4, 5.

Thigpen, C. H., & Cleckley, H. (1957). *The three faces of Eve.* Kingsport, TN: Kingsport Press.

Thigpen, C. H., & Cleckley, H. M. (1984). On the incidence of multiple personality disorder: A brief communication. *International Journal of Clinical and Experimental Hypnosis, 32,* 63–66.

Thomas, A., Chess, S., & Birch, H. G. (1968). *Temperament and behavior disorders in children.* New York: New York University Press.

Thomas, A., & Sillen, S. (1972). *Racism and psychiatry.* New York: Brunner/Mazel.

Thomason, B. T., Brantley, P. J., Jones, G. N., Dyer, H. R., & Morris, J. L. (1992). The relationship between stress and disease activity in rheumatoid arthritis. *Journal of Behavioral Medicine, 15,* 215–220.

Thompson, J. K. (1986). Larger than life. *Psychology Today, 20,* 39–44.

Thoreson, C. E., & Powell, L. H. (1992). Type A behavior pattern: New perspectives on theory, assessment, and intervention. *Journal of Consulting and Clinical Psychology, 60,* 595–604.

Thorndike, R. L., Hagen, E. P., & Sattler, J. M. (1986). *The Stanford-Binet intelligence scale: Guide for administration and scoring* (3rd ed.). Chicago: Riverside.

Thorpe, G., & Burns, L. (1983). *The agoraphobic syndrome.* Chichester, England: Wiley.

Tienari, P. (1963). Psychiatric illness in identical twins. *Acta Psychiatrica Scandinavica, 39* (Suppl. 171).

Tierney, J. (1988, July 3). Research finds lower-level workers bear brunt of workplace stress. *Seattle Post Intelligencer,* pp. K1–K3.

Tiffany, S. T. (1990). A cognitive model of drug urges and drug-use behavior: Role of automatic and nonautomatic processes. *Psychological Review, 97,* 147–168.

Tizard, B. (1962). The personality of epileptics: A discussion of the evidence. *Psychological Bulletin, 59,* 1906–2010.

Tjosvold, D., & Tjosvold, M. M. (1983). Social psychological analysis of residences for mentally retarded persons. *American Journal of Mental Deficiency, 88,* 28–40.

Tobin, J. J., & Friedman, J. (1983). Spirits, shamans, and nightmare death: Survivor stress in a Hmong refugee. *American Journal of Orthopsychiatry, 53,* 439–448.

Tolan, P., Chertok, F., Keys, C., & Jason, L. (1990). Conversing about theories, methods, and community research. In P. Tolan, C. Keys, F. Chertok, & L. Jason (Eds.), *Researching community psychology* (pp. 3–8). Washington, DC: American Psychological Association.

Torgersen, S. (1983). Genetic factors in anxiety disorders. *Archives of General Psychiatry, 40,* 1085–1089.

Toro, P. A. (1986). A comparison of natural and professional help. *American Journal of Community Psychology, 14,* 147–160.

Toro, P. A. & Wall, D. D. (1991). Research on homeless persons: Diagnostic comparisons and practice implications. *Professional psychology: Research and practice, 22,* 479–488.

Toufexis, A. (1989, January 23). A not-so-happy anniversary. *Time,* p. 54.

Treiber, F. A., McCaffrey, F., Musante, L., Rhodes, T., Davis, H., Strong, W. B., & Levy, M. (1993). Ethnicity, family history of hypertension and patterns of hemodynamic reactivity in boys. *Psychosomatic Medicine, 55,* 70–77.

Triandis, H. C. (1983). Essentials of studying cultures. In D. Landis & R. W. Brislin (Eds.), *Handbook of intercultural training.* New York: Pergamon Press.

Trimble, J. E. (1991). The mental health service and training needs of American Indians. In H. F. Myers, P. Wohlford, L. P. Guzman, & R. J. Echemendia, *Ethnic minority perspectives on clinical training and services in psychology* (pp. 43–48). Washington, DC: American Psychological Association.

Tross, S., & Hirsch, D. A. (1988). Psychological distress and neuropsychological complications of HIV infection and AIDS. *American Psychologist, 43*(11), 929–934.

Tsoi, W. F. (1990). Developmental profile of 200 male and 100 female transsexuals in Singapore. *Archives of Sexual Behavior, 19,* 595–605.

Tsuang, M. T., Winokur, G., & Crowe, R. (1980). Morbidity risks of schizophrenia and affective disorders among first degree relatives of patients with schizophrenia, mania, depression, and surgical conditions. *British Journal of Psychiatry, 137,* 497–504.

Tuckman, J., Kleiner, R., & Lavell, M. (1959). Emotional content of suicide notes. *American Journal of Psychiatry, 16,* 59–63.

Turkheimer, E., & Parry, C. D. H. (1992). Why the gap? *American Psychologist, 47,* 646–655.

Turkington, C. (1987). Special talents. *Psychology Today,* vol. 21, pp. 42–46.

Turner, J. A., & Clancy, S. (1988). Comparison of operant behavioral and cognitive-behavioral group treatment for chronic low back pain. *Journal of Consulting and Clinical Psychology, 56,* 261–266.

Turner, S. M., Beidel, D. C., Nathan, R. S. (1985). Biological factors in obsessive-compulsive disorders. *Psychological Bulletin, 97,* 430–450.

Turner, S. M., Beidel, D. C., & Townsley, R. M. (1990). Social phobia: Relationship to shyness. *Behaviour Research and Therapy, 28,* 497–505.

Turner, S. M., Beidel, D. C., & Townsley, R. M. (1992). Social phobia: A comparison of specific and generalized subtypes and avoidant personality disorder. *Journal of Abnormal Psychology, 101,* 326–331.

Turner, S. M., Jacob, R. G., & Morrison, R. (1984). Somatoform and factitious disorders. In H. E. Adams and P. B. Sutker (Eds.), *Comprehensive handbook of psychiatry* (pp. 307–348). New York: Plenum Press.

Turner, W. J., & Merlis, A. (1962). Clinical correlations between electroencephalography and antisocial behavior. *Medical Times, 90,* 505–511.

Tyler, F. B., Brome, D. R., & Williams, J. E. (1991). *Ethnic validity, ecology, and psychotherapy: A psychosocial competence model.* New York: Plenum Press.

Tynes, L. L., White, K., & Steketee, G. S. (1990). Towards a new nosology of obsessive-compulsive disorder. *Comprehensive Psychiatry, 31,* 465–480.

Tyrer, P., Lee, I., & Alexander, J. (1980). Awareness of cardiac function in anxious, phobic, and hypochondriacal patients. *Psychological Medicine, 10,* 171–174.

Ubell, E. (1989, December 3). They're closing in on mental illness. *Parade Magazine,* pp. 6–7.

Udwin, O. (1993). Annotation: Children's reactions to traumatic events. *Journal of Child Psychology and Psychiatry, 34,* 115–127.

Uhlenhuth, E. H., Balter, M. B., Mellinger, G. D., Cisin, I. H., & Clinthorne, J. (1983). Symptom checklist syndromes in the general population. *Archives of General Psychiatry, 40,* 1167–1173.

Ullmann, L. P., & Krasner, L. (1965). Introduction. In L. P. Ullmann & L. Krasner (Eds.), *Case studies in behavior modification.* New York: Holt, Rinehart & Winston.

Ullmann, L. P., & Krasner, L. (1975). *A psychological approach to abnormal behavior* (2nd ed.). Englewood Cliffs, NJ: Prentice-Hall.

United States Public Health Service. (1986). *Surgeon general's report on acquired immune deficiency syndrome.* Washington, DC: U.S. Department of Health and Human Services.

University of Minnesota. (1977). *Epilepsy and the school age child.* Minneapolis, MN: State of Minnesota.

Update (1988): Sudden unexplained death syndrome among southeast Asian refugees—United States. *Morbidity and Mortality Weekly Report, 37,* 569–570.

U.S. Bureau of the Census. (1988). *Statistical abstract of the United States* (108th ed.). Washington, DC: U.S. Government Printing Office.

U.S. Department of Commerce (1991). *1990 Census Profile.* Washington, DC: U.S. Bureau of the Census.

U.S. Department of Health, Education and Welfare. (1971). *The alcoholism report: The authoritative newsletter for professionals.* Washington, DC: U.S. Government Printing Office.

U.S. Department of Health and Human Services. (1985). *Toward a national plan for the chronically mentally ill.* Washington, DC: U.S. Government Printing Office.

U.S. Department of Health and Human Services. (1991). *Depression: What you need to know.* Rockville, MD: NIMH 60-FL-1485-0.

Vaillant, G. E. (1975). Sociopathy as a human process: A viewpoint. *Archives of General Psychiatry, 32,* 178–183.

Vaillant, G. E., & Milofsky, E. S. (1982). The etiology of alcoholism. *American Psychologist, 37,* 494–503.

Vaillant, G. E., & Perry, J. C. (1985). Personality disorders. In H. I. Kaplan & B. J. Sadock (Eds.), *Comprehensive textbook of psychiatry* (4th ed., pp. 958–986). Baltimore: Williams & Wilkins.

Valenstein, E. S. (1986). *Great and desperate cures: The rise and decline of psychosurgery and other radical treatments for mental illness.* New York: Basic Books.

Van Der Molen, G. M., Van Den Hout, M. A., Vroemen, J., Lousberg, H., & Griez, E. (1986). Cognitive determinants of lactate-induced anxiety. *Behaviour Research and Therapy, 24,* 677–680.

Van Evra, J. P. (1983). *Psychological disorders of children and adolescents.* Boston: Little, Brown.

Van Horn, J. D., & McManus, I. C. (1992). Ventricular enlargement in schizophrenia. *British Journal of Psychiatry, 160,* 687–697.

Van Pragg, H. M. (1983). CSF 5-H1AA and suicide in non-depressed schizophrenics, *Lancet, 2,* 977–978.

Van Putten, T., Philip, R. A., May, M. D., & Marder, S. R. (1984). Response to antipsychotic medication: The doctor's and the consumer's view. *American Journal of Psychiatry, 141,* 16–19.

Vandenbos, G. R., Cummings, N. A., & Deleon, P. H. (1992). A century of psychotherapy: Economic and environmental influences. In D. K. Freedheim (Ed.), *History of psychotherapy* (pp. 65–102). Washington, DC: American Psychological Association.

Vanderlinden, J., Norre, J. & Vandereycken, W. (1992). *A practical guide to the treatment of bulimia nervosa.* New York: Brunner/Mazel.

Vartianinen, E., Dianjun, D., Marks, J. S., Korhonen, H., Guanyi, G., Ze-Yu, G., Koplan, J. P., Pietinen, P., Guang-Lin, W., Williamson, D., & Nissinen, A. (1991). Mortality, cardiovascular risk factors, and diet in China, Finland, and the United States. *Public Health Reports, 106,* 41–46.

Vaughn, C., & Leff, J. (1981). Patterns of emotional response in relatives of schizophrenic patients. *Schizophrenia Bulletin, 7,* 43–45.

Vazquez, M. I., & Buceta, J. M. (1993). Effectiveness of self-management programmes and relaxation training in the treatment of bronchial asthma: Relationships with trait anxiety and emotional attack triggers. *Journal of Psychosomatic Medicine, 37*, 71–81.

Vega, W., & Rumbaut, R.G. (1991). Ethnic minorities and mental health. *Annual Review of Sociology, 17*, 351–383.

Venter, A., Lord, C., & Schopler, E. (1992). A follow-up study of high-functioning autistic children. *Journal of Child Psychology and Psychiatry, 33*, 489–507.

Visintainer, M. A., Volpicelli, J. R., & Seligman, M. E. P. (1982). Tumor rejection in rats after inescapable or escapable shock. *Science, 216*, 437–439.

Visser, S., & Bouman, T. K. (1992). Cognitive-behavioural approaches in the treatment of hypochondriasis: Six single case cross-over studies. *Behaviour Research and Therapy, 30*, 301–306.

Vita, A., Dieci, M., Giobbio, G. M., Azzone, P., Garbini, M., Sacchetti, E., Cesana, B. M., & Cazzullo, C. L. (1991). CT scan abnormalities and outcome in chronic schizophrenia. *American Journal of Psychiatry, 148*, 1577–1579.

Vogel, G., Vogel, F., McAbee, R., & Thurmond, A. (1980). Improvement of depression by REM sleep deprivation. *Archives of General Psychiatry, 37*, 247–253.

Vogler, R. E., & Bartz, W. R. (1983). *The better way to drink*. New York: Simon & Schuster.

Volden, J., & Lord, C. (1991). Neologisms and idiosyncratic language in autistic speakers. *Journal of Autism and Developmental Disorders, 21*, 109–130.

Volkmar, F. R., Cicchetti, D. V., Dykens, E., Sparrow, S. S., Leckman, J. F., & Cohen, D. J. (1988). An evaluation of the Autism Behavior checklist. *Journal of Autism and Developmental Disorders, 18*, 81–97.

Volkow, N. D., Wolf, A. P., Van Gelder, P., Brodie, J. D., Overall, J. E., Camcro, R., & Gomez-Mont, F. (1987). Phenomenological correlates of metabolic activity in 18 patients with chronic schizophrenia. *American Journal of Psychiatry, 144*, 151–158.

Wachtel, P. L. (1977). *Psychoanalysis and behavior therapy*. New York: Basic Books.

Wachtel, P. L. (1982). Vicious circles: The self and the rhetoric of emerging and unfolding. *Contemporary Psychoanalysis, 18*, 280–282.

Wahba, M., Donlon, P. T., & Mendow, A. (1981). Cognitive changes in acute schizophrenia with brief neuroleptic treatment. *American Journal of Psychiatry, 138*, 1307–1310.

Wakefield, J. (1988). Female primary orgasmic dysfunctions: Masters and Johnson versus DSM-III-R on diagnosis and incidence. *Journal of Sex Research, 24*, 363–377.

Wakefield, J. C. (1992). The concept of mental disorder. *American Psychologist, 47*, 373–388.

Walder, C. P., McCraken, J. S., Herbert, M., James, P. T., & Brewitt, N. (1987). Psychological intervention in civilian flying phobia. *British Journal of Psychiatry, 151*, 494–498.

Waldstein, S. R., Manuk, S. B., Ryan, C. M., & Muldoon, M. F. (1991). Neurophysiological correlates of hypertension: Review and methodological considerations. *Psychological Bulletin, 110*, 451–468.

Walen, S., Hauserman, N. M., & Lavin, P. J. (1977). *Clinical guide to behavior therapy*. Baltimore: Williams & Wilkins.

Walker, E. A., Katon, W. J., Neraas, K., Jemelka, R. P., & Massoth, D. (1992). Dissociation in women with chronic pelvic pain. *American Journal of Psychiatry, 149*, 534–537.

Walker, H. M., Shinn, M. R., O'Neill, R. E., & Ramsey, E. (1987). A longitudinal assessment of the development of antisocial behavior in boys: Rationale, methodology, and first-year results. *Remedial and Special Education, 8*, 7–16.

Walker, L. A. (1991). Their spirit lifts them. *Parade Magazine, January 6*, 18–20.

Walker, L. E. (1991). Post-traumatic stress disorder in women: Diagnosis and treatment of battered woman syndrome. *Psychotherapy, 28*, 21–29.

Walker, N. (1968). *Crime and insanity in England: The historical perspective*. Edinburgh, Scotland: Edinburgh University Press.

Wallace, C., Nelson, C., Liberman, R., Aitchison, R., Lukoff, D., Elder, J., & Ferris, C. (1980). A review and critique of social skills training with schizophrenic patients. *Schizophrenia Bulletin, 6*, 42–64.

Waller, G. (1991). Sexual abuse as a factor in eating disorders. *British Journal of Psychiatry, 159*, 664–671.

Ward, C. H., Beck, A. T., Mendelson, M., Mock, J. E., & Erbaught, J. K. (1962). The psychiatric nomenclature: Reasons for diagnostic disagreement. *Archives of General Psychiatry, 7*, 198–205.

Warheit, G. J., Longino, C. F., & Bradsher, J. E. (1991). Sociocultural aspects. In J. Sadavoy, L. W. Lazarus, & L. F. Jarvik (Eds.), *Comprehensive review of geriatric psychiatry* (pp. 99–116). Washington, DC: American Psychiatric Press.

Warner, R. (1986). Hard times and schizophrenia. *Psychology Today*, vol. 20, 50–51.

Warren, C. A. B. (1982). *The court as a last resort: Mental illness and the law*. Chicago: University of Chicago Press.

Warwick, H. M. C., & Marks, I. M. (1988). Behavioural treatment for illness phobia and hypochondriasis. *British Journal of Psychiatry, 152*, 239–241.

Wasserman, E., & Gromisch, D. (1981). *Survey of clinical pediatrics*. New York: McGraw-Hill.

Watkins, B., & Bentovim, A. (1992). The sexual abuse of male children and adolescents: A review of current research. *Journal of Child Psychology and Psychiatry, 33*, 197–248.

Watkins, E. C., & Peterson, P. (1986). Psychiatric epidemiology: Its relevance for counselors. *Journal of Counseling and Development, 65*, 57–59.

Watkins, J. G., & Watkins, H. H. (1990). Dissociation and displacement: Where goes the "ouch?" *American Journal of Clinical Hypnosis, 33*, 1–10.

Watson, C. G., & Buranen, C. (1979). The frequencies of conversion reaction symptoms. *Journal of Abnormal Psychology, 88*, 209–211.

Watson, J. B., & Rayner, R. (1920). Conditioned emotional responses. *Journal of Experimental Psychology, 3*, 1–14.

Watzlawick, P., Weakland, J., & Fisch, R. (1974). *Change: Principles of problem formation and problem resolution.* New York: Norton.

Weakland, J. H. (1960). The "double-bind" hypothesis of schizophrenia and three-party interaction. In D. D. Jackson (Ed.), *The etiology of schizophrenia.* New York: Basic Books.

Webster, J. S., & Scott, R. P. (1983). The effects of self-instruction training in attention deficit following head injury. *Clinical Neuropsychology, 5*, 69–74.

Webster-Stratton, C. (1991). Annotation: Strategies for helping families with conduct disordered children. *Journal of Child Psychology and Psychiatry, 32*, 1047–1062.

Wechsler, D. (1981a). *Manual for the Wechsler Adult Intelligence Scale-Revised (WAIS-R).* New York: Psychological Corporation.

Wechsler, D. (1981b). *Wechsler Adult Intelligence Scale.* New York: Harcourt, Brace, Jovanovich.

Weddington, W. W. (1979). Single case study: Conversion reaction in an 82-year-old man. *Journal of Nervous and Mental Diseases, 167*, 368–369.

Weeks, S. J., & Hobson, R. P. (1987). The salience for facial expression for autistic children. *Journal of Child Psychology and Psychiatry, 28*, 137–152.

Weene, K. A. (1993). Is childhood sexual abuse a risk factor for bulimia? *American Journal of Psychiatry, 150*, 357.

Wehr, S. H., & Kaufman, M. E. (1987). The effects of assertive training on performance in highly anxious adolescents. *Adolescence, 22*, 195–205.

Weiden, P. J., Mann, J. J., Haas, G., Mattson, M., & Frances, A. (1987). Clinical nonrecognition of neuroleptic-induced movement disorders: A cautionary study. *American Journal of Psychiatry, 144*, 1148–1553.

Weile, E. F. (1960). On social psychological questions in suicidal personalities. *Psychological Research, 11*, 37–44.

Weinberg, T. S. (1987). Sadomasochism in the United States: A review of recent sociological literature. *Journal of Sex Research, 23*, 50–69.

Weiner, B. (1975). On being sane in insane places: A process (attributional) analysis and critique. *Journal of Abnormal Psychology, 84*, 433–441.

Weiner, B. A. (1985). Insanity evaluation. In S. J. Brakel, J. Parry, & B. A. Weiner (Eds.), *Mental disability and criminal law* (pp. 693–801). Chicago: American Bar Association.

Weiner, H. (1991). From simplicity to complexity (1950–1990): The case of peptic ulceration—II. Animal studies. *Psychosomatic Medicine, 53*, 491–516.

Weiner, H., Thaler, M., Reisner, M. F., & Mirsky, I. A. (1957). Etiology of duodenal ulcer: 1. Relation of specific psychological characteristics to rate of gastric secretion. *Psychosomatic Medicine, 19*, 1–10.

Weiner, I. B. (Ed.). (1976). *Individual psychotherapy. Clinical methods in psychology.* New York: Wiley.

Weiner, I. W. (1969). The effectiveness of suicide prevention programs. *Mental Hygiene, 53*, 357–373.

Weintraub, W. (1981). Compulsive and paranoid personalities. In J. R. Lion (Ed.), *Personality disorders: Diagnosis and management.* Baltimore: Williams & Wilkins.

Weiss, B., Weisz, J. R., Politano, M., Carey, M., Nelson, W. M., & Finch, A. J. (1992). Relations among self-reported depressive symptoms in clinic referred children versus adolescents. *Journal of Abnormal Psychology, 101*, 391–397.

Weiss, D. S. (1988). Personality assessment. In H. H. Goldman (Ed.), *Review of general psychiatry* (pp. 221–232). Norwalk, CT: Appleton & Lange.

Weiss, J. M., Glazer, H. I., & Pohorecky, L. A. (1975). Coping behavior and neurochemical changes: Alternative explanation for the original "learned helplessness" experiments. In G. Serban & A. Ling (Eds.), *Relevance of the animal model to the human.* New York: Plenum.

Weissberg, M. (1993). Multiple personality disorder and iatrogenesis: The cautionary tale of Anna O. *International Journal of Clinical and Experimental Hypnosis, XLI*, 15–34.

Weissberg, R. P., Cowen, E. L., Lotyczewski, B. S., & Gesten, E. L. (1983). The primary mental health project: Seven consecutive years of program outcome research. *Journal of Consulting and Clinical Psychology, 51*, 100–107.

Weissman, M. M., & Klerman, G. L. (1977). Sex differences and the epidemiology of depression. *Archives of General Psychiatry, 34*, 98–111.

Weisz, J. R., Weiss, B., & Donenberg, G. R. (1992). The lab versus the clinic: Effects of child and adolescent psychotherapy. *American Psychologist, 12*, 1578–1585.

Weitz, S. (1977). *Sex roles: Biological, psychological, and social foundations.* New York: Oxford University Press.

Welgan, P. R. (1974). Learned control of gastric acid secretions in ulcer patients. *Psychosomatic Medicine, 36,* 411–419.

Welkowitz, L. A., Papp, L. A., Cloitre, M., Liebowitz, M. R., Martin, L. Y., & Gorman, J. M. (1991). Cognitive-behavioral therapy for panic disorder delivered by psychopharmacologically oriented clinicians. *Journal of Nervous and Mental Disease, 179,* 473–477.

Wells, C. E. (1978). Role of stroke in dementia. *Stroke, 9,* 1–3.

Wells, C. E. (1985). Organic syndromes: Delirium. In H. I. Kaplan & B. J. Sadock (Eds.), *Comprehensive textbook of psychiatry/IV* (pp. 838–851). Baltimore: Williams & Wilkins.

Wender, P. H., & Klein, D. F. (1981, February). The promise of biological psychiatry. *Psychology Today,* vol. 15, pp. 25–41.

Wender, P. H., Rosenthal, D., Rainer, J. D., Greenbill, L., & Sarlan, M. B. (1977). Schizophrenics' adopting parents. *Archives of General Psychiatry, 34,* 777–784.

Werner, A. (1975). Sexual dysfunction in college men and women. *American Journal of Psychiatry, 132,* 164–168.

Werry, J. S., Methuen, R. J., & Fitzpatrick, J. (1983). The interrater reliability of DSM-III in children. *Journal of Abnormal Child Psychology, 11,* 341–354.

Westen, D. (1991). Cognitive-behavioral interventions in the psychoanalytic psychotherapy of borderline personality disorders. *Clinical Psychology Review, 11,* 211–230.

Westermeyer, J. (1987). Public health and chronic mental illness. *American Journal of Public Health, 77,* 667–668.

Wexler, L., Weissman, M. M., & Kasl, S. V. (1978). Suicide attempts 1970–1975: Updating a United States study and comparison with international trends. *British Journal of Psychiatry, 132,* 180–185.

Whalen, C. K., & Henker, B. (1991). Therapies for hyperactive children: Comparisons, combinations, and compromises. *Journal of Consulting and Clinical Psychology, 59,* 126–137.

Wheat, W. D. (1960). Motivational aspects of suicide in patients during and after psychiatric treatment. *Southern Medical Journal, 53,* 273.

White, J. L. (1984). *The psychology of blacks.* Englewood Cliffs, NJ: Prentice-Hall.

White, M. (1983). Anorexia nervosa: A transgenerational system perspective. *Family Process, 22,* 255–273.

Whitehead, W. E. (1993). Gut feelings: Stress and the GI tract. In D. Goleman and J. Gurin (Eds.), *Mind/Body medicine* (pp. 161–175). New York: Consumer Reports Books.

Whitehead, W. E., Winget, C., Fedoravicius, A. S., Wooley, S., & Blackwell, B. (1982). Learned illness behavior in patients with irritable bowel syndrome and peptic ulcer. *Digestive Diseases and Sciences, 27,* 202–208.

Whitehill, M., DeMeyer-Gapin, S., & Scott, T. J. (1976). Stimulus seeking in antisocial preadolescent children. *Journal of Abnormal Psychology, 85,* 101–104.

Whitman, B. Y., Graves, B., & Accardo, P. (1987). Mentally retarded parents in the community: Identification method and needs assessment survey. *American Journal of Mental Deficiency, 91,* 636–638.

Whittenmore, H. (1992). He Broke the Silence. *Parade Magazine,* Sept. 20, p. 8, 10.

Wickramasekera, I. (1976). Aversive behavior rehearsal for sexual exhibitionism. *Behavioral Therapy, 1,* 167–176.

Widiger, T. A. (1992). Generalized social phobia versus avoidant personality disorder: A commentary on three studies. *Journal of Abnormal Psychology, 101,* 340–343.

Widiger, T. A., Frances, A. J., Pincus, H. A., Davis, W. W., & First, M. B. (1991). Toward an empirical classification for the DSM-IV. *Journal of Abnormal Psychology, 100,* 280–288.

Widiger, T. A., and Shea, T. (1991). Differentiation of Axis I and Axis II disorders. *Journal of Abnormal Psychology, 100,* 399–406.

Widiger, T. A., and Spitzer, R. L. (1991). Sex bias in the diagnosis of personality disorders: Conceptual and methodological issues. *Clinical Psychology Review, 11,* 1–22.

Widom, C. S. (1976). Interpersonal and personal construct systems in psychopaths. *Journal of Consulting and Clinical Psychology, 44,* 614–623.

Widom, C. S. (1977). A methodology for studying noninstitutionalized psychopaths. *Journal of Consulting and Clinical Psychology, 45,* 674–683.

Wiedl, K. H., & Schottner, B. (1991). Coping with symptoms related to schizophrenia. *Schizophrenia Bulletin, 17,* 525–538.

Wiener, A. (1992). The Dissociative Experiences Scale. *American Journal of Psychiatry, 149,* 143.

Wiens, A. N. (1983). The assessment interview. In I. B. Weiner (Ed.), *Clinical methods in psychology.* New York: John Wiley.

Wig, N. N., Menon, D. K., & Bedig, H. (1987). Expressed emotion and schizophrenia in North India: I. Cross-cultural transfer of ratings of relatives' expressed emotion. *British Journal of Psychiatry, 151,* 156–173.

Wiggins, J. (1979). Attractive notion. *APA Monitor, 10,* 2.

Wiggins, J. S., and Picus, A. L. (1989). Conceptions of personality disorders and dimensions of personality. *Psychological Assessment: A Journal of Consulting and Clinical Psychology, 1,* 305–316.

Wijsman, M. (1990). Linkage analysis of alcoholism: Problems and solutions. In C. R. Cloninger & H. Begleiter (Eds.), *Genetics and biology of alcoholism* (pp. 317–

326). Cold Spring Harbor, NY: Cold Spring Harbor Laboratory Press.

Wild, C. (1965). Creativity and adaptive regression. *Journal of Personality and Social Psychology, 2,* 161–169.

Wilding, T. (1984). Is stress making you sick? *American Health, 6,* 2–5.

Williams, J. B., & Spitzer, R. L. (1983). The issue of sex bias in DSM-III: A critique of "A woman's view of DSM-III" by Marcie Kaplan. *American Psychologist, 38,* 793–799.

Williams, J. H. (1977). *Psychology of women: Behavior in a biosocial context.* New York: Norton.

Williams, J. M. (1984). Cognitive-behaviour therapy for depression: Problems and perspectives. *British Journal of Psychiatry, 145,* 254–262.

Williams, L. M., & Finkelhor, D. (1990). The characteristics of incestuous fathers: A review of recent studies. In W. L. Marshall, D. R. Laws, & H. E. Barbaree (Eds.), *Handbook of sexual assault. Issues, theories, and treatment of the offender* (pp. 231–256). New York: Plenum Press.

Williams, R. (1974). The problem of match and mismatch. In L. Miller (Ed.), *The testing of black children.* Englewood Cliffs, NJ: Prentice-Hall.

Williams, R. B., Benson, H., & Follick, M. J. (1985). To the editor. *New England Journal of Medicine, 312,* 1356–1357.

Williams, R. B. Jr., Barefoot, J. C., Haney, T. L., Harrell, F. E., Jr., Blumenthal, J. A., Pryor, D. B., & Peterson, B. (1988). Type A behavior and angiographically documented coronary atherosclerosis in a sample of 2,289 patients. *Psychosomatic Medicine, 50,* 139–152.

Williamson, D. A., Cubic, B. A., & Gleaves, D. H. (1993). Equivalence of body image disturbances in anorexia and bulimia nervosa. *Journal of Abnormal Psychology, 102,* 177–180.

Willis, M. J. (1982). The impact of schizophrenia on families: One mother's point of view. *Schizophrenia Bulletin, 8,* 617–619.

Willison, G., & Masson, R. (1986). The role of touch in therapy: An adjunct to communications. *Journal of Counseling and Development, 65,* 497–500.

Wilson, G. T. (1984). Clinical issues and strategies in the clinical practice of behavior therapy. In C. M. Franks, G. T. Wilson, K. D. Brownell, & P. Kendall (Eds.), *Annual review of behavior therapy: Theory and practice, 8.* New York: Guilford Press.

Wilson, G. T., & O'Leary, K. D. (1980). *Principles of behavior therapy.* Englewood Cliffs, NJ: Prentice-Hall.

Wilson, M. S., & Meyer, E. (1962). Diagnostic consistency in a psychiatric liaison service. *American Journal of Psychiatry, 19,* 207–209.

Wilson, P. (1982). Combined pharmacological and behav-

ioural treatment of depression. *Behaviour Research and Therapy, 20,* 173–184.

Wincze, J. P., Bansal, S., & Malamud, M. (1986). Effects of medrox progesterone acetate on subjective arousal, arousal to erotic stimulation, and nocturnal penile tumescence in male sex offenders. *Archives of Sexual Behavior, 15,* 293–305.

Wincze, J. P., Hoon, E. F., & Hoon, P. W. (1978). Multiple measure analysis of women experiencing low sexual arousal. *Behaviour Research and Therapy, 16,* 43–49.

Wing, J. K. (1980). Social psychiatry in the United Kingdom: The approach to schizophrenia. *Schizophrenia Bulletin, 6,* 557–565.

Wing, L., & Gould, J. (1979). Severe impairment of social interaction and associated abnormalities in children: Epidemiology and classification. *Journal of Autism and Developmental Disorders, 9,* 11–29.

Winnett, R. L., Bornstein, P. H., Cogsuell, K. A., & Paris, A. E. (1987). Cognitive-behavioral therapy for childhood depression: A levels-of-treatment approach. *Journal of Child and Adolescent Psychotherapy, 4,* 283–286.

Winokur, G., Clayton, P. J., & Reich, T. (1969). *Manic depressive illness.* St. Louis: Mosby.

Winokur, G., Reich, T., Rimmer, J., & Pitts, F. (1970). Alcoholism III: Diagnosis and familial psychiatric illness in 259 alcoholic probands. *Archives of General Psychiatry, 23,* 104–111.

Wise, R. A. (1988). The neurobiology of craving: Implications for understanding and treatment of addiction. *Journal of Abnormal Psychology, 97,* 118–132.

Wittkower, E. C., & Rin, H. (1965). Cultural psychiatric research. In W. Caudell & T. Lin (Eds.), *Mental health research in Asia and the Pacific.* Honolulu: East-West Center Press.

Wolf, L. E. M., & Crowther, J. H. (1983). Personality and eating habit variables as predictors of severity of binge eating and weight. *Addictive Behavior, 8,* 335–344.

Wolfensberger, W. (1988). Common assets of mentally retarded people that are commonly not acknowledged. *Mental Retardation, 26,* 63–70.

Wolff, R., & Rapoport, J. (1988). Behavioral treatment of childhood obsessive-compulsive disorder. *Behavior Modification, 12,* 252–266.

Wolkin, A., Angrist, B., Wolf, A., Brodier, J. D., Wolkin, B., Jaeger, J., Camro, R., & Retrosen, J. (1988). Low frontal glucose utilization in chronic schizophrenia: A replication study. *American Journal of Psychiatry, 145,* 251–253.

Wolpe, J. (1973). *The practice of behavior therapy.* New York: Pergamon.

Wolpe, J. (1982). *The practice of behavior therapy* (3rd ed.). Elmsford, NY: Pergamon Press.

Wolpe, J. (1985). *Psychotherapy by reciprocal inhibition.* Stanford, CA: Stanford University Press.

Wolpe, J., & Abrams (1991). Post-traumatic stress disorder overcome by eye-movement desensitization. *Journal of Behaviour Therapy and Experimental Psychiatry, 22,* 39–43.

Wood, C. (1986). The hostile heart. *Psychology Today, 20,* 10–12.

Wood, J. M., Bootzin, R. R., Rosenhan, D., Nolen-Hoeksema, S., & Jourden, F. (1992). Effects of the 1989 San Francisco earthquake on frequency and content of nightmares. *Journal of Abnormal Psychology, 101,* 219–224.

World Health Organization. (1973a). *Manual of the international statistical classification of diseases, injuries and causes of death* (Vol. 1). Geneva: World Health Organization.

World Health Organization. (1973b). *Report on the international pilot study of schizophrenia* (Vol. 1). Geneva: World Health Organization.

World Health Organization. (1975). *Schizophrenia: A multinational study.* Geneva: World Health Organization.

World Health Organization. (1981). *Current state of diagnosis and classification in the mental health field.* Geneva: World Health Organization. Used by permission of the World Health Organization, Geneva.

World Health Organization. (1987). The Dexamethasone Suppression Test in depression. *British Journal of Psychiatry, 150,* 459–462.

Wright, L. (1978). A method for predicting sequelae to meningitis. *American Psychologist, 33,* 1037–1039.

Wrightsman, L. S. (1972). *Social psychology in the seventies.* Monterey, CA: Brooks/Cole.

Wyler, A. R., Masuda, M., & Holmes, T. H. (1971). Magnitude of the life events and seriousness of illness. *Journal of Psychosomatic Medicine, 33,* 115–122.

Yager, J., Landsverk, J., & Edelstein, C. K. (1987). A 20-month follow-up of 628 women with eating disorders, I: Course and severity. *American Journal of Psychiatry, 144,* 1172–1177.

Yalom, I. D. (1970). *The theory and practice of group psychotherapy.* New York: Basic Books.

Yarnold, P. R., & Grimm, L. G. (1982). Time urgency among coronary-prone individuals. *Journal of Abnormal Psychology, 91,* 175–177.

Yassa, R., & Jeste, D. V. (1992). Gender differences in tardive dyskinesia: A critical review of the literature. *Schizophrenia Bulletin, 18,* 701–715.

Yates, A. (1983). Behavior therapy and psychodynamic psychotherapy: Basic conflict or reconciliation and integration? *British Journal of Clinical Psychology, 22,* 107–125.

Yates, A. J. (1958). The application of learning theory to the treatment of tics. *Journal of Abnormal and Social Psychology, 56,* 175–182.

Yates, A. J. (1970). *Behavior Therapy.* New York: Wiley & Sons.

Yates, W. R. (1991). Transient hypochondriasis: A new somatoform diagnosis? *Archives of General Psychiatry, 48,* 955.

York, D., Borkovec, T. D., Lasey, M., & Stern, R. (1987). Effects of worry and somatic anxiety induction on thoughts, emotion, and physiological activity. *Behaviour Research and Therapy, 25,* 523–526.

Young, A. H., Blackwood, D. H. R., Roxborough, H., McQueen, J. K., Martin, M. J., & Kean, D. (1991). A magnetic resonance imaging study of schizophrenia: Brain structure and clinical symptoms. *British Journal of Psychiatry, 158,* 158–164.

Young, E. C., & Kramer, B. M. (1991). Characteristics of age-related language decline in adults with Down syndrome. *Mental Retardation, 29,* 75–79.

Young, M. (1980). Attitudes and behavior of college students relative to oral-genital sexuality. *Archives of Sexual Behavior, 9,* 61–67.

Youngren, M. A., & Lewinsohn, P. M. (1980). The functional relation between depression and problematic interpersonal behavior. *Journal of Abnormal Psychology, 89,* 333–341.

Youngstrom, N. (1991). Spotting serial killer difficult, experts note. *APA Monitor, 22,* No. 10, 32.

Yu-Fen, H., & Neng, T. (1981). Transcultural investigation of recent symptomatology of schizophrenia in China. *American Journal of Psychiatry, 138,* 1484–1486.

Yurchenco, H. (1970). *A mighty hard road: The Woody Guthrie story.* New York: McGraw-Hill.

Zajonc, R. B. (1975). Birth order and intelligence: Dumber by the dozen. *Psychology Today, 8,* 37–43.

Zantal-Weiner, K. (1988). Early intervention services for pre-school children. *Teaching Exceptional Children, 54,* 61–62.

Zax, M., & Cowen, E. L. (1972). *Abnormal psychology.* New York: Holt, Rinehart & Winston.

Zax, M., & Spector, G. A. (1974). *An introduction to community psychology.* New York: Wiley.

Zeiss, A. M., Rosen, G. M., & Zeiss, R. A. (1977). Orgasm during intercourse: A treatment strategy for women. *Journal of Consulting and Clinical Psychology, 45,* 891–895.

Zeiss, R. A. (1977). Self-directed treatment for premature ejaculation: Preliminary case reports. *Journal of Behavior Therapy and Experimental Psychiatry, 8,* 87–91.

Zelt, D. (1981). First person account: The messiah quest. *Schizophrenia Bulletin, 7,* 527–531.

Zentall, S. S., & Zentall, T. R. (1983). Optimal stimulation: A model of disordered activity and performance in normal and deviant children. *Psychological Bulletin, 94,* 446–471.

Zerbin-Rudin, E. Genetic research and the theory of schizophrenia. *International Journal of Mental Health, 1,* 42–62.

Zigler, E. (1967). Familial mental retardation: A continuing dilemma. *Science, 155,* 292–298.

Zigler, E., & Bergman, W. (1983). Discerning the future of early childhood intervention. *American Psychologist, 38,* 893–905.

Zigler, E., Taussig, C. & Black, K. (1992). Early childhood intervention: A promising preventative for juvenile delinquency. *American Psychologist, 47,* 997–1006.

Zigman, W. B., Schupf, N., Lubin, R. A., & Silverman, W. P. (1987). Premature regression of adults with Down syndrome. *American Journal of Mental Deficiency, 92,* 161–168.

Zilbergeld, B. (1983). *The shrinking of America.* Boston: Little, Brown.

Zilboorg, G., & Henry, G. W. (1941). *A history of medical psychology.* New York: Norton.

Zimbardo, P. (1977). *Shyness: What is it, what to do about it.* Reading, MA: Addison-Wesley.

Zipursky, R. B., Lim, K. O., & Pfefferbaum, A. (1991). Brain size in schizophrenia. *Archives of General Psychiatry, 48,* 179–180.

Zito, J. M., Craig, T. J., Wanderling, J., & Siegel, C. (1987). Pharmaco-epidemiology in 136 hospitalized schizophrenic patients. *American Journal of Psychiatry, 144,* 778–782.

Zubin, J. (1978). But is it good for science? *Clinical Psychologist, 31*(1), 5–7.

Zubin, J., & Ludwig, A. M. (1983). What is schizophrenia? *Schizophrenia Bulletin, 9,* 331–334.

Zubin, J., & Spring, B. (1977). Vulnerability—a new view of schizophrenia. *Journal of Abnormal Psychology, 86,* 103–126.

Zubin, J., Steinhauer, S. R., & Condray, R. (1992). Vulnerability to relapse in schizophrenia. *British Journal of Psychiatry, 161,* 13–18.

Zucker, K. J. (1990). Gender identity disorders in children: Clinical descriptions and natural history. In R. Blanchard & B. W. Steiner (Eds.), *Clinical management of gender identity disorders in children and adults* (pp. 1–24). Washington, DC: American Psychiatric Press.

Zuger, B. (1984). Early effeminate behavior in boys: Outcome and significance for homosexuality. *Journal of Nervous and Mental Disease, 172,* 90–97.

Zuger, B. (1987). Childhood cross-gender behavior and adult homosexuality. *Archives of Sexual Behavior, 16,* 85–87.

Zullow, H. M., Oettingen, G., Peterson, C., & Seligman, M. E. (1988). Pessimistic explanatory style in the historical record: Caving LBJ, presidential candidates, and East versus West Berlin. *American Psychologist, 43,* 673–682.

Zverina, J., Lachman, M., Pondelickova, J., & Vanek, J. (1987). The occurrence of atypical sexual experience among various female patient groups. *Archives of Sexual Behavior, 16,* 321–326.

Credits

Credits *(continued from copyright page)*

Chapter 1: **p. 4:** G. Cloyd/Taurus Photos, Inc. **p. 5:** Catherine Karnow/Woodfin Camp & Associates. **p. 7:** *left* William Carter/Photo Researchers, Inc. *right* UPI/Bettmann Newsphotos. **p. 11:** Rod Aydelotte/Waco Tribune Herald/Sygma. **p. 13:** Joseph Schuyler/Stock, Boston. **p. 19:** Neg. no. 312263 (Photo by Julius Kirschner) Courtesy Department Library Services. American Museum of Natural History. **p. 20:** Eglise des Cordeliers/Franziskanerkirche, Fribourg (Switzerland). **p. 23:** Giraudon/Art Resource. **p. 24:** National Archives.

Chapter 2: **p. 34:** AP/Wide World Photos. **p. 37:** *Figure 2.2* From Laird and Thompson, *Psychology.* © 1992 by Houghton Mifflin Company. Used with permission. **pp. 38 and 39:** *Figures 2.3 and 2.4* From Laird and Thompson, *Psychology.* © 1992 by Houghton Mifflin Company. Used with permission. **p. 39:** *Table 2.1* From Laird and Thompson, *Psychology.* © 1992 by Houghton Mifflin Company. Used with permission. **p. 40:** Gerry Davis/Phototake NYC. **p. 42:** Archive/Photo Researchers, Inc. **p. 44:** *left* © The Stock Market/Barbara Kirk. *right* Laura Dwight/Peter Arnold, Inc. **p. 45:** *left* © Stacy Pick 1988/Stock, Boston. *right* Richard Hutchings, Photo Researchers, Inc. **p. 49:** National Library of Medicine. **p. 50:** *left* UPI/Bettmann Newsphotos. *right* The Bettmann Archives. **p. 57:** *left* Landmark Photos. *right* The Bettmann Archives. **p. 60:** © Diane M. Lowe/Stock, Boston **p. 61:** *Extract* From May, Rollo, *Existential Psychology.* © 1961 by Rollo May. Used by permission of Random House, Inc.

Chapter 3: **p. 71:** Peter Vandermark/Stock, Boston. **p. 73:** *left* Courtesy of Mr. Franklin H. Avers, reprinted from Norman L. Munn. *Psychology: The Fundamentals of Human Adjustment.* Houghton Mifflin Co., 1946, p. 267. *right* Peter Vandermark/Stock, Boston. **p. 74:** Blair Seitz/Photo Researchers, Inc. **p. 76:** © Bob Daemmrich/Stock, Boston. **p. 81:** *Focus 3.1* Adapted from Ellis, A., *Reason and Emotion in Psychotherapy.* © 1962 by Lyle Stuart, Inc. Used with permission. **p. 81:** Institute for Rational-Emotive Therapy. **p. 84:** Donald Meichenbaum. **p. 91:** Lawrence Migdale/Stock, Boston.

Chapter 4: **p. 106:** Jerry Howard/Positive Images. **p. 107:** Rorschach H.: Psychodiagnostics. © 1921 Verlag Hans Huber, Bern (renewed 1948). **p. 108:** © 1971 by the President and Fellows of Harvard College. **p. 111:** © Dan McCoy/Rainbow. **p. 112:** *Table 4.2* From Marvin R. Goldfried and Gerald C. Davison, *Clinical Behavior Therapy.* © 1976 by Holt, Rinehart & Winston, Inc. Reprinted by permission of the authors. **p. 114:** *Figure 4.1* As taken from the Bender® Visual Motor Gestalt Test, published by American Orthopsychiatric Assn., © 1938. Used with permission. **p. 115:** © The Stock Market/Henley & Savage. **p. 118:** Historical Picture Service, Chicago. **pp. 120–121:** *Table 4.3* Summarized from Dahlstrom, W. G., and Welsh, G. S. (1965). *An MMPI Handbook.* Minneapolis: University of Minnesota Press. Used by permission. **p. 125:** Frank Siteman/Southern Light. **p. 129:** *Table 4.4* Simulated items similar to those from the Wechsler Adult Intelligence Scale-Revised. © 1981, 1955 by The Psychological Corporation. Reproduced by permission. All rights reserved.

Chapter 5: **p. 138:** © Richard Nowitz/Phototake NYC. **p. 142:** © The Stock Market/Henley & Savage. **p. 146:** Christopher Brown/Stock, Boston. **p. 150:** Dawson Jones, Inc./Stock, Boston. **p. 156:** © Martin Rogers/Stock, Boston.

Chapter 6: **p. 163:** Used with permission American Cancer Society, Inc. **p. 165:** Scala/Art Resource. **p. 166:** © Joseph Giannetti/Stock, Boston. **p. 172:** © William McCoy/Rainbow. **p. 173:** Jeff Albertson/Stock, Boston. **p. 174:** Norman Rowan/Stock, Boston. **p. 181:** © Susan Lapides. **p. 182:** © Carol Palmer. **p. 190:** Martha Gershen/Photo Researchers, Inc. **p. 192:** Bob Daemmrich/Stock, Boston. **p. 193:** *Figure 6.2* Reprinted with permission of Brunner/Mazel, Inc. and the author from "Conceptualizing Post-traumatic Stress Disorder," by Bonnie Green, John Wilson, and Jacob Lindy in *Trauma and Its Wake*, Vol. 1 by Charles R. Figley, Ph.D.

Chapter 7: **p. 199:** © Bard Martin/The Image Bank. **p. 200:** Dan McCoy/Rainbow. **p. 210:** PEOPLE Weekly © 1989 Deborah Lex. **p. 211:** Alan Carey/The Image Works, Inc. **p. 216:** Willie Hill, Jr./The Image Works. **p. 220:** Francoise Sauze/Science Photo Library/Photo Researchers, Inc.

Name Index

Bryant, R. A., 214
Bryant-Waugh, R., 522, 526
Buceta, J. M., 245
Buchanan, A., 532
Buchanan, R. W., 452
Buchsbaum, M. S., 452
Buckner, H. T., 327
Bühler, F. K., 435
Buhrmester, D., 510, 511
Bulhan, H. A., 601
Bull, J., 487
Bullard-Bates, P. C., 474
Bundy, T., 266, 272
Bunney, W. E., 378
Buono, A., 612
Burack, J. H., 234
Buranen, C., 215
Burchard, J. D., 594
Burgess, A. W., 329, 334, 335, 336, 351
Burkhart, B. R., 335
Burman, B., 457
Burns, L., 172
Burt, C., 32
Burt, D. B., 507
Burton, A., 629
Buss, A. H., 9, 38
Butcher, J. N., 109
Butler, G., 170, 171, 181
Butler, R. N., 481, 482, 494
Butler, R. W., 424
Butterfield, E. C., 528
Byer, C. O., 326

Cade, J. F. J., 26
Cadoret, R. J., 269, 303
Caeser, J., 488
Cain, C., 269
Caldwell, R. A., 589
Calhoun, K. S., 335, 412
California Board of Medical Quality Assurance, 630
Callanan, P., 624
Cameron, R., 559
Campbell, M. K., 506
Campbell, R. J., 381
Campbell, S. B., 508, 517
Camus, A., 61
Caplan, P. J., 128, 257, 602
Cappell, H., 301
Cardena, E., 205
Carey, G., 269
Carey, W. B., 517
Carlisle, J. M., 333
Carlson, B. E., 590
Carlson, C. L., 511
Carlson, E. B., 191
Carlson, G. A., 519
Carlson, K., 308
Carmelli, D., 240

Carone, B. J., 436
Carr, A. T., 186
Carr, E. G., 76, 502, 556
Carroll, A., 520
Carroll, D., 248
Carson, C. C., 350
Carson, N. D., 402
Carson, R. C., 119, 127, 421
Carstensen, L. L., 402, 483
Casas, J. M., 32, 33
Cash, T. F., 166
Cassel, C. A., 327
Cassel, J., 598
Cassens, H. L., 220
Cassileth, B. R., 238
Catania, J., 627
Cautela, J. R., 313, 555
Centers for Disease Control, 227, 342
Cerletti, U., 538
Cesaroni, L., 498, 499
Chadwick, 425
Chaika, E., 429
Channabasavanna, S. M., 324
Chapman, J. P., 109
Chapman, L. J., 109
Charcot, J-M., 25
Check, J. V. P., 337, 338
Chemtob, C. M., 407
Chesler, P., 52, 604, 631
Chess, S., 247, 517
Chivas, A., 210
Chodoff, P., 205, 206
Chodorow, N., 52
Chollar, S., 511
Christensen, D., 501
Christiansen, K. O., 269
Christison, G. W., 460
Chu, F. D., 587
Chung, R., 367
Ciompi, L., 436
Clancy, J., 328
Clancy, S., 221
Claridge, G., 139
Clark, D. M., 168
Clark, K. B., 599
Clark, M., 168, 243, 245, 482
Clark, M. K., 599
Clark, R., 37
Clarke, A. D. B., 531
Clarke, A. M., 531
Clarkin, J. F., 262
Clayton, P. J., 376
Cleary, C. P., 130
Cleary, J., 170, 512
Cleckley, H., 204
Cleckley, H. M., 205
Cleckley, J., 265, 266, 275
Clementz, B. A., 453

Clemmensen, L. H., 324
Clinthorne, J. K., 542
Clinton, W., 353
Clomipramine Collaborative Study Group, 187
Cloninger, C. R., 37, 137
Clooney, R., 16
Coates, J., 301
Coates, S., 323
Coates, T., 627
Coates, T. J., 369
Cobb, E. J., 594
Cobb, S., 598
Cobbs, P., 9
Coelho, G. V., 58
Coffman, J. A., 115
Cohen, B. M., 444
Cohen, D. J., 519
Cohen, E. D., 627
Cohen, M. J., 247
Cohen, S., 233
Cohen, S. L., 398
Cohn, L. D., 525
Cole, J. O., 540, 543, 544
Cole, W. C., 200
Collinge, W. B., 601
Comas-Diaz, L., 585
Comings, B. G., 187
Comings, D. E., 137, 187
Commander, M., 520
Commission on Obscenity and Pornography, 338
Committee on Drug Abuse of the Council on Psychiatric Services, 287, 300, 301
Committee on the Review of Medicines, 170
Committee on Women in Psychology of the American Psychological Association, 630
Compton, W. M., III, 167, 171
Conaway, 628
Condray, R., 454
Conger, J. J., 306
Conn, D. K., 478, 480
Conners, M. E., 136, 139, 525
Consensus Development Panel, 511
Cook, E. W., III, 77
Coombs, D. W., 411
Coons, D., 483
Coons, P. M., 148, 155, 204, 205, 206, 207, 208, 209
Cooper, A., 292, 308
Cooper, A. J., 351
Cooper, J. E., 421
Cooper, J. R., 37
Cooper, M. J., 522, 523
Cooper, M. L., 314
Corazzini, J. G., 566

Hekmat, H., 181
Heller, K., 582, 587, 598
Helms, J. E., 113
Hemingway, E., 16, 397
Hemsley, D., 424
Hendin, H., 190
Henker, B., 511, 512
Henley, N., 631
Hennard, G., 618
Henry, G. W., 18, 21
Henryk-Gutt, R., 244
Herbert, J. D., 173
Herlicky, B., 624
Herman, I., 395
Herman, J., 329, 338
Herman, S., 338
Hernandez, J., 215
Hernandez, P., 9
Hernstein, R., 32, 153
Hersen, M., 129, 215, 384, 557, 587
Hershkowitz, S., 324
Hess, E. P., 210
Heston, L. L., 446, 447
Hetherington, C. R., 479
Hibbert, G., 168
Higgitt, A., 542
Hilker, R. J., 232
Hill, C. E., 566
Hill, D., 270
Hillyer, J., 362
Himmelhoch, J., 384
Himmelnoch, J. M., 557
Hinckley, J., Jr., 612, 614, 632
Hinshaw, S., 514
Hipple, J. L., 615
Hipple, L. B., 615
Hippocrates, 18, 19, 20, 24, 29
Hirsch, B. J., 598
Hirsch, D. A., 485
Hirschfeld, R. M., 381
Hirschfield, R. M., 396
Hirschman, L., 329, 338
Hirschman, R., 337, 341
Hite, S., 319, 348
Ho, D. Y. F., 501
Ho, E. D. F., 501
Ho, M. K., 93
Hobbs, N., 586
Hoberman, H. M., 367, 372
Hobson, R. P., 502
Hoch, Z., 348, 349
Hochron, S., 245, 247
Hodges, W. F., 589
Hodgeson, R., 554, 557
Hodgson, R., 185
Hodgson, R. J., 186
Hoehn-Saric, R., 187
Hoffman, D., 500, 501
Hoffman, M. A., 627

Hoffman, P. L., 303
Hogarty, G. E., 461, 465
Hogue, L., 616
Hohmann, A. A., 541
Holahan, C. J., 368
Holcomb, H. H., 115
Holden, C., 128, 257
Holden, N. L., 432
Hollender, M. H., 219
Hollon, S. D., 26, 384, 385
Holmes, T. H., 230, 231
Holmes, T. S., 230
Holmstrom, L. L., 334, 335, 351
Holroyd, J., 52, 630, 631
Holstrom, L., 336
Holt, R. R., 62
Holzberg, J. D., 594
Hood, J., 401
Hoon, E. F., 350
Hoon, P. W., 350
Hope, D. A., 173
Hoppe, C. M., 511
Horne, A. M., 566
Horne, R. L., 522, 538
Horney, K., 50, 54
Horning, C. D., 171
Horowitz, M. J., 489
Horwath, E., 171
Horwitz, A. V., 9
Hostetter, A. M., 369
Hovanitz, C. A., 246, 249
Howard, R., 7, 423
Howell, C. T., 508
Howell, J. G., 506
Hsu, L. K., 524
Hu, L., 604
Hubbard, F., 526
Huber, G., 437, 454
Huber, S. J., 484
Hudgens, A., 221
Hudson, J. I., 136, 139, 190, 522, 525
Huerta, E., 525
Hugdahl, K., 177, 178, 179
Hughes, H., 184
Hull, J. C., 292
Humphrey, D., 414
Hunt, M. M., 331, 337
Hunter, R., 18, 487
Hurtig, A. L., 323
Hutchens, T. A., 512
Hutchings, B., 269
Hutchinson, C. P., 524
Hymovitz, P., 543
Hynd, G. W., 511, 512

Idupuganti, S., 422
Igra, A., 242
Innocent VIII, 21
Irwin, A., 530

Irwin, M., 235
Isenberg, S. A., 245, 247
Israelsen, H., 501
Ivanoff, J., 346
Ivey, 628

Jackson, A., 555
Jackson, D., 91
Jackson, M., 139
Jackson v. Indiana, 615
Jacob, R. G., 217
Jacobs, M., 596
Jacobson, E., 248, 554
Jacobson, L., 130
Jacobson, N. S., 372
Jaenicke, C., 519
Jaffe, H. W., 343
Jaffee, D., 337, 340
Jahoda, M., 58
James, G. D., 241
James, W., 16, 23
Janford, E. E., 532
Janoff-Bulman, R., 191, 192, 194
Jansen, A., 523
Janssen, K., 249
Janus, C. L., 341, 346, 355
Janus, S. S., 341, 346, 355
Jason, L. A., 590
Jasper, H. H., 490
Jawed, S. Y., 212
Jay, S. M., 215
Jefferson, T., 58
Jekelis, A. W., 350
Jellinek, E. M., 294
Jenike, M. A., 187
Jenkins, J. H., 456
Jenkins, S., 508
Jenner, F. A., 366
Jennings, J. R., 229
Jennison, J. H., 479
Jensen, A., 32, 153
Jessor, R., 304
Jessor, S. L., 304
Jeste, D. V., 464
Jimenez, T., 392, 393, 400
Jobes, D. A., 395, 400, 401
Johnson, C., 391, 393
Johnson, D. A. W., 461
Johnson, D. L., 590
Johnson, F., 620
Johnson, J., 171
Johnson, J. H., 232
Johnson, R. E., 402
Johnson, V. E., 149, 340, 341, 342, 344, 346, 347, 348, 349, 351, 352, 354, 355
Johnson, W. G., 33, 484
Johnston, L. D., 290, 295, 300, 307
Johnston, R., 594

Subject Index